HEATH

ALGEBRA 2

AN INTEGRATED APPROACH

Roland E. Larson

Timothy D. Kanold

Lee Stiff

McDougal Littell

Evanston, Illinois   Boston ◆ Dallas

About the Cover

The cover shows mathematics used in aeronautics and air safety. The background is a photograph of an airplane above the clouds in a rainbow sky. The photo inset shows two air traffic controllers at work in an airport's air traffic control station.

The equations $B = 10 \log_{10} \dfrac{I}{I_0}$ and $I = \dfrac{10}{r^2}$ relate the intensity of sound, I, to the level of sound, B, and the distance from the source of the sound, r. Knowing such relationships is important when designing safe working conditions for airport employees. A person's hearing could be permanently damaged if the level of sound is too great. The equation $S = 136.4\sqrt{p} + 4.5$ relates the indicated airspeed, S, of an airplane to the difference, p, between the static and dynamic pressures. Understanding such relationships is an important part of preparation for a career as an airplane pilot or an aeronautical engineer.

As you read the text, you will find information that is directly related to the cover.

Acknowledgments

Editorial Development Jane Bordzol, Rita Campanella, Anne M. Collier, Peter R. Devine, Tamara Trombetta Gorman, Marc Hurwitz, Albert Jacobson, Barbara M. Kelley, Savitri Kaur Khalsa, Pearl Ling, Marlys Mahajan, James O'Connell, George J. Summers, Folkert Van Karssen
Marketing/Advertising Jo DiGiustini, Phyllis D. Lindsay, Richard Ravich, Debbie R. Secrist
Design Robert Botsford, Pamela Daly, Leslie Dews, Robin Herr, Cynthia Maciel, Joan Williams
Production Sandra Easton, Lalia Nuzzolo, Mark Tricca

Author Acknowledgments

In Algebra 2, we have included numerous examples and exercises that use real-life data. This would not have been possible without the help of many people and organizations. Our wholehearted thanks goes to all for their time and effort.

We tried to use the data accurately—to give honest and unbiased portrayals of real-life situations. In the cases where models were fit to data, we used the least-squares method. In all cases, the square of the correlation coefficient, r^2, was at least 0.95. In most cases, it was 0.99 or greater.

(Acknowledgments continue following the Index.)

Published simultaneously in Canada

Printed in the United States of America

International Standard Book Number: 0-669-43394-2

2 3 4 5 6 7 8 9 10 VHP 02 01 00 99 98 97

Roland E. Larson is Professor of Mathematics at the Behrend College of Pennsylvania State University in Erie. He is a member of NCTM and a highly successful author of many high school and college mathematics textbooks. Several of his D.C. Heath college titles have proved to be top choices for senior high school mathematics courses.

Timothy D. Kanold is Chairman of Mathematics and Science and a teacher at Adlai Stevenson High School in Prairie View, Illinois. He is the 1986 recipient of the Presidential Award for Excellence in Mathematics Teaching, as well as the 1991 recipient of the Outstanding Young Alumni Award from Illinois State University. A member of NCTM, he served on NCTM's *Professional Standards for Teaching Mathematics* Commission and is a member of the Regional Services Committee.

Lee Stiff is an Associate Professor of Mathematics Education in the College of Education and Psychology of North Carolina State University at Raleigh. He has taught mathematics at the high school and middle school levels. He is a member of the NCTM Board of Directors, served on NCTM's *Professional Standards for Teaching Mathematics* Commission, and is a member of the *Committee for a Comprehensive Mathematics Education of Every Child.*

REVIEWERS AND CONTRIBUTORS

Linda Bailey
Putnam City Schools
Oklahoma City, OK

Pat Beck
Putnam City North High School
Oklahoma City, OK

Larry Demetrak
San Marin High School
Novato, CA

Charleen M. DeRidder
Knox County Schools
Knoxville, TN

Melanie Donnell
Russellville High School
Russellville, AR

Joseph P. Dooley
Upper Darby High School
Upper Darby, PA

David J. Enterlin
Upper Darby High School
Upper Darby, PA

M. Jayne Fleener
University of Oklahoma
Norman, OK

Gail Gonyo
Adirondack Community College
Queensbury, NY

Wanda Heflin
Russellville High School
Russellville, AR

Karen Humble
Western Oaks Junior High School
Oklahoma City, OK

Regina D. Kiczek
Ferris High School
Jersey City, NJ

Fran Kormes
Harry S. Truman High School
Levittown, PA

Chicha Lynch
Capuchino High School
San Bruno, CA

Elizabeth J. Manes
Harry S. Truman High School
Levittown, PA

Deanna Mauldin
Liberty Bell Middle School
Johnson City, TN

Terry McBroom
San Marin High School
Novato, CA

Dominic Mendalla
Capuchino High School
San Bruno, CA

Dennis H. Noe
School District of Waukesha
Waukesha, WI

Dean Orfanedes
Capuchino High School
San Bruno, CA

Jennifer J. Penley
Liberty Bell Middle School
Johnson City, TN

Susan Shumate
Edmond Public Schools
Edmond, OK

Sharon Siegel
Dodgen Middle School
Marietta, GA

Linda Tassano
San Marin High School
Novato, CA

John Wellington
Upper Darby High School
Upper Darby, PA

There are many ways to study algebra. After years of teaching and guiding students through algebra courses, we have compiled a list of learning ideas that will help you take responsibility for your own success. These ideas will take some time and effort—but they work!

Do the Homework: Learning algebra is like learning to play the piano or basketball. You cannot become skilled by just watching someone else do it. You must also do it yourself. When you start a new exercise set, understanding is much more important than speed. Your *ultimate* goal is to be able to solve the problems accurately and efficiently.

Prepare for Class: After completing your homework assignment, and before attending your next class, read the next portion of the text that is to be covered. This takes a lot of self-discipline, but it pays off.

Keep a Journal: Each day do a self-analysis in which you reflect on your learning of algebra. Ask yourself these questions: What were the major goals and tasks of the class? Why did I learn it? What procedures should I know to successfully do the problems? This type of reflection, combined with your completed attempt at the homework, will help to develop your confidence.

Participate in Class: As you are reading the text, communicating in class, or practicing problems, write down any questions you have about the material. Then ask your teacher.

Taking Notes: Take notes in class, especially on definitions, rules, and model examples. Then, as part of your homework, read through your notes—adding any explanations that are necessary to make your notes understandable to you. Highlight important aspects of the lesson, too.

Find a Study Partner: When you get stuck on a problem, it helps to be able to try to work with someone else. Even if you think you are giving more help than you are getting, you will find that teaching others is one of the best ways to learn.

Remember, math is not a spectator sport—it's a valuable tool you can use in everyday life! We believe that our book will help you to see, feel, and understand the wonderful value of Algebra.

ROLAND E. LARSON   TIMOTHY D. KANOLD   LEE STIFF

Real-Life Applications

Look through this list for things that interest you. Then find out how they are used with algebra.

Accounting   20, 22, 28, 807, 824
Advertising   127, 155, 214, 337, 451
Aerospace   351, 393, 720
Agriculture   22, 83, 112, 135, 163, 185, 451, 459, 580
Animal/Insect Studies   8, 23, 35, 42, 46, 48, 53, 167, 193, 323, 332, 382, 386, 388–389, 410, 425, 445, 451, 504, 511, 741, 749, 786, 809, 827
Archaeology   238, 497
Architecture   106, 241, 249, 462, 476, 479
Arts   147, 220, 272, 356, 520, 603, 617, 688, 691, 721, 725, 794, 810
Astronomy   234, 350, 370, 505, 585, 588, 618, 628, 649, 720, 725
Banking   326, 422, 424, 437, 439, 450, 553, 560, 800
Biology   36, 46, 167, 366, 668, 741, 756, 784, 786, 827
Business   26, 51, 83, 98, 124, 126, 142, 153, 155, 179, 184, 195, 214, 221, 234, 256, 290, 294–295, 307, 310, 351, 358, 365, 403–404, 430, 433, 447, 451, 468, 471, 483, 485–486, 490, 506, 523, 632, 634–635, 640, 807, 812, 824
Chemistry   14, 23, 40, 166, 212, 214, 411, 417, 424, 439, 451, 525, 530, 791
Communications   247, 267, 270, 310, 337, 580, 789, 799–800
Construction   25, 256, 707, 821–822
Consumer   8, 75, 82, 142, 148, 166, 184, 293, 307, 310, 317, 505, 546, 656
Cryptography   198–199, 201
Earth Science   713, 751
Economics   166, 176, 195, 290, 295, 353
Education   13, 73, 176, 179, 296, 327, 330, 358, 394, 446, 793, 810, 825
Electronics   418, 526, 529
Engineering   393, 497, 531, 600, 690, 707
Entertainment   42, 98, 105, 141–142, 155, 218, 225, 290, 319, 330, 379, 445, 522, 538, 574, 627, 698
Environomental Science   5, 28, 54, 133, 190, 355, 447, 525, 528, 566, 572, 751

Finance   22, 82, 91, 108, 126, 135, 139, 141–142, 174, 273, 287, 293–294, 303–304, 326, 352–353, 356, 401, 437, 439, 450, 468, 546, 555–560, 564, 642, 658–665, 668–669, 800, 807, 818, 824
Forensic Science   428
Fractals   261, 263
Game Theory   797, 802–803, 814, 816–818, 820–821
Geography   42, 66, 68, 75, 98, 192, 240, 281, 336, 506, 699, 714, 736, 742
Geology/Mining   68, 276, 415
Government   52, 89, 221, 269, 385, 424, 439, 492, 505, 798, 806, 825
History   75, 117, 505, 512
Home Economics   98, 372
Insurance   818, 821
Law Enforcement   76
Library Science   394
Mechanics   705, 726
Medical   49, 68, 214, 279, 311, 357, 379, 442, 446, 522, 552, 801
Meteorology   7, 42, 88, 103, 303, 336, 383, 386, 410, 478, 543, 595, 739, 741, 806, 826
Military   492, 523
Music   53, 150, 162, 373, 525, 546, 554, 714, 733, 764
Nautical Science   363
Navigation   609, 718
Nutrition/Fitness   65, 91, 112, 184, 499
Oceanography   24, 48, 393, 408, 439
Optics   735, 762, 765
Photography   220, 417, 547
Physics   36, 91, 143, 231, 234, 254, 269, 337, 373, 393, 417–418, 424, 430, 478, 520, 528–531, 536, 564–565, 574–575, 578, 580, 593, 612, 647, 649, 669, 707, 721, 733, 748, 768
Physiology   48, 98, 109, 388, 536, 742, 774
Population   13, 140, 166, 202, 269, 281, 319, 328–329, 331, 338, 431, 439, 461, 501, 505, 523, 550, 643, 741, 783, 787, 797, 825
Publishing   9, 11, 91, 149, 327, 461

Recreation   27, 160, 357

Retailing   8, 75, 80, 82, 91, 138, 142, 148, 166, 184, 268–269, 293, 461, 490, 499–500, 510, 625, 774, 819, 822

Sociology   50, 466

Sports   7, 27–28, 32, 48, 52–54, 96, 105, 112, 142, 150, 166, 178, 182, 208, 218, 221, 225, 234, 240, 249, 256, 303, 332, 365, 404, 425, 478, 500, 503, 539, 544, 586, 587, 602, 627, 656, 696, 698, 708, 717, 720, 792, 799–800, 809, 826

Testing   123, 417, 504, 511, 791

Time Management   329

Topography   3, 7, 681, 683–684, 711

Transportation   127, 135, 527, 565, 609, 720

Travel   162, 225, 232, 235, 357, 379, 507, 815

"Modeling puts a mathematical overlay on the real world. It's attainable, reasonable, straight-forward, and it fits with the topics at hand. Real-world connections make ALGEBRA meaningful for all students and promotes success at all levels."

Lee Stiff   Timothy D. Kanold   Roland E. Larson

TABLE OF CONTENTS

CHAPTER 1 — Review of Basic Algebra

Problem Solving in Every Lesson
Chapter 1 reviews the key problem solving steps used throughout Algebra 1. Chapters 1–3 review the first seven chapters of Algebra 1 and introduce additional enriching models and applications.

▥ Chapter Overview	1
1.1 Real Numbers and Number Operations D	2
1.2 Algebraic Expressions and Models D,F,G	9
▥ Mixed Review	15
▥ Career Interview: Architect	15
▥ Using a Scientific Calculator or Graphing Calculator	16
1.3 Solving Linear Equations G	18
1.4 Problem-Solving Strategies D	24
▥ Mid-Chapter Self-Test	30
1.5 Literal Equations and Formulas F,G	31
1.6 Solving Linear Inequalities F	37
◆ Investigating Solutions of Inequalities	37
▥ Mixed Review	43
1.7 Solving Absolute Value Equations and Inequalities D,F	44
1.8 Exploring Data: Tables and Graphs D	50
▥ Chapter Summary	56
▥ Chapter Review D,F,G	57
▥ Chapter Test	61

CHAPTER 2 — Linear Equations

Emphasis on Graphing and Coordinate Geometry
Chapter 2 revisits the graphing techniques of quick graphs, coordinate geometry, and the power of graphing calculators introduced and developed in Algebra 1 and integrates them throughout Algebra 2.

▥ Chapter Overview	63
2.1 The Graph of an Equation C,D,F	64
2.2 Slope and Rate of Change C,D,F	70
▥ Mixed Review	77
▥ Milestones: Mathematical Symbols	77
2.3 Quick Graphs of Linear Equations C,F	78
▥ Using a Graphing Calculator	84
2.4 Writing Equations of Lines C,D,F	86
▥ Mid-Chapter Self-Test	93
2.5 Graphing Linear Inequalities in Two Variables C,F,G	94
▥ Mixed Review	100
2.6 Graphs of Absolute Value Equations C,F	101
2.7 Exploring Data: Fitting a Line to Data C,D,F	107
◆ Investigating a Best-Fitting Line	107
▥ Chapter Summary	114
▥ Chapter Review C,D,F	115
▥ Chapter Test	119

C Integrates Coordinate Geometry　　**D** Integrates Data Analysis
F Integrates Functions　　**G** Integrates Geometry

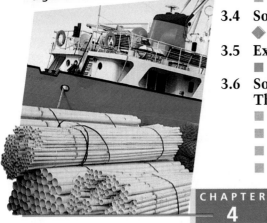

Integrating Technology
Algebra 2 integrates graphing calculator technology throughout the program in lessons, in exercises, and in the "Using a Graphing Calculator" feature — one per chapter — allowing you to continually explore, discover, and reinforce algebraic concepts.

CHAPTER 3

Systems of Linear Equations and Inequalities

■ Chapter Overview   121
3.1 Solving Linear Systems by Graphing c,d,f   122
  ■ Using a Graphing Calculator   128
3.2 Solving Linear Systems Algebraically c,d,f   130
  ■ Mixed Review   137
  ■ Career Interview: Air Traffic Controller   137
3.3 Problem Solving Using Linear Systems c,f   138
  ■ Mid-Chapter Self-Test   144
3.4 Solving Systems of Linear Inequalities c,d,f   145
  ◆ Investigating the Graph of a System   145
3.5 Exploring Data: Linear Programming c,d,f   151
  ■ Mixed Review   156
3.6 Solving Systems of Linear Equations in Three Variables d   157
  ■ Chapter Summary   165
  ■ Chapter Review c,d,f   166
  ■ Chapter Test   169
  ■ Cumulative Review c,d,f   170

CHAPTER 4

Matrices and Determinants

■ Chapter Overview   173
4.1 Exploring Data: Matrix Operations d   174
4.2 Matrix Multiplication d   180
  ■ Mixed Review   186
  ■ Milestones: Arthur Cayley   186
4.3 Determinants c,d   187
  ■ Using a Graphing Calculator   194
4.4 Identity and Inverse Matrices d   196
  ◆ Investigating Inverse Matrices   196
  ■ Mid-Chapter Self-Test   203
4.5 Solving Systems Using Inverse Matrices d   204
  ■ Mixed Review   209
4.6 Solving Systems Using Augmented Matrices d   210
4.7 Solving Systems Using Cramer's Rule d   216
  ■ Chapter Summary   222
  ■ Chapter Review c,d   223
  ■ Chapter Test   227

CHAPTER
5

Quadratic Equations and Parabolas

▪ Chapter Overview	229
5.1 Solving Quadratic Equations by Finding Square Roots C,F,G	230
5.2 Parabolas: Graphs of Quadratic Equations C,F,G	236
▪ Using a Graphing Calculator	242
▪ Mixed Review	244
▪ Career Interview: Epidemiologist	244
5.3 Completing the Square C,F,G	245
▪ Mid-Chapter Self-Test	251
5.4 The Quadratic Formula C,D,F,G	252
5.5 Complex Numbers	258
▪ Mixed Review	264
5.6 Solving Any Quadratic Equation C,D,F,G	265
◆ Investigating Real Solutions of Quadratics	266
5.7 Graphs of Quadratic Inequalities C,D,F	271
▪ Chapter Summary	277
▪ Chapter Review C,D,F	278
▪ Chapter Test	281

CHAPTER
6

Functions

▪ Chapter Overview	283
6.1 Relations and Functions C,D,F,G	284
6.2 Function Operations C,D,F,G	291
▪ Mixed Review	297
▪ Milestones: Fractals	297
6.3 Inverse Functions C,D,F,G	298
▪ Mid-Chapter Self-Test	305
6.4 Special Functions C,F	306
▪ Using a Graphing Calculator	312
6.5 Transformations of Graphs of Functions C,F	314
◆ Investigating Horizontal and Vertical Shifts	314
▪ Mixed Review	320
6.6 Recursive Functions and Finite Differences D,F	321
6.7 Exploring Data: Measures of Central Tendency D	327
▪ Chapter Summary	333
▪ Chapter Review C,D,F,G	334
▪ Chapter Test	339
▪ Cumulative Review C,D,F	340

C Integrates Coordinate Geometry   **D** Integrates Data Analysis
F Integrates Functions   **G** Integrates Geometry

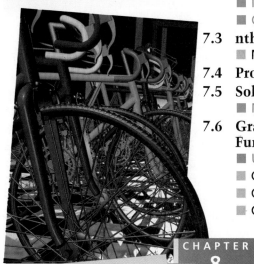

Integrating Data Analysis
In Chapter 7, the "Exploring Data" lesson, as in most of the chapters in Algebra 2, integrates authentic data to model real life and to develop data analysis techniques.

CHAPTER 7 — Powers, Roots, and Radicals

▓	Chapter Overview	345
7.1	**Properties of Exponents** D,G	346
◆	Investigating Operations with Powers	346
7.2	**Exploring Data: Compound Interest and Exponential Growth** C,D,F	352
▓	Mixed Review	359
▓	Career Interview: Contractor	359
7.3	**nth Roots and Rational Exponents** G	360
▓	Mid-Chapter Self-Test	367
7.4	**Properties of Roots and Real Numbers** D,G	368
7.5	**Solving Radical Equations** C,D,F,G	374
▓	Mixed Review	380
7.6	**Graphing Square Root and Cube Root Functions** C,D,F,G	381
▓	Using a Graphing Calculator	388
▓	Chapter Summary	390
▓	Chapter Review C,D,F	391
▓	Chapter Test	395

CHAPTER 8 — Exponential and Logarithmic Functions

Modeling Algebra in Real Life
Algebra 2 uses an abundance of applications to model algebra in real life and to develop critical thinking. Chapter 8 explores the laws of exponents and follows with the study of exponential and logarithmic functions.

▓	Chapter Overview	397
8.1	**Exponenetial Functions** C,D,F	398
◆	Investigating Irrational Exponents	400
8.2	**Logarithmic Functions** C,F	405
▓	Mixed Review	412
▓	Milestones: Logarithms	412
8.3	**Properties of Logarithms** D	413
▓	Mid-Chapter Self-Test	419
8.4	**The Natural Base** e C,D,F	420
8.5	**Natural Logarithms** C,F	428
▓	Using a Graphing Calculator	432
8.6	**Solving Exponential and Logarithmic Equations** D,F	434
▓	Mixed Review	440
8.7	**Exploring Data: Logistics Growth Functions** C,D,F	441
▓	Using a Graphing Calculator	447
▓	Chapter Summary	448
▓	Chapter Review C,D,F	449
▓	Chapter Test	453

CHAPTER 9
Polynomials and Polynomial Functions

■ Chapter Overview		455
9.1	**Operations with Polynomials** D,F,G	456
9.2	**Graphs of Polynomial Functions** C,F,G	463
	■ Using a Graphing Calculator	470
	■ Mixed Review	472
	■ Career Interview: Nursing Home Director	472
9.3	**Factoring Polynomials and Solving Polynomial Equations** D,G	473
	◆ Investigating Factoring Patterns	473
9.4	**Polynomial Division, Factors, and Remainders** C,D,F,G	480
	■ Mid-Chapter Self-Test	487
9.5	**Finding Rational Zeros** C,D,F	488
	■ Mixed Review	493
9.6	**Connections: Zeros, Factors, and Solutions** C,F	494
9.7	**Exploring Data: Measures of Dispersion** D	501
	■ Chapter Summary	508
	■ Chapter Review C,D,F	509
	■ Chapter Test	513
	■ Cumulative Review C,F	514

CHAPTER 10
Rational Functions

■ Overview		517
10.1	**Graphs of Rational Functions** C,D,F	518
	■ Using a Graphing Calculator	524
10.2	**Inverse and Joint Variation** C	526
	■ Mixed Review	532
	■ Milestones: Abel and Galois	532
10.3	**Multiplying and Dividing Rational Expressions** G	533
	◆ Investigating Simplification Strategies	533
	■ Mid-Chapter Self-Test	540
10.4	**Solving Rational Equations** C,D,F	541
10.5	**Addition, Subtraction, and Complex Fractions**	548
	■ Mixed Review	554
10.6	**Exploring Data: The Algebra of Finance** D	555
	■ Chapter Summary	561
	■ Chapter Review C,D,F,G	562
	■ Chapter Test	567

C Integrates Coordinate Geometry   **D** Integrates Data Analysis
F Integrates Functions   **G** Integrates Geometry

Quadratic Relations

■ Chapter Overview	569
11.1 Parabolas C,D,F,G	570
11.2 Circles and Points of Intersection C,F,G	576
◆ Investigating Points of Intersection	577
■ Mixed Review	582
■ Career Interview: Sales Coordinator	582
11.3 Ellipses C,G	583
■ Mid-Chapter Self-Test	589
11.4 Hyperbolas C,D,F,G	590
11.5 Translations of Conics C,D,F	597
■ Mixed Review	603
■ Using a Graphing Calculator	604
11.6 Classifying Conics C,D,F	606
■ Chapter Summary	614
■ Chapter Review C,D,F	615
■ Chapter Test	619

Sequences and Series

■ Chapter Overview	621
12.1 Sequences and Series F,G	622
12.2 Arithmetic Sequences and Series C,F	629
■ Mixed Review	636
■ Milestones: Gödel's Proof	636
12.3 Geometric Sequences and Series D,F,G	637
■ Mid-Chapter Self-Test	644
12.4 Infinite Geometric Series D,F,G	645
12.5 The Binomial Theorem D	651
◆ Investigating Pascal's Triangle	652
■ Mixed Review	657
12.6 Exploring Data: The Algebra of Finance D	658
■ Using a Programmable or Graphing Calculator	664
■ Chapter Summary	666
■ Chapter Review D,F	667
■ Chapter Test	671
■ Cumulative Review C,D,F,G	672

CHAPTER
13

Trigonometric Ratios and Functions

Trigonometry
Chapters 13 and 14 introduce trigonometric functions — with special emphasis on modeling real-life applications using trigonometry.

■ Chapter Overview		677
13.1	**Right Triangle Trigonometry** G,T	678
13.2	**Angles of Rotation and Radian Measure** D,G,T	685
	■ Mixed Review	692
	■ Career Interview: Dermatologist	692
13.3	**Evaluating Trigonometric Functions** C,G,T	693
	■ Using a Graphing Calculator	700
	■ Mid-Chapter Self-Test	702
13.4	**Inverse Trigonometric Functions** D,G,T	703
	◆ Investigating Inverse Trig Functions	703
13.5	**The Law of Sines** D,G,T	709
	■ Mixed Review	715
13.6	**The Law of Cosines** G,T	716
	■ Chapter Summary	722
	■ Chapter Review G,T	723
	■ Chapter Tests	727

CHAPTER
14

Trigonometric Graphs, Identities, and Equations

■ Chapter Overview		729
14.1	**Graphs of Sine and Cosine Functions** D,F,T	730
	◆ Investigating Sine and Cosine Graphs	730
14.2	**Translations and Reflections of Graphs** C,F,T	737
	■ Mixed Review	743
	■ Milestones: Unsolved Problems	743
14.3	**Trigonometric Identities** T	744
	■ Using a Graphing Calculator	750
	■ Mid-Chapter Self-Test	752
14.4	**Solving Trigonometric Equations** D,F,G,T	753
14.5	**Sum and Difference Formulas** F,T	760
	■ Mixed Review	765
14.6	**Double- and Half-Angle Formulas** C,F,T	766
	■ Chapter Summary	772
	■ Chapter Review C,F,T	773
	■ Chapter Test	777
	■ Cumulative Review C,G,T	778

C Integrates Coordinate Geometry   **D** Integrates Data Analysis
F Integrates Functions   **G** Integrates Geometry   **T** Integrates Trigonometry

Probability Chapter 15 explores the concepts of probability and statistics.

CHAPTER 15 Probability and Statistics

■ Chapter Overview		781
15.1 Introduction to Probability D,G		782
15.2 Counting Methods: Permutations D,G		788
■ Mixed Review		795
■ Career Interview: Illustrator		795
15.3 Counting Methods: Combinations D,G		796
■ Using a Graphing Calculator		802
■ Mid-Chapter Self-Test		804
15.4 Probability, Unions, and Intersections D		805
15.5 Independent Events D		811
◆ Investigating Random Numbers		811
■ Mixed Review		816
15.6 Expected Value D,G		817
■ Chapter Summary		823
■ Chapter Review D,G		824
■ Chapter Test		828

Properties, Models, Transformations, Formulas	830
Glossary	836
Student Handbook	846
Technology Appendix	856
Selected Answers	868
Index	931
Acknowledgments	942

Interactive Technology The following program is available for use with this textbook:

■ Larson Interactive Real-Life Investigations for Algebra 2
available on CD-ROM or diskette (Macintosh or Windows)

Chapter 1	Animal Voices and Hearing	**Chapter 2**	Working Men and Women
Chapter 3	Retail Sales of Companies	**Chapter 4**	Cryptograms
Chapter 5	Fractals	**Chapter 6**	Communication
Chapter 7	Growth of Animals	**Chapter 8**	Half-Life and Radioactivity
Chapter 9	Volume of a Box	**Chapter 10**	Air Resistance and Parachutes
Chapter 11	Comets	**Chapter 12**	Banking and Personal Finance
Chapter 13	Skyscrapers	**Chapter 14**	Meteorology
Chapter 15	Genes		

Review of Basic Algebra

LESSONS

1.1 Real Numbers and
Number Operations
▪ 2

1.2 Algebraic Expressions
and Models ▪ 9

1.3 Solving Linear
Equations ▪ 18

1.4 Problem-Solving
Strategies ▪ 24

1.5 Literal Equations and
Formulas ▪ 31

1.6 Solving Linear
Inequalities ▪ 37

1.7 Solving Absolute
Value Equations and
Inequalities ▪ 44

1.8 Exploring Data:
Tables and Graphs
▪ 50

*The National Aeronautics and
Space Administration (NASA) is
working on a replacement for
the space shuttle. The current
shuttle is propelled into orbit by
expensive rockets that are used
only once. NASA is designing a
shuttle system whose rockets
could be reused.*

Temperature Conversions

When the space shuttle leaves its orbit and enters Earth's atmosphere, the air friction produces tremendous heat. Temperatures on the wings can reach 2750°F. To write degrees Fahrenheit as degrees Celsius, you can use the formula $C = \frac{5}{9}(F - 32)$.

$$C = \frac{5}{9}(2750 - 32) = 1510°$$

To write from degrees Celsius as degrees Fahrenheit, use the formula $F = \frac{9}{5}C + 32$.

$$F = \frac{9}{5}(1510) + 32 = 2750°$$

1.1

Real Numbers and Number Operations

What you should learn:

Goal 1 How to use the real number line to graph and order real numbers

Goal 2 How to use the properties of real numbers

Why you should learn it:

An understanding of real numbers and their properties is the basic building block to all of mathematics.

Goal 1   Using the Real Number Line

The numbers used in algebra are **real numbers.** They can be pictured as points on a horizontal line called the **real number line.** The point labeled *0* is the **origin.** Points to the left of 0 represent **negative numbers,** and points to the right of 0 represent **positive numbers.** Zero is neither positive nor negative.

The scale marks on a number line are equally spaced and represent **integers.** An integer is either negative, zero, or positive.

$$\{..., -3, -2, -1, 0, 1, 2, 3, ...\} \quad \textit{Integers}$$

Negative   Zero Positive

Enclosing numbers in braces { } indicates that they form a **set.** The three dots on each side indicate that the list continues in each direction without end. Here are some other important **subsets** of real numbers.

Whole Numbers: 0, 1, 2, 3, . . .

Rational Numbers: Numbers such as $\frac{1}{2}$ and $-\frac{3}{1}$ that can be written as the ratio of two integers

Irrational Numbers: Real numbers such as $\sqrt{2}$ or π, that are not rational

The point on a number line that corresponds to a number is its **graph.** Graphing the number is called **plotting** the point.

Example 1   *Graphing Numbers on a Number Line*

Sketch the graph of the real numbers $-\frac{2}{3}$, $\sqrt{2}$, and $\frac{5}{2}$.

Solution   To begin, write each number in decimal form.

$$-\frac{2}{3} \approx -0.67 \qquad \sqrt{2} \approx 1.41 \qquad \frac{5}{2} = 2.5$$

The real number line can be used to order real numbers.

2 is less than 5   −1 is greater than −4

The **inequality symbols** $<$, $\leq$, $>$, and $\geq$ can be used to show the order of two numbers.

Verbal Statement	Inequality	Number Line Interpretation
2 is *less* than 5.	$2 < 5$	2 is to the *left* of 5.
−1 is *greater* than −4.	$-1 > -4$	−1 is to the *right* of −4.

Both statements, $2 < 5$ and $5 > 2$, give the same information.

Topography

Draw a Diagram

Example 2   *Ordering Real Numbers*

The lowest elevation in Mexico is −33 feet (33 feet below sea level) near Mexicali. The highest elevation is 18,701 feet at Orizaba. Order the following locations in *increasing* order according to their elevations.

Cancún (20)	Durango (6189)	Guadalajara (505)
La Paz (43)	Mexicali (−33)	Morelia (6386)
Monterrey (1765)	Orizaba (18,701)	Torreón (3740)

Solution   Begin by plotting the elevations on a number line.

From the number line, you can see that the order is

Mexicali (−33)	Cancún (20)	La Paz (43)
Guadalajara (505)	Monterrey (1765)	Torreón (3740)
Durango (6189)	Morelia (6386)	Orizaba (18,701)

■

Two points on a number line that are the same distance from the origin but are on opposite sides of the origin are **opposites.** For instance, −4 and 4 are opposites. Zero is a special case and is its own opposite. In general, the opposite of a is $-a$ and the opposite of $-a$ is $-(-a) = a$.

1. If a is positive, then its opposite, $-a$, is negative.
2. The opposite of 0 is 0.
3. If a is negative, then its opposite, $-a$, is positive.

Goal 2 Using Properties of Real Numbers

Four operations with real numbers are addition, subtraction, multiplication, and division. *Addition* and *multiplication* are the basic operations and are used to define the other two. Their properties are listed below.

Properties of Addition and Multiplication

Let a, b, and c be any real numbers.

Name of Property	Addition Properties	Multiplication Properties
1. Closure	$a + b$ is a real number.	ab is a real number.
2. Commutative	$a + b = b + a$	$ab = ba$
3. Associative	$(a + b) + c = a + (b + c)$	$(ab)c = a(bc)$
4. Identity	$a + 0 = a, 0 + a = a$	$a \cdot 1 = a, 1 \cdot a = a$
5. Inverse	$a + (-a) = 0$	$a \cdot \frac{1}{a} = 1, a \neq 0$

Properties Relating Addition and Multiplication

6. **Left Distributive Property** $a(b + c) = ab + ac$
   Right Distributive Property $(a + b)c = ac + bc$

The **reciprocal** of a is $\frac{1}{a}$, provided a is not zero. Zero has no reciprocal.

Subtraction is defined as *adding the opposite,*

$$a - b = a + (-b) \qquad \textit{Definition of subtraction}$$

and *division* is defined as *multiplying by the reciprocal.*

$$\frac{a}{b} = a \cdot \frac{1}{b} \qquad \textit{Definition of division}$$

Example 3   *Operations with Real Numbers*

a. The **sum** of -12 and 14 is

$$-12 + 14 = 2.$$

b. The **difference** of 5 and -13 is

$$5 - (-13) = 5 + 13 = 18.$$

c. The **product** of -3 and -11 is

$$(-3)(-11) = 33.$$

d. The **quotient** of -42 and 14 is

$$\frac{-42}{14} = -3.$$ ∎

This "wind farm" near Palm Springs, California, consists of 4000 windmills that generate electricity. The states with the greatest wind power potential are shown in the table below.

Real Life
Conservation

States with the Greatest Wind Power Potential

(Percents represent potential of total electrical use in the United States.)

North Dakota	11%
Texas	11%
Kansas	10%
Montana	9%
South Dakota	9%
Nebraska	8%
Oklahoma	7%
Minnesota	7%
Wyoming	6%
Iowa	5%
Colorado	4%
New Mexico	4%

Example 4   *Operations with Real Numbers*

One barrel of oil can generate 545 kilowatt-hours of electricity. In 1990, the 17,000 windmills in California could generate up to 1.5 million kilowatt-hours per hour. At peak capacity, how many barrels of oil could be saved each hour? Operating at 75% of peak efficiency, how many barrels of oil could be saved in a year? *(Source: U.S. Department of Energy)*

Solution

$$\text{Barrels of oil} = \frac{\text{Kilowatt-hours per hour (from the wind)}}{545 \text{ kilowatt-hours per hour, per barrel}}$$

$$= \frac{1,500,000}{545}, \text{ or about 2752 barrels per hour}$$

Operating at 75% of peak capacity for a year, the savings would be the following.

$$(0.75)\left(\frac{2752 \text{ barrels}}{\text{hour}}\right)\left(\frac{24 \text{ hours}}{\text{day}}\right)\left(\frac{365 \text{ days}}{\text{year}}\right) \approx \frac{18 \times 10^6 \text{ barrels}}{\text{year}} \blacksquare$$

Communicating about ALGEBRA

▶ SHARING IDEAS about the Lesson

A. Four million 500-kilowatt windmills in the states listed in the table could generate 91% of the total electrical use. If this were done, how many windmills would be in North Dakota? (*Hint:* It is not 11% of 4 million.)

B. How many barrels of oil would be saved each hour if 4 million 500-kilowatt windmills were operating at 75% capacity?

EXERCISES

Guided Practice

▶ **CRITICAL THINKING about the Lesson**

1. Is zero a positive number, a negative number, or neither? Is zero an integer?

2. Give examples of real numbers that are whole numbers, integers, rational numbers, and irrational numbers.

3. Which of the following is *false?* Explain.
  a. Every whole number is an integer.
  b. Every integer is a rational number.
  c. No integer is an irrational number.
  d. Every rational number is an integer.

4. Leon is 16 and Neesha is 18. Which of the following is *false?*
Explain.
  a. (Leon's age) < (Neesha's age)
  b. (Neesha's age) ≤ (Neesha's age)
  c. (Neesha's age) ≥ (Leon's age)
  d. (Leon's age) > (Leon's age)

5. Which of the following "associative properties" are true? Explain
your answer.
  a. *Addition:* $(a + b) + c = a + (b + c)$
  b. *Subtraction:* $(a - b) - c = a - (b - c)$
  c. *Multiplication:* $(a \cdot b) \cdot c = a \cdot (b \cdot c)$
  d. *Division:* $(a \div b) \div c = a \div (b \div c)$

6. *Factor Analysis*   Find the unit of measure for the product. Explain
your reasoning.
$$\left(\frac{3 \text{ pounds}}{1 \text{ square inch}}\right)\left(\frac{144 \text{ square inches}}{1 \text{ square foot}}\right)\left(\frac{1 \text{ ton}}{2000 \text{ pounds}}\right)\left(\frac{25 \text{ dollars}}{1 \text{ ton}}\right)$$

Independent Practice

**In Exercises 7–12, plot the numbers on the real number line. Then decide
which is greater.**

7. $\frac{1}{2}$ and -3
8. 5 and $\frac{2}{3}$
9. $\sqrt{3}$ and 1
10. -6 and $\sqrt{2}$
11. $-\frac{7}{3}$ and $\sqrt{5}$
12. 0 and $-\sqrt{6}$

In Exercises 13–16, write the numbers in decreasing order.

13. $1, -4, -\sqrt{3}, 9, \frac{1}{3}$
14. $\sqrt{13}, \frac{5}{2}, -\frac{7}{16}, 1, 10$
15. $-\frac{5}{2}, -\sqrt{5}, 4, 0, \frac{3}{2}$
16. $-20, -0.5, -\sqrt{6}, 4.75, \frac{1}{3}$

In Exercises 17–24, state the property that is illustrated.

17. $(2 \cdot 4) \cdot 9 = 2(4 \cdot 9)$
18. $6 \cdot 5 = 5 \cdot 6$
19. $3 + 1 = 1 + 3$
20. $7 \cdot \frac{1}{7} = 1$
21. $4 + (-4) = 0$
22. $(8 + 7) + 2 = 8 + (7 + 2)$
23. $2(3 + 12) = 2 \cdot 3 + 2 \cdot 12$
24. $9(1) = 9$

25. What is the sum of 64 and -5?

26. What is the sum of -14 and -7?

27. What is the difference of -18 and 6?

28. What is the difference of 4 and -7?

29. What is the product of 12 and 2?

30. What is the product of -16 and 3?

31. What is the quotient of 3 and $\frac{1}{2}$?

32. What is the quotient of 16 and $\frac{4}{3}$?

33. *Football Coaches* In 1990, the ten National Football League coaches with the most wins (in regular season games through 1990) are listed in alphabetical order. Order the coaches (in decreasing order) according to the number of wins. Who is the coach in the picture?

This NFL coach has had the most wins in regular season games.

Coach	Wins	Coach	Wins
Paul Brown	166	Tom Landry	250
Bud Grant	158	Chuck Noll	177
George Halas	319	Steve Owen	151
Chuck Knox	155	Don Shula	269
Earl Lambeau	226	Hank Stram	131

34. *Low Temperatures of Cities* The lowest temperatures ever recorded in various cities are listed below. Order the cities in increasing order by their lowest temperatures.

City	Low Temp.	City	Low Temp.
Baltimore, MD	$-7°F$	Honolulu, HI	$53°F$
Cincinnati, OH	$-25°F$	Indianapolis, IN	$-22°F$
Columbia, SC	$-1°F$	Jackson, MS	$2°F$
Great Falls, MT	$-43°F$	Phoenix, AZ	$17°F$
Hartford, CT	$-26°F$	Seattle, WA	$0°F$

35. *A Close Call* The temperature of air drops about 3°F for each 1000-foot increase in altitude. About how much had the temperature dropped when Glaisher and Coxwell reached an altitude of 25,000 feet? If the temperature at sea level was 60°F, what was the temperature at 25,000 feet?

In September 1862, James Glaisher, a meteorologist, and Henry Coxwell, a professional balloonist, went up in their hot-air balloon much higher than they had expected. At 25,000 feet, Glaisher became unconscious from lack of oxygen. To get the balloon to descend, Coxwell climbed up the rigging above the basket, but when he grasped the ice-cold hoop, his hands became too numb to pull the valve cord. Finally, he was able to pull the cord with his teeth. The balloon then began to descend, and both men made it safely back to Earth.

36. *Ouch!*   The white-headed woodpecker's skull is specially designed to protect its brain from the force of continual pecking. This woodpecker pecks at a rate of 18 pecks per second. If you heard one pecking on a tree for 4 seconds, then 3 seconds, then 2 seconds, and then 4 seconds, how many times did it peck the tree? Show how the Distributive Property can be used to find the answer.

Integrated Review

In Exercises 37–40, decide whether the real number is rational or irrational.

37. 0.25 **38.** $-\sqrt{3}$ **39.** $\sqrt{7}$ **40.** 13

In Exercises 41–44, place the correct inequality symbol between the numbers.

41. $-2 \boxed{?} 1$ **42.** $2 \boxed{?} \sqrt{6}$ **43.** $3 \boxed{?} \sqrt{10}$ **44.** $-5 \boxed{?} -\frac{7}{2}$

In Exercises 45–48, state the opposite of the number.

45. 14 **46.** -6 **47.** $-\sqrt{5}$ **48.** 19.9

In Exercises 49–52, state the reciprocal of the number.

49. -31 **50.** $\frac{10}{11}$ **51.** $-\frac{5}{7}$ **52.** 14

In Exercises 53 and 54, find the product and its unit of measure.

53. $\left(\dfrac{50 \text{ miles}}{1 \text{ hour}}\right)\left(\dfrac{5280 \text{ feet}}{1 \text{ mile}}\right)\left(\dfrac{1 \text{ hour}}{3600 \text{ seconds}}\right)$

54. $\left(\dfrac{7 \text{ dollars}}{1 \text{ hour}}\right)\left(\dfrac{40 \text{ hours}}{1 \text{ week}}\right)\left(\dfrac{52 \text{ weeks}}{1 \text{ year}}\right)$

Exploration and Extension

UPC Codes   **In Exercises 55 and 56, use the following information.**

Packaged products sold in the United States have a Universal Product Code (UPC) or bar code as shown at the right. The following algorithm is used on the first eleven digits and the result should equal the twelfth digit, called the check digit.

First Digit · 0 ‖25215‖04658‖ 2 · Check Digit

Using the algorithm on this UPC produces
$(0 + 5 + 1 + 0 + 6 + 8)(3) + (2 + 2 + 5 + 4 + 5) = 78$.
The next highest multiple of 10 is 80, so $80 - 78 = 2$,
which is the check digit.

- Add the odd-numbered positions together. Multiply by 3.
- Add the even-numbered positions together.
- Add the results of steps 1 and 2.
- Subtract the result of step 3 from the next highest multiple of 10.

55. Does a UPC of 0 76737 20012 9 check? Explain.

56. Does a UPC of 0 41800 48700 3 check? Explain.

1.2 Algebraic Expressions and Models

What you should learn:

Goal 1 How to evaluate an algebraic expression

Goal 2 How to use algebraic expressions as models of real-life situations

Why you should learn it:

You can model many real-life situations with algebraic expressions, such as the average cost of children's books for the last ten years.

Real Life
Children's Books

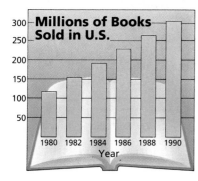

Goal 1 Evaluating Algebraic Expressions

A **variable** is a letter that is used to represent one or more numbers. Any number used to replace a variable is the **value of the variable.** An **algebraic expression** is a collection of numbers, variables, operations, and grouping symbols.

When the variables in an algebraic expression are replaced by numbers, you are **evaluating** the expression. The resulting number is called the **value of the expression.** To evaluate a variable expression, use the following *flowchart*.

| Write algebraic expression. | $\longrightarrow$ | Substitute values of variables. | $\longrightarrow$ | Simplify. |

The parts of an expression that form a sum, a product, or a quotient have special names.

Sum: $4x$ and 3 are the **terms** of $4x + 3$.
Product: 4 and x are the **factors** of $4x$.
Quotient: $3x$ is the **numerator** and 8 is the **denominator** of the fraction $\frac{3x}{8}$.

Example 1 shows how an algebraic expression can be used as a **model** of a real-life situation.

Example 1 *Algebraic Expressions as Models*

For 1980 through 1990, the number, B (in millions), of children's books that were sold in the United States can be modeled by $B = 18.7t + 119$ where $t = 0$ represents 1980. Use the model to approximate the number of children's books sold in 1985. *(Source: Book Industry Times)*

Solution If $t = 0$ represents 1980, then $t = 5$ represents 1985.

$B = 18.7t + 119$ *Model for number of books sold*

$B = 18.7(5) + 119$ *Substitute 5 for t.*

$B = 212.5$ *Simplify.*

About 212.5 million children's books were sold in 1985. ■

Exponents are used to represent repeated factors in multiplication. For instance, the expression 2^5 represents the number that you obtain when 2 is used as a factor 5 times.

$$2^5 = \underbrace{2 \cdot 2 \cdot 2 \cdot 2 \cdot 2}_{\text{5 factors of 2}}$$

This expression is read as "2 to the 5th power." The number 2 is the **base,** and the number 5 is the **exponent.** The exponent represents the number of times the base is used as a factor. For *a number to the first power,* usually the exponent 1 is not written. For instance, 2^1 is written simply as 2.

An exponent applies only to the number, variable, or expression that is immediately to its left. In the expression $3x^4$, the base is x, not $3x$. In the expression $(3x)^4$, the base is $3x$.

An established **order of operations** helps avoid confusion when simplifying numerical expressions.

Order of Operations

1. First, do operations that occur within grouping symbols using Rules 2–4.
2. Next, evaluate powers.
3. Then do multiplications and divisions from left to right.
4. Finally, do additions and subtractions from left to right.

Example 2   *Evaluating Expressions Using Order of Operations*

a. $-4 + 2(-2 + 5)^2 = -4 + 2(3)^2$ *Add within parentheses.*

$= -4 + 2(9)$ *Evaluate the power.*

$= -4 + 18$ *Multiply.*

$= 14$ *Add.*

b. $(-4 + 2)(-2 + 5)^2 = (-2)(3)^2$ *Add within parentheses.*

$= (-2)(9)$ *Evaluate the power.*

$= -18$ *Multiply.*

c. $5 - 12 \div 3 - 7 = 5 - 4 - 7$ *Divide first.*

$= -6$ *Subtract from left to right.* ∎

Over one half of the adults in the United States read at least one book for enjoyment each year. Reading books to children increases the likelihood that the children will read for enjoyment as adults. (Source: National Endowment for the Arts)

Real Life
Children's Books

Goal 2 Writing Algebraic Expressions as Models

Example 3 *Creating a Real-Life Model*

For 1980 through 1990, the average price, *p*, of a children's book can be modeled by $p = 0.2t + 3.3$ where $t = 0$ represents 1980. Use this model *and* the model given in Example 1 to find a model for the total sales (in millions of dollars) from children's books for 1980 through 1990. Then use the model to find the total sales in 1988.

Solution   Let *S* represent yearly sales in millions of dollars.

| Total yearly sales | = | Number sold each year | · | Average price per book each year |

$$S = (18.7t + 119)(0.2t + 3.3)$$

To find the total sales in 1988, substitute 8 for *t* in this model.

$S = (18.7t + 119)(0.2t + 3.3)$ *Total sales model*

$\quad = (18.7 \cdot 8 + 119)(0.2 \cdot 8 + 3.3)$ *Substitute 8 for t.*

$\quad = (268.6)(4.9), \text{ or } 1316.14$ *Simplify.*

The total sales of children's books in 1988 was about $1316 million (or about $1.3 billion). ∎

Communicating about ALGEBRA

▶ **SHARING IDEAS about the Lesson**

Use a Model   Use the model in Example 3 to construct a bar graph showing the total sales from children's books (in millions of dollars) for 1980 through 1990.

EXERCISES

▶ **CRITICAL THINKING about the Lesson**

1. Give an example of an algebraic expression for which the value of the expression is positive regardless of the value of the variable.
2. Describe the difference between the terms of an expression and the factors of an expression.
3. Identify the terms of $6x^3 - 17x + 5$.
4. Identify the factors of $10xy$.
5. Write a verbal description of the expression $(x^3 + 1)^2$.
6. Explain how the Order of Operations is used to evaluate $3 - 8^2 \div 4 + 1$.

Independent Practice

In Exercises 7–16, evaluate the expression.

7. $x - 5$ when $x = 3$
8. $7y + 2$ when $y = 5$
9. $50a - 2b + 6$ when $a = 2$ and $b = 20$
10. $16p - 32q + 5$ when $p = 2$ and $q = 1$
11. $m + 2(m - 5)$ when $m = 25$
12. $60n(2 - n)$ when $n = 3$
13. $2x \div (13 - 9y)$ when $x = 14$ and $y = \frac{1}{3}$
14. $(5 + y) \div (6x)$ when $x = 10$ and $y = 7$
15. $(20a - 1) \div b$ when $a = 2$ and $b = 13$
16. $(60b \div 5) + c$ when $b = \frac{1}{2}$ and $c = 11$

In Exercises 17–20, evaluate $12x \div (x - 1)$ for the given value of x.

17. $x = 7$
18. $x = 0$
19. $x = 3$
20. $x = 10$

In Exercises 21–24, use a calculator to evaluate the expression. If necessary, round your result to two decimal places.

21. $65.1z - 0.4$ when $z = 1.2$
22. $5.7 - 26.3z$ when $z = 80.0$
23. $15(0.5p + q)$ when $p = 31.5$ and $q = 0.8$
24. $\dfrac{2.01p - q}{16.87q}$ when $p = 7.7$ and $q = 7.1$

In Exercises 25–30, write the expression using exponents.

25. y squared
26. seven cubed
27. x to the third power
28. three to the rth power
29. $z \cdot z \cdot z \cdot z \cdot z \cdot z$
30. $16 \cdot 16 \cdot 16 \cdot 16$

In Exercises 31–36, evaluate the expression.

31. s^2 when $s = 12$
32. m^5 when $m = 2$
33. $(2a)^2 + 4$ when $a = 3$
34. $(4r)^3 + 10$ when $r = \frac{1}{2}$
35. $11(b + d)^2$ when $b = 1$ and $d = 9$
36. $x^2 + y^2$ when $x = 5$ and $y = 6$

In Exercises 37–44, evaluate the expression.

37. $6 - 3 + 1$ **38.** $10 + 12 - 24$ **39.** $20 \div 5 + 5 \cdot 4$ **40.** $13 \cdot 4 - 2$

41. $1 + 7 \cdot 4 - 5$ **42.** $23 - 3 \cdot 6 \div 9$ **43.** $4 - (6 \cdot 2)^2 + 2$ **44.** $2 \cdot (13 - 9) \div 6$

Geometry **In Exercises 45–48, find an expression for the area of the figure. Then evaluate for the given value(s) of the variable(s).**

45. $n = 80$ **46.** $a = 5, b = 4$ **47.** $x = 10, y = 3$ **48.** $x = 9$

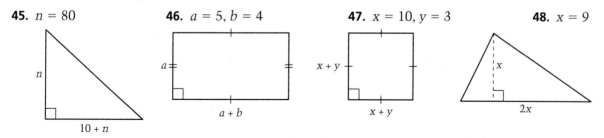

Average Salaries **In Exercises 49–52, use the following information.**

For 1980 through 1994, the average salary, A (in 1000's of dollars), of assistant principals at public high schools can be modeled by

$A = 2.2t + 25$

where $t = 0$ represents 1980. During the same years, the average salary, P, (in 1000's of dollars), of principals at public high schools followed the model

$P = 2.6t + 29.$

49. Approximate a high school assistant principal's salary in 1992.

50. Approximate a high school principal's salary in 1992.

51. Write a model that gives the ratio of A to P.

52. Evaluate the model found in Exercise 51 when $t = 0$ and $t = 4$. Describe the results in words.

(Source: Educational Research Service)

Population of Hawaii **In Exercises 53 and 54, use the following information.**

For 1980 through 1994, the population, P (in 1000's), of Hawaii can be modeled by

$P = 15.5(t + 62)$

where $t = 0$ represents 1980. *(Source: U.S. Bureau of the Census)*

53. What was the population in 1993?

54. What was the population increase from 1980 to 1993?

Integrated Review

In Exercises 55–60, use a calculator to perform the given operations. If necessary, round your answers to two decimal places.

55. $19.5 \div 6.4$

56. $210 \cdot 3.7$

57. $65.16 \cdot 0.27$

58. $0.14 \div 10.8$

59. $8.05 \div 0.001 + 2$

60. $10.61 \cdot 5 - 2.3$

Geometry **In Exercises 61–63, find the volume of the solid.**

61. Prism $V = lwh$

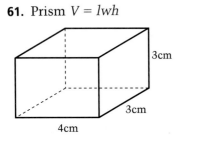
3cm
3cm
4cm

62. Cone $V = \frac{1}{3}\pi r^2 h$

5in.
2in.

63. Sphere $V = \frac{4}{3}\pi r^3$

3ft

64. *Molecular Man* During a break between experiments at the IBM Almaden Research Center in San Jose, California, scientist Peter Zeppenfeld made a tiny figure out of 28 molecules. His "Molecular Man" is only 200 billionths of an inch tall and 100 billionths of an inch from hand to hand. Express these dimensions in scientific notation. How many Molecular Men could stand side by side within one inch?

To create "Molecular Man," Zeppenfeld sprayed carbon monoxide gas onto a platinum surface cooled to −269°C. He then probed 28 carbon monoxide molecules, one at a time, into position. (Source: Popular Science)

65. *College Entrance Exam Sample* If on a certain day only 28 of 32 students were present for a gym class, what percent of the class was absent?
a. 4%   **b.** 12.5%   **c.** 25%   **d.** 28%   **e.** 87.5%

66. *College Entrance Exam Sample* Let $\boxed{x}$ represent the number of different pairs of positive integers whose product is x. For example, $\boxed{16} = 3$ because there are 3 different pairs of positive integers whose product is 16: 16 × 1, 8 × 2, and 4 × 4. What does $\boxed{36}$ equal?
a. 5   **b.** 6   **c.** 8   **d.** 10   **e.** 12

Exploration and Extension

67. *Going from Room to Room* The floor plan at the right shows five rooms. Some of the rooms have four doors and some have five doors. Is it possible to find an (unbroken) path through each door without going through any door twice? Explain your answer.

1. Multiply: $\left(\frac{1}{2}\right)\left(\frac{2}{3}\right)\left(\frac{3}{4}\right)$.

2. Add: $\frac{1}{2} + \frac{1}{3}$.

3. Subtract: $\frac{1}{2} - \frac{1}{3}$.

4. Divide: $\frac{1}{2} \div \frac{1}{3}$.

5. What number is 14% of 35?

6. 17.6 is what percent of 80?

7. Evaluate $2x^2 - 3x$ when $x = -1$. **(1.2)***

8. Evaluate $2x^2 \div 3x$ when $x = -1$. **(1.2)**

9. Multiply: $(1.25 \times 10^2)(2.5 \times 10^{-1})$.

10. Divide: $(1.25 \times 10^2) \div (2.5 \times 10^{-1})$.

11. Evaluate $-2x^3$ when $x = -2$. **(1.2)**

12. Evaluate $\left(\frac{1}{5}\right)^n$ when $n = 4$. **(1.2)**

13. Simplify: $4 + 6 \div 2 - 1$.

14. Simplify: $-2 \cdot 4 - 2$. **(1.2)**

15. Write in increasing order: $-2, 3, 0, -3$. **(1.1)**

16. Write in decreasing order: $-\frac{1}{2}, -\frac{1}{4}, -\frac{1}{3}, -\frac{1}{5}$. **(1.1)**

17. Is -2 a solution of $4x^2 + 16 = 0$?

18. Is 2 a solution of $x^1 - 1 = 0$?

19. Write in exponential form: $2 \cdot 2 \cdot x \cdot x \cdot x$. **(1.2)**

20. Simplify: $-3(x + 4) + 5(x - 2)$. **(1.2)**

*Refers to lesson in which skill was taught. Exercises without lesson references review skills taught in previous mathematics courses.

Career Interview

Architect

Heidi Johnson is an architect who designs buildings and the space in and around them. Her designs and drawings can range from an entire town square to the detail of a doorknob or hinge.

Q: *What led you into this career?*

A: Before becoming an architect, I was teaching special needs students. The classrooms were often pretty depressing. That is how my interest in space and its impact on people developed. I wanted to design buildings and space that uplift or educate people rather than hinder them.

Q: *Does having a math background help you on the job?*

A: Yes, it helps. I work with different scales to measure and draw both interior and exterior spaces. Architectural design has a lot of mathematical applications.

Q: *What have you learned on the job?*

A: I have learned that culture often impacts the definition of space relationship. For example, in our culture a door has a specific size in relation to a room. In another country, however, that relationship may be very different. So it is necessary for us to be culturally sensitive when working on international projects.

This book includes many examples and exercises that are best done with a calculator. Most of these can be done with a scientific calculator *or* a graphing calculator. (Some require a graphing calculator.) Occasionally sample keystrokes for calculations will be given. These keystroke sequences, however, may not agree precisely with the steps required by *your* calculator. So be sure you are familiar with your own calculator.

Example 1   Evaluating Expressions on a Calculator

Expression	Keystrokes	Display	
a. $-4 - 5$	4 [+/−] [−] 5 [=]	−9	Scientific
$-4 - 5$	[(−)] 4 [−] 5 [ENTER]	−9	Graphing
b. $-3^2 + 4$	3 [x^2] [+/−] [+] 4 [=]	−5	Scientific
$-3^2 + 4$	[(−)] 3 [x^2] [+] 4 [ENTER]	−5	Graphing
c. $(-3)^2 + 4$	[(] 3 [+/−] [)] [x^2] [+] 4 [=]	13	Scientific
$(-3)^2 + 4$	[(] [(−)] 3 [)] [x^2] [+] 4 [ENTER]	13	Graphing ∎

On a scientific calculator, notice the difference between the change sign key [+/−] and the subtraction key [−]. On a graphing calculator, the negation key [(−)] and the subtraction key [−] may not perform the same operations.

Example 2   Evaluating Expressions on a Calculator

Expression	Keystrokes	Display	
a. $24 \div 2^3$	24 [÷] 2 [y^x] 3 [=]	3	Scientific
$24 \div 2^3$	24 [÷] 2 [∧] 3 [ENTER]	3	Graphing
b. $(24 \div 2)^3$	[(] 24 [÷] 2 [)] [y^x] 3 [=]	1728	Scientific
$(24 \div 2)^3$	[(] 24 [÷] 2 [)] [∧] 3 [ENTER]	1728	Graphing
c. $\dfrac{5}{4 + 3 \cdot 2}$	5 [÷] [(] [(] 4 [+] 3 [×] 2 [)] [)] [=]	0.5	Scientific
$\dfrac{5}{4 + 3 \cdot 2}$	5 [÷] [(] [(] 4 [+] 3 [×] 2 [)] [)] [ENTER]	0.5	Graphing ∎

Some scientific and most graphing calculators are programmable. This means that you can write and store a program or algorithm in the calculator, such as a program that would calculate the volume of a right circular cylinder. The formula for the volume is

$$V = \pi r^2 h$$

where r is the radius and h is the height.

Keystroke instructions for programming this formula into a *TI-82*, Casio *fx-9700GE*, and Sharp *EL-9300C* are listed on page 856.

If you use one of these programs to find the volume of the cylinder shown at the right, you should get a volume of about 226.2 cubic units, as shown below.

```
prgmVOLUME
ENTER RADIUS
?3
ENTER HEIGHT
?8
THE VOLUME IS
          226.1946711
```

Exercises

In Exercises 1–4, write an expression that corresponds to the calculator keystrokes.

1. $(\,(-)\, 4 \,)\, \wedge\, 2$ [ENTER]

2. $7 \div (\,(\, (-)\, 3 - 5 \,)$ [ENTER]

3. $(\,1 + 4 \,)\, \wedge\, (-)\, 1$ [ENTER]

4. $3 \times (\,5 - 2 \,)$ [ENTER]

In Exercises 5–12, use a calculator to evaluate the expression. Round the result to three decimal places.

5. $3(5.3 - 4.1^2)^2$

6. $(-3.7 - 5.2)^3$

7. $(0.21 + 5.23)^{-1}$

8. $\frac{4}{3}\pi(4^2)$

9. $2075(1 + 0.65)^4$

10. $\frac{9.2 - 4.5}{0.6}$

11. $\frac{3.4}{-7.2 - 8.4}$

12. $\frac{1 + 3(4^2)}{7.25}$

13. Enter a program similar to those listed on page 856 on a graphing calculator. (See the calculator's manual to learn how to enter the program.) Then use the program to find the volume of several cylinders, including the one shown below.

14. Write a graphing calculator program that will evaluate the volume of a rectangular prism. Then use the program to find the volume of several prisms, including the one shown below.

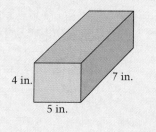

1.3

Solving Linear Equations

What you should learn:

Goal 1 How to solve a linear equation

Goal 2 How to use linear equations to answer questions about real-life situations

Why you should learn it:

You can model many real-life situations with linear equations, such as your weekly pay, when you are working for an hourly wage.

Goal 1 Solving a Linear Equation

An **equation** is a statement that two expressions are equal. A **linear equation** in x is an equation in which x appears to the first power. A number is a **solution** of an equation if the statement is true when the number is substituted for the variable. For instance, 9 is a solution of the linear equation

$$2x - 5 = 13$$

because $2(9) - 5 = 13$ is a true statement. Two equations are **equivalent** if they have the same solutions. For instance, the equations $x - 4 = 1$ and $x = 5$ are equivalent because both have the number 5 as their only solution. The following transformations produce equivalent equations and can be used to **solve an equation.**

Transformations That Produce Equivalent Equations

1. *Add* the same number to both sides.
2. *Subtract* the same number from both sides.
3. *Multiply* both sides by the same nonzero number.
4. *Divide* both sides by the same nonzero number.
5. *Simplify* one or both sides.
6. *Interchange* the two sides.

Example 1 *Solving a Linear Equation*

Solve $\frac{2}{5}x + 7 = 13$.

Solution This solution can be found by isolating the variable on one side of the equation.

$$\frac{2}{5}x + 7 = 13 \qquad \textit{Rewrite original equation.}$$

$$\frac{2}{5}x = 6 \qquad \textit{Subtract 7 from both sides.}$$

$$x = \frac{5}{2}(6) \qquad \textit{Multiply both sides by } \frac{5}{2}.$$

$$x = 15 \qquad \textit{The solution is 15.}$$

Check this by substituting 15 into the original equation.   ■

Example 2 — Solving a Linear Equation

Solve $8x + 15 = -4x + 51$.

Solution

$$8x + 15 = -4x + 51 \qquad \text{\textit{Rewrite original equation.}}$$
$$12x + 15 = 51 \qquad \text{\textit{Add 4x to both sides.}}$$
$$12x = 36 \qquad \text{\textit{Subtract 15 from both sides.}}$$
$$x = 3 \qquad \text{\textit{Divide both sides by 12.}}$$

Check: You can check the solution by substituting 3 for x in the original equation.

$$8x + 15 = -4x + 51 \qquad \text{\textit{Rewrite original equation.}}$$
$$8(3) + 15 \overset{?}{=} -4(3) + 51 \qquad \text{\textit{Substitute 3 for x.}}$$
$$39 = 39 \qquad \text{\textit{The solution checks.}} \quad \blacksquare$$

Example 3 — Solving a Linear Equation

Solve $15(1 - x) = -3(-x - 2)$.

Solution

$$15(1 - x) = -3(-x - 2) \qquad \text{\textit{Rewrite original equation.}}$$
$$15 - 15x = 3x + 6 \qquad \text{\textit{Distributive Property}}$$
$$15 = 18x + 6 \qquad \text{\textit{Add 15x to both sides.}}$$
$$9 = 18x \qquad \text{\textit{Subtract 6 from both sides.}}$$
$$\tfrac{1}{2} = x \qquad \text{\textit{Divide both sides by 18.}}$$

The solution is $\tfrac{1}{2}$. Check this in the original equation. $\quad \blacksquare$

Example 4 — Solving a Linear Equation

$$\tfrac{1}{3}(14x + 9) = 11 - 5(x - 3) \qquad \text{\textit{Original equation}}$$
$$\tfrac{1}{3}(14x + 9) = 11 - 5x + 15 \qquad \text{\textit{Distributive Property}}$$
$$\tfrac{1}{3}(14x + 9) = 26 - 5x \qquad \text{\textit{Combine like terms.}}$$
$$14x + 9 = 78 - 15x \qquad \text{\textit{Multiply both sides by 3.}}$$
$$29x + 9 = 78 \qquad \text{\textit{Add 15x to both sides.}}$$
$$29x = 69 \qquad \text{\textit{Subtract 9 from both sides.}}$$
$$x = \tfrac{69}{29} \qquad \text{\textit{Divide both sides by 29.}}$$

The solution is $\tfrac{69}{29}$. Check this in the original equation. $\quad \blacksquare$

BakeryCorp *in Miami, Florida, is a bakery that supplies baked goods to restaurants. The business was started in 1986 by three brothers: (clockwise from left) Luis, Juan, and José Lacal. During the first five years, sales approximately doubled each year. In 1991, BakeryCorp paid its employees between $4.50 and $7.00 per hour for the first 40 hours per week and time and a half for overtime.*

(**Source:** Your Company Magazine)

Real Life
Accounting

Example 5 *Finding the Number of Hours Worked*

Model the weekly earnings of a baker who earns $7 an hour at *BakeryCorp* and works *at least* 40 hours a week. How many hours would the baker work in a week to earn $332.50?

Solution

Verbal Model	Hourly wage	·	40 hours	+ 1.5 ·	Hourly wage	·	Overtime hours

Labels Hourly wage = 7   (dollars)
Total hours worked in week = t (hours)
Overtime hours = $t - 40$ (hours)

Expression $7(40) + 1.5(7)(t - 40)$

The number of hours worked to earn $332.50 in a week is found by solving the following linear equation.

$$332.50 = 7(40) + 1.5(7)(t - 40)$$
$$332.50 = 280 + 10.5t - 420$$
$$472.50 = 10.5t$$
$$45 = t \quad \text{(total hours worked in week)}$$

■

Communicating about **A L G E B R A**

▷ **SHARING IDEAS about the Lesson**

Suppose the baker in Example 5 earns $6.50 per hour (regular pay rate). How many hours must the employee work in one week to earn $318.50? Explain.

EXERCISES

Guided Practice

▶ **CRITICAL THINKING about the Lesson**

In Exercises 1 and 2, decide whether the equations are equivalent.

1. $x - 5 = 5$ and $x = 0$

2. $4x = 2$ and $x = 0.5$

3. Which of the following transformations of the equation $-2x = 3 + 1$ does not produce an equivalent equation? Explain.
   a. Simplify the right side.   **b.** Divide both sides by -2.   **c.** Square both sides.

4. Is -4 the only solution of $2x + 9 = 1$? Explain your answer.

Independent Practice

In Exercises 5–10, describe the transformations you could use to solve the equation.

5. $x + 8 = -3$

6. $\frac{1}{7}x = 2$

7. $-\frac{5}{2}x = 4$

8. $x - 4 = 0$

9. $\frac{x}{3} = 2$

10. $5 = -x$

In Exercises 11–16, check whether the number is a solution of the equation.

11. $5 - t = 7$, -2

12. $9 + 5t = -6$, 4

13. $-4x = 24$, -8

14. $2y = -22$, 10

15. $6x + 1 = 7$, 1

16. $3x - 11 = 1$, 4

In Exercises 17–22, solve the equation.

17. $16x = 8$

18. $x - 7 = 18$

19. $8x - 1 = 15$

20. $5x + 9 = 4$

21. $6 - 2x = 5$

22. $10 + 7x = 24$

In Exercises 23–40, solve the equation. Check your solution.

23. $13x = 52$

24. $\frac{x}{2} = -5$

25. $-\frac{x}{3} = 6$

26. $-5x = 30$

27. $\frac{1}{2}x - 12 = 4$

28. $3x + 5 = 17$

29. $2x + 3 = x - 7$

30. $5x - 4 = 2x + 6$

31. $3(x - 2) = 6(5 + x)$

32. $2(3 - x) = 16(x + 1)$

33. $4(x + 5) = 6(2x - 1)$

34. $-2(4 + 3x) = 3(x - 2)$

35. $3(x - 2) + 6 = 4(2 - x)$

36. $7(x + 1) = 1 - 2(5 - x)$

37. $2(3x - 1) = 5 - (x + 3)$

38. $-4(3 + x) + 5 = 4(x + 3)$

39. $-(x + 2) - 2x = -2(x + 1)$

40. $-(x - 1) + 10 = -3(x - 2)$

In Exercises 41 and 42, find the dimensions of the figure.

41. Area $= 504$

42. Perimeter $= 23$

43. *Summer Jobs*   You have two summer jobs. In the first job, you work 40 hours a week and earn $6.25 an hour. The second one, you earn $5.50 an hour and can work as many hours as you want. If you want to earn $316 a week, how many hours must you work at your second job?

44. *Car Repair*   The bill for the repair of your car was $415. The cost for parts was $265. The cost for labor was $25 per hour. How many hours did the repair work take?

75 Years of Tractors   **In Exercises 45–48, use the following information.**

In 1917, a *Case* tractor was steam-powered. It used 20 chunks of hardwood per hour as a fuel and took $1\frac{1}{2}$ hours to start. The 1991 *Case Magnum 7140* is diesel-powered. It uses 11 gallons of fuel per hour and has a start-up time of 10 seconds. *(Source: J. I. Case Corp)*

You can find some other comparisons between these two *Case* tractors by using the given clues.

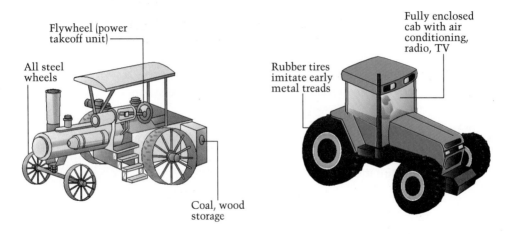

Flywheel (power takeoff unit)

All steel wheels

Coal, wood storage

Fully enclosed cab with air conditioning, radio, TV

Rubber tires imitate early metal treads

45. The 1991 tractor has a horsepower of 195, which is 5 less than 4 times the horsepower of the 1917 tractor. What was the horsepower of the 1917 tractor?

46. The maximum speed of the 1991 tractor is 19.6 miles per hour, which is 1.2 more than 8 times the maximum speed of the 1917 tractor. What was the maximum speed of the 1917 tractor?

47. In 1917, the *Case* company made 65 tractors, which is 35 less than one hundredth of the *Magnum 7140* tractors made in 1991. How many were made in 1991?

48. The height of the rear wheels of the 1917 tractor is the same as the height of the front wheels of the 1991 tractor. The 1917 tractor's front wheels were 22 inches shorter than the rear wheels. The 1991 tractor's front wheels are 10 inches shorter than its rear wheels. The average wheel height for the 1991 model is 71 inches. Find the heights of the front and rear wheels of each model.

49. Dry Ice Dry ice is solid carbon dioxide that changes to a gas at $-78.5°C$. What is the "melting point" of dry ice in degrees Fahrenheit?

50. Hot Dog Your dog's temperature is $38.4°C$. Does it have a fever? Explain.

The normal body temperature of a dog is 101.5°F.

Integrated Review

In Exercises 51–56, evaluate the expression.

51. $2(3 - 5x)$ when $x = 3$

52. $-3(x + 3)$ when $x = -2$

53. $5x - (x + 3)$ when $x = -5$

54. $4 + (x - 4)$ when $x = 9$

55. $7 + 3(2x - 9)$ when $x = -1$

56. $13x - 2(x + 3)$ when $x = -5$

In Exercises 57–62, simplify the expression.

57. $3x - 4(x - 3)$

58. $5(x - 4) + 3$

59. $9[x + 3(4 + x)] - 1$

60. $10 - [8(5 - x) + 2]$

61. $2 + [3(x + 4) - 10]$

62. $[2(5x + 3) + 4] - 3$

63. College Entrance Exam Sample If the following numbers are arranged from least to greatest, what will be their correct order?

I. $\frac{9}{13}$ **II.** $\frac{13}{9}$ **III.** 70% **IV.** $\frac{1}{0.70}$

a. II, I, III, IV **b.** III, II, I, IV **c.** III, IV, I, II **d.** II, IV, III, I
e. I, III, IV, II

64. College Entrance Exam Sample If $\frac{2}{3} + \frac{3}{4} + \frac{5}{6} + P = 3$, then $P = \boxed{?}$.

a. $\frac{4}{3}$ **b.** $\frac{3}{4}$ **c.** $\frac{2}{3}$ **d.** $\frac{1}{2}$ **e.** $\frac{1}{3}$

Exploration and Extension

Round-Off Error **In Exercises 65 and 66, solve the equation in the following two ways. Explain why the two solutions are different.**

- Find the exact solution as a fraction. Then write it as a decimal, rounded to two decimal places.
- Write each coefficient as a decimal, rounded to two decimal places. Then solve the equation.

65. $\frac{1}{9}x = 20 + \frac{1}{10}x$

66. $\frac{9}{20}x - \frac{4}{9}x = 60$

1.4

Problem-Solving Strategies

What you should learn:

Goal How to use problem-solving strategies to solve real-life problems

Why you should learn it:

You can use algebra to solve many real-life problems, such as those related to water pressure, building a railroad line, and starting your own business.

Goal **Problem-Solving Strategies**

In this lesson, you will review some of the most common strategies for solving real-life problems.

Problem-Solving Strategies

- **Guess** a reasonable solution. **Check** the guess. **Revise** the guess and continue until a correct solution is found.
- **Make a table** using the data from a problem. **Look for a pattern.** Use the pattern to complete the table and solve.
- **Draw a diagram** that shows the facts from the problem. Use the diagram to visualize the action of the problem. Use algebra to find a solution. Then check the solution.

Each of these strategies can be used alone or in combination with the strategy for creating algebraic models. The key steps in creating an algebraic model are as follows.

| Write a verbal model. | → | Assign labels. | → | Write an algebraic model. | → | Solve the algebraic model. | → | Answer the question. |

Real Life
Scuba Diving

Water weighs 62.4 pounds per cubic foot. The water pressure at a depth, d (in feet), is 62.4d pounds per square foot.

Example 1 *Exploring Arctic Waters*

To study life in arctic waters, scientists worked in a submerged Sub-Igloo station in Resolute Bay in northern Canada. The water pressure at the floor of the station was 2184 pounds per square foot. How deep was the station floor?
(Source: National Geographic Society)

Solution

| **Verbal Model** | Water pressure | = | Weight of water per cubic foot | · | Depth of station |

Labels
Water pressure = 2184   (pounds per square foot)
Weight of water = 62.4   (pounds per cubic foot)
Depth of station = x (feet)

Equation $2184 = 62.4x$ *Linear model*

       $35 = x$ *Divide both sides by 62.4.*

The station floor was 35 feet deep. ■

In 1862, two railroad companies were given the rights to build a railroad connecting Omaha, Nebraska, with Sacramento, California. The Central Pacific Company began building eastward from Sacramento in 1863. Twenty-four months later the Union Pacific Company began building westward from Omaha.

Problem Solving
Draw a Diagram

├── 1590 mi ──┤
Central Pacific

Union
Pacific

Sacramento   Omaha
      Promontory

Example 2   *The First Transcontinental Railroad*

The Central Pacific Company averaged 8.75 miles of track per month. The Union Pacific Company averaged 20 miles of track per month. The photo shows the two companies meeting in Promontory, Utah, as the 1590 miles of track were completed. When was the photo taken? How many miles of track did each company build?

Solution

Verbal Model	Total miles of track	=	Miles per month	·	Number of months	+	Miles per month	·	Number of months

Central Pacific   Union Pacific

Labels
Total miles of track = 1590   (miles)
Central Pacific rate = 8.75   (miles per month)
Central Pacific time = t (months)
Union Pacific rate = 20   (miles per month)
Union Pacific time = $t - 24$ (months)

Equation

$1590 = 8.75t + 20(t - 24)$ *Linear model*

$1590 = 8.75t + 20t - 480$ *Distributive Property*

$2070 = 28.75t$ *Add 480 to both sides.*

$72 = t$ *Divide both sides by 28.75.*

The construction took 72 months (6 years) from the time the Central Pacific Company began. Thus, the photo was taken in 1869. The number of miles built by each company is:

Central Pacific: (8.75 miles per month)(72 months) = 630 mi

Union Pacific: (20 miles per month)(48 months) = 960 mi   ■

Example 3   *Starting a Small Business*

You have started a small business making papier-mâché sculptures. Your cost per sculpture is only $0.50. (The ingredients are water, flour, carpenter's glue, newspaper, wire, and paint.) Your pieces sell for $12.50 at an arts-and-crafts shop, and you receive 50% of the selling price. Each sculpture takes about 2 hours to complete. If you spend 16 hours a week working on the sculptures, how many weeks will you work to earn a profit of $400?

Solution   Because you receive $6.25 for each sculpture, your profit per sculpture is $5.75. Working 16 hours a week, you can make 8 sculptures per week.

Verbal Model	Total profit	=	Profit per sculpture	·	Sculptures per week	·	Number of weeks

Labels   Total profit = 400   (dollars)
Profit per sculpture = 5.75   (dollars per sculpture)
Sculptures per week = 8   (sculptures per week)
Number of weeks = x (weeks)

Equation $400 = 5.75(8)(x)$ *Linear model*

$400 = 46x$ *Simplify*

$8.7 \approx x$ *Divide both sides by 46.*

It will take you about 9 weeks to make a profit of $400.   ∎

Communicating about ALGEBRA

▶ **SHARING IDEAS about the Lesson**

Use a Diagram   The house plans at the left show a house whose shape is a regular octagon. (The 8 sides have the same length.)

A. Approximate the length, x (in feet), of each side of the house by solving the following linear equation.
$$43.5 = \frac{\sqrt{2}x}{2} + x + \frac{\sqrt{2}x}{2} \text{ or } 43.5 = \frac{2\sqrt{2}x + 2x}{2}$$
Explain how the Pythagorean Theorem can be used to obtain this equation. (What do you know about the green triangle in the diagram?)

B. Partition the house into two trapezoids and one rectangle. Then use these shapes to approximate the area of the house.

43.5 ft
Deck
8 ft
Living room
43.5 ft
Bedroom
Kitchen   Bath   Bath
Bedroom
Porch   Entry   Bedroom
MAIN FLOOR

EXERCISES

Guided Practice

▶ **CRITICAL THINKING about the Lesson**

Girl Scout Cookies   **In Exercises 1–4, use the following information.**

Your sister is selling Girl Scout cookies for $2.60 a box. Your family bought 6 boxes. How many more boxes of cookies must she sell in order to collect $130? Use the following verbal model.

$$\boxed{\begin{array}{c}\text{Boxes}\\\text{sold}\end{array}} \cdot \boxed{\begin{array}{c}\text{Price}\\\text{per}\\\text{box}\end{array}} + \boxed{\begin{array}{c}\text{Boxes}\\\text{to be}\\\text{sold}\end{array}} \cdot \boxed{\begin{array}{c}\text{Price}\\\text{per}\\\text{box}\end{array}} = \boxed{\begin{array}{c}\text{Total}\\\text{sales}\end{array}}$$

1. Assign labels to each part of the verbal model. Indicate the units of measure.
2. Use the labels to translate the verbal model into an algebraic equation.
3. Solve the equation.
4. Answer the question.

Independent Practice

Sailing on the Seine   **In Exercises 5–8, use the following information.**

You are on a boat traveling the navigable portion of the Seine River. The boat's average speed is 32 kilometers per hour. How long will the boat ride take? Use the following verbal model.

$$\boxed{\begin{array}{c}\text{Distance}\\\text{traveled}\end{array}} = \boxed{\begin{array}{c}\text{Rate of}\\\text{boat}\end{array}} \cdot \boxed{\begin{array}{c}\text{Time}\\\text{traveled}\end{array}}$$

5. Assign labels for each part of the verbal model.
6. Use the labels to translate the verbal model into an algebraic equation.
7. Solve the equation.
8. Answer the question.

The Seine River flows under more than 30 bridges in Paris, France. The entire length of the river is 764 kilometers, but only 547 kilometers can accommodate boats.

Relay Race   **In Exercises 9–12, use the following information.**

You are the last runner in a relay race. The baton is passed to you 16 seconds after your opponents pass theirs. If you run 5.5 yards per second and tie your opponent, who runs 5 yards per second, how long did it take you to run your portion of the race? Use the following verbal model.

| Your rate | · | Your time | = | Opponent's rate | · | Opponent's time |

9. Assign labels to each part of the verbal model.

10. Use the labels to translate the verbal model into an algebraic equation.

11. Solve the equation.

12. Answer the question.

Environmental Hazard   **In Exercises 13 and 14, use the following information.**

You are attending a wedding in Cedar City, Utah. As the bride and groom prepare to go to the wedding reception, helium balloons are released in the air. The wind is blowing as shown on the map at the right. The radius of the blue circle is 1000 miles, and the radius of the green circle is 2000 miles. After 24 hours, the balloons fall to Earth due to the loss of helium.

13. What wind speed will allow the balloons to reach the Atlantic Ocean?

14. Suppose the balloons remain in the air for 36 hours. What wind speed will allow the balloons to reach the Atlantic Ocean?

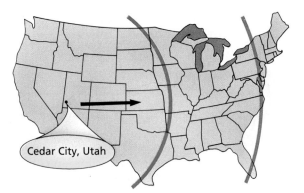

Cedar City, Utah

If a helium balloon travels as far as the ocean before falling to Earth, it can be mistaken as food by fish or sea mammals, who can die from ingesting it.

15. *Hang Gliding*   You are taking hang gliding lessons. The cost of the first lesson is one and a half times the cost of each additional lesson. You spend $260 for six lessons. How much did each lesson cost?

16. *Typing Papers*   Some of your classmates ask you to type their English papers throughout a 10-week summer course. How much should you charge for each page if you want to earn enough to pay for the hang gliding classes in Exercise 15 and have $50 left for spending money? You estimate that you can type 20 pages a week.

17. *Density of Liquids*   You are assigned a project in science class. You must use a hydrometer to measure the density of different liquids and then determine the specific gravity of the liquid. If you measure the density of ethanol to be 49 pounds per cubic foot, what is its specific gravity?

18. *Boyle's Law*   The Irish scientist Robert Boyle (1627–1691) performed an experiment in which he varied the volume, V, and pressure, P, of a fixed quantity of air. (The temperature was kept constant.) Here are the actual data from the experiment.

V (in.³)	48	40	32	24
P (in. of Hg)	29.1	35.3	44.2	58.8

V (in.³)	20	16	12
P (in. of Hg)	70.7	87.2	117.5

The equation that relates V and P is an example of what is now called *Boyle's Law*. What is the equation?

The specific gravity of a liquid is the ratio of its density to the density of water (which is 62.4 pounds per cubic foot). Of two liquids, the one with the lower specific gravity will float on top of the other. The liquids in this photo (from top to bottom) are oil and vinegar.

Integrated Review

In Exercises 19–24, find the resulting unit of measure.

19. $\dfrac{\text{meters}}{\text{minutes}} \cdot \text{minutes}$

20. $\dfrac{\text{hours}}{\text{week}} \cdot \text{weeks}$

21. feet + feet

22. liters − liters

23. $\dfrac{\text{yards}}{\text{second}} \cdot \text{seconds} - \text{yards}$

24. $\dfrac{\text{dollars}}{\text{hour}} \cdot \text{hours} + \text{dollars}$

In Exercises 25–30, solve the equation.

25. $6.7x = 93.1$

26. $9.3 = 2.8y$

27. $3y + 4.4 = 9.3y + 6$

28. $4.1 - 5.3x = 12.9x$

29. $3.1x = 7.5 - 1.9x$

30. $6y - 4.2 = 12$

Exploration and Extension

You Be the Teacher   Create a real-life problem similar to those in Exercises 5–18. The problem should require a solver to use a linear equation. Pick a subject that is interesting to you. Use algebra to solve your problem.

Take this test as you would take a test in class. The answers to the exercises are given in the back of the book.

1. Write the numbers in increasing order: $4, -2, -3, -\frac{3}{2}, 0, 3, \frac{1}{2}$.
   (1.1)

2. Plot -3 and -2 on the real number line. Which is greater? **(1.1)**

3. What is the product of $\frac{2}{3}$ and $-\frac{2}{3}$? **(1.1)**

4. What is the sum of $\frac{2}{3}$ and $-\frac{2}{3}$? **(1.1)**

5. Evaluate $6 - 4 \div 12 + 8 \div 6$. **(1.2)**

6. Evaluate $12 \cdot 2 - 2 \cdot 6$. **(1.2)**

In Exercises 7–10, evaluate the expression. (1.2)

7. $-3x^2 + 4x$ when $x = -2$

8. $-a(a - 3)$ when $a = 1$

9. $\dfrac{-2(y + 1)}{16 - 2y^2}$ when $y = 4$

10. $\dfrac{ab - 1}{ab + 1}$ when $a = -2$ and $b = 2$

In Exercises 11 and 12, evaluate the expression. Round the result to two decimal places. (1.2)

11. $1.34(x - 9.21)^2$ when $x = 4.13$.

12. $\dfrac{1.67 - t}{4t + 1}$ when $t = 0.32$.

In Exercises 13–16, solve the equation. (1.3)

13. $x - 6 = 3x + 2$

14. $3(a - 1) = 5 - a$

15. $7 = 7(2b + 5) - 6(b + 8)$

16. $-2(4t - 7) = 3(t - 10)$

In Exercises 17–19, find the area of the blue region. (In Exercise 18, each of the yellow regions are quarter circles.) (1.2)

17.

2cm
3cm
4cm

18.
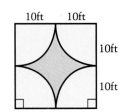
10ft   10ft
10ft
10ft

19.
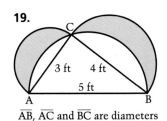
C
3 ft   4 ft
5 ft
A   B
$\overline{AB}, \overline{AC}$ and $\overline{BC}$ are diameters

20. From 1980 through 1990, the prize money, P (in $1000's), for the singles champions at the U.S. Tennis Open can be modeled by

    $P = 30.2t + 35.8$

    where $t = 0$ represents 1980. According to this model, when will the prize money be $500,000?
    (Source: United States Tennis Association) **(1.4)**

Prize Money per Champion (U.S. Open)

Thousands
$350
$300
$250
$200
$150
$100
$50
$0
0 1 2 3 4 5 6 7 8 9 10
Year (0 ↔ 1980)

1.5 Literal Equations and Formulas

What you should learn:

Goal How to solve a literal equation for a specific variable, and how to evaluate it for specified values of the other variables

Why you should learn it:

To estimate a value in a formula, you can solve for that variable and substitute known values for the other variables.

Connections
Geometry

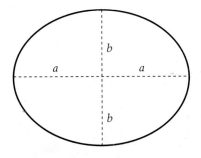

The longest chord of an ellipse is its major axis. The shortest chord through its center is its minor axis.

Goal Solving a Literal Equation

A **literal equation** is an equation that has more than one variable. For instance, $5x + 2y = 7$ is a literal equation because it has two variables, x and y. The word *literal* comes from the Latin word for "letter." You can solve a literal equation for any one of its variables.

Solve for x	Solve for y
$5x + 2y = 7$	$5x + 2y = 7$
$5x = 7 - 2y$	$2y = 7 - 5x$
$x = \dfrac{7 - 2y}{5}$	$y = \dfrac{7 - 5x}{2}$

Example 1 *The Area of an Ellipse*

The area, A, of an ellipse is given by the formula $A = \pi ab$, where a and b are half the lengths of the major and minor axes, respectively.

a. Solve this formula for a.

b. Use the result to find the length of the major axis of an ellipse whose area is 15 square inches and whose minor axis has a length of 4 inches.

Solution

a. $A = \pi ab$ *Formula for area*

$\dfrac{A}{\pi b} = a$ *Divide both sides by πb.*

This gives the length of the semimajor axis in terms of the area and the length of the semiminor axis.

b. Substitute $A = 15$ and $b = 2$ into the formula for a.

$a = \dfrac{A}{\pi b}$ *Formula for a*

$= \dfrac{15}{\pi(2)}$ *Substitute 15 for A and 2 for b.*

≈ 2.39 *Simplify.*

The length of a is about 2.39 inches, so the major axis has a length of about 4.78.

The Pythagorean Theorem of Baseball *is a formula for approximating the ratio of the number of wins to the total games played.*

Let R be the number of runs scored during the season, A be the number of runs allowed the opponents, W be the number of games won, and T be the number of games played. These four variables are related by

$$\frac{R^2}{R^2 + A^2} \approx \frac{W}{T}.$$

(*Source:* Inside Sports)

Sports Estimating

Example 2   *Approximating the Number of Wins in Baseball*

a. Solve the formula $\frac{R^2}{R^2 + A^2} \approx \frac{W}{T}$ for W.

b. In 1990, the Pittsburgh Pirates scored 733 runs and gave up 619 runs. How many of its 162 games would you estimate the team to have won?

Solution

a. $\dfrac{R^2}{R^2 + A^2} \approx \dfrac{W}{T}$ *Pythagorean Theorem of Baseball*

$\dfrac{TR^2}{R^2 + A^2} \approx W$ *Multiply both sides by T.*

b. Substitute $R = 733$, $A = 619$, and $T = 162$.

$$W \approx \frac{TR^2}{R^2 + A^2}$$
$$= \frac{162(733^2)}{733^2 + 619^2}$$
$$= 95$$

The formula would estimate the number of wins to be 95 (which, as it happens, is exactly the number of games the Pittsburgh Pirates won in 1990.) ∎

The graph at the left shows the estimated number of wins for all 26 American League and National League baseball teams for 1990. For 15 of the teams, the formula gives a number of wins within three of the actual number.

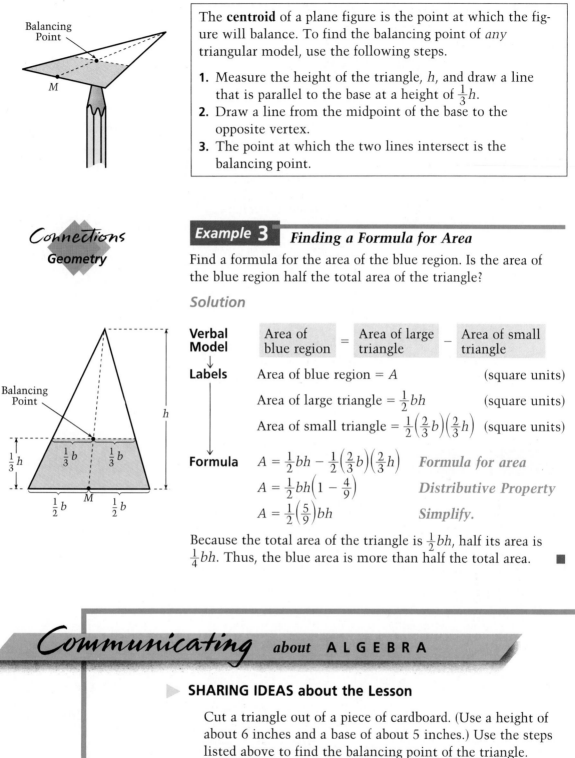

Balancing
Point

M

The **centroid** of a plane figure is the point at which the figure will balance. To find the balancing point of *any* triangular model, use the following steps.

1. Measure the height of the triangle, h, and draw a line that is parallel to the base at a height of $\frac{1}{3}h$.

2. Draw a line from the midpoint of the base to the opposite vertex.

3. The point at which the two lines intersect is the balancing point.

Connections
Geometry

Example 3   *Finding a Formula for Area*

Find a formula for the area of the blue region. Is the area of the blue region half the total area of the triangle?

Solution

Verbal Model	Area of blue region	$=$	Area of large triangle	$-$	Area of small triangle

Labels   Area of blue region $= A$ (square units)

Area of large triangle $= \frac{1}{2}bh$ (square units)

Area of small triangle $= \frac{1}{2}\left(\frac{2}{3}b\right)\left(\frac{2}{3}h\right)$ (square units)

Formula $A = \frac{1}{2}bh - \frac{1}{2}\left(\frac{2}{3}b\right)\left(\frac{2}{3}h\right)$ *Formula for area*

$A = \frac{1}{2}bh\left(1 - \frac{4}{9}\right)$ *Distributive Property*

$A = \frac{1}{2}\left(\frac{5}{9}\right)bh$ *Simplify.*

Because the total area of the triangle is $\frac{1}{2}bh$, half its area is $\frac{1}{4}bh$. Thus, the blue area is more than half the total area. ∎

Communicating about **ALGEBRA**

▶ **SHARING IDEAS about the Lesson**

Cut a triangle out of a piece of cardboard. (Use a height of about 6 inches and a base of about 5 inches.) Use the steps listed above to find the balancing point of the triangle. Then test your result by balancing the triangle on the *eraser* of a pencil. (If you measured *very* carefully, the triangle could balance on the *point* of the pencil.)

EXERCISES

Guided Practice

▶ **CRITICAL THINKING about the Lesson**

1. Which of the following sentences can be written as a literal equation? Explain.
   a. The time it takes to drive 20 miles to the store is equal to 20 divided by the speed.
   b. The height of the mast of the sailboat is 12.5 meters.

Geometry   In Exercises 2–4, match the formula for volume, *V*, with the figure. Describe the measurement represented by each variable (other than *V*).

2. $V = \frac{1}{3}b^2h$

  a. **Sphere**

3. $V = \frac{1}{3}\pi r^2 h$

  b. **Pyramid**

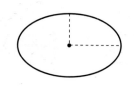

4. $V = \frac{4}{3}\pi r^3$

  c. **Cone**

Independent Practice

Geometry   In Exercises 5–10, match the formula for area, *A*, with the figure. Describe the length represented by each variable (other than *A*).

5. $A = \pi ab$

6. $A = \pi r^2$

7. $A = \frac{1}{2}bh$

8. $A = LW$

9. $A = bh$

10. $A = \frac{1}{2}(b_1 + b_2)h$

  a. **Trapezoid**

  b. **Ellipse**

  c. **Triangle**

  d. **Parallelogram**

  e. **Circle**

  f. **Rectangle**

In Exercises 11–20, solve for the indicated variable.

11. *Volume of a right circular cylinder*
    Solve for h: $V = \pi r^2 h$

12. *Perimeter of a rectangle*
    Solve for W: $P = 2L + 2W$

13. *Circumference of a circle*
    Solve for r: $C = 2\pi r$

14. *Volume of a general cone*
    Solve for A: $V = \frac{1}{3}Ah$

15. *Area of a trapezoid*
    Solve for b_2: $A = \frac{1}{2}(b_1 + b_2)h$

16. *Discount*
    Solve for L: $S = L - rL$

17. *Conversion from Fahrenheit to Celsius*
    Solve for F: $C = \frac{5}{9}(F - 32)$

18. *Profit*
    Solve for C: $P = R - C$

19. *Investment at simple interest*
    Solve for P: $A = P + Prt$

20. *Investment at compound interest*
    Solve for P: $A = P(1 + r)^t$

In Exercises 21–23, solve the formula for the indicated variable. Then evaluate the variable for the given values. (Include units of measure in your result.)

21. Area of a circular ring:
    $A = 2\pi pw$. Solve for p.
    Find p given $A = 22$ cm^2
    and $w = 2$ cm.

22. Surface area of a cylinder: $S = 2\pi rh + 2\pi r^2$.
    Solve for h. Find h given
    $S = 105$ in.^{2} and $r = 3$ in.

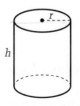

23. Perimeter of a pond:
    $P = 2\pi r + 2x$. Solve
    for r. Find r if $P = 75$ ft
    and $x = 20$ ft.

24. *Forager Honeybees*   A forager honeybee spends about three weeks becoming accustomed to the immediate surroundings of its hive, and then the rest of its life collecting pollen and nectar. A forager's flight muscles can last only about 500 miles—after that the bee dies. The total number of miles, T, a forager can fly in its lifetime, L (in days), can be modeled by

    $$T = m(L - 21)$$

    where m is the number of miles it flies each day. A hardworking forager honeybee can fly about 55 miles each day. About how long does it live?

A Leaky Faucet **In Exercises 25–27, use the following information.**

Suppose that a leaky faucet continues to drip at the same rate for one year. Let v be the volume of water dripping from the faucet in t minutes and let V be the volume dripping in one year. Since there are about 525,600 minutes in a year, the three variables are related by the proportion

$$\frac{v}{t} = \frac{V}{525,600}.$$

25. You have a leaky faucet at home that fills an 8-ounce glass (0.03 gallon) in 12 minutes. How much water would drip from this faucet in one year?

26. An average bath uses 25 gallons of water. In one year, how many baths are "lost" through the leaky faucet?

27. An average 10-minute shower uses 50 gallons of water. In a year, how many showers are "lost"?

Integrated Review

In Exercises 28–33, solve the equation.

28. $3d + 16 = d - 4$

29. $5 - x = 23 + 2x$

30. $10(y - 1) = y + 4$

31. $p - 16 + 4 = 4(2 - p)$

32. $x(2 - 6 \cdot 2) = 5x + 30$

33. $12 = z(2 \cdot 6 \div 3)$

In Exercises 34–39, evaluate the expression.

34. $a - 11b + 2$ when $a = 61$ and $b = 7$

35. $\frac{1}{2}c + \frac{5}{2}d - 7$ when $c = 20$ and $d = 4$

36. $15x + 8y$ when $x = \frac{1}{2}$ and $y = \frac{1}{3}$

37. $80\left(n - \frac{1}{4}m\right)$ when $n = 13$ and $m = 5$

38. $\frac{1}{5}(p + q) - 7$ when $p = 5$ and $q = 3$

39. $\frac{1}{10}\left(20g + \frac{1}{3}h\right)$ when $g = 6$ and $h = 6$

Exploration and Extension

Cells **In Exercises 40 and 41, use the following information.**

The surface-to-volume quotient, Q, of a living cell is related to the cell's ability to interact with its environment to obtain nourishment. If the surface area is small compared to its volume, the cell could not survive. Consider a spherical cell of radius r. Its surface-to-volume quotient is given by

$$Q = \frac{4\pi r^2}{\frac{4}{3}\pi r^3}.$$

Escheichia coli

40. Measured in centimeters, a typical spherical cell's surface-to-volume quotient is 2400. What is the radius of such a cell?

41. Measured in centimeters, an *Escheichia coli* cell has a surface-to-volume ratio of 30,000. The cell is approximately spherical. What is its radius? (About 78,000 of these cells could fit within the period at the end of this sentence.)

1.6

Solving Linear Inequalities

What you should learn:

Goal 1 How to solve simple and compound inequalities

Goal 2 How to use inequalities to solve real-life problems

Why you should learn it:

You can model many real-life situations with inequalities, such as a range of frequencies for the human voice

Goal 1 Solving Inequalities

A **solution of an inequality** in one variable is any value of the variable that makes the inequality true. Most inequalities have many solutions. For instance, -2, 0, $\frac{1}{2}$, 0.872, and 1 are some of the many solutions of $x \le 1$.

The **graph** of a linear inequality in one variable is the graph on the real number line of all solutions of the inequality. For instance, here are the graphs of two inequalities. Notice that an open dot is used for $<$ or $>$ and a solid dot is used for $\le$ or $\ge$.

Graph of $x < 2$ **Graph of $x \ge -1$**

LESSON INVESTIGATION

■ Investigating Solutions of Inequalities

Partner Activity Look at the six transformations listed on page 18. Discuss which of these transformations can be used to solve a linear inequality. Test your conclusions by solving the following inequalities

a. $3x + 5 \le -4$ **b.** $4 - 2x > 6$ **c.** $\frac{1}{2}(x - 2) \ge 3$

Do any of the transformations listed on page 18 *not* work with inequalities? Explain.

Study Tip

When solving a linear inequality, the goal is to isolate the variable on one side using transformations that produce **equivalent** inequalities. In the transformations at the right, notice that when you multiply or divide both sides by a negative number, you must reverse the inequality sign. For instance, to reverse $<$, replace it with $>$.

Transformations That Produce Equivalent Inequalities

1. *Add* the same number to both sides.
2. *Subtract* the same number from both sides.
3. *Multiply* both sides by the same *positive* number.
4. *Divide* both sides by the same *positive number.*
5. *Multiply* both sides by the same *negative* number and reverse the inequality.
6. *Divide* both sides by the same *negative* number and reverse the inequality.

Example **1** *Solving a Simple Linear Inequality*

Solve $3y - 8 < 10$.

Solution

$$3y - 8 < 10 \qquad \textit{Rewrite original inequality.}$$

$$3y < 18 \qquad \textit{Add 8 to both sides.}$$

$$y < 6 \qquad \textit{Divide both sides by 3.}$$

The solution is *all real numbers less than 6.* As a check, try several numbers that are less than 6 in the original inequality. (*Also*, try checking some numbers that are greater than or equal to 6 to see that they are *not* solutions of the original inequality.) The graph of this inequality is shown at the left. ■

Example **2** *Solving a Simple Linear Inequality*

Solve $3x - 2 \le 5x - 3$.

Solution

$$3x - 2 \le 5x - 3 \qquad \textit{Rewrite original inequality.}$$

$$3x \le 5x - 1 \qquad \textit{Add 2 to both sides.}$$

$$-2x \le -1 \qquad \textit{Subtract 5x from both sides.}$$

$$x \ge \tfrac{1}{2} \qquad \textit{Divide both sides by } -2 \textit{ and reverse inequality.}$$

The solution is *all real numbers greater than or equal to $\tfrac{1}{2}$.* Check several numbers that are greater than or equal to $\tfrac{1}{2}$ in the original inequality. The graph of this inequality is shown at the left. ■

A **compound inequality** is two simple inequalities joined by "or" or "and." Here are two examples.

Graph	**Verbal Phrase**	**Inequality**
−1 0 1 2 3 4 5 6	All real numbers that are greater than or equal to 1 *and* less than 3. (This inequality can also be written as $1 \le x$ *and* $x < 3$.)	$1 \le x < 3$
−4 −2 0 2 4	All real numbers that are less than −2 *or* greater than or equal to 1.	$x < -2 \quad \text{or} \quad x \ge 1$

The inequality $a < x < b$ is read as "*x is between a and b.*" The inequality $a \le x \le b$ is read as "*x is between a and b, inclusive.*"

The transformations used to solve a compound linear inequality are the same as those used to solve a simple linear inequality.

Example 3   *Solving a Compound Linear Inequality*

Solve $-4 \le 2t - 6 \le 12$.

Solution   To solve this inequality, you must isolate the variable t between the two inequality signs.

$-4 \le 2t - 6 \le 12$	*Rewrite original inequality.*
$2 \le\ \ \ 2t\ \ \ \le 18$	*Add 6 to each expression.*
$1 \le\ \ \ \ t\ \ \ \ \le 9$	*Divide each expression by 2.*

Because t is between 1 and 9 inclusive, the solution is *all real numbers that are greater than or equal to 1 <u>and</u> less than or equal to 9.* Check several numbers between 1 and 9 in the original inequality. The graph is shown below.

Example 4   *Solving a Compound Linear Inequality*

Solve $4x + 3 < 7$ *or* $3x - 8 > 7$.

Solution   A solution of this compound inequality is a solution of *either* of its simple parts, so you should solve each part separately.

Solution of First Inequality:

$4x + 3 < 7$	*Rewrite first inequality.*
$4x < 4$	*Subtract 3 from both sides.*
$x < 1$	*Divide both sides by 4.*

Solution of Second Inequality:

$3x - 8 > 7$	*Rewrite second inequality.*
$3x > 15$	*Add 8 to both sides.*
$x > 5$	*Divide both sides by 3.*

The solution is *all real numbers that are less than 1 <u>or</u> greater than 5.* The graph is shown below.

In most parts of the United States, people add antifreeze to automobile cooling systems. The antifreeze lowers the freezing point of the coolant and raises the boiling point. (The changes in freezing and boiling points depend on the amount and type of antifreeze that is added.)

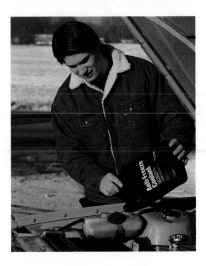

Goal 2 Using Inequalities to Solve Problems

Real Life
Chemistry

Example 5 *Finding the Freezing and Boiling Points*

You have added enough antifreeze to your car's cooling system to lower the freezing point to $-35°C$ and raise the boiling point to $125°C$. The coolant will remain a liquid as long as the temperature, C (in degrees Celsius), satisfies the inequality $-35 < C < 125$. Write this inequality in degrees Fahrenheit.

Solution Let F represent the temperature in degrees Fahrenheit and use the formula $C = \frac{5}{9}(F - 32)$.

$-35 <\quad C\quad < 125$ *Rewrite original inequality.*

$-35 < \frac{5}{9}(F - 32) < 125$ *Replace C by $\frac{5}{9}(F - 32)$.*

$-63 <\quad F - 32\quad < 225$ *Multiply each expression by $\frac{9}{5}$.*

$-31 <\quad F\quad < 257$ *Add 32 to each expression.*

The coolant will remain liquid between $-31°F$ and $257°F$. ■

Communicating about ALGEBRA

▶ **SHARING IDEAS about the Lesson**

Solve the following inequalities. Sketch the graph of each solution and explain your steps.

A. $3x + 5 \le 10$ **B.** $-4x + 6 \le 3x - 15$

C. $-5 \le 2x + 5 < 7$ **D.** $3x - 4 < 8$ or $3x - 4 > 23$

EXERCISES

▶ **CRITICAL THINKING about the Lesson**

In Exercises 1 and 2, write an inequality that corresponds to the phrase.

1. All real numbers less than or equal to -5

2. All real numbers less than 7 and greater than or equal to -2

3. *True or False?* Multiplying both sides of an inequality by the same number produces an equivalent inequality. Explain.

4. Write a verbal phrase that describes $x > -1$.

5. Sketch the graph of $x < 3$.

6. Sketch the graph of $1 \leq x < 5$.

Independent Practice

In Exercises 7–10, write an inequality for the verbal sentence.

7. x is less than 9.

8. 18 is less than or equal to a.

9. x is greater than 4 and less than 6.

10. y is greater than or equal to -5 and less than 0.

In Exercises 11–14, match the inequality with its graph.

11. $x \geq 4$

12. $x \geq 4$ or $x < -4$

13. $-4 < x < 4$

14. $x < 4$

a.
$$\xleftarrow{\quad} \overset{-4\ -3\ -2\ -1\ \ 0\ \ 1\ \ 2\ \ 3\ \ 4}{+\!+\!+\!+\!+\!+\!+\!+\!\bullet} \xrightarrow{} x$$

b.
$$\xleftarrow{\quad} \overset{-4\ -3\ -2\ -1\ \ 0\ \ 1\ \ 2\ \ 3\ \ 4}{\bullet\!+\!+\!+\!+\!+\!+\!+\!\bullet} \xrightarrow{} x$$

c.
$$\xleftarrow{\quad} \overset{-4\ -3\ -2\ -1\ \ 0\ \ 1\ \ 2\ \ 3\ \ 4}{+\!+\!+\!+\!+\!+\!+\!+\!\bullet} \xrightarrow{} x$$

d.
$$\xleftarrow{\quad} \overset{-4\ -3\ -2\ -1\ \ 0\ \ 1\ \ 2\ \ 3\ \ 4}{\bullet\!+\!+\!+\!+\!+\!+\!+\!\bullet} \xrightarrow{} x$$

In Exercises 15–20, decide whether the number is a solution of the inequality.

15. $3y - 4 < 10, 5$

16. $x + 4 > 9, 5$

17. $7 - n \geq 3, 4$

18. $\frac{1}{2}x - 3 \leq -3, 4$

19. $-1 < 2x \leq 8, 4$

20. $-4 < w + 4 < 6, 0$

In Exercises 21–32, solve the inequality.

21. $6t + 7 > 11$

22. $4 + x \leq 19$

23. $9 - k < 4$

24. $3 - 2x \geq 15$

25. $2h - 3 \geq 6 - h$

26. $-x + 5 < 3x + 1$

27. $-3 \leq x - 3 \leq 6$

28. $-14 < 2j + 3 \leq 6$

29. $4 \leq -3x - 1 \leq 9$

30. $-3 \leq -x + 5 \leq 0$

31. $-1 < -2x + 1 \leq 5$

32. $-7 \leq 5y - 2 < 3$

In Exercises 33–38, solve the inequality. Then sketch its graph.

33. $4 \leq r + 5 \leq 5$

34. $x - 1 \leq 5$ or $x + 3 \geq 10$

35. $x - 4 < 0$ or $x - 6 \geq 4$

36. $-3 < 2x - 3 \leq 17$

37. $m + \frac{1}{2} \leq -3$ or $m - 3 > -2$

38. $0 \leq \frac{1}{3}x - 1 \leq 3$

The first Ferris wheel ever built was designed by the American mechanical engineer George Ferris (1859–1896) for use at the Columbian Exposition (World's Fair) in Chicago in 1893, and later used at the World's Fair in St. Louis in 1904. It had a diameter of 250 feet, and each of its 36 cars could hold 60 passengers.

39. *Ferris Wheels*   Write an inequality that represents the number, n, of people on a single Ferris wheel.

40. *Centipedes*   The longest species of centipede known measures about 33 centimeters. The shortest centipede recorded measures only about 0.5 centimeters. Write an inequality that represents the length of a centipede. Then graph the inequality.

41. *Eclipses*   The greatest number of eclipses possible in a year is 7. This happened in 1935, when 5 solar and 2 lunar eclipses occurred. The smallest number of eclipses possible in a year is 2, both of which must be solar. Write an inequality that represents the number of eclipses in a year. Sketch the inequality.

42. *Entertainers*   The highest-paid American entertainer in 1990 was Bill Cosby, who was paid $55 million during that year. Write an inequality that describes the salary of any American entertainer in 1990. (Although Cosby makes his money in entertainment, he holds a doctorate in education.)

Bats   **In Exercises 43–45, use the following information.**

The range of a human's voice frequency, h (in cycles per second), is about $85 \leq h \leq 1100$. The range of a human's hearing frequency, H, is about $20 \leq H \leq 20{,}000$.

43. The relationship between a human's voice frequency and a bat's voice frequency, b, is $h = 85 + \frac{203}{22{,}000}(b - 10{,}000)$. Find the range of a bat's voice frequency.

44. The relationship between a human's hearing frequency and a bat's hearing frequency, B, is $H = 20 + \frac{999}{5950}(B - 1000)$. Find the range of a bat's hearing frequency.

45. If a bat flies into your room and you scream, will it hear you? If you scare the bat and it screams, will you hear it? Explain.

In Exercises 46–51, solve the equation.

46. $5 + 2x = 19$ **47.** $-5x + 6 = 1 + 9x$ **48.** $3x - 9 = 2x - 12$

49. $8 + x = -5x - 20$ **50.** $6 - 2x = 7x - 4$ **51.** $4x - 13 = 5 - x$

52. *Powers of Ten*   Which is the best estimate of the average annual income for an American family in 1990?
    a. $\$3 \times 10^2$ **b.** $\$3 \times 10^3$ **c.** $\$3 \times 10^4$ **d.** $\$3 \times 10^5$

53. *Powers of Ten*   Which is the best estimate of the diameter of an automobile tire?
    a. 2.4×10^0 in.   **b.** 2.4×10^1 in.   **c.** 2.4×10^2 in.   **d.** 2.4×10^3 in.

54. *College Entrance Exam Sample*   If $6565 = 65(x + 1)$, then $x = \boxed{?}$.
    a. 10   **b.** 11   **c.** 100   **d.** 101   **e.** 1001

55. *College Entrance Exam Sample*   If $x = 2$ and $y = -1$, what is the value of $\dfrac{x - y}{x + y}$?
    a. -3 **b.** -1 **c.** $\frac{1}{3}$ **d.** 1   **e.** 3

Exploration and Extension

In Exercises 56 and 57, write a compound inequality that is equivalent to the given inequality.

56. $x^2 < 25$ **57.** $x^2 < 16$

58. A number is in the **intersection** of two sets if it is in each set. Sketch the graphs of $2x - 5 > -9$ and $5x + 4 < 29$. Write a compound inequality that describes the intersection of the graphs.

Mixed REVIEW

1. What is one fifth of 120?   **2.** What is the ratio of 5 feet to 3 feet?

3. Add: $-1.45 + 2.55$.   **4.** Multiply: $12^2 \cdot 12^3$.

5. What is the reciprocal of $-\frac{2}{3}$?   **(1.1)**   **6.** What is the opposite of $-\frac{2}{3}$?   **(1.1)**

7. Write in scientific notation: 1,540,000.   **8.** Write in scientific notation: 0.0014.

9. Is -4 a solution of $5 - (x + 2) = 3$?   **(1.2)**   **10.** Is 12 a solution of $-2(x - 3) - (x + 1) = 31$?   **(1.2)**

11. Solve $5(x - 2) = -2(x + 1)$.   **(1.3)**   **12.** Solve $-\frac{1}{2}(x + 1) = 5x - 6$.   **(1.3)**

13. Find the volume: cube with 3-inch sides.   **(1.5)**   **14.** Find the area: circle with 2-inch radius.   **(1.5)**

15. Is -2 a solution of $-4x + 1 \le 9$?   **(1.3)**   **16.** Is -3 a solution of $-9x - 15 < 15$?   **(1.3)**

17. Solve and graph: $-2 \le -2x < 2$.   **(1.6)**   **18.** Evaluate $\frac{2}{3}x$ when $x = \frac{3}{2}$.   **(1.2)**

1.7

Solving Absolute Value Equations and Inequalities

What you should learn:

Goal 1 How to solve absolute value equations and inequalities

Goal 2 How to use absolute value inequalities in real-life settings

Why you should learn it:

You can model many problems, such as those dealing with a range of acceptable measurements, with absolute value equations and inequalities.

Goal 1 **Solving Equations and Inequalities**

The **absolute value** of a number, x, is the distance the number is from 0.

$$|x| = \begin{cases} x, & \text{if } x \text{ is positive.} \\ 0, & \text{if } x = 0. \\ -x, & \text{if } x \text{ is negative.} \end{cases}$$

Example

$|4| = 4$
$|0| = 0$
$|-2| = -(-2) = 2$

To solve an absolute value equation, remember that the expression inside the absolute value symbols can be either positive or negative. For instance, the solution of $|x| = 5$ is $x = 5$ or $x = -5$.

Example 1 *Solving an Absolute Value Equation*

Solve $|2x - 3| = 7$.

Solution

$|2x - 3| = 7$		*Rewrite original equation.*
$2x - 3 = 7$	or $2x - 3 = -7$	*Expression can be 7 or −7.*
$2x = 10$	or $2x = -4$	*Add 3 to both sides.*
$x = 5$	or $x = -2$	*Divide both sides by 2.*

The equation has two solutions: 5 and −2. Check these solutions by substituting each into the original equation. ∎

An absolute value *inequality* such as $|x - 2| < 4$ can be solved by rewriting it as a compound inequality.

Transformations of Absolute Value Inequalities

1. The inequality $|ax + b| < c$ means that $ax + b$ is *between* $-c$ and c. This is equivalent to $-c < ax + b < c$.

2. The inequality $|ax + b| > c$ means that $ax + b$ is *not between* $-c$ and c inclusive. This is equivalent to $ax + b < -c$ or $ax + b > c$.

In the first transformation, $<$ could be replaced by $\leq$, adjusting inclusiveness. Similarly, in the second transformation, $>$ could be replaced by $\geq$.

Example 2 *Solving an Absolute Value Inequality*

Solve $|2x - 3| < 5$.

Solution

$|2x - 3| < 5$	*Rewrite original inequality.*
$-5 < 2x - 3 < 5$	*Write equivalent compound inequality.*
$-2 < \quad 2x \quad < 8$	*Add 3 to each expression.*
$-1 < \quad x \quad < 4$	*Divide each expression by 2.*

The solution is *all real numbers that are greater than -1 <u>and</u> less than 4.* The graph is shown below.

Example 3 *Solving an Absolute Value Inequality*

Solve $|3x + 4| \geq 10$.

Solution   This absolute value inequality is equivalent to the following compound inequality.

$$3x + 4 \leq -10 \quad or \quad 3x + 4 \geq 10$$

Solve First Inequality:

$3x + 4 \leq -10$	*Rewrite first inequality.*
$3x \leq -14$	*Subtract 4 from both sides.*
$x \leq -\frac{14}{3}$	*Divide both sides by 3.*

Solve Second Inequality:

$3x + 4 \geq 10$	*Rewrite first inequality.*
$3x \geq 6$	*Subtract 4 from both sides.*
$x \geq 2$	*Divide both sides by 3.*

The solution is *all real numbers that are less than or equal to $-\frac{14}{3}$ <u>or</u> greater than or equal to 2.* The graph is shown below.

The pit organs of a rattlesnake can detect temperature changes that are as little as 0.005°F. By moving its head back and forth, a rattlesnake can detect warm prey, even in the dark.

Goal 2 Using Absolute Value Inequalities

Example 4 Creating a Model

To test the accuracy of a rattlesnake's "pit-organ sensory system," a biologist blindfolded a rattlesnake and presented the snake with a warm "target." The snake was on-target 17 times out of 36. In fact, the snake was within 5° of the target for 30 of the strikes. Let A represent the number of degrees by which the snake is off-target. Then $A = 0$ represents a strike that is aimed directly at the target. Positive values of A represent strikes to the right of the target, and negative values of A represent strikes to the left of the target. Use the diagram at the left to write an absolute-value inequality that describes the interval in which the 36 strikes occurred.

Solution From the diagram, you can see that the snake was never off by more than 15° in either direction. This can be represented by the compound inequality $-15 \leq A \leq 15$.

As an absolute value inequality, the interval in which the strikes occurred can be represented by $|A| \leq 15$. ■

Communicating about ALGEBRA

▶ **SHARING IDEAS about the Lesson**

Write absolute value inequalities that are equivalent to the following compound inequalities. Explain your strategy.

A. $-3 \leq x \leq 3$

B. $x \leq -2$ or $x \geq 2$

C. $0 < x < 6$

D. $x < 0$ or $x > 8$

EXERCISES

▶ **CRITICAL THINKING about the Lesson**

1. The absolute value of a number cannot be negative. How, then, can the absolute value of a be $-a$?

2. The absolute value of a can be defined as the distance from a to the origin on the real number line. Illustrate this definition with $a = -3$ and with $a = 4$.

3. The graph of the inequality $|x - 3| < 2$ can be described as *all real numbers that are within 2 units of 3*. Give a similar description of the graph of $|x - 4| < 1$.

4. The graph of the inequality $|y - 1| > 3$ can be described as *all real numbers that are greater than 3 units from 1*. Give a similar description of the graph of $|y + 2| > 4$. (Hint: $x + 2 = x - (-2)$.)

Independent Practice

In Exercises 5–8, decide whether the number is a solution of the equation.

5. $|4x + 5| = 10$, 2   **6.** $|2x - 16| = 10$, 3   **7.** $|6 - 2w| = 2$, 4   **8.** $|\frac{1}{2}x + 4| = 8$, 6

In Exercises 9–12, transform the absolute value equation into two linear equations.

9. $|x - 10| = 17$ **10.** $|7 - 2t| = 5$

11. $|4x + 1| = \frac{1}{2}$ **12.** $|22k + 6| = 9$

In Exercises 13–18, solve the equation.

13. $|9 + 2x| = 7$ **14.** $|4 - 6x| = 2$

15. $|\frac{1}{4}m - 9| = 6$ **16.** $|\frac{3}{5}x + 2| = 11$

17. $|20 - 3x| = 7$ **18.** $|20 - 9q| = 5$

In Exercises 19–22, transform the absolute value inequality into a compound inequality.

19. $|y + 5| < 3$ **20.** $|6x + 7| \le 5$ **21.** $|7 - 2h| \ge 9$ **22.** $|8 - x| > 25$

In Exercises 23–30, solve the inequality.

23. $|d + 1| \le 6$ **24.** $|11 - x| < 20$ **25.** $|14 - 5x| > 8$ **26.** $|18 + \frac{1}{2}x| \ge 10$

27. $|2x + 3| \ge 26$ **28.** $|7r + 3| < 11$ **29.** $|19 + j| < 2$ **30.** $|7 + 8x| > 5$

In Exercises 31–34, sketch the graph of the inequality.

31. $\left|\frac{1}{4}p - \frac{1}{3}\right| \le \frac{1}{3}$ **32.** $|x + 1| \le 27$ **33.** $|x - 8| > 14$ **34.** $|6 - 5c| < 9$

35. *Accuracy of Measurements*   In woodshop class, you must cut several pieces of wood to within $\frac{3}{16}$ inch of the teacher's specifications. Let $(s - x)$ represent the difference between the specification, s, and the measured length, x, of a cut piece. Write an absolute value inequality that describes the values of x that are within specifications. One of the pieces of wood is specified to be $s = 5\frac{1}{8}$ inches. Describe the acceptable lengths for this piece.

36. *The Mile Run*   The average time to run a mile for members of your gym class is 7 minutes 4 seconds. You want your time to be within 5 seconds of the class average. Rewrite the class average as seconds, then write and solve an absolute value inequality for the difference between your time, t, and the class average.

Hand Measurements   **In Exercises 37 and 38, use the following information.**

In a sampling conducted by the United States Air Force, the right-hand dimensions of 4000 Air Force men were measured. (The information could be used when designing control panels, keyboards, gloves, and so on.)

37. Ninety-five percent of the palm widths, p (in inches), were solutions of the inequality $|p - 3.49| \le 0.26$. Sketch the graph of this inequality.

38. Ninety-nine percent of the palm widths were solutions of the inequality $|p - 3.49| \le 0.37$. Sketch the graph of this inequality. How many of the 4000 men had palm widths that are solutions of the inequality $|p - 3.49| > 0.37$?

39. *Body Temperature*   Physicians consider an adult's body temperature to be normal if it is between 97.6°F and 99.6°F. Write an absolute value inequality that describes this normal temperature range.

40. *Green Ocean Plants*   Green plants can live in the ocean only at depths of 0 to 100 feet. Find an absolute value inequality describing the possible depth range of green plants in an ocean.

Show Collies   **In Exercises 41 and 42, use the following information.**

The American Kennel Club had developed guidelines for judging the features of various breeds of dogs. For collies, the guidelines specify that the weight should be between 60 and 75 pounds for males and between 50 and 65 pounds for females.
(Source: American Kennel Club)

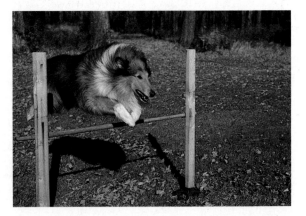

41. Write an absolute value inequality for the recommended weight of a female collie.

42. Write an absolute value inequality for the recommended weight of a male collie.

In Exercises 43–48, match the inequality with its graph.

43. $-\frac{1}{2} < x \leq \frac{3}{4}$

44. $1 \leq 2x + 3 < 5$

45. $3 < x + 4 \leq 5$

46. $-4 \leq x - 7 \leq -2$

47. $\frac{1}{3} < x + \frac{2}{3} \leq \frac{7}{6}$

48. $-17 < 17x \leq 34$

In Exercises 49–54, solve the equation.

49. $7x - \frac{1}{4} = 2$

50. $25 - x = 16x$

51. $\frac{10}{11}x + 5 = -\frac{5}{11}$

52. $18x + \frac{1}{2} = 13x$

53. $6 - 2x = 40x$

54. $35 + 3x = 10x$

In Exercises 55–60, solve the inequality.

55. $-5x \leq 65$

56. $6x < 4 - 12x$

57. $10 > 6 - 2x$

58. $13 \leq 5x - 2$

59. $\frac{1}{2} + \frac{3}{4}x < 10$

60. $-\frac{6}{5}x - \frac{1}{3} \geq \frac{2}{3}$

Exploration and Extension

American Doctors   **In Exercises 61 and 62, use the following information.**

The table at the right shows the number, N, of practicing medical doctors per 100,000 people in each of the 50 states in 1988.
(Source: U.S. Bureau of Census)

61. The range of N within the 50 states is given by the compound inequality

$$120 \leq N \leq 325.$$

Write an absolute value inequality that is equivalent to this compound inequality.

62. Drop the five lowest and five highest values of N. Complete the following statement: *Eighty percent of the values of N can be described by the compound inequality*

$$\boxed{?} \leq N \leq \boxed{?}.$$

Write an absolute value inequality that is equivalent to the compound inequality.

AK-138	HI- 225	ME- 173	NJ- 234	SD- 138
AL-151	IA- 145	MI- 180	NM-173	TN-187
AR-144	ID- 120	MN-212	NV- 158	TX- 169
AZ-191	IL- 210	MO-190	NY- 307	UT-177
CA-242	IN- 151	MS- 125	OH-191	VA- 204
CO-202	KS- 169	MT-150	OK- 145	VT- 244
CT-296	KY- 161	NC- 179	OR- 196	WA-206
DE- 191	LA- 184	ND-167	PA- 227	WI- 181
FL- 203	MA-322	NE- 168	RI- 244	WV-164
GA-167	MD-325	NH-186	SC- 156	WY-134

1.8

Exploring Data: Tables and Graphs

What you should learn:

Goal How to organize data by using tables and graphs

Why you should learn it:

Real-life problems can involve hundreds of pieces of information. Data-organization techniques help you to see patterns in the data.

Goal **Organizing Data**

The world we live in is becoming more and more complex. Almost every day of your life you will be given **data** that describe real-life situations. (The word *data* is plural, and it means information, facts, or numbers that describe something. The singular form, *datum*, is seldom used.)

A collection of data is easier to understand when it is organized in a table or in a graph. There is no "best way" to organize data, but there are many good ways. This lesson illustrates several types of tabular and graphic presentations: tables, frequency distributions, line plots, bar graphs, circle graphs, time-line graphs, and picture graphs.

Real Life
Family Size

Example 1 *Making a Frequency Distribution and Line Plot*

Thirty-two students in a class were asked how many brothers and sisters they have (including half brothers, half sisters, stepbrothers, and stepsisters). The results were as follows.

0, 2, 0, 1, 1, 3, 4, 0, 0, 3, 2
1, 1, 6, 0, 3, 0, 2, 1, 2, 6, 1
3, 0, 2, 1, 5, 7, 1, 2, 0, 4

Construct a frequency distribution and a line plot for this data.

Solution In the frequency distribution, each tally mark represents one response. In the line plot, each × represents one response.

Number	Tally	Frequency
7	|	1
6	||	2
5	|	1
4	||	2
3	||||	4
2	⫫ |	6
1	⫫ |||	8
0	⫫ |||	8

Frequency Distribution

Line plot

Connections

Fast-Food Sales

Example 2 — *Making a Bar Graph and a Circle Graph*

The table shows the ten fast-food companies in the United
States that had the greatest sales in 1990. Construct a double
bar graph that shows the number of outlets and the sales of
each company. Then construct a circle graph that shows each
company's percent of the total amount sold by the ten companies. *(Source: Restaurants and Institutions 400)*

Rank	Company	Number of Outlets	Sales ($ billions)
1.	McDonald's	11,162	17.3
2.	Burger King	6,051	5.7
3.	Kentucky Fried Chicken	7,945	5.3
4.	Pizza Hut	7,410	4.1
5.	Wendy's	3,755	3.0
6.	Hardee's	3,231	2.9
7.	Domino's Pizza	5,220	2.5
8.	Dairy Queen	5,206	2.2
9.	Taco Bell	3,125	2.1
10.	Arby's	2,247	1.3

Solution — The double bar graph is shown below. The circle
graph is shown at the left.

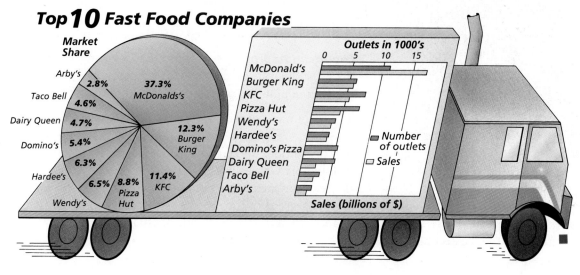

Top 10 Fast Food Companies

Real Life
Women's Rights

Example 3 *Creating a Time Line*

On August 18, 1920, the Nineteenth Amendment to the United States Constitution was ratified. This amendment gave women in each state the right to vote. Before the Nineteenth Amendment, each state was allowed to decide whether women could vote. Find the dates that women achieved full voting rights in each state. Then create a time line to show the results.

Solution Wyoming was the first state in 1869 to grant full voting rights to women. By the time South Dakota, Oklahoma, and Michigan granted voting rights in 1918, the women's suffrage movement had gained enough support to pass the Nineteenth Amendment. ∎

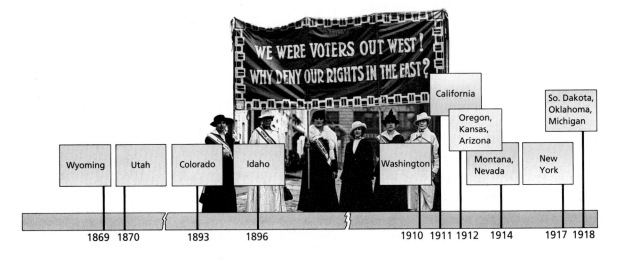

Communicating about **ALGEBRA**

▶ **SHARING IDEAS about the Lesson**

Choose an Appropriate Graph For each set of data, choose the most appropriate graph—bar or double bar graph, circle graph, line plot, or time line. Justify your answer.

A. The number of gold and silver medals won by North and South American countries in the 1992 Olympics
B. The number of countries participating in each of the Olympic Games from 1960 to the present
C. The year each sport became an Olympic event
D. The percent of the medals that were won by participants from each of the seven continents

EXERCISES

Guided Practice

▶ **CRITICAL THINKING about the Lesson**

1. Give an example of a collection of data that you could organize using a line plot.

2. *Student Council Election*   Which of the techniques discussed in this lesson do you think is best suited to organizing the results of a student council election? Explain.

3. *Favorite Music*   Each of your classmates was asked to select their favorite type of music from these choices: classical, jazz, country, rock, and rap. How would you organize the results?

4. *Pizza Prices*   Which would give a better picture of the price of a cheeze pizza at pizza shops—a frequency distribution or a bar graph? Explain.

Independent Practice

5. *Fishing Trip*   On each day of your three-week summer vacation in Alaska, you went fishing. At the end of each day, you recorded the number of legal-size fish you caught. The results are shown in the table at the right. Construct a frequency distribution and a line plot for this data.

S	M	T	W	T	F	S
5	7	4	5	2	3	4
3	4	6	2	7	6	1
5	1	3	6	2	4	3

6. *Band Practice*   On each day except Sundays for two weeks, the band director recorded the attendance of his band. Construct a frequency distribution and line plot for the results.

M	T	W	T	F	S
299	298	300	300	297	300
300	299	295	296	300	299

7. *Endangered Species*   In 1990, 405 animal species were endangered in the United States. Construct a circle graph that shows each category's percent of the total number of endangered species.

(Source: U.S. Fish and Wildlife Service)

Amphibians/Reptiles	16
Arachnids/Insects	12
Birds	57
Clams/Snails	49
Fish	53
Mammals	36
Plants	182

The Florida panther is on the top-ten list of endangered species published by **Defenders of Wildlife.**

8. *You're Kidding, Aren't You?* In 1985, a typical daily serving for each New York Giants football player during training camp included about 2.6 pounds of prime rib, 1.1 pounds of chicken, 0.3 pound of fish, 0.3 pound of vegetables, 0.5 pound of fruit, and 1.1 pounds of pasta. In 1990, this menu changed to 2.1 pounds of prime rib, 1.6 pounds of chicken, 1.1 pounds of fish, 0.7 pound of vegetables, 1.3 pounds of fruit, and 2.1 pounds of pasta. Construct a double bar graph that shows the pounds of each type of food for 1985 and 1990. *(Source: Dick Rossi, New York Giants)*

United States Shopping Malls   **In Exercises 9–12, use the following information.**

The list shows the ten largest shopping malls in the United States completed by 1990. *(Source: International Council of Shopping Centers)*

Shopping Mall	Square Feet
Del Amo Fashion Center (Calif.)	3,000,000
The Galleria (Tex.)	2,808,000
South Coast Plaza & Town (Calif.)	2,600,000
Lakewood Center Mall (Calif.)	2,498,000
Roosevelt Field Mall (N.J.)	2,264,000
Sawgrass Mills (Fla.)	2,200,000
Randall Park Mall (Ohio)	2,097,000
Woodfield (Ill.)	2,000,000
Northwest Plaza (Mo.)	1,868,000
Franklin Mills (Penn.)	1,800,000

9. Construct a bar graph that represents the sizes of the ten largest malls completed by 1990.

10. What percent of the total shopping center space in the United States is represented by the ten shopping malls in the table?

11. Use the graph at the right to estimate the number of shopping malls in the United States in 1970 and 1980.

12. What was the average number of square feet in a shopping mall in the United States in 1990?

Retail space for shopping centers in 1990 was 4.5 billion square feet—18 sq. ft. for every person in the U.S.A.
(Source: International Council of Shopping Centers.)

13. *Landfills in Vermont* In 1987, Vermont put 328,200 tons of solid waste into its 64 landfills. The types of material put into the landfills are shown in the circle graph. Use the graph to estimate the weight of the cardboard.
(Source: Vermont Agency of Natural Resources)

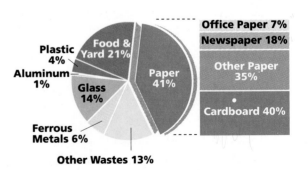

House Wren Nest   **In Exercises 14 and 15, use the following information.**

Wrens are very eccentric in their selection of building materials. A house wren's nest was taken apart for analysis, and the following was found among the nesting materials.
(Source: **America's Favorite Backyard Birds,** *Simon and Schuster, 1983)*

52 Hairpins	188 Nails
4 Thumbtacks	13 Staples
21 Pins	4 Pencil leads
6 Paper clips	52 Wires
1 Buckle	2 Hooks
3 Trash bag twists	2 Odds and ends

14. What percent of the items were nails?

15. What percent of the items were staples?

Of the 63 types of wrens in the world, 7 are native to the Eastern United States.
(Source: **Peterson's Field Guide of Eastern Birds***)*

In Exercises 16–21, solve the inequality.

16. $9 + 3x \leq 1 - x$

17. $1 + 4x > x - 5$

18. $-12 < 3x - 1 \leq 3$

19. $2 \leq 5 + 7x \leq 6$

20. $|x + 4| \geq 4$

21. $|3 - x| < 21$

22. *The First Thirteen States*   The Constitution of the United States was signed by representatives of the original thirteen colonies on September 17, 1787. Each colony, however, was not admitted into the union as a state until it had ratified (approved by vote) the Constitution. The dates of admission into the union are shown in the table. Create a time-line graph for this data.

23. *The Next Seven States*   Use a reference source to find the dates of the next seven states that were admitted to the union: Vermont, Kentucky, Tennessee, Ohio, Louisiana, Indiana, and Mississippi. Make a time-line graph of these data. Did you use the same scale as in Exercise 22?

State	Date of Admission
1. Delaware	December 7, 1787
2. Pennsylvania	December 12, 1787
3. New Jersey	December 18, 1787
4. Georgia	January 2, 1788
5. Connecticut	January 9, 1788
6. Massachusetts	February 6, 1788
7. Maryland	April 28, 1788
8. South Carolina	May 23, 1788
9. New Hampshire	June 21, 1788
10. Virginia	June 25, 1788
11. New York	July 26, 1788
12. North Carolina	November 21, 1789
13. Rhode Island	May 29, 1790

Chapter Summary

What did you learn?

1. Add, subtract, multiply, and divide real numbers. **(1.1, 1.2)**
2. Evaluate an algebraic expression. **(1.2)**
3. Solve
   - a linear equation. **(1.3)**
   - a literal equation for one of its variables. **(1.5)**
   - an absolute value equation. **(1.7)**
4. Solve and graph
   - a linear inequality. **(1.6)**
   - an absolute value inequality. **(1.7)**

5. Create algebraic models for real-life situations. **(1.1–1.7)**
6. Use problem-solving strategies to solve real-life problems. **(1.4)**

7. Use tables and graphs to organize data. **(1.8)**

Why did you learn it?

The *primary* use of algebra is to create mathematical models for real-life situations that can be used to answer questions about those situations. As you continue your study of algebra, you should recognize that almost every facet of life uses some mathematics. Most people know that business, science, construction, engineering, and computer science use a lot of mathematics. But other fields such as history, art, music, politics, and psychology also use mathematics. For this book, we have chosen applications of mathematics from many different fields. We hope that we have chosen many that interest you.

How does it fit into the bigger picture of algebra?

This first chapter reviewed several basic skills and strategies from Algebra 1. From that course, you should remember that algebra is much more than just solving equations that contain letters (or variables). Other algebraic skills include extending the rules of arithmetic to form the rules of algebra, simplifying algebraic expressions, creating and using mathematical models in real-life settings, and organizing information with tables and graphs.

You practiced using these skills in this chapter, and you will continue expanding them throughout this course.

In Exercises 1–6, plot the numbers on the real number line. Then state which is greater. (1.1)

1. $\frac{2}{3}$ and $\frac{3}{4}$

2. $\frac{6}{7}$ and $\frac{5}{6}$

3. -4 and -3

4. -5 and -5.1

5. $\sqrt{3}$ and 1.7

6. $-\sqrt{2}$ and -1.4

In Exercises 7–12, write the numbers in increasing order. (1.1)

7. $-2, -0.5, 0, 0.5, -1.5, 1$

8. $-1.2, 0.6, -0.2, 1.4, 0.61, -0.1$

9. $\frac{1}{3}, -\frac{1}{2}, \frac{2}{3}, -\frac{1}{4}, \frac{2}{5}, -\frac{1}{8}$

10. $\frac{1}{3}, 0.33, \frac{3}{10}, \frac{3}{11}, 0.34, \frac{3}{8}$

11. $-\sqrt{2}, 1.41, -1.42, \sqrt{2}, -1.41, 1.42$

12. $\pi, \frac{22}{7}, 3.1416, \frac{355}{113}, 3.14, \frac{311}{99}$

In Exercises 13 and 14, find the product. (1.1)

13. $\left(\dfrac{80 \text{ kilometers}}{1 \text{ hour}}\right)\left(\dfrac{1000 \text{ meters}}{1 \text{ kilometer}}\right)\left(\dfrac{1 \text{ hour}}{60 \text{ minutes}}\right)\left(\dfrac{1 \text{ minute}}{60 \text{ seconds}}\right)$

14. $\left(\dfrac{20 \text{ dollars}}{1 \text{ ton}}\right)\left(\dfrac{1 \text{ ton}}{2000 \text{ pounds}}\right)\left(\dfrac{1 \text{ pound}}{16 \text{ ounces}}\right)\left(\dfrac{100 \text{ cents}}{1 \text{ dollar}}\right)$

In Exercises 15–20, evaluate the expression. (1.2)

15. $-2b^2$ when $b = -2$

16. $7x - 8x^3$ when $x = -1$

17. $5\sqrt{y} + 2$ when $y = 4$

18. $|2x - 5|$ when $x = 2.1$

19. $\dfrac{3ab^2 + 1}{3a^2b - 1}$ when $a = 2$ and $b = -2$

20. $\dfrac{4x - 3y}{3x - 4y}$ when $x = 2$ and $y = 3$

In Exercises 21–24, evaluate the expression. (1.1)

21. $-3 - 6 \div 2 - 12$

22. $7 - (3 \cdot 4)2 + 8$

23. $12 - 3 \cdot 2 + 5$

24. $-4 - 5 - 2 \cdot 3^2$

In Exercises 25–28, find the area of the blue region. (1.2)

25. Triangle   **26.** Circle   **27.** Ellipse   **28.** Trapezoid

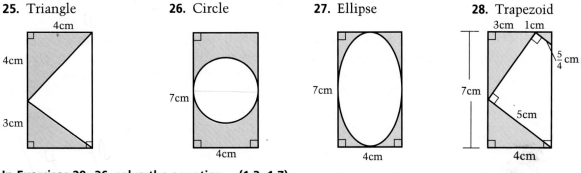

In Exercises 29–36, solve the equation. (1.3, 1.7)

29. $-5x + 3 = 18$

30. $-2(x - 4) = 12$

31. $3(x - 6) = 6x + 3$

32. $-4x - 4 = 3(2 - x)$

33. $|x| = 3$

34. $|x + 1| = 4$

35. $|2x - 3| = 5$

36. $-2|3x - 1| = -8$

In Exercises 37–42, solve and graph the inequality. (1.7)

37. $2x - 3 < 5$

38. $-3x + 4 \geq 2x + 19$

39. $-3 \leq 2x + 1 < 5$

40. $3x + 1 < -2$ or $3x + 1 > 7$

41. $|2x - 5| < 9$

42. $|3x + 4| \geq 2$

Scouting Helicopter   **In Exercises 43 and 44, use the following information.**

In 1991, Boeing Helicopters and Sikorsky Aircraft were awarded a $30 billion contract to build the United States Army's new scouting helicopter. Each two-person chopper will be equipped with night vision and will be able to fly 1250 nautical miles before refueling. The first of nearly 1300 helicopters is scheduled for production in 1998.
*(Source: **Popular Science**)*

43. A nautical mile is 6080 feet. How many (standard) miles will the new scouting helicopter be able to fly before refueling?

44. Approximate the average cost of each scouting helicopter.

Lettuce   **In Exercises 45 and 46, use the following information.**

For 1970 through 1990, the average price, p (in dollars), of a pound of lettuce can be modeled by $p = 0.19 + 0.023t$, where $t = 0$ represents 1970. The total amount, L (in billions of pounds), of lettuce consumed in the United States can be modeled by $L = 4.5 + 0.05t$.
*(Source: **U.S. Department of Agriculture**)*

45. According to these models, during which year will the average price of lettuce be $0.765?

46. Approximate the total sales in lettuce in the United States in 1990.

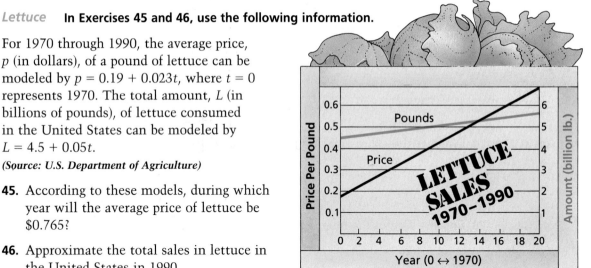

In Exercises 47–50, find the volume of the solid. (1.2)

47. Sphere

48. Cone

49. Cylinder

50. Rectangular Prism

In Exercises 51 and 52, solve the literal equation for _y_. (1.5)

51. $7x + 3y = 9$

52. $-3xy + 4y = 10$

53. *Louisiana and Georgia*   The range of recorded temperatures, L (in °F), in Louisiana is $-16 \leq L \leq 114$. The range of recorded temperatures, G, in Georgia is related to those in Louisiana by $L = G + 1$. What is the range of recorded temperatures in Georgia?

54. *Union Membership*   Use the graph at the right to approximate the percent of American workers who were members of unions in 1985 and in 1993.
(Source: Bureau of Labor Statistics)

In 1994, 87 million full-time salaried and wage workers were employed in the United States.

55. *Overtime*   If you are paid $12 an hour for up to 40 hours per week and time and a half for overtime, how many hours would you have to work in a week to earn $624? Create a bar graph that shows your weekly pay for working overtime between 0 and 8 hours.

56. *License Plate Colors*   Use the graph at the right to create a circle graph that shows the colors used on automobile license plates in the United States. *(Source: USA Today)*

57. *Number of License Plates*   In 1993, 10,613,000 vehicles were registered in New Mexico, Maryland, and Georgia. New Mexico had 3000 less than two fifths of the number in Maryland. Georgia had 52,000 less than 4 times the number in New Mexico. How many registered motor vehicles were in each of these three states?
(Source: U.S. Federal Highway Administration)

58. *Muscular Dystrophy Telethon*   Use the graph below to estimate the amount of money raised by the Muscular Dystrophy Telethon in 1988.
(Source: Muscular Dystrophy Association)

59. *Muscular Dystrophy*   Duchenne dystrophy is the most common form of muscular dystrophy. It is very rare in females (women who carry the defective gene rarely develop the disease), but it occurs in about one out of 3000 males. In 1992, about two million male babies were born in the United States. Approximately how many had Duchenne muscular dystrophy?

The Muscular Dystrophy Association Labor Day Telethon results.

The Race to the South Pole In Exercises 60–63, use the following information.

In 1911, the Norwegian explorer Roald Amundsen and the English explorer Robert Scott both wanted to be the first human to reach the South Pole. Going by different routes (of about 900 miles each), the two explorers raced teams of men, dogs, and horses over the frozen land. Amundsen started on October 19 and averaged about 15.8 miles per day. Scott started on November 1 and averaged about 11.6 miles per day.

60. On which day did Amundsen's team reach the South Pole?

61. On which day did Scott's team reach the South Pole?

62. Because it is covered with a thick ice cap, Antarctica has the greatest average elevation of any of Earth's seven continents. The thickness, I (in feet), of the ice cap varies between 0 and 15,700. Write a compound inequality for the thickness of Antarctica's ice cap. Then, write the compound inequality as an absolute value inequality.

63. The temperature, F (in degrees Fahrenheit), in Antarctica can be described by $-128.6 \le F \le 50$. Write an inequality for the temperature range in degrees Celsius.

64. *Penguins* The emperor penguin is the largest species of penguins—adults have heights of up to 45 inches. The heights (in inches) of the other species are king (37), Adelie (29), chinstrap (27), gentoo (29), macaroni (27), royal (24), rockhopper (22), crested (26), fiordland (22), black-footed (27), Peruvian (25), Magellan (27), Galápagos (21), yellow-crowned (29), little (16), Chathan Island little (15), and white-flippered (16). Create a bar graph to represent the heights of the 18 species.

65. *Kings and Emperors* Although king penguins are almost as tall as emperor penguins, the kings weigh only half of what the emperors weigh. Let K be the average weight (in pounds) of an adult king penguin and let E be the average weight (in pounds) of an adult emperor penguin. If $K + E = 99$, find K and E.

Chapter TEST

1. Plot $-\frac{4}{3}$ and $-\frac{3}{4}$ on the real number line. Which is greater?

2. Write the numbers in decreasing order: $-0.1, -0.6, 0.3, -0.5, 0.4$.

3. Evaluate $8 - 4 \div 2 - 1$.

4. Simplify $3(x - 8) - 2(x + 5)$.

5. Evaluate $-2b^2 + 4ab$ when $a = 3$ and $b = -1$.

6. Evaluate $\frac{1}{4}x + \frac{1}{3}y$ when $x = 3$ and $y = 2$.

In Exercises 7–10, solve the equation.

7. $2x + 19 = 5(x + 2)$

8. $1.2n = 2.3n - 2.20$

9. $|2x + 7| = 3$

10. $|5x + 11| = 9$

11. Solve the literal equation $5xy + 2x = 3$ for y.

12. Solve the literal equation $a^2b + 2b = 12$ for b.

In Exercises 13–16, solve and graph the inequality.

13. $5x - 2 \le 7$

14. $1 < 2x - 3 < 5$

15. $|1 - 2x| \le 3$

16. $|-x + 3| > 4$

In Exercises 17 and 18, find the area of the blue region.

17.

18.

19. In 1990, the average sales tax percent in Connecticut, Illinois, Rhode Island, and Tennessee was 6%. The sales tax in Connecticut, Rhode Island, and Tennessee was, respectively, 2.5%, 1%, and 0.5% more than the sales tax in Illinois. What was the sales tax percent in each state?

20. Of the Broadway shows running at the end of 1990, those that had the most performances were *Cats* (3427), *Les Misérables* (1527), *Phantom of the Opera* (1224), *Black and Blue* (805), *Grand Hotel* (473), *Gypsy* (468), *A Few Good Men* (465), *City of Angels* (439), *Aspects of Love* (305), and *Piano Lesson* (295). Create a bar graph to represent these data. *(Source: Variety)*

Cast member in Cats

21. Let x represent the total number of performances of *Cats* at the end of 1991. In 1991, the show had at most 312 performances. Write an inequality that describes the possible values of x.

Linear Equations

LESSONS

2.1 The Graph of an
Equation ▪ 64

2.2 Slope and Rate of
Change ▪ 70

2.3 Quick Graphs of
Linear Equations ▪ 78

2.4 Writing Equations of
Lines ▪ 86

2.5 Graphing Linear
Inequalities in Two
Variables ▪ 94

2.6 Graphs of Absolute
Value Equations
▪ 101

2.7 Exploring Data:
Fitting a Line to Data
▪ 107

*Water-ski jumping is performed
competitively in many parts of
the country.*

Real Life
Water Skiing

$$\text{Slope} = \frac{\text{Rise}}{\text{Run}} = \frac{6}{21} = \frac{2}{7}$$

In tournament water-ski jumping, the ramp rises to a height of 6 feet on a ramp that is 21 feet long. Skiers leave the ramp at about 35 miles per hour and can travel over 130 feet before hitting the water.

The steepness of the ski ramp can be measured by its slope. The slope is the ratio of its height (the rise) to the length of its base (the run).

2.1

The Graph of an Equation

What you should learn:

Goal 1 How to sketch a graph using a table of values

Goal 2 How to identify equations whose graphs are horizontal or vertical lines

Why you should learn it:

You can use a coordinate plane to visualize the relationship between two variables.

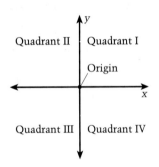

Goal 1 Sketching the Graph of an Equation

A **coordinate plane** is formed by two perpendicular real number lines. The horizontal line is the **horizontal axis,** or **x-axis,** and the vertical line is the **vertical axis,** or **y-axis.** The point at which the two lines meet is the **origin,** and the axes divide the plane into four parts called **quadrants.**

Each point in a coordinate plane corresponds to an **ordered pair** of real numbers. For an ordered pair, the first number is the **horizontal coordinate** and the second number is the **vertical coordinate.** For instance, the ordered pair $(4, -1)$ has a horizontal coordinate of 4 and a vertical coordinate of -1.

$$\underbrace{\text{Horizontal}}_{\text{coordinate}} \quad (4, -1) \quad \underbrace{\text{Vertical}}_{\text{coordinate}}$$

An ordered pair (x, y) is a **solution** of an equation in x and y if the equation is true when the values of x and y are substituted into the equation. The **graph** of an equation in x and y is the collection of *all* points (x, y) whose coordinates are **solutions** of the equation. For instance, since $(4, -1)$ is a solution of $y = -2x + 7$, you know that $(4, -1)$ is a point on the graph of $y = -2x + 7$. To sketch the graph of an equation, construct a *table of values,* graph enough solutions to recognize a pattern, and then connect the points.

Example 1 *Sketching the Graph of an Equation*

Sketch the graph of $y = -2x + 7$.

Solution Begin by constructing a table of values for $y = -2x + 7$.

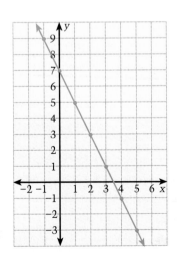

Choose *x.*	−1	0	1	2	3	4	5
Evaluate *y.*	9	7	5	3	1	−1	−3

With this table of values, you have found seven solutions.

$(-1, 9), (0, 7), (1, 5), (2, 3), (3, 1), (4, -1), (5, -3)$

By plotting the points, you can see that they all lie on a line. The line through the points is the *graph* of the equation. ■

Goal 2 Identifying Equations of Lines

The point-plotting technique shown in Example 1 is useful when sketching the graph of an unfamiliar equation. Some equations, however, occur so often that you can learn to recognize their graphs and sketch a "quick graph." Two types of equations whose graphs are easy to recognize are equations of the form $x = a$ or $y = b$.

> **Equations of Horizontal and Vertical Lines**
> **1.** In a coordinate plane, the graph of $x = a$ is a **vertical line.**
> **2.** In a coordinate plane, the graph of $y = b$ is a **horizontal line.**

Example 2 Sketching Horizontal and Vertical Lines

Sketch the graphs of $x = 4$ and $y = -2$. Find the coordinates of the point of intersection of the two graphs.

Solution The graph of $x = 4$ is a vertical line and the graph of $y = -2$ is a horizontal line because the solutions must be of the following form.

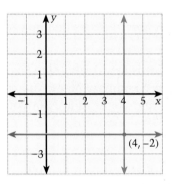

Vertical line: $x = 4$

| x must be 4. | y can have any value. |

$(4, y)$

Horizontal line: $y = -2$

| x can have any value. | y must be -2. |

$(x, -2)$

The point of intersection of the graphs must have an x-coordinate of 4 *and* a y-coordinate of -2. Thus the point is $(4, -2)$. ■

Real Life
Nutrition

Example 3 Creating a Model

For 1980 through 1990, the per capita consumption, p (in pounds), of canned white potatoes in the United States is shown in the table. Write a model that approximates the number of pounds of canned white potatoes eaten per year by an American. Let $t = 0$ represent 1980.
(Source: U.S. Department of Agriculture)

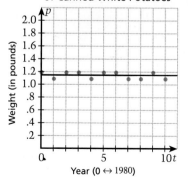

Annual Per Capita Consumption of Canned White Potatoes

Weight (in pounds)

Year (0 ↔ 1980)

Year, t	0	1	2	3	4	5	6	7	8	9	10
Pounds, p	1.2	1.1	1.2	1.2	1.1	1.2	1.2	1.1	1.1	1.2	1.1

Solution Each year the consumption was either 1.1 or 1.2 lb per person. Thus a reasonable model would be $p = 1.15$. ■

The Homestead Act, passed by Congress in 1862, allowed Americans or new immigrants the right to obtain 160 acres of public land, called a quarter, because it formed a quarter of a square mile. In many of the midwestern states, the lines that marked adjoining square-mile sections became roads and county borders. The map at the right shows the county lines in Iowa. They were drawn so that no one would live more than one day's buggy ride from their county seat.

Connections
Geography

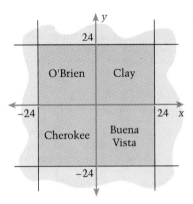

Example 4 *Finding the Boundary Lines of a County*

On the map above, a coordinate plane has been superimposed over four counties, O'Brien, Clay, Cherokee, and Buena Vista, in northwestern Iowa. Find equations that approximate the boundaries of these four counties. The scale on the coordinate plane is 1 mile to each unit. How many sections and quarters are in each of the four counties?

Solution   Each of the four counties is approximately square, 24 miles by 24 miles. For the given coordinate plane, the north and south boundaries of the four counties are horizontal lines given by

$$y = 24, \ y = 0, \text{ and } y = -24.$$

The east and west boundaries are vertical lines given by

$$x = 24, \ x = 0, \text{ and } x = -24.$$

Each county contains about 576 sections. Since a section has four quarters, each county has 2304 quarters.   ■

Communicating about **ALGEBRA**

▶ **SHARING IDEAS about the Lesson**

Sketch the graph of each equation.

A. $y = -3$ **B.** $y = 2x - 4$ **C.** $y = -x + 3$

D. What is the equation of the x-axis? What is the equation of the y-axis?

EXERCISES

Guided Practice

▶ **CRITICAL THINKING about the Lesson**

1. Plot the point $(-1, 3)$ in a coordinate plane.
2. Plot the point $(6, -2)$ in a coordinate plane.
3. Construct a table of values for $y = 3x - 9$. Then use the table to sketch the graph of $y = 3x - 9$. Can you sketch the *entire* graph? Explain.
4. What does *quadrant* mean?
5. Explain how to sketch a quick graph of $x = -5$.
6. Explain how to sketch a quick graph of $y = 2$.

Independent Practice

In Exercises 7–12, plot the point in a coordinate plane. In which quadrant does the point lie? (Points on an axis are not in any of the quadrants.)

7. $(5, -1)$ **8.** $(4, 9)$ **9.** $(-6, -2)$ **10.** $(-3, 0)$ **11.** $(0, 5)$ **12.** $(-1, 2)$

In Exercises 13–18, find three points on the graph of the equation. (There are many such points.)

13. $y = x + 5$ **14.** $y = -6x - 8$ **15.** $y = 5x - 1$

16. $y = -8x + 3$ **17.** $y = -3x + 4$ **18.** $y = 9x + 2$

In Exercises 19–24, match the equation with its graph.

19. $x = 3$ **20.** $y = -x - 3$ **21.** $y = -2x + 1$

22. $y = x - 5$ **23.** $y = x + 1$ **24.** $y = 3$

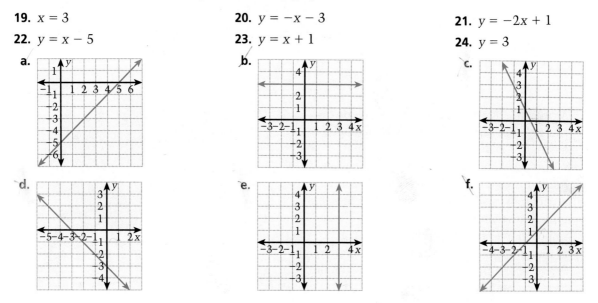

In Exercises 25–32, sketch the graph of the equation.

25. $y = x - 5$ **26.** $y = -x + 8$ **27.** $y = 2x + 5$ **28.** $y = 4x - 3$

29. $y = -4x + 2$ **30.** $y = 3x + 1$ **31.** $y = 3x - 4$ **32.** $y = -2x - 4$

In Exercises 33–36, sketch both lines on the coordinate plane. Then find the coordinates of the point at which the two lines intersect.

33. $x = -2, y = 5$ **34.** $y = 0, x = -10$

35. $y = 1, x = 8$ **36.** $x = 11, y = 6$

In Exercises 37–40, write an equation for the line.

37. The x-coordinate of each point on the line is -4.

38. The x-coordinate of each point on the line is 6.

39. The y-coordinate of each point on the line is 1.

40. The y-coordinate of each point on the line is -12.

In Exercises 41–44, write equations for the horizontal and vertical lines that pass through the point.

41. $(10, 0)$ **42.** $(-4, 15)$

43. $(-5, -3)$ **44.** $(6, -9)$

Mount St. Helens before the eruption.

45. *Physician's Services* For 1985 through 1993, the average amount, p (in dollars), spent by an American on physician's services is shown in the table. The table also shows the average amount, h (in dollars), spent by an American on all health services. Let r represent the ratio of p to h, and let t represent the year, with $t = 5$ representing 1985. Calculate the value of r for each year, t. Graph your results, and write a model that approximates the relationship between r and t.
(Source: U.S. Health Care Financing Administration)

Year, t	5	6	7	8	9	10	11	12	13
Physician's Services, p	231	256	282	310	329	356	373	398	411
Health Services, h	942	1023	1115	1212	1324	1447	1511	1597	1693

46. *Mount St. Helens* Mount St. Helens is a volcano in Washington that had been dormant for many years. In 1980, the volcano erupted, causing great damage for many miles around the volcano. The map at the right shows the affected region. Each unit on the coordinate plane that is superimposed over the map represents 2 miles. Is the point $(-4, 2)$ in the damaged region? Write equations for the sides of a rectangle that enclose the damaged area.

El Escorial   In Exercises 47 and 48, use the following information.

El Escorial, a monumental creation of Philip II of Spain, was completed in 1584. It is located in the Guadarrama Mountains near Madrid. A combination church, monastery, palace, mausoleum, college, and library, El Escorial is almost a city in itself.

47. A coordinate plane has been superimposed over the floor plan of El Escorial so that the main gate lies at the origin. Each unit on the coordinate plane represents 50 feet. Approximate the number of square feet in El Escorial.

48. Philip II often joined the monks in their devotions in the High Choir located at $(0, 7.25)$. Philip's apartment was located at $(1.25, 12)$. About how many feet did Philip walk from his apartment to High Choir? Explain your reasoning.

Integrated Review

49. Evaluate $-6x - 22$ when $x = 1$.

50. Evaluate $-14x + 8$ when $x = 2$.

In Exercises 51–54, find the value for _y_ when _x_ has the given value.

51. $y = x - 16$, $x = 9$

52. $y = -2x + 8$, $x = -10$

53. $y = 2x + 11$, $x = 0$

54. $y = x - 20$, $x = -20$

In Exercises 55 and 56, copy and complete the table.

55. $y = 3x - 5$

x	−3	−2	−1	0	1	2	3
y	?	?	?	?	?	?	?

56. $y = -8x + 11$

x	−3	−2	−1	0	1	2	3
y	?	?	?	?	?	?	?

In Exercises 57–60, solve the equation for _y_.

57. $4x + y = 10$

58. $x - 6y = 12$

59. $6x + 2y = 9$

60. $4x + 5y = 20$

Exploration and Extension

In Exercises 61 and 62, find the point of intersection of the two lines.

61. $y = -5x + 9$ and $x = 12$

62. $y = 3x - 14$ and $y = 4$

2.2

Slope and Rate of Change

What you should learn:

Goal 1 How to find the slope of a line and to identify parallel and perpendicular lines from their slopes

Goal 2 How to interpret slope as a rate of change

Why you should learn it:

You can model many real-life situations using slope—interpreting it either geometrically or as a rate of change.

Goal 1 **Finding the Slope of a Line**

The **slope** of a nonvertical line is the number of units the line rises (or falls) for each unit of horizontal change.

The line shown below at the left rises 2 units for each unit of horizontal change from left to right. Thus this line has a slope of 2. Two points on a line are all that is needed to determine its slope, which is represented by the letter "*m*."

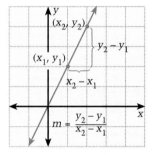

The Slope of a Line

The **slope,** *m*, of the nonvertical line passing through the points (x_1, y_1) and (x_2, y_2) is

$$m = \frac{y_2 - y_1}{x_2 - x_1}.$$

The numerator is read as "*y* sub 2 minus *y* sub 1" and is called the **rise.** The denominator is read as "*x* sub 2 minus *x* sub 1" and is called the **run.** The slope of a vertical line is not defined.

Line rises,
positive slope.

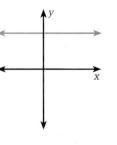

Line is horizontal,
zero slope.

Line falls,
negative slope.

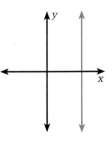

Line is vertical,
undefined slope.

Example 1   *Finding the Slope of a Line*

Find the slope of the line containing $(-3, 4)$ and $(2, 1)$.

Solution   Let $(x_1, y_1) = (-3, 4)$ and $(x_2, y_2) = (2, 1)$.

$$m = \frac{y_2 - y_1}{x_2 - x_1} \quad \begin{array}{l}\leftarrow \textit{Rise: Difference of y-values} \\ \leftarrow \textit{Run: Difference of x-values}\end{array}$$

$$= \frac{1 - 4}{2 - (-3)} \qquad \textit{Substitute values.}$$

$$= \frac{-3}{2 + 3} \qquad \textit{Simplify.}$$

$$= -\frac{3}{5} \qquad \textit{Simplify.} \qquad \blacksquare$$

In Example 1, notice that the line falls from left to right, and the slope of the line is negative. This suggests one of the important uses of slope—to decide whether y decreases, increases, or is constant as x increases.

Classification of Lines by Slope

1. A line with positive slope *rises* from left to right. $(m > 0)$
2. A line with negative slope *falls* from left to right. $(m < 0)$
3. A line with slope zero *is horizontal.* $(m = 0)$
4. A line with undefined slope *is vertical.*   (m is undefined.)

The slope of a line tells you more than whether the line rises, falls, or is horizontal. It also tells you the steepness of the line. For two lines with positive slopes, the line with the greater slope is steeper. For two lines with negative slopes, the line with the slope of greater absolute value is steeper.

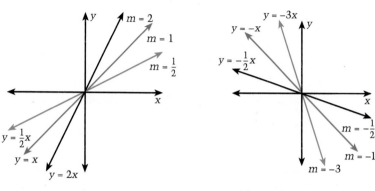

Lines with positive slopes   *Lines with negative slopes*

Two lines in a plane are **parallel** if they do not intersect. Two lines in a plane are **perpendicular** if they intersect to form a right angle. Slope can be used to determine whether two (nonvertical) lines are parallel or perpendicular.

Slopes of Parallel and Perpendicular Lines

Consider two different, nonvertical lines with slopes of m_1 and m_2.

1. The lines are parallel if and only if they have the same slope.

$m_1 = m_2$ *Parallel lines*

2. The lines are perpendicular if and only if their slopes are negative reciprocals of each other.

$m_1 = -\dfrac{1}{m_2}$ *Perpendicular lines*

The phrase "if and only if" is used in mathematics as a way to write two **converse** statements as a single statement. For instance, the two statements in property 1 above are *if two lines are parallel, then they have the same slope* and its converse *if two lines have the same slope, then they are parallel.*

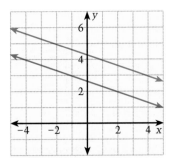

Example **2**	*Deciding Whether Lines are Parallel or Perpendicular*

Decide whether the two lines are parallel, perpendicular, or neither.

Line 1	Line 2
a. Contains $(1, 4)$, $(2, 7)$	Contains $(-2, 1)$, $(1, 0)$
b. Contains $(-2, 5)$, $(4, 3)$	Contains $(-1, 3)$, $(2, 2)$

Solution

a. The slopes of the two lines are

$$m_1 = \frac{7 - 4}{2 - 1} = 3 \text{ and } m_2 = \frac{0 - 1}{1 - (-2)} = -\frac{1}{3}.$$

Because m_1 and m_2 are the negative reciprocals of each other, you can conclude that the lines are perpendicular. The graphs of these two lines are shown at the left.

b. The slopes of the two lines are

$$m_1 = \frac{3 - 5}{4 - (-2)} = -\frac{1}{3} \text{ and } m_2 = \frac{2 - 3}{2 - (-1)} = -\frac{1}{3}.$$

Because $m_1 = m_2$, you can conclude that the lines are parallel. The graphs of these two lines are shown at the left. ∎

In real-life problems, slope is often used to describe a **constant rate of change** or an **average rate of change.** These rates include units of measure, such as miles per hour or dollars per year.

Connections
Education

Example 3 *Slope as a Rate of Change*

In 1980, 3.5% of the doctorates in engineering were awarded to women. By 1990, 8.5% were earned by women. Find the average rate of change in the percent of engineering doctorates earned by women from 1980 to 1990. *(Source: National Research Council)*

Solution   Let p represent the percent of engineering doctorates who were women and let t represent the year. The two given data points are represented by (t_1, p_1) and (t_2, p_2).

| First year | First percent | | Second year | Second percent |

$(t_1, p_1) = (1980, 3.5)$ $(t_2, p_2) = (1990, 8.5)$

The formula for slope will give the average rate of change.

$$\text{Rate of change} = \frac{p_2 - p_1}{t_2 - t_1} \quad \begin{array}{l} \leftarrow \textit{Difference of percents} \\ \leftarrow \textit{Difference of years} \end{array}$$

$$= \frac{8.5 - 3.5}{1990 - 1980} \quad \textit{Substitute values.}$$

$$= \frac{5}{10}, \text{ or } 0.5 \quad \textit{Simplify.}$$

From 1980 through 1990, the *average rate of change* in the percent of engineering doctorates awarded to women was a half percent per year, although the exact changes varied slightly. ∎

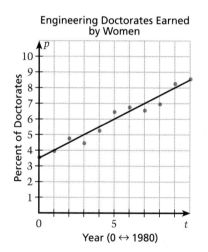

Engineering Doctorates Earned
by Women

Percent of Doctorates

Year (0 ↔ 1980)

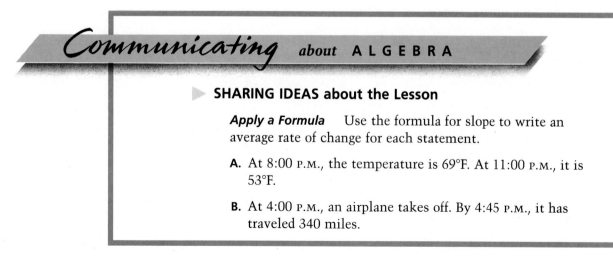

Communicating about **ALGEBRA**

▶ **SHARING IDEAS about the Lesson**

Apply a Formula   Use the formula for slope to write an average rate of change for each statement.

A. At 8:00 P.M., the temperature is 69°F. At 11:00 P.M., it is 53°F.

B. At 4:00 P.M., an airplane takes off. By 4:45 P.M., it has traveled 340 miles.

EXERCISES

▶ **CRITICAL THINKING about the Lesson**

1. Describe in your own words what is meant by the slope of a nonvertical line. Explain how your description relates to the definition of *slope*.

2. Tell all you know about the slope of a line that falls from left to right, the slope of a line that rises from left to right, and the slope of a horizontal line.

3. Which line is steeper?
   a. Line 1: through $(-4, 0)$ and $(2, 3)$
   b. Line 2: through $(0, 2)$ and $(1, 4)$

4. How can you decide, using slope, whether two nonvertical lines are parallel? perpendicular?

Independent Practice

In Exercises 5–8, estimate the slope of the line if it exists.

 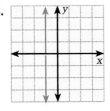

5.   **6.**   **7.**   **8.**

In Exercises 9–14, sketch the line containing the given point that has the given slope.

9. $(-3, 1)$, $m = 2$

10. $(10, 4)$, m is undefined.

11. $(4, 0)$, $m = -1$

12. $(-6, 1)$, $m = 4$

13. $(6, 5)$, $m = 0$

14. $(9, -12)$, $m = -\frac{1}{2}$

In Exercises 15–26, draw the line segment with the given endpoints. Then find the slope of the segment.

15. $(3, 1)$, $(6, -4)$

16. $(1, -5)$, $(2, 7)$

17. $(16, -3)$, $(2, 8)$

18. $(-12, -9)$, $(1, -8)$

19. $(4, 5)$, $(-1, 9)$

20. $(3, -6)$, $(2, 10)$

21. $(4, 2)$, $(-14, 3)$

22. $(-4, 1)$, $(-5, 2)$

23. $(-2, 6)$, $(10, 0)$

24. $(-15, 8)$, $\left(-9, \frac{1}{2}\right)$

25. $\left(\frac{3}{4}, -8\right)$, $(2, -5)$

26. $(11, 7)$, $(12, -10)$

In Exercises 27–30, match the pair of points with the description of the line containing the pair of points.

27. $(2, 3)$, $(-15, 5)$

28. $(8, -12)$, $(9, 2)$

29. $(-4, 7)$, $(-4, 4)$

30. $(4, -3)$, $(-20, -3)$

a. The line is horizontal.

b. The line falls to the right.

c. The line rises to the right.

d. The line is vertical.

In Exercises 31 and 32, decide which line is steeper.

31. a. Line 1 contains $(-3, 4)$ and $(1, 6)$.
   b. Line 2 contains $(1, -5)$ and $(6, 2)$.

32. a. Line 1 contains $(6, 1)$ and $(-4, 4)$.
   b. Line 2 contains $(-2, 3)$ and $(-1, -6)$.

In Exercises 33–36, decide whether the lines are parallel, perpendicular, or neither.

33. Line 1 contains $(1, 7)$ and $(-3, -5)$.
   Line 2 contains $(-6, -20)$ and $(0, -2)$.

34. Line 1 contains $(4, -4)$ and $(-16, 1)$.
   Line 2 contains $(1, 5)$ and $(5, 21)$.

35. Line 1 contains $(3, -13)$ and $(22, 4)$.
   Line 2 contains $(6, 2)$ and $(-8, 9)$.

36. Line 1 contains $(20, 3)$ and $(0, -7)$.
   Line 2 contains $(6, -4)$ and $(12, -1)$.

In Exercises 37 and 38, find the average rate of change between the two points. List the units of measure.

37. $(3, 2)$ and $(7, 18)$
   x is measured in hours.
   y is measured in dollars.

38. $(0, 3)$ and $(3, 15)$
   x is measured in minutes.
   y is measured in miles.

39. *Average Speed*   At 10:00 A.M., you are 150 miles from home. At 4:00 P.M., you are 390 miles from home. Find your average speed. (Assume you are traveling directly away from home.)

40. *Spending Your Paycheck*   On the day after payday, you have $200. Eight days after payday, you have $46. At what average rate are you spending?

41. *Leaning Tower of Pisa*   When it was built, the Leaning Tower of Pisa in Italy was 180 feet tall. Since then, one side of the base has sunk 1 foot into the ground, causing the top of the tower to lean 16 feet off-center. Approximate the slope of the leaning side of the tower.

42. *Cheops's Great Pyramid*   The Great Pyramid is the largest of the Egyptian pyramids. When it was built, it was 481 feet tall and had a square base with 755-foot sides. The pyramid has *two* different slopes—one along its sides and the other along its edges. Which slope is steeper? Explain. (*Hint:* You need the Pythagorean Theorem to find the slope along the pyramid's edges.)

43. *Law Enforcement*   The percent of female law enforcement officers in the United States rose from 10.9 in 1986 to 16.0 in 1993. What was the average rate of change in the percent of women in law enforcement?   *(Source: U.S. Department of Labor)*

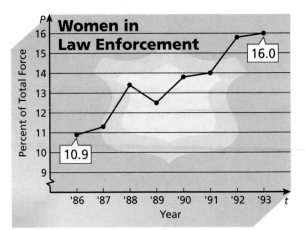

44. In 1986, 14.9% of all food servers in the United States were men. By 1994, this percent had risen to 21.4%. What was the average rate of change in the percent of male food servers?   *(Source: U.S. Bureau of Labor Statistics)*

Integrated Review

In Exercises 45–50, plot the points in the coordinate plane.

45. $(5, 1), (4, 5)$

46. $(1, 8), (7, -6)$

47. $\left(-\frac{1}{2}, 3\right), (-14, 3)$

48. $(1, 0), (7, -1)$

49. $(-2, -2), (1, 0)$

50. $(3, 7), (-4, 5)$

In Exercises 51–56, find two points on the graph of the equation. (There are many such points.)

51. $y = \frac{1}{4}x + 6$

52. $y = -\frac{1}{2}x - 4$

53. $y = 6x - 4$

54. $y = 3x + 4$

55. $y = -9x + 3$

56. $y = -x + 8$

57. *College Entrance Exam Sample*   From 9:00 A.M. to 2:00 P.M., the temperature rose at a constant rate from $-14°F$ to $+36°F$. What was the temperature at noon?

 a. $-4°F$ **b.** $+6°F$ **c.** $+16°F$ **d.** $+26°F$ **e.** $+31°F$

58. *College Entrance Exam Sample*   If $40,404 + x = 44,444$, then $40,404 - 10x = \boxed{?}$.

 a. -4.04 **b.** 0 **c.** 4 **d.** 4.04 **e.** 40.4

Exploration and Extension

59. Find x so that the line containing $(1, 1)$ and $(x, -2)$ will have a slope of 6.

60. Find y so that the line containing $(1, 1)$ and $(4, y)$ will have a slope of -1.

61. The graph of the equation $3x + 5y = 30$ is a line. Explain how you could use the formula for slope to find the slope of the line.

62. A circle of radius 5 has its center at $(0, 0)$. A line is tangent to the circle at $(3, 4)$. What is the slope of the line?

1. Write 2,580,000 in scientific notation.
2. 41.4 is 36% of what number?
3. Simplify: $-3(x - 2) + 4x + 5(2x - 6)$. **(1.2)**
4. Write in increasing order: $-\frac{2}{3}, -\frac{4}{5}, -\frac{3}{4}$.
5. Evaluate $3x^2$ when $x = 3$. **(1.2)**
6. Simplify: $\frac{1}{2}x - \frac{1}{3}x + \frac{1}{6}x$. **(1.2)**
7. Write the ratio of 27 to 54 in simplest form. **(1.1)**
8. Subtract $3x - 9$ from $2x + 4$. **(1.2)**
9. Divide: $(3.4 \times 10^{-1}) \div (1.7 \times 10^{-2})$.
10. Solve $3x - 4 = 5x + 6$. **(1.3)**
11. Solve $|2x - 7| = 3$. **(1.7)**
12. Solve $2|x - 7| = 3$. **(1.7)**
13. Plot the points: $(-1, 2), (1, -3)$. **(2.1)**
14. Write 24 as a product of prime numbers.
15. Solve $3x^2y + 2y = 12$ for y. **(1.5)**
16. Find the area of a circle of radius 4 feet.
17. Evaluate $3a^2b^3$ when $a = 2$ and $b = -3$. **(1.2)**
18. Write in exponential form: $2x \cdot 2x \cdot 2x$. **(1.2)**
19. Find the slope of the line through $(-3, 4)$ and $(2, -5)$. **(2.2)**
20. What is the slope of a horizontal line? **(2.2)**

Milestones MATHEMATICAL SYMBOLS

```
450        1500              1550              1600              1650        1700
```

First use in print of + and – signs

Oughtred introduces multiplication sign (×)

Leibniz introduces multiplication symbol (•)

The language of algebra as it appears in this book evolved over the centuries. The first algebraic equations were written in words and diagrams. An equation written in 1545 as *cubus $\bar{p}$ 6 rebus aequalis 20* is today written as $x^3 + 6x = 20$. Different symbols were introduced and adopted over time.

It is believed that our Hindu-Arabic numeral system was developed between the 4th and 7th centuries in India. Through commerce, conquest, and academic study, its use spread but only began to replace Roman numerals in Europe in the 13th century.

The minus and plus signs were first used in Germany in 1489. The plus sign (+) evolved from a shorthand notation of the Latin word *et,* meaning "and". The equal sign (=), the square root notation ($\sqrt{}$), and variables were introduced in the 1500's in Europe. In 1631, William Oughtred introduced the use of × to indicate multiplication. Gottfried Wilhelm von Leibniz thought it was easily confused with the variable x and proposed the dot symbol ($\cdot$) in 1698.

1521   I□e 32C° – 320 numeri
$x^2 + 32x = 320$

1525   Sit 1₂ aequatus 12 ℛ – 36
$x^2 = 12x - 36$

1553   2 ℛ A + 2⅛. aequata. 4335
$2x A + 2x^2 = 4,335$

1557   14. ℭ. + .15. ℺ = 71. ℺
$14x + 15 = 71$

1572   I. p. 8. Eguale à 20
$x^6 + 8x^3 = 20$

1585   3② + 4 egales à 2① + 4
$3x^2 + 4 = 2x + 4$

1631   aaa – 3 bba = + 2 ccc
$x^3 - 3b^2x = 2c^3$

Differences continue to exist in the written language of mathematics among countries. Find out what some of these differences are.

2.3 Quick Graphs of Linear Equations

What you should learn:

Goal 1 How to use intercepts to sketch a quick graph of a line

Goal 2 How to use the slope-intercept form of a line to sketch a quick graph

Why you should learn it:

You can use graphs to see relationships between variables, such as the profits from the sale of two different items.

Goal 1 Using Intercepts to Sketch a Line

A **linear equation** in x and y is of the form $Ax + By = C$. This type of equation is called linear because its graph is always a line (unless both A and B are zero).

In Lesson 2.1, you sketched the graph of a linear equation by creating a table of values, plotting the corresponding points, and drawing the graph through the points. In this lesson, you will study two quicker ways to sketch such a graph.

One way is to find the points at which the graph intersects the x-axis and the y-axis.

Intercepts of a Line
Consider the line given by $Ax + By = C$.

1. The **x-intercept** of the line is the value of x when $y = 0$. To find the x-intercept, let $y = 0$ and solve for x in $Ax = C$.
2. The **y-intercept** of the line is the value of y when $x = 0$. To find the y-intercept, let $x = 0$ and solve for y in $By = C$.

Note: We can speak of the x-intercept as a or the point $(a, 0)$, and the y-intercept as b or the point $(0, b)$.

Example 1 *Sketching a Graph Using Intercepts*
Sketch the line given by $3x + 5y = 15$.

Solution First find the intercepts.

x-Intercept (Let $y = 0$.)

$$3x + 5y = 15$$
$$3x + 5(0) = 15$$
$$x = 5$$
x-intercept is 5.

y-Intercept (Let $x = 0$.)

$$3x + 5y = 15$$
$$3(0) + 5y = 15$$
$$y = 3$$
y-intercept is 3.

To sketch the line, plot the intercepts, and draw a line through them. In the graph shown at the left, note that the x-intercept is $(5, 0)$ and the y-intercept is $(0, 3)$.

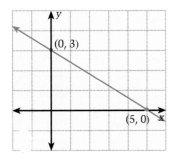
Quick graph using intercepts

Goal 2 Using the Slope-Intercept Form

A second way to sketch a quick graph of a line requires that you write the equation in slope-intercept form.

> ### Slope-Intercept Form of the Equation of a Line
> The linear equation
>
> Slope   y-Intercept
>
> $y = mx + b$
>
> is written in **slope-intercept form.** The slope of the line is m. The y-intercept is b.

To sketch a quick graph of a line, first write the equation in slope-intercept form (by solving for y). Next, graph the y-intercept. Finally, use the slope to find a second point on the line.

Example 2   *Using Slope and y-Intercept to Graph*

Sketch the graph of $x + 2y = 4$.

Solution   Begin by solving the equation for y.

$$x + 2y = 4 \qquad \textit{Original equation}$$

$$2y = -x + 4 \qquad \textit{Subtract x from both sides.}$$

$$y = -\frac{1}{2}x + 2 \qquad \textit{Divide both sides by 2.}$$
$$\underset{m}{} \qquad \underset{b}{}$$

You can sketch the line as follows. First, graph the y-intercept at $(0, 2)$. Then locate a second point by moving 2 units to the right and 1 unit down. Finally, draw the line through the two points.

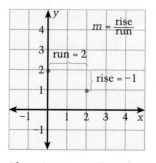

Plot y-intercept, then use the slope to find a second point.

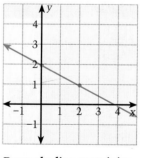

Draw the line containing the two points.

Retail markup rates vary greatly. They depend on the store and the item that is being sold. For instance, typical retail markup rates are 9% for gasoline, 14% for new cars, 25% for groceries, 70% for clothes, and 100% for jewelry. These rates are based on cost; the same rates based on retail price would be 8.3%, 12.3%, 20%, 41.2%, and 50%.

Connections
Retail Sales

Example 3 — *Creating a Linear Model*

You are the manager of a convenience store. Based on retail prices, your markup rate on gasoline is 8.3% and your average markup rate on food and other store items is 20%. Write a model that shows the amounts of gasoline and food you could sell during a week to obtain a total markup of $1000.

Solution

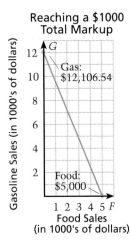

Reaching a $1000 Total Markup

Gasoline Sales (in 1000's of dollars)

Gas: $12,106.54

Food: $5,000

Food Sales (in 1000's of dollars)

Verbal Model	Markup rate	·	Gas sales	+	Markup rate	·	Food sales	=	Total markup

Labels
Markup rate for gas = 0.083   (% as decimal)
Gas sales = G (dollars)
Markup rate for food = 0.2   (% as decimal)
Food sales = F (dollars)
Total markup = 1000   (dollars)

Equation $0.083G + 0.2F = 1000$ *Linear model*

This equation has many solutions that can be seen from its graph. For instance, selling $5000 worth of food and no gasoline is one solution. Selling $12,106.54 worth of gasoline and no food is another solution. ■

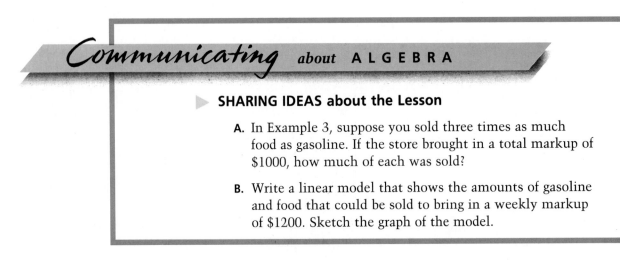

Communicating about **ALGEBRA**

▶ **SHARING IDEAS about the Lesson**

A. In Example 3, suppose you sold three times as much food as gasoline. If the store brought in a total markup of $1000, how much of each was sold?

B. Write a linear model that shows the amounts of gasoline and food that could be sold to bring in a weekly markup of $1200. Sketch the graph of the model.

EXERCISES

Guided Practice

▶ **CRITICAL THINKING about the Lesson**

1. Why is an equation written in the form $Ax + By = C$ called a *linear* equation?

2. Describe the intercepts of a graph. How do you find the intercepts of a graph?

3. Find the intercepts of the line $3x - 6y = 12$.

4. Find the slope and *y*-intercept of the line $y = -4x - 2$.

5. Which of the two quick-graph techniques discussed in the lesson would you use to sketch the graph of $3x + 4y = 24$? Explain.

6. Which of the two quick-graph techniques discussed in the lesson would you use to sketch the graph of $y = -2x + 4$? Explain.

Independent Practice

In Exercises 7–12, find the *x*-intercept and *y*-intercept of the line.

7. $16x + 2y = 8$

8. $-x + 7y = 21$

9. $3x - 8y = 9$

10. $5x - 10y = 10$

11. $21x + 7y = -7$

12. $-2x + 5y = 12$

In Exercises 13–18, match the equation with its graph.

13. $5x + y = 10$

14. $-2x + 8y = 24$

15. $9x + 3y = 18$

16. $x - 2y = 5$

17. $2x + 8y = -24$

18. $3x - 6y = 18$

a.

b.

c.

d.

e.

f.

In Exercises 19–24, sketch the line with the given intercepts. (For one exercise, the intercepts do not determine a single line. Which is it and why?)

19. *x*-intercept: 1
y-intercept: 4

20. *x*-intercept: -7
y-intercept: -5

21. *x*-intercept: -2
y-intercept: 5

22. *x*-intercept: 4
y-intercept: -2

23. *x*-intercept: -3
y-intercept: -1

24. *x*-intercept: 0
y-intercept: 0

In Exercises 25–30, sketch the line. Label the coordinates of the *x*-intercepts and *y*-intercepts.

25. $x - y = 4$

26. $2x + y = 6$

27. $3x + 4y = -12$

28. $5x - 15y = 15$

29. $6x - 3y = 9$

30. $-2x + 5y = 5$

In Exercises 31–36, write the slope-intercept form of the equation. Identify the slope and *y*-intercept.

31. $8x + 2y = 1$

32. $-4x + 2y = -1$

33. $-13x + y = 2$

34. $10x + y = 9$

35. $-x + 2y = -8$

36. $-x + 3y = 15$

In Exercises 37–42, sketch the line using the slope and *y*-intercept.

37. $y = 4x + 4$

38. $y = -3x + 2$

39. $y = \frac{5}{6}x - 1$

40. $y = \frac{5}{2}x - 5$

41. $y = -\frac{1}{2}x + 6$

42. $y = -\frac{3}{4}x + 2$

43. *Ladder Safety*   In the book *Fix It Fast, Fix It Right*, the following ladder-safety feature is given.

> *"Adjust the ladder until it is at least one quarter of the ladder height from the wall. For example, a 12-foot ladder should be at least 3 feet from the wall."*

What is the maximum slope that this book is recommending for a ladder? Why do you think it is unsafe to set up a ladder with a steeper slope?

(Source: Fix It Fast, Fix It Right, ©1991, Rodale Press)

44. *Fund-Raiser*   The members of the marching band are selling pizzas and submarine sandwiches as a fund-raising project. Their goal is to make $1000 profit. They will receive $2.75 profit for every pizza sold and $1.50 profit for every sub sold. Write a model that shows the different numbers of pizzas and subs the band members must sell to achieve their goal.

45. *Ticket Prices*   Student tickets at your high school football game cost $2 each. Non-student tickets cost $5 each. The ticket sales at the homecoming game totaled $6800. Write a model that shows the different numbers of students and adults who could have attended the game.

46. *Wheelchair Ramp*   A recommended maximum slope for a wheelchair ramp is $\frac{1}{10}$. What does this mean? If a business was to install a wheelchair ramp that rose 16 inches (the height of two steps), what would be the minimum horizontal length of the ramp?

47. Is $(1, -2)$ a solution of $-3x + 2y = 7$?

48. Is $(5, 7)$ a solution of $6x - 4y = 2$?

In Exercises 49–54, let $y = 0$ and solve for x.

49. $2x - y = 16$

50. $-4x + 16y = 21$

51. $-6x + 10y = 15$

52. $3x - 5y = 15$

53. $-x + 27y = 9$

54. $5x + 12y = 144$

In Exercises 55–60, solve for y.

55. $6x - 4y = 16$

56. $9x - 3y = 20$

57. $-5x + 3y = 9$

58. $-x + 5y = 15$

59. $x - 4y = 10$

60. $2x - 8y = 5$

In Exercises 61–66, sketch the line by creating a table of values.

61. $y = x - 5$

62. $y = -x + 7$

63. $y = 2x + 1$

64. $y = 4x - 9$

65. $y = -5x - 2$

66. $y = -8x - 9$

Exploration and Extension

67. *Herb Garden*   You are planning an herb garden. The garden has 120 inches of "row space." The parsley seedlings each need 8 inches of row space and the garlic bulbs each need 6 inches of row space. Write a model that shows the numbers of parsley and garlic plants that will fit in your garden. If you want 6 parsley plants, how many garlic bulbs can you plant?

68. *Car Wash*   You own a car wash. You charge $6 for a wash and $7 for a wash-and-wax. At the end of a busy day, total sales were $2258. Write a model that shows the different number of car washes and wash-and-waxes that could have been sold during the day. If 170 cars got a wash-and-wax, how many got washes only?

69. What kind of line has no x-intercept?

70. What kind of line has no y-intercept?

In Exercises 71 and 72, write an equation for the line.

71.

72.

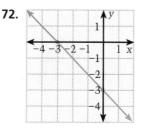

A graphing calculator or computer can be used to sketch the graph of an equation. For instance, the screen at the right shows the graph of $x + 2y = 4$. Keystroke instructions for sketching this graph on a *TI-82*, Casio *fx-9700GE*, and Sharp *EL-9300C* are listed on page 857.

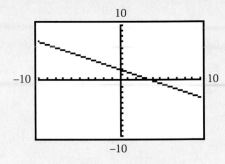

A standard viewing rectangle uses least x and y values of −10 and greatest x and y values of 10.

Using a graphing calculator to sketch a graph is fairly easy, but there are three ideas you must remember.

• Solve the equation for y in terms of x.

• Describe the viewing rectangle by entering the least and greatest x and y values and the scale (units per mark). This is called *setting the Window or Range*.

• Use parentheses if you are unsure of the calculator's order of operations.

After sketching the graph, you might want a better view of some part of the graph. For instance, if you want a closeup view of the point where the line $y = -\frac{1}{2}x + 2$ crosses the *x*-axis, you could enter new settings to produce a different viewing rectangle, as show below.

Cooperative Learning

Partner Activity Without showing your partner, enter an equation of the form

$$y = ax + b$$

into a graphing calculator. Choose an equation whose intercepts are both visible in a standard viewing rectangle. Then give the graphing calculator to your partner. His or her goal is to find the equation of the line. To do this, your partner is allowed to use only the trace key.

After your partner has found the equation of the line, switch roles and repeat the activity.

Changing the range setting to get a better view of a portion of a graph is called *zooming in* on the graph. Graphing calculators have a zoom key that will automatically change the setting to give you a close-up view of any part of the display. You can use the zoom feature to approximate the solution of an equation graphically.

Example 1   Approximating the Solution of an Equation

Use a graphing calculator to approximate the solution of

$$-340.5(x - 7.2) = 512.4(x + 13.7).$$

Solution   To begin, rewrite the equation with 0 on one side.

$$-340.5(x - 7.2) - 512.4(x + 13.7) = 0$$

Then, set y equal to the nonzero side of the equation and sketch the graph of

$$y = -340.5(x - 7.2) - 512.4(x + 13.7).$$

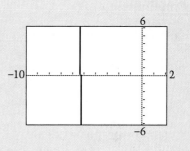

The solution of the original equation is the x-intercept of the graph of this equation. Notice that the graph (shown above) is almost vertical. The x-intercept of the line is approximately -5.4. ∎

Exercises

In Exercises 1–6, use a graphing calculator to sketch the graph of the equation. For 1–3, use the standard range (-10 to 10 by units of 1 for both x and y). For 4–6, use the indicated range.

1. $y = -3x + 5$

2. $y = 2x - 6$

3. $x - 3y = -2$

4. $y = 2x - 17$
  RANGE
  Xmin=-2 Ymin=-20
  Xmax=12   Ymax=2
  Xscl=1   Yscl=1

5. $y = -x + 30$
  RANGE
  Xmin=-5 Ymin=-5
  Xmax=35   Ymax=35
  Xscl=5   Yscl=5

6. $y = 0.2x + 1.8$
  RANGE
  Xmin=-10 Ymin=-1
  Xmax=2   Ymax=3
  Xscl=1   Yscl=1

In Exercises 7–10, use a graphing calculator to sketch the graph of the equation. Choose a range setting that makes both intercepts visible.

7. $y = 3.7x - 20$ **8.** $y = -1.54x + 63.4$ **9.** $y = -12.7x - 19.2$ **10.** $y = 1.4x + 208$

In Exercises 11 and 12, use a graphing calculator to approximate the solution.

11. $9.1(2x - 12.1) = 15.6x + 24.7$ **12.** $1.4(2.1x - 5.8) = -0.2(x + 19.1)$

2.4

Writing Equations of Lines

What you should learn:

Goal 1 How to write equations of lines

Goal 2 How to use equations of lines to solve real-life problems

Why you should learn it:

You can model many real-life situations with a linear equation, especially those involving direct variation.

Goal 1   Writing Equations of Lines

In Lesson 2.3, you learned to find the slope and y-intercept of a line whose equation is given. In this lesson, you will study the reverse process. That is, you will learn to write an equation of a line using one of the following: the slope and y-intercept of the line, the slope and a point on the line, or two points on the line.

Writing an Equation of a Line

1. Given the slope, m, and the y-intercept, b, use the equation

$y = mx + b$.   *Slope-intercept form*

2. Given the slope, m, and a point, (x_1, y_1), use the equation

$y - y_1 = m(x - x_1)$.   *Point-slope form*

3. Given two points, (x_1, y_1) and (x_2, y_2), use the formula

$m = \dfrac{y_2 - y_1}{x_2 - x_1}$

to find the slope, m. Then use the point-slope form with either of the given points to find an equation of the line.

Example 1   *Using the Slope-Intercept Form to Write an Equation*

Write an equation of the line shown at the left.

Solution   Since the line intersects the y-axis at $(0, -3)$, the y-intercept, b, is -3. From the graph, you see that the slope is

$m = \dfrac{\text{rise}}{\text{run}} = \dfrac{4}{3}$.

Using the slope and y-intercept of the line, you can write

$y = mx + b$ *Slope-intercept form*

$y = \dfrac{4}{3}x - 3$ *Substitute $\frac{4}{3}$ for m and -3 for b.*

An equation of the line is $y = \dfrac{4}{3}x - 3$.   ∎

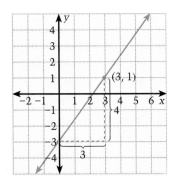

Example 2

Using the Point-Slope Form to Write an Equation

Write an equation of the line containing the point (1, 2) with a slope of $-\frac{1}{2}$.

Solution Using the point-slope form, with $(x_1, y_1) = (1, 2)$ and $m = -\frac{1}{2}$, you can write the following.

$$y - y_1 = m(x - x_1) \quad \textit{Point-slope form}$$
$$y - 2 = -\frac{1}{2}(x - 1) \quad \textit{Substitute for m, } x_1 \textit{, and } y_1.$$

Once you have used the point-slope form to find an equation, you can simplify your result to the slope-intercept form, as follows.

$$y - 2 = -\frac{1}{2}(x - 1) \quad \textit{Point-slope form}$$
$$y - 2 = -\frac{1}{2}x + \frac{1}{2} \quad \textit{Distributive Property}$$
$$y = -\frac{1}{2}x + \frac{5}{2} \quad \textit{Slope-intercept form}$$

Graphic Check   Try sketching the graph of the line containing the point (1, 2) with a slope of $-\frac{1}{2}$. From your graph, does it appear that the y-intercept is $\frac{5}{2}$? ■

Remember that the point-slope form, $y - y_1 = m(x - x_1)$, has *two* minus signs. Be sure to account for these signs when the coordinates (x_1, y_1) involve negative numbers.

Example 3

Using Two Given Points to Write an Equation

Write an equation of the line shown at the left.

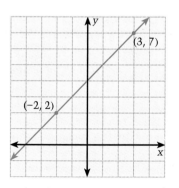

Solution   Since the line passes through $(x_1, y_1) = (-2, 2)$ and $(x_2, y_2) = (3, 7)$, its slope is the following.

$$m = \frac{y_2 - y_1}{x_2 - x_1} = \frac{7 - 2}{3 - (-2)}$$
$$= \frac{5}{5}, \text{ or } 1$$

To find an equation of the line, use the point-slope form and then simplify, as follows.

$$y - y_1 = m(x - x_1) \quad \textit{Point-slope form}$$
$$y - 2 = 1(x - (-2)) \quad \textit{Substitute for m, } x_1 \textit{ and } y_1.$$
$$y - 2 = x + 2 \quad \textit{Simplify.}$$
$$y = x + 4 \quad \textit{Slope-intercept form} \quad ■$$

Goal 2 Using Equations of Lines in Real Life

Two variable quantities that have the same rate or ratio, regardless of the values of the variables, have **direct variation.** For instance, if the ratio of y to x is k, then you can write $\frac{y}{x} = k$. By multiplying both sides of the equation by x, you obtain $y = kx$.

Direct Variation

The variables x and y **vary directly** if for a constant k

$$\frac{y}{x} = k \text{ or } y = kx.$$

The number k is the **constant of variation.**

Connections
Meteorology

Example 4 *Creating a Linear Model for Direct Variation*

Hailstones are formed when frozen raindrops are caught in updrafts and carried into high clouds containing supercooled water droplets. The radius, r (in inches), of a hailstone varies directly with the time, t (in seconds), that the hailstone is in the high cloud. After a hailstone has been in a certain cloud for 10 seconds, the radius of the hailstone is 0.5 inch. Write a linear model that gives the radius of the hailstone in terms of the time, t.

Hailstones can be very large. For instance, on July 12, 1984, hailstones as big as tennis balls fell in a storm in Munich, Germany.

Solution

$$r = kt \qquad \textit{Model for direct variation}$$
$$0.5 = k(10) \qquad \textit{Substitute 0.5 for r, 10 for t.}$$
$$0.05 = k \qquad \textit{Divide both sides by 10.}$$

The model is $r = 0.05t$. (To grow to the size of a tennis ball, with a radius of about 1.25 inches, a hailstone would have to remain in the cloud for about 25 seconds.) ■

In 1973, Barbara Jordan became the first African-American woman from a southern state to serve in the United States Congress. The graph shows that between 1970 and 1990 the number of African-American women holding elective office increased at a linear rate.

African-American Women Holding Elected Office

(20, 1950)

(0, 130)

Year (0 ↔ 1970)

Number of Elected Office Holders

Real Life
Political Science

Example 5 ▸ *Writing a Linear Model*

In 1970, 130 African-American women held elected offices. By 1990, the number had increased to 1950. Write a linear model for the number, n, of African-American women who held elected offices between 1970 and 1990. (Let $t = 0$ represent 1970.) *(Source: Joint Center for Political and Economic Studies)*

Solution You can find two points on the line.

In 1970, the value of n was 130: one point is (0, 130).

In 1990, the value of n was 1950: second point is (20, 1950).

The n-intercept, b, is 130. The slope of the line is

$$m = \frac{1950 - 130}{20 - 0} = \frac{1820}{20} = 91.$$

Using the slope-intercept form, the equation is $n = 91t + 130$. ∎

Communicating about **ALGEBRA**

▸ **SHARING IDEAS about the Lesson**

A. If x and y vary directly and are related by the linear equation $y = kx$, is (0, 0) a point on the graph? Explain.

B. What is the slope of the line? In direct variation problems, what is another name for the slope?

C. Suppose that $y = 24$ when $x = 3$. What is the value of k? Explain your steps.

EXERCISES

Guided Practice

▶ **CRITICAL THINKING about the Lesson**

1. You are given the slope of a line and a point on the line. How can you find an equation of the line?

2. You are given the slope of a line and the y-intercept of the line. How can you find an equation of the line?

3. You are given the x-intercept and y-intercept of a line. How can you find an equation of the line?

4. Give a real-life example of two variable quantities that vary directly.

Independent Practice

In Exercises 5–10, write an equation of the line.

5.

6.

7.

8.

9.

10.

In Exercises 11–16, write an equation of the line containing the given point that has the given slope.

11. $(0, 3)$, $m = -\frac{1}{2}$

12. $(4, 0)$, $m = 4$

13. $(-8, 1)$, $m = 10$

14. $(6, 7)$, $m = \frac{2}{3}$

15. $\left(\frac{1}{2}, -2\right)$, $m = -\frac{4}{3}$

16. $(3, -4)$, $m = \frac{2}{5}$

In Exercises 17–19, write an equation of the line passing through the two points.

17. $(7, 6)$ and $(10, 15)$

18. $(4, 11)$ and $(5, 9)$

19. $(-9, 9)$ and $(0, 1)$

In Exercises 20–25, the values of x and y vary directly and one pair of values for x and y are given. Write an equation that relates the variables.

20. $x = 2$, $y = 5$

21. $x = -4$, $y = 6$

22. $x = -5$, $y = 10$

23. $x = 12$, $y = 3$

24. $x = 0.1$, $y = 0.9$

25. $x = 1$, $y = 0.5$

26. *Mirror Length*   To be able to see your complete reflection in a flat mirror that is hanging on a vertical wall, the mirror must have a minimum length of m inches. (Moving closer or farther back *doesn't* change the amount you see.) The value of m varies directly with your height, h (in inches). A person 69 inches tall requires a $34\frac{1}{2}$-inch mirror. Find a linear model for the minimum mirror length in terms of the person's height. What is the minimum length that you need to see your own full reflection? Explain.

Mirror

m

27. *Burning Calories*   The number of Calories, c, a person burns and the time, t (in minutes), the person spends performing an activity vary directly. A 150-pound person can burn off 75 Calories (one cup of lowfat milk) by sitting in class for 50 minutes. Write a linear model that relates c and t. How long must a 150-pound person sit in class to burn off 545 Calories (a chicken pot pie)?

28. *Bookstore Sales*   For 1986 through 1991, retail sales of American bookstores increased at a rate that was approximately linear. In 1986, the retail sales were $4.9 billion. In 1991, the retail sales were $7.9 billion. Write a linear model for the retail sales, s (in billions of dollars), of American bookstores from 1986 to 1991. Let $t = 0$ represent 1986.
(Source: American Booksellers Association)

Bookstore Sales
(in billions of dollars)

4.9 5.3 6.0 6.5 7.3 7.9

'86 '87 '88 '89 '90 '91

29. *Magazine Titles*   From 1980 through 1991, the number, m, of magazines published in the United States increased at an approximately linear rate. In 1980, 1456 magazines were published and in 1991, 2276. Write a linear model for the number of magazines being published. (Let $t = 0$ represent 1980.) How many would you expect to be published in 1995? *(Source: Wilkofsky Gruen Associates)*

Running the IRS   **In Exercises 30 and 31, use the following information.**

The graph at the right shows the cost, C (in billions of dollars), to run the Internal Revenue Service from 1980 to 1990.
(Source: Internal Revenue Service)

30. Write a linear model for the average cost. Let $t = 0$ represent 1980 and estimate the cost of running the IRS in 1995.

31. In 1989, the IRS collected about 9.5 trillion dollars. What percent of this was spent running the IRS?

Cost of Collecting our Taxes
Total cost of running the IRS (in billions)

$5.5

$5

$3

$2.3

$1

'80 '82 '84 '86 '88 '90

In Exercises 32–37, find the slope of the line containing the points.

32. $(1, 6), (6, 1)$ **33.** $(3, 9), (0, -6)$ **34.** $(8, -3), (7, 8)$

35. $(2, 5), (9, 4)$ **36.** $(6, 1), (-8, 2)$ **37.** $(7, 2), (3, 2)$

In Exercises 38–41, match the equation with its graph.

38. $y = -x + 4$ **39.** $y = -\frac{1}{2}x - 6$ **40.** $y = 2x - 6$ **41.** $y = -2x + 3$

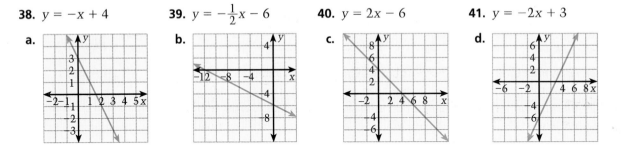

In Exercises 42–47, find the *x*-intercept and *y*-intercept of the line.

42. $4x + 2y = 7$ **43.** $-x + 8y = 21$

44. $9x - y = 18$ **45.** $5x - 9y = 5$

46. $-12x + 8y = 72$ **47.** $-3x - 6y = 10$

48. *Powers of Ten*   Which is the best estimate of the number of times your heart beats in an hour?

a. 4×10^3 **b.** 4×10^4
c. 4×10^5 **d.** 4×10^6

49. *Powers of Ten*   Which is the best estimate of the ratio of the area of Africa to the area of the United States?

a. 3×10^{-2} **b.** 3×10^{-1}
c. 3×10^0 **d.** 3×10^1

50. Find an equation of the line containing the point $(4, 6)$ that is parallel to the line containing the points $(6, -6)$ and $(10, -4)$.

51. Find an equation of the line containing the point $(1, -1)$ that is perpendicular to the line containing the points $(4, 2)$ and $(-4, 0)$.

52. *Research*   Use a library or some other reference source to find an example of a real-life situation that can be modeled by a linear equation whose graph does not contain the origin. Describe the situation, sketch a graph of your results, and list the source of your information.

Take this test as you would take a test in class. The answers to the exercises are given in the back of the book.

1. Plot the points in a coordinate plane: $(-3, 5)$, $(4, -1)$, $(0, 2)$. **(2.1)**

2. Construct a table of values for $y = -4x + 12$.
   (Use $-3, -2, -1, 0, 1, 2, 3$ as x-values.) **(2.1)**

In Exercises 3–5, find the slope of the line containing the points. (2.2)

3. $(2, 5)$, $(4, 8)$

4. $(-3, 4)$, $(2, -2)$

5. $(-2, 5)$, $(4, 5)$

6. An airplane is flying from Owensboro, Kentucky, straight to Cincinnati, Ohio. At 1:40 P.M., the plane is 120 miles from Cincinnati. At 2:20 P.M., the airplane is 30 miles from Cincinnati. What is the average speed of the airplane? **(2.2)**

In Exercises 7 and 8, state whether the lines are parallel, perpendicular, or neither. (2.2)

7. $2x - 4y = 8$, $-x + 2y = 4$

8. $2x - 4y = 8$, $2x + y = 4$

In Exercises 9 and 10, find the intercepts of the line. (2.3)

9. $-4x + 6y = 36$

10. $y = -5x + 20$

In Exercises 11 and 12, state the slope of the line and the *y*-intercept. (2.3)

11. $3x - 2y = 4x + 5$

12. $0 = 5x - 4y + 40$

In Exercises 13 and 14, sketch the line. (2.3)

13. $4x + 2y = 9$

14. $y = -\frac{2}{3}x + 3$

15. Write an equation of the line containing $(4, -2)$ and $(-2, 0)$. **(2.4)**

16. Write an equation of the line with a slope of $\frac{1}{4}$ and a *y*-intercept of 4. **(2.4)**

17. Write an equation of the line containing $(3, -2)$ that has a slope of $\frac{1}{5}$. **(2.4)**

18. In 1980, Americans made an average of 2.5 phone calls per month to friends and relatives living more than 100 miles away. In 1990, the average was 4.1 phone calls per month. Estimate the average number of such phone calls per month for 1993. *(Source: Roper Poll)* **(2.2)**

19. The area, A (in square inches), of a rectangle varies directly with its width, w (in inches). When the width is 4 inches, the area is 12 square inches. Write an equation that relates A and w. **(2.4)**

20. Use the graph at the right to find the average rate of change per year in individual contributions to public television from 1981 to 1990. *(Source: Public Broadcasting Service)* **(2.2)**

Public TV Viewer Support
Average Annual Contribution

$34 $34 $42 $42 $45 $48 $49 $51 $50 $52

'81 '82 '83 '84 '85 '86 '87 '88 '89 '90

2.5 Graphing Linear Inequalities in Two Variables

What you should learn:

Goal 1 How to graph a linear inequality in two variables

Goal 2 How to use a linear inequality in two variables to model real-life situations

Why you should learn it:

You can model many real-life problems with linear inequalities in two variables, such as the "safe surfacing" times and depths for scuba divers.

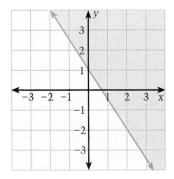

Goal 1 Graphing Inequalities

A **linear inequality** in x and y is an inequality that can be written in one of the following forms

$$ax + by < c, \ ax + by \leq c, \ ax + by > c, \ ax + by \geq c$$

where a and b are not both 0. An ordered pair (x, y) is a **solution** of a linear inequality in x and y if the inequality is true when a and b are substituted for x and y, respectively. For instance, $(-2, 12)$ is a solution of $5x + y < 3$ because $5(-2) + 12 = 2$, which is less than 3.

Example 1 *Checking Solutions of Inequalities*

Check whether the ordered pairs are solutions of $3x + 2y \geq 2$.

a. $(0, 0)$ **b.** $(2, -1)$ **c.** $(0, 2)$

Solution

(x, y)	Substitute	Conclusion
a. $(0, 0)$	$3(0) + 2(0) = 0 < 2$	$(0, 0)$ is not a solution.
b. $(2, -1)$	$3(2) + 2(-1) = 4 \geq 2$	$(2, -1)$ is a solution.
c. $(0, 2)$	$3(0) + 2(2) = 4 \geq 2$	$(0, 2)$ is a solution. ■

The **graph of an inequality** is the graph of the solutions of the inequality. For instance, the graph of $3x + 2y \geq 2$ is shown at the left. Every point in the shaded region is a solution of the inequality, and every other point in the plane is not.

To sketch the graph of a linear inequality in two variables, first sketch the line given by the corresponding equation. (Use a *dashed* line for inequalities with $<$ or $>$ and a *solid* line for inequalities with $\leq$ or $\geq$.) This line separates the coordinate plane into two **half-planes.**

- In one of the half-planes, all points are solutions of the inequality.
- In the other half-plane, no point is a solution.

You can decide whether the points in an entire half-plane satisfy the inequality by testing *one* point in the half-plane.

Example 2 Sketching the Graph of a Linear Inequality

Sketch the graphs of the linear inequalities.

a. $y \geq 3$ **b.** $x < 2$

Solution

a. For $y \geq 3$, sketch the *(solid)* horizontal line

$$y = 3. \quad \textit{Horizontal line}$$

Next test a point. The origin $(0, 0)$ is *not* a solution and it lies below the line. Therefore, the graph of $y \geq 3$ is all points on or above the line $y = 3$.

b. For $x < 2$, sketch the *(dashed)* vertical line

$$x = 2. \quad \textit{Vertical line}$$

Next test a point. The origin $(0, 0)$ *is* a solution, and it lies to the left of the line. Therefore, the graph of $x < 2$ is all points to the left of the line $x = 2$. ∎

To sketch a line that is neither horizontal nor vertical, you may want to write the line in slope-intercept form first.

Example 3 Writing in Slope-Intercept Form

Sketch the graph of $-x + y < 5$.

Solution The corresponding equation is $-x + y = 5$. To sketch this line, first write the equation in slope-intercept form, $y = x + 5$.

Then sketch the (dashed) line that has a slope of 1 and a y-intercept of 5. The origin $(0, 0)$ *is* a solution of $-x + y < 5$, and it lies below the line. Therefore, the graph is all points below the line. (Try checking another point below the line. Any one you choose will satisfy the inequality.)

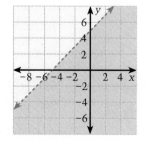

∎

Notice that the origin is used as a test point for each inequality. You can use any point that is not on the line. The origin is often convenient because it is easy to evaluate expressions in which 0 is substituted for each variable.

Goal 2 Using Linear Inequalities in Real Life

Real Life
Scuba Diving

Example 4   *Using Linear Inequalities in Real Life*

The time, t (in minutes), that a scuba diver can remain at a depth, d (in feet), *without* having to decompress while surfacing is given by the following inequalities.

For depths between 60 and 90 feet: $t \le 120 - d$

For depths between 90 and 130 feet: $t \le 75 - \frac{1}{2}d$

Sketch the graph of these inequalities. Does a diver with a depth and time of (80, 50) need to decompress? How about a diver with a depth and time of (100, 20)?

(Source: U.S. Navy Standard Air Decompression Tables)

Time Limits for Scuba Divers

Solution   The graph is shown at the left. The diver with a depth and time of (80, 50) was at a depth of 80 feet for 50 minutes. The maximum time allowed at a depth of 80 feet (without decompressing) is $120 - 80 = 40$ minutes. Therefore, this diver should use decompression stages when surfacing. The diver with a depth and time of (100, 20) does not need to decompress. Why? ■

Communicating about ALGEBRA

▶ **SHARING IDEAS about the Lesson**

Sketch the graphs of the following. Explain your steps.

A. $3x \le 4$ **B.** $-y \ge -2$ **C.** $2x - 3y < 6$

EXERCISES

Guided Practice

▶ **CRITICAL THINKING about the Lesson**

1. Why is $ax + by < c$ called a *linear inequality*?
2. Is the ordered pair $\left(\frac{5}{6}, 0\right)$ a solution of $6x + y < 5$? Explain.
3. Would you use a dashed line or a solid line for the graph of $ax + by < c$? for the graph of $ax + by \leq c$? Explain.
4. *True or False?* The graph of $y < 3x + 4$ is the set of all points in the coordinate plane that lie *below* the line $y = 3x + 4$. Explain.

Independent Practice

In Exercises 5–12, check whether each ordered pair is a solution of the inequality.

5. $x + 2y \leq -3$, $(0, 3)$, $(-5, 1)$

6. $5x - y > 2$, $(-5, 0)$, $(5, 23)$

7. $12x + 4y \geq 3$, $(1, -3)$, $(0, 2)$

8. $\frac{1}{2}x - 7y \leq 5$, $(20, 1)$, $(4, -2)$

9. $-8x - 3y < 5$, $(-1, 1)$, $(3, -9)$

10. $21x - 10y > 4$, $(2, 3)$, $(-1, 0)$

11. $-x - y \leq -10$, $(-3, -7)$, $(5, 4)$

12. $4x + 5y < 6$, $\left(\frac{1}{2}, 1\right)$, $\left(\frac{1}{2}, -1\right)$

In Exercises 13–16, write an equation (in slope-intercept form) that corresponds to the given inequality.

13. $10x + 5y > 2$

14. $13x - y < 6$

15. $-2x - 3y \leq 1$

16. $\frac{1}{2}x + \frac{3}{4}y \geq 4$

In Exercises 17–24, sketch the graph of the inequality.

17. $x \leq 4$

18. $-x > 3$

19. $-y < 50$

20. $y \leq -\frac{1}{3}$

21. $12y > -6$

22. $2x \geq -\frac{5}{2}$

23. $7x \geq \frac{7}{3}$

24. $6y < 12$

In Exercises 25–28, match the inequality with its graph.

25. $-x + y > -2$

26. $-x + y \leq 2$

27. $x + 2y > -4$

28. $-2x + y < 4$

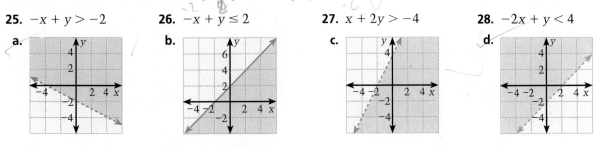

In Exercises 29–36, sketch the graph of the inequality.

29. $y < \frac{3}{4}x - 5$

30. $y \geq 2x + 10$

31. $4x + 12y > 3$

32. $-6x + y \geq 3$

33. $x - 5y \leq 15$

34. $7x - 7y > -21$

35. $9x + 3y \leq -1$

36. $2x + 4y < -8$

37. *San Juan*   The lowest temperature ever recorded in San Juan, Puerto Rico, is 60°F. Write an inequality for T representing San Juan's recorded temperatures. Sketch the graph of the inequality in a coordinate plane. Use T on the vertical axis and t, representing years, on the horizontal axis.

38. *Tap Dancing*   The fastest rate ever recorded for tap dancing in the United States is 28 taps per second by Michael Flatley of Palos Park, Illinois, on May 9, 1989. Let r represent the recorded rate (taps per second of a tap dancer). Write an inequality for r. Sketch the graph of the inequality in a coordinate plane. Use r on the vertical axis and t on the horizontal axis. *(Source: Guinness Book of Records)*

39. *Roasting a Turkey*   The time, t (in minutes), that it takes at 350°F to roast a turkey weighing p pounds is given by these inequalities:

For a turkey up to 6 pounds: $t \geq 20p$

For a turkey over 6 pounds: $t \geq 15p + 30$

Sketch the graphs of these inequalities. What are the coordinates for a 12-pound turkey that has been roasting for 3 hours and 40 minutes? Is this turkey fully cooked?

40. *Pizza and Soda Pop*   You and some friends go out for pizza. Together you have $26. You want to order two large pizzas with cheese at $8 each. Each additional topping costs $0.40, and each small soft drink costs $0.80. Write an inequality that represents the number of toppings, x, and drinks, y, that your group can afford. Sketch the graph of the inequality. What are the coordinates for an order of 6 soft drinks and two large pizzas with cheese, each with 3 additional toppings? Is this a solution of the inequality? (Assume there is no sales tax.)

Getting a Workout   **In Exercises 41 and 42, use the following information.**

The heart rate, r (in beats per minute), of a person in normal health is related to the person's age, A (in years). The relationship between r and A is given by the inequality $r \leq 220 - A$.

41. Sketch the graph of $r \leq 220 - A$. (Use A on the horizontal axis and use r on the vertical axis.)

42. Physiologists recommend that during a workout, a person should strive to increase his or her heart rate to 75% of the maximum rate for the person's age. Sketch the graph of $r = 0.75(220 - A)$ on the same coordinate plane used in Exercise 41. Write a short paragraph that describes how the graphs could be used.

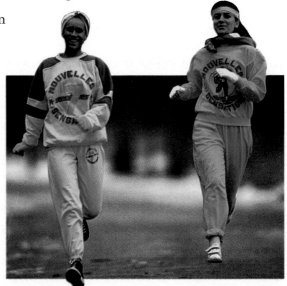

In Exercises 43–46, decide whether the ordered pair is a solution of the equation.

43. $3x - \frac{1}{2}y = 5$, $(-2, 0)$, $(6, 2)$

44. $x - 3y = 10$, $(0, 7)$, $(1, 2)$

45. $-11x + y = 1$, $(1, 10)$, $(4, 4)$

46. $-2x - 12y = 6$, $\left(5, \frac{1}{3}\right)$, $(-3, 0)$

In Exercises 47–50, write the equation in slope-intercept form.

47. $14x + 2y = 1$

48. $6x - y = 4$

49. $-9x - 3y = 12$

50. $-4x + 16y = -2$

In Exercises 51–54, sketch the graph of the equation.

51. $-x + y = 3$

52. $3x - y = -1$

53. $x + 2y = 6$

54. $-16x + 4y = -4$

55. *Cutting Circles from a Square*   You are cutting circles out of square pieces of sheet metal, 8 inches by 8 inches. How much of the sheet metal must you waste in each case if you cut 1, 4, 9, and 16 circles, as shown in the following diagram?

56. *Cutting More Circles from a Square*   You are given a square piece of sheet metal that is $5\frac{1}{4}$ inches by $5\frac{1}{4}$ inches. You are asked to cut as many penny-size circles from the sheet as possible. How many can you cut? How much of the sheet metal must you waste?

In Exercises 57–60, write the inequality whose graph is shown.

57.

58.

59.

60.

61. For which values of x is the graph of $y = 2x + 2$ below the x-axis? Describe how you could use the graph of this line to graphically solve the inequality $2x + 2 < 0$.

62. Write four different inequalities whose intersection is the blue region shown at the right.

- Each point in the blue region must be a solution of all four inequalities.
- Each point that is not in the blue region must *not* be a solution of at least one of the four inequalities.

63. Graph the equation $y = 3x - 4$. For which half-plane is $y < 3x - 4$? Explain how you can determine which half-plane is the solution without graphing.

Mixed **REVIEW**

1. Write in decimal form: 6.13×10^{-3}.

2. Divide $\frac{2}{3}$ by $\frac{4}{5}$.

3. Write the reciprocal of $-\frac{3}{5}$. **(1.1)**

4. Write the opposite of $-\frac{3}{5}$. **(1.1)**

5. Solve $3(x - 2) - 4x = -2(5 - x)$. **(1.3)**

6. Simplify: $3(x - 2) - 4x + 2(5 - x)$. **(1.2)**

7. What is the ratio of 2 feet to 42 inches?

8. Sketch the graph of $2x - y = 5$. **(2.1)**

9. Simplify: $\frac{5}{2}x - \frac{5}{4}x + x$. **(1.2)**

10. Divide $[9 - (-6)]$ by $[-2 - (-3)]$. **(1.1)**

11. Solve $|-3x + 4| = 12$. **(1.7)**

12. Solve $3x - 5 \le 2x - 7$. **(1.6)**

13. Solve $8nm^2 - 4mn = 16$ for n. **(1.5)**

14. Thirty-four is what percent of eighty-five?

15. Find the slope of the line $-5x + 3y = 8$. **(2.2)**

16. Write in slope-intercept form: $4x - 12y = 18$. **(2.3)**

17. At a speed of 34 feet per second, how far will you travel in 1 minute? **(2.2)**

18. You traveled 72 miles in 84 minutes. What was your average speed (in miles per hour)? **(2.2)**

19. Find an equation of the line passing through $(-4, 5)$ and $(3, -12)$. **(2.4)**

20. x and y vary directly. When $x = 5$, $y = 2$. Find an equation relating x and y. **(2.4)**

2.6 Graphs of Absolute Value Equations

What you should learn:

Goal 1 How to graph absolute value equations

Goal 2 How to use graphs of absolute value equations to answer questions about real-life situations

Why you should learn it:

You can model some real-life images such as the Transamerica Pyramid in San Francisco, with graphs of absolute-value equations.

Goal 1 Graphing Absolute Value Equations

The absolute value of a number can be defined as follows.

$$|x| = \begin{cases} x, & \text{if } x > 0. \\ 0, & \text{if } x = 0. \\ -x, & \text{if } x < 0. \end{cases}$$

Example

$|2| = 2$

$|0| = 0$

$|-4| = -(-4) = 4$

In this lesson, you will learn to sketch the graph of absolute value equations. To begin, let's look at the graph of $y = |x|$. By constructing a table of values and plotting points, you can see that the graph is **V**-shaped and opens up. The corner point of the graph is its **vertex.** The vertex of this graph is $(0, 0)$.

x	y = |x|
−4	4
−3	3
−2	2
−1	1
0	0
1	1
2	2
3	3
4	4

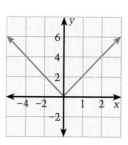

Other absolute value graphs in two variables are also **V**-shaped. Some open up and some open down. Here are some examples.

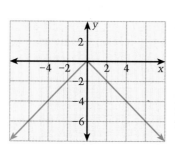

Graph of $y = -|x|$:
Vertex at (0, 0), opens down.

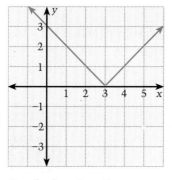

Graph of $y = |x - 3|$:
Vertex at (3, 0), opens up.

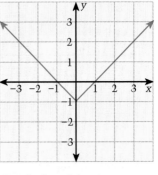

Graph of $y = |x| - 1$:
Vertex at (0, −1), opens up.

The following guidelines can help you sketch the graph of an absolute value equation.

Sketching the Graph of an Absolute Value Equation

To sketch the graph of $y = a|bx + c| + d$, use the following steps.

1. Find the x-coordinate of the vertex by finding the value of x for which $bx + c = 0$.
2. Construct a table of values, using the x-coordinate of the vertex, some x-values to its left, and some to its right.
3. Plot the points given in the table. Connect the points with a V-shaped graph, opening up if a is positive, down if a is negative.

Example 1   *Graphing an Absolute Value Equation*

Sketch the graph of $y = -|x - 2| + 3$.

Solution

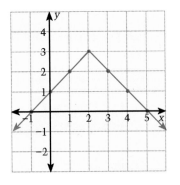

1. The x-coordinate of the vertex is 2 because that is the value of x for which $x - 2 = 0$.
2. Construct a table, using x-values to the left and right of 2.

Vertex ↓

x	-1	0	1	2	3	4	5
$y = -\|x - 2\| + 3$	0	1	2	3	2	1	0

3. Plot the points. Notice that the vertex is at $(2, 3)$. Draw a V-shaped graph (opening down) through the points. ■

Example 2   *Graphing an Absolute Value Equation*

Sketch the graph of $y = |2x + 1| - 4$.

Solution

1. The x-coordinate of the vertex is $-\frac{1}{2}$ because that is the value of x for which $2x + 1 = 0$.
2. Construct a table, using x-values to the left and right of $-\frac{1}{2}$.

Vertex ↓

x	-3	-2	-1	$-\frac{1}{2}$	0	1	2
$y = \|2x + 1\| - 4$	1	-1	-3	-4	-3	-1	1

3. Plot the points. Notice that the vertex is at $\left(-\frac{1}{2}, -4\right)$. Then draw a V-shaped graph through the points. ■

Connections
Meteorology

Example 3 *Finding the Total Amount of Rainfall*

a. It is raining at a steady rate of $r = 0.5$ inch per hour for 2 hours. What is the total rainfall?

b. A rainstorm lasts for two hours, building up from a drizzle to a heavy rain, then dropping back to a drizzle. The rate, r, of the rain (in inches per hour) is given by

$$r = -0.5|t - 1| + 0.5; \quad 0 \le t \le 2$$

where t is the time in hours. What is the total rainfall?

Solution In both cases, the total amount of rainfall can be found geometrically. In the first case, the rate is *constant*, and the total rainfall corresponds to the area of a rectangle. In the second case, the rate *varies*, and the total rainfall corresponds to the area of a triangle.

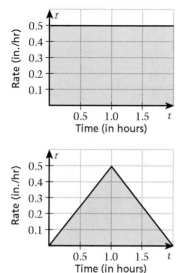

a. The total rainfall, T (in inches), is

$$T = \left(0.5 \frac{\text{inches}}{\text{hour}}\right)(2 \text{ hours}) = 1 \text{ inch.}$$

Notice that this can be interpreted geometrically as the area of a rectangle that is 0.5 unit high and 2 units long.

b. In this case, the rate of the rain varies according to the equation $r = -0.5|t - 1| + 0.5$. To find the total rainfall, sketch the graph of this equation. Then find the area of the triangle formed by the x-axis and the graph.

$$T = \tfrac{1}{2}(\text{base})(\text{height}) = \tfrac{1}{2}(2)(0.5) = 0.5 \text{ inch.} \quad \blacksquare$$

Communicating about **ALGEBRA**

▶ **SHARING IDEAS about the Lesson**

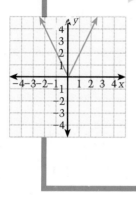

Compare Graphs Sketch the graph of each equation on the same coordinate plane. How does the shape of each compare to the graph of $y = |2x|$ shown at the left? How does the position of each compare to the graph at the left? Use translations and reflections in your comparisons.

A. $y = |2x - 4|$

B. $y = |2x - 4| + 1$

C. $y = -|2x - 4| + 1$

EXERCISES

▶ **CRITICAL THINKING about the Lesson**

1. Explain in your own words why $|x|$ can equal either x, 0, or $-x$. Give an example of a value of x for which $|x| = -x$.

2. Which value (a, b, c, or d) determines whether the vertex of the graph of $y = a|bx + c| + d$ shows a maximum or a minimum value for y? Explain.

3. What is the x-coordinate of the vertex of $y = |x - 5| + 1$? Which x-values would you use to construct a table of values?

4. Sketch the graph of $y = |x - 5| + 1$.

Independent Practice

In Exercises 5–8, match the equation with its graph. Describe how the graph relates to the graph of $y = |x|$.

5. $y = |x| + 4$ **6.** $y = |x| - 4$ **7.** $y = |x + 4|$ **8.** $y = |x - 4|$

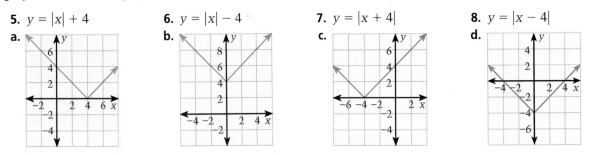

In Exercises 9–20, find the vertex of the graph.

9. $y = |x| + 1$

10. $y = -|x| - 5$

11. $y = |x - 1| + 3$

12. $y = |x + 3| - 10$

13. $y = -|x - 2| - 12$

14. $y = -|x + 14| - 1$

15. $y = |2x + 4| + 3$

16. $y = -2|4x - 1| + 16$

17. $y = 3\left|\frac{1}{2}x - 3\right| + 6$

18. $y = -3\left|\frac{1}{9}x + 5\right| - 5$

19. $y = -2|5 - 2x| + 6$

20. $y = -|16 - 6x| + 9$

In Exercises 21–24, match the equation with its graph.

21. $y = -|x + 2| - 4$ **22.** $y = |x - 4| - 2$ **23.** $y = |x - 2| + 4$ **24.** $y = -|x + 4| + 2$

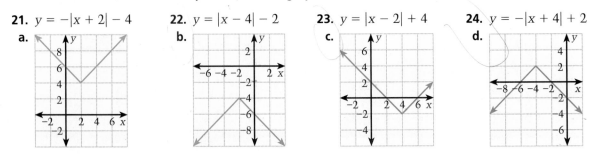

In Exercises 25–28, complete the table. Describe the pattern of symmetry.

25. $y = |x + 2|$

x	−5	−4	−3	−2	−1	0	1
y	?	?	?	?	?	?	?

26. $y = |x| - 5$

x	−3	−2	−1	0	1	2	3
y	?	?	?	?	?	?	?

27. $y = 2|x - 1| + 3$

x	−2	−1	0	1	2	3	4
y	?	?	?	?	?	?	?

28. $y = -|2x + 3| - 10$

x	$-\frac{9}{2}$	$-\frac{7}{2}$	$-\frac{5}{2}$	$-\frac{3}{2}$	$-\frac{1}{2}$	$\frac{1}{2}$	$\frac{3}{2}$
y	?	?	?	?	?	?	?

In Exercises 29–44, sketch the graph of the equation.

29. $y = |x - 5|$ **30.** $y = |x| - 5$ **31.** $y = |x| + 7$ **32.** $y = -|x - 8| + 3$

33. $y = -|x + 2| + 9$ **34.** $y = -|x - 8| - 9$ **35.** $y = |5 - x| + 4$ **36.** $y = -|10 - x| + 4$

37. $y = |2x| + 3$ **38.** $y = \left|\frac{1}{3}x\right| - 9$ **39.** $y = |3x - 1|$ **40.** $y = \left|\frac{1}{2}x + 6\right|$

41. $y = -4|2x + 1|$ **42.** $y = 2|x + 3| - 9$ **43.** $y = -2|9 - 2x| + 3$ **44.** $y = -|6 - 5x| - 4$

New Album Release   **In Exercises 45–47, use the following information.**

A musical group's new album is released. Weekly sales, *s* (in thousands), increase steadily for a while and then decrease as given by the model

$$s = -2|t - 22| + 44$$

where *t* is the time in weeks.

45. Sketch the graph of the sales model.

46. Estimate the total number of albums sold during the first 44 weeks. Did the album "go gold"? Did it "go platinum"? Explain.

47. Would the group have sold more albums during the 44 weeks if it had sold 20,000 albums per week? Give a geometric interpretation of your answer.

48. *Playing Billiards*   You are trying to shoot the eight-ball into the corner pocket as shown. Imagine that a coordinate plane is superimposed over the pool table so that the points (10, 0) and (0, 5) are two corner pockets. The eight-ball follows the path given by $y = \frac{5}{4}|x - 6|$. Do you make your shot? Sketch a graph of the equation. At what point does the eight-ball bank off the first side of the table?

The Recording Industry Association of America presents a gold album to artists whose album sells over 500,000 copies. A platinum album is given for an album that sells over 1,000,000 copies.

In Exercises 49–52, the coordinates in the table of values are solutions of either a linear equation or an absolute value equation. Plot the points and sketch the graph. Then find an equation of the graph.

49.

x	0	1	2	3	4
y	1	0	−1	0	1

50.

x	−1	0	1	2	3
y	$-\frac{3}{2}$	$-\frac{1}{2}$	$\frac{1}{2}$	$\frac{3}{2}$	$\frac{5}{2}$

51.

x	−3	−2	−1	0	1
y	−4	−3	−2	−1	−2

52.

x	$\frac{1}{2}$	$\frac{3}{4}$	1	$\frac{5}{4}$	$\frac{3}{2}$
y	−2	−1	0	1	2

In Exercises 53–56, evaluate the expression.

53. $2|x - 10| + 5$ when $x = -4$

54. $6 - \frac{1}{2}|x - 5|$ when $x = -3$

55. $10 + \frac{1}{4}|7 - x|$ when $x = 15$

56. $3|x| + 4|1 - x|$ when $x = 6$

Exploration and Extension

Hitting Red Lights   **In Exercises 57 and 58, use the following information.**

When a red traffic light turns green, you accelerate at a constant rate to a speed of 60 feet per second (about 41 mph), then decelerate steadily to stop at the next traffic light. Your speed, r (in feet per second), is given by $r = -10|t - 6| + 60$, where t is the time in seconds.

57. Sketch the graph of the equation. How many seconds did it take you to reach the second light?

58. What is the distance between the two lights? (Your rate was not constant, but you can use a geometric model to find the distance.)

Transamerica Pyramid   **In Exercises 59 and 60, use the following information.**

The Transamerica Pyramid is an office building in San Francisco. It is about 850 feet tall and about 160 feet wide at its base.

59. What is the slope of the sides of the building?

60. Imagine that a coordinate plane has been superimposed over a head-on picture of the building. In the coordinate plane, each unit represents one foot, and the origin is at the center of the building's base. Write an absolute value equation whose graph is the V-shaped edges of the building.

2.7 Exploring Data: Fitting a Line to Data

What you should learn:

Goal 1 How to fit a line to a set of data and to write an equation for the line

Goal 2 How to identify whether a set of data shows positive or negative correlation, or no correlation

Why you should learn it:

You can use the equation of a best-fitting line to investigate trends in data and to make predictions.

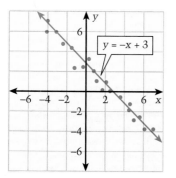

Goal 1 Fitting a Line to Data

In Lesson 2.4, you studied how to find an equation of the line that passes through *two* points. For this type of problem, there is always only one line—because two points determine exactly one line.

In this lesson, you will study problems that involve *several* data points. Usually there is no single line that passes through all the data points, so you try to find the line that best fits the data. This is called the **best-fitting line.** For instance, in the graph shown below, the line given by $y = -x + 3$ is the best-fitting line for the data points.

There are several ways to find the best-fitting line for a given set of data points whose graph suggests a linear relationship. One way is to use a graphing calculator or computer and formulas from a branch of mathematics called statistics. The statistical formula can *find* the best-fitting line. In this lesson, however, you will use a graphical approach, which *approximates* the best-fitting line.

LESSON INVESTIGATION

■ Investigating a Best-Fitting Line

Partner Activity With your partner, use the following steps to approximate a best-fitting line.

1. Carefully plot the following points on graph paper.

$(-3, 3.4)$, $(-2, 3.8)$, $(-1, 4.2)$, $(0, 4.7)$, $(0, 5.1)$, $(1, 5.4)$, $(1, 5.8)$, $(2, 7.1)$, $(2, 7.4)$, $(3, 8.0)$, $(4, 9.1)$, $(4, 9.6)$, $(5, 10.2)$, $(6, 12.1)$, $(7, 14.0)$

2. Use a ruler to sketch the line that you think best approximates the data points.

3. Locate two points on the line and approximate the x-coordinate and y-coordinate of each point. (These don't have to be two of the original data points.)

4. Use the technique described in Lesson 2.4 to find an equation of the line that passes through the two points in Step 3.

Real Life

Finance

Example 1   *Approximating a Best-Fitting Line*

The 1990 earnings per share and dividends per share for 35 electric utility companies (in the central United States) are shown in the table. Approximate the best-fitting line for this data. Let e represent the earnings per share. Let d represent the dividend per share. What can you conclude from the result? *(Source: The Value Line Investment Survey)*

Solution   To begin, think of each of the data pairs as an *ordered pair*. For instance, the first pair of numbers in the table is represented by the ordered pair (1.67, 1.73). Next, draw a scatter plot for the ordered pairs. Then sketch the line that best fits the points, as shown below.

Earnings (e)	Dividend (d)
1.67	1.73
1.73	1.46
1.77	1.48
1.79	1.42
1.84	1.63
1.90	1.60
1.92	1.83
1.97	1.46
1.99	1.56
1.99	1.67
2.00	1.72
2.00	1.65
2.00	1.86
2.23	1.74
2.23	1.56
2.25	1.80
2.38	2.20
2.48	1.60
2.55	2.35
2.56	2.00
2.58	1.80
2.69	2.46
2.74	2.10
2.77	1.74
2.79	2.30
3.02	1.90
3.26	1.78
3.32	2.62
3.38	2.51
3.45	2.81
3.54	2.28
3.70	2.50
3.79	2.76
4.12	2.40
4.40	2.96

The next step is to find two points that lie on the best-fitting line. From the graph, you might choose the points (1.7, 1.5) and (3.7, 2.5). The slope of the line passing through these two points is

$$m = \frac{d_2 - d_1}{e_2 - e_1} = \frac{2.5 - 1.5}{3.7 - 1.7} = \frac{1.0}{2.0} = 0.5.$$

To find an equation of the line, use the point-slope form.

$d - d_1 = m(e - e_1)$	*Point-slope form*
$d - 1.5 = 0.5(e - 1.7)$	*Substitute values of m, e_1, d_1.*
$d = 0.5e - 0.85 + 1.5$	*Add 1.65 to both sides.*
$d = 0.5e + 0.65$	*Solve for d.*

From this equation, you can conclude two general results. As the utility companies earned more per share, they tended to pay a higher dividend per share. Another result is that the typical dividend was about half the earnings per share *plus* 65¢. ∎

Normal human babies sleep more than half of their first year of life. A typical newborn sleeps about 16 hours a day, and a typical one-year-old sleeps about 13 hours a day.

(Source: Scientific American)

Connections
Physiology

Example 2 *Comparing Sleep to Age*

The data in the table shows the age, t (in years), and the number of hours, h, slept in a day by 28 infants who are less than one year old. Approximate the best-fitting line for this data.

Solution To begin, sketch a scatter plot as shown.

Age (yrs)	Sleep (hrs)	Age (yrs)	Sleep (hrs)
0.03	15.0	0.52	14.4
0.05	15.8	0.69	13.2
0.05	16.4	0.70	14.1
0.08	16.2	0.75	14.2
0.10	14.9	0.80	13.4
0.11	14.8	0.82	14.3
0.19	14.7	0.82	13.2
0.21	14.5	0.86	13.9
0.26	15.4	0.90	13.7
0.34	15.2	0.91	13.1
0.35	15.3	0.94	13.7
0.35	14.4	0.97	12.7
0.44	13.9	0.98	13.7
0.52	13.4	0.98	13.6

Infant Sleep Requirements

Next sketch the line that appears to fit the points best, and locate two points on the line: (0.05, 15.8) and (0.8, 13.4). The slope of the line passing through these two points is

$$m = \frac{h_2 - h_1}{t_2 - t_1} = \frac{13.4 - 15.8}{0.8 - 0.05} = \frac{-2.4}{0.75} = -3.2.$$

Use the point-slope form to find the equation of the line.

$h - h_1 = m(t - t_1)$	*Point-slope form*
$h - 15.8 = -3.2(t - 0.05)$	*Substitute values of m, t_1, h_1.*
$h = -3.2t + 0.16 + 15.8$	*Add 15.8 to both sides.*
$h = -3.2t + 15.96$	*Solve for h.* ∎

Positive Correlation

Negative Correlation

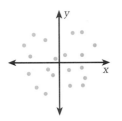

No Correlation

Goal 2 Positive and Negative Correlations

Three scatter plots are shown at the left. In the first, x and y have a **positive correlation,** which means that the points can be approximated by a line with a *positive slope.* In the second, x and y have a **negative correlation,** which means that the points can be approximated by a line with a *negative slope.* In the third, there is **no correlation** between x and y.

We have been talking about the best-fitting line. Sometimes, however, the best-fitting line isn't a very *good* fit. In statistics, the **correlation coefficient,** r, is used as a measure of how well a collection of data points can be modeled by a line. Correlation coefficients range between -1 and 1. The closer $|r|$ is to 1, the better the line fits the points. (There is more to the story than this—lines that are nearly horizontal have r-values that are close to 0. You can learn more about correlation in a statistics course.) The formula for r is

$$r = \frac{\text{Sum of } (x_i - \overline{x})(y_i - \overline{y})}{\sqrt{[\text{Sum of } (x_i - \overline{x})^2] \cdot [\text{Sum of } (y_i - \overline{y})^2]}}$$

where $\overline{x}$ is the average x-value and $\overline{y}$ is the average y-value.

Communicating about ALGEBRA

▶ SHARING IDEAS about the Lesson

Year	Math Research
1980	$ 91
1981	$118
1982	$128
1983	$134
1984	$151
1985	$184
1986	$185
1987	$205
1988	$212
1989	$230
1990	$245

The total amount, m (in millions of dollars), spent by the federal government on mathematics research from 1980 through 1990 is shown in the table.
(Source: U.S. National Science Foundation)

A. Sketch a scatter plot. Let $t = 0$ represent 1980. From your scatter plot, do m and t appear to have a positive correlation, a negative correlation, or no correlation?

B. Sketch the best-fitting line. Locate two points on the line. (Your two points may or may not be the same as the points chosen by classmates.) Use the two points you chose to find an equation of the line.

C. Use the equation that you found to predict the amount the federal government will spend for mathematics research in 1995.

EXERCISES

Guided Practice

▶ **CRITICAL THINKING about the Lesson**

1. Do the points in the scatter plot at the right have a positive correlation or a negative correlation? Explain.

2. Find an equation of the line that you think best fits the points.

3. Suppose you were given the shoe sizes, s, and the heights, h, of one hundred 25-year-old men. Do you think that s and h would have a positive correlation, a negative correlation, or no correlation? Explain.

4. Suppose you were given the incomes, i, and the percents of income, p, spent on food for one hundred families. Do you think i and p would have a positive correlation, a negative correlation, or no correlation? Explain.

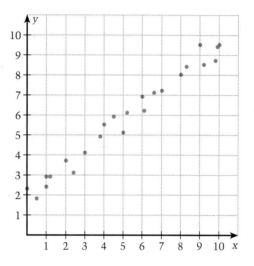

Independent Practice

In Exercises 5–8, state whether x and y have a positive correlation, a negative correlation, or no correlation.

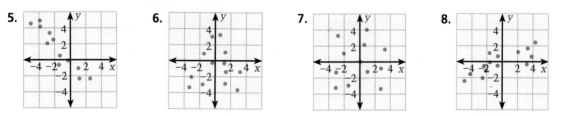

5.   **6.**   **7.**   **8.**

In Exercises 9–12, write an equation of the line that you think best fits the scatter plot.

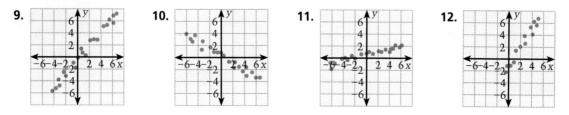

9.   **10.**   **11.**   **12.**

In Exercises 13 and 14, construct a scatter plot for the given data. Then find an equation of the line that you think best fits the data.

13.

x	−2	−1	0	0.5	1	2	2.5	3.5	4	4.5
y	5	3	3.5	1.5	2	0	−2	−3.5	−2	−3.5

14.

x	−2	−1	−0.5	0	0.5	1	2	3	3.5	4
y	1.25	1.5	1.5	2	1.75	2	2.5	2.5	2.75	3.25

15. *Home Computers*   The table lists the number of households, c (in millions), in the United States that owned computers between 1984 and 1991. Approximate the best-fitting line for this data. Let t represent the year, with $t = 4$ corresponding to 1984. If this pattern was to continue, how many households would own computers in 1993? *(Source: Electronics Industry Association)*

Year	1984	1985	1986	1987	1988	1989	1990	1991
Households	6.0	11.3	14.2	16.2	19.2	21.3	25.3	26.6

16. *Laying More Eggs*   Between 1920 and 1990, improvements in poultry science produced hens that laid more eggs. The average number of eggs produced per hen per week for several years is shown in the graph. Find an equation of the line that you think best fits the data. *(Source: United States Department of Agriculture)*

Average Weekly Egg Production

Number of Eggs per Hen

(60, 4.4)

Year (0 ↔ 1920)

17. *Ice Cream*   For 1986 through 1990, the percent, p, of low-calorie and/or low-fat ice cream sold in the United States increased as shown in the table. Approximate the best-fitting line for this data. (Let t represent the year, with $t = 6$ corresponding to 1986.) If this were to continue, what percent of ice cream sold in 1994 would be low-calorie and/or low-fat? *(Source: A.C. Nielson)*

Year	Percent
1986	6
1987	8
1988	12
1989	19
1990	25

18. *100-Meter Sprint*   A person who is running a 100-meter sprint was clocked several times during the sprint. The velocities, v (in meters per second), and the accelerations, a (in meters per second per second), are shown in the scatter plot at the right. Find an equation of the line that you think best fits this data. What can you conclude from the result? *(Source: Mathematics in Sport ©1984 Halsted Press)*

One Hundred Meter Sprint

Acceleration (in m/sec²)

Velocity (in m/sec)

In Exercises 19–22, find the slope of the line containing the points.

19. $(6, -9), (7, 7)$ **20.** $(6, 7), (-5, 5)$ **21.** $(5, 0), (-5, 1)$ **22.** $(3, -3), (-2, 1)$

In Exercises 23–26, find an equation of the line containing the points.

23. $(7, 2), (8, 9)$ **24.** $(9, 4), (-8, 3)$ **25.** $(4, -8), (7, 5)$ **26.** $(2, 1), (7, -3)$

Exploration and Extension

Correlation Coefficient   **In Exercises 27–30, match the correlation coefficient with the scatter plot. Explain your reasoning.**

27. $r = 0.93$ **28.** $r = 0.99$ **29.** $r = -0.64$ **30.** $r = -0.95$

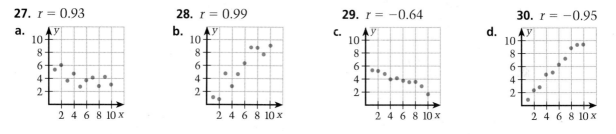

Correlation Coefficient   **In Exercises 31–34, use the following information.**

The scatter plot at the right has five points. Find the correlation coefficient for these points by following the instructions in the exercises.

31. Find $\bar{x}$, the mean (average) of the x-values.

32. Find $\bar{y}$, the mean of the y-values.

33. Complete the table and find the totals of the third, sixth, and seventh columns.

34. Use the formula given in the lesson to calculate the correlation coefficient, r.

x_i	$x_i - \bar{x}$	$(x_i - \bar{x})^2$	y_i	$y_i - \bar{y}$	$(y_i - \bar{y})^2$	$(x_i - \bar{x})(y_i - \bar{y})$
0	?	?	12	?	?	?
10	?	?	22	?	?	?
20	?	?	30	?	?	?
30	?	?	38	?	?	?
40	?	?	54	?	?	?

In Exercises 35 and 36, find the correlation coefficient, r, for the data.

35. $(-5, 5), (-4, 3), (-2, 2), (-1, -1), (3, -5)$ **36.** $(-20, -12), (-10, -7), (4, -3), (10, 0), (20, 5)$

2 Chapter Summary

What did you learn?

Skills

1. Plot points in a coordinate plane. **(2.1)**
2. Use a table of values to sketch the graph of an equation. **(2.1)**
3. Find the slope of a line
   - given two points on the line. **(2.2)**
   - given an equation of the line. **(2.3)**
4. Sketch the graph of a line
   - using intercepts. **(2.3)**
   - using the slope-intercept form. **(2.3)**
5. Write an equation of a line
   - given its slope and y-intercept. **(2.4)**
   - given its slope and a point on the line. **(2.4)**
   - given two points on the line. **(2.4)**
6. Sketch the graph of a linear inequality. **(2.5)**
7. Sketch the graph of an absolute value equation. **(2.6)**

Strategies

8. Use linear equations and inequalities to solve real-life problems. **(2.1–2.7)**

Exploring Data

9. Approximate the equation of the best-fitting line for related data. **(2.7)**

Why did you learn it?

Many relationships in real life are linear or approximately linear. By recognizing the relationship between two variables, you can learn more about the real-life situation. You can also make reasonable predictions of future trends. For instance, if a city's population has been increasing for the past 10 years at an approximately linear rate, you can find the average rate of change and use it to predict the population for the next 5 years. This use of linear models is important for businesses and city governments.

How does it fit into the bigger picture of algebra?

In Chapter 2, you studied linear equations and inequalities in two variables. A linear equation in x and y is an equation that can be written in the form $Ax + By = C$. In a coordinate plane, the graph of a linear equation is a line.

Using the coordinate plane to create geometric models of equations is an important part of algebra. Throughout this chapter, you translated geometric statements into algebraic statements, such as when you were given two points in a coordinate plane and found an equation of the line containing them. You also translated algebraic statements into geometric relationships, such as when you sketched the graph of an equation or inequality.

In Exercises 1–6, plot the points in a coordinate plane. In which quadrant does each point lie? **(2.1)**

1. $(5, 1)$, $(-4, 0)$

2. $(2, -3)$, $(1, -8)$

3. $(4, -6)$, $(3, 8)$

4. $(4, 1)$, $(-4, 3)$

5. $(2, -2)$, $(8, 6)$

6. $(7, 9)$, $(0, 2)$

In Exercises 7 and 8, find the average rate of change per year. **(2.2)**

7. A business had a profit of $58,000 in 1989 and a profit of $74,000 in 1993.

8. In 1790, each state was allowed one Congressman in the House of Representatives for every 33,000 citizens. In 1990, each Congressman or Congresswoman represented 555,000 citizens.

In Exercises 9–14, sketch the graph of the equation. **(2.1)**

9. $x = 4$

10. $y = -1$

11. $y = x - 5$

12. $y = -x + 9$

13. $y = -3x + 6$

14. $y = 2x + 7$

In Exercises 15–18, find the slope of the line containing the points. **(2.2)**

15. $(1, -3)$, $(6, 7)$

16. $(5, -3)$, $(0, 12)$

17. $(2, 2)$, $(8, -1)$

18. $(9, 1)$, $(-5, 2)$

In Exercises 19–22, find the *x*-intercept and *y*-intercept of the line. **(2.3)**

19. $2x - 5y = 20$

20. $6x - y = 36$

21. $-x + 4y = 16$

22. $-9y - 12x = 27$

In Exercises 23–28, write the equation in slope-intercept form. Then sketch the line. **(2.3)**

23. $x - y = 9$

24. $2x - 10y = 15$

25. $2x + 8y = 24$

26. $-4x + 5y = 16$

27. $-3x - 7y = 1$

28. $-x + 9y = 30$

In Exercises 29–34, write an equation of the line containing the points. **(2.4)**

29. $(7, 0)$, $(9, 6)$

30. $(6, 5)$, $(-7, 4)$

31. $(3, -7)$, $(8, 2)$

32. $(0, 7)$, $(5, 3)$

33. $(8, 5)$, $(-3, 2)$

34. $(-8, 5)$, $(9, 14)$

In Exercises 35 and 36, *x* and *y* vary directly. Find an equation that relates *x* and *y*. **(2.4)**

35. $y = 10$ when $x = 1$

36. $y = 4$ when $x = 6$

In Exercises 37–42, sketch the graph of the inequality. **(2.5)**

37. $2x < 6$

38. $4y \geq 9$

39. $y \geq x + 5$

40. $y < -x + 4$

41. $x + 8y < 1$

42. $3x + y < 9$

In Exercises 43–46, sketch the graph of the equation.   (2.6)

43. $y = |3x| + 5$ **44.** $y = |x| + 3$ **45.** $y = |x - 4| + 3$ **46.** $y = |x + 7| - 12$

In Exercises 47–58, match the equation or inequality with its graph.   (2.5, 2.6)

47. $y = -\frac{1}{2}x + 2$ **48.** $y = \frac{1}{2}x - 2$ **49.** $y = 2$ **50.** $x = -2$

51. $y = |x + 4| - 1$ **52.** $y = -|x + 4| + 1$ **53.** $y = |x - 1| + 4$ **54.** $y = -|x + 1| - 4$

55. $2x < 4$ **56.** $3y > 6$ **57.** $2x + 3y < 6$ **58.** $2x - y > 4$

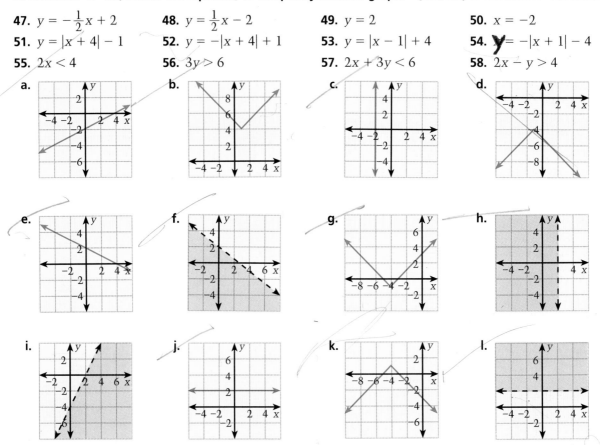

Medical School Applicants   **In Exercises 59 and 60, use the following information.**

The graph at the right shows the number of applicants, a, and the number of students accepted, s, at American medical schools in the years from 1982 through 1990. Let t represent the year, with $t = 2$ corresponding to 1982.
(Source: Association of American Medical Colleges)

59. Find the average annual rate of change in the number of applications to medical schools between 1982 and 1990.

60. Find an equation for the number of applicants accepted to medical schools per year between 1982 and 1990.

Getting Into Medical School

Thousands of Students

40 — 36,000

30

29,000

20

Applicants

10

17,000

Accepted

0

1982   1984   1986   1988   1990

Year

The Tomb of Tutankhamen   **In Exercises 61–63, use the following information.**

Tutankhamen served as king of Egypt from the age of nine to about the age of eighteen. His underground 4-room tomb was discovered in 1922. The tomb contained over 5000 objects, including many art objects. In the diagram at the right, a coordinate plane has been superimposed over the tomb. Each unit in the coordinate plane represents 5 feet.

61. If you walk from the doorway at the foot of the steps to the point (4, 7.5), where are you standing?

62. Approximate the area of the burial chamber.

63. Each of the 16 steps are $\frac{3}{4}$-foot high and $\frac{3}{4}$-foot wide. Find the slope of the staircase.

Oxygen Use   **In Exercises 64–67, use the following information.**

While at rest, a person in normal health inhales about 12.5 liters of oxygen per minute of which about 0.5 liter is absorbed by the blood through the person's lungs. The rest is dispelled when the person exhales. The amount, A (in liters), of oxygen used varies directly with the amount, I (in liters), that is inhaled.

64. Write an equation that relates the amount of oxygen absorbed, A, and the amount inhaled, I.

65. The maximum amount of oxygen that a person's body is capable of using is about 3.5 liters per minute. (This would normally occur during heavy exercise.) At this rate, how much oxygen would be inhaled each minute?

66. How much oxygen does your body absorb in a normal day?

67. During photosynthesis, 1 square foot of plant surface produces about 0.1 liter of oxygen per minute. Photosynthesis occurs only during daylight. Approximate the number of square feet of plant surface needed to replenish the oxygen that your body absorbs in 24 hours. Assume a day has 12 hours of sunlight.

Plants produce oxygen during photosynthesis.

Low-Profile Tires   In Exercises 68–70, use the following information.

Automobile tires sold in the United States have codes that give information about the tire. For instance, the meaning of P 205/60 R 13 85H is given at the right.

A 75% ratio of tire height to width is standard, 70% is low-profile, and 60% is ultralow-profile.

- <u>P</u>assenger car
- <u>205</u> mm ≈ cross section width
- <u>60</u>% ratio of tire height to width
- <u>R</u>adial tire
- <u>13</u> inch wheel diameter
- <u>85</u> load index
- <u>H</u> speed rating

Standard tire
P 195/75 R 14

7.72 in.
(196 mm) wide

Width of rim
5.50 in. (140mm)

Low profile tire
P 205/70 R 14

7.99 in.
(203 mm) wide

Width of rim
5.50 in. (140mm)

Ultra-low profile tire
P 225/60 R 14

8.78 in.
(223 mm) wide

Width of rim
6.00 in. (152 mm)

68. As recommended by *Motor Trend* magazine, the maximum width, W (in millimeters), of a tire for your car varies directly with the width, r (in millimeters), of the rim of one of the car's wheels. For a rim width of 152 millimeters, *Motor Trend* recommends a tire be no wider than 215 millimeters. Write an inequality that relates the maximum tire width, W, with the wheel width, r.

69. The speedometer on a car depends on the number of wheel revolutions per minute. Changing the size of the tires on a car can alter the accuracy of the car's speedometer. Let d be the diameter (in inches) of the tire. Let R be the number of revolutions per minute. Then the speed, s (in miles per hour), is given by the following.

$$s = \left(\frac{R \text{ rev}}{\text{min}}\right)\left(\frac{\pi d \text{ in.}}{\text{rev}}\right)\left(\frac{1 \text{ ft}}{12 \text{ in.}}\right)\left(\frac{1 \text{ mile}}{5280 \text{ ft}}\right)\left(\frac{60 \text{ min}}{1 \text{ hr}}\right)$$
$$= \frac{1}{1056}\pi R d \text{ miles per hour}$$

The standard tire has a diameter of $d = 14 + 2(0.75)(7.72) \approx 25.6$ in. If your speedometer was set for this tire and you switched to the low-profile tire shown, would the readings on your speedometer become too high or too low? Explain.

70. The load index, I, used on tires can be used to find the maximum load, L, that should be placed on the tire as shown in the scatter plot. Is the relationship between I and L linear? Explain.

Recommended Maximum Load

Load (in pounds) vs. Load Index

Chapter TEST

1. Find the slope of the line containing $(-1, 3)$ and $(-4, 5)$.

2. At 3:10 P.M. a skydiver jumps from an airplane at an altitude of 15,000 feet. At 3:10:26 P.M., at an altitude of 4200 feet, the skydiver opens the parachute. What was the skydiver's average speed during the 26-second free-fall?

3. Sketch the graph of $-6x + 2y = 4$.

4. What is the slope of $2x + 4y = 15$?

5. What is the y-intercept of the line $-3x + 5y = 25$?

6. What is the x-intercept of the line $8x - 7y = 16$?

In Exercises 7 and 8, decide whether the lines are parallel, perpendicular, or neither.

7. $-3x - 5y = 10, -3x + 5y = 10$

8. $-3x - 5y = 10, -5x + 3y = 10$

9. Write an equation of the line containing $(5, -2)$ and $(7, -3)$.

10. Write an equation of the line that passes through $(1, 4)$ and is perpendicular to the line $y = -3x + 1$.

11. Sketch the graph of $4x - 7y \geq 28$.

12. Sketch the graph of $y \leq -2$.

13. Sketch the graph of $y = |x - 3| - 1$.

14. Sketch the graph of $y = -2|x + 1| + 3$.

In Exercises 15–18, match the inequality with its graph.

15. $3x - 2y \leq 4$
16. $-3x + 2y \leq 4$
17. $3x + 2y \geq 4$
18. $3x - 2y \geq 4$

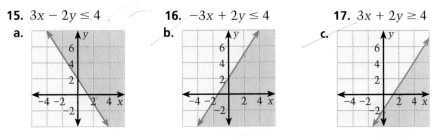

19. The height, b (in feet), that a basketball will bounce on a hardwood floor varies directly with the height, h (in feet), from which the ball is *dropped.* A basketball dropped from a height of 5 feet will bounce 2.8 feet. Write an equation that relates b and h.

20. You begin walking downtown. After 3 minutes you are $1\frac{1}{4}$ miles from your destination. Is this enough information to determine your average speed? Explain.

21. The scatter plot shows the number, s (in millions), of time-share owners of condominiums and houses worldwide for 1980 through 1990. Let t represent the year, with $t = 0$ corresponding to 1980. Write an equation of a line that you think best fits this data. *(Source: American Resort and Residential Development Association)*

Time-Share Owners Worldwide

Millions of Owners

$(0 \leftrightarrow 1980)$

Systems of Linear Equations and Inequalities

3.1 Solving Linear Systems by Graphing ▪ 122

3.2 Solving Linear Systems Algebraically ▪ 130

3.3 Problem Solving Using Linear Systems ▪ 138

3.4 Solving Systems of Linear Inequalities ▪ 145

3.5 Exploring Data: Linear Programming ▪ 151

3.6 Solving Systems of Linear Equations in Three Variables ▪ 157

The commercial harbor in San Juan, Puerto Rico, channels the country's exports to the rest of the world.

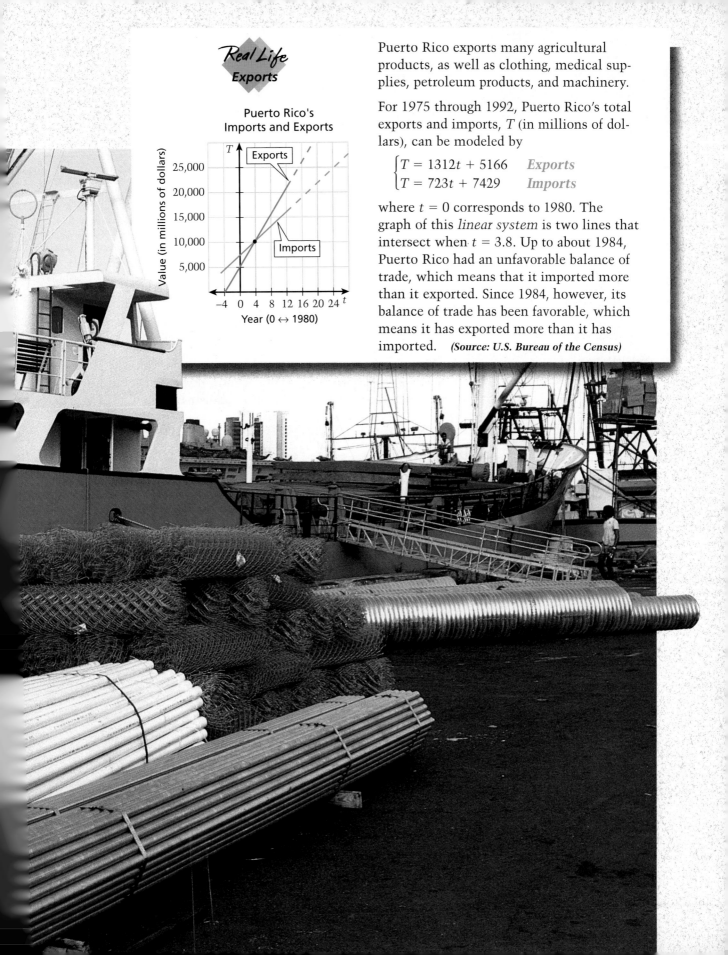

Real Life
Exports

Puerto Rico's Imports and Exports

Value (in millions of dollars)

25,000
20,000
15,000
10,000
5,000

Exports

Imports

−4 0 4 8 12 16 20 24 t

Year (0 ↔ 1980)

Puerto Rico exports many agricultural products, as well as clothing, medical supplies, petroleum products, and machinery.

For 1975 through 1992, Puerto Rico's total exports and imports, T (in millions of dollars), can be modeled by

$$\begin{cases} T = 1312t + 5166 & \textit{Exports} \\ T = 723t + 7429 & \textit{Imports} \end{cases}$$

where $t = 0$ corresponds to 1980. The graph of this *linear system* is two lines that intersect when $t = 3.8$. Up to about 1984, Puerto Rico had an unfavorable balance of trade, which means that it imported more than it exported. Since 1984, however, its balance of trade has been favorable, which means it has exported more than it has imported. *(Source: U.S. Bureau of the Census)*

3.1

Solving Linear Systems by Graphing

What you should learn:

Goal 1 How to graph and solve a system of linear equations in two variables

Goal 2 How to use a system of linear equations in two variables to answer questions about a real-life situation

Why you should learn it:

You can use a system of linear equations as a model to find the number of test items answered correctly and incorrectly on a standardized test.

Goal 1 Graphing and Solving a System

A **system of two linear equations in two variables** x and y consists of two equations of the following form.

$$\begin{cases} Ax + By = C & \textit{Equation 1} \\ Dx + Ey = F & \textit{Equation 2} \end{cases}$$

A **solution** of a system of linear equations in two variables is an ordered pair (x, y) that is a solution of both equations.

A system of two linear equations in two variables can have exactly one solution, no solution, or infinitely many solutions. To see why this is true, consider the following graphs.

A system of linear equations whose graph is intersecting lines has exactly one solution.

A system of linear equations whose graph is two parallel lines has no solution.

A system of linear equations whose graph is the same line has infinitely many solutions.

Example 1 *Checking a Solution*

Check that $(1, 3)$ is a solution of the system.

$$\begin{cases} 5x - 3y = -4 & \textit{Equation 1} \\ x + 2y = 7 & \textit{Equation 2} \end{cases}$$

Solution To check $(1, 3)$ as a solution, substitute 1 for x and 3 for y in each equation.

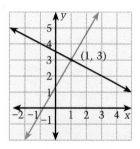

Equation 1 check: $5(1) - 3(3) = 5 - 9 = -4$

Equation 2 check: $(1) + 2(3) = 1 + 6 = 7$

To check the solution graphically, sketch a quick graph of each equation. The coordinates of the point of intersection will be the solution. ∎

The **graph of a system** can be used to approximate the solution of the system. Be sure to check such a solution algebraically to ensure that the coordinates of the point are exact.

Example 2 The Graph-and-Check Method

Solve the system: $\begin{cases} 4x + 5y = -3 & \textbf{\textit{Equation 1}} \\ -x + y = 3 & \textbf{\textit{Equation 2}} \end{cases}$

Solution To sketch the two lines, first write the equations in slope-intercept form.

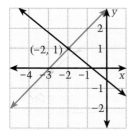

$\begin{cases} y = -\frac{4}{5}x - \frac{3}{5} & \textbf{\textit{Equation 1}} \\ y = x + 3 & \textbf{\textit{Equation 2}} \end{cases}$

The two lines seem to intersect at $(-2, 1)$. To check, substitute -2 for x and 1 for y in *each* equation of the original system.

$$4(-2) + 5(1) \overset{?}{=} -3 \qquad\qquad -(-2) + 1 \overset{?}{=} 3$$
$$-3 = -3 \;\textbf{\textit{(checks)}} \qquad\qquad 3 = 3 \;\textbf{\textit{(checks)}} \quad\blacksquare$$

Real Life
College Entrance Exam

Example 3 Writing a Linear System as a Model

On a college entrance exam, you answered 80 of the 85 questions. Each correct answer adds 1 point to your raw score, each unanswered question adds nothing, and each incorrect answer subtracts $\frac{1}{4}$ point. Your raw score was 70. How many questions did you answer correctly?

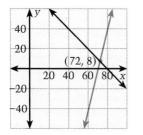

Solution

Verbal Model

$$\boxed{\text{Number correct}} + \boxed{\text{Number incorrect}} = \boxed{\text{Questions answered}}$$

$$\boxed{\substack{1 \\ \text{point}}} \cdot \boxed{\substack{\text{Number} \\ \text{correct}}} + \boxed{\substack{-\frac{1}{4} \\ \text{point}}} \cdot \boxed{\substack{\text{Number} \\ \text{incorrect}}} = \boxed{\substack{\text{Raw} \\ \text{score}}}$$

Labels
Number correct $= x$ (Questions)
Number incorrect $= y$ (Questions)
Total answered $= 80$ (Questions)
Raw score $= 70$ (Points)

System $\begin{cases} x + y = 80 & \textbf{\textit{Equation 1}} \\ x - \frac{1}{4}y = 70 & \textbf{\textit{Equation 2}} \end{cases}$

Sketch the graph of the system. The two lines appear to intersect at $(72, 8)$. This solution *checks* with the original problem.

$$72 + 8 = 80 \qquad \textbf{\textit{You answered 80 questions.}}$$
$$1(72) - \left(\frac{1}{4}\right)(8) = 70 \qquad \textbf{\textit{Your raw score was 70.}}$$

Thus you answered 72 questions correctly. $\blacksquare$

In 1992, there were about 20 million businesses in the United States. Of these, 15.5 million were owned by a sole proprietor, that is, a single person or family. The circle graph at the right shows the percents of these businesses in each revenue category.
(Source: Internal Revenue Service)

Revenues of Sole Proprietorships

9.4%   0.9%
8.2%   0.4%
11.7%
67.1%

☐ Under $25,000
☐ $25,000–$49,999
☐ $50,000–$99,999
☐ $100,000–$499,999
☐ $500,000–$999,999
☐ $1,000,000 or more

Goal 2 Using Linear Systems as Real-Life Models

Linear systems can be used to find the *break-even point* of a business. For a new business, the break-even point occurs when the *revenue* (the income from sales) is equal to the *cost* (the amount the business has spent).

Real Life
Business

Example 4 *Finding the Break-Even Point*

You have purchased a flower shop. The previous owner's records for the past three years show the average monthly cost was $5400. The average monthly revenue was $8600. You paid $153,600 for the shop. If monthly costs and revenues remain the same, how long will it take to break even?

Solution   Let R represent the revenue you bring in during the first t months. A model for the revenue is $R = 8600t$.

Let C represent your cost, including purchase price, during the first t months. A model for the cost is $C = 5400t + 153,600$.

By sketching the graphs of both equations on the same coordinate plane, it appears that the revenue and cost equations intersect at 48 months. Substituting $t = 48$ in either equation will give the other coordinate, 412.8. Thus your break-even point occurs at 48 months, at which time you will have spent and taken in the same amount: $412,800.   ■

Flower Shop Costs and Revenues

Thousands of Dollars

(48, 412.8)

Cost

Revenue

10 20 30 40 50 t
Time (in months)

Communicating about ALGEBRA

▶ **SHARING IDEAS about the Lesson**

Solve the linear systems graphically. Explain your steps.

A. $\begin{cases} 3x - 4y = 5 \\ -2x + y = -5 \end{cases}$ **B.** $\begin{cases} 3x - 4y = 5 \\ -3x + 4y = -5 \end{cases}$ **C.** $\begin{cases} 3x - 4y = 5 \\ -3x + 4y = 5 \end{cases}$

EXERCISES

Guided Practice

▶ **CRITICAL THINKING about the Lesson**

1. The graph of a system of two linear equations in two variables is a pair of lines. How can you use the graph to decide how many solutions the linear system has?

2. A linear system can have exactly one solution, no solution, or infinitely many solutions. Explain why a linear system in two variables cannot have exactly two solutions.

3. Sketch the graph of the following system and use the graph to find the solution. Check the solution algebraically.

$$\begin{cases} x + 5y = -1 \\ x + 4y = 0 \end{cases}$$

In Exercises 4–6, match the linear system with its graph. How many solutions does the system have?

4. $\begin{cases} 2x - y = -5 \\ x + 2y = 0 \end{cases}$

5. $\begin{cases} -2x + 3y = 12 \\ 2x - 3y = 6 \end{cases}$

6. $\begin{cases} 2x - y = 5 \\ -4x + 2y = -10 \end{cases}$

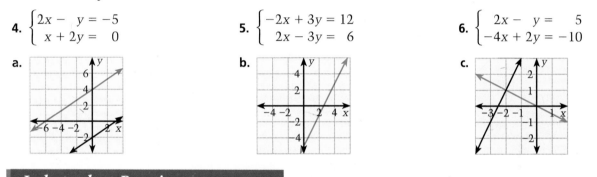

a.

b.

c.

Independent Practice

In Exercises 7–12, how many solutions does the linear system have?

7. $\begin{cases} 24x - 9y = 3 \\ 8x - 3y = 1 \end{cases}$

8. $\begin{cases} x + 4y = 9 \\ -2x + y = 0 \end{cases}$

9. $\begin{cases} 2x + 8y = 16 \\ -3x + 6y = 30 \end{cases}$

10. $\begin{cases} -x + 3y = 3 \\ 2x - 6y = 30 \end{cases}$

11. $\begin{cases} 2x + y = -1 \\ -4x - 2y = -5 \end{cases}$

12. $\begin{cases} -x + 2y = 16 \\ 4x - 8y = -64 \end{cases}$

In Exercises 13–18, decide whether the ordered pair is a solution of the linear system. Use an algebraic check.

13. $(5, -2)$
$\begin{cases} 5x - y = 27 \\ -3x + 4y = -23 \end{cases}$

14. $(4, 0)$
$\begin{cases} -x + 6y = 4 \\ 3x + y = 12 \end{cases}$

15. $(9, 1)$
$\begin{cases} 2x - 9y = 9 \\ -x + 8y = 17 \end{cases}$

16. $(-3, 3)$
$\begin{cases} 2x - 4y = -18 \\ 4x - 2y = -18 \end{cases}$

17. $(-2, -7)$
$\begin{cases} 4x - 3y = 13 \\ 7x - y = -7 \end{cases}$

18. $(8, 9)$
$\begin{cases} -2x + 4y = -20 \\ 3x + y = 33 \end{cases}$

In Exercises 19–24, decide whether the ordered pair is a solution of the linear system. Use a graphic check.

19. $(0, 3)$

$$\begin{cases} x + 2y = 8 \\ 2x + y = -3 \end{cases}$$

20. $(4, 4)$

$$\begin{cases} -x + 2y = 4 \\ -3x + 4y = 4 \end{cases}$$

21. $(2, -1)$

$$\begin{cases} -x + 2y = -4 \\ y = -1 \end{cases}$$

22. $\left(\frac{2}{3}, 0\right)$

$$\begin{cases} -3x + 2y = 2 \\ 3x + 2y = -2 \end{cases}$$

23. $(1, 4)$

$$\begin{cases} -5x + y = -1 \\ -3x + y = 1 \end{cases}$$

24. $(3, 4)$

$$\begin{cases} 3x + 4y = 12 \\ -4x + 3y = -3 \end{cases}$$

In Exercises 25–36, sketch the graph of the linear system. Use your graph to estimate the solution. Check your estimate algebraically.

25. $\begin{cases} x + 2y = 0 \\ -x + y = -3 \end{cases}$

26. $\begin{cases} -2x + y = 5 \\ x + y = 8 \end{cases}$

27. $\begin{cases} 2x + y = 4 \\ x + y = 3 \end{cases}$

28. $\begin{cases} 3x + 4y = -8 \\ -5x + y = -25 \end{cases}$

29. $\begin{cases} 3x + y = 9 \\ -3x + y = 3 \end{cases}$

30. $\begin{cases} 2x + y = 13 \\ x - y = 5 \end{cases}$

31. $\begin{cases} y = \frac{1}{6}x - 2 \\ y = -\frac{1}{6}x + 2 \end{cases}$

32. $\begin{cases} y = 3x \\ y = x + 2 \end{cases}$

33. $\begin{cases} 2x + y = -5 \\ x - 2y = 0 \end{cases}$

34. $\begin{cases} x + 4y = -24 \\ x - 4y = 24 \end{cases}$

35. $\begin{cases} x - 3y = -3 \\ 2x + y = 8 \end{cases}$

36. $\begin{cases} x - 2y = 0 \\ x + 2y = 4 \end{cases}$

37. *Investing in Two Funds*   A total of \$4500 is invested in two funds paying 4% and 5% annual interest. The combined annual interest is \$210. How much of the \$4500 is invested in each fund?

38. *Exam Score*   You answered 82 questions out of 85 on a college entrance exam. Your raw score was 67. Use the information in Example 3 to find the number of questions you answered correctly.

39. *Break-Even Analysis*   Your family is planning to open a restaurant. You need an initial investment of \$85,000. Each week your costs will be about \$7400. If your weekly revenue is \$8000, how many weeks will it take to break even?

40. *Vietnam Veterans Memorial*   "The Wall" in Washington, D.C., designed by Maya Ling Lin when she was a student at Yale University, has two vertical, triangular sections of black granite with a common side. The top of each section is level with the ground. The bottoms of the two sections can be modeled by the equations $y = \frac{2}{25}x - 10$ and $y = -\frac{5}{61}x - 10$, when the x-axis is superimposed on the top of the wall. Each unit in the coordinate system represents 1 foot. How deep is the memorial at the point where the two sections meet? How long is each section?

The Vietnam Veterans Memorial honors all the men and women who served in the Vietnam War.

41. *Airport Runways* A small airport has two runways that intersect. (The runway in use depends on wind conditions.) A coordinate plane is superimposed over the airport, with the origin at the control tower. The endpoints of the center line of one runway are at $(-1, -6)$ and $(3, 2)$. The endpoints of the center line of the other runway are at $(-3, -4)$ and $(6, 2)$. Find equations for the lines that contain the runways. Then sketch the lines and find the point of intersection.

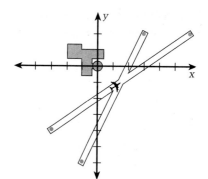

Advertising Expenditures **In Exercises 42–44, use the following information.**

The graph at the right shows advertising expenses in the United States as a percent of the gross national product. The dashed portions of the graphs are predictions.
(Source: American Demographics)

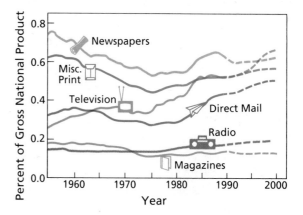

42. When did television advertising expenses surpass direct-mail advertising expenses?

43. When did radio advertising expenses surpass magazine advertising expenses?

44. When are television advertising expenses predicted to surpass newspaper advertising expenses?

Integrated Review

In Exercises 45–50, state whether the ordered pair is a solution of the equation.

45. $2x + 3y = 9$, $(1, 4)$

46. $-x + 5y = 12$, $(3, 3)$

47. $16x + 2y = 12$, $(-2, 10)$

48. $\frac{1}{2}x + \frac{1}{6}y = 2$, $(10, -18)$

49. $-\frac{3}{4}x + y = -2$, $(2, -\frac{1}{2})$

50. $6x + 7y = -4$, $(-3, 2)$

In Exercises 51–53, rewrite the equation in slope-intercept form.

51. $-7x + 2y = 6$

52. $3x + y = -10$

53. $4x - y = 13$

In Exercises 54–56, graph the equation.

54. $y = -4x - 5$

55. $y = \frac{1}{2}x + 4$

56. $2x + y = 10$

Exploration and Extension

In Exercises 57 and 58, describe a technique *other than graphing* that could be used to solve the linear system.

57. $\begin{cases} y = x + 2 \\ y = 4 \end{cases}$

58. $\begin{cases} y = 3x - 6 \\ x = 2 \end{cases}$

A graphing calculator or computer can be used to graph a system of linear equations. For instance, the screen at the right shows the graph of the following system.

$$\begin{cases} 3x - 4y = 2 & \textit{Equation 1} \\ 5x + 6y = 16 & \textit{Equation 2} \end{cases}$$

Note that the two lines appear to intersect at the point (2, 1). To check this, substitute 2 for x and 1 for y in each equation.

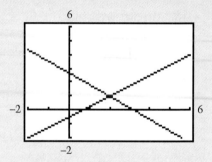

Graph of a System of Linear Equations.

The first step in using a graphing calculator to sketch the graph of a linear system is to solve each equation for y.

$$\begin{cases} y = \dfrac{3}{4}x - \dfrac{1}{2} & \textit{Equation 1} \\ y = -\dfrac{5}{6}x + \dfrac{8}{3} & \textit{Equation 2} \end{cases}$$

Next find settings for a viewing rectangle that shows the point of intersection. You may have to try a few before you obtain a viewing rectangle that shows the portion of the graph you want to see. For this particular system, you can use a setting in which both x and y vary between -2 and 6.

Keystroke instructions for sketching these graphs on a TI-82, Casio fx-9700GE, and Sharp EL-9300C are listed on page 858.

Cooperative Learning

Partner Activity Use a graphing calculator to sketch the graph of the following system of linear equations.

$$\begin{cases} 6x + 2y = 13 & \textit{Equation 1} \\ 3x - 3y = 12 & \textit{Equation 2} \end{cases}$$

The coordinates of the solution are rational numbers. Try finding the *exact* solution using only the trace and zoom keys on your graphing calculator. Check your solution by substituting it into the equations in the original system.

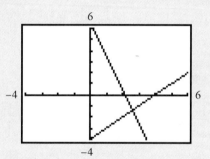

Some models using linear systems call for *exact* solutions. For others, however, an *approximate* solution is sufficient. For instance, suppose two linear models represent two different trends in population. It is not reasonable to expect such a model to produce an answer like "August 16, 1992." Rather, you expect the model to be accurate enough to produce an answer like "sometime in 1992" or "about midyear in 1992."

Example: Approximating the Solution of a Linear System

The following models for the total exports and imports of Puerto Rico (in millions of dollars) for 1975 through 1992 were given on page 121.

$$\begin{cases} T = 1312t + 5166 & \textit{Exports} \\ T = 723t + 7429 & \textit{Imports} \end{cases}$$

(t is the year, with $t = 0$ representing 1980.) Use a graphing calculator to approximate the year in which Puerto Rico's exports began to exceed its imports.

Solution   Graphing calculators use x and y as variables, so you first need to rewrite the equations using x and y. (The variables T and θ, used by a graphing calculator, are for other types of graphs and should not be used for linear systems.)

$$\begin{cases} y = 1312x + 5166 & \textit{Exports} \\ y = 723x + 7429 & \textit{Imports} \end{cases}$$

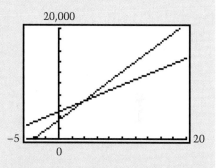

After entering these equations in the calculator and setting an appropriate range, you can obtain the graph shown at the right. From the graph, you can see that the exports began to exceed the imports around 1984. (The *trace* key can help you approximate the point of intersection.) ∎

Exercises

In Exercises 1–4, use a graphing calculator to sketch the graph of the system. Approximate the solution and check your answer algebraically.

1. $\begin{cases} y = -2x + 2 \\ y = \frac{1}{2}x - \frac{11}{2} \end{cases}$ 2. $\begin{cases} y = 3x + 11 \\ y = \frac{1}{3}x + \frac{19}{3} \end{cases}$ 3. $\begin{cases} 7x - 8y = 5 \\ 5x + 4y = 23 \end{cases}$ 4. $\begin{cases} 10x + 11y = 24 \\ 9x - 6y = -42 \end{cases}$

5. **Per Capita Income**   For 1987 through 1994, the per capita incomes, y, in Nevada and New Hampshire can be modeled by

$$\begin{cases} y = 1077t + 9035 & \textit{Nevada} \\ y = 712t + 13{,}324 & \textit{New Hampshire} \end{cases}$$

where t is the year, with $t = 7$ corresponding to 1987. Use a graphing calculator to approximate the year in which the per capita income of Nevada surpassed that of New Hampshire.   *(Source: Bureau of Economic Analysis)*

3.2 Solving Linear Systems Algebraically

What you should learn:

Goal 1 How to use algebraic methods to solve a linear system

Goal 2 How to use a linear system to answer questions about a real-life situation

Why you should learn it:

You can model many real-life situations with a linear system, such as the numbers of sheep and cattle grazing on national forest land during the last twenty years.

Goal 1 Using Algebraic Methods

In this lesson, you will study two algebraic methods for solving a linear system. The first is called **substitution.**

The Substitution Method for Solving a Linear System

1. *Solve* one of the equations for one of its variables.
2. *Substitute* this expression into the other equation and solve for the other variable.
3. *Substitute* this value in the revised first equation and solve.
4. *Check* the solution in each of the original equations.

Example 1 The Substitution Method

Solve the linear system.

$$\begin{cases} -2x + y = 8 & \text{Equation 1} \\ 3x + y = -2 & \text{Equation 2} \end{cases}$$

Solution Begin by solving for y in either of the equations.

$$y = 2x + 8 \qquad \textit{Revised Equation 1}$$

Substitute this expression for y in Equation 2 and solve for x.

$$3x + y = -2 \qquad \textit{Equation 2}$$
$$3x + (2x + 8) = -2 \qquad \textit{Substitute 2x + 8 for y.}$$
$$5x = -10 \qquad \textit{Simplify.}$$
$$x = -2 \qquad \textit{Solve for x.}$$

You now know that the value of x in the solution is -2. To find the value of y, substitute the value of x into the revised Equation 1.

$$y = 2x + 8 \qquad \textit{Revised Equation 1}$$
$$y = 2(-2) + 8 \qquad \textit{Substitute -2 for x.}$$
$$y = 4 \qquad \textit{Solve for y.}$$

The solution is $(-2, 4)$. Check it in the original system. ∎

When using the substitution method, you will obtain the same solution (x, y) whether you solve for y first or x first. Thus you should begin by solving for the variable that has a coefficient of 1.

Solve for x first here:

$$\begin{cases} 5x - 3y = 2 \\ x + 2y = 3 \end{cases}$$

Solve for y first here:

$$\begin{cases} -4x + y = 0 \\ 2x - 3y = -10 \end{cases}$$

If neither variable has a coefficient of 1, you can still use the substitution method by writing an equivalent equation that does have a coefficient of 1. In such cases, however, the **linear combination method** may be better.

Linear Combination Method for Solving a Linear System

1. *Arrange* the equations with like terms in columns.
2. *Obtain* coefficients for x (or y) that differ only in sign by multiplying each term of one or both equations by an appropriate number.
3. *Add* the equations and solve for the remaining variable.
4. *Substitute* the value obtained in step 3 into either of the original equations and solve for the other variable.
5. *Check* the solution in each of the original equations.

Example 2 **The Linear Combination Method**

Solve the linear system.

$$\begin{cases} 5x + 4y = 6 & \textit{Equation 1} \\ -2x - 3y = -1 & \textit{Equation 2} \end{cases}$$

Solution One way to obtain coefficients for y that differ only in sign is by multiplying the first equation by 3 and the second equation by 4. Add the results to obtain an equation that has only one variable, x.

$$
\begin{array}{rcll}
5x + 4y = 6 & \longrightarrow & 15x + 12y = 18 & \textit{Multiply by 3.} \\
-2x - 3y = -1 & \longrightarrow & -8x - 12y = -4 & \textit{Multiply by 4.} \\
\hline
& & 7x \qquad\quad = 14 & \textit{Add the equations.}
\end{array}
$$

Therefore $x = 2$. By substituting this value in the second equation, you can solve for y.

$$-2x - 3y = -1 \qquad \textit{Equation 2}$$

$$-2(2) - 3y = -1 \qquad \textit{Substitute 2 for x.}$$

$$y = -1 \qquad \textit{Solve for y.}$$

The solution is $(2, -1)$. Check it in the original system. ■

The linear systems in Examples 1 and 2 each have exactly one solution. Remember, however, that some linear systems have no solution and some have infinitely many solutions.

Example 3 *A Linear System with No Solution*

Solve the linear system.

$$\begin{cases} 3x - 2y = 5 & \textit{Equation 1} \\ -6x + 4y = 7 & \textit{Equation 2} \end{cases}$$

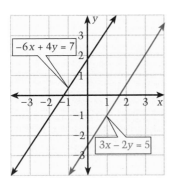

Solution You can use any of the three methods to solve the system. Using the graphing method, it appears that the two equations graph as parallel lines. Using either the substitution or linear combination method, you obtain a false "equation." For instance, the linear combination method produces the following.

$$\begin{array}{llll} 3x - 2y = 5 & \longrightarrow & 6x - 4y = 10 & \textit{Multiply by 2.} \\ -6x + 4y = 7 & \longrightarrow & -6x + 4y = 7 & \textit{Equation 2} \\ \hline & & 0 = 17 & \textit{Sum of equations} \end{array}$$

Because the statement $0 = 17$ is not true, you can conclude that there is no solution. ∎

Using the substitution method or the linear combination method for a linear system with infinitely many solutions produces an equation such as $3 = 3$ or $0 = 0$. For instance, by adding the equations in the linear system

$$\begin{cases} 3x - 2y = 5 & \textit{Equation 1} \\ -3x + 2y = -5 & \textit{Equation 2} \end{cases}$$

you obtain $0 = 0$, which indicates that both equations graph as the same line. Every point on the line is a solution.

The federal government protects and manages about 300,000 square miles of national forest in the United States and Puerto Rico. (This is more than the combined areas of California and Nevada.) Some of the grass-covered areas of national forests are leased to ranchers for grazing cattle and sheep.

Goal 2 Using a Linear System as a Model

Example 4 *Grazing in National Forests*

For 1970 through 1990, the number, y (in 1000's), of cattle and sheep that grazed on national forest land can be modeled by the following equations. (Let $t = 0$ represent 1970.)

$$y = 1600 - 11t \quad \textit{Cattle}$$

$$y = 1650 - 30t \quad \textit{Sheep}$$

In 1970, more sheep than cattle were grazing in national forests. When did this change? *(Source: National Forest Service)*

Solution This system can be solved using substitution.

$$y = 1650 - 30t \qquad \textit{Equation 2}$$

$$(1600 - 11t) = 1650 - 30t \qquad \textit{Substitute 1600} - 11t \textit{ for y.}$$

$$19t = 50 \qquad \textit{Subtract 1600 and add 30t.}$$

$$t \approx 2.6 \qquad \textit{Solve for t.}$$

Thus according to this model, the number of grazing sheep fell below the number of grazing cattle around 1972 or 1973. ∎

Grazing on National Forest Land

Communicating about **ALGEBRA**

▶ SHARING IDEAS about the Lesson

Comparing Methods Sketch the graph of the linear system. Then use substitution and linear combinations to solve the system. Compare the merits of each method.

A. $\begin{cases} 4x - 3y = 2 \\ 5x + 2y = -1 \end{cases}$ B. $\begin{cases} 4x - y = 2 \\ 5x + 2y = 9 \end{cases}$

EXERCISES

▶ **CRITICAL THINKING about the Lesson**

1. Describe how you would use substitution to solve the system.

$$\begin{cases} 13x + 5y = 2 \\ x - 4y = 10 \end{cases}$$

2. Describe how you would use a linear combination to solve the system.

$$\begin{cases} 6x - 5y = 30 \\ -4x + 2y = 7 \end{cases}$$

3. Suppose you used substitution to solve a linear system and obtained the equation $-4 = -4$. What could you conclude?

4. Suppose you used substitution to solve a linear system and obtained the result $12 = 0$. What could you conclude?

In Exercises 5 and 6, which method would you use to solve the linear system? Explain.

5. $\begin{cases} 5x + 3y = -1 \\ -4x + 2y = 3 \end{cases}$

6. $\begin{cases} 5x + 3y = 1 \\ -4x + y = 6 \end{cases}$

Independent Practice

In Exercises 7–12, use substitution to solve the linear system.

7. $\begin{cases} 2x + y = 9 \\ 3x - 4y = 8 \end{cases}$

8. $\begin{cases} 3x + 5y = 12 \\ x + 4y = 11 \end{cases}$

9. $\begin{cases} x - 9y = 25 \\ 6x - 5y = 3 \end{cases}$

10. $\begin{cases} 2x + y = -9 \\ 3x + 5y = 4 \end{cases}$

11. $\begin{cases} 2x + 3y = -6 \\ 3x + 2y = 25 \end{cases}$

12. $\begin{cases} -x + 3y = 18 \\ 4x - 2y = 8 \end{cases}$

In Exercises 13–18, use a linear combination to solve the system.

13. $\begin{cases} -2x + 7y = 10 \\ x - 3y = -3 \end{cases}$

14. $\begin{cases} 2x - y = 2 \\ -5x + 4y = -2 \end{cases}$

15. $\begin{cases} 3x + 11y = 4 \\ -2x - 6y = 0 \end{cases}$

16. $\begin{cases} -9x + 5y = 1 \\ 3x - 2y = 2 \end{cases}$

17. $\begin{cases} 7x + 20y = 11 \\ 3x + 10y = 5 \end{cases}$

18. $\begin{cases} 2x - y = 3 \\ 9x - 6y = 6 \end{cases}$

In Exercises 19–24, sketch the graph of the system. Then use any convenient method to solve the system.

19. $\begin{cases} x - y = 10 \\ 3x - 2y = 25 \end{cases}$

20. $\begin{cases} -7x + 5y = 0 \\ 14x - 8y = 2 \end{cases}$

21. $\begin{cases} 4x + 3y = 1 \\ -3x - 6y = 3 \end{cases}$

22. $\begin{cases} -4x - 10y = 12 \\ x + 5y = 2 \end{cases}$

23. $\begin{cases} 5x + 16y = 15 \\ -2x - 4y = 1 \end{cases}$

24. $\begin{cases} 4x + y = 2 \\ 6x + 3y = 0 \end{cases}$

In Exercises 25–28, how many solutions does the linear system have? Explain.

25. $\begin{cases} 3x + y = 12 \\ 2x + 2y = 4 \end{cases}$

26. $\begin{cases} 6x - y = 5 \\ 12x - 2y = 3 \end{cases}$

27. $\begin{cases} x - 2y = 1 \\ 3x - 6y = 2 \end{cases}$

28. $\begin{cases} 3x - y = -3 \\ -3x + y = 2 \end{cases}$

29. *World Food Production*   For comparison purposes, the United Nations classifies countries as *developed* or *developing.* In 1990, the developed countries were Australia, Canada, all European countries, Israel, Japan, New Zealand, South Africa, the Soviet Union, and the United States. Based on an index for which *100* represents the food production in 1980, the food production, *y*, of developed and developing countries can be modeled by

$$\begin{cases} y = \frac{6}{5}t + 88 & \textit{Developed countries} \\ y = \frac{11}{5}t + 78 & \textit{Developing countries} \end{cases}$$

where $t = 0$ represents 1970. In 1970, food production was greater in developed countries. When did this change?
(Source: United Nations)

This kibbutz in Israel grows peppers in greenhouses to conserve water.

30. *World Fuel Production*   For 1980 through 1990, the coal production in the world, *C* (in millions of metric tons), and crude petroleum production, *P* (in millions of metric tons), can be modeled by the following equations. (Let $t = 0$ represent 1980.)

$C = 86.5t + 2728$ *Coal production*

$P = -27.5t + 2979$ *Petroleum production*

During which year were the production levels equal?
(Source: United Nations)

31. *New York City Subway*   The map shows a section of the New York City subway system. The portion of the track shown in blue lies approximately on the line given by $11x + 6y = 110$. From Central Park through most of the downtown area, the Avenue of the Americas is straight and lies on the line given by $-13x + 7y = 25$. (Each unit in the coordinate system represents a quarter mile.) Find the coordinates of the point at which the subway track goes under the Avenue of the Americas.

32. *Paying the IRS*   In 1990, the federal income tax, *I*, for a single person whose taxable income, *x*, was less than $97,620 was given by the following equations.

$I = 0.15x,$ *if* $x \leq A.$

$I = 0.28x - 2528.5,$ *if* $A \leq x \leq B.$

$I = 0.33x - 4881,$ *if* $B \leq x \leq 97,620.$

At what taxable income level, *A*, did a person move from the 15% *tax bracket* to the 28% tax bracket? At what taxable income level, *B*, did a person move from the 28% tax bracket to the 33% tax bracket? Explain your answer.

In Exercises 33–38, solve the equation.

33. $5x + 6(1 + x) = 17$ **34.** $x - 8 - 5x = 10$ **35.** $x - 10x + 4 = 10$

36. $9 - 3x + x = 15$ **37.** $7 - 4x + 3 + 2x = 6$ **38.** $3x + 3 - 5x = 17$

In Exercises 39–44, decide whether the ordered pair is a solution of the system.

39. $(4, -2)$

$$\begin{cases} 2x - y = 6 \\ -x + 3y = 14 \end{cases}$$

40. $(1, 0)$

$$\begin{cases} 6x - 2y = 6 \\ -5x + 3y = -5 \end{cases}$$

41. $(1, 5)$

$$\begin{cases} x + y = 6 \\ 3x - y = -2 \end{cases}$$

42. $(-4, -7)$

$$\begin{cases} -x - 7y = 46 \\ x + y = -11 \end{cases}$$

43. $(-3, -6)$

$$\begin{cases} x - 6y = 33 \\ -2x - y = 0 \end{cases}$$

44. $(-6, 2)$

$$\begin{cases} 10x + 13y = -34 \\ -15x - 17y = 56 \end{cases}$$

In Exercises 45–50, solve for y.

45. $2x + 9y = 36$ **46.** $4x + 9y = 16$ **47.** $16x + 3y = 24$

48. $x - 14y = 28$ **49.** $-5x + 10y = 14$ **50.** $-8x + 9y = 16$

Eating Together **In Exercises 51 and 52, use the following information.**

The chart at the right shows the percents of Americans (18 years old and older) who eat breakfast with other people in their home and the percents who eat an evening meal with other people in their home. People who live alone are not included in these data.

(Source: Roper Organization)

51. Find the ratio of the breakfast percent to the evening meal percent for each of the four age groups. What do you notice about the ratios?

52. How would you explain the differences in eating habits shown by the four age groups?

Exploration and Extension

53. Find the point of intersection of the line $y = 2x - 1$ and the line that passes through $(4, 1)$ and is perpendicular to $y = 2x - 1$.

Creating Your Own Linear Systems **In Exercises 54–56, write a linear system that produces the given number of solutions. Use $y = -\frac{1}{2}x - 3$ as one of the equations.**

54. One solution **55.** No solution **56.** Infinitely many solutions

1. Evaluate $3x - 2y$ when $x = -1$ and $y = 2$. **(1.2)**

2. Write in slope-intercept form: $-2x + 3y = 10$. **(2.3)**

3. Write in decimal form: 3.14×10^4.

4. Add: $\frac{2}{3} + \frac{1}{3} + \frac{4}{3}$

5. Solve $-3(x - 2) = 2(5 - x)$. **(1.3)**

6. Solve $|2x - 5| = 3$. **(1.7)**

7. Sketch the graph of $y = 3x - 4$. **(2.3)**

8. Sketch the graph of $y = |x - 2| - 2$. **(2.6)**

9. Sketch the graph of $y \le -\frac{1}{2}x + 3$. **(2.5)**

10. Solve $-3x + 4 \le 2x + 24$. **(1.6)**

11. What is 49% of 135?

12. What is the reciprocal of $-\frac{1}{7}$?

13. Write 30 as the product of prime numbers.

14. For which type of line is slope not defined? **(2.2)**

15. Solve $3xy + 4y = 8$ for y. **(1.5)**

16. Find the volume of a cube with 3-foot edges.

17. Write an equation of the horizontal line through $(-5, 6)$. **(2.1)**

18. Write an equation of the vertical line through $(-5, 6)$. **(2.1)**

19. Write an equation of the line through $(2, -3)$ and $(-1, 0)$. **(2.4)**

20. What is the slope of a line that is perpendicular to $2x - 5y = 6$? **(2.2)**

Career Interview

Air Traffic Controller

Terry Gilbert is an air traffic controller at the control center in Chicago, which supervises the area that extends from Green Bay, Wisconsin, to Champagne, Illinois, to Detroit, Michigan, to Iowa City, Iowa. Over 2 million planes fly within this corridor annually!

Q: What do you do as a controller?

A: O'Hare Airport, located within the center's airspace, is rated as an 80-plane-per-hour site. Controllers must balance the incoming load so that all 80 planes do not arrive within the first 5 minutes! We also keep track of the landing slots. That is, which slots are used, how often each is used, and whether each is used on a timely basis.

Q: How much of the actual math is done by radar?

A: Airplanes on radar are tagged to show the plane's altitude, code number, direction, and speed.

Q: How much mental math and estimation do you use?

A: Controllers often calculate distances, and climb and descent rates mentally. So good mental math and estimation skills are essential.

3.3

Problem Solving Using Linear Systems

Real Life
Retail Sales

Goal | **Linear Systems as Real-Life Models**

You have already modeled some real-life situations with linear systems. Remember that the key steps are writing a *verbal model*, assigning *labels*, writing an *algebraic model*, *solving* the algebraic model, and *answering* the original question.

| Write a verbal model. | → | Assign labels. | → | Write an algebraic model. | → | Solve the model. | → | Answer the question. |

When you write a linear system to model a real-life problem, remember also that you have *three* methods for solving the system: graphing, substitution, and linear combination.

Example 1 *Finding the Price per Item*

You and several other people are helping your aunt move. At lunch, you volunteer to go out to buy sandwiches. You get 6 chicken sandwiches and 6 beef sandwiches for $30. Later in the afternoon, everyone is hungry again. You go to the same shop and buy 4 chicken sandwiches and 8 beef sandwiches for $30.60. What was the price of each type of sandwich? (Assume sales tax is included in the price.)

Solution

Verbal Model $6 \cdot \boxed{\text{Price of chicken}} + 6 \cdot \boxed{\text{Price of beef}} = \boxed{30.00}$

$4 \cdot \boxed{\text{Price of chicken}} + 8 \cdot \boxed{\text{Price of beef}} = \boxed{30.60}$

Labels Price of chicken sandwich $= c$ (dollars)
Price of beef sandwich $= b$ (dollars)

System $\begin{cases} 6c + 6b = 30 & \textit{Equation 1} \\ 4c + 8b = 30.6 & \textit{Equation 2} \end{cases}$

Using the linear combination method, you can multiply the first equation by 2, multiply the second equation by -3, and add the results. The solution is $2.35 per chicken sandwich and $2.65 per beef sandwich. ■

Your automobile insurance premium depends on many factors: your age, where you live, the value of your car, the type of car, and your driving record. Of course, it also depends on the amount of coverage you obtain. At the right is a typical annual insurance premium schedule for a $15,000 car driven by a 16-year-old driver in 1991.

Liability, L (in $1000's)
Premium = 480 + 0.31L

Collision Deductible, D (in dollars)
Premium = 692 − 0.49D

Real Life
Insurance

Example 2 *Buying Automobile Insurance*

You are quoted a total annual premium of $1154 for automobile insurance. This premium gives liability coverage of L thousand dollars and collision coverage that has a deductible of D dollars. The insurance agent tells you that if you are willing to increase your collision deductible by $400, then you can get *five times* the liability coverage and still save $72 a year on your premium. What was the amount of the deductible and the amount of liability coverage in the first quote? (Use the premium schedule given above.)

Solution

First Quote: $\underbrace{480 + 0.31L}_{\text{Liability premium}} + \underbrace{692 - 0.49D}_{\text{Collision premium}} = 1154$

Second Quote: $\underbrace{480 + 0.31(5L)}_{\text{Liability premium}} + \underbrace{692 - 0.49(D + 400)}_{\text{Collision premium}} = 1154 - 72$

After simplifying these two equations, you can obtain the following linear system.

$$\begin{cases} 0.31L - 0.49D = -18 & \text{\textit{Equation 1}} \\ 1.55L - 0.49D = 106 & \text{\textit{Equation 2}} \end{cases}$$

Using the linear combination method (multiply the first equation by −1 and add the result to the second equation), you can determine that the solution is $L = 100$ and $D = 100$. Thus, the first quote was for liability coverage of $100,000 with a $100 collision deductible. The second was for liability coverage of $500,000 with a $500 collision deductible. By raising your deductible, you can afford to carry a higher liability coverage. ■

Example 3   *Comparing Two Populations*

In 1980, the population of Illinois was 11,427,000, and the population of Florida was 10,195,000. In 1990, the population of Illinois was 11,467,000, and the population of Florida was 13,003,000. Over the ten-year period, both populations increased at a rate that was approximately linear. Estimate the year that the population of Florida surpassed the population of Illinois. *(Source: United States Census Bureau)*

Solution   Let t represent the year, with $t = 0$ corresponding to 1980. The rate of change of Illinois's population was

$$\frac{(1990 \text{ population}) - (1980 \text{ population})}{10 - 0} = \frac{40,000}{10}$$
$$= 4000 \text{ people/year.}$$

The rate of change of Florida's population was

$$\frac{(1990 \text{ population}) - (1980 \text{ population})}{10 - 0} = \frac{2,808,000}{10}$$
$$= 280,800 \text{ people/year.}$$

Using the slope-intercept form, the linear models for the populations, P, of the two states are as follows.

$$\begin{cases} P = 4,000t + 11,427,000 & \textit{Illinois} \\ P = 280,800t + 10,195,000 & \textit{Florida} \end{cases}$$

The graph of the system is shown at the left. From the graph, you can see that the population of Florida surpassed the population of Illinois around 1984 or 1985. ∎

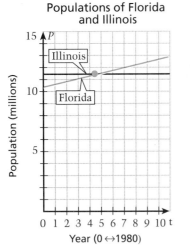

Populations of Florida and Illinois

Communicating about ALGEBRA

▷ SHARING IDEAS about the Lesson

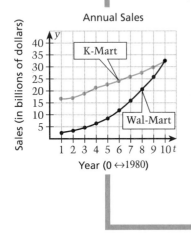

The scatter plot at the left shows the annual revenue, y (in billions of dollars), for K Mart Corporation and Wal-Mart Stores for 1981 through 1990.
(Source: K Mart Corporation and Wal-Mart Stores)

A. In 1990, the total revenue for Wal-Mart was $32.6 billion, and the total revenue for K Mart was $32.1 billion. How early do you think you could have predicted that Wal-Mart's revenue would exceed K Mart's? Explain.

B. Estimate K Mart's revenue in 1995. Estimate Wal-Mart's revenue in 1995. Explain the process you used.

EXERCISES

Guided Practice

▶ **CRITICAL THINKING about the Lesson**

Soccer Victory   **In Exercises 1–4, use the following information.**

A soccer team bought ice-cream cones to celebrate a victory. The total cost of 12 double cones and 8 single cones was $17. A double cone cost $0.25 more than a single cone. What was the price of each type of cone?

1. Write a verbal model for this problem.

2. Assign labels to the verbal model.

3. Use the labels to write a linear system that represents the problem.

4. Solve the system and answer the question.

Independent Practice

5. *Forgotten Luggage*   Your aunt and uncle have been visiting at your home. Five minutes after they drive away, you realize that they forgot their luggage. You happen to know that they drive slowly, so you get in your car and drive to catch up with them. Your average speed is 10 miles an hour faster than their average speed, and you catch up with them in 25 minutes. How fast did you drive? Use the following verbal model.

Verbal Model	Your speed	=	Their speed	+	10 miles per hour

Your speed	·	Your time in hours	=	Their speed	·	Their time in hours

6. *Auditing the Books*   You run an accounting business that specializes in auditing (verifying accounting records). One of your auditors is working on the payroll records for a company with 75 employees. Some are part-time and some are full-time. After working for three days, your auditor tells you that the audit is completed for half of the full-time employees, but there are still 50 employee records to audit. After your auditor leaves your office, you wonder how many of the employees are full-time and how many are part-time. Use the following verbal model to find out.

Verbal Model	Number of full-time employees	+	Number of part-time employees	=	75

	$\frac{1}{2}$ Number of full-time employees	+	Number of part-time employees	=	50

7. *Tables and Chairs*   You invited 56 people to your graduation party. You can afford to rent 5 tables, round and/or rectangular (each costing the same). Each round table can seat 8 people and each rectangular table can seat 12 people. How many round and rectangular tables should you rent?

8. *Collecting Sports Cards*   You collect baseball and football cards. Your uncle has an old collection of 360 cards that he gives to you. The collection has more baseball cards than football cards. In fact, it has 30 more baseball cards than *twice* the number of football cards. How many of each type are in your uncle's collection?

9. *Cable Television*   Your family receives basic cable television and one movie channel for $39 a month. Your neighbor receives basic cable and two movie channels for $45.50. What is the monthly charge for basic cable? (Assume that each movie channel has the same monthly charge.)

10. *Hotel Rates*   A hotel has 260 rooms—some singles and some doubles. The singles cost $35 and the doubles cost $60. Because of a math teachers' convention, all of the hotel rooms are occupied. The sales for this night are $14,000. How many of each type of room does the hotel have?

DALE MURPHY
OUTFIELD
BRAVES

Collecting is one of the most common hobbies in America.

11. *Buying Automobile Insurance*   You are quoted a total annual premium of $1111.50 for automobile insurance. This premium gives a coverage of L thousand dollars for liability and collision coverage with a deductible of D dollars. The insurance agent tells you that if you are willing to double your collision deductible, you can increase your liability by $500,000 and add only $32.50 to your annual premium. What were the amounts of the liability and the deductible in the first quote? (Use the premium schedule given at the top of page 139.)

12. *A Historical Puzzle*   You can find the years of Napoleon's birth and death by solving the following system. How old was Napoleon when he crossed the Alps?

$$\begin{cases} 3x - 2y = 1665 \\ -4x + 3y = -1613 \end{cases}$$

13. *Clothing and Food Costs*   The Consumer Price Index (CPI) is used to measure the rate of inflation. From 1980 to 1988, the CPI for clothing increased from 90.9 to 115.4. (This means that clothing that cost $90.90 in 1980 would have cost $115.40 in 1988.) From 1980 to 1988, the CPI for food increased from 86.8 to 118.2. Use a graph to estimate the year that the CPI for clothing and food were the same. What does the graph tell you about the rate of inflation for these two items?

This etching is one interpretation of Napoleon crossing the Alps in 1797.

14. *Appliances*   In 1978, 35% of U.S. households owned a dishwasher but only 8% owned a microwave oven. By 1993, 84% of the households owned a microwave oven and 45% owned a dishwasher. Use a graph to estimate the first year in which more homes owned a microwave oven than a dishwasher.   *(Source: Energy Information Administration)*

Integrated Review

In Exercises 15–17, solve the system by graphing.

15. $\begin{cases} x + 2y = 13 \\ -2x + y = 9 \end{cases}$

16. $\begin{cases} 3x - 2y = 3 \\ x - y = -1 \end{cases}$

17. $\begin{cases} 2x + 3y = -12 \\ -3x + 2y = 5 \end{cases}$

In Exercises 18–20, solve the system by substitution.

18. $\begin{cases} x - 3y = 13 \\ 3x + 2y = 41 \end{cases}$

19. $\begin{cases} 3x + y = -1 \\ 4x + 5y = 6 \end{cases}$

20. $\begin{cases} 7x - 2y = 41 \\ 2x + y = 7 \end{cases}$

In Exercises 21–23, solve the system by using a linear combination.

21. $\begin{cases} 2x - 6y = -30 \\ x + 4y = 2 \end{cases}$

22. $\begin{cases} 3x + 2y = 6 \\ -5x - 4y = -8 \end{cases}$

23. $\begin{cases} 2x + 3y = -8 \\ 5x - 9y = 13 \end{cases}$

Exploration and Extension

Types of Apes   **In Exercises 24 and 25, use the puzzle at the right, which contains the names of all four types of apes hidden within it.**

24. Find equations of the lines that contain the words *gorilla, chimpanzee,* and *orangutan.*

25. The name of the fourth type of ape lies on a line that intersects two of the lines found in Exercise 24. What is it?

```
18 O C H Y E T O S B K A B R O N R Y O
   M B U K A C W P E L K T M R N I S C
16 P A N S S I H Y L O N E O Z E M N N
   K B N G E J L I N B B E S I R A L L
14 S B C I A U R E M P I P E Q T T S W
   A I M I D O O A N P D R T U U E A D
12 D M O R G T N E A Y A O G I R S P E
   K W I Y O I M A S T T N O P R T M L
10 H I S E R B B O O J A E Z A I U I D
   N O N K G R U B N R L E Y E K V B R
 8 I R E G T O T E O O U G H P E F H A
   A F E T K R U S T N A O A M L P O P
 6 J I P Z A O R C H I P R Z T G W C O
   I Q U S N O N I L L O Y M O N K E Y
 4 T E P B A B I G A B N S L A U R I E
   G R A P E A P E E W R I L A J O G N
 2 R S N A K E O H P L O H K B B B O N
   T E N A R O N G E T A N G I F L H O
    2   4   6   8  10  12  14  16  18 x
```

Take this test as you would take a test in class. The answers to the exercises are given in the back of the book.

In Exercises 1–3, match the linear system with its graph. How many solutions does the system have? **(3.1)**

1. $\begin{cases} 3x - 4y = 2 \\ -x + 3y = 1 \end{cases}$

2. $\begin{cases} -x + y = 3 \\ 2x - 2y = -6 \end{cases}$

3. $\begin{cases} x + 2y = 3 \\ -2x - 4y = 3 \end{cases}$

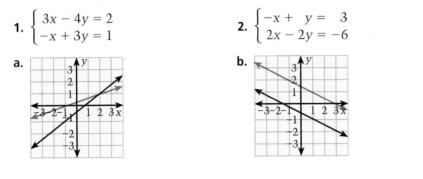

a.   b.   c.

In Exercises 4–6, sketch the graph of the linear system. Then solve the system. **(3.1)**

4. $\begin{cases} 3x - 4y = 2 \\ -x + 3y = 1 \end{cases}$

5. $\begin{cases} -x + y = 3 \\ 2x - 2y = -6 \end{cases}$

6. $\begin{cases} x + 2y = 3 \\ -2x - 4y = 3 \end{cases}$

In Exercises 7–9, use substitution to solve the system. **(3.2)**

7. $\begin{cases} 5x - 3y = 7 \\ x + 6y = -4 \end{cases}$

8. $\begin{cases} 3x + 5y = 1 \\ -2x + y = 10 \end{cases}$

9. $\begin{cases} 6x - 4y = 10 \\ -3x + 2y = 5 \end{cases}$

In Exercises 10–12, use a linear combination to solve the system. **(3.2)**

10. $\begin{cases} 2x + y = 12 \\ 3x - y = 13 \end{cases}$

11. $\begin{cases} 5x - 3y = 18 \\ 4x - 6y = 0 \end{cases}$

12. $\begin{cases} 3x - 4y = 10 \\ 4x - 5y = 13 \end{cases}$

13. How can \$12,600 be split between two investments, one paying 6% annually and one paying 8% annually, so that the amounts of interest from the two investments are equal? **(3.1)**

14. Halley's Comet appears about every 75 years. One appearance was the year Mark Twain was born. The next appearance was the year he died. The sum of these two years is 3745. In what year did Mark Twain die? **(3.3)**

15. The measures of the two acute angles of a right triangle differ by 18 degrees. What are their measures? **(3.3)**

16. A company purchases injection-mold equipment to make plastic knives, forks, and spoons. The cost of the equipment was \$82,800 and the cost of making a package is \$0.36. The company sells each package for \$1.08. How many packages must be sold for the company to break even? **(3.1)**

Plastic Production

3.4 Solving Systems of Linear Inequalities

What you should learn:

Goal 1 How to graph a system of linear inequalities to find the solution to the system

Goal 2 How to use a system of linear inequalities to model a real-life situation

Why you should learn it:

You can model many real-life situations that involve area, such as regions of a map or floor plan, with systems of linear inequalities.

Goal 1 Graphing a System of Inequalities

A **solution of a system of linear inequalities** is an ordered pair that is a solution of each inequality in the system. The **graph of a system** is the graph of all solutions in the system.

LESSON INVESTIGATION

■ Investigating the Graph of a System

Partner Activity Three graphs of linear inequalities are shown below. Write the linear inequality for each graph. Then describe and sketch the graph of the system composed of the three inequalities.

Example 1 *Graphing a System of Linear Inequalities*

Sketch the graph of the system of linear inequalities.

$$\begin{cases} x < 3 & \textit{Inequality 1} \\ y \geq -2 & \textit{Inequality 2} \\ y < x + 1 & \textit{Inequality 3} \end{cases}$$

Solution The graph of $x < 3$ is the half-plane lying to the left of the vertical line $x = 3$. The graph of $y \geq -2$ is the half-plane lying above the horizontal line $y = -2$. The graph of $y < x + 1$ is the half-plane lying below the diagonal line $y = x + 1$. The graph of the system is the **intersection** of these three half-planes. ∎

After graphing a system of linear inequalities, you can find each **vertex** (corner point). For instance, the graph at the left has three vertices: $(-3, -2)$, $(3, 4)$, and $(3, -2)$.

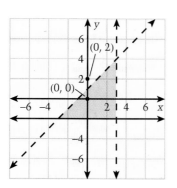

The point $(0, 0)$ is in the graph of the system. The point $(0, 2)$ is not.

Here are some guidelines that may help you sketch the graph of a system of linear inequalities.

> **Graphing a System of Linear Inequalities**
> 1. Sketch the line that corresponds to each inequality. (Use a dashed line for inequalities with $<$ or $>$ and a solid line for inequalities with $\leq$ or $\geq$.)
> 2. Lightly shade the half-plane that is the graph of each linear inequality. (Colored pencils may help you distinguish the different half-planes.)
> 3. The graph of the system is the intersection of each of the half-planes. (If you used colored pencils, it is the region that has been shaded with *every* color.)

Example 2 *Graphing a System of Linear Inequalities*

Sketch the graph of the system of linear inequalities.

$$\begin{cases} x \leq 3 & \textit{Inequality 1} \\ x > 1 & \textit{Inequality 2} \end{cases}$$

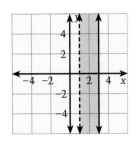

Solution   The graph of the first inequality is the half-plane *to the left of and including* the vertical line $x = 3$. The graph of the second inequality is the half-plane *to the right* of the vertical line $x = 1$.

$$x = 3 \quad \textit{Right boundary}$$
$$x = 1 \quad \textit{Left boundary}$$

The graph of the system is the vertical strip *between* the two vertical lines (where $x \leq 3$ *and* $x > 1$) and includes the line on the right. (Note that this graph has no vertices.) ∎

Example 3 *Graphing a System of Linear Inequalities*

Sketch the graph of the system of linear inequalities. Find the vertices of the graph.

$$\begin{cases} y \leq -\frac{1}{2}x + 2 & \textit{Inequality 1} \\ y \geq 0 & \textit{Inequality 2} \\ x \geq 0 & \textit{Inequality 3} \end{cases}$$

Solution   The graph of the first inequality is the half-plane *below and including* the line $y = -\frac{1}{2}x + 2$. The graph of the second inequality is the half-plane above and including the x-axis, and the graph of the third inequality is the half-plane to the right of and including the y-axis. The vertices of the graph are $(0, 0)$, $(0, 2)$, and $(4, 0)$. ∎

Goal 2 Linear Inequalities as Real-Life Models

Art Museums

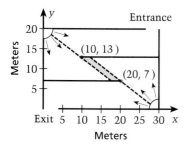

Each unit in the coordinate system represents 1 meter.

Example 4 *Writing a System of Linear Inequalities*

An art museum has installed an electronic surveillance system. In one hall, two cameras were installed at opposite corners, as shown in the diagram. To increase display space, however, the museum also built two temporary walls, each 20 meters long. Write a system of inequalities that describes the region of the room not visible to the cameras.

Solution   The region that is not visible to either camera is shaded blue in the diagram. The line passing through the points (0, 20) and (10, 13) represents the left boundary of the region. The line passing through the points (30, 0) and (20, 7) represents the right boundary. The upper and lower boundaries are given by the lines $y = 7$ and $y = 13$. Using these equations, you can write the following system of inequalities.

$$\begin{cases} y \geq -\dfrac{7}{10}x + 20 & \text{Left boundary} \\ y \leq -\dfrac{7}{10}x + 21 & \text{Right boundary} \\ y \leq \quad 13 & \text{Upper boundary} \\ y \geq \quad 7 & \text{Lower boundary} \end{cases}$$ ■

Communicating about ALGEBRA

▶ SHARING IDEAS about the Lesson

Sketch the graph of the system of equations. Then mark and label the vertices of the region. Explain your steps.

A. $\begin{cases} x < 4 \\ y > 1 \\ y < x + 1 \end{cases}$ **B.** $\begin{cases} 4x + 3y \leq 12 \\ x \geq 0 \\ y \geq 0 \end{cases}$ **C.** $\begin{cases} x + 3y \geq 6 \\ 3x + 2y \leq 18 \\ y \leq 3 \end{cases}$

EXERCISES

Guided Practice

▶ **CRITICAL THINKING about the Lesson**

1. Sketch the graph of the system of linear inequalities.

$$\begin{cases} y \leq x + 2 \\ y \leq -x + 2 \\ y \geq 0 \end{cases}$$

In Exercises 2–5, decide whether the ordered pair is a solution of the system of linear inequalities. Justify your answer algebraically and graphically.

$$\begin{cases} x \geq -1 \\ y < 2 \\ y > 2x + 2 \end{cases}$$

2. $(-1, 0)$ **3.** $(0, 0)$ **4.** $(-1, 1)$ **5.** $\left(-\frac{1}{2}, 1\right)$

6. Explain how to find the vertices of the graph of a system of linear inequalities.

Independent Practice

In Exercises 7–12, match the system of inequalities with its graph.

7. $\begin{cases} y > x \\ x > -3 \\ y \leq 0 \end{cases}$ **8.** $\begin{cases} y \leq 4 \\ y > -2 \end{cases}$ **9.** $\begin{cases} y < x \\ y > -3 \\ x \leq 0 \end{cases}$

10. $\begin{cases} x \leq 3 \\ y < 1 \\ y \geq -x + 1 \end{cases}$ **11.** $\begin{cases} y > -1 \\ x \geq -3 \\ y \leq -x + 1 \end{cases}$ **12.** $\begin{cases} y > -4 \\ y \leq 2 \end{cases}$

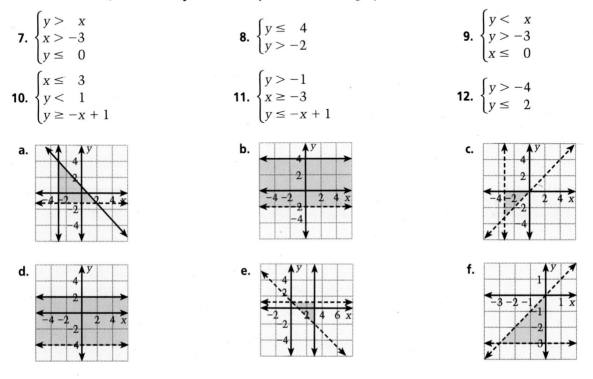

a.   **b.**   **c.**

d.   **e.**   **f.**

In Exercises 13–24, sketch the graph of the system of linear inequalities.

13. $\begin{cases} x < 3 \\ x > -2 \end{cases}$

14. $\begin{cases} y > -1 \\ y \leq 2 \end{cases}$

15. $\begin{cases} y \leq 4 \\ y > 1 \\ x \geq -3 \end{cases}$

16. $\begin{cases} y < 4 \\ x > -4 \\ y > x \end{cases}$

17. $\begin{cases} y > -5 \\ x \leq 2 \\ y \leq x + 2 \end{cases}$

18. $\begin{cases} y \leq -1 \\ x \leq 2 \\ y \leq x + 2 \end{cases}$

19. $\begin{cases} y \geq 2x - 3 \\ y > -5x - 8 \end{cases}$

20. $\begin{cases} y \leq x + 3 \\ y \leq -\frac{1}{2}x - 1 \end{cases}$

21. $\begin{cases} x + y > 3 \\ 4x + y < 4 \end{cases}$

22. $\begin{cases} 2x - y \geq 2 \\ 5x - y \geq 2 \end{cases}$

23. $\begin{cases} x + y \geq -10 \\ x > -1 \\ y < 1 \end{cases}$

24. $\begin{cases} 2x - y \leq -1 \\ x - 2y \geq -8 \\ y \leq 4 \end{cases}$

In Exercises 25–30, sketch the graph of the system of linear inequalities. Mark and label each vertex of the graph.

25. $\begin{cases} x - 3y \geq -1 \\ 4x - 2y \leq 1 \\ x > -3 \end{cases}$

26. $\begin{cases} 3x - 4y > -20 \\ 3x + 4y < 7 \\ y \geq -2 \end{cases}$

27. $\begin{cases} 2x - 3y > -6 \\ 5x - 3y < 3 \\ x + 3y > -3 \end{cases}$

28. $\begin{cases} x - 4y > 0 \\ x + y \leq 1 \\ x + 3y > -1 \end{cases}$

29. $\begin{cases} x + y \leq 4 \\ x + y \geq -1 \\ x - y \geq -2 \\ x - y \leq 2 \end{cases}$

30. $\begin{cases} y < 4 \\ y > -8 \\ 2x - y \geq -4 \\ 2x + y \leq 6 \end{cases}$

In Exercises 31–34, write a system of linear inequalities for the region shown.

31.

32.

33.

34.

35. *Morning Snacks*   You are a counselor at a summer day camp, and have been sent to buy drink boxes and boxes of raisins for the campers' morning snack. Each box of raisins costs $0.10 and each juice box costs $0.40. You have $26, and you want to buy enough so that each camper will have at least one box of raisins and one juice box. There are at most 40 campers. Write a system of linear inequalities that shows the various numbers of boxes of raisins and juice boxes that you could buy. (You don't have to spend all the money.) Sketch a graph of the system.

36. *Research Paper Bibliography*   You have been assigned a research paper. The guidelines specify that you must have at least ten sources in the bibliography, no more than three of which can be encyclopedias. Write a system of inequalities that describes the various number of encyclopedia sources and other sources that you could use. Graph this system.

37. *Swimming Safety*   The diagram shows a cross section of a roped-off swimming area at a beach. Write a system of inequalities that describes the cross section. (Each unit in the coordinate system represents 1 foot.)

38. *A View of the Chorus*   The diagram shows the chorus platform on a stage. Write a system of inequalities that describes the part of the audience that can see the full chorus. (Each unit in the coordinate system represents 1 meter.)

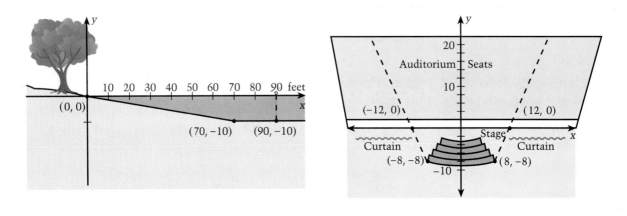

Integrated Review

In Exercises 39–44, sketch the graph of the inequality.

39. $y > -\frac{1}{2}x + 6$

40. $y < x - 56$

41. $y \le 5x - 1$

42. $y > 9 + 16x$

43. $9x - y > 16$

44. $4x + 2y \le 9$

In Exercises 45–50, solve the linear system.

45. $\begin{cases} x - 2y = 16 \\ -2x - y = -2 \end{cases}$

46. $\begin{cases} 5x - 4y = -11 \\ -2x + y = 5 \end{cases}$

47. $\begin{cases} -4x + y = 5 \\ 3x - 2y = -15 \end{cases}$

48. $\begin{cases} 3x - 5y = 5 \\ 4x + 3y = 26 \end{cases}$

49. $\begin{cases} -2x - 3y = 3 \\ 3x + 7y = 13 \end{cases}$

50. $\begin{cases} 9x - 7y = 25 \\ -3x + 2y = -11 \end{cases}$

51. *College Entrance Exam Sample*   If $820 + R + S - 610 = 342$ and $R = 2S$, then $S = \boxed{?}$.
  a. 44   **b.** 48   **c.** 132   **d.** 184   **e.** 192

52. *College Entrance Exam Sample*   If $x + y = 8p$ and $x - y = 6q$, then $x = \boxed{?}$.
  a. $7pq$ **b.** $4p + 3q$ **c.** pq **d.** $4p - 3q$ **e.** $8p + 6q$

Exploration and Extension

Technology   In Exercises 53 and 54, use a graphing calculator to sketch the system of inequalities. Use the trace feature to estimate the vertex.

53. $\begin{cases} y \le 9.2x + 12.1 \\ y > -4.1x - 2.0 \end{cases}$

54. $\begin{cases} y > 5.3x - 3.6 \\ y \le -2.1x + 18.8 \end{cases}$

3.5

Exploring Data: Linear Programming

What you should learn:

Goal 1 How to solve a linear programming problem

Goal 2 How to use linear programming to answer questions about real-life situations

Why you should learn it:

You can model many business problems about maximizing costs or minimizing expenses using linear programming.

Goal 1 A Linear Programming Problem

Many real-life problems involve a process called **optimization,** which means finding the minimum or maximum value of some quantity. In this lesson, you will study one type of optimization process called **linear programming.**

A linear programming model consists of a system of linear inequalities called **constraints** and an **objective quantity** that can be minimized or maximized. To find the minimum or maximum value of the objective quantity, first find all the vertices of the graph of the constraint inequalities. Then, evaluate the objective quantity at each vertex. The least of these values is the minimum for the entire region and the greatest of these values is the maximum for the region (provided the objective quantity has a minimum and maximum value).

Example 1 *Solving a Linear Programming Problem*

Find the minimum value and maximum value of

$$C = 4x + 5y \quad \textit{Objective quantity}$$

subject to the following constraints.

$$\begin{cases} x \geq 0 \\ y \geq 0 \quad \textit{Constraints} \\ x + y \leq 6 \end{cases}$$

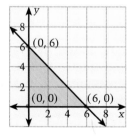

Solution To find the minimum and maximum values of C, evaluate $C = 4x + 5y$ at each of the three vertices of the graph.

At $(0, 0)$: $C = 4(0) + 5(0) = 0$ *Minimum value of C*

At $(6, 0)$: $C = 4(6) + 5(0) = 24$

At $(0, 6)$: $C = 4(0) + 5(6) = 30$ *Maximum value of C*

The minimum value of C is 0, when $x = 0$ and $y = 0$.
The maximum value of C is 30, when $x = 0$ and $y = 6$. ∎

In Example 1, try evaluating C at the other feasible points in the graph of the constraints. No matter which point you choose, the value of C will be greater than or equal to 0 and less than or equal to 30.

Example 2 — Solving a Linear Programming Problem

Find the minimum value and maximum value of

$$C = 3x + 4y \quad \textit{Objective quantity}$$

subject to the following constraints.

$$\begin{cases} x \geq 2 \\ x \leq 5 \\ y \geq 1 \\ y \leq 6 \end{cases} \quad \textit{Constraints}$$

Solution The graph of the constraint inequalities is shown at the left. The four vertices are (2, 1), (2, 6), (5, 1), and (5, 6). To find the minimum and maximum values of C, evaluate $C = 3x + 4y$ at each of the four vertices.

At (2, 1): $C = 3(2) + 4(1) = 10$ *Minimum value of C*

At (2, 6): $C = 3(2) + 4(6) = 30$

At (5, 1): $C = 3(5) + 4(1) = 19$

At (5, 6): $C = 3(5) + 4(6) = 39$ *Maximum value of C*

The minimum value of C is 10. It occurs when $x = 2$ and $y = 1$. The maximum value of C is 39. It occurs when $x = 5$ and $y = 6$. ■

Example 3 — Solving a Linear Programming Problem

Find the minimum value and maximum value of

$$C = 6x + 7y \quad \textit{Objective quantity}$$

subject to the following constraints.

$$\begin{cases} x \geq 0 \\ y \geq 0 \\ 4x + 3y \geq 24 \\ x + 3y \geq 15 \end{cases} \quad \textit{Constraints}$$

Solution The graph of the system of linear inequalities is shown at the left. The three vertices are (0, 8), (3, 4), and (15, 0). To find the minimum and maximum values of C, evaluate $C = 6x + 7y$ at each of the three vertices.

At (0, 8): $C = 6(0) + 7(8) = 56$

At (3, 4): $C = 6(3) + 7(4) = 46$ *Minimum value of C*

At (15, 0): $C = 6(15) + 7(0) = 90$

The minimum value of C is 46. It occurs when $x = 3$ and $y = 4$. There is no maximum value. (The graph of the constraints is unbounded.) ■

Goal 2 Modeling with Linear Programming

Process A earns a profit of $80 per set and Process B earns a profit of $40 per set.

Example 4 *Finding the Maximum Profit*

You own a factory that makes metal patio sets using two processes. The hours of unskilled labor, machine time, and skilled labor *per patio set* are given in the table. You can use up to 4000 hours of unskilled labor, up to 1500 hours of machine time, and up to 2300 hours of skilled labor. How many patio sets should you make by each process to maximize profits?

	Assembly Hours	
	Process A	*Process B*
Unskilled labor	10	1
Machine time	1	3
Skilled labor	5	2

Solution Let a and b represent the number made with each process. To maximize profits, P, use the objective quantity

$P = 80a + 40b$. *Profit: $80 for Process A, $40 for Process B*

The constraints are as follows. The graph is at the left.

$$\begin{cases} 10a + b \le 4000 & \textit{Unskilled labor: Up to 4000 hours} \\ a + 3b \le 1500 & \textit{Machine time: Up to 1500 hours} \\ 5a + 2b \le 2300 & \textit{Skilled labor: Up to 2300 hours} \\ a \ge 0 & \textit{Cannot produce a negative amount.} \\ b \ge 0 & \textit{Cannot produce a negative amount.} \end{cases}$$

The profit at each vertex of the graph is as follows.

At (0, 500): $P = \$20,000$ At (400, 0): $P = \$32,000$
At (300, 400): $P = \$40,000$ At (0, 0): $P = \$0$
At (380, 200): $P = \$38,400$

The maximum profit is obtained by making 300 patio sets with Process A and 400 patio sets with Process B. ∎

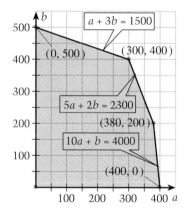

Communicating about ALGEBRA

▶ SHARING IDEAS about the Lesson

Vary the Conditions In Example 4, how many patio sets should you produce by each process if the profit per patio set is as follows?

A. Process A: $80
Process B: $30

B. Process A: $110
Process B: $10

EXERCISES

Guided Practice

▶ **CRITICAL THINKING about the Lesson**

1. How is the *objective quantity* used in a linear programming problem? How is the system of constraint inequalities used?

2. In a linear programming problem, which ordered pairs should be tested to see whether they produce a minimum value?

In Exercises 3 and 4, use the graph at the right.

3. What are the vertices of the region?

4. What is the minimum and maximum value of the objective quantity $C = 5x + 7y$?

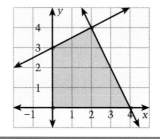

Independent Practice

In Exercises 5–8, you are given the graph of the constraint inequalities. What are the minimum and maximum values of the objective quantity?

5. $C = x - y$ 6. $C = x + 3y$ 7. $C = 2x + 5y$ 8. $C = 9x - 2y$

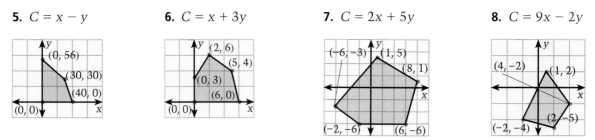

In Exercises 9–20, find the minimum and maximum values of the objective quantity.

9. **Objective quantity:**
   $C = -2x + y$

   Constraints:
   $$\begin{cases} x \geq -5 \\ x \leq 4 \\ y \geq -1 \\ y \leq 3 \end{cases}$$

10. **Objective quantity:**
    $C = 5x + 4y$

    Constraints:
    $$\begin{cases} x \leq -2 \\ x \geq -4 \\ y \geq 1 \\ y \leq 6 \end{cases}$$

11. **Objective quantity:**
    $C = x + 4y$

    Constraints:
    $$\begin{cases} x \geq 0 \\ x \leq 12 \\ y \leq 10 \\ 2x + 3y \geq 24 \end{cases}$$

12. **Objective quantity:**
    $C = 6x + 2y$

    Constraints:
    $$\begin{cases} x \geq 0 \\ x \leq 5 \\ y \geq 0 \\ 4x - y \geq 1 \end{cases}$$

13. **Objective quantity:**
    $C = 2x + y$

    Constraints:
    $$\begin{cases} x \geq 0 \\ y \geq 2 \\ 2x + y \leq 10 \\ x - 3y \geq -3 \end{cases}$$

14. **Objective quantity:**
    $C = 3x + y$

    Constraints:
    $$\begin{cases} x \geq 0 \\ y \geq 0 \\ 2x - 5y \geq 0 \\ 2x - 5y \leq 2 \end{cases}$$

15. Objective quantity:

$C = 3x + 2y$

Constraints:

$$\begin{cases} x \geq 0 \\ y \geq 0 \\ x + 3y \leq 15 \\ 4x + y \leq 16 \end{cases}$$

16. Objective quantity:

$C = 6x + 4y$

Constraints:

$$\begin{cases} x \geq 0 \\ y \geq 0 \\ x + 6y \leq 30 \\ 6x + y \leq 40 \end{cases}$$

17. Objective quantity:

$C = 10x + 3y$

Constraints:

$$\begin{cases} x \geq 0 \\ y \geq 0 \\ -x + y \geq 0 \\ 2x + y \geq 4 \\ 2x + y \leq 13 \end{cases}$$

18. Objective quantity:

$C = 5x + 2y$

Constraints:

$$\begin{cases} x \geq 0 \\ y \geq 0 \\ y \leq 8 \\ x + y \leq 14 \\ 5x + y \leq 50 \end{cases}$$

19. Objective quantity:

$C = 4x + 3y$

Constraints:

$$\begin{cases} x \geq 0 \\ y \geq 0 \\ 2x + 3y \geq 6 \\ 3x - 2y \leq 9 \\ x + 5y \leq 20 \end{cases}$$

20. Objective quantity:

$C = 3x + 6y$

Constraints:

$$\begin{cases} x \geq 0 \\ y \geq 0 \\ x + 4y \geq 4 \\ x + y \geq 2 \end{cases}$$

21. *Finding the Maximum Profit* For each unit of a product made by Process A, you make $50 profit. For each unit of a product made by Process B, you make $55 profit. How many units should you make by each process to obtain a maximum profit?

	Assembly Hours		
	Process A	*Process B*	*Maximum Hours*
Unskilled labor	1	6	2700
Machine time	3	1	1500
Skilled labor	1	1	700

22. *Inventory Control* You are the assistant manager of an appliance store. Next month you will order two types of stereo systems. How many of each model should you order to minimize the cost?

- *Model A:* Your cost is $300. Your profit is $40.
- *Model B:* Your cost is $400. Your profit is $60.
- You expect a profit of at least $4800.
- You expect to sell at least 100 units.

23. *Magician* Your school has contracted with a professional magician to perform at the school. The school has guaranteed an attendance of at least 1000 and total ticket receipts of at least $4800. The tickets are $4 for students and $6 for nonstudents, of which the magician receives $2.50 and $4.50, respectively. What is the minimum amount of money the magician could receive?

In Exercises 24–29, sketch the graph of the inequality.

24. $2x - 4y > 7$ **25.** $-3x + 5y \le 5$ **26.** $x + 9y \le 27$

27. $2x - 7y > 3$ **28.** $12x + 16y \ge 33$ **29.** $5x + 4y \ge -15$

30. *Powers of Ten* Which is the best estimate for the area of Mississippi?
  a. 4.8×10^3 mi^2 **b.** 4.8×10^4 mi^2 **c.** 4.8×10^5 mi^2 **d.** 4.8×10^6 mi^2

31. *Powers of Ten* Which is the best estimate for the speed of a jet aircraft?
  a. 4.8×10^0 mph **b.** 4.8×10^1 mph **c.** 4.8×10^2 mph **d.** 4.8×10^3 mph

Exploration and Extension

In Exercises 32 and 33, use the following information.

When the maximum (or minimum) occurs at two consecutive vertices in a linear programming problem, it occurs at any point on the line segment connecting the two vertices. Illustrate this result with each of the following.

32. Objective quantity: $C = 2x + 2y$

Constraints: $\begin{cases} y \le 4 \\ x \le 5 \\ x + y \le 6 \end{cases}$

33. Objective quantity: $C = 5x - y$

Constraints: $\begin{cases} y \ge -1 \\ x \le 3 \\ -5x + y \le 4 \end{cases}$

Mixed REVIEW

1. Simplify: $-(2x - 5) + 4(x + 3)$. **(1.2)**

2. Simplify: $\frac{1}{4}(2x - 1) - \frac{3}{4}(2x + 1)$. **(1.2)**

3. Rewrite 854 feet as miles.

4. Rewrite 1.34 meters as centimeters.

5. Evaluate: $\frac{1}{2}(3) - \frac{2}{3}(4)$.

6. Evaluate: $\frac{5}{6} + \frac{1}{2}$.

7. Round to 3 decimal places: 4.04641.

8. Solve $5x - (x - 4) = -2(x + 4)$. **(1.3)**

9. Solve $2|x - 1| \ge 6$. **(1.7)**

10. Solve $-3(x - 4) \ge -2x + 5$. **(1.6)**

11. The sum of which two consecutive whole numbers is 37? **(1.3)**

12. Find the area of a triangle whose height is 4 inches and whose base is 5 inches.

13. Sketch the graph of $2y - 4x + 7 = 0$. **(2.1)**

14. What is the opposite of $\frac{1}{3}$? **(1.1)**

15. 14.4 is 15% of what number?

16. Divide 1.4×10^3 by 2.8×10^4.

17. Find the slope of the line $-3x + 5y = 2$. **(2.2)**

18. Sketch the graph of $y \ge \frac{3}{4}x + \frac{1}{4}$. **(2.5)**

19. Solve $\begin{cases} 2x - 4y = 5 \\ -2x + 3y = -4 \end{cases}$. **(3.2)**

20. Solve $\begin{cases} -3x - 5y = -1 \\ 4x + 2y = 6 \end{cases}$. **(3.2)**

3.6 Solving Systems of Linear Equations in Three Variables

What you should learn:

Goal 1 How to solve a system of linear equations in three variables

Goal 2 How to use a linear system in three variables to answer questions about real-life situations

Why you should learn it:

You can model many real-life situations with a system of linear equations in three variables, such as data about three groups of people.

Goal 1 Solving a System in Three Variables

In this lesson, you will learn a technique for solving a **system of three linear equations** in three variables, such as these:

$$\begin{cases} x - 2y + 2z = 9 \\ -x + 3y = -4 \\ 2x - 5y + 3z = 16 \end{cases} \qquad \begin{cases} x - 2y + 2z = 9 \\ y + 2z = 5 \\ z = 3 \end{cases}$$

The linear system on the right is in **triangular form,** which means that its three equations follow a stair-step pattern, *and* each equation has 1 as the coefficient of its first nonzero term.

A **solution** of a linear system in x, y, and z is an **ordered triple** (x, y, z) that is a solution of each equation in the system. Finding the set of all solutions is called **solving** the system. A linear system in triangular form is easier to solve than a system that is not in that form as the next example shows.

Example 1 *Solving a Linear System That Is in Triangular Form*

Solve the system.

$$\begin{cases} x - 2y + 2z = 9 & \textit{Equation 1} \\ y + 2z = 5 & \textit{Equation 2} \\ z = 3 & \textit{Equation 3} \end{cases}$$

Solution From Equation 3, you know the value of z. To solve for y, substitute 3 for z in Equation 2.

$$y + 2(3) = 5 \qquad \textit{Substitute 3 for z.}$$
$$y = -1 \qquad \textit{Solve for y.}$$

Next substitute -1 for y and 3 for z in Equation 1.

$$x - 2(-1) + 2(3) = 9 \qquad \textit{Substitute } -1 \textit{ for y and 3 for z.}$$
$$x = 1 \qquad \textit{Solve for x.}$$

The solution is $x = 1$, $y = -1$, and $z = 3$, which can be written as the *ordered triple* $(1, -1, 3)$. Check this solution by substituting into each equation in the original system.

Equation 1 check: $(1) - 2(-1) + 2(3) = 1 + 2 + 6 = 9$
Equation 2 check: $(-1) + 2(3) = -1 + 6 = 5$ ∎

Two linear systems are **equivalent** if they have the same set of solutions. To solve a system that is not in triangular form, first rewrite it as an *equivalent* system in triangular form.

> ## Equivalent Systems of Equations
>
> Each of the following **row operations** on a system of linear equations produces an *equivalent* system of linear equations.
>
> **1.** Interchange two equations.
> **2.** Multiply one of the equations by a nonzero constant.
> **3.** Add a multiple of one of the equations to another equation to replace the latter equation.

Rewriting a system of linear equations into triangular form usually involves a *chain* of equivalent systems, each of which is obtained by using one of the three basic row operations. This process is called **Gaussian elimination,** after the German mathematician Carl Friedrich Gauss (1777–1855).

Example 2   *Using Elimination to Solve a System*

Solve the system.

$$\begin{cases} x - 2y + 2z = 9 & \text{\textit{Equation 1}} \\ -x + 3y = -4 & \text{\textit{Equation 2}} \\ 2x - 5y + 3z = 16 & \text{\textit{Equation 3}} \end{cases}$$

Solution   Work from the upper left-hand corner. Save the x in the upper left-hand corner and eliminate the other x's from the first column.

$$\begin{cases} x - 2y + 2z = 9 \\ y + 2z = 5 \longleftarrow \\ 2x - 5y + 3z = 16 \end{cases}$$

Add the first equation to the second to obtain a new second equation.

$$\begin{cases} x - 2y + 2z = 9 \\ y + 2z = 5 \\ -y - z = -2 \longleftarrow \end{cases}$$

Add -2 times the first equation to the third to obtain a new third equation.

All but the first x has been eliminated from the first column. Next you need to eliminate y from the third equation.

$$\begin{cases} x - 2y + 2z = 9 \\ y + 2z = 5 \\ z = 3 \longleftarrow \end{cases}$$

Add the second equation to the third to obtain a new third equation.

The system is now in triangular form. In fact, it is the same triangular system we solved in Example 1. Thus the solution is $x = 1$, $y = -1$, and $z = 3$, or the ordered triple $(1, -1, 3)$. ■

A second way to solve a system of three linear equations in three variables is to use *linear combinations.*

Example 3 **Using Linear Combinations**

Solve the system.

$$\begin{cases} 3x + 2y + 4z = 11 & \textit{Equation 1} \\ 2x - y + 3z = 4 & \textit{Equation 2} \\ 5x - 3y + 5z = -1 & \textit{Equation 3} \end{cases}$$

Solution   The goal is to eliminate one of the variables in two of the given equations. This is done by adding multiples of two equations as demonstrated below.

$$\begin{array}{ll} \begin{array}{l} 3x + 2y + 4z = 11 \\ \underline{4x - 2y + 6z = 8} \\ 7x + 10z = 19 \end{array} & \begin{array}{l} \textit{Add 2 times the second} \\ \textit{equation to the first.} \\ \textit{New Equation 1} \end{array} \end{array}$$

$$\begin{array}{ll} \begin{array}{l} 5x - 3y + 5z = -1 \\ \underline{-6x + 3y - 9z = -12} \\ -x - 4z = -13 \end{array} & \begin{array}{l} \textit{Add} -3 \textit{ times the second} \\ \textit{equation to the third.} \\ \textit{New Equation 2} \end{array} \end{array}$$

This produces a system of linear equations in two variables.

$$\begin{cases} 7x + 10z = 19 & \textit{New Equation 1} \\ -x - 4z = -13 & \textit{New Equation 2} \end{cases}$$

Using any of the methods described in the previous sections, you solve this system and determine that $x = -3$ and $z = 4$. Finally, by substituting these values into any of the three original equations, you can solve for y.

$$\begin{array}{ll} 2x - y + 3z = 4 & \textit{Equation 2} \\ 2(-3) - y + 3(4) = 4 & \textit{Substitute } -3 \textit{ for x and 4 for z.} \\ y = 2 & \textit{Simplify and solve for y.} \end{array}$$

Therefore the solution is $x = -3$, $y = 2$, and $z = 4$, or the ordered triple $(-3, 2, 4)$. ■

You know that a linear system in two variables can have exactly one solution, no solution, or an infinite number of solutions. The same is true of a linear system in *three* variables. (A geometric interpretation of this is shown on page 164.)

The systems in Examples 1, 2, and 3 each have exactly one solution. Try solving the following systems. Can you see how to tell how many solutions the system has?

No Solution

$$\begin{cases} x + y - 2z = 5 \\ x + 2y + z = 8 \\ 2x + 3y - z = 1 \end{cases}$$

Many Solutions

$$\begin{cases} x + y - 2z = 5 \\ x + 2y + z = 8 \\ 2x + 3y - z = 13 \end{cases}$$

Real Life
Recreation

Emerson High School holds seven dances each year. Three of these are "open"—any student in Grades 10–12 can attend. The total attendance and the percent of each class that attended the open dances is shown in the table.

Example 4 *Finding Class Enrollments*

Use the information in the table. How many sophomores, juniors, and seniors attend Emerson High School?

	Sophomores	Juniors	Seniors	Total
Homecoming	40%	80%	80%	488
Winter Holiday	80%	40%	40%	412
Spring Fling	50%	70%	80%	491

Solution Let x, y, and z represent the number of sophomores, juniors, and seniors, respectively. The information in the table can be used to create a system of linear equations.

$$\begin{cases} 0.4x + 0.8y + 0.8z = 488 & \text{\textit{Equation 1}} \\ 0.8x + 0.4y + 0.4z = 412 & \text{\textit{Equation 2}} \\ 0.5x + 0.7y + 0.8z = 491 & \text{\textit{Equation 3}} \end{cases}$$

You can use elimination to solve this linear system. Begin by multiplying each term in the first and second equations by 2.5, and each term in the third equation by 10.

$$\begin{cases} x + 2y + 2z = 1220 \\ 2x + y + z = 1030 \\ 5x + 7y + 8z = 4910 \end{cases}$$

Now use elimination to write the system in triangular form.

$$\begin{cases} x + 2y + 2z = 1220 \\ y + z = 470 \\ z = 220 \end{cases}$$

Using substitution, you can find the solution to be $x = 280$ (sophomores), $y = 250$ (juniors), and $z = 220$ (seniors). ∎

Communicating about **ALGEBRA**

▶ **SHARING IDEAS about the Lesson**

Solve each system. Justify each step.

A. $\begin{cases} x - 3z = -2 \\ 3x + y - 2z = 5 \\ 2x + 2y + z = 4 \end{cases}$ **B.** $\begin{cases} x + y + z = 6 \\ 2x - y + z = 3 \\ 3x - z = 0 \end{cases}$

EXERCISES

Guided Practice

▶ **CRITICAL THINKING about the Lesson**

In Exercises 1 and 2, solve the linear system.

1. $\begin{cases} 2x - y + 2z = 5 \\ y + z = 4 \\ z = 1 \end{cases}$

2. $\begin{cases} x + y - z = 4 \\ y + z = 4 \\ z = 2 \end{cases}$

3. Add -2 times Equation 1 to Equation 2. What effect does this operation have?

$\begin{cases} x - 3y + 4z = 4 & \textbf{Equation 1} \\ 2x - 5y + 3z = -1 & \textbf{Equation 2} \\ 3y - 4z = -5 & \textbf{Equation 3} \end{cases}$

4. Add 3 times Equation 2 to Equation 3. What effect does this operation have?

$\begin{cases} x - 2y - 2z = -4 & \textbf{Equation 1} \\ y + z = 3 & \textbf{Equation 2} \\ -3y - 4z = -13 & \textbf{Equation 3} \end{cases}$

In Exercises 5 and 6, write the system in triangular form.

5. $\begin{cases} 2x + 10y + 2z = 6 \\ y + z = 1 \\ y + 2z = 3 \end{cases}$

6. $\begin{cases} x + 5y - 3z = 2 \\ -x - 7y + 4z = -2 \\ 2x + 4y = 10 \end{cases}$

Independent Practice

In Exercises 7–12, solve the linear system.

7. $\begin{cases} x + 4y + z = 12 \\ y - 3z = -7 \\ z = 3 \end{cases}$

8. $\begin{cases} x + 2z = 30 \\ y + z = 12 \\ z = 1 \end{cases}$

9. $\begin{cases} x + y - 3z = -20 \\ -3y + 2z = 5 \\ z = 4 \end{cases}$

10. $\begin{cases} x - y + z = 14 \\ y + z = 15 \\ z = 7 \end{cases}$

11. $\begin{cases} x + 2y - 5z = 10 \\ y + 2z = 2 \\ z = -1 \end{cases}$

12. $\begin{cases} x + y - z = 17 \\ y + z = 1 \\ z = -3 \end{cases}$

In Exercises 13–16, perform the indicated row operation. Write the equivalent system.

13. Interchange Equations 1 and 3.

$\begin{cases} 4x + y - 3z = 19 & \textbf{Equation 1} \\ -2x + 2y - z = 12 & \textbf{Equation 2} \\ x + y - z = 39 & \textbf{Equation 3} \end{cases}$

14. Multiply Equation 1 by $\frac{1}{2}$.

$\begin{cases} 2x + 3y - z = 9 & \textbf{Equation 1} \\ -3x + y - 2z = 14 & \textbf{Equation 2} \\ 4x - 3y + 9z = 36 & \textbf{Equation 3} \end{cases}$

15. Add -2 times Equation 1 to Equation 2.

$\begin{cases} x - 3y + 4z = 24 & \textbf{Equation 1} \\ 2x + y - 2z = 30 & \textbf{Equation 2} \\ -3x - 2y + z = 46 & \textbf{Equation 3} \end{cases}$

16. Add 4 times Equation 1 to Equation 2.

$\begin{cases} x + 3y - 4z = 12 & \textbf{Equation 1} \\ -4x - y + 3z = 26 & \textbf{Equation 2} \\ 2x + y + z = 46 & \textbf{Equation 3} \end{cases}$

In Exercises 17–20, write the system of linear equations in triangular form.

17. $\begin{cases} x - y + 2z = 15 \\ -2x + 2y - 3z = -25 \\ y + 2z = 9 \end{cases}$

18. $\begin{cases} x - y + 2z = -1 \\ 2x - 2y + 2z = -8 \\ y + 3z = 15 \end{cases}$

19. $\begin{cases} x - y - 3z = 1 \\ x - z = -4 \\ 3x = -15 \end{cases}$

20. $\begin{cases} x + y - z = 0 \\ 2x + 2y - z = 1 \\ 3x + 4y = -2 \end{cases}$

In Exercises 21–28, solve the system of equations. Check your solution.

21. $\begin{cases} x + 9y + z = 20 \\ x + 10y - 2z = 18 \\ 3x + 27y + 2z = 58 \end{cases}$

22. $\begin{cases} x + 3y + 2z = 41 \\ 2x + 8y - 2z = 60 \\ -2x - 8y + z = -66 \end{cases}$

23. $\begin{cases} 2x - 4y + 2z = 16 \\ -2x + 5y + 2z = -34 \\ x - 2y + 2z = 4 \end{cases}$

24. $\begin{cases} 2x + 2y - 6z = -6 \\ x + y - 2z = 0 \\ -2x - y + 8z = 19 \end{cases}$

25. $\begin{cases} -x + y - 3z = -4 \\ 3x - 2y + 8z = 14 \\ 2x - 2y + 5z = 7 \end{cases}$

26. $\begin{cases} -x + 2y + 4z = 10 \\ 2x - 3y - 7z = -13 \\ 2x - 4y - 6z = -24 \end{cases}$

27. $\begin{cases} 2x + 6y - 4z = 8 \\ 3x + 10y - 7z = 12 \\ -2x - 6y + 5z = -3 \end{cases}$

28. $\begin{cases} 3x - 6y + 3z = 18 \\ 2x - 3y + 4z = 6 \\ 2x - 3y + 5z = 4 \end{cases}$

29. *School Orchestra* The table shows the percents of each section of the North High School orchestra that were chosen to participate in the city orchestra, the county orchestra, and the state orchestra. Thirty members of the city orchestra, 17 members of the county orchestra, and 10 members of the state orchestra are from North. How many members are in each section of North High's orchestra?

	Section		
	String	Wind	Percussion
City orchestra	40%	30%	50%
County orchestra	20%	25%	25%
State orchestra	10%	15%	25%

30. *It's Going to Be a Long Ride* To prepare for a field trip by bus, you and two friends buy some snacks. From the information at the right, can you determine the price per pound for popcorn, granola, and dried fruit? Explain.

Shopper	Popcorn	Granola	Dried Fruit	Total Price
You	1 lb	$\frac{1}{2}$ lb	$\frac{1}{2}$ lb	$5.97
Greg	$1\frac{1}{3}$ lb	$\frac{1}{2}$ lb	$\frac{3}{2}$ lb	$9.91
Sara	$\frac{1}{3}$ lb		2 lb	$6.83

31. *County Fair* A dairy makes three types of cheddar cheese—mild, medium, and sharp—and sells the cheese in three booths at the county fair. At the beginning of one day, each booth was stocked with the same amount of each type of cheese but the total amount was different for each booth. By the end of the day, the dairy had sold 62 pounds of mild, 216 pounds of medium, and 162 pounds of sharp. The percents sold *of the amounts each booth was given* are shown in the table. How much of each type of cheddar was given to each booth?

	Booth 1	Booth 2	Booth 3
Mild	10%	20%	20%
Medium	30%	70%	80%
Sharp	20%	50%	70%

Integrated Review

In Exercises 32–37, solve the linear system.

32. $\begin{cases} x + 3y = 16 \\ 9x - 5y = -16 \end{cases}$

33. $\begin{cases} 6x - 5y = 11 \\ -9x + 6y = -15 \end{cases}$

34. $\begin{cases} 2x - y = 32 \\ x + y = 4 \end{cases}$

35. $\begin{cases} 5x - y = 28 \\ x + 3y = -4 \end{cases}$

36. $\begin{cases} -3x + 2y = 24 \\ x - 4y = -28 \end{cases}$

37. $\begin{cases} -4x + 3y = 15 \\ -x + y = 6 \end{cases}$

In Exercises 38–41, evaluate the expression.

38. $2x + 3y + 3z$ when $x = 2$, $y = -2$, $z = 5$

39. $-3x + 2y + z$ when $x = -1$, $y = 8$, $z = 1$

40. $x - 4y - z$ when $x = 4$, $y = -5$, $z = 6$

41. $-5x + 2y - z$ when $x = -2$, $y = 3$, $z = -7$

Exploration and Extension

42. Decide whether the linear system has exactly one solution, no solution, or an infinite number of solutions. Explain how you arrived at your decision.

$$\begin{cases} x + 3y + z = 26 \\ y + z = 10 \\ x + y - z = 4 \end{cases}$$

43. Which values should be given to a, b, and c so that the linear system has $(-1, 2, -3)$ as its only solution?

$$\begin{cases} x + 2y - 3z = a \\ -x - y + z = b \\ 2x + 3y - 2z = c \end{cases}$$

Solutions of equations with three variables can be pictured with a **three-dimensional coordinate system.** To construct such a system, begin with the xy-coordinate plane in a horizontal position. Then draw the z-axis as a vertical line through the origin.

Every ordered triple (x, y, z) corresponds to a point in the three-dimensional coordinate system. For instance, the points corresponding to $(-2, 5, 4)$, $(2, -5, 3)$, and $(3, 3, -2)$ are shown at the right.

The **graph** of an equation in three variables consists of all points (x, y, z) that are solutions of the equation. The graph of a linear equation in three variables is a *plane*. Sketching graphs in a three-dimensional coordinate system is difficult because the sketch itself is only two-dimensional.

One technique for sketching a plane is to find the three points at which the plane intersects the axes. For instance, the plane given by

$$3x + 2y + 4z = 12$$

intersects the x-axis at the point $(4, 0, 0)$, the y-axis at the point $(0, 6, 0)$, and the z-axis at the point $(0, 0, 3)$. By plotting these three points, connecting them with line segments, and shading the resulting triangular region, you can picture a portion of the graph, as shown at the right.

Plane: $3x + 2y + 4z = 12$

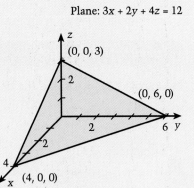

The graph of a system of three linear equations in three variables consists of *three* planes. When these planes intersect in a single point, the system has exactly one solution. When the three planes have no point in common, the system has no solution. When the three planes contain a common line, the system has infinitely many solutions.

Exactly One Solution *No Solution* *Infinitely Many Solutions*

Chapter Summary

3

What did you learn?

Skills

1. Solve a system of linear equations in two variables
   - by graphing. **(3.1)**
   - by substitution. **(3.2)**
   - by linear combination. **(3.2)**
2. Solve a system of linear equations in three variables. **(3.6)**
3. Identify the number of solutions of a linear system. **(3.1, 3.6)**
4. Solve a system of linear inequalities. **(3.4)**
5. Solve a linear programming problem. **(3.5)**

Strategies

6. Use a system of linear equations to model a real-life situation. **(3.1–3.3)**
7. Use a system of linear inequalities to model a real-life situation. **(3.4)**

Exploring Data

8. Use linear programming to solve a real-life problem. **(3.5)**

Why did you learn it?

Systems of linear equations and systems of linear inequalities occur often as models of real-life situations. One common application is the use of a system of linear equations to compare the rate of change of two quantities. For instance, you might want to compare the total revenue for selling x units of a product with the total cost of selling y units of the product. Another common application is finding original data. For instance, you might want to find the total number of sophomores, juniors, and seniors when you know the dance attendance patterns.

Writing equations of lines and inequalities are the basic modeling skills you need for solving problems in this chapter.

How does it fit into the bigger picture of algebra?

In this chapter, you continued your study of linear equations and inequalities. Here, instead of working with a single equation or inequality, you worked with systems of two or more equations or inequalities.

You investigated the three basic techniques of solving a system of linear equations: graphing, substitution, and linear combinations. By now, you should recognize the advantages and disadvantages of each technique.

Most of this chapter dealt with linear systems in two variables. In real life, however, many applications of linear systems contain more than two variables. You explored such systems in the last lesson of the chapter.

In Exercises 1–3, decide whether the ordered pair is a solution of the linear system. (3.1)

1. $(-9, 2)$
$$\begin{cases} -x + 2y = 5 \\ 2x - 4y = 8 \end{cases}$$

2. $(1, 5)$
$$\begin{cases} 2x + 3y = 17 \\ -x + 2y = 11 \end{cases}$$

3. $(-2, -1)$
$$\begin{cases} 7x + 2y = -16 \\ -6x + 9y = 3 \end{cases}$$

In Exercises 4–6, sketch the graph of the linear system. Use the graph to approximate the solution. Then check your solution algebraically. (3.1)

4. $\begin{cases} x + y = 2 \\ -3x + 4y = 36 \end{cases}$

5. $\begin{cases} -x + 2y = 11 \\ 3x - 2y = -13 \end{cases}$

6. $\begin{cases} -4x + y = 2 \\ x - 2y = -11 \end{cases}$

In Exercises 7–12, use substitution or a linear combination to solve the linear system. Then check your solution graphically. (3.2)

7. $\begin{cases} x - 4y = 20 \\ 2x + 5y = 1 \end{cases}$

8. $\begin{cases} 9x - 5y = -30 \\ x + 3y = 18 \end{cases}$

9. $\begin{cases} x + 3y = -2 \\ -3x + y = 6 \end{cases}$

10. $\begin{cases} -x + y = -14 \\ 2x - 3y = 33 \end{cases}$

11. $\begin{cases} 2x + 3y = -7 \\ -4x - 5y = 13 \end{cases}$

12. $\begin{cases} 2x - 2y = -8 \\ 7x + 6y = 11 \end{cases}$

In Exercises 13–15, sketch the graph of the system of inequalities and find the vertices of the graph. (3.5)

13. $\begin{cases} x \geq 0 \\ y \geq 0 \\ x + 2y \leq 24 \\ 4x + y \leq 40 \end{cases}$

14. $\begin{cases} x \geq 0 \\ y \geq 0 \\ -x + 2y \leq 8 \\ 3x + 2y \leq 24 \end{cases}$

15. $\begin{cases} x \geq 0 \\ x \leq 5 \\ y \geq 0 \\ y \leq 3 \end{cases}$

In Exercises 16–18, find the minimum value and maximum value of the objective quantity. (3.5)

16. Objective quantity:
$C = 5x + 2y$

Constraints:
$$\begin{cases} x \geq 3 \\ y \geq 2 \\ 3x + 2y \leq 22 \end{cases}$$

17. Objective quantity:
$C = 4x + 2y$

Constraints:
$$\begin{cases} y \geq 0 \\ -3x + y \leq 4 \\ x + 5y \leq 180 \\ 16x - y \leq 288 \end{cases}$$

18. Objective quantity:
$C = x + 4y$

Constraints:
$$\begin{cases} x \geq 0 \\ y \geq 0 \\ -2x + y \leq 10 \\ 4x - y \leq 20 \\ 5x + 2y \leq 38 \end{cases}$$

In Exercises 19–21, solve the linear system. (3.6)

19. $\begin{cases} x - 2y + z = 33 \\ y + 2z = 5 \\ z = 4 \end{cases}$

20. $\begin{cases} x + y + 3z = 20 \\ 2x + 4y + 5z = 30 \\ x + y + 4z = 26 \end{cases}$

21. $\begin{cases} 3x - 6y + z = 0 \\ 3x - 4y - 4z = 15 \\ -6x + 8y + 9z = -33 \end{cases}$

22. *Wearing Makeup*   In a 1991 survey of American women, x percent said they wore makeup regularly and y percent said they wore makeup occasionally. The number who wore makeup regularly was 23% more than the number who wore makeup occasionally. What percent said they wore makeup regularly? What percent said they wore makeup occasionally?
(Source: Roper Organization)

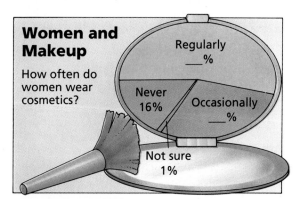

Women and Makeup

How often do women wear cosmetics?

Regularly ___%

Never 16%

Occasionally ___%

Not sure 1%

23. *Single-Parent Dads*   The sum of the numbers of single-parent fathers in 1970, 1980, and 1990 is 2,433,000. The sum for 1980 and 1990 is 2,040,000. There were 1,350,000 single-parent fathers in 1990. Express this information as a system of three linear equations in three variables. (Let x, y, and z represent the number of single-parent fathers in the United States in 1970, 1980, and 1990, respectively.) Solve the system.
(Source: U.S. Bureau of Census)

24. *Waiting to Remarry*   From 1970 through 1988, the average number of years, R, that an American waited to remarry (after divorce or death of a spouse) is given by

$$\begin{cases} R = 0.067t + 2.9 & \textit{Women} \\ R = 0.072t + 2.3 & \textit{Men} \end{cases}$$

where t is the year, with $t = 0$ corresponding to 1970. Sketch the graph of this system. Do the two lines intersect between $t = 0$ and $t = 18$? **(Source: National Center for Health Statistics)**

25. *Why Ice Floats*   Most liquids contract as they cool. This is true of pure water, however, only as it cools to 39°F. Between 39°F and 32°F, pure water expands as it cools. This is the reason ice floats—its density is less than the density of liquid water. As salt is added to water, it loses this property gradually. In fact, water that is more than 2.5% salt continues to contract as it cools until it finally freezes. (Icebergs float because they are broken off from glaciers, which are formed from fresh water.) Write a system of linear inequalities that models the temperature and saltiness of water that expands as it cools.

Behavior of Salt Water

Temperature (°F)

Water contracts as it cools

Water expands as it cools

$(0, 39)$

$(2.5, 29)$

$(0, 32)$ Ice

Percent Salt

Pearl Necklace In Exercises 26 and 27, use the following information.

If the pearls shown at the right are strung to form a graduated pearl necklace, it would just fit within the graph of the system

$$
\begin{cases}
y \le \frac{1}{60}x + \frac{1}{10} \\
y \ge -\frac{1}{60}x - \frac{1}{10} \\
y \le -\frac{1}{60}x + \frac{3}{10} \\
y \ge \frac{1}{60}x - \frac{3}{10} \\
x \ge -3 \\
x \le 15
\end{cases}
$$

where x and y are measured in inches.

26. How long is the necklace?

27. Approximate the diameter of the largest pearl in the necklace.

Growing a Pearl In Exercises 28–30, use the following information.

Pearls are grown by oysters and other mollusks that produce a lustrous substance called *nacre*. A pearl is formed when a foreign object is embedded in the mollusk. The mollusk reacts by slowly covering the object with layer upon layer of nacre. In a cultured oyster pearl, a spherical nucleus is embedded in an oyster. Most cultured oyster pearls are grown in Japan. The nuclei, however, come mainly from the nacre of freshwater mussels in Camden, Tennessee.

28. The radius, R (in millimeters), of a cultured pearl depends on the radius of the nucleus and the time, t (in months), the nucleus is left in the oyster. The relationship between R and t is indicated by:

$$
\begin{cases}
R = \frac{1}{30}t + 2 & \textit{Nucleus radius: 2 mm} \\
R = \frac{1}{30}t + 3 & \textit{Nucleus radius: 3 mm} \\
R = \frac{1}{30}t + 4 & \textit{Nucleus radius: 4 mm} \\
R = \frac{1}{30}t + 5 & \textit{Nucleus radius: 5 mm}
\end{cases}
$$

Sketch the graph of this system. Do the lines intersect?

29. From the linear system given in Exercise 28, how much does a cultured pearl increase in radius each month?

30. Some natural pearls have grown in oysters for as long as 20 years. Estimate the diameter of such a pearl if its nucleus radius is 2 mm.

Growing freshwater mussels in Tennessee

In Exercises 1–3, solve the linear system. Check your solution graphically.

1. $\begin{cases} y = -\dfrac{3}{2}x + \dfrac{7}{2} \\ y = \dfrac{5}{7}x - \dfrac{8}{7} \end{cases}$

2. $\begin{cases} x + 2y = 10 \\ 2x - 3y = -8 \end{cases}$

3. $\begin{cases} 4x - 5y = 3 \\ 3x - 2y = 4 \end{cases}$

In Exercises 4–6, sketch the graph of the system of inequalities. Label the vertices.

4. $\begin{cases} x \geq 0 \\ y \geq 0 \\ x + y \leq 5 \end{cases}$

5. $\begin{cases} x \leq 5 \\ x \geq 1 \\ y \leq 7 \\ y \geq -2 \end{cases}$

6. $\begin{cases} x \geq 0 \\ y \geq 0 \\ 2x + y \leq 12 \\ -x + 4y \leq 20 \end{cases}$

In Exercises 7–9, find the minimum and maximum values of the objective quantity.

7. Objective quantity:
$C = 2x + 3y$

Constraints:
$\begin{cases} x \geq 1 \\ y \geq 1 \\ x + y \leq 5 \end{cases}$

8. Objective quantity:
$C = 8x + 7y$

Constraints:
$\begin{cases} x \geq 0 \\ y \geq 0 \\ x + y \leq 7 \\ 4x + 3y \leq 24 \end{cases}$

9. Objective quantity:
$C = 3x + 4y$

Constraints:
$\begin{cases} x + y \geq 8 \\ x + y \leq 9 \\ x + 2y \leq 16 \\ 2x + y \leq 16 \end{cases}$

In Exercises 10–12, solve the linear system.

10. $\begin{cases} x + 3y - 4z = 9 \\ y + 2z = 8 \\ z = 1 \end{cases}$

11. $\begin{cases} x + 2y - 6z = 23 \\ x + 3y + z = 4 \\ 2x + 5y - 4z = 24 \end{cases}$

12. $\begin{cases} -x + 2y - 7z = -17 \\ 4x + 6y + 18z = 20 \\ 3x - y - 3z = -7 \end{cases}$

13. Your hourly wage at a grocery store is greater after 6:00 P.M. than during the day. One week you work 18 daytime hours and 22 evening hours, and earn $264. The next week you work 30 daytime hours and 10 evening hours, and earn $240. What is the daytime hourly rate? What is the evening hourly rate?

14. In 1990, the aquariums with the greatest attendance were the Sea Worlds in Florida, California, and Texas. The total attendance at these three was 10,200,000. Sea World of Florida had 300,000 more than Sea World of California. Sea World of California had 1,200,000 more than Sea World of Texas. What was the 1990 attendance of each?

(Source: American Association of Zoological Parks and Aquariums)

15. Write a system of linear inequalities to model the region shown at the right.

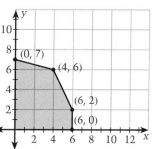

In Exercises 1–4, solve the equation.

1. $3(x + 4) = (2 - x)7$

2. $\frac{1}{4}|x + 2| = 3$

3. $|3x - 4| = 15$

4. $3x - 2(x + 6) = 13 - x$

5. *Simple Interest* Solve the formula $A = P + Prt$ for r. Then use the result to find the value of r when $A = \$575$, $P = \$500$, and $t = 3$ years.

In Exercises 6–8, solve the inequality.

6. $4x - (2 + 3x) \geq 14$

7. $\frac{1}{2}|2x - 3| \leq 13$

8. $\left|\frac{1}{4}x + 3\right| > 5$

In Exercises 9–12, write an equation of the indicated line. Then sketch its graph.

9. Slope: $\frac{2}{3}$, Point: $(0, 3)$

10. Slope: -4, y-intercept: -1

11. Two points: $(-3, 2)$, $(8, -1)$

12. Two points: $(-0.5, 6)$, $(0.25, 5)$

In Exercises 13–15, sketch the graph of the linear inequality.

13. $3x - 5y < 15$

14. $\frac{1}{4}x + 2y \geq 6$

15. $\frac{1}{3}y - x > 7$

In Exercises 16–18, sketch the graph of the absolute value equation.

16. $y = 3|x - 2| + 4$

17. $y = \frac{1}{7}|x + 6| - 3$

18. $y = -\left|\frac{3}{2}x + 2\right| + 5$

In Exercises 19–24, solve the system of equations.

19. $\begin{cases} 3x + 5y = 0 \\ y = -\frac{3}{2} \end{cases}$

20. $\begin{cases} \frac{1}{4}x + \frac{2}{3}y = 7 \\ y = 4 \end{cases}$

21. $\begin{cases} -4x + 8y = 4 \\ 3x + \frac{1}{2}y = 10 \end{cases}$

22. $\begin{cases} 3x + 2y - 2z = 13 \\ 4y + 8z = 20 \\ 3z = 6 \end{cases}$

23. $\begin{cases} 8x - 2y + z = 32 \\ 6x + \frac{1}{2}y + \frac{1}{4}z = 26 \\ x + y - 5z = -14 \end{cases}$

24. $\begin{cases} -4x - 3y + 5z = 1 \\ 4x + 8y - 6z = 10 \\ 5x - y + 7z = -24 \end{cases}$

In Exercises 25 and 26, sketch the graph of the system of linear inequalities. Label each vertex of the graph.

25. $\begin{cases} 2x + y \leq 4 \\ 5x + y \leq 8 \\ x \geq 0 \\ y \geq 0 \end{cases}$

26. $\begin{cases} 4x - y > -6 \\ x + 2y < 6 \\ 4x - 3y < 9 \end{cases}$

27. *Breakfast Calories* For breakfast, you had 1 cup of oatmeal, 1 cup of lowfat milk, and 1 cup of orange juice, for a total of 375 calories. Your brother had 2 cups of oatmeal, 2 cups of lowfat milk, and 1 cup of orange juice, for a total of 640 calories. Your sister had 1 cup of oatmeal, $\frac{3}{4}$ cup of lowfat milk, and $\frac{1}{2}$ cup of orange juice, for a total of 290 calories. How many calories are in 1 cup of oatmeal, 1 cup of lowfat milk, and 1 cup of orange juice?

Hewlett-Packard   **In Exercises 28–31, use the following information.**

Sales, S (in millions of dollars), for the Hewlett-Packard Company from
1980 through 1990 are given in the table.
(Source: Hewlett-Packard Company)

Year	1980	1981	1982	1983	1984	1985
Sales	$3099	$3578	$4254	$4710	$6044	$6505

Year	1986	1987	1988	1989	1990
Sales	$7102	$8090	$9831	$11,899	$13,233

28. Sketch a scatter plot. Let $t = 0$ represent 1980.

29. Do S and t have a positive correlation, a negative correlation, or no
correlation?

30. Sketch the best-fitting line. Write an equation for the line.

31. Estimate the 1994 sales for the Hewlett-Packard Company.

32. *National Parks*   The ten most popular national parks are listed in
the table with their 1990 attendance. Construct a circle graph that
shows each park's percentage of the total attendance.

National Park	Attendance	National Park	Attendance
Great Smokies, NC & TN	8,333,600	Yellowstone, WY	2,644,400
Acadia, ME	5,441,000	Rocky Mountain, CO	2,502,900
Grand Canyon, AZ	3,966,200	Zion, UT	1,998,900
Yosemite, CA	3,308,200	Shenandoah, VA	1,873,800
Olympic, WA	2,737,600	Glacier, MT	1,821,500

33. *Maximum Profit*   Your company produces cabinets using two different processes. The number of assembly hours required for each
process are listed in the table. You can use up to 3000 hours of
machine time, up to 3600 hours of skilled labor, and up to 3600
hours of unskilled labor. The profit from Process A is $50 per cabi-
net and the profit from Process B is $70 per cabinet. How many
cabinets should you make with each process to obtain a maximum
profit?

	Assembly hours	
	Process A	Process B
Machine time	1	2
Skilled labor	2	2
Unskilled labor	3	1

Matrices and Determinants

LESSONS

4.1 Exploring Data:
Matrix Operations
▪ 174

4.2 Matrix
Multiplication ▪ 180

4.3 Determinants ▪ 187

4.4 Identity and Inverse
Matrices ▪ 196

4.5 Solving Systems
Using Inverse
Matrices ▪ 204

4.6 Solving Systems
Using Augmented
Matrices ▪ 210

4.7 Solving Systems
Using Cramer's
Rule ▪ 216

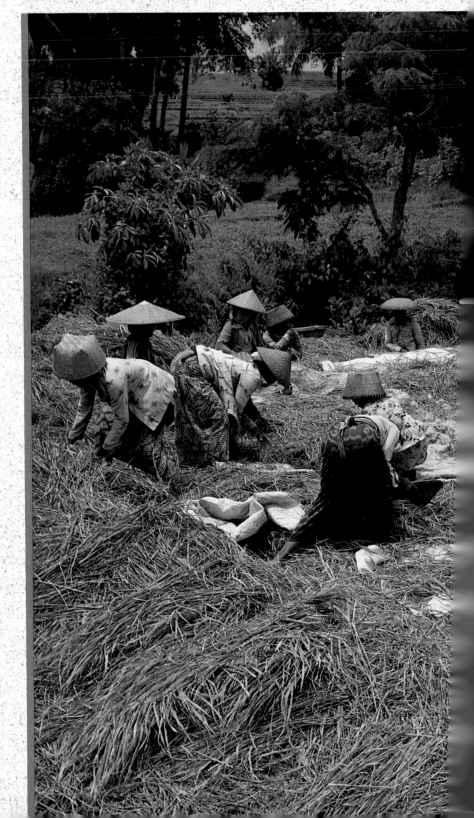

New varieties of high-yield rice have helped reduce food shortages in Asia and the South Pacific. These farmers are harvesting rice in Bali, Indonesia.

Real Life
Food Production

Percent of Crop Grown in Each Country

	Wheat	Rice	Corn
China	16.6%	37.2%	13.6%
India	8.7%	18.9%	1.7%
C.I.S.	17.2%	0.5%	2.6%
U.S.	10.6%	1.3%	43.6%

During the mid 1960's, the population in developing nations was growing fast. Keeping the burgeoning population fed seemed an impossible task in these countries, until the introduction of high-yield varieties of wheat and rice. This produced what is known as the "green revolution." By the 1980's, some of these countries, such as China and India, were accumulating surpluses.

By 1990, China and India were two of the largest grain-producing countries in the world. The matrix at the left lists the percent of the world's wheat, rice, and corn produced in 1990 by the top four grain producers—China, the Commonwealth of Independent States (formerly the Soviet Union), India, and the United States.

Exploring Data:
Matrix Operations

What you should learn:

Goal 1 How to organize data into matrices and to work with them, using addition, subtraction, and scalar multiplication

Goal 2 How to use matrices in real-life settings

Why you should learn it:

You can use matrices to organize many types of real-life data, such as income tax tables, nutrition charts, and accounting spreadsheets.

Goal 1 Organizing Data in a Matrix

A **matrix** is a rectangular arrangement of numbers in rows and columns. For instance, the matrix below has two rows and three columns. The **order** of this matrix is 2×3 (read "2 by 3"). A **row matrix** is a matrix that has only one row. A **column matrix** has only one column, and a **square matrix** has the same number of rows and columns.

$$\begin{bmatrix} 6 & 2 & -1 \\ -2 & 0 & 5 \end{bmatrix}$$

The numbers in a matrix are its **entries.** In the above matrix, the entry in the second row and third column is 5. A **zero matrix** is a matrix whose entries are all zero.

Two matrices (*matrices* is the plural of *matrix*) are equal if the entries in corresponding positions are equal.

$$\begin{bmatrix} 5 & 0 \\ -\frac{4}{4} & \frac{3}{4} \end{bmatrix} = \begin{bmatrix} 5 & 0 \\ -1 & 0.75 \end{bmatrix} \qquad \begin{bmatrix} -2 & 6 \\ 0 & -3 \end{bmatrix} \neq \begin{bmatrix} -2 & 6 \\ -3 & 0 \end{bmatrix}$$

Think of a matrix as a type of table used to organize data.

Real Life
Consumer Finance

Example 1   *Reading the Entries of a Matrix*

The monthly payment for a car loan depends on the annual interest rate, the amount of the loan, and the length of the loan. The matrix shows different monthly payments for a 12% annual interest rate. How much more interest would you pay for a 12% auto loan of $15,000 if you took the loan for 5 years instead of 3 years?

Monthly Payment	36 Months	48 Months	60 Months
$10,000	$332.14	$253.34	$222.48
$15,000	$498.22	$395.01	$333.67
$20,000	$664.29	$526.68	$444.89

Solution   For 3 years, you would make 36 payments of $498.22 for a total of $17,935.92. The total interest would be $2935.92. For 5 years, you would make 60 payments of $333.67 for a total of $20,020.20. The total interest would be $5020.20. Thus, you would pay $2084.28 more in interest. ■

To add or subtract matrices, you simply add or subtract corresponding entries, as shown in Example 2.

Example 2   *Adding and Subtracting Matrices*

a. $\begin{bmatrix} 5 & -3 \\ -3 & 4 \\ 0 & 7 \end{bmatrix} + \begin{bmatrix} -2 & 1 \\ 3 & 0 \\ 4 & -3 \end{bmatrix} = \begin{bmatrix} 5 + (-2) & -3 + 1 \\ -3 + 3 & 4 + 0 \\ 0 + 4 & 7 + (-3) \end{bmatrix}$

$$= \begin{bmatrix} 3 & -2 \\ 0 & 4 \\ 4 & 4 \end{bmatrix}$$

b. $\begin{bmatrix} 8 & 3 \\ -4 & 0 \end{bmatrix} - \begin{bmatrix} 2 & -7 \\ -6 & 1 \end{bmatrix} = \begin{bmatrix} 8 - 2 & 3 - (-7) \\ -4 - (-6) & 0 - 1 \end{bmatrix}$

$$= \begin{bmatrix} 6 & 10 \\ 2 & -1 \end{bmatrix}$$ ∎

You can add or subtract matrices only if they have the same orders. You cannot, for instance, add a matrix that has three rows to a matrix that has only two rows.

Matrix addition is associative and commutative. This means that three or more matrices can be added in any order. If A, B, and C are matrices of the same order, these properties can be stated as follows:

$(A + B) + C = A + (B + C)$ *Associative Property*

$A + B = B + A$ *Commutative Property*

In matrix algebra, a real number is often called a **scalar.** To *multiply a matrix by a scalar,* you multiply each entry in the matrix by the scalar. Multiplication of a matrix by a scalar obeys the Distributive Property.

$c(A + B) = cA + cB$ *Distributive Property (Addition)*

$c(A - B) = cA - cB$ *Distributive Property (Subtraction)*

Example 3   *Multiplying a Matrix by a Scalar*

a. $4 \begin{bmatrix} -2 & 0 \\ 4 & -1 \end{bmatrix} = \begin{bmatrix} 4(-2) & 4(0) \\ 4(4) & 4(-1) \end{bmatrix}$

$$= \begin{bmatrix} -8 & 0 \\ 16 & -4 \end{bmatrix}$$

b. $-2\left(\begin{bmatrix} 1 & -2 \\ 0 & 3 \end{bmatrix} + \begin{bmatrix} -4 & 5 \\ 6 & -8 \end{bmatrix} \right) = -2 \begin{bmatrix} -3 & 3 \\ 6 & -5 \end{bmatrix}$

$$= \begin{bmatrix} 6 & -6 \\ -12 & 10 \end{bmatrix}$$ ∎

Real Life
College Costs

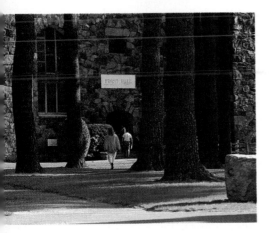

From 1991 to 1994, college costs at private 4-year universities increased by about 21% per year.

Example 4 — *Finding the Total Cost of College*

The matrices below show the average yearly cost of tuition and room and board at colleges in the United States between 1991 and 1994. Use matrix addition to find a matrix showing the totals of these fees. *(Source: U.S. National Center for Educational Statistics)*

Tuition	1991	1992	1993	1994
Public 4-Year University	2159	2410	2604	2822
Private 4-Year University	11379	12192	13055	13812
Public 4-Year College	1707	1933	2192	2368
Private 4-Year College	8389	9053	9533	10151
Public 2-Year College	824	937	1025	1114

Room and Board	1991	1992	1993	1994
Public 4-Year University	3425	3641	3838	3887
Private 4-Year University	5124	5587	5843	6215
Public 4-Year College	3296	3527	3548	3791
Private 4-Year College	3832	4136	4348	4551
Public 2-Year College	2644	2686	2774	2892

Solution The Total Charges matrix is as follows.

Total Charges	1991	1992	1993	1994
Public 4-Year University	5584	6051	6442	6709
Private 4-Year University	16503	17779	18898	20027
Public 4-Year College	5003	5460	5740	6159
Private 4-Year College	12221	13189	13881	14702
Public 2-Year College	3468	3623	3799	4006

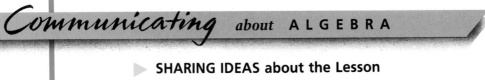

Communicating about **A L G E B R A**

▶ **SHARING IDEAS about the Lesson**

A. Use the following matrices and scalar to show that $c(A + B) = cA + cB$.

$$A = \begin{bmatrix} 4 & -5 \\ -2 & 8 \end{bmatrix}, \quad B = \begin{bmatrix} -3 & 7 \\ 8 & 2 \end{bmatrix}, c = 2$$

B. Give a *convincing* argument that the general property $c(A + B) = cA + cB$ is true for *any* scalar c and *any* 2×2 matrices A and B.

EXERCISES

▶ **CRITICAL THINKING about the Lesson**

1. Give an example of a row matrix, a column matrix, a 4×3 matrix.

2. To add two matrices, what must be true of their orders?

3. What is the order of $\begin{bmatrix} 10 & 4 & 2 & 4 \\ -2 & 0 & 1 & 7 \\ 3 & 1 & -9 & 6 \end{bmatrix}$?

4. Are the two matrices equal? Explain. $\begin{bmatrix} -6 & \frac{1}{2} \\ 0 & -2 \\ 1 & 5 \end{bmatrix} \stackrel{?}{=} \begin{bmatrix} -6 & 0.5 \\ 0 & 2 \\ 1 & 5 \end{bmatrix}$

5. Add: $[2 \quad 1 \quad 3 \quad 5] + [0 \quad -4 \quad 3 \quad -2]$.

6. Multiply the matrix by the scalar: $-2 \begin{bmatrix} 4 & 6 \\ 1 & 0 \end{bmatrix}$.

Independent Practice

In Exercises 7–10, state the order of the matrix.

7. $\begin{bmatrix} 5 & -3 & 3 \\ 1 & 5 & 1 \\ 0 & 6 & -9 \end{bmatrix}$
8. $\begin{bmatrix} 1 & -2 \\ 6 & 9 \\ 9 & 2 \\ 4 & 1 \end{bmatrix}$
9. $\begin{bmatrix} 5 & 9 & -3 & 6 \\ 3 & 1 & 4 & 10 \end{bmatrix}$
10. $\begin{bmatrix} 1 & 4 & 10 & 6 \\ 2 & 3 & -1 & 9 \\ -8 & 9 & -3 & -8 \end{bmatrix}$

In Exercises 11–18, perform the indicated operation, if possible. If not possible, state the reason.

11. $\begin{bmatrix} 1 & 2 \\ -3 & 1 \end{bmatrix} + \begin{bmatrix} 1 & 5 \\ 2 & 0 \end{bmatrix}$

12. $\begin{bmatrix} 4 & 2 \\ -9 & 5 \end{bmatrix} - \begin{bmatrix} 2 & 8 \\ 4 & 8 \end{bmatrix}$

13. $\begin{bmatrix} 7 & -3 & 2 \\ 0 & 8 & 1 \\ 8 & 6 & -6 \end{bmatrix} + \begin{bmatrix} 1 & 0 & -5 \\ 0 & 8 & 7 \\ -7 & 9 & 6 \end{bmatrix}$

14. $\begin{bmatrix} 1 & -6 \\ 9 & 7 \\ 5 & 6 \end{bmatrix} + \begin{bmatrix} 0 & -4 & 8 \\ 5 & 2 & 5 \\ 3 & 9 & -8 \end{bmatrix}$

15. $\begin{bmatrix} 0 & -8 \\ 3 & 0 \\ -4 & 2 \end{bmatrix} - \begin{bmatrix} 5 & 4 \\ 2 & 5 \\ -7 & -5 \end{bmatrix}$

16. $\begin{bmatrix} 2 & -1 & 7 \\ 5 & 8 & 2 \end{bmatrix} - \begin{bmatrix} 2 & 9 & 3 \\ -5 & 2 & -2 \end{bmatrix}$

17. $\begin{bmatrix} -6 & 8 & 5 \\ 4 & -4 & 7 \end{bmatrix} - \begin{bmatrix} 4 & 2 \\ 8 & -4 \\ 3 & 3 \end{bmatrix}$

18. $\begin{bmatrix} 9 & 1 & 6 \\ -5 & 0 & 9 \\ 2 & -2 & 3 \end{bmatrix} + \begin{bmatrix} 9 & 0 & 4 \\ -4 & 6 & 8 \\ 3 & -5 & -6 \end{bmatrix}$

In Exercises 19–22, multiply the matrix by the scalar.

19. $-3 \begin{bmatrix} 1 & -3 & 6 \\ 9 & -1 & 4 \end{bmatrix}$
20. $4 \begin{bmatrix} 0 & -7 \\ 5 & 3 \end{bmatrix}$
21. $-8 \begin{bmatrix} 0 & \frac{1}{2} \\ -2 & -1 \\ 4 & 3 \end{bmatrix}$
22. $2 \begin{bmatrix} 1 & -1 & 0 \\ 6 & 3 & 1 \\ 3 & 2 & 9 \end{bmatrix}$

In Exercises 23–27, simplify the expression.

23. $\left(\begin{bmatrix} 4 & 0 \\ -1 & 5 \end{bmatrix} - \begin{bmatrix} 6 & -2 \\ 3 & 4 \end{bmatrix}\right) + \begin{bmatrix} 3 & 5 \\ -1 & 8 \end{bmatrix}$

24. $\begin{bmatrix} 3 & 2 \\ -2 & 0 \\ 1 & 6 \end{bmatrix} - \left(\begin{bmatrix} 9 & -1 \\ 2 & -3 \\ 3 & 8 \end{bmatrix} + \begin{bmatrix} -7 & 4 \\ 5 & -1 \\ 3 & -2 \end{bmatrix}\right)$

25. $-4\left(\begin{bmatrix} 5 & 1 & -3 \\ 4 & 0 & -1 \\ -3 & 9 & 6 \end{bmatrix} - \begin{bmatrix} 1 & 8 & -2 \\ 4 & -6 & 0 \\ 3 & -1 & 5 \end{bmatrix}\right)$

26. $6\begin{bmatrix} 6 & 4 \\ 9 & -3 \\ 5 & 11 \end{bmatrix} - 2\left(\begin{bmatrix} 1 & 0 \\ 5 & 3 \\ 9 & 4 \end{bmatrix} + \begin{bmatrix} 5 & 2 \\ 7 & 3 \\ 9 & -4 \end{bmatrix}\right)$

27. $\left(\begin{bmatrix} -2 & 0 & 5 \\ 5 & 1 & 9 \\ 7 & 2 & -1 \end{bmatrix} + 2\begin{bmatrix} 6 & -4 & 0 \\ 9 & 5 & 4 \\ -1 & 0 & 7 \end{bmatrix}\right) - \begin{bmatrix} 4 & 6 & 3 \\ -1 & 0 & 2 \\ 5 & 9 & 1 \end{bmatrix}$

In Exercises 28 and 29, solve for x.

28. $\begin{bmatrix} 2x & 8 \\ 4 & -6 \end{bmatrix} + \begin{bmatrix} 3 & -2 \\ -1 & 5 \end{bmatrix} = \begin{bmatrix} 5 & 6 \\ 3 & -1 \end{bmatrix}$

29. $\begin{bmatrix} 3 & 6 \\ 8 & -5 \end{bmatrix} - \begin{bmatrix} 8 & 1 \\ 10 & -4x \end{bmatrix} = \begin{bmatrix} -5 & 5 \\ -2 & 19 \end{bmatrix}$

In Exercises 30 and 31, solve for x, y, and z.

30. $\begin{bmatrix} x \\ 0 \\ 0 \end{bmatrix} + \begin{bmatrix} 2y \\ y \\ 0 \end{bmatrix} + \begin{bmatrix} z \\ -z \\ 2z \end{bmatrix} = \begin{bmatrix} 5 \\ 3 \\ 6 \end{bmatrix}$

31. $\begin{bmatrix} 2x \\ 0 \\ 0 \end{bmatrix} + \begin{bmatrix} -4y \\ 3y \\ 0 \end{bmatrix} + \begin{bmatrix} 2z \\ 6z \\ z \end{bmatrix} = \begin{bmatrix} 2 \\ 0 \\ -1 \end{bmatrix}$

32. *Designated Hitter Rule*   The designated hitter rule in major league baseball applies only to the American League. The matrix below gives the percentages of the responses from the American League (AL) and National League (NL) fans when asked how they would treat the rule if they were league commissioners. From each league, 190 fans were surveyed. How many from each league said they would ban the designated hitter rule? How many from each league said they would expand it to the National League?

Designated Hitter Rule?	NL Fans	AL Fans
Ban the rule.	72%	24%
Expand to NL.	20%	53%
Leave as is.	8%	23%

Dodger Stadium Video   **In Exercises 33 and 34, use the following information.**

The video display at Dodger Stadium is made up of 3- by 3-inch modules. Each module contains 4 pixels. (A pixel is formed by 4 small cathode ray tubes.)

33. The giant screen is rectangular: 25 feet by 30 feet. How many pixels are on the screen?

34. What is the order of the "pixel-matrix" shown?

35. *Sizes of Football Fields* The matrix shows the standard widths and lengths (in feet) of four types of football fields. What is the difference in the area of a college football field and an arena football field?

Football Field Sizes	Width	Length
Arena Football	85	198
U.S. College Football	160	360
U.S. Professional Football	160	360
Canadian Football	195	450

Teachers' Salaries **In Exercises 36–37, use the following information.**

The matrices at the right list teachers' salaries in a certain Pennsylvania school district from the 1990–1991 school year to the 1993–1994 school year. The codes at the top of each matrix classify a teacher according to the number of graduate credits earned. The numbers to the left represent a teacher's current year of service to the district.

36. Suppose that in 1990, you accepted a teaching position in this school district. Your beginning code is A, but by the 1993–94 year you have earned enough graduate credits to be classified as a code B. What would be your total salary for your first four years of teaching?

37. Suppose that you had reached code B by your second year of teaching. What would be your total salary for your first four years of teaching?

1990–91	A	B	C
1	19,894	19,994	20,094
2	20,671	20,771	20,871
3	21,448	21,548	21,648
4	22,225	22,325	22,425

1991–92	A	B	C
1	20,525	20,625	20,725
2	21,375	21,475	21,575
3	22,225	22,325	22,425
4	23,075	24,025	23,275

1992–93	A	B	C
1	22,475	22,575	22,675
2	23,325	23,425	23,525
3	24,175	24,275	24,375
4	25,025	25,125	25,225

1993–94	A	B	C
1	24,525	24,625	24,725
2	25,375	25,475	25,575
3	26,225	26,325	26,425
4	27,075	27,175	27,275

Integrated Review

In Exercises 38–41, simplify the expression.

38. $10(5 - 1) - 5$

39. $6 + 2(1 - 6)$

40. $4(-3 + 7) + 9$

41. $10 - (5 + 9)$

42. What number is 24% of 700?

43. What number is 86% of 250?

44. 228 is what percent of 380?

45. 63 is what percent of 84?

Exploration and Extension

46. *Getting a Raise* The hourly wage of an employee at a restaurant depends on the employee's job description and the number of months the employee has worked. The matrix at the right shows the wage rates before the employees won a 5% wage hike. Write the new wage matrix.

Hourly Wage (in dollars)	Three Months	Six Months	Twelve Months
Regular Employee	5.00	5.10	5.35
Assistant Supervisor	5.75	5.85	6.10

4.2

Matrix Multiplication

What you should learn:

Goal 1 How to multiply two matrices

Goal 2 How to use matrix multiplication to answer questions about real-life situations

Why you should learn it:

You can model many real-life situations with matrix multiplication, such as data on a spreadsheet.

Goal 1 — Multiplying Two Matrices

The **matrix multiplication** of A and B is defined only if the number of columns in A equals the number of rows in B. For instance, the product AB of the matrices below is defined since A has two columns (3×2) and B has two rows (2×2).

$$A = \begin{bmatrix} -1 & 3 \\ 4 & -2 \\ 5 & 0 \end{bmatrix} \quad \text{and} \quad B = \begin{bmatrix} -3 & 2 \\ -4 & 1 \end{bmatrix}$$

If A is an $m \times n$ matrix and B is an $n \times p$ matrix, then the product AB is an $m \times p$ matrix.

Example 1 — *Finding the Product of Two Matrices*

Find the product: $\begin{bmatrix} -1 & 3 \\ 4 & -2 \\ 5 & 0 \end{bmatrix} \begin{bmatrix} -3 & 2 \\ -4 & 1 \end{bmatrix}$.

Solution Since A is a 3×2 matrix and B is a 2×2 matrix, the product AB is defined and is a 3×2 matrix. To find the entry in the first row and first column of AB, multiply corresponding entries in the first row of A and the first column of B. Then add.

$$(-1)(-3) + (3)(-4) = -9$$

$$\begin{bmatrix} -1 & 3 \\ 4 & -2 \\ 5 & 0 \end{bmatrix} \begin{bmatrix} -3 & 2 \\ -4 & 1 \end{bmatrix} = \begin{bmatrix} -9 & \square \\ \square & \square \\ \square & \square \end{bmatrix}$$

By continuing this pattern, you can obtain the following.

$$AB = \begin{bmatrix} -1 & 3 \\ 4 & -2 \\ 5 & 0 \end{bmatrix} \begin{bmatrix} -3 & 2 \\ -4 & 1 \end{bmatrix}$$

$$= \begin{bmatrix} (-1)(-3) + (3)(-4) & (-1)(2) + (3)(1) \\ (4)(-3) + (-2)(-4) & (4)(2) + (-2)(1) \\ (5)(-3) + (0)(-4) & (5)(2) + (0)(1) \end{bmatrix}$$

$$= \begin{bmatrix} -9 & 1 \\ -4 & 6 \\ -15 & 10 \end{bmatrix}$$

Be sure you understand that for the product of two matrices to be defined, the number of columns of the first matrix must equal the number of rows of the second matrix. That is, in the diagram below, the two blue numbers must match. Note also that the outside two numbers give the order of the product.

$$
\begin{array}{ccc}
A & \cdot & B & = & AB \\
m \times n & & n \times p & & m \times p
\end{array}
$$

equal

order of AB

Example 2   *Finding the Product of Two Matrices*

a.
$$
\begin{bmatrix} 1 & 0 & 3 \\ 2 & -1 & -2 \end{bmatrix}
\begin{bmatrix} -2 & 4 & 2 \\ 1 & 0 & 0 \\ -1 & 1 & -1 \end{bmatrix}
=
\begin{bmatrix} -5 & 7 & -1 \\ -3 & 6 & 6 \end{bmatrix}
$$
$$
2 \times 3 \qquad\qquad 3 \times 3 \qquad\qquad 2 \times 3
$$

b.
$$
\begin{bmatrix} 3 & 4 \\ -2 & 5 \end{bmatrix}
\begin{bmatrix} 1 & 0 \\ 0 & 1 \end{bmatrix}
=
\begin{bmatrix} 3 & 4 \\ -2 & 5 \end{bmatrix}
$$
$$
2 \times 2 \quad\; 2 \times 2 \qquad 2 \times 2
$$

c.
$$
\begin{bmatrix} 1 & -2 & -3 \end{bmatrix}
\begin{bmatrix} 2 \\ -1 \\ 1 \end{bmatrix}
=
\begin{bmatrix} 1 \end{bmatrix}
$$
$$
1 \times 3 \qquad 3 \times 1 \;\; 1 \times 1
$$

d.
$$
\begin{bmatrix} 2 \\ -1 \\ 1 \end{bmatrix}
\begin{bmatrix} 1 & -2 & -3 \end{bmatrix}
=
\begin{bmatrix} 2 & -4 & -6 \\ -1 & 2 & 3 \\ 1 & -2 & -3 \end{bmatrix}
$$
$$
3 \times 1 \qquad 1 \times 3 \qquad\qquad 3 \times 3
$$

■

Notice in Parts **c** and **d** of Example 2 that the products AB and BA are *not the same*. Matrix multiplication is not, in general, commutative. That is, for most matrices, $AB \neq BA$.

Properties of Matrix Multiplication

Let A, B, and C be matrices and let c be a scalar.

1. $A(BC) = (AB)C$ *Associative Property*
2. $A(B + C) = AB + AC$ *Left Distributive Property*
3. $(A + B)C = AC + BC$ *Right Distributive Property*
4. $c(AB) = (cA)B = A(cB)$

Goal 2 Using Matrix Multiplication in Real Life

Real Life
Softball Expenses

Example 3 Finding the Total Cost

Two softball teams submit equipment lists to their sponsors.

	Bats	Balls	Gloves
Women's Team	12	45	15
Men's Team	15	38	17

If a bat costs \$21, a ball costs \$4, and a glove costs \$30, use matrices to find the total cost of equipment for each team.

Solution To begin, write the equipment list and the cost per item in matrix form.

Equipment	Bats	Balls	Gloves		Cost	Dollars
Women's Team	12	45	15		Bats	21
Men's Team	15	38	17		Balls	4
					Gloves	30

The total cost for each team can now be obtained by multiplying the equipment matrix by the cost matrix.

$$\begin{bmatrix} 12 & 45 & 15 \\ 15 & 38 & 17 \end{bmatrix} \begin{bmatrix} 21 \\ 4 \\ 30 \end{bmatrix} = \begin{bmatrix} 12(21) + 45(4) + 15(30) \\ 15(21) + 38(4) + 17(30) \end{bmatrix} = \begin{bmatrix} 882 \\ 977 \end{bmatrix}$$

The total cost of equipment for the women's team is \$822, and the total cost of equipment for the men's team is \$977. ■

Communicating about ALGEBRA

▶ **SHARING IDEAS about the Lesson**

Two competing companies offer cable television to a city with 100,000 households. Company A has 25,000 subscribers and Company B has 30,000. (The other 45,000 households do not subscribe.) The percent changes in cable subscriptions each year are shown below. Explain how matrix multiplication can be used to find the number of subscribers each company will have in one year.

Percent Changes	From Company A	From Company B	From Nonsubscriber
To Company A	0.70	0.15	0.15
To Company B	0.20	0.80	0.15
Nonsubscriber	0.10	0.05	0.70

EXERCISES

▶ **CRITICAL THINKING about the Lesson**

1. Is matrix multiplication defined for the matrices shown? Explain your answer.

$$\begin{bmatrix} 2 & -1 & 5 \\ 1 & 0 & 4 \end{bmatrix} \text{ and } \begin{bmatrix} 0 & 6 \\ -1 & 4 \\ 1 & 2 \end{bmatrix}$$

2. In the following matrix multiplication, find the missing entry.

$$\begin{bmatrix} 4 & 2 \\ 1 & 0 \\ 6 & 2 \\ -1 & 3 \end{bmatrix} \begin{bmatrix} 1 & -1 & 0 \\ 0 & 5 & 2 \end{bmatrix} = \begin{bmatrix} 4 & \boxed{?} & 4 \\ 1 & -1 & 0 \\ 6 & 4 & 4 \\ -1 & 16 & 6 \end{bmatrix}$$

3. A is a 6×1 matrix. B is a 1×2 matrix. Which of the matrix products is defined, AB or BA? Explain.

4. *True or False?* $\begin{bmatrix} 5 & 3 \\ -3 & 5 \end{bmatrix} \begin{bmatrix} 2 & 0 \\ 0 & 1 \end{bmatrix} = \begin{bmatrix} 2 & 0 \\ 0 & 1 \end{bmatrix} \begin{bmatrix} 5 & 3 \\ -3 & 5 \end{bmatrix}$ Explain.

Independent Practice

In Exercises 5–12, state whether the matrix product *AB* is defined. If so, state the order of the product.

5. Order of A: 2×3, Order of B: 3×1
6. Order of A: 1×4, Order of B: 4×5
7. Order of A: 3×2, Order of B: 3×5
8. Order of A: 5×5, Order of B: 5×4
9. Order of A: 5×4, Order of B: 4×2
10. Order of A: 3×2, Order of B: 3×4
11. Order of A: 8×3, Order of B: 3×4
12. Order of A: 5×1, Order of B: 1×3

In Exercises 13–22, find the product. If it is not defined, state the reason.

13. $\begin{bmatrix} 1 & 2 \\ -4 & 3 \end{bmatrix} \begin{bmatrix} 4 & 1 \\ 0 & -1 \end{bmatrix}$

14. $\begin{bmatrix} 6 & 1 \\ 0 & 2 \end{bmatrix} \begin{bmatrix} 1 & 1 \\ -5 & 3 \end{bmatrix}$

15. $\begin{bmatrix} 7 & 1 & 1 \\ 0 & 2 & 6 \\ 3 & -2 & 1 \end{bmatrix} \begin{bmatrix} 0 & 1 & 4 \\ 5 & -2 & 1 \\ -3 & 1 & -8 \end{bmatrix}$

16. $\begin{bmatrix} 3 & 0 & 3 \\ 1 & 2 & 1 \\ 2 & -1 & 0 \end{bmatrix} \begin{bmatrix} 1 & 0 & 0 \\ 4 & 1 & 1 \\ -5 & 0 & 2 \end{bmatrix}$

17. $\begin{bmatrix} 2 & 8 & 1 \\ 0 & 5 & -2 \end{bmatrix} \begin{bmatrix} 0 & 1 & -1 \\ 8 & 2 & 4 \end{bmatrix}$

18. $\begin{bmatrix} 5 & -2 \\ 0 & 2 \\ 1 & 1 \end{bmatrix} \begin{bmatrix} 3 & 0 \\ 6 & 2 \end{bmatrix}$

19. $\begin{bmatrix} -3 & 2 & -5 \\ 4 & -6 & 3 \end{bmatrix} \begin{bmatrix} 4 \\ 1 \\ 0 \end{bmatrix}$

20. $\begin{bmatrix} 0 & 1 & 0 \\ 6 & -3 & 1 \\ -1 & 4 & -2 \end{bmatrix} \begin{bmatrix} 6 & 7 & 1 \\ 2 & 10 & 5 \\ 1 & -10 & 9 \end{bmatrix}$

21. $\begin{bmatrix} 5 \\ 0 \\ 1 \end{bmatrix} [4 \quad 2 \quad -10]$

22. $[3 \quad 1 \quad 1] \begin{bmatrix} 2 \\ -6 \\ 0 \end{bmatrix}$

In Exercises 23 and 24, solve for *x* and *y*.

23. $\begin{bmatrix} -2 & 1 & 2 \\ 3 & 2 & 4 \\ 0 & -2 & 4 \end{bmatrix} \begin{bmatrix} 1 & 3 \\ x & 2 \\ 3 & -1 \end{bmatrix} = \begin{bmatrix} 6 & -6 \\ 19 & 9 \\ 8 & y \end{bmatrix}$

24. $\begin{bmatrix} 4 & 1 & 3 \\ -2 & x & 1 \end{bmatrix} \begin{bmatrix} 9 & -2 \\ 2 & 1 \\ -1 & 4 \end{bmatrix} = \begin{bmatrix} y & 5 \\ -13 & 11 \end{bmatrix}$

In Exercises 25–30, simplify the expression.

25. $2 \begin{bmatrix} 4 & 2 \\ 6 & -3 \end{bmatrix} \begin{bmatrix} 1 & -4 \\ 0 & 2 \end{bmatrix}$

26. $-3 \begin{bmatrix} -5 & 3 \\ 1 & 2 \end{bmatrix} \begin{bmatrix} 0 & -3 \\ 2 & 4 \end{bmatrix}$

27. $\begin{bmatrix} 6 & -4 \\ 0 & -2 \end{bmatrix} \begin{bmatrix} 2 & -3 \\ 3 & 1 \end{bmatrix} + \begin{bmatrix} 6 & -4 \\ 0 & -2 \end{bmatrix} \begin{bmatrix} -1 & 1 \\ 3 & 2 \end{bmatrix}$

28. $\begin{bmatrix} 2 & -1 \\ 4 & 5 \end{bmatrix} \begin{bmatrix} 2 & 0 \\ -3 & 1 \end{bmatrix} + \begin{bmatrix} 2 & -1 \\ 4 & 5 \end{bmatrix} \begin{bmatrix} -3 & 4 \\ 5 & -1 \end{bmatrix}$

29. $\begin{bmatrix} 1 & 3 & 4 \\ 0 & -3 & -5 \\ 2 & 5 & 1 \end{bmatrix} \left(\begin{bmatrix} 2 & 4 & 0 \\ -1 & 3 & 2 \\ 2 & -2 & 1 \end{bmatrix} + \begin{bmatrix} -3 & 1 & 9 \\ 8 & 3 & 4 \\ 4 & -3 & 0 \end{bmatrix} \right)$

30. $\left(\begin{bmatrix} 4 & 2 & 1 \\ 1 & -1 & 3 \\ 0 & -3 & 2 \end{bmatrix} + \begin{bmatrix} -1 & 3 & 4 \\ 0 & -2 & 3 \\ 4 & 1 & 2 \end{bmatrix} \right) \begin{bmatrix} 0 & -5 & 4 \\ 1 & 3 & 9 \\ -3 & 1 & 3 \end{bmatrix}$

31. *Roses, Carnations, and Lilies* You and your cousin decide to make two bouquets: one for your mother and one for your grandparents. The number of roses, carnations, and lilies that will be in your mother's and your grandparents' bouquets is shown in the matrix. Each rose costs $3, each carnation costs $1.25, and each lily costs $4. Your cousin agrees to share the cost of your grandparents' bouquet. Show how matrix multiplication can be used to determine your cousin's share of the cost.

Number of Flowers	Roses	Carnations	Lilies
Mother's Bouquet	4	5	3
Grandparents' Bouquet	6	4	3

32. *Eating Healthy* The matrix shows the results of a survey taken by *USA Today*. In the survey, people were asked why they tried to eat a healthful diet. The survey results show the percent of answers by 8900 women and 7000 men. Show how matrix multiplication can be used to find how many people answered in each of the three categories.

Why Eat Healthy?	Women	Men
To look better	0.6	0.4
To live longer	0.36	0.53
I don't eat healthy	0.04	0.07

33. *World Grain Production*   The percents of the total 1990 world production of wheat, rice, and corn grown by the four countries that grow the most grain are given in the matrix on page 172. The total 1990 world production (in thousands of metric tons) of wheat, rice, and corn was 535,842, 475,533, and 480,609, respectively. Show how matrix multiplication can be used to find how many metric tons of the three grains were grown in each of the four countries. *(Source: United Nations)*

Integrated Review

In Exercises 34–37, state the order of the matrix.

34. $\begin{bmatrix} 5 & 6 & 1 \\ 4 & 2 & -4 \\ -1 & 5 & 0 \\ 0 & -2 & 3 \end{bmatrix}$ **35.** $\begin{bmatrix} 6 & -1 & 6 \\ 9 & 0 & 5 \\ -2 & 4 & 3 \end{bmatrix}$ **36.** $\begin{bmatrix} 1 & -4 & 3 & 4 \\ 9 & 6 & -3 & 7 \end{bmatrix}$ **37.** $\begin{bmatrix} 4 & -1 & 5 & -4 & 0 \\ 3 & 0 & -6 & 1 & 8 \end{bmatrix}$

In Exercises 38–43, state whether the operation is possible. If the operation is not possible, state the reason. If the operation is possible, state the order of the resulting matrix.

38. Add a 2×3 matrix to a 3×2 matrix.

39. Subtract a 4×4 matrix from a 4×2 matrix.

40. Add a 1×3 matrix to a 3×2 matrix.

41. Subtract a 2×3 matrix from a 2×3 matrix.

42. Multiply a 6×4 matrix by a 4×6 matrix.

43. Multiply a 1×3 matrix by a 3×4 matrix.

Exploration and Extension

In Exercises 44–47, use the given matrices and the scalar $c = 4$ to illustrate the property.

$$A = \begin{bmatrix} 1 & 3 \\ 9 & -1 \end{bmatrix} \quad B = \begin{bmatrix} 6 & 3 \\ 4 & 2 \end{bmatrix} \quad C = \begin{bmatrix} 2 & 0 \\ 4 & -2 \end{bmatrix}$$

44. *Associative Property:*
   $A(BC) = (AB)C$

45. *Left Distributive Property:*
   $A(B + C) = AB + AC$

46. *Right Distributive Property:*
   $(A + B)C = AC + BC$

47. *Property of Scalar Multiplication:*
   $c(AB) = (cA)B = A(cB)$

1. Simplify $-2(3) + (-4)(-6) + 3(-5)$. **(1.1)**

2. Simplify $-3\left(\frac{2}{3}\right) + 4\left(\frac{1}{3}\right) - 2\left(-\frac{4}{3}\right)$. **(1.1)**

3. 39 is 150% of what number?

4. Write 3.24×10^{-3} in decimal form.

5. Simplify $\frac{4}{5} - \frac{2}{3} + 4$.

6. Evaluate $-3x^2 + 4x$ when $x = -2$. **(1.2)**

7. What is the slope of the line $-4x + 6y = 5$? **(2.2)**

8. Find the intercepts of the line $3y - x = 4$. **(2.3)**

9. What is the reciprocal of $-\frac{3}{5}$? **(1.1)**

10. What is the opposite of $-\frac{3}{5}$? **(1.1)**

11. Find the slope of the line through $(0, 2)$ and $(-3, 4)$. **(2.2)**

12. Find an equation of the line that passes through $(7, 2)$ with a slope of -3. **(2.4)**

13. Add: $\begin{bmatrix} 2 & -1 \\ -3 & 0 \end{bmatrix} + \begin{bmatrix} 5 & 6 \\ 2 & -4 \end{bmatrix}$. **(4.1)**

14. Multiply: $\begin{bmatrix} 2 & -1 \\ -3 & 0 \end{bmatrix}\begin{bmatrix} 5 & 6 \\ 2 & -4 \end{bmatrix}$. **(4.2)**

15. Solve $|-x + 4| < 3$. **(1.7)**

16. Solve $-3(5 + x) = 2(9 - x)$. **(1.3)**

17. Sketch the graph of $y = -3x + 2$. **(2.3)**

18. Sketch the graph of $2x - 3y \le 6$. **(2.5)**

19. Solve: $\begin{cases} 2x - 3y = 1 \\ -x - 7y = -11 \end{cases}$. **(3.2)**

20. Solve the system: $\begin{cases} x + y = 34 \\ x - y = 2 \end{cases}$. **(3.2)**

Milestones ARTHUR CAYLEY

1800	1820	1840	1860	1880	1900
	Arthur Cayley born		Elected to chair at Cambridge	"The Collected Mathematical Papers" began publication	

The invention of matrices is credited to Arthur Cayley. Born in England in 1821, Cayley grew up doing complex computations for amusement. He attended the University of Cambridge, studying languages and mathematics. Upon graduation in 1842, he received a 3-year appointment to Trinity College at Cambridge. He went on to study law and was admitted to the bar in 1849. While practicing law, Cayley continued his research in mathematics. Cayley returned to Cambridge in 1863 when he was elected to the new Sadlerian Chair of Pure Mathematics.

Cayley investigated many topics in modern mathematics. He developed matrix algebra, worked on group theory, and studied hyperspace. He was influential in getting Cambridge to accept women students. A prolific writer, Cayley authored more than 900 papers and notes that were published in 14 volumes from 1889 through 1898 in *The Collected Mathematical Papers*.

Arthur Cayley introduced matrices and their operations in an 1858 memoir.

Find out what mathematical field Werner Heisenberg developed. How did Cayley's work help him?

4.3 Determinants

What you should learn:

Goal 1 How to evaluate the determinant of a 2 × 2 or a 3 × 3 matrix

Goal 2 How to use determinants to solve real-life problems

Why you should learn it:

You can use the determinant of a matrix to answer real-life problems, such as finding the area of a triangle in a coordinate plane.

Goal 1 Evaluating Determinants

Recall from Lesson 4.1 that a *square* matrix has the same number of rows and columns. Associated with each square matrix is a real number called its **determinant.** In this lesson, you will learn to evaluate the determinant of a 2 × 2 matrix and a 3 × 3 matrix.

Determinant of a 2 × 2 Matrix

The **determinant** of the matrix $\begin{bmatrix} a & b \\ c & d \end{bmatrix}$ is $\begin{vmatrix} a & b \\ c & d \end{vmatrix} = ad - cb.$

The following diagram shows that the determinant of a 2 × 2 matrix is equal to the difference of the products of the entries on the two diagonals.

$$\begin{vmatrix} a & b \\ c & d \end{vmatrix} = ad - cb.$$

Example 1 *Evaluating the Determinant of a 2 × 2 Matrix*

Evaluate the determinant of each matrix.

a. $\begin{bmatrix} 2 & -3 \\ 1 & 4 \end{bmatrix}$ **b.** $\begin{bmatrix} -1 & 2 \\ 2 & -4 \end{bmatrix}$ **c.** $\begin{bmatrix} 1 & 3 \\ 2 & 5 \end{bmatrix}$

Solution

a. $\begin{vmatrix} 2 & -3 \\ 1 & 4 \end{vmatrix} = 2(4) - 1(-3) = 8 + 3 = 11$

b. $\begin{vmatrix} -1 & 2 \\ 2 & -4 \end{vmatrix} = (-1)(-4) - 2(2) = 4 - 4 = 0$

c. $\begin{vmatrix} 1 & 3 \\ 2 & 5 \end{vmatrix} = 1(5) - 2(3) = -1$

Although vertical bars are used to denote both determinants and absolute value, notice in Example 1 that the determinant of a matrix can be positive, zero, or negative.

The determinant of a 3 × 3 matrix is more difficult to evaluate than the determinant of a 2 × 2 matrix. Two methods are common. The first is **expansion by minors,** which expresses the determinant of a 3 × 3 matrix in terms of three 2 × 2 determinants.

Determinant of a 3 × 3 Matrix (Expansion by Minors)

The determinant of the matrix $\begin{bmatrix} a & b & c \\ d & e & f \\ g & h & i \end{bmatrix}$ is

$$\begin{vmatrix} a & b & c \\ d & e & f \\ g & h & i \end{vmatrix} = a \begin{vmatrix} a & b & c \\ d & e & f \\ g & h & i \end{vmatrix} - b \begin{vmatrix} a & b & c \\ d & e & f \\ g & h & i \end{vmatrix} + c \begin{vmatrix} a & b & c \\ d & e & f \\ g & h & i \end{vmatrix}$$

$$= a \begin{vmatrix} e & f \\ h & i \end{vmatrix} - b \begin{vmatrix} d & f \\ g & i \end{vmatrix} + c \begin{vmatrix} d & e \\ g & h \end{vmatrix}.$$

This pattern shows expansion by minors *along the first row*. Patterns for expanding along other rows or columns are similar. The *sign pattern* for expanding along the first or third row or column is "+ − +." The sign pattern for the second row or column is "− + −."

Example 2 *Evaluating the Determinant of a 3 × 3 Matrix*

Evaluate the determinant of $\begin{bmatrix} -1 & 1 & 2 \\ 0 & 2 & 3 \\ 3 & 4 & 2 \end{bmatrix}$.

Solution   Expanding by minors along the *first* row, you obtain the following.

$$\begin{vmatrix} -1 & 1 & 2 \\ 0 & 2 & 3 \\ 3 & 4 & 2 \end{vmatrix} = (-1)\begin{vmatrix} 2 & 3 \\ 4 & 2 \end{vmatrix} - (1)\begin{vmatrix} 0 & 3 \\ 3 & 2 \end{vmatrix} + (2)\begin{vmatrix} 0 & 2 \\ 3 & 4 \end{vmatrix}$$

$$= (-1)(4 - 12) - (1)(0 - 9) + (2)(0 - 6)$$

$$= 8 + 9 - 12, \text{ or } 5$$

In Example 2, expansion by minors along the *second* row would yield

$$\begin{vmatrix} -1 & 1 & 2 \\ 0 & 2 & 3 \\ 3 & 4 & 2 \end{vmatrix} = -(0)\begin{vmatrix} 1 & 2 \\ 4 & 2 \end{vmatrix} + (2)\begin{vmatrix} -1 & 2 \\ 3 & 2 \end{vmatrix} - (3)\begin{vmatrix} -1 & 1 \\ 3 & 4 \end{vmatrix}$$

$$= 0 - 16 + 21 = 5.$$

The second method for evaluating the determinant of a 3 × 3 matrix is called the **diagonals method.** To apply this method, it is easier to copy the first and second columns of the matrix to form fourth and fifth columns. The determinant is then obtained by adding the products of three diagonals and subtracting the products of three diagonals, as shown in the following diagram.

Second, subtract these products.

$$\begin{vmatrix} a & b & c \\ d & e & f \\ g & h & i \end{vmatrix} \begin{matrix} a & b \\ d & e \\ g & h \end{matrix} = aei + bfg + cdh - gec - hfa - idb$$

First, add these products.

Example **3** **Evaluating the Determinant of a 3 × 3 Matrix**

Evaluate the determinant of $\begin{bmatrix} 0 & 2 & 1 \\ 3 & -1 & 2 \\ 4 & -4 & 1 \end{bmatrix}$.

Solution

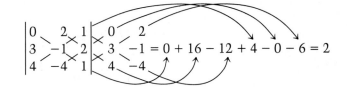

$$\begin{vmatrix} 0 & 2 & 1 \\ 3 & -1 & 2 \\ 4 & -4 & 1 \end{vmatrix} \begin{matrix} 0 & 2 \\ 3 & -1 \\ 4 & -4 \end{matrix} = 0 + 16 - 12 + 4 - 0 - 6 = 2$$

Goal **2** Using Determinants in Real-Life Situations

A determinant can be used to find the area of a triangle whose vertices are points in a coordinate plane.

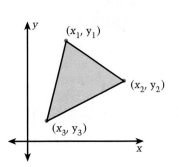

Area of a Triangle

The area of a triangle with vertices (x_1, y_1), (x_2, y_2), and (x_3, y_3) is given by

$$\text{area} = \pm\frac{1}{2}\begin{vmatrix} x_1 & y_1 & 1 \\ x_2 & y_2 & 1 \\ x_3 & y_3 & 1 \end{vmatrix}$$

where the symbol (±) indicates that the appropriate sign should be chosen to yield a positive value.

Gypsy moths are native to France. In 1869, however, some were accidentally brought to the United States. Since then, the gypsy moth population has increased greatly and has done great damage to forests, especially in the northeastern United States.

Real Life
Forestry

Example 4 *Finding the Area of a Triangular Region*

A large region of forest has been infected with gypsy moths. The region is roughly triangular, as shown in the map at the left. From the northern vertex of the region, the distance to the other vertices is 20 miles south and 28 miles east (for vertex C), and 25 miles south and 10 miles east (for vertex B). Approximate the number of square miles in this region.

Solution Begin by superimposing a coordinate plane on the map. The vertices of the triangular region are $(x_1, y_1) = (0, 0)$, $(x_2, y_2) = (10, -25)$, and $(x_3, y_3) = (28, -20)$.

$$\text{Area} = \pm \frac{1}{2} \begin{vmatrix} x_1 & y_1 & 1 \\ x_2 & y_2 & 1 \\ x_3 & y_3 & 1 \end{vmatrix}$$

$$= \pm \frac{1}{2} \begin{vmatrix} 0 & 0 & 1 \\ 10 & -25 & 1 \\ 28 & -20 & 1 \end{vmatrix}$$

$$= \pm \frac{1}{2} \left(0 \begin{vmatrix} -25 & 1 \\ -20 & 1 \end{vmatrix} - 0 \begin{vmatrix} 10 & 1 \\ 28 & 1 \end{vmatrix} + 1 \begin{vmatrix} 10 & -25 \\ 28 & -20 \end{vmatrix} \right)$$

$$= \pm \frac{1}{2} (0 - 0 + (1)(-200 + 700))$$

$$= 250 \text{ square miles.} \qquad \blacksquare$$

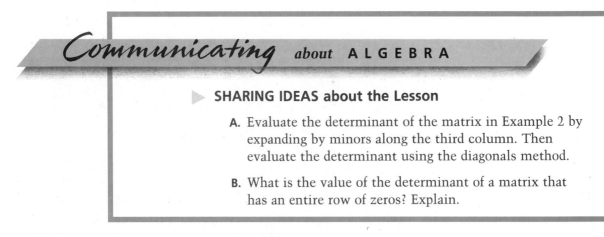

Communicating about ALGEBRA

▷ **SHARING IDEAS about the Lesson**

A. Evaluate the determinant of the matrix in Example 2 by expanding by minors along the third column. Then evaluate the determinant using the diagonals method.

B. What is the value of the determinant of a matrix that has an entire row of zeros? Explain.

EXERCISES

▶ **CRITICAL THINKING about the Lesson**

1. Evaluate the determinant of $\begin{bmatrix} 0 & 1 \\ 6 & 2 \end{bmatrix}$.

2. Can two different matrices have the same determinant? If so, give an example.

3. Evaluate the determinant of the matrix in two ways: $\begin{bmatrix} 1 & -2 & 4 \\ 0 & 0 & -3 \\ 2 & 1 & -2 \end{bmatrix}$

   - Expand by minors along the first row.
   - Expand by minors along the second row.

   Which is easier? Why?

4. Use the diagonals method to evaluate. $\begin{vmatrix} 5 & -2 & -4 \\ 0 & 1 & -2 \\ 3 & -2 & 4 \end{vmatrix}$

Independent Practice

In Exercises 5–16, evaluate the determinant of the matrix.

5. $\begin{bmatrix} -4 & 2 \\ -6 & 3 \end{bmatrix}$

6. $\begin{bmatrix} 9 & 0 \\ 4 & -3 \end{bmatrix}$

7. $\begin{bmatrix} 8 & 3 \\ -1 & 2 \end{bmatrix}$

8. $\begin{bmatrix} -6 & 11 \\ -6 & 5 \end{bmatrix}$

9. $\begin{bmatrix} 1 & 7 \\ 2 & 9 \end{bmatrix}$

10. $\begin{bmatrix} 1 & 4 \\ 6 & 8 \end{bmatrix}$

11. $\begin{bmatrix} -4 & 1 \\ 7 & -2 \end{bmatrix}$

12. $\begin{bmatrix} 5 & 0 \\ -2 & 5 \end{bmatrix}$

13. $\begin{bmatrix} 3 & 4 \\ 2 & -1 \end{bmatrix}$

14. $\begin{bmatrix} 9 & -3 \\ 6 & -2 \end{bmatrix}$

15. $\begin{bmatrix} 0 & -3 \\ 4 & 1 \end{bmatrix}$

16. $\begin{bmatrix} 12 & 6 \\ 3 & 1 \end{bmatrix}$

In Exercises 17–22, evaluate the determinant of the matrix. (Expand by minors along the indicated row or column.)

17. Expand along row 1.
$\begin{bmatrix} 5 & 0 & 2 \\ 1 & 4 & -1 \\ 3 & 2 & 0 \end{bmatrix}$

18. Expand along row 3.
$\begin{bmatrix} 10 & 4 & 2 \\ -8 & 1 & -1 \\ 2 & 3 & 2 \end{bmatrix}$

19. Expand along row 2.
$\begin{bmatrix} 6 & 2 & 1 \\ 5 & 6 & -3 \\ -1 & 2 & 2 \end{bmatrix}$

20. Expand along column 3.
$\begin{bmatrix} 1 & 2 & 1 \\ -3 & 3 & -1 \\ 2 & 1 & 0 \end{bmatrix}$

21. Expand along column 2.
$\begin{bmatrix} 10 & 0 & 1 \\ 6 & 0 & 4 \\ -1 & 5 & 5 \end{bmatrix}$

22. Expand along column 1.
$\begin{bmatrix} 1 & -4 & 3 \\ 0 & 10 & -12 \\ -1 & 2 & -2 \end{bmatrix}$

In Exercises 23–26, use the diagonals method to evaluate the determinant of the matrix.

23. $\begin{bmatrix} 12 & 4 & -6 \\ 2 & 1 & 3 \\ 1 & 0 & -2 \end{bmatrix}$

24. $\begin{bmatrix} 5 & -8 & 4 \\ 4 & 2 & 1 \\ 1 & 1 & 2 \end{bmatrix}$

25. $\begin{bmatrix} 0 & 3 & 2 \\ 10 & 14 & 2 \\ 1 & -1 & 6 \end{bmatrix}$

26. $\begin{bmatrix} 1 & 20 & 1 \\ 0 & 5 & 1 \\ 1 & 15 & -2 \end{bmatrix}$

27. Write a 3 × 3 matrix that has a row of zeros. Then evaluate its determinant. State a generalization about the determinant of a 3 × 3 matrix that has a column of zeros.

28. Write a 3 × 3 matrix that has two rows that are the same. Then evaluate its determinant. State a generalization about the determinant of a 3 × 3 matrix that has two rows that are the same.

In Exercises 29–32, show that the determinant of the matrix is zero. Exercises 27 and 28 indicate two quick ways to recognize 3 × 3 matrices whose determinants are zero. State some other ways.

29. $\begin{bmatrix} 1 & 2 & 3 \\ 2 & 4 & 6 \\ -1 & 0 & 8 \end{bmatrix}$ **30.** $\begin{bmatrix} 4 & -5 & 0 \\ 3 & -1 & 0 \\ -2 & 7 & 0 \end{bmatrix}$ **31.** $\begin{bmatrix} 5 & 2 & 2 \\ -3 & -4 & -4 \\ 8 & 3 & 3 \end{bmatrix}$ **32.** $\begin{bmatrix} -2 & -6 & 3 \\ 1 & 3 & -4 \\ 3 & 9 & 1 \end{bmatrix}$

In Exercises 33–35, use a determinant to find the area of the triangle.

33. **34.** **35.**

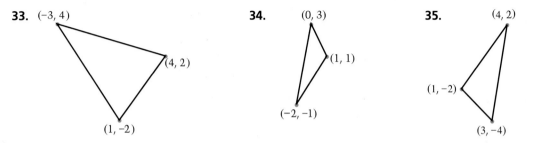

In Exercises 36–38, use two determinants to find the area of the region.

36. **37.** **38.**

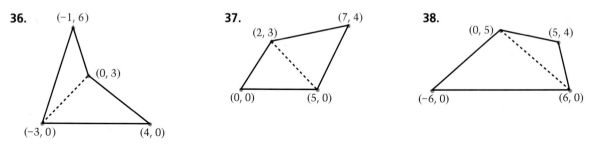

39. *The Bermuda Triangle*   The Bermuda Triangle is a large triangular region in the Atlantic Ocean. Many ships and planes have been lost in this region. The triangle is formed by imaginary lines connecting Bermuda, Puerto Rico, and a point near Melbourne, Florida. Estimate the coordinates of these three locations on the map. Then use a determinant to estimate the number of square miles in the Bermuda Triangle. (*Hint:* Each unit on the map represents 47 miles.)

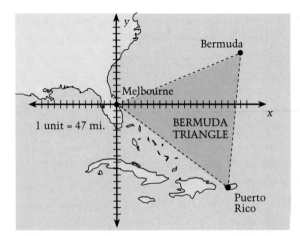

40. *Wetland Breeding Area* Black-necked stilts are birds that live throughout Florida and surrounding areas but breed mostly in the triangular region shown at the right. Each unit of the coordinate system represents a mile. Estimate the area of this region.

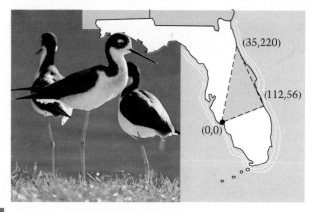

(35,220)

(112,56)

(0,0)

Integrated Review

In Exercises 41 and 42, illustrate the following property of determinants.
"If A and B are square matrices, then |AB| = |A||B|."

41. $\begin{bmatrix} 5 & 6 \\ -1 & 3 \end{bmatrix}\begin{bmatrix} 6 & 2 \\ 7 & -1 \end{bmatrix}$

42. $\begin{bmatrix} -4 & 7 \\ 0 & 5 \end{bmatrix}\begin{bmatrix} -6 & -3 \\ 1 & 2 \end{bmatrix}$

43. *Powers of Ten* Which best estimates the distance between Virginia Beach, Virginia, and Malibu Beach, California?
a. 3×10^2 miles **b.** 3×10^3 miles **c.** 3×10^4 miles **d.** 3×10^5 miles

44. *Powers of Ten* Which best estimates the length of a pencil?
a. 160×10^{-2} cm **b.** 160×10^{-1} cm **c.** 160×10^0 cm **d.** 160×10^1 cm

45. *College Entrance Exam Sample* The symbol $\triangle$ represents one of the four basic operations of arithmetic. It has the following properties.
- If a and b are real numbers, $a \triangle b = b \triangle a$.
- If a is a real number, then $a \triangle 0 = a$.
Which operation(s) must $\triangle$ represent?
a. + only **b.** $\times$ only **c.** + or $\times$ **d.** $-$ **e.** $\div$

46. *College Entrance Exam Sample* For all real numbers a, let $\widehat{x}$ be defined by $\widehat{x} = x^2 - 1$. Which of the following is equal to the product of $\widehat{3}$ and $\widehat{4}$?
a. $\widehat{12}$ **b.** $\widehat{11}$ **c.** $\widehat{10}$ **d.** $\widehat{9}$ **e.** $\widehat{7}$

Exploration and Extension

47. Use a determinant to find the area of the "triangle" whose vertices are $(-2, 4)$, $(4, 1)$, and $(8, -1)$. Based on your result, make a conjecture about the three points.

48. *Collinearity Test* Use the result of Exercise 47 to state a test that determines whether the points (x_1, y_1), (x_2, y_2), and (x_3, y_3) are collinear (lie on the same line).

49. *Determinant Form of Equation of a Line* Give a geometric argument why the equation at the right is an equation of the line through the points (x_1, y_1) and (x_2, y_2). Use this form to find an equation of the line containing $(2, 5)$ and $(6, -3)$.

$$\begin{vmatrix} x & y & 1 \\ x_1 & y_1 & 1 \\ x_2 & y_2 & 1 \end{vmatrix} = 0$$

Most graphing calculators can perform matrix algebra. That is, they can add, subtract, and multiply matrices, multiply a matrix by a scalar, find the determinant of a matrix, and find the inverse of a matrix. (The inverse of a matrix is introduced in Lesson 4.4.)

Keystroke instructions for entering and adding matrices with a *TI-82*, Casio *fx-9700GE*, and Sharp *EL-9300C* are listed on page 859.

Cooperative Learning

Partner Activity   Enter the following matrix in a graphing calculator

$$A = \begin{bmatrix} 1 & 0.4 & 0.3 \\ 0 & 0.3 & 0.2 \\ 0 & 0.3 & 0.5 \end{bmatrix}$$

Then calculate the following powers of A by repeatedly multiplying A by itself.

$$A^1 = \begin{bmatrix} 1.0000 & 0.4000 & 0.3000 \\ 0.0000 & 0.3000 & 0.2000 \\ 0.0000 & 0.3000 & 0.5000 \end{bmatrix} \qquad A^2 = \begin{bmatrix} 1.0000 & 0.6100 & 0.5300 \\ 0.0000 & 0.1500 & 0.1600 \\ 0.0000 & 0.2400 & 0.3100 \end{bmatrix}$$

$$A^3 = \begin{bmatrix} 1.0000 & 0.7420 & 0.6870 \\ 0.0000 & 0.0930 & 0.1100 \\ 0.0000 & 0.1650 & 0.2030 \end{bmatrix} \qquad A^4 = \begin{bmatrix} 1.0000 & 0.8287 & 0.7919 \\ 0.0000 & 0.0609 & 0.0736 \\ 0.0000 & 0.1104 & 0.1345 \end{bmatrix}$$

$$A^5 = \begin{bmatrix} 1.0000 & 0.8862 & 0.8617 \\ 0.0000 & 0.0404 & 0.0490 \\ 0.0000 & 0.0735 & 0.0893 \end{bmatrix} \qquad A^6 = \begin{bmatrix} 1.0000 & 0.9244 & 0.9081 \\ 0.0000 & 0.0268 & 0.0326 \\ 0.0000 & 0.0488 & 0.0594 \end{bmatrix}$$

$$A^7 = \begin{bmatrix} 1.0000 & 0.9497 & 0.9389 \\ 0.0000 & 0.0178 & 0.0216 \\ 0.0000 & 0.0325 & 0.0394 \end{bmatrix} \qquad A^8 = \begin{bmatrix} 1.0000 & 0.9666 & 0.9594 \\ 0.0000 & 0.0118 & 0.0144 \\ 0.0000 & 0.0216 & 0.0262 \end{bmatrix}$$

With your partner, discuss any pattern you see. As the matrix A is raised to higher and higher powers, which matrix do the powers appear to be approaching? Explain how to use a graphing calculator to test your conjecture.

Many matrices used to solve problems in engineering, business, and science have several rows and columns. Because it is so easy to make a mistake, people who work with such matrices almost always use technology to do the actual matrix calculations. Matrices have always been a powerful type of mathematical model—especially for problems that have a lot of data. With technology available to do the calculations, matrices have also become a *practical* type of mathematical model.

Example: Finding the Market Share

Two cable television companies compete in a city with 100,000 households. Company A has 25,000 subscribers and Company B has 30,000. (The other 45,000 households do not subscribe.) The percent changes in cable subscriptions each year are shown in the following **transition** matrix. How many subscribers will each company have in one year? In two years? (This is the same problem discussed on page 182.)

Percent Changes	From Company A	From Company B	From Nonsubscriber
To Company A	0.70	0.15	0.15
To Company B	0.20	0.80	0.15
To Nonsubscriber	0.10	0.05	0.70

Solution The matrix giving the present number of subscribers is shown at the right.

$$\begin{bmatrix} 25{,}000 \\ 30{,}000 \\ 45{,}000 \end{bmatrix} \begin{array}{l} \textit{Company A} \\ \textit{Company B} \\ \textit{Nonsubscriber} \end{array}$$

To find the number of subscribers in one year, multiply the "subscriber matrix" by the transition matrix.

$$\begin{bmatrix} 0.70 & 0.15 & 0.15 \\ 0.20 & 0.80 & 0.15 \\ 0.10 & 0.05 & 0.70 \end{bmatrix} \begin{bmatrix} 25{,}000 \\ 30{,}000 \\ 45{,}000 \end{bmatrix} = \begin{bmatrix} 28{,}750 \\ 35{,}750 \\ 35{,}500 \end{bmatrix} \begin{array}{l} \textit{Company A} \\ \textit{Company B} \\ \textit{Nonsubscriber} \end{array}$$

To find the number of subscribers in two years, multiply this new subscriber matrix by the transition matrix.

$$\begin{bmatrix} 0.70 & 0.15 & 0.15 \\ 0.20 & 0.80 & 0.15 \\ 0.10 & 0.05 & 0.70 \end{bmatrix} \begin{bmatrix} 28{,}750 \\ 35{,}750 \\ 35{,}500 \end{bmatrix} = \begin{bmatrix} 30{,}812.5 \\ 39{,}675.0 \\ 29{,}512.5 \end{bmatrix} \begin{array}{l} \textit{Company A} \\ \textit{Company B} \\ \textit{Nonsubscriber} \end{array} \blacksquare$$

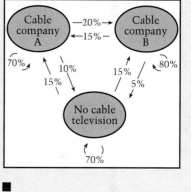

Exercises

In Exercises 1–3, use a graphing calculator to multiply the matrices.

1. $\begin{bmatrix} 3 & -2 & 12 \\ 0 & -6 & -9 \\ 8 & -7 & 10 \end{bmatrix} \begin{bmatrix} 9 & 8 \\ 9 & -3 \\ 9 & -5 \end{bmatrix}$

2. $\begin{bmatrix} 2 & 0 & 5 \\ 1 & 3 & 7 \\ 0 & 3 & 2 \end{bmatrix} \begin{bmatrix} 1 & 1 & 2 \\ 2 & 4 & 3 \\ 3 & 6 & 5 \end{bmatrix}$

3. $\begin{bmatrix} -2 & 2 & 3 \\ 1 & -1 & 0 \\ 0 & 1 & 4 \end{bmatrix} \begin{bmatrix} -4 & -5 & 3 \\ -4 & -8 & 3 \\ 1 & 2 & 0 \end{bmatrix}$

In Exercises 4–5, use a graphing calculator to evaluate the determinant of the matrix.

4. $\begin{bmatrix} 2 & 4 & 7 \\ -3 & 5 & 8 \\ 10 & 2 & -9 \end{bmatrix}$

5. $\begin{bmatrix} 8 & -7 & -7 \\ 2 & 5 & -5 \\ -8 & 7 & 7 \end{bmatrix}$

6. *Market Share* In Example 1 above, how many subscribers will each company have in five years? Is the market stabilizing for each company? Explain.

4.4

Identity and Inverse Matrices

What you should learn:

Goal 1 How to find and use the inverse of a 2 × 2 matrix

Goal 2 How to use inverse matrices in real-life settings

Why you should learn it:

You can use inverse matrices in many settings, such as in solving systems of linear equations and in decoding cryptograms.

Goal 1   **Using the Inverse of a 2 × 2 Matrix**

For real numbers, the number 1 is the multiplicative identity because for any real number a, $1 \cdot a = a$ and $a \cdot 1 = a$. For 2 × 2 matrices, the **multiplicative identity** is

$$I = \begin{bmatrix} 1 & 0 \\ 0 & 1 \end{bmatrix}.$$

Try multiplying any 2 × 2 matrix A by this identity. What do you obtain?

LESSON INVESTIGATION

■ **Investigating Inverse Matrices**

Partner Activity The real numbers 2 and $\frac{1}{2}$ are multiplicative inverses of each other because their product is equal to the multiplicative identity, 1. Which two of the following matrices are inverses of each other? Explain.

$$A = \begin{bmatrix} 3 & 1 \\ -5 & 2 \end{bmatrix} \qquad B = \begin{bmatrix} 3 & -1 \\ -5 & 2 \end{bmatrix} \qquad C = \begin{bmatrix} 2 & 1 \\ 5 & 3 \end{bmatrix}$$

Study Tip

The **inverse** of a matrix A is written as A^{-1}. This notation is similar to that used for real numbers because a^{-1} is the inverse of the nonzero real number a.

The Inverse of a 2 × 2 Matrix

The inverse of the matrix $A = \begin{bmatrix} a & b \\ c & d \end{bmatrix}$ is

$$A^{-1} = \frac{1}{|A|} \begin{bmatrix} d & -b \\ -c & a \end{bmatrix} = \frac{1}{ad - cb} \begin{bmatrix} d & -b \\ -c & a \end{bmatrix}, \quad ad - cb \neq 0.$$

Example 1   *Finding the Inverse of a 2 × 2 Matrix*

Find the inverse of $A = \begin{bmatrix} 2 & 4 \\ 1 & 3 \end{bmatrix}$.

Solution

$$A^{-1} = \frac{1}{6 - 4} \begin{bmatrix} 3 & -4 \\ -1 & 2 \end{bmatrix} = \begin{bmatrix} \frac{3}{2} & -2 \\ -\frac{1}{2} & 1 \end{bmatrix}$$

Check this by showing that $AA^{-1} = I$ and $A^{-1}A = I$. ■

Example 2 *Solving a Matrix Equation*

Solve the matrix equation for the 2×2 matrix X.

$$\underbrace{\begin{bmatrix} 11 & 5 \\ 2 & 1 \end{bmatrix}}_{A} X = \underbrace{\begin{bmatrix} 4 & -1 \\ 2 & 0 \end{bmatrix}}_{B} \quad \textit{Matrix equation} \quad AX = B$$

Solution   Begin by finding the inverse of A.

$$A^{-1} = \frac{1}{11 - 10} \begin{bmatrix} 1 & -5 \\ -2 & 11 \end{bmatrix} = \begin{bmatrix} 1 & -5 \\ -2 & 11 \end{bmatrix}$$

To solve the equation for X, multiply both sides of the equation by A^{-1} *on the left.*

$$\begin{bmatrix} 1 & -5 \\ -2 & 11 \end{bmatrix}\begin{bmatrix} 11 & 5 \\ 2 & 1 \end{bmatrix} X = \begin{bmatrix} 1 & -5 \\ -2 & 11 \end{bmatrix}\begin{bmatrix} 4 & -1 \\ 2 & 0 \end{bmatrix} \quad A^{-1}AX = A^{-1}B$$

$$\begin{bmatrix} 1 & 0 \\ 0 & 1 \end{bmatrix} X = \begin{bmatrix} -6 & -1 \\ 14 & 2 \end{bmatrix} \quad\quad IX = A^{-1}B$$

$$X = \begin{bmatrix} -6 & -1 \\ 14 & 2 \end{bmatrix} \quad\quad X = A^{-1}B$$

■

Some 2×2 matrices do not have an inverse. You can tell whether a matrix has an inverse by evaluating its determinant. If the determinant of A is zero, then A does not have an inverse. If the determinant is nonzero, then A has an inverse.

The inverse of a 3×3 matrix can be very difficult to compute. Of course, if you have a calculator that will compute inverse matrices, then the task is simplified.

Example 3 *Verifying the Inverse of a 3 × 3 Matrix*

Show that

$$B = \begin{bmatrix} 1 & -1 & 0 \\ 1 & 0 & -1 \\ 6 & -2 & -3 \end{bmatrix} \text{ is the inverse of } A = \begin{bmatrix} -2 & -3 & 1 \\ -3 & -3 & 1 \\ -2 & -4 & 1 \end{bmatrix}.$$

Solution

$$BA = \begin{bmatrix} 1 & -1 & 0 \\ 1 & 0 & -1 \\ 6 & -2 & -3 \end{bmatrix}\begin{bmatrix} -2 & -3 & 1 \\ -3 & -3 & 1 \\ -2 & -4 & 1 \end{bmatrix} = \begin{bmatrix} 1 & 0 & 0 \\ 0 & 1 & 0 \\ 0 & 0 & 1 \end{bmatrix}$$

$$AB = \begin{bmatrix} -2 & -3 & 1 \\ -3 & -3 & 1 \\ -2 & -4 & 1 \end{bmatrix}\begin{bmatrix} 1 & -1 & 0 \\ 1 & 0 & -1 \\ 6 & -2 & -3 \end{bmatrix} = \begin{bmatrix} 1 & 0 & 0 \\ 0 & 1 & 0 \\ 0 & 0 & 1 \end{bmatrix}$$

Because both products are equal to the 3×3 identity matrix, you can conclude that B is the inverse of A. ■

A *cryptogram* is a message written according to a secret code. (The Greek word *kryptos* means *"hidden."*) The following technique uses matrices to encode and decode messages.

To begin, assign a number to each letter in the alphabet (with 0 assigned to a blank space).

0 = __	6 = F	12 = L	18 = R	24 = X
1 = A	7 = G	13 = M	19 = S	25 = Y
2 = B	8 = H	14 = N	20 = T	26 = Z
3 = C	9 = I	15 = O	21 = U	
4 = D	10 = J	16 = P	22 = V	
5 = E	11 = K	17 = Q	23 = W	

The message is converted to numbers and partitioned into 1×2 *uncoded row matrices*. For instance, the message "STOP NOW" would be converted to the following row matrices.

$$[19 \quad 20] \quad [15 \quad 16] \quad [0 \quad 14] \quad [15 \quad 23]$$
$$\text{S} \quad \text{T} \quad\quad \text{O} \quad \text{P} \quad\quad \underline{} \quad \text{N} \quad\quad \text{O} \quad \text{W}$$

To encode a message, choose a 2×2 matrix A that has an inverse and multiply the uncoded row matrices (on the right) by A to obtain *coded row matrices*.

The text of the Rosetta Stone is written in Greek, Egyptian demotic, and hieroglyphics. Modern methods of cryptography were used to "break the code" of the hieroglyphs.

Real Life
Cryptography

Example 4 *Encoding a Message*

Use the matrix $A = \begin{bmatrix} -1 & 2 \\ 2 & -3 \end{bmatrix}$ to encode the message "STOP NOW."

Solution The coded row matrices are obtained by multiplying each of the uncoded row matrices (listed above) by the matrix A.

Uncoded Row Matrix	Encoding Matrix A	Coded Row Matrix
$[19 \quad 20]$	$\begin{bmatrix} -1 & 2 \\ 2 & -3 \end{bmatrix}$ =	$[21 \quad -22]$
$[15 \quad 16]$	$\begin{bmatrix} -1 & 2 \\ 2 & -3 \end{bmatrix}$ =	$[17 \quad -18]$
$[0 \quad 14]$	$\begin{bmatrix} -1 & 2 \\ 2 & -3 \end{bmatrix}$ =	$[28 \quad -42]$
$[15 \quad 23]$	$\begin{bmatrix} -1 & 2 \\ 2 & -3 \end{bmatrix}$ =	$[31 \quad -39]$

The coded message is 21, -22, 17, -18, 28, -42, 31, -39. ■

For those who do not know the matrix A, decoding the crypto-gram in Example 4 is difficult. (When larger coding matrices are used, decoding is even more difficult.) But for an authorized receiver who knows the matrix A, decoding is simple. The receiver need only multiply the coded row matrices (on the right) by A^{-1} to retrieve the uncoded row matrices.

Problem Solving
Work Backward

Example 5 *Decoding a Message*

Use the inverse of $A = \begin{bmatrix} -1 & 2 \\ 2 & -3 \end{bmatrix}$ to decode the message

$$-9,\ 23,\ -6,\ 16,\ 26,\ -39,\ 13,\ -12,\ 45,\ -65.$$

Solution To decode the message, partition the message into groups of two numbers to form coded row matrices. Then multiply each coded row matrix by A^{-1} (on the right) to obtain the decoded row matrices.

Coded Row Matrix	Decoding Matrix A^{-1}		Decoded Row Matrix
$[-9 \quad 23]$	$\begin{bmatrix} 3 & 2 \\ 2 & 1 \end{bmatrix}$	$=$	$[19 \quad 5]$
$[-6 \quad 16]$	$\begin{bmatrix} 3 & 2 \\ 2 & 1 \end{bmatrix}$	$=$	$[14 \quad 4]$
$[26 \quad -39]$	$\begin{bmatrix} 3 & 2 \\ 2 & 1 \end{bmatrix}$	$=$	$[0 \quad 13]$
$[13 \quad -12]$	$\begin{bmatrix} 3 & 2 \\ 2 & 1 \end{bmatrix}$	$=$	$[15 \quad 14]$
$[45 \quad -65]$	$\begin{bmatrix} 3 & 2 \\ 2 & 1 \end{bmatrix}$	$=$	$[5 \quad 25]$

From the uncoded row matrices, read the message as follows.

$$[19 \quad 5] \quad [14 \quad 4] \quad [0 \quad 13] \quad [15 \quad 14] \quad [5 \quad 25]$$
$$\text{S} \quad \text{E} \quad \text{N} \quad \text{D} \quad - \quad \text{M} \quad \text{O} \quad \text{N} \quad \text{E} \quad \text{Y} \quad \blacksquare$$

Communicating about **ALGEBRA**

▷ **SHARING IDEAS about the Lesson**

Use the inverse of $\begin{bmatrix} 3 & -4 \\ -2 & 3 \end{bmatrix}$ to decode the message.

$$-4,\ 7,\ -23,\ 35,\ -26,\ 39,\ 15,\ -20,\ 31,\ -36,\ -38,\ 57,\ -21,$$
$$33,\ 20,\ -20,\ 75,\ -100$$

EXERCISES

Guided Practice

▶ **CRITICAL THINKING about the Lesson**

1. What is the multiplicative identity for 2×2 matrices? For 3×3 matrices?

2. For two 2×2 matrices, A and B, to be inverses of each other, what must be true of AB and BA?

3. Are A and B inverses of each other? Justify your answer.
$$A = \begin{bmatrix} 0 & -\frac{1}{2} \\ 2 & 5 \end{bmatrix} \quad \text{and} \quad B = \begin{bmatrix} 5 & \frac{1}{2} \\ -2 & 0 \end{bmatrix}$$

4. Find the inverse of matrix A below.
$$A = \begin{bmatrix} -4 & 3 \\ -3 & 2 \end{bmatrix}$$

5. Does $\begin{bmatrix} 6 & -3 \\ -2 & 1 \end{bmatrix}$ have an inverse? Explain.

6. How do you solve $\underbrace{\begin{bmatrix} 2 & 3 \\ 3 & 4 \end{bmatrix}}_{A} X = \underbrace{\begin{bmatrix} 1 & 3 \\ 2 & -1 \end{bmatrix}}_{B}$ for X?

Independent Practice

In Exercises 7 and 8, decide whether the matrices are inverses of each other.

7. $\begin{bmatrix} 3 & 2 \\ 7 & 5 \end{bmatrix}$ and $\begin{bmatrix} 5 & -2 \\ -7 & 3 \end{bmatrix}$

8. $\begin{bmatrix} 9 & -2 \\ 5 & -1 \end{bmatrix}$ and $\begin{bmatrix} -1 & 2 \\ -5 & 9 \end{bmatrix}$

In Exercises 9–16, find the inverse of the matrix.

9. $\begin{bmatrix} 7 & -4 \\ -5 & 3 \end{bmatrix}$

10. $\begin{bmatrix} 5 & 2 \\ 2 & 1 \end{bmatrix}$

11. $\begin{bmatrix} 8 & 17 \\ -1 & -2 \end{bmatrix}$

12. $\begin{bmatrix} -4 & -3 \\ 3 & 2 \end{bmatrix}$

13. $\begin{bmatrix} 6 & -2 \\ 7 & -2 \end{bmatrix}$

14. $\begin{bmatrix} 3 & 2 \\ 4 & 1 \end{bmatrix}$

15. $\begin{bmatrix} 11 & -5 \\ 3 & -1 \end{bmatrix}$

16. $\begin{bmatrix} 7 & 4 \\ 3 & 2 \end{bmatrix}$

In Exercises 17–22, solve the matrix equation.

17. $\begin{bmatrix} -5 & -13 \\ 2 & 5 \end{bmatrix} X = \begin{bmatrix} 3 & 1 \\ -4 & 0 \end{bmatrix}$

18. $\begin{bmatrix} 12 & 7 \\ 5 & 3 \end{bmatrix} X = \begin{bmatrix} 2 & -1 \\ 3 & 2 \end{bmatrix}$

19. $\begin{bmatrix} 2 & 4 \\ 0 & 1 \end{bmatrix} X = \begin{bmatrix} 4 & 0 & 6 \\ 3 & -1 & 5 \end{bmatrix}$

20. $\begin{bmatrix} -6 & -3 \\ 3 & 1 \end{bmatrix} X = \begin{bmatrix} 9 & 12 & 0 \\ -4 & 5 & -2 \end{bmatrix}$

21. $\begin{bmatrix} 4 & 7 \\ 1 & 2 \end{bmatrix} X + \begin{bmatrix} 2 & 7 \\ -3 & 4 \end{bmatrix} = \begin{bmatrix} 6 & 2 \\ -2 & 3 \end{bmatrix}$

22. $\begin{bmatrix} -7 & -9 \\ 4 & 5 \end{bmatrix} X + \begin{bmatrix} 3 & 4 \\ 4 & -3 \end{bmatrix} = \begin{bmatrix} 1 & 9 \\ 6 & -6 \end{bmatrix}$

In Exercises 23–26, decide whether the matrix has an inverse.

23. $\begin{bmatrix} 8 & 2 & 0 \\ 4 & 1 & -1 \\ 0 & 0 & 4 \end{bmatrix}$

24. $\begin{bmatrix} 2 & -1 & 2 \\ 1 & 0 & -1 \\ 3 & 2 & -1 \end{bmatrix}$

25. $\begin{bmatrix} 5 & 1 & 0 \\ 2 & 3 & -2 \\ 1 & 3 & 1 \end{bmatrix}$

26. $\begin{bmatrix} 4 & -2 & 0 \\ 0 & 2 & 0 \\ 5 & 1 & 3 \end{bmatrix}$

In Exercises 27–30, decide whether the matrices are inverses of each other.

27. $\begin{bmatrix} 0 & 2 & -1 \\ 5 & 2 & 3 \\ 7 & 3 & 4 \end{bmatrix}$ and $\begin{bmatrix} -1 & -11 & 8 \\ 1 & 7 & -5 \\ 1 & 14 & -10 \end{bmatrix}$ **28.** $\begin{bmatrix} 11 & 2 & -8 \\ 4 & 1 & -3 \\ -8 & -1 & 6 \end{bmatrix}$ and $\begin{bmatrix} 3 & -4 & 2 \\ 0 & 2 & 1 \\ 4 & -5 & 3 \end{bmatrix}$

29. $\begin{bmatrix} 1 & 3 & 1 \\ 1 & 2 & 2 \\ 1 & 0 & 3 \end{bmatrix}$ and $\begin{bmatrix} 6 & -9 & 4 \\ -1 & 2 & -1 \\ -2 & 2 & -1 \end{bmatrix}$ **30.** $\begin{bmatrix} 10 & 2 & -25 \\ 4 & 1 & -10 \\ -9 & -2 & 23 \end{bmatrix}$ and $\begin{bmatrix} 3 & 4 & 5 \\ -2 & 5 & 0 \\ 1 & 2 & 2 \end{bmatrix}$

In Exercises 31–34, use a graphing calculator to find the inverse of the matrix.

31. $\begin{bmatrix} -3 & 4 & 9 \\ 1 & 0 & 0 \\ 5 & 3 & 7 \end{bmatrix}$ **32.** $\begin{bmatrix} -7 & 0 & -6 \\ -4 & 1 & 3 \\ 11 & -3 & -10 \end{bmatrix}$ **33.** $\begin{bmatrix} -2 & 1 & -1 \\ 2 & 0 & 4 \\ 0 & 2 & 5 \end{bmatrix}$ **34.** $\begin{bmatrix} 2 & 1 & -2 \\ 5 & 3 & 0 \\ 4 & 3 & 8 \end{bmatrix}$

Encoding Messages **In Exercises 35–38, use the matrix to encode the message.**

35. $A = \begin{bmatrix} 1 & -2 \\ -1 & 3 \end{bmatrix}$, BREAK A LEG

36. $A = \begin{bmatrix} 1 & 2 \\ 1 & 3 \end{bmatrix}$, KNOCK ON WOOD

37. $A = \begin{bmatrix} 2 & 3 \\ 1 & 2 \end{bmatrix}$, GET WELL SOON

38. $A = \begin{bmatrix} 2 & -3 \\ -1 & 2 \end{bmatrix}$, COME TO DINNER

Decoding Messages **In Exercises 39–42, use the following information.**

Primitive humans were skilled at making tools and jewelry from stone, bones, wood, and ivory. Use the inverse of

$$\begin{bmatrix} 5 & 2 \\ 3 & 1 \end{bmatrix}$$

to decode each message. Then match the message with an artifact made by primitive people in Europe.   *(Source: U.S. News and World Report)*

39. 111, 40, 129, 48, 125, 50, 95, 37, 82, 32, 47, 16, 100, 40

40. 47, 16, 42, 15, 67, 24, 100, 40, 85, 33, 48, 17, 63, 25, 30, 11

41. 55, 19, 85, 33, 42, 14, 40, 15, 56, 20, 82, 29

42. 57, 21, 119, 46, 24, 8, 120, 45, 112, 41

a.   **b.**   **c.**   **d.**

Integrated Review

In Exercises 43–46, simplify the matrix.

43. $-4\begin{bmatrix} 3 & 6 & 4 \\ 9 & 4 & 3 \\ -2 & 1 & 2 \end{bmatrix}$

44. $\begin{bmatrix} 1 & 2 & 5 \\ 0 & 4 & 10 \\ -10 & 6 & 5 \end{bmatrix} - 2\begin{bmatrix} 4 & 3 & 1 \\ -1 & 1 & 7 \\ -5 & 6 & 4 \end{bmatrix}$

45. $\begin{bmatrix} 1 & 2 & 0 \\ 3 & 2 & -1 \\ -3 & -1 & 4 \end{bmatrix}\begin{bmatrix} 6 & 1 & -2 \\ 4 & 3 & 1 \\ 0 & 4 & -1 \end{bmatrix}$

46. $\begin{bmatrix} 1 & -3 & 4 \\ 0 & 2 & -2 \\ 3 & 1 & 4 \end{bmatrix}\begin{bmatrix} -1 & 3 & 2 \\ -2 & 1 & -1 \\ 0 & 4 & 2 \end{bmatrix}$

In Exercises 47–50, evaluate the determinant of the matrix.

47. $\begin{bmatrix} 10 & 15 \\ 1 & 4 \end{bmatrix}$

48. $\begin{bmatrix} -5 & -3 \\ 9 & 4 \end{bmatrix}$

49. $\begin{bmatrix} 9 & 0 & 10 \\ 0 & 4 & 3 \\ -1 & 2 & 1 \end{bmatrix}$

50. $\begin{bmatrix} 4 & 2 & 3 \\ -4 & 1 & 0 \\ 0 & 0 & 5 \end{bmatrix}$

Exploration and Extension

51. The inverse of $A = \begin{bmatrix} a & b & c \\ d & e & f \\ g & h & i \end{bmatrix}$ is $A^{-1} = \dfrac{1}{|A|}\begin{bmatrix} \begin{vmatrix} e & f \\ h & i \end{vmatrix} & -\begin{vmatrix} b & c \\ h & i \end{vmatrix} & \begin{vmatrix} b & c \\ e & f \end{vmatrix} \\ -\begin{vmatrix} d & f \\ g & i \end{vmatrix} & \begin{vmatrix} a & c \\ g & i \end{vmatrix} & -\begin{vmatrix} a & c \\ d & f \end{vmatrix} \\ \begin{vmatrix} d & e \\ g & h \end{vmatrix} & -\begin{vmatrix} a & b \\ g & h \end{vmatrix} & \begin{vmatrix} a & b \\ d & e \end{vmatrix} \end{bmatrix}.$

Use this formula to find the inverse of $\begin{bmatrix} 1 & 0 & -2 \\ 0 & 2 & 4 \\ 2 & 1 & -1 \end{bmatrix}$.

52. *City and Suburban Living*   The following matrix equation describes the population changes in a city and its suburbs between 1980 and 1990.

$$\underbrace{\begin{bmatrix} 0.8 & 0.1 \\ 0.2 & 0.9 \end{bmatrix}}_{A}\underbrace{\begin{bmatrix} x \\ y \end{bmatrix}}_{X} + \underbrace{\begin{bmatrix} 22{,}000 \\ 37{,}000 \end{bmatrix}}_{B} - \underbrace{\begin{bmatrix} 42{,}500 \\ 27{,}500 \end{bmatrix}}_{C} = \underbrace{\begin{bmatrix} 211{,}200 \\ 282{,}200 \end{bmatrix}}_{D} \begin{matrix} \longleftarrow \textit{City} \\ \longleftarrow \textit{Suburbs} \end{matrix}$$

The first row of each matrix refers to the city population, and the second row refers to the suburban population.

A: Transition matrix (shows population changes between city and suburb)
X: 1980 population matrix
B: New births and people who moved in from another area
C: Deaths and people who moved away to another area
D: 1990 population matrix

How many people lived in the city and its suburbs in 1980? Is the city losing population to the suburbs? Explain.

Take this test as you would take a test in class. The answers to the exercises are given in the back of the book.

In Exercises 1–6, perform the matrix operations. (4.1, 4.2)

1. $\begin{bmatrix} 2 & -3 & 5 \\ 0 & 2 & -2 \end{bmatrix} + \begin{bmatrix} 4 & 5 & 0 \\ -2 & -3 & 8 \end{bmatrix}$

2. $\begin{bmatrix} 5 & -2 \\ 4 & 1 \end{bmatrix} - \begin{bmatrix} 0 & -2 \\ 4 & -2 \end{bmatrix}$

3. $4\begin{bmatrix} 5 & -3 & 6 \\ 9 & -4 & 0 \\ -2 & 3 & 7 \end{bmatrix}$

4. $-\frac{1}{2}\begin{bmatrix} 4 \\ 6 \\ -8 \end{bmatrix} + 2\begin{bmatrix} -3 \\ 4 \\ 0 \end{bmatrix}$

5. $\begin{bmatrix} 2 & -1 & 3 \\ 2 & 4 & 0 \end{bmatrix}\begin{bmatrix} 1 & 0 \\ 9 & -3 \\ 2 & -5 \end{bmatrix}$

6. $\begin{bmatrix} 1 & 0 & 0 \\ 0 & 1 & 0 \\ 0 & 0 & 1 \end{bmatrix}\begin{bmatrix} -2 & 7 & 9 \\ 4 & -2 & -7 \\ 9 & 8 & 2 \end{bmatrix}$

7. Evaluate $\begin{vmatrix} 5 & 6 \\ -1 & 2 \end{vmatrix}$. **(4.3)**

8. Evaluate $\begin{vmatrix} -1 & 3 & 5 \\ 0 & 1 & 3 \\ -2 & 2 & 1 \end{vmatrix}$. **(4.3)**

9. Find the inverse of $\begin{bmatrix} -2 & 3 \\ -4 & 5 \end{bmatrix}$. **(4.4)**

10. Solve the equation. **(4.5)**

$$\begin{bmatrix} 2 & -3 \\ 3 & -4 \end{bmatrix}\begin{bmatrix} x \\ y \end{bmatrix} = \begin{bmatrix} -8 \\ -9 \end{bmatrix}$$

11. Which is the inverse of $\begin{vmatrix} 1 & 2 & 1 \\ 2 & 1 & 1 \\ 0 & 1 & 1 \end{vmatrix}$? **(4.4)**

$\begin{bmatrix} 0 & \frac{1}{2} & -\frac{1}{2} \\ 1 & -\frac{1}{2} & -\frac{1}{2} \\ 1 & \frac{1}{2} & \frac{3}{2} \end{bmatrix}$ or $\begin{bmatrix} 0 & \frac{1}{2} & -\frac{1}{2} \\ 1 & -\frac{1}{2} & -\frac{1}{2} \\ -1 & \frac{1}{2} & \frac{3}{2} \end{bmatrix}$

12. Find the area of the triangle. **(4.3)**

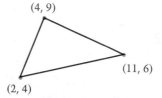

(4, 9)

(11, 6)

(2, 4)

13. A company has two stores. The incomes and expenses (in dollars) for the two stores for the first two quarters of the year are shown in the matrices. Write a matrix that shows each store's profit for the first six months of the year. **(4.1)**

1st Quarter	Income	Expenses
Store 1	400,000	280,000
Store 2	320,000	240,000

2nd Quarter	Income	Expenses
Store 1	420,000	320,000
Store 2	340,000	250,000

14. A company keeps three types of sweatshirts in stock at each of its two stores. Use matrix multiplication to find a matrix that gives the inventory value of the sweatshirts at each store. **(4.2)**

Inventory	Type A	Type B	Type C
Store 1	25	32	34
Store 2	15	24	16

Type	Price (in dollars)
Type A	14
Type B	16
Type C	18

4.5

Solving Systems Using Inverse Matrices

What you should learn:

Goal 1 How to solve systems of linear equations using inverse matrices

Goal 2 How to use systems of linear equations to solve real-life problems

Why you should learn it:

You can use matrices to solve real-life problems that can be modeled with systems of linear equations.

Goal 1 Solving Systems Using Matrices

A system of linear equations can be written as a *single* matrix equation. Here is an example.

Linear System

$$\begin{cases} 2x - 3y = 10 \\ -5x + 8y = -26 \end{cases}$$

Matrix Equation

$$\underbrace{\begin{bmatrix} 2 & -3 \\ -5 & 8 \end{bmatrix}}_{A} \underbrace{\begin{bmatrix} x \\ y \end{bmatrix}}_{X} = \underbrace{\begin{bmatrix} 10 \\ -26 \end{bmatrix}}_{B} \qquad AX = B$$

The matrix A is the **coefficient matrix** of the system. X is the **matrix of variables,** and B is the **matrix of constants.**

Solution of a Linear System

Let $AX = B$ represent a system of linear equations. If the determinant of A is nonzero, then the linear system has exactly one solution, which is given by $X = A^{-1}B$.

Example 1 *Using an Inverse Matrix to Solve a Linear System*

Use an inverse matrix to solve the linear system.

$$\begin{cases} 2x - 3y = 10 \\ -5x + 8y = -26 \end{cases}$$

Solution Begin by writing the equation in matrix form.

$$\begin{bmatrix} 2 & -3 \\ -5 & 8 \end{bmatrix} \begin{bmatrix} x \\ y \end{bmatrix} = \begin{bmatrix} 10 \\ -26 \end{bmatrix}$$

Then, find the inverse of the coefficient matrix A.

$$A^{-1} = \frac{1}{16 - 15} \begin{bmatrix} 8 & 3 \\ 5 & 2 \end{bmatrix} = \begin{bmatrix} 8 & 3 \\ 5 & 2 \end{bmatrix}$$

Finally, multiply the matrix of constants by A^{-1} (on the left) to obtain the solution.

$$X = A^{-1}B = \begin{bmatrix} 8 & 3 \\ 5 & 2 \end{bmatrix} \begin{bmatrix} 10 \\ -26 \end{bmatrix} = \begin{bmatrix} 2 \\ -2 \end{bmatrix} = \begin{bmatrix} x \\ y \end{bmatrix}$$

The solution of the system is $x = 2$ and $y = -2$. ■

Using an inverse matrix to solve a linear system *by hand* is not particularly efficient, especially with linear systems that have more than two variables. If, however, you have access to a calculator or computer that does matrix algebra, then using inverse matrices is quite efficient.

Connections
Technology

Example 2   ***Using a Graphing Calculator to Solve a Linear System***

Use a matrix equation and a graphing calculator to solve the linear system.

$$\begin{cases} 2x + 3y + z = -1 & \text{Equation 1} \\ 3x + 3y + z = 1 & \text{Equation 2} \\ 2x + 4y + z = -2 & \text{Equation 3} \end{cases}$$

Solution   The matrix equation that represents the system is

$$\begin{bmatrix} 2 & 3 & 1 \\ 3 & 3 & 1 \\ 2 & 4 & 1 \end{bmatrix} \begin{bmatrix} x \\ y \\ z \end{bmatrix} = \begin{bmatrix} -1 \\ 1 \\ -2 \end{bmatrix}.$$

Using a graphing calculator, you can find the inverse of the matrix A to be

$$A^{-1} = \begin{bmatrix} -1 & 1 & 0 \\ -1 & 0 & 1 \\ 6 & -2 & -3 \end{bmatrix}.$$

To find the solution, multiply B by A^{-1} (on the left).

$$X = A^{-1}B = \begin{bmatrix} -1 & 1 & 0 \\ -1 & 0 & 1 \\ 6 & -2 & -3 \end{bmatrix} \begin{bmatrix} -1 \\ 1 \\ -2 \end{bmatrix} = \begin{bmatrix} 2 \\ -1 \\ -2 \end{bmatrix} = \begin{bmatrix} x \\ y \\ z \end{bmatrix}$$

The solution is $x = 2$, $y = -1$, $z = -2$.   ∎

When you use a graphing calculator to solve the system of linear equations in Example 2, you don't have to display the matrix A^{-1} to find the solution. Simply enter the matrices A and B. Then, multiply B by A^{-1} to obtain the solution.

MATRIX[A] 3×3	MATRIX[B] 3×1	[A]⁻¹ [B]
[2 3 1]	[-1]	[[2]
[3 3 1]	[1]	[-1]
[2 4 1]	[-2]	[-2]]
Enter matrix A.	*Enter matrix B.*	*Multiply B by A⁻¹.*

When you use this method, remember that it only works if the matrix A has an inverse. If A does not have an inverse, then the system has either no solution or many solutions and you should use a different solution technique.

Real Life
Investment Strategy

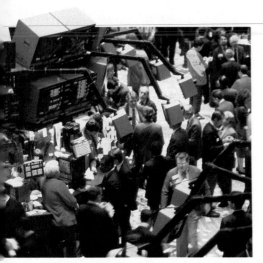

Investors in the stock market often try to keep a diversified portfolio of stocks. This means that they will own some stocks that they believe will pay high returns, and others that are likely to pay average or even below-average returns. Typically stocks that have the potential for higher returns also are a greater risk.

Example 3 ***Dividing an Investment among Three Stocks***

You have $30,000 to invest in the three stocks shown below. You want an average annual return of 9%. Because Stock X is a high-risk stock, you want the combined investment in Stock Y and Stock Z to be 4 times the amount invested in Stock X. How much should you invest in each type of stock?

Stock	Expected Return
Stock X	12%
Stock Y	9%
Stock Z	8%

Solution Let x, y, and z be the three investment amounts.

$$\begin{cases} x + y + z = 30{,}000 & \textit{Total investment: \$30,000} \\ 0.12x + 0.09y + 0.08z = 2{,}700 & \textit{Avg. return: 0.09(30,000)} \\ 4x - y - z = 0 & \textit{(y + z) is 4 times x.} \end{cases}$$

The coefficient matrix and matrix of constants are

$$A = \begin{bmatrix} 1 & 1 & 1 \\ 0.12 & 0.09 & 0.08 \\ 4 & -1 & -1 \end{bmatrix} \quad \text{and} \quad B = \begin{bmatrix} 30{,}000 \\ 2{,}700 \\ 0 \end{bmatrix}.$$

Using a graphing calculator, you can find the solution to be

$$X = A^{-1}B = \begin{bmatrix} 0.2 & 0 & 0.2 \\ -8.8 & 100 & -0.8 \\ 9.6 & -100 & 0.6 \end{bmatrix} \begin{bmatrix} 30{,}000 \\ 2{,}700 \\ 0 \end{bmatrix} = \begin{bmatrix} 6{,}000 \\ 6{,}000 \\ 18{,}000 \end{bmatrix}.$$

The solution is $x = \$6000$, $y = \$6000$, and $z = \$18{,}000$. ∎

Communicating about **ALGEBRA**

▶ **SHARING IDEAS about the Lesson**

Use an inverse matrix to solve each linear system. Solve the first by hand and use a graphing calculator to solve the second.

A. $\begin{cases} 5x + 2y = 21 \\ 4x + 3y = 35 \end{cases}$

B. $\begin{cases} x + 3y - 5z = -3 \\ x - 2y - z = 12 \\ x + 3y - z = 18 \end{cases}$

EXERCISES

▶ **CRITICAL THINKING about the Lesson**

1. Write the linear system $\begin{cases} 6x - y = 0 \\ x + 3y = 5 \end{cases}$ as a matrix equation.

2. Is $\begin{bmatrix} 28 \\ -10 \\ -7 \end{bmatrix}$ a solution of $\begin{bmatrix} 3 & 7 & 2 \\ -2 & -5 & -1 \\ 0 & 1 & -2 \end{bmatrix} \begin{bmatrix} x \\ y \\ z \end{bmatrix} = \begin{bmatrix} 0 \\ 1 \\ 4 \end{bmatrix}$? Explain.

3. If $|A| \neq 0$, what is the solution to $AX = B$?

4. Explain how to use an inverse matrix to solve $\begin{cases} -3x + y + 5z = 2 \\ x - z = 1. \\ 2y + 3z = 2 \end{cases}$

Independent Practice

In Exercises 5–10, write the linear system as a matrix equation.

5. $\begin{cases} 2x - 4y = 7 \\ -3x + y = 12 \end{cases}$

6. $\begin{cases} x + 9y = 20 \\ 2x - 4y = 15 \end{cases}$

7. $\begin{cases} 2x - 5y = 12 \\ x - 3y = -3 \end{cases}$

8. $\begin{cases} x - 2y + 3z = 14 \\ 2x + y - 2z = 16 \\ -3x - 5y + 9z = 36 \end{cases}$

9. $\begin{cases} 3x - y + 4z = 16 \\ 2x + 4y - z = 10 \\ x - y + 3z = 31 \end{cases}$

10. $\begin{cases} x + y - z = 0 \\ 2x -   z = 1 \\ y + z = 2 \end{cases}$

In Exercises 11–19, use an inverse matrix to solve the linear system.

11. $\begin{cases} 3x + y = 5 \\ 5x + 2y = 9 \end{cases}$

12. $\begin{cases} x + y = 2 \\ 7x + 8y = 21 \end{cases}$

13. $\begin{cases} 2x + 7y = -53 \\ x + 3y = -22 \end{cases}$

14. $\begin{cases} 8x + 5y = 38 \\ 3x + 2y = 14 \end{cases}$

15. $\begin{cases} -2x - 3y = -26 \\ 3x + 4y = 36 \end{cases}$

16. $\begin{cases} 5x - 7y = 54 \\ 2x - 4y = 30 \end{cases}$

17. $\begin{cases} x + 2y = -9 \\ -2x - 3y = 14 \end{cases}$

18. $\begin{cases} -5x + 3y = -52 \\ 3x + 2y = 32 \end{cases}$

19. $\begin{cases} 3x - 7y = -16 \\ -2x + 4y = 8 \end{cases}$

In Exercises 20–22, the inverse of the coefficient matrix is given. Use the inverse to solve the linear system.

20. $\begin{cases} -2x + y + z = 0 \\ x + 2z = 9 \\ x - 2y - 9z = -31 \end{cases}$

$A^{-1} = \begin{bmatrix} 4 & 7 & 2 \\ 11 & 17 & 5 \\ -2 & -3 & -1 \end{bmatrix}$

21. $\begin{cases} x + 9y + z = 20 \\ x + 10y - 2z = 18 \\ 3x + 27y + 2z = 58 \end{cases}$

$A^{-1} = \begin{bmatrix} -74 & -9 & 28 \\ 8 & 1 & -3 \\ 3 & 0 & -1 \end{bmatrix}$

22. $\begin{cases} 2x - 4y + 2z = 16 \\ -2x + 5y + 2z = -34 \\ x - 2y + 2z = 4 \end{cases}$

$A^{-1} = \begin{bmatrix} 7 & 2 & -9 \\ 3 & 1 & -4 \\ -\frac{1}{2} & 0 & 1 \end{bmatrix}$

23. $\begin{cases} 3x + 2y \phantom{{}+ z} = 13 \\ 3x + 2y + z = 13 \\ 2x + y + 3z = 9 \end{cases}$

24. $\begin{cases} -x + y - 3z = -4 \\ 3x - 2y + 8z = 14 \\ 2x - 2y + 5z = 7 \end{cases}$

25. $\begin{cases} 2x + 6y - 4z = 8 \\ -3x + 10y - 7z = 12 \\ -2x - 6y + 5z = -3 \end{cases}$

26. $\begin{cases} 2x \phantom{{}+ y} + z = 2 \\ 5x - y + z = 5 \\ -x + 2y + 2z = 0 \end{cases}$

27. $\begin{cases} 5x + 4y + z = 14 \\ 5x + 2y \phantom{{}+ z} = 3 \\ 2x + 5y + 2z = 24 \end{cases}$

28. $\begin{cases} x + y - 2z = 5 \\ -2x + z = 2 \\ -9x - 2y + z = -1 \end{cases}$

29. *Summer Olympics*   The 1996 Summer Olympics were held in Atlanta, Georgia. In 1991, the planned budget for the event was $1162 million. The budget contained three categories: operating expenses, e, facilities construction, c, and surplus, s. The amount allowed for operating expenses was the same as the total amount allowed for facilities construction and surplus combined. The budget committee estimated that 14% of the total budget would be surplus. Write a linear system that represents this information. Solve the linear system to find the amount of money budgeted for each category.

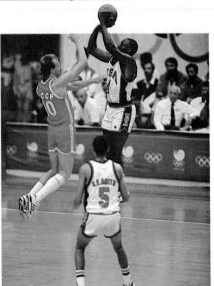

30. *Gross State Product*   The 1991 gross state product of Nebraska can be classified into: services, s, agricultural products, a, and industrial goods, i. The total gross state product was $35 billion. Services and agriculture made up sixth sevenths, and services produced five and one fifth times as much as industry. Write a linear system that represents this information. Solve the system to find the value of agricultural goods, industrial goods, and services in 1991.   *(Source: U.S. Bureau of Economic Analysis)*

31. *Stock Investment*   You have $20,000 to invest in three types of stocks. You expect the annual returns on Stock X, Stock Y, and Stock Z to be 12%, 10%, and 6%, respectively. You want the combined investment in Stock Y and Stock Z to be three times the amount invested in Stock X. How much should you invest in each type of stock to obtain an average return of 9%?

32. *Bowling*   In 1993, the total membership in the American Bowling Congress, Women's Bowling Congress, and Young American Bowling Alliance was about 5 million. The American Bowling Congress and Women's Bowling Congress membership made up 90% of the total. The Young American Bowling Alliance and the Women's Bowling Congress made up 54% of the total. What was the membership in each bowling organization?

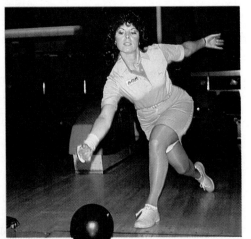

Integrated Review

In Exercises 33–36, solve the linear system by any convenient method.

33. $\begin{cases} 6x + 4y = 8 \\ 3x + 3y = 9 \end{cases}$ **34.** $\begin{cases} 4x - 2y = 0 \\ 2x - y = -1 \end{cases}$ **35.** $\begin{cases} x - 3y + z = 7 \\ y - z = 2 \\ x - 3y - z = 11 \end{cases}$ **36.** $\begin{cases} x + 3y + z = 1 \\ x + 5y + 2z = -1 \\ 2x + 6y + 3z = 2 \end{cases}$

In Exercises 37 and 38, solve the matrix equation.

37. $\begin{bmatrix} 0 & 1 \\ -1 & 4 \end{bmatrix} \begin{bmatrix} x \\ y \end{bmatrix} = \begin{bmatrix} 2 \\ 9 \end{bmatrix}$

38. $\begin{bmatrix} 5 & 4 \\ 4 & 3 \end{bmatrix} \begin{bmatrix} x \\ y \end{bmatrix} = \begin{bmatrix} 7 \\ 6 \end{bmatrix}$

Exploration and Extension

39. *Decoding a Message* Use the inverse of $A = \begin{bmatrix} 1 & 0 & 5 \\ 1 & 2 & 0 \\ 1 & 1 & 3 \end{bmatrix}$ to

decode the message: 37, 45, 80, 16, 12, 56, 35, 17, 138.

40. Solve the linear system, using the given inverse of the coefficient matrix.

$\begin{cases} x + 6y + 3z - 3w = 2 \\ 2x + 7y + z + 2w = 5 \\ x + 5y + 3z - 3w = 3 \\ -6y - 2z + 3w = 6 \end{cases}$ $A^{-1} = \begin{bmatrix} 40 & -3 & -33 & 9 \\ 1 & 0 & -1 & 0 \\ -39 & 3 & 33 & -8 \\ -24 & 2 & 20 & -5 \end{bmatrix}$

Mixed REVIEW

1. Solve $7x - 4 = -2x + 14$. **(1.3)**

2. Solve $\frac{1}{2}(-5x + 3) = \frac{3}{2}(-x + 2)$. **(1.3)**

3. Evaluate $y - 2z$ when $y = 1$ and $z = 2$. **(1.2)**

4. Find the slope of the line $3x - 4y = 9$. **(2.3)**

5. Simplify $\frac{4}{5}(25) - \frac{3}{5}(30) + \frac{2}{5}(45)$.

6. Write in decimal form: 3.56×10^{-2}.

7. Solve $3x + 4 \le 5x - 8$.

8. Evaluate $-3w^2 + 4w$ when $w = -2$. **(1.2)**

9. Sketch the graph of $y = -2x + 5$. **(2.1)**

10. Sketch the graph of $y \le \frac{1}{2}x - 2$. **(2.5)**

11. Sketch the graph of $|x - 3| \le 2$. **(2.6)**

12. Find the area of a circle of radius 4 feet.

13. Solve the system: $\begin{cases} 3x - 2y = 8 \\ -2x + 5y = 2 \end{cases}$ **(3.2)**

14. Solve the system: $\begin{cases} -x - 5y = 33 \\ 3x + 4y = -22 \end{cases}$ **(3.2)**

15. Add: $\begin{bmatrix} -2 & 5 & 3 \\ 0 & -3 & -4 \end{bmatrix} + \begin{bmatrix} -4 & -2 & -5 \\ 2 & -6 & 7 \end{bmatrix}$. **(4.1)**

16. Add: $\begin{bmatrix} -1 & 0 \\ 2 & -3 \end{bmatrix} + \begin{bmatrix} -2 & 4 \\ 1 & -7 \end{bmatrix}$. **(4.1)**

17. Multiply: $\begin{bmatrix} -9 & 4 \\ 7 & -3 \end{bmatrix} \begin{bmatrix} 3 & 4 \\ 7 & 9 \end{bmatrix}$. **(4.1)**

18. Multiply: $\begin{bmatrix} -8 & 4 \\ 4 & -2 \end{bmatrix} \begin{bmatrix} 1 & 2 \\ 2 & 4 \end{bmatrix}$. **(4.2)**

4.6 Solving Systems Using Augmented Matrices

What you should learn:

Goal 1 How to use an augmented matrix to solve a system of linear equations

Goal 2 How to use a system of linear equations to solve real-life problems

Why you should learn it:

Solving linear systems with augmented matrices is the preferred computer technique for systems of linear equations with many variables and equations.

Goal 1 Using an Augmented Matrix

A matrix derived from a system of linear equations is the **augmented matrix** of the system.

Linear System

$$\begin{cases} x - 4y + 3z = 5 \\ -x + 3y - z = -3 \\ 2x \quad\quad - 4z = 6 \end{cases}$$

Augmented Matrix

$$\begin{bmatrix} 1 & -4 & 3 & \vdots & 5 \\ -1 & 3 & -1 & \vdots & -3 \\ 2 & 0 & -4 & \vdots & 6 \end{bmatrix}$$

The first three columns of the augmented matrix show the coefficients of x, y, and z in the linear system. (Note the use of 0 for the missing y-variable in the third equation.) The fourth column in the augmented matrix shows the constant terms in the linear system.

Recall from Lesson 3.6 the three operations that can be used on a system of linear equations in order to produce an equivalent system:

1. Interchange two equations.
2. Multiply an equation by a nonzero constant.
3. Add a multiple of an equation to another equation.

In matrix terminology, these three operations correspond to **elementary row operations.** An elementary row operation on an augmented matrix of a given linear system produces a new augmented matrix corresponding to a new (but equivalent) linear system. Two matrices are **row-equivalent** if one can be obtained from the other by a sequence of elementary row operations.

> **Elementary Row Operations**
>
> Any of the following elementary row operations performed on an augmented matrix will produce a matrix that is row-equivalent to the original matrix.
>
> **1.** Interchange two rows.
> **2.** Multiply a row by a nonzero constant.
> **3.** Add a multiple of a row to another row.

In Lesson 3.6, you learned how to use elimination to solve a linear system—first write the system in triangular form, then use substitution to solve for each variable. With matrices, you use the same basic approach. One difference is that with matrices, you do not need to keep writing the variables.

Example 1 — *Using Elementary Row Operations to Solve a System*

Linear System

$$\begin{cases} x - 2y + 2z = 9 \\ -x + 3y = -4 \\ 2x - 5y + z = 10 \end{cases}$$

Augmented Matrix

$$\left[\begin{array}{ccc:c} 1 & -2 & 2 & 9 \\ -1 & 3 & 0 & -4 \\ 2 & -5 & 1 & 10 \end{array}\right]$$

Add the first equation to the second equation.

Add the first row to the second row $(R_1 + R_2)$.

$$\begin{cases} x - 2y + 2z = 9 \\ y + 2z = 5 \\ 2x - 5y + z = 10 \end{cases}$$

$R_1 + R_2 \longrightarrow \left[\begin{array}{ccc:c} 1 & -2 & 2 & 9 \\ 0 & 1 & 2 & 5 \\ 2 & -5 & 1 & 10 \end{array}\right]$

Add -2 times the first equation to the third equation.

Add -2 times the first row to the third row.

$$\begin{cases} x - 2y + 2z = 9 \\ y + 2z = 5 \\ -y - 3z = -8 \end{cases}$$

$-2R_1 + R_3 \longrightarrow \left[\begin{array}{ccc:c} 1 & -2 & 2 & 9 \\ 0 & 1 & 2 & 5 \\ 0 & -1 & -3 & -8 \end{array}\right]$

Add the second equation to the third equation.

Add the second row to the third row.

$$\begin{cases} x - 2y + 2z = 9 \\ y + 2z = 5 \\ -z = -3 \end{cases}$$

$R_2 + R_3 \longrightarrow \left[\begin{array}{ccc:c} 1 & -2 & 2 & 9 \\ 0 & 1 & 2 & 5 \\ 0 & 0 & -1 & -3 \end{array}\right]$

Multiply the third equation by -1.

Multiply the third row by -1.

$$\begin{cases} x - 2y + 2z = 9 \\ y + 2z = 5 \\ z = 3 \end{cases}$$

$-R_3 \longrightarrow \left[\begin{array}{ccc:c} 1 & -2 & 2 & 9 \\ 0 & 1 & 2 & 5 \\ 0 & 0 & 1 & 3 \end{array}\right]$

At this point, you can use substitution to find that the solution is $x = 1$, $y = -1$, and $z = 3$. ■

Although elementary row operations are simple to perform, they involve a lot of arithmetic. Because it is easy to make a mistake, we suggest that you get in the habit of noting the elementary row operations performed in each step so that you can go back and check your work. The notation we use to denote each elementary row operation is to write an abbreviated version of the row operation to the left of the *row that has been changed.*

Goal **2** Using Linear Systems in Real-Life Settings

Real Life
Metallurgy

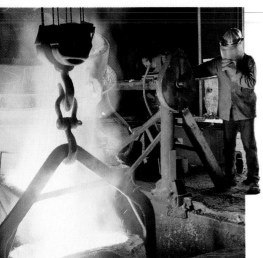

The properties of pure iron can be altered by adding other elements to form iron alloys. Elements that are often added are carbon, chromium, silicon, and nickel.

Example 2 *Solving a Mixture Problem*

Three iron *alloys* contain the following percents of carbon, chromium, and iron.

	Alloy X	Alloy Y	Alloy Z
Carbon	1%	1%	4%
Chromium	0%	15%	3%
Iron	99%	84%	93%

You have 15 tons of carbon, 39 tons of chromium, and 546 tons of iron. How much of each type of alloy can you make?

Solution   Let x, y, and z be the amount of each iron alloy. You can model the situation with the following linear system.

$$\begin{cases} 0.01x + 0.01y + 0.04z = 15 & \textit{Carbon} \\ \qquad\quad\; 0.15y + 0.03z = 39 & \textit{Chromium} \\ 0.99x + 0.84y + 0.93z = 546 & \textit{Iron} \end{cases}$$

The augmented matrix for this system is as follows.

$$\begin{bmatrix} 0.01 & 0.01 & 0.04 & \vdots & 15 \\ 0 & 0.15 & 0.03 & \vdots & 39 \\ 0.99 & 0.84 & 0.93 & \vdots & 546 \end{bmatrix}$$

After applying several elementary row operations, you obtain the following augmented matrix, which is in triangular form.

$$\begin{bmatrix} 1 & 1 & 4 & \vdots & 1500 \\ 0 & 1 & \frac{1}{5} & \vdots & 260 \\ 0 & 0 & 1 & \vdots & 300 \end{bmatrix} \longrightarrow \begin{cases} x + y + 4z = 1500 \\ \qquad y + \frac{1}{5}z = 260 \\ \qquad\qquad\; z = 300 \end{cases}$$

Using substitution, the solution is $x = 100$, $y = 200$, and $z = 300$. Thus, you can make 100 tons of Alloy X, 200 tons of Alloy Y, and 300 tons of Alloy Z. (Alloys X, Y, and Z are types of wrought iron, stainless steel, and cast iron, respectively.) ■

Communicating about **ALGEBRA**

▶ **SHARING IDEAS about the Lesson**

Use an augmented matrix to solve each linear system.

A. $\begin{cases} x - 3y = 5 \\ -2x - 4y = 20 \end{cases}$ **B.** $\begin{cases} x + y + 2z = 1 \\ 3x - y - z = 2 \\ 2x + 3y + 4z = 4 \end{cases}$

EXERCISES

▶ **CRITICAL THINKING about the Lesson**

1. Describe the three elementary row operations that can be performed on an augmented matrix.

2. What is meant by saying that two augmented matrices are row-equivalent?

3. Are the following augmented matrices row-equivalent? Justify your answer.

$$\begin{bmatrix} 1 & 2 & -2 & \vdots & 8 \\ -2 & -3 & 7 & \vdots & -2 \\ 1 & 2 & -1 & \vdots & 2 \end{bmatrix} \text{ and } \begin{bmatrix} 1 & 2 & -2 & \vdots & 8 \\ 0 & 1 & 3 & \vdots & 14 \\ 0 & 0 & 1 & \vdots & -6 \end{bmatrix}$$

4. What elementary row operation does $-3R_1 + R_3$ denote? Which row can it replace? Explain.

Independent Practice

In Exercises 5–7, write the augmented matrix for the linear system.

5. $\begin{cases} x + 3y - z = 16 \\ 4x - 6y = 9 \\ 2y - 3z = 12 \end{cases}$

6. $\begin{cases} -x - 3y + 2z = 8 \\ 2x + y - 3z = 9 \\ x - 3z = 10 \end{cases}$

7. $\begin{cases} 2x - y + 3z = 4 \\ -3x - z = 1 \\ x - 3y + z = 5 \end{cases}$

In Exercises 8–10, write the linear system that is represented by the augmented matrix. Then use substitution to solve the system.

8. $\begin{bmatrix} 1 & 1 & 2 & \vdots & -5 \\ 0 & 1 & 5 & \vdots & 2 \\ 0 & 0 & 1 & \vdots & 4 \end{bmatrix}$

9. $\begin{bmatrix} 1 & -6 & 4 & \vdots & 7 \\ 0 & 1 & -8 & \vdots & -2 \\ 0 & 0 & 1 & \vdots & 0 \end{bmatrix}$

10. $\begin{bmatrix} 1 & 2 & -2 & \vdots & 1 \\ 0 & 1 & -3 & \vdots & -8 \\ 0 & 0 & 1 & \vdots & 6 \end{bmatrix}$

In Exercises 11–19, use an augmented matrix to solve the linear system.

11. $\begin{cases} x + 3y + z = 3 \\ x + 5y + 5z = 1 \\ 2x + 6y + 3z = 8 \end{cases}$

12. $\begin{cases} 3x + 6y + 6z = 3 \\ x + 3y + 10z = -10 \\ x + 2y + 5z = -11 \end{cases}$

13. $\begin{cases} y - 5z = 15 \\ x + 2y - z = 7 \\ -3x - y + 2z = 10 \end{cases}$

14. $\begin{cases} 2x - 10y + 3z = -20 \\ x - 3y + 7z = 0 \\ x - 5y + z = -10 \end{cases}$

15. $\begin{cases} 2x + 4y + 5z = 5 \\ x + 3y + 3z = 2 \\ 2x + 4y + 4z = 2 \end{cases}$

16. $\begin{cases} x - y + 3z = 6 \\ x - 2y = 5 \\ 2x - 2y + 5z = 9 \end{cases}$

17. $\begin{cases} x + 2z = 4 \\ x + y + z = 6 \\ 3x + 3y + 4z = 28 \end{cases}$

18. $\begin{cases} -2x - 2y - 15z = 0 \\ x + 2y + 2z = 18 \\ 3x + 3y + 22z = 2 \end{cases}$

19. $\begin{cases} 2x + 10y = 28 \\ x + 3y + 4z = 22 \\ x + 5y - z = 10 \end{cases}$

20. *Brochure Mailing* An art gallery is mailing brochures to 1960 people to promote the gallery's annual exhibition. The envelopes were addressed by hand with calligraphy (decorative handwriting). You began addressing envelopes early. Later Rosa started, and finally Rafael started. Together you and Rafael addressed 1680 envelopes and together Rosa and Rafael addressed 840 envelopes. How many did each of you address?

21. *Toy Factory* You are working at a toy factory using two machines that can assemble plastic boats. You and two other employees, Jamie and Lan, take turns operating the machines. On Monday, Jamie and you operate the machines and produce 10,200 boats. On Tuesday, Jamie and Lan operate the machines and produce 10,100 boats. On Wednesday, Lan and you operate the machines and produce 9900 boats. The rates at which each of you work is the same each day. How many boats can each of you produce in a day?

22. *Dental Fillings* Dentists use mixtures of amalgam for silver fillings. The matrix shows the amounts of copper, mercury, and silver-tin that can be used to make two types of amalgam and one other mixture (which is not used in dental work). You have 320 grams of copper, 6140 grams of mercury, and 3540 grams of a silver-tin alloy. How much of each mixture can you make?

Percent by Weight	I	II	III
Copper	0.02	0.02	0.06
Mercury	0.46	0.48	0.94
Silver-Tin	0.52	0.50	0.00

Very pure gold is mixed with other metals such as silver and copper to make jewelry.

23. *Gold Alloys* Gold jewelry is seldom made of pure gold because pure gold is soft and expensive. Instead, gold is mixed with other metals to produce a harder, less expensive gold alloy. The amount of gold (by weight) in an alloy is measured in karats. Anything made of 24-karat gold is 100% gold. An 18-karat gold mixture is 75% gold, and so on. Three gold alloys contain the percents of gold, copper, and silver shown in the matrix. You have 20,144 grams of gold, 766 grams of copper, and 1990 grams of silver. How much of each alloy can you make?

Percent by Weight	Alloy X	Alloy Y	Alloy Z
Gold	94%	92%	80%
Copper	4%	2%	4%
Silver	2%	6%	16%

In Exercises 24–27, use substitution to solve the linear system.

24. $\begin{cases} x - y - 2z = 3 \\ 2y + 3z = 8 \\ z = 2 \end{cases}$

25. $\begin{cases} 2x + y + z = 10 \\ - y + 9z = 28 \\ z = 3 \end{cases}$

26. $\begin{cases} 2x - y - 3z = 16 \\ 3y + z = 8 \\ z = -7 \end{cases}$

27. $\begin{cases} 6x - 3y + 4z = -11 \\ 5y - z = 14 \\ z = 1 \end{cases}$

In Exercises 28–31, perform the operation on the linear system.

28. Add -4 times the first equation to the second equation.

$\begin{cases} x - 2y + z = 7 \\ 4x + 2y - z = 3 \\ x + y - 5z = 13 \end{cases}$

29. Interchange the first and third equations.

$\begin{cases} 2x + y + z = -3 \\ 3x - 2y + 4z = 9 \\ x + 2y - 2z = -13 \end{cases}$

30. Multiply the first equation by $-\frac{1}{3}$.

$\begin{cases} -3x + y - 2z = -11 \\ x - 3y + z = 5 \\ 2x + 2y - z = -2 \end{cases}$

31. Add 3 times the first equation to the second equation.

$\begin{cases} x - y + 2z = 10 \\ -3x + y - z = -11 \\ 2x - 2y + z = 11 \end{cases}$

In Exercises 32–35, check whether the values of *x*, *y*, and *z* form a solution of the linear system.

32. $x = 1$, $y = -3$, $z = 2$

$\begin{cases} x - y + 3z = 10 \\ 2x + y - 2z = -5 \\ -x + 2y + z = -5 \end{cases}$

33. $x = 5$, $y = 0$, $z = -2$

$\begin{cases} -x + 2y + z = -7 \\ 3x - y + 2z = 11 \\ 4x + y - 3z = 26 \end{cases}$

34. $x = 4$, $y = 9$, $z = -1$

$\begin{cases} 2x + y - 3z = 18 \\ 4x - 2y + z = -5 \\ x - 3y - z = -23 \end{cases}$

35. $x = -1$, $y = 4$, $z = 3$

$\begin{cases} -3x - y + 4z = 11 \\ 6x + y - z = -5 \\ x - 2y + 3z = 0 \end{cases}$

36. The solution of the system represented by the augmented matrix is $x = -20$, $y = 24$, and $z = -16$. What is the value of a?

$$\begin{bmatrix} 1 & 2 & 1 & \vdots & 12 \\ 1 & 3 & a & \vdots & 4 \\ 3 & 6 & 4 & \vdots & 20 \end{bmatrix}$$

37. Use an augmented matrix to solve the linear system.

$\begin{cases} a + 2b - 6c + d = 12 \\ -2a - 3b + 9c + d = -19 \\ a + 2b - 5c + 2d = 15 \\ 2a + 4b - 12c + 3d = 24 \end{cases}$

4.7

Solving Systems Using Cramer's Rule

What you should learn:

Goal 1 How to use Cramer's rule to solve a system of linear equations

Goal 2 How to use linear systems to solve real-life problems

Why you should learn it:

You can model many real-life problems with systems of linear equations, which can be solved using Cramer's rule.

Goal 1 Using Cramer's Rule

So far you have studied several methods for solving a linear system. In this lesson, you will learn one more method— called **Cramer's rule,** named after Gabriel Cramer (1704– 1752). This rule uses determinants to express the solution of a linear system. To see how Cramer's rule works, consider the following linear system.

$$\begin{cases} ax + by = c \\ dx + ey = f \end{cases}$$

If $ae - bd$ is not zero, the solution of the system is

$$x = \frac{ce - fb}{ae - db} \text{ and } y = \frac{af - dc}{ae - db}.$$

The denominator for x and y is the determinant of the *coefficient matrix* of the system. The numerators are the determinants of the matrices formed by using the column of constants as replacements for the coefficients of either x or y. A similar pattern gives the solution of a linear system with three equations and three variables.

Cramer's Rule

Consider a linear system whose coefficient matrix has a determinant D. If $D \neq 0$, then the system has exactly one solution.

1. The solution of $\begin{cases} ax + by = c \\ dx + ey = f \end{cases}$ is $x = \dfrac{\begin{vmatrix} c & b \\ f & e \end{vmatrix}}{\begin{vmatrix} a & b \\ d & e \end{vmatrix}}$ and $y = \dfrac{\begin{vmatrix} a & c \\ d & f \end{vmatrix}}{\begin{vmatrix} a & b \\ d & e \end{vmatrix}}.$

2. The solution of $\begin{cases} ax + by + cz = d \\ ex + fy + gz = h \\ ix + jy + kz = l \end{cases}$ is

$$x = \frac{\begin{vmatrix} d & b & c \\ h & f & g \\ l & j & k \end{vmatrix}}{\begin{vmatrix} a & b & c \\ e & f & g \\ i & j & k \end{vmatrix}}, \quad y = \frac{\begin{vmatrix} a & d & c \\ e & h & g \\ i & l & k \end{vmatrix}}{\begin{vmatrix} a & b & c \\ e & f & g \\ i & j & k \end{vmatrix}}, \text{ and } z = \frac{\begin{vmatrix} a & b & d \\ e & f & h \\ i & j & l \end{vmatrix}}{\begin{vmatrix} a & b & c \\ e & f & g \\ i & j & k \end{vmatrix}}.$$

Example 1 — Using Cramer's Rule for a 2 × 2 System

Solve using Cramer's rule: $\begin{cases} 4x - 2y = 10 \\ 3x - 5y = 11 \end{cases}$.

Solution The determinant of the coefficient matrix is:

$$\begin{vmatrix} 4 & -2 \\ 3 & -5 \end{vmatrix} = -20 - (-6) = -14.$$

Since this determinant is not 0, you can apply Cramer's rule.

$$x = \frac{\begin{vmatrix} 10 & -2 \\ 11 & -5 \end{vmatrix}}{-14} = \frac{(-50) - (-22)}{-14} = \frac{-28}{-14} = 2$$

$$y = \frac{\begin{vmatrix} 4 & 10 \\ 3 & 11 \end{vmatrix}}{-14} = \frac{44 - 30}{-14} = \frac{14}{-14} = -1$$

The solution is $x = 2$ and $y = -1$. Check this solution in the original system. ∎

Example 2 — Using Cramer's Rule for a 3 × 3 System

Use Cramer's rule to solve $\begin{cases} -x + 2y - 3z = 1 \\ 2x + \quad\ z = 0. \\ 3x - 4y + 4z = 2 \end{cases}$

Solution The determinant of the coefficient matrix is

$$\begin{vmatrix} -1 & 2 & -3 \\ 2 & 0 & 1 \\ 3 & -4 & 4 \end{vmatrix}\begin{matrix} -1 & 2 \\ 2 & 0 \\ 3 & -4 \end{matrix} = 0 + 6 + 24 - 0 - 4 - 16 = 10.$$

Since this determinant is not 0, you can apply Cramer's rule.

$$x = \frac{\begin{vmatrix} 1 & 2 & -3 \\ 0 & 0 & 1 \\ 2 & -4 & 4 \end{vmatrix}}{10} = \frac{8}{10} = \frac{4}{5}$$

$$y = \frac{\begin{vmatrix} -1 & 1 & -3 \\ 2 & 0 & 1 \\ 3 & 2 & 4 \end{vmatrix}}{10} = \frac{-15}{10} = -\frac{3}{2}$$

$$z = \frac{\begin{vmatrix} -1 & 2 & 1 \\ 2 & 0 & 0 \\ 3 & -4 & 2 \end{vmatrix}}{10} = \frac{-16}{10} = -\frac{8}{5}$$

The solution is $x = \frac{4}{5}$, $y = -\frac{3}{2}$, and $z = -\frac{8}{5}$. Check this solution in the original system. ∎

Goal 2 Using Linear Systems in Real Life

Real Life
Media Research

Example 3 *World Series and Super Bowl Viewers*

The total viewing audience of the 1990 World Series and Super Bowl XXV was 109.75 million. The total female viewing audience was about 47.38 million. Determine the number of viewers for each of these sporting events.

(Source: Nielsen Media Research)

Solution Let x be the number of people who watched the 1990 World Series, and let y be the number of people who watched Super Bowl XXV. From the bar graph, you can write the following system.

$$\begin{cases} 0.41x + 0.44y = 47.38 \\ 0.59x + 0.56y = 62.37 \end{cases}$$

Using Cramer's rule, the solution of the system is as follows.

$$x = \frac{\begin{vmatrix} 47.38 & 0.44 \\ 62.37 & 0.56 \end{vmatrix}}{\begin{vmatrix} 0.41 & 0.44 \\ 0.59 & 0.56 \end{vmatrix}} = \frac{26.5328 - 27.4428}{0.2296 - 0.2596} = \frac{-0.91}{-0.03} \approx 30.33$$

$$y = \frac{\begin{vmatrix} 0.41 & 47.38 \\ 0.59 & 62.37 \end{vmatrix}}{\begin{vmatrix} 0.41 & 0.44 \\ 0.59 & 0.56 \end{vmatrix}} = \frac{25.5717 - 27.9542}{0.2296 - 0.2596} = \frac{-2.3825}{-0.03} \approx 79.42$$

Therefore, approximately 30.33 million people watched the 1990 World Series, and approximately 79.42 million people watched Super Bowl XXV. ■

Communicating about ALGEBRA

▶ **SHARING IDEAS about the Lesson**

Use Cramer's rule to solve each linear system.

A. $\begin{cases} 4x - 3y = -2 \\ 2x - 9y = 19 \end{cases}$ **B.** $\begin{cases} x + 3y = -20 \\ 5x - y = 12 \end{cases}$

C. $\begin{cases} 2x - 3y + 3z = 0 \\ x + 2y - 3z = 5 \\ 4x - 5y - 6z = 5 \end{cases}$

EXERCISES

Guided Practice

▶ **CRITICAL THINKING about the Lesson**

1. To use Cramer's rule to solve a linear system, what must be true of the determinant of the coefficient matrix?

2. Complete the solution of $\begin{cases} x + 2y = 4 \\ 3x - y = 1 \end{cases}$. $x = \dfrac{\begin{vmatrix} \boxed{?} & 2 \\ \boxed{?} & -1 \end{vmatrix}}{\begin{vmatrix} 1 & 2 \\ 3 & -1 \end{vmatrix}}$ and $y = \dfrac{\begin{vmatrix} 1 & \boxed{?} \\ 3 & \boxed{?} \end{vmatrix}}{\begin{vmatrix} 1 & 2 \\ 3 & -1 \end{vmatrix}}$

3. Use Cramer's rule to solve $\begin{cases} 6x - 8y = 4 \\ 4x - 5y = -4 \end{cases}$.

4. Complete the solution of $\begin{cases} 10x - y + 3z = 3 \\ 4x + y - z = 1 \\ 5x + 3y + 2z = -1 \end{cases}$.

$x = \dfrac{\begin{vmatrix} \boxed{?} & -1 & 3 \\ \boxed{?} & 1 & -1 \\ \boxed{?} & 3 & 2 \end{vmatrix}}{\begin{vmatrix} 10 & -1 & 3 \\ 4 & 1 & -1 \\ -5 & 3 & 2 \end{vmatrix}}$, $y = \dfrac{\begin{vmatrix} 10 & \boxed{?} & 3 \\ 4 & \boxed{?} & -1 \\ 5 & \boxed{?} & 2 \end{vmatrix}}{\begin{vmatrix} 10 & -1 & 3 \\ 4 & 1 & -1 \\ 5 & 3 & 2 \end{vmatrix}}$, and $z = \dfrac{\begin{vmatrix} 10 & -1 & \boxed{?} \\ 4 & 1 & \boxed{?} \\ 5 & 3 & \boxed{?} \end{vmatrix}}{\begin{vmatrix} 10 & -1 & 3 \\ 4 & 1 & -1 \\ 5 & 3 & 2 \end{vmatrix}}$

Independent Practice

In Exercises 5–7, find the determinant of the coefficient matrix.

5. $\begin{cases} 4x + y = 19 \\ -3x + 3y = 10 \end{cases}$

6. $\begin{cases} 5x - 3y = 6 \\ 2x + 7y = 18 \end{cases}$

7. $\begin{cases} 3x + 4y + z = 17 \\ 2x + 3y + 2z = 15 \\ x + y = 4 \end{cases}$

In Exercises 8–13, use Cramer's rule to solve the linear system.

8. $\begin{cases} 2x + y = 12 \\ 5x + 3y = 27 \end{cases}$

9. $\begin{cases} x - 4y = 22 \\ 2x - 7y = 39 \end{cases}$

10. $\begin{cases} x + 4y = 12 \\ 2x + 5y = 18 \end{cases}$

11. $\begin{cases} 4x - y = -2 \\ -2x + y = 3 \end{cases}$

12. $\begin{cases} x - 2y = 11 \\ 2x + 5y = -14 \end{cases}$

13. $\begin{cases} 2x - 4y = 7 \\ -x + y = 1 \end{cases}$

In Exercises 14–16, use Cramer's rule to write the determinant form of the solution. (You do not need to evaluate the determinants.)

14. $\begin{cases} x - y + 10z = 2 \\ 3x + z = 4 \\ 7x + 2y + z = 0 \end{cases}$

15. $\begin{cases} 4x + 2z = 3 \\ -x + 2y + 5z = -1 \\ 3x + y - 7z = 10 \end{cases}$

16. $\begin{cases} 2x + 6y - z = 4 \\ 3x + y + 2z = -4 \\ 6x - y + 3z = 1 \end{cases}$

In Exercises 17–25, use Cramer's rule to solve the linear system.

17. $\begin{cases} x + 3y - z = 8 \\ 2x - y + 2z = 0 \\ -3x + y - 3z = -2 \end{cases}$

18. $\begin{cases} x + 2z = -3 \\ x - y + 2z = -4 \\ 2x - 3y + z = -3 \end{cases}$

19. $\begin{cases} x + 2y - 3z = -2 \\ x - y + z = -1 \\ 3x + 4y - 4z = 4 \end{cases}$

20. $\begin{cases} x + 3y - z = 1 \\ -2x - 6y + z = -3 \\ 3x + 5y - 2z = 4 \end{cases}$

21. $\begin{cases} 3x + 2y - 5z = -10 \\ 6x - z = 8 \\ -y + 3z = -2 \end{cases}$

22. $\begin{cases} x + 2y + z = 9 \\ x + y + z = 3 \\ 5x - 2z = -1 \end{cases}$

23. $\begin{cases} 2x - 2y + 5z = 1 \\ -8x + z = -6 \\ x + y - 2z = 1 \end{cases}$

24. $\begin{cases} 4x + y + 6z = -4 \\ 2x + 2y + 4z = 1 \\ -x - y + z = -5 \end{cases}$

25. $\begin{cases} x + y - z = 2 \\ 6x + 4y + 3z = 4 \\ 3x + 6z = -3 \end{cases}$

In Exercises 26–31, use any convenient method to solve the linear system. Explain why you chose the method.

26. $\begin{cases} 3x + y + z = 6 \\ x - 4y + 2z = -1 \\ x - 3y + z = 0 \end{cases}$

27. $\begin{cases} x - 2y + 3z = -2 \\ -x + 3y - z = 2 \\ 2x - y + 2z = 6 \end{cases}$

28. $\begin{cases} x - y + 2z = 6 \\ -2x + 3y - z = -7 \\ 3x + 2y + 2z = 5 \end{cases}$

29. $\begin{cases} 2x + y - 3z = 2 \\ x - 2y + 4z = 4 \\ 3x - y + 2z = 7 \end{cases}$

30. $\begin{cases} x + 6y + 4z = -1 \\ y + 2z = 5 \\ z = 2 \end{cases}$

31. $\begin{cases} x = 3 \\ 2x + y = 3 \\ 3x + 2y + z = 3 \end{cases}$

32. **Western Painter** Charles Russell (1864–1926) is one of America's best-known western painters and sculptors. A self-taught artist, he started painting when he was x years old. During the next y years before he died, he completed over 4500 works of art that depict the life of the early settlers and Native Americans in the American and Canadian west. Find the values of x and y by solving the following linear system. (Use Cramer's rule.) How many years had Russell been painting when he completed the painting at the right?

$$\begin{cases} x + y = \boxed{?} \\ 40x - 22y = 0 \end{cases}$$

Captain Meriwether Meeting the Shoshones
by Charles Russell, 1888.

33. **Camera Bugs** Americans take an average of about 41.6 million photographs each day. Of these, x are color photographs and y are black-and-white. The value of x is 31.2 million more than the value of y. What is the average number of color photographs taken each day? What is the average number of black-and-white photographs taken each day? Show how Cramer's rule can be used to answer the question. *(Source: Photo Marketing Association International)*

34. *Senators* Each state in the United States has two senators. In 1990, about 44 million Americans of voting age (voters and nonvoters) could name both senators from their state. About 41 million could name only one of their senators. Let x represent the number of Americans of voting age who were voters and let y represent the number who were nonvoters. Use the graph at the right to write a system of linear equations in x and y. Then use Cramer's rule to solve the system.

Can You Name Your Senators?

One Correct   Both Correct   Don't Know/Wrong

35. *Shoe Purchases* The graph shows the percents (by age group) of the total amounts spent on three types of shoes in 1988. For instance, 18% of the total amount spent on gym shoes was spent by the 14–17 age group, 10% was spent by the 18–24 age group, and 16% was spent by the 25–34 age group. In 1988, the amount (in millions of dollars) spent on *all three* types of shoes is shown in the matrix. How many dollars worth of gym shoes, jogging shoes, and walking shoes were sold in 1988?

Percent of Shoe Sales

Amount ($ millions)	Spent on Shoes
14–17	200.4
18–24	154.5
25–34	361.8

Integrated Review

In Exercises 36–39, evaluate the determinant of the matrix.

36. $\begin{bmatrix} 10 & 7 \\ 5 & 3 \end{bmatrix}$

37. $\begin{bmatrix} 4 & 2 \\ 1 & 4 \end{bmatrix}$

38. $\begin{bmatrix} 3 & -5 & 5 \\ 1 & 2 & -2 \\ 6 & 0 & 0 \end{bmatrix}$

39. $\begin{bmatrix} 2 & 1 & 0 \\ 4 & 6 & -1 \\ 5 & 4 & -2 \end{bmatrix}$

Top Spectator Sports In Exercises 40 and 41, use the following information.

In 1990, about 1240 sports fans were asked to choose their favorite sport to watch in person or on t.v. Of these fans, 35% said football, 16% said baseball, and 15% said basketball.

40. How many of the fans chose basketball?

41. How many of the fans chose football?

Exploration and Extension

42. Solve for x: $\begin{vmatrix} 11 & x \\ 7 & 6 \end{vmatrix} = 3$

43. Solve for x: $\begin{vmatrix} 5 & 7 \\ x & -6 \end{vmatrix} = -2$

Chapter Summary

What did you learn?

Skills

1. Perform matrix operations.
   - Add and subtract matrices. **(4.1)**
   - Multiply a matrix by a scalar. **(4.1)**
   - Multiply two matrices. **(4.2)**
2. Find the determinant of a square matrix. **(4.3)**
3. Find the inverse of a square matrix. **(4.4)**
4. Solve a linear system
   - using an inverse matrix. **(4.5)**
   - using an augmented matrix. **(4.6)**
   - using Cramer's rule. **(4.7)**

Strategies

5. Use matrices and determinants to model real-life situations. **(4.1–4.4)**
6. Use a system of linear equations to model a real-life situation. **(4.5–4.7)**

Exploring Data

7. Use matrices to organize data. **(4.1)**

Why did you learn it?

In this chapter, you studied two basic uses of matrices. One is to organize real-life data. Often matrices used for this can be added, subtracted, or multiplied by another matrix or a scalar to help answer questions about real-life situations.

The second basic use of matrices and determinants is to solve a linear system. In this chapter, you studied three ways of solving a linear system: using the inverse matrix, using an augmented matrix, and using Cramer's rule.

How does it fit into the bigger picture of algebra?

Two important uses of a matrix are to organize data and to solve a system of linear equations. You learned to use matrices in both of these ways in this chapter.

Just like real numbers, matrices can be added or multiplied. All matrices have opposites (so you can subtract), and some matrices have inverses. The rules for operating with matrices form part of *the algebra of matrices*. Some of the properties of this algebra are similar to the properties in the algebra of real numbers. Others, however, are not. For example, in Lesson 4.2, you saw that the product of two matrices depends on the order in which the two matrices are multiplied. In other words, matrix multiplication is *not* commutative.

In Exercises 1–8, perform the matrix operation(s). (4.1)

1. $\begin{bmatrix} 0 & 1 & -5 \\ 4 & 1 & 6 \end{bmatrix} + \begin{bmatrix} 10 & 3 & 11 \\ -2 & 8 & 3 \end{bmatrix}$

2. $\begin{bmatrix} 15 & 4 \\ 3 & 12 \end{bmatrix} - \begin{bmatrix} 0 & 9 \\ 2 & 7 \end{bmatrix}$

3. $\begin{bmatrix} 5 & 1 & 10 \\ -1 & 0 & 0 \\ 2 & 3 & 4 \end{bmatrix} - \begin{bmatrix} 6 & 7 & 3 \\ 0 & 14 & 6 \\ 1 & -1 & 2 \end{bmatrix}$

4. $\begin{bmatrix} 6 & 10 \\ 9 & 6 \\ 4 & -1 \end{bmatrix} + \begin{bmatrix} 2 & 1 \\ 0 & 7 \\ 4 & 7 \end{bmatrix}$

5. $3\begin{bmatrix} 4 & 6 & -1 \\ 10 & -5 & 2 \\ 2 & 11 & 1 \end{bmatrix}$

6. $8\begin{bmatrix} 3 & 2 & 0 & 1 \\ 5 & 3 & 3 & 6 \\ -9 & 4 & 2 & 0 \end{bmatrix}$

7. $-2\left(\begin{bmatrix} 6 & 4 \\ 0 & 3 \end{bmatrix} - \begin{bmatrix} 5 & 10 \\ 1 & 3 \end{bmatrix}\right)$

8. $-3\left(\begin{bmatrix} 4 & 7 \\ 1 & -2 \end{bmatrix} + \begin{bmatrix} 3 & -5 \\ 6 & 0 \end{bmatrix}\right)$

In Exercises 9–14, write the product as a single matrix. (4.2)

9. $\begin{bmatrix} 1 & 0 \\ 4 & 9 \end{bmatrix}\begin{bmatrix} -1 & 1 \\ 3 & 2 \end{bmatrix}$

10. $\begin{bmatrix} 2 & 15 \\ 3 & 10 \end{bmatrix}\begin{bmatrix} -5 & 12 \\ 1 & 0 \end{bmatrix}$

11. $\begin{bmatrix} 6 & 6 & 0 \\ 1 & -1 & 5 \end{bmatrix}\begin{bmatrix} -6 & 1 & 4 \\ 5 & -2 & 1 \\ 3 & -8 & 0 \end{bmatrix}$

12. $\begin{bmatrix} 4 & -1 & 3 \\ 7 & 10 & -3 \\ 1 & 2 & -5 \end{bmatrix}\begin{bmatrix} 0 & 1 \\ 9 & 2 \\ 12 & 0 \end{bmatrix}$

13. $\begin{bmatrix} 10 & 2 & 1 & 5 \end{bmatrix}\begin{bmatrix} 1 \\ 0 \\ -2 \\ 3 \end{bmatrix}$

14. $\begin{bmatrix} 6 & 2 & 1 & -3 \end{bmatrix}\begin{bmatrix} 0 \\ 5 \\ 4 \\ 3 \end{bmatrix}$

In Exercises 15–22, evaluate the determinant of the matrix. (4.3)

15. $\begin{bmatrix} 6 & -3 \\ 2 & 1 \end{bmatrix}$

16. $\begin{bmatrix} -2 & -6 \\ 1 & 4 \end{bmatrix}$

17. $\begin{bmatrix} 9 & 1 \\ -3 & 2 \end{bmatrix}$

18. $\begin{bmatrix} 4 & 1 \\ 0 & 6 \end{bmatrix}$

19. $\begin{bmatrix} 2 & 1 & 5 \\ -1 & 6 & 3 \\ 2 & -4 & 2 \end{bmatrix}$

20. $\begin{bmatrix} -3 & 1 & 0 \\ 2 & -1 & 1 \\ 0 & 3 & 4 \end{bmatrix}$

21. $\begin{bmatrix} 2 & -3 & 4 \\ 0 & 1 & -2 \\ 1 & 2 & -3 \end{bmatrix}$

22. $\begin{bmatrix} 3 & -2 & 1 \\ 4 & -2 & 1 \\ 0 & 3 & -2 \end{bmatrix}$

In Exercises 23 and 24, use a determinant to find the area of the triangle. (4.3)

23.

24.

In Exercises 25–30, find the inverse of the matrix. **(4.4)**

25. $\begin{bmatrix} 7 & 3 \\ 5 & 2 \end{bmatrix}$ **26.** $\begin{bmatrix} 2 & 3 \\ 7 & 11 \end{bmatrix}$ **27.** $\begin{bmatrix} 2 & 2 \\ 1 & 3 \end{bmatrix}$

28. $\begin{bmatrix} 2 & -2 \\ 4 & -3 \end{bmatrix}$ **29.** $\begin{bmatrix} 8 & -3 \\ 4 & -2 \end{bmatrix}$ **30.** $\begin{bmatrix} 6 & 10 \\ 2 & 4 \end{bmatrix}$

In Exercises 31 and 32, decide whether the matrices are inverses of each other. **(4.4)**

31. $\begin{bmatrix} 1 & -1 & -3 \\ 5 & 2 & 1 \\ -3 & -1 & 0 \end{bmatrix}, \begin{bmatrix} 1 & 3 & 5 \\ -3 & -9 & -16 \\ 1 & 4 & 7 \end{bmatrix}$ **32.** $\begin{bmatrix} -2 & 0 & -3 \\ -7 & 1 & -11 \\ -3 & 0 & -4 \end{bmatrix}, \begin{bmatrix} -4 & 0 & 3 \\ 5 & -1 & -1 \\ 3 & 0 & -2 \end{bmatrix}$

In Exercises 33–36, solve the matrix equation. **(4.5)**

33. $\begin{bmatrix} 3 & -1 \\ 5 & 2 \end{bmatrix}\begin{bmatrix} x \\ y \end{bmatrix} = \begin{bmatrix} -3 \\ 2 \end{bmatrix}$ **34.** $\begin{bmatrix} 5 & 6 \\ 4 & 5 \end{bmatrix}\begin{bmatrix} x \\ y \end{bmatrix} = \begin{bmatrix} 1 \\ -5 \end{bmatrix}$

35. $\begin{bmatrix} -1 & -1 \\ 4 & 2 \end{bmatrix}\begin{bmatrix} x \\ y \end{bmatrix} + \begin{bmatrix} -1 \\ 2 \end{bmatrix} = \begin{bmatrix} -5 \\ 0 \end{bmatrix}$ **36.** $\begin{bmatrix} 0 & 1 \\ 2 & 4 \end{bmatrix}\begin{bmatrix} x \\ y \end{bmatrix} - \begin{bmatrix} 10 \\ -3 \end{bmatrix} = \begin{bmatrix} -8 \\ 5 \end{bmatrix}$

In Exercises 37 and 38, use the matrix $\begin{bmatrix} 4 & 0 \\ -1 & 2 \end{bmatrix}$ to encode the message.

37. MAKE A WISH   **38.** SPECIAL DELIVERY

In Exercises 39 and 40, use the inverse of $\begin{bmatrix} 2 & -1 \\ 3 & -1 \end{bmatrix}$ to decode the message. **(4.5)**

39. 44, -15, 3, -1, 80, -32, 39, -17, 3, -1, 12, -4, 77, -26

40. 53, -24, 40, -18, 24, -8, 46, -17, 32, -16, 15, -7, 98, -39

In Exercises 41–43, use an inverse matrix to solve the linear system. (Use a graphing calculator for Exercises 42 and 43.) **(4.5)**

41. $\begin{cases} x - 3y = 10 \\ 2x + 5y = -2 \end{cases}$ **42.** $\begin{cases} x + 4y + 2z = 1 \\ -x + 5y + 2z = 3 \\ 4x + z = -5 \end{cases}$ **43.** $\begin{cases} -5x + 4y + 2z = 2 \\ y - 3z = -6 \\ -4x + 3y + 2z = 1 \end{cases}$

In Exercises 44–46, use an augmented matrix to solve the linear system. **(4.6)**

44. $\begin{cases} x - y - 5z = 1 \\ 2x - y - 6z = 2 \\ 2x - 2y - 9z = -1 \end{cases}$ **45.** $\begin{cases} x + 3y - 5z = 2 \\ x + 4y - 9z = 3 \\ 2x + 6y - 9z = 6 \end{cases}$ **46.** $\begin{cases} x - y - 4z = 3 \\ -x + 3y - z = -1 \\ x - y + 5z = 3 \end{cases}$

In Exercises 47–49, use Cramer's rule to solve the linear system. **(4.6)**

47. $\begin{cases} 2x - 3y = -17 \\ 3x + 4y = 0 \end{cases}$ **48.** $\begin{cases} x + 5y = -16 \\ 5x - 2y = -4 \end{cases}$ **49.** $\begin{cases} x + 2y + z = -2 \\ 2x - y - 3z = 1 \\ -3x + y - 2z = -7 \end{cases}$

50. *Rod Woodson*   In 1989, Rod Woodson led the National Football League on kick-off returns with 982 yards in 36 carries. Let x represent the total return yardages for Woodson during the first half of the 1989 season, and let y represent his total return yardages during the second half of the season. Use an inverse matrix to solve the following linear system for x and y.

$$\begin{cases} x + y = 982 \\ 3x - 2y = 461 \end{cases}$$

51. *Stock Investment*   You have $18,000 to invest in three types of stocks. You expect the annual returns on Stock X, Stock Y, and Stock Z to be 10%, 9%, and 6%. You want the combined investment in Stock Y and Stock Z to be twice the amount invested in Stock X. How much should you invest in each type of stock to obtain an average return of 8%?

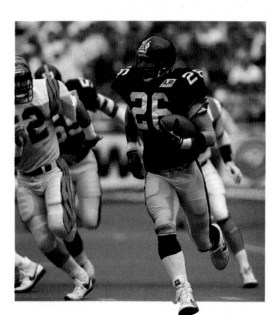

Rod Woodson

In Exercises 52 and 53, find the area of the blue region. (The area of the rectangle is 24 square units.)

52.

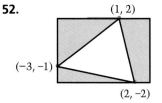

(1, 2)
(−3, −1)
(2, −2)

53.

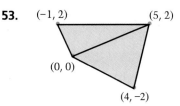

(−1, 2)   (5, 2)
(0, 0)
(4, −2)

54. *Summer Vacations*   More summer vacations were taken by Americans in 1991 than in 1988, but the vacations were shorter. The percents of vacations lasting 1 night, 2–3 nights, and 4 nights or more for the two summers are shown in the bar graph at the right. In 1988 and 1991 combined, a total of 53.9 million summer vacations lasted 1 night, and a total of 130.9 million lasted 2–3 nights. How many summer vacations were taken in 1988? In 1991?

(Source: U.S. Travel Data Center)

Flags of the World   **In Exercises 55–58, use the following information.**

Each of the following matrices contains the flags of nine countries.
Your goal is to match each country to its flag.

Matrix A

1. Indonesia
2. Chile
3. Norway
4. Iceland
5. Thailand
6. Netherlands
7. France
8. Denmark
9. Panama

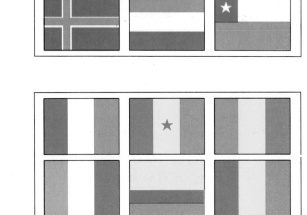

Matrix B

1. Ivory Coast
2. Italy
3. Senegal
4. Mali
5. Hungary
6. Chad
7. Colombia
8. Guinea
9. Cameroon

55. Solve the matrix equation

$$\begin{bmatrix} 1 & 1 & 2 \\ 3 & 1 & 0 \\ -2 & 0 & 3 \end{bmatrix}\begin{bmatrix} a & b & c \\ d & e & f \\ g & h & i \end{bmatrix} = \begin{bmatrix} 19 & 28 & 10 \\ 27 & 30 & 8 \\ -4 & 4 & 4 \end{bmatrix}.$$

56. Use the clues given by the solution of Exercise 55 to match the countries to the flags in Matrix A.

57. Solve the matrix equation

$$\begin{bmatrix} 1 & 1 & 2 \\ 3 & 1 & 0 \\ -2 & 0 & 3 \end{bmatrix}\begin{bmatrix} a & b & c \\ d & e & f \\ g & h & i \end{bmatrix} = \begin{bmatrix} 13 & 28 & 22 \\ 7 & 16 & 30 \\ 11 & 21 & -4 \end{bmatrix}.$$

58. Use the clues given by the solution of Exercise 57 to match the countries to the flags in Matrix B.

Chapter TEST

In Exercises 1–4, perform the matrix operation(s).

1. $2\left(\begin{bmatrix} 1 & 5 & -6 \\ 2 & 0 & 3 \end{bmatrix} - \begin{bmatrix} 6 & 2 & -1 \\ 9 & 9 & 5 \end{bmatrix}\right)$

2. $-2\left(\begin{bmatrix} 1 & 12 \\ -6 & -7 \end{bmatrix} + \begin{bmatrix} 4 & -8 \\ 2 & 4 \end{bmatrix}\right)$

3. $\begin{bmatrix} 3 & 1 & 0 \\ -1 & 9 & -4 \\ 2 & 3 & 0 \end{bmatrix}\begin{bmatrix} -1 \\ 4 \\ 2 \end{bmatrix}$

4. $\begin{bmatrix} 0 & 1 & 0 \\ 2 & -1 & 1 \\ 0 & 2 & -1 \end{bmatrix}\begin{bmatrix} -1 & 2 & 0 \\ 4 & 6 & 0 \\ 1 & 0 & 1 \end{bmatrix}$

In Exercises 5–7, evaluate the determinant of the matrix and find the inverse matrix.

5. $\begin{bmatrix} 7 & -2 \\ -3 & 4 \end{bmatrix}$

6. $\begin{bmatrix} -6 & 2 \\ 24 & -8 \end{bmatrix}$

7. $\begin{bmatrix} -2 & -1 \\ 1 & -1 \end{bmatrix}$

In Exercises 8–10, evaluate the determinant of the matrix. Which two of the three matrices are inverses of each other?

8. $\begin{bmatrix} 4 & 10 & -1 \\ 11 & 28 & -4 \\ -6 & -15 & 2 \end{bmatrix}$

9. $\begin{bmatrix} -4 & -5 & -12 \\ 2 & 2 & 5 \\ 3 & 0 & 2 \end{bmatrix}$

10. $\begin{bmatrix} -2 & -1 & 3 \\ -2 & 4 & 3 \\ 0 & 1 & -1 \end{bmatrix}$

In Exercises 11–16, use the indicated method to solve the linear system. (*Hint:* For Exercise 14, use the information from Exercises 8–10.)

11. Inverse Matrix
$\begin{cases} 3x + 2y = -8 \\ -2x + 5y = 18 \end{cases}$

12. Augmented Matrix
$\begin{cases} x - 3y = 17 \\ 9x + 6y = 21 \end{cases}$

13. Cramer's Rule
$\begin{cases} -4x + 5y = -10 \\ 5x - 6y = 13 \end{cases}$

14. Inverse Matrix
$\begin{cases} 4x + 10y - z = -3 \\ 11x + 28y - 4z = 1 \\ -6x - 15y + 2z = -1 \end{cases}$

15. Augmented Matrix
$\begin{cases} x + y - 2z = 4 \\ -2x - 3y + 4z = -2 \\ x + y - 3z = 5 \end{cases}$

16. Cramer's Rule
$\begin{cases} x + y = 2 \\ 2y - z = 0 \\ -x - y + z = -1 \end{cases}$

17. Use the inverse of $\begin{bmatrix} 4 & 3 \\ 1 & 1 \end{bmatrix}$ to decode the message.

61, 51, 96, 77, 19, 19, 29, 28, 14, 14, 60, 45

18. Write a 3×3 matrix that has no entries that are zero, but whose determinant is zero.

19. You have 296 ounces of tin, 271 ounces of lead, and 5 ounces of silver. How much of Alloy X, Alloy Y, and Alloy Z can you make?

Percents	Alloy X	Alloy Y	Alloy Z
Tin	20%	10%	80%
Lead	78%	88%	20%
Silver	2%	2%	0%

20. Find the area of the red triangle in the stained glass.

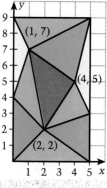

LESSONS

5.1 Solving Quadratic Equations by Finding Square Roots • 230

5.2 Parabolas: Graphs of Quadratic Equations • 236

5.3 Completing the Square • 245

5.4 The Quadratic Formula • 252

5.5 Complex Numbers • 258

5.6 Solving Any Quadratic Equation • 265

5.7 Graphs of Quadratic Inequalities • 271

The Brooklyn Bridge connects two boroughs of New York City: Manhattan and Brooklyn. Designed by the American engineer John Roebling, it was completed in 1883. At the time, the Brooklyn Bridge was the longest suspension bridge in the world.

Cables

Roadbed

200

100

−600 −400 −200 200 400 600

East River

The center span of the Brooklyn Bridge is 1595 feet long and is suspended from cables that are 16 inches in diameter. The towers rise 154 feet above the roadbed. The shape of the suspension cables can be represented by the *quadratic model*

$$y = 0.000243x^2$$

where x and y are measured in feet. In this model, the roadbed lies along the x-axis.

5.1

Solving Quadratic Equations by Finding Square Roots

What you should learn:

Goal 1 How to solve a quadratic equation by finding square roots

Goal 2 How to use quadratic equations as models of real-life situations

Why you should learn it:

You can model many real-life situations with quadratic equations, such as the height of an object as it falls.

Goal 1 Solving a Quadratic Equation

A **quadratic equation** in x is an equation that can be written in the **standard form**

$$ax^2 + bx + c = 0$$

where a, b, and c are real numbers ($a \neq 0$). The number a is the **leading coefficient.** In this lesson, you will solve quadratic equations of the form $ax^2 + c = 0$.

Recall from Algebra 1 that all positive real numbers have two square roots: the **positive square root** and the **negative square root.** Square roots are written with the **radical symbol** $\sqrt{}$. (The number inside a radical symbol is the **radicand**.)

Solving $x^2 = d$ by Finding Square Roots

1. If d is positive, then $x^2 = d$ has two solutions: $x = \pm\sqrt{d}$.

2. The equation $x^2 = 0$ has one solution: $x = 0$.

3. If d is negative, then $x^2 = d$ has no *real-number* solution.

(The case in which d is negative will be discussed in Lesson 5.5. There you will learn about solutions that are not real numbers.)

The symbol $\pm\sqrt{d}$ is read: "plus or minus the square root of d."

Example 1 *Solving Quadratic Equations*

Solve $3x^2 = 21$.

Solution

$3x^2 = 21$	*Rewrite original equation.*
$x^2 = 7$	*Divide both sides by 3.*
$x = \pm\sqrt{7}$	*Find square roots.*

The solutions are $\sqrt{7}$ and $-\sqrt{7}$. Check these in the original equation. To do that, you need to use the properties that $(\sqrt{d})(\sqrt{d}) = d$ and $(-\sqrt{d})(-\sqrt{d}) = d$. ∎

Connections
Physics

Problem Solving
Make a Table

This accident killed 14 people. The toll would have been greater, but it was a drizzly Saturday morning and most of the building's 15,000 office workers were at home.

Goal 2 Using Quadratic Equations in Real Life

When an object (with little air resistance) is dropped, its speed continually *increases*. The height, h (in feet), of such an object is given by the model

$$h = -16t^2 + s \qquad \textit{Falling-Object Model}$$

where s is the height from which the object was dropped and t is the number of seconds it has fallen. This model works on Earth, but not on planets with different gravity.

Example 2   *Finding the Time a Falling Object Takes*

At 9:55 A.M. on Saturday, July 28, 1945, a terrible airplane accident occurred. A B-25 bomber crashed into the 78th and 79th floors of the Empire State Building in New York City. Hundreds of pieces of debris fell 975 feet to the streets below. How much time after hearing the crash did the people on the street have to get out of the way?

Solution   Because the debris dropped from a height of 975 feet, the model for its height is $h = -16t^2 + 975$. The table gives the heights at different times in seconds.

Time, t	0	1	2	3	4	5	6	7	7.8
Height, h	975	959	911	831	719	575	399	191	2

From the table, you can see that the debris would take about 8 seconds to hit the ground. Because the sound of the crash would take about 1 second to reach the ground (sound travels at about 1100 feet per second), you can conclude that people had about 7 seconds to get out of the way of the falling debris.

Another way to determine how long it took the debris to hit the ground is to solve the quadratic equation for the time that gives a height of $h = 0$ feet.

$-16t^2 + 975 = h$	*Falling-object model*
$-16t^2 + 975 = 0$	*Substitute 0 for h.*
$975 = 16t^2$	*Add $16t^2$ to both sides.*
$\dfrac{975}{16} = t^2$	*Divide both sides by 16.*
$\sqrt{\dfrac{975}{16}} = t$	*Find the positive square root.*
$7.8 \approx t$	*Use a calculator.*

Since it took about 1 second to hear the crash, you can conclude that the people on the street had about 7 seconds to get out of the way. ■

5.1 ▪ *Solving Quadratic Equations by Finding Square Roots*   **231**

Real Life
Travel Plans

Example 3   *Using the Pythagorean Theorem*

You are in downtown Milwaukee and want to drive to Menomonee Falls. You are considering two options. You could drive 9 miles north on Interstate 43 and then 9 miles west on Brown Deer, *or* you could drive northwest on Fond du Lac Avenue. You can average 55 miles per hour on Interstate 43, then 40 miles per hour on Brown Deer, and 45 miles per hour on Fond du Lac. How much time would each route take?

Solution   The time it would take on I-43 and Brown Deer is:

$$\text{time} = \underbrace{\frac{9 \text{ miles}}{55 \text{ miles per hour}}}_{\text{Interstate 43}} + \underbrace{\frac{9 \text{ miles}}{40 \text{ miles per hour}}}_{\text{Brown Deer}}$$

$$\approx 0.164 + 0.225 = 0.389 \text{ hours} \approx 23 \text{ minutes.}$$

To find the distance, c (in miles), on Fond du Lac Avenue, use the Pythagorean Theorem.

$c^2 = a^2 + b^2$	*Pythagorean Theorem*
$c^2 = 9^2 + 9^2$	*Substitute 9 for a and 9 for b.*
$c^2 = 162$	*Simplify.*
$c = \sqrt{162}$	*Find positive square root.*
$c \approx 12.73 \text{ miles}$	*Use a calculator.*

The time it will take you on Fond du Lac Avenue is

$$\text{time} = \frac{12.73 \text{ miles}}{45 \text{ miles per hour}} \approx 0.28 \text{ hours} \approx 17 \text{ minutes.} \quad \blacksquare$$

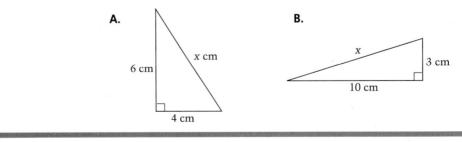

Communicating about **A L G E B R A**

▶ **SHARING IDEAS about the Lesson**

Use a Geometry Theorem   Use a radical to write the *exact* length of *x*. Then write approximate lengths correct to the nearest 0.01 cm.

A.

6 cm, x cm, 4 cm

B.

x, 3 cm, 10 cm

EXERCISES

Guided Practice

▶ **CRITICAL THINKING about the Lesson**

1. Write the quadratic equation $3 - 2x = -4x^2$ in standard form. What is its leading coefficient?

In Exercises 2–4, solve the equation. If the equation has no real-number solutions, explain why.

2. $2x^2 + 4 = 0$

3. $x^2 + 3 = 3$

4. $3x^2 = 12$

Independent Practice

In Exercises 5–16, solve the equation.

5. $2x^2 = 32$

6. $3x^2 = 27$

7. $\frac{1}{3}x^2 = 4$

8. $\frac{2}{3}x^2 = 6$

9. $4x^2 - 5 = 9$

10. $6x^2 + 3 = 16$

11. $-x^2 + 9 = 2x^2 - 6$

12. $-x^2 + 2 = x^2 + 1$

13. $3x^2 - 7 = 2(x^2 + 3)$

14. $\frac{1}{2}x^2 - 5 = 13$

15. $\frac{2}{3}x^2 + 6 = 18$

16. $\frac{1}{4}x^2 + 1 = 33$

In Exercises 17–22, solve the equation. Round the solutions to two decimal places.

17. $7x^2 + 4 = 12$

18. $x^2 - 7 = 3$

19. $3x^2 - 5 = 9$

20. $-\frac{1}{2}x^2 + 5 = 2$

21. $2x^2 + 3 = 10$

22. $5x^2 - 8 = 1$

23. *Geometry* The surface area of a cube is 326 square meters. How long is each edge?

24. *Geometry* The surface area of a sphere is 576π square inches. Find the radius.

$S = 4\pi r^2$

Geometry **In Exercises 25 and 26, use the Pythagorean Theorem to find x.**

25.

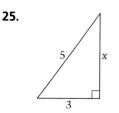

26.

Falling Object   **In Exercises 27 and 28, find the time it takes an object to hit the ground when it is dropped from a height of *s*.**

27. $s = 25$ feet

28. $s = 64$ feet

Falling on Mars   **In Exercises 29 and 30, use the following information.**

The height, h (in feet), of a falling object on Mars after t seconds is given by

$$h = -6t^2 + s.$$

29. Suppose one of the rocks scooped up by the Viking I space probe fell back to Mars' surface from a height of 72 feet. About how long would it take to reach the surface?

30. If the same rock was dropped from the same height on Earth, how long would it take to reach Earth's surface?

On July 20, 1976, the Viking I space probe landed on Mars and scooped up samples of rock. This photo shows Viking I orbiting Mars.

31. *Looking at the Horizon*   At sea, the distance, d (in miles), that you can see to the horizon depends on your height. If your eyes are h feet above sea level, then the approximate distance you can see to the horizon is given by

$$d^2 = \frac{3}{2}h.$$

Solve this equation for d. A 6-foot person is standing on the seashore. About how far out to sea can the person see?

32. *Period of a Pendulum*   The *period* of a pendulum is the time the pendulum takes to swing back and forth. The period, t (in seconds), of a pendulum of length d (in inches) is given by

$$d = 9.78t^2.$$

The longest pendulum in the world is part of a clock on a building in Tokyo, Japan. This pendulum is about 74 feet (888 inches) long. What is the period of this pendulum?
(Source: Guinness Book of World Records)

33. *PGA Prize Money*   From 1970 to 1990, the prize money, P (in dollars), at the Professional Golf Association Championship can be approximated by the model $P = 2875t^2 + 200,000$ where t is the year, with $t = 0$ corresponding to 1970. During which year was the prize money first over $1,350,000? **1976**
(Source: Professional Golf Association)

34. *Company Profit*   From 1980 to 1991, the profit, P (in dollars), of a company could be modeled by $P = 9400t^2 + 525,000$ where $t = 0$ represents 1980. According to this model, when would the company have a profit of $2,615,000?

35. Stair Steps Find the distance between the edges of two consecutive steps in the stairs shown below. Approximate the length of the handrail shown above the stairs.

36. Taking a Trip You are driving from Deerfield to Campbellsport in Ohio. Highway 14 is under construction, so you drive 5.5 miles north on Route 225, then 5.8 miles west on Interstate 76. How many miles longer is this route than taking Highway 14?

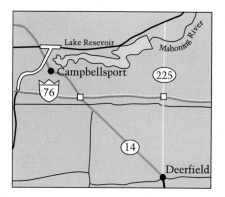

Integrated Review

In Exercises 37–42, evaluate the expression.

37. $3x^2 + 9x - 4$ when $x = 3$ **38.** $x^2 - 5x + 12$ when $x = 4$ **39.** $\sqrt{x} - 12$ when $x = 49$

40. $x - \sqrt{x} + 5$ when $x = 4$ **41.** $\frac{1}{2}x^2 - x + 1$ when $x = 1$ **42.** $-\frac{1}{3}x^2 + 6x - 1$ when $x = 12$

In Exercises 43–48, solve the equation.

43. $5x + 3 = 18$ **44.** $-x + 4 = 13$ **45.** $-\frac{1}{3}x - 7 = 1$

46. $\frac{1}{2}x - 5 = 17$ **47.** $-4x + 11 = -9$ **48.** $9x - 5 = 13$

49. Powers of Ten Which best estimates the weight of a house cat?
   a. 1.0×10^{-1} lb   **b.** 1.0×10^{0} lb   **c.** 1.0×10^{1} lb   **d.** 1.0×10^{2} lb

50. Powers of Ten Which best estimates the volume of an automobile fuel tank?
   a. 1.5×10^{0} gal   **b.** 1.5×10^{1} gal   **c.** 1.5×10^{2} gal   **d.** 1.5×10^{3} gal

---

Exploration and Extension

51. Complete the table and plot the points on a coordinate system.

x	−3	−1	0	1	3
$y = -x^2 + 1$	?	?	?	?	?

52. Use the graph to approximate the solutions of $-x^2 + 1 = -3$.

53. Confirm your results by solving the equation algebraically.

5.2

Parabolas: Graphs of Quadratic Equations

What you should learn:

Goal 1 How to graph a quadratic equation

Goal 2 How to use the graph of a quadratic equation in a real-life setting

Why you should learn it:

You can use the graph of a quadratic equation to model real-life shapes, such as the foundation of *Pueblo Bonita* in Chaco Canyon, New Mexico.

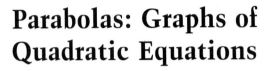

Goal 1 Graphing a Quadratic Equation

In this lesson, you will study the graphs of equations of the form

$$y = ax^2 + bx + c, \quad a \neq 0.$$

This equation is quadratic (second degree) in x and linear (first degree) in y. For simplicity, however, we will call the equation a **quadratic equation.**

The graph of a quadratic equation is U-shaped and is called a **parabola.** If the leading coefficient a is negative, the parabola opens *down.* If the leading coefficient is positive, the parabola opens *up.* On a parabola that opens up, the lowest point is the **vertex.** On a parabola that opens down, the highest point is the vertex. The vertical line passing through the vertex is the **axis of symmetry.** This line divides a parabola into two symmetrical parts, which are mirror images of each other. Here are two examples of quadratic equations.

$y = -x^2 + 9$	$y = x^2 - 2x + 1$
Leading coefficient: $a = -1$	Leading coefficient: $a = 1$
Parabola opens down.	Parabola opens up.
Vertex: $(0, 9)$	Vertex: $(1, 0)$
Axis of symmetry: $x = 0$	Axis of symmetry: $x = 1$

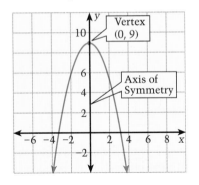

Graph of a Quadratic Equation

The graph of $y = ax^2 + bx + c$ is a parabola.

1. If a is positive, the parabola opens up. If a is negative, the parabola opens down.
2. The x-coordinate of the vertex is $-\frac{b}{2a}$.
3. The axis of symmetry is the vertical line $x = -\frac{b}{2a}$.

To sketch the graph of a quadratic equation, first find the x-coordinate of the vertex. Then construct a table of values, using x-values to the left and right of the vertex. Finally, plot the points and connect them with a U-shaped graph.

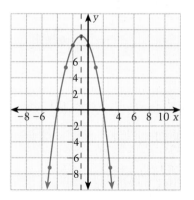

Example 1

Sketching the Graph of a Quadratic Equation

Sketch the graph of $y = -x^2 - 2x + 8$.

Solution In the standard form $ax^2 + bx + c$, the coefficients are $a = -1$, $b = -2$, and $c = 8$. The x-coordinate of the vertex is

$$-\frac{b}{2a} = -\frac{-2}{2(-1)} = -1. \quad \textit{x-coordinate of vertex}$$

Using x-values to the left and right of this x-value, construct a table of values.

				Vertex				

x	-5	-4	-3	-2	-1	0	1	2	3
y = -x² - 2x + 8	-7	0	5	8	9	8	5	0	-7

The vertex is $(-1, 9)$ and the axis of symmetry is $x = -1$. Plot the points given in the table and connect them with a parabola that opens down. ∎

The graph in Example 1 has x-intercepts at $(-4, 0)$ and $(2, 0)$. The y-intercept occurs at $(0, 8)$.

Example 2

Sketching the Graph of a Quadratic Equation

Sketch the graph of $y = x^2 - 4x - 5$.

Solution For this quadratic equation, $a = 1$, $b = -4$, and $c = -5$. The x-coordinate of the vertex is

$$-\frac{b}{2a} = -\frac{-4}{2(1)} = 2. \quad \textit{x-coordinate of vertex}$$

Using x-values to the left and right of this x-value, construct a table of values.

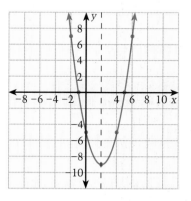

			Vertex			

x	-2	-1	0	2	4	5	6
y = x² - 4x - 5	7	0	-5	-9	-5	0	7

The vertex is $(2, -9)$ and the axis of symmetry is $x = 2$. Plot the points given in the table and connect them with a parabola that opens up. ∎

The graph in Example 2 has x-intercepts at $(-1, 0)$ and $(5, 0)$. The y-intercept occurs at $(0, -5)$. You can verify this from the graph.

The Anasazi Indians, ancestors of today's Pueblo Indians, built multistory buildings in Chaco Canyon, New Mexico. The largest of these "Great Houses" is Pueblo Bonito. The shape of its foundation is approximately parabolic, with a base (at the top of the photo) of about 500 feet and a height of about 300 feet.
(Source: Scientific American)

Goal 2 Using Quadratic Models in Real Life

Real Life
Archaeology

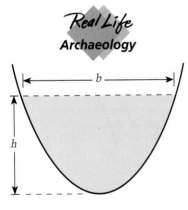

Example 3 *Finding the Area of a Parabolic Region*

The area of a region formed by a parabola (that opens up or down) and a horizontal line segment (the base) is

$$\text{area} = \tfrac{2}{3}bh$$

where b is the length of the base and h is the height. Use this formula to approximate the area of *Pueblo Bonito*.

Solution The area is given by

$$\text{area} = \tfrac{2}{3}(500)(300) = 100,000 \text{ square feet.} \quad \blacksquare$$

Communicating about **ALGEBRA**

▶ **SHARING IDEAS about the Lesson**

The parabola shown at the left is given by

$$y = 0.0048x^2 - 300.$$

A. Find the x-intercepts and y-intercepts of the parabola.

B. Find the area of the shaded region.

C. A drawing of *Pueblo Bonito* has been superimposed over the parabolic area. Do you think the approximation found in Example 3 is too large, too small, or just about right? Explain.

EXERCISES

▶ **CRITICAL THINKING about the Lesson**

1. Describe the graph of $y = ax^2 + bx + c$. What is the name of this type of graph?

2. Does the graph of $y = 3x^2 - x - 2$ open up or down? Explain.

3. Find the coordinates of the vertex of the parabola given by $y = -x^2 + 4x$. Explain your steps.

4. The table shows several x-values and y-values for a quadratic equation. Explain how you can use the table to find the x-intercepts and y-intercepts of the graph of the equation.

x	−2	−1	0	1	2	3	4
y	−8	−3	0	1	0	−3	−8

Independent Practice

In Exercises 5–10, decide whether the parabola opens up or down.

5. $y = -x^2 + 4x - 2$

6. $y = 2 - 10x^2$

7. $y = -6 + x^2 - 5x$

8. $y = 2x^2 - 5x - 6$

9. $y = -3x + 2 + 5x^2$

10. $y = 6 - x^2 + 7x$

In Exercises 11–16, find the vertex and axis of symmetry of the parabola.

11. $y = -2x^2 + 5x - 10$

12. $y = 3x^2 + 6x - 2$

13. $y = 4x^2 - 2x + 1$

14. $y = -x^2 - 2x - 3$

15. $y = 10x^2 - 20x - 15$

16. $y = 7x^2 + 2x - 10$

In Exercises 17–22, complete the table. Then use the table to find the x- and y-intercepts of the graph.

17. $y = -x^2 - 2x + 3$

x	−4	−3	−2	−1	0	1	2
y	?	?	?	?	?	?	?

18. $y = x^2 - 4$

x	−3	−2	−1	0	1	2	3
y	?	?	?	?	?	?	?

19. $y = 3x^2 - 12$

x	−3	−2	−1	0	1	2	3
y	?	?	?	?	?	?	?

20. $y = -x^2 - 10x - 24$

x	−6	−5	−4	−3	−2	−1	0
y	?	?	?	?	?	?	?

21. $y = x^2 - 8x + 12$

x	0	1	2	3	4	5	6	7
y	?	?	?	?	?	?	?	?

22. $y = -x^2 + 4x + 12$

x	−4	−2	0	2	4	6	8
y	?	?	?	?	?	?	?

In Exercises 23–28, match the equation with its graph.

23. $y = x^2 - 2$ **24.** $y = x^2 + 4x - 1$ **25.** $y = -x^2 - 4x - 3$

26. $y = x^2 + 2$ **27.** $y = -x^2 + 4x + 1$ **28.** $y = -x^2 + 2$

a.

b.

c.

d.

e.

f.
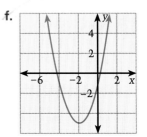

In Exercises 29–40, sketch the graph of the equation.

29. $y = x^2 - 2x + 6$ **30.** $y = x^2 + 8x + 16$ **31.** $y = -x^2 + 6x - 9$

32. $y = -x^2 - 2x - 3$ **33.** $y = x^2 + 14x + 45$ **34.** $y = x^2 - 4x + 7$

35. $y = -\frac{1}{4}x^2 + 4$ **36.** $y = \frac{1}{4}x^2 - 4$ **37.** $y = -\frac{1}{4}x^2 + x + 3$

38. $y = -\frac{1}{6}x^2 + 6$ **39.** $y = -\frac{1}{3}x^2 + 3$ **40.** $y = -\frac{1}{3}x^2 + 4x - 9$

41. *Area of Mongolia*   The map below shows the country of Mongolia. Each tic mark on the coordinate system represents 60 miles. Use the map to estimate the area of Mongolia. Explain your procedure.

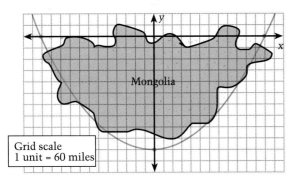

Grid scale
1 unit = 60 miles

42. *Area of a Lake*   The map below shows the tip of Lake Michigan superimposed on a coordinate system. Each tic mark represents about 12.5 miles. Use the map to estimate the area of the lake south of Milwaukee and Grand Haven. Explain.

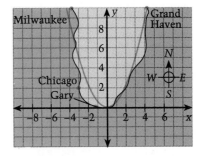

43. *Kicking a Football*   A football player kicked a 41-yard punt. The path of the ball was modeled by $y = -0.035x^2 + 1.4x + 1$, where x and y are measured in yards. What was the maximum height of the ball? The player kicked the football toward midfield from the 18 yard line. Over which yard line was the ball when it was at its maximum height?

Golden Gate Bridge   **In Exercises 44–46, use the following information.**

The shape of each suspension cable on the Golden Gate Bridge (in San Francisco) can be approximated by either of the models

$$y = \frac{1}{9000}x^2 + 5$$

or

$$y = \frac{1}{9000}(x - 2100)^2 + 5$$

where x and y are measured in feet. (The roadbed of the bridge lies on the x-axis.)

44. Sketch the graph of each model.

45. In each model, what are the coordinates of the lowest point on the cable?

46. The span between the two towers is 4200 feet. How high above the roadbed are the cables connected to the towers?

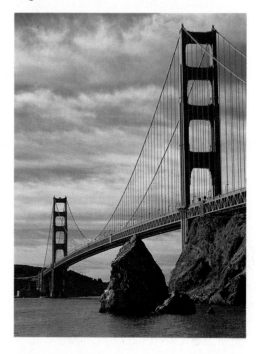

Integrated Review

In Exercises 47–52, sketch the graph.

47. $y = -2x + 3$

48. $y = 10x - 5$

49. $y = 5x - 7$

50. $y = -6x + 3$

51. $2x + 5y = 10$

52. $x - 2y = -8$

In Exercises 53–58, solve the equation.

53. $-3x^2 = -9$

54. $2x^2 + 5 = 9$

55. $6x^2 + 3 = 3$

56. $4x^2 = 0$

57. $\frac{1}{2}x^2 - 7 = 1$

58. $\frac{1}{7}x^2 - 2 = 5$

59. *College Entrance Exam Sample*   In a right triangle, the ratio of the legs is 1 to 2. The area of the triangle is 25 square units. What is the length of the hypotenuse?

a. $\sqrt{5}$ b. $5\sqrt{5}$ c. $5\sqrt{3}$ d. $10\sqrt{3}$ e. $25\sqrt{5}$

60. *College Entrance Exam Sample*   What is the total length of the line segments in the drawing at the right?

a. 10   b. $\sqrt{17} + \sqrt{6}$ c. $2(\sqrt{13} + \sqrt{5})$ d. $2(\sqrt{15} + \sqrt{7})$

Exploration and Extension

In Exercises 61 and 62, sketch the graphs of the two equations. Then find the area of the region that is bounded by the two graphs.

61. $y = 0$ and $y = x^2 - 9$

62. $y = 0$ and $y = -x^2 + 36$

You can use the zoom feature of a graphing calculator to approximate the solutions of an equation to any desired accuracy. The four graphs below show four steps in approximating the positive solution of

$$x^2 - 5 = 0.$$

Here, the approximation is $x \approx 2.237$. (The exact solution is $x = \sqrt{5}$.)
By repeated zooming, you can obtain whatever accuracy you need.

1.

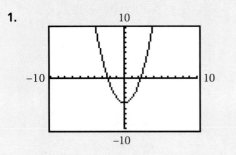

Sketch the graph of $y = x^2 - 5$.

2.

Zoom once and Trace to get a better view of the positive x-intercept. (The viewing rectangle will change automatically.)

3.

Zoom a second time and Trace to get an even better view. Use the cursor keys to determine that the x-intercept is about 2.24.

4.

Zoom a third time. Use the trace feature to find the y-value that is closest to 0. The corresponding x-value, which is 2.237, is your approximation.

Many equations can be solved by find the x-intercepts of a related equation in x and y. For instance, the above screens show how to solve the equation

$$x^2 - 5 = 0 \quad \textit{Equation in x}$$

by finding the x-intercepts of the graph of

$$y = x^2 - 5. \quad \textit{Equation in x and y}$$

You will encounter this technique again in Chapters 8, 10, and 14.

Example: Using a Graphing Calculator to Approximate a Solution

On the kite shown at the right, the length of $\overline{AB}$ is 39 inches. The combined length of $\overline{AC}$ and $\overline{CB}$ is 50 inches. How long are $\overline{AC}$ and $\overline{CB}$?

Solution   Let x represent the length of $\overline{CB}$. Because the combined length of $\overline{AC}$ and $\overline{CB}$ is 50 inches, it follows that the length of $\overline{AC}$ is $50 - x$. Using the Pythagorean Theorem, you can write the following equation.

$$x^2 + (50 - x)^2 = 39^2$$
$$x^2 + 2500 - 100x + x^2 = 1521$$
$$2x^2 - 100x + 979 = 0$$

To solve this equation with a graphing calculator, sketch the graph of $y = 2x^2 - 100x + 979$ and approximate the x-intercepts of the graph. Using the zoom feature as described on page 242, you can approximate the x-intercepts to be 13.36 and 36.64. Since $BC < AC$, the length of $\overline{CB}$ is approximately 13.36 inches, and the length of $\overline{AC}$ is approximately 36.64 inches. ■

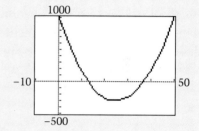

Exercises

In Exercises 1–8, use a graphing calculator to approximate the solutions of the equation to one decimal place.

1. $3x^2 - 5x - 7 = 0$

2. $-x^2 - 6x + 12 = 0$

3. $\frac{1}{2}x^2 + 12x + 5 = 0$

4. $\frac{4}{5}x^2 - 7x - 9 = 0$

5. $-0.3x^2 - 4.2x + 8.1 = 0$

6. $4.2x^2 + 5.6x + 1.3 = 0$

7. $15x^2 + 15.4x - 6.8 = 0$

8. $0.4x^2 + 1.2x - 3.2 = 0$

Geometry   **In Exercises 9 and 10, solve for x, as in the example.**

9.

10.

1. Simplify: $2(x^2 - x) - 3(2x - 7)$. **(1.2)**
2. Find the intercepts of $3x - 7y = 21$. **(2.3)**
3. Solve $|x - 7| < 3$. **(1.7)**
4. Solve $-3|x - 4| \leq -6$. **(1.7)**
5. What is 15% of 36?
6. Multiply: $\frac{2}{3} \cdot \frac{9}{16}$.
7. Find the slope of $3x - 4y = 2x - 10$. **(2.2)**
8. Solve $-3(x - 5) + (4x - 5) = 4x - 2$. **(1.3)**
9. Solve $(x + 3)^2 < 4$. **(1.6)**
10. Solve $|2x - 5| = 9$. **(1.7)**
11. Solve for y: $2xy + 3y = x$. **(1.5)**
12. Evaluate: $(3 \cdot 4 - 2) - (3^2 - 8)$. **(1.2)**
13. Sketch the graph of $-4 < x < 1$. **(1.6)**
14. Sketch the graph of $x < -2$ or $x > 3$. **(1.6)**
15. Solve $|x + 7| \leq 2$. **(1.7)**
16. Solve $\begin{cases} 2x - 3y = 20 \\ 5x + 2y = -7 \end{cases}$ **(3.2)**
17. Evaluate $3 \begin{bmatrix} 2 & 5 \\ -1 & 3 \end{bmatrix}$. **(4.1)**
18. Find the determinant of $\begin{bmatrix} 2 & 5 \\ -1 & 3 \end{bmatrix}$. **(4.3)**
19. What is the radius of a circle with a circumference of 24 inches?
20. An object dropped from 49 feet will hit the ground in how many seconds? **(5.1)**

Career Interview

Epidemiologist

Nancy Dreyer is an epidemiologist who specializes in studies relating to the causes of human diseases. "Part of my job is to use math and logic to determine the appropriate research needed to address specific concerns."

Q: *What math did you take in school?*
A: In high school, I took Algebra 1, Algebra 2, and Geometry. In graduate school, I took statistics courses; I especially remember biostatistics where I learned how to evaluate data and make comparisons using statistical tools, such as means and medians.

Q: *How do you use math on the job?*
A: I use math to calculate disease rates among different groups, and then apply rate ratios for comparisons. Or in drug related studies, I use math to describe the differences in side effects between groups.

Q: *How much mental math and estimation do you use?*
A: I use mental math and estimation all the time. You can't just assume that answers from computers are always correct. You have to check the accuracy of each answer. I use mental math and estimation to check myself, so I can find mistakes before anyone else does.

5.3 Completing the Square

What you should learn:

Goal 1 How to solve a quadratic equation by completing the square

Goal 2 How to use "completing the square" to solve real-life problems

Why you should learn it:

You can use quadratic equations to solve many real-life problems, such as finding the dimensions of some rectangles.

Goal 1 Solving by Completing the Square

In this lesson, you will solve quadratic equations by **completing the square.** Before doing that, however, let's look at some examples of *expanding a binomial* by squaring it.

Square of Binomial   Perfect-Square Trinomial

$$(x + 3)^2 = x^2 + 6x + 9$$
$$(x - 4)^2 = x^2 - 8x + 16$$

In each case, the constant term of the trinomial is the square of half of the coefficient of the trinomial's x-term.

Perfect-Square Trinomial   Square of Binomial

$$x^2 + bx + \left(\frac{b}{2}\right)^2 \qquad \left(x + \frac{b}{2}\right)^2$$

$$\underbrace{\qquad}_{(\text{half of } b)^2}$$

Thus, to make the expression $x^2 + bx$ a perfect square, you must add $\left(\frac{1}{2}b\right)^2$ to the expression.

When completing the square to solve a quadratic equation, remember that you *must preserve the equality.* When you add a constant to one side of the equation, be sure to add the same constant to the other side of the equation.

Example 1 Completing the Square: Leading Coefficient Is 1

Solve $x^2 - 4x + 2 = 0$ by completing the square.

Solution

$$x^2 - 4x + 2 = 0 \qquad \textit{Rewrite original equation.}$$

$$x^2 - 4x = -2 \qquad \textit{Subtract 2 from both sides.}$$

$$x^2 - 4x + (-2)^2 = -2 + 4 \qquad \textit{Add } (-2)^2 = 4 \textit{ to both sides.}$$

$$\underbrace{\qquad}_{(\text{half of } -4)^2}$$

$$(x - 2)^2 = 2 \qquad \textit{Binomial squared}$$

$$x - 2 = \pm\sqrt{2} \qquad \textit{Take square roots.}$$

$$x = 2 \pm \sqrt{2} \qquad \textit{Add 2 to both sides.}$$

The equation has two solutions: $2 + \sqrt{2}$ and $2 - \sqrt{2}$. ∎

If the leading coefficient of the quadratic is not 1, you should divide both sides of the equation by this coefficient *before* completing the square.

Example 2 *Completing the Square: Leading Coefficient Is Not 1*

Solve $4x^2 + 2x - 5 = 0$ by completing the square.

Solution

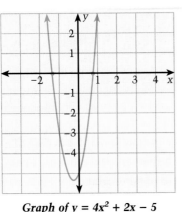

Graph of $y = 4x^2 + 2x - 5$

$$4x^2 + 2x - 5 = 0 \qquad \textit{Rewrite original equation.}$$

$$4x^2 + 2x = 5 \qquad \textit{Add 5 to both sides.}$$

$$x^2 + \frac{1}{2}x = \frac{5}{4} \qquad \textit{Divide both sides by 4.}$$

$$x^2 + \frac{1}{2}x + \left(\frac{1}{4}\right)^2 = \frac{5}{4} + \frac{1}{16} \qquad \textit{Add } \left(\frac{1}{4}\right)^2 = \frac{1}{16} \textit{ to both}$$
$$\underbrace{\qquad\qquad}_{\left(\text{half of } \frac{1}{2}\right)^2} \qquad \textit{sides.}$$

$$\left(x + \frac{1}{4}\right)^2 = \frac{21}{16} \qquad \textit{Binomial squared}$$

$$x + \frac{1}{4} = \pm\frac{\sqrt{21}}{4} \qquad \textit{Find square roots.}$$

$$x = -\frac{1}{4} \pm \frac{\sqrt{21}}{4} \qquad \textit{Solve for x.}$$

The equation has two solutions: $-\dfrac{1}{4} + \dfrac{\sqrt{21}}{4}$ and $-\dfrac{1}{4} - \dfrac{\sqrt{21}}{4}$.

■

Checking solutions that have fractions and square roots is cumbersome. A graphing check is usually more efficient. For instance, in Example 2, the solutions of $4x^2 + 2x - 5 = 0$ are

$$-\frac{1}{4} + \frac{\sqrt{21}}{4} \approx 0.9 \quad \text{and} \quad -\frac{1}{4} - \frac{\sqrt{21}}{4} \approx -1.4.$$

From the graph of $y = 4x^2 + 2x - 5$ at the left, you can see that the x-intercepts are about -1.4 and 0.9.

Connections

Technology

A graphing check is especially efficient with a graphing calculator. The graph below shows the display screen from a graphing calculator. Note that the scale on the x-axis has been set with tick marks that are 0.1 units apart.

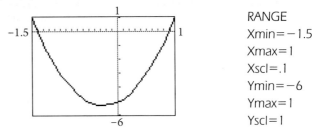

RANGE
Xmin=−1.5
Xmax=1
Xscl=.1
Ymin=−6
Ymax=1
Yscl=1

Goal 2 Using Completing-the-Square in Real Life

Real Life
Television

Example 3 *Finding the Dimensions of a Rectangle*

Television screens are usually measured by the length of the diagonal. The oversized television at the left has a 60-inch diagonal. The screen is 12 inches wider than it is high. Find the dimensions of the screen.

Solution Use the Pythagorean Theorem to write a model.

Verbal Model

Square of height	$+$	Square of width	$=$	Square of diagonal

Labels

Height $= x$ (inches)

Length $= x + 12$ (inches)

Diagonal $= 60$ (inches)

Equation

$$x^2 + (x + 12)^2 = 60^2 \qquad \textit{Pythagorean Theorem}$$

$$x^2 + x^2 + 24x + 144 = 3600 \qquad \textit{Expand the binomial.}$$

$$2x^2 + 24x = 3456 \qquad \textit{Subtract from both sides.}$$

$$x^2 + 12x = 1728 \qquad \textit{Divide both sides by 2.}$$

$$x^2 + \underbrace{12x + (6)^2}_{\text{(half of 12)}^2} = 1728 + 36 \qquad \textit{Add } 6^2 = 36 \textit{ to both sides.}$$

$$(x + 6)^2 = 1764 \qquad \textit{Binomial squared}$$

$$x + 6 = \pm 42 \qquad \textit{Find square roots.}$$

$$x = -6 \pm 42 \qquad \textit{Solve for x.}$$

$$x = 36 \text{ or } -48 \qquad \textit{Simplify.}$$

Choosing the positive solution, you can conclude that the height of the picture is 36 inches. The width of the picture is 48 inches (because it is 12 inches wider than it is high). ■

Communicating about **ALGEBRA**

▶ **SHARING IDEAS about the Lesson**

Solve the equation by completing the square. Explain your steps *and* use a graphic check.

A. $x^2 - 8x + 10 = 0$ **B.** $-2x^2 - 8x - 6 = 0$

EXERCISES

Guided Practice

▶ **CRITICAL THINKING about the Lesson**

1. Which of the following is a perfect-square trinomial? Explain.

    a. $x^2 - 4x + 4$ **b.** $x^2 - 6x + 6$

2. Write the perfect-square trinomial $x^2 - 8x + 16$ as the square of a binomial.

3. For the equations at the right, describe each step used to complete the square. What is the missing value in the *completed-square form?*

$$x^2 + 8x + 2 = 0$$
$$x^2 + 8x = -2$$
$$x^2 + 8x + (4)^2 = -2 + 16$$
$$(x + \boxed{?})^2 = 14$$

4. What term must be added to $x^2 - 10x$ to complete the square?

5. Write $2x^2 + 6x = 1$ in completed-square form. Explain your steps.

6. Describe two methods for checking the solutions of a quadratic equation.

Independent Practice

In Exercises 7–12, write the trinomial as the square of a binomial.

7. $x^2 - 2x + 1$ **8.** $x^2 + 24x + 144$ **9.** $x^2 + 14x + 49$

10. $x^2 + \frac{4}{3}x + \frac{4}{9}$ **11.** $x^2 - x + \frac{1}{4}$ **12.** $x^2 - 12x + 36$

In Exercises 13–18, solve the equation by completing the square.

13. $x^2 + 10x + 24 = 0$ **14.** $x^2 - 4x + 3 = 0$ **15.** $x^2 - 2x - 15 = 0$

16. $x^2 + 4x - 1 = 0$ **17.** $x^2 + 6x - 4 = 0$ **18.** $x^2 - 2x + 5 = 0$

In Exercises 19–24, solve the equation. Check your results graphically.

19. $2x^2 - 6x - 5 = 0$ **20.** $-3x^2 + 3x + 4 = 0$ **21.** $3x^2 + 9x + 1 = 0$

22. $2x^2 - 10x - 6 = 0$ **23.** $-5x^2 - 5x + 9 = 0$ **24.** $4x^2 - 16x - 10 = 0$

Geometry   **In Exercises 25 and 26, find the dimensions of the figure.**

25. Triangle Area = 12 cm^2 **26.** Rectangle Area = 160 ft^2

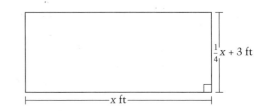

27. *Cutting across the Lawn* On the sidewalk, the walk from the high school to the junior high school is 400 meters. By cutting across the lawn, the walking distance is shortened to 300 meters. How long is each part of the L-shaped sidewalk?

28. *More Grass to Mow* Your home is built on a square lot. To add more space to your yard, you purchase an additional 4 feet along the side of the property. The area of the lot is now 9600 square feet. What are the dimensions of the new lot?

29. *Pulling a Boat into the Dock* A windlass is used to pull a boat to the dock. The rope is attached to the boat at a point 15 feet below the level of the windlass. Find the distance from the boat to the dock when the rope is 75 feet.

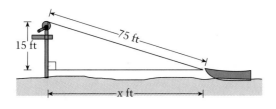

30. *Fencing in a Corral* You have 200 feet of fencing to enclose two adjacent rectangular corrals. The total area of the enclosed region is 1400 feet. What are the dimensions of each corral? (The corrals are the same size.)

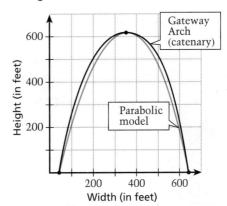

Gateway Arch **In Exercises 31 and 32, use the following information.**

The Gateway Arch in St. Louis, Missouri, was designed in the shape of a *catenary* (a ∪-shaped curve that resembles a parabola). The outer edge of the arch can be approximated by the equation

$$y = \frac{-2}{315}x^2 + \frac{92}{21}x - \frac{880}{7}$$

where x and y are measured in feet.

31. Find the x-intercepts of the graph. How wide is the arch?

32. How high is the arch? How does the parabolic model differ from the arch's actual shape?

In Exercises 33–38, expand the binomial.

33. $(x + 6)^2$

34. $(x - 1)^2$

35. $\left(x - \frac{1}{3}\right)^2$

36. $(x + 5)^2$

37. $(2x - 1)^2$

38. $(3x - 2)^2$

In Exercises 39–44, decide whether the numbers are solutions of the equation.

39. $x^2 + 8x + 16 = 0, -4$

40. $x^2 - 4x + 4 = 0, 2$

41. $x^2 - 6x + 9 = 0, -3$

42. $x^2 - 18x + 81 = 0, 9$

43. $x^2 - \frac{3}{2}x + \frac{9}{16} = 0, \frac{3}{2}$

44. $x^2 + \frac{2}{9}x + \frac{1}{81} = 0, \frac{1}{9}$

In Exercises 45–50, sketch the graph of the equation.

45. $y = x^2 - 4x + 8$

46. $y = x^2 - 6x + 14$

47. $y = -x^2 - 8x - 17$

48. $y = x^2 + 10x + 28$

49. $y = -x^2 - 2x + 2$

50. $y = x^2 - 14x + 47$

Exploration and Extension

Finding the Vertex of a Parabola   **In Exercises 51 and 52, use the following information.**

The equation $y = a(x - h)^2 + k$ is written in *completed-square form*. In this form, the coordinates of the vertex of the graph are (h, k). Completing the square can be used to write a quadratic equation in completed-square form. When you do this, you complete the square by *adding and subtracting* the same quantity. Here is an example.

$$y = x^2 - 6x + 11 \qquad \textit{Standard form}$$
$$y = [x^2 - 6x + (-3)^2] + 11 - (-3)^2 \quad \textit{Add and subtract } (-3)^2$$
$$\textit{from the right side.}$$
$$y = (x - 3)^2 + 2 \qquad \textit{Completed-square form}$$

51. Write $y = x^2 - 2x + 5$ in completed-square form. Then find the coordinates of the vertex of the graph.

52. Write $y = x^2 + 4x + 5$ in completed-square form. Then find the coordinates of the vertex of the graph.

In Exercises 53–55, match the equation with its graph.

53. $y = (x - 1)^2 + 3$

54. $y = (x - 1)^2$

55. $y = (x - 1)^2 - 3$

a.   **b.**   **c.**

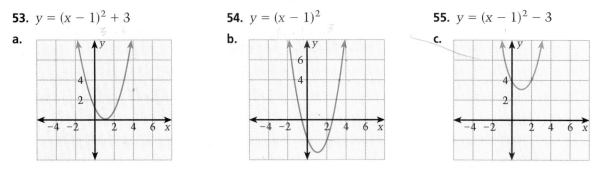

Take this test as you would take a test in class. The answers to the exercises are given in the back of the book.

In Exercises 1–3, solve the equation.   (5.1)

1. $4x^2 = 28$

2. $\frac{2}{5}x^2 = 6$

3. $x^2 - 2x + 3 = 8 - 2x$

In Exercises 4–6, solve the equation by completing the square.   (5.3)

4. $x^2 + 8x + 3 = 0$

5. $x^2 - 10x - 4 = 0$

6. $3x^2 + 4x - 1 = 0$

In Exercises 7–9, find the vertex and the axis of symmetry of the parabola.   (5.2, 5.3)

7. $y = 2x^2 - 4x + 3$

8. $y = 6x^2 + 3x$

9. $y = (x - 7)^2 + 5$

In Exercises 10–12, sketch the graph of the parabola.   (5.2, 5.3)

10. $y = x^2 + 4x + 7$

11. $y = (x + 2)^2 - 5$

12. $y = -\frac{1}{3}x^2 - 4x - 8$

13. What must be added to $x^2 + 8x$ to make the expression a perfect square trinomial?   **(5.3)**

14. Rewrite $y = x^2 + 12x + 29$ in completed square form.   **(5.3)**

15. The area of a circle is 20π square inches. To the nearest hundredth, what is the radius?   **(5.1)**

16. A skydiver jumps from a plane at an altitude of 7000 feet. What is the approximate altitude of the diver after 15 seconds of free fall?   **(5.1)**

17. A ladder is leaning against a building. The base of it is 6 feet from the base of the building, and the top of it touches the building at a point that is 21 feet above the ground. How long is the ladder?   **(5.1)**

18. The parabola $y = x^2 + 6x$ has x-intercepts at $(-6, 0)$ and $(0, 0)$. What is the area between the parabola and the x-axis?   **(5.2)**

19. The period, t (in seconds), of a pendulum is given by $d = 9.78t^2$, where d is the length of the pendulum in inches. A grandfather clock with a 60-inch pendulum is running fast. The clock is adjusted by lengthening the pendulum $\frac{1}{2}$ inch. To the nearest hundredth of a second, how much has the period changed?   **(5.1)**

20. When looking at the ocean, the distance, d (in miles), you can see to the horizon is given by $d^2 = \frac{3}{2}h$, where h is the height of the viewer (in feet above sea level). To the nearest mile, how far can a sailor see by climbing a 60 foot mast?   **(5.1)**

5.4 The Quadratic Formula

What you should learn:

Goal 1 How to use the quadratic formula to solve quadratic equations

Goal 2 How to use quadratic models in real-life settings

Why you should learn it:

You can use quadratic equations to model many real-life situations, such as the height of an object as it falls.

Goal 1 Using the Quadratic Formula

In Lesson 5.3, you solved quadratic equations by completing the square for *each problem.* However, completing the square *once* for the standard quadratic equation $ax^2 + bx + c = 0$ produces a formula for the solutions of any quadratic equation. The formula for the solutions is called the **quadratic formula.**

> **The Quadratic Formula**
>
> Let a, b, and c be real numbers such that $a \neq 0$. The solutions of the quadratic equation $ax^2 + bx + c = 0$ are
> $$x = \frac{-b \pm \sqrt{b^2 - 4ac}}{2a}.$$

Remember this formula: *The opposite of b, plus or minus the square root of b squared minus 4ac, all divided by 2a.*

Remember that *before* you can apply the quadratic formula, you must first write the equation in standard form, $ax^2 + bx + c = 0$.

Example 1 *Writing in Standard Form First*

Solve $3x^2 + 5x = 6$.

Solution

$$3x^2 + 5x = 6 \qquad \text{\textit{Rewrite original equation.}}$$

$$3x^2 + 5x - 6 = 0 \qquad \textit{a = 3, b = 5, c = -6}$$

$$x = \frac{-5 \pm \sqrt{5^2 - 4(3)(-6)}}{2(3)} \qquad \textit{Quadratic formula}$$

$$x = \frac{-5 \pm \sqrt{97}}{6} \qquad \textit{Simplify.}$$

The equation has two solutions.

$$x = \frac{-5 + \sqrt{97}}{6} \approx 0.81 \quad \text{and} \quad x = \frac{-5 - \sqrt{97}}{6} \approx -2.47$$

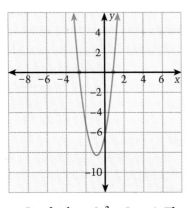

Graph of $y = 3x^2 + 5x - 6$. The x-intercepts are approximately 0.81 and −2.47.

The expression $b^2 - 4ac$ under the radical in the quadratic formula is the **discriminant** of $ax^2 + bx + c$.

$$\boxed{Discriminant}$$

$$x = \frac{-b \pm \sqrt{b^2 - 4ac}}{2a} \quad \textit{Quadratic formula}$$

The discriminant of a quadratic equation indicates how many real-number solutions the equation has.

The Number of Real-Number Solutions of a Quadratic Equation

Consider the quadratic equation $ax^2 + bx + c = 0$.

1. If $b^2 - 4ac$ is positive, then the equation has two solutions.
2. If $b^2 - 4ac$ is zero, then the equation has one solution.
3. If $b^2 - 4ac$ is negative, then the equation has no *real-number* solution. (The equation does have two solutions that are not real numbers. You will study this case in Lesson 5.6.)

Example 2 *Finding the Number of Solutions*

$ax^2 + bx + c = 0$	Discriminant $b^2 - 4ac$	Number of Real-Number Solutions
a. $x^2 - 4x + 5 = 0$	$(-4)^2 - 4(1)(5) = -4$	None
b. $x^2 - 4x + 4 = 0$	$(-4)^2 - 4(1)(4) = 0$	One
c. $x^2 - 4x + 3 = 0$	$(-4)^2 - 4(1)(3) = 4$	Two

Using the quadratic formula, the solution to Part **b** is
$$x = \frac{4 \pm \sqrt{(-4)^2 - 4(1)(4)}}{2(1)} = \frac{4 \pm 0}{2} = 2.$$
Similarly, you can use the quadratic formula to find the solutions in Part **c** to be 1 and 3. ∎

In Example 2, note that the number of solutions can be changed by just changing the value of c. A graph can help you see why this occurs. By changing the value of c, you can move the graph of $y = x^2 - 4x + c$ up or down in the coordinate plane. If the graph is moved too high, it won't have an x-intercept and the equation $x^2 - 4x + c = 0$ won't have a real-number solution.

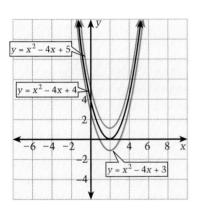

$y = x^2 - 4x + 5$ *Graph above x-axis (no x-intercepts)*

$y = x^2 - 4x + 4$ *Graph touches x-axis (one x-intercept)*

$y = x^2 - 4x + 3$ *Graph crosses x-axis (two x-intercepts)*

Goal **2** Using Quadratic Models in Real Life

In Lesson 5.1, you studied the model for the height (in feet) of a falling object that is *dropped*. For an object that is *thrown* down or up, the model needs an extra term. Problems that use either of these models are **vertical motion** problems.

Vertical Motion Models

$h = -16t^2 + s$ Height after object is *dropped*

$h = -16t^2 + vt + s$ Height after object is *thrown*

Labels
h = height   (feet)
t = time in motion   (seconds)
s = initial height (when $t = 0$)   (feet)
v = initial velocity (when $t = 0$)   (feet per second)

Be sure you understand that v is the velocity, not the speed. Velocity can be positive (moving up), negative (moving down), or zero (not moving). Speed is the absolute value of velocity.

Baton Tossing

Example **3** *Vertical Motion Problem*

When the baton twirler releases the baton into the air, the twirler's hand is 5 feet above the ground. The twirler will catch the baton when it falls back to a height of 6 feet. How many seconds is the baton in the air?

Solution   When the baton is thrown up, its initial velocity is $v = 30$ feet per second. The initial height is $s = 5$ feet. The twirler will catch the baton when the height is 6 feet.

$$h = -16t^2 + 30t + 5 \quad \textit{Vertical motion model}$$

$$6 = -16t^2 + 30t + 5 \quad \textit{Substitute 6 for h.}$$

$$16t^2 - 30t + 1 = 0 \quad \textit{a = 16, b = -30, c = 1}$$

$$t = \frac{30 \pm \sqrt{836}}{32} \quad \textit{Quadratic formula}$$

$$t \approx 1.84 \text{ or } 0.03$$

Thus the twirler has less than 2 seconds to catch the baton. ∎

When the baton twirler tosses the baton into the air, its initial velocity is 30 feet per second.

Communicating about **ALGEBRA**

▶ **SHARING IDEAS about the Lesson**

A. Find values of c so that the equation $x^2 - 8x + c = 0$ will have no solution, one solution, and two solutions.

B. Give a graphical interpretation of your Part A answers.

EXERCISES

Guided Practice

▶ **CRITICAL THINKING about the Lesson**

1. State the quadratic formula *in words*.

2. What is the discriminant of $ax^2 + bx + c = 0$? How is the discriminant related to the number of solutions of $ax^2 + bx + c = 0$?

3. What are the missing numbers in the solutions of the equation? How many solutions does the equation have? Explain your answer.

$$2x^2 + 10x - 5 = 0 \quad x = \frac{\boxed{?} \pm \sqrt{100 - 4\boxed{?} \cdot \boxed{?}}}{4}$$

4. Compare the two vertical motion models, $h = -16t^2 + s$ and $h = -16t^2 + vt + s$.

Independent Practice

In Exercises 5–8, write the equation in standard form.

5. $5 - 3x^2 = 7x + x^2$

6. $4x^2 - 10 = -13x - 7x$

7. $12x + 1 = 6 - 30x^2$

8. $2x^2 + x - 3 = 4x^2 - 5$

In Exercises 9–14, state the discriminant of the quadratic equation.

9. $3x^2 - 8x + 12 = 0$

10. $6x^2 + 9x - 4 = 0$

11. $15x^2 - 10x + 1 = 0$

12. $4x^2 + x - 20 = 0$

13. $3x^2 - 6x + 3 = 0$

14. $5x^2 - 12x + 10 = 0$

In Exercises 15–20, use the discriminant to determine the number of real solutions of the equation.

15. $x^2 + x + 1 = 0$

16. $3x^2 - 6x + 1 = 0$

17. $20x^2 - 10x + 5 = 0$

18. $-2x^2 - 5x - 6 = 0$

19. $-7x^2 - 8x - 10 = 0$

20. $-2x^2 + 3x - 1 = 0$

In Exercises 21–30, use the quadratic formula to solve the equation.

21. $-5x^2 - 15x + 10 = 0$

22. $4x^2 - 6x + 2 = 0$

23. $-9x - 1 = -9x^2$

24. $10x^2 + 15x + 5 = -2.5x$

25. $-13x^2 - 9x + 4 = 5 + 2x^2 - x$

26. $7x^2 + x = 12x^2 - 3x + 2$

27. $11x^2 + 4 = 2 - 7x^2 + 11x$

28. $x - x^2 = 1 - 6x^2$

29. $4x - 2 = -3x^2 + 3x$

30. $12x^2 - 9x + 1 = 10x^2 + 10x + 7$

In Exercises 31–34, solve the equation. Round to two decimal places.

31. $5.1x^2 - 0.33x - 0.1 = 0$

32. $6.3x^2 + 10.08x + 0.99 = 0$

33. $3.2x^2 - 0.01 = 15.1 + 3.3x$

34. $17.02x - 3x^2 = 4.01x^2 - 1.5$

In Exercises 35–38, find values of c such that the equation has two real-number solutions, one real-number solution, and no real-number solution.

35. $x^2 - 6x + c = 0$ **36.** $x^2 - 12x + c = 0$ **37.** $x^2 + 8x + c = 0$ **38.** $x^2 + 2x + c = 0$

Geometry   **In Exercises 39 and 40, use the quadratic formula to find the dimensions of the figure.**

39. Rectangle Area $= 58.14$ in.^{2}

x in.

$x + 6.3$ in.

40. Ellipse Area $= 9.02$ (area of ellipse is πab)

x

$x + 19$

41. *Hitting Baseballs*   You are hitting baseballs. When tossing the ball into the air, your hand is 5 feet above the ground. You hit the ball when it falls back to a height of 4 feet. If you toss the ball with an initial velocity of 25 feet per second, how much time will pass before you hit the ball?

42. *Cellular Phones*   For 1987 through 1994, the number of cellular phone subscribers, s (in millions), in the United States can be approximated by the model

$$s = 0.52t^2 - 7.94t + 31.87$$

where $t = 7$ represents 1987. In which year did cellular phone companies have about 7.5 million subscribers? *(Source: Cellular Telecommunications Industry Association)*

Cellular Phone Subscribers

Subscribers (in millions)

'87 '88 '89 '90 '91 '92 '93 '94

Year

43. *Conveyor Belt*   Gravel is falling 4 feet from one conveyor belt to another. Because of the way the conveyor belt is constructed, the gravel is given a slight downward velocity (-1.4 feet per second). How long does it take each piece of gravel to fall from the upper belt to the lower belt?

44. *Boat Owners*   For 1983 to 1993, the number, b (in millions), of recreational boats owned in the United States can be approximated by the model

$$b = -0.01t^2 + 0.59t + 11.28$$

where $t = 3$ represents 1983. In what year were 15.8 million recreational boats owned? *(Source: National Marine Manufacturers Association)*

Boat Owners (in millions)

Recreational Boat Owners

3 4 5 6 7 8 9 10 11 12 13

Year (3 ↔ 1983)

In Exercises 45–54, solve the equation using the most convenient method. Round to the nearest hundredth.

45. $6x^2 - x + 1 = x^2 - x + 4$

46. $2x^2 + 5x - 9 = -10$

47. $4.5x^2 - 3x = 0.33 - 2.1x^2$

48. $16x - 3x^2 - 7 = -6x^2 + 10x$

49. $-5x^2 - 4 = x^2 - 10x$

50. $-10x^2 + 2x - 5 = -6 - 6x^2 + 2x$

51. $6.7x^2 + 30x - 0.04 = 1.7$

52. $-5x^2 + 21.2x = 10.2x - 6.01$

53. $3x^2 + 5x - 10 = 11 + 5x$

54. $-2x^2 + 2x - 2 = -9x^2 - 5x$

55. *College Entrance Exam Sample*   In the figure, the diameter of the small circle is AC and the diameter of the large circle is AD. If $AB = BC = CD$, what is the ratio of the area of the shaded region to the area of the smaller circle?

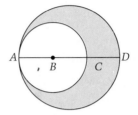

   a. $1:1$ **b.** $3:2$ **c.** $4:3$

   d. $5:4$ **e.** $9:4$

56. *College Entrance Exam Sample*   In the figure, square $PQRS$ is divided into four smaller squares. If the area of the shaded region is 3, what is the area of $PQRS$?

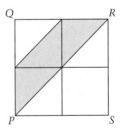

   a. 8   **b.** 7   **c.** 6   **d.** 5   **e.** 1

Compact Disks and Records   **In Exercises 57 and 58, use the following information.**

For 1986 through 1990, the number of compact disks, C (in millions), and the number of record albums, R (in millions), sold in the United States can be approximated by the models $C = 4.3t^2 - 9.8t - 42.7$ and $R = -28.8t + 301$ where $t = 6$ represents 1986.

(Source: Recording Industry Association of America)

57. How many compact disks were sold in 1986? How many record albums were sold in 1986?

58. During which year was the number of compact disks sold approximately equal to the number of record albums sold?

In Exercises 59 and 60, sketch the graph of each equation. Use your graph to approximate the points at which the two graphs intersect. Describe an algebraic procedure for finding the points of intersection.

59. $\begin{cases} x + 3y = 11 \\ x^2 - 3y = -5 \end{cases}$

60. $\begin{cases} x + 2y = -7 \\ -x - y^2 = -17 \end{cases}$

5.5

Complex Numbers

What you should learn:

Goal 1 How to identify, add, subtract, and multiply imaginary and complex numbers

Goal 2 How to plot complex numbers in the complex plane

Why you should learn it:

You can use the complex plane to illustrate relationships between complex numbers, such as in fractal geometry.

Goal 1 Imaginary and Complex Numbers

You have seen that some quadratic equations have no real-number solutions. For instance, the quadratic equation $x^2 + 1 = 0$ has no real-number solution because no real number x can be squared to produce -1. To overcome this problem, mathematicians created an expanded system of numbers using the **imaginary unit** i, defined as

$$i = \sqrt{-1}. \quad \textit{Imaginary unit } i$$

Note that $i^2 = -1$. The imaginary unit i can be used to write the square root of *any* negative number.

Imaginary Numbers

If a is a positive real number, then $\sqrt{-a}$ is an **imaginary number** and

$$\sqrt{-a} = i\sqrt{a}. \quad \textit{Imaginary number}$$

The imaginary number $i\sqrt{a}$ has the property that $(i\sqrt{a})^2 = -a$.

Example 1 *Writing Imaginary Numbers*

Use the imaginary unit i to write the solutions of $x^2 = -3$.

Solution

$$\begin{aligned}
x^2 &= -3 && \textit{Rewrite original equation.} \\
x &= \pm\sqrt{-3} && \textit{Take square root.} \\
x &= \pm i\sqrt{3} && \textit{Write with imaginary unit.}
\end{aligned}$$

The two solutions are $i\sqrt{3}$ and $-i\sqrt{3}$.

Check:

$$\begin{aligned}
x^2 &= -3 & x^2 &= -3 \\
(i\sqrt{3})^2 &\stackrel{?}{=} -3 & (-i\sqrt{3})^2 &\stackrel{?}{=} -3 \\
-3 &= -3 \quad \textbf{\textit{Check}} & -3 &= -3 \quad \textbf{\textit{Check}}
\end{aligned}$$ ■

A **complex number** is a number that is the sum of a real number and an imaginary number. Each complex number can be written in the **standard form**, $a + bi$.

Complex Numbers

For any real numbers a and b, the number

$$a + bi$$

is a **complex number.** If $b = 0$, then the complex number is a real number. Two complex numbers $a + bi$ and $c + di$ are **equal** if $a = c$ and $b = d$.

To add (or subtract) two complex numbers, add (or subtract) the real and imaginary parts of the numbers.

$$\textbf{Sum: } (a + bi) + (c + di) = (a + c) + (b + d)i$$

$$\textbf{Difference: } (a + bi) - (c + di) = (a - c) + (b - d)i$$

Example 2   *Adding and Subtracting Complex Numbers*

a. $(3 - i) + (2 + 3i) = 3 - i + 2 + 3i$
$$= 3 + 2 - i + 3i$$
$$= (3 + 2) + (-1 + 3)i$$
$$= 5 + 2i$$

b. $2i + (-4 - 2i) = 2i - 4 - 2i$
$$= -4 + 2i - 2i$$
$$= -4$$

c. $3 - (-2 + 3i) + (-5 + i) = 3 + 2 - 3i - 5 + i$
$$= 3 + 2 - 5 - 3i + i$$
$$= 0 - 2i$$
$$= -2i \qquad \blacksquare$$

The following properties of real numbers hold for complex numbers as well.

Associative Properties of Addition and Multiplication

Commutative Properties of Addition and Multiplication

Distributive Property of Multiplication over Addition

Example **3**   *Multiplying Complex Numbers*

a. $i \cdot -3i = -3i^2 = -3(-1) = 3$

b. $i(4 + 3i) = 4i + 3i^2$ *Distributive Property*

$= 4i + 3(-1)$ $i^2 = -1$

$= -3 + 4i$ *Standard form*

c. $(2 - i)(4 + 3i) = (2 - i)(4) + (2 - i)(3i)$

$= 8 - 4i + 6i - 3i^2$

$= 8 - 4i + 6i - (-3)$

$= 8 - 4i + 6i + 3$

$= 11 + 2i$ ∎

Goal **2**   **The Complex Number Plane**

Most applications of complex numbers are either theoretical or very technical, and are therefore not appropriate for this text. However, to give you some idea of how complex numbers can be used, consider their role in **fractal geometry.**

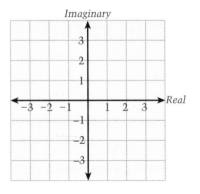

Just as every real number corresponds to a point on the real line, every complex number can be made to correspond to a point in a plane called the **complex plane.** In the complex plane, the horizontal axis is the **real axis,** and the vertical axis is the **imaginary axis.**

Don't worry about confusing the complex plane with the standard coordinate plane. This lesson is the *only* one in the book that uses complex planes—*all* other coordinate planes in the book are standard coordinate planes whose points are ordered pairs of *real numbers.*

Example **4**   *Plotting Complex Numbers in the Complex Plane*

Plot the complex numbers in the complex plane.

a. $2 - 3i$ **b.** $-1 + 2i$ **c.** $2i$

Solution

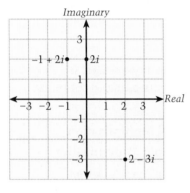

a. To plot the complex number $2 - 3i$, move (from the origin) two units to the right on the real axis and 3 units down.

b. To plot the complex number $-1 + 2i$, move (from the origin) one unit to the left and 2 units up.

c. To plot the complex number $2i$, move (from the origin) two units up.   ∎

People who understand fractal geometry can use the complex plane to draw stunning pictures, called **fractals.** The most famous such picture is called the **Mandelbrot set,** after the Polish-born mathematician Benoit Mandelbrot.

In the picture below, the Mandelbrot set is the black region in the complex plane. Each point in one of the colored regions is *not* in the set. (The reason for assigning colors to points not in the set is too complicated to mention here.)

Connections
Fractal Geometry

Example 5   *The Mandelbrot Set*

Decide whether the complex number is in the Mandelbrot set.

a. -1 **b.** $\frac{1}{2}i$ **c.** $1 + i$

Solution

a. The point that represents -1 is on the real axis, one unit to the left of the origin. This number *is* in the Mandelbrot set.
b. The point that represents $\frac{1}{2}i$ is on the imaginary axis, one-half unit above the origin. It *is also* in the Mandelbrot set.
c. The point that represents $1 + i$ is one unit to the right and one unit above the origin. It is *not* in the Mandelbrot set. ∎

Communicating about **ALGEBRA**

▶ **SHARING IDEAS about the Lesson**

A. Is a real number also a complex number? Explain.
B. The rule for adding two complex numbers is sometimes called the parallelogram rule. Graph the complex numbers $2 + i$ and $1 + 3i$ in the complex plane. Then graph their sum. How are the three points and the origin related to a parallelogram?

EXERCISES

Guided Practice

▶ **CRITICAL THINKING about the Lesson**

1. Does the equation $x^2 = -1$ have a real-number solution? Does it have solutions that are not real numbers? Explain.
2. Rewrite $\sqrt{-4}$ using the imaginary unit i.

In Exercises 3–6, perform the indicated operation.

3. $(i\sqrt{2})^2$ **4.** $(4 + 3i) + (-2 - 2i)$ **5.** $i(-2 + 2i)$ **6.** $(1 - i)(4 + 2i)$

7. Is $-i\sqrt{2}$ a solution of $x^2 + 2 = 0$? Justify your answer.
8. Plot the complex number $2 - 3i$ in the complex plane.

Independent Practice

In Exercises 9–14, write the number using the imaginary unit *i*.

9. $\sqrt{-9}$ **10.** $\sqrt{-4}$ **11.** $-\sqrt{-25}$

12. $-\sqrt{-1}$ **13.** $\sqrt{-5}$ **14.** $-\sqrt{-15}$

In Exercises 15–20, simplify the expression.

15. $2i^2$ **16.** $(2i)^2$ **17.** $-i^2$

18. $(\sqrt{-6})^2$ **19.** $(\sqrt{-10})^2$ **20.** $(i\sqrt{3})^2$

In Exercises 21–26, decide whether the complex number is a solution of the equation.

21. $x^2 = -9, 3i$ **22.** $x^2 = -14, 14i$ **23.** $x^2 + 9 = 8, -i$

24. $x^2 - 4 = 2, i\sqrt{2}$ **25.** $x^2 + 10 = 3, 7i$ **26.** $x^2 + 5 = -5, -i\sqrt{10}$

In Exercises 27–32, solve the equation.

27. $x^2 = -4$ **28.** $x^2 = -5$ **29.** $-3x^2 + 1 = 7$

30. $4x^2 + 15 = 3$ **31.** $6x^2 + 5 = 2x^2 + 1$ **32.** $x^2 = 7x^2 + 1$

In Exercises 33–44, perform the indicated operations.

33. $(3 + 2i) + (9 + i)$ **34.** $(9 + 2i) + (3 - i)$ **35.** $(-4 + i) + (i - 4)$

36. $(1 + i) + (7 - 4i)$ **37.** $(5 - 3i) - (-1 + i)$ **38.** $(2 - i) - (5 + i)$

39. $(1 - 3i) - (8 + i)$ **40.** $(-4 + 6i) - (-3 + 12i)$ **41.** $(30 - i) - (18 + 6i) + 3i^2$

42. $(3 - 36i) + (7 + 28i) + i$ **43.** $-i + (9 - 2i) - (5 + 7i)$ **44.** $(8 - i) + (5 + 13i) - 2i^2$

In Exercises 45–56, perform the indicated multiplication.

45. $i(1 + i)$

46. $i(2 - i)$

47. $-i(5 + 2i)$

48. $3i(1 - 2i)$

49. $2i(6 + i)$

50. $-8i(6 + i)$

51. $(3 + i)(2 + i)$

52. $(2 + 7i)(4 - 2i)$

53. $(1 + 4i)(2 - i)$

54. $(9 - 10i)(-8 + 3i)$

55. $(-7 - i)(3 + 2i)$

56. $(-14 + 6i)(1 - i)$

In Exercises 57–62, simplify the expression.

57. $4i(1 + i) + (6 + 2i)$

58. $(6 + 6i) - 3i^2(1 - 2i)$

59. $i^2[(1 + 4i) - (2 - 3i)]$

60. $i(7 - 3i)(2 + 10i)$

61. $10i(2 - 2i)(5 + i)$

62. $3i[2i(1 + i) - (2 - 10i)]$

In Exercises 63–68, graph the complex number in the complex plane.

63. $3 - i$

64. $4 + 2i$

65. $-2 + 5i$

66. $-10 - 4i$

67. $-3i$

68. $2 - 12i$

Fractals　**In Exercises 69–72, use the following information.**

Trace the Mandelbrot set on page 261 on a piece of paper. Then evaluate the expressions and mark the locations of the results on your tracing. This shows where each enlargement (pictured below) is found. The colors of the enlargements are not necessarily those used on page 261.

69. *Cos Antenna* $(6.2 - 1.2i) - (7.6 - 1.2i)$

70. *Star Factory* $-\frac{1}{170}(3 + 5i)(8 + 15i)$

71. *Lightning* $(1 + 0.5i)(0.396 + 0.822i)$

72. *Spanish Lace* $2i(0.1 + 0.36i)$

In Exercises 73–78, simplify the expression.

73. $-3(2x + 3)$ **74.** $4(-3a + b)$ **75.** $\frac{1}{2}s(s - 3)$

76. $-\frac{1}{4}t(2t - 8)$ **77.** $x(-3x + 1)$ **78.** $-2y(2y + 7)$

In Exercises 79–84, solve the equation.

79. $x^2 - 2x = 1$ **80.** $3x^2 - 5x + 2 = 0$ **81.** $16x^2 = 4$

82. $3x - 5x^2 = -7$ **83.** $30x^2 - 10x - 1 = 0$ **84.** $-8x^2 - 2x + 5 = 1$

Exploration and Extension

Powers of i   **In Exercises 85–88, raise the imaginary unit i to various powers, then find and use a pattern.**

85. Complete the table.

i	i^2	i^3	i^4	i^5	i^6	i^7	i^8
i	-1	$-i$	?	?	?	?	?

86. Describe the pattern in the second row of the table.

87. Use the pattern to evaluate i^{26}.   **88.** Use the pattern to evaluate i^{52}.

Mixed REVIEW

1. Solve $7x^2 = 28$. **(5.1)**

2. Write $(x + 2)^2$ as a trinomial. **(5.3)**

3. Find the y-intercept of $y = 3x^2 + 8$. **(5.2)**

4. Find the x-intercept of $y = \frac{2}{3}x - 4$. **(2.3)**

5. Find the area of the region between the graphs of $y = x^2 - 4$ and $y = 0$. **(5.2)**

6. Divide: $\frac{4}{9} \div \frac{8}{27}$.

7. Write 5,320,000 in scientific notation.

8. Write 0.000048 in scientific notation.

9. Solve $|3x - 2| > 5$. **(1.7)**

10. 12 is 6% of what number?

11. Solve $\frac{3}{2}x^2 + 8 = \frac{26}{3}$. **(5.1)**

12. Solve for a: $a^2bc - a^2 - b = 2$. **(1.5)**

13. Sketch the graph of $y = -|x + 2| + 4$. **(2.6)**

14. Find the vertex of $y = (x - 5)^2 - 7$. **(5.2)**

15. Write $y = x^2 + 4x - 7$ in completed square form. **(5.3)**

16. Find the axis of symmetry of $y = 5x^2 - 9x + 4$. **(5.2)**

17. A stone dropped into a well hits the water after 2 sec. How deep is the well?

18. In order of length, the sides of a right triangle measure 8, x, and 12. Find x. **(5.1)**

19. Multiply: $\begin{bmatrix} 3 & 1 \\ 0 & 2 \end{bmatrix}\begin{bmatrix} 1 & 3 \\ -2 & 4 \end{bmatrix}$. **(4.2)**

20. Find the inverse of $\begin{bmatrix} 2 & -4 \\ 1 & -1 \end{bmatrix}$. **(4.3)**

5.6 Solving Any Quadratic Equation

What you should learn:

Goal 1 How to solve any quadratic equation (even ones that have complex-number solutions)

Goal 2 How to use complex numbers and programmable calculators to solve real-life problems

Why you should learn it:

You can solve *any* quadratic equation by using complex numbers. In real-life settings, these solutions must be interpreted to fit the context.

Goal 1 Solving Any Quadratic Equation

In Lesson 5.4, you learned that if the discriminant of the quadratic equation $ax^2 + bx + c = 0$ is negative, then the equation has no *real-number* solution, but it does have two *complex-number* solutions.

You can find the complex solutions in the same way you find real solutions—by using the quadratic formula. For instance, the solutions of $x^2 + 2x + 2 = 0$ are as follows.

$$x = \frac{-2 \pm \sqrt{2^2 - 4(1)(2)}}{2(1)} \qquad \textit{Quadratic formula}$$

$$= \frac{-2 \pm \sqrt{-4}}{2} \qquad \textit{Simplify.}$$

$$= \frac{-2 \pm 2i}{2} \qquad \textit{Write with imaginary unit.}$$

$$= \frac{2(-1 \pm i)}{2} \qquad \textit{Distributive Property}$$

$$= -1 \pm i \qquad \textit{Divide common factor.}$$

The two solutions are $-1 + i$ and $-1 - i$. You can check this solution by substituting it into the original equation. For instance, you can check $-1 + i$ as follows.

$$(-1 + i)^2 + 2(-1 + i) + 2 = 1 - 2i - 1 - 2 + 2i + 2 = 0$$

Example 1 *Finding Complex-Number Solutions*

Solve $x^2 - 3x + \frac{5}{2} = 0$.

Solution

$$x = \frac{3 \pm \sqrt{(-3)^2 - 4(1)\left(\frac{5}{2}\right)}}{2(1)} \qquad \textit{Quadratic Formula}$$

$$= \frac{3 \pm \sqrt{-1}}{2} \qquad \textit{Simplify.}$$

$$= \frac{3 \pm i}{2} \qquad \textit{Write with imaginary unit.}$$

$$= \frac{3}{2} \pm \frac{1}{2}i \qquad \textit{Write in standard form.}$$

The two solutions are $\frac{3}{2} + \frac{1}{2}i$ and $\frac{3}{2} - \frac{1}{2}i$. ■

You can program a graphing calculator to find the real solutions of a quadratic equation. The keystroke instructions for doing this on a *TI-82*, Casio *fx-9700GE*, and Sharp *EL-9300C* are listed on page 861.

LESSON INVESTIGATION

■ Investigating Real Solutions of Quadratics

Partner Activity Enter one of the programs listed on page 861 in a graphing calculator. The program is written to solve any quadratic equation of the form

$$ax^2 + bx + c = 0. \quad \textit{Quadratic equation}$$

After entering the program, use it to find the real solutions of the following equations. In each case, give a graphical interpretation of the number of real solutions.

$$x^2 + 6x + 3 = 0, \quad x^2 + 6x + 9 = 0, \quad x^2 + 6x + 15 = 0$$

Connections
Technology

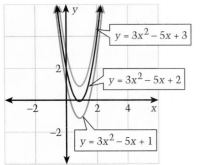

Example **2** *Finding Real Solutions*

Use one of the programs listed on page 861 to solve the equations.

a. $3x^2 - 5x + 1 = 0$ **b.** $3x^2 - 5x + 2 = 0$ **c.** $3x^2 - 5x + 3 = 0$

Solution

a. Running the program with $A = 3$, $B = -5$, and $C = 1$ produces two real solutions that are approximately 1.434 and 0.232. Using the quadratic formula, the *exact* solutions are $\frac{5}{6} \pm \frac{\sqrt{13}}{6}$.

b. Running the program with $A = 3$, $B = -5$, and $C = 2$ produces two real solutions that are 1 and approximately 0.667. The exact solutions are 1 and $\frac{2}{3}$.

c. Running the program with $A = 3$, $B = -5$, and $C = 3$ produces the display "No Real Solution." In this case the solutions are not real numbers. Using the quadratic formula, you can find the solutions to be $\frac{5}{6} \pm \frac{\sqrt{11}}{6}i$. ■

During the 1960's and 1970's, most homes in the United States had television antennas. With the introduction of cable television, however, fewer homes needed a television antenna.

Real Life

Television

Example 3 **Interpreting Complex Solutions**

For 1970 through 1990, the sales, A (in millions of dollars), of television and FM antennas in the United States is given by

$$A = -0.2t^2 + 3.5t + 70$$

where t represents the year, with $t = 0$ corresponding to 1970. According to this model, during which year did the sales of antennas reach $95 million?

Solution

$$A = -0.2t^2 + 3.5t + 70$$

$$95 = -0.2t^2 + 3.5t + 70$$

$$0.2t^2 - 3.5t + 25 = 0$$

$$t = \frac{3.5 \pm \sqrt{(3.5)^2 - 4(0.2)(25)}}{2(0.2)}$$

$$t = \frac{3.5 \pm \sqrt{-7.75}}{0.4}$$

Because the discriminant is negative, the equation has no real solutions. In no year did antenna sales reach $95 million. This conclusion is supported by the graph at the left. Note that the graph of $A = -0.2t^2 + 3.5t + 70$ is a parabola that opens down. The maximum sales occurred around 1979. ∎

Sales of Antennas

Sales (in millions of dollars)

Year (0 ↔ 1970)

Communicating about **ALGEBRA**

▶ **SHARING IDEAS about the Lesson**

Find an equation of a parabola with the given description.

A. The parabola opens down and has no x-intercepts.

B. The parabola opens up and has no x-intercepts.

EXERCISES

▶ **CRITICAL THINKING about the Lesson**

1. One of the following equations has two real solutions, one has one real solution, and one has no real solutions. Which is which?
   a. $4x^2 - 8x + 5 = 0$ **b.** $4x^2 - 8x + 4 = 0$ **c.** $4x^2 - 8x + 3 = 0$

2. Write $\dfrac{4 \pm \sqrt{-2}}{6}$ in standard complex-number form.

3. Solve $2x^2 + 6x + 5 = 0$.

4. *New Style of Jeans* The monthly sales, S (in thousands of pairs), of a new style of jeans can be modeled by

   $S = -\dfrac{3}{4}t^2 + 6t + 51$

   where $t = 0$ corresponds to the first month of sales. In which month were 64 thousand pairs of jeans sold? Explain your answer algebraically and graphically.

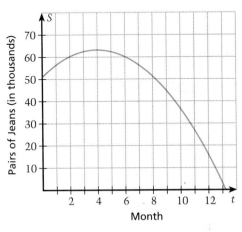

Sales of Jeans

Independent Practice

In Exercises 5–10, decide whether the complex number is a solution of the equation.

5. $x^2 - 2x + 2 = 0$, $1 + i$

6. $x^2 - 4x + 5 = 0$, $2 + i$

7. $x^2 - 2x + 5 = 0$, $1 + 2i$

8. $x^2 - 2x + 5 = 0$, $1 - 2i$

9. $x^2 - 2x + 10 = 0$, $1 + 3i$

10. $x^2 - 2x + 10 = 0$, $1 - 3i$

In Exercises 11–22, solve the equation.

11. $-x^2 + 5x - 9 = 0$

12. $6x^2 - 7x + 3 = 0$

13. $x^2 + 2x + 7 = 0$

14. $-5x^2 + 10x - 6 = 0$

15. $-4x^2 + 6x - 3 = 0$

16. $x^2 - x + 1 = 0$

17. $-3x^2 - 5x - 3 = 0$

18. $2x^2 + 12x + 19 = 0$

19. $16x - x^2 = -4 - 22x^2$

20. $x + 2x^2 + 1 = -1 - x$

21. $13x^2 - 5 = x + 10x^2 - 8$

22. $7x^2 - 4 - x = 6x^2 - 10$

Technology **In Exercises 23–28, use a programmable calculator to find all real solutions of the equation.**

23. $16x^2 - 10x + 1 = 0$

24. $3x^2 + 7x - 2 = 0$

25. $4x^2 + 5x + 11 = 0$

26. $-9x^2 + 8x - 1 = 0$

27. $8x^2 - 6x + 6 = 0$

28. $-14x^2 - 12x - 4 = 0$

29. *Fencing the Yard*   A friend's family has built a fence around three sides of their property. (See figure.) In total, they used 550 feet of fencing. By their calculations, the lot is one acre (43,560 square feet). Is this correct? Explain your answer.

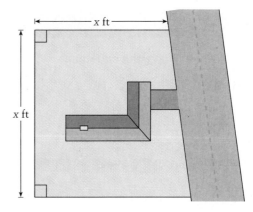

30. *More Fencing*   You have 100 feet of fencing. Do you have enough fencing to enclose a rectangular region whose area is 630 square feet? How about a circular region whose area is 630 square feet? Explain.

31. *High School Enrollment*   Randall Curtain High School's enrollment, E, decreased from 1955 to 1975. In 1975, the enrollment began to increase. For 1955 through 1995, the enrollment can be modeled by $E = 0.37t^2 - 14.8t + 460$ where $t = 5$ corresponds to 1955. In what year was enrollment down to 300 students? Explain your answer algebraically and graphically.

32. *Grocery Sales*   In 1975, your uncle opened a neighborhood grocery store. For 1975 through 1995, his annual sales, S (in millions of dollars), could be modeled by $S = -0.015t^2 + 0.36t + 0.5$ where $t = 5$ represents 1975. During which years were the annual sales $2,300,000? During which year were the annual sales $2,750,000? Explain your answers algebraically and graphically.

33. *United States Postal Service Revenue*
For 1980 through 1994, the postal service's revenue, R (in millions of dollars), for fourth-class mail can be approximated by the model

$R = 5.16t^2 - 36.68t + 822.51$

where $t = 0$ represents 1980. Construct a table that shows the revenue for each year. From the table, did the annual revenue drop as low as $750 million from 1980 through 1994? What happens when you try to solve the equation $750 = 5.16t^2 - 36.68t + 822.51$?
(Source: U.S. Postal Service)

34. *Sale of Electricity*   For 1970 through 1992, the sale of electricity, S (in billions of dollars), in the United States can be modeled by the equation

$S = -0.22t^2 + 9.38t + 105.21$

where $t = 0$ represents 1980. In what year did electricity sales reach $150 billion?   *(Source: U.S. Energy Information Administration)*

Integrated Review

In Exercises 35–40, solve the equation.

35. $-10x^2 + 16 = 30$

36. $5 - x^2 = 10 + 4x^2$

37. $2x^2 + 9 = -2x^2$

38. $7x^2 + 56 = 3x^2 - 8$

39. $x^2 - 17 = 13 - x^2$

40. $-3x^2 - 7 = -3$

In Exercises 41–44, use the quadratic formula to solve the equation.

41. $x^2 - 3x + x = 0$

42. $-2x^2 + 12x - x = 0$

43. $-3x^2 + x + 10 = 0$

44. $15x - 6x^2 = 12x - 14x^2 - 2$

In Exercises 45–50, sketch the graph of the equation.

45. $y = 2x^2 + x + 5$

46. $y = x^2 - 3x + 1$

47. $y = 6x^2 - x + 2$

48. $y = 7x^2 + x - 2$

49. $y = x^2 + 5x - 4$

50. $y = -8x^2 + 10x - 5$

Exploration and Extension

51. *Morse Code*   For some values of d, the equation

$$2x^2 - 16.8x + 37.64 = d$$

has at least one real solution. For other values of d, the equation has no real solution. Complete the following tables by placing a dot (•) if the equation has at least one real solution and a dash (■) if the equation has no real solution. After completing the tables, use the International Morse Code at the right to find the five-letter word that is being spelled.

d	4.2	10.1	13.5	6.3
Code	?	?	?	?

d	6.0	5.0	0.0
Code	?	?	?

d	11.25	−1.0	12.0
Code	?	?	?

d	7.2	2.2	8.0
Code	?	?	?

d	1.6	10.5	−7.2	2.0
Code	?	?	?	?

5.7 Graphs of Quadratic Inequalities

What you should learn:

Goal 1 How to sketch the graph of a quadratic inequality

Goal 2 How to use quadratic inequalities in real-life modeling

Why you should learn it:

You can model many real-life situations with quadratic equations, such as some of the unusual shapes found in corporate logos.

Goal 1 The Graph of a Quadratic Inequality

In this lesson, you will study the following four types of **quadratic inequalities.**

$$y < ax^2 + bx + c \qquad y \le ax^2 + bx + c$$

$$y > ax^2 + bx + c \qquad y \ge ax^2 + bx + c$$

The **graph** of any such inequality consists of the graph of all solutions (x, y) of the inequality. The steps used to sketch the graph of a quadratic inequality are similar to those used to sketch the graph of a linear inequality. (See Lesson 2.5.)

Sketching the Graph of a Quadratic Inequality

1. Sketch the graph of the parabola $y = ax^2 + bx + c$. (Use a *dashed* parabola for inequalities with $<$ or $>$ and a *solid* parabola for inequalities with $\le$ or $\ge$.)

2. Test a point inside the U-shape and one outside the U-shape.

3. Only one of the test points will be a solution. Shade the region that contains this test point.

Example 1 Sketching the Graph of a Quadratic Inequality

Sketch the graph of $y < 3x^2 - 6x$.

Solution The parabola $y = 3x^2 - 6x$ has a vertex at $(1, -3)$. Its dashed graph is shown at the left. Choose a point inside the U-shape, say $(1, 0)$, and a point outside the U-shape, say $(3, 0)$.

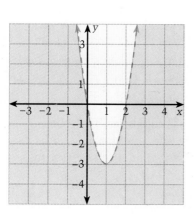

Point	Test the Point	Conclusion
$(1, 0)$	$0 \overset{?}{<} 3(1)^2 - 6(1)$	Because 0 *is not* less than or equal to -3, the ordered pair $(1, 0)$ is not a solution.
$(3, 0)$	$0 \overset{?}{<} 3(3)^2 - 6(3)$	Because 0 *is* less than 9, the ordered pair $(3, 0)$ is a solution.

Thus the graph must be the region outside the U-shape. ∎

Many organizations have a logo that is designed to be easily recognized. For example, the logo for the company that publishes this book is shown at the bottom of the spine on the outside cover of the book.

Goal **2** Using Quadratic Inequalities in Real Life

Real Life
Design

Example **2** *Sketching the Graph of an Inequality*

You are using a computer to create a logo for a company called Magic World. Each of the four green and yellow regions can be described as the *intersection* of the graphs of two quadratic inequalities. Create one of these by sketching the graphs of the following inequalities.

$$y \geq x^2 \quad \text{and} \quad y \leq -x^2 + 2x + 4$$

Solution The parabola $y = x^2$ opens up and has its vertex at the origin. The graph of the inequality

$$y \geq x^2$$

is the region on and inside the parabola. The parabola $y = -x^2 + 2x + 4$ opens down and has its vertex at (1, 5). The graph of the inequality

$$y \leq -x^2 + 2x + 4$$

is the region on and inside the parabola.

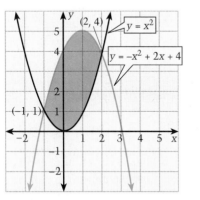

You can see from the coordinate plane at the left that the intersection of these two graphs is a region that has the shape of the green regions in the logo for Magic World. ■

Sketch the graphs of the following inequalities. Does the intersection of these two graphs look like one of the green regions in the logo or does it look like one of the yellow regions in the logo?

$$y \geq x^2 + 4x + 4 \quad \text{and} \quad y \leq -x^2 - 6x + 4$$

Example 3 *Take-Home Pay*

In 1990, the monthly take-home pay, y (in dollars), for a person claiming four *income-tax deductions* can be modeled by

$$y = -0.000025x^2 + 0.85x$$

where x represents the monthly gross pay (in dollars). Describe the deductions claimed by a person whose take-home pay is given by one of the following inequalities.

(Source: Hooper International Accounting Software, based on a state and local income-tax rate of 3.1%)

$$y > -0.000025x^2 + 0.85x$$

$$y < -0.000025x^2 + 0.85x$$

Solution The graphs of the two inequalities are shown below. For the graph at the left, the monthly take-home pay is greater than that of a person who claims four deductions, so the person must be claiming *more than four deductions*. For the graph at the right, the monthly take-home pay is less than that of a person who claims four deductions, so the person must be claiming *less than four deductions*. ■

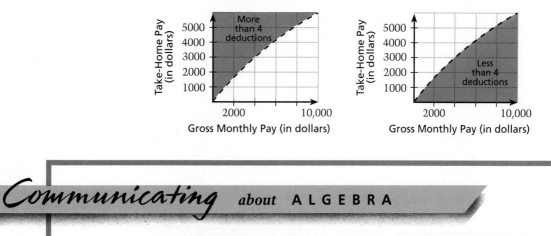

Communicating about ALGEBRA

▶ **SHARING IDEAS about the Lesson**

Match each inequality with its graph. Explain your choices.

A. $y \le -x^2 + 2x$

B. $y \le -x^2 + 4x - 3$

C. $y \le -x^2 + 6x - 8$

EXERCISES

▶ **CRITICAL THINKING about the Lesson**

In Exercises 1–4, use the inequality $y \le 4x^2 - 3x + 1$.

1. What are the coordinates of the lowest point in the graph?

2. Sketch the graph of the parabola $y = 4x^2 - 3x + 1$.

3. Test two points in the coordinate plane—one inside the parabola and one outside.

4. Use the result of your test in Exercise 3 to shade the graph of the inequality.

Independent Practice

In Exercises 5–10, determine whether the ordered pair is a solution of the inequality.

5. $y > -x^2 + x + 4$, $(1, 6)$

6. $y \ge -x^2 - 5x + 3$, $(2, -10)$

7. $y \le 3x^2 - x - 1$, $(-1, 5)$

8. $y < 4x^2 - x + 5$, $(0, 5)$

9. $y \ge -\frac{1}{2}x^2 + 2x - 4$, $(4, -2)$

10. $y \le -x^2 + 9x + 7$, $(-1, 3)$

In Exercises 11–16, match the inequality with its graph.

11. $y \le -x^2 + 3x + 5$

12. $y > -x^2 - 6x - 2$

13. $y > -2x^2 + 3x + 5$

14. $y \ge 2x^2 + 3x - 5$

15. $y \le \frac{1}{2}x^2 + 3x + 2$

16. $y > x^2 - 3x - 5$

a.

b.

c.

d.
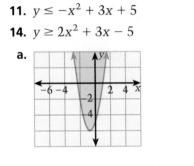

e.

f.

In Exercises 17–28, sketch the graph of the inequality.

17. $y > x^2 - x + 10$

18. $y \ge 5x^2 + 10x + 7$

19. $y \le -2x^2 + 4x - 1$

20. $y < 3x^2 - 18x + 2$

21. $y > 3x^2 + 12x$

22. $y \ge x^2 - 20x + 90$

23. $y \ge 6x^2 + 36x + 50$

24. $y < -x^2 + 14x - 7$

25. $y \ge -2x^2 + 4x + 8$

26. $y < -3x^2 + 30x - 50$

27. $y < -x^2 + 6x - 2$

28. $y \le 4x^2 + 16x$

In Exercises 29–34, sketch the intersection of the graphs of the inequalities.

29. $y > x^2 - 6x + 9$
$y < -x^2 + 6x - 3$

30. $y \geq 3x^2 - 12x + 12$
$y \leq -x^2 + 4x$

31. $y \geq x^2 - 2x + 2$
$y < x^2 - 8x + 20$

32. $y \geq 2x^2$
$y \leq -2x^2 - 8x + 2$

33. $y > x^2 + 2x - 4$
$y > x^2 - 4x - 1$

34. $y < -3x^2 + 6x + 7$
$y \leq -2x^2 + 16x - 22$

35. *The Sleepy Hare* You are using a computer to create a logo for The Sleepy Hare restaurant. The logo you have designed is shown at the right. Sketch the intersections of the graphs of the inequalities. Which region represents the hare's right ear? Which region represents the hare's left ear?

a. $y \leq -0.4x^2 + 8x - 30$
$y \geq 0.4x^2 - 12x + 90$

b. $y \leq -0.4x^2 + 8x - 30$
$y \geq 0.4x^2 - 4x + 10$

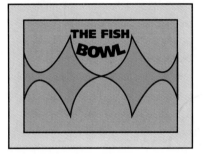

36. *The Fish Bowl* You are using a computer to create a logo for an aquarium supplies store called The Fish Bowl. The logo is the intersection of the graphs of *eight* inequalities.

$y \leq x^2 + 10x + 25.25$ $x \leq 6$

$y \geq -x^2 - 10x - 25.25$ $x \geq -6$

$y \leq x^2 - 10x + 25.25$ $y \leq 0.25x^2$

$y \geq -x^2 + 10x - 25.25$ $y \geq -0.25x^2$

Sketch the graphs of these inequalities and label each of the borders with its equation. What are the coordinates of the upper and lower points of the fins of each fish?

37. *United States Water Use* For 1940 through 1980, the daily water use, W (in billions of gallons), in the United States followed the quadratic model

$W = 0.063t^2 + 5.69t + 133.24$

where $t = 0$ represents 1940. Suppose this model had been used to predict the water use for 1980 through 1990. The actual use in 1985 was 400 billion gallons. Was this less or more than the predicted consumption for 1985? Explain. *(Source: Water Resources Activities in the United States)*

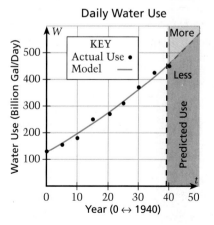

Daily Water Use

38. *Chicago Fire* A coordinate system has been super-imposed on the map at the right, with $(0, 0)$ at the fire's origin. Which of the inequalities below, used with $y \geq -\frac{9}{5}x + 9$ and $y \geq 7$, approximates the north side region of Chicago that was burned in the fire?

a. $y \geq x^2 - 2x + 7$

b. $y \geq -\frac{3}{4}x^2 + 3x + 20$

c. $y \leq x^2 - 2x + 7$

d. $y \leq -\frac{3}{4}x^2 + 3x + 20$

In October 1871, the Great Chicago Fire started on the southwest side of the city, raced north, and crossed the river to the north side. The fire covered the area shaded on the map.

Integrated Review

In Exercises 39–42, sketch the graph of the equation.

39. $y = 2x^2 - 8x + 12$

40. $y = x^2 - 12x + 39$

41. $y = -6x^2 + 1$

42. $y = 5x^2 + 10x + 7$

In Exercises 43–48, decide whether the ordered pair is a solution of the inequality.

43. $y > x + 1$, $(-2, -3)$

44. $y > -2x + 4$, $(4, 1)$

45. $y \leq -x - 3$, $(1, 1)$

46. $y < 2x + 3$, $(-3, -1)$

47. $y \geq \frac{1}{2}x - 2$, $(1, 3)$

48. $y \leq -\frac{1}{4}x - 1$, $(5, 0)$

In Exercises 49–54, sketch the graph of the inequality.

49. $y \leq 10x - 5$

50. $y < \frac{1}{2}x - 8$

51. $y > -x + 3$

52. $y \leq 2x - 5$

53. $y \leq \frac{1}{4}x - 4$

54. $y \geq x + 11$

Exploration and Extension

Geometry **In Exercises 55 and 56, find the area of the intersection of the graphs of the inequalities.** $\left(\text{Use the formula } A = \frac{2}{3}bh.\right)$

55. $y \geq \frac{1}{9}x^2 + \frac{4}{3}x + 1$
$y \leq 1$

56. $y \leq -\frac{1}{15}x^2 + 2x + 5$
$y \geq 5$

Chapter Summary

What did you learn?

Skills

1. Solve a quadratic equation
  - by finding square roots. **(5.1)**
  - by completing the square. **(5.3)**
  - by using the quadratic formula. **(5.4, 5.6)**

2. Check a solution of a quadratic equation
  - algebraically. **(5.1, 5.4, 5.6)**
  - graphically. **(5.3)**

3. Use the discriminant to find the number of solutions of a quadratic equation. **(5.4, 5.6)**

4. Sketch the graph of a quadratic equation in two variables. **(5.2)**
  - Find the vertex of a parabola. **(5.2)**
  - Find the intercepts of a parabola. **(5.2)**

5. Add, subtract, and multiply complex numbers. **(5.5)**
  - Plot complex numbers in the complex plane. **(5.5)**
  - Write complex solutions in standard form. **(5.6)**

Strategies

6. Use quadratic equations to model real-life situations. **(5.1–5.7)**

Why did you learn it?

One of your goals in Algebra 2 is to become familiar with different types of equations and inequalities. You have now studied three types of equations in one and two variables: linear equations and inequalities, absolute value equations and inequalities, and quadratic equations and inequalities.

In this chapter, you studied examples of real-life situations that can be modeled with quadratic equations. For instance, you studied falling-object problems, parabolic-shaped regions, and quantities that are related to time by a quadratic model.

How does it fit into the bigger picture of algebra?

In this chapter, you studied quadratic equations in one variable and in two variables. A quadratic equation in one variable contains the square of the variable. You solved these equations by finding square roots, by completing the square, and by using the Quadratic Formula.

The graph of a quadratic equation in two variables, such as $y = x^2 - 4$, is a parabola. Solving equations such as these often relies on the algebra-geometry connection between equations in one and two variables. For instance, the equation $x^2 - 4 = 0$ has two solutions, which correspond to the two x-intercepts of the graph of $y = x^2 - 4$.

Chapter REVIEW

In Exercises 1–3, solve the equation. (5.1)

1. $\frac{1}{3}x^2 = 12$

2. $-x^2 - 7 = -56$

3. $3 - x^2 = 5x^2 - 9$

In Exercises 4–9, sketch the graph of the equation. (5.2)

4. $y = x^2 + 4x - 7$

5. $y = 5x^2 + 20x - 18$

6. $y = 2x^2 + 6x - 1$

7. $y = 4x^2 - 32x + 20$

8. $y = -x^2 + x - 5$

9. $y = x^2 - 3x + 2$

In Exercises 10–15, solve the equation by completing the square. (5.3)

10. $x^2 + 4x - 1 = 0$

11. $x^2 + 3x - 2 = 0$

12. $2x^2 + 4x + 1 = 3$

13. $3x^2 - 6x + 2 = 5$

14. $3x^2 - x + 7 = 4 - 4x$

15. $4x^2 + 10x + 1 = -3 - 6x$

In Exercises 16–18, state the number of real solutions of the equation. (5.4)

16. $5x^2 + x - 4 = 0$

17. $3x^2 + 6x + 3 = 0$

18. $-x^2 + 7x - 2 = 0$

In Exercises 19–24, solve the equation by using the quadratic formula. (5.4)

19. $1 - 6x^2 = 5x + 3x^2$

20. $4x^2 - 2 = -6x + 5$

21. $3x + 2 - 10x^2 = 2x - 9x^2$

22. $16x + 6x^2 + 5 = 4$

23. $2.2x^2 - 3x + 1 = 0.9$

24. $5.6 - x = 4 + x + 3.3x^2$

In Exercises 25–30, find the real solutions by using the most convenient method. (5.3, 5.4)

25. $1.4x^2 + 0.2x - 1 = 0$

26. $4x^2 + 5 = 9$

27. $x^2 - 2x + 1 = 0$

28. $x^2 + 5x - 7 = 0$

29. $3x^2 + 2x - 2 = 0$

30. $-6x^2 + 2x - 0.3 = 0$

In Exercises 31–39, perform the indicated operation(s). (5.5)

31. $(4 + i) + (-6 - 3i)$

32. $(-3 + i) + (11 - 8i)$

33. $(1 + 3i) - (4 - i)$

34. $(7 + 6i) - (15 + 9i)$

35. $-5(3 + i) - (1 - 2i)$

36. $6i(2 + i) + (4 - 2i)$

37. $(2 + 3i)(1 + i)$

38. $(1 - 5i)(-7 - 10i)$

39. $(1 + 2i)(3 + i) + i$

In Exercises 40–42, graph the complex number in the complex plane. (5.5)

40. $2 - 3i$

41. $-3 - 2i$

42. $1 + 9i$

In Exercises 43–48, solve the equation. (Give complex solutions in standard form.) (5.6)

43. $2x^2 + 3x + 4 = 0$

44. $6x^2 - x + 1 = 0$

45. $3x^2 + 7x = -10$

46. $-6x^2 - 5x = 2$

47. $5x^2 - 2 = 4x^2 - 6x$

48. $3x^2 = 2x^2 - 2x - 1$

In Exercises 49–54, sketch the graph of the inequality. (5.7)

49. $y \le 3x^2 - 6x - 1$

50. $y < 2x^2 - 4x - 4$

51. $y \ge x^2 - 4x + 4$

52. $y \le \frac{1}{2}x^2 + 4x - 2$

53. $y > 2x^2 - 8x + 11$

54. $y > 5x^2 + \frac{2}{5}x + 4$

55. *Truck Off the Road* Two tow trucks have attached cables to another truck that has gone through a guardrail. Find the length of each tow truck's cable.

30 ft

60 ft

20 ft

50 ft

56. *Pickup Lift* The end of the beam on the pickup is x feet above the ground. Find this height by solving the equation $(x - 4)^2 + 18^2 = 22^2$.

22 ft

x ft

4 ft

18 ft

Medicaid Payments **In Exercises 57 and 58, use the following information.**

For 1970 through 1990, the total amount, M (in billions of dollars), spent on Medicaid can be modeled by

$M = 0.13t^2 + 0.58t + 5.8$ *Federal share*

$M = 0.06t^2 + 0.26t + 2.5$ *State share*

where $t = 0$ represents 1970.

(Source: National Association of State Budget Officers)

57. During which year was the federal government's share of Medicaid payments approximately $28 billion? Explain your answer algebraically and graphically.

Medicaid Expenditures

Medicaid (in billions of dollars)

100

80

60

40

20

Federal

State

4   8   12   16   20   24   t

Year (0 ↔ 1970)

58. In 1990, a review commission of the National Association of State Budget Offices projected the 1995 Medicaid spending by the federal government to be $155 billion and by the state governments to be $67 billion. Did the review commission use the quadratic models given above, or another model to make the projections? Explain.

59. *Contact Lens* The shape and thickness of a contact lens depends on the vision correction that is needed. The intersection of the following inequalities describes a typical contact lens cross section. (x and y are measured in millimeters.) Sketch the region. How wide is the contact lens? How thick is it?

$y \leq -0.065x^2 + 2.34$

$y \geq -0.055x^2 + 1.98$

Population of Madagascar   **In Exercises 60 and 61, use the following information.**

For 1970 through 1990, the population, P (in thousands), of Madagascar can be modeled by

$$P = 6.4t^2 + 135t + 6750$$

where $t = 0$ represents 1970.
(Source: United Nations)

60. During which year was the population of Madagascar 8,740,000?

61. According to this model, when will the population of Madagascar reach 16,560,000?

The central part of Madagascar was once covered with rain forest. When the forest was destroyed, millions of cubic feet of soil eroded.

Rain Forests of Madagascar   **In Exercises 62 and 63, use the following information.**

Madagascar has an area of about 226,660 square miles. The number of square miles (in thousands) of rain forest in 1955 and in 1985 can be found by solving the equation

$$x^2 - 96x + 2048 = 0.$$

(Source: National Geographic)

62. What percent of Madagascar's area was rain forest in 1955? What percent was rain forest in 1985?

63. The cross section of a hill is modeled by a quadratic equation, as shown in the diagram. How wide is the hill? How high is it? What is its volume? (In the diagram, x and y are measured in feet.)

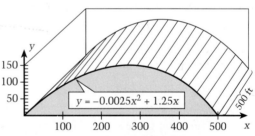

$y = -0.0025x^2 + 1.25x$

64. *Jumping from Branch to Branch*   One branch on a tree is 6 feet directly above another. A lemur on the lower branch jumps up toward the higher branch with an initial velocity of 18 feet per second. The lemur is 18 inches tall. Will it reach the higher branch? Explain.

Many of Madagascar's forest animals, such as this ring-tailed lemur, are endangered because of the dwindling forest areas.

In Exercises 1 and 2, solve the equation by completing the square.

1. $x^2 + 6x - 3 = 0$

2. $2x^2 - 8x + 3 = 0$

In Exercises 3 and 4, solve the equation by the quadratic formula.

3. $3x^2 - 6x + 2 = 0$

4. $5x^2 - 2x + 1 = 0$

In Exercises 5–10, simplify the expression.

5. $(2 + 7i) + (3 - 6i)$

6. $(3 + 4i) - (1 - 3i)$

7. $i(4i - 5)$

8. $(2 + 3i)(3 - 4i)$

9. i^{42}

10. $i^{15} \cdot i^{20}$

In Exercises 11 and 12, state the number of real solutions of the equation.

11. $3x^2 - 5x + 3 = 0$

12. $9x^2 - 6x + 1 = 0$

In Exercises 13–16, sketch the graph of the equation or inequality.

13. $y = 2x^2 - 8x + 5$

14. $y = (x + 3)^2 - 2$

15. $y > x^2 + 2x - 3$

16. $y \geq -x^2 + 6x - 7$

17. Find the value of the discriminant of $5x^2 - 6x + 2 = 0$.

18. For what values of c will $2x^2 - 9x + c = 0$ have two real solutions?

19. Find the axis of symmetry of the graph of $y = 2x^2 - 10x + 7$.

20. Write $y = x^2 + 8x + 7$ in completed square form.

21. A ball was thrown upward from the top of a tower at a velocity of 28 feet per second. The ball hit the ground at the base of the tower 4 seconds later. How high is the tower?

22. For 1980 through 1995, the annual sales, S (in thousands of dollars), of a photography studio can be modeled by $S = -\frac{1}{8}t^2 + 3t + 42$, where $t = 0$ represents 1980. During which year did the studio have sales of \$59,500? During which year did the studio have sales of \$65,500?

23. A rectangular stage in a park is being decorated for a Fourth of July celebration. The stage has an area of 450 square feet. Is 80 feet of skirting material enough to create a skirt that covers all four sides of the stage?

24. You are hanging a rectangular mirror in your room so that one diagonal of the mirror is parallel to the base of the wall. The diagonal of the mirror is 15 inches long. The width of the mirror is three inches shorter than its length. What are the dimensions of the mirror?

Functions

L E S S O N S

6.1 Relations and
Functions ▪ 284

6.2 Function
Operations ▪ 291

6.3 Inverse Functions
▪ 298

6.4 Special Functions
▪ 306

6.5 Transformations
of Graphs
of Functions ▪ 314

6.6 Recursive Functions
and Finite
Differences ▪ 321

6.7 Exploring Data:
Measures of Central
Tendency ▪ 327

Whether a musical tone is high-pitched or low-pitched depends on the frequency of the sound wave. In a pipe organ, such as the one in Milwaukee, Wisconsin, shown here, the pitch is determined by the length of the pipe that is sounded.

Tone Produced by
Length of Pipe

Frequency of Tone
(in vibrations/sec)

200

100

5   10   15   20   25   30 L

Length (in ft)

The pitch of a musical tone sounded by a pipe organ depends on the length of the pipe. An open-ended pipe that is L feet long will produce a pitch with a frequency, f (in vibrations per second), of

$$f = \frac{1100}{2L}$$

where 1100 feet per second is the speed of sound. For example, an 8-foot pipe would have a frequency of about 68.75 vibrations per second, which is roughly two octaves below middle C.

Because the frequency, f, is determined by the length, L, f is called a *function* of the length.

6.1 Relations and Functions

What you should learn:

Goal 1 How to identify a relation and a function

Goal 2 How to identify real-life relations that are functions

Why you should learn it:

You can use functions to describe many relationships in science and social studies, such as the life expectancy of currency.

Goal 1 Identifying Relations and Functions

A **relation** between two variables x and y is a set of ordered pairs. The x-values are the **inputs,** or the **domain,** and the y-values are the **outputs,** or the **range.** Here is an example.

Domain

$$\{(0,-2), (0, 2), (3,-1), (3, 1), (4, 0)\}$$

Range

For this relation, the domain is the set $\{0, 3, 4\}$, and the range is the set $\{-2, 2, -1, 1, 0\}$.

A relation may be described by a set of ordered pairs, a graph, a mapping diagram, a table, an equation, or a verbal sentence.

Example 1 Describing a Relation

The above relation was described as a set of ordered pairs. Here are some other ways to describe the same relation.

a. Graph

b. Mapping Diagram

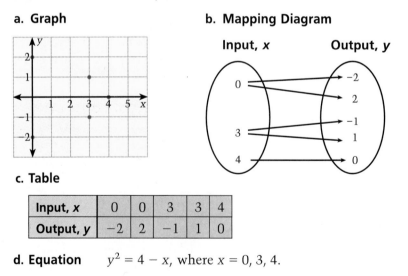

c. Table

Input, *x*	0	0	3	3	4
Output, *y*	−2	2	−1	1	0

d. Equation $y^2 = 4 - x$, where $x = 0, 3, 4$.

You can find the y-values that correspond to a given x-value by substituting the x-value in the equation. For instance, when $x = 0$, $y = \pm 2$. ∎

A relation between x and y is a **function** of x if each value of x corresponds to *exactly one* value of y. From this definition, you can see that the relation in Example 1 is *not* a function of x because two y-values may correspond to the same x-value. For instance, when $x = 0$, y has the values of -2 and 2.

Example 2   Identifying Functions

a. The relation

$$\{(0,-5),\ (0, 5),\ (3,-4),\ (3, 4),\ (4,-3),\ (4, 3),\ (5, 0)\}$$

describes seven points that lie on a circle of radius 5. This relation is *not* a function because two y-values correspond to each of the x-values, 0, 3, and 4. For instance, when $x = 3$, y has the values of -4 and 4. The domain and range of the relation are as follows.

$\{0, 3, 4, 5\}$ *Domain: Set of x-values*

$\{-5, 5,-4, 4,-3, 3, 0\}$ *Range: Set of y-values*

b. The relation

$$\{(-5, 0),\ (-4, 3),\ (-3, 4),\ (0, 5),\ (3, 4),\ (4, 3),\ (5, 0)\}$$

also describes seven points that lie on a circle of radius 5. This relation, however, *is* a function because each x-value corresponds to exactly one y-value. The domain and range are as follows.

$\{-5,-4,-3, 0, 3, 4, 5\}$ *Domain: Set of x-values*

$\{0, 3, 4, 5\}$ *Range: Set of y-values*   ■

The graph of a relation can help you see whether the relation is a function. If you can find one vertical line that passes through two points of the relation, then the relation is *not* a function.

Graph of Example 2a

Relation is not a function because at least one vertical line contains two points.

Graph of Example 2b

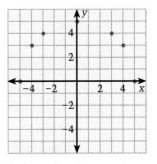

Relation is a function because no two points lie on any one vertical line.

Functions are often described by equations. For example, the equation $y = 4x - 3$ describes y as a function of x. By giving this function the name "f", you can use **function notation.**

Input	Output	Equation
x	$f(x)$	$f(x) = \underbrace{4x - 3}$

$$\uparrow$$
input output

The symbol $f(x)$ is read as the "value of f at x," or simply "f of x." Note that $f(x)$ is another name for y.

To find $f(x)$ for a given value of x is to **evaluate** the function f by substituting an input value into the equation and simplifying. When an equation is used to describe a function, the domain is the set of all x-values that make sense in the equation.

x-value	Function value, $f(x) = 4x - 3$
$x = 0$	$f(0) = 4 \cdot 0 - 3 = 0 - 3 = -3$
$x = 1$	$f(1) = 4 \cdot 1 - 3 = 4 - 3 = 1$
$x = 2$	$f(2) = 4 \cdot 2 - 3 = 8 - 3 = 5$

Up to this point in the text, parentheses have been used to represent multiplication. The function notation $f(x)$ is a *different* use of parentheses. Remember that $f(x)$ means "the value of f at x." It does not mean "f times x."

Example 3   *Evaluating a Function*

Evaluate the function $f(x) = -x^2 - 3x + 5$ at the given x-values.

a. $x = -1$ **b.** $x = 4$

Solution

a. To find the value of $f(x)$ when $x = -1$, substitute -1 for x in the equation that describes the function.

$f(x) = -x^2 - 3x + 5$	*Equation for f*
$f(-1) = -(-1)^2 - 3(-1) + 5$	*Substitute −1 for x.*
$= -1 + 3 + 5, \text{ or } 7$	*Simplify.*

b. To find the value of $f(x)$ when $x = 4$, substitute 4 for x in the equation that describes the function.

$f(x) = -x^2 - 3x + 5$	*Equation for f*
$f(4) = -(4)^2 - 3(4) + 5$	*Substitute 4 for x.*
$= -16 - 12 + 5, \text{ or } -23$	*Simplify.* ∎

Although f is often used as the name of a function, other letters such as g or h can also be used.

Real Life
Currency

| Example **4** | *Identifying Relations That Are Functions* |

a. The average life span of United States currency is a function of the value of the currency. For instance, a $1 bill has an average life span of 1.5 years, a $5 bill has an average life span of 2 years, etc. *(Source: Bureau of Engraving and Printing)*

Value, *x*	$1	$5	$10	$20	$50	$100
Life Span, *y*	1.5 yrs	2 yrs	3 yrs	4 yrs	5 yrs	9 yrs

Real Life
Business

b. For 1980–1985, the dividend per share was not a function of the earnings per share for PepsiCo, Inc. In 1980 and in 1982, the company earned $0.36 per share, but the dividend was $0.14 in 1980 and $0.18 in 1982. *(Source: PepsiCo, Inc.)*

Earnings, *E*	$0.36	$0.40	$0.36	$0.33	$0.38	$0.50
Dividend, *D*	$0.14	$0.16	$0.18	$0.18	$0.19	$0.20

Communicating about ALGEBRA

▶ **SHARING IDEAS about the Lesson**

Does the mapping diagram represent a function? Explain.

A.

| ① | ② | ③ | ④ | ⑤ | ← *Input* |
| ③ | ④ | ⑤ | ⑥ | ⑦ | ← *Output* |

B.

| ① | ② | ③ | ④ | ⑤ | ← *Input* |
| ③ | ④ | ⑤ | ⑥ | ⑦ | ← *Output* |

EXERCISES

▶ **CRITICAL THINKING about the Lesson**

1. Do the mapping diagram and graph describe the same relation? Explain.

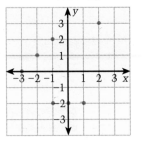

2. Describe in your own words which types of relations are functions.

3. Is the relation described by the table a function? Why or why not? Justify your answer graphically.

Input, x	-3	-2	-1	0	1	2	3	4
Output, y	2	1	-2	-2	-1	0	2	2

4. Which set of ordered pairs describes a function? Explain.

$A = \{(-2, 2), (0, 5), (1, 6), (1, 7), (2, -1), (3, 2)\}$
$B = \{(0, 1), (2, -1), (3, 2), (4, 2), (5, 3), (-5, 1)\}$

Independent Practice

In Exercises 5–8, find the domain and range of the relation.

5. $\{(1, 5), (-2, 8), (0, 4), (-1, 5), (2, 8)\}$

6. $\left\{\left(-\frac{1}{2}, 0\right), (4, 3), (4, -3), (0, 1), (0, -1)\right\}$

7. $\{(4, 1), (7, 2), (7, -2), (3, 0), (4, -1)\}$

8. $\{(0, -1), (1, 2), (-1, 0), (-2, 5), (2, 9)\}$

In Exercises 9–12, sketch a graph of the relation.

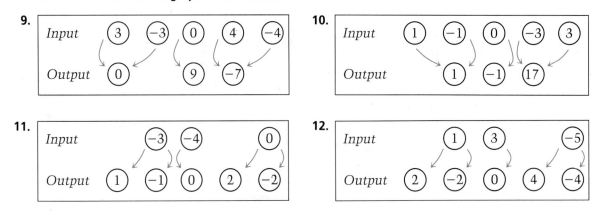

In Exercises 13–16, use a table to describe the relation.

13.

14.

15.

16.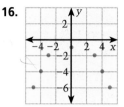

In Exercises 17–20, use a mapping diagram to describe the relation.

17.

18.

19.

20.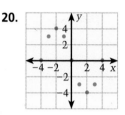

21. Which of the relations in Exercises 13–16 are functions?

22. Which of the relations in Exercises 17–20 are functions?

In Exercises 23–26, determine whether the relation is a function.

23. $\{(0,-5),\ (1,3),\ (2,2),\ (0,4),\ (-5,6),\ (3,4)\}$

24. $\{(-1,6),\ (-1,3),\ (2,4),\ (0,3),\ (1,2),\ (3,1)\}$

25. $\left\{\left(-10,\tfrac{1}{2}\right),\ (-6,1),\ \left(-4,\tfrac{3}{2}\right),\ (-2,2),\ (2,0),\ (0,1)\right\}$

26. $\{(0,-5),\ (5,4),\ (6,6),\ (1,-5),\ (7,7),\ (2,3)\}$

In Exercises 27–34, find the indicated value of $f(x)$.

27. $f(x) = x - 9,\ f(3)$

28. $f(x) = -x^2 + 3,\ f(-1)$

29. $f(x) = x^2 - 3x + 2,\ f(-2)$

30. $f(x) = 3x^2 - x - 1,\ f(4)$

31. $f(x) = \tfrac{1}{2}x^2 - 4x,\ f(1)$

32. $f(x) = \tfrac{-2}{3}x^2 - x + 5,\ f(6)$

33. $f(x) = x^2 - 2x - 4,\ f\left(\tfrac{1}{2}\right)$

34. $f(x) = -x^2 + 4x + 3,\ f\left(-\tfrac{1}{2}\right)$

35. *Geometry* The volume of a cube with edges of length x is given by the function $f(x) = x^3$. Find $f(5)$. Explain what $f(5)$ represents.

36. *Geometry* The volume of a regular tetrahedron with edge length e is given by the function $f(e) = \tfrac{\sqrt{2}}{12}e^3$. Find $f(2)$. Explain what $f(2)$ represents.

Cubes and tetrahedrons are only two possible shapes for dice.

37. *Peanut Production*   For 1984 through 1991, the peanut production, P (in billions of pounds), in the United States is shown in the
table. The table also shows the average yield, y (in pounds per acre).
Was the peanut production a function of average yield? Explain.

Year	1984	1985	1986	1987	1988	1989	1990	1991
Average Yield, y	2880	2805	2400	2335	2440	2440	1895	2596
Production, P	4.44	4.13	3.71	3.60	4.00	4.00	3.62	5.09

38. *New Movie Releases*   The graph at the
right shows the number of new major
movies released from 1985 through 1990.
Is the number of movies a function of the
year? Explain.

Integrated Review

In Exercises 39–42, complete the table.

39. $y = 7x^2 + 4x - 10$

x	-3	-2	-1	0	1	2
y	?	?	?	?	?	?

40. $y = x^2 + \frac{1}{2}x + 6$

x	-2	-1	0	1	2	3	4
y	?	?	?	?	?	?	?

41. $y = -x^2 + 5x + 5$

x	0	1	2	3	4	5	6
y	?	?	?	?	?	?	?

42. $y = 3x^2 + 10x - 2$

x	-5	-4	-3	-2	-1	0	1
y	?	?	?	?	?	?	?

In Exercises 43–46, sketch the graph of the equation.

43. $y = x^2 - 2x + 6$ **44.** $y = x^2 + 10x + 15$ **45.** $y = 2x^2 - 4x - 1$ **46.** $y = -4x^2 - 16x - 15$

Exploration and Extension

47. Let y be a prime factor of x (y is a factor of x and also a prime
number), where x and y are positive integers. Draw a mapping diagram for the inputs and outputs below. Then decide whether the
relation is a function.

Input x: 2, 3, 4, 5, 6, 7, 8

Output y: 2, 3, 4, 5, 6, 7, 8

6.2

Function Operations

What you should learn:

Goal 1 How to perform operations with functions

Goal 2 How to use function operations in real-life situations

Why you should learn it:

You can model many real-life situations with function operations, such as the application of successive discounts.

Goal 1 Performing Function Operations

So far in the book, you have performed addition and multiplication with real numbers, matrices, and complex numbers. These operations can also be performed with functions. Here are some examples that use the functions

$$f(x) = 3x \quad \text{and} \quad g(x) = x - 5.$$

The domain for both f and g is the set of all real numbers. When an equation is used to describe a function, the domain is the set of all x-values that make sense in the equation.

Operation	Resulting Function	Domain
Addition	$f(x) + g(x) = 3x + (x - 5)$ $= 4x - 5$	All real numbers
Subtraction	$f(x) - g(x) = 3x - (x - 5)$ $= 2x + 5$	All real numbers
Multiplication	$f(x) \cdot g(x) = 3x(x - 5)$ $= 3x^2 - 15x$	All real numbers
Division	$f(x) \div g(x) = \dfrac{3x}{x - 5}$	All real numbers except $x = 5$

Note that the domain of the quotient of f and g does not include 5, because that would produce a denominator of zero.

Example 1 *Finding the Domain of a Function*

a. The domain of $f(x) = -3x^2 + 4x + 5$ is the set of all real numbers.

b. The domain of $g(t) = \sqrt{t}$ is the set of nonnegative real numbers, because the square root of a negative number is not a real number. (Unless stated otherwise, you can assume that function values are real numbers.)

c. The domain of

$$h(x) = \frac{3}{x - 4}$$

is the set of all real numbers *except* 4. The number 4 is not in the domain because the denominator cannot be zero. ∎

A fifth operation that is performed with functions is called **composition.**

> ### The Composition of Two Functions
> The **composition** of the function f with the function g is given by
>
> $$h(x) = f(g(x)).$$

A good way to find the composition of two functions is to use three steps, *working from the inside out.* For instance, if $f(x) = 4x + 2$ and $g(x) = x - 3$, then the composition of f with g, $f(g(x))$, can be found as follows.

$$g(x)$$

1. Substitute formula for $g(x)$. $f(g(x)) = f(\overbrace{x - 3})$

$$f(\square) = 4\square + 2$$

2. Apply formula for $f(x)$. $f(g(x)) = \overbrace{4(x - 3) + 2}$

3. Simplify. $f(g(x)) = 4x - 10$

Example 2 *Finding the Composition of Functions*
Find the composition of $f(x) = 4x$ with $g(x) = 2 - x$.

Solution

$$g(x)$$

$f(g(x)) = f(\overbrace{2 - x})$ *Substitute $2 - x$ for $g(x)$.*

$= 4(2 - x)$ *Apply $f(\square) = 4\square$.*

$= 8 - 4x$ *Simplify.* ∎

Example 3 *Finding the Composition of Functions*
Find the composition of $g(x) = 2 - x$ with $f(x) = 4x$.

Solution

$$f(x)$$

$g(f(x)) = g(\overbrace{4x})$ *Substitute $4x$ for $f(x)$.*

$= 2 - (4x)$ *Apply $g(\square) = 2 - \square$.*

$= 2 - 4x$ *Simplify.* ∎

Notice in Examples 2 and 3 that the composition of f with g is not the same as the composition of g with f.

Real Life
Consumer Finance

Example 4 *Comparing Composition Orders*

The regular price of a certain new car is $15,800. The dealer-ship advertised a factory rebate of $1500 *and* a 12% discount. Compare the sale price obtained by subtracting the rebate first, then taking the discount, with the sale price obtained by taking the discount first, then subtracting the rebate.

Solution Using function notation, where x is the price of the car, the price after rebate, $f(x)$, and the price after discount, $g(x)$, can be represented by

$$f(x) = x - 1500 \quad \textit{Rebate of \$1500}$$

$$g(x) = 0.88x \quad \textit{Discount of 12\%}$$

Rebate First: If you subtract the rebate first, the sale price is given by the composition of g with f.

$$g(f(15{,}800)) = g(15{,}800 - 1500) \quad \textit{Subtract the rebate first.}$$

$$= g(14{,}300) \quad \textit{Simplify.}$$

$$= 0.88 \cdot 14{,}300 \quad \textit{Take discount.}$$

$$= \$12{,}584 \quad \textit{Simplify.}$$

Discount First: If you take the discount first, the sale price is given by the composition of f with g.

$$f(g(15{,}800)) = f(0.88 \cdot 15{,}800) \quad \textit{Take the discount first.}$$

$$= f(13{,}904) \quad \textit{Simplify.}$$

$$= 13{,}904 - 1500 \quad \textit{Subtract rebate.}$$

$$= \$12{,}404 \quad \textit{Simplify.}$$

Thus given an option, you should take the discount first. ■

Car dealers often offer two types of incentives to buyers. One is a factory rebate, *which is a dollar amount that is subtracted from the price of the car. The other is a percent* discount *that is taken off the price of the car.*

Communicating *about* **ALGEBRA**

▶ **SHARING IDEAS about the Lesson**

A car dealership is offering a rebate of $1200 *and* a discount of 15% on the purchase of some new cars. Represent the sales price after each type of discount by writing a function for each. Then use composition of functions to express each sale price. What is the difference in the cost of a new car whose regular price is $18,400?

EXERCISES

Guided Practice

▶ **CRITICAL THINKING about the Lesson**

1. What is the domain of $f(x) = 6x - 21$?

2. What is the domain of $f(x) = \dfrac{3x + 2}{x - 5}$?

3. Name the five function operations discussed in this lesson.

4. Consider the functions $f(x) = x + 1$ and $g(x) = 3x$. Find the compositions $f(g(x))$ and $g(f(x))$. Are they the same?

Independent Practice

In Exercises 5–12, find the domain and range of the function.

5. $f(x) = x + 1$

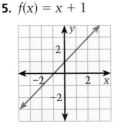

6. $f(x) = x^2 - x$

7. $f(x) = 2x^2 - x + 1$

8. $f(x) = 1 - x^2$

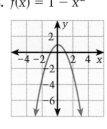

9. $f(x) = \sqrt{x - 3}$

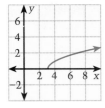

10. $f(x) = \sqrt{x + 1}$

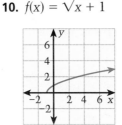

11. $f(x) = \dfrac{4}{x + 1}$

12. $f(x) = \dfrac{x - 3}{x + 3}$

In Exercises 13–20, let $f(x) = x + 1$ and $g(x) = 2x$. Write and simplify an equation for $h(x)$.

13. $h(x) = f(x) + g(x)$

14. $h(x) = f(x) - g(x)$

15. $h(x) = 2f(x) - g(x)$

16. $h(x) = \frac{1}{2}g(x) + f(x)$

17. $h(x) = f(x) \cdot g(x)$

18. $h(x) = g(x) \cdot f(x)$

19. $h(x) = g(x) \div f(x)$

20. $h(x) = f(x) \div g(x)$

In Exercises 21–26, find $f(g(x))$ and $g(f(x))$.

21. $f(x) = x + 1$ and $g(x) = 2x$

22. $f(x) = 2x + 1$ and $g(x) = x - 3$

23. $f(x) = x^2$ and $g(x) = x - 1$

24. $f(x) = x^2 - 1$ and $g(x) = x + 2$

25. $f(x) = x - 3$ and $g(x) = x + 3$

26. $f(x) = -x^2 - 1$ and $g(x) = x + 5$

In Exercises 27–34, let $f(x) = 2x - 8$ and $g(x) = x^2$. Write an equation for $h(x)$. Then describe the domain of h.

27. $h(x) = 2f(x)$ **28.** $h(x) = f(x) + g(x)$ **29.** $h(x) = g(x) - f(x)$ **30.** $h(x) = 6g(x)$

31. $h(x) = f(x) \div g(x)$ **32.** $h(x) = f(x) \cdot g(x)$ **33.** $h(x) = f(g(x))$ **34.** $h(x) = g(f(x))$

35. *Winter Coat Sale*   You have a coupon for $50 off the price of a winter coat. When you arrive at the store, you find that the coats are on sale for 20% off. Use function notation to describe the cost with your coupon and the cost with the 20% discount.

36. Would you pay less for the coat in Exercise 35 if you used your coupon after the discount? Explain.

37. *Sales Bonus*   You are a sales representative for a clothing manufacturer. You are paid an annual salary plus a bonus of 2% of your sales *over* $200,000. Consider two functions: $f(x) = x - 200,000$ and $g(x) = 0.02x$. If x is greater than $200,000$, which of the following represents your bonus? Explain.
   a. $f(g(x))$ **b.** $g(f(x))$

38. *A Bridge over Troubled Waters*   You are standing on a bridge over a calm pond and drop a pebble, causing ripples of concentric circles in the water. The radius (in feet) of the outer ripple is given by $r(t) = 0.6t$, where t is time in seconds after the pebble hits the water. The area of a circle is given by the function $A(r) = \pi r^2$. Find an equation for the composite function $A(r(t))$. What is the input and output of this composite function?

39. *Weekly Production Cost*   The weekly cost of producing x units in a manufacturing process is given by the function $C(x) = 60x + 750$. The number of units produced in t hours during a week is given by $x(t) = 50t$, $0 \le t \le 40$. Find, simplify, and interpret $C(x(t))$.

Dogs and Cats   **In Exercises 40 and 41, use the following information.**

For 1982 through 1990, the numbers of dogs, d (in millions), and cats, c (in millions), in the United States can be modeled by the following functions. (Let $t = 2$ represent 1982.)

     Dogs: $d(t) = 0.875t + 46.25$

     Cats: $c(t) = 2.5t + 38$

(Source: Market Research Corporation of America)

40. How many dogs were there in 1982?

41. Find, simplify, and interpret the sum of $d(t)$ and $c(t)$.

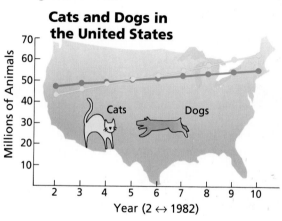

Cats and Dogs in the United States

Extending the School Year   **In Exercises 42 and 43, use the following information.**

Polls were taken in 1982 and in 1991 to determine whether American adults think the school year should be extended. The results can be represented by the following functions, where the function values are percents in decimal form. (Let $t = 2$ represent 1982.)

Favor: $f(t) = 0.0156t + 0.3389$

Oppose: $g(t) = -0.0122t + 0.5544$

Don't Know: $h(t) = -0.0034t + 0.1067$

(Source: Gallup Poll)

Should the School Year Be Extended?

42. What percent favored extending the school year in 1982? In 1991?

43. Find and interpret the sum of $f(t)$, $g(t)$, and $h(t)$.

Integrated Review

In Exercises 44–55, let $f(x) = x - 4$ and $g(x) = -x + 6$. Find the indicated value.

44. $f(3) + g(3)$

45. $f(1) - g(1)$

46. $-3f(3)$

47. $10 + g(6)$

48. $f(2) \cdot g(2)$

49. $f(5) \cdot g(5)$

50. $f(-4) \div g(-4)$

51. $f(4) \div g(4)$

52. $f(g(2))$

53. $g(f(0))$

54. $g(f(1))$

55. $f(g(-3))$

56. *College Entrance Exam Sample*   Fill in the box with either $<$, $>$, or $=$.

| Percent of increase when a $10.00 price is increased by $1.00 | ? | Percent of increase when a $15.00 price is increased by $1.50 |

57. *College Entrance Exam Sample*   In a certain army post, 30% of the enlistees are from New York State, and 10% of these are from New York City. What percent of the enlistees in the post are from New York City?

a. 0.03%   **b.** 0.3%   **c.** 3%   **d.** 13%   **e.** 20%

Exploration and Extension

58. Find $f(x)$ and $g(x)$ such that $f(g(x)) = (x + 1)^2$.

59. Find $f(x)$ and $g(x)$ such that $g(f(x)) = \sqrt{x - 5}$.

60. For most functions f and g that are different, the composite functions $f(g(x))$ and $g(f(x))$ are also different. Find two functions f and g, such that f and g are different, but $f(g(x))$ and $g(f(x))$ are the same.

1. Find all integers such that $-4 < x < 3$.
2. Add: $\frac{2}{3} + \frac{3}{4}$.
3. Simplify: $(3.6 \times 10^6) \div (1.2 \times 10^3)$.
4. Solve $(x - 5)^2 = 16$.
5. Sketch the graph of $y = (x + 3)^2 - 4$. **(5.3)**
6. Find the y-intercept: $y = 3x^2 - 7x + 2$. **(2.3)**
7. Add: $(3a + 4b - c) + (a + 6b + 4c)$.
8. Sketch the graph of $y = \frac{2}{5}x - 3$. **(2.1)**
9. Solve for x: $ax + by = cx$. **(1.5)**
10. Find the vertex of $y = 3|x - 2| + 7$. **(2.6)**
11. Find the intercepts of $y = x^2 + x - 6$. **(5.3)**
12. Has $2x^2 - 4x - 5 = 0$ any real solutions? **(5.4)**
13. Solve $x^2 = -49$. **(5.5)**
14. Solve $9x^2 = 49$. **(5.1)**
15. Simplify: $(0.03)(8.2)$.
16. Write the reciprocal of $\frac{5}{16}$.
17. Write an equation of the line parallel to $y = \frac{3}{4}x + 7$, through $(2, 1)$. **(2.2)**
18. Find the area of the triangle with vertices at $(0, 4)$, $(4, 6)$, and $(2, 1)$. **(4.3)**
19. Solve $\begin{bmatrix} 2 & 1 \\ 0 & -1 \end{bmatrix} X = \begin{bmatrix} 7 & -4 \\ -1 & 0 \end{bmatrix}$. **(4.4)**
20. Write $y = x^2 + 8x + 13$ in completed square form. **(5.3)**

Milestones FRACTALS

| 700 | 500 | 300 | 100 B.C. | A.D.100 | 300 | 500 | 700 | 900 | 1100 | 1300 | 1500 | 1700 | 1900 | 2100 | 2300 |

Euclidean Geometry   Fractal Geometry

The literal translation of the word *geometry* is *earth measurement*. Euclidean geometry measures, or describes quantitatively, many of the shapes found in the natural world, such as circles, spheres, and cones. However, it doesn't describe shapes in nature such as clouds, coastlines, and mountain ranges. Until very recently it was thought that such shapes could not be described in mathematical terms.

In the 1970's, Benoit Mandelbrot discovered that these shapes do have a pattern in their irregularity. He found these shapes are made up of smaller parts that are scaled-down versions of the shape itself. These parts are made up of yet smaller parts that again resemble the shape and so on through numerous reductions. Once the smallest shape that repeats is quantified, computers are helpful in generating the larger image. Mandelbrot coined the term *fractal* for these shapes and for the geometry used to describe them.

By R. F. Voss; from the Fractal Geometry of Nature by Benoit B. Mandelbrot, 1982

The study of fractals involves the concept of chaos. Find out what this is.

6.3

Inverse Functions

What you should learn:

Goal 1 How to identify inverse relations and inverse functions and to verify that two functions are inverses of each other

Goal 2 How to use inverse functions in real-life situations

Why you should learn it:

You can model many pairs of situations with pairs of inverse functions. For example, you could find the sum of the measures of the angles of a polygon given the number of sides, or find the number of sides given the sum of the measures of the angles.

Goal 1 Finding Inverses

The **inverse** of a relation is the set of ordered pairs obtained by switching the coordinates of each ordered pair in the relation. Here is an example.

$\{(0,-3), (1,-1), (2, 1), (3, 3), (4, 5)\}$ *Original relation*

$\{(-3, 0), (-1, 1), (1, 2), (3, 3), (5, 4)\}$ *Inverse relation*

The graph of the inverse is the **reflection** of the graph of the original relation. The mirror of the reflection is the line $y = x$.

Graph of Original Relation   **Graph of Inverse Relation**

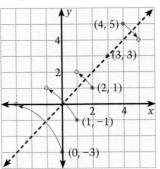

To find the inverse of a relation that is given by an equation in x and y, switch the roles of x and y in the equation.

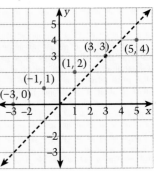

The graphs of $y = 2x - 3$ and $x = 2y - 3$ are reflections of each other in the line $y = x$.

Example 1   *Finding an Inverse Relation*

Find an equation for the inverse of the relation $y = 2x - 3$.

Solution   Begin with the original equation. Then switch the roles of x and y.

$y = 2x - 3$ *Original equation*

$x = 2y - 3$ *Switch the roles of x and y to find an equation for the inverse relation.*

Be sure you see that these two equations are *not* equivalent. When finding an equation of an inverse relation, you are forming a *different* equation whose solutions reflect the switching of x and y. You can confirm this by sketching their graphs. ■

The inverse of a function is found in the same way you find the inverse of a relation (because a function is simply a special type of relation). It is important to realize, however, that the inverse of a function may not itself be a function.

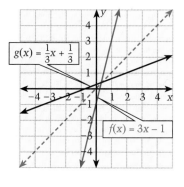

Example 2 Finding the Inverse of a Function

Find the inverse of the function $f(x) = 3x - 1$. Is the inverse a function of x?

Solution To begin, replace $f(x)$ by y. Then switch x and y in the equation.

$$f(x) = 3x - 1 \quad \textit{Original function}$$

$$y = 3x - 1 \quad \textit{Replace f(x) by y.}$$

$$x = 3y - 1 \quad \textit{Switch x and y to obtain inverse.}$$

Thus the inverse relation is given by the linear equation $x = 3y - 1$. To check whether this equation describes a function of x, sketch its graph—it helps to write the equation in slope-intercept form, $y = \frac{1}{3}x + \frac{1}{3}$. Because no vertical line intersects the graph twice, you can conclude that the inverse relation is itself a function. In such cases, function notation is usually used to describe the inverse.

$$g(x) = \frac{1}{3}x + \frac{1}{3} \quad \textit{Inverse function}$$

$\blacksquare$

Example 3 An Inverse Relation That Is Not a Function

Find the inverse of the function $f(x) = x^2 + 1$. Is the inverse a function of x?

Solution

$$f(x) = x^2 + 1 \quad \textit{Original function}$$

$$y = x^2 + 1 \quad \textit{Replace f(x) by y.}$$

$$x = y^2 + 1 \quad \textit{Switch x and y to obtain inverse.}$$

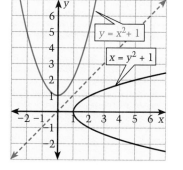

Thus the inverse relation is given by the quadratic equation $x = y^2 + 1$. By constructing a table of values, you can graph this equation, as shown at the left. Notice that the graph does not pass the vertical line test for functions. Thus this inverse relation is *not* a function, and you cannot use function notation to represent the inverse relation. $\blacksquare$

The graph of a function can tell you whether the inverse is also a function. If no *horizontal line* intersects the graph of f twice, then the inverse of f is itself a function. Why?

If g is the inverse of f, then it is also true that f is the inverse of g. This means the functions f and g are inverses of each other. You can verify that two functions defined by equations are inverses of each other by using composition of functions.

Using Composition to Verify Inverse Functions

If the functions f and g are inverses of each other, then

$$f(g(x)) = x \quad \text{and} \quad g(f(x)) = x.$$

Example 4   *Verifying Inverse Functions*

Verify that the functions from Example 2 are inverses of each other.

$$f(x) = 3x - 1 \quad \text{and} \quad g(x) = \tfrac{1}{3}x + \tfrac{1}{3}$$

Solution

$$
\begin{aligned}
f(g(x)) &= f\!\left(\tfrac{1}{3}x + \tfrac{1}{3}\right) && \textit{Substitute } \tfrac{1}{3}x + \tfrac{1}{3} \textit{ for } g(x). \\
&= 3\!\left(\tfrac{1}{3}x + \tfrac{1}{3}\right) - 1 && \textit{Apply } f(\square) = 3\square - 1. \\
&= 3\!\left(\tfrac{1}{3}x\right) + 3\!\left(\tfrac{1}{3}\right) - 1 && \textit{Distributive Property} \\
&= x + 1 - 1 && \textit{Simplify.} \\
&= x && \textit{Simplify.}
\end{aligned}
$$

$$
\begin{aligned}
g(f(x)) &= g(3x - 1) && \textit{Substitute } 3x - 1 \textit{ for } f(x). \\
&= \tfrac{1}{3}(3x - 1) + \tfrac{1}{3} && \textit{Apply } g(\square) = \tfrac{1}{3}\square + \tfrac{1}{3}. \\
&= \tfrac{1}{3}(3x) - \tfrac{1}{3}(1) + \tfrac{1}{3} && \textit{Distributive Property} \\
&= x - \tfrac{1}{3} + \tfrac{1}{3} && \textit{Simplify.} \\
&= x && \textit{Simplify.}
\end{aligned}
$$

Because both compositions produce x, you can conclude that the functions f and g are inverses of each other. ∎

When working with inverse functions, it helps to think of one as "undoing" the operations performed by the other. For instance, the functions

$$f(x) = 4x \quad \text{and} \quad g(x) = \tfrac{1}{4}x$$

are inverses because if you multiply x by 4 and then multiply the result by $\tfrac{1}{4}$, you come back to x. Similarly, the functions $f(x) = x + 5$ and $g(x) = x - 5$ are inverses. The first function adds 5 to x, and the second function subtracts 5, which brings you back to x.

A formula from geometry states that the sum, S (in degrees), of the angles of an n-sided polygon is S = 180n − 360.

Triangle: 180°

Quadrilateral: 360°

Pentagon: 540°

Hexagon: 720°

Heptagon: 900°

Octagon: 1080°

Connections
Geometry

A stop sign is a familiar example of an octagon.

Example 5 *Rewriting a Formula*

The formula $S = 180n - 360$ gives the sum of the angles of an n-sided polygon, where n is the input and S the output. Solve the formula for n so that S is the input and n the output.

Solution Solve for n in terms of S.

$$n = \tfrac{1}{180}S + 2 \qquad \textit{S is input, n is output.}$$

This "inverse" formula could be used to find the number of sides of a polygon when you are given the sum, S, of its angles. For example, a polygon whose interior angles have a sum of 1800° has $n = \tfrac{1}{180}(1800) + 2 = 12$ sides. ∎

You could write the formulas in Example 5 as the inverse functions $f(x) = 180x - 360$ and $g(x) = \tfrac{1}{180}x + 2$. But when the variables have applications, letters that are easily associated with the quantities being measured are often used.

Communicating *about* **ALGEBRA**

▶ **SHARING IDEAS about the Lesson**

Find the inverse of the function. Is the inverse itself a function? Use a graph to help explain your answer.

A. $f(x) = \tfrac{2}{3}x - 4$ **B.** $f(x) = \tfrac{1}{2}x^2 + 3$

EXERCISES

▶ **CRITICAL THINKING about the Lesson**

1. Describe how to find the inverse relation of a relation given by a set of ordered pairs. Give an example.

2. Describe how to find the inverse relation of a relation given by an equation in x and y. Give an example.

3. Find an equation that represents the inverse of the function $f(x) = \frac{1}{2}x - 4$. Sketch the graphs of f and its inverse. Is the inverse of f a function?

4. The graphs of $f(x) = -|x| - 1$ and the inverse of f are shown at the right. Is the inverse of f a function of x? Explain.

5. How is the graph of a relation related to the graph of its inverse?

6. Verify that $f(x) = 2x + 4$ and $g(x) = \frac{1}{2}x - 2$ are inverses of each other.

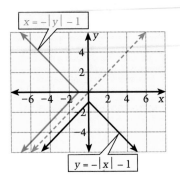

Independent Practice

In Exercises 7–10, find the inverse of the relation.

7. $\{(1, 5), (4, -3), (1, 9), (0, -1)\}$

8. $\{(0, -4), (-4, 3), (3, 2), (2, 1)\}$

9. $\{(-3, 1), (-2, 2), (-1, 0), (3, 3)\}$

10. $\{(1, -4), (3, -2), (0, -6), (-3, 2)\}$

In Exercises 11–14, match the graph with the graph of its inverse.

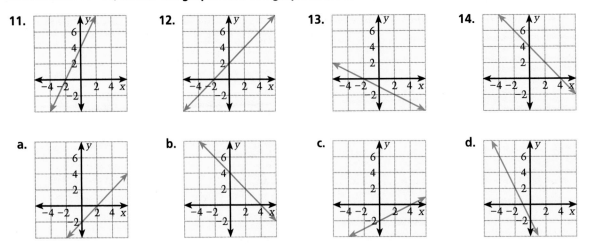

In Exercises 15–22, write an equation for the inverse of the relation.

15. $y = -3x + 5$ **16.** $y = 2x - 3$ **17.** $y = x + 4$ **18.** $y = -5x + 9$

19. $y = 12x - 6$ **20.** $y = -13x + 6$ **21.** $y = 4x - 1$ **22.** $y = 9x - 14$

In Exercises 23–30, sketch the function and its inverse in the same coordinate plane. Is the inverse a function of x?

23. $f(x) = x + 3$ **24.** $f(x) = -x + 2$ **25.** $f(x) = 3x + 4$ **26.** $f(x) = 2x^2 + 4$

27. $f(x) = x^2 + 1$ **28.** $f(x) = -x^2 + 3$ **29.** $f(x) = -x^2 - 4$ **30.** $f(x) = \frac{1}{2}x + 9$

In Exercises 31–34, sketch the graph of the function. Use the graph of f to decide whether the inverse of f is a function of x.

31. $f(x) = x + 1$ **32.** $f(x) = -2x^2 - 1$ **33.** $f(x) = x^2 - 2$ **34.** $f(x) = |x| - 1$

In Exercises 35–40, verify that f and g are inverses of each other.

35. $f(x) = x + 9$, $g(x) = x - 9$

36. $f(x) = -x + 4$, $g(x) = -x + 4$

37. $f(x) = 2x - 1$, $g(x) = \frac{1}{2}x + \frac{1}{2}$

38. $f(x) = \frac{1}{2}x + 2$, $g(x) = 2x - 4$

39. $f(x) = -3x + \frac{1}{2}$, $g(x) = -\frac{1}{3}x + \frac{1}{6}$

40. $f(x) = -4x + 8$, $g(x) = -\frac{1}{4}x + 2$

41. *Temperature Conversion*   The formula to convert temperature in degrees Celsius to temperature in degrees Fahrenheit is

$F = \frac{9}{5}C + 32.$

For this formula, C is the input and F is the output. Rewrite the formula so that F is the input and C is the output.

42. *Geometry*   The height h of an equilateral triangle with sides of length s is

$h = \frac{\sqrt{3}s}{2}.$

Rewrite the formula so that the height is the input and the length of the sides is the output.

43. *Bowling Handicap*   You belong to a bowling league in which each bowler's handicap, H, is determined by his or her average, A, according to the following formula.

$H = 0.8(200 - A)$

(If the bowler's average is over 200, the handicap is 0.) Rewrite this formula so that the handicap is the input and the average is the output. If your handicap is 32, what is your average?

44. *State Sales Tax*   In a state that has a 6% sales tax, the total cost, C, of a taxable item that has a price of p is $C = 0.06p + p$. Rewrite this formula so that C is the input and p is the output.

Tax-Freedom Day **In Exercises 45 and 46, use the following information.**

Tax-Freedom Day is the day of the year that the average taxpayer will have earned enough money to pay his or her total federal, state, and local taxes. The table gives the number of the Tax-Freedom Day in each state (and the District of Columbia) in 1990. *(Source: Tax Foundation)*

AK–129	FL–122	LA–122	NC–122	OK–125	VA–120
AL–119	GA–119	MA–128	ND–117	OR–115	VT–120
AR–115	HI–137	MD–132	NE–115	PA–126	WA–125
AZ–124	IA–116	ME–123	NH–109	RI–127	WI–123
CA–124	ID–114	MI–123	NJ–129	SC–123	WV–120
CO–117	IL–125	MN–128	NM–130	SD–109	WY–120
CT–132	IN–117	MO–121	NV–123	TN–119	
DC–143	KS–122	MS–110	NY–143	TX–118	
DE–138	KY–119	MT–116	OH–124	UT–118	

45. Let T represent the total federal, state, and local taxes for the average taxpayer in Tennessee. Let I represent the taxpayer's total 1990 income. Which of the following equations describes the relationship between T and I?

a. $T = \frac{119}{365}I$ **b.** $I = \frac{119}{365}T$

46. Explain the differences in the numbers in the table.

Integrated Review

In Exercises 47–50, write the equation in slope-intercept form.

47. $x = 2y - 3$ **48.** $x = 9y + 18$ **49.** $x = y + 2$ **50.** $x = -2y - 6$

In Exercises 51–54, sketch the graph of the equation. Is y a function of x?

51. $y = x$ **52.** $y = x^2$ **53.** $x = y^2$ **54.** $x = |y|$

In Exercises 55–58, find $f(g(x))$.

55. $f(x) = \frac{1}{2}x,\quad g(x) = 3x + 2$ **56.** $f(x) = x + 1,\quad g(x) = 2x - 6$

57. $f(x) = x^2 - 6,\quad g(x) = -10x$ **58.** $f(x) = -5x + 1,\quad g(x) = 2x$

Exploration and Extension

59. Is it possible for a relation that is not a function to have an inverse that is a function? Why or why not?

60. True or False?   The function $f(x) = 2 - x$ is its own inverse. Explain.

61. *Geometry*   Find the area of the polygon formed by the graphs of $y = 4 - x$, $f(x) = 8 - 2x$, and the inverse of f.

62. *Geometry*   Find the area of the polygon formed by the graphs of $y = 2 - x$, $y = 6 - x$, $f(x) = x + 2$, and the inverse of f.

Take this test as you would take a test in class. The answers to the exercises are given in the back of the book.

1. Express the relation $\{(2, 3), (4, 7), (4, 12), (5, 3), (6, 8)\}$ as a mapping. **(6.1)**

2. Sketch the graph of $\{(0, -4), (1, 0), (2, 1), (3, 5), (4, 1)\}$. **(6.1)**

3. Which is *not* the graph of a function? **(6.1)**

a.

b.

c.
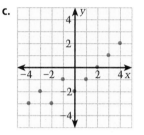

4. Given $f(x) = 2x^2 + 5x + 2$, find $f(-3)$. **(6.1)**

5. Is $\{(-2, 1), (-1, 2), (-1, 3), (0, 4), (3, 5)\}$ a function? Explain. **(6.1)**

6. Find the domain and range of
   $\{(-4, 1), (-3, 2), (-2, 3), (-1, 4), (0, 5)\}$. **(6.1)**

In Exercises 7–9, find the domain of the function. (6.2)

7. $f(x) = \dfrac{x-5}{x+2}$

8. $h(x) = 4x^2$

9. $k(x) = \sqrt{x-7}$

In Exercises 10–12, find the range of the function. (6.2)

10. $k(x) = x^2 + 9$

11. $f(x) = (x+5)^2 + 3$

12. $h(x) = \sqrt{x+16}$

In Exercises 13–15, use $f(x) = x^2$ and $g(x) = 4x - 6$ to find $h(x)$. (6.2, 6.3)

13. $h(x) = f(x) - g(x)$

14. $h(x) = f(g(x))$

15. $h(x)$ is the inverse of $g(x)$.

In Exercises 16–18, use the following information. With a coupon, if you purchase one spaghetti dinner at the regular price, x, you can purchase the second dinner at half price. (6.2)

16. Write a function, $P(x)$, for the price of the two spaghetti dinners.

17. Write a function, $C(x)$, that represents the total amount spent for the two dinners. In the total price, include a 15% tip (based on the full regular price of two dinners), and a 7% sales tax.

18. Evaluate the function in Exercise 17 when x is $5.

In Exercises 19 and 20, use the following information. After giving a 75-point test, a teacher adjusts the test scores by adding 7 points to each student's score. After adding the 7 points, each student is given a percent score (based on 75 possible points). (6.3)

19. Write a function that inputs the original point score and outputs the percent score.

20. Find the inverse of the function in Exercise 19. Use this inverse to find the original score of a student whose percent score is 89%.

6.4

Special Functions

What you should learn:

Goal 1 How to use special functions, such as compound functions and step functions

Goal 2 How to use these functions in real-life situations

Why you should learn it:

You can model many situations with compound functions, such as the changing costs of mobile homes in the United States.

Goal 1 Using Special Functions

In the first three lessons of this chapter, a single equation represented each function. In many real-life problems, however, functions may be represented by a combination of equations. Such functions are called **compound functions.** For example, the compound function given by

$$f(x) = \begin{cases} 2x - 1, & x \leq 1 \\ x^2 - 2x + 1, & x > 1 \end{cases}$$

is defined by two equations. One equation gives the values of $f(x)$ when x is less than or equal to 1, and the other equation gives the values of $f(x)$ when x is greater than 1.

Example 1 Using a Compound Function

Sketch the graph of the compound function. What is $f(-2)$? What is $f(3)$?

$$f(x) = \begin{cases} -x^2 + 2, & x < 0 \\ x + 2, & x \geq 0 \end{cases}$$

Solution To the left of the y-axis, the graph of the function is a parabola that opens down and whose vertex is $(0, 2)$. To the right of the y-axis, the graph is a line that has a slope of 1 and a y-intercept of 2. To sketch the graph of the function, you can lightly draw both graphs. Then darken the portion of the graph that represents the function, as shown at the left.

To find the value of the function when $x = -2$, use the first equation.

$$f(-2) = -(-2)^2 + 2 = -4 + 2 = -2$$

To find the value of the function when $x = 3$, use the second equation.

$$f(3) = 3 + 2 = 5$$

In Example 1, the left and right portions of the graph of the compound function connect at the point $(0, 2)$. Try sketching the graph of the compound function listed at the top of the page. Do the left and right portions of its graph connect? ∎

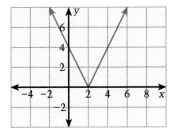

Example 2

Writing an Absolute Value Function as a Compound Function

Write the *absolute value function* $f(x) = |2x - 4|$ as a compound function.

Solution For $x < 2$, the values of $2x - 4$ are negative, and for $x > 2$, the values of $2x - 4$ are positive. Thus, the function could be written as follows.

$$f(x) = \begin{cases} -(2x - 4), & x < 2 \\ 2x - 4, & x \geq 2 \end{cases}$$

The graph of the function is shown at the left. ■

Some compound functions are defined by many different equations. One special type is called a **step function** because its graph looks like stair steps.

Real Life

Postage Rates

Example 3 — Sketching the Graph of a Step Function

The cost, C, of using an overnight delivery service to send a package depends on the weight, x (in ounces), of the package. The following step function gives the cost for packages that weigh less than 1 pound. Sketch the graph of this function.

$$C = \begin{cases} 8.50, & 0 < x < 2 \\ 9.75, & 2 \leq x < 4 \\ 12.00, & 4 \leq x < 6 \\ 13.25, & 6 \leq x < 8 \\ 15.50, & 8 \leq x < 10 \\ 16.75, & 10 \leq x < 12 \\ 18.00, & 12 \leq x < 14 \\ 19.25, & 14 \leq x < 16 \end{cases}$$

Cost of Overnight Delivery

Weight (in ounces)

Solution The graph consists of horizontal line segments. The endpoints of the line segments are represented by either open dots or solid dots. For instance, the first line segment has an open dot on the left because you cannot send a package that weighs 0 ounces. The first line segment also has an open dot on the right because a 2-ounce package does *not* cost $8.50, but $9.75 (which is symbolized by the solid dot on the left of the second line segment). ■

Goal 2 | **Using Special Functions in Real Life**

Real Life
Housing Cost

Example 4 The Price of a Mobile Home

For 1975 through 1994, the average cost, C, of a new mobile home in the United States can be modeled by the compound function

$$C = \begin{cases} 19{,}600 + 1800t, & -5 \le t < 0 \\ 19{,}600 + 297t + 46t^2, & 0 \le t \le 14 \end{cases}$$

where $t = 0$ represents 1980. Sketch the graph of this compound function. Use the graph to describe the change in the average cost of a mobile home.

(Source: U.S. Bureau of Census Construction Reports)

Cost of Mobile Homes

Price (in thousands of dollars)

Year (0 ↔ 1980)

Solution To the left of the y-axis, the graph is a line, and to the right of the y-axis, the graph is a parabola. From the graph, you can see that between 1975 and 1980, the average cost of a mobile home was increasing at a constant rate. Between 1980 and 1994, however, the average cost began increasing according to a quadratic model. ∎

Communicating *about* **ALGEBRA**

▶ **SHARING IDEAS about the Lesson**

Sketch the graph of each function. Explain the steps you used.

A. $f(x) = \begin{cases} -2x^2 + 4, & x \le 0 \\ 2x^2 + 4, & x > 0 \end{cases}$ **B.** $f(x) = \begin{cases} 4, & 0 \le x < 3 \\ 5, & 3 \le x < 6 \\ 6, & 6 \le x < 9 \end{cases}$

EXERCISES

Guided Practice

▶ **CRITICAL THINKING about the Lesson**

1. Give an example of a compound function. Draw its graph.

In Exercises 2 and 3, consider the function $f(x) = |10 - 2x|$.

2. Write $f(x)$ as a compound function.

3. Sketch the graph of f. What is $f(3)$? What is $f(6)$?

4. Give an example of a step function. Draw its graph.

Independent Practice

In Exercises 5–8, evaluate the function for the given value of *x*.

$$f(x) = \begin{cases} -x^2 - 2x, & x < -1 \\ x + 2, & x \geq -1 \end{cases}$$

5. $f(-3)$ **6.** $f(0)$ **7.** $f(-1)$ **8.** $f(3)$

In Exercises 9–12, evaluate the function for the given value of *x*.

$$g(x) = \begin{cases} -2x - 1, & x \leq 1 \\ -x^2 + 3x - 5, & x > 1 \end{cases}$$

9. $g(1)$ **10.** $g(-2)$ **11.** $g(4)$ **12.** $g(0)$

In Exercises 13–18, sketch the graph of the function.

13. $f(x) = \begin{cases} x + 5, & x < -2 \\ x^2 + 2x + 3, & x \geq -2 \end{cases}$ **14.** $g(x) = \begin{cases} 2x, & x \leq 2 \\ -2x^2 + 3x + 6, & x > 2 \end{cases}$

15. $h(x) = \begin{cases} \frac{1}{4}x - 2, & x \leq 4 \\ x^2 - x - 13, & x > 4 \end{cases}$ **16.** $f(x) = \begin{cases} x^2 - 4x + 5, & x < 3 \\ -2x + 8, & x \geq 3 \end{cases}$

17. $f(x) = \begin{cases} x^2 + 4x - 20, & x < 3 \\ -x + 4, & x \geq 3 \end{cases}$ **18.** $f(x) = \begin{cases} \frac{1}{2}x^2 - x + 7, & x \leq -4 \\ 2x + 11, & x > -4 \end{cases}$

In Exercises 19–22, match the equation with its graph.

19. $f(x) = |x - 6|$ **20.** $f(x) = |-x + 4|$ **21.** $f(x) = |-2x - 8|$ **22.** $f(x) = \left| \frac{1}{2}x + 4 \right|$

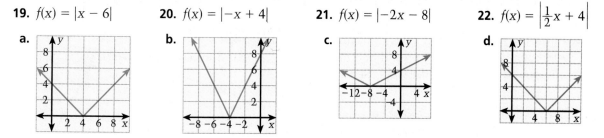

In Exercises 23–28, write the absolute value function as a compound function.

23. $f(x) = |x + 2|$

24. $f(x) = |-x + 5|$

25. $f(x) = |-2x - 6|$

26. $f(x) = \left|\frac{1}{2}x - 3\right|$

27. $f(x) = \left|\frac{1}{3}x - 1\right|$

28. $f(x) = |-3x + 6|$

In Exercises 29–31, sketch the graph of the step function.

29. $y = \begin{cases} 4, & -2 \le x < 3 \\ 6, & 3 \le x < 5 \\ 9, & 5 \le x < 6 \\ 12, & 6 \le x < 10 \end{cases}$

30. $y = \begin{cases} 10, & 0 \le x < 1 \\ 4, & 1 \le x < 2 \\ 1, & 2 \le x < 3 \\ -3, & 3 \le x < 4 \end{cases}$

31. $y = \begin{cases} 4.6, & -3 \le x < -1 \\ 2.1, & -1 \le x < 2 \\ 0, & 2 \le x < 3 \\ -3.1, & 3 \le x < 5 \end{cases}$

32. *Summer Job*   You are working at a summer job that pays time and a half for overtime. That is, if you work more than 40 hours per week, your hourly wage for the extra hours is 1.5 times the normal hourly wage of $5.50. Write a compound function that gives your weekly pay, P, in terms of the number of hours, x, you work.

33. *Silk-screen T-Shirts*   A silk-screen shop has the following price schedule for silk-screen T-shirts.

- An initial charge of $10 to create the silk-screen.
- $8.50 per shirt for orders of 25 or fewer shirts.
- $7.75 per shirt for orders of more than 25 shirts.

Write a compound function that gives the cost, C, for an order of x shirts. Sketch the graph of this function.

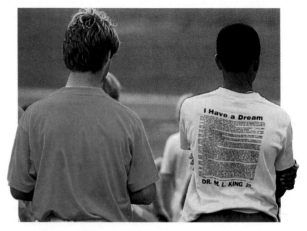

34. *Telephone Call*   The cost, C, of a t-minute telephone call from Bogalusa, Louisiana, to Biloxi, Mississippi, is given by the following step function. (The rates are based on an evening call in 1991.) Sketch the graph of this function. What is the cost of a call that lasts 20 minutes and 35 seconds?

$$C = \begin{cases} 0.28, & 0 < t \le 1 \\ 0.28 + 1(0.18), & 1 < t \le 2 \\ 0.28 + 2(0.18), & 2 < t \le 3 \\ 0.28 + 3(0.18), & 3 < t \le 4 \\ 0.28 + 4(0.18), & 4 < t \le 5 \\ \vdots & \vdots \end{cases}$$

35. *Photocopy Rates*   The cost, C, of making x photocopies is given by the compound function at the right. Sketch the graph of this function.

$$C = \begin{cases} 0.10x, & 0 < x \le 25 \\ 0.08x, & 25 < x \le 100 \\ 0.06x, & 100 < x \le 250 \\ 0.04x, & 250 < x \end{cases}$$

36. Why would it not make sense to order 240 photocopies with this rate schedule?

Health and Research In Exercises 37 and 38, match the compound function given in the exercise with its graph. Then answer the questions.

37. For 1970 through 1990, the total health expenses, H (in billions of dollars), in the United States can be modeled by

$$H = \begin{cases} t^2 + 6.4t + 76, & 0 \le t < 10 \\ 36.5t - 125, & 10 \le t \le 20 \end{cases}$$

where $t = 0$ represents 1970. What were the expenses in 1975? in 1985?

38. For 1970 through 1990, the total amount, R (in billions of dollars), spent on research and development in the United States can be modeled by

$$R = \begin{cases} 0.31t^2 + 0.25t + 26.5, & 0 \le t < 10 \\ -0.26t^2 + 15.3t - 67, & 10 \le t \le 20 \end{cases}$$

where $t = 0$ represents 1970. How much was spent on research and development in 1970? In 1980? In 1990?

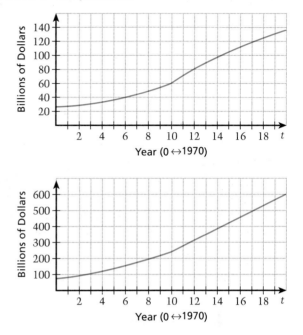

Integrated Review

In Exercises 39–44, sketch the graph of the equation.

39. $y = -\frac{1}{2}x + 6$ **40.** $y = 2x + 9$ **41.** $y = x^2 + 6x - 9$

42. $y = -2x^2 - x + 4$ **43.** $y = -\frac{1}{2}x^2 + 4x + 10$ **44.** $y = 3x^2 - x + 9$

In Exercises 45–50, find the indicated value of $f(x)$.

45. $f(x) = x - 2, \quad f(3)$ **46.** $f(x) = -\frac{1}{2}x + 3, \quad f(4)$ **47.** $f(x) = x^2 - x, \quad f(-1)$

48. $f(x) = x^2 - 5x, \quad f(5)$ **49.** $f(x) = 3x^2 - x - 7, \quad f(-5)$ **50.** $f(x) = 3x^2 + 4x - 6, \quad f(-3)$

Exploration and Extension

51. *Writing a Compound Function* In the coordinate plane at the right, the equations for the graphs are as follows.

A: $y = -\frac{1}{4}x^2 + 2x + 4$
B: $y = 2x - 12$
C: $y = -2x + 36$
D: $y = -\frac{1}{4}x^2 + 10x - 92$

Write a compound function that describes the entire graph.

After finding an equation that represents the inverse of a function, you can use a graphing calculator to verify that the graph of the inverse is a reflection (in the line $y = x$) of the graph of the original function. For instance, to verify graphically that the functions

$$f(x) = 2x + 3 \quad \text{and} \quad g(x) = \frac{1}{2}(x - 3)$$

are inverses of each other, you can sketch the graph of f, the graph of g, and the graph of $y = x$, all on the same screen. The graph of g should be the mirror image (in the line $y = x$) of the graph of f.

Because the display screens on most graphing calculators are not square, you will not obtain a true reflection with a standard setting. You need to use a **square setting,** in which the ratio of (Ymax − Ymin) to (Xmax − Xmin) is equal to the ratio of the screen height to the screen width. On most graphing calculators, this ratio is two thirds.

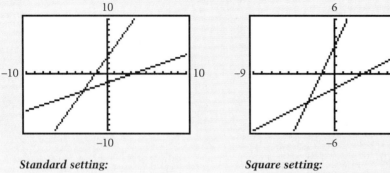

Standard setting:
Graph is distorted.

Square setting:
Graph is not distorted.

Another case for which it is helpful to use a square setting is to sketch graphs of two perpendicular lines.

Example 1: Using a Square Setting for Perpendicular Lines

Sketch the graphs of $y = -3x + 12$ and $y = \frac{1}{3}x + 2$. Choose a viewing rectangle that shows the two lines intersecting at right angles.

Solution If you sketch the two lines with a standard setting, you can see that they intersect at the point $(3, 3)$. The angles formed by the two lines at the point, however, do not appear to be right angles. (Try this with your own graphing calculator.) To eliminate the distortion in the graph, change to a square setting, such as $-9 \leq x \leq 9$ and $-6 \leq y \leq 6$. For this setting, there is no distortion, and the lines are shown to be perpendicular. ■

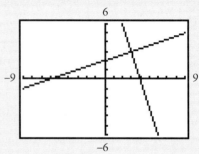

Example 2:   Sketching the Graph of a Circle

Sketch the graphs of the functions

$$f(x) = \sqrt{36 - x^2} \quad \text{and} \quad g(x) = -\sqrt{36 - x^2}$$

on the same coordinate plane. What recognizable shape do the graphs form?

Solution   Begin by changing the range to the square setting given by $-9 \le x \le 9$ and $-6 \le y \le 6$. Then sketch the graphs of both functions. As shown at the right, the two graphs form the upper and lower portions of a circle. The center of the circle is the origin, and the radius of the circle is 6.

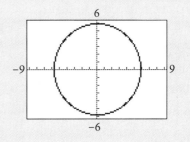

Notice that the entire circle could not be represented by a single function, because it does not pass the vertical line test. The domain and range of each function are as follows.

Domain of f: $-6 \le x \le 6$ *Range of f:* $0 \le y \le 6$
Domain of g: $-6 \le x \le 6$ *Range of g:* $-6 \le y \le 0$ ■

Exercises

In Exercises 1–6, find the inverse of the function. Then use a graphing calculator to verify that the graph of the inverse is a reflection (in the line $y = x$) of the graph of *f*. Use a square setting.

1. $f(x) = 4x - 9$

2. $f(x) = -\frac{1}{2}x + 5$

3. $f(x) = \frac{2}{3}x - 6$

4. $f(x) = -3x + 8$

5. $f(x) = -2.5x + 5$

6. $f(x) = 0.35x - 4$

7. Find an equation of the line that passes through the point $(2, -3)$ and is perpendicular to the line $4x - 5y = 8$. Then use a graphing calculator to sketch the graph of each line. Use a square setting.

8. Find an equation of the line that passes through the point $(-1, 4)$ and is perpendicular to the line $-2x + 3y = 4$. Then use a graphing calculator to sketch the graph of each line. Use a square setting.

In Exercises 9–12, sketch the graphs of both functions on the same display screen. (Use a square setting.) State the domain and range of each function. Then use a formula from geometry to find the area of the region enclosed by the two graphs.

9. $f(x) = \sqrt{25 - x^2}, g(x) = -\sqrt{25 - x^2}$

10. $f(x) = \frac{2}{3}\sqrt{81 - x^2}, g(x) = -\frac{2}{3}\sqrt{81 - x^2}$

11. $f(x) = 6 - |x|, \quad -6 \le x \le 6$
$g(x) = -6 + |x|, \quad -6 \le x \le 6$

12. $f(x) = 3 + \frac{1}{2}x - \frac{1}{2}|x|, \quad -6 \le x \le 6$

$g(x) = -3 + \frac{1}{2}x + \frac{1}{2}|x|, \quad -6 \le x \le 6$

6.5 Transformations of Graphs of Functions

What you should learn:

Goal 1 How to use translations and reflections to sketch the graph of a function

Goal 2 How to use transformations of graphs of functions in real-life settings

Why you should learn it:

Translations and reflections provide a quick way of sketching graphs of functions.

Goal 1   Using Translations and Reflections

Many functions have graphs that are **geometric transformations** of the graphs of simpler functions. For instance, the graph of $g(x) = x^2 + 1$ is a shift of the graph of $f(x) = x^2$ *upward* by one unit. In function notation, g and f are related by

$$g(x) = x^2 + 1 = f(x) + 1. \quad \textit{Upward shift of 1}$$

LESSON INVESTIGATION

■ **Investigating Horizontal and Vertical Shifts**

Partner Activity Use a graphing calculator to sketch the graph of $f(x) = x^2$ using a standard viewing rectangle. Then with your partner, write equations for the following graphs.

a. Graph of g: Shift the graph of f up 2 units.
b. Graph of g: Shift the graph of f down 3 units.
c. Graph of g: Shift the graph of f left 1 unit.
d. Graph of g: Shift the graph of f right 4 units.

In general, discuss how you can alter an equation so that its graph is shifted horizontally or vertically.

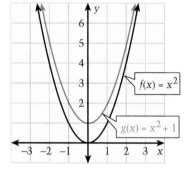

Shift the graph of f up 1 unit to get the graph of g.

The list below summarizes the various **horizontal shifts** and **vertical shifts** (or translations) of the graphs of functions.

Vertical and Horizontal Shifts

Let c be a positive real number. **Vertical** and **horizontal shifts** of the graph of f are represented as follows.

1. Vertical shift of c units *upward*: $g(x) = f(x) + c$
2. Vertical shift of c units *downward*: $g(x) = f(x) - c$
3. Horizontal shift of c units *to the right*: $g(x) = f(x - c)$
4. Horizontal shift of c units *to the left*: $g(x) = f(x + c)$

Example 1 *Shifts of the Graphs of Functions*

Use the graph of $f(x) = x^2$ to sketch the graph of each function.

a. $g(x) = x^2 - 2$

b. $h(x) = (x + 3)^2$

Solution

a. To sketch the graph of $g(x) = x^2 - 2$, shift the graph of $f(x) = x^2$ *downward* by 2 units.

b. To sketch the graph of $h(x) = (x + 3)^2$, shift the graph of $f(x) = x^2$ *to the left* by 3 units.

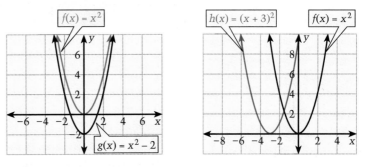

a. *Shift downward of 2 units*   **b.** *Shift left of 3 units*

Some graphs can be obtained from a *combination* of vertical and horizontal shifts, as shown in the next example. ◼

Example 2 *Shifts of the Graphs of Functions*

Use the graph of $f(x) = |x|$ to sketch the graph of each function.

a. $g(x) = |x - 3| + 1$

b. $h(x) = |x + 2| - 3$

Solution

a. To sketch the graph of $g(x) = |x - 3| + 1$, shift the graph of $f(x) = |x|$ by 3 units *to the right* and 1 unit *upward.*

b. To sketch the graph of $h(x) = |x + 2| - 3$, shift the graph of $f(x) = |x|$ by 2 units *to the left* and 3 units *downward.*

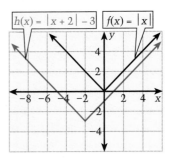

a. *Right shift of 3 units,*
    upward shift of 1 unit

b. *Left shift of 2 units,*
    downward shift of 3 units ◼

The reflection of the hill and tree is seen in the lake.

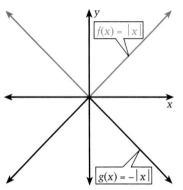

A second type of transformation is a **reflection.** For instance, if you imagine that the x-axis represents a mirror, then the graph of $g(x) = -|x|$ is the mirror image (or reflection) of the graph of $f(x) = |x|$.

> **Reflection in the x-Axis**
>
> If $g(x) = -f(x)$, then the graph of g is a reflection in the x-axis of the graph of f.

Example 3 *Reflections of the Graphs of Functions*

Use the graph of $f(x) = x^2$ to sketch the graph of each function.
a. $g(x) = -x^2$ **b.** $h(x) = -(x-3)^2$

Solution

a. To sketch the graph of $g(x) = -x^2$, reflect the graph of $f(x) = x^2$ in the x-axis.

b. To sketch the graph of $h(x) = -(x-3)^2$, first shift the graph of $f(x) = x^2$ by 3 units *to the right*. Then reflect the result in the x-axis.

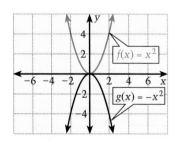

a. *Reflection in the x-axis*

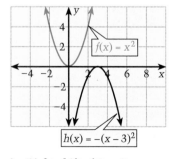

b. *Right shift of 3 units, reflection in the x-axis*

Goal **2** Using Transformation of Graphs

Real Life
Consumer Spending

| *Example* **4** | *Shifting a Graph* |

For 1970 through 1990, the amount of money, $f(t)$ (in billions of dollars), that Americans spent on radios, televisions, recordings, and musical instruments can be modeled by

$$f(t) = 8.4 + 0.125t^2$$

where $t = 0$ represents 1970. Rewrite this model so that $t = 0$ represents 1980. *(Source: U.S. Bureau of Economic Analysis)*

Solution In the formula for f, $t = 10$ represents 1980. You want to obtain a formula in which $t = 0$ represents 1980. Therefore, you need to shift the graph 10 units *to the left.* The resulting model is

$$g(t) = 8.4 + 0.125(t + 10)^2. \quad \textit{t = 0 represents 1980.}$$

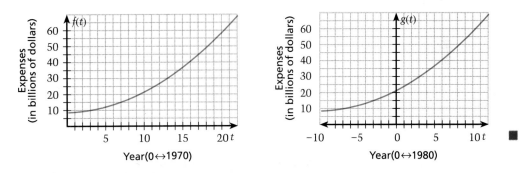

Communicating about ALGEBRA

▶ **SHARING IDEAS about the Lesson**

Each of the graphs represents a transformation of the graph of $f(x) = x^2$. Find an equation for each graph. Explain your reasoning.

A.　　　　**B.**　　　　**C.**

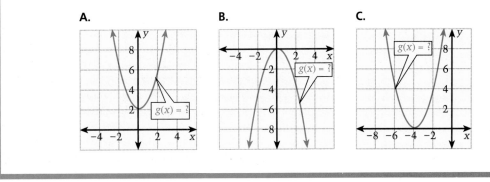

EXERCISES

Guided Practice

▶ **CRITICAL THINKING about the Lesson**

1. Describe the four types of shifts of the graph of a function.

2. How are the graphs of $f(x)$ and $g = -f(x)$ related?

3. Use a shift to sketch the graph of $h(x) = (x + 2)^2$.

4. Use a reflection to sketch the graph of $g(x) = -|x|$.

In Exercises 5–8, match the function with its graph.

5. $f(x) = |x - 3|$ **6.** $f(x) = |x| + 2$ **7.** $f(x) = -(x - 2)^2$ **8.** $f(x) = (x + 2)^2 - 2$

a.

b.

c.

d.
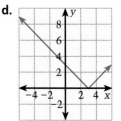

Independent Practice

In Exercises 9–16, compare the graph of g to the graph of $f(x) = x^2$.

9. $g(x) = x^2 + 3$ **10.** $g(x) = x^2 + 9$ **11.** $g(x) = x^2 - 1$ **12.** $g(x) = x^2 - 3$

13. $g(x) = (x - 8)^2$ **14.** $g(x) = (x + 4)^2$ **15.** $g(x) = (x + 5)^2$ **16.** $g(x) = (x - 7)^2$

In Exercises 17–20, show how f and g are related by writing an equation of the form $g(x) = f(\boxed{?})$ or $g(x) = f(x) + \boxed{?}$.

17. $f(x) = x^2$
    $g(x) = (x + 1)^2$

18. $f(x) = |x|$
    $g(x) = |x - 9|$

19. $f(x) = |x|$
    $g(x) = |x| - 3$

20. $f(x) = x^2$
    $g(x) = x^2 + 4$

In Exercises 21–24, match the equation with its graph.

21. $y = (x - 4)^2$ **22.** $y = x^2 + 4$ **23.** $y = |x| + 4$ **24.** $y = |x + 4|$

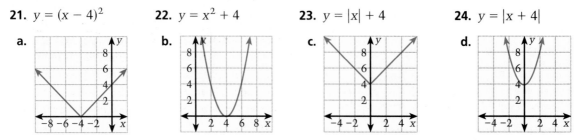

In Exercises 25–42, sketch the graph of the function.

25. $f(x) = |x| + 1$

26. $f(x) = |x + 2|$

27. $f(x) = x^2 + 2$

28. $f(x) = |x + 5| + 1$

29. $f(x) = |x - 2| + 5$

30. $f(x) = (x + 3)^2$

31. $f(x) = (x - 5)^2 + 4$

32. $f(x) = |x - 4| - 3$

33. $f(x) = |x + 6| - 3$

34. $f(x) = -|x|$

35. $f(x) = -(x - 1)^2$

36. $f(x) = -(x^2 + 1)$

37. $f(x) = -(x + 5)^2$

38. $f(x) = -(x + 3)^2 + 1$

39. $f(x) = (x - 2)^2 + 4$

40. $f(x) = -|x + 3| - 3$

41. $f(x) = (x + 7)^2 - 1$

42. $f(x) = -|x - 1| + 4$

In Exercises 43–46, match the equation with its graph.

43. $y = -|x - 3|$

44. $y = -|x - 2|$

45. $y = -(x + 2)^2$

46. $y = -(x - 3)^2$

a.

b.

c.

d.

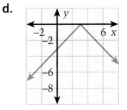

Cable Television Systems   **In Exercises 47–49, use the following information.**

For 1970 through 1994, the number of cable television systems, $C(t)$, in the United States can be modeled by

$$C(t) = 14t^2 + 63.2t + 2500$$

where $t = 0$ represents 1970.
(Source: Television and Cable Factbook)

47. Rewrite the model so that $t = 0$ represents 1980. Describe the shift from the original model to this one.

48. Rewrite the model so that $t = 0$ represents 1990. Describe the shift from the original model to this one.

49. Approximate the average number of subscribers of cable television in 1993.

50. *Civilian Population of United States* For 1950 through 1994, the civilian population, P (in thousands), in the United States can be modeled by

$$P = -8t^2 + 2767t + 150{,}000$$

where $t = 0$ represents 1950. Rewrite this model so that $t = 0$ represents 1970.
(Source: U.S. Bureau of the Census)

Cable television began in the United States in the 1950's. The cables are connected to large antennas that receive the television signals. In 1994, there were 60.5 million cable television subscribers in the United States.

In Exercises 51–56, sketch the graph of the function.

51. $f(x) = x^2 + x - 4$

52. $f(x) = 2x^2 - 8x + 1$

53. $f(x) = 3x^2 + 6x + 5$

54. $f(x) = x^2 - 4x + 3$

55. $f(x) = 6x^2 - 24x + 10$

56. $f(x) = x^2 - 2x + 5$

57. *Powers of Ten*   Which best estimates the 1990 federal income tax for a single person who had no dependents and earned $20,000?

    a. $\$2.2 \times 10^0$ **b.** $\$2.2 \times 10^1$ **c.** $\$2.2 \times 10^2$ **d.** $\$2.2 \times 10^3$

58. *Powers of Ten*   Which best estimates the weight of a newborn child?

    a. 1.1×10^0 oz   **b.** 1.1×10^1 oz   **c.** 1.1×10^2 oz   **d.** 1.1×10^3 oz

Exploration and Extension

More about Reflections   **In Exercises 59 and 60, use the following information.**

The graph of $y = f(-x)$ is a reflection of the graph of f in the y-axis. Use this fact to sketch the graph of the function.

59. $g(x) = (-x + 2)^2$

60. $g(x) = (-x - 1)^2$

Mixed REVIEW

1. Subtract: $\frac{4}{5} - \frac{2}{3}$.

2. Simplify: $(4.8 \times 10^4)(1.6 \times 10^{-2})$.

3. Solve $|x - 2| > 4$.   **(1.7)**

4. Solve for x: $ax^2 + b = y$.   **(1.5)**

5. Find the intercepts of $y = (x - 3)^2 - 5$.   **(2.3)**

6. Simplify: $(3a^2b^4)(4a^3b)$.

7. Sketch the graph of $5x + 2y + 4 = 0$.   **(2.1)**

8. Sketch the graph of $y = x^2 + 4x - 1$.   **(5.2)**

9. Subtract: $(4x - 2y + 3) - (x - 8y + 2)$.

10. Write $y = 4x^2 - 8x + 3$ in completed square form.   **(5.3)**

In Exercises 11–16, use $f(x) = 2x$ and $g(x) = 3x - 9$ to write an equation for $h(x)$.

11. $h(x) = \frac{1}{3}g(x) + f(x)$ **(6.2)**

12. $h(x) = f(x) - g(x)$ **(6.2)**

13. $h(x) = f(x) \cdot g(x)$ **(6.2)**

14. $h(x) = g(f(x))$ **(6.2)**

15. $h(x)$ is the inverse of $g(x)$.   **(6.3)**

16. $h(x) = f(g(x))$ **(6.2)**

17. Simplify: $\dfrac{8x^2y^4}{12x^5y}$.

18. Write an equation of the line perpendicular to $y = -\frac{2}{3}x - 11$ through $(-1, 3)$.   **(2.2)**

19. With what velocity must an arrow be shot straight up, to return in 8 sec?   **(5.4)**

20. Find the area of the region enclosed between $y = 9$ and $y = x^2 - 6x + 9$.   **(5.2)**

6.6

Recursive Functions and Finite Differences

What you should learn:

Goal 1 How to identify and classify recursive functions

Goal 2 How to use recursive functions as real-life models

Why you should learn it:

You can model many real-life situations with recursive functions, such as Fibonacci's famous rabbit problem.

Goal 1 Identifying Recursive Functions

A **recursive function** is a function whose domain is the set of nonnegative integers (or sometimes the set of positive integers). To indicate that the domain is this set and not the set of real numbers, n is usually used as the variable.

A recursive function can be defined by stating the value of the function at 0 and by giving an equation for the value of the function at n in terms of the value of the function at $n - 1$.

A well-known example of a recursive function is the **factorial function.** It is defined as follows. (The exclamation mark is read "factorial.")

$$0! = 1 \qquad \textit{State the value of n! at n = 0.}$$

$$n! = n \cdot (n - 1)! \qquad \textit{Define n! in terms of (n - 1)!.}$$

To evaluate a function that is defined recursively, first evaluate the function at 0, then at 1, then at 2, and so on.

$$0! = 1 \qquad \textit{The value of 0! is given.}$$

$$1! = 1 \cdot 0! = 1 \cdot 1 = 1 \qquad \textit{Use 0! to find 1!.}$$

$$2! = 2 \cdot 1! = 2 \cdot 1 = 2 \qquad \textit{Use 1! to find 2!.}$$

$$3! = 3 \cdot 2! = 3 \cdot 2 = 6 \qquad \textit{Use 2! to find 3!.}$$

$$4! = 4 \cdot 3! = 4 \cdot 6 = 24 \qquad \textit{Use 3! to find 4!.}$$

Example 1 *Evaluating a Recursive Function*

Use the following definition to find the value of $f(4)$.

$$f(1) = 3 \quad \text{and} \quad f(n) = f(n - 1) + n$$

Solution

$$f(1) = 3 \qquad \textit{The value of f(1) is given.}$$

$$f(2) = f(1) + 2 = 3 + 2 = 5 \qquad \textit{Use f(1) to find f(2).}$$

$$f(3) = f(2) + 3 = 5 + 3 = 8 \qquad \textit{Use f(2) to find f(3).}$$

$$f(4) = f(3) + 4 = 8 + 4 = 12 \qquad \textit{Use f(3) to find f(4).} \qquad \blacksquare$$

The **first differences** of a recursive function are found by subtracting consecutive values of the function. The **second differences** are found by subtracting consecutive first differences. The first and second differences of the function in Example 1 are as follows.

n	1	2	3	4	5	6
$f(n)$	3	5	8	12	17	23

First differences   2   3   4   5   6

Second differences   1   1   1   1

For this function, the second differences are all the same nonzero number. When this happens, the function has a quadratic model. (If the first differences are all the same number, then the function has a linear model.) The next example shows you how to find the quadratic model for the function given in Example 1.

Example 2   *Finding a Quadratic Model*

Find a quadratic model whose values are $f(1) = 3$, $f(2) = 5$, and $f(3) = 8$.

Solution   You know the model has the form

$$f(n) = an^2 + bn + c.$$

By substituting 1, 2, and 3 for n, you can obtain a system of three linear equations in three variables.

$f(1) = a(1^2) + b(1) + c = 3$ *Substitute 1 for n.*

$f(2) = a(2^2) + b(2) + c = 5$ *Substitute 2 for n.*

$f(3) = a(3^2) + b(3) + c = 8$ *Substitute 3 for n.*

You now have a system of three equations in a, b, and c.

$$\begin{cases} a + b + c = 3 & \textit{Equation 1} \\ 4a + 2b + c = 5 & \textit{Equation 2} \\ 9a + 3b + c = 8 & \textit{Equation 3} \end{cases}$$

Using the techniques discussed in Chapters 3 and 4, you can find the solution to be $a = \frac{1}{2}$, $b = \frac{1}{2}$, and $c = 2$. Thus a quadratic model is

$$f(n) = \frac{1}{2}n^2 + \frac{1}{2}n + 2.$$

Try checking the values of $f(1)$, $f(2)$, and $f(3)$.   ■

Notice that the constant second differences were used to conclude that the function in Example 1 *has* a quadratic model. To *find* the model, three values of n were used to create a system of three linear equations.

Goal 2 Using Recursive Functions in Real Life

The numbers given by the recursive function in Example 3 are called Fibonacci numbers. They are named after the Italian mathematician Leonardo of Pisa (c. 1170–1250), also called Fibonacci.

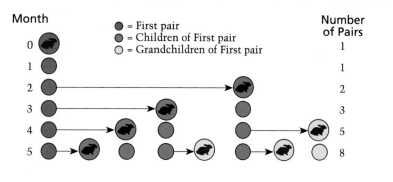

Month		Number of Pairs
	● = First pair	
	● = Children of First pair	
	○ = Grandchildren of First pair	
0		1
1		1
2		2
3		3
4		5
5		8

Problem Solving
Look for a Pattern

Example 3 Using a Recursive Function

Fibonacci proposed this rabbit problem: *Begin with one pair of newborn rabbits. Suppose that when a pair of rabbits is two months old, they begin to produce a new pair of rabbits each month. If none of the rabbits ever die, how many pairs of rabbits will there be in the nth month?*

Solution The above diagram shows the number of pairs of rabbits in months 0 through 5. Fibonacci answered the question with a recursive function, in which $f(n)$ is the number of pairs in the nth month.

$$f(0) = 1 \qquad f(1) = 1$$
$$f(n) = f(n - 2) + f(n - 1)$$

The following calculations confirm the definition.

$f(0) = 1$ *The value of f(0) is given.*

$f(1) = 1$ *The value of f(1) is given.*

$f(2) = 1 + 1 = 2$ *Use f(0) + f(1) to find f(2).*

$f(3) = 1 + 2 = 3$ *Use f(1) + f(2) to find f(3).*

$f(4) = 2 + 3 = 5$ *Use f(2) + f(3) to find f(4).*

$f(5) = 3 + 5 = 8$ *Use f(3) + f(4) to find f(5).* ∎

Communicating *about* ALGEBRA

▶ **SHARING IDEAS about the Lesson**

Find the Fibonacci numbers through $f(9)$. Find the first and second differences for these ten numbers. Do they have a linear or quadratic model? Explain.

EXERCISES

▶ **CRITICAL THINKING about the Lesson**

1. Give an example of a recursive function.

2. Find the value of $f(5)$.
$f(0) = 1$
$f(n) = f(n - 1) + n - 1$

3. Find the value of $f(7)$.
$f(1) = 1$
$f(2) = 2$
$f(n) = f(n - 2) + f(n - 1)$

4. Find the first and second differences for the following values of $f(n)$.

n	0	1	2	3	4	5
$f(n)$	3	2	3	6	11	18

5. Can the function whose values are given in Exercise 4 be described with a linear or quadratic model? Explain.

6. Does the following function have a linear or quadratic model? Explain.

$f(0) = 0$
$f(n) = f(n - 1) + 3n$

Independent Practice

In Exercises 7–18, find the first five values of the recursive function.

7. $f(0) = 1$
$f(n) = f(n - 1) + 2$

8. $f(1) = 4$
$f(n) = n + f(n - 1) + 2$

9. $f(0) = 0$
$f(n) = f(n - 1) + n^2$

10. $f(0) = -3$
$f(n) = |f(n - 1)| - 10$

11. $f(1) = 2$
$f(n) = [f(n - 1)]^2 + 1$

12. $f(0) = 7$
$f(n) = n^2 - f(n - 1)$

13. $f(1) = 10$
$f(n) = 4f(n - 1)$

14. $f(0) = 3$
$f(n) = [f(n - 1)]^2 - 2$

15. $f(0) = 4$
$f(n) = n^2 + 3n - f(n - 1)$

16. $f(0) = 4$
$f(1) = 2$
$f(n) = f(n - 1) - f(n - 2)$

17. $f(0) = 0$
$f(1) = 2$
$f(n) = f(n - 1) + 2f(n - 2)$

18. $f(1) = 1$
$f(2) = 2$
$f(n) = f(n - 1) \cdot f(n - 2)$

In Exercises 19–24, find the first seven values of the function. Then use the values to find the first differences of the function.

19. $f(0) = 3$
$f(n) = n^2 - f(n - 1)$

20. $f(0) = 1$
$f(n) = [f(n - 1)]^2 + 1$

21. $f(1) = 0$
$f(n) = f(n - 1) + 3$

22. $f(1) = 2$
$f(n) = n - f(n - 1)$

23. $f(1) = -2$
$f(n) = |f(n - 1)| - n^2$

24. $f(3) = -1$
$f(n) = -f(n - 1) + 3$

In Exercises 25–30, find the first seven values of the function. Then use the values to calculate the second differences of the function.

25. $f(1) = 3$
$f(n) = f(n - 1) - n$

26. $f(0) = 1$
$f(n) = n^2 - f(n - 1)$

27. $f(0) = 0$
$f(n) = -3[f(n - 1)] + 5$

28. $f(1) = 0$
$f(n) = f(n - 1) + (n - 1)^2$

29. $f(3) = 9$
$f(n) = f(n - 1) + n^2 - n$

30. $f(2) = -3$
$f(n) = -2f(n - 1)$

In Exercises 31–36, state whether the function has a linear or quadratic model or neither.

31. $f(0) = 0$
$f(n) = f(n - 1) + n$

32. $f(0) = 2$
$f(n) = [f(n - 1)]^2$

33. $f(1) = 2$
$f(n) = f(n - 1) + 2$

34. $f(1) = 0$
$f(n) = f(n - 1) + 2n$

35. $f(0) = 1$
$f(n) = f(n - 1) + n^2$

36. $f(0) = 0$
$f(n) = f(n - 1) - 1$

In Exercises 37–42, find a linear model that has the indicated values.

37. $f(1) = 1, \quad f(2) = 3$

38. $f(0) = 4, \quad f(2) = 6$

39. $f(4) = 1, \quad f(1) = 7$

40. $f(2) = 2, \quad f(4) = 1$

41. $f(1) = 1, \quad f(2) = 6$

42. $f(1) = 6, \quad f(4) = 15$

In Exercises 43–50, find a quadratic model that has the indicated values.

43. $f(0) = 3, \quad f(1) = 3, \quad f(4) = 15$

44. $f(0) = 7, \quad f(1) = 6, \quad f(3) = 10$

45. $f(0) = -3, \quad f(2) = 1, \quad f(4) = 9$

46. $f(0) = 3, \quad f(2) = 0, \quad f(6) = 36$

47. $f(0) = 4, \quad f(1) = -2, \quad f(2) = -14$

48. $f(0) = 4, \quad f(1) = 2, \quad f(2) = -2$

49. $f(0) = -3, \quad f(1) = 4, \quad f(3) = 30$

50. $f(0) = 1, \quad f(1) = 3, \quad f(2) = 15$

In Exercises 51–56, find a linear or quadratic model for the function.

51. $f(0) = 2$
$f(n) = 2 + f(n - 1)$

52. $f(1) = 2$
$f(n) = f(n - 1) + 3$

53. $f(1) = 0$
$f(n) = f(n - 1) + 4n$

54. $f(1) = 3$
$f(n) = 5 + f(n - 1)$

55. $f(0) = 0$
$f(n) = f(n - 1) - 2n$

56. $f(1) = 1$
$f(n) = f(n - 1) + 3n$

57. *Diagonals of a Polygon*   The number of diagonals, $f(n)$, of an n-sided polygon is given by the following function. Write the first six values of the function. Find a quadratic model for the function.

$f(3) = 0$
$f(n) = f(n - 1) + n - 2$

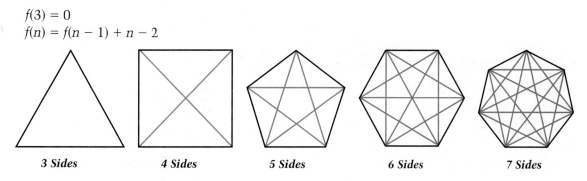

3 Sides   4 Sides   5 Sides   6 Sides   7 Sides

58. *Triangular Numbers*   The diagram at the right shows the first four triangular numbers. The nth triangular number is given by the following function. Write the first eight values of the function. Decide whether the function has a linear or quadratic model. If it does, find the model.

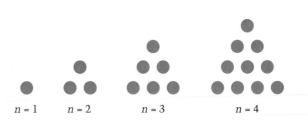

$n = 1$ $n = 2$ $n = 3$ $n = 4$

$f(1) = 1$
$f(n) = f(n - 1) + n$

59. *Savings*   Your savings account earns 0.005% monthly (6% annually). Each month you deposit $20. The balance at the beginning of the nth month is given by the following recursive function.

$f(1) = 20$
$f(n) = 20 + 1.005f(n - 1)$

Find the balances at the beginning of each of the first 12 months. Can this function be represented by a linear model or a quadratic model?

60. The values of the following recursive function form better and better approximations of a simple fraction. What is the fraction?

$f(0) = \dfrac{3}{10}$
$f(n) = f(n - 1) + \left(\dfrac{1}{10}\right)^n \left(\dfrac{3}{10}\right)$

Integrated Review

In Exercises 61–66, evaluate the function as indicated.

61. $f(x) = x - 3, \quad f(-6)$

62. $f(x) = 3x - 2, \quad f(-1)$

63. $f(x) = x^2 + 9, \quad f(-1)$

64. $f(x) = -2x^2 + 5, \quad f(8)$

65. $f(x) = |x + 3|, \quad f(4)$

66. $f(x) = (x - 3)^2 + 7, \quad f(-3)$

In Exercises 67–72, solve the system of equations.

67. $\begin{cases} x - 3y = 13 \\ 3x + y = -1 \end{cases}$

68. $\begin{cases} 2x - 3y = 61 \\ -x + 5y = -83 \end{cases}$

69. $\begin{cases} \frac{1}{2}x - y = -5 \\ -x + 3y = -5 \end{cases}$

70. $\begin{cases} x + y + z = -1 \\ 2x - y + 4z = -4 \\ 5x + 3y - z = 7 \end{cases}$

71. $\begin{cases} -x + 3y + 4z = 5 \\ x \quad\quad - z = 1 \\ 2x - y + 2z = 15 \end{cases}$

72. $\begin{cases} -x - 2y + 4z = 13 \\ 2x + y - z = 1 \\ x - y + 2z = 8 \end{cases}$

Exploration and Extension

In Exercises 73 and 74, find a recursive function whose values agree with those given in the table. (There is more than one correct solution.)

73.

n	0	1	2	3	4	5
$f(n)$	3	5	7	9	11	13

74.

n	0	1	2	3	4	5
$f(n)$	3	8	15	24	35	48

6.7

Exploring Data: Measures of Central Tendency

What you should learn:

Goal 1 How to find the mean, median, mode, and quartiles of a set of numbers

Goal 2 How to use measures of central tendency to answer questions about real-life situations

Why you should learn it:

You can use the mean, median, or mode of a set of data to represent a "typical" number of the data.

Connections
Reading

Goal 1 Measures of Central Tendency

There are three commonly used **measures of central tendency** for a collection of numbers.

1. The **mean,** or average, of n numbers is the sum of the numbers divided by n.
2. The **median** of n numbers is the middle number when the numbers are written in order. (If n is even, the median is the average of the two middle numbers.)
3. The **mode** of n numbers is the number that occurs most frequently.

These three measures can be different, *or* they can all be the same. For example, the numbers 1, 2, 2, 3, 4, 4, 4, 5, 6, 6, 7 have a mean of $\frac{44}{11} = 4$, a median of 4, and a mode of 4.

Many collections of numbers that are taken from real life have bar graphs that are *bell-shaped* (or nearly bell-shaped). For such collections, the mean, median, and mode are approximately equal.

Example 1 *Comparing Central Tendencies*

One of the ways that the reading level of material is assessed is to count the letters in each word and find the average word length of the material. The number of words of different lengths in the poem "A Visit from St. Nicholas," by Clement Clarke Moore, is shown in the bar graph at the left. Find the mean, median, and mode of these data.

Solution The poem has 544 words. To find the mean word length, multiply each word length by its *frequency* and divide the result by 544.

$$\text{mean} = \frac{38(1) + 89(2) + 141(3) + \cdots + 15(8) + 10(9)}{544}$$

$$= \frac{2076}{544}, \text{ or about } 3.8.$$

The median word length is 4 because the middle two word lengths (numbers 272 and 273) are both 4. The word length mode is 3 because there are more 3 letter words than words of any other length. ∎

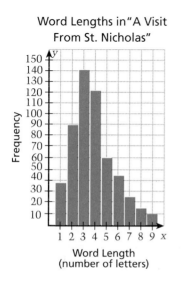

Word Lengths in "A Visit From St. Nicholas"

Frequency (y-axis): 10 to 150
Word Length (number of letters) (x-axis): 1 2 3 4 5 6 7 8 9

The median of an ordered collection of numbers roughly partitions the collection into two halves: numbers below the median and numbers above the median. The **first quartile** is the median of the lower half. The **second quartile** is the median of the entire collection. The **third quartile** is the median of the upper half. Quartiles roughly partition an ordered collection into four **quarters.**

Example 2 *Finding the Quartiles of a Collection of Numbers*

The percent of the population of each state (including the District of Columbia and Puerto Rico) that is 18 years old or younger is given in the table. Find the first, second, and third quartiles for these data.

AK—32.0	FL—22.7	LA—29.4	NC—25.2	OK—27.2	UT—37.3
AL—27.2	GA—28.0	MA—22.6	ND—27.3	OR—24.8	VA—24.4
AR—27.1	HI—26.2	MD—24.8	NE—26.4	PA—23.7	VT—25.3
AZ—27.3	IA—25.2	ME—25.2	NH—25.3	PR—28.4	WA—25.6
CA—26.5	ID—30.3	MI—26.5	NJ—23.7	RI—23.1	WI—26.2
CO—26.3	IL—25.9	MN—26.0	NM—29.8	SC—27.3	WV—25.5
CT—23.5	IN—26.3	MO—25.5	NV—25.2	SD—27.6	WY—29.4
DC—22.3	KS—26.2	MS—29.8	NY—24.3	TN—25.6	
DE—25.2	KY—26.3	MT—27.4	OH—26.0	TX—29.6	

Solution   There are 52 numbers in the collection. Begin by ordering the numbers. Then form the quartiles by breaking the numbers into 4 groups of 13 each.

First quarter: 22.3, 22.6, 22.7, 23.1, 23.5, 23.7, 23.7, 24.3, 24.4, 24.8, 24.8, 25.2, 25.2

Second quarter: 25.2, 25.2, 25.2, 25.3, 25.3, 25.5, 25.5, 25.6, 25.6, 25.9, 26.0, 26.0, 26.2

Third quarter: 26.2, 26.2, 26.3, 26.3, 26.3, 26.4, 26.5, 26.5, 27.1, 27.2, 27.2, 27.3, 27.3

Fourth quarter: 27.3, 27.4, 27.6, 28.0, 28.4, 29.4, 29.4, 29.6, 29.8, 29.8, 30.3, 32.0, 37.3

From the above grouping, you can see that the first quartile is 25.2, the second quartile (or median) is 26.2, and the third quartile is 27.3.

A **box-and-whisker plot** can be used to present a graphic summary of the information found in Example 2.

22.3   25.2 26.2 27.3   37.3

Scheduled Time	12 to 17 yr	18 to 29 yr	Free Time	12 to 17 yr	18 to 29 yr
Classes	18.1	4.1	Visiting, social	4.4	7.8
Homework	3.1	3.4	Conversation	2.6	3.1
Work-related	2.8	29.0	Correspondence	0.4	0.4
Cleaning, laundry	2.2	3.2	Organizations, meetings	1.2	0.5
Yard and garden	2.4	1.4	Church, synagogue	1.0	0.5
Shopping	2.4	2.4	Travel	2.5	2.8
Travel (shopping)	1.5	1.9	Sports and sports events	4.1	2.1
Services	0.5	0.7	Walking outdoors	2.0	1.9
Child care	1.2	1.8	Games and hobbies	3.9	1.6
Adult care	0.6	0.6	Other recreation	1.0	0.5
Meals	9.0	9.1	Cultural events	0.3	0.4
Bathing, dressing	6.4	6.8	Movies	0.6	0.7
Sleep	62.6	55.9	Radios, records	0.9	0.7
Naps	1.3	1.7	Television	17.7	14.2
Travel (school/work)	3.4	2.4	Reading	1.3	1.9
Other	5.8	3.4	Relaxing, thinking	0.8	1.1

Real Life
Time Management

Example 3 *Interpreting Measures of Central Tendency*

The data in the above table show the mean hours per week that two groups of young Americans spend on their activities. The "12 to 17 yr" and "18 to 29 yr" categories represents *un-married* Americans between the given ages. Which activities show significantly different uses of time between the two groups? How could you explain the differences? **(Source: American Demographics, 1991)**

Solution Two clear differences are the times spent in class and at work. This seems reasonable because most Americans between the ages of 12 and 17 attend school each year, whereas most Americans between the ages of 18 and 29 attend school for only a portion of those years. ∎

Communicating about **ALGEBRA**

▶ **SHARING IDEAS about the Lesson**

What are some other comparisons that you can make for Americans aged 12-to-17 and 18-to-29 from the table above?

EXERCISES

▶ **CRITICAL THINKING about the Lesson**

1. Define the mean, median, and mode of a set of *n* numbers in your own words.

In Exercises 2–4, use the following set of numbers.

{34, 35, 40, 31, 34, 34, 31, 38, 29, 35, 35, 32, 37, 33, 34, 37, 37, 35, 34, 32}

2. Find the mean, median, and mode of the data.

3. Find the first, second, and third quartiles of the data.

4. Construct a box-and-whisker plot for the numbers.

Independent Practice

5. *Reading Levels* The Preamble to the Constitution of the United States of America contains 52 words. The blue bars in the bar graph represent the number of words of different lengths in the Preamble. The green bars represent the number of words of different lengths (of the first 52 words) in *Green Eggs and Ham* by Dr. Seuss. Find the mean word length of each set of 52 words. Compare the reading levels of the two passages.

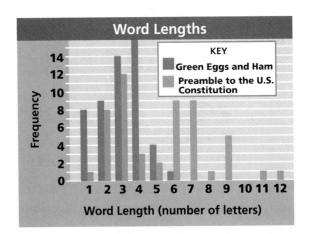

6. *Prime-Time Viewers* The numbers (in millions) of Americans who watched television during prime time in the fall of 1990 is shown in the graph at the right. What was the mean number of viewers per night? What was the median number of viewers per night?
(Source: Nielsen Media Research)

7. *Wedding Cake* The table below shows the prices in nine regions of the United States for a wedding cake that serves 300. Find the mean, median, and mode of these prices. *(Source: How to Have a Big Wedding on a Small Budget, 1990, Writer's Digest Books)*

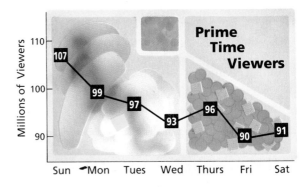

Region	Cost	Region	Cost	Region	Cost
Northwestern	$340	Central Mountain	$325	Northeastern (urban)	$400
California (urban)	400	Midwestern	255	Northeastern (rural)	350
California (rural)	225	Southwestern	400	Southeastern	290

8. *Birthday Months*   The table shows numbers (in millions) of living Americans who were born in each of the 12 months. Construct a box-and-whisker plot.

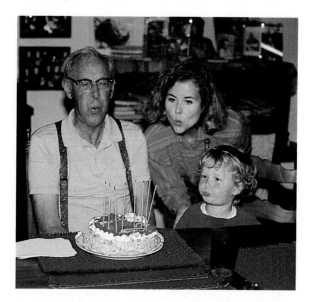

Month	Number	Month	Number
January	21.2	July	20.4
February	20.4	August	21.2
March	22.2	September	22.8
April	20.0	October	17.4
May	21.4	November	19.0
June	20.0	December	20.4

9. *Greeting Cards*   The table shows a greeting card company's monthly sales (in thousands of dollars) for one year. Construct a box-and-whisker plot and a bar graph for the data. Which do you think gives a better picture of the monthly sales? Why?

Month	Sales	Month	Sales
January	260	July	262
February	284	August	262
March	275	September	279
April	272	October	281
May	310	November	276
June	288	December	300

Super Bowl Scores   **In Exercises 10–12, use the following information.**

The table shows the final score of each Super Bowl game from 1967 to 1990. (1967 was the year of the first Super Bowl.)

Year	1967	1968	1969	1970	1971	1972	1973	1974
Score	35–10	33–14	16–7	23–7	16–13	24–3	14–7	24–7

Year	1975	1976	1977	1978	1979	1980	1981	1982
Score	16–6	21–17	32–14	27–10	35–31	31–19	27–10	26–21

Year	1983	1984	1985	1986	1987	1988	1989	1990
Score	27–17	38–9	38–16	46–10	39–20	42–10	20–16	55–10

10. Find the margin of victory for each Super Bowl. Then find the mean, median, and modes of the margins of victory.

11. Find the first, second, and third quartiles for the margins of victory.

12. Construct two box-and-whisker plots: one for the winning scores and one for the losing scores.

Sports Injuries   **In Exercises 13 and 14, use the following information.**

The following table shows the percent of sports participants who are injured each year. *(Source: Consumer Products Safety Commission)*

Sport	Percent	Sport	Percent
Archery	1.4%	Racquetball	1.0%
Baseball	9.8	Roller-skating	1.9
Basketball	5.4	Snow-skiing	1.1
Bicycling	2.4	Soccer	4.2
Football	9.6	Swimming	0.3
Golf	0.4	Tennis	0.4
Ice-skating	0.5	Water-skiing	0.4

13. Find the mean and median of the data.   **14.** Construct a box-and-whisker plot for the data.

Polar Bears   **In Exercises 15 and 16, use the following information.**

The following list shows the weights (in pounds) of 20 adult male polar bears that were weighed by a Norwegian scientific team.

952   937   932   1062   925   964   954
980   1022   872   1030   992   1005   928
925   1078   978   1026   1002   894

15. Which measure of central tendency do you think best describes the average weight of an adult male polar bear? Explain.

16. Construct a box-and-whisker plot of the data.

Integrated Review

College Entrance Exam Samples   **In Exercises 17 and 18, use the following information.**

The graph at the right compares the test scores of five students on two different tests.

17. For which student was the change in scores from test I to test II the greatest?
   a. *A*   **b.** *B*   **c.** *C*   **d.** *D*   **e.** *E*

18. What was the mean of the scores of the five students on test II?
   a. 60   **b.** 65   **c.** 68   **d.** 70   **e.** 72

Test Score Correlations

Exploration and Extension

19. *Prices*   Create a list of 8 prices so that the mean is $20 and the median is $18.

20. *Days*   Create a list of data so that the mean is 5 days and the median is 6 days.

6 Chapter Summary

What did you learn?

Skills

1. Identify relations and functions. **(6.1)**
   - Use function notation. **(6.1)**
2. Perform operations with functions. **(6.2)**
3. Find the inverse of a relation. **(6.3)**
   - Decide whether an inverse relation is a function. **(6.3)**
4. Evaluate compound functions and step functions. **(6.4)**
5. Use translations and reflections to graph functions. **(6.5)**
6. Evaluate recursive functions. **(6.6)**
   - Use first and second differences to decide whether a recursive function has a linear or quadratic model. **(6.6)**

Strategies

7. Use functions to model real-life situations. **(6.1–6.6)**

Exploring Data

8. Find measures of central tendency for data. **(6.7)**
9. Sketch box-and-whisker plots to represent data. **(6.8)**

Why did you learn it?

One of the primary uses of algebra is to create and use models of real-life situations. Often the model is a function. For instance, the equation $V = \frac{4}{3}\pi r^3$ shows how the volume of a sphere is related to the radius of the sphere. This equation describes the volume, V, as a function of the radius, r.

As you study the remaining chapters of the book, you will encounter many references to functions. Remember that a function is simply a special type of relation. Moreover, most functions are specified by equations such as $f(x) = 3x - 4$ or $g(x) = x^2 - 4x + 1$.

How does it fit into the bigger picture of algebra?

This chapter explored functions. A function is a special type of relationship between two variables in which each input value corresponds to exactly one output value. For instance, the area of a circle is a function of its radius. You can think of the radius of a circle as input and the area of the circle as output. If someone gives you the radius, r, of a circle, you know the area is $A = \pi r^2$.

Now you should be able to use function notation, perform operations with functions, and sketch graphs of functions.

The last lesson in the chapter discussed measures of central tendency and box-and-whisker plots.

Chapter REVIEW

In Exercises 1–4, state whether the relation is a function. (6.1)

1.

2.

3.

4.

In Exercises 5–10, find the indicated value of $f(x)$. (6.1)

5. $f(x) = 10x + 2,\quad f(-1)$

6. $f(x) = -x^2 - 5,\quad f(-3)$

7. $f(x) = -6x^2 + 13,\quad f(-2)$

8. $f(x) = 2x^2 + \frac{1}{2}x - 1,\quad f(4)$

9. $f(x) = \frac{1}{3}x^2 - 3x + 1,\quad f(6)$

10. $f(x) = -x^2 - 4x + 3,\quad f(10)$

In Exercises 11–16, find the domain of the function. (6.2)

11. $f(x) = \dfrac{10x - 4}{x - 1}$

12. $f(x) = \sqrt{-x}$

13. $f(x) = \dfrac{\sqrt{x}}{5}$

14. $f(x) = \dfrac{x^2}{3 - x}$

15. $f(x) = -16x^2 + 2$

16. $f(x) = \dfrac{x^2 + 3}{x - 2}$

In Exercises 17–25, let $f(x) = 2x - 4$ and $g(x) = x - 1$. Write and simplify an equation for $h(x)$. (6.2)

17. $h(x) = f(x) + g(x)$

18. $h(x) = f(x) - g(x)$

19. $h(x) = f(x) - 3g(x)$

20. $h(x) = \frac{1}{2}f(x) + 2g(x)$

21. $h(x) = f(x) \cdot g(x)$

22. $h(x) = f(x) \div g(x)$

23. $h(x) = g(x) \div f(x)$

24. $h(x) = f(g(x))$

25. $h(x) = g(f(x))$

In Exercises 26–28, find the inverse of the function. (6.3)

26. $f(x) = 11x + 22$

27. $f(x) = \frac{1}{2}(x - 10)$

28. $f(x) = \frac{1}{3}(-6x + 2)$

In Exercises 29–34, sketch the graph of the function and its inverse on the same coordinate plane. (6.3)

29. $f(x) = x^2 - 1$

30. $f(x) = \frac{1}{2}x - 4$

31. $f(x) = x - 10$

32. $f(x) = 2x + 1$

33. $f(x) = -2x + 7$

34. $f(x) = -x^2$

In Exercises 35–38, verify that the two functions are inverses of each other. (6.3)

35. $f(x) = 2x - 5,\quad g(x) = \frac{1}{2}x + \frac{5}{2}$

36. $f(x) = -\frac{1}{2}x + 7,\quad g(x) = -2x + 14$

37. $f(x) = 3x + 6,\quad g(x) = \frac{1}{3}x - 2$

38. $f(x) = \frac{1}{3}x + 8,\quad g(x) = 3x - 24$

39. Evaluate $f(3)$. **(6.4)**

$$f(x) = \begin{cases} -3x^2 + 10, & x < 3 \\ x - 20, & x \ge 3 \end{cases}$$

40. Evaluate $f(-2)$. **(6.4)**

$$f(x) = \begin{cases} x^2 + 2x - 1, & x \le 1 \\ 3 - x, & x > 1 \end{cases}$$

In Exercises 41–46, sketch the graph of the function. **(6.4)**

41. $y = \left| \frac{1}{2}x + 3 \right|$

42. $y = |3x - 6|$

43. $f(x) = \begin{cases} 2x + 2, & x \le 2 \\ \frac{1}{4}x^2 + x + 1, & x > 2 \end{cases}$

44. $f(x) = \begin{cases} x^2 - 6, & x < 0 \\ \frac{1}{2}x - 6, & x \ge 0 \end{cases}$

45. $f(x) = \begin{cases} -3, & 0 \le x < 2 \\ -1, & 2 < x \le 4 \\ 0, & 4 < x \le 6 \\ 3, & 6 < x \le 8 \end{cases}$

46. $f(x) = \begin{cases} -1, & -2 \le x \le 4 \\ 2, & 4 < x \le 6 \\ 4, & 6 < x \le 20 \\ 6, & 20 < x \le 30 \end{cases}$

In Exercises 47–58, use shifts and reflections to sketch the graph of the function. **(6.5)**

47. $y = x^2 - 6$

48. $y = (x + 7)^2$

49. $y = |x + 10|$

50. $y = |x| - 7$

51. $y = x^2 + 12$

52. $y = -x^2 + 1$

53. $y = -(x - 2)^2$

54. $y = -|x - 4|$

55. $y = -|x| + 9$

56. $y = (x - 2)^2 + 3$

57. $y = -|x + 3| - 2$

58. $y = -(x - 1)^2 + 1$

In Exercises 59–62, find the first five values of the recursive function. **(6.6)**

59. $f(1) = 4$
$f(n) = f(n - 1) + n + 6$

60. $f(1) = -3$
$f(n) = |f(n - 1)| - 4$

61. $f(0) = 1$
$f(n) = [f(n - 1)]^2 + 1$

62. $f(2) = 2$
$f(n) = 6 - [f(n - 1)]^2$

In Exercises 63–66, match the function with its graph. Then find a linear or quadratic model for the function. **(6.6)**

63. $f(0) = 0$
$f(n) = f(n - 1) + 2$

64. $f(1) = 0$
$f(n) = f(n - 1) + n$

65. $f(0) = 10$
$f(n) = f(n - 1) - n$

66. $f(1) = 12$
$f(n) = f(n - 1) - 3$

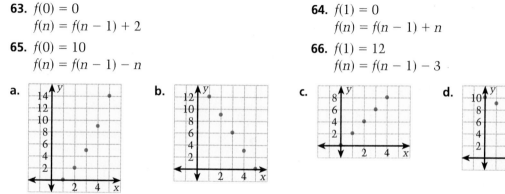

In Exercises 67–74, match the function with its graph. (6.4, 6.5)

67. $f(x) = -2x + 1$

68. $f(x) = (x - 1)^2 + 1$

69. $f(x) = |x - 1| + 1$

70. $f(x) = -(x - 2)^2$

71. $f(x) = \begin{cases} -2x + 1, & x < 0 \\ x + 1, & x \geq 0 \end{cases}$

72. $f(x) = \begin{cases} x^2, & x < 0 \\ -x^2, & x \geq 0 \end{cases}$

73. $f(x) = \begin{cases} 2, & 0 \leq x < 1 \\ 3, & 1 \leq x \leq 2 \end{cases}$

74. $f(x) = \begin{cases} 2, & 0 \leq x \leq 1 \\ 3, & 1 < x \leq 2 \end{cases}$

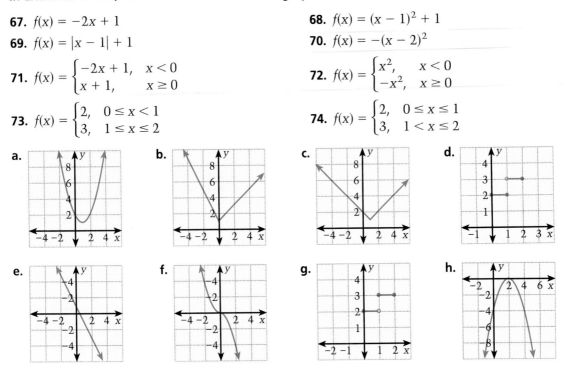

Temperatures in Phoenix **In Exercises 75 and 76, use the following information.** (6.7)

For each month of the year, the average daily high temperature in degrees Fahrenheit in Phoenix, Arizona, is shown in the table.

Month	Temperature	Month	Temperature	Month	Temperature
January	52.3	May	77.0	September	84.6
February	56.1	June	86.5	October	92.3
March	60.6	July	92.3	November	60.6
April	68.0	August	89.9	December	53.5

75. Find the mean, median, and mode of these data.

76. Find the first, second, and third quartiles for these data.

77. *Geometry* The radius, $r(x)$, of a circle inscribed in an equilateral triangle with sides of length x is given by the function

$$r(x) = \frac{\sqrt{3}}{6}x.$$

Evaluate $r(18)$. Explain in words what the value $r(18)$ represents. Explain how the formula for $r(x)$ can be derived.

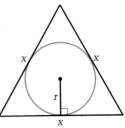

78. *Sled Riding* A person's velocity, v (in meters per second), while sliding down a hill on a sled depends on several things, such as the slope of the hill, the type of snow, and the type of sled. The following model approximates the velocity of the person sliding down the hill shown at the right.

$$v = \sqrt{19.6h}$$

In this model, h is the change in height (in meters) measured from the top of the hill. Rewrite this equation so that velocity is the input and height is the output. What is the value of h when the velocity is 14 meters per second?

79. *Call or Write?* Over the past half century, telephone calls have far exceeded letters as a means of personal communication in the United States. From 1952 through 1988, the average number, P, of phone calls made in a year, can be approximated by

$$P = 1.2t^2 + 430$$

where $t = 0$ represents 1952. Rewrite this model so that $t = 0$ represents 1980.

Average Number of Phone Calls
(1952–1988)

Year $(0 \leftrightarrow 1952)$

Local Television Ads **In Exercises 80–83, use the following information.**

For 1950 through 1990, the total expenses, T (in millions of dollars), for local television advertisements can be modeled by

$$T = \begin{cases} 225t + 2450, & 0 \leq t \leq 18 \\ 930t - 10{,}240, & 18 < t \leq 25 \\ 2324t - 45{,}090, & 25 < t \leq 32 \\ 3900t - 95{,}522, & 32 < t \leq 40 \end{cases}$$

where $t = 0$ represents 1950.
(Source: McCann-Erickson, Inc.)

80. Approximate the total expense for 1960.

81. Approximate the total expense for 1970.

82. Approximate the total expense for 1980.

83. Approximate the total expense for 1990.

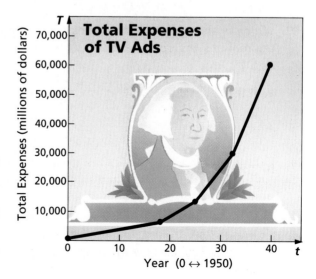

Total Expenses of TV Ads

Year $(0 \leftrightarrow 1950)$

In Exercises 84–91, use the following information.

The map shows the center of population in the contiguous United States for each of the census years from 1790 through 1990. For each exercise, use the following functions.

$f(x) = 800 + 300x, \quad g(x) = 990 - 200x \qquad$ *h(x) is the inverse of g(x)*

Find the year that the center of population was at (or near) the indicated town. Each exercise represents a town from a different state. Name the state.

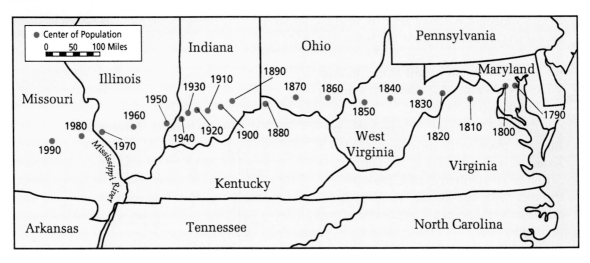

84. Mascoutah: $\frac{1}{10}f(3) + 1800$

85. Clarksburg: $-8 \cdot \dfrac{f(5)}{g(5)}$

86. Middleburg: $f(4) - g(4)$

87. Davisville: $g(f(-4)) - 79{,}000$

88. Hebron: $4080 + f(g(5))$

89. Poole's Island: $f(0) + g(0)$

90. Chillicothe: $\frac{1}{100}f(2) \cdot g(2) - 6400$

91. Whitehall: $384h(-10)$

92. Which of the compound functions has a graph that most resembles the roof of a covered wagon?

a. $f(x) = \begin{cases} \frac{1}{3}|x - 9| + 5, & 6 \leq x < 12 \\ \frac{1}{3}|x - 15| + 5, & 12 \leq x \leq 18 \end{cases}$

b. $g(x) = \begin{cases} 6, & 6 \leq x < 9 \\ 5, & 9 \leq x < 15 \\ 6, & 15 \leq x \leq 18 \end{cases}$

c. $h(x) = \begin{cases} \frac{1}{9}x^2 - 2x + 14, & 6 \leq x < 12 \\ \frac{1}{9}x^2 - \frac{10}{3}x + 30, & 12 \leq x \leq 18 \end{cases}$

1. Which, if any, of the following are graphs of functions?

a.

b.

c.

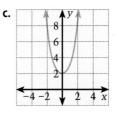

In Exercises 2–4, find the domain and range of the function.

2. $f(x) = \sqrt{x + 2}$

3. $f(x) = \dfrac{4}{x - 3}$

4. $f(x) = x^2 + 3$

5. Find the inverse of $\{(-4, -1), (-3, 0), (-2, 1), (0, 2)\}$.

6. Use $f(x) = x^2 - 7$ and $g(x) = |x| + 2$ to write the equation for $g(f(x))$.

In Exercises 7–9, sketch the inverse of the function. Is the inverse a function?

7. $f(x) = \frac{1}{2}x + 2$

8. $g(x) = |x - 2| + 3$

9. $h(x) = (x - 2)^2 - 1$

10. Given that $f(x)$ and $g(x)$ are inverse functions, find $f(g(7))$.

11. Write $f(x) = |3x - 12|$ as a compound function.

12. Sketch the graph of $f(x) = \begin{cases} |x + 2| - 2, & \text{if } x < 0 \\ -x^2 + 4x, & \text{if } x \geq 0 \end{cases}$.

13. Given $f(x) = x^2$, write an equation $g(x)$ where $g(x)$ is the graph of $f(x)$ shifted 4 units to the right and down 8 units.

14. Given $f(1) = 2$ and $f(n) = 2f(n - 1) - 1$, find $f(6)$.

In Exercises 15 and 16, write a linear or quadratic model for the function.

15.

n	1	2	3	4	5
$f(n)$	−2	−1	1	4	8

16.

n	1	2	3	4	5
$f(n)$	−1	1	3	5	7

17. Lead poisonings in Massachusetts children under 6 years of age from 1985 through 1990 can be modeled by $f(t) = 0.3t^2 - 53.8t + 2415$, where $f(t)$ is the number of cases found per 1000 people and $t = 85$ represents 1985. Using this model, about how many cases per 1000 were found in 1990? *(Source: Boston Globe)*

18. For 1990, the ratio of per capita highway miles traveled to rail miles traveled is given for several countries. Compute the mean, first with and then without, the ratio for the United States. *(Source: World Monitor)*

Austria	7	France	7	Poland	1	Sweden	10
Belgium	8	Italy	7	Portugal	5	United States	158
Britain	10	Netherlands	9	Spain	6	West Germany	11

In Exercises 1–4, perform the indicated matrix operation.

1. $5\begin{bmatrix} 3 & -4 & \frac{1}{2} \\ -6 & 7 & 2 \end{bmatrix} + \begin{bmatrix} -8 & 22 & 6 \\ \frac{3}{2} & -10 & 3 \end{bmatrix}$

2. $\begin{bmatrix} 0 & 17 \\ 8 & 4 \\ -10 & 5 \end{bmatrix} - \frac{1}{3}\begin{bmatrix} 6 & 7 \\ 3 & -2 \\ -5 & 21 \end{bmatrix}$

3. $\begin{bmatrix} 5 & 1 \\ 6 & 0 \\ 8 & 3 \end{bmatrix}\begin{bmatrix} 2 & 1 \\ -4 & 7 \end{bmatrix}$

4. $\begin{bmatrix} 7 & 5 & 0 \\ 1 & 2 & -4 \\ -8 & 7 & 1 \end{bmatrix}\begin{bmatrix} -3 \\ 2 \\ 6 \end{bmatrix}$

In Exercises 5 and 6, evaluate the determinant of the matrix. Then find the inverse of the matrix.

5. $\begin{bmatrix} 4 & 7 \\ 2 & 1 \end{bmatrix}$

6. $\begin{bmatrix} 3 & -2 \\ 1 & 0 \end{bmatrix}$

In Exercises 7 and 8, evaluate the determinant of the matrix.

7. $\begin{bmatrix} -3 & 11 & 6 \\ 4 & -2 & 7 \\ 5 & 0 & 1 \end{bmatrix}$

8. $\begin{bmatrix} -1 & 1 & 2 \\ 6 & 2 & 5 \\ -3 & 8 & -9 \end{bmatrix}$

In Exercises 9 and 10, decide whether the matrices are inverses of each other.

9. $\begin{bmatrix} 0 & 2 & -3 \\ 5 & 8 & 4 \\ 2 & 3 & 2 \end{bmatrix}$ and $\begin{bmatrix} -4 & 13 & -32 \\ 2 & -6 & 15 \\ 1 & -4 & 10 \end{bmatrix}$

10. $\begin{bmatrix} 11 & 8 & -28 \\ 3 & 2 & -7 \\ -7 & -5 & 18 \end{bmatrix}$ and $\begin{bmatrix} -1 & 4 & 0 \\ 5 & -2 & 7 \\ 1 & 1 & 2 \end{bmatrix}$

In Exercises 11–14, solve the linear system using an inverse matrix, an augmented matrix, or Cramer's Rule.

11. $\begin{cases} 3x - 2y = -7 \\ -5x + y = 14 \end{cases}$

12. $\begin{cases} 4x + 5y = 11 \\ -3x + 2y = 32 \end{cases}$

13. $\begin{cases} 3x + 4z = -1 \\ -3x + 2y - z = -6 \\ x + 4y + 2z = -9 \end{cases}$

14. $\begin{cases} 5x - y + 6z = -3 \\ -2x + 2y - z = 0 \\ 4x + 3y + 2z = 7 \end{cases}$

In Exercises 15–18, solve the quadratic equation.

15. $x^2 + 7x + 42 = -5x + 6$

16. $4x^2 - 121 = 0$

17. $3x^2 + 2x - 10 = 0$

18. $5x^2 + 5 = -5x^2 + 11x + 11$

In Exercises 19–22, use the discriminant to find the number of real solutions of the quadratic equation.

19. $3x^2 + 4x - 10 = 0$

20. $-2x^2 + 3x - 4 = 0$

21. $2x^2 - 4x + 2 = 0$

22. $5x^2 + 4x + 4 = 0$

In Exercises 23–25, sketch the graph of the quadratic equation.

23. $y = 3x^2 + 6x - 9$

24. $y = -x^2 + 2x - 1$

25. $y = -4x^2 + 3x - 5$

In Exercises 26–28, solve the quadratic equation.

26. $\frac{1}{2}x^2 - 3x + 5 = 0$

27. $-3x^2 + 4x - 3 = 0$

28. $x^2 + x + 2 = 0$

In Exercises 29–32, perform the indicated operations.

29. $3i(4 - 3i) + i^2(1 + 2i)$

30. $(3 - i) + 2(4 + 2i)$

31. $4i(7 - 2i)(2 - i)$

32. $(3i)^2 - 6i(2 - 3i)$

In Exercises 33 and 34, sketch the graph of the quadratic inequality.

33. $y \geq 3x^2 + 20x + 12$

34. $y < -x^2 + 6x - 8$

In Exercises 35–38, match the function with its graph.

35. $f(x) = |x - 3| + 3$

36. $f(x) = \begin{cases} x + 3, & x > -3 \\ -x - 3, & x \leq -3 \end{cases}$

37. $f(x) = -(x - 2)^2 + 4$

38. $f(x) = \begin{cases} 6x + 1, & x \geq 0 \\ -2x^2 + 1, & x < 0 \end{cases}$

a.

b.

c.

d.
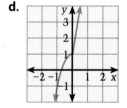

In Exercises 39–42, let $f(x) = 3x + 3$ and $g(x) = -4x + 1$. Write and simplify an equation for $h(x)$.

39. $h(x) = \frac{1}{3}f(x) - g(x)$

40. $h(x) = f(x) + g(x)$

41. $h(x) = f(x) \cdot g(x)$

42. $h(x) = f(g(x))$

In Exercises 43 and 44, sketch the graph of the function and its inverse on the same coordinate plane.

43. $f(x) = \frac{1}{4}x - 6$

44. $f(x) = 2x + 3$

In Exercises 45 and 46, find the first five values of the recursive function.

45. $f(2) = 4$
$f(n) = f(n - 1) - 2$

46. $f(1) = 1$
$f(n) = [f(n - 1)]^2 + 5$

In Exercises 47–50, evaluate the factorial.

47. $5!$

48. $6!$

49. $7!$

50. $8!$

51. *High-School Memories*   Five hundred high-school students and 500 parents of high-school students were asked to name the most memorable part of high school. The matrix gives the percent (in decimal form) of those who thought friendship, sports, or classes were memorable. Show how matrix multiplication can be used to find the total number of people who answered that friendship, sports, or classes were the most memorable. *(Source: 1991 Harris Poll)*

Which is Most Memorable?

	Friendship	Sports/Activities	Teachers/Classes
Students	0.34	0.28	0.13
Parents	0.18	0.33	0.15

52. *Library Book Sale*   The library is having its annual book sale. Pat spent $7.00 on books, Chris spent $5.50, and Mike spent $4.50. The matrix below shows the number of books each one bought. Use an augmented matrix to determine the prices that the library charged for books.

Books

	Price A	Price B	Price C
Pat	1	2	3
Chris	2	3	1
Mike	3	0	2

The Great Wall of China   **In Exercises 53–56, use the following information.**

The height of the Great Wall of China varies from 15 feet to 39 feet.

53. If you dropped a ball from the maximum height of the wall, how many seconds would it take to reach the ground?

54. If another ball was dropped from the minimum height, how long would it take to reach the ground?

55. Someone finds the second ball at the base of the wall and tosses it straight up from a height of 4 feet with an initial velocity of 16 feet per second. Does the ball reach the minimum height of the wall?

56. If the ball is tossed at twice the velocity of that in Exercise 55, does it reach the minimum height?

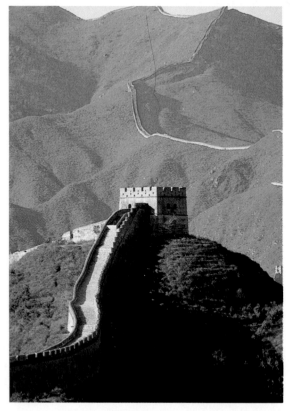

The Great Wall of China has a main-line length of 2,150 miles with spurs and branches totaling 1,780 miles. Erected by hand, it is the longest structure ever built.

In Exercises 57 and 58, use the following information.

The table gives the 1995 cotton yield (in pounds per acre) for twelve states.   *(Source: Agricultural Statistics Board)*

Alabama	382
Arizona	1006
Arkansas	637
California	843
Georgia	635
Louisiana	614
Mississippi	624
Missouri	559
North Carolina	504
Oklahoma	190
Tennessee	531
Texas	378

All parts of a cotton plant are useful. The lint is used to make fiber. The cottonseed provides oil. The stalks and leaves are plowed under to improve soil structure.

57. What is the average yield per acre for these states?

58. Construct a box-and-whisker plot to represent the data.

Farm Foods   **In Exercises 59–62, use the following information.**

For 1980 through 1993, the amount, $f(t)$ (in billions of dollars), American consumers spent on farm foods can be modeled by

$$f(t) = \begin{cases} 15t + 268, & 0 \le t < 7 \\ -1.4t^2 + 48t + 105.6, & 7 \le t \le 13 \end{cases}$$

where $t = 0$ represents 1980.   *(Source: U.S. Department of Agriculture)*

59. How much did consumers spend on farm foods in 1985?

60. How much did consumers spend on farm foods in 1992?

61. Sketch a graph of the function f.

62. During which year was $373 billion spent on farm foods? Which equation did you use to obtain the answer? Could you have used the other equation?

Farm Land   **In Exercise 63, use the following information.**

For 1980 through 1994, the total amount (in millions of acres) of farm land in the United States can be modeled by

$$f(t) = 0.14t^2 - 6.76t + 1040$$

where $t = 0$ represents 1980.   *(Source: U.S. Department of Agriculture)*

63. Rewrite this model so that $t = 0$ represents 1990.

Powers, Roots, and Radicals

LESSONS

7.1 Properties of
Exponents ▪ 346

7.2 Exploring Data:
Compound Interest
and Exponential
Growth ▪ 352

7.3 nth Roots
and Rational
Exponents ▪ 360

7.4 Properties of Roots
of Real Numbers
▪ 368

7.5 Solving Radical
Equations ▪ 374

7.6 Graphing Square Root
and Cube Root
Functions ▪ 381

*The scene shown on this page is
from the prize-winning com-
puter-animated film* Red's
Dream. *Storage of computer
graphic images requires a tremendous amount of computer
memory.*

Real Life
Computer Graphics

Memory Needed for High Resolution Graphics

High resolution graphics, which have 36 pixels per centimeter and use 3 bytes of memory per pixel, need the following number of bytes to store a picture that is y centimeters high and $\frac{4}{3}y$ centimeters wide.

$$x = \underbrace{(36)(y)}_{\substack{\textit{Number of} \\ \textit{pixels high}}} \cdot \underbrace{(36)\left(\tfrac{4}{3}y\right)}_{\substack{\textit{Number of} \\ \textit{pixels wide}}} \cdot \underbrace{(3)}_{\substack{\textit{Bytes per} \\ \textit{pixel}}} = 5184y^2 \text{ bytes}$$

Solving this equation for y in terms of x produces

$$y = \frac{1}{72}\sqrt{x}.$$

From the graph, you can see that half a megabyte of memory (500,000 bytes) can store a picture that is about 9.8 centimeters high. With a full megabyte of memory, you can store a picture that is about 13.9 centimeters high.

7.1

Properties of Exponents

What you should learn:

Goal 1 How to use properties of exponents to evaluate and simplify exponential expressions

Goal 2 How to use powers as models in real-life problems

Why you should learn it:

You can use models containing powers for many real-life situations, such as volume measurements.

Goal 1 **Using Properties of Exponents**

Recall that the expression a^n, when n is a positive integer, represents the number that you obtain when a is used as a factor n times. The number a is the **base,** and the number n is the **exponent.** The expression a^n is called a **power** and is read as "a to the nth power."

LESSON INVESTIGATION

■ Investigating Operations with Powers

Partner Activity Here are two examples of multiplying and dividing powers.

Multiplying Powers

$$2^4 \cdot 2^2 = 2 \cdot 2 \cdot 2 \cdot 2 \cdot 2 \cdot 2 = 2^6$$

Dividing Powers

$$\frac{3^5}{3^3} = \frac{3 \cdot 3 \cdot \cancel{3} \cdot \cancel{3} \cdot \cancel{3}}{\cancel{3} \cdot \cancel{3} \cdot \cancel{3}} = 3^2$$

With your partner, write several other examples of multiplying and dividing powers. Then describe a rule for multiplying powers and a rule for dividing powers. Check that your rules fit each of your examples.

Study Tip

Rather than simply trying to memorize the rules at the right, we suggest that you try to see that each rule makes sense. For instance, the investigation above shows how to make sense of the rules for the product and quotient of powers.

Properties of Exponents

Let a and b be real numbers and let m and n be integers.

1. $a^m \cdot a^n = a^{m+n}$ *Product of Powers Property*

2. $(a^m)^n = a^{m \cdot n}$ *Power of a Power Property*

3. $(ab)^m = a^m b^m$ *Power of a Product Property*

4. $a^{-n} = \dfrac{1}{a^n}$, $a \neq 0$ *Negative Power Property*

5. $a^0 = 1$, $a \neq 0$ *Zero Power Property*

6. $\dfrac{a^m}{a^n} = a^{m-n}$, $a \neq 0$ *Quotient of Powers Property*

7. $\left(\dfrac{a}{b}\right)^m = \dfrac{a^m}{b^m}$, $b \neq 0$ *Power of a Quotient Property*

The properties of exponents may be used to simplify both real numbers and variable expressions.

Example 1   *Using Properties of Exponents*

a. $(-3)(-3)^5 = (-3)^{1+5}$

$\qquad = (-3)^6$

$\qquad = 729$

b. $[(-2)^3]^3 = (-2)^{3 \cdot 3}$

$\qquad = (-2)^9$

$\qquad = -512$

c. $(3^2xy)^4 = (3^2)^4 \cdot x^4 \cdot y^4$

$\qquad = 3^8 \cdot x^4 \cdot y^4$

$\qquad = 6561x^4y^4$

d. $4^{-3} \cdot 4^3 = 4^{-3+3}$

$\qquad = 4^0$

$\qquad = 1$ ■

Expressions involving negative powers may be rewritten with positive powers by using the Negative Power Property.

Example 2   *Using Properties of Exponents*

a. $(3^{-2})^2 = 3^{-2 \cdot 2}$

$\qquad = 3^{-4}$

$\qquad = \dfrac{1}{3^4}$

$\qquad = \dfrac{1}{81}$

b. $x^3 \cdot \dfrac{1}{x^5} = \dfrac{x^3}{x^5}$

$\qquad = x^{3-5}$

$\qquad = x^{-2}$

$\qquad = \dfrac{1}{x^2}$

c. $\dfrac{6^2 \cdot 6}{6^5} = \dfrac{6^3}{6^5}$

$\qquad = 6^{-2}$

$\qquad = \dfrac{1}{6^2}$

$\qquad = \dfrac{1}{36}$

d. $\left(\dfrac{2}{3}\right)^{-2} = \dfrac{2^{-2}}{3^{-2}}$

$\qquad = \dfrac{3^2}{2^2}$

$\qquad = \dfrac{9}{4}$ ■

Example 3   *Simplifying an Expression*

Simplify $\dfrac{4x^3y}{10x^2} \cdot \dfrac{5x^3y}{y^3}$.

Solution

$\dfrac{4x^3y}{10x^2} \cdot \dfrac{5x^3y}{y^3} = \dfrac{(4x^3y)(5x^3y)}{(10x^2)(y^3)}$ *Multiply fractions.*

$\qquad = \dfrac{20x^6y^2}{10x^2y^3}$ *Product of Powers Property*

$\qquad = 2x^4y^{-1}$ *Quotient of Powers Property*

$\qquad = \dfrac{2x^4}{y}$ *Write with positive exponents.*   ■

Goal 2 Using Powers to Solve Real-Life Problems

Real Life
Estimation

Example 4 Comparing Two Volumes

A store is having a contest to guess the number of regular-sized playing marbles in a large jar. The jar is cylindrical with a radius of 6 inches and a height of 15 inches. How many marbles would you guess are in the jar?

Solution To make your guess, you use some playing marbles and a cylindrical container that you have at home. First, you measure the radius of a marble to be $\frac{3}{10}$ inch, which means that each marble has a volume of

$$\frac{4}{3}\pi\left(\frac{3}{10}\right)^3 \text{ cubic inches.}$$

Next, you count the number of marbles that will fit into your cylindrical container that has a radius of $\frac{3}{2}$ inches and a height of $\frac{11}{2}$ inches. You find that the container holds 180 marbles. Thus, the ratio of marble volume to container volume is

$$\frac{\text{Marble volume}}{\text{Container volume}} = \frac{180 \cdot \frac{4}{3}\pi\left(\frac{3}{10}\right)^3}{\pi\left(\frac{3}{2}\right)^2\left(\frac{11}{2}\right)} = \frac{144}{275} \approx 52.4\%.$$

Finally, you guess that 52.4% of the volume of the large contest jar is filled with marbles.

$$\text{Number of marbles} \approx \frac{(0.524)(15\pi6^2)}{\frac{4}{3}\pi\left(\frac{3}{10}\right)^3} \approx 7860$$

Your guess is that 7860 marbles are in the contest jar. ∎

Communicating about ALGEBRA

▶ **SHARING IDEAS about the Lesson**

A. Use the properties of exponents to help complete the missing steps in Example 4. That is, show that

$$\frac{180 \cdot \frac{4}{3}\pi\left(\frac{3}{10}\right)^3}{\pi\left(\frac{3}{2}\right)^2\left(\frac{11}{2}\right)} = \frac{144}{275}.$$

B. If 1000 marbles will fill a cube that is 6 inches on each edge, approximately how many marbles will fill a cube that is 12 inches on each edge? Explain your reasoning.

EXERCISES

▶ **CRITICAL THINKING about the Lesson**

1. How do you read the expression $\frac{x^3}{y^4}$?

In Exercises 2–5, simplify the expression. State each property of exponents used.

2. $2a^2 \cdot a^6$

3. $\frac{a^{-3}}{a}$

4. $(a^2)^3$

5. $\left(\frac{1}{a}\right)^{-2}$

6. Use a calculator to evaluate $(2.15)^7$. Round your result to two decimal places.

In Exercises 7–10, identify the base and the exponent of the expression.

7. 3^4

8. $\left(\frac{1}{4}\right)^3$

9. x^3

10. 2^{-3}

In Exercises 11–38, simplify the expression.

11. $(2)^3(2)^5$

12. $(-3)^2(-3)^1$

13. $\left(\frac{1}{2}\right)^2\left(\frac{1}{2}\right)^{-2}$

14. $3\left(\frac{2}{3}\right)^3\left(\frac{3}{2}\right)^2$

15. $x^4 \cdot x^{-2}$

16. $3y^2 \cdot y^2$

17. $(4^3)^2$

18. $(6^2)^{-2}$

19. $(x^{-3})^5$

20. $(y^4)^3$

21. $(x^3y)^4$

22. $(2xy^3)^{-2}$

23. $(-3x^2)^2$

24. $(x^2y^2)^{-1}$

25. $4x^{-1}y$

26. $xy^{-2}x$

27. $3x^0y^4$

28. $-2x^{-2}y^0$

29. $\frac{4^3}{4^1}$

30. $\frac{x^3}{x^{-1}}$

31. $\frac{x^{-3}y}{xy^{-2}}$

32. $\frac{2x^2y^7}{6xy^{-1}}$

33. $\frac{6x}{5y} \cdot \frac{y^2x^{-2}}{x^3}$

34. $\frac{-3x^5}{x^{13}} \cdot \frac{2x^{10}y}{15y^2}$

35. $\frac{-12xy}{7x^4} \cdot \frac{21x^5y^2}{4y}$

36. $\frac{xy^9}{3y^{-2}} \cdot \frac{-7y}{21x^5}$

37. $\frac{y^{10}}{2x^3} \cdot \frac{20x^{14}}{xy^6}$

38. $\frac{5x^{-2}}{3x} \cdot \frac{2y^3}{x^{10}}$

In Exercises 39–47, use properties of exponents to solve for x.

Sample: $\quad 2^x2^4 = 2^2$
$$2^{x+4} = 2^2$$
$$x + 4 = 2$$
$$x = -2$$

39. $4^x4^2 = 4^5$

40. $\frac{a^2}{a^x} = a^{-3}$

41. $x^{-1} = \frac{1}{4}$

42. $x^{-2} = 9$

43. $\frac{x^2}{3} \cdot \frac{1}{x} = 4$

44. $\frac{x^6}{2x^{-2}} \cdot \frac{10}{x^7} = 20$

45. $\frac{x^{16}y^2}{2x^{12}y} \cdot \frac{3}{x^3y} = \frac{9}{2}$

46. $\frac{12x^5a^2}{2x^4} \cdot \frac{2a}{3a^2} = -12$

47. $\frac{2kx^4}{5k^2x} \cdot 25kx^{-1} = \frac{1}{10}$

48. *Geometry*   Find an expression for the area of the rectangle.

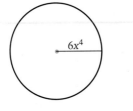

x^4

$4x^4$

49. *Geometry*   Find an expression for the area of the circle.

$6x^4$

50. *Kepler's Third Law*   In 1619, Johannes Kepler, a German astronomer, discovered that the period, T (in years), of each planet in our solar system is related to the planet's mean distance, R (in astronomical units), from the sun by the equation

$$\frac{T^2}{R^3} = k.$$

Test Kepler's equation for the nine planets in our solar system, using the table at the right. (Astronomical units relate the other planets' periods and mean distances to Earth's period and mean distance.) Do you get approximately the same value for k for each planet?

Planet	T	R
Mercury	0.241	0.387
Venus	0.615	0.723
Earth	1.000	1.000
Mars	1.881	1.523
Jupiter	11.861	5.203
Saturn	29.457	9.541
Uranus	84.008	19.190
Neptune	164.784	30.086
Pluto	248.350	39.507

51. *Discovering a Planet*   Suppose that you discovered a planet whose mean distance from the sun is 48.125 astronomical units. Use the results of Exercise 50 to find the period of this planet in days. (The period of Earth is 365.25 days.)

52. *Pluto*   Find the ratio of Pluto's mean distance (from the sun) to Mercury's mean distance.

53. *Pluto*   If you draw a diagram of our solar system in which Mercury's mean distance from the sun is represented by 1 inch, how many inches would be needed to represent Pluto's mean distance from the sun?

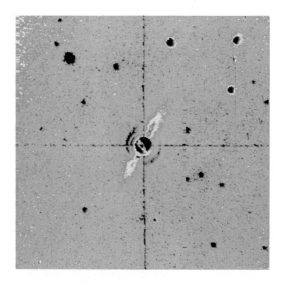

The first visual evidence of a solar system other than our own was recorded in 1984 by the Las Campanas Observatory in Chile.

54. *National Park Spending* For 1985 through 1994, the total expenditures, M (in millions of dollars), for all the national parks in the United States can be modeled by

$$M = 575(1.066)^t$$

where $t = 5$ represents 1985. What was the total expenditure in 1985? In 1993?
(Source: U.S. National Park Service)

55. *Aerospace Sales* For 1980 through 1993, new orders, O (in billions of dollars), in the aerospace industry can be modeled by

$$O = \begin{cases} 68.7(1.1)^t, & 0 \le t < 10 \\ 386.87 - 24.03t, & 10 \le t \le 13 \end{cases}$$

where $t = 0$ represents 1980. What was the value of new orders in 1988? In 1990?
(Source: U.S. Bureau of Census)

A National Park Service range guides students in a nature studies program.

Integrated Review

In Exercises 56–59, evaluate the expression.

56. $x^4 y^2$ when $x = 2$ and $y = 3$

57. $2x^3 + 6y^5$ when $x = 3$ and $y = -1$

58. $x^4 - xy - y^2$ when $x = -5$ and $y = 4$

59. $3x^2 + 4xy - 2y^2$ when $x = 4$ and $y = -10$

60. *Powers of Ten* Which best estimates the number of hours that a person sleeps in a year?
a. 3.0×10^1 **b.** 3.0×10^2 **c.** 3.0×10^3 **d.** 3.0×10^4

61. *Powers of Ten* Which best estimates the number of cubic inches in a 12-ounce soda pop can?
a. 2.2×10^1 **b.** 2.2×10^2 **c.** 2.2×10^3 **d.** 2.2×10^4

Exploration and Extension

62. *Geometry* When the radius of a sphere is doubled, how much is the volume increased? Justify your answer algebraically.

63. *Geometry* The volume of a circular cone is $V = \frac{1}{3}\pi r^2 h$, where r is the radius of the base and h is the height. Write a formula for the volume of a circular cone whose height is equal to the diameter of its base. (Use the letters V and r in your formula.) Use the formula to find the volume of a cone whose height and diameter are each 10 centimeters.

7.2

Exploring Data: Compound Interest and Exponential Growth

What you should learn:

Goal 1 How to use the formulas for compound interest and exponential growth and decay formulas

Goal 2 How to solve real-life problems modeled by exponential growth formulas

Why you should learn it:

You can use exponential models for many problems, such as those measuring acidity with the pH scale.

Real Life
Finance

Goal 1 Using Exponential Formulas

Simple interest is paid only on the initial *principal*. Compound interest* is paid on the initial principal and on previously earned interest.

> **Compound Interest**
>
> Consider an initial principal of P deposited in an account that pays interest at an annual rate of r, compounded n times per year. The *balance, A,* in the account after t years is
>
> $$A = P\left(1 + \frac{r}{n}\right)^{nt}.$$

Example 1 *Finding the Balance in an Account*

Assume $1000 is deposited in an account that pays 8% annual interest compounded quarterly. What is the balance after one year?

Solution The number of compoundings per year is $n = 4$. This means that the account earns $\frac{r}{n} = 2\%$ interest each quarter. You can find the balance after one year in two ways. One way is to find the balance at the end of each quarter.

Finding the Balance after Each Quarter:

$1000.00(1.02) = \$1020.00$ *1st Quarter Balance*

$1020.00(1.02) = \$1040.40$ *2nd Quarter Balance*

$1040.40(1.02) = \$1061.21$ *3rd Quarter Balance*

$1061.21(1.02) = \$1082.43$ *4th Quarter Balance*

Another way is to apply the compound interest formula:

$$A = 1000\left(1 + \frac{0.08}{4}\right)^{4 \cdot 1} = 1000(1.02)^4 = \$1082.43$$

The balance at the end of one year is $1082.43. Notice that if the account paid simple interest, the balance at the end of one year would be $1000(1.08) = \$1080.00$.

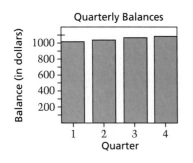

Quarterly Balances

Balance (in dollars) — 1000, 800, 600, 400, 200 / Quarter 1, 2, 3, 4

The formula for compound interest shows you four ways to increase the balance, *A*, in a savings account: increase the initial principal *P*, increase the interest rate *r*, increase the time *t*, or increase the number of compoundings per year *n*.

Real Life

Finance

Example 2 *Comparing Quarterly and Monthly Compounding*

Assume $5000 is deposited in an account that pays 6% annual interest. Find the balance after 25 years if the interest is
a. compounded quarterly.   **b.** compounded monthly.

Solution

a. If the interest is compounded quarterly, the balance at the end of 25 years would be

$$A = 5000 \left(1 + \frac{0.06}{4}\right)^{4 \cdot 25} \quad \textit{P = 5000, r = 0.06, n = 4, t = 25}$$

$$= 5000(1.015)^{100} \quad \textit{Simplify.}$$

$$= \$22,160.23 \quad \textit{Use a calculator.}$$

b. If the interest is compounded monthly, the balance at the end of 25 years would be

$$A = 5000 \left(1 + \frac{0.06}{12}\right)^{12 \cdot 25} \quad \textit{P = 5000, r = 0.06, n = 12, t = 25}$$

$$= 5000(1.005)^{300} \quad \textit{Simplify.}$$

$$= \$22,324.85 \quad \textit{Use a calculator.}$$

Notice that more frequent compoundings produce a greater balance. ■

The formula for compound interest can be used to find the value of other quantities that increase by the same percent over equal time intervals.

Real Life

Inflation

Housing Inflation

$179,700

$20,000

Value of House (in $1000s)

150

100

50

0   10   20   30   40

Year (0 ↔ 1950)

Example 3 *Finding the Value of a House*

You have inherited a house that was purchased for $20,000 in 1950. It is now 1995, and the value of the house increased by approximately 5% each year. What is the value of the house now?

Solution Using *P* = 20,000, *r* = 0.05, *n* = 1, and *t* = 45, you can apply the formula for compound interest to obtain a 1995 value of

$$A = 20,000(1 + 0.05)^{45}$$

$$= 20,000(1.05)^{45}$$

$$\approx \$179,700.$$

The house is now (in 1995) worth about $179,700. ■

Modeling Exponential Growth and Decay

Compound interest is an example of exponential growth.

Exponential Growth and Decay

Let a and C be real numbers, with $C > 0$. The models for **exponential growth** and **exponential decay** are as follows.

$y = Ca^x$ *Exponential growth model, $a > 1$*

$y = Ca^x$ *Exponential decay model, $0 < a < 1$*

Example 4   *Classifying Exponential Models*

Classify the model as exponential growth or exponential decay.

a. $y = 3\left(\frac{1}{2}\right)^x$

b. $y = 2\left(\frac{3}{2}\right)^x$

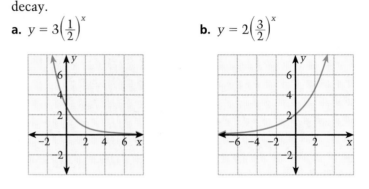

Solution

a. Because the base, $a = \frac{1}{2}$, is less than 1, this model represents exponential decay. Notice from the graph that the values of y decrease as the values of x increase.

b. Because the base, $a = \frac{3}{2}$, is greater than 1, this model represents exponential growth. Notice from the graph that the values of y increase as the values of x increase. ■

To sketch the graph of an exponential growth or decay model, construct a table of values, graph the points, and then connect the points with a curve. For instance, the following tables could be used to sketch the graphs shown in Example 4.

a.

x	-2	-1	0	1	2
$y = 3\left(\frac{1}{2}\right)^x$	12	6	3	$\frac{3}{2}$	$\frac{3}{4}$

b.

x	-2	-1	0	1	2
$y = 2\left(\frac{3}{2}\right)^x$	$\frac{8}{9}$	$\frac{4}{3}$	2	3	$\frac{9}{2}$

The map at the right shows the pH levels of rain in the United States. The acid in the rain is the result of pollutants in the air—especially those from burning gasoline, coal, and oil. The brown and purple areas on the map indicate regions with low alkalinity in the surface water. Because an acid can neutralize alkalinity, these areas are very susceptible to harm from acid rain.

Real Life
Acid Rain

	Solution	pH
Acid	Hydrochloric acid	0
	Stomach acid	1
	Lemon juice	2
	Vinegar	3
	Tomato juice	4
	Coffee	5
	Milk	6
	Pure water	7
	Egg white	8
	Baking soda	9
	Hand soap	10
	Household ammonia	11
	Washing soda	12
Base	Oven cleaner	13
	Sodium hydroxide	14

Example 5 *Using an Exponential Model*

To test whether a solution is a *base* (such as baking soda) or an *acid* (such as vinegar), chemists have devised a test called the pH test. The test measures the concentration of hydrogen ions (in moles per liter) in the solution.

$$\text{Concentration of hydrogen ions} = \left(\frac{1}{10}\right)^{\text{pH}}$$

Pure water has a pH of 7. Solutions with pH values greater than 7 are bases and solutions with pH values less than 7 are acids. Normal rain has a pH value of about 5.5. Which parts of the United States have rain that is at least 10 times the acidity of normal rain? *(Source: Scientific American)*

Solution A pH of 4.5 is ten times more acidic than a pH of 5.5. To see this, you can write the following ratio.

$$\frac{4.5 \text{ pH}}{5.5 \text{ pH}} = \frac{\left(\frac{1}{10}\right)^{4.5}}{\left(\frac{1}{10}\right)^{5.5}} = \left(\frac{1}{10}\right)^{-1} = \frac{1}{\frac{1}{10}} = 10$$

The northeastern portion of the United States has rain with pH values that are 4.5 or lower, which means that its rain has at least 10 times the acidity of normal rain. ∎

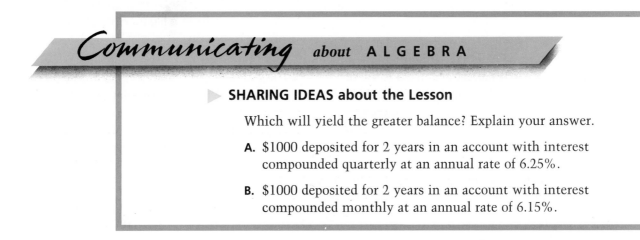

Communicating about **ALGEBRA**

▶ **SHARING IDEAS about the Lesson**

Which will yield the greater balance? Explain your answer.

A. $1000 deposited for 2 years in an account with interest compounded quarterly at an annual rate of 6.25%.

B. $1000 deposited for 2 years in an account with interest compounded monthly at an annual rate of 6.15%.

EXERCISES

▶ **CRITICAL THINKING about the Lesson**

1. What is the difference between simple and compound interest?

2. *Comparing Balances*   Which will yield the larger balance in one year? Explain.
   a. $3000 at 6% annual interest, compounded twice a year
   b. $3000 at 6% annual interest, compounded four times a year

3. *Balance in an Account* $2000 is deposited in an account that pays 8% annual interest, compounded monthly. What is the balance in five years?

4. *Balance in an Account* $2000 is deposited in an account that pays 8% annual interest, compounded annually. What is the balance in five years?

5. Is $y = 5\left(\frac{6}{5}\right)^x$ a model for exponential growth or decay? Explain.

6. Is $y = \frac{1}{4}\left(\frac{3}{4}\right)^x$ a model for exponential growth or decay? Explain.

Independent Practice

7. *Balance in an Account* $800 is deposited in an account that pays 9% annual interest, compounded annually. Find the balance after four years.

8. *Balance in an Account* $100 is deposited in an account that pays 6% annual interest, compounded annually. Find the balance after five years.

9. *Balance in an Account* $2250 is deposited in an account that pays 6% annual interest, compounded quarterly. Find the balance after ten years.

10. *Balance in an Account* $1800 is deposited in an account that pays 5% annual interest, compounded monthly. Find the balance after one year.

11. *How Much to Deposit?*   How much must you deposit in an account that pays 6.25% interest, compounded annually, to have a balance of $700 after two years?

12. *How Much to Deposit?*   How much must you deposit in an account that pays 8% annual interest, compounded monthly, to have a balance of $1000 after one year?

13. *Inheritance*   You have inherited an emerald ring that had an appraised value of $2400 in 1960. It is now 1996, and the appraised value of the ring has increased by approximately 6% each year. What is the value now?

14. *Fine Art*   Vincent Van Gogh's painting "Irises" was auctioned for $53.9 million dollars in 1987. Suppose that it sold for $50 in 1889, when it was painted. Assuming exponential growth, by what percent did its value increase each year?

In Exercises 15–18, state whether the function is a model of exponential growth or exponential decay.

15. $y = \frac{1}{3}(2)^x$

16. $y = 6\left(\frac{1}{5}\right)^x$

17. $A = 100(1.05)^x$

18. $y = 0.05(10)^x$

In Exercises 19–22, match the function with its graph.

19. $y = \frac{3}{2}(5)^x$

20. $y = 5\left(\frac{4}{3}\right)^x$

21. $y = 2\left(\frac{1}{3}\right)^x$

22. $y = 3(0.75)^x$

a.   b.   c.   d.

In Exercises 23–28, copy and complete the table of values and sketch the graph of the exponential function.

23. $y = 4\left(\frac{1}{2}\right)^x$

x	-3	-2	-1	0	1	2
y						

24. $y = 2\left(\frac{1}{4}\right)^x$

x	-3	-2	-1	0	1	2
y						

25. $y = \frac{1}{3}(3)^x$

x	-3	-2	-1	0	1	2	3
y							

26. $y = 10(2)^x$

x	-3	-2	-1	0	1	2	3
y							

27. $A = 2000(1.02)^{4t}$

t	1	2	3	4	5	6
A						

28. $A = 2000(1.08)^t$

t	1	2	3	4	5	6
A						

29. *Recreational Books*   Of the total amounts of money spent on recreation for 1970 through 1990, the percent, P, spent on books and maps can be modeled by

$$P = 2.94(1.07)^t$$

where $t = 0$ represents 1970. Sketch the graph of this model.

(Source: U.S. Bureau of Economic Analysis)

30. *Wheelchairs*   For 1980 through 1990, the total amount, E (in billions of dollars), spent on health appliances such as eyeglasses, hearing aids, and wheelchairs can be approximated by the model

$$E = 4.9(1.1)^t$$

where $t = 0$ represents 1980. Sketch the graph of this model.

(Source: U.S. Health Care Financing Administration)

Modern lightweight wheelchairs give greater freedom to physically challenged people.

31. *Teachers' Salaries* For 1980 through 1990, the average salary, S (in thousands of dollars), of public school teachers in the United States can be modeled by $S = 1.5t + 16$ ($t = 0$ represents 1980). During that time, the average inflation rate was 6.2% per year. Did the average salary keep up with inflation? Explain.

32. *Miners' Wages* For 1980 to 1990, the average hourly wage, M (in dollars), of miners in the United States can be modeled by $M = -0.045t^2 + 0.8t + 9.2$ where $t = 0$ represents 1980. During that period of time, the average rate of inflation was 6.2% per year. Did the average wage keep up with inflation? Explain.

Teachers' Salaries

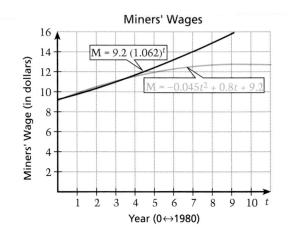

Miners' Wages

Integrated Review

In Exercises 33–36, evaluate the expression.

33. $6\left(\dfrac{4}{5}\right)^3$

34. $\dfrac{1}{3}\left(\dfrac{1}{2}\right)^7$

35. $250(1.06)^{15}$

36. $1024\left(\left(\dfrac{1}{2}\right)^2\right)^4$

37. *College Entrance Exam Sample* Suppose that the average cost of a new home increased from 1969 to 1978 by the same percent that it increased from 1960 to 1969. Use the graph at the right to approximate the average cost of a new home in 1978.

  a. $35,000 **b.** $31,000 **c.** $28,000
  d. $25,000 **e.** $24,000

Average Cost of a New Home

Exploration and Extension

38. *Population Growth* In 1980, the population of Shady Bridge was 2500. Each year between 1980 and 1993, the population increased by 1.8%. Write a model for the population, P, in year, t, where $t = 0$ represents 1980.

39. *Population Growth* Sketch the graph of the model in Exercise 38. During which year did the population surpass 3000?

1. 24 is what percent of 120?

2. Solve $|x - 7| > 2$. **(1.6)**

3. Solve $|2x - 4| = 8$. **(1.7)**

4. In which quadrant is $(-3, 8)$? **(2.1)**

5. Find the intercepts of $\frac{x}{7} + \frac{y}{3} = 1$. **(2.3)**

6. Sketch the graph of $y \le \frac{2}{3}x + 5$. **(2.5)**

7. Solve $2(3x - 5) - (2x - 3) = x + 2$. **(1.3)**

8. Find the intercepts of $y = -2|x - 4| + 6$. **(2.6)**

9. Find the domain of $f(x) = \dfrac{3}{\sqrt{x - 4}}$. **(6.2)**

10. Write the inverse of $y = \frac{2}{3}x + 4$. **(6.3)**

11. Simplify: $4.7 \times 10^3 + 8.9 \times 10^3$.

12. Simplify: $(2 \times 10^{-2})(6 \times 10^4)$.

13. Find the vertex of $y = 4|x - 3| + 8$. **(2.6)**

14. If $f(1) = -1$ and $f(n + 1) = [f(n)]^2 - 3$, find $f(4)$. **(6.6)**

15. Write the equation for the line passing through $(2, -4)$ and $(3, 1)$.

16. State the area of a triangle whose base is 3 units greater than its height, h. **(1.2)**

17. Solve $\begin{cases} 2x + 3y = 6 \\ 4x + 4y = \frac{10}{3} \end{cases}$ **(3.2)**

18. For what values of c will $y = 3x^2 - 7x + c$ have no x-intercepts? **(5.4)**

Career Interview

Contractor

James Simko is a general contractor. His work involves the design, construction, and renovation of residential buildings, and he oversees all aspects of running the business.

Q: *Were you a good math student?*

A: I didn't think I was a particularly good math student. I didn't expect to use much math in my career, because at that time I was more interested in the humanities.

Q: *What math skill do you now apply in your work?*

A: I enjoyed geometry, but after college, I hardly used it. When I started this job, the geometric formulas I learned in school came to life. I can use the formulas instead of making guesses!

Q: *Is it important to know other math skills?*

A: I do cost estimates when bidding on a project. These estimates are legally binding, so there isn't any room for errors. Even when I use a calculator or a computer program, I still need to understand the calculations and to have a sense of what is reasonable.

Q: *How do you know if you are successful in your job?*

A: I know I'm successful when the company is profitable. That comes from a combination of good management and communication skills.

7.3

*n*th Roots and Rational Exponents

What you should learn:

Goal 1 How to evaluate *n*th roots of real numbers using radical notation and rational exponent notation

Goal 2 How to use *n*th roots to solve real-life problems

Why you should learn it:

You can model many situations with *n*th roots, such as the lengths of the sides of regular polyhedrons.

Goal 1 Evaluating *n*th Roots

You know how to find the square roots of a number. For instance, $\pm\sqrt{5}$ are square roots of 5 because $(\sqrt{5})^2 = 5$ and $(-\sqrt{5})^2 = 5$.

In this lesson, you will study other types of roots of numbers: cube roots, fourth roots, fifth roots, and so on. For instance, 2 is a cube root of 8 because $2^3 = 8$. Similarly, -3 and 3 are fourth roots of 81 because $(-3)^4 = 81$ and $3^4 = 81$.

---

nth Roots of a Real Number

Let *n* be an integer greater than 1. If $b^n = a$, then *b* is an *n*th root of *a*. (Notice below that *n*th roots can be written using either radicals or rational exponents.)

1. If *n* is *odd*, then *a* has one *n*th root.

$b = \sqrt[n]{a}$ *Radical notation*

$b = a^{1/n}$ *Rational exponent notation*

2. If *n* is *even* and *a* is positive, then *a* has two *n*th roots.

$b = \pm\sqrt[n]{a}$ *Radical notation*

$b = \pm a^{1/n}$ *Rational exponent notation*

Example 1   *Using Radical Notation for nth Roots*

a. $\sqrt[3]{64} = 4$ because $4^3 = 64$.

b. $\sqrt[4]{81} = 3$ because $(3^4) = 81$.

c. $\sqrt[5]{-32} = -2$ because $(-2)^5 = -32$. ∎

Example 2   *Using Rational Exponent Notation*

a. $16^{1/2} = 4$ because $4^2 = 16$.

b. $(-27)^{1/3} = -3$ because $(-3)^3 = -27$.

c. $625^{1/4} = 5$ because $5^4 = 625$. ∎

Most calculators have a square root key but do not have keys for other roots. Thus, when using a calculator to approximate an nth root, you should first rewrite the nth root using a rational exponent. Then use the calculator's power key.

Connections
Technology

Example 3 *Approximating Roots with a Calculator*

To approximate $\sqrt[3]{5}$, write the expression as $5^{1/3}$. Then use the power key as follows.

Expression	Keystrokes	Display	
$5^{1/3}$	5 $\boxed{y^x}$ $\boxed{(}$ 1 $\boxed{\div}$ 3 $\boxed{)}$ $\boxed{=}$	1.70998	*Scientific*
$5^{1/3}$	5 $\boxed{\wedge}$ $\boxed{(}$ 1 $\boxed{\div}$ 3 $\boxed{)}$ $\boxed{=}$	1.70998	*Graphing*

Rounded to two decimal places, the value is $\sqrt[3]{5} \approx 1.71$. ■

A rational exponent doesn't have to be of the form $\frac{1}{n}$. Rational numbers such as $\frac{3}{2}$ and $-\frac{1}{2}$ can also be used as exponents.

Rational Exponents

Let $a^{1/n}$ be an nth root of a and let m be a positive integer.

1. $a^{m/n} = (a^{1/n})^m$

2. $a^{-1/n} = \dfrac{1}{a^{1/n}}$, $a \neq 0$

3. $a^{-m/n} = \dfrac{1}{a^{m/n}} = \dfrac{1}{(a^{1/n})^m}$, $a \neq 0$

Example 4 *Evaluating Expressions with Rational Exponents*

a. $4^{3/2} = (4^{1/2})^3 = 2^3 = 8$

b. $9^{-1/2} = \dfrac{1}{9^{1/2}} = \dfrac{1}{3}$

c. $8^{2/3} = (8^{1/3})^2 = 2^2 = 4$

d. $32^{-3/5} = \dfrac{1}{32^{3/5}}$

$\qquad = \dfrac{1}{(32^{1/5})^3} = \dfrac{1}{2^3} = \dfrac{1}{8}$ ■

Connections
Technology

Example 5 *Using a Calculator to Evaluate Rational Exponents*

a. $6^{3/4} \approx 3.834$ *Use a calculator.*

b. $8^{-1/5} \approx 0.660$ *Use a calculator.* ■

A polyhedron is a geometric solid whose faces are polygons. A regular polyhedron has sides that are congruent regular polygons that make equal angles with each other. There are only five such polyhedrons—the five Platonic solids. Their names and the approximate formulas for their volumes in terms of the length of an edge a are given at the right.

Tetrahedron:
$V \approx 0.11785a^3$

Cube:
$V = a^3$

Octahedron:
$V \approx 0.47140a^3$

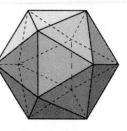

Dodecahedron:
$V \approx 7.66312a^3$

Icosahedron:
$V \approx 2.18169a^3$

Goal 2 Using *n*th Roots in Real-Life Problems

Connections
Geometry

Example 6 *Finding the Length of an Edge of a Polyhedron*

The uncut diamond shown at the left weighs 616 carats. It has the shape of an octahedron. Approximate the length of each edge of this diamond. (A 1-carat diamond has a mass of $\frac{1}{5}$ gram.)

Solution The mass of the diamond in grams is $\frac{1}{5}(616)$, or about 123.2. Since the density of diamond is 3.513 grams per cubic centimeter, the volume of the diamond is

$$\text{volume} = \frac{\text{mass}}{\text{density}} = \frac{123.2 \text{ grams}}{3.513 \text{ g/cm}^3} \approx 35.07 \text{ cubic centimeters.}$$

Using the formula for the volume of an octahedron, you can solve for the length of an edge as follows.

$V \approx 0.47140a^3$	*Volume of octahedron*
$35.07 \approx 0.47140a^3$	*Substitute 35.07 for V.*
$74.40 \approx a^3$	*Divide both sides by 0.47140.*
$\sqrt[3]{74.40} \approx a$	*Find cube root.*
$4.2 \approx a$	*Use a calculator.*

The density of diamond is 3.513 grams per cubic centimeter.

Each edge of the diamond is about $\sqrt[3]{74.40} \approx 4.2$ centimeters. ■

The Olympias *was built in 1987. It is a reconstruction of a trireme (a Greek galley ship). The people shown are volunteers who operated the ship's triple set of oars.*

Real Life

Nautical Science

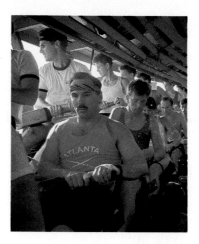

Example 7   *Finding the Speed of a Ship*

The speed, s (in knots), of the *Olympias*, was found to be related to the power, P (in kilowatts), generated by the rowers by the model $P = 0.03s^3$. The volunteer crew of the *Olympias* was able to generate a maximum power of 10.5 kilowatts. What was its greatest speed? *(Source: Scientific American)*

Solution

$P = 0.03s^3$	*Cubic model*
$10.5 = 0.03s^3$	*Substitute 10.5 for P.*
$350 = s^3$	*Divide both sides by 0.03.*
$\sqrt[3]{350} \approx s$	*Find cube root.*
$7 \approx s$	*Use a calculator.*

The greatest speed attained by the *Olympias* was about 7 knots (about 8 miles per hour). ▪

Communicating about **ALGEBRA**

▶ SHARING IDEAS about the Lesson

A. Find the length of an edge of a cube that has a volume of 14 cubic feet.

B. Find the length of an edge of a tetrahedron that has a volume of 8 cubic inches.

C. If the volunteer crew of the *Olympias* could have matched the power output of the crew of the U.S. Navy light racing cutters (21.8 kilowatts), how fast could the *Olympias* have traveled?

EXERCISES

Guided Practice

▶ **CRITICAL THINKING about the Lesson**

1. Is 4 a cube root of 64? Is -4? Explain.

2. Is 4 a square root of 16? Is -4? Explain.

3. Evaluate $\sqrt[3]{125}$ and $\sqrt[4]{10{,}000}$.

4. Evaluate $(-125)^{1/3}$ and $\sqrt[4]{-10{,}000}$.

5. *Geometry*   The Unisphere, which was the symbol of the 1964 World's Fair in New York City, has a volume of approximately 1,440,000 cubic feet. Approximate the radius of the Unisphere.

6. Evaluate $27^{-2/3}$ without a calculator. Check your result with a calculator.

Unisphere, Flushing Meadows Park, New York

Independent Practice

In Exercises 7–12, rewrite the expression using rational exponents.

7. $\sqrt[5]{12}$ 8. $\sqrt[3]{9}$ 9. $\sqrt[9]{16}$ 10. $\sqrt[4]{29}$ 11. $\sqrt[4]{2}$ 12. $\sqrt[7]{3}$

In Exercises 13–18, rewrite the expression using radical notation.

13. $4^{1/3}$ 14. $5^{1/7}$ 15. $10^{1/6}$

16. $7^{1/3}$ 17. $3^{1/4}$ 18. $6^{1/4}$

In Exercises 19–24, use radical notation to write all of the indicated roots.

19. Cube root(s) of 3   20. Fifth root(s) of 14   21. Sixth root(s) of 9

22. Ninth root(s) of 216   23. Fourth root(s) of 10   24. Tenth root(s) of 110

Technology   **In Exercises 25–42, evaluate the expression using a calculator. Round the result to two decimal places, when appropriate.**

25. $\sqrt[3]{125}$ 26. $\sqrt[3]{729}$ 27. $\sqrt[5]{-32{,}768}$

28. $\sqrt[4]{81}$ 29. $\sqrt[4]{256}$ 30. $\sqrt[3]{216}$

31. $15{,}625^{1/6}$ 32. $2401^{1/4}$ 33. $-243^{1/5}$

34. $-512^{1/3}$ 35. $1024^{1/5}$ 36. $1024^{1/10}$

37. $\sqrt[3]{9}$ 38. $\sqrt[4]{108}$ 39. $\sqrt[5]{118}$

40. $\sqrt[7]{210}$ 41. $\sqrt[6]{6}$ 42. $\sqrt[3]{-96}$

In Exercises 43–54, evaluate the expression without using a calculator.

43. $16^{-3/2}$

44. $4^{7/2}$

45. $81^{3/4}$

46. $64^{-2/3}$

47. $125^{2/3}$

48. $-8^{5/3}$

49. $-27^{4/3}$

50. $9^{3/2}$

51. $8^{2/3}$

52. $25^{3/2}$

53. $100^{3/2}$

54. $256^{3/4}$

Technology **In Exercises 55–60, use a calculator to evaluate the expression. Round the result to three decimal places.**

55. $4^{2/3}$

56. $8^{3/8}$

57. $10^{-1/3}$

58. $9^{-1/4}$

59. $16^{-4/5}$

60. $26^{-3/4}$

61. *Geometry* Find the length of an edge of an icosahedron that has a volume of 21 cubic centimeters.

62. *Geometry* Find the length of an edge of a dodecahedron that has a volume of 30 cubic feet.

63. *Lawn Bowling* The target ball in lawn bowling is called the jack. It weighs about 283 grams and is made of wood whose density is 2.11 grams per cubic centimeter. What is the radius of a jack?

64. *Water Balloon* You fill a spherical balloon with one pint of water. What is the radius of the water balloon? (*Hint:* 1 pint = 28.875 cubic inches.)

Lawn bowling is an ancient game in which players roll balls at a white target ball. About 20 nations have lawn bowling associations.

65. *Spectator Sports* For 1980 through 1990, the admission receipts, S (in billions of dollars), for spectator sports in the United States can be modeled by

$$S = 2.84 + 0.014t^3$$

where $t = 0$ represents 1985. In what year were the receipts approximately $3.2 billion?

66. *Cement Production* For 1980 through 1990, the world production of cement, C (in millions of metric tons), can be modeled by

$$C = 868 + \frac{1}{2}t^3$$

where $t = 0$ represents 1980. In what year were about 868 million metric tons of cement produced? 900 million metric tons?

Concrete is used in most construction projects, such as La Grand Arche in Paris.

67. *Douglas Fir* The volume, V (in cubic feet), of wood in the main trunk of a Douglas fir can be approximated by the model $V = 50r^3$, where r is the radius of the trunk at the base of the tree. Assume that the trunk of a Douglas fir has the shape of a tall, slender right circular cone. What is the ratio of the tree's height to its radius?

68. *Doyle Log Rule* The Doyle Log Rule is a formula for approximating the number of board feet, B, in a circular log that is L feet long and has a radius of r inches.

$$B \approx \left(\frac{r-2}{2}\right)^2 L$$

What was the approximate radius of a 20-foot log that produced 5000 board feet of lumber?

Lumber mills use different log-sawing patterns when cutting large logs than when cutting small logs, as shown in the diagrams at the right. The patterns are designed to produce as many board feet as possible from a log. One board foot is the amount of wood in a 1-inch thick piece of lumber that is 12 inches square.

Douglas firs produce more lumber than any other type of North American tree.

Integrated Review

In Exercises 69–72, simplify the expression.

Sample: $\sqrt{72} = \sqrt{36} \cdot \sqrt{2} = 6\sqrt{2}$

69. $\sqrt{20}$ **70.** $\sqrt{180}$ **71.** $\sqrt{54}$ **72.** $\sqrt{216}$

In Exercises 73–76, evaluate the expression.

73. $4x^6$ when $x = 2$ **74.** x^4 when $x = 5$ **75.** 4^x when $x = 3$ **76.** 10^{-x} when $x = 2$

In Exercises 77–80, solve the equation for x.

77. $25 = 16x^2$ **78.** $13x^2 = 39$ **79.** $2x^2 + 5 = 13$ **80.** $512 = 2x^2$

Exploration and Extension

In Exercises 81 and 82, solve the equation for x.

81. $x^7 - 5x^2 = 0$ **82.** $x^4 - 9x = 0$

Take this test as you would take a test in class. The answers to the exercises are given in the back of the book.

In Exercises 1–3, simplify the expression. **(7.1)**

1. $\dfrac{a^4 b^0 c^{-3}}{a^2 b^{-7} c}$

2. $\left(\dfrac{a^2}{b^3}\right)^5 \cdot \left(\dfrac{b}{a^5}\right)^2$

3. $\dfrac{(a^2 b^3)^4}{(ab^{-2})^{-3}}$

In Exercises 4–6, evaluate the expression. **(7.3)**

4. $(-8)^{2/3}$

5. $81^{-3/4}$

6. $\sqrt[4]{16}$

In Exercises 7–9, rewrite using only positive exponents. **(7.1)**

7. $\dfrac{15^{-2} 3^{-3}}{5^{-2}}$

8. $2(6^{-2})(3)(4^2)$

9. $\dfrac{2^{-3}}{8^{-2}}$

In Exercises 10 and 11, copy and complete the table of values. **(7.2)**

10.

x	-2	-1	0	1	2
$y = 4\left(\frac{2}{3}\right)^x$	?	?	?	?	?

11.

x	-2	-1	0	1	2
$y = 3(4^x)$	?	?	?	?	?

12. Rewrite $3^{1/2}$ using radical notation. **(7.3)**

13. Rewrite $\sqrt[3]{7}$ using rational exponents. **(7.3)**

14. Use radical notation to write all fourth roots of 90. **(7.3)**

15. In 1980, the population of a town was 12,000. If the population increases by 4% each year, what would the population be in 1995? **(7.2)**

16. $2000 is deposited in an account that earns 6% annual interest, compounded monthly. Find the balance after 10 years. **(7.2)**

17. How much money must be deposited in an account paying 8% annual interest, compounded quarterly, to have $3585 in the account after 11 years? **(7.2)**

18. 100 grams of radioactive actinium decays according to the model $A = 100(2)^{-0.05t}$ where A is the amount (in grams) and t is the time (in years). Find the amount remaining after 5 years. How long does it take for half of the actinium to decay? **(7.2)**

19. For 1980 through 1990, home sales of personal computers can be modeled by the equation $y = 0.05(1.37)^t + 2.6$, where y is sales in millions and $t = 0$ represents 1980. Using the model, estimate the sales for 1995. (*Source:* USA Today) **(7.2)**

20. In the early 1400s, a plague took the lives of about one-third of the population of Europe. Had the plague not occurred, the estimated world population, y (in billions), for the years between 1400 and 1900 can be modeled by $y = 0.003(2.05)^t + 0.514$ where $t = 4$ represents 1400, $t = 5$ represents 1500, and so on. Using the model, estimate the world population in 1900, had the plague not occurred. **(7.2)**

Properties of Roots of Real Numbers

What you should learn:

Goal 1 How to use properties of roots to evaluate and simplify expressions containing radicals and rational exponents

Goal 2 How to use properties of roots to solve real-life problems

Why you should learn it:

You can model many problems with expressions containing roots, such as ratios of areas or volumes.

Goal 1 Using Properties of Roots

You can use the definition of rational exponents to show that the properties of exponents presented in Lesson 7.1 also apply to these exponents.

Properties of Roots

Let a and b be real numbers and let m and n be rational numbers.

Property	**Example**
1. $a^m \cdot a^n = a^{m+n}$	$2^{1/2} \cdot 2^{3/2} = 2^{(1/2 + 3/2)} = 2^2 = 4$
2. $(a^m)^n = a^{m \cdot n}$	$(4^{3/2})^2 = 4^{(3/2 \cdot 2)} = 4^3 = 64$
3. $(a \cdot b)^m = a^m \cdot b^m$	$(4 \cdot 9)^{1/2} = 4^{1/2} \cdot 9^{1/2} = 2 \cdot 3 = 6$
4. $\dfrac{a^m}{a^n} = a^{m-n},\ a \neq 0$	$\dfrac{5^{3/2}}{5^{1/2}} = 5^{(3/2 - 1/2)} = 5^1 = 5$
5. $\left(\dfrac{a}{b}\right)^m = \dfrac{a^m}{b^m},\ b \neq 0$	$\left(\dfrac{27}{8}\right)^{1/3} = \dfrac{27^{1/3}}{8^{1/3}} = \dfrac{3}{2}$
6. $a^{-m} = \dfrac{1}{a^m},\ a \neq 0$	$4^{-1/2} = \dfrac{1}{4^{1/2}} = \dfrac{1}{2}$

For rational exponents, the third and fifth properties above are often shown in radical notation.

$$\sqrt[m]{a \cdot b} = \sqrt[m]{a} \cdot \sqrt[m]{b} \qquad \textit{Product Property}$$

$$\sqrt[m]{\frac{a}{b}} = \frac{\sqrt[m]{a}}{\sqrt[m]{b}} \qquad \textit{Quotient Property}$$

Example 1 *Using Properties of Roots*

a. $3^{1/2} \cdot 3^{1/4} = 3^{3/4}$

b. $\dfrac{1}{2^{-1/2}} = 2^{1/2}$

c. $\dfrac{2}{2^{1/3}} = \dfrac{2^1}{2^{1/3}}$
$= 2^{2/3}$

d. $(3^{1/2} \cdot 2^{1/3})^2 = (3^{1/2})^2 \cdot (2^{1/3})^2$
$= 3 \cdot 2^{2/3}$

e. $2^{1/3} \cdot 4^{1/3} = (2 \cdot 4)^{1/3}$
$= 8^{1/3}$
$= 2$

f. $(5^4 \cdot 3^4)^{1/4} = ((5 \cdot 3)^4)^{1/4}$
$= (15^4)^{1/4}$
$= 15$ ■

Example 2 *Simplifying Radical Expressions*

a. $\sqrt[3]{3} \cdot \sqrt[3]{9} = \sqrt[3]{3 \cdot 9} = \sqrt[3]{27} = 3$

b. $\dfrac{\sqrt{50}}{\sqrt{2}} = \sqrt{\dfrac{50}{2}} = \sqrt{25} = 5$

c. $\sqrt[3]{4} \cdot \sqrt{4} = 4^{1/3} \cdot 4^{1/2} = 4^{(1/3+1/2)} = 4^{5/6}$ ■

Applying the properties of roots to expressions involving variables can be difficult—especially with even roots such as $\sqrt{x^2}$ and $\sqrt[4]{x^4}$. In these cases, an absolute value sign is necessary to ensure that the result will be positive when the variable is negative.

$$\sqrt[n]{x^n} = x \qquad \textit{n is odd.}$$

$$\sqrt[n]{x^n} = |x| \qquad \textit{n is even.}$$

Example 3 *Simplifying Expressions Involving Variables*

a. $\sqrt[3]{8x^3} = \sqrt[3]{8}\sqrt[3]{x^3} = 2x$

b. $\sqrt{4x^2} = \sqrt{4}\sqrt{x^2} = 2|x|$

c. $x^{1/2} \cdot x^{3/2} = x^2$ ■

In the radical expression $c\sqrt[n]{a}$, the number a is the **radicand,** and the number n is the **index.** Two radical expressions are **like radicals** if they have the same index and the same radicand. For instance, $\sqrt[3]{2}$ and $4\sqrt[3]{2}$ are like radicals. To add or subtract like radicals, use the Distributive Property.

Sum: $\qquad \sqrt[3]{2} + 4\sqrt[3]{2} = (1 + 4)\sqrt[3]{2} = 5\sqrt[3]{2}$

Difference: $\quad \sqrt[3]{2} - 4\sqrt[3]{2} = (1 - 4)\sqrt[3]{2} = -3\sqrt[3]{2}$

Example 4 *Adding and Subtracting Roots and Radicals*

a. $\sqrt[4]{5} + 6\sqrt[4]{5} = 7\sqrt[4]{5}$

b. $5(4^{1/3}) - 2(4^{1/3}) = 3(4^{1/3})$

c. $\sqrt{8} + \sqrt{2} = \sqrt{4 \cdot 2} + \sqrt{2}$

$\qquad\qquad = \sqrt{4} \cdot \sqrt{2} + \sqrt{2}$

$\qquad\qquad = 2\sqrt{2} + \sqrt{2}$

$\qquad\qquad = 3\sqrt{2}$ ■

Real Life
Astronomy

Example 5 *Finding the Volume of a Sphere*

Find the ratio of the volume of the moon to the volume of Earth.

Solution The surface area and volume of a sphere are given by $S = 4\pi r^2$ and $V = \frac{4}{3}\pi r^3$, where r is the radius. Begin by solving for each radius.

Moon Radius	**Earth Radius**
$S = 4\pi r^2$	$S = 4\pi r^2$
$4,668,868\pi = 4\pi r^2$	$62,835,320\pi = 4\pi r^2$
$1,167,217 = r^2$	$15,708,830 = r^2$
$(1,167,217)^{1/2} = r$	$(15,708,830)^{1/2} = r$

The ratio of the volume of the moon to the volume of Earth is as follows.

$$\frac{\text{Volume of moon}}{\text{Volume of Earth}} = \frac{\frac{4}{3}\pi((1,167,217)^{1/2})^3}{\frac{4}{3}\pi((15,708,830)^{1/2})^3}$$

$$= \frac{(1,167,217)^{3/2}}{(15,708,830)^{3/2}}$$

$$= \left(\frac{1,167,217}{15,708,830}\right)^{3/2} \approx 0.02$$

Thus the volume of the moon is about 2% or $\frac{1}{50}$ the volume of Earth. ∎

The surface area of the moon is 4,668,868π square miles. The surface area of Earth is 62,835,320π square miles. If the moon were placed on top of the United States, its diameter would span more than three-fourths of the distance between the east and west coasts.

Communicating about **ALGEBRA**

▶ **SHARING IDEAS about the Lesson**

Use the given surface areas to find the indicated ratios.

Ping-Pong Ball:	2.24π in.^{2}	Tennis Ball:	6.28π in.^{2}
Golf Ball:	2.84π in.^{2}	Baseball:	7.56π in.^{2}
Billiard Ball:	4.24π in.^{2}	Softball:	17.12π in.^{2}

A. Find the ratio of the volume of a Ping-Pong ball to the volume of a billiard ball.

B. Find the ratio of the volume of a tennis ball to the volume of a golf ball.

C. Find the ratio of the volume of a baseball to the volume of a softball.

EXERCISES

▶ **CRITICAL THINKING about the Lesson**

In Exercises 1–4, simplify the expression.

1. $\sqrt[6]{4}\sqrt[3]{4}$

2. $8^{3/2} \cdot 2^{3/2}$

3. $\dfrac{x}{x^{1/5}}$

4. $\dfrac{\sqrt[3]{24}}{\sqrt[3]{3}}$

5. Are $2\sqrt[3]{3}$ and $2\sqrt[3]{4}$ like radicals? Explain.

6. In the expression $10\sqrt[4]{7}$, identify the radical, the radicand, and the index.

Independent Practice

In Exercises 7–42, simplify the expression.

7. $(3)^{1/4} \cdot (3)^{3/4}$

8. $\sqrt[3]{4} \cdot \sqrt[3]{16}$

9. $\sqrt[4]{20} \cdot \sqrt[4]{\dfrac{4}{5}}$

10. $(-9)^{1/7}(-9)^{3/7}$

11. $\left(\dfrac{1}{3}\right)^{1/5} \cdot \left(\dfrac{1}{3}\right)^{3/5}$

12. $(2^{1/2})^{2/3}$

13. $(4^{1/3})^{9/4}$

14. $-(8^{5/4})^{6/5}$

15. $-(6^{4/3})^{3/7}$

16. $\left(\dfrac{2}{3}\right)^{5/3} \cdot \left(\dfrac{2}{3}\right)^{1/3}$

17. $(1296x)^{1/4}$

18. $\dfrac{4^{1/5}}{-4^{3/5}}$

19. $(243y)^{1/5}$

20. $\left(\dfrac{96}{16}\right)^{3}$

21. $\dfrac{2^{1/5}}{2^{6/5}}$

22. $\sqrt[7]{128x^7y}$

23. $\left(\dfrac{100}{64}\right)^{3}$

24. $(32x)^{1/5}$

25. $\dfrac{9^{2/3}}{9^{1/6}}$

26. $\dfrac{12^{10/8}}{12^{-3/8}}$

27. $\sqrt[4]{256x}$

28. $\sqrt[3]{512x}$

29. $\sqrt[5]{\dfrac{7776}{243}}$

30. $\sqrt[3]{32x} \cdot \sqrt[3]{2}$

31. $\dfrac{1}{6^{-1/2}}$

32. $\dfrac{1}{x^{-5/4}}$

33. $(4^{1/4} \cdot 4^{1/3})^2$

34. $(6^{2/3} \cdot 6^{1/4})^{12/11}$

35. $\dfrac{\sqrt[3]{648}}{\sqrt[3]{3}}$

36. $\dfrac{\sqrt[5]{2048}}{\sqrt[5]{2}}$

37. $\sqrt[4]{6x^4}$

38. $\sqrt[3]{27xy^3}$

39. $\sqrt[5]{32x^5}$

40. $\sqrt[6]{2x^6}$

41. $\sqrt[3]{2x^6}$

42. $\sqrt[3]{8x^9}$

Technology   In Exercises 43–54, use a calculator to evaluate the expression. Then simplify the expression and use a calculator to evaluate the simplified expression. **Compare your results.**

43. $\sqrt[3]{14} \cdot \sqrt[3]{13}$

44. $\sqrt[8]{3} \cdot \sqrt[8]{5}$

45. $6^{1/4} \cdot 6^{4/5}$

46. $(5^{6/7})^{1/2}$

47. $(6^{-3})^{5/3}$

48. $3^{1/8} \cdot 3^{3/5}$

49. $(6^{1/4} \cdot 6^{4/5})^{1/7}$

50. $(2^{5/7} \cdot 2^{4/3})^{3/5}$

51. $(9^{1/2} \cdot 9^{2/3})^{1/6}$

52. $(5^{1/3} \cdot 5^{2/5})^{3/2}$

53. $\sqrt[5]{11 \cdot 14}$

54. $\sqrt[5]{3 \cdot 160}$

In Exercises 55–66, simplify the expression (if possible).

55. $\sqrt[4]{5} + 4\sqrt[4]{5}$

56. $\sqrt[7]{7} + 6\sqrt[7]{7}$

57. $4\sqrt[9]{6} - 6\sqrt[9]{6}$

58. $-3\sqrt[5]{2} + 10\sqrt[5]{2}$

59. $\sqrt[4]{768} - 3\sqrt[4]{3}$

60. $\sqrt[3]{6} + \sqrt[3]{48}$

61. $\sqrt[3]{270} + 2\sqrt[3]{10}$

62. $\sqrt[3]{14} - \sqrt[3]{112}$

63. $\sqrt[5]{1701} + 4\sqrt[5]{7}$

64. $2\sqrt[4]{176} + 5\sqrt[4]{11}$

65. $\sqrt[5]{160} - \sqrt[5]{1215}$

66. $\sqrt[3]{375} + \sqrt[3]{81}$

67. Geometry   The areas of the circles below are 15 square centimeters and 20 square centimeters. Find the ratio of the radius of the small circle to the radius of the large circle.

68. Geometry   The volume of the sphere and the circular cylinder shown below are each 4 cubic feet. What is the ratio of the radius of the sphere to the radius of the circular cylinder?

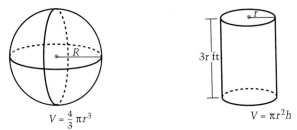

$V = \frac{4}{3}\pi r^3$ $V = \pi r^2 h$

Strength-to-Weight Efficiency   **In Exercises 69 and 70, use the following information.**

Young's Modulus   Young's Modulus, named after the English scientist Thomas Young (1773–1829), is a measure of flexibility. Materials with a large Young's modulus are stiff. Materials with a small Young's modulus are flexible. The table gives the Young's modulus and density (in grams per cubic centimeter) of seven materials. The *strength-to-weight efficiency* of a column is $\frac{1}{d}\sqrt{E}$ and of a panel is $\frac{1}{d}\sqrt[3]{E}$.

Material	Steel	Aluminum	Brick	Bone	Concrete	Oak	Spruce
Young's Modulus, E	210,000	73,000	21,000	18,000	15,000	12,000	10,000
Density, d	7.8	2.8	3.0	3.0	2.5	0.65	0.35

69. Which of the materials has the greatest strength-to-weight efficiency as a column? Which has the least?

70. Which of the materials has the greatest strength-to-weight efficiency as a panel? Which has the least?

71. *Quilts*   Find a radical expression that represents the total perimeter of the red triangles in the quilt at the right. Simplify the expression.

72. *Quilts*   Find a radical expression that represents the total perimeter of the blue triangles. Simplify the expression.

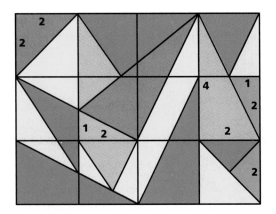

The musical note A-440 (above middle C) has a frequency of 440 vibrations per second. The frequency, F, of any note can be found by the equation

$$F = 440 \cdot 2^{n/12}$$

where n represents the number of black and white keys below or above the given note and A-440.

73. Approximate the lowest and highest frequencies of a trumpet.

74. Describe the pattern of the frequencies of successive notes of the same letter.

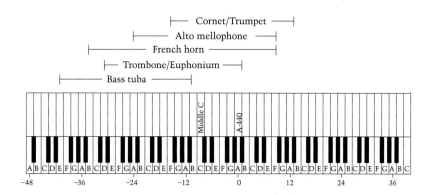

Integrated Review

In Exercises 75–82, simplify the expression.

75. $x^4 \cdot x^7$

76. $x^4 x^{-8}$

77. $(x^3)^5$

78. $\dfrac{x}{x^{-10}}$

79. $x^{-3} x^2$

80. $(x^7)^8$

81. $\dfrac{x^2}{x^9}$

82. $x^2 \cdot x^5$

In Exercises 83–90, evaluate the expression.

83. $(-3)^{1/3}$

84. $2^{1/4}$

85. $16^{1/6}$

86. $27^{2/3}$

87. $\sqrt[3]{200}$

88. $\sqrt[3]{56}$

89. $\sqrt[4]{14}$

90. $\sqrt[4]{625}$

Exploration and Extension

In Exercises 91 and 92, solve for a and b.

91. $\dfrac{3^a \cdot 5^b}{5^{1/2} \cdot 3^{5/6}} = 5^{1/6} 3^{1/3}$

92. $\dfrac{2^b (6^{1/2} \cdot 6^a)^4}{2^5} = \dfrac{6^{10}}{2^6}$

7.5

Solving Radical Equations

What you should learn:

Goal 1 How to solve equations that have radicals and rational exponents

Goal 2 How to use radical equations to solve real-life problems

Why you should learn it:

You can model many real-life situations with radical expressions, such as the distance between two points.

Goal 1 Solving a Radical Equation

To solve a **radical equation**—one that contains radicals or rational exponents—you try to eliminate the radicals and obtain a linear or quadratic equation. Then you can solve the new equation using the standard procedures. The following property plays a key role.

Raising Both Sides of an Equation to the nth Power

If $a = b$, then $a^n = b^n$.

Before raising both sides of an equation to the nth power, you must isolate the radical expression on one side of the equation.

Example 1 *Solving a Radical Equation*

Solve $\sqrt[3]{x} - 2 = 0$.

Solution

$$\sqrt[3]{x} - 2 = 0 \qquad \textit{Rewrite original equation.}$$

$$\sqrt[3]{x} = 2 \qquad \textit{Add 2 to both sides.}$$

$$(\sqrt[3]{x})^3 = 2^3 \qquad \textit{Cube both sides.}$$

$$x = 8 \qquad \textit{Simplify.}$$

The solution is 8. Check this in the original equation. ∎

Example 2 *Solving an Equation Containing Exponents*

Solve: $x^{3/2} = 27$.

$$(x^{3/2})^{2/3} = 27^{2/3} \qquad \textit{Raise both sides to } \tfrac{2}{3} \textit{ power.}$$

$$x = (27^{1/3})^2 \qquad \textit{Apply properties of exponents.}$$

$$x = 9 \qquad \textit{Simplify.}$$

The solution is 9. Check this in the original equation. ∎

Raising both sides of an equation to the nth power may introduce **extraneous** (or false) **solutions.** So when you use this procedure, it is critical that you check each solution in the *original* equation. For instance, squaring both sides of the equation

$$\sqrt{x} = -1$$

produces $x = 1$. This result, however, is extraneous. The original equation has no real-number solution.

Example 3 — Solving a Radical Equation

Solve $\sqrt{3x - 8} + 1 = 3$.

Solution

$\sqrt{3x - 8} + 1 = 3$	*Rewrite original equation.*
$\sqrt{3x - 8} = 2$	*Subtract 1 from both sides.*
$(\sqrt{3x - 8})^2 = 2^2$	*Square both sides.*
$3x - 8 = 4$	*Simplify.*
$3x = 12$	*Add 8 to both sides.*
$x = 4$	*Divide both sides by 3.*

Check

$\sqrt{3x - 8} + 1 = 3$	*Rewrite original equation.*
$\sqrt{3(4) - 8} \stackrel{?}{=} 2$	*Substitute 4 for x.*
$\sqrt{4} \stackrel{?}{=} 2$	*Simplify.*
$2 = 2$	*Solution checks.*

The solution is 4. ■

The **geometric mean** of a and b is $\sqrt{ab}$. For instance, the geometric mean of 2 and 18 is $\sqrt{2 \cdot 18} = \sqrt{36} = 6$.

Example 4 — Using the Geometric Mean

The geometric mean of 4 and a is 20. What is a?

Solution

$$\text{Geometric mean} = \sqrt{a \cdot 4}$$
$$20 = \sqrt{4a}$$
$$20^2 = (\sqrt{4a})^2$$
$$400 = 4a$$
$$100 = a$$

Since $a = 100$, the geometric mean of 4 and 100 is 20. ■

Radicals are also used to find the distance between two points in a coordinate plane. Suppose you were asked to find the distance between the points $A(2, 2)$ and $B(6, 5)$. How would you do it? One way is to locate point $C(6, 2)$ so that $\triangle ABC$ is a right triangle. Then find the lengths of the two legs and use the Pythagorean Theorem.

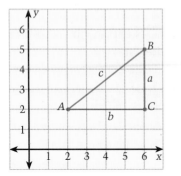

$a = 5 - 2 = 3$ *Length of $\overline{BC}$*

$b = 6 - 2 = 4$ *Length of $\overline{AC}$*

$c = \sqrt{a^2 + b^2}$ *Pythagorean Theorem*

$c = \sqrt{3^2 + 4^2}$ *Substitute $a = 3$ and $b = 4$.*

$c = \sqrt{25}$ *Simplify.*

$c = 5$ *Simplify.*

By performing this process with two general points (x_1, y_1) and (x_2, y_2), you can obtain the Distance Formula.

The Distance Formula

The distance d between the points (x_1, y_1) and (x_2, y_2) is

$$d = \sqrt{(x_2 - x_1)^2 + (y_2 - y_1)^2}.$$

Example 5   *Using the Distance Formula*

The distance between $(0, -3)$ and $(x, 4)$ is $\sqrt{65}$. What is x?

Solution   Let $(x_1, y_1) = (0, -3)$ and $(x_2, y_2) = (x, 4)$.

$\sqrt{65} = \sqrt{(0 - x)^2 + (-3 - 4)^2}$

$\sqrt{65} = \sqrt{x^2 + 49}$

$65 = x^2 + 49$

$16 = x^2$

$\pm 4 = x$

There are two solutions: $x = -4$ and $x = 4$. A graphic check is shown below.

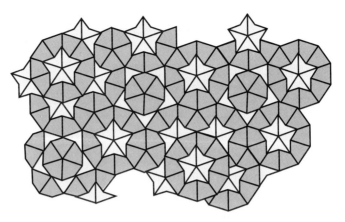

This tile pattern is made with Penrose's two simple shapes—one shaped like a kite and the other like an arrowhead. Although these tiles can be used to cover the plane, every such covering is nonrepeating!

Goal 2 Solving Radical Equations in Real Life

Example 6   Using the Distance Formula

In the early 1970's, Roger Penrose, an English physicist, discovered two tiling shapes whose dimensions involve the *golden ratio*. In the diagram at the left, find the value of c.

Solution   Let $(x_1, y_1) = (0, c)$ and let $(x_2, y_2) = (\sqrt{5} - 2, 0)$. Using the Distance Formula, you can solve for c as follows.

$$d = \sqrt{(x_2 - x_1)^2 + (y_2 - y_1)^2}$$
$$\sqrt{14 - 6\sqrt{5}} = \sqrt{(\sqrt{5} - 2 - 0)^2 + (0 - c)^2}$$
$$14 - 6\sqrt{5} = (\sqrt{5} - 2)^2 + (-c)^2$$
$$14 - 6\sqrt{5} = (5 - 2\sqrt{5} - 2\sqrt{5} + 4) + c^2$$
$$5 - 2\sqrt{5} = c^2$$
$$\sqrt{5 - 2\sqrt{5}} = c$$

The value of c is $\sqrt{5 - 2\sqrt{5}}$.   ∎

Communicating about ALGEBRA

▶ **SHARING IDEAS about the Lesson**

A. The **golden ratio** is $\dfrac{\sqrt{5} + 1}{2}$. In the diagram, show that the ratio of b to a is the golden ratio.

B. The golden ratio can also be written as $\dfrac{2}{\sqrt{5} - 1}$. Show that this is equivalent to the form in Part **A** by multiplying the numerator and denominator by $(\sqrt{5} + 1)$ and simplifying.

EXERCISES

▶ **CRITICAL THINKING about the Lesson**

1. Describe a general strategy for solving a radical equation.
2. Solve $\sqrt[3]{2x + 10} + 1 = 3$. Explain your steps.
3. Find the geometric mean of 3 and 6.
4. Find the distance between $(6, 1)$ and $(-2, 5)$ in two ways: use the Distance Formula and use the Pythagorean Theorem.

Independent Practice

In Exercises 5–10, check whether the value is a solution of the equation.

5. $\sqrt{x} - 4 = 4, \quad x = 64$ **6.** $2(x - 3)^{1/2} = 12, \quad x = 39$ **7.** $(x + 4)^{3/2} - 60 = 4, \quad x = 12$

8. $4(2x + 1)^{2/3} = 36, \quad x = 13$ **9.** $\sqrt[3]{4x} + 9 = 3, \quad x = -54$ **10.** $2\sqrt[4]{2x + 1} + 2 = 0, \quad x = 0$

In Exercises 11–40, solve the equation. Check for extraneous solutions.

11. $\sqrt{x} = 20$

12. $x^{1/2} = 5$

13. $y^{1/3} - 7 = 0$

14. $x^{2/3} + 13 = 17$

15. $\sqrt[4]{2x} + 2 = 6$

16. $2x^{3/4} = 54$

17. $\sqrt{a + 100} = 25$

18. $\sqrt[3]{b + 12} = 5$

19. $(x - 2)^{3/2} = -8$

20. $(8x)^{1/2} + 6 = 0$

21. $(3y + 5)^{1/2} - 3 = 4$

22. $\sqrt[3]{5z - 4} + 7 = 10$

23. $\sqrt[4]{x + 2} + 9 = 14$

24. $2(x + 4)^{2/3} = 8$

25. $\sqrt{x^2 + 5} = x + 3$

26. $\sqrt{x^2 - 4} = x - 2$

27. $\sqrt{x + 3} = \sqrt{2x - 1}$

28. $\sqrt{3t + 1} = \sqrt{t + 15}$

29. $\sqrt{3y - 5} - 3\sqrt{y} = 0$

30. $\sqrt{2u + 10} - 2\sqrt{u} = 0$

31. $\sqrt[3]{3x - 4} = \sqrt[3]{x + 10}$

32. $2\sqrt[3]{10 - 3x} = \sqrt[3]{2 - x}$

33. $\sqrt[3]{2x + 15} - \sqrt[3]{x} = 0$

34. $\sqrt[4]{2x} + \sqrt[4]{x + 3} = 0$

35. $\sqrt{2x} = x - 4$

36. $\sqrt{x} = x - 6$

37. $\sqrt{8x + 1} = x + 2$

38. $\sqrt{3x + 7} = x + 3$

39. $\sqrt{2t + 3} = 3 - \sqrt{2t}$

40. $\sqrt{x + 3} - \sqrt{x - 1} = 1$

In Exercises 41 and 42, find x.

41. The geometric mean of 2 and x is $3\sqrt{6}$.

42. The geometric mean of x and 6 is $4\sqrt{3}$.

In Exercises 43–45, find the distance between the two points.

43. $(0, 1), (1, 5)$ **44.** $(-2, 6), (3, 6)$ **45.** $(3, 7), (9, -1)$

In Exercises 46–48, find all values of x for which the distance between the given points is d.

46. $(5, -8), (x, -11)$
$d = 3\sqrt{2}$

47. $(-3, 2), (-10, x)$
$d = \sqrt{53}$

48. $(3, x), (5, 7)$
$d = 2\sqrt{17}$

49. *Geometry*   In a right triangle, a line segment is drawn from the vertex of the right angle, perpendicular to the hypotenuse. Let h represent the length of the segment and let x and y represent the lengths of the two parts of the hypotenuse. One of these lengths is the geometric mean of the other two lengths. Which is it? Explain.

50. *Geometry*   In the diagram at the right, the rectangle whose sides have lengths x and 6 is similar to the rectangle whose sides have lengths 24 and x. Which of the three lengths (6, 24, and x) is the geometric mean of the other two lengths? Explain your answer and then use the result to solve for x.

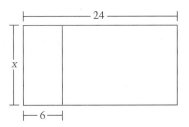

Wisconsin   **In Exercises 51 and 52, use the following information.**

A grid is superimposed on the map of Wisconsin at the right. Each unit of the grid represents 10.5 miles.

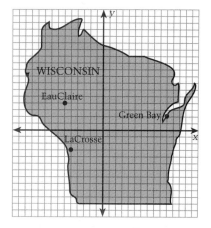

51. Approximate the distance in miles between La Crosse and Green Bay. How long would a flight from La Crosse to Green Bay take traveling at 225 m.p.h.?

52. Approximate the distance in miles between Eau Claire and La Crosse. What is the minimum time necessary to walk from Eau Claire to La Crosse walking at a rate of 5 miles per hour?

53. *Public Television*   For 1970 through 1990, the average number, h, of broadcast hours per year per public television station can be modeled by $h = \sqrt{-91{,}150t^2 + 3{,}187{,}200t + 4{,}255{,}600}$ where $t = 0$ represents 1970. In which year was the average equal to 5420 hours?

54. *Women in Medicine*   For 1980 through 1990, the percent, p, of Doctor of Medicine (MD) degrees earned each year by women can be modeled by

$$p = \sqrt{3.3t^2 + 50.7t + 528.4}$$

where t represents the year with $t = 0$ corresponding to 1980. In what year were 28% of the MD degrees earned by women?

In 1981, Dr. Alexa Canady became the first African-American woman to become a neurosurgeon in the United States. She now directs neurosurgery at Children's Hospital of Michigan in Detroit.

Integrated Review

In Exercises 55–62, simplify the expression.

55. $[(3x)^4]^{1/2}$ **56.** $[(4x)^{1/2}]^{-3}$ **57.** $(\sqrt[5]{6x^3})^3$ **58.** $(64)^{1/3} \cdot (64)^{1/3}$

59. $(-8)^{2/3}$ **60.** $(\sqrt[6]{64x^7})^{-1}$ **61.** $(13)^{3/2} \cdot (13)^{-5/2}$ **62.** $(\sqrt[3]{27x})^4$

63. *College Extrance Exam Sample*   In the diagram, ABC is a right triangle with $AB = 6$ and $AC = 7$. What does BC equal?

   a. 1   **b.** $\sqrt{13}$ **c.** 6   **d.** $\sqrt{39}$ **e.** $\sqrt{78}$

64. *College Entrance Exam Sample*   The lengths of the sides of a triangle are 6 in., 8 in., and 10 in. A rectangle equal in area to that of the triangle has a width of 3 in. What is the perimeter of the rectangle (in in.)?

   a. 11   **b.** 16   **c.** 22   **d.** 24   **e.** 30

Exploration and Extension

Collinear Points   **In Exercises 65 and 66, use the following information.**

Three points are collinear if the sum of the distances between two pairs of the points is equal to the distance between the third pair. Use this to help you decide whether the three points lie on a line.

65. $(0, 5)$, $(1, 7)$, $(2, 9)$ **66.** $(0, 2)$, $(-2, 3)$, $(2, -1)$

Mixed REVIEW

1. For $f(x) = x^3$, find $f(f(x))$. **(6.2)**

2. Find the inverse of $g(x) = 3x - 1$. **(6.3)**

3. Find $\frac{3}{7}$ of 56.

4. $52\frac{1}{2}$ is $\frac{5}{8}$ of what?

5. Given $f(x) = 4^{-x}$, find $f(-2)$. **(7.1)**

6. Simplify: $(3x^2y^3)^4$. **(7.1)**

7. 3×10^{-3} is 6% of what?

8. Simplify: $\left(\frac{1}{2}\right)^{-4}$. **(7.1)**

9. Simplify: $\dfrac{8x^3y^{-5}z^3}{27xyz^5}$. **(7.1)**

10. Simplify: $\dfrac{(1762.4)^0 x^{-5}}{x^{-8}}$. **(7.1)**

11. Write $\left(\frac{1}{3}\right)^4$ using negative exponents. **(7.1)**

12. Sketch the graph of $y \leq -|x + 4| + 3$. **(5.7)**

13. Find the vertex of $y = 2x^2 - 8x + 5$. **(5.2)**

14. Find the vertex of $y = |x - 2| + 1$. **(6.5)**

15. Sketch the graph of $y = (-x - 3)^2$. **(6.5)**

16. Sketch the graph of $y = -|x - 2| - 3$. **(6.5)**

17. Write a model for the function containing $(-1, -3)$, $(0, -2)$, $(1, 0)$, and $(2, 3)$. **(6.6)**

18. Solve $\begin{bmatrix} 2 & 3 \\ 1 & 0 \end{bmatrix} X = \begin{bmatrix} 1 & 6 \\ -1 & 0 \end{bmatrix}$. **(4.4)**

7.6 Graphing Square Root and Cube Root Functions

What you should learn:

Goal 1 How to graph square root and cube root functions

Goal 2 How to use square root and cube root functions to solve real-life problems

Why you should learn it:

You can model many real-life situations with square root functions, such as the Beaufort scale.

Goal 1 Graphing Radical Functions

In this lesson, you will study graphs of functions of the form

$$f(x) = \sqrt{x - a} + b \quad \text{and} \quad f(x) = \sqrt[3]{x - a} + b.$$

Each of these functions has graphs that are translations of the following two graphs.

Square Root: $f(x) = \sqrt{x}$

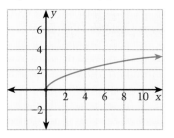

Domain: $x \geq 0$
Range: $y \geq 0$

Cube Root: $f(x) = \sqrt[3]{x}$

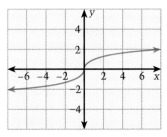

Domain: *All real numbers*
Range: *All real numbers*

Example 1 Graphing a Square Root Function

Sketch the graphs of $g(x) = \sqrt{x - 3}$ and $h(x) = -\sqrt{x - 3}$ on the same coordinate plane.

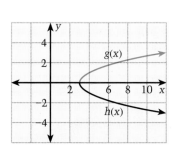

Solution To sketch the graph of g, draw the graph of $f(x) = \sqrt{x}$ three units to the right of the origin. To sketch the graph of h, reflect the graph of g in the x-axis. A table of values can help you locate several points on each graph.

x	3	4	5	6	7
$g(x) = \sqrt{x - 3}$	0	1	$\sqrt{2} \approx 1.4$	$\sqrt{3} \approx 1.7$	2
$h(x) = -\sqrt{x - 3}$	0	−1	$-\sqrt{2} \approx -1.4$	$-\sqrt{3} \approx -1.7$	−2

The domain of both g and h is $x \geq 3$. The range of g is $y \geq 0$, and the range of h is $y \leq 0$. ∎

Notice that the two graphs together form a parabola. The parabola can be represented by the single equation $y^2 = x - 3$, but this equation does not define y as a function of x. (Why?)

Example **2** **Sketching the Graph of a Cube Root Function**

Sketch the graph of $g(x) = \sqrt[3]{x + 2} + 1$.

Solution To sketch the graph of g, draw the graph of $f(x) = \sqrt[3]{x}$ shifted two units to the left and one unit up. A table of values can help you locate several points on the graph.

x	−4	−3	−2	−1	0	1
$g(x) = \sqrt[3]{x + 2} + 1$	−0.26	0	1	2	2.26	2.44

Each of the domain and range of g is all real numbers. ∎

Goal **2** Using Square and Cube Root Functions

Real Life
Zoology

Example **3** **Graphing a Cube Root Function**

The shoulder height, h (in feet), of a male African elephant can be modeled by the equation

$$h = \sqrt[3]{13t} + 3, \quad 0 \le t$$

where t is the age of the elephant in years. Sketch the graph of this equation.

Solution To sketch the graph, construct a table of values, graph the points, and connect the points with a smooth curve.

t	0	1	3	10	15	40
$h = \sqrt[3]{13t} + 3$	3	5.4	6.4	8	8.8	11

The graph is shown below. ∎

Elephants grow slowly and are among the longest lived animals. A newborn male African elephant measures about 3 feet high at the shoulders. A fully-grown male (about 40 years old) measures about 11 feet high at the shoulders.

Elephant Age and Height

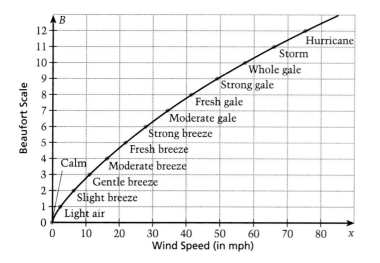

Beaufort Scale and Wind Effects

0 Smoke rises vertically.
1 Smoke shows wind direction.
2 Wind felt on face.
3 Leaves move, flags extend.
4 Paper, small branches move.
5 Small trees sway, flags ripple.
6 Large branches sway, flags beat.
7 Large trees sway, walking is difficult.
8 Twigs break, walking is hindered.
9 Slight roof damage
10 Severe damage, trees uprooted
11 Widespread damage
12 Devastation

*The **Beaufort scale** was devised by Francis Beaufort in 1805 to measure wind speeds. The scale is numbered from 0 to 12, and represents wind speeds in the open, 33 feet above ground.*

Real Life
Meteorology

Example 4 *Graphing a Square Root Function*

The Beaufort scale, B, can be modeled by the function

$$B = 1.9\sqrt{x + 8} - 5.4$$

where x is the speed of the wind in miles per hour. Sketch the graph of this function.

Solution To sketch the graph, construct a table of values, graph the points, and connect the points with a smooth curve.

Speed, *x*	0	3.30	7.15	11.55	16.50	22.00	28.05
Scale, *B*	0	1	2	3	4	5	6

Speed, *x*	34.65	41.80	49.50	57.75	66.55	75.90
Scale, *B*	7	8	9	10	11	12

The graph is shown above. ■

Communicating about ALGEBRA

▶ **SHARING IDEAS about the Lesson**

Sketch the graphs of the functions. Explain the procedure you used.

A. $f(x) = \sqrt{x - 5} - 2$ **B.** $f(x) = \sqrt[3]{x + 2} + 3$

EXERCISES

Guided Practice

▶ **CRITICAL THINKING about the Lesson**

1. Which of the graphs at the right is the graph of a square root function and which is the graph of a cube root function? Explain.

   a.

   b.

2. Compare the graph of $g(x) = \sqrt[3]{x} - 10$ to the graph of $f(x) = \sqrt[3]{x}$.

3. Copy and complete the table. What are the domain and range of the function?

x	−2	−1	0	1	2
$y = -\sqrt{x + 2}$	?	?	?	?	?

4. Sketch the graph of the function in Exercise 3.

Independent Practice

In Exercises 5–10, compare the graph of g to the graph of f.

5. $f(x) = \sqrt{x}$ and $g(x) = -\sqrt{x + 16}$

6. $f(x) = \sqrt{x}$ and $g(x) = \sqrt{x} + 15$

7. $f(x) = \sqrt[3]{x}$ and $g(x) = -\sqrt[3]{x} - 9$

8. $f(x) = \sqrt[3]{x}$ and $g(x) = -\sqrt[3]{x + 2}$

9. $f(x) = \sqrt{x}$ and $g(x) = \sqrt{x - 10} - 1$

10. $f(x) = \sqrt[3]{x}$ and $g(x) = \sqrt[3]{x + 7} - 4$

In Exercises 11–16, match the function with its graph.

11. $f(x) = \sqrt[3]{x} - 1$

12. $f(x) = \sqrt[3]{x - 3} - 1$

13. $f(x) = \sqrt{x + 3} + 1$

14. $f(x) = -\sqrt[3]{x} - 1$

15. $f(x) = \sqrt{x} - 1$

16. $f(x) = \sqrt{x} - 3$

a.

b.

c.

d.

e.

f.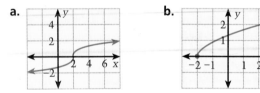

In Exercises 17–34, sketch the graph of the function. State the domain and range of the function.

17. $f(x) = \sqrt{x - 1}$

18. $g(x) = \sqrt{x + 2}$

19. $f(x) = \sqrt[3]{x - 5}$.

20. $g(x) = (x + 1)^{1/3}$

21. $g(x) = \sqrt[3]{x} + 1$

22. $h(x) = \sqrt{x} + 4$

23. $f(x) = (x - 1)^{1/2} + 7$

24. $f(x) = \sqrt[3]{x - 2} + 4$

25. $h(x) = -\sqrt[3]{x} + 4$

26. $f(x) = \sqrt[3]{x - 6} + 2$

27. $f(x) = -\sqrt{x + 5}$

28. $g(x) = \sqrt{x + 2} + 5$

29. $f(x) = -x^{1/2} - 3$

30. $f(x) = -\sqrt[3]{x - 1}$

31. $h(x) = (x - 10)^{1/3} + 2$

32. $f(x) = -\sqrt{x - 1} + 1$

33. $g(x) = 2\sqrt{x + 4}$

34. $f(x) = 3(x - 2)^{1/3}$

Congressional Aides   **In Exercises 35–38, use the following information.**

Each member of the United States Congress has a staff of congressional aides. For 1930 through 1990, the number of aides, A, assigned to members of the House of Representatives can be modeled by the function

$$A = 1220\sqrt[3]{t - 42} + 4900.$$

where $t = 0$ represents 1930.

35. In what year were about 4900 aides assigned to members of the House of Representatives?

36. In what year were about 7340 aides assigned to members of the House of Representatives?

37. Sketch the graph of the function

$$A = 1220\sqrt[3]{t - 42} + 4900.$$

38. The House of Representatives has 435 members. Write a function that gives the average number of congressional aides per representative. Sketch the graph of this function.

Members of Congress appoint young people (between 14 and 18 years old) to work as congressional pages. Pages attend a special high school from 6:30 A.M. to 9:45 A.M.

39. *Geometry*   Write a function that gives the radius, r, of a circle in terms of the circle's area, A. Sketch the graph of this function.

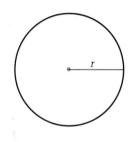

40. *Geometry*   Write a function that gives the radius, r, of a sphere in terms of the sphere's volume, V. Sketch the graph of this function.

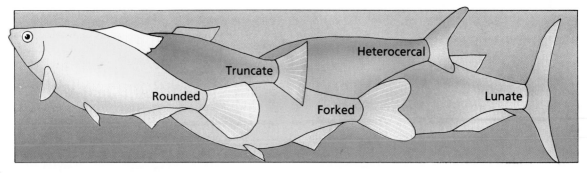

The aspect ratio of a fish's tail fin depends on the shape of the fin. (The aspect ratio is defined to be the ratio of the square of the fin height to the fin area.) The truncate tail fin, like that of salmon or bass, has an aspect ratio of 3. The forked tail fin, like that of herring or yellowtail, has an aspect ratio of 5.

Fish Tail Fins   **In Exercises 41 and 42, use the following information.**

The tail fin height, h, of a fish is related to the tail fin area, A, and the aspect ratio, r, by the model

$$h = \sqrt{rA}.$$

41. Write a function that gives the tail fin height of a salmon in terms of the tail fin area. Then sketch the graph of the function.

42. Write a function that gives the tail fin height of a herring in terms of the tail fin area. Then sketch the graph of the function.

Storms at Sea   **In Exercises 43 and 44, use the following information.**

The *fetch*, f (in nautical miles), of the wind at sea is the distance over which the wind is blowing. The minimum fetch required to create a "fully developed" storm is related to the wind speed, S (in knots), by the model

$$S = 4.6\sqrt[3]{f + 16}.$$

43. Sketch the graph of this function.

44. If the wind is blowing at 25 knots, what is the minimum fetch required to create a fully developed storm?

In Exercises 45–50, evaluate the expression.

45. $\sqrt[3]{x}$ when $x = 125$

46. $\sqrt{x - 3}$ when $x = 52$

47. $\sqrt{x^2 + x - 29}$ when $x = 10$

48. $\sqrt[3]{x^2 + 28}$ when $x = -6$

49. $\sqrt[4]{x - 4} - 6$ when $x = 20$

50. $\sqrt{3x - 15} + \sqrt[3]{x}$ when $x = 8$

In Exercises 51–56, match the function with its graph.

51. $f(x) = |x + 4|$

52. $f(x) = |x| - 4$

53. $f(x) = x^2 - 4$

54. $f(x) = \sqrt[3]{x + 4}$

55. $f(x) = \sqrt{x} - 4$

56. $f(x) = (x - 4)^2$

a.

b.

c.

d.

e.

f.

Reflections in the y-Axis   **In Exercises 57 and 58, use the following information.**

The graph of $y = f(-x)$ is a reflection of the graph of f in the y-axis. Use this result to sketch the graph of the function. State the domain and range of the function.

57. $g(x) = \sqrt{-x} + 1$

58. $h(x) = \sqrt[3]{-x} - 1$

In Exercises 59 and 60, write an equation for the function whose graph is given.

59.

60.

A graphing calculator can be used to investigate the graphs of functions of the form

$$y = x^n.$$

For instance, to produce the screen shown at the right, a graphing calculator was used to sketch the first-quadrant portions of the graphs of the following functions.

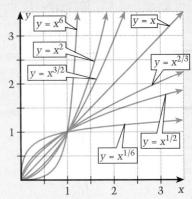

$$y = x^1$$

$y = x^6$	$y = x^3$	$y = x^2$	$y = x^{3/2}$	*Concave up*
$y = x^{1/6}$	$y = x^{1/3}$	$y = x^{1/2}$	$y = x^{2/3}$	*Concave down*

Notice that if $n = 1$, the graph of $y = x^n$ is a line that makes an angle of $45°$ with the x-axis. If $n > 1$, the graph is **concave up.** If $0 < n < 1$, the graph is **concave down.**

Example 1: Sketching the Graph of a Model

The chest circumferences, C (in inches), of five different species of adult primates (tamarins, squirrel monkeys, vervet monkeys, macaques, and baboons) were compared to their weights, W (in pounds). From 32 sets of measurements, the relationship between C and W was modeled by

$$C = 5W^{37/100}.$$

Sketch the graph of this model for weights between 0 pounds and 40 pounds. *(Source: Scientific American)*

Solution   Using a graphing calculator, you can obtain the graph shown at the right. ∎

Macaques are a type of rhesus monkey. The Golden Macaques, as shown, are a rare coloring for these monkeys.

Example 2: Finding a Mathematical Model

Most graphing calculators are capable of fitting power models of the form $y = ax^b$ to data. The table below lists the length, x (in inches), and diameter, y (in inches), of several sizes of common nails. Find a power model for these data.

Length, x	1.00	2.00	3.00	4.00	5.00	6.00
Diameter, y	0.070	0.111	0.146	0.176	0.204	0.231

2 Penny
Nail
Length is 1 in.

60 Penny
Nail
Length is 6 in.

Solution   Begin by entering the data into a graphing calculator. Keystrokes for doing this on a *TI-82*, Casio *fx-9700GE*, and Sharp *EL-9300C* are listed on page 862. After running the power regression program, you should obtain

$$a \approx 0.07 \quad \text{and} \quad b \approx 0.67.$$

Because $\frac{2}{3} \approx 0.67$, you can write the model as follows.

$$y = 0.07x^{2/3} \quad \blacksquare$$

Exercises

In Exercises 1–4, sketch the first-quadrant portion of the graph of each function. State whether each graph is concave up or concave down.

1. $y = x^5, y = x^{1/5}$ 　　**2.** $y = x^4, y = x^{1/4}$ 　　**3.** $y = x^{4/3}, y = x^{3/4}$ 　　**4.** $y = x^{6/5}, y = x^{5/6}$

5. *Galloping Speed of Animals*   Four-legged animals run with two types of motion: trotting and galloping. An animal that is trotting has at least one foot on the ground at all times. When an animal is galloping, sometimes all four feet are off the ground. The number of strides per minute at which an animal breaks from a trot to a gallop depends on the animal's weight. Use the table to find an equation of the form $y = ax^b$ that relates the lowest galloping speed, y (in strides per minute), with the weight of the animal, x (in pounds). Use a graphing calculator to graph the model.

Weight, x	25	35	50	75	500	1000
Galloping Speed, y	191.5	182.7	173.8	164.2	125.9	114.2

7

Chapter Summary

What did you learn?

Skills

1. Use properties of exponents
   - to perform operations with powers. **(7.1, 7.4)**
   - to simplify expressions. **(7.1, 7.4)**
2. Recognize exponential growth and decay models. **(7.2)**
3. Find the nth roots of a number. **(7.3)**
   - Use rational exponent notation. **(7.3)**
   - Use radical notation. **(7.3)**
4. Solve equations that contain radicals or roots. **(7.5)**
5. Sketch graphs of square root functions and cube root functions. **(7.6)**

Strategies

6. Use exponential growth and decay in real-life problems. **(7.2)**
7. Use roots and radicals in real-life problems. **(7.3–7.5)**

Exploring Data

8. Solve compound interest problems. **(7.2)**

Why did you learn it?

Many models of real-life situations involve exponents and roots. For instance, the length of the edge of a cube is the cube root of the volume of the cube.

In this chapter, you studied whole number exponents, integer exponents, and rational exponents. The ability to use all these exponents is an important skill—one that you will need as long as you study and use mathematics.

How does it fit into the bigger picture of algebra?

The square root of 2 can be written with the familiar radical notation as $\sqrt{2}$, or it can be written as $2^{1/2}$. The second notation uses a *rational exponent*. The advantage of the rational exponent notation is that the standard properties of exponents can be used to simplify radicals or perform operations involving radicals.

The chapter began by reviewing properties of integer exponents. In Lessons 7.3 and 7.4, these properties were extended to rational exponents. In the last two lessons, you learned how to solve *radical equations* and sketch the graphs of *radical functions*.

Chapter REVIEW

In Exercises 1–16, simplify the expression. **(7.1)**

1. $(5)^2(5)^6$ **2.** $(3)^5(3)^7$ **3.** $x^{-5} \cdot x^4$ **4.** $y^3 \cdot y^{-6}$

5. $(y^4)^{-3}$ **6.** $(10^{-4})^6$ **7.** $(6x)^2$ **8.** $(14x)^3$

9. $3x^0 y$ **10.** $\dfrac{x^{-4}}{x^{-6}}$ **11.** $\dfrac{x^5}{x^7}$ **12.** $4x^4 y^0$

13. $\dfrac{y^6}{6x^4} \cdot \dfrac{18x}{x^2 y}$ **14.** $\dfrac{9x^2 y}{y^3} \cdot \dfrac{xy^3}{3x}$ **15.** $\dfrac{4y^2}{x^2} \cdot \dfrac{x^3}{2y^4}$ **16.** $\dfrac{5x^2}{y^{-2}} \cdot \dfrac{1}{25xy}$

17. *Balance in an Account*   A principal of $500 is deposited in an account that pays 7% interest, compounded annually. Find the balance after 5 years. **(7.2)**

18. *Balance in an Account*   A principal of $800 is deposited in an account that pays 6% interest, compounded quarterly. Find the balance after 8 years. **(7.2)**

19. *How Much to Deposit?*   How much must you deposit in an account that pays 8% interest, compounded monthly, to have a balance of $1000 after 10 years? **(7.2)**

20. *How Much to Deposit?*   How much must you deposit in an account that pays 6% interest, compounded quarterly, to have a balance of $2000 after 20 years? **(7.2)**

In Exercises 21–24, complete the table. **(7.2)**

21.

x	−2	−1	0	1	2
$y = 2\left(\frac{1}{2}\right)^x$	?	?	?	?	?

22.

x	−2	−1	0	1	2
$y = \frac{1}{2}(4)^x$	?	?	?	?	?

23.

x	−2	−1	0	1	2
$y = \frac{1}{3}\left(\frac{3}{2}\right)^x$	?	?	?	?	?

24.

x	−2	−1	0	1	2
$y = -2\left(\frac{1}{3}\right)^x$	?	?	?	?	?

In Exercises 25–32, evaluate the expression without using a calculator. **(7.4)**

25. $\sqrt[4]{625}$ **26.** $(243)^{1/5}$ **27.** $(729)^{1/6}$ **28.** $\sqrt[3]{64}$

29. $(512)^{-1/3}$ **30.** $(27)^{-1/3}$ **31.** $\sqrt[4]{16}$ **32.** $\sqrt[5]{-32}$

In Exercises 33–44, simplify the expression. **(7.4)**

33. $(5)^{1/4}(5)^{-9/4}$ **34.** $((5)^{1/3})^{3/4}$ **35.** $\sqrt[3]{16} \cdot \sqrt[3]{\frac{1}{4}}$ **36.** $(81x)^{1/4}$

37. $\left(\dfrac{200}{8}\right)^{1/3}$ **38.** $\dfrac{2^{1/9}}{2^{5/6}}$ **39.** $(6^{1/2} \cdot 2^{1/3})^6$ **40.** $\sqrt[6]{4x^6}$

41. $3\sqrt[3]{6} - 9\sqrt[3]{6}$ **42.** $5\sqrt[3]{17} + 4\sqrt[3]{17}$ **43.** $\sqrt[4]{7} + 2\sqrt[4]{1792}$ **44.** $4\sqrt[5]{3} + \sqrt[5]{729}$

In Exercises 45–52, solve the equation if possible. (7.5)

45. $\sqrt{x} + 3 = 4$

46. $\sqrt{x} - 9 = 1$

47. $3(x - 4)^{1/2} + 5 = 11$

48. $2\sqrt{x + 5} + 5 = 7$

49. $-4\sqrt{2x - 1} - 10 = 6$

50. $-2(3x + 4)^{1/2} - 3 = 21$

51. $\sqrt[3]{x - 4} + 6 = 4$

52. $2(x + 3)^{1/3} - 5 = 1$

Geometric Mean   **In Exercises 53 and 54, find x.** (7.5)

53. The geometric mean of 8 and x is 16.

54. The geometric mean of 14 and x is 28.

In Exercises 55–58, find all values of x for which the distance between the given points is d. (7.5)

55. $(3, x), (-2, 4); d = 6$

56. $(10, x), (2, 4); d = 10$

57. $(6, 10), (1, x); d = 13$

58. $(8, 12), (x, 4); d = 17$

In Exercises 59–64, match the function with its graph. (7.2, 7.6)

59. $f(x) = 3\left(\dfrac{1}{2}\right)^x$

60. $f(x) = \sqrt{x - 7}$

61. $f(x) = \sqrt[3]{x + 7}$

62. $f(x) = \dfrac{1}{2}(2)^x$

63. $f(x) = \sqrt{x} + 2$

64. $f(x) = \sqrt[3]{x} - 2$

a.

b.

c.

d.

e.

f.

In Exercises 65–76, sketch the graph of the function. (7.2, 7.6)

65. $f(x) = 5\left(\dfrac{3}{4}\right)^x$

66. $g(x) = (x - 11)^{1/2}$

67. $h(x) = \dfrac{1}{3}(2)^x$

68. $f(x) = \dfrac{1}{2}(6)^x$

69. $f(x) = \sqrt{x} + 15$

70. $g(x) = 9\left(\dfrac{1}{3}\right)^x$

71. $g(x) = (x - 7)^{1/3}$

72. $f(x) = \sqrt[3]{x} + 16$

73. $f(x) = \sqrt{x - 9} + 3$

74. $h(x) = \sqrt[3]{x + 4} - 9$

75. $h(x) = (x + 2)^2 - 4$

76. $h(x) = -(x - 3)^2 + 9$

77. *R&D*   For 1970 through 1990, the average cost of research and development, C (in thousands of dollars per scientist or engineer), can be modeled by $C = 61 + 0.33t^2 - 12.88(2.7)^{-t}$ where $t = 0$ represents 1970. Approximate the average cost in 1980.
(Source: U.S. National Science Foundation)

78. *Fish Catch*   For 1970 through 1990, the total amount of fish caught, F (in millions of metric tons), in the world can be modeled by $F = 67 + 0.005t^3$, where t represents the year with $t = 0$ corresponding to 1970. In what year were approximately 72 million metric tons of fish caught? *(Source: Statistical Office of the United Nations)*

79. *Car Advertising*   For 1970 through 1990, the amount, A (in millions of dollars), spent on automotive advertising in the United States can be modeled by $A = 0.52(t^{5/2}) + 90$ where $t = 0$ represents 1970. In what year was approximately $471 million spent on automotive advertising?

Airspeed   **In Exercises 80 and 81, use the following information.**

Airplane speeds are measured in three different ways: *indicated airspeed*, *true airspeed*, and *ground speed.* The indicated airspeed is the airspeed given by an instrument called an airspeed indicator. The true airspeed is the speed of the airplane relative to the wind. The ground speed is the speed of the airplane relative to the ground. (For instance, if a plane were flying at a true airspeed of 200 knots into a headwind of 50 knots, then the ground speed would be 150 knots.)

80. The indicated airspeed, S (in knots), of an airplane is given by an airspeed indicator that measures the difference, p (in inches of mercury), between the static and dynamic pressures. The relationship between S and p is given by the model

$$S = 136.4\sqrt{p} + 4.5.$$

Construct a table of values for this function and sketch its graph.

81. An airplane pilot can approximate the true airspeed, T (in knots), by

$$T = \left(1 + \frac{A}{50,000}\right)S$$

where A is the altitude (in feet) and S is the indicated airspeed (in knots). A plane is flying at an altitude of 20,000 feet and the differential pressure is 2.05 (inches of mercury). What is its true airspeed?

Pilots do not usually calculate their airspeed, but they should know how to estimate it in emergencies.

Library Statistics   **In Exercises 82–85, simplify the expression to find the indicated library statistic. (The statistics refer to college and university libraries in the United States in 1990.)**

82. *Total Number of Libraries:*

$$\frac{10^6}{2^4} \cdot \frac{2^3}{10^2}$$

83. *Total Number of Employees:*

$$2000\sqrt[3]{24389}$$

84. *Total Expenses (Millions of Dollars):*

$$\left(\frac{4 \cdot 25^3}{36^{-1}}\right)^{1/2}$$

85. *Total Number of Books (in Millions):*

$$\frac{\sqrt[3]{8^{11}}}{\sqrt[3]{8^2}} + \sqrt[3]{8}$$

86. *Largest Public Library*   The ten-story Harold Washington Library Center opened in 1991 in Chicago, Illinois. If all the bookshelves in this library were laid end to end, they would stretch from Chicago to Belvidere, Illinois. How many miles would they stretch? (Each unit on the coordinate axes represents about 3.3 mi.)

87. *Overdue Book*   According to the *Guinness Book of World Records*, the record for an overdue library book was set in 1955 when a book that had been borrowed from the Sidney Sussex College Library in Cambridge, England, was returned. The book had been borrowed for x years where x is a solution of

$$\sqrt{\frac{x}{2}} = 12.$$

When was the book borrowed?

88. *Masters Degrees*   For 1975 through 1990, the number of library and archival science masters degrees, L, earned in the United States can be modeled by

$$L = 670\sqrt{280 - 31.6t + t^2}$$

where $t = 5$ represents 1975. In which year (prior to 1990) were approximately 5360 masters degrees in library and archival science earned?

The Harold Washington Library Center in Chicago, Illinois.

1. The geometric mean of x and 18 is $6\sqrt{3}$. Find x.

2. Find the distance between $(4, -6)$ and $(1, 2)$.

3. A circle has a center at $(-4, 2)$ and a radius of $5\sqrt{2}$. Find all possible values of x such that $(3, x)$ is a point on the circle.

4. Simplify: $\left(\dfrac{x^2 y}{y^{-4}}\right)^2 \cdot \dfrac{x^0 y^{-6}}{y^2}$.

5. Sketch the graph of $y = \sqrt{x + 4} - 2$.

6. Sketch the graph of $y = \sqrt[3]{x} - 2$.

In Exercises 7–12, simplify the expression.

7. $\sqrt[3]{27x^3}$

8. $2^{3/4} \cdot 2^{1/2}$

9. $(8^{1/2})^{2/3}$

10. $\sqrt[5]{64x^{10}}$

11. $3\sqrt[4]{2} + 5\sqrt[4]{2}$

12. $\sqrt[3]{28} + \sqrt[3]{224}$

In Exercises 13–18, solve the equation.

13. $\sqrt{x^2 + 7} = x + 1$

14. $\sqrt{x^2 + 16} = \sqrt{x^2 - 5x + 1}$

15. $\sqrt{11 - x} - 2\sqrt{x + 9} = 0$

16. $\sqrt{x + 4} = x - 8$

17. $\sqrt[3]{2x} = \sqrt[3]{x - 4}$

18. $x^{2/3} = 9$

19. In the figure at the right, x is the geometric mean of the lengths of the shorter side of the small rectangle and the longer side of the large rectangle. Find x.

20. The geometric mean of two numbers equals one half the first number. If the first number is 8, what is the second number?

21. The surface area of Venus is 5×10^8 square kilometers and the surface area of Mars is 1.43×10^8 square kilometers. Find the ratio of the surface area of Venus to the surface area of Mars.

22. $4000 is deposited in an account that earns 6% annual interest, compounded monthly. What is the balance after 8 years?

23. A 70,000-gallon swimming pool is leaking water at the rate of 10% per week. Write a model for the volume of water, W (in gallons), in the pool after t weeks. If none of the water is replaced, how much will remain after 4 weeks?

24. In 1990, the sales, y (in billions of dollars), of portable computers were predicted to increase, based on the model $y = 6(1.25)^t - 3.75$, where $t = 0$ represents 1990. What are the predicted sales for the year 2000? *(Source: USA Today)*

CHAPTER 8

Exponential and Logarithmic Functions

LESSONS

8.1 Exponential
Functions ▪ 398

8.2 Logarithmic
Functions ▪ 405

8.3 Properties of
Logarithms ▪ 413

8.4 The Natural Base e
▪ 420

8.5 Natural Logarithms
▪ 426

8.6 Solving Exponential
and Logarithmic
Equations ▪ 434

8.7 Exploring Data:
Logistics Growth
Functions ▪ 441

*Monteca is a jazz fusion band
from Toronto, Canada. They use
a combination of standard and
electronic instruments.*

Sound Intensity and Decibels

Sound Level (in decibels)

Intensity (in watts/cm²)

The level of sound, B (in decibels), is related to the intensity of the sound, I (in watts per square centimeter), by the logarithmic equation

$$B = 10 \log_{10} \frac{I}{I_0},$$

where I_0 is an intensity of 10^{-16} watts per square centimeter, corresponding roughly to the faintest sound that can be heard by human beings.

Prolonged exposure to noises of 85 decibels or greater can cause hearing loss. Above 100 decibels, even brief exposure can be damaging.

(Source: Time Magazine)

8.1

Exponential Functions

Goal 1 How to graph exponential functions and evaluate exponential expressions

Goal 2 How to use exponential functions as models for real-life problems

Why you should learn it:

You can model many real-life problems with exponential models, such as the depreciating value of a car as it ages.

Goal 1 **Graphing Exponential Functions**

In Lesson 7.2, you studied the graphs of basic exponential functions of the form $f(x) = Ca^x$. If $0 < a < 1$, then the graph represents exponential decay. If $a > 1$, then the graph represents exponential growth.

Exponential Decay: $f(x) = \left(\frac{1}{2}\right)^x$ **Exponential Growth:** $f(x) = 3^x$

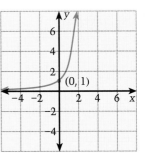

In this lesson, you will study vertical shifts, horizontal shifts, and reflections of these two basic types of graphs.

Example 1 *Using Vertical Shifts to Sketch Graphs*

Sketch the graph of each function.

a. $g(x) = \left(\frac{1}{2}\right)^x + 1$ **b.** $h(x) = 3^x - 2$

Solution

a. To sketch the graph of g, shift the graph of $f(x) = \left(\frac{1}{2}\right)^x$ upward by 1 unit.

b. To sketch the graph of h, shift the graph of $f(x) = 3^x$ downward by 2 units.

Example 2 **Using Horizontal Shifts**

Sketch the graph of each function.

a. $g(x) = 2^{x+3}$
b. $h(x) = 2^{x-2}$

Solution

a. To sketch the graph of g, shift the graph of $f(x) = 2^x$ to the left 3 units.
b. To sketch the graph of h, shift the graph of $f(x) = 2^x$ to the right 2 units.

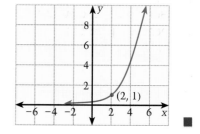

Each graph in Examples 1 and 2 shows a single vertical shift or a single horizontal shift. Example 3 shows how combinations of shifts and reflections can be used to sketch the graph of a function.

Example 3 **Using Reflection and Shifts**

Sketch the graph of each function.

a. $g(x) = -\left(\frac{1}{2}\right)^x + 4$
b. $h(x) = -2^{x-2} + 2$

Solution

a. To sketch the graph of g, reflect the graph of $f(x) = \left(\frac{1}{2}\right)^x$ in the x-axis. Then shift the graph upward 4 units.
b. To sketch the graph of h, shift the graph of $f(x) = 2^x$ 2 units to the right. Then reflect the graph in the x-axis and shift 2 units upward.

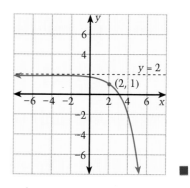

When the graph of an exponential function is sketched over the entire x-axis, you are assuming that *any* real number can be used as an exponent. What, however, does it mean to raise a number to an irrational power, such as $\sqrt{2}$?

Study Tip

Here are some definitions of powers that you have already studied.

Positive Integer Exponent:

$$a^n = \underbrace{a \cdot a \cdot a \cdots a}_{n \text{ factors}}$$

Zero Exponent:

$$a^0 = 1$$

Rational Exponent:

$$a^{1/n} = \sqrt[n]{a}$$

Negative Exponent:

$$a^{-n} = \frac{1}{a^n}$$

LESSON INVESTIGATION

■ Investigating Irrational Exponents

Partner Activity Use a calculator to evaluate the powers. Round your results to five decimal places.

$3^{14/10}$

$3^{141/100}$

$3^{1414/1000}$

$3^{14,142/10,000}$

$3^{141,421/100,000}$

$3^{1,414,214/1,000,000}$

Each of these powers has a rational exponent, which means that it can be defined by

$$a^{m/n} = \left(\sqrt[n]{a}\right)^m.$$

With your partner, discuss how you can use these powers to define the power $3^{\sqrt{2}}$, which has an irrational exponent.

Example 4   *Evaluate Powers That Have Irrational Exponents*

Use a calculator to evaluate the power. Round the result to 3 decimal places.

a. $3^{\sqrt{2}}$ **b.** $3^{-\pi}$

Solution

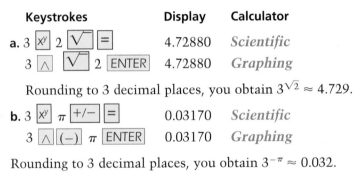

Keystrokes	Display	Calculator
a. 3 x^y 2 $\sqrt{}$ =	4.72880	*Scientific*
3 ∧ $\sqrt{}$ 2 ENTER	4.72880	*Graphing*

Rounding to 3 decimal places, you obtain $3^{\sqrt{2}} \approx 4.729$.

b. 3 x^y π +/− =	0.03170	*Scientific*
3 ∧ (−) π ENTER	0.03170	*Graphing*

Rounding to 3 decimal places, you obtain $3^{-\pi} \approx 0.032$.   ■

Goal 2 Using Exponential Models in Real Life

Real Life
Automobiles

Example 5 — Exponential Decay Model

Suppose that you purchased a new car for $20,000 in 1990. If the value of the car decreases by 16% each year to 84% of its previous value, what will the car be worth in 1996? In 1998?

Solution   One way to solve this problem is to create an exponential decay model. Let V represent the value of the car and let $t = 0$ represent 1990. Using the exponential decay model, you can write the following.

$$V = Ca^t \quad \textit{Exponential decay model}$$

$$= \boxed{\begin{matrix}\text{Initial} \\ \text{Value}\end{matrix}}\,(0.84)^t$$

$$= 20{,}000(0.84)^t$$

With this model, you can determine that the value of the car in 1996 is

$$V = 20{,}000(0.84)^6 \approx \$7026 \quad \textit{Value in 1996}$$

and the value in 1998 is

$$V = 20{,}000(0.84)^8 \approx \$4958. \quad \textit{Value in 1998}$$

The graph of $V = 20{,}000(0.84)^t$ is shown below.

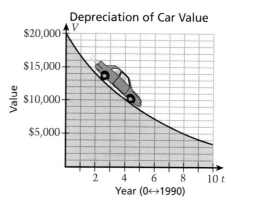

Depreciation of Car Value

Communicating about ALGEBRA

▶ **SHARING IDEAS about the Lesson**

Sketch the graph of the function. Explain your steps.

A. $f(x) = 2^{x-2} - 1$ **B.** $f(x) = -3^{x+1} + 4$

EXERCISES

Guided Practice

▶ **CRITICAL THINKING about the Lesson**

1. Compare the graphs of $f(x) = 5^x$ and $g(x) = 5^x - 3$.

2. Compare the graphs of $f(x) = 3^x$ and $g(x) = -3^{x+2}$.

3. Use a calculator to evaluate $5^{\sqrt{3}}$. Round the result to 3 decimal places.

4. Write an expression that could be the limit of the following sequence.

$$2^{3.1}, \ 2^{3.14}, \ 2^{3.142}, \ 2^{3.1416}, \ 2^{3.14159}, \ 2^{3.141593}, \ \ldots$$

Independent Practice

In Exercises 5–12, compare the graphs of f and g.

5. $f(x) = \left(\frac{1}{2}\right)^x$

    $g(x) = \left(\frac{1}{2}\right)^x - 2$

6. $f(x) = 4^x$

    $g(x) = 4^{x-1}$

7. $f(x) = 5^x$

    $g(x) = 5^x + 6$

8. $f(x) = \left(\frac{1}{5}\right)^x$

    $g(x) = \left(\frac{1}{5}\right)^x + 10$

9. $f(x) = \left(\frac{1}{3}\right)^x$

    $g(x) = -\left(\frac{1}{3}\right)^{x+4}$

10. $f(x) = 2^x$

    $g(x) = -2^x + 9$

11. $f(x) = 8^x$

    $g(x) = 8^{x-4} + 5$

12. $f(x) = 10^x$

    $g(x) = 10^{x+2} - 2$

In Exercises 13–20, match the function with its graph.

13. $f(x) = \left(\frac{1}{2}\right)^x - 4$

14. $f(x) = 4^{x-1}$

15. $f(x) = \left(\frac{1}{2}\right)^{x-4}$

16. $f(x) = 4^x + 1$

17. $f(x) = (4)^{x+1}$

18. $f(x) = \left(\frac{1}{2}\right)^{x+4}$

19. $f(x) = (4)^x - 1$

20. $f(x) = \left(\frac{1}{2}\right)^x + 4$

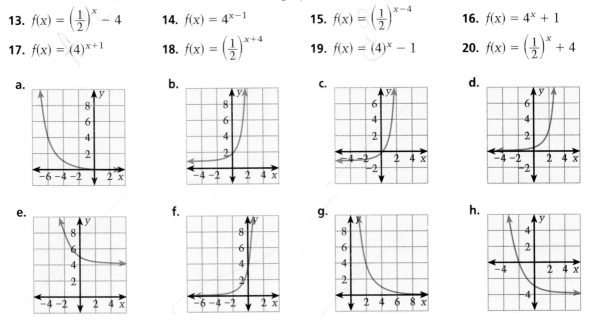

In Exercises 21–36, sketch the graph of the function.

21. $f(x) = \left(\frac{2}{3}\right)^x + 2$ **22.** $f(x) = 2^{x-5}$ **23.** $f(x) = \left(\frac{1}{4}\right)^{x-1}$ **24.** $f(x) = 2^x - 5$

25. $f(x) = 5^{x+3}$ **26.** $f(x) = 4^{x-4}$ **27.** $f(x) = 5^x - 4$ **28.** $f(x) = \left(\frac{3}{4}\right)^x + 1$

29. $f(x) = -\left(\frac{1}{3}\right)^x$ **30.** $f(x) = -6^x$ **31.** $f(x) = -2^{x+2}$ **32.** $f(x) = -\left(\frac{1}{2}\right)^x + 4$

33. $f(x) = -\left(\frac{1}{2}\right)^{x-3} + 7$ **34.** $f(x) = -2^{x-8} + 1$ **35.** $f(x) = -5^{x+1} - 2$ **36.** $f(x) = 4^{x+3} - 3$

Technology   **In Exercises 37–44, use a calculator to evaluate the expression. Round your result to three decimal places.**

37. $5^{\sqrt{5}}$ **38.** $21^{\sqrt{11}}$ **39.** 6^{π} **40.** $7^{-\pi}$

41. $2^{\sqrt{3}}$ **42.** $13^{2\pi}$ **43.** $4^{\pi/3}$ **44.** $18^{\sqrt{6}}$

45. *Technology*   In the following sequence of powers, which power is the first to approximate $4^{\sqrt{3}}$ accurately to 5 decimal places?

    a. $4^{1.732}$ **b.** $4^{1.7321}$ **c.** $4^{1.73205}$ **d.** $4^{1.732051}$ **e.** $4^{1.7320508}$

46. *Technology*   In the following sequence of powers, which power is the first to approximate 6^{π} accurately to 1 decimal places?

    a. $6^{3.1}$ **b.** $6^{3.14}$ **c.** $6^{3.142}$ **d.** $6^{3.1416}$ **e.** $6^{3.14159}$

In Exercises 47 and 48, write an exponential model that describes the situation.

47. *Increase in Value*   In 1985, you bought a sculpture for $380. Each year, t, the value, v, of the sculpture increases by 8%.

48. *Decrease in Value*   In 1990, you bought a television for $600. Each year, t, the value, v, of the television decreases by 6%.

49. *Automobile Depreciation*   If the value of a new $19,000 car that you bought in 1991 decreases by 14% each year, what will the car be worth in 1995? In 1998? Sketch the graph of the exponential decay model.

Elvis Presley has been awarded more gold records by the recording industry than any other individual musician.

50. *Business Revenue*   In 1980, your business had a revenue of $30,000. Each year after that, the revenue increased by 15%. What was the revenue in 1990? In 1992? Sketch the graph of the exponential growth model.

51. *Record Albums*   Record albums increased in popularity until about 1980. For 1985 through 1994, however, the number, n (in millions), of record albums sold each year can be modeled by

$$n = 817.75(0.732)^t$$

where $t = 5$ represents 1985. How many were sold in 1990? What might explain why the sale of record albums decreased so rapidly after 1985? *(Source: Recording Industry Association of America)*

Record Albums

Number Sold (in millions) / Year (5 ⟷ 1985)

52. Recreational Boats From 1970 through 1990, the number of recreational boats, B (in millions), in the United States can be modeled by $B = 6.65(1.04)^t + 2$, where $t = 0$ represents 1970. Sketch the graph of this function. How many recreational boats were owned in the United States in 1984? *(Source: National Marine Manufacturers Association)*

Integrated Review

In Exercises 53–60, sketch the graph of the function.

53. $f(x) = (x + 8)^2$ **54.** $f(x) = -x^2 + 2$ **55.** $f(x) = |x| + 3$ **56.** $f(x) = |x + 2|$

57. $f(x) = \sqrt{x - 9}$ **58.** $f(x) = \sqrt{x} + 9$ **59.** $f(x) = \sqrt[3]{x} + 4$ **60.** $f(x) = \sqrt[3]{x + 1}$

In Exercises 61–64, decide whether the function represents exponential growth or exponential decay.

61. $f(x) = \left(\frac{1}{4}\right)^x$ **62.** $f(x) = (6)^x$

63. $f(x) = \left(\frac{3}{2}\right)^x$ **64.** $f(x) = \left(\frac{2}{3}\right)^x$

65. Powers of Ten Which best approximates the length of an F-18 Hornet fighter airplane?
a. 5.6×10^{-1} ft   **b.** 5.6×10^0 ft
c. 5.6×10^1 ft   **d.** 5.6×10^2 ft

66. Powers of Ten Which best approximates the length of an aircraft carrier?
a. 10.9×10^0 ft   **b.** 10.9×10^1 ft
c. 10.9×10^2 ft   **d.** 10.9×10^3 ft

Exploration and Extension

The Natural Base **In Exercises 67–70, use the following information.**

The number $e \approx 2.71828$ is called the natural base. Use this approximation of e to evaluate the powers in Exercises 67–70. Round the results to two decimal places.

67. 5^e **68.** e^{-4} **69.** $(e)^{-\frac{1}{3}}$ **70.** $\left(\frac{1}{2}\right)^e$

71. The Natural Exponential Function Copy and complete the table using $e \approx 2.71828$. Round your answers to two decimal places.

x	−3	−2	−1	0	1	2	3
e^x	?	?	?	?	?	?	?

72. The Natural Exponential Function Use the result of Exercise 71 to sketch the graph of $f(x) = e^x$.

8.2 Logarithmic Functions

What you should learn:

Goal 1 How to evaluate logarithmic expressions and graph logarithmic functions

Goal 2 How to use logarithms in real-life situations

Why you should learn it:

You can model many real-life situations with logarithmic models, such as the slope of a beach relative to the size of the sand particles.

Goal 1 Evaluating Logarithmic Expressions

You know that $2^2 = 4$ and $2^3 = 8$, but for what value of y does

$$2^y = 6?$$

Because $2^2 < 6 < 2^3$, you would expect the solution to be between 2 and 3. To answer this question exactly, mathematicians defined *logarithms*. In terms of a logarithm, $y = \log_2 6 \approx 2.585$.

> **Definition of Logarithm to Base *a***
>
> Let a and x be positive numbers, $a \neq 1$. The **logarithm of *x* with base *a*** is denoted by $\log_a x$ and is defined as follows.
>
> $$\log_a x = y \quad \text{if and only if} \quad a^y = x$$
>
> The expression $\log_a x$ is read as the "log base a of x." The function $f(x) = \log_a x$ is the **logarithmic function with base *a*.**

This definition tells you that the equations $\log_a x = y$ and $a^y = x$ are equivalent. The first is in logarithmic form, and the second is in exponential form.

Example 1 Rewriting Exponential and Logarithmic Equations

Logarithmic Form	Exponential Form
a. $\log_2 16 = 4$	$2^4 = 16$
b. $\log_{10} 10 = 1$	$10^1 = 10$
c. $\log_3 1 = 0$	$3^0 = 1$
d. $\log_{10} 0.1 = -1$	$10^{-1} = 0.1$
e. $\log_2 6 \approx 2.585$	$2^{2.585} \approx 6$

Be sure you see that a logarithm is defined as an exponent. Thus, to evaluate the expression $\log_3 9$, you should ask the question "3 to what power gives 9?" Because the answer is 2, it follows that $\log_3 9 = 2$.

Example 2 **Evaluating Logarithms**

Evaluate the logarithms.

a. $\log_4 16$ **b.** $\log_5 1$
c. $\log_4 2$ **d.** $\log_3(-1)$

Solution In each case, note the question asked.

a. 4 to what power gives 16?

$$4^2 = 16 \longrightarrow \log_4 16 = 2$$

b. 5 to what power gives 1?

$$5^0 = 1 \longrightarrow \log_5 1 = 0$$

c. 4 to what power gives 2?

$$4^{\frac{1}{2}} = 2 \longrightarrow \log_4 2 = \frac{1}{2}$$

d. There is no power of 3 that gives -1. (Think of the graph of $y = 3^x$.) Therefore, $\log_3(-1)$ is undefined. ∎

There are some special logarithm values that you should learn to recognize.

Special Logarithm Values

Let a and x be positive real numbers such that $a \neq 1$.

1. $\log_a 1 = 0$ because $a^0 = 1$.
2. $\log_a a = 1$ because $a^1 = a$.
3. $\log_a a^x = x$ because $a^x = a^x$.

The logarithmic function with base 10 is called the **common logarithmic function.** On most scientific calculators, this function can be evaluated with the key $\boxed{log}$. To use a calculator to evaluate logarithms to other bases, you can use the **change of base formula.**

$$\log_a x = \frac{\log_{10} x}{\log_{10} a} \quad \textit{Change of Base Formula}$$

Connections
Technology

Example 3 **Using a Calculator to Evaluate a Logarithm**

Evaluate $\log_2 6$.

Solution Using the change of base formula, you can write

$$\log_2 6 = \frac{\log_{10} 6}{\log_{10} 2} \approx \frac{0.778}{0.301} \approx 2.585.$$ ∎

By definition, the functions $f(x) = a^x$ and $g(x) = \log_a x$ are inverses of each other. This means the graph of $g(x) = \log_a x$ is a reflection of the graph of $f(x) = a^x$ in the line $y = x$.

Example 4 Sketching the Graph of a Logarithmic Function

Sketch the graph of $g(x) = \log_2 x$.

Solution One way to sketch the graph is to construct a table of values, plot the points, and connect the points with a smooth curve.

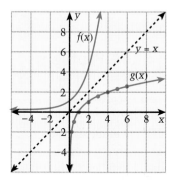

	Without Calculator					With Calculator		
x	$\frac{1}{4}$	$\frac{1}{2}$	1	2	4	3	5	6
log₂ x	-2	-1	0	1	2	1.58	2.32	2.58

Another way to sketch the graph of g is to reflect the graph of $f(x) = 2^x$ in the line $y = x$. The graph is shown at the left. ∎

From the graph of $g(x) = \log_2 x$, you can see that the domain of the function is the set of positive numbers and the range is the set of all real numbers.

Example 5 Sketching the Graph of a Logarithmic Function

Sketch the graph of $f(x) = \log_{10} x$.

Solution

	Without Calculator				With Calculator		
x	$\frac{1}{100}$	$\frac{1}{10}$	1	10	2	5	8
log₁₀ x	-2	-1	0	1	0.301	0.699	0.903

The graph is shown below. Notice how slowly the graph rises for $x > 1$. On this graph, you would need to move out to $x = 1000$ before the graph rises to $y = 3$.

The slope of a beach depends on the size of its sand particles. If the sand is very coarse, the slope of the beach will be steeper than if the sand is fine. The photo shows a coral sand beach in St. Thomas, Virgin Islands. Because the sand is fine, the beach has a gentle slope.

Goal 2 Using Logarithms in Real-Life Problems

Real Life
Oceanography

Diameter (in mm)	Type of Sand Particle
4	Pebble
2	Granule
1	Very coarse sand
0.5	Coarse sand
0.25	Medium sand
0.125	Fine sand
0.0625	Very fine sand

Example 6 *Evaluating a Logarithmic Function*

The slope, s, of a beach is related to the average diameter, d (in millimeters), of the sand particles on the beach by the model

$$s = 0.159 + 0.118 \log_{10} d.$$

Find the slope of the beach if the average diameter of the sand is 0.25 millimeter.

Solution If $d = 0.25$, then the slope of the beach is

$s = 0.159 + 0.118 \log_{10} 0.25$ *Substitute 0.25 for d.*

$\approx 0.159 + 0.118(-0.602)$ *Use a calculator.*

$\approx 0.09.$

The slope of the beach is about 0.09. This is a gentle slope that has a rise of only 9 meters for a run of 100 meters. ■

Communicating about ALGEBRA

▶ **SHARING IDEAS about the Lesson**

Match the function with its graph. Explain your reasoning.

A. $f(x) = \log_3 x$ **B.** $f(x) = \log_4 x$ **C.** $f(x) = \log_5 x$

EXERCISES

Guided Practice

▶ **CRITICAL THINKING about the Lesson**

1. Write the expression symbolically, "logarithm of 3 with base 2."
2. Rewrite $\log_3 x = 1.7$ in exponential form.
3. Rewrite $4^x = 8$ in logarithmic form.
4. Evaluate $\log_{25} 5$ without a calculator.
5. Use the change of base formula to evaluate $\log_6 7$ with a calculator.
6. In the coordinate plane at the right, identify the graph of $f(x) = 5^x$ and the graph of $g(x) = \log_5 x$.

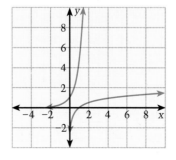

Independent Practice

In Exercises 7–14, write the equation in exponential form.

7. $\log_3 27 = 3$ **8.** $\log_4 256 = 4$ **9.** $\log_6 36 = 2$ **10.** $\log_6 216 = 3$

11. $\log_2 32 = 5$ **12.** $\log_8 64 = 2$ **13.** $\log_5 125 = 3$ **14.** $\log_1 1 = 3$

In Exercises 15–22, write the equation in logarithmic form.

15. $3^5 = 243$ **16.** $10^{0.12} \approx 1.318$ **17.** $4^{-1} = \frac{1}{4}$ **18.** $16^{-\frac{1}{2}} = \frac{1}{4}$

19. $4^3 = 64$ **20.** $13^2 = 169$ **21.** $9^{\frac{2}{3}} \approx 4.327$ **22.** $6^4 = 1296$

In Exercises 23–34, evaluate the expression without using a calculator.

23. $\log_5 25$ **24.** $\log_9 9^{-0.56}$ **25.** $\log_{12} 1$ **26.** $\log_9 81$

27. $\log_4 4^{\frac{5}{6}}$ **28.** $\log_4 2$ **29.** $\log_{\frac{1}{2}} \frac{1}{2}$ **30.** $\log_5(-25)$

31. $\log_2 \frac{1}{8}$ **32.** $\log_9 \frac{1}{3}$ **33.** $\log_4(-4)$ **34.** $\log_{10} 10$

In Exercises 35–38, estimate a range of values for the expression. Then evaluate using the change of base formula.

35. $\log_4 5$ **36.** $\log_2 5$ **37.** $\log_6 3$ **38.** $\log_3 10$

In Exercises 39–46, use a calculator to evaluate the expression.

39. $\log_2 9$ **40.** $\log_4 7$ **41.** $\log_{1.4} 10$ **42.** $\log_5 2$

43. $\log_3 20$ **44.** $\log_{0.8} 10$ **45.** $\log_6 -3$ **46.** $\log_{\frac{1}{4}} 6$

In Exercises 47–58, solve the equation for x.

47. $\log_3 81 = x$ **48.** $\log_2 256 = x$ **49.** $\log_6 x = -1$ **50.** $\log_x 343 = 3$

51. $\log_3 x = 5$ **52.** $\log_4 x = 2$ **53.** $\log_x 64 = 3$ **54.** $\log_x 243 = 5$

55. $\log_x 256 = 8$ **56.** $\log_5 x = 1$ **57.** $\log_2(x + 1) = 1$ **58.** $\log_5(x - 4) = 0$

In Exercises 59–62, find the inverse of the function.

59. $f(x) = \log_6 x$ **60.** $f(x) = 8^x$ **61.** $f(x) = \left(\frac{1}{3}\right)^x$ **62.** $f(x) = \log_{\frac{1}{2}} x$

In Exercises 63–66, match the function with its graph.

63. $f(x) = 1 + \log_2 x$ **64.** $f(x) = \log_2 x$ **65.** $f(x) = 1 + \log_4 x$ **66.** $f(x) = \log_4 x$

a.   **b.**   **c.**   **d.**

In Exercises 67–78, sketch the graph of the function.

67. $f(x) = \log_5 x$ **68.** $f(x) = \log_3 x$ **69.** $f(x) = 1 + \log_2 x$ **70.** $f(x) = 2 + \log_{10} x$

71. $f(x) = \log_8 x$ **72.** $f(x) = -1 + \log_3 x$ **73.** $f(x) = \log_{10} 10x$ **74.** $f(x) = \log_8 2x$

75. $f(x) = \log_2(x - 1)$ **76.** $f(x) = \log_{10}(x - 2)$ **77.** $f(x) = \log_3(x + 2)$ **78.** $f(x) = \log_4(x + 3)$

79. *American Elk*   The antler spread, a (in inches), and shoulder height, h (in inches), of an adult male elk are related approximately by the model

$$h = 116 \log_{10}(a + 40) - 176.$$

Approximate the shoulder height of a male American elk.

80. *Tornadoes*   Most tornadoes last less than an hour and travel less than 20 miles. The speed of the wind, S (in miles per hour), near the center of the tornado is related to the distance the tornado travels, d (in miles), by the model

$$S = 93 \log_{10} d + 65.$$

On March 18, 1925, a large tornado struck Missouri, Illinois, and Indiana, covering a distance of 220 miles. Approximate the speed near the center of this tornado.

81. *Horn of Gabriel*   A portion of the three-dimensional mathematical figure called the horn of Gabriel is shown at the right. The area of the cross section (in the coordinate plane) of the horn is given by

$$A \approx \frac{2}{\log_{10} 2.71828}.$$

Approximate this area.

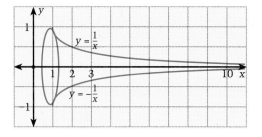

Male American elks grow antlers with a spread of about 5 feet.

Carbon Dating   **In Exercises 82 and 83, use the following information.**

Sunlight produces radioactive carbon (carbon-14), which is absorbed by living plants and animals. Once the plant or animal dies, it stops absorbing carbon-14. Using carbon-14's half-life of 5700 years, scientists can approximate the age of plant or animal fossils by measuring the fossil's concentration, C, of carbon-14 atoms. For living things, C is given a value of 1. Thus, C is related to the number of years, t (since the plant or animal died), by the model $t = 5700 \log_{\frac{1}{2}} C$.

82. For a particular plant fossil, the concentration of carbon-14 atoms is one tenth of what it was when the plant was alive. About how long ago did the plant die?

83. A particular animal fossil has $\frac{1}{8}$ of the carbon-14 atoms that it had when the animal was alive. How long ago did the animal die?

Hundreds of figures, like this 170-foot giant, were etched in the desert near Blythe, California, by prehistoric natives of California. In 1952, historians concluded that the figures were created between the sixteenth and nineteenth centuries. Later, carbon dating of organic matter that grew on the gravel showed that they were created about A.D. 900.

Integrated Review

In Exercises 84–88, sketch the graph of the function.

84. $y = 3^x$ **85.** $y = \left(\frac{1}{3}\right)^x$ **86.** $y = 4^x - 3$ **87.** $y = 4^{x-2}$ **88.** $y = \left(\frac{1}{2}\right)^x + 3$

89. *College Entrance Exam Sample*   A baseball team has won 40 games out of 60 played. It has 32 more games to play. How many of these must the team win to obtain a 75% win record for the year?
   a. 26   **b.** 29   **c.** 28   **d.** 30   **e.** 32

90. *College Entrance Exam Sample*   The enrollment at a university was 3000 in 1950 and 12,000 in 1975. By what percent did the enrollment increase?
   a. 125%   **b.** 25%   **c.** 300%   **d.** 400%   **e.** 3%

Exploration and Extension

91. *Change of Base*   Use the formula $\log_a x = \dfrac{\log_b x}{\log_b a}$ to verify that $\log_a b = \dfrac{1}{\log_b a}$.

In Exercises 92 and 93, verify the equation without using a calculator.

92. $\log_2 4 = \dfrac{1}{\log_4 2}$

93. $\log_5 125 = \dfrac{1}{\log_{125} 5}$

Mixed REVIEW

1. Simplify: $(a^2b^0c^4)(a^{-5}b^{-3}c^{-2})$. **(7.1)**

2. Simplify: $\sqrt{x^2}$. **(7.4)**

3. Simplify: $\sqrt[3]{-27}$. **(7.4)**

4. Simplify: $\sqrt{50a^2b^5}$. **(7.4)**

5. Simplify: $(3^{2/3})^{3/5}$. **(7.4)**

6. Simplify: $\sqrt{3} \cdot \sqrt{6}$. **(7.4)**

7. Simplify: $(3i^4)(2i^3)$. **(5.5)**

8. Solve $\sqrt{5x+1} - 2 = 4$. **(7.5)**

9. In which quadrant is $(5, -2)$? **(2.6)**

10. Find the slope of $3x - 4y = -2$. **(2.2)**

11. Find the vertex of $y = 2|x - 7| + 5$. **(2.5)**

12. Find the distance from $(3, 5)$ to $(6, 1)$. **(7.5)**

13. For $f(1) = -1$ and $f(n + 1) = 2(-1)^n f(n)$, find $f(4)$. **(6.6)**

14. For $f(x) = x - 3$ and $g(x) = x^2 + 2$, find $g(f(x))$. **(6.2)**

15. Find the geometric mean of 4 and 16. **(7.5)**

16. Sketch the graph of $y = 4(x + 3)^2 - 1$. **(5.2)**

17. Simplify: $\dfrac{\sqrt[5]{64}}{\sqrt[5]{2}}$. **(7.4)**

18. Find the domain of $y = \dfrac{2}{\sqrt{x - 3}}$. **(6.2)**

19. \$1200 saved at 8% compounded quarterly will be how much in 6 years?

20. Write an equation of the line passing through $(2, -5)$ and $(-1, -3)$. **(2.4)**

Milestones LOGARITHMS

```
1600        1620              1640              1660              1680              1700
Napier introduces logarithms  Briggs publishes common logarithm tables   Recognition of relationship between
                                                                          logarithms and exponents
```

As the field of mathematics grew through the centuries, so did the need for computational tools. In 1614, a Scotsman, John Napier, introduced logarithms. Logarithms made it possible to use addition and subtraction in place of multiplication and division. Pierre-Simon Laplace said the invention of logarithms, "by shortening the labors, doubled the life of the astronomer."

Henry Briggs, an English geometry professor, was excited by Napier's work and traveled to Scotland to meet him. They decided that a convenient logarithm system would be based on the number 10. From their visit, came the system of common logarithms. In 1624, Briggs published a book of logarithms of the numbers between 1 and 20,000 and from 90,000 to 100,000.

The invention of logarithms was remarkable in many ways. It made decimals, which were slowly coming into use, a necessity. Any discussion of logarithms is certain to include exponents, but their relationship was not recognized until 1685.

John Napier

Find out who developed logarithms independently in Switzerland shortly after Napier developed them in Scotland.

8.3

Properties of Logarithms

What you should learn:

Goal 1 How to use properties of logarithms

Goal 2 How to use logarithms to solve real-life problems

Why you should learn it:

You can model many real-life situations with logarithms, such as the intensity of earthquakes as measured by the Richter scale.

Goal 1   Using Properties of Logarithms

Since the logarithm function with base a is the inverse of the exponential function with base a, it makes sense that each property of exponents should have a corresponding property of logarithms. For instance, the exponential property $a^0 = 1$ has the corresponding logarithmic property $\log_a 1 = 0$.

In this lesson, you will study the properties of logarithms that correspond to the following three properties of exponents.

1. $a^n a^m = a^{n+m}$ **2.** $\dfrac{a^n}{a^m} = a^{n-m}$ **3.** $(a^n)^m = a^{nm}$

Properties of Logarithms

Let a, u, and v be positive numbers such that $a \neq 1$, and let n be any real number.

1. $\log_a(uv) = \log_a u + \log_a v$ *Product Property*

2. $\log_a \dfrac{u}{v} = \log_a u - \log_a v$ *Quotient Property*

3. $\log_a u^n = n \log_a u$ *Power Property*

Note that there is no general property of logarithms that can be used to simplify $\log_a(u + v)$. For instance, $\log_a(u + v)$ does not equal $\log_a u + \log_a v$.

Example 1   *Demonstrating Properties of Logarithms*

Use $\log_{10} 2 \approx 0.301$ and $\log_{10} 3 \approx 0.477$ to approximate the following.

a. $\log_{10} \dfrac{2}{3}$ **b.** $\log_{10} 6$ **c.** $\log_{10} 9$

Solution

a. $\log_{10} \dfrac{2}{3} = \log_{10} 2 - \log_{10} 3 \approx 0.301 - 0.477 = -0.176$

b. $\log_{10} 6 = \log_{10}(2 \cdot 3) = \log_{10} 2 + \log_{10} 3$
$\approx 0.301 + 0.477 = 0.778$

c. $\log_{10} 9 = \log_{10}(3^2) = 2 \log_{10} 3 \approx 2(0.477) = 0.954$ ∎

When using the properties of logarithms, you may find that it helps to remember verbal forms of the properties. For instance, the verbal form of $\log_a(uv) = \log_a u + \log_a v$ is "The log of a product is the sum of the logs of the factors." Similarly, the verbal form of $\log_a \frac{u}{v} = \log_a u - \log_a v$ is "The log of a quotient is the difference of the logs of the numerator and denominator."

Example 2 *Rewriting the Logarithm of a Product*

Use the properties of logarithms to rewrite $\log_{10} 7x^3$.

Solution

$$\log_{10} 7x^3 = \log_{10} 7 + \log_{10} x^3 \qquad \textit{Product Property}$$
$$= \log_{10} 7 + 3 \log_{10} x \qquad \textit{Power Property} \qquad \blacksquare$$

When a logarithmic expression is rewritten as in Example 2, it is called expanding the expression. The reverse procedure is demonstrated in Example 3 and is called condensing a logarithmic expression.

Example 3 *Condensing a Logarithmic Expression*

Condense $\log_{10} x - \log_{10} 3$.

Solution

$$\log_{10} x - \log_{10} 3 = \log_{10} \tfrac{x}{3} \qquad \textit{Quotient Property} \qquad \blacksquare$$

Example 4 *Expanding a Logarithmic Expression*

Expand $\log_2 3xy^2$.

Solution

$$\log_2 3xy^2 = \log_2 3 + \log_2 x + \log_2 y^2 \qquad \textit{Product Property}$$
$$= \log_2 3 + \log_2 x + 2 \log_2 y \qquad \textit{Power Property} \qquad \blacksquare$$

Example 5 *Condensing a Logarithmic Expression*

Condense $\log_{10} 2 - 2 \log_{10} x$.

Solution

$$\log_{10} 2 - 2 \log_{10} x = \log_{10} 2 - \log_{10} x^2 \qquad \textit{Power Property}$$
$$= \log_{10} \frac{2}{x^2} \qquad \textit{Quotient Property}$$
$$\blacksquare$$

The Richter scale is used to measure the magnitude of an earthquake. The magnitude, R, of an earthquake of intensity I is given by $R = \log_{10} I$, where the intensity is a measure of the wave energy of an earthquake per unit of area. The photo at the right shows the devastation caused by the San Francisco Earthquake of 1989, which measured 7.1 on the Richter scale.

Goal 2 Using Logarithms to Solve Problems

Real Life
Geology

Example 6 *Using Properties of Logarithms*

Find the intensity per unit of area for the earthquakes listed.
a. Great San Francisco Earthquake in 1906, $R = 8.3$
b. San Francisco Bay Area Earthquake in 1989, $R = 7.1$

Solution
a. Using the formula $R = \log_{10} I$ and $R = 8.3$, you can write $8.3 = \log_{10} I$ or

$$I = 10^{8.3} \approx 199{,}526{,}000.$$

b. Using $R = 7.1$, you can write $7.1 = \log_{10} I$ or

$$I = 10^{7.1} \approx 12{,}589{,}000.$$

Note that an increase of 1.2 units on the Richter scale (from 7.1 to 8.3) represents an intensity change by a factor of

$$\frac{199{,}526{,}000}{12{,}589{,}000} \approx 16.$$

In other words, the earthquake in 1906 had an intensity about 16 times greater than that of the one in 1989. ■

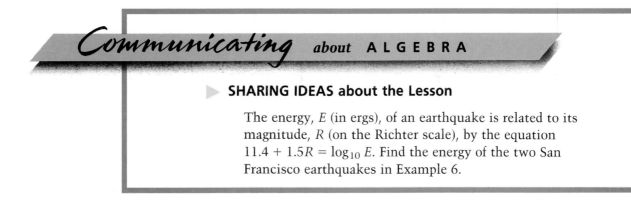

Communicating about **A L G E B R A**

▶ **SHARING IDEAS about the Lesson**

The energy, E (in ergs), of an earthquake is related to its magnitude, R (on the Richter scale), by the equation $11.4 + 1.5R = \log_{10} E$. Find the energy of the two San Francisco earthquakes in Example 6.

EXERCISES

▶ **CRITICAL THINKING about the Lesson**

1. Which is equivalent to $\log_{10}\left(\frac{5}{7}\right)^2$? Explain.

   a. $2(\log_{10} 5 - \log_{10} 7)$ **b.** $\dfrac{2 \log_{10} 5}{\log_{10} 7}$

2. Use a property of logarithms to help evaluate $\log_3 27^5$.

3. Use $\log_2 5 \approx 2.322$ and $\log_2 3 \approx 1.585$ to approximate $\log_2 15$.

4. Which is equivalent to $\log_6(2x^2 + 5)$? Explain.

   a. $\log_6 2x^2 + \log_6 5$ **b.** $\log_6 2x^2 \cdot \log_6 5$ **c.** Neither **a** nor **b** is equivalent.

Independent Practice

In Exercises 5–8, use $\log_{10} 3 \approx 0.477$ and $\log_{10} 12 \approx 1.079$ to approximate the value of the expression. Use a calculator to verify your results.

5. $\log_{10} 4$ **6.** $\log_{10} \frac{1}{4}$ **7.** $\log_{10} 36$ **8.** $\log_{10} 144$

In Exercises 9–24, expand the expression.

9. $\log_2 3x$ **10.** $\log_8 16x$ **11.** $\log_{10} 2x^3$ **12.** $\log_3 x^3$

13. $\log_4 \frac{6}{5}$ **14.** $\log_5 9$ **15.** $\log_6 \frac{10}{3}$ **16.** $\log_3 6xy$

17. $\log_{10} 7x^3yz$ **18.** $\log_6 36x^2$ **19.** $\log_2 x^{1/2}y^3$ **20.** $\log_3 12^{2/3}x^7$

21. $\log_{10} \sqrt{x}$ **22.** $\log_2 \sqrt[3]{x}$ **23.** $\log_{10} \sqrt[3]{x^2}$ **24.** $\log_2 \sqrt{4x}$

In Exercises 25–38, condense the expression.

25. $\log_5 6 - \log_5 4$ | **26.** $\log_3 13 + \log_3 3$

27. $2 \log_{10} x + \log_{10} 5$ | **28.** $5 \log_4 12 - 5 \log_4 2$

29. $3 \log_3 19 - 3 \log_3 38$ | **30.** $\log_7 48 - 4 \log_7 2$

31. $\log_{10} 8 + \log_{10} x + 2 \log_{10} y$ | **32.** $\log_{10} 6 - 3 \log_{10} \frac{1}{3}$

33. $6 \log_8 2 + 2 \log_8 x + 2 \log_8 y$ | **34.** $\log_3 2 + \frac{1}{2} \log_3 y$

35. $10 \log_{10} x + \frac{2}{3}\log_{10} 64$ | **36.** $2 \log_{10} 9 + 5 \log_{10} x + \log_{10} \frac{1}{3}$

37. $2(\log_5 18 - \log_5 3) + \frac{1}{2} \log_5 \frac{1}{16}$ | **38.** $\frac{1}{3} \log_4 27 - \left(2 \log_4 6 - \frac{1}{2} \log_4 81\right)$

In Exercises 39–46, use properties of logarithms to solve for *x*.

39. $\log_4 2 - \log_4 x = \log_4 \frac{2}{3}$ | **40.** $\log_3 6 = \log_3 3 + \log_3 x$

41. $\log_4 5 = \log_4 10 - \log_4 x$ | **42.** $\log_3 3 = \log_3 x - \log_3 3$

43. $\log_3 8 = x \log_3 2$ | **44.** $\log_{10} 16 = x \log_{10} 2$

45. $\log_2 x = \frac{1}{2} \log_2 4$ | **46.** $\frac{1}{3} \log_4 x = \log_4 4$

Molecular Transport   **In Exercises 47–49, use the following information.**

The energy, E (in kilocalories per gram molecule), required to transport a substance from the outside to the inside of a living cell is given by

$$E = 1.4(\log_{10} C_2 - \log_{10} C_1),$$

where C_1 is the concentration of the substance outside the cell and C_2 is the concentration inside the cell.

47. Condense the given equation.

48. The concentration of a particular substance inside a cell is twice the concentration outside the cell. How much energy is required to transport the substance from outside to inside the cell?

49. The concentration of a particular substance inside a cell is six times the concentration outside the cell. How much energy is required to transport the substance from outside to inside the cell?

50. *Human-Memory Model*   Students in a ninth grade class were given an exam on French vocabulary words. During the next two years, the same students were retested several times. The average score, S, of the class can be modeled by

$$S = 90 - \log_{10}(t + 1)^{15},$$

where t is the time in months since the original exam. Expand this model. What was the average score after 1 year?

Photography   **In Exercises 51 and 52, use the following information.**

The f-stops on a 35-millimeter camera control the amount of light that enters a camera. Let s be a measure of the amount of light that strikes the film and let f be the f-stop. Then s and f are related by the model

$$s = \log_2 f^2.$$

51. The table shows the first eight f-stops on a 35-millimeter camera. Copy and complete the table and describe the pattern.

f	1.414	2.000	2.828	4.000
s	?	?	?	?

f	5.657	8.000	11.314	16.000
s	?	?	?	?

52. Many 35-millimeter cameras have nine f-stops. What do you think the ninth f-stop is? Explain your reasoning.

The two top photos were taken with an f-stop of 2. With that setting, the camera could not be focused on both near and far subjects. The bottom photo was taken with an f-stop of 16. With that setting, all figures appear in focus.

Intensity of Sound **In Exercises 53–56, use the following information.**

The level of sound, B (in decibels), is related to the intensity of the sound, I (in watts per square centimeter), by the model

$$B = 10 \log_{10} \frac{I}{I_0},$$

where I_0 is an intensity of 10^{-16} watts per square centimeter, corresponding roughly to the faintest sound that can be heard by humans.

Decibel Level	Example
130	Jet airplane takeoff
120	Riveting machine
110	Rock concert
100	Boiler shop
90	Subway train
80	Average factory
70	City traffic
60	Conversation
50	Average home
40	Quiet library
30	Soft whisper
20	Quiet room
10	Rustling leaf
0	Hearing threshold

53. What is the sound intensity in an average home?

54. What is the sound intensity of city traffic?

55. Sound levels above 120 decibels can cause pain. What is the intensity for such a sound?

56. What is the intensity of a jet airplane takeoff?

Integrated Review

In Exercises 57–64, evaluate the expression without a calculator.

57. $\log_3 243$ **58.** $\log_2 16$ **59.** $\log_4 16$ **60.** $\log_3 27$

61. $\log_4 256$ **62.** $\log_5 125$ **63.** $\log_2 32$ **64.** $\log_4 1024$

In Exercises 65–70, evaluate the expression.

65. $\log_{10} x$ when $x = 5$ **66.** $\log_{10} 2x$ when $x = 2$ **67.** $3 \log_{10}\left(\frac{1}{2}x\right)$ when $x = 6$

68. $\log_6 x$ when $x = 9$ **69.** $\log_3 3x$ when $x = 2$ **70.** $\log_4 x^2$ when $x = 4$

Exploration and Extension

In Exercises 71 and 72, sketch the graph of the function.

71. $y = \log_{10} 2x - \log_{10} 2$ **72.** $y = \log_4 8x + \log_4 2x$

73. True or False? Explain. $(\log_8 6 - \log_8 3) + \log_8 2 = \log_8 6 - (\log_8 3 + \log_8 2)$

74. True or False? Explain. $2(\log_5 4 - \log_5 3) = \log_5 4^2 - \log_5 3^2$

Take this test as you would take a test in class. The answers to the exercises are given in the back of the book.

In Exercises 1–3, sketch the graph of the function. (8.1)

1. $h(x) = \left(\frac{1}{3}\right)^x - 4$

2. $h(x) = 5^x + 7$

3. $h(x) = 4^{x-2} + 1$

In Exercises 4–6, write the equation in exponential form. (8.2)

4. $\log_2 8 = 3$

5. $\log_5 5 = 1$

6. $\log_7 1 = 0$

In Exercises 7–9, write the equation in logarithmic form. (8.2)

7. $6^0 = 1$

8. $7^1 = 7$

9. $4^3 = 64$

In Exercises 10–15, evaluate the expression, if possible. (8.2)

10. $\log_2 32$

11. $\log_3 0$

12. $\log_3 \frac{1}{27}$

13. $\log_9 9$

14. $\log_2(-8)$

15. $\log_{10} 17$

In Exercises 16–18, expand the expression. (8.3)

16. $\log_{10} 6x$

17. $\log_{10} \frac{3}{a}$

18. $\log_{10} x^4$

In Exercises 19–21, condense the expression. (8.3)

19. $\log_{10} 3 + \log_{10} x$

20. $\log_{10} 7 - \log_{10} b$

21. $4 \log_{10} y$

In Exercises 22–27, use the properties of logarithms to solve for x. (8.2, 8.3)

22. $\log_4 x = 3$

23. $\log_x 64 = 6$

24. $\log_3(x - 2) = 4$

25. $\log_2 x + \log_2 5 = 4$

26. $x \log_4 8 = 3$

27. $\frac{1}{3} \log_9 x = \frac{1}{2}$

28. Sketch the graph of $g(x) = \log_{10} x$. **(8.2)**

29. Given $\log_5 x = 2$, evaluate $\log_x 5$. **(8.2)**

30. 1000 trout fry introduced into a lake are expected to increase at the rate of 37% per year for six years. If that expectation is true, what will be the trout population after six years? **(8.1)**

31. For 1900 to 1990, the population, p (in millions), of the southern states can be modeled by $y = 10 + 15.6(1.195)^t$, where $t = 0$ represents 1900, $t = 1$ represents 1910, and so on. Use the model to estimate the population in The South in 1990.
(Source: U.S. Bureau of Census) **(8.1)**

32. Use the formula $R = \log_{10} I$, where R is the measurement on the Richter scale, to determine the ratio of the intensity, I, of the Mexico City aftershock to the intensity of the earthquake. **(8.3)**

On September 19, 1985, an earthquake measuring R = 8.1 shook Mexico City.

8.4

The Natural Base e

What you should learn:

Goal 1 How to use the number e as a base of an exponential function

Goal 2 How to use the natural base e in real-life problems

Why you should learn it:

Many business and scientific models use the natural base e, such as the formula for compounding interest continually.

Goal 1 Using the Natural Base e

Much of the history of mathematics is marked by the discovery of special types of numbers such as the counting numbers, zero, negative numbers, π, and imaginary numbers.

In this lesson, you will study one of the most famous numbers of modern times. Like π and i, the number is denoted by a letter. The number is called the **natural base e,** or the **Euler number,** after its discoverer, Leonhard Euler (1707–1783).

The Natural Base e

The natural base e is defined to be

$$e = \frac{1}{0!} + \frac{1}{1!} + \frac{1}{2!} + \frac{1}{3!} + \frac{1}{4!} + \frac{1}{5!} + \cdots$$

$$= 1 + 1 + \frac{1}{2} + \frac{1}{6} + \frac{1}{24} + \frac{1}{120} + \cdots$$

$$\approx 2.718281828459.$$

The number e is irrational—its decimal representation does not terminate or follow a repeating pattern.

A function of the form $f(x) = Ce^{bx}$ is a natural-base exponential function, or a base-e exponential function. To evaluate this function, you need a calculator. For instance, to evaluate e^2 on a graphing calculator, you can enter

[2nd] [e^x] 2 [ENTER].   *Display is 7.389056099.*

Example 1 *The Graph of a Base e Function*

Sketch the graph of $f(x) = e^x$.

Solution You can begin by constructing a table of values.

x	-2	-1.5	-1	-0.5	0	0.5	1	1.5	2
e^x	0.14	0.22	0.37	0.61	1	1.65	2.72	4.48	7.39

By plotting points and connecting them with a smooth curve, you can obtain the graph shown at the left. ∎

420   *Chapter 8 ▪ Exponential and Logarithmic Functions*

Example 2 — *Simplifying Natural Base Expressions*

a. $e^2 \cdot e^3 = e^{2+3} = e^5$

b. $\dfrac{6e^2}{2e} = 3e^{2-1} = 3e$

c. $(2e^{-1})^2 = 2^2 e^{-2} = 4e^{-2} = \dfrac{4}{e^2}$　■

The graph of the function $f(x) = Ce^{bx}$ represents exponential growth if b is positive and exponential decay if b is negative.

Example 3 — *Graphs of Natural Base Exponential Functions*

Sketch the graph of each function.

a. $f(x) = 0.5e^{0.6x}$　　　　**b.** $g(x) = 0.5e^{-0.6x}$

Solution

a. The graph of f is an example of exponential growth. The domain of the function is all real numbers, and the range is all positive numbers.

b. The graph of g is an example of exponential decay. The domain of the function is all real numbers, and the range is all positive numbers.

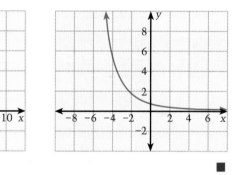

■

The x-axis is a horizontal asymptote of the graph of both functions in Example 3 because if you move far to the left on the graph of $f(x) = 0.5e^{0.6x}$ or far to the right on the graph of $g(x) = 0.5e^{-0.6x}$, you get closer and closer to the x-axis. For instance, when $x = 25$, the value of $g(x)$ is

$$g(25) = 0.5e^{-0.6(25)}$$

$$\approx 0.00000015.$$

In general, the graph of $f(x) = Ce^{bx} + d$ has the line $y = d$ as its horizontal asymptote. For instance, the graph of $f(x) = e^x + 3$ is shown at the left. Its horizontal asymptote is the line $y = 3$.

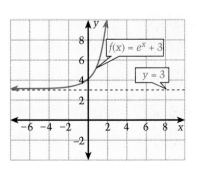

Goal 2 Using the Natural Base e in Real Life

In Lesson 7.2, you studied the formula for the value of an investment in which interest is compounded n times per year.

$$A = P\left(1 + \frac{r}{n}\right)^{nt} \quad \textit{Compounded n times per year}$$

In this formula, A is the balance, P is the initial principal, r is the annual interest rate, n is the number of times the interest is compounded in a year, and t is the number of years. Another common investment formula for compound interest is

$$A = Pe^{rt}. \quad \textit{Compounded continuously}$$

Here the interest is **continuously compounded interest,** and it is roughly equivalent to compounding every second.

Real Life
Banking

Example 4 · *Finding Continuously Compounded Interest*

You deposit $10,000 in an account that pays 6% interest. Find the balance after 10 years if the interest is compounded
a. quarterly.   **b.** continuously.

Solution

a. Compounding quarterly yields a balance of

$$A = 10,000\left(1 + \frac{0.06}{4}\right)^{4(10)} = 10,000(1.015)^{40} \approx \$18,140.18.$$

b. Compounding continuously yields a balance of

$$A = 10,000e^{0.06(10)} = 10,000e^{0.6} \approx \$18,221.19.$$

Thus by compounding continuously, you would obtain a balance that is $81.01 greater than compounding quarterly. This is a characteristic of continuous compounding—it produces a balance that is greater than or equal to the balance obtained by compounding n times per year. ∎

Communicating about ALGEBRA

▶ **SHARING IDEAS about the Lesson**

Sketch the graph of the function. Classify the graph as showing exponential growth or exponential decay.

A. $f(x) = 0.2e^{0.4x}$ **B.** $f(x) = 0.3e^{-0.2x}$

EXERCISES

▶ **CRITICAL THINKING about the Lesson**

1. True or False? $e = \frac{271801}{99990}$. Explain your reasoning.

2. Simplify $\frac{5e^3}{20e^{-2}}$. Check your result with a calculator.

3. Sketch the graph of $f(x) = \frac{1}{2}e^{3x}$. Is this function an example of exponential growth or exponential decay?

4. State the horizontal asymptote of the graph shown at the right. (The function is $f(x) = 2e^x - 2$.)

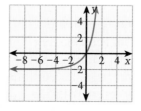

Independent Practice

In Exercises 5–12, use a calculator to evaluate the expression. Round your answer to three decimal places.

5. e^5 **6.** e^3 **7.** $e^{-3/4}$ **8.** $e^{1.2}$

9. $e^{1/2}$ **10.** $e^{1/3}$ **11.** $e^{3.2}$ **12.** $e^{-1/2}$

In Exercises 13–24, simplify the expression.

13. $e^2 \cdot e^4$ **14.** $3e^{-2}e^6$ **15.** $e^x \cdot 4e^{2x+1}$ **16.** $\frac{e^x}{2e}$

17. $\frac{4e^x}{e^{4x}}$ **18.** $e^6 \cdot e^x \cdot e^{-2x}$ **19.** $(3e^{-3x})^{-1}$ **20.** $\left(\frac{1}{2}e^{-3}\right)^3$

21. $(2e^{5x})^2$ **22.** $(10e^{0.5x})^{-4}$ **23.** $\sqrt{4e^2x}$ **24.** $\sqrt[3]{64e^6x}$

In Exercises 25–28, decide whether the function is an example of exponential growth or exponential decay.

25. $f(x) = 3e^{2x}$ **26.** $f(x) = e^{-4x}$ **27.** $f(x) = 4e^{-2x}$ **28.** $f(x) = \frac{1}{9}e^{8x}$

In Exercises 29–32, match the equation with its graph.

29. $f(x) = e^{-2x} + 1$ **30.** $f(x) = 2e^{-x} - 3$ **31.** $f(x) = e^{-3x} - 1$ **32.** $f(x) = 2e^x - 3$

a.

b.

c.

d.

In Exercises 33–44, sketch the graph of the function.

33. $f(x) = 2e^x$ **34.** $f(x) = \frac{1}{2}e^x$ **35.** $f(x) = e^{-x}$ **36.** $f(x) = e^{-4x}$

37. $f(x) = 1.3e^{-0.5x}$ **38.** $f(x) = 3e^{2x} + 2$ **39.** $f(x) = \frac{2}{3}e^x - 1$ **40.** $f(x) = 0.1e^{-x}$

41. $f(x) = 2e^{-1.4x} + 3$ **42.** $f(x) = e^{-3.5x}$ **43.** $f(x) = 0.1e^{2x} - 4$ **44.** $f(x) = \frac{4}{3}e^x + 1$

45. *Continuous Compounding* $600 is deposited in an account that pays 7% annual interest, compounded continuously. What is the balance after 5 years?

46. *Continuous Compounding* $1250 is deposited in an account that pays 6.5% annual interest, compounded continuously. What is the balance after 8 years?

47. *Comparing Types of Compounding* $3000 is deposited in an account that pays 5% annual interest. Compare the balance at the end of 10 years for continuous compounding of interest with the balance for quarterly compounding.

48. *Effective Yield*   The sign at the right is in a bank lobby. What is meant by the effective yield of a savings account?

> ### Our Savings Accounts Pay 6.25% Interest Compounded Continuously
>
> *Effective Yield: 6.45%*

49. *Air Pressure*   The air pressure, P, at sea level is about 14.7 pounds per square inch. As the altitude, h (in feet above sea level), increases, the air pressure decreases. The relationship between air pressure and altitude can be modeled by

$$P = 14.7e^{-0.00004h}.$$

Mount Everest in Tibet and Nepal rises to a height of 29,108 feet above sea level. What is the air pressure at the peak of Mount Everest? What is the ratio of the air pressure at your school to the air pressure at the peak of Mount Everest?

50. *Radioactive Decay*   One hundred grams of radium is stored in a container. The amount of radium, R (in grams), present after t years is given by $R = 100e^{-0.00043t}$ How much of the radium will remain after 10,000 years?

51. *Radioactive Decay*   Sketch the graph of the model in Exercise 50.

52. *Postal Service Expenses*   The amount of money, M (in millions of dollars), spent by the United States Postal Service from 1975 through 1990 can be modeled by $M = 8679e^{0.079t}$, where $t = 5$ represents 1975. Estimate the amount the United States Postal Service spent in 1986.

Pierre and Marie Curie discovered radium. They jointly won a Nobel prize in physics in 1903.

In Exercises 53–56, simplify the expression.

53. $5^{2x}(5^{-x})$

54. $\dfrac{4^{5x}}{4^{2x}}$

55. $(4^{2x})^5$

56. $\left(\dfrac{2^x}{3^x}\right)^{-1}$

57. *Comparing Exponential Growth Curves*
Match the function with its graph. Explain your reasoning.

$f(x) = \left(\dfrac{5}{2}\right)^x$

$g(x) = 3^x$

$h(x) = e^x$

$k(x) = 2^x$

58. *Comparing Exponential Decay Curves*
Match the function with its graph. Explain your reasoning.

$f(x) = \left(\dfrac{1}{2}\right)^x$

$g(x) = \left(\dfrac{1}{3}\right)^x$

$h(x) = e^{-x}$

$k(x) = 3^{-x}$

59. *Alligators*   Let A be the number of pounds of alligator meat sold in Louisiana from 1980 to 1990. Let $t = 0$ represent 1980. Compare the values given by $A = 100{,}835(1.2755)^t$ to the actual data represented by the graph.

60. *Minor League Attendance*   Let A be the average season attendance per team in minor league baseball from 1955 to 1990. Let $t = 0$ represent 1970. Compare the model $A = 93{,}285(1.01473)^t$ to the actual data represented by the graph.

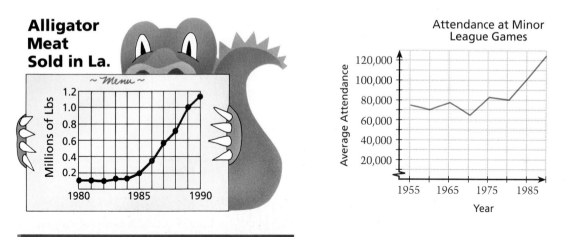

61. Find the first several values of the recursive function. What number is being approached by the values of the recursive function?

$f(0) = \dfrac{1}{0!}, \quad f(n) = f(n-1) + \dfrac{1}{n!}$

62. Complete the table. The function values appear to be getting closer and closer to what number?

n	10^0	10^1	10^2	10^3	10^4	10^5	10^6
$f(n) = \left(1 + \dfrac{1}{n}\right)^n$	?	?	?	?	?	?	?

8.5

Natural Logarithms

What you should learn:

Goal 1 How to evaluate natural logarithmic expressions and graph natural logarithmic functions

Goal 2 How to use natural logarithmic functions as real-life models

Why you should learn it:

You can model many real-life situations with natural logarithmic functions, such as the time an object takes to cool to the temperature of a new environment.

Goal 1 Graphing Natural Log Functions

In Lesson 8.4, the number e was used as a base for an exponent. It is also used as a base for a logarithm, called the **natural base logarithm,** or simply the **natural logarithm.**

> **Natural Logarithm**
>
> If x is a positive real number, then the natural logarithm of x is denoted by
>
> $\log_e x$ or $\ln x$.
>
> (The second notation is more common.) A function given by $f(x) = a + \ln bx$ is called a natural logarithmic function.

Many calculators have a special key for evaluating natural logarithms. For example, to evaluate ln 2 on a graphing calculator, you can use the keystrokes

ln 2 ENTER.   *Display is 0.6931471806.*

Example 1 *Graphing the Natural Log Function*

Sketch the graph of $f(x) = \ln x$.

Solution   You can begin by constructing a table of values.

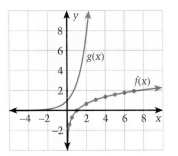

x	0.25	0.5	1	2	3	4	5	6	7
ln x	−1.39	−0.69	0	0.69	1.10	1.39	1.61	1.79	1.95

By plotting points and connecting them with a smooth curve, you can obtain the graph of $f(x)$ shown at the left. The domain of the function is the positive real numbers. The range is all real numbers. ∎

The functions $f(x) = \ln x$ and $g(x) = e^x$ are inverses of each other. This can be verified by observing that the graph of f is the reflection of the graph of g in the line $y = x$. In such a reflection, the x-axis (the horizontal asymptote of the graph of g) becomes the y-axis (the vertical asymptote of the graph of f).

Example 2 **Using Logarithmic Properties to Evaluate Natural Logarithms**

a. $\ln 1 = 0$ because $e^0 = 1$ **b.** $\ln e = 1$ because $e^1 = e$

c. $\ln e^2 = 2$ **d.** $\ln e^{-3} = -3$ ∎

Example 3 **Expanding and Condensing Natural Logarithms**

a. $\ln 3x = \ln 3 + \ln x$

b. $\ln x^3 y = \ln x^3 + \ln y = 3 \ln x + \ln y$

c. $\ln x - \ln 2 = \ln \dfrac{x}{2}$ ∎

Example 4 **Sketching the Graph of a Natural Logarithmic Function**

Sketch the graph of $f(x) = 3 - \ln(x - 2)$.

Solution   The domain of the function is all real numbers that are greater than 2. Thus you can begin by constructing a table of values that uses several x-values greater than 2.

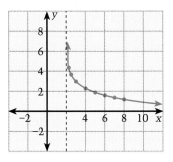

x	2.25	2.5	3	4	5	6	7	8
3 − ln(x − 2)	4.39	3.69	3	2.31	1.90	1.61	1.39	1.21

By plotting points and connecting them with a smooth curve, you obtain the graph shown at the left. The range of the function is all real numbers. The vertical line $x = 2$ is a vertical asymptote of the graph. ∎

In Lesson 8.2, you used a change-of-base formula to evaluate logarithms in bases other than 10 that used common logarithms. A similar formula exists for natural logarithms.

$$\log_a x = \frac{\ln x}{\ln a} \qquad \textit{Change-of-base formula}$$

Example 5 **Using the Change-of-Base Formula**

Use a calculator to evaluate $\log_3 12$.

Solution   Using natural logarithms, you can write

$$\log_3 12 = \frac{\ln 12}{\ln 3} \approx \frac{2.4849}{1.0986} \approx 2.262.$$

You can check the result by raising 3 to the 2.262 power. The result should be approximately 12. ∎

Forensic scientists work in crime laboratories of police departments. Modern crime laboratories use computers and scientific analysis to examine clues.

Goal 2 Using Natural Logarithms in Real Life

Real Life

Forensic Science

Example 6 *Estimating the Time of Death*

At 8:30 A.M., a coroner was called to the home of a person who had died during the night. In order to estimate the time of death, the coroner took the person's body temperature twice. At 9:00 A.M. the temperature was 85.7°F and at 9:30 A.M. the temperature was 82.8°F. The room temperature stayed constant at 70°F. Find the approximate time of death.

Solution   To estimate the time of death, the coroner used Newton's law of cooling

$$kt = \ln \frac{T - S}{T_0 - S}, \quad \textit{Newton's law of cooling}$$

where k is a constant, S is the temperature of the surrounding air, and t is the time it takes for the body temperature to cool from $T_0 = 98.6$ to T. From the first temperature reading, the coroner could obtain $kt \approx -0.6$. From the second temperature reading, the coroner could obtain $k\left(t + \frac{1}{2}\right) \approx -0.8$. Solving these two equations for k and t produces $k = -0.4$ and $t = 1.5$. Therefore, the coroner could approximate that the first temperature reading took place 1.5 hours after death, which implies that the death occurred at about 7:30 A.M. ■

Communicating about ALGEBRA

▶ **SHARING IDEAS about the Lesson**

Show how you can use the following equations to conclude that $k \approx -0.4$ and $t \approx 1.5$ in Example 6.

1st Temperature Reading   **2nd Temperature Reading**

$$kt = \ln \frac{85.7 - 70}{98.6 - 70} \qquad k\left(t + \frac{1}{2}\right) = \ln \frac{82.8 - 70}{98.6 - 70}$$

EXERCISES

Guided Practice

▶ **CRITICAL THINKING about the Lesson**

1. Explain why $\ln e = 1$.

2. Explain why $\ln e^6 = 6$.

3. Sketch the graph of $f(x) = -\ln(x)$. What is the domain of the function? What is the range? How is its graph related to the graph of $f(x) = \ln x$ at the right?

4. Explain how to use natural logarithms to evaluate $\log_6 10$.

Independent Practice

In Exercises 5–7, evaluate the expression without using a calculator.

5. $\ln e^4$

6. $\ln e^{-2}$

7. $\ln\left(\dfrac{1}{e^3}\right)$

In Exercises 8–16, use a calculator to evaluate the expression.

8. $\ln 1.4$

9. $\ln 15$

10. $2 \ln 3$

11. $3.2 \ln 8$

12. $4 \ln 6 + 5$

13. $2 - 5 \ln \dfrac{1}{2}$

14. $\ln 6 - \ln 9$

15. $\ln 2 + \ln 16$

16. $6 \ln 3.3 + 2 \ln 1.5$

In Exercises 17–22, expand the expression.

17. $\ln \dfrac{8}{6x}$

18. $\ln 3xy^2$

19. $\ln 16x^2$

20. $\ln \dfrac{2xy}{x^2}$

21. $\ln \dfrac{2y^7}{x^3}$

22. $\ln 32x^5y$

In Exercises 23–28, condense the expression.

23. $\ln 16 - \ln 4$

24. $\ln 20 + 2 \ln \dfrac{1}{2} + \ln x$

25. $3 \ln 5 - (\ln 15 - \ln 3)$

26. $4 \ln 3 - \ln 9$

27. $3 \ln x + \ln y + \ln 10$

28. $2(\ln 2 - \ln x) + (\ln x - \ln 4)$

In Exercises 29–32, match the function with its graph.

29. $f(x) = \ln(x + 1)$

30. $f(x) = 4 - \ln(x + 4)$

31. $f(x) = \ln\left(x - \dfrac{3}{2}\right)$

32. $f(x) = -\dfrac{3}{2} \ln x$

a.

b.

c.

d.

In Exercises 33–44, sketch the graph of the function.

33. $f(x) = -\ln x$

34. $f(x) = -2 \ln x$

35. $f(x) = 5 + \ln x$

36. $f(x) = \ln x - 4$

37. $f(x) = \ln(x + 9)$

38. $f(x) = -\ln(x - 2)$

39. $f(x) = -10 - \ln(x + 4)$

40. $f(x) = \ln(x + 2) - 1$

41. $f(x) = 1 + \ln(x + 6)$

42. $f(x) = 2 - \ln(x - 1)$

43. $f(x) = \frac{4}{3} \ln(x - 1)$

44. $f(x) = \frac{5}{2} \ln(x + 2)$

In Exercises 45–50, use natural logarithms to rewrite the expression. Then use a calculator to evaluate the expression. Round the result to three decimal places.

45. $\log_2 9$

46. $\log_2 180$

47. $\log_5 4.2$

48. $\log_5 30$

49. $\log_8 \sqrt{3}$

50. $\log_2 1.5$

Making Ice Cubes   **In Exercises 51–53, use the following information.**

You place a tray of 60°F water into a freezer that is set at 0°F. The water cools according to Newton's law of cooling

$$kt = \ln \frac{T - S}{T_0 - S},$$

where T is the temperature (in °F), t is the number of hours the tray is in the freezer, S is the temperature of the surrounding air, and T_0 is the original temperature of the water.

51. If the water freezes in 4 hours, what is the constant k? (Hint: Water freezes at 32°F.)

52. Suppose you lower the temperature in the freezer to -10°F. At this temperature, how long will it take for the ice cubes to form?

53. Suppose the initial temperature of the water is 50°F. If the freezer temperature is 0°F, how long will it take for the ice cubes to form?

54. *Thawing Steaks*   A package of frozen steaks is taken out of the freezer and left at room temperature. The temperature, T (in °F), of the package is related to the time, t (in hours), by the model

$$t = -3.8 \ln \frac{T - 70}{24 - 70}.$$

How long will it take the package to reach a temperature of 60°F?

55. *National Park Salaries*   For 1981 through 1990, the amount, A (in millions of dollars), spent on salaries and wages for National Park Service employees can be modeled by

$$A = 286.52 + 7.25t + 27.51 \ln t,$$

where $t = 1$ represents 1981. About how much was spent on salaries and wages in 1984?

National Park Service Ranger

56. *Median Age of Americans*   For 1980 through 2030, the median age, M (in years), of Americans is predicted to follow the population model

$$M = 19.17 + 0.107t + 4.028 \ln t,$$

where $t = 10$ represents 1980. According to this model, will the median age be increasing or decreasing? Explain.

Integrated Review

In Exercises 57–60, identify the asymptote of the graph of the function.

57. $f(x) = \ln(x + 5)$

58. $f(x) = e^x + 3$

59. $f(x) = e^x - 2$

60. $f(x) = 2 - \ln(x - 1)$

In Exercises 61–64, expand the expression.

61. $\log_{10} \left(\dfrac{x}{y} \right)^2$

62. $\log_4 21x^4$

63. $\log_6 81y^2$

64. $\log_2 \dfrac{16}{x^3 y}$

In Exercises 65–68, condense the expression.

65. $\log_3 6 + \log_3 \frac{1}{2}$

66. $\log_2 3 - \log_2 5$

67. $5(\log_{10} 4 - \log_{10} 2)$

68. $2 \log_{10} x + 3 \log_{10} y$

Exploration and Extension

Logarithmic Spiral   **In Exercises 69 and 70, use the following information.**

The shape of the seashell fossil shown at the right is a logarithmic spiral. Consider a point, P at $(1, 0)$, on the positive x-axis. To form the spiral, the point moves counterclockwise around the origin. The distance, r, between the point and the origin is given by

$$r = e^{0.001745\theta},$$

where θ (the Greek letter *theta*) is the number of degrees through which the point has spiraled.

69. What is the distance between the point and the origin when the point has spiraled through 45°?

70. Write the given equation in logarithmic form. Use the result to find the number of degrees that correspond to an r-value of 2.

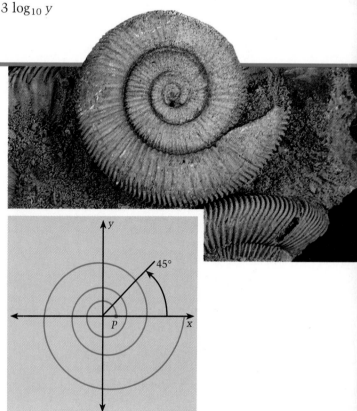

A graphing calculator can be used to fit exponential and logarithmic models of the form

$$y = a(b^x) \quad \text{and} \quad y = a + b \ln x$$

to data. For details on the actual keystrokes, consult the user's manual that accompanies your graphing calculator.

Example 1: Finding an Exponential Model

For 1950 through 1990, the total amount, y (in billions of dollars), of life insurance in the United States is shown in the table. Use a graphing calculator to find an exponential model that approximates these data.

(Source: American Council of Life Insurance)

Year	1950	1955	1960	1965	1970	1975	1980	1985	1990
Amount	234	373	586	901	1402	2314	3541	6053	9198

Solution   Let $x = 0$ represent 1950. Then enter the following coordinates into the statistical data bank of the calculator.

(0, 234), (5, 373), (10, 586), (15, 901), (20, 1402)
(25, 2314), (30, 3541), (35, 6053), (40, 9198)

After running the exponential regression program, the display should read $a \approx 231.5$ and $b \approx 1.0963$. (The correlation of $r \approx 0.9998$ tells you that the fit is very good.) Thus a model for these data is

$$y = 231.5(1.0963)^x.$$

The graph below compares the actual data with the model. ∎

Year (0↔1950)

Example 2:   Finding a Logarithmic Model

A savings account contains $1000, which earns 5% annual interest, compounded continuously. The number of years, y, the money must be left in the account for it to grow to a balance of x dollars is given in the table. Find a logarithmic model for these data.

Balance, x	1000	2000	3000	4000	5000	6000	7000
Years, y	0	13.86	21.97	27.73	32.19	35.84	38.92

Continuously Compounded Savings

Solution   To find a logarithmic model for these data, enter the seven ordered pairs from the table into the statistical data bank of the calculator. Then run the "logarithmic regression" program. The display should read $a \approx -138.2$ and $b \approx 20$. (The correlation of $r \approx 1$ tells you that the fit is nearly perfect.) Thus the model for these data is $y = -138.2 + 20 \ln x$. The graph at the right compares the actual data with the model. ∎

Exercises

In Exercises 1–4, sketch a scatter plot of the data. Then find an exponential or logarithmic model that approximates the data.

1.

x	1	2	3	4	5	6	7	8	9	10
y	0.58	0.66	0.76	0.87	1.01	1.16	1.33	1.53	1.76	2.02

2.

x	1	2	3	4	5	6	7	8	9	10
y	2.42	2.93	3.54	4.29	5.19	6.28	7.59	9.19	11.12	13.45

3.

x	1	2	3	4	5	6	7	8	9	10
y	2.00	2.35	2.55	2.69	2.80	2.90	2.97	3.04	3.10	3.15

4.

x	1	2	3	4	5	6	7	8	9	10
y	5.00	4.58	4.34	4.17	4.03	3.92	3.83	3.75	3.68	3.62

5. *Liz Claiborne, Inc.*   The table shows the annual sales, y (in millions of dollars), for Liz Claiborne, Inc., from 1981 through 1990. Sketch a scatter plot of the data. (Let $x = 1$ represent 1981.). Then find an exponential or a logarithmic model that approximates the data. Use your model to estimate the 1991 sales. *(Source: Liz Claiborne, Inc.)*

Year	1981	1982	1983	1984	1985	1986	1987	1988	1989	1990
Sales, y	116.8	165.7	228.7	391.3	556.6	813.5	1053.3	1184.2	1410.7	1728.9

8.6

Solving Exponential and Logarithmic Equations

What you should learn:

Goal 1 How to solve exponential and logarithmic equations

Goal 2 How to use exponential and logarithmic equations to answer questions about real life

Why you should learn it:

You can solve an exponential equation to solve many real-life problems, such as the length of time your money must be invested to double your principal.

Goal 1 Solving Equations

Consider the exponential equation $2^x = 32$. To solve this equation, you can rewrite it as

$$2^x = 2^5,$$

from which you can conclude that $x = 5$. Suppose, however, that you were asked to solve the equation $2^x = 7$. To solve for x in this equation, you can take the logarithm with base 2 of both sides to obtain the following.

$$2^x = 7 \qquad \textit{Rewrite original equation.}$$

$$\log_2 2^x = \log_2 7 \qquad \textit{Take log with base 2 of both sides.}$$

$$x = \log_2 7 \qquad \textit{Simplify.}$$

The last step uses one of the inverse properties of exponents and logarithms.

Inverse Properties of Exponents and Logarithms

Let a be a positive real number, $a \neq 1$.

Base a	**Base e**
1. $\log_a a^x = x$	$\ln e^x = x$
2. $a^{\log_a x} = x$	$e^{\ln x} = x$

Example 1 Solving an Exponential Equation

Solve $e^x = 72$.

Solution

$$e^x = 72 \qquad \textit{Rewrite original equation.}$$

$$\ln e^x = \ln 72 \qquad \textit{Take ln of both sides.}$$

$$x = \ln 72 \qquad \textit{Simplify.}$$

$$x \approx 4.277 \qquad \textit{Use a calculator.}$$

The solution is $x = \ln 72$. Check this in the original equation. ∎

Example 2 *Solving an Exponential Equation*

Solve $10^x + 5 = 60$.

Solution

$$10^x + 5 = 60 \qquad \textit{Rewrite original equation.}$$

$$10^x = 55 \qquad \textit{Subtract 5 from both sides.}$$

$$\log_{10} 10^x = \log_{10} 55 \qquad \textit{Take log of both sides.}$$

$$x = \log_{10} 55 \qquad \textit{Simplify.}$$

$$x \approx 1.740 \qquad \textit{Use a calculator.}$$

The solution is $x = \log_{10} 55$. Check this in the original equation. ∎

Example 3 *Solving an Exponential Equation*

Solve $4e^{2x} = 5$.

Solution

$$4e^{2x} = 5 \qquad \textit{Rewrite original equation.}$$

$$e^{2x} = \frac{5}{4} \qquad \textit{Divide both sides by 4.}$$

$$\ln e^{2x} = \ln \frac{5}{4} \qquad \textit{Take ln of both sides.}$$

$$2x = \ln \frac{5}{4} \qquad \textit{Simplify.}$$

$$x = \frac{1}{2} \ln \frac{5}{4} \qquad \textit{Divide both sides by 2.}$$

$$x \approx 0.112 \qquad \textit{Use a calculator.}$$

The solution is $x = \frac{1}{2} \ln \frac{5}{4}$. Check this in the original equation. ∎

To solve a logarithmic equation such as

$$\ln x = 3 \qquad \textit{Logarithmic form}$$

write the equation in exponential form as follows.

$$e^{\ln x} = e^3 \qquad \textit{Exponentiate both sides.}$$

$$x = e^3 \qquad \textit{Exponential form}$$

This procedure is called exponentiating both sides of an equation.

Example 4 ▸ Solving a Logarithmic Equation

Solve $5 + 2 \ln x = 4$.

Solution

$$5 + 2 \ln x = 4 \qquad \textit{Rewrite original equation.}$$

$$2 \ln x = -1 \qquad \textit{Subtract 5 from both sides.}$$

$$\ln x = -\frac{1}{2} \qquad \textit{Divide both sides by 2.}$$

$$e^{\ln x} = e^{-1/2} \qquad \textit{Exponentiate both sides.}$$

$$x = e^{-1/2} \qquad \textit{Simplify.}$$

$$x \approx 0.607 \qquad \textit{Use a calculator.}$$

The solution is $x = e^{-1/2}$. Check this in the original equation.
∎

Example 5 ▸ Solving a Logarithmic Equation

Solve $2 \log_{10} 3x = 4$.

Solution

$$2 \log_{10} 3x = 4 \qquad \textit{Rewrite original equation.}$$

$$\log_{10} 3x = 2 \qquad \textit{Divide both sides by 2.}$$

$$10^{\log_{10} 3x} = 10^2 \qquad \textit{Exponentiate both sides.}$$

$$3x = 100 \qquad \textit{Simplify.}$$

$$x = \frac{100}{3} \qquad \textit{Divide both sides by 3.}$$

$$x \approx 33.333 \qquad \textit{Simplify.}$$

The solution is $x = \frac{100}{3}$. Check this solution in the original equation.
∎

When solving exponential or logarithmic equations, the following properties are useful. Can you see where these properties were used in the examples in this lesson?

Properties of Exponential and Logarithmic Equations

Let a be a positive real number.

1. $a^x = a^y$
   if and only if $x = y$.

2. $\log_a x = \log_a y$
   if and only if $x = y$.

Real Life
Finance

Interest rates paid by banks and other savings institutions have varied considerably over the past 20 years. Moreover, interest rates depend on the type of savings account. Typically, passbook accounts pay lower interest rates than certificates of deposit (which require committing a deposit for a specified period of time).

Example 6 *Doubling Time*

You have deposited $500 in an account that pays 6.75% interest, compounded continuously. How long will it take for your money to double?

Solution Using the formula for continuous compounding, you can write

$$A = Pe^{rt} = 500e^{0.0675t}.$$

To find the time required for the balance to double, let $A = 1000$ and solve the resulting equation for t.

$500e^{0.0675t} = 1000$	*Let A = 1000.*
$e^{0.0675t} = 2$	*Divide both sides by 500.*
$\ln e^{0.0675t} = \ln 2$	*Take ln of both sides.*
$0.0675t = \ln 2$	*Simplify.*
$t = \dfrac{1}{0.0675} \ln 2$	*Divide both sides by 0.0675.*
$t \approx 10.27$	*Use a calculator.*

The balance in the account will double after approximately 10.27 years. This result is shown visually in the graph below.

Time (in years)

Communicating about **ALGEBRA**

▶ **SHARING IDEAS about the Lesson**

Solve the following equations. Explain your steps.

A. $4 + 2(3^{2x}) = 12$ **B.** $-3 + 2\ln(x - 3) = 2$

EXERCISES

▶ **CRITICAL THINKING about the Lesson**

1. Explain how to solve $2^x = 10$ by taking the log of both sides of the equation.

2. Explain how to solve $\log_{10} x = 2.4$ by exponentiating both sides of the equation.

3. Which is the correct set of steps in solving $\log_3 4x = 6$? Explain.

   a. $\log_3 4x = 6$
   $$e^{\log_3 4x} = e^6$$
   $$4x = e^6$$
   $$x = \frac{1}{4}e^6$$

   b. $\log_3 4x = 6$
   $$3^{\log_3 4x} = 3^6$$
   $$4x = 3^6$$
   $$x = \frac{1}{4}(3)^6$$

4. Solve $\ln x = 0.5$. Explain your steps.

In Exercises 5–10, decide whether the *x*-value is a solution of the equation.

5. $\ln x = 31$, $x = e^{31}$

6. $\log_5 \frac{1}{2}x = 17$, $x = 2e^{17}$

7. $3 - \log_8 3x = 1$, $x = \frac{64}{3}$

8. $\ln 5x = 4$, $x = \frac{1}{4}e^5$

9. $2e^x = 4$, $x = \ln 2$

10. $e^x + 2 = 18$, $x = \log_2 16$

In Exercises 11–28, solve the exponential equation.

11. $e^x = 12$

12. $2^x = 1.5$

13. $4^x - 5 = 3$

14. $10^{2x} + 3 = 8$

15. $6e^{-x} = 3$

16. $\frac{1}{2}e^{3x} = 20$

17. $5(2)^{3x} - 4 = 13$

18. $1.2e^{-5x} + 2.6 = 3$

19. $-12e^{-x} + 8 = 7$

20. $\frac{2}{3}(3)^{4x} + \frac{1}{3} = 4$

21. $6^{0.1x} + 5 = 10$

22. $\left(\frac{1}{4}\right)^x - \frac{3}{5} = 1$

23. $\frac{1}{2}(8)^{2x} + 2 = 9$

24. $\frac{1}{4}(3)^{-x} - 18 = 18$

25. $10^{-12x} + 6 = 100$

26. $12 + 3(3)^{0.1x} = 16$

27. $4 - 2e^x = -23$

28. $-16 + 0.2(10)^x = 35$

In Exercises 29–46, solve the logarithmic equation.

29. $\ln x = 4$

30. $\log_2 x = -1$

31. $\log_{10} 2x = 1.5$

32. $\ln \frac{1}{2}x = \frac{1}{4}$

33. $4 \log_3 x = 28$

34. $16 \ln x = 30$

35. $1 - 2 \ln x = -4$

36. $\frac{1}{3} \log_2 x + 5 = 7$

37. $2 \ln(-x) + 7 = 14$

38. $8 + 9 \log_{10} x = 3$

39. $3 \log_5 5x = 9$

40. $\frac{1}{2} \log_6 16x = 3$

41. $15 + 2 \log_2 x = 31$

42. $6 \ln 4x - 1 = 14$

43. $-5 + 2 \ln 3x = 5$

44. $2 \log_2 2x = 19$

45. $10 \ln 100x - 3 = 117$

46. $6.5 \log_5 3x = 20$

47. Compound Interest You deposit $1000 in an account that pays 5% annual interest, compounded continuously. How long will it take for the balance to reach $1500?

48. Compound Interest You deposit $2000 in an account that pays 7.5% interest, compounded quarterly. How long will it take for the balance to reach $2400?

49. Doubling Time You deposit $200 in an account that pays 7% annual interest, compounded continuously. How long will it take for the balance to double?

50. Tripling Time You deposit $600 in an account that pays 6% annual interest, compounded monthly. How long will it take for the balance to triple?

51. Municipal Waste For 1960 through 1986, the amount of municipal waste, W (in pounds per person per day), processed for energy recovery in the United States can be approximated by the equation $W = 0.007e^{0.0051t^2}$, where $t = 0$ represents 1960. In what year did the amount of waste reach 0.22 pound per person?

52. Population of Colonial America The first permanent colony in America was established in Jamestown, Virginia, in 1607. For 1610 through 1780, the population, P (in thousands), in colonial America can be modeled by

$$P = 242.4e^{0.00008t^2} - 244,$$

where $t = 10$ represents 1610. When was the population about 345 thousand?

53. Oceanography Oceanographers use the density, d (in grams per cubic centimeter), of seawater to obtain information about the circulation of water masses and the rates at which waters of different densities mix. For water with a salinity of 30%, the water temperature, T (in degrees Celsius), is related to the density by

$$T = 7.9 \ln(1.0245 - d) + 61.84.$$

Find the densities of the subantarctic water and the antarctic bottom water shown in the diagram.

This cross section shows complex currents at various depths in the South Atlantic Ocean off Antarctica.

54. Muon Decay A muon is an elementary particle that is similar to an electron, but much heavier. Muons are unstable—they quickly decay to form electrons and other particles. In an experiment conducted in 1943, the number of muon decays, m (of an original 5000 muons), was related to the time T (in microseconds), by the model $T = 15.7 - 2.48 \ln m$. How many decays were recorded when T was equal to 2.5 microseconds?

Integrated Review

In Exercises 55–60, evaluate the expression for the given value of x.

55. $6 \ln 2x$, $x = 10$

56. $\frac{1}{2} \log_2(-x)$, $x = -5$

57. $6 + e^{4x}$, $x = \frac{2}{3}$

58. $21 - 5 \log_{10} x$, $x = 16$

59. $0.05 \log_3 6x$, $x = 12$

60. $10e^{-x}$, $x = 5$

Your Gasoline Dollar **In Exercises 61 and 62, use the following information.**

The circle graph at the right shows what happens to each dollar spent on gasoline in the United States. *(Source: Computer Petroleum)*

61. Suppose you spend $16 for gasoline. How much of that goes for federal tax?

62. Suppose gasoline costs $1.39 per gallon. How much of the per-gallon price goes to the gasoline dealer?

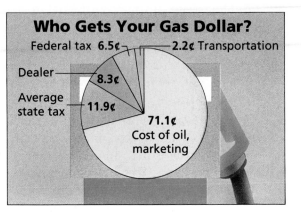

Who Gets Your Gas Dollar?

Federal tax 6.5¢ — 2.2¢ Transportation
Dealer — 8.3¢
Average state tax — 11.9¢
71.1¢ Cost of oil, marketing

Exploration and Extension

63. *Technology* Use a graphing calculator to sketch the graphs of $f(x) = x$, $g(x) = \ln e^x$, and $h(x) = e^{\ln x}$ on the same coordinate plane. What can you conclude about each function?

Mixed **R E V I E W**

1. Simplify: $\sqrt[3]{x^3}$. **(7.4)**

2. Simplify: $\sqrt[5]{64}$. **(7.4)**

3. Simplify: $\sqrt[3]{24a^6b^{14}}$. **(7.4)**

4. Simplify: $\sqrt[3]{9} \cdot \sqrt[3]{15}$. **(7.4)**

5. Simplify: $(2 + 3i)(4 - 5i)$. **(5.5)**

6. Simplify: $(16^{1/3})^{3/4}$. **(7.4)**

7. For $f(x) = 2^x$, find $f(-1)$. **(6.1)**

8. Write $(3a - 2)(2a + 5)$ as a trinomial.

9. Write the inverse of $f(x) = 3x - 1$. **(6.3)**

10. Find the vertex of $y = 3(x + 4)^2 - 7$. **(5.2)**

11. Solve $\sqrt[3]{7a + 1} - 4 = 0$. **(7.5)**

12. Sketch the graph of $y < \frac{3}{4}x - 5$. **(2.5)**

13. Find the geometric mean of $2a^5$ and $8a^3$. **(7.5)**

14. Find the distance from $(-4, -1)$ to $(2, -3)$. **(7.5)**

15. Sketch the graph of $|x - 5| < 3$. **(1.7)**

16. Solve $2x^2 - 3x + 5 = 0$. **(5.4)**

17. Simplify: $\dfrac{a^2b^{-3}}{c^0b^{-2}} \cdot \left(\dfrac{a^{-2}c}{b^{-3}}\right)^4$. **(7.1)**

18. Find the domain of $y = \dfrac{3}{x^2 + 4}$. **(6.2)**

19. $4000 saved at 6% compounded monthly is how much in 5 years? **(7.2)**

20. A rock dropped from a 400-ft bridge hits the water in how many seconds? **(5.1)**

8.7

Exploring Data: Logistics Growth Functions

What you should learn:

Goal 1 How to graph a logistics growth function

Goal 2 How to use logistics growth functions to answer questions about real-life situations

Why you should learn it:

You can model many types of growth using logistics functions, such as the spread of an infectious disease in a small environment.

Connections
Technology

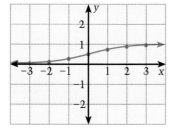

Goal 1 Graphing Logistics Growth Functions

Four common types of mathematical models involving exponential or logarithmic functions are as follows.

1. Exponential Growth: $\quad y = a^x, 1 < a \qquad y = e^{bx}, 0 < b$
2. Exponential Decay: $\quad y = a^x, 0 < a < 1 \quad y = e^{-bx}, 0 < b$
3. Logarithmic: $\qquad\qquad y = \log_{10} bx \qquad y = \ln bx$
4. Logistics Growth: $\qquad y = \dfrac{1}{1 + be^{-cx}}$

You have already studied the first three models. In this lesson, you will study the fourth model.

Logistics growth models are used to represent populations or quantities whose rate of growth changes—from an increasingly rapid growth to a decreasingly rapid growth. An example would be a bacteria culture allowed to grow initially under ideal conditions, followed by less favorable conditions that inhibit growth.

Example 1 *Graphing a Logistics Growth Function*

Sketch the graph of $f(x) = \dfrac{1}{1 + e^{-x}}$.

Solution As usual, begin by using a calculator to construct a table of values.

x	−3	−2	−1	0	1	2	3
f(x)	0.05	0.12	0.27	0.50	0.73	0.88	0.95

Plot the points given by the table of values and connect the points with a smooth curve to obtain the graph at the left.

The domain of the function is all real numbers. The range of the function is $0 < y < 1$. The x-axis is a horizontal asymptote of the graph (to the left), and the line $y = 1$ is a horizontal asymptote of the graph (to the right). ∎

In Example 1, notice that the graph is rising more and more rapidly until it reaches the y-axis. At that point, the graph continues to rise, but at a slower and slower rate. Eventually, for large values of x, the graph is nearly horizontal.

Epidemics are a major threat to human, animal, and plant populations. The worst in recent times was the global influenza epidemic of 1918 and 1919. About 20 million people died worldwide, including about one-half million people in the United States.

Goal 2 Using Logistics Growth Models

Real Life
Epidemiology

Example 2 *Spread of a Virus*

On a college campus of 5000 students, one student returned from vacation with a contagious three-day flu virus. The spread of the virus through the student body can be modeled by

$$y = \frac{5000}{1 + 4999e^{-0.8t}},$$

where y is the total number infected after t days. How many students will have been infected by the end of five days? Sketch a graph of this function.

Solution After five days, the number infected is

$$y = \frac{5000}{1 + 4999e^{-0.8t}} \qquad \textit{Logistics growth model}$$

$$= \frac{5000}{1 + 4999e^{-0.8(5)}} \qquad \textit{Substitute 5 for t.}$$

$$= \frac{5000}{1 + 4999e^{-4}} \qquad \textit{Simplify.}$$

$$\approx 54. \qquad \textit{Use a calculator.}$$

In a similar way, you can compute other values of y, as shown in the table. By plotting the values and connecting them with a smooth curve, you obtain the graph shown at the left.

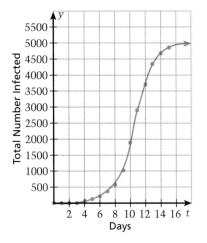

t	0	1	2	3	4	5	6	7
y	1	2	5	11	24	54	119	257

t	8	9	10	11	12	13	14	15
y	537	1057	1868	2851	3735	4340	4680	4851

Real Life
Social Science

The ages at which women and men marry vary from time to time and from country to country. From 1970 to 1990, the median age of American women and men at their first marriage increased by about 3 years.

Example 3   *Median Age of First Marriages*

For 1970 through 1990, the median age, A, of Americans at their first marriage can be modeled by

$$A = 20.4 + \frac{3.1}{1 + 43e^{-0.36t}} \quad \textbf{Women}$$

$$A = 22.4 + \frac{3.3}{1 + 63e^{-0.36t}} \quad \textbf{Men}$$

where $t = 0$ represents 1970. Find the median age of women and men at their first marriage in **(a)** 1970, **(b)** 1980, and **(c)** 1990. *(Source: U.S. Center for Health Statistics)*

Average Age at First Marriage

Solution

	Women	**Men**

a. 1970:

$$20.4 + \frac{3.1}{1 + 43e^{-0.36(0)}} \approx 20.5 \qquad 22.4 + \frac{3.3}{1 + 63e^{-0.36(0)}} \approx 22.5$$

b. 1980:

$$20.4 + \frac{3.1}{1 + 43e^{-0.36(10)}} \approx 21.8 \qquad 22.4 + \frac{3.3}{1 + 63e^{-0.36(10)}} \approx 23.6$$

c. 1990:

$$20.4 + \frac{3.1}{1 + 43e^{-0.36(20)}} \approx 23.4 \qquad 22.4 + \frac{3.3}{1 + 63e^{-0.36(20)}} \approx 25.6$$
∎

Communicating about **A L G E B R A**

▶ **SHARING IDEAS about the Lesson**

Sketch the graphs of the logistics growth functions. Explain your steps. What are the horizontal asymptotes of each graph?

A. $f(x) = \dfrac{2}{1 + e^{-0.5x}}$ **B.** $g(x) = \dfrac{5}{1 + e^{-0.2x}}$

EXERCISES

Guided Practice

▶ **CRITICAL THINKING about the Lesson**

In Exercises 1–4, use the function $f(x) = \dfrac{4}{1 + 4e^{-x}}$.

1. Complete the table of values for the function.

x	−3	−2	−1	0	1	2	3
f(x)	?	?	?	?	?	?	?

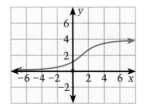

2. What kind of mathematical model is the function?

3. Estimate the horizontal asymptotes of the graph.

4. What are the function's domain and range?

Independent Practice

In Exercises 5–10, identify the type of mathematical model.

5. $f(x) = \ln 2x$

6. $f(x) = e^{-0.11x}$

7. $f(x) = \dfrac{10}{1 + 6e^{-0.5x}}$

8. $f(x) = 4 \log_2(0.5x)$

9. $f(x) = 2000(1.05)^x$

10. $f(x) = 2.04e^{0.8x}$

In Exercises 11–14, match the function with its graph.

11. $f(x) = \dfrac{2}{1 + e^{-2x}}$

12. $f(x) = \dfrac{3}{1 + e^{-x}}$

13. $f(x) = \dfrac{5}{1 + e^{-0.5x}}$

14. $f(x) = \dfrac{3}{1 + e^{-x}} + 1$

a. b. c. d.

In Exercises 15–26, sketch the graph. Identify the horizontal asymptotes.

15. $f(x) = \dfrac{1}{1 + 2e^{-2x}}$

16. $f(x) = \dfrac{1}{1 + 0.8e^{-x}}$

17. $f(x) = \dfrac{5}{1 + e^{-10x}}$

18. $f(x) = \dfrac{4}{1 + 3e^{-3x}}$

19. $f(x) = \dfrac{4}{1 + 0.05e^{-1.2x}}$

20. $f(x) = \dfrac{2}{1 + 2e^{-x}}$

21. $f(x) = \dfrac{10}{1 + 4e^{-x}} - 4$

22. $f(x) = \dfrac{3}{1 + e^{-8x}} + 1$

23. $f(x) = \dfrac{8}{1 + e^{-1.02x}} + 4$

24. $f(x) = \dfrac{4}{1 + 5e^{-4x}} - 2$

25. $f(x) = \dfrac{6}{1 + 0.8e^{-2x}} - 6$

26. $f(x) = \dfrac{12}{1 + 2e^{-x}} + 1$

27. *Stocking a Lake*   A lake has been stocked with 500 trout. During the next several years, the trout population, P, in the lake can be modeled by

$$P = \frac{10,000}{1 + 19e^{-0.2t}},$$

where t is the time in years. Sketch the graph of this model. What is the maximum number of trout that the lake can support? Explain.

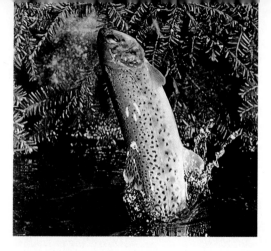

28. *Endangered Species*   One hundred animals of an endangered species have been released into a game preserve that has a carrying capacity of 1000 animals. The population, P, of the herd can be modeled by

$$P = \frac{1000}{1 + 9e^{-0.16t}},$$

where t is the time in years. What is the population after 5 years?

29. *Discontinued Advertising*   In 1980, the manufacturer of Lotus Egg Rolls decided to discontinue all advertising of the product. After that, the annual sales, S (in dollars), can be modeled by

$$S = \frac{500,000}{1 + 0.6e^{0.05t}},$$

where $t = 0$ represents 1980. Did the sales increase or decrease after 1980? Approximate the sales in 1992.

30. *Videocassette Prices*   For 1980 through 1990, the average price, p (in dollars), of a prerecorded videocassette in the United States can be modeled by

$$p = 65.5 - \frac{49.5}{1 + 127e^{-1.175t}},$$

where $t = 0$ represents 1980. Sketch the graph of this function. Explain why the average price was decreasing during the 1980's. *(Source: Paul Kagan Associates, Inc.)*

31. *Videocassette Sales*   For 1980 through 1990, the number, x (in thousands), of prerecorded videocassettes sold in the United States can be modeled by

$$x = 1630 + \frac{82,100}{1 + 1506e^{-1.22t}},$$

where $t = 0$ represents 1980. Use the model given in Exercise 30 to find the total revenue (in $1000s) for prerecorded videocassettes in 1980, 1985, and 1990.
(Source: Paul Kagan Associates, Inc.)

32. *High School Graduates*   For 1980 through 1990, the percent, P, of Americans who had not completed high school can be modeled by

$$P = 33.8 - \frac{10.3}{1 + 25.8e^{-0.833t}},$$

where $t = 0$ represents 1980. What percentage of Americans did not complete high school in 1988? Did the percentage increase or decrease during the 1980's?

Integrated Review

In Exercises 33–36, match the function with its graph. State the domain and range.

33. $f(x) = 2e^x - 3$ **34.** $f(x) = 2\ln(x + 3)$ **35.** $f(x) = -2^x + 3$ **36.** $f(x) = \dfrac{2}{1 + 2e^{-1.5x}}$

a.   **b.**   **c.**   **d.**

37. *College Entrance Exam Sample*
Which is the best approximation of
$5 - \sqrt{32.076} + 1.00017^3$?
  a. 9   **b.** 7   **c.** 5   **d.** 3   **e.** 0

38. *College Entrance Exam Sample*
Which fraction is greater than $\frac{3}{4}$?
  a. $\frac{35}{71}$ **b.** $\frac{13}{20}$ **c.** $\frac{71}{101}$ **d.** $\frac{19}{24}$ **e.** $\frac{15}{20}$

Exploration and Extension

39. *Flu Epidemic*   In a small town, one person has a flu virus. The virus' spread through the population is modeled by

$y = \dfrac{1000}{1 + 990e^{-0.7t}}$, where y is the total number infected after t days.

In how many days will 818 people be infected with the virus?

40. *World Population*   The graph at the right shows the population, P (in billions), of the world as projected by the Population Reference Bureau. The bureau's projection can be modeled by

$$P = \frac{11.14}{1 + 1.101e^{-0.051t}},$$

where $t = 0$ represents 1990. If this model is accurate, what is the maximum world population?

Projected World Population

In Lesson 8.6, you studied how to solve exponential and logarithmic equations by hand. The strategies discussed in that lesson work well for equations such as $2e^{-x} + 5 = 7$ or $\log_{10}(3x - 2) = 8$. Equations that have more than one type of expression, however, cannot usually be solved in such a straightforward manner. For instance, it is not easy to solve the equation $\ln x = x - 2$ by hand. To solve such equations, we usually rely on technology such as a computer or a graphing calculator.

Example: Using a Graphing Calculator to Solve an Equation

For 1980 through 2030, the median age, M, of Americans is predicted to follow the model

$$M = 19.17 + 0.107t + 4.028 \ln t,$$

where $t = 10$ represents 1980. (See Exercise 56, Lesson 8.5.) In 1980 the median age was about 30 (half of all Americans were 30 years old or younger). By 1990, the median age had risen to about 33. According to this model, when will the median age be 40?

Solution   To answer this question, solve the equation

$$40 = 19.17 + 0.107t + 4.028 \ln t.$$

On a graphing calculator, you can sketch the graphs of $y = 40$ and $y = 19.17 + 0.107x + 4.028 \ln x$ and find the point at which the two graphs intersect. From the calculator display shown at the right, you can see that the two graphs intersect when x is about 49. Thus, the median age will be 40 in about 2019. ∎

Exercises

In Exercises 1–6, use a graphing calculator to approximate the solution(s) of the equation. (Some equations may have no solutions.)

1. $\ln x = x - 2$

2. $\log_{10} x = x^2 - 3$

3. $2 \ln x = -x + 4$

4. $e^x = -x + 3$

5. $2^x = x^2$

6. $e^x = 2 + \ln x$

7. *National Park Salaries*   For 1981 through 1990, the amount, A (in millions of dollars), spent on salaries and wages for National Park Service employees can be modeled by $A = 286.52 + 7.25t + 27.51 \ln t$, where $t = 1$ represents 1981. (See Exercise 55, Lesson 8.5.) During which year was the amount spent on salaries and wages about $367 million?

Chapter Summary

What did you learn?

Skills

1. Evaluate and graph an exponential function
- with base a. **(8.1)**
- with natural base e. **(8.4)**

2. Evaluate and graph a logarithmic function
- with base a. **(8.2)**
- with natural base e. **(8.5)**

3. Use properties of logarithms. **(8.3, 8.5)**

4. Solve exponential or logarithmic equations. **(8.6)**

Strategies

5. Use exponential models to solve real-life problems. **(8.1–8.7)**

6. Use logarithmic models to solve real-life problems. **(8.2–8.6)**

Exploring Data

7. Use logistics growth functions as real-life models. **(8.7)**

Why did you learn it?

Many quantities in real life are related exponentially. For instance, in savings accounts in which the interest is compounded continuously, the balances are related to the time by the exponential equation $A = Pe^{rt}$. Other quantities in real life such as the decibel level and intensity of sound are related by logarithmic equations.

Exponential functions and logarithmic functions are inverses of each other. They form an important part of advanced mathematics—especially calculus and probability.

How does it fit into the bigger picture of algebra?

In this chapter, you studied exponential functions and their inverses, called logarithmic functions. Exponential functions are used in real-life situations to model growth that increases by the same percent over equal periods of time. For instance, if you receive a 5% increase in salary each year, your salary could be modeled by an exponential function. (Remember from Chapter 2 that quantities that increase by the same amount over equal periods of time are modeled by linear, not exponential, functions.)

Any positive number other than 1 can be used as a base for an exponential or a logarithmic function. There is, however, a special number that is often used. This important number, called e, is used in the last four lessons of the chapter.

In Exercises 1–9, use a calculator to evaluate the expression. Round your result to three decimal places. (8.1)

1. 8^π

2. $2^{-\sqrt{3}}$

3. $\log_6 10$

4. $\left(\frac{1}{2}\right)^\pi$

5. $\ln 4$

6. $\ln 23$

7. $e^{4.2}$

8. $e^{-2.1}$

9. π^e

In Exercises 10–15, evaluate the expression without using a calculator. (8.2)

10. $\log_2 16$

11. $\log_4 64$

12. $\log_2(-1)$

13. $\log_2 \frac{1}{8}$

14. $\log_3 \frac{1}{9}$

15. $\log_6 1$

In Exercises 16–18, write the equation in exponential form. (8.2)

16. $\log_5 125 = 3$

17. $\log_3 81 = 4$

18. $\log_4 1024 = 5$

In Exercises 19–21, write the equation in logarithmic form. (8.2)

19. $2^5 = 32$

20. $6^3 = 216$

21. $25^{-1/2} = \frac{1}{5}$

In Exercises 22–27, simplify the expression. (8.4)

22. $e^{x-3} \cdot e^{3x}$

23. $4e^{x^2} \cdot 2e^{2x+1}$

24. $\frac{5e^{2x}}{e}$

25. $\frac{e^{-3}}{3e^{2x}}$

26. $(2e^{-4x})^2$

27. $\left(6e^{20x} \cdot \frac{1}{2}e^{-10x}\right)^2$

In Exercises 28–33, expand the expression. (8.5)

28. $\log_{10} 5x^3$

29. $\ln\left(\frac{2x}{x^2}\right)^3$

30. $\ln \frac{7x}{3}$

31. $\log_3 6xy^2$

32. $\log_2 \frac{4x}{3}$

33. $\ln \frac{x^5 y^{-2}}{2y}$

In Exercises 34–39, condense the expression. (8.5)

34. $2 \ln 3 - \ln 5$

35. $\log_2 x + \frac{1}{2} \log_2 9$

36. $\log_4 3 + 3 \log_4 2$

37. $\frac{1}{3} \log_6 8 + \log_6 x + 2 \log_6 y$

38. $\frac{1}{2} \ln 4 + 2(\ln 6 - \ln 2)$

39. $-\frac{3}{2}(\log_{10} x + 2 \log_{10} 2)$

In Exercises 40–48, solve the equation. (8.6)

40. $\log_4 x = 3$

41. $\ln x = 5$

42. $\log_x 256 = 4$

43. $10^x = 4.3$

44. $e^x = 6$

45. $\log_x 729 = 3$

46. $3e^{-x} - 4 = 9$

47. $10 + 0.1e^{3x} = 18$

48. $2(3)^{2x} = 5$

In Exercises 49–54, identify the type of mathematical model. (8.1, 8.2, 8.7)

49. $f(x) = \dfrac{66}{1 + e^{2x}}$

50. $f(x) = e^{-4x}$

51. $f(x) = \ln(x + 3)$

52. $f(x) = \log_{10} x + 4$

53. $f(x) = 10\left(\frac{1}{2}\right)^x$

54. $f(x) = 4 + \dfrac{1}{1 + e^x}$

In Exercises 55–62, match the function with its graph. State the domain and range. (8.1, 8.2, 8.7)

55. $f(x) = 2e^x - 1$

56. $f(x) = -\ln x + 2$

57. $f(x) = -2^x + 4$

58. $f(x) = \dfrac{4}{1 + e^{3x}} - 2$

59. $f(x) = \ln(x + 3)$

60. $f(x) = \log_3 2x$

61. $f(x) = \dfrac{2}{1 + e^{-2x}}$

62. $f(x) = e^{x-1}$

In Exercises 63–74, sketch the graph of the function. (8.1, 8.2, 8.7)

63. $f(x) = 3^{x-2}$

64. $f(x) = \log_3(2x)$

65. $f(x) = \log_{10}(4x)$

66. $f(x) = 2^x + 5$

67. $f(x) = e^{x+5}$

68. $f(x) = -4^x + 2$

69. $f(x) = 3 \log_5 x$

70. $f(x) = -e^x + 3$

71. $f(x) = 3 \ln x + 4$

72. $f(x) = 2e^x - 3$

73. $f(x) = \dfrac{3}{1 + e^{-0.5x}} - 1$

74. $f(x) = \dfrac{2}{1 + e^{2x}} + 1$

75. *Compound Interest*   You deposit $1500 in an account that pays 6.5% annual interest, compounded continuously. Find the balance after 10 years.

76. *Compound Interest*   You deposit $300 in an account that pays 7% annual interest, compounded continuously. Find the balance after 20 years.

77. *Doubling Time*   You deposit $500 in an account that pays 6% annual interest, compounded continuously. How long before your balance doubles? Would a larger deposit double in a shorter time? Explain.

78. *Compound Interest*   You deposit $2500 in an account that pays 7.5% annual interest, compounded quarterly. How long will it take for your balance to become $3000? Would a larger deposit increase by $500 in a shorter time? Explain.

79. *Chemical Reaction* The rate, R, of many chemical reactions can be modeled by $R = ke^{-4727/(T+273)}$, where T is the temperature in degrees Celsius and k is a constant. The chemical reactions that take place when a cake is baked can be approximated by this model. Find the ratio of the chemical reaction rates of batter placed in a 200°C oven to batter placed in a 150°C oven.

80. *Deer Herd* The state Parks and Wildlife Department releases 100 deer into a wilderness area. The population, P, of the herd can be modeled by

$$P = \frac{500}{1 + 4e^{-0.36t}},$$

where t is measured in years. Find the population after 5 years. What is the maximum number of deer that the wilderness area can support?

Fruits and Vegetables **In Exercises 81–83, use the following information.**

The pH of a material is a measure of its acidity or alkalinity. A material with a pH of 7 is neutral. A material with a pH less than 7 is an acid. The pH of a material is given by

$$pH = \log_{10} \frac{1}{H},$$

where H is the concentration of hydrogen ions in moles per liter. The pH values of several fruits and vegetables are shown in the table.

Fruit	pH	Fruit	pH
Apples	3.1	Lemons	2.3
Asparagus	5.6	Oranges	3.5
Cabbage	5.3	Pears	3.8
Cherries	3.6	Potatoes	5.8
Corn	6.3	Pumpkins	5.0
Grapes	4.0	Tomatoes	4.2

81. What is the concentration of hydrogen ions in apples?

82. What is the concentration of hydrogen ions in pumpkins?

83. What is the ratio of the concentration of hydrogen ions in lemons to the concentration of hydrogen ions in grapes?

84. *Car Advertising Expenses* For 1970 through 1990, the amount of money, A (in billions of dollars), spent by new car dealerships on advertising their product line can be modeled by

$$A = 0.11e^{0.2t} + 0.3,$$

where $t = 0$ represents 1970. In what year was about $4.3 billion spent by new car dealerships?

The Stone of the Fifth Sun In Exercises 85–94, use the following information.

This Stone of the Fifth Sun, uncovered in 1790 in Mexico City, is a depiction of the Aztec cosmos. In each exercise, evaluate the function at $x = 2$. Then arrange the function values in ascending order to find the animal or object that is depicted in each of the ten day signs numbered below. (*Hint:* Some of the functions are easier to evaluate if they are first simplified.)

85. Deer: $d(x) = 1 + \dfrac{1}{1 + e^{3x}}$

86. Eagle: $e(x) = \dfrac{e^x}{12e^{-2x}}$

87. Flower: $f(x) = 6^x \cdot 6^4$

88. Grass: $g(x) = \dfrac{3}{1 + e^{-2x}}$

89. Jaguar: $j(x) = (5e^{-2x})^{-1}$

90. Lizard: $l(x) = \ln 4 - 2 \ln x$

91. Monkey: $m(x) = e^{-4x} \cdot e^9$

92. Rabbit: $r(x) = \log_5 5 + \log_5 3x$

93. Serpent: $s(x) = \log_4 3x - \log_4(x + 2)$

94. Wind: $w(x) = 2 \log_2 x - \log_2 8$

In Exercises 1–3, sketch the graph of the function.

1. $f(x) = e^{-x}$

2. $f(x) = \ln(x - 2)$

3. $f(x) = \dfrac{1}{1 + e^{-x}}$

In Exercises 4–6, simplify the expression.

4. $(2e^{-4})(3e^2)$

5. $\dfrac{-6e^x}{2e^2}$

6. $\sqrt{4e^6x^2}$

In Exercises 7–9, evaluate the expression. If appropriate, round your result to three decimal places.

7. $\ln e^3$

8. $\log_3 \dfrac{1}{9}$

9. $\log_6 \sqrt{5}$

In Exercises 10–12, expand the expression.

10. $\ln \dfrac{7x}{2}$

11. $\log_{10} 4x^2$

12. $\ln \dfrac{3x}{4y^2}$

In Exercises 13–15, condense the expression.

13. $\log_4 24 - \log_4 6$

14. $\ln 7 + \ln 8$

15. $3 \ln x - 2 \ln y$

In Exercises 16–18, solve the equation. Round your result to three decimal places.

16. $3e^{5x} = 8$

17. $3 \ln 5x = 27$

18. $\log_5 3x = 4$

19. Write $\ln 5 = x$ in exponential form.

20. Write $e^x = 17$ in logarithmic form.

21. \$4000 is deposited in an account that earns 7% annual interest, compounded continuously. Find the balance at the end of 5 years.

22. Money is deposited in an account that earns 7% annual interest, compounded continuously. How long will it take for the balance to double?

23. For 1980 through 1990, the sales, S (in thousands of dollars), of electronic keyboards can be modeled by

$$y = \dfrac{70}{1 + 0.67e^{-2.2(t-6)}} + 45$$

where $t = 0$ represents 1980. Use the model to estimate the sales of electronic keyboards in 1989.
(Source: USA Today)

24. For 1978 through 1988, the sales, S (in thousands of units), of VCRs can be modeled by

$$y = 0.14(1.78)^t$$

where $t = 1$ represents 1978. Use the model to estimate the year in which 8000 units were sold. *(Source: Electronic Market Data Book)*

25. The ice trays of a freezer are filled with water at 53°F. The freezer maintains a temperature of 20°F. According to Newton's Law of Cooling, the water temperature, T, is related to the time, t (in hours), by the equation

$$kt = \ln\dfrac{T - 20}{53 - 20}.$$

After 1 hour, the water temperature in the ice trays is 40°F. Use the fact that $T = 40$ when $t = 1$ to find how long it takes the water to freeze.

CHAPTER

9

Polynomials and Polynomial Functions

LESSONS

9.1 Operations with Polynomials • 456

9.2 Graphs of Polynomial Functions • 463

9.3 Factoring Polynomials and Solving Polynomial Equations • 473

9.4 Polynomial Division, Factors, and Remainders • 480

9.5 Finding Rational Zeros • 488

9.6 Connections: Zeros, Factors, and Solutions • 494

9.7 Exploring Data: Measures of Dispersion • 501

Rectangular prisms are among the most common structures in our environment, as this photograph of Oahu, Hawaii shows. Yet they give rise to surprising relationships, such as the one described on the opposite page.

Each of the boxes shown has a square base. If a side of the base is x inches, then the height of the box was made to be $h = 54x^{-1} - \frac{1}{2}x$ inches. This implies that the surface area, S, of each box is the same!

$$S = 2x^2 + 4xh = 2x^2 + 4x\left(54x^{-1} - \frac{1}{2}x\right) = 216$$

The volumes of the boxes, however, differ greatly. The volume, V, of each is given by

$$V = x^2\left(54x^{-1} - \frac{1}{2}x\right) = 54x - \frac{1}{2}x^3.$$

In Lesson 9.2, you will be asked to sketch the graph of this *polynomial equation*.

	x	h	S	V
A.	3.0	16.50	216	148.5
B.	4.0	11.50	216	184.0
C.	4.5	9.75	216	197.4
D.	5.0	8.30	216	207.5
E.	6.0	6.00	216	216.0
F.	8.0	2.75	216	176.0
G.	9.0	1.50	216	121.5

9.1

Operations with Polynomials

What you should learn:

Goal 1 How to add, subtract, and multiply polynomials

Goal 2 How to use polynomial operations to solve real-life problems

Why you should learn it:

You can combine two polynomial models to get a new polynomial model, such as using the difference between consumer spending for an item and the cost of its raw materials to find the cost of processing, packaging, and marketing the item.

Goal 1 Adding, Subtracting, and Multiplying

An expression whose terms are of the form $a_k x^k$, where k is a nonnegative integer, is a *polynomial in x*. The real number a_k is the **coefficient** of x^k, and the integer k is the **degree** of $a_k x^k$. For instance, the degree of $a_2 x^2$ is two, the degree of $a_1 x$ is one, and the degree of the **constant term** a_0 is zero. (The coefficient a_k is read as "a sub k.")

Definition of Polynomial in x

A polynomial in x is an expression of the form

$$a_n x^n + \cdots + a_2 x^2 + a_1 x + a_0.$$

If $a_n \neq 0$, then the polynomial is of **degree** n, and the number a_n is called the **leading coefficient.** A polynomial that is written with descending powers of x is in **standard form.** Polynomials with one, two, or three terms are called **monomials, binomials,** or **trinomials,** respectively.

To add or subtract polynomials, add or subtract the coefficients of terms with the same degree. You can use a horizontal or vertical format.

Example 1 *Adding and Subtracting Polynomials*

a. $(2x^2 + 3x) - (3x^2 + x - 4) = 2x^2 + 3x - 3x^2 - x + 4$
$$= -x^2 + 2x + 4$$

b.
$$\begin{aligned} & 4x^3 + 5x^2 - 9x - 3 \\ + & 5x^3 - 2x^2 \qquad\;\; + 2 \\ \hline & 9x^3 + 3x^2 - 9x - 1 \end{aligned}$$
■

A common mistake is to forget to change signs correctly when subtracting one polynomial from another. Here is an example.

Wrong Signs

$$(x^2 - 3x + 4) - (x^2 + 5x - 1) \neq x^2 - 3x + 4 - x^2 + 5x - 1$$

A basic type of polynomial multiplication is that of multiplying a polynomial by a monomial. Here is an example.

$$(6x)(3x^2 + 4x - 1) = (6x)(3x^2) + (6x)(4x) - (6x)(1)$$
$$= 18x^3 + 24x^2 - 6x$$

To multiply two binomials, you can use both left and right Distributive Properties.

$$(2x + 3)(5x - 1) = 2x(5x - 1) + 3(5x - 1)$$
$$= (2x)(5x) - (2x)(1) + (3)(5x) - (3)(1)$$
$$= 10x^2 - 2x + 15x - 3$$

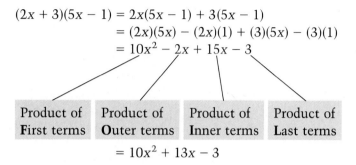

| Product of **First terms** | Product of **Outer terms** | Product of **Inner terms** | Product of **Last terms** |

$$= 10x^2 + 13x - 3$$

This technique for mentally multiplying two binomials in a single step is called using the **FOIL pattern.**

To multiply two polynomials that have three or more terms, remember that *each term of one polynomial must be multiplied by each term of the other polynomial.* This can be done using either a vertical or horizontal format.

Example 2   *Multiplying Polynomials (Vertical Format)*

Multiply: $(x - 3)(4 + 2x - x^2)$.

Solution   Begin by writing each polynomial in standard form.

$$
\begin{array}{rl}
-x^2 + 2x + 4 & \textit{Standard form} \\
\times x - 3 & \textit{Standard form} \\
\hline
3x^2 - 6x - 12 \longleftarrow & -3(-x^2 + 2x + 4) \\
-x^3 + 2x^2 + 4x \longleftarrow & x(-x^2 + 2x + 4) \\
\hline
-x^3 + 5x^2 - 2x - 12 & \textit{Simplified form} \quad\blacksquare
\end{array}
$$

Example 3   *Multiplying Polynomials (Horizontal Format)*

Multiply: $(x - 3)(3x^2 - 2x - 4)$.

Solution

$$(x - 3)(3x^2 - 2x - 4) = (x - 3)(3x^2) - (x - 3)(2x) - (x - 3)(4)$$
$$= 3x^3 - 9x^2 - 2x^2 + 6x - 4x + 12$$
$$= 3x^3 - 11x^2 + 2x + 12 \quad\blacksquare$$

Try using a vertical format and compare your results.

Some binomial products occur so frequently that it is worth memorizing their special product patterns. You can verify each of these products by multiplying. Here is an example.

$$(u - v)^3 = (u - v)(u - v)^2$$
$$= (u - v)(u^2 - 2uv + v^2)$$
$$= u^3 - 3u^2v + 3uv^2 - v^3$$

Special Product Patterns

Sum and Difference   *Example*
$(u + v)(u - v) = u^2 - v^2$ $(x + 4)(x - 4) = x^2 - 16$

Square of a Binomial   *Example*
$(u + v)^2 = u^2 + 2uv + v^2$ $(x + 3)^2 = x^2 + 6x + 9$
$(u - v)^2 = u^2 - 2uv + v^2$ $(3x - 2)^2 = 9x^2 - 12x + 4$

Cube of a Binomial   *Example*
$(u + v)^3 = u^3 + 3u^2v + 3uv^2 + v^3$ $(x + 2)^3 = x^3 + 6x^2 + 12x + 8$
$(u - v)^3 = u^3 - 3u^2v + 3uv^2 - v^3$ $(x - 1)^3 = x^3 - 3x^2 + 3x - 1$

Connections
Geometry

Example 4   *A Polynomial Model for Volume*

A rectangular box has sides whose lengths (in inches) are $(x + 2)$, $(x - 2)$, and $(2x + 1)$. Write a polynomial model, in standard form, for the volume of the box. Then use the model to find the volume when x is equal to 5 inches.

Solution

Verbal Model   Volume $=$ Length $\cdot$ Width $\cdot$ Height

Labels   Volume $= V$ (cubic inches)
      Length $= x + 2$ (inches)
      Width $= x - 2$ (inches)
      Height $= 2x + 1$ (inches)

Model $V = (x + 2)(x - 2)(2x + 1)$
          $= (x^2 - 4)(2x + 1)$
          $= 2x^3 + x^2 - 8x - 4$

When x is 5 inches, the volume is

$$V = 2(5^3) + 5^2 - 8(5) - 4$$
$$= 250 + 25 - 40 - 4$$
$$= 231 \text{ cubic inches.}$$

Check: When $x = 5$ inches, the box has dimensions 7 inches by 3 inches by 11 inches. The volume is

$$(7 \text{ inches})(3 \text{ inches})(11 \text{ inches}) = 231 \text{ cubic inches.}$$ ■

The world's major sources of food are barley, cassava, corn, millet, oats, potato, rice, rye, sorghum, soybeans, sweet potato, and wheat. Some people consume these foods directly. Americans, however, tend to prefer ready-to-eat forms (pasta, bread) or converted forms (meats, eggs). This preference, as you see in Example 5, is costly.

Goal 2 Using Polynomials as Real-Life Models

Real Life
Agriculture

Example 5 — Consumer Expenses for Farm Foods

For 1980 through 1990, the total amount, A (in billions of dollars), spent by Americans for farm foods can be modeled by

$$A = -0.035t^2 + 15.9t + 267.6$$

where $t = 0$ represents 1980. The amount, F (in billions of dollars), paid to farmers can be modeled by

$$F = 0.156t^2 + 0.475t + 81.5.$$

Find a model that represents the amount that was spent on processing, packaging, and marketing the food.

Solution

Let M represent the amount (in billions of dollars) spent on processing, packaging, and marketing the food. To find a model for M, subtract the amount paid to farmers from the total amount.

$$M = A - F$$
$$= (-0.035t^2 + 15.9t + 267.6) - (0.156t^2 + 0.475t + 81.5)$$
$$= -0.191t^2 + 15.425t + 186.1$$

The graphs of all three models are shown at the left. ∎

Food Purchases

Billions of Dollars
400 — A
300
200 — M
100 — F

2 4 6 8 10
Year (0 ↔ 1980)

Communicating about **ALGEBRA**

▶ **SHARING IDEAS about the Lesson**

Perform the indicated polynomial operations. Explain your steps.

A. $(3x^3 - 4x + 5) + (3x^2 + 6x)$ **B.** $(2x - 5)(3x - 9)$
C. $(-x^2 + x - 4) - (2x^2 + 3x - 4)$ **D.** $(x - 5)(x + 5)(2x - 1)$

EXERCISES

▶ **CRITICAL THINKING about the Lesson**

1. Identify the degree, the leading coefficient, and the other coefficients of $-3x^3 + x^2 + 1$.

2. Find two second-degree polynomials whose sum is a first-degree polynomial.

3. Use the FOIL pattern to multiply: $(7x - 1)(2x + 3)$.

4. Use a vertical format to multiply: $(6x + 1)(2x^2 - 3x + 2)$.

In Exercises 5–8, write the polynomial in standard form.

5. $(x + 2)^2$ **6.** $(x - 1)^3$ **7.** $(2x - 1)(2x + 1)$ **8.** $(x - 3)^2$

Independent Practice

In Exercises 9–16, state whether the expression is a polynomial.

9. $2x - x^{-1}$ **10.** $14x + 3$ **11.** $\sqrt{6x^2 + 1}$ **12.** 9

13. $\dfrac{2}{x^2 + 1}$ **14.** 2^x **15.** $(x - 2)^2$ **16.** $\log_{10}(x^2 + 3)$

In Exercises 17–22, write the polynomial in standard form. Then state its degree.

17. $14 + x + 13x^2$ **18.** $\dfrac{2}{3}x - \dfrac{5}{3}x^2$ **19.** $-1 + x^2 + 6x^3$

20. $x^3 + 5x - 2x^2 + 2$ **21.** $-3x^2 + 3 - x^3$ **22.** $-4x^3 + 6x^2 - 19x + 18$

In Exercises 23–36, perform the indicated operation.

23. $(6x^2 + 1) + (5x^2 - 4)$ **24.** $(2x^3 + 11x + 2) - (x^3 - 2x + 7)$

25. $(x^2 - 3x + 3) - (x^2 + x - 1)$ **26.** $(14 - 16x) + (10x - 5)$

27. $(8x^3 - 1) - (20x^3 + 2x^2 - x - 5)$ **28.** $6x - (22x + 3 - 36x^2 + x^3)$

29. $(4x^2 - 15x + 16) + (2x - 20)$ **30.** $(7x^3 - 2 + x^2 + 13x) - (4x^3 + 10)$

31. $(-3x^3 + 4x - 9) - (2x^3 + x^2 - x)$ **32.** $(6x^2 - 18x + 3) - (14x^2 - 12x + 9)$

33. $(15 - 10x^3 - 2x^2 + x) - (x^2 + 7x)$ **34.** $(50x - 3) - (8x^3 + 9x^2 + 2x + 4)$

35. $(4x - 33 + 9x^2) + (20x^3 - 19x + 3)$ **36.** $(12x^3 - 5x^2 - 70x + 1) + (-17x^3 + 56x)$

In Exercises 37–48, perform the indicated operations.

37. $x(x^2 + 9x - 5)$ **38.** $12x^2(x - 8)$ **39.** $-2x(x + 4)$

40. $2x(3x^2 - x + 6)$ **41.** $(x - 2)(x - 4)$ **42.** $(x + 8)(x - 1)$

43. $(x + 3)(x^2 - x + 2)$ **44.** $(x + 9)(x^2 - 6x + 4)$ **45.** $(2x - 1)(3x^3 - x + 3)$

46. $(6x + 2)(2x^2 + x + 1)$ **47.** $(x + 9)(x^2 - 2x + 6)$ **48.** $(2x - 3)(4x^2 - 3x + 3)$

In Exercises 49–57, write the polynomial in standard form.

49. $(x - 9)(x + 9)$

50. $(x + 2)(x - 2)$

51. $(x + 5)^2$

52. $(x - 3)^2$

53. $(x - 4)^3$

54. $(x + 6)^3$

55. $(x + 1)^3$

56. $(3x + 4)^2$

57. $(2x - 1)^2$

In Exercises 58–60, find the area of the blue region.

58.

59.

60.

61. *Age Distribution*   For 1980 through 1994, the population, P (in thousands), of the United States can be modeled by

$$P = 2348t + 226{,}427$$

where $t = 0$ represents 1980. The number, S (in thousands), of people 65 years or older can be modeled by

$$S = -3.53t^2 + 595t + 25{,}584.$$

Write a model that represents the number, y (in thousands), of people under age 65. How many people were under age 65 in 1990?
(Source: U.S. Bureau of Census)

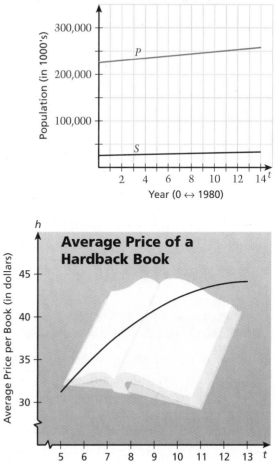

Age Distribution

Population (in 1000's)

Year (0 ↔ 1980)

62. *Hardback Book Revenue*   For 1985 through 1993, the average price for a hardback book, h (in dollars), can be modeled by

$$h = -0.195t^2 + 5.13t + 10.41$$

where $t = 5$ represents 1985. The total number, x (in millions), of hardback books sold in the United States can be modeled by

$$x = -0.316t^2 + 5.49t + 588.$$

Write a model that represents the total revenue, R (in millions of dollars), received from hardback books. What was the revenue in 1991?
(Source: Book Industry Study Group)

Average Price of a Hardback Book

Average Price per Book (in dollars)

Year (5 ↔ 1985)

John Hancock Center **In Exercises 63 and 64, use the following information.**

Each of the four sides of the 100-story John Hancock Center in Chicago, Illinois, are shaped like trapezoids. The height of the building is 28 feet less than 7 times the length of the base along Michigan Avenue. The length of the roof on the Michigan Avenue side of the building is 65 feet shorter than the length of the base below it.

63. The area of the side of the John Hancock Center that faces Michigan Avenue is 149,327.5 square feet. What is the length of the base along Michigan Avenue? How tall is the building?

64. The area of the rectangular roof is 16,000 square feet. What are its dimensions?

Integrated Review

In Exercises 65–68, simplify the expression.

65. $e^{-2} \cdot e^4$ **66.** $(-2)^{x+1}(-2)^3$ **67.** $3^x \cdot 3^2$ **68.** $e^9 \cdot e^{-9}$

69. *Powers of Ten*   Which best approximates the volume of a stack of 12 *National Geographic* magazines?
   a. 2.6×10^0 in.^{3} **b.** 2.6×10^1 in.^{3} **c.** 2.6×10^2 in.^{3} **d.** 2.6×10^3 in.^{3}

70. *Powers of Ten*   Which best approximates the volume of the interior of an automobile?
   a. 1.4×10^2 ft^3 **b.** 1.4×10^3 ft^3 **c.** 1.4×10^4 ft^3 **d.** 1.4×10^5 ft^3

In Exercises 71–76, simplify the expression.

71. $6y^2 + 3y + 3 + y^2$ **72.** $17x^2 - 5 + 3x - 9x^2$ **73.** $x^2 + 2 - (x - 3 + x^2)$

74. $2(6x - 3x^3) - 4(x^3 - 9x)$ **75.** $x^3 + x^2 - 2x^3 + 3x + 4$ **76.** $-10y^3 - 3y + 12y + y^2 + 4y^3$

Exploration and Extension

77. What must you add to $3x^2 - x + 5$ to obtain $-x^2 - 4x + 1$?

78. What must you subtract from $x^3 + 3x - 2$ to obtain $x^3 - x^2 + 1$?

In Exercises 79 and 80, solve for *a*, *b*, and *c*.

79. $(4x^2 + bx + 9) - (ax^2 + 3x - 2) = 2x^2 + x + c$

80. $3x(ax^2 - 5) + (bx + cx^2) = x^3 + 2x^2 - x$

9.2

Graphs of Polynomial Functions

What you should learn:

Goal 1 How to sketch the graph of a polynomial function

Goal 2 How to use polynomial functions as models of real-life situations

Why you should learn it:

You can use a graph to help you visualize the relationships in a polynomial model, such as the model for the amounts of charitable contributions.

Goal 1 Sketching a Polynomial Function

A function of the form

$$f(x) = a_n x^n + a_{n-1} x^{n-1} + \cdots + a_1 x + a_0, \qquad a_n \neq 0$$

is a **polynomial function** of degree n. You know how to sketch the graph of a polynomial function of degree 0, 1, or 2.

Function	Degree	Graph
$f(x) = a$	0	Horizontal line
$f(x) = ax + b$	1	Line of slope a
$f(x) = ax^2 + bx + c$	2	Parabola

The graphs of polynomial functions of degree greater than 2 are more difficult to sketch, as the graphs below illustrate. In this lesson, however, you will learn to recognize some of their basic features. With these features, point-plotting, and intercepts, you will be able to make reasonably accurate sketches by hand. Of course, if you have a graphing calculator or graphing software for a computer, then the task is easier.

Features of Graphs of Polynomial Functions

1. The graph of a polynomial function is **continuous.** This means that the graph has no breaks—you could sketch the graph without lifting your pencil from the paper.
2. The graph of a polynomial function has only smooth turns. A function of degree n has *at most* $n - 1$ turns.
3. If the leading coefficient of the polynomial function is positive, then the graph rises to the right. If the leading coefficient is negative, then the graph falls to the right.

$f(x) = -\frac{1}{3}x^3 + x - \frac{2}{3}$

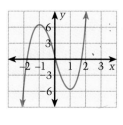

$f(x) = 3x^3 - 9x + 1$

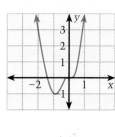

$f(x) = 3x^4 + 4x^3$

$f(x) = x^5 - 5x^3 + 4x$

The polynomial functions that have the simplest graphs are the monomial functions $f(x) = a_n x^n$. When n is *even* the graph is similar to the graph of $f(x) = x^2$. When n is *odd* the graph is similar to the graph of $f(x) = x^3$. Moreover, the greater the value of n, the flatter the graph of a monomial is on the interval $-1 \le x \le 1$.

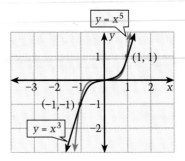

For n even, the graph of $y = x^n$ is tangent to the x-axis at the origin.

For n odd, the graph of $y = x^n$ crosses the x-axis at the origin.

Example 1 Sketching Transformations of Monomial Functions

a. *Reflection*   To sketch the graph of $g(x) = -x^5$ reflect the graph of $f(x) = x^5$ in the x-axis.

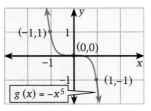

b. *Vertical shift*   To sketch the graph of $g(x) = x^4 + 1$ shift the graph of $f(x) = x^4$ up one unit.

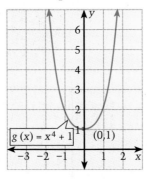

c. *Horizontal shift*   To sketch the graph of $g(x) = (x + 1)^3$ shift the graph of $f(x) = x^3$ one unit to the left (see left).   ■

The y-intercept of the graph of a function occurs when $x = 0$. The x-intercepts are the **zeros** of the function. At an x-intercept, the value of the function is zero.

Example 2   *Sketching a Cubic Polynomial Function*

Sketch the graph of $f(x) = x^3 - 9x$.

Solution   Because the leading coefficient is positive, you know that the graph rises to the right. Also, because the degree of the polynomial function is 3, you know that the graph can have at most two turns. Using these general observations with the values given in the table, you can sketch the graph as shown at the left. Notice that the function has three zeros: -3, 0, and 3.

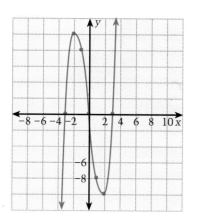

x	-4	-3	-2	-1	0	1	2	3	4
$f(x)$	-28	0	10	8	0	-8	-10	0	28

If the degree of a polynomial function is even, then its graph has the same behavior to the left and right. For instance, the graph of $f(x) = x^4$ rises to the right and rises to the left.

If the degree is odd, the graph has opposite behaviors to the right and left. For instance, the graph of $f(x) = -x^3$ falls to the right and rises to the left.

Example 3   *Identifying the Left and Right Behavior*

a. Because the leading coefficient of $f(x) = -x^3 + 4x$ is negative, the graph falls to the right. Because the degree is odd, the graph rises to the left.

b. Because the leading coefficient of $f(x) = x^4 - 5x^2 + 4$ is positive, the graph rises to the right. Because the degree is even, the graph rises to the left.

c. Because the leading coefficient of $f(x) = x^5 - x$ is positive, the graph rises to the right. Because the degree is odd, the graph falls to the left.

a.

b.   **c.**

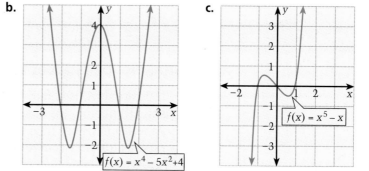

Real Life
Social Science

Example 4 *Charitable Contributions*

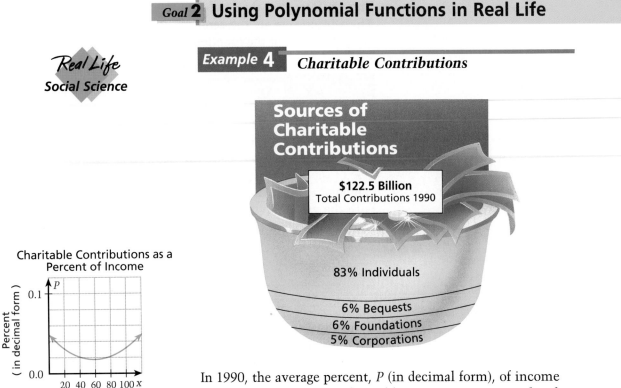

Sources of Charitable Contributions

$122.5 Billion
Total Contributions 1990

83% Individuals

6% Bequests
6% Foundations
5% Corporations

Charitable Contributions as a
Percent of Income

Percent
(in decimal form)

0.1

0.0

20 40 60 80 100 *x*
Income (in $1000's)

In 1990, the average percent, *P* (in decimal form), of income that Americans gave to charitable organizations was related to their income, *x* (in thousands of dollars), by the model

$$P = 0.000014x^2 - 0.001529x + 0.05855, \qquad 5 \le x \le 100.$$

Use this model to write a model for the average amount given.
(Source: **Giving and Volunteering in the United States***)*

Solution To find the average amount, *A*, that an individual gave to charity, you can multiply the average percent-of-income model by the income (1000*x*) to obtain

$$A = 1000x(0.000014x^2 - 0.001529x + 0.05855)$$
$$= 0.014x^3 - 1.529x^2 + 58.55x, \qquad 5 \le x \le 100.$$

The graphs of both models are shown at the left. ∎

Amount of Charitable
Contributions

Amount Given to Charity
(in dollars)

6000
5000
4000
3000
2000
1000

20 40 60 80 100 *x*
Income (in $1000's)

Communicating about **A L G E B R A**

▶ **SHARING IDEAS about the Lesson**

In Example 4, is it fair to say that in 1990 Americans whose annual income was about $55,000 gave less to charity than Americans whose income was lower or higher? Give reasons for your conclusion.

EXERCISES

Guided Practice

▶ **CRITICAL THINKING about the Lesson**

1. Explain what is meant by a continuous graph.

2. Name a feature of the graph of $f(x) = |x|$ that is *not* shared by graphs of polynomial functions.

3. Does the graph of $f(x) = 13x^4 - 3x$ rise or fall to the right? How can you tell?

4. Which is the graph of $f(x) = 2x^5 - 2$? Explain.

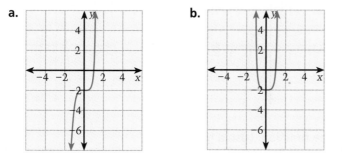

a.   **b.**

5. How is the graph of $g(x) = x^4 + 3$ related to the graph of $f(x) = x^4$?

6. Find the zeros of $f(x) = x^2 + 2x - 15$.

Independent Practice

In Exercises 7–10, describe the transformation of g that would produce f.

7. $f(x) = (x - 5)^3$
  $g(x) = x^3$

8. $f(x) = x^4 + 3$
  $g(x) = x^4$

9. $f(x) = -x^6$
  $g(x) = x^6$

10. $f(x) = (x + 1)^5$
  $g(x) = x^5$

In Exercises 11–14, state the maximum number of turns in the graph.

11. $f(x) = 2x^5 - x + 6$

12. $f(x) = \frac{1}{2}x^3 + 1$

13. $f(x) = x^4 + 9x - 1$

14. $f(x) = -2x^6 + 3x + 7$

In Exercises 15–24, describe the left and right behaviors of the graph.

15. $f(x) = -5x^4$

16. $f(x) = -x^2$

17. $f(x) = 2x^2$

18. $f(x) = 10x^3$

19. $f(x) = -x^6 + 2x^3 - x$

20. $f(x) = \frac{1}{2}x^5 + 4x^2$

21. $f(x) = x^5 - 4x^4 + 4x^2 + 3$

22. $f(x) = -x^5 + 3x^3 + x$

23. $f(x) = 6x^7 - 3x^3 + 2x - 3$

24. $f(x) = 3x^6 - x - 11$

In Exercises 25–30, match the function with its graph.

25. $f(x) = x^3 - 5x$

26. $f(x) = -x^4 + x + 4$

27. $f(x) = -x^3 + 2x^2$

28. $f(x) = -x^5 + 3x^3 + 1$

29. $f(x) = x^5 - 3x^3 + 2$

30. $f(x) = x^4 - 4x^2 + x$

a.

b.

c.

d.

e.

f.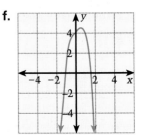

In Exercises 31–48, sketch the graph of the function. (Use a graphing calculator for Exercises 43–48.)

31. $f(x) = -x^3$

32. $f(x) = -x^4$

33. $f(x) = x^5 + 1$

34. $f(x) = x^4 - 2$

35. $f(x) = (x + 2)^4$

36. $f(x) = (x - 4)^3$

37. $f(x) = -(x - 3)^3$

38. $f(x) = -(x + 2)^5$

39. $f(x) = (x + 2)^4 - 6$

40. $f(x) = (x + 1)^3 + 3$

41. $f(x) = -x^5 - 2$

42. $f(x) = -x^4 + 8$

43. $f(x) = -x^3 + 4x^2$

44. $f(x) = x^5 + x^2 - 10x - 6$

45. $f(x) = x^3 - 8x^2 + x - 1$

46. $f(x) = x^5 + x$

47. $f(x) = x^5 + 3x^3 - x$

48. $f(x) = x^4 - 2x + 6$

In Exercises 49–51, find the zeros of the function.

49. $f(x) = x^2 + 9x - 4$

50. $f(x) = 2x^2 - 2x - 1$

51. $f(x) = -2x^2 - 3x + 6$

52. *Maximum Volume*   The volume of each of the boxes on page 455 is given by $V = 54x - \frac{1}{2}x^3$, where x is the length of each side of the base. Sketch the graph of this function. Which box has the greatest volume?

53. *Stock Ownership Plans*   From 1975 through 1990, the number of employee stock ownership plans, S, in the United States can be modeled by $S = 4.2t^3 - 148t^2 + 2210t - 6380$, where $t = 5$ represents 1975. Sketch the graph of this function. How many plans were there in 1982?

54. *Clothes Cleaning Services*   From 1980 through 1990, the annual revenue, R (in millions of dollars), for laundry and dry cleaning can be modeled by $R = 12.2(t^4 - 16.3t^3 + 86t^2 - 92t + 754)$ where $t = 0$ represents 1980. Sketch the graph of this function. What was the revenue in 1988?

55. *Making a Box* An open box is to be made from a 10-in. by 12-in. piece of cardboard by cutting x-in. squares from each corner and folding up the sides. Write a function giving the volume of the box in terms of x. Sketch the graph of the function and use it to approximate the value of x that produces the greatest volume.

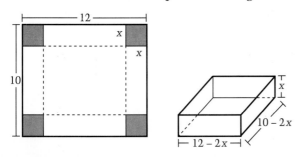

56. *Putting a Lid on It* Using a 10-in. by 12-in. piece of cardboard, you construct a box with a lid, as shown. Write a function that gives the volume in terms of x. Sketch the graph and use it to approximate the value of x that produces the greatest volume.

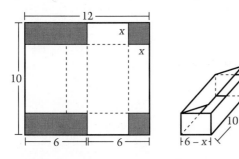

Integrated Review

In Exercises 57—62, sketch the graph of the function.

57. $f(x) = 6$

58. $f(x) = -x + 2$

59. $f(x) = \frac{1}{2}x - 1$

60. $f(x) = x^2 - 2x + 6$

61. $f(x) = -x^2 + 4x - 3$

62. $f(x) = -2x^2 - x + 1$

63. *College Entrance Exam Sample* In the equation $y = x^2 + rx - 3$, for what value of r will $y = 11$ when $x = 2$?

    a. 6   **b.** 5   **c.** 4   **d.** $3\frac{1}{2}$ **e.** 0

64. *College Entrance Exam Sample* If a cubic inch of metal weighs 2 pounds, a cubic foot of the same metal weighs how many pounds?

    a. 8   **b.** 24   **c.** 96   **d.** 288   **e.** 3456

Exploration and Extension

In Exercises 65–68, find a polynomial function that has only the given zeros.

65. $2, -1$

66. $0, 1, 2$

67. $1, -3, -1, 0$

68. $2, -2, 3, -3$

Sketching the graph of a polynomial function with a graphing calculator can be tricky. The problem is in finding screen boundaries that will display the basic shape of the graph. For instance, both of the screens below show a portion of the graph of $f(x) = 4x^3 + 2x^2 - x + 12$. The screen on the left, however, is not as good a view for seeing the basic characteristics of the graph as the screen on the right.

Example 1:   Sketching the Graph of a Polynomial Function

For 1970 through 1990, the amount, P (in millions of dollars), spent for public elementary and secondary schools can be modeled by

$$P = -0.2t^4 + 15t^3 - 53t^2 + 4667t + 40{,}724$$

where $t = 0$ represents 1970. For private schools, the total amount, R (in millions of dollars), can be modeled by

$$R = -0.2t^4 + 6t^3 - 19t^2 + 261t + 2508.$$

Find bounds for x and y that will show the relevant portions of the graphs of both models.

Solution   Because the models represent the years from 1970 through 1990, you can set the horizontal bounds to be

$0 \le t \le 20.$ ***Horizontal bounds***

When $t = 20$, the value of P is 200,864 and the value of R is 16,128. Because it is reasonable to assume that the expenses were increasing, you can set the vertical bounds to be

$0 \le y \le 210{,}000.$ ***Vertical bounds***

The graph is shown at the right.   ■

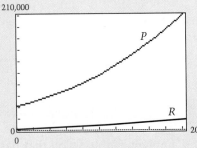

One of the reasons that polynomial functions are important is that they can be used as approximations for other types of functions. (If you go on to study calculus, you will encounter this use of polynomials.)

Example 2: Comparing the Graphs of Two Functions

The graph of the polynomial function

$$f(x) = 1 + x + \frac{1}{2}x^2 + \frac{1}{6}x^3 + \frac{1}{24}x^4 + \frac{1}{120}x^5 + \frac{1}{720}x^6$$

can be used as an approximation of the graph of $g(x) = e^x$. Find bounds for x and y for which the graphs of f and g appear to be the same.

Solution   Using trial and error, you can find the graphs to be close to each other over the interval $-2.5 \le x \le 2.5$. ■

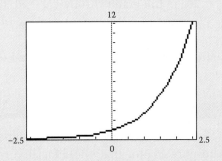

Exercises

In Exercises 1–6, find bounds for x and y that display the basic characteristics of the graph of the polynomial function.

1. $f(x) = x^3 + 6x^2 - 11x + 3$

2. $f(x) = -x^3 + 25x^2 + 4$

3. $f(x) = x^4 - 5x^2 + 6$

4. $f(x) = -x^4 - 3x^3 + x^2 - x + 5$

5. $f(x) = x^5 - 10x^4 + 35x^3 - 50x^2 + 24x$

6. $f(x) = -x^5 + 5x^3 - 4x + 10$

7. Sketch the graph of $f(x) = (x - 1)(x - 2)(x - 3)$. What are the zeros?

8. Find bounds for x and y for which the graphs of f and g appear the same.

$$f(x) = 1 - x^2 + x^4 - x^6 + x^8 - x^{10} \quad \text{and} \quad g(x) = \frac{1}{x^2 + 1}$$

9. *Company Profit*   For 1980 through 1992, the profit, P (in millions of dollars), for a company can be modeled by

$$P = -t^3 + 10t^2 + 3t + 204$$

where $t = 0$ represents 1980. Find appropriate bounds for x and y for the graph of this function. For which year (between 1980 and 1992) was the profit the greatest?

1. Sketch $f(x) = 3x^2 - 12x + 5$. **(5.2)**
2. Solve $|3x - 4| = 6$. **(1.7)**
3. Subtract: $\frac{4}{5} - \frac{2}{7}$.
4. Solve $3x^2 - 2x + 1 = 0$. **(5.6)**
5. Simplify: $(2 + 3i)^2$. **(5.5)**
6. Simplify: $\sqrt{48a^2b^4c^7}$. **(7.4)**
7. Evaluate $16^{3/4}$. **(7.3)**
8. Find the y-intercept of $f(x) = 5^x - 3$. **(8.1)**
9. Sketch $f(x) = \left(\frac{1}{7}\right)^x + 2$. **(8.1)**
10. Find the x-intercept of $f(x) = e^{x+3}$. **(8.1)**
11. Find the y-intercept of $y = \dfrac{1}{1 + e^{-x}}$. **(8.7)**
12. Find the geometric mean of 4 and 27. **(7.5)**
13. Sketch $f(x) = \log_{10}(x - 5)$. **(8.2)**
14. Evaluate $e^{\ln 4}$. **(8.6)**
15. Expand $\ln \dfrac{8x}{3}$. **(8.3)**
16. Solve: $\log_7 x = 5$. **(8.2)**
17. Find the distance from $(2, -5)$ to $(-6, -2)$. **(7.5)**
18. \$2000 at 8% compounded continuously is how much in 10 years? **(8.4)**
19. Write an equation of the line through $(4, -5)$ perpendicular to $y = -\frac{2}{3}x + 4$. **(2.4)**
20. Is the graph through $(1, -3)$, $(2, -1)$, $(3, 2)$, and $(4, 3)$ linear, quadratic, or neither? **(6.6)**

Career Interview

Administrator

Nancy Hsu is the administrator of a nursing home. "I am like a mayor. I am responsible for the whole facility, from keeping budgets to planning menus to conducting fire drills."

Q: *What math did you take in school?*
A: I love math. I took algebra, trigonometry, and calculus in high school and more calculus in college.

Q: *Does having a math background help you on the job?*
A: All the time. Recently I was figuring out how much cleaning solution to order each month. I had to consider the quantity needed per gallon per room per month and also the storage space available.

Q: *How has new technology changed your job experiences?*
A: Computer spreadsheet programs save me the most time. I can plan and respond to budget changes instantly. For example, if there is a 10% budget cut, the spreadsheet shows me the impact immediately.

Q: *Are mental math and estimation strategies helpful?*
A: Mental math and estimation allow me to respond to a situation or question quickly and with reasonable accuracy.

Q: *What would you like to tell kids about math?*
A: Think of mathematics as a language, like learning French or Spanish. To be good at it, you need to practice.

9.3

Factoring Polynomials and Solving Polynomial Equations

What you should learn:

Goal 1 How to factor polynomial expressions and equations

Goal 2 How to use factoring to solve real-life problems

Why you should learn it:

You can model many real-life situations with polynomials that can be factored, such as the model for the velocity that a basketball player must achieve to make a slam dunk.

Goal 1 Factoring Expressions and Equations

LESSON INVESTIGATION

■ Investigating Factoring Patterns

Partner Activity From Algebra 1, remember that **factoring** a polynomial means to write it as the product of polynomials of lesser degrees. With your partner, use the factoring techniques you learned in Algebra 1 to factor each of the following. In each case, describe the factoring pattern.

1. Common monomial	$3x^2 + 6x$
2. Difference of Squares	$4x^2 - 9$
3. Perfect-Square Trinomial	$x^2 - 8x + 16$
4. Factorable Trinomial	$x^2 - 4x + 3$

Example 1 *Factoring Polynomials Completely*

a. $3x - 12x^3 = 3x(1 - 4x^2)$ *Common monomial*

$\quad\quad\quad\quad = 3x(1 - 2x)(1 + 2x)$ *Difference of squares*

b. $16x^4 - 81 = (4x^2 - 9)(4x^2 + 9)$ *Difference of squares*

$\quad\quad\quad = (2x - 3)(2x + 3)(4x^2 + 9)$ *Difference of squares*

c. $2x^3 + 12x^2 + 18x = 2x(x^2 + 6x + 9)$ *Common monomial*

$\quad\quad\quad\quad\quad\quad = 2x(x + 3)^2$ *Perfect-square trinomial*

d. $6x^2 + 21x + 9 = 3(2x^2 + 7x + 3)$ *Common monomial*

$\quad\quad\quad\quad\quad = 3(2x + 1)(x + 3)$ *Factorable trinomial*

e. $x^4 - 4x^2 + 3 = (x^2 - 1)(x^2 - 3)$ *Factorable trinomial*

$\quad\quad\quad\quad = (x - 1)(x + 1)(x^2 - 3)$ *Difference of squares* ■

Study Tip

A polynomial with integer coefficients is completely factored with respect to the integers if it cannot be further factored using integer coefficients.

None of the polynomials in Example 1 can be factored further without using fractions, irrational numbers, or imaginary numbers.

$$2x - 3 = 2\left(x - \frac{3}{2}\right)$$ *Requires fractions.*

$$x^2 - 3 = (x - \sqrt{3})(x + \sqrt{3})$$ *Requires irrational numbers.*

$$4x^2 + 9 = (2x - 3i)(2x + 3i)$$ *Requires imaginary numbers.*

Special Factoring Patterns

Sum of Two Cubes
$$u^3 + v^3 = (u + v)(u^2 - uv + v^2)$$
   Example: $x^3 + 8 = (x + 2)(x^2 - 2x + 4)$

Difference of Two Cubes
$$u^3 - v^3 = (u - v)(u^2 + uv + v^2)$$
   Example: $27x^3 - 1 = (3x - 1)(9x^2 + 3x + 1)$

Factoring by Grouping
$$au^3 + acu^2 + bu + bc = au^2(u + c) + b(u + c) = (au^2 + b)(u + c)$$
   Example: $x^3 + 2x^2 + 3x + 6 = x^2(x + 2) + 3(x + 2)$
$$= (x^2 + 3)(x + 2)$$

Example 2   *Factoring the Sum or Difference of Cubes*

Factor the polynomials.
a. $x^3 - 27$ **b.** $3x^3 + 192$

Solution

a. $x^3 - 27 = x^3 - 3^3$ *Difference of cubes*
$$= (x - 3)(x^2 + 3x + 9)$$

b. $3x^3 + 192 = 3(x^3 + 4^3)$ *Sum of cubes*
$$= 3(x + 4)(x^2 - 4x + 16)$$ ■

Example 3   *Factoring by Grouping*

Factor the polynomials.
a. $4x^3 - 6x^2 + 10x - 15$ **b.** $x^3 - 2x^2 - 4x + 8$

Solution

a. $4x^3 - 6x^2 + 10x - 15 = 2x^2(2x - 3) + 5(2x - 3)$
$$= (2x^2 + 5)(2x - 3)$$

b. $x^3 - 2x^2 - 4x + 8 = (x^3 - 2x^2) - (4x - 8)$
$$= x^2(x - 2) - 4(x - 2)$$
$$= (x - 2)(x^2 - 4)$$
$$= (x - 2)(x - 2)(x + 2)$$
$$= (x - 2)^2(x + 2)$$ ■

The **Zero Product Property** states that if the product of two factors is zero, then one (or both) of the factors must be zero.

Zero Product Property

Let a and b be real numbers. If $ab = 0$, then $a = 0$ or $b = 0$.

This property connects factoring to solving equations. For instance, to solve the equation

$$(2x + 1)(x - 4) = 0$$

you can use the Zero Product Property to conclude that either $(2x + 1)$ or $(x - 4)$ must be zero. Setting $2x + 1$ equal to zero produces the solution $x = -\frac{1}{2}$. Setting $x - 4$ equal to zero produces the solution $x = 4$.

The Zero Product Property can be generalized to include equations with more than two factors, as shown in Example 4.

Example 4 *Solving a Polynomial Equation by Factoring*

Solve $3x^4 = 48x^2$.

Solution   The basic approach is to write the polynomial equation in standard form first (with zero on the right side of the equation), factor the left side, and then set each factor equal to zero.

$$3x^4 = 48x^2 \qquad \textit{Given equation}$$

$$3x^4 - 48x^2 = 0 \qquad \textit{Collect terms on left side.}$$

$$3x^2(x^2 - 16) = 0 \qquad \textit{Common monomial factor}$$

$$3x^2(x + 4)(x - 4) = 0 \qquad \textit{Difference of two squares}$$

$$\left.\begin{array}{l} 3x^2 = 0 \longrightarrow x = 0 \\ x + 4 = 0 \longrightarrow x = -4 \\ x - 4 = 0 \longrightarrow x = 4 \end{array}\right\} \begin{array}{l} \textit{Zero} \\ \textit{Product} \\ \textit{Property} \end{array}$$

The equation has three solutions: 0, −4, and 4. Check these solutions in the original equation. ■

When solving the equation shown in Example 4, some people like to divide both sides of the equation by 3. This does help simplify the equation a little. Remember, however, that you cannot divide both sides of an equation by a variable such as $3x^2$. Doing this would "lose" $x = 0$ as one of the solutions.

Goal 2 Using Factoring in Real-Life Problems

**World Trade Center,
New York City**

Example 5 *A Trip to the World Trade Center*

Each of the twin towers of the World Trade Center in New York City has a volume of 1,695,744 cubic meters. One of the tour guides at the World Trade Center, who is a Michael Jordan fan, likes to tell tour groups the following riddle. From these clues, can you find the dimensions of each tower?

Each tower of the World Trade Center is 207 times as tall as Michael Jordan. The base of each tower is square. To find the length of each side of the base, subtract 1 meter from Michael Jordan's height and multiply the result by 64.

Solution Let x represent Michael Jordan's height (in meters).

Verbal Model

| Volume | = | Height | · | Length | · | Width |

Labels

Volume = 1,695,744	(cubic meters)
Height = $207x$	(meters)
Length = $64(x - 1)$	(meters)
Width = $64(x - 1)$	(meters)

Equation $1,695,744 = 207x \cdot 64(x - 1) \cdot 64(x - 1)$

You can solve this equation as follows.

$$207x(64^2)(x - 1)^2 = 1,695,744 \quad \text{\textit{Model for volume}}$$

$$x(x - 1)^2 = 2 \quad \text{\textit{Divide both sides by} } 207(64^2).$$

$$x^3 - 2x^2 + x - 2 = 0 \quad \text{\textit{Standard form}}$$

$$x^2(x - 2) + (x - 2) = 0 \quad \text{\textit{Factor by grouping.}}$$

$$(x - 2)(x^2 + 1) = 0 \quad \text{\textit{Factored form}}$$

From the factored form, you can see that $x = 2$. So Michael Jordan's height is 2 meters. Thus each tower is 414 meters high and has a base that is 64 meters square. ∎

Communicating about ALGEBRA

▶ SHARING IDEAS about the Lesson

Solve the equations by factoring. Explain your steps.

A. $x^3 - 2x^2 = 9x - 18$ **B.** $x^4 - 29x^2 + 100 = 0$

EXERCISES

Guided Practice

▶ **CRITICAL THINKING about the Lesson**

1. What does it mean for a polynomial with integer coefficients to be completely factored with respect to the integers? Give an example of such a second-degree polynomial that cannot be further factored with respect to the integers.

In Exercises 2–5, factor completely with respect to the integers.

2. $81x^4 - 1$ **3.** $16x^3 - 64x$ **4.** $1 - 64x^3$ **5.** $2x^3 - 8x^2 + 3x - 12$

6. What is wrong with the following solution steps?

$2x^4 - 18x^2 = 0$	*Original equation*
$2x^2(x^2 - 9) = 0$	*Common monomial factor*
$2x^2(x + 3)(x - 3) = 0$	*Difference of squares*
$(x + 3)(x - 3) = 0$	*Divide both sides by $2x^2$.*
$x + 3 = 0 \longrightarrow x = -3$	*Zero-Product Property*
$x - 3 = 0 \longrightarrow x = 3$	*Zero-Product Property*

Independent Practice

In Exercises 7–14, find the missing factor.

7. $10x^4 - 40x^2 = (\ ?\ )(x + 2)(x - 2)$ **8.** $8x^3 - 18x = 2x(2x + 3)(\ ?\ )$

9. $6x^3 + 9x = 3x(\ ?\ )$ **10.** $18x^3 - 6x^2 + 3x = (\ ?\ )(6x^2 - 2x + 1)$

11. $3x^3 + 24 = 3(\ ?\ )(x^2 - 2x + 4)$ **12.** $16x^3 - 54 = 2(2x - 3)(\ ?\ )$

13. $3x^3 + 12x^2 + 2x + 8 = (\ ?\ )(x + 4)$ **14.** $14x^3 + 7x^2 + 10x + 5 = (7x^2 + 5)(\ ?\ )$

In Exercises 15–50, factor completely with respect to the integers.

15. $9x^2 - 4$	**16.** $3x^2 - 48$	**17.** $x^3 - 8$	**18.** $x^3 + 64$
19. $216x^3 + 1$	**20.** $125x^3 - 1$	**21.** $200x^2 - 50$	**22.** $32x^3 - 4$
23. $128x^3 - 2$	**24.** $8x^3 - 64$	**25.** $3x^3 + 81$	**26.** $40x^3 - 5$

27. $x^3 + x^2 + x + 1$	**28.** $30x^3 + 40x^2 + 3x + 4$	**29.** $x^3 + 2x^2 + 5x + 10$
30. $x^3 - 2x^2 + 4x - 8$	**31.** $9x^3 + 18x^2 + 7x + 14$	**32.** $-2x^3 - 4x^2 - 3x - 6$
33. $2x^3 + 4x^2 + 4x + 8$	**34.** $18x^3 + 30x^2 + 3x + 5$	**35.** $2x^3 - 2x^2 + 5x - 5$
36. $2x^3 + 3x^2 - 32x - 48$	**37.** $5x^3 - 20x^2 + 3x - 12$	**38.** $18x^3 - 2x^2 + 27x - 3$
39. $7x^3 + 14x^2 + 7x$	**40.** $3x^2 - 24x + 48$	**41.** $2x^3 - 4x^2 - 3x + 6$
42. $6x^3 - 18x^2 - 2x + 6$	**43.** $3x^3 - 24$	**44.** $x^3 + 125$
45. $3x^4 - 300x^2$	**46.** $28x^3 - 7x$	**47.** $3x^4 + 3x^3 + 6x^2 + 6x$
48. $x^4 + 12x^3 + 4x^2 + 48x$	**49.** $10x^3 - 20x^2 - 2x + 4$	**50.** $18x^3 - 9x^2 - 18x + 9$

In Exercises 51–62, find all real-number solutions.

51. $x^2 - 3x = 0$

52. $2x^3 - 6x^2 = 0$

53. $x^2 + 8x + 16 = 0$

54. $x^2 - 4x + 4 = 0$

55. $x^3 - 15x^2 + 75x - 125 = 0$

56. $x^3 + 3x^2 + 3x + 1 = 0$

57. $2x^2 - x = 3$

58. $x^2 + 3x = 10$

59. $x^3 + 3x^2 - 2x - 6 = 0$

60. $x^4 + 7x^3 - 8x - 56 = 0$

61. $x^3 + 2x^2 - x = 2$

62. $x^3 - x^2 + 2x = 2$

Making a Slam Dunk **In Exercises 63–65, use the following information.**

A basketball hoop is 10 feet above the playing floor. To make a "slam dunk," a player must jump high enough to reach $10\frac{1}{2}$ feet. The November, 1991 issue of *Popular Mechanics* analyzed the mechanics of a slam dunk as follows.

"If you take a person's height, H (in feet), subtract the distance from the top of the head to the shoulder (about 1 foot), and then add half of the result (about one arm's length), you obtain the formula $R = \frac{3}{2}(H - 1)$, where R is the person's standing reach in feet."

Using this model, the initial velocity, v (in feet per second), at which a person must jump to make a slam dunk is given by

$$\frac{21}{2} - \frac{3}{2}(H - 1) = \frac{1}{64}v^2$$

63. Copy and complete the table.

Height, H	5.5	6.0	6.5	7.0	7.5
Reach, R	?	?	?	?	?
Velocity, v	?	?	?	?	?

64. Popular Mechanics states that "perhaps the most amazing dunker in professional basketball is 5'7" Spud Webb, of the Atlanta Hawks." With what initial velocity must Webb jump to make a slam dunk?

65. Let h (in feet) be the distance between a player's shoes and the floor and let v be the initial velocity in feet per second. Then h and v are related by the equation $h = -16t^2 + vt$. What is Spud Webb's minimum hang time—the time that he must be in the air to make a slam dunk?

66. *Weather Balloon* A heavy piece of equipment falls from a weather balloon that is 1600 feet above the ground. Let h be the height (in feet) above ground of the piece of equipment. Use factoring and the vertical motion model $h = -16t^2 + 1600$ to find the time, t (in seconds), that the piece of equipment takes to hit the ground.

67. *Room Dimensions* A rectangular room has an area of 160 square feet. The length of the room is 6 feet more than its width. Find the dimensions of the room.

68. *Big Ben* Big Ben is the name of a famous bell in a clock tower in London and also the name of its clock tower. Let x represent one-third the diameter of Big Ben, the bell. The volume of Big Ben, the clock tower (not counting the belfry) is 336,000 cubic feet. What are the dimensions of the clock tower if it has a square base? What is the diameter of the bell at its widest place?

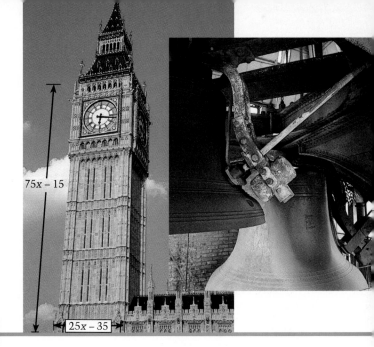

$75x - 15$

$25x - 35$

Integrated Review

In Exercises 69–74, write in standard polynomial form.

69. $(x + 4)^2$ **70.** $(x - 2)^2$

71. $(x - 3)^3$ **72.** $(x + 1)^3$

73. $(x + 9)^3$ **74.** $(x - 5)^3$

In Exercises 75–78, find all real and imaginary solutions.

75. $2x^2 + 2x - 60 = 0$ **76.** $x^2 + x + 1 = 0$

77. $4x^2 + x - 3 = 0$ **78.** $3x^3 - 18x = 0$

Exploration and Extension

In Exercises 79 and 80, find all integers b such that the trinomial can be factored using integer coefficients.

79. $x^2 + bx + 15$ **80.** $x^2 + bx - 12$

In Exercises 81 and 82, find all real and imaginary solutions of the equation.

81. $9x^5 - 4x^3 + 9x^2 - 4 = 0$

82. $x^5 - 4x^3 + 8x^2 - 32 = 0$

83. *Geometry* The cube at the right is formed by four solids: I, II, III, and IV. Explain how the figure can be used as a geometric factoring model for the *difference of two cubes* factoring pattern.

$$a^3 - b^3 = (a - b)(a^2 + ab + b^2)$$
$$= (a - b)a^2 + (a - b)ab + (a - b)b^2$$

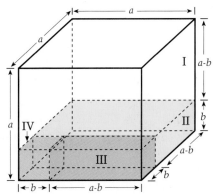

9.4

Polynomial Division, Factors, and Remainders

What you should learn:

Goal 1 How to divide polynomials using long division and synthetic division and relating the quotient to the Remainder Theorem and the Factor Theorem

Goal 2 How to use polynomial division in real-life problems

Why you should learn it:

You can factor many polynomial models to find other solutions, such as alternate prices that will give the same amount of profit.

Goal 1 Dividing Polynomials

There are two algorithms for polynomial division: *long division* and *synthetic division*. Of the two, synthetic division is quicker, but long division is more general—it will work for divisors of any degree. (Synthetic division works *only* for divisors of the form $x \pm k$.) An example of how long division can be used to divide $x^2 + 3x + 5$ by $x + 1$ is shown.

$$
\begin{array}{r}
x + 2 \leftarrow \text{Quotient} \\
\text{Divisor} \longrightarrow x + 1 \overline{)x^2 + 3x + 5} \leftarrow \text{Dividend} \\
\underline{x^2 + x} \\
2x + 5 \\
\underline{2x + 2} \\
3 \leftarrow \text{Remainder}
\end{array}
$$

You can write this result as follows.

$$
\underbrace{\frac{\overbrace{x^2 + 3x + 5}^{\text{Dividend}}}{\underbrace{x + 1}_{\text{Divisor}}}} = \overbrace{x + 2}^{\text{Quotient}} + \frac{\overbrace{3}^{\text{Remainder}}}{\underbrace{x + 1}_{\text{Divisor}}}
$$

If there is a zero remainder, then the divisor *divides evenly* into the dividend.

Example 1 *Long Division of Polynomials*

Divide $2x^4 + 4x^3 - 5x^2 + 2x - 3$ by $x^2 + 2x - 3$.

Solution

$$
\begin{array}{r}
2x^2 + 1 \\
x^2 + 2x - 3 \overline{)2x^4 + 4x^3 - 5x^2 + 2x - 3} \\
\underline{2x^4 + 4x^3 - 6x^2} \\
x^2 + 2x - 3 \\
\underline{x^2 + 2x - 3} \\
0
\end{array}
$$

This result can be written as follows.

$$
\frac{2x^4 + 4x^3 - 5x^2 + 2x - 3}{x^2 + 2x - 3} = 2x^2 + 1
$$

∎

When the divisor is of the form $x \pm k$, an abbreviated form of long division, called **synthetic division,** can be used. The pattern for synthetic division of a cubic polynomial is summarized below.

Synthetic Division (of a Cubic Polynomial)

To divide $ax^3 + bx^2 + cx + d$ by $x - k$, use the following pattern. (The pattern for higher-degree polynomials is similar.)

Coefficients of Quotient   (in decreasing order)

Vertical Pattern: Add terms.
Diagonal Pattern: Multiply by k.

Note: k can be positive or negative. For instance, if you divide by $(x + 2) = (x - (-2))$, then $k = -2$.

Example 2   *Using Synthetic Division*

Use synthetic division to divide $x^4 - 10x^2 + 2x + 3$ by $x - 3$.

Solution   When setting up the synthetic division array, you must include a zero for each "missing" term in the dividend.

$$
\begin{array}{r|rrrrr}
3 & 1 & 0 & -10 & 2 & 3 \\
  &   & 3 & 9 & -3 & -3 \\
\hline
  & 1 & 3 & -1 & -1 & 0 \leftarrow \text{Remainder: } 0
\end{array}
$$

Quotient: $x^3 + 3x^2 - x - 1$

In fractional form, you can write the result as follows.

$$\frac{x^4 - 10x^2 + 2x + 3}{x - 3} = x^3 + 3x^2 - x - 1$$

You can check this result by multiplying. That is,

$$(x - 3)(x^3 + 3x^2 - x - 1) = x^4 - 10x^2 + 2x + 3.$$

The use of long division to obtain the same result is shown at the left.   ■

Be sure you see that synthetic division works *only* for divisors of the form $x - k$. You cannot, for example, use synthetic division to divide a polynomial by a quadratic such as $x^2 + 4$. For that, you would have to use long division.

$$
\begin{array}{r}
x^3 + 3x^2 - x - 1 \\
x - 3 \overline{)\, x^4 \quad\quad - 10x^2 + 2x + 3} \\
\underline{x^4 - 3x^3} \\
3x^3 - 10x^2 \\
\underline{3x^3 - 9x^2} \\
-x^2 + 2x \\
\underline{-x^2 + 3x} \\
-x + 3 \\
\underline{-x + 3} \\
0
\end{array}
$$

The remainder obtained when dividing has an interesting connection to polynomial functions.

Remainder Theorem

If a polynomial $f(x)$ is divided by $(x - k)$, then the remainder is
$r = f(k)$.

Example 3 *Evaluating a Polynomial by the Remainder Theorem*

Evaluate $f(x) = 3x^3 + 8x^2 + 5x - 7$ at $x = -2$.

Solution Begin by using synthetic division.

$$
\begin{array}{r|rrrr}
-2 & 3 & 8 & 5 & -7 \\
   &   & -6 & -4 & -2 \\
\hline
   & 3 & 2 & 1 & -9
\end{array}
$$

Because the remainder is -9, you can conclude from the Remainder Theorem that $f(-2) = -9$. ∎

Factor Theorem

A polynomial $f(x)$ has a factor $(x - k)$ if and only if $f(k) = 0$.

Example 4 *Using Synthetic Division to Find Factors of a Polynomial*

Given that $f(x) = 2x^3 + 11x^2 + 18x + 9$ has $x = -3$ as a zero, factor $f(x)$.

Solution Because $f(-3) = 0$, you know that $(x - (-3))$, which is equal to $(x + 3)$, is a factor of $f(x)$. Using synthetic division produces the following.

$$
\begin{array}{r|rrrr}
-3 & 2 & 11 & 18 & 9 \\
   &   & -6 & -15 & -9 \\
\hline
   & 2 & 5 & 3 & 0
\end{array}
$$

Thus you can write

$$2x^3 + 11x^2 + 18x + 9 = (x + 3)(2x^2 + 5x + 3)$$
$$= (x + 3)(2x + 3)(x + 1).$$

The complete factorization is $(x + 3)(2x + 3)(x + 1)$. ∎

In business, the demand function gives the price per unit as a function of the number of units sold. The demand function whose graph is shown at the immediate right is $p = 40 - 5x^2$, where p is in dollars and x is measured in millions of units. Note that to increase sales, the price must decrease. The revenue, R, (in millions of dollars) is given by

$$R = xp = x(40 - 5x^2).$$

Real Life
Business

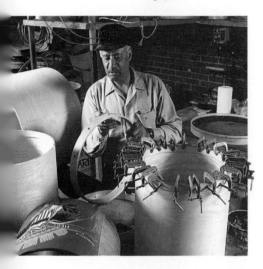

Economic models are used by both large and small businesses, such as this company in Essex, Conn., that handcrafts drums.

Example 5 *Making a Profit*

The cost of producing the product whose demand function is shown above is $15 per unit. The total cost, C (in millions of dollars), of producing x million units is $15x$. The total profit, P (in millions of dollars), for selling these x million units is

$$P = R - C = x(40 - 5x^2) - 15x = -5x^3 + 25x.$$

By selling 1,600,000 units ($x = 1.6$) at $27.20 each, the company made a profit of $19,520,000 ($P = 19.52$). Find a smaller unit sales that would have produced the same profit.

Solution Let $P = 19.52$ and solve the resulting equation.

$$-5x^3 + 25x = 19.52 \quad \text{or} \quad -5x^3 + 25x - 19.52 = 0$$

Because one solution is $x = 1.6$, you know that $(x - 1.6)$ is a factor of the left side of the equation. Using synthetic division, you can factor the left side to obtain

$$(x - 1.6)(-5x^2 - 8x + 12.2) = 0.$$

Using the Quadratic Formula, solve $-5x^2 - 8x + 12.2 = 0$. The company could have made the same profit by selling approximately 955,000 units ($x \approx 0.955$) at $39.09 each. ∎

Communicating about ALGEBRA

▶ **SHARING IDEAS about the Lesson**

In Example 5, approximate the maximum profit that the company could have made. What price per unit should the company charge to obtain a maximum profit?

EXERCISES

▶ **CRITICAL THINKING about the Lesson**

1. Write the result of the long division at the right in fractional form.

2. Does $x^2 - 3$ divide evenly into

   $4x^4 + x^3 - 12x^2 + 3x$?

   Justify your answer.

3. What kind of divisor is required for synthetic division?

$$\begin{array}{r} 2x^2 + 3x - 1 \\ x - 1\overline{)2x^3 + x^2 - 4x + 2} \\ \underline{2x^3 - 2x^2} \\ 3x^2 - 4x \\ \underline{3x^2 - 3x} \\ -x + 2 \\ \underline{-x + 1} \\ 1 \end{array}$$

4. Write the polynomial divisor, dividend, and quotient that the synthetic division below represents.

$$\begin{array}{r|rrr} 1 & 2 & 6 & 0 & -8 \\ & & 2 & 8 & 8 \\ \hline & 2 & 8 & 8 & 0 \end{array}$$

5. Evaluate $f(x) = 2x^3 + 6x^2 - 8$ at $x = 1$.

6. Factor $2x^3 + 6x^2 - 8$ completely.

In Exercises 7–18, use long division. Write the result in fractional form.

7. $(x^2 + 7x - 2) \div (x - 2)$

8. $(2x^2 + x - 1) \div (x + 4)$

9. $(3x^2 + 9x + 1) \div (x + 3)$

10. $(x^2 - 5x + 4) \div (x - 1)$

11. $(4x^4 + 5) \div (x^2 + 1)$

12. $(x^3 + 6x^2 - 5x + 20) \div (x^2 + 5)$

13. $(6x^4 + 2x^3 + 5x^2 + 3x) \div (3x^2 + x - 2)$

14. $(10x^3 + 27x^2 + 14x + 5) \div (x^2 + 2x)$

15. $(2x^3 + 3x^2 - 4x - 7) \div (x^2 - 2)$

16. $(2x^4 + 2x^3 - 10x - 9) \div (x^3 + x^2 - 5)$

17. $(5x^4 + 18x^3 + 10x^2 + 3x) \div (x^2 + 3x)$

18. $(x^4 + 3x^3 - 5x^2 - 8x + 6) \div (x^2 + 2x - 6)$

In Exercises 19–30, use synthetic division. Write the result in fractional form.

19. $(x^3 - 7x + 6) \div (x - 2)$

20. $(x^3 - 28x - 48) \div (x + 4)$

21. $(4x^2 + 3x - 3) \div (x + 1)$

22. $(7x^2 + 4x + 3) \div (x + 2)$

23. $(2x^2 + 7x + 8) \div (x - 2)$

24. $(4x^2 - 6x) \div (x - 2)$

25. $(x^2 + 9) \div (x + 3)$

26. $(x^2 + 3) \div (x + 3)$

27. $(10x^4 + 5x^3 + 4x^2 - 9) \div (x + 1)$

28. $(x^4 - 2x^3 - 70x + 20) \div (x - 5)$

29. $(2x^4 - 6x^3 + x^2 - 3x - 3) \div (x - 3)$

30. $(4x^4 + 5x^3 + 2x^2 - 1) \div (x + 1)$

In Exercises 31–36, use the Remainder Theorem to evaluate the function.

31. $f(x) = 4x^2 - 10x - 21$ at $x = 5$

32. $f(x) = 6x^3 - x^2 - 16x$ at $x = 2$

33. $f(x) = 2x^2 - 2x + x + 1$ at $x = 4$

34. $f(x) = 4x^4 + x^2 + 6x + 2$ at $x = -1$

35. $f(x) = 5x^4 + 2x^3 - 20x - 6$ at $x = 2$

36. $f(x) = x^2 - 26x + 7$ at $x = 5$

In Exercises 37–42, find the missing factors.

37. $x^3 - 8x^2 + 4x + 48 = (x - 4)(\,?\,)(\,?\,)$

38. $2x^3 - 14x^2 - 56x - 40 = (x - 10)(\,?\,)(\,?\,)$

39. $x^3 + 2x^2 - 5x - 6 = (x + 3)(\,?\,)(\,?\,)$

40. $x^3 - 13x^2 + 24x + 108 = (x + 2)(\,?\,)(\,?\,)$

41. $6x^3 - 24x^2 - 42x + 60 = 2(x - 5)(\,?\,)(\,?\,)$

42. $x^4 + 14x^3 + 51x^2 + 54x = x(x + 9)(\,?\,)(\,?\,)$

Geometry   **In Exercises 43–45, you are given an expression for the volume of the solid shown. Find an expression for the missing dimension.**

43. $V = 3x^3 + 8x^2 - 45x - 50$ **44.** $V = x^3 + 18x^2 + 80x + 96$ **45.** $V = 2x^3 + 17x^2 + 40x + 25$

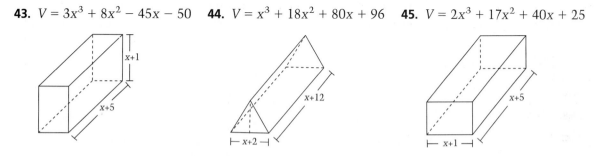

Points of Intersection   **In Exercises 46–48, find all points of intersection of the two graphs. One intersection occurs at $x = 1$.**

46.   **47.**   **48.**

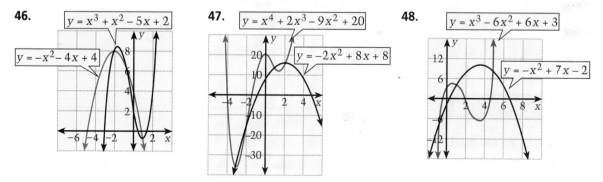

49. *Company Profit*   The demand function for a type of camera is given by the model $p = 100 - 8x^2$ where p is measured in dollars and x is measured in millions of units. The production cost is $25 per camera. A sale of 2.5 million cameras produced a profit of $62.5 million. What other amount of cameras could the company sell to make the same profit?

50. *Company Profit*   Suppose the company described in Example 5 on page 483 had sold 200,000 units. How much profit did the company make? Would any fewer unit sales produce the same profit? Would any larger unit sales produce the same profit? Explain.

Integrated Review

In Exercises 51–56, factor completely.

51. $3x^2 - 27$

52. $2x^3 + 54$

53. $2x^2 - 18x - 20$

54. $9 - 36x^2$

55. $12x^3 - 12x^2 + 3x - 3$

56. $2x^3 + 4x^2 + 12x + 24$

57. *Eating Pasta*   In 1990, the retail sales of pasta in the United States totaled about $1.3 billion. How much was spent on spaghetti and linguini? How much was spent on noodles? (*Source: National Pasta Association*)

58. *Eating Salad*   1000 people were asked how often they eat salad. Of those surveyed, how many eat salad once or twice a day? Less than once a month?

(*Source: The Association for Dressings and Sauces*)

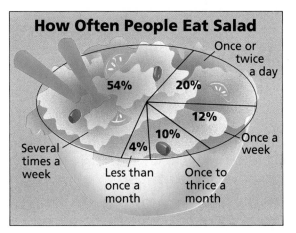

Exploration and Extension

In Exercises 59 and 60, factor completely.

59. $x^4 - 2x^3 - 17x^2 + 18x + 72$

60. $x^4 - 11x^3 + 42x^2 - 64x + 32$

61. *Counterfeit Coins*   You are given ten stacks of silver dollars. Each stack contains ten coins. Nine of the stacks are completely genuine and one is completely counterfeit. You are told that a genuine silver dollar weighs 26.7 grams and a counterfeit silver dollar weighs 27.7 grams. You are given a scale and are allowed to weigh any number of coins, but you are allowed *only one* weighing! How many coins should you weigh to be sure of identifying the counterfeit stack?

Take this test as you would take a test in class. The answers to the exercises are given in the back of the book.

In Exercises 1–4, perform the indicated operation. **(9.1)**

1. $(3x^3 - 4x^2 + 7) + (5x^2 - 7x - 4)$

2. $(8x^4 - 3x^2 + 7x) - (x^4 - 5x^3 - 3x^2 + 2)$

3. $3x^2(2x^3 - 4x^2 + 5)$

4. $(3x - 7)(2x + 1)$

In Exercises 5 and 6, sketch the graph of the function. **(9.2)**

5. $f(x) = x^3$

6. $f(x) = (x - 2)^4$

In Exercises 7–10, completely factor the polynomial with respect to the integers. **(9.3)**

7. $16x^2 - 9$

8. $6x^3 - 21x^2$

9. $4x^2 - 20x + 25$

10. $8x^3 - 125$

In Exercises 11 and 12, find all real-number solutions. **(9.3)**

11. $12x^2 + 7x = 10$

12. $16x^4 - 81 = 0$

In Exercises 13 and 14, use long division to write the quotient. **(9.4)**

13. $(10x^2 - 11x - 6) \div (2x - 3)$

14. $(12x^4 - 5x^2 - 3) \div (3x^2 + 1)$

In Exercises 15 and 16, use synthetic division to write the quotient. **(9.4)**

15. $(3x^4 + 12x^3 - 5x^2 - 18x + 8) \div (x + 4)$

16. $(x^3 - 2x^2 - 9) \div (x - 3)$

17. Use the remainder theorem to evaluate $f(x) = 3x^3 - 7x^2 + 4x - 2$ when $x = -2$. **(9.4)**

18. Completely factor $x^3 - 5x^2 - 2x + 24$, given that $(x - 4)$ is a factor. **(9.4)**

19. For 1910 through 1990, the number, $f(t)$, of representatives from New England in the House of Representatives can be modeled by $f(t) = -1.17t + 32.9$, where $t = 1$ represents 1910, $t = 2$ represents 1920, and so on. The number of representatives from California can be modeled by $g(t) = 4.9t + 5.2$. Write a linear function that models the number of representatives from New England and California combined. *(Source: Boston Globe)* **(9.1)**

20. The playhouse shown at the right has a total volume of $9x^3 + 46x^2 + 59x + 6$ cubic feet. Find the missing dimension of the playhouse. **(9.4)**

21. The demand function of a product is given by $p = 20 - 2x^2$, where p is the unit price in dollars and x is measured in millions of units. The cost of producing the product is $8 per unit. Write a polynomial for the total profit, P (in millions of dollars), of selling x million units. **(9.1)**

9.5

Finding Rational Zeros

What you should learn:

Goal 1 How to find the rational zeros of a polynomial function

Goal 2 How to use the zeros of a polynomial function to solve real-life problems

Why you should learn it:

You can model many real-life situations with polynomial models that have rational zeros, such as the model for the actual and projected number of home computers in the United States.

Goal 1 Using the Rational-Zero Test

The real-number zeros of a polynomial function are either rational or irrational. (Remember that a rational number is one that can be written as the quotient of two integers.) For instance, the function $f(x) = x^2 - 3x - 4$ has two rational zeros: -1 and 4. On the other hand, the function $f(x) = x^2 - 2$ has no rational zeros—its two zeros, $\pm\sqrt{2}$, are both irrational.

In this lesson, you will learn to use the Rational-Zero Test to compile a list that will include all rational zeros of a polynomial function with integer coefficients. By testing the numbers in the list, you can find the zeros that are rational.

The Rational-Zero Test

Consider a polynomial $f(x) = a_n x^n + \cdots + a_1 x + a_0$ with *integer* coefficients. Every rational zero of f has the form

$$\frac{p}{q} = \frac{\text{Factor of constant term, } a_0}{\text{Factor of leading coefficient, } a_n}.$$

Example 1 *Using the Rational-Zero Test*

Find the rational zeros of $f(x) = x^4 - x^3 - 5x^2 + 3x + 6$.

Solution The leading coefficient is 1, and the constant term is 6. Thus the rational zeros are of the following form.

$$\textit{Possible rational zeros: } \frac{\pm 1, \pm 2, \pm 3, \pm 6}{\pm 1}$$

Using synthetic division and the Remainder Theorem, you can determine that two of the *possible* rational zeros are *actual* zeros: $x = -1$ and $x = 2$. This implies that $(x + 1)$ and $(x - 2)$ are factors of $f(x)$.

$$f(x) = (x + 1)(x - 2)(x^2 - 3)$$

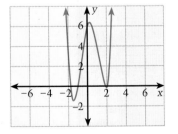

From this factorization, you can see that f has only two rational zeros. (The other two zeros, $\pm\sqrt{3}$, are irrational.) The graph of f is shown at the left. ■

In Example 1, synthetic division was used to test each rational zero. Remember that when you find a zero, you can also find the factorization associated with the zero by the Factor Theorem. Here is what we mean.

$$
\begin{array}{r|rrrr}
-1 & 1 & -1 & -5 & 3 & 6 \\
  &   & -1 & 2 & 3 & -6 \\
\hline
  & 1 & -2 & -3 & 6 & 0
\end{array}
\qquad \text{Test } -1 \text{ as a zero.}
$$

$$(x + 1)(x^3 - 2x^2 - 3x + 6)$$

$$
\begin{array}{r|rrrr}
2 & 1 & -2 & -3 & 6 \\
  &   & 2 & 0 & -6 \\
\hline
  & 1 & 0 & -3 & 0
\end{array}
\qquad \begin{array}{l} \text{Test 2 as a zero of} \\ x^3 - 2x^2 - 3x + 6. \end{array}
$$

$$(x + 1)(x - 2)(x^2 - 3)$$

When the leading coefficient is not 1, the list of possible rational zeros can increase dramatically. In such cases the search can be shortened by making a rough sketch of the function—either by hand or on a graphing calculator.

Finding the first zero is often the hardest part. After that, the search is simplified by using the lower-degree polynomial obtained in synthetic division.

Example 2 Using the Rational-Zero Test

Find all the real zeros of the function

$$f(x) = 10x^3 - 15x^2 - 16x + 12.$$

Solution Since the leading coefficient is 10 and the constant term is 12, you have a long list of possible rational zeros.

$$\text{Possible rational zeros: } \frac{\pm 1,\ \pm 2,\ \pm 3,\ \pm 4,\ \pm 6,\ \pm 12}{\pm 1,\ \pm 2,\ \pm 5,\ \pm 10}$$

With so many possibilities (32, in fact), it is worth your time to sketch the graph of the function. From the graph, it looks like three reasonable choices would be $x = -\frac{6}{5}$, $x = \frac{1}{2}$, and $x = 2$. Testing these by synthetic division shows that only $x = 2$ works.

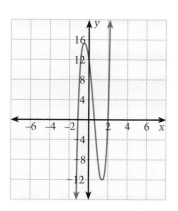

$$
\begin{array}{r|rrrr}
2 & 10 & -15 & -16 & 12 \\
  &   & 20 & 10 & -12 \\
\hline
  & 10 & 5   & -6 & 0
\end{array}
$$

From this result, a factored form is

$$f(x) = (x - 2)(10x^2 + 5x - 6).$$

Using the Quadratic Formula, you can determine that the other two zeros are irrational numbers.

$$x = \frac{-5 + \sqrt{265}}{20} \approx 0.5639 \quad \text{and} \quad x = \frac{-5 - \sqrt{265}}{20} \approx -1.0639 \quad \blacksquare$$

Real Life
Computer Purchases

The first home computer, the Altair, was introduced in 1975. It did not sell well, however, because it came as a kit. In 1977, two American students, Steve Wozniak and Steve Jobs (shown above) founded the highly successful Apple Computer Company. Since then, millions of Americans have purchased home computers.

| **Example 3** | *Solving a Polynomial Equation* |

For 1985 through 1995, the actual and projected number, C (in millions), of home computers sold in the United States can be modeled by

$$C = 0.0092(t^3 + 8t^2 + 40t + 400)$$

where $t = 0$ represents 1990. During which year are 8.51 million computers projected to be sold? *(Source: Dataquest)*

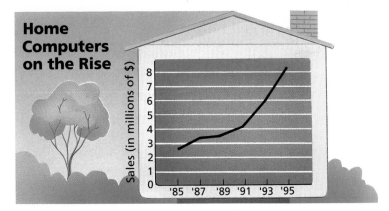

Home Computers on the Rise

Solution Let $C = 8.51$ and solve the resulting equation.

$$0.0092(t^3 + 8t^2 + 40t + 400) = 8.51$$
$$t^3 + 8t^2 + 40t + 400 = 925$$
$$t^3 + 8t^2 + 40t - 525 = 0$$

From the Rational-Zero Test, you can determine that 5 is a solution. To check, substitute $t = 5$ into the original model.

$$C = 0.0092(5^3 + 8(5^2) + 40(5) + 400) = 8.51$$

Thus the sales are projected to be 8.51 million in 1995. ■

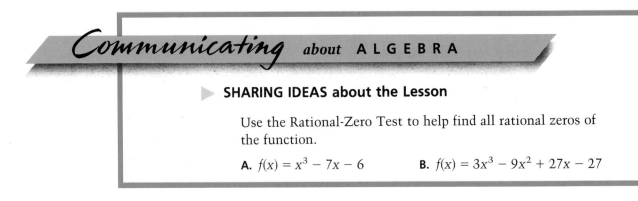

Communicating about **A L G E B R A**

▶ **SHARING IDEAS about the Lesson**

Use the Rational-Zero Test to help find all rational zeros of the function.

A. $f(x) = x^3 - 7x - 6$ **B.** $f(x) = 3x^3 - 9x^2 + 27x - 27$

EXERCISES

Guided Practice

▶ **CRITICAL THINKING about the Lesson**

1. List the possible rational zeros given by the Rational-Zero Test for $f(x) = 3x^3 - 6x^2 + 7x - 2$.

2. Factor $x^3 - 3x^2 - 6x + 8$ completely.   3. Factor $x^3 + 4x^2 - x - 4$ completely.

In Exercises 4–6, find all real zeros of the polynomial function.

4. $y = 4x^3 - 12x^2 - x + 15$ 5. $y = -4x^3 + 15x^2 - 8x - 3$ 6. $y = -3x^3 + 20x^2 - 36x + 16$

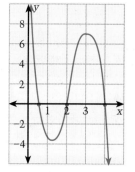

Independent Practice

In Exercises 7–10, list the possible rational zeros given by the Rational-Zero Test.

7. $f(x) = x^3 - 2x^2 + x - 3$

8. $g(x) = 2x^3 + 5x^2 - 6x - 10$

9. $f(x) = 2x^5 + x^2 + 16$

10. $h(x) = 3x^3 - 5x - 24$

In Exercises 11–20, find all rational zeros of the function.

11. $g(x) = x^3 + 2x^2 - 11x - 12$

12. $f(x) = x^3 + x^2 - 10x + 8$

13. $f(x) = x^3 - 8x^2 - 23x + 30$

14. $g(x) = x^3 - 9x^2 + 15x + 25$

15. $f(x) = x^3 - 7x^2 + 2x + 40$

16. $g(x) = x^3 - x^2 - 21x + 45$

17. $f(x) = 2x^3 + 4x^2 - 2x - 4$

18. $g(x) = 3x^3 + 12x^2 + 3x - 18$

19. $h(x) = 2x^3 - 5x^2 - 14x + 8$

20. $f(x) = 3x^3 - 3x + x^2 - 1$

In Exercises 21–30, find all real zeros of the function.

21. $g(x) = x^3 + x^2 - 2x - 2$

22. $f(x) = x^3 + 6x^2 - 6x - 36$

23. $h(x) = x^3 + 2x^2 - 9x - 18$

24. $f(x) = x^3 + 9x^2 - 4x - 36$

25. $g(x) = 2x^3 - x^2 - 32x + 16$

26. $f(x) = 2x^3 + x^2 - 50x - 25$

27. $h(x) = x^4 + 9x^3 + 5x^2 - 27x - 24$

28. $g(x) = 5x^4 + 11x^3 - 48x^2 - 110x - 20$

29. $f(x) = x^5 + 5x^4 + 2x^3 - 22x^2 - 35x - 15$

30. $f(x) = x^5 - x^4 - 7x^3 + 7x^2 + 12x - 12$

31. Portable Personal Computers For 1990 through 2000, the predicted sales, S (in millions of dollars), of portable personal computers in the United States can be modeled by

$$S = -2.6t^4 + 80t^3 - 219t^2 + 1710t + 3000$$

where $t = 0$ represents 1990. In what year are the sales predicted to be approximately $52,200 million?

32. Defense-Related Jobs In 1991, the United States Department of Defense announced that it was beginning to cut back military and defense-related jobs. The planned cutback was to take place over a five-year period. The number of jobs remaining, J (in thousands), can be modeled by

$$J = 12t^3 - 100t^2 + 5100$$

where $t = 1$ represents 1991. In what year was the number of jobs remaining projected to be 4,100,000?

33. United States Exports For 1980 through 1994, the total exports, E (in billions of dollars), can be modeled by

$$E = -0.21t^3 + 6.32t^2 - 27.9t + 239$$

where $t = 0$ represents 1980. In what year were the total exports about $312.76 billion? *(Source: U.S. Bureau of the Census)*

34. Education Donations For 1983 through 1993, the amount of private donations, D (in millions of dollars), allocated to education can be modeled by

$$D = -2.98t^3 + 92t^2 + 6159$$

where $t = 3$ represents 1983. In what year did about $14,258 million of charitable contributions go to education? *(Source: AAFRC Trust for Philanthropy)*

Integrated Review

In Exercises 35–40, sketch the graph of the function.

35. $g(x) = x^4 + 9$

36. $f(x) = x^2 - 3x + 7$

37. $h(x) = x^3 - x^2 + 2x - 4$

38. $h(x) = (x + 4)^3 + 2$

39. $g(x) = x^4 - 2x^3 + x - 3$

40. $f(x) = x^4 - 2x^3 - x - 3$

In Exercises 41–46, perform the indicated division.

41. $(x^4 - 2x^3 + 4x^2 + x - 4) \div (x - 1)$

42. $(x^3 + 6x^2 + 5x - 6) \div (x + 2)$

43. $(x^3 - 4x^2 + 4x - 3) \div (x - 3)$

44. $(x^4 + 3x^3 - x^2 - 4x - 3) \div (x + 3)$

45. $(x^6 + x^5 - x^3 - x^2 + 3x + 3) \div (x + 1)$

46. $(x^5 - 2x^4 - x^2 + 7x - 10) \div (x - 2)$

In Exercises 47–50, one of the zeros of the polynomial is $x = 2$. Use this fact to completely factor the polynomial.

47. $x^3 - 2x^2 - x + 2$

48. $x^3 + 3x^2 - 4x - 12$

49. $x^3 - 4x^2 + x + 6$

50. $x^3 + 4x^2 - 39x + 54$

51. *Powers of Ten*   Which best estimates the length (in millimeters) of the world's smallest bird as shown at the right?

a. 5.5×10^0 **b.** 5.5×10^1
c. 5.5×10^2 **d.** 5.5×10^3

52. *Powers of Ten*   Which best estimates the weight (in ounces) of a new "Number 2" pencil?

a. 2.5×10^{-2} **b.** 2.5×10^{-1}
c. 2.5×10^0 **d.** 2.5×10^1

Exploration and Extension

In Exercises 53–56, find a polynomial function that has only the given zeros.

53. $2, \pm\sqrt{3}$

54. $\pm\sqrt{2}, 1, 2$

55. $0, 1, \pm i$

56. $1, 2, 3, 4$

Mixed REVIEW

1. Multiply: $(2x - 3)(4x + 5)$. **(9.1)**

2. Factor $4x^2 - 25$. **(9.3)**

3. Factor $15x^2 - 31x + 10$. **(9.3)**

4. Sketch $f(x) = (x - 4)(x - 1)(x + 3)$. **(9.2)**

5. Solve $x^4 - 81 = 0$. **(9.3)**

6. Sketch $f(x) = 2^{x-3}$. **(8.1)**

7. Sketch $f(x) = \ln(x - 3)$. **(8.2)**

8. Write $e^{x-6} = 8$ in logarithmic form. **(8.4)**

9. Evaluate $\log_3 27$. **(8.2)**

10. Evaluate $\ln e^9$. **(8.6)**

11. Find the y-intercept of $y = \log_2(x + 8)$. **(8.2)**

12. Find the y-intercept of $y = -3 + \log_4 x$. **(8.2)**

13. Condense $5 \ln x + \frac{1}{2} \ln y - \ln 2$. **(8.3)**

14. Solve $\log_{10}(x - 3) = 2$. **(8.2)**

15. Solve $e^{3x-4} = 7$. **(8.6)**

16. Solve for y: $2 \ln y - x = 2$. **(8.6)**

17. Find the y-intercept of $f(x) = 5x^4 + 2x^3 - 7x + 8$. **(2.3)**

18. Find the slope of the line through $(-4, -1)$ and $(2, -8)$. **(2.2)**

19. Solve $\begin{cases} 3x + 2y = 1 \\ 7x + 3y = -2 \end{cases}$. **(3.2)**

20. Sketch the solution of $-4 < 2x + 5 < 2$. **(2.5)**

9.6

Connections: Zeros, Factors, and Solutions

What you should learn:

Goal 1 How to look at zeros of polynomial functions, factors of polynomials, and solutions of polynomial equations to see their connections

Goal 2 How to use polynomials to solve real-life problems

Why you should learn it:

You can use polynomial models for many real-life situations, such as the model for the volume of the blocks of concrete found in the remains of Caesarea harbor.

Goal 1 Viewing Polynomials in Three Ways

In this chapter, we have talked about polynomials, polynomial functions, and polynomial equations. These are closely related.

Zeros, Factors, and Solutions

Let $f(x) = a_n x^n + \cdots + a_1 x + a_0$ be a polynomial function. The following statements are equivalent.

1. k is a zero of the polynomial function f.
2. $(x - k)$ is a factor of the polynomial $f(x)$.
3. k is a solution of the polynomial equation $f(x) = 0$.

These three statements are equivalent for *any real or complex* number. For *real* numbers, a fourth equivalent statement can be added: $(k, 0)$ is an x-intercept of the graph of f.

Example 1 *Zeros, Factors, Solutions, and x-Intercepts*

a. The polynomial function $f(x) = x^3 - x^2 - 4x + 4$ has three zeros: $-2, 1, 2$.

$$f(-2) = (-2)^3 - (-2)^2 - 4(-2) + 4 = -8 - 4 + 8 + 4 = 0$$
$$f(1) = (1)^3 - (1)^2 - 4(1) + 4 = 1 - 1 - 4 + 4 = 0$$
$$f(2) = (2)^3 - (2)^2 - 4(2) + 4 = 8 - 4 - 8 + 4 = 0$$

b. The polynomial $x^3 - x^2 - 4x + 4$ factors as the product of three linear factors.

$$x^3 - x^2 - 4x + 4 = (x + 2)(x - 1)(x - 2)$$

c. The polynomial equation $x^3 - x^2 - 4x + 4 = 0$ has three solutions: $-2, 1$, and 2. (Check them!)

d. Because all three zeros of f are real, they show up as x-intercepts of the graph of f.

$$(-2, 0), (1, 0), \text{ and } (2, 0)$$

(Complex zeros of a polynomial function do not show up as x-intercepts of the graph of the function.) ∎

The following theorem is called the **Fundamental Theorem of Algebra.** Its beauty lies in the simplicity of its statement and its strong, logical appeal.

Carl Friederich Gauss

> ## The Fundamental Theorem of Algebra
> Counting complex and repeated solutions, an *n*th-degree polynomial equation has *exactly n* solutions.

Note: The Fundamental Theorem of Algebra is often stated as "Any polynomial equation of degree 1 or greater has at least one complex number solution." This version is equivalent to the one stated above. (Remember that each real number is also a complex number.)

The Fundamental Theorem of Algebra was proved by the great German mathematician Carl Friederich Gauss (1777–1855) when he was only 22 years old. The proof of this theorem marked the end of an era for algebra. The theorem told mathematicians that the set of complex numbers contains all possible solutions of polynomial equations. After 1799, it was unnecessary (at least for solving polynomial equations) to hunt for new types of numbers.

Example 2   *Demonstrating the Fundamental Theorem of Algebra*

a. The first-degree polynomial equation $x - 4 = 0$ has exactly *one* solution: $x = 4$.

b. Counting repeated solutions, the second-degree polynomial equation

$$x^2 - 6x + 9 = 0$$
$$(x - 3)(x - 3) = 0$$

has exactly *two* solutions: $x = 3$ and $x = 3$.

c. The third-degree polynomial equation

$$x^3 + 4x = 0$$
$$x(x - 2i)(x + 2i) = 0$$

has exactly *three* solutions: $x = 0$, $x = 2i$, and $x = -2i$.

d. The fourth-degree polynomial equation

$$x^4 - 1 = 0$$
$$(x - 1)(x + 1)(x - i)(x + i) = 0$$

has exactly *four* solutions: $x = 1$, $x = -1$, $x = i$, and $x = -i$.

■

Because each solution of a polynomial equation corresponds to a linear factor of the polynomial, the Fundamental Theorem of Algebra can also be stated in terms of factors of a polynomial.

Linear Factorization Theorem

A polynomial of degree n has exactly n linear factors

$$f(x) = a_n(x - k_1)(x - k_2) \cdots (x - k_n)$$

where $k_1, k_2, \ldots, k_n$ are complex numbers and a_n is the leading coefficient of $f(x)$.

Example 3 **Finding the Zeros of a Polynomial Function**

Write $f(x) = x^5 + x^3 + 2x^2 - 12x + 8$ as the product of linear factors and list all of its zeros.

Solution   The possible rational zeros are ± 1, ± 2, ± 4, and ± 8. Synthetic division produces the following.

$$
\begin{array}{r|rrrrrr}
1 & 1 & 0 & 1 & 2 & -12 & 8 \\
  &   & 1 & 1 & 2 & 4 & -8 \\
\hline
  & 1 & 1 & 2 & 4 & -8 & 0
\end{array}
\quad \textit{1 is a zero.}
$$

$$
\begin{array}{r|rrrrr}
1 & 1 & 1 & 2 & 4 & -8 \\
  &   & 1 & 2 & 4 & 8 \\
\hline
  & 1 & 2 & 4 & 8 & 0
\end{array}
\quad \textit{1 is a repeated zero.}
$$

$$
\begin{array}{r|rrrr}
-2 & 1 & 2 & 4 & 8 \\
   &   & -2 & 0 & -8 \\
\hline
   & 1 & 0 & 4 & 0
\end{array}
\quad \textit{-2 is a zero.}
$$

From the results of the synthetic division, you can write

$$
\begin{aligned}
f(x) &= (x - 1)(x - 1)(x + 2)(x^2 + 4) \\
     &= (x - 1)(x - 1)(x + 2)(x - 2i)(x + 2i).
\end{aligned}
$$

This factorization gives the following five zeros:

$1, 1, -2, 2i,$ and $-2i$.

Note from the graph of f that the *real* zeros are the only ones that appear as x-intercepts. ∎

In Example 3, the zeros $2i$ and $-2i$ are **complex conjugates.** The complex zeros of a polynomial function with *real* coefficients always occur in complex conjugate pairs. That is, if $a + bi$ is a solution, then $a - bi$ must also be a solution.

The building of the port of Caesarea, around 30 B.C., was the first known use of hydraulic concrete—concrete that will set up in water. Caesarea was located in Israel, which at the time was a province of Rome. Recent archeological finds include the large block of hydraulic concrete shown.

Real Life
Engineering

Example 4 *Solving a Polynomial Equation*

In 1980, archaeologists at the ruins of Caesarea discovered a huge hydraulic concrete block. The block had a volume of 330 cubic yards. (A typical concrete driveway to a house would use about 5 cubic yards.) The dimensions of the block were x yards by $5x + 1$ yards by $7x + 1$ yards. How high was the block?

Solution

Verbal Model	Volume $=$ Height $\cdot$ Length $\cdot$ Width	
Labels	Volume $= 330$	(cubic yards)
	Height $= x$	(yards)
	Length $= 5x + 1$	(yards)
	Width $= 7x + 1$	(yards)
Equation	$330 = x(5x + 1)(7x + 1)$	
	$0 = 35x^3 + 12x^2 + x - 330$	
	$0 = (x - 2)(35x^2 + 82x + 165)$	

The equation has only one real solution: $x = 2$. Thus the block was 2 yards high. The dimensions of the block were 2 by 11 by 15, which produces a volume of 330 cubic yards. ■

Communicating about ALGEBRA

▶ **SHARING IDEAS about the Lesson**

A graphing calculator was used to sketch the graph of the equation in Example 4, $f(x) = 35x^3 + 12x^2 + x - 330$. What are the scales on the x-axis and y-axis? Are all of the x-intercepts shown in the graph? Explain.

EXERCISES

Guided Practice

▶ **CRITICAL THINKING about the Lesson**

1. Two of the zeros of $f(x) = x^3 - 6x^2 - 16x + 96$ are 4 and -4. Explain why the third zero must also be a real number. Using only the constant of the polynomial, what must the other zero be? Explain.

2. How many solutions does the equation $x^5 + x - 3 = 0$ have? Explain.

3. Find the zeros of $f(x) = x^4 + x^2 - 12$.

4. State the Linear Factorization Theorem in your own words.

5. At the right is the graph of $f(x) = 2x^4 + 2x^3 - 9x^2 - 2x + 7$. How many real zeros does the graph have? How many are complex?

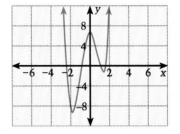

Independent Practice

In Exercises 6–11, decide whether the given x-value is a zero of the function.

6. $f(x) = x^3 - x^2 + 3x - 3$, $x = 1$
7. $f(x) = x^3 + 4x^2 + 3x + 12$, $x = 3$
8. $f(x) = x^4 - x + 4$, $x = 0$
9. $f(x) = x^3 + 3x^2 + x + 3$, $x = -3$
10. $f(x) = x^3 - 2x^2 + 4x - 8$, $x = 2i$
11. $f(x) = x^3 - 2x^2 + x - 2$, $x = -i$

In Exercises 12–19, write a polynomial function that has the given zeros and has a leading coefficient of 1.

12. 2, 1, 5
13. 1, -3, 4
14. -6, 4, 2
15. 6, -2, 2
16. 5, i, $-i$
17. $3i$, $-3i$, 4
18. 3, -3, $2i$, $-2i$
19. i, $-i$, $2i$, $-2i$

In Exercises 20–23, write a polynomial function whose graph has the given x-intercepts and has a leading coefficient of 1.

20. $(4, 0)$, $(1, 0)$
21. $(-2, 0)$, $(5, 0)$
22. $(-3, 0)$, $(2, 0)$
23. $(9, 0)$, $(-1, 0)$

In Exercises 24–35, write the polynomial as a product of linear factors.

24. $x^4 + x^3 - 19x^2 + 11x + 30$
25. $x^4 + 3x^3 - 2x^2 - 12x - 8$
26. $x^3 - x^2 - 2x$
27. $x^3 + 5x^2 - 9x - 45$
28. $x^4 - 5x^2 - 36$
29. $x^3 - x^2 + 9x - 9$
30. $x^3 - x^2 + 16x - 16$
31. $x^3 + 3x^2 + 25x + 75$
32. $x^4 - x^3 - 5x^2 - x - 6$
33. $x^4 - x^3 + 2x^2 - 4x - 8$
34. $2x^4 - 7x^3 - 27x^2 + 63x + 81$
35. $x^3 - 2x^2 + 25x - 50$

36. *Harvard Step Test*   A group of people were given the Harvard Step Test to determine their physical fitness. Each person was asked to step up onto a one-foot box, then step down, repeatedly, for five minutes. At the end of the test, each person was given a score, S, determined by the rate at which their pulse returned to normal. The scores of the people in the group were found to be related to the amounts of their blood hemoglobin, x (in grams per 100 milliliters of blood), by the model $S = -0.015x^3 + 0.6x^2 - 2.4x + 19$. Approximate the amount of hemoglobin in the blood of a person who scored 40 on the Harvard Step Test.

37. *Grocery Store Revenue*   A neighborhood grocery store has been open for 25 years. During that time, the store's annual revenue, R (in millions of dollars), can be modeled by

$$R = \frac{1}{10,000}(-t^4 + 12t^3 - 77t^2 + 600t + 13,650)$$

where $t = 0$ represents the store's first year. In what years did the revenue reach $1.5 million?

Silkworm Puzzle   **In Exercises 38–43, find the sum of the real zeros of the function. Then use the sum to complete the fact about silkworms.**

When the casing of a silkworm's cocoon is unraveled, a single unbroken thread of silk results.

38. Adult silkworm length (in inches): $f(x) = x^4 - 3x^3 - 27x^2 - 3x - 28$

39. Number of times a silkworm sheds its skin: $f(x) = 2x^3 - 8x^2 + x - 4$

40. Number of breathing vents on a silkworm: $f(x) = x^3 - 9x^2 + 4x - 36$

41. Number of species of wild silkworms (in hundreds):

$f(x) = x^4 - 5x^3 + 3x^2 - 45x - 54$

42. Average silkworm life span (in days):

$f(x) = x^4 - 26x^3 + 168x^2 - 262x + 119$

43. Ratio of adult-to-birth weight (in 1000's):

$f(x) = x^4 - 10x^3 + 28x^2 - 40x + 96$

For 1980 through 1990, the sales, S (in millions of dollars), of snow skiing equipment can be modeled by

$$S = 0.42t^4 - 9.7t^3 + 72.3t^2 - 134t + 378,$$

where $t = 0$ represents 1980.

44. Use a graphing calculator to sketch the graph. Was there a year in which sales were about \$664 million? Explain.

45. Was there a year in which sales were about \$280 million? Explain.

Integrated Review

In Exercises 46–53, find all the zeros of the function.

46. $f(x) = x^3 - 7x^2 + 7x + 15$

47. $f(x) = 2x^3 + 3x^2 - 3x - 2$

48. $f(x) = x^3 - 4x^2 - 15x + 18$

49. $f(x) = x^3 + 13x^2 + 48x + 36$

50. $f(x) = 2x^3 - 15x^2 - 47x - 30$

51. $f(x) = x^4 + 4x^3 + 3x^2 - 4x - 4$

52. $f(x) = x^4 + 3x^3 - 18x^2 - 32x + 96$

53. $f(x) = x^4 - 15x^2 - 10x + 24$

54. *College Entrance Exam Sample*   If $z = -x$ and $x \neq 0$, what are all values of y for which $(x + y)^2 + (y + z)^2 = 2x^2$?
   a. 0   **b.** 0, 1   **c.** $-1, 0, 1$ **d.** All positive numbers
   e. There are no values of y for which the equation is true.

55. *College Entrance Exam Sample*   A *perfect square* is an integer whose square root is an integer. The numbers 16, 25, and 36 are perfect squares. If a and b are perfect squares, which of the following is *not* necessarily a perfect square?
   a. $25a$ **b.** a^2 **c.** a^3 **d.** ab **e.** $a - b$

Exploration and Extension

56. Write a third-degree polynomial, two of whose zeros are 1 and i.

57. Write a fourth-degree polynomial, two of whose zeros are $2i$ and $-3i$.

58. The graph of

$$f(x) = x^5 - 2x^3 - 2x^2 - 3x - 2$$

is shown at the right. Find all the zeros of the function.

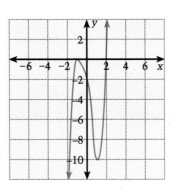

9.7

Exploring Data: Measures of Dispersion

What you should learn:

Goal 1 How to find the range of a collection of numbers

Goal 2 How to find the standard deviation of a collection of numbers

Why you should learn it:

You can use the range and standard deviation to describe many collections of data, such as the quality control data for the color brightness of paper.

Goal 1 Finding the Range

You already know several ways to display a collection of data, a frequency distribution, a bar graph, or a box-and-whisker plot. You also know how to find the mean, median, mode, and quartiles for a collection of numbers. In this lesson, you will study two **measures of dispersion** of a collection of numbers: the *range* and the *standard deviation*. Each of these gives you an idea of how much the numbers in the collection vary.

The **range** of a collection of numbers is the difference between the largest and smallest values in the collection. For instance, the range of the collection 2, 3, 4, 6, 9 is $9 - 2 = 7$.

Example 1 *Finding the Range of a Set of Numbers*

Three employees at a frozen yogurt store were each asked by their manager to fill a dozen 8-ounce cups of yogurt. The manager weighed each of the cups and recorded the following results. Which employee(s) had the most consistent record?

Sean	Eric	Jody
6.5, 7.0, 9.0	8.0, 7.0, 10.0	7.0, 8.0, 8.0
9.0, 8.0, 7.0	11.0, 7.5, 5.0	7.5, 8.0, 8.5
7.5, 9.5, 9.0	9.5, 5.0, 10.5	10.0, 8.0, 7.5
9.5, 7.0, 7.0	9.0, 7.5, 6.0	8.0, 8.0, 7.5

Solution One way to answer the question is to calculate the range for each set of measurements.

Sean's range: $9.5 - 6.5 = 3$ ounces
Eric's range: $11.0 - 5.0 = 6$ ounces
Jody's range: $10.0 - 7.0 = 3$ ounces

Judging from the ranges of each, Sean's and Jody's performances were more consistent than Eric's. ∎

In Example 1, notice that the mean of each set of measurements was 8 ounces. (Try checking this.) Their abilities to consistently fill cups with 8 ounces of yogurt, however, varied. From this example, you can see that two collections of numbers with the same mean can have very different dispersion patterns.

Goal 2 Finding the Standard Deviation

The range of a collection of numbers is only a simple measure of its dispersion. In Example 1, for instance, the range was not able to distinguish between Sean's and Jody's performance. To obtain a more sophisticated measure of dispersion, statisticians use the *standard deviation*.

Standard Deviation of a Collection of Numbers

The **standard deviation** of $x_1, x_2, x_3, \ldots, x_n$ is

$$s = \sqrt{\frac{(x_1 - \overline{x})^2 + (x_2 - \overline{x})^2 + \cdots + (x_n - \overline{x})^2}{n}}$$

where $\overline{x}$ is the mean of $x_1, x_2, \ldots,$ and x_n.

Example 2 *Finding the Standard Deviation of a Collection of Numbers*

The standard deviations for the sets of measurements given in Example 1 are as follows. (The mean for each is $\overline{x} = 8$.)

$$\textit{Sean: } s = \sqrt{\frac{(6.5 - 8)^2 + (7.0 - 8)^2 + \cdots + (7.0 - 8)^2}{12}}$$

$$= \sqrt{\frac{14}{12}} \approx 1.080$$

$$\textit{Eric: } s = \sqrt{\frac{(8.0 - 8)^2 + (7.0 - 8)^2 + \cdots + (6.0 - 8)^2}{12}}$$

$$= \sqrt{\frac{46}{12}} \approx 1.958$$

$$\textit{Jody: } s = \sqrt{\frac{(7.0 - 8)^2 + (8.0 - 8)^2 + \cdots + (7.5 - 8)^2}{12}}$$

$$= \sqrt{\frac{6}{12}} \approx 0.707$$

A larger standard deviation tells you that the numbers in the collection are more "spread out"—the dispersion is greater. A smaller standard deviation tells you that the numbers in the collection are more tightly grouped. Thus, using standard deviation as a measure, the employee with the most consistent record was Jody. The bar graphs at the left confirm that Eric's measurements are more spread out than Sean's, and Sean's are more spread out than Jody's. ■

Calculating the standard deviation using the formula given in its definition can be tedious (and may involve significant round-off error). The following alternate formula is easier to use. This formula is *equivalent* to the formula on page 502.

Alternate Formula for Standard Deviation

$$s = \sqrt{\frac{x_1^2 + x_2^2 + \cdots + x_n^2}{n} - \bar{x}^2}$$

Example 3 — Finding Standard Deviation with the Alternate Formula

The heights (in inches) of 20 members of a high school football team are given below. Find the mean and standard deviation of the heights.

64.0, 66.0, 66.5, 68.0, 68.5, 70.0, 70.0, 70.5, 71.0, 71.5
71.5, 72.0, 72.0, 72.5, 73.0, 73.0, 74.0, 74.5, 76.0, 78.0

Height of 20 Football Players

Solution   The mean height for the team is

$$\bar{x} = \frac{64.0 + 66.0 + \cdots + 76.0 + 78.0}{20} = \frac{1422.5}{20} = 71.125 \text{ inches.}$$

Using the alternate formula, the standard deviation is

$$s = \sqrt{\frac{64.0^2 + 66.0^2 + \cdots + 76.0^2 + 78.0^2}{20} - (71.125)^2}$$
$$\approx \sqrt{5069.7375 - 5058.7656} \approx 3.31 \text{ inches.}$$

Note in the bar graph that most of the heights lie within 1 standard deviation of the mean. That is, most of the heights lie between 67.815 and 74.435. ■

Communicating about **ALGEBRA**

> **SHARING IDEAS about the Lesson**
>
> Find the range and standard deviation of each collection.
>
> **A.** The weights (in pounds) of ten giant pandas: 302, 310, 331, 298, 348, 305, 314, 284, 321, 337
>
> **B.** The age (in years) of ten giant pandas: 3.4, 4.2, 8.6, 5.1, 3.6, 2.8, 7.1, 4.4, 5.2, 5.6

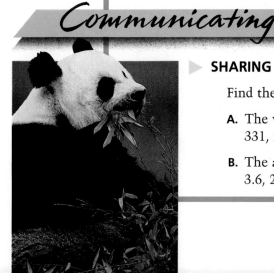

EXERCISES

▶ **CRITICAL THINKING about the Lesson**

1. Give an example of two collections of four numbers, each with a mean of 5. Choose the numbers so that one collection has a range of 3 and the other has a range of 7. Which has the greater standard deviation?

2. The following box-and-whisker plots represent two collections of numbers. Which collection has the greater range? Explain.

   a.

   3   5 6   8   10

   b.

   5 6   8   10 11

3. *Test Scores*   The following bar graphs represent two collections of test scores. Which collection has the smaller standard deviation? Explain.

   a.

   b.

4. *Test Scores*   Find the standard deviation of the collection of test scores you chose in Exercise 3. If you received a score of 98 on the test, would your score have been within one standard deviation of the mean score?

In Exercises 5–8, find the range and standard deviation of the data.

5. 5.6, 5.6, 5.7, 5.8, 5.8, 5.8, 5.9, 6.1

6. 100, 156, 158, 159, 162, 165, 170, 190

7. 0, 0.1, 0.1, 0.3, 0.6, 0.6, 0.7, 0.8

8. 201, 201, 203, 205, 208, 210, 211, 220

9. *Squirrel Tails*   The average tail lengths (in inches) of ten types of squirrels are shown in the list. Find the range and standard deviation of these lengths.

Western gray squirrel	12	Apache fox squirrel	11
Tassel-eared squirrel	8.5	Red squirrel	6
Eastern gray squirrel	10	Chickaree	5
Arizona gray squirrel	12	Southern flying squirrel	4
Eastern fox squirrel	14	Northern flying squirrel	5

10. *Brothers and Sisters*   A class of 28 students took a survey of the number of brothers and sisters each student had. Find the range and standard deviation of the results.

0 0 0 0 0 1 1 1 1 1 1 1 1 2
2 2 2 2 2 2 2 2 2 3 3 3 4 6

11. *Grocery Shopping*   Over the past year, your parents went grocery shopping once every two weeks. The costs of the groceries were as follows. What is the range of these costs? What is the mean?

$210.55 $178.60 $197.22 $181.23 $172.45 $201.74 $211.38 $199.71 $193.30
$202.01 $190.64 $180.13 $180.95 $192.76 $219.82 $220.70 $192.02 $194.40
$195.06 $202.36 $185.12 $198.46 $194.62 $204.28 $198.54 $188.60

12. *Moons of the Planets*   The numbers of known moons for the nine planets in our solar system are shown in the table. Find the range and standard deviation of these data.

Mercury	0	Mars	2	Uranus	15
Venus	0	Jupiter	16	Neptune	8
Earth	1	Saturn	17	Pluto	1

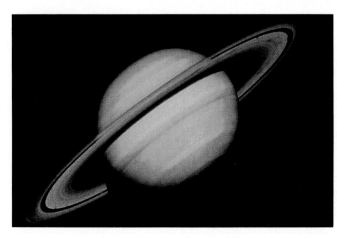

Each of the moons in our solar system has been named—except for our moon. It is simply called the moon. For instance, the names of the 17 moons of Saturn are Atlas, Calypso, Dione, Enceladus, Epimetheus, Helene, Hyperion, Janus, Japetus, Mimas, Pandora, Phoebe, Prometheus, Rhea, Telesto, Tethys, and Titan.

President's Ages   **In Exercises 13–16, use the following information.**

The ages of the first 40 Presidents of the United States at the time of their inaugurations are given in the list.

42, 43, 46, 47, 48, 49, 50, 51, 51, 51, 51, 51, 52, 52
54, 54, 54, 54, 55, 55, 55, 55, 56, 56, 56, 57, 57, 57
57, 58, 60, 61, 61, 61, 62, 64, 64, 65, 68, 69

13. What is the range of the ages?

14. What is the mean of the ages?

15. The sum of the squares of the ages is 126,703. Use this to find the standard deviation of the ages.

16. Ronald Reagan was the oldest to be inaugurated as president. John F. Kennedy, at age 43, was the youngest to be *elected.* Use a library or some other reference source to find who was the youngest person to become President.

17. *Color Brightness of Paper*   A company that manufactures paper pulls ten samples from one roll of paper and ten samples from another roll. The color brightness of each sample is measured with a spectrophotometer. The company's goal is to produce rolls of paper that have the same color brightness throughout the roll. In practice, however, absolute consistency is almost impossible. Judging from the samples, which roll has the more consistent color?

Roll #1: 81.35, 81.24, 81.76, 81.64, 81.77, 81.85, 81.70, 83.24, 83.42, 82.49

Roll #2: 81.73, 81.80, 81.60, 81.69, 81.75, 81.20, 81.75, 81.30, 81.95, 81.44

Rain in New Mexico   **In Exercises 18 and 19, use the following information.**

The tables list the average number of days with rain or snow in Albuquerque and Roswell, New Mexico. Find the mean and standard deviation of each collection. Which data set is more consistent?

18. *Albuquerque:*

Month	Jan	Feb	Mar	Apr	May	Jun	Jul	Aug	Sept	Oct	Nov	Dec
Days	4	4	4	4	4	4	9	10	5	5	3	4

19. *Roswell:*

Month	Jan	Feb	Mar	Apr	May	Jun	Jul	Aug	Sept	Oct	Nov	Dec
Days	3	4	2	3	4	4	9	7	4	4	2	2

20. *Log Length*   The lengths (in feet) of 30 logs are listed below. What is the mean of their lengths? What percent of the logs have lengths that differ from the mean by more than one standard deviation?

25, 26, 26, 27, 27, 28, 28, 28, 29, 29,
30, 30, 30, 30, 30, 31, 31, 31, 31, 32,
32, 32, 32, 32, 33, 34, 34, 35, 35, 36

Hundreds of logs are shown on their way to a paper pulp mill in Oregon.

21. *College Entrance Exam Sample* In a family of five, the heights of the members are 5 feet 1 inch, 5 feet 7 inches, 5 feet 2 inches, 5 feet, and 4 feet 7 inches. What is the average height?

a. 4′4″ **b.** 5′ **c.** 5′1″ **d.** 5′2″ **e.** 5′3″

22. *College Entrance Exam Sample* A recipe for a cake called for $1\frac{1}{4}$ cups of milk and 3 cups of flour. With this recipe, a cake is baked using 12 cups of flour. How many cups of milk are required?

a. 3 **b.** 4 **c.** 5 **d.** 6 **e.** 7

23. *Postage Prices* Although the price of a first-class stamp rose four cents in 1991, it was still cheaper to mail a letter in the United States than in other major industrialized countries. What was the mean cost of a first-class stamp in the five countries below? *(Source: U.S. Postal Service)*

24. *Overseas Travel* In 1993, about 44 million Americans who traveled abroad spent about 40.5 billion dollars. Use the information below to approximate the average amount spent by each traveler to Canada, to Mexico, and overseas.

(Source: U.S. Travel and Tourism Administration)

Postage Prices

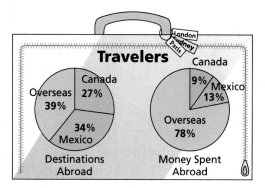

25. *Household Sizes* The following list gives the average number of people per household in 1994 for each of the 50 states. Use a calculator or a computer to find the mean and standard deviation of these data.

AL	2.61	GA	2.67	ME	2.54	NE	2.56	OH	2.59	TX	2.75
AK	2.81	HI	2.99	MD	2.67	NV	2.56	OK	2.56	UT	3.13
AZ	2.66	ID	2.75	MA	2.57	NH	2.61	OR	2.53	VT	2.54
AR	2.58	IL	2.66	MI	2.65	NJ	2.72	PA	2.57	VA	2.60
CA	2.83	IN	2.59	MN	2.60	NM	2.77	RI	2.57	WA	2.56
CO	2.52	IA	2.52	MS	2.74	NY	2.64	SC	2.66	WV	2.53
CT	2.60	KS	2.56	MO	2.56	NC	2.55	SD	2.63	WI	2.62
DE	2.59	KY	2.59	MT	2.58	ND	2.54	TN	2.57	WY	2.62
FL	2.50	LA	2.72								

Which states have household sizes that differ from the mean by more than one standard deviation? By more than two standard deviations?

9

Chapter Summary

What did you learn?

Skills

1. Add, subtract, and multiply polynomials. **(9.1)**
   - Use special product patterns to multiply polynomials. **(9.1)**
2. Sketch the graph of a polynomial function. **(9.2)**
   - Identify basic features of polynomial graphs. **(9.2)**
3. Factor a polynomial.
   - Use special factoring patterns. **(9.3)**
   - Use the Rational-Zero Test. **(9.5)**
4. Divide polynomials.
   - Use long division. **(9.4)**
   - Use synthetic division. **(9.4)**
5. Solve polynomial equations. **(9.3, 9.5, 9.6)**
6. Find zeros of polynomial functions. **(9.2–9.6)**

Strategies

7. Use polynomial models to solve real-life problems. **(9.1–9.6)**

Exploring Data

8. Use measures of dispersion to describe data. **(9.7)**

Why did you learn it?

Polynomial models have been used by people for many hundreds of years— longer than any other type of model. In Algebra 1 and in the first part of Algebra 2, you studied many uses of polynomial models of degree 0, 1, and 2. In this chapter, you have seen that polynomials of degree 3 or more can also be used to model a variety of real-life situations.

One way to create real-life models is to add, subtract, or multiply other models. For instance, to create a model for the profit, P, you can subtract the model for total cost, C, from the model for total revenue, R.

How does it fit into the bigger picture of algebra?

In this chapter, you studied the graphs of *polynomial functions*. You also learned how to find the *x*-intercepts of the graph of a polynomial function by finding the real-number *zeros* of the function. Knowing how to find the real zeros of a polynomial function, you also know how to *find the real solutions of a polynomial equation*. The two problems are essentially the same.

The problem of finding the solutions of a polynomial equation is *the* most classic problem in all of algebra. Because of that, some of the results in this chapter are theoretical in nature. For instance, the chapter contains the *Fundamental Theorem of Algebra*.

In Exercises 1–14, perform the indicated operation. (9.1)

1. $(4x^3 + 2x^2 + 1) + (x^2 + x - 5)$

2. $(x^4 - x + 3) + (x^3 - x^2 - 3x + 4)$

3. $(9x^2 - 3x - 4) - (x^2 + 2x - 1)$

4. $(-3x^3 + 2x^2 - x + 1) - (x^3 + x + 3)$

5. $2x(x^2 + 3x - 4)$

6. $x(x^4 + 2x^2 - 3)$

7. $(x + 6)(x - 6)$

8. $(x + 14)(x - 14)$

9. $(x - 3)(x^2 + x - 7)$

10. $(x + 1)(x^2 + 3x + 1)$

11. $(x + 9)^2$

12. $(x - 10)^2$

13. $(x - 7)^3$

14. $(x + 5)^3$

In Exercises 15–20, match the function with its graph. (9.2)

15. $f(x) = (x + 1)^3 - 6$

16. $f(x) = x^4 - 3x^3 + x - 2$

17. $f(x) = x^5 + 2x^2 - 3x + 1$

18. $f(x) = x^3 + 2x - 1$

19. $f(x) = -x^4 + 2x^3 + 5$

20. $f(x) = -\frac{1}{4}(x + 1)^5 + 2$

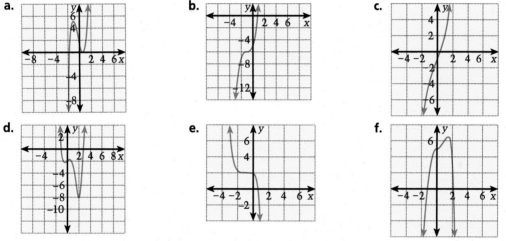

In Exercises 21–32, sketch the graph of the function. (9.2)

21. $f(x) = -x^3 + 5$

22. $f(x) = (x - 7)^3 + 1$

23. $f(x) = (x + 2)^3$

24. $f(x) = -x^3 + 4$

25. $f(x) = (x - 1)^4$

26. $f(x) = x^4 - 3$

27. $f(x) = -(x + 3)^4 + 5$

28. $f(x) = -(x + 6)^3$

29. $f(x) = x^5 + 6$

30. $f(x) = -(x - 2)^5$

31. $f(x) = -x^3 + 4x + 1$

32. $f(x) = x^4 - 5x + 4$

In Exercises 33–44, completely factor the polynomial with respect to the integers. (9.3)

33. $16x^2 - 144$

34. $4x^2 - 49$

35. $125x^3 - 8$

36. $64x^2 + 343$

37. $x^2 - 9x - 22$

38. $x^2 + 8x - 9$

39. $2x^2 - 5x + 2$

40. $3x^2 - 11x - 20$

41. $x^3 - x^2 + 5x - 5$

42. $x^3 - 3x^2 - 5x + 15$

43. $2x^3 - 3x^2 + 4x - 6$

44. $2x^3 + x^2 + 2x + 1$

In Exercises 45–52, find all real solutions of the equation. (9.3)

45. $x^2 - 6x = 27$

46. $x^2 + 9x - 10 = 0$

47. $x^3 + 3x^2 - x - 3 = 0$

48. $x^3 - 4x^2 - 4x + 16 = 0$

49. $x^3 + x^2 - 16x = 16$

50. $x^3 + 6x^2 - 25x = 150$

51. $2x^3 - 3x^2 - 18x + 27 = 0$

52. $4x^3 - 8x^2 - x + 2 = 0$

In Exercises 53–56, divide using long division. (9.4)

53. $(x^3 + 2x^2 - 57x + 54) \div (x + 9)$

54. $(x^3 - 13x^2 + 35x + 49) \div (x - 7)$

55. $(2x^3 - x^2 + 5x - 6) \div (x - 1)$

56. $(x^4 + x^3 + 3x^2 - 9x - 4) \div (x - 5)$

In Exercises 57–64, divide using synthetic division. (9.4)

57. $(x^5 + 3x^4 - x^2 + 6) \div (x + 3)$

58. $(x^4 + 5x^3 - x^2 - 3x - 1) \div (x - 1)$

59. $(2x^4 + 3x^3 + x - 9) \div (x - 1)$

60. $(2x^5 - 6x^2 - 5) \div (x + 5)$

61. $(3x^3 + 2x^2 - x + 4) \div (x + 5)$

62. $(-2x^6 + 3x^4 - x^3 + x - 2) \div (x - 3)$

63. $(x^6 + 3x^3 - 6x^2 + 7) \div (x + 2)$

64. $(6x^3 - 2x^2 - 9x + 6) \div (x - 4)$

In Exercises 65–72, find *all* solutions of the equation. (9.5, 9.6)

65. $x^3 - 9x^2 + 49x - 441 = 0$

66. $x^4 + x^3 - x^2 + x - 2 = 0$

67. $x^3 - x^2 + 16x - 16 = 0$

68. $2x^3 - 3x^2 + 2x - 3 = 0$

69. $x^4 + 2x^3 + x^2 + 8x - 12 = 0$

70. $x^4 - 8x^3 - 8x^2 - 8x - 9 = 0$

71. $2x^4 - 3x^3 + 7x^2 - 9x + 3 = 0$

72. $3x^3 - 2x^2 + 3x = 2$

73. *Grocery Sales*　For 1980 through 1990, the number, G (in thousands), of grocery stores in the United States can be modeled by

$$G = 0.09t^2 - 1.6t + 172.5$$

where $t = 0$ represents 1980. The average sales, S (in thousands of dollars), per grocery store can be modeled by

$$S = -0.5t^2 + 90t + 1190.$$

Write a model that represents the total sales, T (in millions of dollars), for grocery stores in the United States. Use the model to approximate the total sales in 1988. *(Source: U.S. Department of Agriculture)*

74. *Foreign Investment in the United States*　For 1970 through 1990, the total foreign investment, I (in millions of dollars), in the United States can be modeled by

$$I = 13t^4 - 414t^3 + 4958t^2 - 13453t + 13435$$

where $t = 0$ represents 1970. In what year was the investment $327,913 million? *(Source: U.S. Bureau of Economic Analysis)*

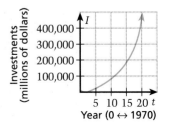

75. *Advertising*   For 1970 through 1990, the total amount, T (in millions of dollars), spent on advertising in the United States can be modeled by

$$T = 257t^2 + 1016t + 19{,}100$$

where $t = 0$ represents 1970. The total amount, L (in millions of dollars), spent on local advertising can be modeled by

$$L = 114t^2 + 434t + 8450.$$

Write a model that represents the total amount, N (in millions of dollars), spent on national advertising. Use the model to approximate the amount spent on national advertising in 1986.

(Source: McCann-Erickson, Inc.)

76. *Red Foxes*   The weights (in pounds) of twenty red foxes is given below. Find the mean, range, and standard deviation for these data.

8.5	9.0	11.0	9.5	10.0
10.5	8.0	9.0	9.0	10.5
9.5	8.5	8.0	10.0	9.0
10.0	9.0	9.5	8.0	8.5

77. *Red Foxes*   What percent of the weights in Exercise 76 lie within one standard deviation of the mean weight?

78. *Market Testing*   To test consumer reaction to a new type of potato chip dip, people in grocery stores were asked to taste the dip and then check the box by the picture that best describes their reaction to the dip. Each of the pictures was assigned a number from -3 to 3. The numbers at the right show the reactions of 25 people to the chip dip. Find the mean and standard deviation of these data.

$+2,$	$-1,$	$+3,$	$+1,$	$+3$
$+1,$	$0,$	$+1,$	$-3,$	-1
$+1,$	$+1,$	$+1,$	$0,$	0
$-2,$	$+3,$	$0,$	$+2,$	$+1$
$-1,$	$+3,$	$+2,$	$-3,$	-1

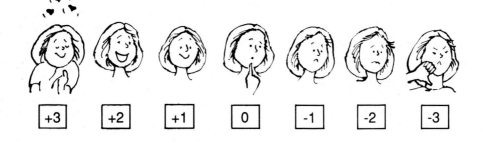

79. *One-Hundred-Year-Old Box*   On April 30, 1989, Benjamin P. Field opened a box that had been in his family since 1889. His father had told him that the box had been sealed on April 30, 1889, and that it contained memorabilia of the centennial of George Washington's first inaugural. The box had a volume of 2280 cubic inches. The box's dimensions were $5x$ inches by $2(x + 1)$ inches by $6x + 1$ inches. What is x? What were the dimensions of the box? (To see what was in the box, look at the September 1989 issue of *National Geographic*.)

Ten Decades in America   **In Exercises 80–89, each of the events, people, or objects is associated with a decade between 1890 and 1990. To find the decade, find the only real zero of the function. Then use the chart below to match the decade with the event, person(s), organization, activity, or object.**

a. 1890–1899	**b.** 1900–1909	**c.** 1910–1919	**d.** 1920–1929
e. 1930–1939	**f.** 1940–1949	**g.** 1950–1959	**h.** 1960–1969
i. 1970–1979	**j.** 1980–1989		

80. The Supremes:
$f(x) = 2x^3 - 16x^2 + x - 8$

81. Wright Brothers:
$f(x) = 2x^3 - x^2 - 4x - 4$

82. Shirley Temple:
$f(x) = x^3 - x^2 - 12x - 40$

83. Compact Discs:
$f(x) = x^3 - 10x^2 + x - 10$

84. United Nations:
$f(x) = x^3 - 6x^2 + 3x - 18$

85. Richie Valens:
$f(x) = 4x^3 - 28x^2 + 3x - 21$

86. World War I:
$f(x) = 3x^3 - 9x^2 + 7x - 21$

87. United States Bicentennial:
$f(x) = 3x^3 - 27x^2 + 4x - 36$

88. Chicago World's Fair:
$f(x) = x^3 - x^2 + 9x - 9$

89. Charleston (the dance):
$f(x) = 2x^3 - 8x^2 + x - 4$

In Exercises 1 and 2, perform the indicated operation.

1. $(4x^3 - 3x^2 + 5) - (x^3 - 2x^2 + x - 7)$ **2.** $(2x - 7)^2$

In Exercises 3 and 4, sketch the graph of the function.

3. $f(x) = x^4 - 2$ **4.** $f(x) = (x - 5)^3$

In Exercises 5 and 6, solve the equation.

5. $x^3 - 10x^2 + 25x = 0$ **6.** $x^4 - 3x^3 + x - 3 = 0$

In Exercises 7 and 8, completely factor the polynomial with respect to the integers.

7. $2x^3 - 2x^2 - 12x$ **8.** $x^4 - 3x^2 - 4$

9. Determine how many x-intercepts the graph of $f(x) = x^3 - x^2 - 3x + 3$ has.

10. Write an equation of a polynomial function that has a leading coefficient of 1 and has $2i$, $-2i$, and 5 as its only zeros.

11. Find $f(4)$ for $f(x) = 5x^4 - 16x^3 - 14x^2 - 11x + 11$.

12. Use long division to divide $(6x^3 - 17x^2 - 5x + 6)$ by $(2x - 1)$.

13. Use synthetic division to divide $(12x^3 + 31x^2 - 17x - 6)$ by $(x + 3)$.

14. Find the x-intercepts of the graph of $f(x) = x^3 - 19x + 30$.

15. Find all zeros of $f(x) = x^3 - 4x^2 + 9x - 36$. (Hint: $3i$ is a solution.)

16. Use the rational zero test to list all *possible* rational zeros of $f(x) = 5x^3 + 19x^2 + 22x + 8$.

17. Which of the possible rational zeros listed in Exercise 16 are actual zeros of $f(x) = 5x^3 + 19x^2 + 22x + 8$?

18. The circle graph at the right shows the approximate number of calories per serving for eight types of pies. Find the mean and the standard deviation of the eight numbers. (Calories are based on a one-eighth serving of a 9-inch pie.)

A Piece Of The Pie
How many calories in your slice of pie? Check the "pie chart" for your favorites

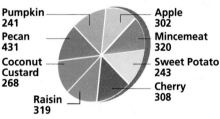

Pumpkin 241   Apple 302
Pecan 431   Mincemeat 320
Coconut Custard 268   Sweet Potato 243
Raisin 319   Cherry 308

In Exercises 19 and 20, use the following information.

The average number of miles driven annually by men and by women can be modeled by

$f(t) = 3.14t^2 + 177.52t + 11{,}660.61$ **Men**
$g(t) = 13.72t^2 - 74.30t + 5421.10$ **Women**

where $t = 0$ represents 1970. *(Source: U.S. Department of Transportation)*

19. In which year did men drive 15,586 miles?   **20.** In which year did women drive 5470 miles?

In Exercises 1–3, simplify the expression.

1. $3\sqrt[5]{5} + 4\sqrt[5]{5}$

2. $7\sqrt[3]{9} - 2\sqrt[3]{72}$

3. $-4\sqrt[4]{405} + \sqrt[4]{80}$

4. Find the geometric mean of 45 and 125.

5. The geometric mean of 27 and x is 9. What's x?

In Exercises 6–11, solve the equation.

6. $\sqrt{x} - 2 = 7$

7. $3x^{1/2} + 4 = 14$

8. $-2\sqrt{x + 5} + 6 = -10$

9. $\frac{1}{2}(x - 6)^{1/3} + 7 = 6$

10. $5\sqrt[3]{x + 2} - 6 = -16$

11. $3(2x + 1)^{1/2} - 4 = 5$

In Exercises 12–14, sketch the graph of the function.

12. $f(x) = 2\left(\frac{1}{4}\right)^x$

13. $f(x) = 3\left(\frac{4}{3}\right)^x$

14. $f(x) = \sqrt{x - 2} + 1$

In Exercises 15–20, solve the equation.

15. $\log_2 x = 3$

16. $\ln x = 10$

17. $3e^x = 8$

18. $10^x = 4$

19. $6 + \frac{1}{2}e^{2x} = 9$

20. $\frac{1}{4}(3)^x = \frac{3}{4}$

In Exercises 21–23, expand the expression.

21. $\log_{10} 3x^2 y^3$

22. $\ln 4xy^2$

23. $\ln\left(\frac{6x}{5y}\right)$

In Exercises 24–26, condense the expression.

24. $\log_7 4 + \log_7 y - 2\log_7 3$

25. $\frac{1}{4}\ln 3 - \ln 4$

26. $\frac{3}{2}(\log_2 x + \log_2 y)$

In Exercises 27–32, sketch the graph of the function.

27. $f(x) = 1 + \ln(x - 2)$

28. $f(x) = e^{x+2} - 4$

29. $f(x) = \log_{10}(4x - 1)$

30. $f(x) = 3\left(\frac{1}{2}\right)^x + 2$

31. $f(x) = (x + 1)^3 + 2$

32. $f(x) = x^4 - 6$

In Exercises 33–38, perform the indicated operation.

33. $(4x^2 + 3x - 1) + (5x^3 + 2x^2 + 5)$

34. $(9x + 3) + (4x^4 - x^3 + 2x + 6)$

35. $(3x^3 + 2x + 7) - (4x^2 - 3x + 2)$

36. $(9x^4 - x^2 + 6) - (x^3 + 5x + 5)$

37. $(2x + 1)(x^3 + 2x - 3)$

38. $(3x - 1)^3$

In Exercises 39 and 40, use long division. In Exercises 41 and 42 use synthetic division.

39. $(x^3 + 3x + 2) \div (x - 7)$

40. $(x^4 + 5x^2 - x - 5) \div (x + 1)$

41. $(2x^3 + 4x^2 - 3x + 1) \div (x - 5)$

42. $(-6x^4 + 3x^3 - x + 6) \div (x + 2)$

In Exercises 43–46, find all solutions of the equation.

43. $2x^3 - 3x^2 - 5x + 6 = 0$

44. $x^4 - 12x^2 + 27 = 0$

45. $2x^4 + x^3 - 8x^2 - x + 6 = 0$

46. $x^4 + 3x^3 - 2x^2 + 6x - 8 = 0$

Depreciation   **In Exercises 47 and 48, use the following information.**

You are an accountant for a company that has just purchased a delivery truck for $30,000. For tax purposes, the truck is to be depreciated using the *double-declining balances method.* With this method, each year the "book-value" of the truck drops by $\frac{2}{n}$ of the previous year's value, where n is the number of years. If the useful life of the truck is estimated to be 5 years, then the book value, V, in year t is given by

$$V = 30{,}000 \cdot \left(1 - \frac{2}{5}\right)^t.$$

47. What is the book value of the delivery truck after 2 years?

48. When is the book value of the truck equal to $3880?

Tennessee   **In Exercises 49 and 50, use the grid superimposed on the map of Tennessee. Each unit of the grid represents 8 miles.**

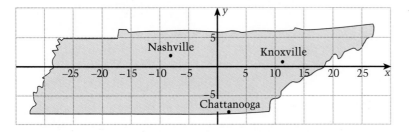

49. You are riding in a "bike-a-thon" fundraiser from Knoxville to Nashville, Tennessee. Your pledges total $12 per mile. How much money will you raise by traveling the entire distance?

50. Approximately how much closer is Chattanooga to Knoxville than Nashville is to Chattanooga?

Acid and Base   **In Exercises 51 and 52, use the formula for pH on page 451.**

51. The pH of cola is 3. What is its concentration of hydrogen ions?

52. Hydrochloric acid secreted by the stomach after a meal has a hydrogen ion concentration of 0.0012 moles per liter. What is the pH of hydrochloric acid?

Major League Baseball   **In Exercises 53 and 54, use the following information.**

For 1982 through 1990, the revenue, R (in millions of dollars), and expenses, E (in millions of dollars), for major league baseball can be modeled by $R = 117t + 113$ and $E = 8t^2 - 29t + 633$ where $t = 3$ represents 1983.

53. In what year did major league baseball have expenses of about $1020 million?

54. In what year did major league baseball have a loss of about 44 million dollars?

CHAPTER
10

Rational Functions

LESSONS

10.1 Graphs of Rational Functions • 518

10.2 Inverse and Joint Variation • 526

10.3 Multiplying and Dividing Rational Expressions • 533

10.4 Solving Rational Equations • 541

10.5 Addition, Subtraction, and Complex Fractions • 548

10.6 Exploring Data: The Algebra of Finance • 555

Fire fighters, such as these in New York City, must handle water that is under great pressure. The speed of this pressurized water in their hoses is inversely proportional to the diameter of the hose.

Speed of Water Flowing at a Rate of 2 ft³/sec

A fire department may use different size hoses for fighting fires. When the water flow remains constant, water flows at a faster speed in a narrower hose than in a wider one. The speed of water, s (in feet per second), varies inversely with the cross-sectional area, A (in square feet), of the hose.

$$s = \frac{k}{A}$$

If a hose has a cross-sectional area of 0.02 square feet, and the speed of water flowing through the hose is 100 feet per second, you can conclude that $k = 2$ cubic feet per second. This means that using the same pump, a hose with a cross-sectional area of 0.05 square feet will flow at a speed of 40 feet per second.

10.1

Graphs of Rational Functions

What you should learn:

Goal 1 How to graph a rational function using asymptotes

Goal 2 How to use rational functions as real-life models

Why you should learn it:

You can model many real-life situations with rational functions, such as average costs over time.

Goal 1 Graphing a Rational Function

A **rational function** is a function of the form

$$f(x) = \frac{p(x)}{q(x)}, \qquad q(x) \neq 0$$

where $p(x)$ and $q(x)$ are polynomials in x. The *domain* of a rational function consists of the values of x for which the denominator $q(x)$ is not zero. For instance, the domain of

$$f(x) = \frac{x + 2}{x - 1}$$

is all real numbers except $x = 1$. When sketching the graph of a rational function, you should give special attention to the shape of the graph near x-values that are not in the domain.

Example 1 Sketching the Graph of a Rational Function

Sketch the graph of $f(x) = \frac{x + 2}{x - 1}$.

Solution Begin by noticing that the domain is all real numbers except $x = 1$. Next construct a table of values, including x-values that are close to 1 on the left *and* on the right.

x-Values to the Left of 1

x	−3	−2	−1	0	0.5	0.9
f(x)	0.25	0	−0.5	−2	−5	−29

x-Values to the Right of 1

x	1.1	1.5	2	3	4	5
f(x)	31	7	4	2.5	2	1.75

Plot the points to the left of 1 and connect them with a smooth curve. Do the same for the points to the right of 1. *Do not* connect the two portions of the graph, which are called **branches**. ∎

For the graph of the function in Example 1, as x approaches 1 from the left, the values of $f(x)$ approach negative infinity. As x approaches 1 from the right, the values of $f(x)$ approach positive infinity.

An **asymptote** of a graph is a line to which the graph becomes arbitrarily close as $|x|$ or $|y|$ increases without bound. In other words, if a graph has an asymptote, then it is possible to move far enough from the origin so that there is almost no difference between the graph and the asymptote.

The graph in Example 1 has two asymptotes: the line $x = 1$ is a **vertical asymptote,** and the line $y = 1$ is a **horizontal asymptote.** Here are some other examples.

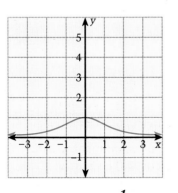

Graph of $f(x) = \dfrac{1}{x^2 + 1}$

Horizontal asymptote: y = 0
Vertical asymptote: None

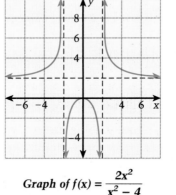

Graph of $f(x) = \dfrac{2x^2}{x^2 - 4}$

Horizontal asymptote: y = 2
Vertical asymptote: x = 2, x = −2

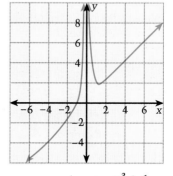

Graph of $f(x) = \dfrac{x^3 + 1}{x^2}$

Horizontal asymptote: None
Vertical asymptote: x = 0

As you can see from these examples, the graph of a rational function may have no horizontal or vertical asymptotes, or it may have several. Here are some guidelines for finding the horizontal and vertical asymptotes of a rational function.

Horizontal and Vertical Asymptotes

Let $f(x) = \dfrac{p(x)}{q(x)}$ where $p(x)$ and $q(x)$ have *no common factors.*

1. The graph of f has a vertical asymptote at *each* real zero of $q(x)$.

2. The graph of f has, at most, one horizontal asymptote.

- If the degree of $p(x)$ is less than the degree of $q(x)$, then the line $y = 0$ is a horizontal asymptote.
- If the degree of $p(x)$ is equal to the degree of $q(x)$, then the line $y = \dfrac{a}{b}$ is a horizontal asymptote, where a is the leading coefficient of $p(x)$ and b is the leading coefficient of $q(x)$.
- If the degree of $p(x)$ is greater than the degree of $q(x)$, then the graph has no horizontal asymptote.

Try applying these guidelines to the three graphs shown above.

The work of the Dutch artist M. C. Escher (1889–1972) has intrigued many people. Escher's drawings involve repeated patterns and optical illusions. For instance, the Escher piece at the right, Drawing Hands, shows the impossible, but fun to look at, illusion of two hands drawing each other.

Goal 2 Using Rational Functions in Real Life

Real Life
Business

Example 2 Finding the Average Cost

As a fund-raising project, your math club is publishing a calendar with an Escher drawing on the cover. The cost of photography, typesetting, printing, and using the Escher drawing is $850. In addition to these one-time charges, the *unit cost* of printing each calendar is $3.25. Let x represent the number of calendars that your club has printed. Write a model that represents the average cost per calendar.

Average Cost per Calendar

Solution The total cost, C, of printing x calendars is $C = 3.25x + 850$. The average cost, A, per calendar for printing x calendars is given by

$$A = \frac{3.25x + 850}{x}.$$

From the graph at the left, notice that the average cost decreases as the number of calendars increases. ∎

Communicating about ALGEBRA

▶ **SHARING IDEAS about the Lesson**

A. Use the model in Example 2. Copy and complete the table.

Number of calendars, x	10	100	1000	10,000
Average cost, A (in dollars)	?	?	?	?

B. What is the horizontal asymptote of the graph shown in Example 2? What is the real-life significance of this asymptote?

EXERCISES

Guided Practice

▶ **CRITICAL THINKING about the Lesson**

1. Explain what is meant by "the domain of a rational function."

2. Complete the table for $f(x) = \dfrac{x^2 + 1}{2x^2 - 4}$. Then sketch the graph of f.

x	-4	-2	-1.6	-1.4	-1	0	1	1.4	1.6	2	4
$f(x)$	?	?	?	?	?	?	?	?	?	?	?

3. Give an example of a rational function whose graph has two vertical asymptotes: $x = 1$ and $x = 5$.

In Exercises 4–6, identify all horizontal and vertical asymptotes of the graph of the function.

4. $f(x) = \dfrac{10x^2 + 3}{5x^2}$

5. $f(x) = \dfrac{3x^4 - 2}{2x - 1}$

6. $f(x) = \dfrac{4x^2}{8x^3 - 1}$

Independent Practice

In Exercises 7–12, state the domain of the function.

7. $f(x) = \dfrac{3x}{x + 16}$

8. $f(x) = \dfrac{9}{2x - 4}$

9. $f(x) = \dfrac{x + 4}{x^2 + 2x + 1}$

10. $f(x) = \dfrac{x + 6}{(x + 1)(x - 8)}$

11. $f(x) = \dfrac{1 + x}{1 - x}$

12. $f(x) = \dfrac{2}{x^2 - 4x - 12}$

13. Complete the table for $f(x) = \dfrac{x - 2}{x - 3}$.

x	2	2.5	2.75	3.25	3.5	4
$f(x)$	?	?	?	?	?	?

14. Complete the table for $f(x) = \dfrac{x + 2}{x - 2}$.

x	1	1.5	1.75	2.25	2.5	3
$f(x)$	?	?	?	?	?	?

In Exercises 15–26, identify all horizontal and vertical asymptotes of the graph of the function.

15. $f(x) = \dfrac{1}{x - 5}$

16. $f(x) = \dfrac{x}{x^2 - 9}$

17. $f(x) = \dfrac{7x}{x^3 + 1}$

18. $f(x) = \dfrac{3x^2 - 1}{x^3}$

19. $f(x) = \dfrac{6x^2 + 3}{x - 1}$

20. $f(x) = \dfrac{5x^3 - 4}{x^2 + 4x - 5}$

21. $f(x) = \dfrac{3x^3 + 30}{2x^3}$

22. $f(x) = \dfrac{2x^2 + x - 9}{3x^2 - 12}$

23. $f(x) = \dfrac{12x^4 + 10x - 3}{3x^4}$

24. $f(x) = \dfrac{13x^4 + x^2}{6x + 3}$

25. $f(x) = \dfrac{4x^2}{x^3 - x^2 - 2x}$

26. $f(x) = \dfrac{11x}{5x^3 + 40}$

In Exercises 27–30, match the function with its graph.

27. $f(x) = \dfrac{x + 3}{x - 2}$ **28.** $f(x) = \dfrac{-8}{x^2 - 4}$ **29.** $f(x) = \dfrac{3}{x + 2}$ **30.** $f(x) = \dfrac{x - 3}{2x + 4}$

a. **b.** **c.** **d.**

In Exercises 31–42, sketch the graph of the function.

31. $f(x) = \dfrac{2x - 6}{x + 4}$ **32.** $f(x) = \dfrac{-5}{x + 9}$ **33.** $f(x) = \dfrac{3}{4x + 10}$

34. $f(x) = \dfrac{5x + 1}{x^2 - 1}$ **35.** $f(x) = \dfrac{3x^2 + 4x + 4}{x^2 - 5x - 6}$ **36.** $f(x) = \dfrac{-3x^2}{2x + 6}$

37. $f(x) = \dfrac{3x^3 + 1}{4x^3 - 32}$ **38.** $f(x) = \dfrac{5 - x}{4x^2 - 3x - 1}$ **39.** $f(x) = \dfrac{x^2 - 6x - 9}{x^3 + 27}$

40. $f(x) = \dfrac{-2x^2}{x^2 - 9}$ **41.** $f(x) = \dfrac{x^2 - 10x + 24}{3x}$ **42.** $f(x) = \dfrac{x^3 + 5x^2 - 1}{x^2 - 4x}$

Renting Videos   **In Exercises 43 and 44, use the following information.**

You have purchased a VCR for $180. You also joined a video rental store where you can rent movies for $3 each.

43. Write a model that represents your average cost per movie (including the price of the VCR). Sketch the graph of this model. What is the horizontal asymptote and what does it represent?

44. Suppose that the cost of admission to a movie theater is $6.00. How many videos must you rent to make your average cost per video less than $6.00?

45. *Hospital Costs*   For 1970 to 1990, the average daily cost, C (in dollars), per patient at a community hospital can be modeled by

$$C = \frac{746{,}676 + 16{,}557t}{10{,}000 - 864t + 22.8t^2}$$

where $t = 0$ represents 1970. Sketch the graph of this model. Would you expect this model to continue to represent patient costs through the year 2010? Explain.

In 1990, Americans rented about 6 million movie videos each day, about twice the number of tickets sold at movie theaters.

46. *Hotel Revenue*   For 1970 through 1990, the total revenue, R (in billions of dollars), from hotels and motels can be modeled by

$$R = \frac{3200 + 270t}{1000 - 33t}$$

where $t = 0$ represents 1970. Sketch the graph of this model. Would you expect this model to continue to represent hotel and motel revenue through the year 2000? Explain.

Integrated Review

In Exercises 47–50, perform the indicated division.

47. $(6x^3 + 9x - 4) \div (x + 4)$

48. $(9x^3 - 2x^2 + x - 2) \div (x - 1)$

49. $(2x^4 - 3x^3 - x^2 + 9) \div (x + 1)$

50. $(x^5 - 6x^3 - 2x^2 + 5x - 6) \div (x + 3)$

In Exercises 51–53, completely factor the polynomial with respect to the integers.

51. $x^4 + 2x^3 + 6x^2 + 18x - 27$

52. $2x^3 - x^2 - 2x + 1$

53. $3x^4 - 9x^2 - 12$

54. *Women Military Pilots*   Find the ratio of the total number of women military pilots (in the Air Force, Army, Navy, and Marines in 1991) to the total number of men military pilots. Use the graph at the right.

55. *Women Executives*   In 1991, women made up only 2.6% of the top corporate officers at Fortune 500 companies. Find the ratio of the number of women who were top corporate officers to the number of men who were top corporate officers.

Exploration and Extension

Slant Asymptotes   **In Exercises 56 and 57, use the information below to find the slant asymptote of the graph of the function. Then sketch the graph of the function and the slant asymptote.**

If the degree of the numerator of a *rational function* is exactly one more than the degree of the denominator, the graph of the function has a slant asymptote. For example, the graph of

$$f(x) = \frac{x^2 + x}{x - 2} = x + 3 + \frac{6}{x - 2}$$

has the line $y = x + 3$ as a slant asymptote.

56. $f(x) = \dfrac{x^2 - x - 2}{x - 1}$

57. $f(x) = \dfrac{x^2 + 5x + 8}{x + 3}$

Most graphing calculators have two graphing modes: a *connected mode* and a *dot mode.* The connected mode works well for graphs of functions that are continuous (have no holes or breaks). The connected mode does not, however, work well for the graphs of many rational functions because they often have two or more disconnected branches. To correct this problem, change the calculator to dot mode.

In the graphs shown below, notice that the graph on the left has a vertical line at approximately $x = 1$. This line is *not* part of the graph—it is simply the calculator's attempt at connecting the two branches of the graph.

Connected Mode   **Dot Mode**

Graph of $f(x) = \dfrac{x + 1}{x - 1}$ Graph of $f(x) = \dfrac{x + 1}{x - 1}$

Example 1:   Investigating Asymptotic Behavior

Some people think that the graph of a rational function cannot cross its horizontal asymptote. This, however, is not true. Use a graphing calculator to sketch the graph of

$$f(x) = \frac{2x^2 - 3x + 5}{x^2 + 1}$$

and its horizontal asymptote $y = 2$ on the screen. Find the x-value at which the graph crosses its horizontal asymptote.

Solution   From the screen below, it appears that the graph crosses the horizontal line $y = 2$ when $x = 1$. You can confirm this by substituting $x = 1$ in the function.

$$f(1) = \frac{2(1^2) - 3(1) + 5}{1^2 + 1} = \frac{4}{2} = 2 \quad \blacksquare$$

Example 2:   Pollution Level of a Pond

Some organic waste has fallen into a pond. Part of the decomposition process includes oxidation, whereby oxygen that is dissolved in the pond water is combined with decomposing material. Let $L = 1$ represent the normal oxygen level in the pond and let t represent the number of weeks after the waste is dumped. The oxygen level in the pond can be modeled by

$$L = \frac{t^2 - t + 1}{t^2 + 1}.$$

Sketch the graph of this model and use the graph to explain how the oxygen level changed during the 15 weeks after the waste was dumped.

Solution   The screen at the right shows the graph of the model and the line $L = 1$ (the normal oxygen level). From the graph, you can see that the oxygen dropped to 50% of its normal level after 1 week. Then, during the next several weeks, the oxygen level gradually returned to normal. By the end of the 15th week, the oxygen level had reached 93% of normal. ■

Oxygen Level of Pond

Exercises

In Exercises 1–6, find ranges for x and y so that the calculator screen displays the basic characteristics of the graph of the rational function.

1. $f(x) = \dfrac{x - 5}{x + 1}$

2. $f(x) = \dfrac{2x - 5}{x - 4}$

3. $f(x) = \dfrac{x^2 - 1}{x^2 - 4}$

4. $f(x) = \dfrac{2x^2 - 7x + 5}{x^2 + 2x + 1}$

5. $f(x) = \dfrac{x^2 - 5x}{2x^2 + 1}$

6. $f(x) = \dfrac{x^3 - 1}{x^3 + 1}$

7. Use a graphing calculator to sketch the graphs of f and g on the same screen. (Use a range of $-5 \leq x \leq 5$ and $-4 \leq y \leq 20$.)

$$f(x) = x^2 \qquad \text{and} \qquad g(x) = \frac{x^3 + x^2 + 1}{x + 1}$$

Use long division to rewrite $g(x)$. Then use the result to explain why the two graphs are close to each other for large values of $|x|$.

8. *Sale of Long-Playing Albums*   For 1975 to 1990, the number, N (in millions), of long-playing albums sold in the United States can be approximated by the model

$$L = \frac{1000 - 74.41t + 1.45t^2}{2.94 - 0.336t + 0.0125t^2}$$

where $t = 5$ represents 1975. Sketch the graph of this function and use the graph to find the year that the sales peaked.

(Source: Recording Industry Association of America)

10.2

Inverse and Joint Variation

What you should learn:

Goal 1 How to create and use real-life models using inverse variation

Goal 2 How to create and use models of real-life situations that use joint variation

Why you should learn it:

You can model many real-life relationships with joint or inverse variation, such as sound intensity and distance from its source.

Connections
Electronics

Goal 1 Using Inverse Variation

In Lesson 2.4, you studied *direct* variation. Recall that two variable quantities x and y vary directly if, for a constant k,

$$\frac{y}{x} = k \quad \text{or} \quad y = kx. \quad \textit{Direct variation}$$

In this lesson, you will study two other types of variation: *inverse variation* and *joint variation*.

Inverse Variation

The variables x and y **vary inversely** if, for a constant k,

$$yx = k \quad \text{or} \quad y = \frac{k}{x}. \quad \textit{Inverse variation}$$

The number k is the **constant of variation.**

Example 1 *Using Inverse Variation*

The resistance, R, of wire varies inversely with its cross-sectional area, A. A 500-centimeter length of copper wire with a radius of 0.2 centimeter has a resistance of 0.025 ohm. Find the resistance of a copper wire of the same length whose radius is 0.1 centimeter.

Solution Since the wire has a radius of 0.2 centimeter, it has a cross-sectional area of $A = \pi r^2 = \pi(0.2)^2 = 0.04\pi$ cm^2.

$$RA = k \quad \textit{Model for inverse variation}$$

$$(0.025)(0.04\pi) = k \quad \textit{Substitute 0.025 for R; 0.04π for A.}$$

$$0.001\pi = k \quad \textit{Simplify.}$$

Thus an equation that relates R and A is

$$RA = 0.001\pi \quad \text{or} \quad R = \frac{0.001\pi}{A}.$$

The resistance of the piece of copper wire whose radius is 0.1 centimeter is

$$R = \frac{0.001\pi}{(0.1)^2\pi} = \frac{0.001\pi}{0.01\pi} = 0.1 \text{ ohm.} \qquad \blacksquare$$

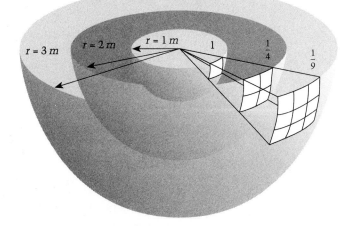

Intensity of sound is measured in watts per square centimeter (or watts per square meter). The intensity of a sound varies inversely with the square of its distance from the source. The diagram suggests why the intensity, at a distance of 3 meters, is one-ninth the intensity at a distance of 1 meter.

Airport Safety

Example 2 Using Inverse Variation

At a distance of 1 meter, the intensity of jet engine noise is 10 watts per square meter. An airport cargo worker is 15 meters from the jet engine. What is the sound intensity at 15 meters?

Solution Let *I* represent the intensity (in watts per square meter) and let *r* represent the distance (in meters). From the information given above, you know that *I* varies inversely as r^2. Thus you can write the following model.

$$Ir^2 = k \quad \textit{Model for inverse variation}$$

$$(10)(1) = k \quad \textit{Substitute 10 for I and 1 for } r^2.$$

$$10 = k \quad \textit{Simplify.}$$

Thus an equation that relates *I* and r^2 is

$$Ir^2 = 10$$

$$I = \frac{10}{r^2}.$$

At a distance of *r* = 15 meters, the intensity is

$$I = \frac{10}{15^2}$$

$$\approx 0.044 \text{ watt per square meter.}$$

This intensity corresponds to about 126 decibels—above the level that can cause damage. (To rewrite this intensity as decibels, see page 418.) ∎

Airport workers wear ear protectors to prevent ear damage from the intensity of jet engine noise.

Joint variation occurs when a quantity varies directly as the product of *two or more* other quantities. For instance, if $z = kxy$, then z varies jointly with the product of x and y.

Real Life
Solar Power

Example 3 *Using Joint Variation*

The horsepower, h, needed for a water pump varies jointly with the well depth, d (in feet), and the rate, r (in gallons per minute). A 55-horsepower motor can pump water from a depth of 150 feet at a rate of 990 gallons per minute. The 1991 *Alternative Energy Sourcebook* has the following description of a pump that runs on solar energy. Estimate the horsepower of this pump.

For your deep-well pumping needs (well depths to 1000 feet at rates of $2\frac{3}{4}$ gallons per minute), we offer the Solarjack Pump water pumping system.

Solution

$$h = krd \qquad \textit{Joint variation model}$$
$$55 = k(990)(150) \qquad \textit{Let h = 55, r = 990, and d = 150.}$$
$$\frac{1}{2700} = k \qquad \textit{Solve for k.}$$

Thus an equation that relates h, r, and d is

$$h = \frac{1}{2700}rd.$$

For a rate of $r = 2.75$ gallons per minute and a depth of $d = 1000$ feet, you would need a motor that has

$$h = \frac{1}{2700}(2.75)(1000)$$
$$\approx 1 \text{ horsepower.} \qquad \blacksquare$$

Communicating about **ALGEBRA**

▶ **SHARING IDEAS about the Lesson**

The Sunraycer, a solar-powered car, has 9500 solar cells to generate electricity for a motor that can deliver up to 4 horsepower. How many solar cells would you estimate are in the Solarjack Pump? To answer the question, did you use direct or inverse variation? Explain.

EXERCISES

▶ **CRITICAL THINKING about the Lesson**

In Exercises 1–4, do *x* and *y* vary directly or inversely?

1. $xy = \frac{1}{2}$

2. $x = \frac{9}{y}$

3. $\frac{x}{y} = 5$

4. $y = 3x$

Distance, Rate, and Time **In Exercises 5 and 6, use the formula *d* = *rt*, where *d* is the distance in miles, *r* is the rate in miles per hour, and *t* is the time in hours.**

5. A car travels a distance of 30 miles. Do the rate and time vary directly or inversely? Explain.

6. A car travels for 30 minutes. Do the distance and rate vary directly or inversely? Explain.

In Exercises 7–9, the variables *x* and *y* vary inversely. Use the given pair of values to find an equation that relates the variables.

7. $x = 3$, $y = -2$

8. $x = 4$, $y = 6$

9. $x = 5$, $y = 1$

In Exercises 10–12, the variable *z* varies jointly with the product of *x* and *y*. Use the given values to find an equation that relates the variables.

10. $x = 3$, $y = 8$, $z = 2$

11. $x = -5$, $y = 2$, $z = \frac{3}{4}$

12. $x = 1$, $y = \frac{1}{2}$, $z = 4$

In Exercises 13–15, find an equation that relates the variables.

13. *Typing Time*   The time, t (in minutes), you need to type a 2000-word paper varies inversely with the rate, r (in words per minute), that you can type. When typing 40 words per minute, you can finish in 50 minutes.

14. *Pressure*   The pressure, P (in pounds per square inch), that a 160-pound person's shoe exerts on the ground when walking varies inversely with the area, A (in square inches), of the sole of the shoe. When the shoes have a sole area of 40 square inches, the pressure is 4 pounds per square inch.

15. *Electrical Resistance*   The resistance, R (in ohms), of a wire varies directly with the length, L (in centimeters), of the wire, and inversely with the cross-sectional area, A (in square centimeters), of the wire. A 500-centimeter piece of copper wire with a radius of 0.2 centimeter has a resistance of 0.025 ohm.

16. Speed of a Whirlpool   A naturally-occurring whirlpool in the Strait of Messina, a channel between Sicily and the Italian mainland, is about 6 feet across at its center, and is said to be large enough to swallow small fishing boats. The speed, s (in feet per second), of the water in the whirlpool varies inversely with the radius, r (in feet). If the water speed is 2.5 feet per second at a radius of 30 feet, what is the speed of the water at a radius of 3 feet?

Many whirlpools occur naturally. This one is on the lake side of the Rance barrage in northern France.

17. Seesaw   To balance a seesaw, the distance, d (in feet), a person is from the fulcrum is inversely proportional to his or her weight, w (in pounds). Roger, who weighs 120 pounds, is sitting 6 feet away from the fulcrum. Ellen weighs 108 pounds. How far from the fulcrum must she sit to balance the seesaw?

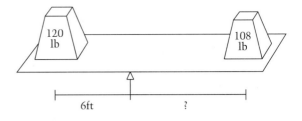

18. Chemistry   The temperature, T (in degrees Kelvin), of an enclosed gas varies jointly with the product of the volume, V (in cubic centimeters), and the pressure, P (in kilograms per square centimeter). The temperature of a gas is 294°K when the volume is 8000 cubic centimeters and the pressure is 0.75 kilogram per square centimeter. What is the temperature when the volume is 7000 cubic centimeters and the pressure is 0.87 kilogram per square centimeter?

19. Simple Interest   The simple interest, I (in dollars), for a savings account is jointly proportional to the product of the time, t (in years), and the principal, P (in dollars). After three months, the interest on a principal of $5000 is $106.25. What is the interest after nine months?

Light Illumination   **In Exercises 20 and 21, use the following information.**

The illumination, I (in luxes), of a surface varies inversely with the square of the distance, d (in meters), from the light source to the surface. One meter away from a certain light, the illumination is 750 luxes. (One lux is equal to 0.093 footcandle.)

20. Write an equation that relates I and d.

21. Find the illumination at a distance of 2 meters.

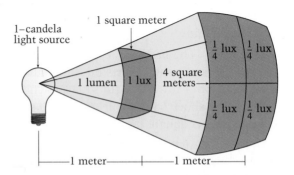

A 200-watt incandescent bulb in a desk lamp provides about 750 luxes (70 footcandles) at the desk's surface.

Lifting an Object   In Exercises 22 and 23, use the following information.

The work, W (in joules), done when lifting an object is jointly proportional to the product of the mass, m (in kilograms), of the object and the height, h (in meters), that the object is lifted. The work done when a 120-kilogram object is lifted 1.8 meters above the ground is 2116.8 joules.

22. Write an equation that relates W, m, and h.

23. How much work is done when lifting a 100-kilogram object 1.5 meters above the ground?

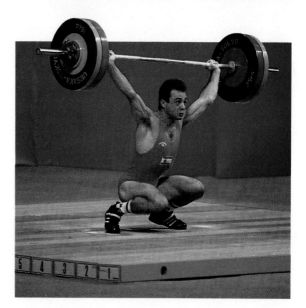

Integrated Review

In Exercises 24–29, sketch the graph of the rational function.

24. $f(x) = \dfrac{x - 5}{2x - 4}$

25. $f(x) = \dfrac{-2}{x + 1}$

26. $f(x) = \dfrac{6}{x - 9}$

27. $f(x) = \dfrac{3x - 4}{x + 2}$

28. $f(x) = \dfrac{x + 2}{x^2 + x - 6}$

29. $f(x) = \dfrac{4x - 1}{x^2 - 9}$

30. *Powers of Ten*   Which best estimates the voltage of common electrical house current?

   a. 1.1×10^{-1} **b.** 1.1×10^{0}

   c. 1.1×10^{1} **d.** 1.1×10^{2}

31. *Powers of Ten*   Which best estimates the number of people who have been president of the United States?

   a. 4.0×10^{-1} **b.** 4.0×10^{0}

   c. 4.0×10^{1} **d.** 4.0×10^{2}

Exploration and Extension

Engineering   In Exercises 32–35, use the following information.

The load, P (in pounds), that can be safely supported by a horizontal beam varies jointly as the product of the width, W (in feet), of the beam and the square of its depth, D (in feet), and inversely as its length, L (in feet).

32. How does P change when the width and length of the beam are doubled?

33. How does P change when the width and depth of the beam are doubled?

34. How does P change when all three of the dimensions are doubled?

35. How does P change when the depth of the beam is halved?

1. Simplify: $(2x^3 - 3x) + (x^3 - 4x)$. **(9.1)**
2. Simplify: $(3x - 4)(2x + 1)$. **(9.1)**
3. Evaluate $\log_3 81^4$. **(8.2)**
4. Evaluate $27^{-2/3}$. **(7.3)**
5. Sketch $f(x) = (x - 3)^5 + 1$. **(9.2)**
6. Sketch $f(x) = e^{x-2} - 4$. **(8.1)**
7. Sketch $y = (x - 5)^2 + 3$. **(5.3)**
8. Sketch $y < 3|x - 2| - 5$. **(2.6)**
9. Solve $|2x + 5| < 3$. **(1.7)**
10. Solve $\sqrt{3x - 2} = 5$. **(7.5)**
11. Solve $|x - 5| > 2$. **(1.7)**
12. Solve $x^{2/3} = 36$. **(7.5)**
13. Factor $6x^2 - 11x - 10$. **(9.3)**
14. Find the intercepts of $\frac{x}{8} - \frac{y}{2} = 1$. **(2.3)**
15. What is 108% of $300?
16. Divide $\frac{3}{8}$ by $\frac{15}{28}$.
17. Find a quadratic function containing $(1, -3)$, $(2, -1)$, $(3, 2)$, and $(4, 6)$. **(6.6)**
18. Find the slope of the line through $(2, -7)$ and $(-5, -1)$. **(2.2)**
19. Given $f(1) = 2$ and $f(n) = f(n - 1) - 3$, find $f(4)$. **(6.6)**
20. For what values of c has $f(x) = 3x^2 - 4x - c$ only one x-intercept? **(5.4)**

Milestones ABEL AND GALOIS

| 1821 | 1822 | 1823 | 1824 | 1825 | 1826 | 1827 | 1828 | 1829 | 1830 | 1831 | 1832 | 1833 | 1834 | 1835 |

Abel's proof published

Galois' proof published

In the exploration of algebra over the centuries, general solutions were found for second-, third-, and fourth-degree polynomial equations. Attempts to find an algebraic solution for the fifth-degree polynomial equation, however, met with failure time and again.

In the early 1800's, Niels Henrik Abel thought he had found the solution for a general fifth-degree equation, but later discovered it contained an error. In 1824, he published a proof that showed that for any degree greater than four, the general polynomial equation could not be solved algebraically. Another young mathematician, Évariste Galois, published a proof in 1831 in which he elaborated on Abel's work to show how to determine whether or not a given equation can be solved algebraically. Of significance in both men's work was the concept of a *group*. Subsequent research in group theory gave mathematicians new ways to explore and describe algebraic structures. The work of Abel and Galois marked the beginning of the modern theory of equations.

Abel

Galois

Which of these events also took place in 1831: Peru's secession from Columbia, Belgium's separation from the Netherlands, or John Quincy Adams' inauguration as president of the United States?

10.3

Multiplying and Dividing Rational Expressions

What you should learn:

Goal 1 How to multiply and divide rational expressions, writing the result in simplest form

Goal 2 How to use rational expressions as real-life models

Why you should learn it:

You can model many real-life situations with rational models, such as the ratio of the surface area of the volume of biological species.

Goal 1 Working with Rational Expressions

A rational expression is in **simplified** (or **simplest**) **form** if its numerator and denominator have no common factors (other than ± 1). To simplify a rational expression, apply the following property.

Simplifying Fractions

Let a, b, and c be nonzero real numbers.

$$\frac{a\cancel{c}}{b\cancel{c}} = \frac{a}{b} \qquad \textit{Divide out common factor of c.}$$

LESSON INVESTIGATION

■ Investigating Simplification Strategies

Partner Activity The simplification property listed above allows you to divide out factors, not terms. With your partner, simplify the following. Discuss your strategy.

a. $\dfrac{x^2 + 4x + 4}{x + 2}$ **b.** $\dfrac{x - 3}{x^2 - 4x + 3}$ **c.** $\dfrac{x^2 - 12x}{12 - x}$

Study Tip

Simplifying a rational expression usually requires two steps. First, factor the numerator and the denominator. Then, divide out any factors that are common to both numerator and denominator.

Example 1   *Simplifying a Rational Expression*

Simplify: $\dfrac{x^2 - 4x - 12}{x^2 - 4}$.

Solution

$$\frac{x^2 - 4x - 12}{x^2 - 4} = \frac{(x + 2)(x - 6)}{(x + 2)(x - 2)} \qquad \textit{Factor numerator and denominator.}$$

$$= \frac{\cancel{(x + 2)}(x - 6)}{\cancel{(x + 2)}(x - 2)} \qquad \textit{Divide out common factor.}$$

$$= \frac{x - 6}{x - 2} \qquad \textit{Simplified form} \qquad ■$$

Multiplying rational expressions is similar to multiplying numerical fractions. In both cases, you multiply numerators, multiply denominators, and write the new fraction in simplest form.

$$\frac{a}{b} \cdot \frac{c}{d} = \frac{ac}{bd}$$

To divide one rational expression by another, multiply the first by the reciprocal of the second.

$$\frac{a}{b} \div \frac{c}{d} = \frac{a}{b} \cdot \frac{d}{c}$$

Example 2 *Multiplying Rational Expressions*

Multiply: $\dfrac{5x^2y}{2xy^3} \cdot \dfrac{6x^3y^2}{10y}$.

Solution

$$\frac{5x^2y}{2xy^3} \cdot \frac{6x^3y^2}{10y} = \frac{30x^5y^3}{20xy^4} \qquad \textit{Multiply numerators and denominators.}$$

$$= \frac{3 \cdot \cancel{10} \cdot \cancel{x} \cdot x^4 \cdot \cancel{y^3}}{2 \cdot \cancel{10} \cdot \cancel{x} \cdot y \cdot \cancel{y^3}} \qquad \textit{Factor and divide out common factors.}$$

$$= \frac{3x^4}{2y} \qquad \textit{Simplified form}$$ ∎

Example 3 *Multiplying Rational Expressions*

Multiply: $\dfrac{4x^2 - 4x}{x^2 + 2x - 3} \cdot \dfrac{x^2 + x - 6}{4x}$.

Solution

$$\frac{4x^2 - 4x}{x^2 + 2x - 3} \cdot \frac{x^2 + x - 6}{4x}$$

$$= \frac{4x(x-1)(x+3)(x-2)}{(x-1)(x+3)(4x)} \qquad \textit{Multiply numerators and denominators.}$$

$$= \frac{\cancel{4x}(\cancel{x-1})(\cancel{x+3})(x-2)}{(\cancel{x-1})(\cancel{x+3})(\cancel{4x})} \qquad \textit{Factor and divide out common factors.}$$

$$= x - 2 \qquad \textit{Simplified form}$$ ∎

The procedure for multiplying fractions can be extended to factors that are not all in fractional form. To do this, rewrite the nonfractional expression as a fraction with a denominator of 1. Here is a simple example.

$$\frac{x+3}{x-2} \cdot (5x) = \frac{x+3}{x-2} \cdot \frac{5x}{1}$$

$$= \frac{(x+3)(5x)}{x-2}$$

$$= \frac{5x(x+3)}{x-2}$$

Example 4   *Dividing Rational Expressions*

Divide: $\dfrac{2x}{3x - 12} \div \dfrac{x^2 - 2x}{x^2 - 6x + 8}$.

Solution

$$\frac{2x}{3x - 12} \div \frac{x^2 - 2x}{x^2 - 6x + 8} = \frac{2x}{3x - 12} \cdot \frac{x^2 - 6x + 8}{x^2 - 2x}$$

$$= \frac{(2x)(x - 2)(x - 4)}{(3)(x - 4)(x)(x - 2)}$$

$$= \frac{(2x)(x - 2)(x - 4)}{(3)(x - 4)(x)(x - 2)}$$

$$= \frac{2}{3} \qquad \blacksquare$$

Example 5   *Dividing a Rational Expression by a Polynomial*

Divide: $\dfrac{x^2 - 3x + 2}{4x^2} \div (x - 1)$.

Solution

$$\frac{x^2 - 3x + 2}{4x^2} \div (x - 1) = \frac{x^2 - 3x + 2}{4x^2} \cdot \frac{1}{x - 1}$$

$$= \frac{(x - 1)(x - 2)}{4x^2(x - 1)}$$

$$= \frac{(x - 1)(x - 2)}{4x^2(x - 1)}$$

$$= \frac{x - 2}{4x^2} \qquad \blacksquare$$

Example 6   *Dividing a Polynomial by a Rational Expression*

Divide: $(2x - 3) \div \dfrac{4x^2 - 9}{x + 5}$.

Solution

$$(2x - 3) \div \frac{4x^2 - 9}{x + 5} = \frac{2x - 3}{1} \cdot \frac{x + 5}{4x^2 - 9}$$

$$= \frac{(2x - 3)(x + 5)}{(2x - 3)(2x + 3)}$$

$$= \frac{(2x - 3)(x + 5)}{(2x - 3)(2x + 3)}$$

$$= \frac{x + 5}{2x + 3} \qquad \blacksquare$$

The geometric model at the right can be used to find an algebraic model for the ratio of the surface area to the volume for a person or animal. The model is created from six rectangular boxes. The dimensions, surface area, S, and volume, V, of each box are shown at the right.

Each arm and leg:
$$S = x^2 + 4(6x^2) = 25x^2$$
$$V = 6x^3$$

Head:
$$S = 5(4x^2) = 20x^2$$
$$V = 8x^3$$

Trunk:
$$S = 2(16x^2) + 4(24x^2) - 4x^2 - 4x^2 = 120x^2$$
$$V = 96x^3$$

Goal 2 Using Rational Expressions in Real Life

Connections

Physics

The greater the ratio of an animal's surface area to its volume, the greater its air resistance when falling through the air.

Example 7 *Comparing Surface Area to Volume*

Find a rational expression that represents the ratio of the surface area to the volume of the geometric model shown above. Simplify the expression. Then evaluate the simplified expression for several values of x, where x is measrued in feet.

Solution

$$\frac{\text{Surface area}}{\text{Volume}} = \frac{4(25x^2) + 20x^2 + 120x^2}{4(6x^3) + 8x^3 + 96x^3}$$

$$= \frac{240x^2}{128x^3}, \quad \text{or} \quad \frac{15}{8x}$$

In the following table, notice that small animals have large ratios and large animals have small ratios.

Animal	Mouse	Squirrel	Cat	Human	Elephant
x	$\frac{1}{24}$	$\frac{1}{12}$	$\frac{1}{6}$	$\frac{2}{5}$	2
Ratio	45	22.5	11.25	4.7	0.9

Communicating about ALGEBRA

▶ **SHARING IDEAS about the Lesson**

A. A mouse and a human each fall 30 feet. Why is the mouse less likely to be hurt?

B. Why do parachutes allow humans to fall from great heights without injury?

EXERCISES

▶ **CRITICAL THINKING about the Lesson**

In Exercises 1 and 2, simplify the expression, if possible.

1. $\dfrac{3x^2}{3x^3 + 21x}$

2. $\dfrac{x^2 + 10x - 4}{x^2 + 10x}$

3. Multiply: $\dfrac{x^2 - x - 2}{3x^2} \cdot \dfrac{3x - 12}{x^2 - 6x + 8}$.

4. Divide: $\dfrac{5x^2 + 10x}{x^2 - x - 6} \div \dfrac{15x^3 + 45x^2}{x^2 - 9}$.

Independent Practice

In Exercises 5–8, simplify the expression.

5. $\dfrac{x^2 + 6x + 9}{x^2 - 9}$

6. $\dfrac{x^2 - 3x + 2}{x^2 + 5x - 6}$

7. $\dfrac{x^2 - 2x - 3}{x^2 - 7x + 12}$

8. $\dfrac{x - 2}{x^3 - x^2 - 4}$

In Exercises 9–20, multiply and simplify.

9. $\dfrac{3xy^3}{x^3y} \cdot \dfrac{y}{6x}$

10. $\dfrac{120x^5}{y^4} \cdot \dfrac{xy}{5x^3}$

11. $\dfrac{16x^3}{5y^9} \cdot \dfrac{x^3y^7}{80xy^2}$

12. $\dfrac{x^{10}y^4}{33x^4} \cdot \dfrac{39x^5}{4y^{10}}$

13. $\dfrac{2x^2 - 10}{x + 1} \cdot \dfrac{x - 4}{4x^2 - 20}$

14. $\dfrac{x^2 + 3x}{x^2 + 6x + 8} \cdot \dfrac{x^2 + x - 2}{4x^3 + 12x^2}$

15. $\dfrac{x - 3}{2x - 8} \cdot \dfrac{6x^2 - 96}{x^2 - 9}$

16. $\dfrac{x^2 - 5x - 6}{4x^5} \cdot \dfrac{x + 2}{x^2 + 3x + 2}$

17. $\dfrac{x^2 + 6x - 7}{x^4 + 8x^3 + 7x^2} \cdot 3x^2$

18. $(x + 2) \cdot \dfrac{x^2 - 9}{x^2 - x - 6}$

19. $(x^2 + 8x + 16) \cdot \dfrac{16x^2 - 64}{x^2 - 16}$

20. $\dfrac{2x^2 - 2}{x^2 - 6x - 7} \cdot (x^2 - 10x + 21)$

In Exercises 21–32, divide and simplify.

21. $\dfrac{x^2 + 4x - 5}{2x^2} \div \dfrac{x - 1}{4x}$

22. $\dfrac{2x^2 - 16x}{x^2 - 9x + 8} \div \dfrac{2x}{5x - 5}$

23. $\dfrac{x^2 + 8x + 16}{x + 2} \div \dfrac{x^2 + 6x + 8}{x^2 - 4}$

24. $\dfrac{x^2 - 8x - 20}{15x^4 - 150x^3} \div \dfrac{x^2 - 9x}{x^2 - 7x - 18}$

25. $\dfrac{x - 3}{x^2 - 5x - 14} \div \dfrac{x^2 - x - 6}{x - 7}$

26. $\dfrac{x^2 + 3x - 4}{x^2 - 4x + 3} \div \dfrac{x + 4}{x - 3}$

27. $\dfrac{x^2 + 10x + 24}{3x^2 + 3x} \div (x + 6)$

28. $\dfrac{x^2 - 14x + 48}{x^2 - 6x} \div (3x - 24)$

29. $(x + 4) \div \dfrac{x^2 - 6x - 40}{x^2 + 3x}$

30. $(x + 1) \div \dfrac{x^2 + 2x + 1}{x^2 + 13x + 12}$

31. $(x^2 + 10x + 25) \div \dfrac{x^2 + 12x + 35}{x^2 - 8x - 105}$

32. $(x^2 + 6x - 16) \div \dfrac{2x^2 + 16x}{x + 2}$

In Exercises 33–40, perform the operations and simplify.

33. $\dfrac{x-11}{2x+10} \div \dfrac{x^2-8x-33}{x+5}$

34. $\dfrac{x^2+3x-10}{x-2} \cdot \dfrac{x^2+3x-10}{x-2} \cdot \dfrac{x+1}{x^2+x-20}$

35. $\dfrac{x^2+12x+20}{4x^2-9} \cdot \dfrac{6x^3-9x^2}{x^3+10x^2} \cdot (2x+3)$

36. $\left[\dfrac{x^2+x-20}{x+1} \div \dfrac{33x^2-132x}{16x+16}\right] \div \dfrac{8x+40}{11x+44}$

37. $(x^2+x-30) \div \dfrac{x^2-11x+30}{x^2+7x+12} \cdot \dfrac{x-6}{x+6}$

38. $\dfrac{x^2-5x-14}{x^3-6x^2-7x} \cdot (x^2-4x-5) \div \dfrac{x^2+x-30}{2x}$

39. $\left[\dfrac{x^2+11x}{x-2} \div (3x^2+6x)\right] \cdot \dfrac{x^2-4}{x+11}$

40. $(x^2+15x) \div \left[\dfrac{x^2+2x-8}{x-2} \cdot \dfrac{x^2+15x}{x+4}\right]$

Geometry **In Exercises 41 and 42, find the ratio of the area of the blue region to the total area. Write your result in simplified form.**

41.

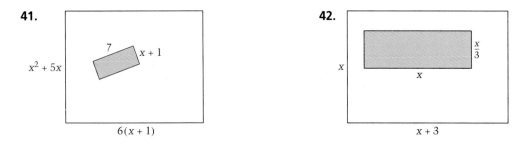

42.

43. *Cost of Tires*   For 1980 through 1992, Alfredo's Autobody Shop spent an average of C dollars per snow tire per year, where

$$C = \dfrac{t+75}{1-0.05t}$$

and $t = 0$ represents 1980. The number, T, of snow tires bought per year by the shop can be modeled by

$$T = \dfrac{500(t+20)}{t+75}.$$

Write a model for the total amount, A, that the shop spent each year on snow tires. How much did the shop spend in 1988?

44. *Drive-In Movies*   For 1980 through 1992, the average monthly revenue, R (in dollars), from admissions at the Sunset Drive-In Theater can be modeled by

$$R = \dfrac{131{,}124 + 3122t}{26-t}$$

where $t = 0$ represents 1980. The average price, p (in dollars), per car can be modeled by

$$p = \dfrac{294+7t}{100-5t}.$$

Write a model for the average number, x, of cars admitted per month to the theater. How many cars were admitted in a month of 1990?

Swimming Pools **In Exercises 45 and 46, use the following information.**

You are considering buying a swimming pool and have narrowed the choices to two—one that is circular and one that is rectangular. The rectangular pool's width is three times its depth. Its length is 6 feet more than its width. The circular pool has a diameter that is twice the width of the rectangular pool, and it is 2 feet deeper.

45. Find the ratio of the circular pool's volume to the rectangular pool's volume.

46. The volume of the rectangular pool is 2592 cubic feet. How many gallons of water are needed to fill the circular pool if 1 gallon ≈ 0.134 ft^3?

Integrated Review

In Exercises 47–52, factor the expression completely with respect to the integers.

47. $x^3 - 9x^2 + 5x - 45$ **48.** $x^3 + 2x^2 + 2x + 4$ **49.** $x^3 - 4x^2 + 9x - 36$

50. $x^3 + x^2 - 16x - 16$ **51.** $2x^3 - 3x^2 + 2x - 3$ **52.** $3x^3 + 6x^2 - 3x - 6$

In Exercises 53–56, simplify the expression.

53. $\dfrac{24x^2y^3}{8x^5y}$ **54.** $\dfrac{3xy^4}{2x^6y}$ **55.** $\dfrac{-9y^2}{3x^3y}$ **56.** $\dfrac{2x^{-1}y}{x^4y^2}$

57. *College Entrance Exam Sample*   If $\dfrac{a}{b} = \dfrac{5}{9}$ and $\dfrac{b}{c} = \dfrac{3}{5}$, then $\dfrac{a}{c} = \boxed{?}$.

    a. $\dfrac{1}{9}$ **b.** $\dfrac{1}{5}$ **c.** $\dfrac{1}{3}$ **d.** $\dfrac{5}{9}$ **e.** $\dfrac{3}{5}$

58. *College Entrance Exam Sample* $[(2x^2y^3)^2]^3 = \boxed{?}$

    a. $4x^4y^6$ **b.** $12x^4y^6$ **c.** $64x^4y^6$ **d.** $64x^{12}y^{18}$ **e.** $64x^{64}y^{216}$

Exploration and Extension

59. Find two pairs of rational expressions with first-degree numerators and first-degree denominators whose product is

$$\frac{2x^2 + 11x - 6}{3x^2 + x - 2}.$$

60. *Technology*   Use a graphing calculator to compare the graphs of the following two functions. What is the domain of each function? Can you find a range setting that shows a difference in the graphs? Explain.

$$f(x) = \frac{x^2 + 3x + 2}{x + 2} \qquad \text{and} \qquad g(x) = x + 1$$

Take this test as you would take a test in class. The answers to the exercises are given in the back of the book.

In Exercises 1–6, sketch the graph of the function. **(10.1)**

1. $f(x) = \dfrac{1}{x + 2}$

2. $f(x) = \dfrac{2}{x^2 + 1}$

3. $f(x) = \dfrac{1}{x^2 - 1}$

4. $f(x) = \dfrac{x}{x + 4}$

5. $f(x) = \dfrac{x^2}{x + 1}$

6. $f(x) = \dfrac{x^2 + 2x - 3}{x - 1}$

In Exercises 7–10, simplify the rational expression. **(10.3)**

7. $\dfrac{x^2 - 2x - 8}{x^2 - 16}$

8. $\dfrac{x^2 - 4x + 4}{2x^2 - 7x + 6}$

9. $\dfrac{6x^6 - 486x^2}{9x^5 + 9x^4 - 108x^3}$

10. $\dfrac{8x^2 - 2x - 15}{10x^2 - 17x + 3}$

In Exercises 11 and 12, multiply and simplify. **(10.3)**

11. $\dfrac{2x^3 - 2x^2 - 12x}{x - 4} \cdot \dfrac{x^2 - 5x + 4}{4x^3 + 4x^2 - 8x}$

12. $\dfrac{8x^2 - 32}{x^3 + x^2} \cdot \dfrac{x^5 - x^4 - 2x^3}{4x^2 - 16x + 16}$

In Exercises 13–16, divide and simplify. **(10.3)**

13. $\dfrac{x^3 - 3x^2}{3x + 6} \div \dfrac{x^3 - 8x^2 + 15x}{6x^2 - 18x - 60}$

14. $\dfrac{6x^3 + 4x^2 - 16x}{3x^2 + 3x - 6} \div \dfrac{45x - 60}{24x^3 + 8x^2 - 32x}$

15. $\dfrac{x^2 + 2x - 3}{3x^2 - x - 2} \div (x + 3)$

16. $(30x^3 - 6x^2) \div \dfrac{15x^2 - 3x}{4x^2 + 4x - 24}$

17. The variables x and y vary inversely. Given that $x = 2$ when $y = -5$, write an equation that relates x and y. **(10.2)**

18. The variable x varies jointly with the product of y and z. Given that $x = 4$ when $y = -1$ and $z = 6$, write an equation that relates the variables. **(10.2)**

19. Consider two people who weigh W_1 pounds and W_2 pounds and are sitting d_1 feet and d_2 feet, respectively, from the center of a seesaw. To balance the see-saw, the people must adjust their distances so that $d_1 W_1 = d_2 W_2$. Rodriguez, who weighs 80 pounds, is sitting 6 feet from the center. Pearl weighs 96 pounds. To balance the seesaw, where should she sit? **(10.2)**

20. For 1956 through 1991, the average cost per year, A, of possessing a United States passport can be modeled by

$$A = \dfrac{18.5t^2 - 310.8t + 5452.2}{-1.2t^2 + 87.2t + 1000}$$

where $t = 0$ represents 1956. Approximate the average cost per year of possessing a United States passport in 1990. **(10.1)**

10.4

Solving Rational Equations

What you should learn:

Goal 1 How to solve equations that contain rational expressions

Goal 2 How to use rational equations to solve real-life problems

Why you should learn it:

Many real-life problems can be modeled by rational equations, such as the year that a rational model for prize money reached a given level.

Goal 1 — Solving Rational Equations

In this lesson, you will learn two basic methods for solving equations that contain rational expressions. The first method works for any rational equation; the second works only for equations in which each side is a single fraction.

The **least common multiple** of two (or more) polynomials is the simplest polynomial that is a multiple of each of the original polynomials. The **least common denominator** of two or more fractions is the least common multiple of the denominators of the fractions.

Example 1   *Least Common Multiple of Polynomials*

Polynomials	Least Common Multiple
a. x and $x - 4$	$x \cdot (x - 4) = x(x - 4)$
b. x^2, $2x$, and $x(x - 3)$	$2 \cdot x \cdot x \cdot (x - 3) = 2x^2(x - 3)$
c. $x^2 - 4$ and $x + 2$	$(x + 2) \cdot (x - 2)$
d. $x^2 - x - 6$ and $x^2 - 2x - 8$	$(x + 2)(x - 3)(x - 4)$ ∎

To solve a rational equation, multiply each term on both sides of the equation by the least common denominator of the terms. Simplify, and solve the resulting polynomial equation.

Example 2   *Solving a Rational Equation*

Solve $\frac{2}{x} + \frac{5}{3} = \frac{7}{x}$.

Solution   The least common denominator is $3x$.

$$\frac{2}{x} + \frac{5}{3} = \frac{7}{x} \qquad \textit{Rewrite original equation.}$$

$$3x\left(\frac{2}{x} + \frac{5}{3}\right) = 3x \cdot \frac{7}{x} \qquad \textit{Multiply both sides by 3x.}$$

$$6 + 5x = 21 \qquad \textit{Simplify.}$$

$$5x = 15 \qquad \textit{Subtract 6x from both sides.}$$

$$x = 3 \qquad \textit{Divide both sides by 5.}$$

The solution is 3. Check this in the original equation. (Or use a graphing calculator to check that the graphs of "each side" intersect when $x = 3$.)   ∎

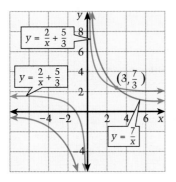

Multiplying both sides of an equation by the least common denominator may introduce extraneous solutions.

Example 3   *An Extraneous Solution*

Solve $\dfrac{5x}{x-2} = 7 + \dfrac{10}{x-2}$.

Solution   The least common denominator is $x - 2$.

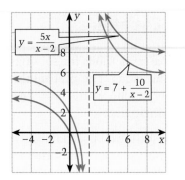

$$\frac{5x}{x-2} = 7 + \frac{10}{x-2}$$

$$(x-2)\cdot\frac{5x}{x-2} = (x-2)(7) + (x-2)\cdot\frac{10}{x-2}$$

$$5x = 7(x-2) + 10$$

$$5x = 7x - 4$$

$$4 = 2x$$

$$x = 2$$

At this point, the solution appears to be 2. After checking 2 in the original equation, however, you can conclude that this "trial solution" is extraneous. Thus, the original equation has no solution. ■

If you have a graphing calculator, try using it to perform a graphic check. Note that the graphs of the two equations do not intersect.

Example 4   *An Equation That Has Two Solutions*

Solve $\dfrac{3x}{x+1} = \dfrac{12}{x^2-1} + 2$.

Solution   The least common denominator is $(x+1)(x-1) = x^2 - 1$.

$$\frac{3x}{x+1} = \frac{12}{x^2-1} + 2$$

$$(x^2-1)\cdot\frac{3x}{x+1} = (x^2-1)\cdot\frac{12}{x^2-1} + (x^2-1)\cdot 2$$

$$(x-1)(3x) = 12 + 2(x^2-1)$$

$$3x^2 - 3x = 12 + 2x^2 - 2$$

$$x^2 - 3x - 10 = 0$$

$$(x+2)(x-5) = 0$$

$$x + 2 = 0 \longrightarrow x = -2$$

$$x - 5 = 0 \longrightarrow x = 5$$

The solutions are -2 and 5. Check these solutions in the original equation. ■

Cross multiplying can be used only for equations that have *exactly one* fraction on each side of the equation.

Example 5 Solving a Rational Equation by Cross Multiplying

Solve $\dfrac{7}{x+3} = \dfrac{x}{4}$.

Solution

$\dfrac{7}{x+3} = \dfrac{x}{4}$	*Rewrite original equation.*
$7(4) = x(x+3)$	*Cross multiply.*
$28 = x^2 + 3x$	*Simplify.*
$0 = x^2 + 3x - 28$	*Standard form*
$0 = (x+7)(x-4)$	*Factor.*
$x = -7 \text{ or } 4$	*Zero Product Property*

The solutions are -7 and 4. Check these solutions in the original equation. ∎

Goal 2 Using Rational Equations in Real Life

Real Life
Meteorology

Example 6 A Temperature Model

The average monthly high temperature in Jackson, Mississippi, can be modeled by

$$T = \frac{-191(t-30)}{t^2 - 16.5t + 114}$$

where T is measured in degrees Fahrenheit and $t = 1, 2, \ldots, 12$ represents the months of the year. During which month is the average monthly high temperature equal to $57.3°$?

Solution

$$\frac{-191(t-30)}{t^2 - 16.5t + 114} = 57.3$$

$$-191(t-30) = 57.3(t^2 - 16.5t + 114)$$

$$-\frac{10}{3}(t-30) = t^2 - 16.5t + 114$$

$$-10t + 300 = 3t^2 - 49.5t + 342$$

$$0 = 3t^2 - 39.5t + 42$$

$$0 = (3t - 3.5)(t - 12)$$

The solutions are 1.17 (January) and 12 (December). The graph at the left confirms these solutions. ∎

Average
Monthly High Temperatures,
Jackson, Mississippi

Temperature (in °F)

Month

The photo shows a contestant in the saddle-bronc event at the Indian rodeo in Gallup, New Mexico. Many rodeo events are dangerous. Fortunately, this rider escaped serious injury.

Total Rodeo Prize Money, 1980–1990

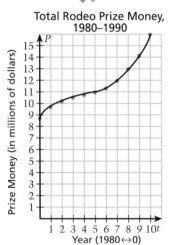

Example 7 — *Solving a Rational Equation*

For 1980 through 1990, the total prize money, P (in millions of dollars), at Professional Rodeo Cowboys Association events can be modeled by

$$P = \frac{69(t^2 + 3t + 30)}{-t^3 + 16t^2 - 15t + 240}$$

where $t = 0$ represents 1980. During which year was the total prize money approximately \$16 million?

Solution You could try to solve this equation algebraically. In doing that, however, you will have to solve a third-degree polynomial equation (which, you know from Chapter 9, can be difficult). In the context of this problem, a graphical approach is much better. After sketching the graph of the equation, as shown at the left, you can see that the total prize money was approximately \$16 million in 1990 (when $t = 10$). ∎

Communicating about ALGEBRA

▶ **SHARING IDEAS about the Lesson**

Use the graph to help find the zeros of the function.

A. $f(x) = \dfrac{2x - 15}{x - 3}$

B. $f(x) = \dfrac{x^2 - 4x - 5}{x^2 + 1}$

EXERCISES

Guided Practice

▶ **CRITICAL THINKING about the Lesson**

1. Describe two methods that can be used to solve a rational equation. Which method is more general? Explain.

2. Find the least common multiple of x, $x^2 + 5x + 6$, and $x + 3$.

3. Use the least common denominator method to solve

$$\frac{3x}{x - 5} = \frac{4 - x}{x - 5} - \frac{4}{x}.$$

4. Use the cross-multiplication method to solve

$$\frac{x}{x^2 - 10} = \frac{3}{2x + 1}.$$

Independent Practice

In Exercises 5–10, find the least common multiple.

5. $(x^2 - 9)$, $(x - 3)$, 3

6. $(x + 5)$, x^2, x

7. $4x$, x^3, $(x - 1)$

8. 1, $3x$, $x(x + 1)$

9. x^2, $2x(x - 2)$, $(x^2 - 4)$

10. $(x - 4)$, $(x^2 - 16)$, x

In Exercises 11–16, determine whether the x-value is a solution of the equation.

11. $\dfrac{3x - 2}{x + 4} = \dfrac{2x}{x + 3}$, -1

12. $\dfrac{x}{2x + 1} = \dfrac{5}{4 - x}$, -1

13. $\dfrac{3x - 1}{x - 2} + 3 = \dfrac{x}{x - 2}$, -2

14. $\dfrac{2x}{x + 3} = 1 - \dfrac{6}{x + 3}$, -3

15. $\dfrac{3}{x(x - 3)} + \dfrac{4}{x} = \dfrac{1}{x - 3}$, 3

16. $\dfrac{x}{x - 5} + 4 = \dfrac{1}{x + 3}$, 4

In Exercises 17–24, find the zeros of the function.

17. $f(x) = \dfrac{x + 2}{x - 2}$

18. $f(x) = \dfrac{2x}{x + 4}$

19. $f(x) = \dfrac{6}{x + 5}$

20. $f(x) = \dfrac{x - 1}{2x - 4}$

21. $f(x) = \dfrac{x^2 - 4}{x^2 + 4x + 3}$

22. $f(x) = \dfrac{x^2 - 4x - 21}{x + 3}$

23. $f(x) = \dfrac{2x^2 + 9x - 5}{2x^2 - 1}$

24. $f(x) = \dfrac{x^2 + 8x + 12}{4x + 1}$

In Exercises 25–48, solve the equation. Check each solution.

25. $\dfrac{10}{x+3}+\dfrac{10}{3}=6$

26. $\dfrac{6}{x}-\dfrac{7x}{5}=\dfrac{x}{10}$

27. $\dfrac{-1}{x-3}=\dfrac{x-4}{x^2-27}$

28. $\dfrac{x}{2x+7}=\dfrac{x-5}{x-1}$

29. $\dfrac{6x}{x+4}+4=\dfrac{2x+2}{x-1}$

30. $\dfrac{7x+1}{2x+5}+1=\dfrac{10x-3}{3x}$

31. $\dfrac{2x}{5}=\dfrac{x^2-5x}{5x}$

32. $\dfrac{x}{x^2-8}=\dfrac{2}{x}$

33. $\dfrac{10}{x^2-2x}+\dfrac{4}{x}=\dfrac{5}{x-2}$

34. $\dfrac{2(x+7)}{x+4}-2=\dfrac{2x+20}{2x+8}$

35. $\dfrac{2}{6x+5}-\dfrac{3}{4(6x+5)}=\dfrac{1}{28}$

36. $3\left(\dfrac{1}{x}+4\right)=2+\dfrac{4}{3x}$

37. $\dfrac{-2}{x-1}=\dfrac{x-8}{x+1}$

38. $\dfrac{8(x-1)}{x^2-4}=\dfrac{4}{x-2}$

39. $\dfrac{x^2+2x+2}{x-1}=\dfrac{2x+3}{x-1}$

40. $\dfrac{2x}{4-x}=\dfrac{x^2}{x-4}$

41. $\dfrac{2x}{x+2}=\dfrac{1}{x^2-4}+1$

42. $\dfrac{6}{x-1}+\dfrac{2x}{x-2}=2$

43. $\dfrac{8}{2x+4}-\dfrac{3x+1}{3x^2+2}=\dfrac{2}{x+2}$

44. $\dfrac{3x}{x+1}=\dfrac{12}{x^2-1}+2$

45. $\dfrac{2x^2-5}{x^2-4}+\dfrac{6}{x+2}=\dfrac{4x-7}{x-2}$

46. $\dfrac{2}{x-10}-\dfrac{3}{x-2}=\dfrac{6}{x^2-12x+20}$

47. $\dfrac{10x^2+x-2}{2x^2-9x-18}=\dfrac{4x}{x-6}+\dfrac{2x-3}{2x+3}$

48. $\dfrac{13x+16}{4x-1}+\dfrac{8x^2+12x+14}{4x^2+11x-3}=\dfrac{24x-8}{x+3}$

49. *Average Cost*   A greeting card manufacturer can produce a dozen cards for $6.50. If the initial investment by the company was $60,000, how many dozen cards must be produced before the average cost per dozen falls to $11.50?

50. *Average Cost*   You invest $40,000 to start a nacho stand in a shopping mall. You can make each basket of nachos for $0.70. How many baskets must you sell before your average cost per basket is $1.50?

Keyboards   **In Exercises 51 and 52, use the following information.**

For 1980 through 1990, the number, P, of conventional pianos sold in the United States can be modeled by

$$P = 223{,}720 - 9480t$$

where $t = 0$ represents 1980. The number, K, of electronic pianos and keyboards sold can be modeled by

$$K = 27{,}820 + 8710t.$$

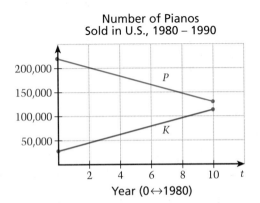

Number of Pianos
Sold in U.S., 1980 – 1990

Year (0↔1980)

51. In what year was the ratio of conventional pianos sold to electronic pianos and keyboards sold equal to 3?

52. In what year does it appear that the number of electronic pianos and keyboards sold will surpass the number of conventional pianos sold?

In Exercises 53–56, match the function with its graph.

53. $f(x) = \dfrac{5}{x - 6}$

54. $f(x) = \dfrac{6}{x + 5}$

55. $f(x) = \dfrac{6x}{x - 5}$

56. $f(x) = \dfrac{2x}{x + 6}$

a.

b.

c.

d.

Photography   **In Exercises 57–60, use the following information.**

The graph below shows the total amount spent by Americans on photofinishing, film, cameras, and other photographic equipment.

Professional wildlife photographers, such as Steven Maka shown above, go to great lengths to photograph wildlife in their natural habitats.

57. What percent of the amount spent by amateur photographers was spent on photofinishing?

58. What percent of the amount spent by amateur photographers was spent on film?

59. Consumers shot about 15.2 billion color prints in 1990, and paid an average of $0.29 for each one printed. How much did consumers spend on color prints?

60. What percent of the photofinishing revenue comes from the sales of color prints?

Exploration and Extension

In Exercises 61 and 62, solve the equation.

61. $\dfrac{6x}{x + 2} - \dfrac{4x^2 - 7x + 25}{x^2 - 4} = \dfrac{x - 5}{x}$

62. $\dfrac{x}{x + 2} - \dfrac{x + 6}{2x} = \dfrac{-2(2x + 3)}{x^2 + 3x + 2}$

10.5

Addition, Subtraction, and Complex Fractions

What you should learn:

Goal 1 How to add and subtract rational expressions and simplify complex fractions

Goal 2 How to use rational expressions as models of real-life situations

Why you should learn it:

You can model many real-life situations with the sum, difference, or ratio of rational functions, such as the difference between the marriage and divorce rates in the United States.

Goal 1   Working with Rational Expressions

As with numerical fractions, the procedure used to add (or subtract) two rational expressions depends upon whether the expressions have *like* or *unlike* denominators.

To add (or subtract) two rational expressions with *like* denominators, simply add (or subtract) their numerators and place the result over the common denominator. For example:

$$\frac{4}{3x} + \frac{5}{3x} = \frac{4+5}{3x} = \frac{9}{3x} = \frac{3}{x} \qquad \textit{Add with like denominators.}$$

$$\frac{2x}{x+3} - \frac{4}{x+3} = \frac{2x-4}{x+3} \qquad \textit{Subtract with like denominators.}$$

To add or subtract rational expressions with *unlike* denominators, first find the least common denominator of the original rational expressions. Then rewrite each expression as an equivalent rational expression using the least common denominator and proceed as with fractions with like denominators.

Example 1   *Adding and Subtracting Rational Expressions*

a. $\dfrac{7}{6x} + \dfrac{5}{8x} = \dfrac{7(4)}{6x(4)} + \dfrac{5(3)}{8x(3)}$ *Rewrite fractions using least common denominator of 24x.*

$\qquad\qquad = \dfrac{28}{24x} + \dfrac{15}{24x}$ *Simplify.*

$\qquad\qquad = \dfrac{28+15}{24x}$ *Add fractions.*

$\qquad\qquad = \dfrac{43}{24x}$ *Simplify.*

b. $\dfrac{3}{x-3} - \dfrac{5}{x+2} = \dfrac{3(x+2)}{(x-3)(x+2)} - \dfrac{5(x-3)}{(x-3)(x+2)}$

$\qquad\qquad = \dfrac{3x+6}{(x-3)(x+2)} - \dfrac{5x-15}{(x-3)(x+2)}$

$\qquad\qquad = \dfrac{(3x+6)-(5x-15)}{(x-3)(x+2)}$

$\qquad\qquad = \dfrac{3x+6-5x+15}{(x-3)(x+2)} = \dfrac{-2x+21}{(x-3)(x+2)}$ ∎

A **complex fraction** is a fraction that contains a fraction in its numerator or denominator. Complex fractions may have numerators or denominators that are the sum or difference of fractions.

To simplify a complex fraction, write its numerator and its denominator as single fractions. Then divide by multiplying by the reciprocal of the denominator.

Example 2   *Simplifying a Complex Fraction*

Simplify $\dfrac{\left(\frac{x}{4} + \frac{3}{2}\right)}{\left(2 - \frac{3}{x}\right)}$.

Solution

$$\frac{\left(\frac{x}{4} + \frac{3}{2}\right)}{\left(2 - \frac{3}{x}\right)} = \frac{\left(\frac{x}{4} + \frac{6}{4}\right)}{\left(\frac{2x}{x} - \frac{3}{x}\right)} \qquad \textit{Find least common denominators.}$$

$$= \frac{\left(\frac{x + 6}{4}\right)}{\left(\frac{2x - 3}{x}\right)} \qquad \textit{Combine fractions in numerator and in denominator.}$$

$$= \frac{x + 6}{4} \cdot \frac{x}{2x - 3} \qquad \textit{Multiply by the reciprocal.}$$

$$= \frac{x(x + 6)}{4(2x - 3)} \qquad \textit{Simplify.} \qquad \blacksquare$$

Another way to simplify a complex fraction is to multiply the numerator and denominator by the least common denominator of *every* fraction in the numerator and denominator.

Example 3   *Simplifying a Complex Fraction*

Simplify $\dfrac{\left(\frac{2}{x + 2}\right)}{\left(\frac{1}{x + 2} + \frac{2}{x}\right)}$.

Solution

$$\frac{\left(\frac{2}{x + 2}\right)}{\left(\frac{1}{x + 2} + \frac{2}{x}\right)} = \frac{\left(\frac{2}{x + 2}\right)(x)(x + 2)}{\frac{1}{x + 2}(x)(x + 2) + \frac{2}{x}(x)(x + 2)}$$

$$= \frac{2x}{x + 2(x + 2)}$$

$$= \frac{2x}{3x + 4} \qquad \blacksquare$$

Marriage (and divorce) rates are often given in the number of marriages (or divorces) per 1000 people. Since 1900, the marriage rate has remained relatively constant—the year with the lowest rate was 1958 (a rate of 8.4) and the year with the highest rate was 1945 (a rate of 12.2). The divorce rate, however, has increased greatly since 1900—from a low of 0.7 in 1900 to a high of 5.3 around 1980.

Goal 2 Using Rational Expressions in Real Life

Real Life
Social Trends

Example 4 *Subtracting Rational Expressions*

For 1975 through 1990, the marriage rate, M (per 1000 people), and the divorce rate, D (per 1000 people), can be modeled by

$$M = 9.6 + \frac{-2t + 48}{t^2 - 25.2t + 178} \qquad \textit{Marriage rate}$$

$$D = 4.4 + \frac{2t + 13}{t^2 - 17t + 106} \qquad \textit{Divorce rate}$$

where $t = 5$ represents 1975. Find a model that gives the difference, R, of marriages and divorces (per 1000 people per year). (You do not need to simplify the model.)

Solution You can find the model for R by subtracting the models for M and D.

$$R = M - D$$

$$= \left(9.6 + \frac{-2t + 48}{t^2 - 25.2t + 178}\right) - \left(4.4 + \frac{2t + 13}{t^2 - 17t + 106}\right)$$

$$= 5.2 + \frac{-2t + 48}{t^2 - 25.2t + 178} - \frac{2t + 13}{t^2 - 17t + 106}$$

Marriage and Divorce Rates, 1975 – 1990

Rate per 1000

12 — Marriages
10
8
6
4 — Divorces
2

5   10   15   20

Year (5↔1975)

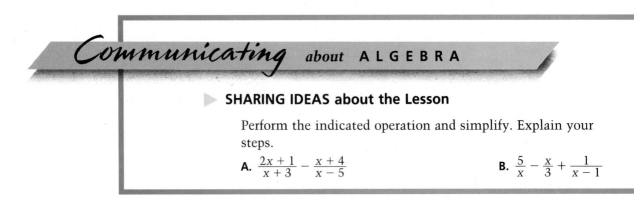

Communicating about **A L G E B R A**

▷ **SHARING IDEAS about the Lesson**

Perform the indicated operation and simplify. Explain your steps.

A. $\dfrac{2x + 1}{x + 3} - \dfrac{x + 4}{x - 5}$

B. $\dfrac{5}{x} - \dfrac{x}{3} + \dfrac{1}{x - 1}$

EXERCISES

▶ CRITICAL THINKING about the Lesson

1. State the least common denominator of $\frac{3}{2x}$, $\frac{7}{x}$, and $\frac{x}{x+4}$. Add the expressions.

2. Which is correct? Which is incorrect? Explain.

   a. $\dfrac{\left(\frac{1}{x}-4\right)}{\left(\frac{5}{3}+\frac{3}{2x}\right)} = \dfrac{\left(\frac{1-4x}{x}\right)}{\left(\frac{10x+9}{6x}\right)}$

   b. $\dfrac{\left(\frac{1}{x}-4\right)}{\left(\frac{5}{3}+\frac{3}{2x}\right)} = \left(\frac{1}{x}-4\right)\cdot\left(\frac{3}{5}+\frac{2x}{3}\right)$

In Exercises 3 and 4, simplify $\dfrac{\left(\frac{x}{5}+\frac{4}{x}\right)}{\left(\frac{6}{5x}+1\right)}$ using the indicated method.

3. Combine the numerator and denominator into single fractions, then divide.

4. Multiply the numerator and denominator by the least common denominator of all fractions, then simplify.

Independent Practice

In Exercises 5–7, state the least common denominator.

5. $\dfrac{18}{2(x+1)}$, $\dfrac{5}{2x}$

6. $\dfrac{2x+3}{9x^2-1}$, $\dfrac{2}{x}$, $\dfrac{8x}{3x+1}$

7. $\dfrac{1}{x(x-5)}$, $\dfrac{32}{x^2-3x-10}$

In Exercises 8–22, perform the operations and simplify.

8. $\dfrac{4}{2x^2}+\dfrac{1}{3x}$

9. $\dfrac{-2}{7x}-\dfrac{5}{4x}$

10. $\dfrac{11}{3(x-5)}-\dfrac{x+1}{3x}$

11. $\dfrac{4x+1}{x^2-4}-\dfrac{3}{x-2}$

12. $\dfrac{4}{7x}-\dfrac{3x^2+x-5}{14x+21}$

13. $\dfrac{3x^2}{x^2-x-30}-\dfrac{3x+5}{x-6}$

14. $\dfrac{2x^2}{3x+5}-\dfrac{14}{x+7}$

15. $\dfrac{12x^2-x+9}{3x+33}-\dfrac{16}{x+11}$

16. $\dfrac{1-3x}{x-6}+\dfrac{2}{2x+1}$

17. $\dfrac{4x}{x+1}+\dfrac{5}{2x-3}-\dfrac{4}{x}$

18. $\dfrac{2}{x+2}-\dfrac{x}{3}-\dfrac{5}{x-2}$

19. $\dfrac{-4x^2+2}{x^2+9x-10}+\dfrac{3}{x+10}$

20. $\dfrac{x^2+x-3}{x^2-12x+32}+\dfrac{3x}{x-8}$

21. $\dfrac{3-4x}{x^2+3x-10}-\dfrac{2}{x+5}$

22. $\dfrac{10x}{3x^2-3}+\dfrac{4}{x-1}+\dfrac{5}{6x}$

10.5 ▪ *Addition, Subtraction, and Complex Fractions* **551**

In Exercises 23–34, simplify the complex fraction.

23. $\dfrac{\left(\dfrac{x}{3} - 4\right)}{\left(5 + \dfrac{1}{x}\right)}$

24. $\dfrac{\left(\dfrac{4}{x} + 2\right)}{\left(\dfrac{1}{2x} - 8\right)}$

25. $\dfrac{\left(\dfrac{3}{x^2} + \dfrac{1}{x}\right)}{\left(2 - \dfrac{4}{5x}\right)}$

26. $\dfrac{\left(16 - \dfrac{1}{x^2}\right)}{\left(\dfrac{1}{4x^2} - 4\right)}$

27. $\dfrac{\left(\dfrac{10}{x + 1}\right)}{\left(\dfrac{1}{2} + \dfrac{3}{x + 1}\right)}$

28. $\dfrac{\left(\dfrac{2}{3x + 15}\right)}{\left(\dfrac{2}{x + 5} + \dfrac{1}{4x + 20}\right)}$

29. $\dfrac{\left(\dfrac{1}{2x + 1} - \dfrac{3}{4(2x + 1)}\right)}{\left(\dfrac{x}{2x + 1}\right)}$

30. $\dfrac{\left(\dfrac{2}{x^2 - 1} + \dfrac{1}{x + 1}\right)}{\left(\dfrac{1}{12x^2 - 3}\right)}$

31. $\dfrac{\left(\dfrac{1}{x + 1} + \dfrac{1}{2}\right)}{\left(\dfrac{3}{2x^2 + 4x + 2}\right)}$

32. $\dfrac{\left(\dfrac{x}{x - 3} - \dfrac{2}{3}\right)}{\left(\dfrac{10}{3x} + \dfrac{x^2}{x - 3}\right)}$

33. $\dfrac{\left(\dfrac{1}{2x} - \dfrac{6}{x + 5}\right)}{\left(\dfrac{x}{x - 5} + \dfrac{1}{x}\right)}$

34. $\dfrac{\left(\dfrac{4}{x^2 - 9} + \dfrac{2}{x - 3}\right)}{\left(\dfrac{1}{x + 3} + \dfrac{1}{x - 3}\right)}$

In Exercises 35–40, solve the equation.

35. $\dfrac{\left(\dfrac{4}{x} + \dfrac{6}{x + 1}\right)}{\left(\dfrac{3}{x + 1} - 5\right)} = -1$

36. $\dfrac{\left(\dfrac{3}{x - 2} + 2\right)}{\left(\dfrac{2x - 3}{x - 2} + \dfrac{2x}{3}\right)} = 1$

37. $\dfrac{\left(x - \dfrac{5x + 3}{x - 1}\right)}{\left(\dfrac{2x}{2x - 2} - \dfrac{x}{2}\right)} = -2$

38. $\dfrac{\left(\dfrac{3x}{x - 1} - \dfrac{4}{x}\right)}{\left(\dfrac{1}{2x} - \dfrac{1}{x}\right)} = 16$

39. $\dfrac{\left(\dfrac{x}{x - 2} + \dfrac{7}{x}\right)}{\left(6 - \dfrac{12}{x}\right)} = -1$

40. $\dfrac{\left(\dfrac{x + 4}{5} - 3\right)}{\left(\dfrac{1}{2} + \dfrac{x + 4}{10}\right)} = -2$

Doctors **In Exercises 41 and 42, use the following information.**

For 1970 to 1990, the number of doctors of medicine, M (in thousands), in the United States can be approximated by

$$M = \dfrac{28{,}390 + 693t}{85 - t},$$

where $t = 0$ represents 1970. The number of doctors of osteopathy, B (in thousands), can be approximated by

$$B = \dfrac{776 - 12t}{55 - 2t}.$$

41. Write an expression for the total number, I, of doctors of medicine (MD) and doctors of osteopathy (DO). Simplify the result.

42. How many MDs and DOs did the United States have in 1985?

Banks In Exercises 43 and 44, use the following information.

For 1970 to 1990, the number of commercial banks, T, in the United States can be modeled by

$$T = \frac{17{,}510(41 + 5t)}{20 + t}$$

where $t = 0$ represents 1970. The number, M, of commercial banks that were members of the Federal Reserve System can be modeled by

$$M = \frac{174{,}720(148 + 5t)}{1174 - t}.$$

43. Write an equation that represents the number, N, of commercial banks that were not members of the Federal Reserve System. Do not simplify the result.

44. How many banks were not members in 1988?

The Federal Reserve System, nicknamed the **Fed**, *is an independent agency of the federal government. The* **Fed** *manages the nation's supply of money and credit and provides services to commercial banks.*

Integrated Review

In Exercises 45–50, find the least common multiple.

45. $x - 7$, x^2, $x(x + 7)$

46. $x + 2$, $x^2 - 4$, x

47. $x^2 - 1$, $x + 1$, x

48. $x - 6$, $x(x - 6)$, x^3

49. x, $x^2(x + 1)$, $x + 1$

50. $9 - x$, x^2, $x + 1$

In Exercises 51–56, solve the equation.

51. $\dfrac{5}{x - 2} = \dfrac{3x + 1}{x - 1}$

52. $\dfrac{11 + x}{x - 1} = \dfrac{-6}{x + 4}$

53. $\dfrac{3x + 2}{x} + \dfrac{3x}{x + 1} = 6$

54. $\dfrac{-6}{x - 2} + \dfrac{6}{x - 1} = -1$

55. $\dfrac{x + 2}{x - 6} + \dfrac{4}{x - 4} = -3$

56. $\dfrac{x + 5}{x - 2} + \dfrac{x}{x - 6} = 5$

57. *Powers of Ten* Which best estimates the length of the tail of the Parson's chameleon shown in the photo? (The twig is about one-half inch thick.)
  a. 5.0×10^{-2} in.
  b. 5.0×10^{-1} in.
  c. 5.0×10^{0} in.
  d. 5.0×10^{1} in.

58. *Powers of Ten* Which best estimates the average mileage of an American automobile (in miles per gallon) in 1990?
  a. 2.0×10^{0}
  b. 2.0×10^{1}
  c. 2.0×10^{2}
  d. 2.0×10^{3}

Exploration and Extension

59. *Country Music Records* Bob's and Helen's favorite pastime is trying to stump each other with puzzles. Can you solve the puzzle?

(Puzzle is from aha! Insight, Martin Gardner, copyright © Scientific American, Inc.)

Bob: *Do you still have your country and western records?*

Helen: *No, I gave half of them, and half a record more, to Suzy.*

Helen: *Then I gave half of what was left, and half a record more, to Joe.*

Helen: *That left me with just one record, which I'll give to you. . . .*

Helen: *. . . If you can tell me how many I began with.*

Bob was puzzled. Suddenly he had an aha! and answered Helen's question.

Mixed REVIEW

1. Simplify: $(5x - 2)^2$. **(9.1)**

2. Simplify: $(8x^3 - 3x^2) - (2x^3 - 4x^2)$. **(9.1)**

3. Sketch $f(x) = (x + 4)^6 - 3$. **(9.2)**

4. Sketch $f(x) = \log_{10}(x - 2)$. **(8.2)**

5. Sketch $|3x - 7| > 4$. **(2.6)**

6. Sketch $f(x) = x^2 + 6x + 4$. **(5.2)**

7. Sketch $f(x) = |x - 4| - 2$. **(2.6)**

8. Sketch $f(x) = -3(x - 5)^2 + 2$. **(5.3)**

9. Factor $49x^2 - 28x + 4$. **(9.3)**

10. Factor $81x^4 - 16$. **(9.3)**

11. Solve $3x^2 - 7x + 1 = 0$. **(5.4)**

12. Solve $3x^3 - 18x^2 + 27x = 0$. **(9.3)**

13. In which quadrant is $(-2, -7)$? **(2.1)**

14. Find 140% of 60.

15. Find the y-intercept of $y = 3|x - 8| + 4$. **(2.3)**

16. Find the distance from $(-5, 1)$ to $(4, 6)$. **(7.5)**

17. The longest sides of a right triangle are 8 ft and 6 ft. Find the third side. **(5.1)**

18. $300 saved at 6% compounded monthly for four years is how much? **(7.2)**

19. Solve $\begin{bmatrix} 2 & -1 \\ 1 & 0 \end{bmatrix} X = \begin{bmatrix} -1 & -1 \\ 0 & 0 \end{bmatrix}$.

20. Find the area of the triangle with vertices $(-3, 5)$, $(4, 4)$ and $(1, -8)$. **(4.3)**

10.6

Exploring Data: The Algebra of Finance

What you should learn:

Goal 1 How to construct an amortization table for a loan

Goal 2 How to find the monthly payment for an installment loan

Why you should learn it:

You will repay most of your consumer loans with monthly installments. Knowing how these installments are computed will ensure that you are not overcharged.

Goal 1 Constructing an Amortization Table

When you receive a loan, you usually are expected to repay it. Most loans are not repaid with a single payment. Instead they are repaid over a period of time with payments called **installments.** This type of loan is an **installment loan,** and the process of repaying the loan is called **amortization.**

The period of time over which the loan is paid is the **term** of the loan. The amount you receive is the **principal.**

Example 1 Constructing an Amortization Table

You borrow $1600.00 and make 11 monthly payments of $144.41 each and one final payment of $144.44. The annual percentage rate is 15%, compounded monthly. Construct an amortization table for this loan. (Assume that repayment begins one month after the loan is obtained.)

Solution Because the annual percentage rate is 15%, the interest for the first month is $I = Prt = 1600(0.15)\left(\frac{1}{12}\right) = \$20.00$. This means $20 of the first payment is interest and the remaining $124.41 reduces the principal. The balance after the first payment is $1600.00 - 124.41 = \$1475.59$.

Payment Number	Balance before Payment	Payment	Interest Payment	Principal Payment	Balance after Payment
1	$1600.00	$144.41	$20.00	$124.41	$1475.59
2	$1475.59	$144.41	$18.44	$125.97	$1349.62
3	$1349.62	$144.41	$16.87	$127.54	$1222.08
4	$1222.08	$144.41	$15.28	$129.13	$1092.95
5	$1092.95	$144.41	$13.66	$130.75	$ 962.20
6	$ 962.20	$144.41	$12.03	$132.38	$ 829.82
7	$ 829.82	$144.41	$10.37	$134.04	$ 695.78
8	$ 695.78	$144.41	$ 8.70	$135.71	$ 560.07
9	$ 560.07	$144.41	$ 7.00	$137.41	$ 422.66
10	$ 422.66	$144.41	$ 5.28	$139.13	$ 283.53
11	$ 283.53	$144.41	$ 3.54	$140.87	$ 142.66
12	$ 142.66	$144.44	$ 1.78	$142.66	$ 0.00

■

Goal 2 Finding a Monthly Payment

> **Monthly Installment Payments**
>
> Consider a monthly installment loan with a principal of P, an annual interest rate of r (in decimal form), and a term of t years. The monthly interest rate is $i = \frac{1}{12}r$ and the monthly payment is
>
> $$M = P\left[\frac{i}{1 - \left(\dfrac{1}{1 + i}\right)^{12t}}\right]$$

From this formula you can see how the monthly payment was calculated for the loan described in Example 1. Using $P = 1600$, $r = 0.15$, $t = 1$, and $i = \frac{1}{12}(0.15) = 0.0125$, you obtain

$$M = (1600)\left[\frac{0.0125}{1 - \left(\dfrac{1}{1 + 0.0125}\right)^{12}}\right] = \$144.41.$$

Because payments are rounded, the final payment will usually differ from the other payments by a few cents.

When obtaining an installment loan, borrowers often decrease the amount of each installment by extending the term of the loan, but this can greatly increase the total interest paid.

Real Life

Home Financing

Example 2 *Comparing Installments with Total Interest Payments*

You are considering a home mortgage for $100,000 with an annual percentage rate of 10.5% and monthly installments. Find the monthly payment for 20 years and 30 years. What is the total interest paid for each term?

Solution

a. Using $P = 100{,}000$, $r = 0.105$, and $t = 20$, you can find the monthly installment to be $998.38. The total interest paid over the 20-year period is

$$240(998.38) - 100{,}000.00 = \$139{,}611.20.$$

b. Using $P = 100{,}000$, $r = 0.105$, and $t = 30$, you can find the monthly installment to be $914.74. The total interest paid over the 30-year period is

$$360(914.74) - 100{,}000.00 = \$229{,}306.40.$$

Increasing the term from 20 to 30 years decreased the monthly payment by only $83.64, but increased the total interest by $89,695.20! ∎

For installment loans over long terms, a large portion of each installment during the early years is the interest. Only a small portion goes toward reducing the principal.

Real Life
Finance

Example 3 *Comparing the Principal Payment with the Interest Payment*

Construct the first 12 months of an amortization table for a home mortgage of $100,000 at 10.5% for 30 years (with monthly payments). How much of the first year's payments are applied against the principal and how much is interest?

Solution The monthly payment for this home mortgage is $914.74, and the amortization table for the first 12 months is shown below.

Payment Number	Balance before Payment	Payment	Interest Payment	Principal Payment	Balance after Payment
1	$100,000.00	$914.74	$875.00	$39.74	$99,960.26
2	$ 99,960.26	$914.74	$874.65	$40.09	$99,920.17
3	$ 99,920.17	$914.74	$874.30	$40.44	$99,879.73
4	$ 99,879.73	$914.74	$873.95	$40.79	$99,838.94
5	$ 99,838.94	$914.74	$873.59	$41.15	$99,797.79
6	$ 99,797.79	$914.74	$873.23	$41.51	$99,756.28
7	$ 99,756.28	$914.74	$872.87	$41.87	$99,714.41
8	$ 99,714.41	$914.74	$872.50	$42.24	$99,672.17
9	$ 99,672.17	$914.74	$872.13	$42.61	$99,629.56
10	$ 99,629.56	$914.74	$871.76	$42.98	$99,586.58
11	$ 99,586.58	$914.74	$871.38	$43.36	$99,543.22
12	$ 99,543.22	$914.74	$871.00	$43.74	$99,499.48

The principal was reduced only $100,000.00 − $99,499.48 = $500.52 at the end of the first year. The total payments for the first year were 12($914.74) = $10,976.88; the portion that went toward interest was $10,976.88 − $500.52 = $10,476.36. ∎

Communicating about ALGEBRA

▶ **SHARING IDEAS about the Lesson**

You are considering a car loan for $12,500. Compare the monthly payments and total interest paid for each loan.

A. A 3-year loan with an 8% annual interest rate.
B. A 3-year loan with a 12% annual interest rate.
C. A 3-year loan with an 18% annual interest rate.

EXERCISES

▶ **CRITICAL THINKING about the Lesson**

Monthly Payment   **In Exercises 1–4, consider a $2000 monthly install-ment loan with an annual interest rate of 12% and a term of one year.**

1. What is the monthly payment?

2. How much of the first month's payment goes toward interest?

3. How much of the first month's payment goes toward principal?

4. What is the balance after the first month's payment?

Independent Practice

Amortization Table   **In Exercises 5–8, construct an amortization table.**

5. You borrow $1200 at an annual interest rate of $10\frac{1}{2}$% to be repaid in eight monthly payments of $139.23 and one final payment of $139.27. (*Hint: $t = \frac{3}{4}$ year.*)

6. You borrow $750 at an annual interest rate of 14% to be repaid in eight monthly payments of $88.27 and one final payment of $88.25.

7. You borrow $5000 at an annual interest rate of 8% to be repaid in 11 monthly payments of $434.94 and one final payment of $434.97.

8. You borrow $400 at an annual interest rate of 15% to be repaid in five monthly payments of $69.61 and one final payment of $69.63.

Monthly Payment   **In Exercises 9–12, find the monthly payment.**

9. A home mortgage for $80,000, with an annual interest rate of 11%, is taken out for a 15-year term.

10. A business loan for $20,000, with an annual interest rate of 12.5%, is taken out for a 10-year term.

11. You borrow $75,000 for 20 years at an annual interest rate of 9%.

12. Your home mortgage is for $50,000, with an annual interest rate of 10%, over a 25-year term.

Home Mortgage   **In Exercises 13–16, use the table of monthly pay-ments to find the total interest payment on a $100,000 home mortgage.**

13. 8% interest, 20 years

14. 8% interest, 30 years

15. 12% interest, 20 years

16. 9% interest, 15 years

	8%	9%	10%	11%	12%
15 years	955.65	1014.27	1074.61	1136.60	1200.17
20 years	836.44	899.73	965.02	1032.19	1101.09
25 years	771.82	839.20	908.70	980.11	1053.22
30 years	733.76	804.62	877.57	952.32	1028.61

17. An installment loan for $2000 to be paid in 12 monthly payments with an annual interest rate of 13%

18. An installment loan for $14,000 to be paid in 18 monthly payments with an annual interest rate of 11% (*Hint:* $t = \frac{3}{2}$ years.)

19. An installment loan for $5500 to be paid in 6 monthly payments with an annual interest rate of 12.5%

20. An installment loan for $8000 to be paid in 9 monthly payments with an annual interest rate of 9.5%

Comparing Two Repayment Plans   **In Exercises 21–24, consider a $2000 loan with an annual interest rate of 12%.**

21. What is the monthly payment for a term of 12 months?

22. What is the monthly payment for a term of 18 months?

23. Find the total interest and the total payment for each term.

24. What is one advantage of each repayment plan?

25. *Fitting a Loan to Your Budget*   You take out a used car loan for $3500 with an annual interest rate of 14%. You want to repay the loan as soon as possible, but you can afford monthly payments of, at most, $100. Which of the following terms should you choose? Explain.
a. 24 months   **b.** 30 months   **c.** 36 months   **d.** 42 months   **e.** 48 months

26. *Fitting a Loan to Your Budget*   You take out a loan for $2600 with an annual interest rate of 18%. You want to repay the loan as soon as possible, but you can afford monthly payments of, at most, $100. Which of the following terms should you choose? Explain.
a. 6 months   **b.** 12 months   **c.** 24 months   **d.** 36 months   **e.** 48 months

27. *Comparing Two Repayment Plans*   You borrow $2000 and have two repayment options. Which has the lesser total payment?
a. One lending source offers the loan for 24 monthly payments at an annual interest rate of 14%.
b. Another lending source offers the loan for 18 monthly payments at an annual interest rate of 16%.

Most monthly payments for personal loans are paid with checks, which are processed at Federal Reserve Banks with machines such as those shown above.

28. *Comparing Two Repayment Plans*   You borrow $20,000 and have two repayment options. Which has the lesser total payment?
a. One lending source offers the loan for 24 monthly payments at an annual interest rate of 8%.
b. Another lending source offers the loan for 36 monthly payments at an annual interest rate of 6%.

29. *Home Mortgage*   You have taken out a home mortgage for $90,000 at 9.5% annual interest for 20 years. You make monthly payments for one year. How much of the total monthly payments made during the first year was interest? What is the balance at the end of the year?

30. *Home Mortgage*   You have taken out a home mortgage for $120,000 at 11% annual interest for 30 years. You make monthly payments for one year. How much of the total monthly payments made during the first year was interest? What is the balance at the end of the year?

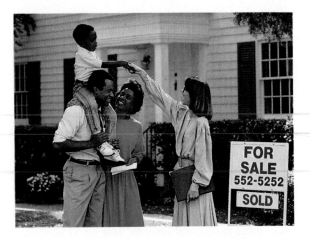

Most people need to obtain a large mortgage to purchase a home. A wise shopper will determine how much of each payment will be applied to the principal.

Integrated Review

31. *Color Television*   You purchased a new color television set. The total price, including a 6% sales tax, was $663.03. What was the price of the television?

32. *Bicycle*   You purchased a new bike. The total price, including a 7% sales tax, was $437.70. What was the price of the bike?

33. *Savings*   In 1991, about 70 million Americans were in the 18-to-34 age group. Using the graph at the right, approximate how many of them saved between $50 and $100 a month.

34. *Savings*   Suppose that each "saver" in Exercise 33 saved $75 a month. How much did the group save in 1991?

Source: The Survey of Consumer Financial Behavior, conducted by the Gallup Organization and Bank Advertising News

Exploration and Extension

35. *Finding the Principal*   You are paying $36.10 each month on a loan with an annual interest rate of 11.5% for a term of 6 years. What was the original amount of the loan?

36. *Finding the Principal*   You are paying $77.71 each month on a loan with an annual interest rate of 9.5%. If the original amount of the loan was $3700, what is the term of your loan?

Chapter Summary

What did you learn?

1. Sketch the graph of a rational function. **(10.1)**
- Find the horizontal and vertical asymptotes. **(10.1)**

2. Perform operations with rational expressions.
- Multiply and divide rational expressions. **(10.3)**
- Add and subtract rational expressions. **(10.5)**

3. Solve rational equations. **(10.4)**

4. Simplify complex fractions. **(10.5)**

5. Use rational models to solve real-life problems. **(10.1–10.5)**

6. Solve inverse variation problems. **(10.2)**

7. Solve joint variation problems. **(10.2)**

8. Find monthly payments for installment loans. **(10.6)**

9. Construct an amortization table for an installment loan. **(10.6)**

Why did you learn it?

The primary characteristic that distinguishes rational functions from polynomial functions is that graphs of rational functions can have horizontal or vertical asymptotes. They can also have discontinuities. (No polynomial function has a horizontal or vertical asymptote or a discontinuity.)

Because rational functions can have horizontal or vertical asymptotes, they can be used to model real-life situations that involve asymptotic behavior. For instance, the average cost of a product can asymptotically approach the unit cost as more and more units are produced.

How does it fit into the bigger picture of algebra?

In this chapter, you studied rational expressions and rational functions. By now you should be able to sketch the graph of a rational function. You have seen that the graphs of many rational functions have horizontal and vertical asymptotes.

You also learned to multiply, divide, add, and subtract rational expressions and solve rational equations. Because a rational expression is the ratio of two polynomials, this chapter provided additional practice with the polynomial operations that you studied in Chapter 9.

In Exercises 1–6, find the horizontal and vertical asymptotes, if any, of the graph of the function.

1. $f(x) = \dfrac{2}{x^2}$

2. $f(x) = \dfrac{1}{x + 4}$

3. $f(x) = \dfrac{3x^2}{4x^2 - 4}$

4. $f(x) = \dfrac{3x^3}{x^3 + 2x^2 - 6x}$

5. $f(x) = \dfrac{5x^2 - 6x + 1}{x - 3}$

6. $f(x) = \dfrac{3x^3 - 7}{4x + 6}$

In Exercises 7–10, match the function with its graph.

7. $f(x) = \dfrac{-4}{2 - x}$

8. $f(x) = \dfrac{x - 5}{x + 3}$

9. $f(x) = \dfrac{-2}{x^2 - 1}$

10. $f(x) = \dfrac{10}{x^2 - 4x - 5}$

a.

b.

c.

d.

In Exercises 11–22, sketch the graph of the function.

11. $f(x) = \dfrac{1}{x^2}$

12. $f(x) = -\dfrac{1}{x}$

13. $f(x) = \dfrac{2}{x - 5}$

14. $f(x) = \dfrac{3}{4 + 3x}$

15. $f(x) = \dfrac{-6x}{x + 2}$

16. $f(x) = \dfrac{3x^2 + 1}{x^2 - 1}$

17. $f(x) = \dfrac{3x^2}{x^2 + 4x + 4}$

18. $f(x) = \dfrac{4x^2 - 1}{x^2 + 8x + 7}$

19. $f(x) = \dfrac{2x^3 - x + 10}{3x^2 + 6x}$

20. $f(x) = \dfrac{4x^4 + x^3 + x - 4}{x^3 - 27}$

21. $f(x) = \dfrac{2x^4 + 1}{x^3 + 64}$

22. $f(x) = \dfrac{5x^2 + 6x - 7}{x - 2}$

In Exercises 23 and 24, the variables x and y vary inversely. Use the given pair of x- and y-values to find an equation that relates the variables.

23. $x = 1,\ y = 5$

24. $x = 4,\ y = 3$

In Exercises 25 and 26, the variable z varies jointly with the product of x and y. Use the given values to find an equation that relates the variables.

25. $z = 4,\ x = 1,\ y = 12$

26. $z = 6,\ x = 6,\ y = 8$

In Exercises 27 and 28, state whether x and y vary directly or inversely.

27.

x	1	2	3	4	5
y	60	30	20	15	12

28.

x	5	4	3	2	1
y	60	48	36	24	12

In Exercises 29–32, simplify the expression.

29. $\dfrac{x^2 - 3x - 10}{x^2 - 4}$
30. $\dfrac{x - 2}{x^2 + 7x - 18}$
31. $\dfrac{x + 5}{x^2 - 4x - 45}$
32. $\dfrac{x^2 - 2x - 8}{x + 2}$

In Exercises 33–44, perform the operations and simplify.

33. $\dfrac{24x^3y^2}{5xy} \cdot \dfrac{10x^2y^4}{3x^4y}$

34. $\dfrac{9xy^5}{2x^2y} \cdot \dfrac{6x^{-1}y}{x^3y^2}$

35. $\dfrac{x^3 + 3x^2 - 10x}{3x^2 + 9x - 30} \cdot (3x - 30)$

36. $\dfrac{x^2 - 3x}{4x^2 - 8x} \cdot (4x^2 - 16)$

37. $\dfrac{x^2 - 2x - 3}{x + 1} \div \dfrac{x^2 + x - 12}{x^2 - 1}$

38. $\dfrac{x - 4}{x^4} \div \dfrac{x^2 + 6x - 40}{x^4 + 9x^3 - 10x^2}$

39. $\dfrac{4x^3 - 40x^2}{2x + 10} \div \dfrac{x^3 - 9x^2 - 10x}{x + 5}$

40. $\dfrac{5x^4 - 50x^3}{x^2 - 3x - 70} \div (5x^3 + 25x^2)$

41. $\dfrac{2x}{x + 3} \cdot \dfrac{x^2 - 9}{5} \div \dfrac{x - 3}{4}$

42. $5x \div \dfrac{1}{x - 6} \cdot \dfrac{x^2 - 9}{x}$

43. $\dfrac{x^2 - 2x - 8}{x - 3} \div \dfrac{x + 2}{x - 3} \cdot \dfrac{x}{x - 4}$

44. $\dfrac{x - 1}{x^2 + 5x + 6} \cdot \dfrac{x^2 + x - 2}{3} \div \dfrac{x - 1}{3x}$

In Exercises 45–54, solve the equation. Check your solutions.

45. $\dfrac{x}{x - 1} = \dfrac{2x + 10}{x + 11}$

46. $\dfrac{2}{3x + 6} = \dfrac{x + 2}{x^2 - 10}$

47. $\dfrac{x + 3}{x} - 1 = \dfrac{1}{x - 1}$

48. $\dfrac{x + 6}{-x} + \dfrac{2x + 1}{x + 3} = 1$

49. $\dfrac{x + 8}{x - 4} + 3 = \dfrac{6(x - 2)}{x - 4}$

50. $\dfrac{x}{x + 2} - 2 = \dfrac{-9}{2x - 3}$

51. $\dfrac{2}{x - 2} - \dfrac{2x}{3} = \dfrac{x - 3}{3}$

52. $\dfrac{x + 6}{x} + 3 = \dfrac{x + 5}{x - 1}$

53. $\dfrac{2x + 4}{x} + \dfrac{x + 2}{x - 2} = \dfrac{3x}{x - 2}$

54. $\dfrac{3x + 2}{x + 1} = 2 - \dfrac{2x + 3}{x + 1}$

In Exercises 55–66, perform the operations and simplify.

55. $\dfrac{6}{x^2 - 4} + \dfrac{x}{x + 4}$

56. $\dfrac{x - 1}{x + 4} + \dfrac{3}{x(x - 4)}$

57. $\dfrac{5x - 1}{x + 3} + \dfrac{9}{x(x + 3)}$

58. $\dfrac{5}{x^2(x - 2)} + \dfrac{x}{x - 2}$

59. $\dfrac{x}{x - 1} - \dfrac{4}{x + 3}$

60. $\dfrac{x + 5}{x - 5} - \dfrac{3}{x + 5}$

61. $\dfrac{x}{x^2 - 16} - \dfrac{x - 2}{x(x + 4)}$

62. $\dfrac{x}{x - 7} - \dfrac{16}{x^2 - 49}$

63. $\dfrac{x - 5}{x^2 - x - 2} - \dfrac{3}{2} + \dfrac{4x + 1}{x + 1}$

64. $\dfrac{x - 2}{5x(x - 1)} + \dfrac{1}{x - 1} - \dfrac{3x + 2}{x^2 + 4x - 5}$

65. $\dfrac{x + 3}{4x - 3} - 2\left(\dfrac{x}{x + 2} + \dfrac{5x}{4x^2 + 5x - 6}\right)$

66. $3\left(\dfrac{10}{x - 4} - \dfrac{x + 3}{2x + 1}\right) + \dfrac{x^2 - 5}{2x^2 - 7x - 4}$

In Exercises 67–72, simplify the complex fraction.

67. $\dfrac{\left(\dfrac{5}{x} - \dfrac{x}{x-1}\right)}{\left(\dfrac{x}{x+1} + \dfrac{6}{x}\right)}$

68. $\dfrac{\left(\dfrac{4+x}{3} + \dfrac{9}{x}\right)}{\left(\dfrac{1}{x+1} - \dfrac{5}{x}\right)}$

69. $\dfrac{\left(\dfrac{x-2}{x+2} + \dfrac{6}{x-2}\right)}{\left(\dfrac{5}{x} - \dfrac{x}{x-2}\right)}$

70. $\dfrac{\left(\dfrac{4}{x} + \dfrac{x-3}{x-1}\right)}{\left(\dfrac{x-1}{x+2} - \dfrac{x+1}{x^2}\right)}$

71. $\dfrac{\left(\dfrac{x-5}{x+4} - \dfrac{x+4}{x-5}\right)}{\left(\dfrac{1}{x-5} + \dfrac{6+x}{x}\right)}$

72. $\dfrac{\left(\dfrac{x-3}{x} + \dfrac{x}{x+4}\right)}{\left(\dfrac{3}{x+4} + \dfrac{x}{5}\right)}$

Geometry **In Exercises 73 and 74, find an expression for the ratio of the area of the blue region to the total area. Then simplify the expression.**

73.

74.

75. *Amortization* You borrow $900 at a 10% annual interest rate. To repay the loan, you make 11 monthly payments of $79.12 and a final payment of $79.16. Construct an amortization table for this loan.

76. *Home Mortgage* You have a home mortgage of $85,000 with an annual interest rate of 11%. What is the monthly payment for a 20-year term? What is the total interest paid over the 20 years?

77. *Principal Payment* You borrow $15,000 at 8% annual interest for 10 years. How much of the first year's monthly installment payments are used to reduce the principal?

78. *Worm and Wheel Gears* For the worm and wheel gears shown at the right, the distance, D, on the perimeter of the wheel that the wheel gear rotates varies jointly with the product of the distance, P, between each tooth on the wheel gear and the number, N, of threads on the worm gear. A wheel gear whose teeth are 0.8 centimeter apart rotates 4 centimeters each time the 5-thread worm gear rotates once. How far would a wheel gear whose teeth are 0.5 centimeter apart rotate each time a 4-thread worm gear rotates once?

79. *Gravitational Force*   The gravitational force, F, between two bodies varies jointly with the product of their masses, m_1 and m_2, and inversely with the square of the distance, r, between the two bodies. For instance, the gravitational force between the moon and Earth is 1.985×10^{20} kilogram-meters per second squared. Use the following values to find an equation that relates F, m_1, m_2, and r.

Mass of moon: $m_1 = 7.354 \times 10^{22}$ kilograms
Mass of Earth:
  $m_2 = 5.979 \times 10^{24}$ kilograms
Distance between moon and Earth:
  $r = 3.844 \times 10^8$ meters

Earth, as photographed by the Apollo II mission while on the moon.

80. *Commercial Airline Revenue*   For 1985 through 1993, the commercial airline revenue from passengers, P (in millions of dollars), and from other sources, R (in millions of dollars), can be modeled by

$$P = \frac{20(173 + 512t)}{1 + 0.089t} \quad \text{and} \quad R = 46.7t^3 - 1398t^2 + 13{,}792t - 34{,}995$$

where $t = 5$ represents 1985. Sketch the graphs of these two models. Which type of revenue increased more from 1985 to 1993, passenger or other sources?   *(Source: Air Transport Association of America)*

81. *Railroad Salaries*   For 1985 through 1993, the average annual salary, S (in dollars), for railroad employees can be modeled by

$$S = \frac{6(5407 - 121t)}{1 - 0.038t}$$

where $t = 5$ represents 1985. The number of railroad employees, N (in thousands), can be modeled by

$$N = \frac{126t + 878}{t}.$$

Write an expression for the total salary (in thousands of dollars) paid to railroad employees. What was the total salary paid in 1991?
(Source: Association of American Railroads)

82. *Dairy Production*   For 1985 through 1994, the average amount of milk, M (in thousands of pounds per cow), produced by American dairy cows can be modeled by

$$M = \frac{11{,}525 + 223t}{1000 - 6.6t}$$

where $t = 5$ represents 1985. In what year was the average amount of milk about 15,000 pounds per cow?   *(Source: U.S. Department of Agriculture)*

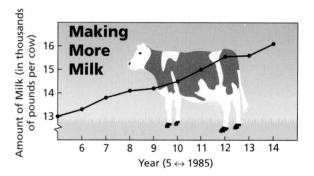

Recycled Paper, Glass, and Aluminum   **In Exercises 83–85, use the following information.**

For 1960 through 1990, the amount (in millions of tons) of paper, P, aluminum, A, and glass, G, that was recycled in the United States can be modeled by

$$P = \frac{215}{40 - t}, \qquad A = \frac{t^3}{25{,}000}, \qquad \text{and} \qquad G = \frac{84 + 15t}{1250 - 33t}$$

where $t = 0$ represents 1960.

83. Sketch the graph of each model.

84. In what year did Americans recycle about 16.5 million tons of paper?

85. In what year did Americans recycle about 0.1 million tons of glass? Was this the same year that 0.1 million tons of aluminum were recycled?

More About Recycling   **In Exercises 86–88, use the following information *and* the information given in Exercises 83–85.**

For 1960 through 1990, one model for the total amount of material, T (in millions of tons), that was recycled in the United States can be written

$$T = \frac{3(t + 330)}{4(40 - t)}$$

where $t = 0$ represents 1960.

86. Of the total recycled materials, write an expression that represents the decimal percent (by weight) that was paper.

87. Of the total recycled materials, write an expression that represents the decimal percent (by weight) that was aluminum.

88. Of the total recycled materials, write an expression that represents the decimal percent (by weight) that was glass.

89. *Nonrecycled Paper*   For 1960 through 1990, the amount of paper, W (in millions of tons) used in the United States can be modeled by

$$W = \frac{5000}{3(51 - t)}$$

where $t = 0$ represents 1960. Write an expression for the amount of paper products used and *not* recycled. Sketch the graph of W and the model for nonrecycled paper on the same coordinate system. What can you conclude from the graphs?

In Exercises 1 and 2, sketch the graph of the equation.

1. $y = \dfrac{3}{x-2}$

2. $y = \dfrac{4}{x^2+4}$

3. The variables x and y vary inversely. When $x = 2$, $y = 4$. Write an equation that relates x and y.

4. The variable x varies jointly with the product of y and z. When $x = 1$ and $y = 2$, $z = 8$. Write an equation that relates x, y, and z.

In Exercises 5–10, perform the operation and simplify.

5. $\dfrac{x^2-4}{x+3} \cdot \dfrac{x^2+4x+3}{2x-4}$

6. $\dfrac{4x-8}{x^2-3x+2} \div \dfrac{3x-6}{x-1}$

7. $\dfrac{3}{5b} + \dfrac{2}{15b}$

8. $\dfrac{5}{x+1} + \dfrac{x-7}{x-2}$

9. $\dfrac{x+1}{3y} - \dfrac{x+2}{6y}$

10. $\dfrac{x-1}{x-2} - \dfrac{x-4}{x+1}$

In Exercises 11–13, solve the equation.

11. $\dfrac{x-3}{8} = \dfrac{2x}{3x+7}$

12. $\dfrac{x}{x+3} + \dfrac{2}{x} = \dfrac{5}{2x}$

13. $\dfrac{\left(3 - \dfrac{2}{x+1}\right)}{\left(3 + \dfrac{3}{x}\right)} = 2$

In Exercises 14 and 15, find the least common multiple.

14. x^2, $x(x-3)$, $(x-3)^2$

15. $x^4 - 3x^3 - 4x^2$, $x^3 - x^2 - 2x$

16. Simplify the complex fraction $\dfrac{\left(1 + \dfrac{3}{x}\right)}{\left(2 - \dfrac{5}{x^2}\right)}$.

17. You are starting a small beekeeping business. You spend $500 for the equipment and the bees. You figure that it will cost $1.25 per pound to collect, clean, bottle, and label the honey. How many pounds must you produce before your average cost per pound is $1.79?

18. From 1970 through 1990, the per capita consumption of red meat, m (in pounds), and boneless chicken, c (in pounds), in the United States can be modeled by $m = -4.4t + 132$ and $c = 0.8t^2 - 1.6t + 37$, where $t = 0$ represents 1970, $t = 1$ represents 1975, and so on. According to these models, in what year was the ratio of red meat consumption to chicken consumption 3 to 1? *(Source: USA Today)*

In Exercises 19 and 20, you take out a 20-year loan for $100,000 at 6% annual interest. You will repay the loan with monthly installments.

19. Calculate the amount of each monthly installment.

20. If you continue making payments each month for 20 years, how much interest will you have paid?

Quadratic Relations

LESSONS

11.1 Parabolas ▪ 570

11.2 Circles and Points of Intersection ▪ 576

11.3 Ellipses ▪ 583

11.4 Hyperbolas ▪ 590

11.5 Translations of Conics ▪ 597

11.6 Classifying Conics ▪ 606

The West Wacker Building in Chicago follows the curve of the Chicago River. It has 36 stories and is 468 feet tall.

Chicago's West Wacker Building, at 333 West Wacker Drive, was designed by the American architect William Pedersen. In a 1986 poll of architects, this building ranked number three in favorite new buildings.

The curved wall of the building follows a bend in the Chicago River. The curve is part of an ellipse given by

$$\frac{x^2}{240^2} + \frac{y^2}{170^2} = 1$$

where x and y are measured in feet. The area of the base is about 24,600 square feet.

11.1

Parabolas

What you should learn:

Goal 1 How to write an equation of a parabola and sketch its graph

Goal 2 How to use parabolas to solve real-life problems

Why you should learn it:

You can model many real-life objects, such as solar collectors, with parabolic models.

Goal 1 Writing an Equation of a Parabola

You already know that the graph of a quadratic function is a *parabola*. In this lesson, you will study properties of parabolas.

A **parabola** is the set of all points (x, y) that are equidistant from a fixed line, the **directrix,** and a fixed point, the **focus.** The midpoint of the segment from the focus perpendicular to the directrix is the **vertex.** The line passing through the focus and the vertex is the **axis.**

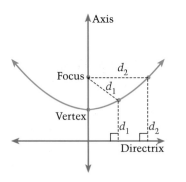

> ### Standard Equation of a Parabola (Vertex at Origin)
> The **standard form of the equation of a parabola** with a vertex at (0, 0) is as follows.
>
> | Equation | Focus | Directrix | |
> |----------|-------|-----------|---|
> | $x^2 = 4py$ | $(0, p)$ | $y = -p$ | *Vertical axis (x = 0)* |
> | $y^2 = 4px$ | $(p, 0)$ | $x = -p$ | *Horizontal axis (y = 0)* |

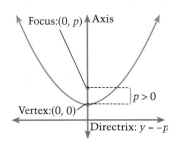

Vertical axis: p > 0

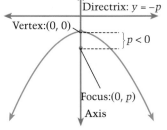

Vertical axis: p < 0

The four ways a parabola can be oriented in the coordinate plane when its axis is horizontal or vertical are shown at right.

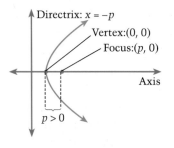

Horizontal axis: p > 0

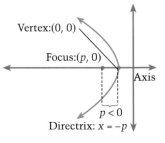

Horizontal axis: p < 0

Example **1** | *Finding the Focus and Directrix*

Find the focus and the directrix of the parabola $y = -2x^2$.

Solution   Since the x-term is squared, you know that the axis is vertical, and the standard form is

$$x^2 = 4py. \qquad \textit{Standard form, vertical axis}$$

You can write the given equation in this form as follows.

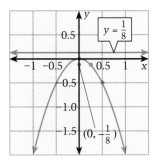

$$-2x^2 = y \qquad \textit{Given equation}$$

$$x^2 = -\frac{1}{2}y \qquad \textit{Divide both sides by } -2.$$

$$x^2 = 4\left(-\frac{1}{8}\right)y \qquad \textit{Standard form}$$

Thus $p = -\frac{1}{8}$. Since p is negative, the parabola opens downward, the focus of the parabola is $(0, p) = \left(0, -\frac{1}{8}\right)$, and the directrix is $y = -p = \frac{1}{8}$. Note that the focus is $\frac{1}{8}$ unit from the vertex, $(0, 0)$. The directrix is also $\frac{1}{8}$ unit from the vertex, but on the side opposite the focus. The directrix is the horizontal line through the point $\left(0, \frac{1}{8}\right)$. ∎

Example **2** | *Writing an Equation and Sketching a Graph*

Write the standard form of the equation of the parabola with vertex at the origin and focus at $(2, 0)$. Sketch the parabola.

Solution   The axis of the parabola is horizontal, through $(0, 0)$, and the focus is at $(p, 0) = (2, 0)$. The standard form of the equation is as follows.

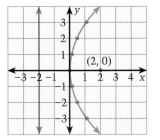

$$y^2 = 4px \qquad \textit{Standard form, horizontal axis}$$

Because $p = 2$, the equation is

$$y^2 = 4(2)x \qquad \textit{Substitute 2 for p.}$$

$$y^2 = 8x. \qquad \textit{Standard form}$$

To sketch the parabola, it helps to write the equation as $x = \frac{1}{8}y^2$ and construct a table of values. From the table, you can sketch the graph shown at the left.

y	-3	-2	-1	0	1	2	3
x	$\frac{9}{8}$	$\frac{1}{2}$	$\frac{1}{8}$	0	$\frac{1}{8}$	$\frac{1}{2}$	$\frac{9}{8}$

∎

Be sure you understand that the term *parabola* is a technical term used in mathematics and does not simply refer to any ∪-shaped curve. For instance, the graph of $y = x^4$ is a ∪-shaped curve but is *not* a parabola.

The world's largest solar-thermal complex, Luz International, is located in California's Mojave Desert. The parabolic mirrors reflect the sun's rays on tubes filled with oil. The heated oil is then used to boil water, which sends steam to a turbine. There are 1.5 million mirrors in the complex. A crew of 20 people works at night to keep the mirrors clean.

Goal 2 Using Parabolas for Real-Life Problems

Solar Energy

In a parabolic reflector, all incoming rays that are parallel to the parabola's axis are directed to the focus.

Example 3 *Farming the Sun*

Cross sections of parabolic mirrors at the solar-thermal complex can be modeled by the equation

$$\frac{1}{25}x^2 = y$$

where x and y are measured in feet. The oil-filled heating tube is located at the focus of the parabola. How high above the vertex of the mirror is the heating tube?

Solution

$$\frac{1}{25}x^2 = y \qquad \text{\textit{Given equation}}$$
$$x^2 = 25y \qquad \text{\textit{Multiply both sides by 25.}}$$
$$x^2 = 4\left(\frac{25}{4}\right)y \qquad \text{\textit{Standard form}}$$

Thus $p = \frac{25}{4} = 6.25$. Since p is positive, the parabola opens upward, and the focus of the parabola is 6.25 feet above the vertex.

Communicating about ALGEBRA

▶ **SHARING IDEAS about the Lesson**

Find the focus and directrix of the parabola. Explain your steps.

A. $y = 2x^2$ **B.** $y = -6x^2$

C. $x = \frac{1}{2}y^2$ **D.** $x = -12y^2$

EXERCISES

Guided Practice

▶ **CRITICAL THINKING about the Lesson**

1. Describe in words the location of a parabola's vertex relative to its focus and directrix.

2. Does the parabola $y^2 = x$ have a horizontal or vertical axis?

3. Write the equation of the directrix of the parabola $x^2 = 4y$.

4. Find the focus of the parabola $y = -\frac{1}{8}x^2$.

5. In which direction does the parabola with vertex at $(0, 0)$ and focus at $(0, 3)$ open?

6. Write an equation of the parabola in Exercise 5. Sketch the parabola.

Independent Practice

In Exercises 7–14, write the equation of the parabola in standard form.

7. $y = 5x^2$

8. $y = -3x^2$

9. $y + 2x^2 = 0$

10. $x = 9y^2$

11. $3y^2 = 2x$

12. $\frac{1}{9}y^2 = 2x$

13. $14y^2 - x = 0$

14. $2y^2 + x = 0$

In Exercises 15–18, decide whether the parabola has a vertical or horizontal axis.

15. $y = -7x^2$

16. $-2x^2 = 5y$

17. $3y^2 = 8x$

18. $x = 9y^2$

In Exercises 19–30, find the focus and the directrix of the parabola.

19. $2x^2 = -y$

20. $4y^2 = x$

21. $x^2 = 8y$

22. $y^2 = 20x$

23. $y^2 = -16x$

24. $x^2 = -36y$

25. $x^2 + 12y = 0$

26. $-80y + 2x^2 = 0$

27. $3y^2 - 12x = 0$

28. $3x^2 - 4y = 0$

29. $-24y + x^2 = 0$

30. $-4x + 9y^2 = 0$

In Exercises 31–38, write the standard form of the equation of the parabola with vertex at the origin and the given focus.

31. $(5, 0)$

32. $(-2, 0)$

33. $(-3, 0)$

34. $(0, 2)$

35. $(-4, 0)$

36. $(2, 0)$

37. $(0, -1)$

38. $(0, -3)$

In Exercises 39–42, match the equation with its graph.

39. $y^2 = 12x$

40. $x^2 = -12y$

41. $x^2 = 12y$

42. $y^2 = -12x$

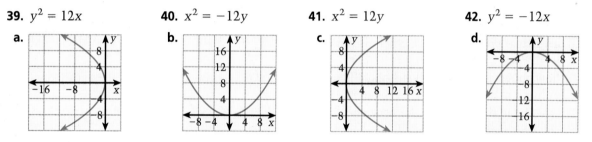

In Exercises 43–54, sketch the parabola.

43. $y^2 = 16x$ **44.** $x^2 = -6y$ **45.** $y^2 = -2x$ **46.** $y^2 = 36x$

47. $x^2 = 8y$ **48.** $y^2 = -10y$ **49.** $x^2 = -20y$ **50.** $x^2 = 14y$

51. $x^2 - 18y = 0$ **52.** $x + \frac{1}{20}y^2 = 0$ **53.** $x - \frac{1}{8}y^2 = 0$ **54.** $5x^2 = 4y$

55. *Television Antenna Dish*   Cross sections of television dish antennas have parabolic shapes. For the dish below, the receiver is located at the focus and is 4 feet above the vertex. Find an equation of a cross section of the dish. (Assume the vertex is at the origin.) Explain how the antenna works.

57. *Gold Rush*   Each second in the *Gold Rush* video game, a gold bar is released from point *F* in any direction, except straight up. At the same time, a gold rusher is released from some point at the bottom of the screen. The gold rusher moves straight up at the same speed as the gold bar. The path *G* represents all possible locations at which the gold rusher intersects the gold bar. Explain why *G* is a parabola. If the point *F* is four units from the bottom of the screen, what is the equation of *G*?

58. *Storage Building*   A storage building for rock salt (for melting ice on roads) has the shape of a *paraboloid*—vertical cross sections are parabolas and horizontal cross sections are circles. An equation of a vertical cross section of the building is $y = -\frac{1}{12}x^2$. If the building is 27 feet high, how much rock salt will it hold? (The volume of a paraboloid is $V = \frac{1}{2}\pi r^2 h$, where *r* is the radius of the base and *h* is the height.)

56. *Automobile Headlights*   The headlights on a car work opposite to the way in which the television dish antenna works. The headlight bulb is at the focus of a parabolic reflector behind it. The bulb is 1.5 inches from the vertex of the reflector. Find an equation of a cross section of the reflector. The reflector is 6 inches wide. How deep is it?

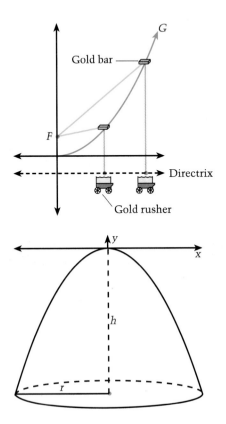

59. *Unzipping a Zipper*   In the picture below, a thumbtack holds tab A fixed at the top of the zipper. Tab B glides along the pole without friction. Explain why the zipper traces out a parabola. Where are the focus and directrix?

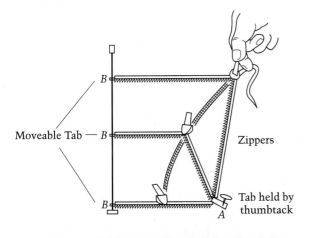

Moveable Tab — B

Zippers

Tab held by thumbtack

60. *Burning Mirror*   The drawing below was taken from a book that was printed in the 17th century. In the drawing, the rays of the sun are shown lighting a candle. Explain why the sun's rays can generate enough heat to do this.

Integrated Review

In Exercises 61–66, sketch the graph of the function.

61. $f(x) = (x + 1)^2$

62. $f(x) = x^2 + 3$

63. $f(x) = x^2 - 4$

64. $f(x) = (x + 2)^2 - 4$

65. $f(x) = (x - 1)^2 + 3$

66. $f(x) = x^2 + 1$

67. *College Entrance Exam Sample*   A rectangular box with a square base contains 6 cubic feet. The height of the box is 18 inches. How many feet are in each edge of the base?

   a. 1   **b.** 2   **c.** $\sqrt{3}$ **d.** $\dfrac{\sqrt{3}}{3}$ **e.** 4

68. *College Entrance Exam Sample*   The surface area of a cube is 150 square feet. What is the volume of the cube in cubic feet?

   a. 30   **b.** 50   **c.** 100   **d.** 125   **e.** 150

Exploration and Extension

In Exercises 69–72, find the points of intersection of the graphs of *f* and *g* by setting *f*(*x*) equal to *g*(*x*) and solving the resulting equation for *x*.

69. $f(x) = 2x^2$
    $g(x) = -2x + 12$

70. $f(x) = 5x^2$
    $g(x) = -15x - 10$

71. $f(x) = -3x^2$
    $g(x) = -9x + 6$

72. $f(x) = -\frac{1}{2}x^2$
    $g(x) = -4x + 6$

Circles and Points of Intersection

What you should learn:

Goal 1 How to write an equation of a circle and sketch its graph

Goal 2 How to use equations and graphs of circles in real-life problems

Why you should learn it:

You can model many real-life situations with circular models, such as finding where two sounds are of equal intensity.

Goal 1 Writing an Equation of a Circle

A **circle** is the set of all points (x, y) that are equidistant from a fixed point, called the **center** of the circle. The distance, r, between the center and any point (x, y) on the circle is the **radius.**

The distance formula can be used to obtain an equation of the circle whose center is the origin and whose radius is r. Because the distance between any point on the circle, (x, y), and the center, $(0, 0)$, is r, you can write the following.

$$\sqrt{(x - 0)^2 + (y - 0)^2} = r \qquad \textit{Distance formula}$$

$$(x - 0)^2 + (y - 0)^2 = r^2 \qquad \textit{Square both sides.}$$

$$x^2 + y^2 = r^2 \qquad \textit{Simplify.}$$

Standard Equation of a Circle (Center at Origin)

The **standard form of the equation of a circle** with center at $(0, 0)$ and radius of r is

$$x^2 + y^2 = r^2.$$

Example 1 Writing an Equation of a Circle

The point $(2, 5)$ is on a circle whose center is the origin. Write the standard form of the equation of the circle.

Solution Because the point $(2, 5)$ is on the circle, the radius of the circle must be the distance between the center and the point $(2, 5)$. Using the distance formula, the radius is

$$r = \sqrt{(2 - 0)^2 + (5 - 0)^2} = \sqrt{4 + 25} = \sqrt{29}.$$

Since the radius is $\sqrt{29}$, use the standard form to write the equation.

$$x^2 + y^2 = r^2 \qquad \textit{Standard form}$$

$$x^2 + y^2 = (\sqrt{29})^2 \qquad \textit{Substitute } \sqrt{29} \textit{ for r.}$$

$$x^2 + y^2 = 29 \qquad \textit{Simplify.}$$

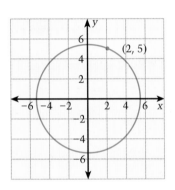

A **point of intersection** of two graphs is a point that lies on both graphs. Two graphs can have no point of intersection, one point, or two or more points.

LESSON INVESTIGATION

■ Investigating Points of Intersection

Partner Activity Find values of r so that the circle $x^2 + y^2 = r^2$ and the line $y = -x + 2$ have the indicated number of points of intersection. If it is not possible, explain why.

a. No points   **b.** 1 point   **c.** 2 points   **d.** 3 points

Study Tip

To find any points of intersection of the graphs of two equations, you can use substitution, as shown in Example 2. The general strategy is to solve for one of the variables in one equation and substitute for that variable in the other equation.

Example 2   *Finding Points of Intersection*

Find the points of intersection of the graphs of

$$x^2 + y^2 = 8 \quad \text{and} \quad y = \tfrac{1}{2}x + 1.$$

Solution   To find the points of intersection, substitute $\tfrac{1}{2}x + 1$ for y in the equation of the circle.

$x^2 + y^2 = 8$	*Equation of circle*
$x^2 + \left(\tfrac{1}{2}x + 1\right)^2 = 8$	*Substitute $\tfrac{1}{2}x + 1$ for y.*
$x^2 + \tfrac{1}{4}x^2 + x + 1 = 8$	*Simplify.*
$\tfrac{5}{4}x^2 + x - 7 = 0$	*Simplify.*
$5x^2 + 4x - 28 = 0$	*Multiply both sides by 4.*
$(x - 2)(5x + 14) = 0$	*Factor.*
$x = 2, -\tfrac{14}{5}$	*Zero Factor Property*

You now know the x-coordinates of the points of intersection. To find the y-coordinates, substitute $x = 2$ and $x = -\tfrac{14}{5}$ into the linear equation $y = \tfrac{1}{2}x + 1$ to conclude that the points of intersection are $(2, 2)$ and $\left(-\tfrac{14}{5}, -\tfrac{2}{5}\right)$. A graphical check, at the left, helps verify the result. ■

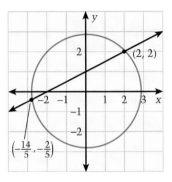

Two electronic speakers are in a room. One is 10 feet from the center of the room and the other is 20 feet from the center, as shown at the right. The speaker that is 20 feet from the center produces twice the intensity as the speaker that is 10 feet from the center.

Real Life
Acoustics

Example 3   *Writing an Equation of a Circle*

Find all points in the room at which the sound from Speaker A has the same intensity as the sound from Speaker B. (Use a two-dimensional model.)

Solution   Let I represent the power of Speaker A at $(10, 0)$. Then $2I$ represents the power of Speaker B at $(20, 0)$. Knowing that the intensity of sound at a point varies inversely as the square of the distance between the point and the source (see page 527), you can conclude that the intensity at a point (x, y) is as follows.

$$\frac{I}{(\sqrt{(x-10)^2+(y-0)^2})^2} \qquad \textit{Intensity from Speaker A}$$

$$\frac{2I}{(\sqrt{(x-20)^2+(y-0)^2})^2} \qquad \textit{Intensity from Speaker B}$$

The points at which these two intensities are equal are given by

$$\frac{I}{(\sqrt{(x-10)^2+(y-0)^2})^2} = \frac{2I}{(\sqrt{(x-20)^2+(y-0)^2})^2}.$$

Simplifying this equation produces $x^2 + y^2 = 200$. Thus at any point on the circle $x^2 + y^2 = 200$, you would hear sound of equal intensity from the two speakers.   ∎

Communicating about **ALGEBRA**

▶ **SHARING IDEAS about the Lesson**

Complete the "missing steps" in Example 3 by showing that the following equation simplifies to $x^2 + y^2 = 200$.

$$\frac{I}{(\sqrt{(x-10)^2+(y-0)^2})^2} = \frac{2I}{(\sqrt{(x-20)^2+(y-0)^2})^2}$$

EXERCISES

▶ **CRITICAL THINKING about the Lesson**

1. What is the radius of the circle $x^2 + y^2 = 1$? Where is the center?

2. Write the standard form of the equation of the circle that passes through $(6, -4)$ and whose center is the origin. Explain the strategy you used.

3. Sketch the graphs of $x^2 + y^2 = 10$ and $y = 2x + 1$ in the same coordinate plane. Are there any points of intersection?

4. Give an algebraic verification of your answer to Exercise 3.

Independent Practice

In Exercises 5–8, write the standard form of the equation of the circle with the given radius and whose center is the origin.

5. $r = 4$ **6.** $r = \frac{1}{2}$ **7.** $r = \sqrt{3}$ **8.** $r = 1 + \sqrt{2}$

In Exercises 9–12, write the standard form of the equation of the circle that passes through the given point and whose center is the origin.

9. $(-2, -4)$ **10.** $(0, 6)$ **11.** $(-5, 1)$ **12.** $(-3, -1)$

In Exercises 13–16, match the equation with its graph.

13. $x^2 + y^2 = 16$ **14.** $x^2 + y^2 = 5$ **15.** $x^2 + y^2 = 4$ **16.** $x^2 + y^2 = 25$

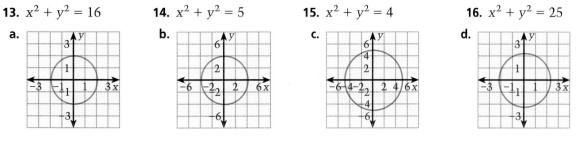

In Exercises 17–28, sketch the graph of the equation.

17. $x^2 + y^2 = 2$ **18.** $x^2 + y^2 = 7$ **19.** $x^2 + y = 0$ **20.** $x^2 + y^2 = 9$

21. $x^2 + y^2 = 36$ **22.** $x^2 + y^2 = 49$ **23.** $x^2 + y^2 = 8$ **24.** $4x^2 + y = 0$

25. $6x^2 + 6y^2 = 144$ **26.** $7x^2 + 7y^2 = 252$ **27.** $20x^2 + 20y^2 = 400$ **28.** $3x^2 + 3y^2 = 48$

In Exercises 29–36, find the points of intersection, if any, of the graphs.

29. $x^2 + y^2 = 1$
$x + y = -1$

30. $x^2 + y^2 = 100$
$x + y = 0$

31. $x^2 + y^2 = 100$
$x + y = 14$

32. $x^2 + y^2 = 9$
$x - 3y = 3$

33. $x^2 + y^2 = 4$
$x - y = 1$

34. $x^2 = -12y$
$2x - y = 15$

35. $x^2 = 8y$
$y = -x$

36. $y^2 = 16x$
$4x - y = -24$

37. *Desert Irrigation*   Each of the circular fields shown at the right has an area of about 2,400,000 square yards. Write an equation that represents the boundary of one of the fields. Let (0, 0) represent the center.

38. *Communications Satellites*   Most communications satellites have *synchronous* orbits, which means they circle the earth at exactly the same speed as Earth is rotating. For a viewer on Earth, such a satellite appears to be stationary. Find an equation that represents the circular orbit of a satellite placed 22,240 miles above Earth. Let (0, 0) represent the center. (The radius of Earth is about 3960 miles.)

This irrigation project in Libya enables farmers to raise crops in the desert. Water from deep wells is pumped to sprinklers that rotate in circular patterns.

Two Lights in a Room   **In Exercises 39 and 40, use the following information.**

A room contains two ceiling lights. In a coordinate system in which the center of the ceiling is the origin, the lights are located at (0, 8) and (0, 16). The light that is farthest from the center of the room is twice as bright as the other light.

39. Find an equation that represents all points on the ceiling that receive the same illumination of light from each source. (*Hint:* Recall from Lesson 10.2 that the illumination of light at a point varies inversely with the square of the distance between the point and the source.)

40. Which of the lights is brighter at the point (8, 8)?

41. *Busing Boundary*   To be eligible to ride the school bus to East High School, a student must live at least 1 mile from the school. Describe the portion of Clark Street for which the residents are *not* eligible to ride the school bus. Use a coordinate system in which the school is at (0, 0) and each unit represents 1 mile.

42. *Geometry*   A theorem from geometry states that if a triangle is inscribed in a circle so that one side of the triangle is a diameter of the circle, then the triangle is a right triangle. Show this theorem is true for the circle $x^2 + y^2 = 100$ and the triangle formed by the lines $y = 0$, $y = \frac{1}{2}x + 5$, and $y = -2x + 20$. (Find the vertices of the triangle and verify that it is a right triangle.)

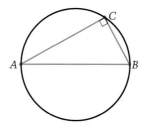

In Exercises 43–48, find the distance between the two points.

43. $(1, 2)$, $(6, 3)$ **44.** $(3, 0)$, $(-1, -2)$ **45.** $(-3, 2)$, $(1, 3)$

46. $(5, -5)$, $(1, 3)$ **47.** $(0, 0)$, $(9, 1)$ **48.** $(4, 3)$, $(-1, 6)$

In Exercises 49–54, find the point of intersection of the lines.

49. $\begin{cases} x + 2y = 1 \\ 2x - 3y = 16 \end{cases}$
50. $\begin{cases} -x + 4y = 11 \\ 3x + 5y = 18 \end{cases}$
51. $\begin{cases} 4x + y = 4 \\ 9x - 5y = -20 \end{cases}$

52. $\begin{cases} 3x + y = 3 \\ -x - 5y = 13 \end{cases}$
53. $\begin{cases} x + 5y = -9 \\ -2x + 3y = -8 \end{cases}$
54. $\begin{cases} 2x + y = -1 \\ x - 3y = 10 \end{cases}$

55. *Powers of Ten*   Which best estimates the diameter of a bicycle tire?
   a. 2.5×10^{-2} in.   **b.** 2.5×10^{-1} in.
   c. 2.5×10^{0} in.   **d.** 2.5×10^{1} in.

56. *Powers of Ten*   Which best estimates the radius of a penny?
   a. 1.0×10^{-1} mm   **b.** 1.0×10^{0} mm
   c. 1.0×10^{1} mm   **d.** 1.0×10^{2} mm

In Exercises 57–60, match the equation with its graph.

57. $|x|^{1/2} + |y|^{1/2} = 1$ **58.** $|x|^{1} + |y|^{1} = 1$ **59.** $|x|^{2} + |y|^{2} = 1$ **60.** $|x|^{4} + |y|^{4} = 1$

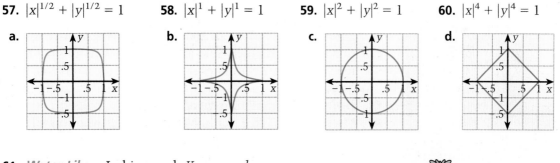

a. **b.** **c.** **d.**

61. *Water Lily*   In his novel, *Kavenaugh*, Henry Wadsworth Longfellow stated the following puzzle about a water lily.

When the stem of the water lily is vertical, the blossom is 10 centimeters above the surface of a lake. If you pull the lily to one side, keeping the stem straight, the blossom touches the water at a spot 21 centimeters from where the stem formerly cut the surface. How deep is the water?

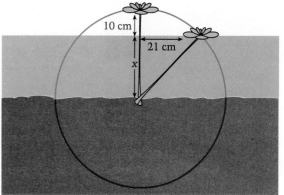

10 cm
21 cm
x

Mixed REVIEW

1. Sketch $-4 < x \le 2$. **(1.6)**

2. Solve $|2x + 3| < 4$. **(1.7)**

3. Write 3.72×10^5 in standard form.

4. Evaluate $f(x) = -x^2$ when $x = -2$. **(6.1)**

5. 15 is $\frac{5}{9}$ of what?

6. Sketch $y = -2x^2 + 4x - 3$. **(5.2)**

7. Find the intercepts of $2x + 4 = x - 4y$. **(5.2)**

8. Find the vertex of $y = 3x^2 - 9x + 5$. **(5.2)**

9. Write the inverse of $f(x) = \frac{2}{3}x - 5$. **(6.3)**

10. Find the slope of $5x + 2y - 7 = 8x - 3y$. **(2.2)**

11. Find $\frac{5}{8}$ of $\frac{4}{15}$.

12. Simplify: $\left(\frac{1}{3}\right)^{-2}$. **(7.1)**

13. Sketch $y = \sqrt[3]{x + 1} - 4$. **(7.6)**

14. Sketch $f(x) = e^{x+5}$. **(8.1)**

15. Evaluate $\log_3 9 - \log_2 8$. **(8.2)**

16. Factor $4x^2 - 20x + 25$. **(9.3)**

17. Solve $\dfrac{x + 6}{3} = \dfrac{6}{5 - x}$. **(10.4)**

18. Add: $\dfrac{x + 2}{x^2 + 2x - 3} + \dfrac{x}{x^2 - 9}$. **(10.5)**

19. If 100 is increased by 10%, and then decreased by 10%, what remains?

20. Solve for y: $\dfrac{x + y}{y} = \dfrac{2x}{5}$. **(1.5)**

Career Interview

Sales Coordinator

Teresa Carrera-Hanley is a sales coordinator in the foreign languages department of a publishing company. "About 60% of my time is spent in schools, talking to teachers and students."

Q: What lead you into this career?
A: I grew up in Ecuador, so Spanish was my first language. In this country, I taught Spanish before moving into publishing. This career combines my business and multi-lingual background.

Q: Did you like math in school?
A: I have always liked math. My grandfather who was Chinese used the abacus to teach me math and to play math games. In school, I earned a lot of respect from my friends because I was good in math. Whenever there was a difficult math problem, everyone would say, "Let's ask Teresa," then we would sit down and solve it together.

Q: Does having a math background help you on the job?
A: I majored in economics in college. My math background was very helpful to me. On the job, I use a lot of statistics. We have many variables to consider when reviewing data. To plan well, I need to interpret the data accurately.

Q: What would you like to tell kids about math?
A: If you don't understand, never hesitate to ask for help.

11.3

Ellipses

What you should learn:

Goal 1 How to write an equation of an ellipse and sketch its graph

Goal 2 How to use ellipses to solve real-life problems

Why you should learn it:

You can model many shapes, such as archways, with elliptical models.

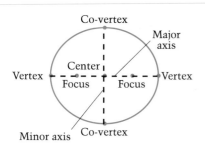

Goal 1 **Writing an Equation of an Ellipse**

An **ellipse** is the set of all points (x, y) such that the sum of the distances between (x, y) and two distinct fixed points, the **focuses** or **foci**, is a constant. The line through the foci intersects the ellipse at two points, the **vertices.** The line segment joining the vertices is the **major axis,** and its midpoint is the **center** of the ellipse. The line segment perpendicular to the major axis at the center is the **minor axis** of the ellipse. The endpoints of the minor axis are the **co-vertices.**

Standard Equation of an Ellipse (Center at Origin)

The **standard form of the equation of an ellipse** with center at $(0, 0)$ and major and minor axes of lengths $2a$ and $2b$, where $a > b$, is as follows.

$$\frac{x^2}{a^2} + \frac{y^2}{b^2} = 1 \quad \textit{Horizontal major axis}$$

$$\frac{x^2}{b^2} + \frac{y^2}{a^2} = 1 \quad \textit{Vertical major axis}$$

The vertices lie on the major axis, a units from the center. The co-vertices lie on the minor axis, b units from the center.

The foci of the ellipse lie on the major axis, c units from the center, where $c^2 = a^2 - b^2$.

The two orientations of an ellipse are shown below.

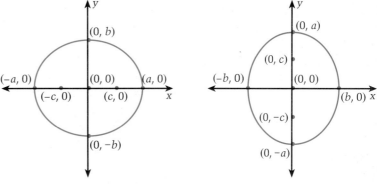

Horizontal major axis   *Vertical major axis*

Example 1 *Writing an Equation of an Ellipse*

Write an equation of the ellipse whose vertices are $(-3, 0)$ and $(3, 0)$ and whose co-vertices are $(0, -2)$ and $(0, 2)$. Find the foci of the ellipse.

Solution   Begin by graphing the four vertices and co-vertices. The center of the ellipse is $(0, 0)$ because that is the point that lies halfway between the vertices (or halfway between the co-vertices). The equation of the ellipse has the form

$$\frac{x^2}{a^2} + \frac{y^2}{b^2} = 1. \quad \textit{Horizontal major axis}$$

The distance between the center and either vertex is $a = 3$. The distance between the center and either co-vertex is $b = 2$. Thus the standard equation of the ellipse is

$$\frac{x^2}{3^2} + \frac{y^2}{2^2} = 1 \quad \text{or} \quad \frac{x^2}{9} + \frac{y^2}{4} = 1.$$

The foci lie on the major axis, c units from the center, where $c^2 = 3^2 - 2^2 = 5$. The coordinates of the foci are $(-\sqrt{5}, 0)$ and $(\sqrt{5}, 0)$. ∎

Goal 2 Using Ellipses in Real-Life Problems

Real Life
Architecture

Example 2   *Building an Archway*

You are responsible for designing an archway whose opening is an ellipse, as shown at the left. The height of the archway is 10 feet and the width is 30 feet. Find an equation of the ellipse and use the equation to sketch an accurate drawing of the archway.

Solution   Locate the origin at the center of the base of the archway. Because the major axis is horizontal, you know that $a = 15$ and $b = 10$, which implies that the equation is

$$\frac{x^2}{15^2} + \frac{y^2}{10^2} = 1 \quad \text{or} \quad \frac{x^2}{225} + \frac{y^2}{100} = 1.$$

To make an accurate sketch of the ellipse, solve this equation for (positive) y, and construct a table of values.

$$y = 10\sqrt{1 - \frac{x^2}{225}}$$

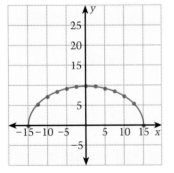

x-value	±15	±12.5	±10	±7.5	±5	±2.5	0
y-value	0	5.53	7.45	8.66	9.43	9.86	10

Using the values in the table, you can sketch the graph shown at the left. ∎

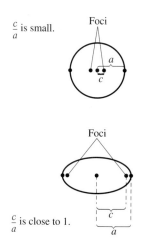

$\frac{c}{a}$ is small.

Foci

$\frac{c}{a}$ is close to 1.

The **eccentricity** of an ellipse is a measure of its ovalness. The eccentricity is given by $\frac{c}{a}$. If the ellipse is nearly circular, then the foci are close to the center and the eccentricity $\frac{c}{a}$ is close to 0. If the ellipse is very elongated, then the foci are close to the vertices and the eccentricity is close to 1.

All planets have elliptical orbits about the sun. (The sun is a focus of the elliptical orbit, *not* the center.) Some orbits, however, are nearly circular. The eccentricity of each is given below. Notice that the orbit of Venus is the most circular and the orbit of Pluto is the most elongated.

Mercury: 0.2055	Venus: 0.0068	Earth: 0.0167
Mars: 0.0934	Jupiter: 0.0484	Saturn: 0.0543
Uranus: 0.0460	Neptune: 0.0082	Pluto: 0.2481

Connections
Astronomy

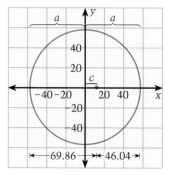

Example 3 *The Orbit of Mercury*

In its orbit, Mercury ranges between 46.04 million kilometers and 69.86 million kilometers from the sun. Use this information to write an equation for the orbit of Mercury.

Solution Notice in the diagram at the left that the greatest and least distances occur at the x-intercepts. Thus you can write a system of linear equations involving a and c.

$$\begin{cases} a - c = 46.04 \\ a + c = 69.86 \end{cases}$$

The solution of this system is $a = 57.95$ and $c = 11.91$. From the relationship $c^2 = a^2 - b^2$, you can conclude that

$$b = \sqrt{a^2 - c^2} \approx 56.71.$$

Thus an equation of the elliptical orbit is

$$\frac{x^2}{(57.95)^2} + \frac{y^2}{(56.71)^2} = 1,$$

where the units for x and y are millions of kilometers. ∎

Communicating *about* ALGEBRA

▶ **SHARING IDEAS about the Lesson**

A. The closest that Pluto gets to the sun is 4.443 billion kilometers. Use this and the eccentricity of Pluto to find the farthest that Pluto gets from the sun.

B. Find an equation for the orbit of Pluto.

EXERCISES

Guided Practice

▶ **CRITICAL THINKING about the Lesson**

In Exercises 1–6, use the graph at the right.

1. Describe the major axis of the ellipse.

2. Describe the minor axis of the ellipse.

3. What are the coordinates of the vertices?

4. What are the coordinates of the co-vertices?

5. What are the coordinates of the foci?

6. Write an equation of the ellipse.

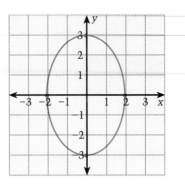

Independent Practice

In Exercises 7–12, find the foci and vertices of the ellipse.

7. $\dfrac{x^2}{25} + \dfrac{y^2}{16} = 1$

8. $\dfrac{x^2}{144} + \dfrac{y^2}{169} = 1$

9. $\dfrac{x^2}{4} + \dfrac{y^2}{36} = 1$

10. $\dfrac{x^2}{9} + \dfrac{y^2}{25} = 1$

11. $\dfrac{x^2}{1} + \dfrac{y^2}{9} = 1$

12. $\dfrac{x^2}{81} + \dfrac{y^2}{9} = 1$

In Exercises 13–18, write the equation in standard form. Find the foci and vertices.

13. $49x^2 + 16y^2 = 784$

14. $49x^2 + 64y^2 = 3136$

15. $4x^2 + 9y^2 = 25$

16. $x^2 + 36y^2 = 4$

17. $\dfrac{x^2}{600} + \dfrac{y^2}{2100} = 150$

18. $\dfrac{x^2}{288} + \dfrac{y^2}{200} = 2$

In Exercises 19–24, find an equation of the ellipse. The center is (0, 0).

19. Vertex: $(0, 6)$
    Co-vertex: $(5, 0)$

20. Vertex: $(0, 5)$
    Co-vertex: $(-4, 0)$

21. Vertex: $(-4, 0)$
    Co-vertex: $(0, 3)$

22. Vertex: $(2, 0)$
    Focus: $(1, 0)$

23. Vertex: $(4, 0)$
    Focus: $(-3, 0)$

24. Vertex: $(0, -6)$
    Focus: $(0, 2)$

In Exercises 25–28, match the equation with its graph.

25. $\dfrac{x^2}{225} + \dfrac{y^2}{100} = 1$

26. $\dfrac{x^2}{121} + \dfrac{y^2}{25} = 1$

27. $\dfrac{x^2}{225} + \dfrac{y^2}{400} = 1$

28. $\dfrac{x^2}{1} + \dfrac{y^2}{25} = 1$

In Exercises 29–40, sketch the ellipse and find its eccentricity.

29. $\dfrac{x^2}{16} + \dfrac{y^2}{36} = 1$

30. $\dfrac{x^2}{4} + \dfrac{y^2}{25} = 1$

31. $\dfrac{x^2}{36} + \dfrac{y^2}{81} = 1$

32. $\dfrac{x^2}{49} + \dfrac{y^2}{121} = 1$

33. $\dfrac{x^2}{4} + y^2 = 100$

34. $\dfrac{x^2}{16} + \dfrac{y^2}{25} = 4$

35. $\dfrac{x^2}{4} + \dfrac{y^2}{6} = 1$

36. $\dfrac{x^2}{9} + \dfrac{y^2}{5} = 1$

37. $64x^2 + 25y^2 = 1600$

38. $400x^2 + 441y^2 = 420^2$

39. $\dfrac{x^2}{4} + \dfrac{4y^2}{9} = 1$

40. $\dfrac{25x^2}{4} + \dfrac{25y^2}{9} = 1$

In Exercises 41–46, find the points of intersection of the graphs.

41. $\dfrac{x^2}{4} + \dfrac{y^2}{9} = 1$
$y = -x - 2$

42. $\dfrac{x^2}{16} + y^2 = 1$
$y = \dfrac{1}{2}(x + 1)$

43. $\dfrac{x^2}{25} + y^2 = 1$
$y = 2x$

44. $\dfrac{x^2}{9} + \dfrac{y^2}{4} = 1$
$y = x$

45. $\dfrac{x^2}{16} + \dfrac{y^2}{4} = 1$
$y = x + 2$

46. $\dfrac{x^2}{100} + \dfrac{y^2}{25} = 1$
$y = -x - 5$

47. *Drawing an Ellipse* You can draw an ellipse with a pencil, paper, string, and two thumbtacks. Place the two thumbtacks at the foci. Tie the string in a loop that is $2(a + c)$ units around. Loop the string around the thumbtacks, pull the string taut with a pencil, and trace a path as shown in the diagram at the right. Explain why the path is an ellipse.

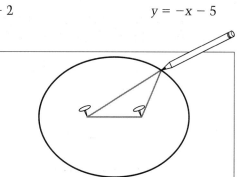

48. *Eccentricity* Suppose you are holding a soda pop can. When the top of the can is facing you, its rim is a circle. When you tip the can, however, the rim of the can appears to become elliptical. What happens to the eccentricity of this "ellipse" the farther you tip the top of the can away from you?

Bicycle Chainwheel **In Exercises 49–51, use the following information.**

The pedals of a bicycle drive a *chainwheel*, which drives a smaller *sprocket wheel* on the rear axle. Many chainwheels are circular. Some, however, are slightly elliptical, which tends to make pedaling easier. The front chainwheel on the bicycle shown at the right is 8 inches at its widest and $7\frac{1}{2}$ inches at its narrowest.

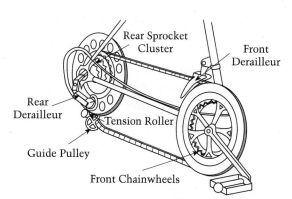

49. Find an equation for the outline of this elliptical chainwheel.

50. What is its eccentricity?

51. What is the area of the chainwheel? (Use $A = \pi ab$ for an ellipse.)

Whispering Gallery **In Exercises 52–54, use the following information.**

Statuary Hall is an elliptical room in the United States Capitol in Washington, D.C. The room is 46 feet wide and 96 feet long. Because of a reflective property of an ellipse, a person standing at one focus can hear even a whisper spoken by a person standing at the other focus. (John Quincy Adams is said to have used this feature of the room to overhear conversations.)

52. Find an equation of the ellipse.

53. How far apart are the two foci?

54. What is the floor area of the room?

55. *Sputnik*   The first artificial satellite to orbit Earth was Sputnik I (launched by the Soviet Union in 1957). The orbit's highest point above Earth's surface was 583 miles, and its lowest point was 132 miles. Find the eccentricity of its orbit. (Use 4000 miles as the radius of Earth.)

56. *Comet's Orbit*   Halley's Comet has an elliptical orbit with the sun at a focus. Its maximum distance from the sun is approximately 35.64 astronomical units and its minimum distance is approximately 0.594 astronomical unit. Find the eccentricity of its orbit. (An astronomical unit is about 93×10^6 miles.)

Integrated Review

In Exercises 57–62, solve the equation for *y*.

57. $\dfrac{x^2}{1} + \dfrac{y^2}{4} = 1$

58. $\dfrac{x^2}{36} + \dfrac{y^2}{64} = 1$

59. $\dfrac{x^2}{4} + \dfrac{y^2}{9} = 1$

60. $\dfrac{x^2}{4} + \dfrac{y^2}{100} = 1$

61. $\dfrac{x^2}{100} + \dfrac{y^2}{81} = 1$

62. $\dfrac{x^2}{25} + \dfrac{y^2}{144} = 1$

In Exercises 63–67, sketch the graph of the equation.

63. $x^2 + y^2 = 81$ **64.** $x^2 = -16y$ **65.** $y^2 = 4x$ **66.** $x^2 + y^2 = 100$ **67.** $y^2 = 20x$

Exploration and Extension

68. *Geometry*   For the ellipse at the right, *a* is half the length of the major axis. Write an expression, in terms of *a*, for the perimeter of each triangle in which one vertex is a focus and the opposite side contains the other focus.

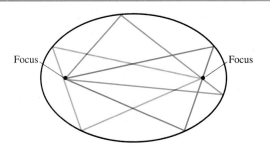

Focus   Focus

Mid-Chapter SELF-TEST

Take this test as you would take a test in class. The answers to the exercises are given in the back of the book.

In Exercises 1 and 2, find the focus and the directrix of the parabola. **(11.1)**

1. $16y = x^2$

2. $-12x = y^2$

In Exercises 3 and 4, write an equation of the parabola whose vertex is at the origin and has the given focus. **(11.1)**

3. $(0,-4)$

4. $\left(\frac{1}{2}, 0\right)$

In Exercises 5–10, sketch the graph of the equation. **(11.1, 11.2, 11.3)**

5. $20y = x^2$

6. $-4x = y^2$

7. $x^2 + y^2 = 49$

8. $4x^2 + 4y^2 = 36$

9. $\dfrac{x^2}{16} + \dfrac{y^2}{4} = 1$

10. $9x^2 + 4y^2 = 36$

11. Write an equation of the circle of radius 5 with center at the origin. **(11.2)**

12. Write an equation of the circle whose center is the origin and passes through the point $(4,-1)$. **(11.2)**

In Exercises 13 and 14, find the foci and the vertices of the ellipse. **(11.3)**

13. $\dfrac{x^2}{9} + \dfrac{y^2}{25} = 1$

14. $9x^2 + 16y^2 = 144$

In Exercises 15–17, find all intersection points. **(11.1, 11.2, 11.3)**

15. $y = \dfrac{1}{12}x^2$

$y = -\dfrac{1}{6}x + \dfrac{2}{3}$

16. $\dfrac{x^2}{4} + \dfrac{y^2}{1} = 1$

$y = x + 1$

17. $x^2 + y^2 = 25$

$y = 10 - 2x$

18. Write the equation in standard form for the ellipse whose co-vertices are $(0, 4)$ and $(0,-4)$ and whose vertices are $(6, 0)$ and $(-6, 0)$. **(11.3)**

19. The moon's orbit about Earth is elliptical. The distance between the moon and Earth varies from 363,000 kilometers to 406,000 kilometers. Find the eccentricity of the moon's orbit. **(11.3)**

20. The jet of water from a fountain forms a parabola. Write an equation for the path the water follows. **(11.1)**

21. A planetarium is sponsoring a craft show in the circular corridor surrounding the auditorium. It is 10 yards from the center of the auditorium to the inside wall of the corridor, and the corridor is 6 yards wide. Write equations for the inside and outside walls of the corridor. **(11.2)**

(5,-10)

11.4

Hyperbolas

What you should learn:

Goal 1 How to write the equation of a hyperbola and graph it using asymptotes

Goal 2 How to use hyperbolas to solve real-life problems

Why you should learn it:

You can use hyperbolic models in real-life situations that require a locus of points for which the difference of the distances to two fixed points is constant.

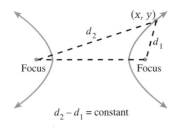

$d_2 - d_1 = \text{constant}$

Goal 1 Writing the Equation of a Hyperbola

The definition of a hyperbola is similar to that of an ellipse. The distinction is that, for an ellipse, the *sum* of the distances between a point on the ellipse and the two fixed points is constant, while, for a hyperbola, the *difference* of these distances is constant.

The line through the *foci* (the two fixed points) intersects the hyperbola at two points, the **vertices.** The line segment joining the vertices is the **transverse axis,** and its midpoint is the **center** of the hyperbola. The graph of a hyperbola has two branches.

Standard Equation of a Hyperbola (Center at Origin)

The **standard form of the equation of a hyperbola** with center at $(0, 0)$ is as follows.

$$\frac{x^2}{a^2} - \frac{y^2}{b^2} = 1 \quad \textit{Horizontal transverse axis}$$

$$\frac{y^2}{a^2} - \frac{x^2}{b^2} = 1 \quad \textit{Vertical transverse axis}$$

The vertices and foci are, respectively, a and c units from the center, and $c^2 = a^2 + b^2$.

The graphs show the two orientations of a hyperbola. Note that a hyperbola has two asymptotes.

Horizontal transverse axis

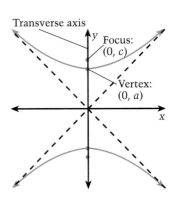

Vertical transverse axis

Example 1   *Writing an Equation of a Hyperbola*

Write an equation of the hyperbola with foci at $(-3, 0)$ and $(3, 0)$ and vertices at $(-2, 0)$ and $(2, 0)$.

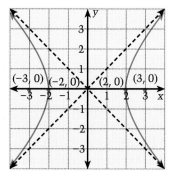

Solution   The center of the hyperbola is the origin and the transverse axis is horizontal. Because the foci are each three units from the center, you can conclude that $c = 3$. Similarly, because the vertices are each two units from the center, you can conclude that $a = 2$. Using these values of a and c, you can write

$$b^2 = c^2 - a^2$$
$$= 3^2 - 2^2 = 9 - 4 = 5$$

which implies that $b = \sqrt{5}$. Because the transverse axis is horizontal, the standard form of the equation is as follows.

$$\frac{x^2}{a^2} - \frac{y^2}{b^2} = 1 \qquad \textit{Horizontal transverse axis}$$

$$\frac{x^2}{2^2} - \frac{y^2}{(\sqrt{5})^2} = 1 \qquad \textit{Substitute } a = 2 \textit{ and } b = \sqrt{5}.$$

$$\frac{x^2}{4} - \frac{y^2}{5} = 1 \qquad \textit{Simplify.}$$ ∎

The asymptotes intersect at the center of the hyperbola and pass through the corners of a rectangle with corners $(\pm a, \pm b)$.

Asymptotes of a Hyperbola (Center at Origin)

The asymptotes of a hyperbola with center at $(0, 0)$ are as follows.

$$y = \frac{b}{a}x \text{ and } y = -\frac{b}{a}x \qquad \textit{Horizontal transverse axis}$$

$$y = \frac{a}{b}x \text{ and } y = -\frac{a}{b}x \qquad \textit{Vertical transverse axis}$$

Horizontal transverse axis

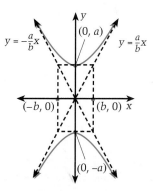

Vertical transverse axis

Example 2   *Sketching a Hyperbola*

Sketch the hyperbola $4x^2 - y^2 = 16$.

Solution   Begin by rewriting the equation in standard form.

$$4x^2 - y^2 = 16 \quad \textit{Given equation}$$

$$\frac{4x^2}{16} - \frac{y^2}{16} = \frac{16}{16} \quad \textit{Divide both sides by 16.}$$

$$\frac{x^2}{2^2} - \frac{y^2}{4^2} = 1 \quad \textit{Standard form}$$

Because the x^2-term is positive, you can conclude that the transverse axis is horizontal. The vertices are $(-2, 0)$ and $(2, 0)$. To sketch the hyperbola, first sketch a rectangle that is centered at the origin, $2a = 4$ units wide and $2b = 8$ units high. Then sketch asymptotes by drawing the lines that pass through opposite corners of the rectangle. Finally, sketch the hyperbola as shown below at the right.

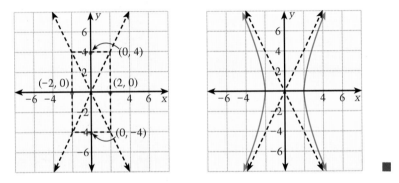

Example 3   *Finding the Foci of a Hyperbola*

Find the foci of the hyperbola having vertices at $(0, -3)$ and $(0, 3)$ and with asymptotes $y = 2x$ and $y = -2x$.

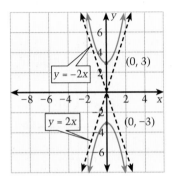

Solution   Because the transverse axis is vertical, the asymptotes are of the form

$$y = \frac{a}{b}x \quad \text{and} \quad y = -\frac{a}{b}x.$$

From the given equations of the asymptotes, it follows that $\frac{a}{b} = 2$, and since $a = 3$, you can conclude that $b = \frac{3}{2}$. Using the equation $c^2 = a^2 + b^2$, you can conclude that

$$c = \sqrt{a^2 + b^2}$$

$$= \sqrt{3^2 + \left(\frac{3}{2}\right)^2} = \sqrt{\frac{45}{4}} = \frac{3}{2}\sqrt{5}.$$

Thus the foci are $\left(0, -\frac{3}{2}\sqrt{5}\right)$ and $\left(0, \frac{3}{2}\sqrt{5}\right)$.

Connections
Physics

Example 4 *Locating an Explosion*

Two microphones, 1 mile apart, recorded an explosion. Microphone A received the sound 2 seconds before Microphone B. Is this enough information to decide where the sound came from?

Solution Because sound travels at 1100 feet per second, you know that the explosion took place 2200 feet farther from B than from A. The set of *all* points that are 2200 feet farther from B than from A is one branch of a hyperbola. Let $(c, 0)$ be the coordinates of A and let $(-c, 0)$ be the coordinates of B. Because A and B are 5280 feet apart, it follows that $c = 2640$. To find the vertex $(a, 0)$, use the fact that

$$(c + a) - (c - a) = 2200.$$

Solving this equation produces $a = 1100$. Finally, you can use the equation $b^2 = c^2 - a^2 = 5{,}759{,}600$ to conclude that the explosion occurred somewhere on the right branch of the hyperbola given by

$$\frac{x^2}{a^2} - \frac{y^2}{b^2} = 1$$

$$\frac{x^2}{1{,}210{,}000} - \frac{y^2}{5{,}759{,}600} = 1.$$

Thus you were not given enough information to determine the exact location of the explosion—only that it came from some point on the hyperbola. ∎

Communicating about **ALGEBRA**

▶ **SHARING IDEAS about the Lesson**

Match the equation with its graph. Explain your reasoning.

A. $x^2 - \dfrac{y^2}{4} = 1$ **B.** $\dfrac{x^2}{4} - y^2 = 1$ **C.** $y^2 - \dfrac{x^2}{4} = 1$

EXERCISES

▶ **CRITICAL THINKING about the Lesson**

In Exercises 1–4, use the graph at the right.

1. State the coordinates of the vertices and foci.

2. Is the transverse axis $x = 0$ or $y = 0$?

3. Write an equation of the hyperbola.

4. Write equations for the asymptotes.

5. Write $y^2 - 4x^2 = 36$ in standard form.

6. Which a, b, c relationship is true for hyperbolas?
   a. $c^2 = a^2 - b^2$ **b.** $c^2 = a^2 + b^2$

Independent Practice

In Exercises 7–12, find the vertices and foci of the hyperbola.

7. $\dfrac{x^2}{9} - \dfrac{y^2}{49} = 1$

8. $\dfrac{x^2}{144} - \dfrac{y^2}{9} = 1$

9. $\dfrac{x^2}{16} - \dfrac{y^2}{4} = 1$

10. $\dfrac{y^2}{36} - \dfrac{x^2}{4} = 1$

11. $\dfrac{y^2}{25} - x^2 = 1$

12. $x^2 - \dfrac{y^2}{49} = 1$

In Exercises 13–18, write the equation in standard form. Find the foci and vertices.

13. $25x^2 - 4y^2 = 100$

14. $y^2 - 64x^2 = 64$

15. $36y^2 - 4x^2 = 9$

16. $16y^2 - 36x^2 + 9 = 0$

17. $y^2 - \dfrac{x^2}{25} = 4$

18. $\dfrac{x^2}{9} - \dfrac{4y^2}{9} = 9$

In Exercises 19–24, write an equation of the hyperbola. Its center is (0, 0).

19. Foci: $(-2, 0), (2, 0)$
    Vertices: $(-1, 0), (1, 0)$

20. Foci: $(-4, 0), (4, 0)$
    Vertices: $(-3, 0), (3, 0)$

21. Foci: $(-9, 0), (9, 0)$
    Vertices: $(-2, 0), (2, 0)$

22. Foci: $(-6, 0), (6, 0)$
    Vertices: $(-4, 0), (4, 0)$

23. Foci: $(0, -9), (0, 9)$
    Vertices: $(0, -7), (0, 7)$

24. Foci: $(0, -2), (0, 2)$
    Vertices: $(0, -1), (0, 1)$

In Exercises 25–28, match the equation with its graph.

25. $\dfrac{x^2}{16} - \dfrac{y^2}{4} = 1$

26. $\dfrac{y^2}{4} - \dfrac{x^2}{2} = 1$

27. $\dfrac{y^2}{16} - \dfrac{x^2}{4} = 1$

28. $\dfrac{x^2}{4} - \dfrac{y^2}{2} = 1$

a.   b.   c.   d.

In Exercises 29–40, find the asymptotes of the hyperbola. Then sketch its graph.

29. $\dfrac{x^2}{25} - \dfrac{y^2}{144} = 1$

30. $\dfrac{x^2}{49} - y^2 = 1$

31. $\dfrac{y^2}{16} - \dfrac{x^2}{9} = 1$

32. $\dfrac{y^2}{9} - \dfrac{x^2}{64} = 1$

33. $\dfrac{x^2}{169} - \dfrac{y^2}{9} = 1$

34. $\dfrac{y^2}{81} - x^2 = 1$

35. $\dfrac{25x^2}{36} - \dfrac{y^2}{121} = 1$

36. $\dfrac{x^2}{49} - \dfrac{9y^2}{4} = 1$

37. $4y^2 - x^2 = 4$

38. $100x^2 - 81y^2 = 8100$

39. $\dfrac{y^2}{25} - \dfrac{x^2}{16} = 16$

40. $x^2 - 25y^2 = 25$

In Exercises 41–46, find the foci of the hyperbola.

41. Vertices: $(-1, 0)$, $(1, 0)$
    Asymptotes: $y = 3x$, $y = -3x$

42. Vertices: $(0, -2)$, $(0, 2)$
    Asymptotes: $y = 2x$, $y = -2x$

43. Vertices: $(0, -5)$, $(0, 5)$
    Asymptotes: $y = 5x$, $y = -5x$

44. Vertices: $(-4, 0)$, $(4, 0)$
    Asymptotes: $y = 2x$, $y = -2x$

45. Vertices: $(0, -6)$, $(0, 6)$
    Asymptotes: $y = \dfrac{3}{4}x$, $y = -\dfrac{3}{4}x$

46. Vertices: $(-3, 0)$, $(3, 0)$
    Asymptotes: $y = \dfrac{4}{3}x$, $y = -\dfrac{4}{3}x$

Geometry   **In Exercises 47 and 48, use the following information.**

The *annular ring* at the right has an inside radius of x and an outside radius of y. Its area is 8π.

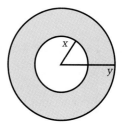

47. Find an equation that represents the relationship between x and y. Sketch the first-quadrant portion of the graph of the equation.

48. Copy and complete the table. What do you notice about the values of y as x increases? Can an annular ring have an area of 8π and an outside radius of 1 million units?

x	0	1	2	3	4	5	10	15	20
y	?	?	?	?	?	?	?	?	?

49. *Thunder*   You and a friend live 4 miles apart and are talking on the phone. You hear a crack of thunder, and 18 seconds later your friend hears the crack. Find an equation that gives the possible places where the lightning could have occurred.

50. *Where Did It Hit?*   You are still on the phone with your friend. After hearing the thunder, your friend says, "I hope that didn't hit the baseball stadium." Knowing that the baseball stadium is 1 mile directly north of you, how can you be sure that lightning didn't hit the stadium?

51. *Hyperbolic Mirror* In a hyperbolic mirror, light rays directed to one focus will be reflected to the other focus. The mirror below has the equation

$$\frac{x^2}{36} - \frac{y^2}{64} = 1.$$

At which point on the mirror will light from the point (0, 10) reflect to the focus?

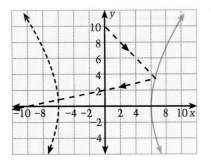

52. *Miniature Golf* You are playing miniature golf. Your golf ball is at $(-15, 25)$. The wall at the end of the enclosed area is part of a hyperbola whose equation is

$$\frac{x^2}{19} - \frac{y^2}{81} = 1.$$

At which point on the wall must your ball hit for it to go into the hole? (The ball bounces off a wall only once.)

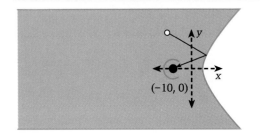

(−10, 0)

Integrated Review

In Exercises 53–60, identify the graph of the equation as a circle, an ellipse, or a hyperbola. Then sketch the graph.

53. $\dfrac{x^2}{25} + \dfrac{y^2}{4} = 1$ **54.** $x^2 + y^2 = 81$ **55.** $x^2 - y^2 = 16$ **56.** $\dfrac{x^2}{4} + \dfrac{y^2}{4} = 1$

57. $\dfrac{x^2}{9} + \dfrac{y^2}{49} = 1$ **58.** $3x^2 - y^2 = 27$ **59.** $x^2 + y^2 = 25$ **60.** $x^2 - 4y^2 = 16$

61. *Powers of Ten* Which best estimates the number of maple leaves that will fill a 32-gallon plastic bag?
  a. 6.0×10^1 **b.** 6.0×10^2
  c. 6.0×10^3 **d.** 6.0×10^4

62. *Powers of Ten* Which best estimates the number of cubic feet in a 32-gallon plastic bag?
  a. 4.3×10^0 **b.** 4.3×10^1
  c. 4.3×10^2 **d.** 4.3×10^3

Those Falling Leaves

A 75-foot maple tree has 500,000-700,000 leaves — enough to fill ten 32-gallon plastic bags.

Exploration and Extension

In Exercises 63 and 64, sketch the graphs of the equations. Find all points of intersection of the graphs.

63. $\dfrac{x^2}{25} + \dfrac{y^2}{9} = 1$ and $\dfrac{x^2}{25} - \dfrac{y^2}{9} = 1$

64. $x^2 + y^2 = 16$ and $-x^2 + \dfrac{y^2}{16} = 1$

11.5

Translations of Conics

What you should learn:

Goal 1 How to write an equation of a parabola with a vertex at (h, k) and an equation of a circle, an ellipse, or a hyperbola with its center at (h, k)

Goal 2 How to use translations to solve real-life problems

Why you should learn it:

If two conics do not share the same center, such as the cam and camshaft of an electric motor, you need to model one of these figures with an equation that is translated from the origin.

Goal 1   Writing Equations of Conics

Parabolas, circles, ellipses, and hyperbolas are called **conic sections** or simply **conics**. In Lessons 11.1 through 11.4, you studied equations of parabolas whose vertex is the origin, and equations of circles, ellipses, and hyperbolas whose center is the origin. In this lesson, you will study equations of conics that have been translated in the coordinate plane.

Standard Form of Equations of Translated Conics

The point (h, k) is the *vertex* of the parabola and the *center* of the other conics.

Circle: $(x - h)^2 + (y - k)^2 = r^2$

	Horizontal axis	**Vertical axis**
Parabola:	$(y - k)^2 = 4p(x - h)$	$(x - h)^2 = 4p(y - k)$
Ellipse:	$\dfrac{(x - h)^2}{a^2} + \dfrac{(y - k)^2}{b^2} = 1$	$\dfrac{(x - h)^2}{b^2} + \dfrac{(y - k)^2}{a^2} = 1$
Hyperbola:	$\dfrac{(x - h)^2}{a^2} - \dfrac{(y - k)^2}{b^2} = 1$	$\dfrac{(y - k)^2}{a^2} - \dfrac{(x - h)^2}{b^2} = 1$

Example 1   *Equations of Translated Conics*

a. $(x - 1)^2 + (y + 2)^2 = 3^2$ *Circle*

b. $\dfrac{(x - 2)^2}{3^2} + \dfrac{(y - 1)^2}{2^2} = 1$ *Ellipse*

c. $\dfrac{(x - 3)^2}{1^2} - \dfrac{(y - 2)^2}{3^2} = 1$ *Hyperbola*

d. $(x - 2)^2 = 4(-1)(y - 3)$ *Parabola*

To write the equation of a (shifted) conic in standard form, complete the square as demonstrated in Examples 2 through 5.

Example 2 *Writing the Standard Form of a Parabola*

Find the vertex and focus of the parabola given by

$$x^2 - 2x + 4y - 3 = 0.$$

Solution

$x^2 - 2x + 4y - 3 = 0$	*Given equation*
$x^2 - 2x = -4y + 3$	*Group terms.*
$x^2 - 2x + 1 = -4y + 3 + 1$	*Add 1 to both sides.*
$(x - 1)^2 = -4y + 4$	*Completed-square form*
$(x - 1)^2 = 4(-1)(y - 1)$	*Standard-form vertical axis*
$(x - h)^2 = 4p(y - k)$	

From the standard form, you can see that $h = 1$, $k = 1$, and $p = -1$. Because the axis is vertical and p is negative, the parabola opens downward. The vertex is $(h, k) = (1, 1)$ and the focus is $(h, k + p) = (1, 0)$. The graph is shown at the left. ∎

Example 3 *Sketching a Circle*

Identify the center and radius of the circle given by the equation, and sketch the circle.

$$4x^2 + 4y^2 + 20x - 16y + 37 = 0$$

Solution Begin by writing the given equation in standard form. To do this, you must complete the square for both the x-terms *and* the y-terms.

$$4x^2 + 4y^2 + 20x - 16y + 37 = 0$$

$$x^2 + y^2 + 5x - 4y + \frac{37}{4} = 0$$

$$(x^2 + 5x + \quad) + (y^2 - 4y + \quad) = -\frac{37}{4}$$

$$\left(x^2 + 5x + \left(\frac{5}{2}\right)^2\right) + (y^2 - 4y + (-2)^2) = -\frac{37}{4} + \frac{25}{4} + 4$$

$$\underbrace{\qquad}_{\left[\frac{1}{2}(5)\right]^2} \qquad \underbrace{\qquad}_{\left[\frac{1}{2}(-4)\right]^2}$$

$$\left(x + \frac{5}{2}\right)^2 + (y - 2)^2 = 1$$

$$(x - h)^2 + (y - k)^2 = r^2$$

The center of the circle is $\left(-\frac{5}{2}, 2\right)$ and the radius of the circle is 1. The graph is shown at the left. ∎

Example 4   *Sketching an Ellipse*

Sketch the ellipse: $x^2 + 4y^2 + 6x - 8y + 9 = 0$.

Solution

$$x^2 + 4y^2 + 6x - 8y + 9 = 0$$
$$(x^2 + 6x + \quad) + (4y^2 - 8y + \quad) = -9$$
$$(x^2 + 6x + \quad) + 4(y^2 - 2y + \quad) = -9$$
$$(x^2 + 6x + 9) + 4(y^2 - 2y + 1) = -9 + 9 + 4(1)$$
$$(x + 3)^2 + 4(y - 1)^2 = 4$$
$$\frac{(x + 3)^2}{4} + \frac{(y - 1)^2}{1} = 1$$
$$\frac{(x - h)^2}{a^2} + \frac{(y - k)^2}{b^2} = 1$$

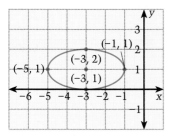

The center is $(h, k) = (-3, 1)$. Because the denominator of the x^2-term is $a^2 = 2^2$, the vertices lie two units to the right and left of the center. Because the denominator of the y^2-term is $b^2 = 1^2$, the co-vertices lie one unit up and down from the center. The graph is shown at the left. ■

Example 5   *Sketching a Hyperbola*

Sketch the hyperbola: $y^2 - 4x^2 + 4y + 24x - 41 = 0$. Also show the asymptotes.

Solution

$$y^2 - 4x^2 + 4y + 24x - 41 = 0$$
$$(y^2 + 4y + \quad) - (4x^2 - 24x + \quad) = 41$$
$$(y^2 + 4y + \quad) - 4(x^2 - 6x + \quad) = 41$$
$$(y^2 + 4y + 4) - 4(x^2 - 6x + 9) = 41 + 4 - 4(9)$$
$$(y + 2)^2 - 4(x - 3)^2 = 9$$
$$\frac{(y + 2)^2}{9} - \frac{4(x - 3)^2}{9} = 1$$
$$\frac{(y + 2)^2}{9} - \frac{(x - 3)^2}{\frac{9}{4}} = 1$$
$$\frac{(y - k)^2}{a^2} - \frac{(x - h)^2}{b^2} = 1$$

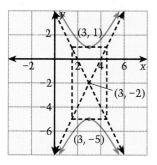

The transverse axis is vertical and the center is $(h, k) = (3, -2)$. Because the denominator of the y^2-term is $a^2 = 3^2$, the vertices lie three units above and below the center. To sketch the hyperbola, draw a rectangle centered at $(3, -2)$ of width $2b = 3$ and height $2a = 6$. Sketch the asymptotes and draw the hyperbola, as shown at the left. ■

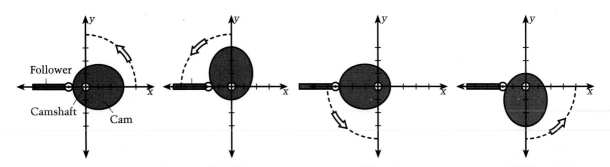

In the above diagram, the camshaft is rotating counterclockwise. An elliptical cam is attached to the camshaft. As the cam rotates, the follower moves back and forth. Thus this cam has changed the direction of the motion from rotational to oscillating (as occurs in a sewing machine).

Goal **2** Using Translations in Real-Life Problems

Real Life
Engineering Design

Example 6 *Finding the Equation of an Ellipse*

In the above diagram, the center of the camshaft is the focus of the elliptical cam. As the follower moves back and forth, it varies between $\frac{1}{2}$ inch and $\frac{3}{2}$ inches from the center of the camshaft. Find an equation of the elliptical cam in its starting position (on the left).

Solution From the diagram at the left, you can see that the length of the major axis of the cam is 2 inches, which implies that $a = 1$. The center of the cam is $\left(\frac{1}{2}, 0\right)$. Because the focus is $\frac{1}{2}$ inch from the center of the cam, you can conclude that $c = \frac{1}{2}$. Using the equation $b^2 = a^2 - c^2$, it follows that $b^2 = \frac{3}{4}$ and $b = \frac{\sqrt{3}}{2}$. Thus the equation of the elliptical cam is:

$$\frac{\left(x - \frac{1}{2}\right)^2}{1^2} + \frac{(y - 0)^2}{\left(\frac{\sqrt{3}}{2}\right)^2} = 1 \text{ or } \left(x - \frac{1}{2}\right)^2 + \frac{y^2}{\frac{3}{4}} = 1.$$

■

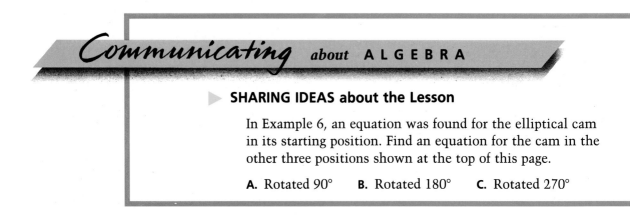

Communicating about **ALGEBRA**

▷ **SHARING IDEAS about the Lesson**

In Example 6, an equation was found for the elliptical cam in its starting position. Find an equation for the cam in the other three positions shown at the top of this page.

A. Rotated 90° **B.** Rotated 180° **C.** Rotated 270°

600 *Chapter 11 ▪ Quadratic Relations*

EXERCISES

▶ **CRITICAL THINKING about the Lesson**

1. What does it mean to "translate a conic in the coordinate plane?"

In Exercises 2–5, identify the type of conic. If the conic is a circle, an ellipse, or a hyperbola, find its center. If the conic is a parabola, find its vertex.

2. $(x - 1)^2 + (y - 2)^2 = 1$

3. $\dfrac{(y - 1)^2}{30} - \dfrac{(x + 1)^2}{25} = 1$

4. $\dfrac{(x - 10)^2}{9} + \dfrac{(y + 2)^2}{4} = 1$

5. $(y - 4)^2 = 4(2)(x - 1)$

6. Write $x^2 + y^2 - 10x + 12y + 37 = 0$ in standard form. Explain your steps. Identify the type of conic.

Independent Practice

In Exercises 7–14, match the equation with its graph.

7. $\dfrac{(x - 2)^2}{4} + \dfrac{(y + 3)^2}{9} = 1$

8. $\dfrac{(x - 2)^2}{9} + \dfrac{(y + 3)^2}{4} = 1$

9. $\dfrac{(x - 2)^2}{9} - \dfrac{(y + 3)^2}{4} = 1$

10. $\dfrac{(x + 2)^2}{4} - \dfrac{(y - 3)^2}{9} = 1$

11. $\dfrac{(x + 2)^2}{9} - \dfrac{(y - 3)^2}{4} = 1$

12. $\dfrac{(x + 2)^2}{9} + \dfrac{(y - 3)^2}{4} = 1$

13. $\dfrac{(x - 2)^2}{4} - \dfrac{(y + 3)^2}{9} = 1$

14. $\dfrac{(x + 2)^2}{4} + \dfrac{(y - 3)^2}{9} = 1$

a.

b.

c.

d.

e.

f.

g.

h.

In Exercises 15–22, find an equation for the conic.

15. *Circle*   Center: $(9, 3)$
Radius: 4

16. *Circle*   Center: $(-3, 1)$
Radius: 2

17. *Parabola*   Vertex: $(1, -2)$
Focus: $(1, 1)$

18. *Parabola*   Vertex: $(3, -2)$
Focus: $(5, -2)$

19. *Ellipse*   Vertices: $(-2, -5)$, $(-2, 4)$
Foci: $(-2, -4)$, $(-2, 3)$

20. *Ellipse*   Vertices: $(-2, 2)$, $(4, 2)$
Co-vertices: $(1, 1)$, $(1, 3)$

21. *Hyperbola*   Vertices: $(8, -4)$, $(8, 4)$
Foci: $(8, -6)$, $(8, 6)$

22. *Hyperbola*   Vertices: $(-10, 3)$, $(10, 3)$
Foci: $(-12, 3)$, $(12, 3)$

**In Exercises 23–26, write the equation of the circle in standard form.
Identify the radius and center and sketch the graph.**

23. $x^2 + y^2 - 2x + 6y + 9 = 0$

24. $x^2 + y^2 - 8x - 20y + 115 = 0$

25. $x^2 + y^2 - 6x - 8y + 24 = 0$

26. $x^2 + y^2 + 10x - 6y + 33 = 0$

**In Exercises 27–30, write the equation of the parabola in standard form.
Identify the vertex and focus and sketch the graph.**

27. $y^2 - 4y + 12x - 8 = 0$

28. $y^2 - 12y + 4x + 4 = 0$

29. $x^2 + 4x - 8y + 12 = 0$

30. $x^2 + 6x - 2y + 13 = 0$

**In Exercises 31–34, write the equation of the ellipse in standard form.
Identify the vertices and foci and sketch the graph.**

31. $25x^2 + y^2 - 100x - 2y + 76 = 0$

32. $x^2 + 4y^2 - 10x - 40y + 121 = 0$

33. $x^2 + 36y^2 - 16x - 72y + 64 = 0$

34. $4x^2 + y^2 - 48x - 4y + 48 = 0$

**In Exercises 35–38, write the equation of the hyperbola in standard form.
Identify the vertices and foci and sketch the graph.**

35. $x^2 - 25y^2 - 14x + 100y - 76 = 0$

36. $9x^2 - y^2 - 72x + 8y + 119 = 0$

37. $-9x^2 + 4y^2 - 36x - 16y - 164 = 0$

38. $-x^2 + y^2 - 2x - 12y + 31 = 0$

39. *Aussie Football*   In Australia, football by *Australian Rules* (or rugby) is played on elliptical fields. The field can be a maximum of 170 yards wide and a maximum of 200 yards long. Let the center of a field of maximum size be represented by the point $(0, 85)$. Write an equation of the ellipse that represents this field. Find the area of the field. *(Source: Oxford Companion to World Sports and Games)*

40. *Geometry*   Find the points of intersection of the circle $(x - 2)^2 + (y - 1)^2 = 100$ and the line $y = -\frac{3}{4}x + \frac{5}{2}$. Show that the line contains a diameter of the circle.

This rugby match is being played on an elliptical field in Melbourne, Australia.

41. *Geometry*   Find an equation of a line that is tangent to the circle $(x + 1)^2 + (y - 3)^2 = 8$ at the point $(1, 1)$.

42. *Designing a Menu*   You are opening a restaurant called the Treetop Restaurant and are using a computer program to design the menu cover. The equation for the tree trunk is $25x^2 - 4y^2 + 80y - 800 = 0$. Write this equation in standard form and then sketch the graph.

The TREETOP

Restaurant
and Lounge

Integrated Review

In Exercises 43–46, solve the equation by completing the square.

43. $x^2 + 4x - 1 = 0$ **44.** $x^2 - 2x - 2 = 0$ **45.** $x^2 - 6x + 4 = 0$ **46.** $x^2 - 4x - 8 = 0$

In Exercises 47–50, sketch the graph of the equation.

47. $x^2 + y^2 = 225$ **48.** $\dfrac{x^2}{25} - \dfrac{y^2}{4} = 1$ **49.** $\dfrac{x^2}{16} + \dfrac{y^2}{144} = 1$ **50.** $\dfrac{y^2}{49} - x^2 = 1$

Exploration and Extension

In Exercises 51 and 52, write the equation in standard form. Then sketch the graph.

51. $9x^2 + y^2 + 36x + 4y + 4 = 0$ **52.** $4x^2 - y^2 - 8x - 6y - 9 = 0$

Mixed REVIEW

1. Divide: $\dfrac{7}{9} \div \dfrac{5}{6}$.

2. Find all intercepts of $y = 3x^2 - 7x + 4$. **(2.3)**

3. Simplify: $\sqrt{72x^2y^3}$. **(7.4)**

4. Find $g(f(x))$ for $f(x) = 4x$, $g(x) = x^2$. **(6.2)**

5. Complete the square: $3x^2 - 12x + 7$. **(5.3)**

6. Find the geometric mean of 3 and 48. **(7.5)**

7. Sketch $f(x) = \ln(x - 5) - 2$. **(8.2)**

8. Expand $\ln\left(\dfrac{5}{8}\right)^3$. **(8.3)**

9. Divide: $\dfrac{2x^3 - 8x^2 + 16x - 30}{x - 3}$. **(9.4)**

10. Find the range of $f(x) = \dfrac{|x|}{\sqrt{x^2}}$. **(6.2)**

11. Solve for x: $3x^2 - 4x + c = 0$. **(5.4)**

12. Solve $3x^4 - 14x^2 + 8 = 0$. **(9.5)**

13. Solve $|4x + 2| > 6$. **(1.7)**

14. Sketch $3y - 2x \le 15$. **(2.5)**

15. Multiply: $\sqrt{-6} \cdot \sqrt{-15}$. **(5.5)**

16. Factor $x^4 + 2x^3 - 13x^2 - 14x + 24$. **(9.4)**

17. Find the focus of $y^2 = x$. **(11.1)**

18. Find the mean: 2, 4, 8, 8, 10, 12. **(9.7)**

19. Solve $\dfrac{x + 4}{3x} + \dfrac{x - 1}{x + 6} = 1$. **(10.4)**

20. Find the center of $x^2 + 4y^2 = 5$. **(11.3)**

When sketching a conic with a graphing calculator, you must remember two things. First, most graphing calculators are set up to sketch the graphs of functions, not relations—so you must first write the relation as one *or more* functions. Second, to obtain graphs with true perspectives (in which circles look like circles), you must use a "square setting." For a graphing calculator whose display screen's height is two thirds of its width, you can obtain a square setting by using

$$\frac{\text{Ymax} - \text{Ymin}}{\text{Xmax} - \text{Xmin}} = \frac{2}{3}. \quad \textit{Square setting}$$

Example 1:   Sketching a Circle with a Graphing Calculator

Use a graphing calculator to sketch the graph of $x^2 + y^2 = 4$.

Solution   Begin by solving the given equation for y.

$$x^2 + y^2 = 4$$
$$y^2 = 4 - x^2$$
$$y = \pm\sqrt{4 - x^2}$$

Next, set the calculator's range setting to $-3 \le x \le 3$ and $-2 \le y \le 2$. Finally, enter the following two equations—one to sketch the top half of the circle and the other to sketch the bottom half of the circle.

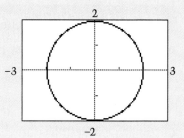

$$y = \sqrt{4 - x^2} \quad \textit{Top half of circle}$$

$$y = -\sqrt{4 - x^2} \quad \textit{Bottom half of circle}$$

The graph is shown at the right.   ■

A graphing calculator can be used to estimate the points of intersection of two graphs. For instance, to find the points of intersection of the line $y = 2x - 2$ and the circle $x^2 + y^2 = 4$, you can show the graph of the line with the graph of Example 1. Using the trace feature, you can approximate the points of intersection to be $(0, -2)$ and $(1.6, 1.2)$. Both points can be verified algebraically as follows.

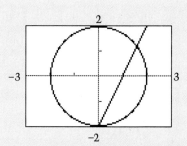

$$x^2 + y^2 = 4 \quad \textit{Given equation of circle}$$

$$x^2 + (2x - 2)^2 = 4 \quad \textit{Substitute } 2x - 2 \textit{ for } y.$$

$$5x^2 - 8x = 0 \quad \textit{Standard form}$$

$$x(5x - 8) = 0 \quad \textit{Factor.}$$

$$\left.\begin{array}{l} x = 0 \\ \text{or } x = \frac{8}{5} \end{array}\right\} \quad \textit{Zero Factor Property}$$

Example 2:   Investigating Asymptotic Behavior

Sketch the hyperbola $\dfrac{(x-2)^2}{3^2} - \dfrac{(y-3)^2}{1^2} = 1$ and its asymptotes on the same display screen.

Solution   To sketch the hyperbola, solve the given equation for y.

$$\frac{(x-2)^2}{3^2} - \frac{(y-3)^2}{1^2} = 1$$

$$\frac{1}{9}(x-2)^2 - 1 = (y-3)^2$$

$$\pm\sqrt{\frac{1}{9}(x-2)^2 - 1} = y - 3$$

$$3 \pm \sqrt{\frac{1}{9}(x-2)^2 - 1} = y$$

The "plus-version" is the equation of the top half of each branch and the "minus-version" is the equation of the bottom half of each branch. The asymptotes of the hyperbola pass through the point $(2, 3)$ with slopes of $\pm\dfrac{b}{a} = \pm\dfrac{1}{3}$.

$$y = \frac{1}{3}(x+7) \quad \text{and} \quad y = \frac{1}{3}(-x+11) \quad \textit{Asymptotes}$$

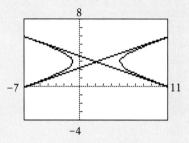

By sketching the hyperbola and the two asymptotes on the same screen, you can see that the hyperbola gets closer to its asymptotes as you move to the right side or left side of the screen. ■

Exercises

In Exercises 1–6, use a graphing calculator to sketch the graph of the equation.

1. $x^2 + y^2 = 16$

2. $\dfrac{x^2}{2^2} + \dfrac{y^2}{5^2} = 1$

3. $\dfrac{y^2}{4^2} - \dfrac{x^2}{6^2} = 1$

4. $(x-1)^2 + (y-2)^2 = 10$

5. $\dfrac{(x+1)^2}{12} + \dfrac{(y-3)^2}{9} = 1$

6. $\dfrac{(x-2)^2}{16} - \dfrac{(y+4)^2}{10} = 1$

In Exercises 7–9, find the points of intersection of the graphs. Use a graphing calculator to verify your result.

7. $(x-4)^2 + (y+2)^2 = 10$
$x + 2y = -5$

8. $\dfrac{4(x+1)^2}{9} + (y-5)^2 = 5$
$x + y = 6$

9. $y^2 = \dfrac{1}{2}x$
$x - 2y = 0$

10. Find the equations of the asymptotes of the hyperbola. Then use a graphing calculator to sketch the hyperbola and the asymptotes on the same display screen.

$$\frac{(x-4)^2}{5^2} - \frac{(y+2)^2}{4^2} = 1$$

11.6

Classifying Conics

What you should learn:

Goal 1 How to classify a conic from its equation

Goal 2 How to use equations of conics to solve mathematical and real-life problems

Why you should learn it:

You can use pairs of quadratic equations to solve many real-life problems, such as locating a ship at sea using the LORAN system of navigation.

Goal 1 Classifying a Conic from Its Equation

The reason that parabolas, circles, ellipses, and hyperbolas are called *conics* or *conic sections* is that each can be formed by the intersection of the plane and a double-napped *cone*, as shown below.

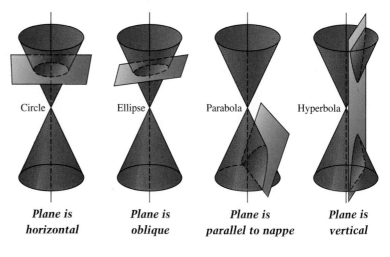

Circle	Ellipse	Parabola	Hyperbola
Plane is horizontal	*Plane is oblique*	*Plane is parallel to nappe*	*Plane is vertical*

Classifying Conics

If the graph of $Ax^2 + Bxy + Cy^2 + Dx + Ey + F = 0$ is a conic, then the type of conic is determined by the **discriminant, $B^2 - 4AC$,** as follows.

1. Ellipse or circle: $B^2 - 4AC < 0$
2. Parabola: $B^2 - 4AC = 0$
3. Hyperbola: $B^2 - 4AC > 0$

In case 1, the graph is a circle if $A = C$.

The equation $Ax^2 + Bxy + Cy^2 + Dx + Ey + F = 0$ is a **general second-degree equation** in x and y. Some second-degree equations in x and y have graphs that are not conics. For instance, the graph of $x^2 + y^2 = 0$ is a single point, and the graph of $x^2 - y^2 = 0$ is a pair of intersecting lines. Graphs of second-degree equations in x and y that are not one of the four "standard" conics are **degenerate conics.**

In a second-degree equation in x and y, if $B \neq 0$ and the graph is a parabola, an ellipse, or a hyperbola, then the axis of the graph in the coordinate plane is neither horizontal nor vertical.

Example 1 *Classifying a Conic*

Classify the conic given by $xy - 1 = 0$.

Solution For this equation, $B = 1$ and $F = -1$. The other coefficients, A, C, D, and E, are zero. The discriminant is

$$B^2 - 4AC = 1^2 - 4(0)(0) = 1 > 0$$

which implies that the graph is a hyperbola. To sketch the graph, write the equation in the form

$$y = \frac{1}{x}$$

and use the strategies described in Lesson 10.1 for sketching the graph of a rational function. The graph is shown at the left. The transverse axis lies on the line $y = x$, and its center is at the origin. ∎

Example 2 *Classifying a Conic*

Classify the conic given by $2x^2 + y^2 - 4x - 4 = 0$.

Solution For this equation, $A = 2$, $B = 0$, and $C = 1$. The discriminant is

$$B^2 - 4AC = 0^2 - 4(2)(1) = -8 < 0 \text{ and } A \neq C$$

which implies that the graph is an ellipse. To sketch the graph of the ellipse, complete the square as follows.

$$2x^2 + y^2 - 4x - 4 = 0$$
$$(2x^2 - 4x) + y^2 = 4$$
$$2(x^2 - 2x) + y^2 = 4$$
$$2(x^2 - 2x + 1) + y^2 = 4 + 2(1)$$
$$2(x - 1)^2 + y^2 = 6$$
$$\frac{(x - 1)^2}{3} + \frac{y^2}{6} = 1$$
$$\frac{(x - h)^2}{b^2} + \frac{(y - k)^2}{a^2} = 1$$

The center is $(h, k) = (1, 0)$. Because the denominator of the y^2-term is $a^2 = 6$, the vertices lie $\sqrt{6}$ units above and below the center. Because the denominator of the x^2-term is $b^2 = 3$, the co-vertices lie $\sqrt{3}$ units to the left and right of the center. The graph is shown at the left. ∎

In Lesson 11.2, you learned how to find points of intersection of a line and a conic by solving a *linear-quadratic system*. The next two examples show how to find the points of intersection of two conics by solving a *quadratic system*.

Example 3 *Solving a Quadratic System by Substitution*

Find the points of intersection of the graphs of the system.

$$x^2 + 4y^2 - 4x - 8y + 4 = 0 \quad \textit{Equation 1}$$

$$x^2 + 4y - 4 = 0 \quad \textit{Equation 2}$$

Solution Because the second equation has no y^2-term, solve that equation for y to obtain $y = 1 - \frac{1}{4}x^2$. Next, substitute this expression for y in the first equation and solve for x.

$$x^2 + 4y^2 - 4x - 8y + 4 = 0$$

$$x^2 + 4\left(1 - \tfrac{1}{4}x^2\right)^2 - 4x - 8\left(1 - \tfrac{1}{4}x^2\right) + 4 = 0$$

$$x^2 + 4 - 2x^2 + \frac{1}{4}x^4 - 4x - \left(8 + 2x^2\right) + 4 = 0$$

$$\tfrac{1}{4}x^4 + x^2 - 4x = 0$$

$$x^4 + 4x^2 - 16x = 0$$

$$x(x - 2)(x^2 + 2x + 8) = 0$$

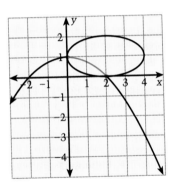

There are two real solutions: $x = 0$ and $x = 2$. The corresponding y-values are $y = 1$ and $y = 0$. Thus the graphs have two points of intersection, $(0, 1)$ and $(2, 0)$, as shown at the left. ∎

Example 4 *Solving a Quadratic System by Elimination*

Find the points of intersection of the graphs of the system.

$$x^2 + y^2 - 16x + 39 = 0 \quad \textit{Equation 1}$$

$$x^2 - y^2 - 9 = 0 \quad \textit{Equation 2}$$

Solution For this system, eliminate the y^2-term by adding the two equations. The resulting equation can be solved for x.

$$2x^2 - 16x + 30 = 0$$

$$2(x - 3)(x - 5) = 0$$

There are two real solutions: $x = 3$ and $x = 5$. The corresponding y-values are $y = 0$ and $y = \pm 4$. Thus the graphs have three points in common, $(3, 0)$, $(5, 4)$, and $(5, -4)$, as shown at the left. ∎

LORAN (long distance radio navigation) uses synchronized pulses sent out by pairs of transmitting stations. By calculating the difference in the times of arrival of the pulses from two stations, the LORAN equipment locates the ship on a hyperbola. By doing the same thing with a second pair of stations, the ship's location will be the intersection of two hyperbolas.

Real Life
Navigation

Example 5 *Finding the Point of Intersection of Two Hyperbolas*

LORAN equipment has calculated a ship's position to be the point of intersection of the graphs of the following hyperbolas. Find the coordinates of the point of intersection.

$$xy - 24 = 0 \quad \textit{Equation 1}$$

$$x^2 - 25y^2 + 100 = 0 \quad \textit{Equation 2}$$

Solution Solve the first equation for y to obtain $y = \frac{24}{x}$. Then substitute this expression for y in the second equation.

$$x^2 - 25y^2 + 100 = 0$$

$$x^2 - 25\left(\frac{24}{x}\right)^2 + 100 = 0$$

$$x^4 + 100x^2 - 14{,}400 = 0$$

$$(x^2 - 80)(x^2 + 180) = 0$$

There are two real solutions: $x = \pm\sqrt{80} \approx \pm 8.94$. From the diagram, the positive solution must represent the x-coordinate of the ship's location. The y-coordinate is $\frac{24}{\sqrt{80}} \approx 2.68$. Thus the ship's position is $(8.94, 2.68)$. ∎

Communicating about **A L G E B R A**

▷ **SHARING IDEAS about the Lesson**

A. Classify the conic $4x^2 + 9y^2 - 16x - 18y - 11 = 0$.

B. Classify the conic $4x^2 - 9y^2 - 16x + 18y - 29 = 0$.

C. Sketch the conics in parts **A** and **B** and find all points of intersection.

EXERCISES

▶ **CRITICAL THINKING about the Lesson**

1. How must a plane intersect a double-napped cone to form a circle? an ellipse? a parabola? a hyperbola?

2. How can the discriminant $B^2 - 4AC$ be used to classify the graph of $Ax^2 + Bxy + Cy^2 + Dx + Ey + F = 0$?

3. Match the equation with one of the figures below. In each case, describe the relationship between the plane and the cone.

   a. $x^2 - y^2 = 0$ **b.** $x + y = 0$ **c.** $x^2 + y^2 = 0$

       Point   **Line**   **Intersecting Lines**

4. If the axis of a parabola, an ellipse, or a hyperbola is horizontal or vertical, what must be true of B in the following equation?

   $$Ax^2 + Bxy + Cy^2 + Dx + Ey + F = 0$$

In Exercises 5 and 6, solve the system. Explain your steps.

5. $x^2 + y^2 - 4y = 0$
   $x^2 + \quad\ y = 0$

6. $x^2 + y^2 - 4x = 0$
   $x^2 - y^2 - 2x = 0$

In Exercises 7–22, classify the conic.

7. $9x^2 + 4y^2 + 36x - 24y + 36 = 0$

8. $x^2 - 9y^2 + 2x - 54y - 80 = 0$

9. $x^2 - 9y^2 + 36y - 72 = 0$

10. $x^2 + y^2 - 10x - 2y + 10 = 0$

11. $16x^2 + 25y^2 - 36x - 50y + 61 = 0$

12. $x^2 + y^2 - 16x + 4y + 67 = 0$

13. $9y^2 - x^2 + 2x + 54y + 62 = 0$

14. $9x^2 + 25y^2 - 36x - 50y + 61 = 0$

15. $x^2 - 2x + 8y + 9 = 0$

16. $y^2 - 4y - 4x = 0$

17. $12x^2 + 20y^2 - 12x + 40y - 37 = 0$

18. $9x^2 - y^2 + 54y + 10y + 55 = 0$

19. $x^2 + y^2 - 4x - 2y - 4 = 0$

20. $36x^2 + 9y^2 + 48x - 36y + 43 = 0$

21. $16y^2 - x^2 + 2x + 64y + 63 = 0$

22. $x^2 - 2x + 8y + 17 = 0$

In Exercises 23–30, match the equation with its graph.

23. $x^2 + 4y^2 - 4x + 8y - 8 = 0$

24. $y^2 - x^2 + 12y + 4x + 31 = 0$

25. $x^2 + 6x + 2y + 5 = 0$

26. $x^2 + y^2 - 4x - 6y - 3 = 0$

27. $x^2 + y^2 + 2x - 2y - 7 = 0$

28. $y^2 - 2y - 4x + 9 = 0$

29. $4x^2 - 9y^2 - 16x - 20 = 0$

30. $25x^2 + 4y^2 + 100x + 16y + 16 = 0$

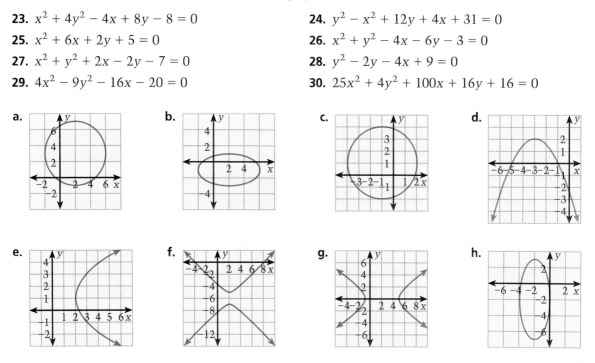

a.   b.   c.   d.
e.   f.   g.   h.

In Exercises 31–42, sketch the graph of the equation.

31. $x^2 + 4x + 4y - 16 = 0$

32. $y^2 - 2x - 20y + 94 = 0$

33. $15x^2 + 15y^2 - 150x - 30y + 330 = 0$

34. $x^2 + y^2 - 20x - 16y + 64 = 0$

35. $16x^2 + y^2 + 160x - 22y + 505 = 0$

36. $4x^2 - 9y^2 + 32x - 144y - 548 = 0$

37. $y^2 - 16x - 14y + 17 = 0$

38. $x^2 + y^2 - 12x - 24y + 36 = 0$

39. $25x^2 + 16y^2 + 50x - 320y + 1225 = 0$

40. $x^2 + 9y^2 - 28x - 36y + 151 = 0$

41. $-25x^2 + y^2 + 50x + 20y + 50 = 0$

42. $4x^2 - y^2 - 8x + 4y - 9 = 0$

In Exercises 43–54, find the points of intersection of the graphs.

43. $16x^2 - y^2 + 16y - 128 = 0$
$\quad\ y^2 - 48x - 16y - 32 = 0$

44. $16x^2 + y^2 - 24y + 80 = 0$
$\quad\ 16x^2 + 25y^2 - 400 = 0$

45. $-x^2 + y^2 + 4x - 6y + 4 = 0$
$\quad\ x^2 + y^2 - 4x - 6y + 12 = 0$

46. $x^2 + y^2 + 8x - 20y + 7 = 0$
$\quad\ x^2 + 9y^2 + 8x + 4y + 7 = 0$

47. $\ 4x^2 + y^2 + 32x - 24y + 64 = 0$
$\quad\ 4x^2 + y^2 + 56x - 24y + 304 = 0$

48. $x^2 - 4y^2 - 20x - 64y - 172 = 0$
$\quad\ 4x^2 + y^2 - 80x + 16y + 400 = 0$

49. $x^2 + y^2 + 2x + 2y = 0$
$\quad\ x^2 + y^2 - 2x - 2y = 0$

50. $x^2 + y^2 + 4x + 3 = 0$
$\quad\ 64x^2 - y^2 - 64 = 0$

51. $x^2 - y^2 - 12x + 12y - 36 = 0$
$\quad\ x^2 + y^2 - 12x - 12y + 36 = 0$

52. $x^2 + y^2 + 36x - 10y + 324 = 0$
$\quad\ x^2 + y^2 + 36x - 20y + 324 = 0$

53. $x^2 + 4y^2 - 2x - 8y + 1 = 0$
$\quad\quad\ x^2 - 2x + 4y + 1 = 0$

54. $\quad\ x^2 + y^2 + 4y - 12 = 0$
$\quad\ x^2 - 16y^2 - 64y - 80 = 0$

55. *Sharpening a Pencil* The sharpened part of the pencil at the right has a conical shape. What type of conic occurs at the intersection of the sharpened cone and each flat side of the pencil? Explain.

56. *Tipping an Hourglass* The hourglass at the right has the shape of a double-napped cone. The hourglass has the same amount of sand inside each nappe. When the hourglass is laid on its side, what type of conic is traced by the top edge of the sand? Explain.

57. *Circles of Apollonius* Apollonius (*circa* 225 B.C.) lived during the classical period of Greece. He proposed the following problem.

Suppose you are given any three nonintersecting circles in a plane. The circles can have different radii, but none of the three should be inside one of the other two. Is it always possible to find a fourth circle that is tangent to each of the three given circles? (Two circles are tangent if their intersection is exactly one point.)

Apollonius showed that it *is* always possible to find a fourth "tangent circle." In fact, he showed that it is always possible to find eight such tangent circles! Two of the solutions are shown below. Find the other six.

Given Three Circles

One Possible Solution

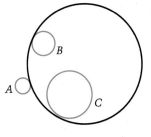

Another Possible Solution

58. *More About Circles* Which of the two solutions shown in Exercise 57 could be represented by the following system of equations? Justify your answer graphically.

$$x^2 + y^2 \qquad\quad - 4y - 4 = 0$$
$$x^2 + y^2 + 5x + y + 6 = 0$$
$$x^2 + y^2 - 2x - 6y + 8 = 0$$
$$x^2 + y^2 - 10x + 6y + 16 = 0$$

59. *Seismographs and Earthquakes* Three seismographs are located at the points $(0, 0)$, $(8, -8)$, and $(11, 10)$, where each unit in the coordinate plane represents 1 mile. An earthquake is recorded by each of the seismographs. The epicenter of the earthquake is 5 miles from the first seismograph, 13 miles from the second, and 10 miles from the third. What are the coordinates of the epicenter? Explain your answer graphically.

60. *Locating an Explosion* Two of your friends live 4 miles apart and on the same "east-west" street, and you live halfway between them. You are all talking on a three-way phone call when you hear an explosion. Six seconds later your friend to the east hears the explosion, and your friend to the north hears it 8 seconds after you do. Find the equations of two hyperbolas that would locate the explosion. (Remember sound travels at a rate of 1100 ft/sec.)

Integrated Review

61. *Telephone Area Codes* What percentage of the 144 possible area codes were in use in 1991?

62. *Delicious Apples* Of the top five varieties of apples picked in 1990, what percent were of the red delicious variety?

Area Codes in Use

90 — 1951
118 — 1961
122 — 1971
122 — 1981
137 — 1991

Year

Most-Picked Apples
Bushels (in millions)

Red Delicious 101
Golden Delicious 36
McIntosh 15
Rome 13
Jonathan 8

63. *College Entrance Exam Sample* If x and y are two different real numbers and $rx = ry$, then $r = \boxed{?}$.

   a. 0   **b.** 1   **c.** $\frac{x}{y}$ **d.** $\frac{y}{x}$ **e.** $x - y$

64. *College Entrance Exam Sample* A cube has 4-inch edges. If each edge is increased by 25%, then the volume is increased by about

   a. 25%   **b.** 48%   **c.** 73%   **d.** 95%   **e.** 122%

Exploration and Extension

Conic Graph Paper **In Exercises 65 and 66, use conic graph paper (shown below).**

65. Sketch a hyperbola whose foci are the centers of the concentric circles. The difference of the distances between each point on the hyperbola and the foci is 10.

66. Sketch an ellipse whose foci are the centers of the concentric circles. The sum of the distances between each point on the ellipse and the foci is 14.

67. Sketch the graph of $x^2 - y^2 + 18x + 8y + 65 = 0$.

68. Sketch the graph of $x^2 + y^2 - 2x + 4y + 5 = 0$.

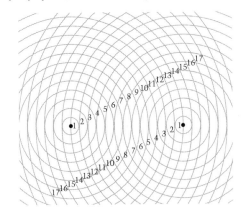

11

Chapter Summary

What did you learn?

Skills

1. Write an equation of a conic.
   - Write an equation of a parabola. **(11.1, 11.5)**
   - Write an equation of a circle. **(11.2, 11.5)**
   - Write an equation of an ellipse. **(11.3, 11.5)**
   - Write an equation of a hyperbola. **(11.4, 11.5)**
2. Find characteristics of conics.
   - Find vertex, focus, and directrix of a parabola. **(11.1, 11.5)**
   - Find center and radius of a circle. **(11.2, 11.5)**
   - Find vertices, foci, and co-vertices of an ellipse. **(11.3, 11.5)**
   - Find vertices, foci, and asymptotes of a hyperbola. **(11.4, 11.5)**
3. Find points of intersection of two graphs.
   - Linear-quadratic systems **(11.2–11.4)**
   - Quadratic systems **(11.6)**
4. Classify the graph of a general second-degree equation. **(11.6)**

Strategies

5. Use conics to solve real-life problems. **(11.1–11.6)**

Why did you learn it?

Conic sections are used in many different types of construction problems. From earlier work with parabolas, you know that suspension bridges include parabolic shapes. In this chapter, you learned that parabolas have reflective properties that can be used in the construction of antennas and light reflectors. You also studied many applications of circles, ellipses, and hyperbolas. For instance, you learned that the navigational system LORAN involves finding the point of intersection of two hyperbolas.

How does it fit into the bigger picture of algebra?

In this chapter, you studied the graphs of quadratic relations of the form

$$Ax^2 + Bxy + Cy^2 + Dx + Ey + F = 0.$$

The graph of a quadratic relation can be a *parabola*, a *circle*, an *ellipse*, or a *hyperbola*. Each of these graphs are called *conic sections* or simply *conics*.

In the first four lessons, you studied properties of the four types of conics. To keep the equations simple, the conics in the first four lessons have their centers (or in the case of a parabola, its vertex) at the origin. In the fifth lesson, you studied equations of conics that have been translated.

In Exercises 1–9, write an equation of the specified conic. (11.1–11.5)

1. *Circle*
Center: $(0, 0)$
Radius: 5

2. *Circle*
Center: $(3, -1)$
Radius: 2

3. *Parabola*
Vertex: $(3, 2)$
Focus: $(1, 2)$

4. *Parabola*
Vertex: $(-1, 2)$
Focus: $(-1, 0)$

5. *Ellipse*
Vertices: $(0, 2)$, $(4, 2)$
Co-vertices: $(2, 3)$, $(2, 1)$

6. *Ellipse*
Vertices: $(-1, 6)$, $(-1, -2)$
Co-vertices: $(1, 2)$, $(-3, 2)$

7. *Ellipse*
Vertices: $(2, 0)$, $(2, 4)$
Foci: $(2, 1)$, $(2, 3)$

8. *Hyperbola*
Vertices: $(2, 0)$, $(6, 0)$
Foci: $(0, 0)$, $(8, 0)$

9. *Hyperbola*
Vertices: $(2, 3)$, $(2, -3)$
Foci: $(2, 5)$, $(2, -5)$

In Exercises 10–15, find the vertex, focus, and directrix of the parabola. (11.1, 11.5)

10. $y = 4x^2$

11. $y = 2x^2$

12. $y^2 = -6x$

13. $y^2 = 3x$

14. $(x - 1) + 8(y + 2)^2 = 0$

15. $(x + 3) + (y - 2)^2 = 0$

In Exercises 16–21, find the center, vertices, and foci of the ellipse. (11.3, 11.5)

16. $\dfrac{x^2}{25} + \dfrac{y^2}{16} = 1$

17. $\dfrac{x^2}{144} + \dfrac{y^2}{169} = 1$

18. $(x + 2)^2 + 4(y + 4)^2 = 1$

19. $\dfrac{(x - 5)^2}{16} + \dfrac{y^2}{9} = 1$

20. $\dfrac{(x - 1)^2}{9} + \dfrac{(y - 5)^2}{25} = 1$

21. $\dfrac{(x + 3)^2}{25} + \dfrac{(y - 1)^2}{36} = 1$

In Exercises 22–27, find the center, vertices, foci, and asymptotes of the hyperbola. (11.4, 11.5)

22. $\dfrac{y^2}{25} - \dfrac{x^2}{144} = 1$

23. $\dfrac{x^2}{36} - \dfrac{y^2}{4} = 1$

24. $\dfrac{(x - 1)^2}{4} - \dfrac{(y + 2)^2}{1} = 1$

25. $\dfrac{(x + 1)^2}{144} - \dfrac{(y - 4)^2}{25} = 1$

26. $(y + 6)^2 - (x - 2)^2 = 1$

27. $\dfrac{(y - 1)^2}{1/4} - \dfrac{(x + 3)^2}{1/9} = 1$

In Exercises 28–31, match the equation with its graph. (11.5)

28. $\dfrac{(x - 3)^2}{9} + \dfrac{(y + 5)^2}{4} = 1$

29. $(x - 5)^2 + (y - 3)^2 = 4$

30. $\dfrac{(x + 3)^2}{9} - \dfrac{(y - 5)^2}{4} = 1$

31. $(y - 3)^2 - (x + 5) = 0$

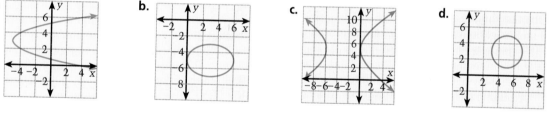

a. **b.** **c.** **d.**

In Exercises 32–40, sketch the graph of the equation.

32. $\dfrac{x^2}{9} + \dfrac{y^2}{49} = 1$

33. $\dfrac{(x+1)^2}{25} - \dfrac{(y+3)^2}{49} = 1$

34. $x^2 + (y-5) = 0$

35. $(y-1)^2 - (x+3) = 0$

36. $(x-3)^2 + (y+7)^2 = 36$

37. $\dfrac{(x-5)^2}{9} + \dfrac{(y+2)^2}{25} = 1$

38. $\dfrac{(x+9)^2}{25} - \dfrac{(y-1)^2}{4} = 1$

39. $\dfrac{(y-4)^2}{16} - \dfrac{(x-1)^2}{4} = 1$

40. $(x+5)^2 + (y-4)^2 = 81$

In Exercises 41–56, write the equation of the conic in standard form. (11.5)

41. $x^2 + 8x - 8y + 16 = 0$

42. $y^2 + 6y - 2x + 9 = 0$

43. $y^2 - 10y - 16x - 7 = 0$

44. $x^2 + 2x - y - 4 = 0$

45. $x^2 + y^2 - 10x + 2y - 74 = 0$

46. $x^2 + y^2 + 8x - 2y + 13 = 0$

47. $x^2 + y^2 + 4x + 8y + 19 = 0$

48. $x^2 + y^2 + 12x + 4y + 39 = 0$

49. $9x^2 + y^2 + 72x - 2y + 136 = 0$

50. $4x^2 + y^2 - 16x + 2y + 1 = 0$

51. $25x^2 + 16y^2 - 50x - 160y + 325 = 0$

52. $144x^2 + y^2 + 576x - 4y + 564 = 0$

53. $y^2 - 4x^2 - 18y - 8x + 76 = 0$

54. $3x^2 - y^2 - 12x - 4y - 1 = 0$

55. $49x^2 - 100y^2 + 98x - 200y - 1276 = 0$

56. $-16x^2 + 36y^2 + 96x - 144y - 16 = 0$

In Exercises 57–64, classify the conic. (11.6)

57. $x^2 + y^2 + 2x - 12y + 28 = 0$

58. $4y^2 - x^2 - 16y - 2x + 3 = 0$

59. $3x^2 - y^2 - 12x - 2y + 5 = 0$

60. $x^2 + 8x - 14y + 16 = 0$

61. $2x^2 + 3y^2 - 12x + 24y + 36 = 0$

62. $x^2 + y^2 - 6x - 2y - 6 = 0$

63. $y^2 - 9y + 2x + 81 = 0$

64. $4x^2 + y^2 + 8x - 4y + 7 = 0$

In Exercises 65–70, find the points of intersection. (11.6)

65. $x^2 + y^2 - 18x + 24y + 200 = 0$
$4x + 3y = 0$

66. $y^2 - 2x - 10y + 31 = 0$
$x - y + 2 = 0$

67. $x^2 + y^2 + 2x - 12y + 12 = 0$
$y^2 + x = 0$

68. $x^2 + 2y^2 + 4x + 8y + 11 = 0$
$y^2 - 40x + 4y - 36 = 0$

69. $4x^2 + y^2 - 48x - 2y + 129 = 0$
$x^2 + y^2 - 2x - 2y - 7 = 0$

70. $9x^2 - 16y^2 + 18x + 153 = 0$
$9x^2 + 16y^2 + 18x - 135 = 0$

71. *Paper Folding*   Draw a dot a few inches from the side of a sheet of paper. Then crease the paper 20 to 30 times, as shown in the diagram. The creases of the paper are tangents of a conic. Is it a parabola or one branch of a hyperbola? Explain.

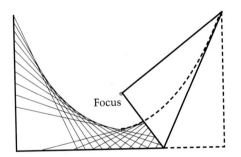

Focus

72. *Purifying Water*   To detoxify the ground water at Livermore National Laboratory in California, water is pumped through tubes that are at the foci of parabolic mirrors. Cross sections of the parabolic mirrors can be modeled by the equation

$$y = \frac{1}{15}x^2$$

where x and y are measured in feet. How far is the tube above the vertex of the mirror?

73. *Archway*   A semi-elliptical arch is to be formed over the entrance to an estate. The arch is to set on pillars that are 10 feet apart and is to have a height atop the pillars of 4 feet. Make an accurate sketch of the arch.

74. *One Man on an Island*   A man lives on an island in a large freshwater lake. Each morning he rides his horse to his gold mine—one mile away. Each evening he rides back to his house. Because he has no well, he always rides to the island's shore to get water on each trip to and from the gold mine. For several weeks, he has been hunting for the shortest path, but no matter how he travels, the distance is always the same. Why?

Pumping station
Contaminated ground water
Reservoir for treated water
Treated water
Parabolic reflective trough

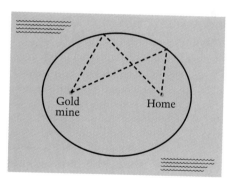

Gold mine
Home

Keeping Sheep   **In Exercises 75 and 76, use the following information.**

The wheel-shaped pen at the right is used in Iceland to hold sheep at shearing time. The inner circle can be approximated by the equation

$$x^2 + y^2 - 250y + 13{,}224 = 0$$

where x and y represent feet. Each individual section outside the inner circle is about 76 feet long.

75. Find the center and radius of the inner circle.

76. Write an equation that represents the outer circle.

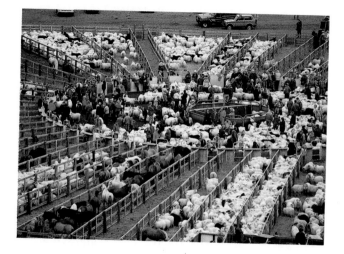

77. *Halley's Comet* Halley's Comet has an elliptical orbit with the sun at one focus. The eccentricity of the orbit is about 0.97. The length of the major axis of the orbit is approximately 36.23 astronomical units. (An astronomical unit is about 93 million miles.) Find an equation for the orbit. Place the center of the orbit at the origin and place the major axis on the x-axis.

78. *The Comet Encke* The comet Encke has an elliptical orbit with the sun at one focus. Encke ranges from 0.34 to 4.08 astronomical units from the sun. Find an equation of the orbit. Place the center of the orbit at the origin and place the major axis on the x-axis.

79. *Pluto and Venus* Pluto and Venus are the two planets whose orbits have the greatest and least eccentricities. Their closest and farthest distances (in miles) from the sun are listed in the table. Find the eccentricity of each planet. Which planet has the more circular orbit?

	Closest	Farthest
Pluto	2,749,600,000	4,582,700,000
Venus	66,800,000	67,700,000

80. *Comets in Our Solar System* Of the 610 comets identified prior to 1970, 245 have elliptical orbits, 295 have parabolic orbits, and 70 have hyperbolic orbits. In each case, the sun lies at the focus of the orbit. Which types of comets pass through our solar system only once? Explain.

Classifying Comets **In Exercises 81 and 82, classify the type of orbit of the comet from its equation. What is the closest distance that the comet gets to the sun? (Each unit represents 1 million miles.)**

81. $9y^2 - 7x^2 + 1170y + 31,725 = 0$

82. $x^2 - 80y = 1600$

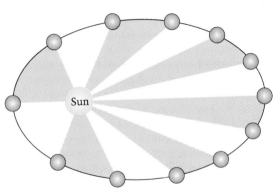

Johannes Kepler, a 17th century German astronomer, discovered that if a ray is extended from the sun to a comet or a planet with an elliptical orbit, the ray sweeps out equal areas in equal times. This principal, called Kepler's Second Law, implies that the comet or planet travels faster as it approaches the sun.

In Exercises 1–4, write the equation of the indicated conic in standard form.

1. Parabola Vertex: $(2, 8)$
Directrix: $y = 4$

2. Circle Center: $(4, -2)$
Radius: 11

3. Ellipse Vertices: $(-4, 6)$, $(8, 6)$
Co-vertices: $(2, 8)$, $(2, 4)$

4. Hyperbola Vertices: $(-3, 2)$, $(7, 2)$
Foci: $(-5, 2)$, $(9, 2)$

In Exercises 5–8, classify the graph as a parabola, circle, ellipse, or hyperbola. Then sketch its graph.

5. $8y = (x - 5)^2$

6. $(x - 3)^2 + (y + 2)^2 = 4$

7. $\dfrac{(x + 4)^2}{4} + \dfrac{(y + 1)^2}{16} = 1$

8. $\dfrac{(x + 4)^2}{9} - \dfrac{(y + 3)^2}{25} = 1$

In Exercises 9–12, classify the graph as a parabola, circle, ellipse, or hyperbola. Then write the equation in standard form.

9. $4x^2 + y = 3$

10. $x^2 - 4x + y^2 + 2y - 4 = 0$

11. $x^2 + 6x + 2y^2 - 8y - 1 = 0$

12. $3x^2 + 6x - 6y^2 + 24y - 33 = 0$

13. Find the vertex and directrix of $x^2 = -16y$.

14. Find the center and radius of $(x + 4)^2 + (y - 6)^2 = 36$.

15. Find the vertices of $\dfrac{(x - 3)^2}{12} + \dfrac{(y - 2)^2}{16} = 1$.

16. Write equations of the asymptotes of $\dfrac{y^2}{4} - \dfrac{x^2}{9} = 1$.

17. Find the points of intersection of $x^2 - y = 0$ and $x^2 + y^2 - 6y + 4 = 0$.

18. An elliptical cam has a shaft mounted at one focus. As it rotates, it lifts a follower from half an inch to two inches above the camshaft center. What is the eccentricity of the cam?

19. A bowl has cross-sections that are parabolic. The equation of a parabolic cross-section is $y = \frac{1}{2}x^2$ where x varies between -4 and 4. Is the focus "inside" or "outside" the bowl? Explain.

20. A light ray from the point $(5, 0)$ is directed toward the focus of a hyperbolic mirror. The mirror has the equation $\frac{1}{9}y^2 - \frac{1}{16}x^2 = 1$. At which point on the mirror will light reflect back to the other focus?

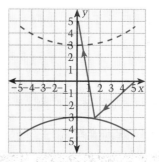

Sequences and Series

LESSONS

12.1 Sequences and Series ▪ 622

12.2 Arithmetic Sequences and Series ▪ 629

12.3 Geometric Sequences and Series ▪ 637

12.4 Infinite Geometric Series ▪ 645

12.5 The Binomial Theorem ▪ 651

12.6 Exploring Data: The Algebra of Finance ▪ 658

The close-up of a daisy head shows the spiraling patterns formed by its florets.

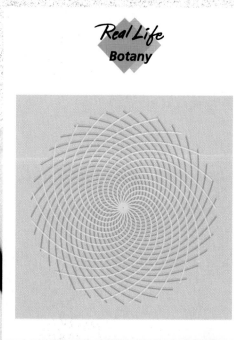

Looking directly into the head of a daisy, you see florets spiraling outward from its center in different directions, forming an intricate pattern. The number of spirals that swirl outward in a clockwise direction is 21. The number of spirals that swirl outward in a counterclockwise direction is 34. When the Fibonacci numbers (see page 323) are listed in order to form the Fibonacci sequence, you see that 21 and 34 are successive numbers:

1, 1, 2, 3, 5, 8, 13, 21, 34, . . .

If you look at the spirals in sunflower heads, pineapple scales, and pinecone brachs, you will again find that their numbers are successive numbers of the Fibonacci sequence.

12.1

Sequences and Series

What you should learn:

Goal 1 How to write and use sequences and series

Goal 2 How to use sequences and series as models of real-life situations

Why you should learn it:

You can model many real-life situations with sequences and series, such as geometric arrangements of items in a display.

Goal 1 Working with Sequences and Series

When we say that a collection of objects is listed "in sequence," we usually mean that the collection is ordered so that it has a first member, a second member, a third member, and so on. In mathematics, the word "sequence" is used in much the same way. Here are two examples.

$$1, 3, 5, 7, \ldots \quad \text{and} \quad \frac{1}{2}, \frac{1}{4}, \frac{1}{8}, \frac{1}{16}, \ldots$$

A Sequence

A **sequence** is a function whose domain is the set of positive integers. The function values

$$a_1, a_2, a_3, a_4, \ldots, a_n, \ldots$$

are the **terms** of the sequence. If the domain consists of the first n positive integers only, then the sequence is a **finite sequence.**

Sometimes it is convenient to include zero in the domain of a sequence and list the terms as

$$a_0, a_1, a_2, a_3, a_4 \ldots$$

Unless otherwise stated, however, you may assume a sequence begins with a_1.

Example 1 Writing Terms in a Sequence

When you are given a formula for the nth term of a sequence, you can find the terms by substituting 1, 2, 3, and so on, for n.

a. Here are the first four terms of the sequence whose nth term is $a_n = 4n - 3$.

$a_1 = 4(1) - 3 = 1$
$a_2 = 4(2) - 3 = 5$
$a_3 = 4(3) - 3 = 9$
$a_4 = 4(4) - 3 = 13$

b. Here are the first four terms of the sequence whose nth term is $a_n = 2 + (-1)^n$.

$a_1 = 2 + (-1)^1 = 2 - 1 = 1$
$a_2 = 2 + (-1)^2 = 2 + 1 = 3$
$a_3 = 2 + (-1)^3 = 2 - 1 = 1$
$a_4 = 2 + (-1)^4 = 2 + 1 = 3$ ∎

Note that simply listing the first few terms is not sufficient to define a sequence—the nth term *must be given*. To see this, consider the following sequences, both of which have the same first three terms.

$$\frac{1}{2}, \frac{1}{4}, \frac{1}{8}, \frac{1}{16}, \cdots, \frac{1}{2^n}, \cdots$$

$$\frac{1}{2}, \frac{1}{4}, \frac{1}{8}, \frac{1}{15}, \cdots, \frac{6}{(n+1)(n^2-n+6)}, \cdots$$

Some very important sequences in mathematics involve factorials. Recall from Lesson 6.6 that $0! = 1$ and

$$n! = 1 \cdot 2 \cdot 3 \cdot 4 \cdots (n-1) \cdot n.$$

Example 2 *Writing Terms of a Sequence Involving Factorials*

Write the first six terms of the sequence whose nth term is $a_n = \frac{30}{n!}$. Begin with $n = 0$.

Solution

$$a_0 = \frac{30}{0!} = \frac{30}{1} = 30 \qquad a_1 = \frac{30}{1!} = \frac{30}{1} = 30$$

$$a_2 = \frac{30}{2!} = \frac{30}{2} = 15 \qquad a_3 = \frac{30}{3!} = \frac{30}{6} = 5$$

$$a_4 = \frac{30}{4!} = \frac{30}{24} = \frac{5}{4} \qquad a_5 = \frac{30}{5!} = \frac{30}{120} = \frac{1}{4}$$ ∎

There is a convenient notation for the sum of the terms of a *finite sequence*. It is called **summation notation** or **sigma notation** because it uses the uppercase Greek letter *sigma*, written as Σ.

Summation Notation

The expression formed by adding the first n terms of a sequence is called a **series** and is represented by

$$\sum_{i=1}^{n} a_i = a_1 + a_2 + a_3 + a_4 + \cdots + a_n$$

where i is called the **index of summation,** n is the **upper limit of summation,** and 1 is the **lower limit of summation.** It is read as "the sum from $i = 1$ to n of a_i."

The index of summation does not have to be i—any letter can be used. Also, the index does not have to begin at 1. For instance, in part b of the next example, the index begins with 3.

Example 3 — Using Summation Notation

a. Let i take on values from 1 to 5 to evaluate the sum.

$$\sum_{i=1}^{5} 3i = 3(1) + 3(2) + 3(3) + 3(4) + 3(5)$$
$$= 3(1 + 2 + 3 + 4 + 5)$$
$$= 3(15)$$
$$= 45$$

b. Let k take on values from 3 to 6 to evaluate the sum.

$$\sum_{k=3}^{6} (1 + k^2) = (1 + 3^2) + (1 + 4^2) + (1 + 5^2) + (1 + 6^2)$$
$$= 10 + 17 + 26 + 37$$
$$= 90$$

c. Let j take on values from 0 to 8 to evaluate the sum.

$$\sum_{j=0}^{8} \frac{1}{j!} = \frac{1}{0!} + \frac{1}{1!} + \frac{1}{2!} + \frac{1}{3!} + \frac{1}{4!} + \frac{1}{5!} + \frac{1}{6!} + \frac{1}{7!} + \frac{1}{8!}$$
$$= 1 + 1 + \frac{1}{2} + \frac{1}{6} + \frac{1}{24} + \frac{1}{120} + \frac{1}{720} + \frac{1}{5040} + \frac{1}{40,320}$$
$$\approx 2.71828$$

This sum is very close to the natural base $e \approx 2.71828$. It can be shown that as more terms of the sequence are added, the sum becomes closer and closer to e. ∎

Goal 2 Using Sequences and Series in Real Life

Connections
Geometry

Example 4 — Finding the Terms of a Sequence

The number of degrees, d_n, in each angle at the tip of the six n-pointed stars shown on this page is given by

$$d_n = \frac{180(n - 4)}{n}, \qquad n \geq 5.$$

Write the first six terms of this sequence.

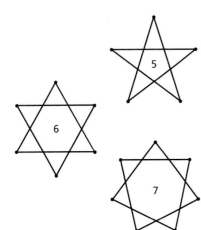

Solution The solution is shown in the table.

n	5	6	7	8	9	10
$\dfrac{180(n-4)}{n}$	36°	60°	$\dfrac{540°}{7} \approx 77.14°$	90°	100°	108°

∎

The sum of the terms of a finite sequence can be found by simply adding the terms. For sequences with many terms, however, adding the terms can be tedious. It is often more efficient to use a formula for the sum of special types of sequences.

Formulas for Special Series

1. $\displaystyle\sum_{i=1}^{n} 1 = n$ **2.** $\displaystyle\sum_{i=1}^{n} i = \frac{1}{2}(n)(n+1)$

3. $\displaystyle\sum_{i=1}^{n} i^2 = \frac{1}{6}(n)(n+1)(2n+1)$

Real Life
Retail Sales

Example 5 *Using a Formula to Find the Sum of a Series*

You are working in the produce department of a grocery store. The manager of the produce department asks you to create a display in which oranges are stacked in a pyramid as shown at the left. The pyramid is to have 16 layers. How many oranges do you need?

Solution To solve the problem, you first need to recognize that the bottom layer has 16^2 oranges, the next layer has 15^2, and so on. This means that the total number of oranges is

$$\sum_{i=1}^{16} i^2 = 1^2 + 2^2 + \cdots + 16^2.$$

One way to find the sum is to add the 16 terms. Another way is to use the formula 3 (shown above).

$$\sum_{i=1}^{16} i^2 = \frac{1}{6}(16)(16+1)(2 \cdot 16 + 1) = \frac{1}{6}(16)(17)(33) = 1496$$

There are 1496 oranges in the stack. Check this by actually adding the number of oranges in each of the 16 layers. ∎

Communicating about ALGEBRA

▶ **SHARING IDEAS about the Lesson**

Find the sum in two ways. First add the terms. Then use one of the formulas shown at the top of this page.

A. $\displaystyle\sum_{i=1}^{15} i$ **B.** $\displaystyle\sum_{i=1}^{10} i^2$

EXERCISES

Guided Practice

▶ **CRITICAL THINKING about the Lesson**

1. Which of the following is a sequence? Which is a series? Explain the difference.

   a. 5, 12, 19, 26, 33, 40   **b.** $5 + 12 + 19 + 26 + 33 + 40$

2. Write the first six terms of the sequence whose nth term is $a_n = 2n$.

3. Write the first six terms of the sequence whose nth term is $a_n = (-1)^{n+1}$.

4. Evaluate the sum $\displaystyle\sum_{i=1}^{4} 2(i-1)$.

Independent Practice

In Exercises 5–28, write the first five terms of the sequence. Begin with $n = 1$.

5. $a_n = 3n - 5$ **6.** $a_n = 4 - n$ **7.** $a_n = n^2 + 2$ **8.** $a_n = (n+1)^2$

9. $a_n = 2^n$ **10.** $a_n = \left(\dfrac{1}{2}\right)^n$ **11.** $a_n = \left(-\dfrac{1}{2}\right)^n$ **12.** $a_n = (-1)^{n-1}$

13. $a_n = \dfrac{n}{n+1}$ **14.** $a_n = \dfrac{n^2}{2n}$ **15.** $a_n = (-2)^n$ **16.** $a_n = (-5)^n$

17. $a_n = n! - 2$ **18.** $a_n = \dfrac{n!}{2}$ **19.** $a_n = \dfrac{3^n}{n!}$ **20.** $a_n = (2n+1)!$

21. $a_n = 2(n!)$ **22.** $a_n = 2(n+2)!$ **23.** $a_n = (n-1)!$ **24.** $a_n = \dfrac{n^2}{n!}$

25. $a_n = 4 + (-1)^n$ **26.** $a_n = 2(-1)^n$ **27.** $a_n = 4 - (-1)^{n+1}$ **28.** $a_n = 2(-1)^{n+1}$

In Exercises 29 and 30, the sequence is defined recursively. Write the first six terms of the sequence. Begin with $n = 0$.

29. $a_0 = 1$
$a_1 = 1$
$a_n = a_{n-2} + a_{n-1}$

30. $a_0 = 1$
$a_n = 3a_{n-1} + 2$

The sequence given by the recursive definition in Exercise 29 is called the Fibonacci sequence (see pages 323 and 621). The terms of the Fibonacci sequence occur as patterns in nature. For instance, from the center of the pine cone shown at the right, there are 8 clockwise spirals and 13 counterclockwise spirals.

In Exercises 31–42, write the series represented by the summation notation. Then evaluate the sum.

31. $\displaystyle\sum_{n=0}^{4} n^2$ **32.** $\displaystyle\sum_{i=0}^{6} (2i + 5)$ **33.** $\displaystyle\sum_{k=1}^{5} (k^2 + 1)$ **34.** $\displaystyle\sum_{j=3}^{7} (6j - 10)$

35. $\displaystyle\sum_{n=1}^{4} n(n + 1)$ **36.** $\displaystyle\sum_{n=0}^{5} 2n^2$ **37.** $\displaystyle\sum_{k=2}^{6} (k! - k)$ **38.** $\displaystyle\sum_{j=0}^{4} \frac{6}{j!}$

39. $\displaystyle\sum_{m=2}^{6} \frac{2m}{2(m - 1)}$ **40.** $\displaystyle\sum_{i=2}^{5} -2i!$ **41.** $\displaystyle\sum_{n=0}^{6} (n! + 10)$ **42.** $\displaystyle\sum_{k=1}^{5} \frac{10k}{k + 2}$

In Exercises 43–46, use summation notation to represent the sum. Use i as the index and begin with $i = 1$.

43. $2 + 4 + 6 + 8 + 10 + 12$

45. $3 + 9 + 27 + 81 + 243$

44. $3 + 5 + 7 + 9 + 11 + 13$

46. $\dfrac{1}{4} + \dfrac{1}{16} + \dfrac{1}{64} + \dfrac{1}{256}$

In Exercises 47–50, use one of the formulas for special series to evaluate the sum.

47. $\displaystyle\sum_{i=1}^{24} 1$ **48.** $\displaystyle\sum_{i=1}^{54} i$ **49.** $\displaystyle\sum_{i=1}^{42} i^2$ **50.** $\displaystyle\sum_{i=1}^{20} i^2$

51. *Towers of Hanoi*   In the puzzle called the Towers of Hanoi, you are asked to move the rings from one peg and stack them *in order* on another peg. You can make as many moves as you want, but each move must consist of moving exactly one ring. Moreover, no ring may be placed on top of a smaller ring. The minimum number of moves required to move n rings is 1 for 1 ring, 3 for 2 rings, 7 for 3 rings, 15 for 4 rings, and 31 for 5 rings. Find a formula for this sequence. What is the minimum number of moves required to move 6 rings?

52. *Soccer Ball*   The number of degrees, a_n, in each angle of a regular n-sided polygon is

$$a_n = \frac{180(n - 2)}{n}, \qquad n \geq 3.$$

The surface of a soccer ball is made of regular hexagons and pentagons. If a soccer ball is taken apart and flattened, as shown at the right, the sides of the hexagons don't meet each other. Use the terms a_5 and a_6 to explain why there are gaps between adjacent hexagons.

53. *Stars* The stars in Example 4 were formed by placing n equally spaced points on a circle and connecting each point with the second point from it on the circle. The stars below are formed in a similar way except each point is connected with the third point from it. For these stars, the number of degrees in a tip is given by

$$d_n = \frac{180(n - 6)}{n}, \quad n \geq 7.$$

Write the first five terms of this sequence.

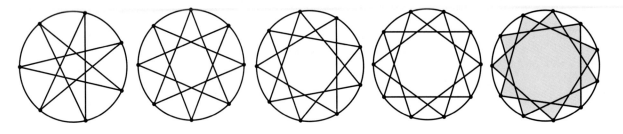

54. *More Stars* If you form the stars by connecting each point with the fourth point from it, you obtain stars with the following numbers of tips and degrees: 9 tips (20°), 10 tips (36°), 11 tips ($49\frac{1}{11}°$), 12 tips (60°). Find a formula for the number of degrees in an n-pointed star.

Integrated Review

In Exercises 55–60, evaluate the expression.

55. $8!$

56. $10!$

57. $\dfrac{18}{3!} - 3$

58. $\dfrac{6!}{80} + 4$

59. $2\left(\dfrac{48}{4!} - \dfrac{60}{5!}\right)$

60. $6!\left(\dfrac{1260}{7!} + \dfrac{3(2!)}{4!}\right)$

In Exercises 61–64, find the first six terms of the sequence defined by the given recursive function.

61. $f(0) = 1$
 $f(n) = 2f(n - 1)$

62. $f(0) = 2$
 $f(n) = n - f(n - 1)$

63. $f(0) = 0$
 $f(1) = 1$
 $f(n) = f(n - 1) - f(n - 2)$

64. $f(0) = 2$
 $f(1) = 5$
 $f(n) = 3f(n - 2) - f(n - 1)$

Exploration and Extension

In Exercises 65–68, find a formula for the nth term of the sequence.

65. $2, 1 + \frac{1}{2}, 1 + \frac{1}{3}, 1 + \frac{1}{4}, 1 + \frac{1}{5}, 1 + \frac{1}{6}, \ldots$

66. $1, \frac{1}{2}, \frac{1}{6}, \frac{1}{24}, \frac{1}{120}, \frac{1}{720}, \ldots$

67. $2, 6, 10, 14, 18, \ldots$

68. $3, 6, 12, 24, 48, 96, \ldots$

12.2

Arithmetic Sequences and Series

What you should learn:

Goal 1 How to find the *n*th term or the sum of an arithmetic series

Goal 2 How to use arithmetic sequences in real-life problems

Why you should learn it:

You can model many real-life situations with arithmetic sequences, such as rows of increasing lengths in some concert halls.

Goal 1 Finding the Terms and the Sum

A sequence whose consecutive terms have a common difference is an **arithmetic sequence.**

An Arithmetic Sequence

The sequence $a_1, a_2, a_3, a_4, \ldots, a_n, \ldots$ is **arithmetic** if there is a number d such that

$$a_2 - a_1 = d, \quad a_3 - a_2 = d, \quad a_4 - a_3 = d$$

and so on. The number d is the common difference of the arithmetic sequence.

Example 1 Examples of Arithmetic Sequences

a. The sequence whose nth term is $4n + 3$ is arithmetic. The common difference between consecutive terms is 4.

$$\underbrace{7, 11,}\ 15, 19, \ldots, 4n + 3, \ldots$$
$$11 - 7 = 4$$

b. The sequence whose nth term is $7 - 5n$ is arithmetic. The common difference between consecutive terms is -5.

$$\underbrace{2, -3,}\ -8, -13, \ldots, 7 - 5n, \ldots$$
$$-3 - 2 = -5$$

c. The sequence whose nth term is $\frac{1}{4}(n + 3)$ is arithmetic. The common difference between consecutive terms is $\frac{1}{4}$.

$$\underbrace{1, \frac{5}{4},}\ \frac{3}{2}, \frac{7}{4}, \ldots, \frac{1}{4}(n + 3), \ldots$$
$$\frac{5}{4} - 1 = \frac{1}{4}$$

■

Every arithmetic sequence has an nth term that is of the form

$$a_n = a_1 + (n - 1)d \quad \textit{nth term of an arithmetic sequence}$$

where d is the common difference of the sequence.

Example 2 **Finding the nth Term**

Find a formula for the nth term of the arithmetic sequence whose first term is 2 and whose common difference is 3.

Solution

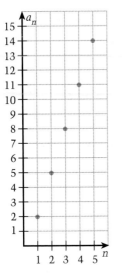

$$a_n = a_1 + (n - 1)d \quad \text{\textit{nth term formula}}$$

$$= 2 + (n - 1)3 \quad \text{\textit{Substitute 2 for } } a_1 \text{ \textit{ and 3 for d.}}$$

$$= 3n - 1 \quad \text{\textit{Simplify.}}$$

The terms of the sequence are as follows.

$$2, 5, 8, 11, 14, \ldots, 3n - 1, \ldots$$

A graph of the sequence is shown at the left. Notice that the points lie on a line. This is true of the graph of *any* arithmetic sequence. ∎

Example 3 **Finding the nth Term**

Find a formula for the nth term of the arithmetic sequence whose common difference is 5 and whose *second* term is 12. What is the eighteenth term of this sequence?

Solution Because the second term is 12 and the common difference is 5, you know that the first term is 7.

$$a_n = a_1 + (n - 1)d \quad \text{\textit{nth term formula}}$$

$$= 7 + (n - 1)5 \quad \text{\textit{Substitute 7 for } } a_1 \text{ \textit{ and 5 for d.}}$$

$$= 5n + 2 \quad \text{\textit{Simplify.}}$$

The eighteenth term of the sequence is $a_{18} = 5(18) + 2 = 92$. ∎

Example 4 **Finding the nth Term**

The fourth term of an arithmetic sequence is 16. The thirteenth term is 43. Write a formula for the nth term.

Solution To obtain the thirteenth term from the fourth term, add the common difference d to the fourth term 9 times.

$$a_{13} = a_4 + 9d$$
$$43 = 16 + 9d$$
$$27 = 9d$$
$$3 = d$$

To obtain the first term, subtract the common difference d from the fourth term 3 times: $a_1 = a_4 - 3(d) = 16 - 9 = 7$. The formula for the nth term is

$$a_n = a_1 + (n - 1)d = 7 + (n - 1)3 = 3n + 4.$$

∎

The expression formed by adding the terms of a finite arithmetic sequence is called an **arithmetic series.** To find the sum of n terms of an arithmetic series, find the average of the first and last terms, $\frac{1}{2}(a_1 + a_n)$, and multiply the result by n.

Here is why the procedure works. Let S represent the sum of the first n terms. You can write the sum S in two ways, and add the results.

$$
\begin{array}{rl}
S = & a_1 + (a_1 + d) + (a_1 + 2d) + \cdots + a_n \\
S = & a_n + (a_n - d) + (a_n - 2d) + \cdots + a_1 \\
\hline
2S = & (a_1 + a_n) + (a_1 + a_n) + (a_1 + a_n) + \cdots + (a_1 + a_n)
\end{array}
$$

From this you can conclude that $2S = n(a_1 + a_n)$, which implies that the sum is $S = \frac{1}{2}n(a_1 + a_n)$.

The Sum of an Arithmetic Series

The sum of an arithmetic series with n terms is

$$
\sum_{i=1}^{n} a_i = n\left(\frac{a_1 + a_n}{2}\right).
$$

This sum can also be written as $\frac{1}{2}n(2a_1 + (n - 1)d)$.

Before using this formula, you should check to be sure that the series is arithmetic.

Example 5 **Evaluating the Sum of an Arithmetic Series**

Find the following sum.

$$1 + 3 + 5 + 7 + 9 + 11 + 13 + 15 + 17 + 19 + 21$$

Solution Because the terms have a common difference of 2, the series is arithmetic. Because the series has 11 terms, its sum is as follows.

$$
\begin{aligned}
\sum_{i=1}^{n} a_i &= 1 + 3 + 5 + 7 + 9 + 11 + 13 + 15 + 17 + 19 + 21 \\
&= n\left(\frac{a_1 + a_n}{2}\right) \\
&= 11\left(\frac{1 + 21}{2}\right) \\
&= 11(11) \\
&= 121
\end{aligned}
$$

The sum of the series is 121. ■

Red Rocks Park is an open-air amphitheater carved out of rock, near Denver, Colorado. The amphitheater has 69 rows of seats. Rows 46 through 69 have seats for 3318 people. The number of seats in the first 45 rows can be modeled by the arithmetic sequence whose nth term is
$$87\tfrac{1}{2} + \tfrac{3}{2}n.$$

Goal 2 Using Arithmetic Series in Real Life

Example 6 Seating Capacity

You are organizing a concert at Red Rocks Park. How much should you charge per ticket in order to receive $50,000 for the ticket sales of a performance that is sold out?

Solution From the information given above, you know that there are 3318 seats in the last 24 rows. To approximate the number of seats in the first 45 rows, you can use the formula for the sum of an arithmetic series.

$$\sum_{i=1}^{45} a_i = 89 + 90\tfrac{1}{2} + 92 + 93\tfrac{1}{2} + \cdots + 155$$
$$= 45\left(\frac{89 + 155}{2}\right)$$
$$= 5490$$

The total number of seats is about $3318 + 5490 = 8808$. To bring in $50,000, you should charge about $\frac{1}{8808}(50,000) \approx$ $5.68 per ticket. ∎

Communicating about ALGEBRA

▶ **SHARING IDEAS about the Lesson**

A. Your job pays $6.50 an hour. After each of the first six years, you receive a raise of $0.50 an hour. Let $a_1 = 6.50$ represent your hourly wage during the first year. Write a formula for your hourly wage during the nth year.

B. Explain how to use the formula for the sum of an arithmetic series to find the sum of the first 100 odd positive integers.

EXERCISES

Guided Practice

▶ **CRITICAL THINKING about the Lesson**

1. What makes a sequence arithmetic?

2. The second and third terms of an arithmetic sequence are 7 and 12, respectively. What is the first term?

3. The fourth term of an arithmetic sequence is 15. The common difference is 2. Write a formula for the nth term of the sequence.

4. The second term of an arithmetic sequence is 10. The eleventh term is 37. What is the sixth term?

5. What is the common difference of the sequence?

   3, 8, 13, 18, 23, . . .

6. Evaluate the sum: $\sum_{i=1}^{4} 5(2i + 3)$.

Independent Practice

In Exercises 7–12, decide whether the sequence is arithmetic.

7. 10, 8, 6, 4, 2, . . .

8. 1, 2, 4, 8, 16, . . .

9. $3, \frac{5}{2}, 2, \frac{3}{2}, 1, \ldots$

10. $\frac{9}{4}, 2, \frac{7}{4}, \frac{3}{2}, \frac{5}{4}, \ldots$

11. $-12, -8, -4, 0, 4, \ldots$

12. $\frac{1}{3}, \frac{2}{3}, \frac{4}{3}, \frac{8}{3}, \frac{16}{3}, \ldots$

In Exercises 13–18, find the common difference of the arithmetic sequence. Write the next term in the sequence.

13. 5, 13, 21, 29, 37, . . .

14. 11, 23, 35, 47, 59, . . .

15. $\frac{1}{3}, \frac{1}{2}, \frac{2}{3}, \frac{5}{6}, 1, \ldots$

16. $3, \frac{11}{3}, \frac{13}{3}, 5, \frac{17}{3}, \ldots$

17. $\frac{7}{2}, \frac{9}{4}, 1, -\frac{1}{4}, -\frac{3}{2}, \ldots$

18. $\frac{5}{2}, \frac{11}{6}, \frac{7}{6}, \frac{1}{2}, -\frac{1}{6}, \ldots$

In Exercises 19–21, find a formula for the nth term of the arithmetic sequence.

19. Common difference: 4
    First term: 1

20. Common difference: 8
    First term: -2

21. Common difference: -2
    Second term: 9

In Exercises 22–27, answer the question about the arithmetic sequence.

22. Common difference: -5
    Second term: 12
    What is the first term?

23. Common difference: 3
    Third term: 6
    What is the sixth term?

24. Common difference: -2
    Fourth term: 1
    What is the tenth term?

25. Common difference: -10
    Sixth term: -20
    What are the first five terms?

26. Fifth term: 6
    Eleventh term: 36
    What are the first four terms?

27. Eighth term: 2
    Nineteenth term: 101
    What are the first four terms?

In Exercises 28–31, match the arithmetic sequence with its graph.

28. $a_n = -\frac{1}{3}n + 2$ **29.** $a_n = 5n - 4$ **30.** $a_n = 2n - 3$ **31.** $a_n = -\frac{1}{2}n + 4$

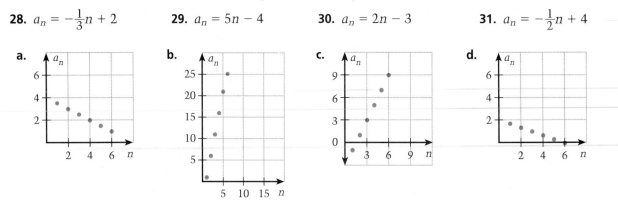

a.

b.

c.

d.

In Exercises 32–39, find the sum of the first n terms of the arithmetic sequence.

32. 8, 20, 32, 44, . . . ; $n = 10$

33. 2, 8, 14, 20, . . . ; $n = 25$

34. $-6, -2, 2, 6, \ldots$; $n = 50$

35. 0.5, 0.9, 1.3, 1.7, . . . ; $n = 10$

36. 40, 37, 34, 31, . . . ; $n = 10$

37. 1.50, 1.45, 1.40, 1.35, . . . ; $n = 20$

38. $a_1 = 100$, $a_{25} = 220$, $n = 25$

39. $a_1 = 15$, $a_{100} = 307$, $n = 100$

In Exercises 40–42, evaluate the sum.

40. $\displaystyle\sum_{i=1}^{20} (3i + 2)$

41. $\displaystyle\sum_{i=1}^{32} (2i + 8)$

42. $\displaystyle\sum_{i=1}^{45} (4i + 9)$

43. *Ticket Prices* There are 20 rows of seats on the main floor of a concert hall: 20 seats in the first row, 21 seats in the second row, 22 seats in the third row, and so on. How much should you charge per ticket in order to obtain $15,000 for the sale of all of the seats on the main floor?

22 seats
21 seats
20 seats

44. *Drilling a Well* A well-drilling company charges $15 for drilling the first foot of a well, $15.25 for drilling the second foot, $15.50 for drilling the third foot, and so on. How much would it cost to have this company drill a 100-foot well?

45. *Pile of Logs* Logs are stacked in a pile as shown below. The top row has 15 logs and the bottom row has 21 logs. How many logs are in the stack?

46. *Brick Pattern* A brick patio has 20 rows of bricks. The first row has 14 bricks and the twentieth row has 33 bricks. How many bricks are in the patio?

←15

←21

33→

14→

47. *Salary Increase* You have accepted a job with a salary of $27,500 the first year. At the end of each year for five years, you receive a $1500 raise. Write a formula for your salary, S_n, during the nth year. What is your total salary during the first six years?

48. *Clock Chimes* A clock chimes once at 1:00, twice at 2:00, three times at 3:00, and so on. The clock also chimes once at 15-minute intervals that are not on the hour. How many times does the clock chime in a 12-hour period?

Integrated Review

In Exercises 49–56, write the first five terms of the sequence.

49. $a_n = 5 + 3n$
50. $a_n = (2^n)n$
51. $a_n = \dfrac{1}{n+1}$
52. $a_n = 1 + 4(n-1)$

53. $a_n = 100 - 3n$
54. $a_n = 2^{n-1}$
55. $a_n = (2 + n) - (1 + n)$
56. $a_n = (-1)^n$

In Exercises 57–60, decide whether the recursive function is linear, quadratic, or neither.

57. $f(0) = 3$
$f(n) = 5 + f(n-1)$

58. $f(1) = 2$
$f(n) = f(n-1) + 2n$

59. $f(1) = 0$
$f(n) = f(n-1) - n^2$

60. $f(0) = 1$
$f(n) = f(n-1) + 13$

61. *Powers of Ten* Which best estimates the height of a 10-story building?
a. 1.2×10^1 ft
b. 1.2×10^2 ft
c. 1.2×10^3 ft
d. 1.2×10^4 ft

62. *Powers of Ten* Which best estimates the volume of this book?
a. 1.2×10^{-1} in.^{3}
b. 1.2×10^0 in.^{3}
c. 1.2×10^1 in.^{3}
d. 1.2×10^2 in.^{3}

Exploration and Extension

63. *Japanese Circle* The Japanese "magic circle" shown at the right is the creation of Seki Kowa, a 17th-century Japanese mathematician. Each set of numbers on a diameter has the same total. Use the magic circle to find the sum of the first 51 positive integers. Check your result using techniques that you studied in this lesson. Can you explain why the magic circle works?

1. Find the inverse $f(x) = x^3 + 2$. **(6.3)**

2. Classify the conic: $6x^2 - 4y^2 = 24$. **(11.6)**

3. Simplify: $\dfrac{3x^4y^{-1}}{x^2} \cdot \dfrac{y^2}{9x^3}$. **(7.1)**

4. Solve $\begin{cases} x + 2y = 8 \\ 4x - y = 5 \end{cases}$. **(3.2)**

5. Factor $x^3 + 5x^2 - 12x - 36$. **(9.3)**

6. Divide $(4x^3 + 3x^2 - 7)$ by $(x - 1)$. **(9.4)**

7. Solve $|4x - 6| \le 3$. **(1.7)**

8. Evaluate $36^{-3/2}$. **(7.3)**

9. Add: $\begin{bmatrix} 2 & 5 \\ -6 & 0 \end{bmatrix} + \begin{bmatrix} -4 & 8 \\ 9 & 7 \end{bmatrix}$. **(4.1)**

10. Multiply: $\begin{bmatrix} \frac{1}{2} & 2 \\ 3 & -1 \end{bmatrix} \begin{bmatrix} 0 & 3 \\ -2 & 0 \end{bmatrix}$. **(4.2)**

11. Solve $\sqrt{x} - \sqrt[4]{2x - 1} = 0$. **(7.5)**

12. Write in logarithmic form $5^{-2} = \frac{1}{25}$. **(8.2)**

13. Expand $\log_6 \dfrac{3x^2}{4}$. **(8.3)**

14. Sketch $y > x^2 + 4x + 3$. **(5.7)**

15. Solve $3mn + 2 = m + n$ for n. **(1.5)**

16. Solve $3x^2 + 4x = 2$. **(5.3)**

17. Write an equation of the line passing through $(-3, 2)$ and $(3, -4)$. **(2.4)**

18. Write an equation of the line that passes through $(1, 1)$ with a slope of $-\frac{1}{4}$. **(2.2)**

19. Find a polynomial equation with leading coefficient of 1 and solutions $2i$, $-2i$, and 1. **(9.6)**

20. Find the mean and median of the numbers: 12, 13, 22, 28, 30, 18, 12, 13, 17, 18. **(6.7)**

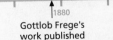

Milestones GÖDEL'S PROOF

| 1870 | 1880 | 1890 | 1900 | 1910 | 1920 | 1930 | 1940 |

1880 Gottlob Frege's work published

First volume of *Principia Mathematica* published

Gödel's proof published

Kurt Gödel

In the late 1800's, a movement began to organize all branches of mathematics similar to the way it is organized in geometry. Efforts were made to identify a complete set of axioms for each branch of mathematics from which all of its theorems and corollaries could be deduced. In 1879, the German mathematician Gottlob Frege published his efforts in two volumes. Alfred North Whitehead and Bertrand Russell made a more complete attempt in the three volumes of *Principia Mathematica*, published between 1910 and 1913. Then, in 1931, a faculty member at the University of Vienna, Kurt Gödel, showed that their goal was unattainable. He proved that a complete set of axioms could never be identified for a branch of mathematics such that all of its propositions could be proven or disproven on the basis of these axioms. Although Gödel effectively closed one avenue of mathematical research, he also pointed out new directions for the future.

In the 1930's and 1940's many mathematicians immigrated to the United States to work and study. Why do you think this was so?

12.3

Geometric Sequences and Series

What you should learn:

Goal 1 How to find the nth term and the sum of a finite geometric series

Goal 2 How to use geometric series in real-life problems

Why you should learn it:

You can model many real-life situations with geometric sequences, such as revenues that increase at a constant percent.

Goal 1 Finding the Terms and the Sum

A sequence whose consecutive terms have a common ratio is a **geometric sequence.**

Definition of a Geometric Sequence

The sequence $a_1, a_2, a_3, a_4, \ldots, a_n, \ldots$ is **geometric** if there is a nonzero number r such that

$$\frac{a_2}{a_1} = r, \quad \frac{a_3}{a_2} = r, \quad \frac{a_4}{a_3} = r$$

and so on. The number r is the *common ratio* of the sequence.

Example 1 *Examples of Geometric Sequences*

a. The first 4 terms of the sequence whose nth term is 2^n are 2, 4, 8, and 16. The common ratio between consecutive terms is 2. Therefore, the sequence is geometric.

$$\underbrace{2, 4,}\, 8, 16, \ldots, 2^n, \ldots$$
$$\frac{4}{2} = 2$$

b. The first 4 terms of the sequence whose nth term is $4(3^n)$ are 12, 36, 108, and 324. The common ratio between consecutive terms is 3. Therefore, the sequence is geometric.

$$\underbrace{12, 36,}\, 108, 324, \ldots, 4(3^n), \ldots$$
$$\frac{36}{12} = 3$$

c. The first 4 terms of the sequence whose nth term is $9\left(-\frac{1}{3}\right)^n$ are $-3, 1, -\frac{1}{3}$, and $\frac{1}{9}$. The common ratio between consecutive terms is $-\frac{1}{3}$. Thus, the sequence is geometric.

$$\underbrace{-3, 1,}\, -\frac{1}{3}, \frac{1}{9}, \ldots, 9\left(-\frac{1}{3}\right)^n, \ldots$$
$$\frac{1}{-3} = -\frac{1}{3}$$

$\blacksquare$

If r is the common ratio of a geometric sequence, then the formula for the nth term of the sequence is

$$a_n = a_1 r^{n-1} \quad \textit{nth term of a geometric sequence}$$

Example **2** **_Finding a Term of a Geometric Sequence_**

Find the fifteenth term of the geometric sequence whose first term is 20 and whose common ratio is 1.05.

Solution   Use the formula for the nth term of the sequence.

$$a_n = a_1 r^{n-1} \qquad \textit{nth term of geometric sequence}$$

$$= 20(1.05)^{n-1} \quad \textit{Substitute 20 for } a_1 \textit{ and 1.05 for } r.$$

The fifteenth term is $a_{15} = 20(1.05)^{14} \approx 39.6$. ■

Example **3** **_Finding a Term of a Geometric Sequence_**

Find the twelfth term of the geometric sequence whose first three terms are 5, 15, and 45.

Solution   The common ratio of this sequence is $r = \frac{15}{5} = 3$. Because the first term is $a_1 = 5$, the formula for the nth term is as follows.

$$a_n = a_1 r^{n-1} \qquad \textit{nth term of geometric sequence}$$

$$= 5(3)^{n-1} \quad \textit{Substitute 5 for } a_1 \textit{ and 3 for } r.$$

The twelfth term is $a_{12} = 5(3)^{11} = 885{,}735$. ■

Example **4** **_Finding a Term of a Geometric Sequence_**

The fourth term of a geometric sequence with positive terms is 125. The tenth term is $\frac{125}{64}$. Find the first term.

Solution   You can obtain the tenth term by multiplying the fourth term by r^6. Because $a_{10} = \frac{125}{64}$ and $a_4 = 125$, you can solve for r as follows.

$$a_{10} = a_4 r^6 \qquad \textit{Multiply } a_4 \textit{ by } r^6 \textit{ to obtain } a_{10}.$$

$$\frac{125}{64} = 125 r^6 \quad \textit{Substitute } \tfrac{125}{64} \textit{ for } a_{10} \textit{ and 125 for } a_4.$$

$$\frac{1}{64} = r^6 \qquad \textit{Divide both sides by 125.}$$

$$\frac{1}{2} = r \qquad \textit{Take sixth root of both sides.}$$

Now, using $r = \frac{1}{2}$, you can solve for the first term of the sequence as follows.

$$a_4 = a_1 r^{4-1} \qquad \textit{Formula for fourth term.}$$

$$125 = a_1 \left(\frac{1}{2}\right)^3 \quad \textit{Substitute 125 for } a_4 \textit{ and } \tfrac{1}{2} \textit{ for } r.$$

$$125 = a_1 \left(\frac{1}{8}\right) \qquad \textit{Simplify.}$$

$$1000 = a_1 \qquad \textit{Multiply both sides by 8.}$$

■

The expression formed by adding the terms of a geometric sequence is called a **geometric series.** You can develop a formula for the sum, S, of a (finite) geometric series as follows.

$$
\begin{aligned}
S &= a_1 + a_1r + a_1r^2 + a_1r^3 + \cdots + a_1r^{n-1} \\
-rS &= \quad\ - a_1r - a_1r^2 - a_1r^3 - \cdots - a_1r^{n-1} - a_1r^n \\
\hline
S(1-r) &= a_1(1-r^n) \quad\quad\quad\quad\quad\quad\quad\quad\quad\quad\quad - a_1r^n
\end{aligned}
$$

By dividing both sides of this equation by $(1-r)$, you can obtain the following formula for S.

The Sum of a Finite Geometric Series

The sum of the geometric series $a_1 + a_1r + a_1r^2 + \cdots + a_1r^{n-1}$ with common ratio $r \neq 1$ is

$$\sum_{i=1}^{n} a_1 r^{i-1} = a_1\left(\frac{1-r^n}{1-r}\right).$$

Example 5 *Finding the Sum of a Geometric Series*

Evaluate the sum.

$$\sum_{i=1}^{12} 4(0.3)^i = 4(0.3) + 4(0.3)^2 + 4(0.3)^3 + \cdots + 4(0.3)^{12}$$

Solution Because $a_1 = 4(0.3)$, $r = 0.3$, and $n = 12$, you can apply the formula for the sum of a geometric series.

$$
\sum_{i=1}^{12} 4(0.3)^i = a_1\left(\frac{1-r^n}{1-r}\right) = 4(0.3)\left(\frac{1-(0.3)^{12}}{1-0.3}\right)
$$
$$
\approx 1.714
$$

Example 6 *Finding the Sum of a Geometric Series*

Evaluate the sum.

$$\sum_{i=0}^{10} 10\left(-\frac{1}{2}\right)^i = 10 + 10\left(-\frac{1}{2}\right) + 10\left(-\frac{1}{2}\right)^2 + \cdots + 10\left(-\frac{1}{2}\right)^{10}$$

Solution By examining the given terms, you can see that the *first term* is $a_1 = 10$, and $r = -\frac{1}{2}$. Moreover, by starting with $i = 0$ and ending with $i = 10$, you are adding $n = 11$ terms.

$$
\sum_{i=0}^{10} 10\left(-\frac{1}{2}\right)^i = a_1\left(\frac{1-r^n}{1-r}\right) = 10\left(\frac{1-\left(-\frac{1}{2}\right)^{11}}{1-\left(-\frac{1}{2}\right)}\right)
$$
$$
\approx 6.670
$$

Connections
Business

Example 7 Finding the Sum of a Geometric Series

For 1981 through 1990, the annual revenue for Rubbermaid, Inc. increased at an average rate of 17.5% per year. Over this 10-year period, the annual revenue, R (in millions of dollars), can be modeled by $R = 361(1.175)^{n-1}$ where $n = 1$ represents 1981. Use this model to approximate the total revenue for Rubbermaid from 1981 to 1990. *(Source: Rubbermaid, Inc.)*

Solution Because the annual revenues are modeled by a geometric sequence, you can approximate the total revenue by using the formula for the sum of a geometric series.

$$\sum_{i=1}^{10} 361(1.175)^{i-1} = 361 + 361(1.175) + \cdots + 361(1.175)^9$$

$$= 361\left(\frac{1 - 1.175^{10}}{1 - 1.175}\right)$$

$$\approx 361\left(\frac{-4.016}{-0.175}\right) \approx 8284$$

The total revenue over the 10-year period was about $8284 million or $8,284,000,000. (Rubbermaid's actual total income over the 10-year period was $8,289,000,000.) ∎

Communicating about **ALGEBRA**

▶ **SHARING IDEAS about the Lesson**

The bar graphs show the annual revenue, R (in millions of dollars), for two companies over a 10-year period. One company's revenue growth followed an arithmetic pattern; the other company's revenue growth followed a geometric pattern. Find a model for each company's revenue and find the total revenue over the 10-year period.

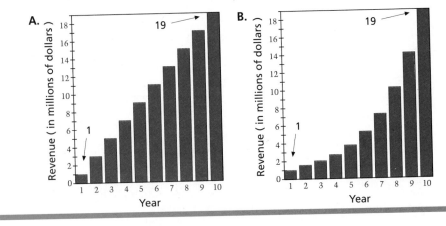

EXERCISES

Guided Practice

▶ **CRITICAL THINKING about the Lesson**

1. What makes a sequence geometric?

2. What is the general formula for the nth term of a geometric sequence?

3. Find the common ratio of the sequence 2, 6, 18, 54, 162, ...

4. Which is the sixth term of the geometric sequence whose third term is 64 and whose common ratio is 4?

   a. $64(4^3)$ **b.** $64(4^4)$ **c.** $64(4^5)$ **d.** $64(4^6)$

5. Find the sum: $\sum\limits_{i=1}^{10} 6\left(\frac{1}{2}\right)^i$.

6. Find the sum: $\sum\limits_{i=0}^{10} 6\left(\frac{1}{2}\right)^i$.

Independent Practice

In Exercises 7–12, decide whether the sequence is arithmetic, geometric, or neither.

7. 5, 15, 45, 135, . . .

8. 1, 4, 9, 16, . . .

9. 3, 12, 21, 30, . . .

10. 1, −2, −5, −8, . . .

11. $\frac{1}{2}, \frac{3}{2}, \frac{9}{2}, \frac{27}{2}, \ldots$

12. −3, −1, 1, 3, . . .

In Exercises 13–18, find the common ratio of the geometric sequence. Then write the next term.

13. 1, −3, 9, −27, . . .

14. 3, 9, 27, 81, . . .

15. 2, 10, 50, 250, . . .

16. 6, −24, 96, −384, . . .

17. $5, -\frac{5}{2}, \frac{5}{4}, -\frac{5}{8}, \ldots$

18. $2, \frac{4}{3}, \frac{8}{9}, \frac{16}{27}, \ldots$

In Exercises 19–24, write the first five terms of the geometric sequence.

19. $a_1 = 2, r = 3$

20. $a_1 = 1, r = \frac{1}{2}$

21. $a_1 = 6, r = 2$

22. $a_1 = 5, r = -\frac{1}{10}$

23. $a_1 = 1, r = -\frac{1}{4}$

24. $a_1 = 1, r = \frac{1}{3}$

In Exercises 25–30, find the indicated term of the geometric sequence.

25. $a_1 = 4, r = \frac{1}{2}, \quad a_{10} = \boxed{?}$

26. $a_1 = 5, r = \frac{3}{2}, \quad a_8 = \boxed{?}$

27. $a_1 = 6, r = -\frac{1}{3}, \quad a_{12} = \boxed{?}$

28. $a_1 = 1, r = -\frac{2}{3}, \quad a_7 = \boxed{?}$

29. $a_1 = 100, r = 2, \quad a_9 = \boxed{?}$

30. $a_1 = 8, r = 4, \quad a_4 = \boxed{?}$

In Exercises 31–34, write a formula for the nth term of the geometric sequence.

31. $1, \frac{3}{2}, \frac{9}{4}, \frac{27}{8}, \ldots$

32. $1, \frac{2}{3}, \frac{4}{9}, \frac{8}{27}, \ldots$

33. $4, 6, 9, \frac{27}{2}, \ldots$

34. 24, 12, 6, 3, . . .

In Exercises 35–43, give the missing information about the geometric sequence.

35. Common ratio: $\frac{1}{2}$
First term: 3
Formula for a_n: ?

36. Common ratio: 4
First term: $\frac{1}{2}$
Formula for a_n: ?

37. Common ratio: $-\frac{1}{3}$
First term: 1
Twelfth term: ?

38. Common ratio: 2
First term: 3
Thirteenth term: ?

39. First term: 4
Fifth term: 324
Eighth term: ?

40. First term: 9
Third term: 1
Tenth term: ?

41. Third term: 64
Seventh term: $\frac{1}{4}$
Common ratio: ?

42. Eighth term: $\frac{1}{9}$
Fifteenth term: 243
Common ratio: ?

43. Third term: 8
Ninth term: $\frac{1}{8}$
Formula for a_n: ?

In Exercises 44–51, evaluate the sum of the finite geometric series.

44. $\sum_{n=1}^{10} 8(2^{n-1})$

45. $\sum_{n=1}^{6} 3(4^{n-1})$

46. $\sum_{i=1}^{10} 8\left(\frac{1}{4}\right)^{i-1}$

47. $\sum_{i=1}^{10} 5\left(\frac{1}{3}\right)^{i-1}$

48. $\sum_{n=1}^{8} 2^{n-1}$

49. $\sum_{n=1}^{8} (-2)^{n-1}$

50. $\sum_{n=0}^{5} 3\left(\frac{3}{2}\right)^{n}$

51. $\sum_{n=0}^{6} 2\left(\frac{4}{3}\right)^{n}$

52. *Student Guaranteed Loans*   For 1982 through 1990, the amount, a_n (in millions of dollars), of guaranteed student loans can be modeled by $a_n = 5650.2(1.2)^{n-1}$ where $n = 2$ represents 1982. Use this model to approximate the total amount of guaranteed student loans for 1982 through 1990. *(Source: Student Loan Marketing Association)*

53. *Geometry*   A square has 16-inch sides. It is partitioned to form a new square by connecting the midpoints of the sides of the original square. Then two of the corner triangles are shaded. This process is repeated five more times. Each time, two of the corner triangles are shaded. The portion of the original square that is shaded on the nth partitioning is $\frac{1}{4}\left(\frac{1}{2}\right)^{n-1}$. Find the total shaded area.

54. *Geometry*   A 27-inch by 27-inch square is partitioned into nine squares and the center square is shaded. Each of the unshaded squares is then partitioned into nine squares and their center squares are shaded. The process is repeated three more times. The portion of the original square that is shaded on the nth partitioning is $\frac{1}{9}\left(\frac{8}{9}\right)^{n-1}$. Find the total shaded area.

In Exercises 55–63, is the sequence arithmetic, geometric, or neither?

55. $\frac{1}{3}$, 1, 3, 9, . . .

56. $\frac{1}{4}$, $\frac{1}{2}$, $\frac{3}{2}$, 2, . . .

57. −5, −3, −1, 1, . . .

58. 2, 1, $\frac{1}{2}$, $\frac{1}{4}$, . . .

59. $\frac{1}{2}$, 1, $\frac{7}{2}$, 5, . . .

60. $\frac{9}{2}$, 1, $\frac{2}{9}$, $\frac{4}{81}$, . . .

61. −5, 1, 3, 6, . . .

62. −4, −2, 2, 4, . . .

63. 0, 1, 2, 4, 8, . . .

In Exercises 64–67, evaluate the sum of the series.

64. $\displaystyle\sum_{i=1}^{4} (6i + 5)$

65. $\displaystyle\sum_{i=1}^{5} 2(0.8)^{i-1}$

66. $\displaystyle\sum_{i=1}^{10} i^2$

67. $\displaystyle\sum_{i=1}^{5} (4 - 2i)$

Native Americans   In Exercises 68–70, use the following data from 1990.

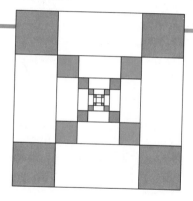

68. Of all Native Americans living in the U.S. in 1990, what percent lived in California?

69. In 1990, the population of New Mexico was 1,515,000. What percent of the population were Native Americans?

70. In 1990, Native Americans represented 4.2% of the population of Arizona. What was the population of Arizona in 1990?

Recently actor Lou Diamond Phillips, who is part Cherokee, produced a documentary on the problems of the 1.5 million Native Americans living in the United States.

Exploration and Extension

71. *Finding a Pattern*   In the large square at the right, four corner squares were drawn and shaded. The sides of each corner square are one-fourth the length of a side of the original square. This process is then repeated in the center square. What portion of the original square is shaded after performing the process five times?

Take this test as you would take a test in class. The answers to the exercises are given in the back of the book.

In Exercises 1–3, decide whether the sequence is arithmetic, geometric, or neither. **(12.2, 12.3)**

1. 4, 10, 20, 34, 52, . . .

2. 11, 7, 3, −1, −5, . . .

3. $-1, \frac{1}{2}, -\frac{1}{4}, \frac{1}{8}, -\frac{1}{16}, \cdots$

In Exercises 4–6, write the first 5 terms of the sequence. Begin with *n* = 1. **(12.1)**

4. $a_n = 3n + 2$

5. $a_n = -3n^2 + 2$

6. $a_n = \frac{n!}{n^2}$

In Exercises 7–9, find a formula for the nth term of the sequence. **(12.2, 12.3)**

7. 4, 10, 16, 22, 28, . . .

8. 6, 12, 24, 48, 96, . . .

9. $\frac{10}{3}, \frac{11}{3}, 4, \frac{13}{3}, \frac{14}{3}, \cdots$

In Exercises 10–12, answer the question about the arithmetic sequence. **(12.2)**

10. Common difference: −4
Second term: 8
What is the 5th term?

11. Common difference: 6
First term: −20
What is the 4th term?

12. Common difference: 2
Tenth term: 15
What is the 15th term?

In Exercises 13–15, answer the question about the geometric sequence. **(12.3)**

13. Common ratio: $\frac{1}{5}$
First term: 10
Write a formula for a_n.

14. Second term: 18
Fifth term: 486
Find the 7th term.

15. Third term: −24
Eighth term: 768
Find the common ratio.

In Exercises 16–18, evaluate the sum of the series. **(12.1–12.3)**

16. $\sum_{n=1}^{44} n$

17. $\sum_{i=0}^{4} \left(\frac{1}{3}\right)^i$

18. $\sum_{n=1}^{16} (4n - 3)$

19. For 1989 through 1994, the amount, a_n (in billions of dollars), of retail sales for general merchandise stores can be modeled by $a_n = 15.66n + 60.28$ where $n = 9$ represents 1989. Use this model to approximate the total retail sales for general merchandise stores for 1989 through 1994. **(12.2)** *(Source: U.S. Bureau of Census)*

20. For 1985 through 1994, the sales, a_n (in millions of dollars), of compact disks can be modeled by $a_n = 251(1.286)^n$ where $n = 5$ represents 1985. Use this model to approximate the total sales of compact disks for 1985 through 1994. **(12.3)**
(Source: U.S. Bureau of Census)

21. For 1989 through 1994, the amount, a_n (in billions of dollars), of sales for bookstores can be modeled by $a_n = 1.2 + 0.6n$ where $n = 9$ represents 1989. Use this model to approximate the total sales for 1989 through 1994. **(12.2)** *(Source: U.S. Bureau of Census)*

12.4

Infinite Geometric Series

What you should learn:

Goal 1 How to find the sum of an infinite geometric series

Goal 2 How to use infinite geometric series as models of real-life problems

Why you should learn it:

You can model many real-life situations with geometric series, such as the total distance traveled by a bouncing ball.

Goal 1   **Summing an Infinite Geometric Series**

It should not surprise you that all *finite* geometric series have a finite sum. You may, however, be surprised that some *infinite* geometric series have a finite sum. Here is an example.

$$\sum_{i=0}^{\infty} 0.3\left(\frac{1}{10}\right)^i = 0.3 + 0.03 + 0.003 + 0.0003 + \cdots$$

$$= 0.3333\ldots$$

$$= \frac{1}{3}$$

To indicate that an **infinite series** has no upper limit of summation, we write the symbol for *infinity*, ∞, in place of the upper limit. This symbol is never used to represent a number. Instead, it is used to indicate a type of unbounded or unending situation. For an infinite series, the infinity symbol is used to indicate that the series is composed of infinitely many terms.

Sum of an Infinite Geometric Series

If $|r| < 1$, then the infinite geometric series

$$a_1 + a_1r + a_1r^2 + a_1r^3 + \cdots + a_1r^{n-1} + \cdots$$

has the sum $\sum_{n=1}^{\infty} a_1r^{n-1} = \dfrac{a_1}{1 - r}$.

If $|r| \geq 1$, then the series has no sum.

Example 1   *Summing an Infinite Geometric Series*

Find the sum.

$$\sum_{n=1}^{\infty} 4(0.6)^{n-1} = 4 + 4(0.6) + 4(0.6)^2 + 4(0.6)^3 + \cdots$$

Solution   For this series, $a_1 = 4$ and $r = 0.6$. Because $|r| < 1$, you can apply the formula for an infinite geometric series.

$$\sum_{n=1}^{\infty} 4(0.6)^{n-1} = \frac{a_1}{1 - r} = \frac{4}{1 - (0.6)} = 10$$

∎

A mathematical *paradox* is an argument in which an apparent untruth has been proved. Many famous paradoxes in mathematics involve infinite geometric series. One is the paradox of *Achilles and the Tortoise.* The paradox was first proposed by the Greek mathematician Zeno (*circa* 480 B.C.).

Connections

Paradoxes

Example 2 *Finding the Sum of an Infinite Series*

Achilles is a heroic character in Greek mythology, thought to run faster than any other living creature. One day, as Achilles is walking in a field, he sees a tortoise that is 100 feet away. The tortoise starts running in a straight line at a speed of 50 feet per second. Achilles starts running at a speed of 100 feet per second. By common sense, you know that Achilles can catch the tortoise—in fact, it should take only two seconds. In the paradox, however, Zeno argues that Achilles can *never* catch the tortoise. His argument is as follows.

Achilles starts running, but when he gets to the position where the tortoise began, the tortoise is no longer there—it is in a new position. So Achilles keeps running, but again when he gets to the new position, the tortoise is no longer there—it is in yet a new position. By this reasoning, Achilles can never catch the tortoise because when Achilles gets to where the tortoise was, the tortoise will have moved to a new position!

How can you resolve this paradox?

Solution The "solution" to this paradox is that it is possible for Achilles, or anyone, to occupy infinitely many positions during a finite length of time. In Achilles' pursuit, the distances traveled between consecutive positions of the tortoise and the times required to reach those positions form geometric series that have finite sums.

Distance (ft)	100	50	25	12.5	6.25	3.125	. . .
Time (sec)	1	0.5	0.25	0.125	0.0625	0.03125	. . .

The total distance traveled and the total time elapsed are as follows.

$$\text{Distance} = \sum_{n=1}^{\infty} 100\left(\frac{1}{2}\right)^{n-1} = \frac{100}{1 - \frac{1}{2}} = 200 \text{ feet}$$

$$\text{Time} = \sum_{n=1}^{\infty} 1\left(\frac{1}{2}\right)^{n-1} = \frac{1}{1 - \frac{1}{2}} = 2 \text{ seconds}$$

The bouncing ball at the right was dropped from a height of 10 feet. Each time it hits the ground, it bounces $\frac{4}{5}$ of its previous height. (Although the ball's path is shown as if it were moving horizontally to the right, its motion is actually straight up and down.)

Physics

Example 3 · Finding the Sum of an Infinite Series

Find the total distance traveled by the bouncing ball above.

Solution The ball first fell 10 feet. It then bounced to a height of $\frac{4}{5}(10) = 8$ feet. After falling 8 feet back to the ground, it bounced to a height of $\frac{4}{5}(8) = \frac{32}{5}$ feet, and so on. The total distance the ball fell is

$$\boxed{\text{Falling distance}} = 10 + 10\left(\frac{4}{5}\right) + 10\left(\frac{4}{5}\right)^2 + \cdots = \frac{10}{1 - \frac{4}{5}} = 50 \text{ feet.}$$

The total distance the ball bounced upwards is

$$\boxed{\text{Bouncing distance}} = 8 + 8\left(\frac{4}{5}\right) + 8\left(\frac{4}{5}\right)^2 + \cdots = \frac{8}{1 - \frac{4}{5}} = 40 \text{ feet.}$$

Thus the total distance traveled by the ball (in both directions) is $50 + 40 = 90$ feet. Did the ball ever stop bouncing? Why?

Communicating about ALGEBRA

▶ **SHARING IDEAS about the Lesson**

A frog at the bottom of a 20-foot well is jumping up the wall, climbing its way to the top. The first jump is 10 feet, the second jump is 5 feet, the third jump is $2\frac{1}{2}$ feet, and so on. At each jump, the frog jumps half of the remaining distance. Each jump takes the frog 1 second. Will the frog ever make it to the top of the well? Explain.

EXERCISES

▶ **CRITICAL THINKING about the Lesson**

1. Write the symbol for *infinity*.

2. Use summation notation to write $a_1 + a_2 + a_3 + \cdots + a_n + \cdots$.

3. Under what condition will $\displaystyle\sum_{i=1}^{\infty} a_1 r^{i-1}$ have a sum?

4. Find the sum of $\displaystyle\sum_{i=1}^{\infty} 4\left(\frac{1}{3}\right)^{i-1}$.

Independent Practice

In Exercises 5–12, decide whether the infinite geometric series has a sum.

5. $\displaystyle\sum_{n=1}^{\infty} 3\left(\frac{3}{2}\right)^{n-1}$

6. $\displaystyle\sum_{n=0}^{\infty} -4\left(\frac{1}{4}\right)^{n}$

7. $\displaystyle\sum_{n=1}^{\infty} \frac{3}{2}\left(\frac{1}{3}\right)^{n-1}$

8. $\displaystyle\sum_{n=1}^{\infty} \frac{2}{3}\left(\frac{4}{3}\right)^{n-1}$

9. $\displaystyle\sum_{n=0}^{\infty} 3\left(-\frac{4}{5}\right)^{n}$

10. $\displaystyle\sum_{n=1}^{\infty} \left(\frac{2}{9}\right)^{n-1}$

11. $\displaystyle\sum_{n=0}^{\infty} 6(2)^{n}$

12. $\displaystyle\sum_{n=1}^{\infty} \left(\frac{6}{5}\right)^{n-1}$

In Exercises 13–28, find the sum (if it has one).

13. $\displaystyle\sum_{n=0}^{\infty} \left(\frac{1}{2}\right)^{n}$

14. $\displaystyle\sum_{n=0}^{\infty} 2\left(\frac{2}{3}\right)^{n}$

15. $\displaystyle\sum_{n=1}^{\infty} \left(-\frac{1}{2}\right)^{n-1}$

16. $\displaystyle\sum_{n=1}^{\infty} \frac{1}{2}(2)^{n-1}$

17. $\displaystyle\sum_{n=0}^{\infty} 4\left(\frac{1}{4}\right)^{n}$

18. $\displaystyle\sum_{n=0}^{\infty} \left(\frac{1}{10}\right)^{n}$

19. $\displaystyle\sum_{n=1}^{\infty} 2\left(\frac{7}{5}\right)^{n-1}$

20. $\displaystyle\sum_{n=0}^{\infty} 4\left(\frac{3}{7}\right)^{n}$

21. $\displaystyle\sum_{n=1}^{\infty} -\frac{1}{6}\left(-\frac{1}{2}\right)^{n-1}$

22. $\displaystyle\sum_{n=1}^{\infty} \frac{1}{2}\left(-\frac{2}{5}\right)^{n-1}$

23. $\displaystyle\sum_{n=0}^{\infty} \frac{1}{12}(-0.12)^{n}$

24. $\displaystyle\sum_{n=1}^{\infty} -\left(-\frac{2}{11}\right)^{n-1}$

25. $\displaystyle\sum_{n=1}^{\infty} 20\left(\frac{4}{5}\right)^{n-1}$

26. $\displaystyle\sum_{n=0}^{\infty} \frac{1}{2}(2)^{n}$

27. $\displaystyle\sum_{n=1}^{\infty} \frac{1}{4}\left(\frac{7}{8}\right)^{n-1}$

28. $\displaystyle\sum_{n=0}^{\infty} -5\left(\frac{1}{5}\right)^{n}$

29. *Stacking Paper*   Start with a piece of paper that is 8 inches by 10 inches. It has a surface area (both sides) of $2(8)(10) = 160$ square inches. Cut a second piece of paper whose length and width are each $\frac{4}{5}$ of the original. It has a surface area of $2\left(\frac{4}{5}\right)(8)\left(\frac{4}{5}\right)(10)$ square inches. Suppose that you could continue this process forever, each time reducing the length and width of the next piece of paper to $\frac{4}{5}$ of the length and width of the previous piece. Would the total surface area of the infinitely many pieces of paper in the stack be finite or infinite? Would the height be finite or infinite? Explain.

30. Length of a Spring The length of the first loop of a spring is 20 inches. The length of the second loop is $\frac{9}{10}$ the length of the first. The length of the third loop is $\frac{9}{10}$ the length of the second, and so on. Suppose the spring has infinitely many loops. Does it have a finite or infinite length? Explain. If it has a finite length, find the length.

31. Superball You drop a superball from a height of 5 feet. After each time it hits the ground, it bounces to $\frac{8}{9}$ of its previous height. What is the total distance that the superball travels before it comes to rest?

32. A Jumping Flea A flea named Argus jumps 12 inches toward another flea, Almo. On the second jump, Argus jumps 6 more inches toward Almo. On the third jump, Argus jumps 3 more inches toward Almo, and so on. Each jump takes one second. Argus keeps getting closer and closer, but cannot quite reach Almo. How far apart were they at the time of Argus's first jump?

33. Thermopane Window A thermopane window is constructed with two parallel pieces of glass, each of which reflects half of the sunlight that hits it from either side. The other half of the sunlight passes through the pane. How much of the sunlight will pass through *both* panes? Explain.

34. Zooming-In The zoom feature on most graphing calculators crops 75% of the width (and 75% of the height) of the previous viewing screen. Let W represent the width of the original screen. The amount of the previous screen's width that is cropped on the nth zoom-in is $(0.75W)(0.25)^{n-1}$. If the zooming could continue forever, the total width that is cropped from the original viewing screen would be given by the sum

$$\sum_{n=1}^{\infty} (0.75W)(0.25)^{n-1}.$$

Find this sum and interpret the result. Then use a graphing calculator to find the number of times it will actually allow you to zoom in. Use the top graph at the right as the original screen.

Original Screen

First Zoom-in

In Exercises 35–42, find the sum (if it has one).

35. $\displaystyle\sum_{n=1}^{5} (2n + 3)$

36. $\displaystyle\sum_{n=0}^{4} (2)^n$

37. $\displaystyle\sum_{n=1}^{6} (5)^n$

38. $\displaystyle\sum_{i=1}^{4} (5i - 2)$

39. $\displaystyle\sum_{n=1}^{6} 4(3)^{n-1}$

40. $\displaystyle\sum_{n=1}^{20} (2)^{n-1}$

41. $\displaystyle\sum_{n=1}^{10} \frac{1}{2}\left(\frac{1}{2}\right)^{n-1}$

42. $\displaystyle\sum_{n=0}^{\infty} 2(3)^n$

43. *College Entrance Exam Sample*   In the figure at the right, ST is tangent to the circle at T. RT is a diameter. If $RS = 12$ and $ST = 8$, what is the area of the circle?
  a. 5π **b.** 8π **c.** 9π **d.** 20π **e.** 40π

44. *College Entrance Exam Sample*   Consider a circle that has the same circumference as the perimeter of a regular hexagon. Each side of the hexagon has a length of 22 inches. Which of the following is the best estimate of the radius of the circle?
  a. 7   **b.** 14   **c.** 21   **d.** 24   **e.** 28

45. *Powers of Ten*   Which best estimates the temperature (in degrees Fahrenheit) of a hot tub?
  a. 1.0×10^0 **b.** 1.0×10^1 **c.** 1.0×10^2 **d.** 1.0×10^3

46. *Powers of Ten*   Which best estimates the diameter (in millimeters) of a high school class ring?
  a. 2.0×10^0 **b.** 2.0×10^1 **c.** 2.0×10^2 **d.** 2.0×10^3

Exploration and Extension

In Exercises 47–50, write the repeated decimal as an infinite series using summation notation. Evaluate the sum and write the sum as the ratio of two integers.

47. 0.11111 . . .

48. 0.4444 . . .

49. 0.363636 . . .

50. 0.212121 . . .

51. You and your friend Lisa begin walking around a $\frac{1}{4}$-mile track. Because Lisa is preparing for a race, she is walking twice as fast as you are. As you start, the two of you are walking side by side. How far will each of you have walked when you are again walking side by side?

12.5

The Binomial Theorem

What you should learn:

Goal 1 How to use the Binomial Theorem to expand a binomial that is raised to a power

Goal 2 How to use the Binomial Theorem in real-life situations

Why you should learn it:

You can use binomial expansions for many real-life problems, such as the probability of a marble rolling into a particular slot of a certain game board.

Goal 1 Using the Binomial Theorem

Recall that a *binomial* is a polynomial that has two terms. In this lesson, you will study a quick method for raising a binomial to a power. To begin, consider the following examples.

$$(x + y)^0 = 1$$
$$(x + y)^1 = x + y$$
$$(x + y)^2 = x^2 + 2xy + y^2$$
$$(x + y)^3 = x^3 + 3x^2y + 3xy^2 + y^3$$
$$(x + y)^4 = x^4 + 4x^3y + 6x^2y^2 + 4xy^3 + y^4$$
$$(x + y)^5 = x^5 + 5x^4y + 10x^3y^2 + 10x^2y^3 + 5xy^4 + y^5$$

For *each* of these expansions, notice the following.

1. $(x + y)^n$ expands to $n + 1$ terms.
2. The first term is x^n and the last term is y^n. Each of these terms has a coefficient of 1.
3. From term to term, the exponents with base x decrease by 1. The exponents with base y increase by 1.
4. The sum of the exponents of each term is n. For instance, in the expansion of $(x + y)^5$, the sum of the exponents of each term is 5.

$$4 + 1 = 5 \qquad 3 + 2 = 5$$
$$(x + y)^5 = x^5 + 5\overbrace{x^4y^1} + 10\overbrace{x^3y^2} + 10x^2y^3 + 5xy^4 + y^5$$

5. The **binomial expansion coefficients** or simply **binomial coefficients** increase and then decrease in a symmetrical pattern. For $(x + y)^5$, the pattern is

$$1 \quad 5 \quad 10 \quad 10 \quad 5 \quad 1.$$

The Binomial Theorem

The binomial expansion of $(x + y)^n$ is

$$(x + y)^n = x^n + nx^{n-1}y + \cdots + \frac{n!}{(n - m)!m!}x^{n-m}y^m + \cdots + nxy^{n-1} + y^n.$$

The coefficient of $x^{n-m}y^m$ is denoted by $\binom{n}{m}$.

Example 1   *Finding Binomial Coefficients*

a. $\begin{pmatrix} 8 \\ 2 \end{pmatrix} = \dfrac{8!}{6!2!} = \dfrac{8 \cdot 7 \cdot 6!}{6! \cdot 2!} = \dfrac{8 \cdot 7}{2 \cdot 1} = 28$

b. $\begin{pmatrix} 10 \\ 3 \end{pmatrix} = \dfrac{10!}{7!3!} = \dfrac{10 \cdot 9 \cdot 8 \cdot 7!}{7! \cdot 3!} = \dfrac{10 \cdot 9 \cdot 8}{3 \cdot 2 \cdot 1} = 120$

c. $\begin{pmatrix} 7 \\ 0 \end{pmatrix} = \dfrac{7!}{7! \cdot 0!} = 1$

d. $\begin{pmatrix} 6 \\ 6 \end{pmatrix} = \dfrac{6!}{0! \cdot 6!} = 1$

Study Tip

When *m* and *n* are not zero, as in parts **a** and **b** in Example 1, the formula for binomial coefficients can be simplified as follows.

$$\begin{pmatrix} 8 \\ 2 \end{pmatrix} = \overset{\text{2 factors}}{\dfrac{8 \cdot 7}{\underset{\text{2 factorial}}{2 \cdot 1}}} = 28$$

$$\begin{pmatrix} 10 \\ 3 \end{pmatrix} = \overset{\text{3 factors}}{\dfrac{10 \cdot 9 \cdot 8}{\underset{\text{3 factorial}}{3 \cdot 2 \cdot 1}}} = 120$$

LESSON INVESTIGATION

■ Investigating Pascal's Triangle

Partner Activity A convenient pattern for writing binomial coefficients is called **Pascal's Triangle,** after the famous French mathematician Blaise Pascal (1623–1662). He was the first to notice that the numbers in this triangle are precisely the same numbers that occur as coefficients in the expansion of $(x + y)^n$ as listed on page 651.

```
              1                    ← Row 0
            1   1                  ← Row 1
          1   2   1                ← Row 2
        1   3   3   1              ← Row 3
      1   4   6   4   1            ← Row 4
    1   5  10  10   5   1          ← Row 5
  1   6  15  20  15   6   1        ← Row 6
1   7  21  35  35  21   7   1      ← Row 7
```

a. With your partner, discuss any patterns you see in the triangle. Write a summary of your discussion.
b. Use your results to write the next two rows of Pascal's Triangle.
c. Find the sum of each of the first six rows of Pascal's Triangle. What is the pattern?

The top row in Pascal's Triangle is **Row 0** because it corresponds to the expansion of $(x + y)^0$. Similarly, the next row is **Row 1,** because it corresponds to the expansion of $(x + y)^1$. In general, **Row *n*** in Pascal's Triangle gives the coefficients of $(x + y)^n$.

Example 2 *Using Pascal's Triangle*

Use Pascal's Triangle to find the following nine binomial coefficients for the expansion of $(x + y)^8$.

$$\binom{8}{0}, \binom{8}{1}, \binom{8}{2}, \binom{8}{3}, \binom{8}{4}, \binom{8}{5}, \binom{8}{6}, \binom{8}{7}, \binom{8}{8}$$

Solution   These nine binomial coefficients represent Row 8 of Pascal's Triangle. Using Row 7 of the triangle, you can calculate the numbers in Row 8, as follows.

Example 3 *Expanding a Binomial Sum*

Expand the binomial $(x + 1)^3$.

Solution   The binomial coefficients in Row 3 of Pascal's Triangle are 1, 3, 3, 1. Therefore, the expansion is as follows.

$$(x + 1)^3 = (1)x^3 + (3)x^2(1) + (3)x(1^2) + (1)(1^3)$$
$$= x^3 + 3x^2 + 3x + 1 \quad \blacksquare$$

In the next examples, notice how any coefficient other than 1 must be raised to a power when writing the expansion.

Example 4 *Expanding a Binomial Difference*

Write the expansion for $(2x - y)^3$.

Solution   The binomial coefficients in Row 4 of Pascal's Triangle are 1, 3, 3, 1. Note the alternating pattern of signs when the binomial is a difference.

$$(2x - y)^3 = (1)(2x)^3 + 3(2x)^2(-y) + 3(2x)(-y)^2 + (1)(-y)^3$$
$$= 8x^3 - 12x^2y + 6xy^2 - y^3 \quad \blacksquare$$

Example 5 *Expanding a Binomial*

Write the expansion for $(x + 3)^4$.

Solution   The binomial coefficients in Row 4 of Pascal's Triangle are 1, 4, 6, 4, 1. Therefore, the expansion is as follows.

$$(x + 3)^4 = (1)x^4 + (4)x^3(3) + (6)x^2(3^2) + (4)x(3^3) + (1)(3^4)$$
$$= x^4 + 12x^3 + 54x^2 + 108x + 81 \quad \blacksquare$$

The model shown at the right is designed to experimentally produce the numbers in Row 7 of Pascal's Triangle. To conduct the experiment, 128 marbles are poured into the funnel at the top. As each marble hits a hexagonal divider, the marble is equally likely to fall to the left or to the right.

Goal 2 Using Binomial Coefficients in Real Life

Connections
Experimental Mathematics

Example 6 *An Experiment Involving Pascal's Triangle*

How many marbles would you expect to fall into the two left-most compartments at the bottom of the apparatus shown above?

Solution Begin by considering how many should fall into the first compartment. Half (or 64) of the 128 marbles that hit hexagon A will fall to the left. Of those, half (or 32) that hit hexagon B will fall to the left. By continuing this pattern, you can conclude that only one marble will fall into the first compartment.

To find the number of marbles that should fall into the second compartment, refer to the second diagram above. The number of marbles falling through each channel is shown in the diagram. From the diagram, you can see that 7 marbles should fall into the second compartment. ∎

Communicating about ALGEBRA

▶ **SHARING IDEAS about the Lesson**

A. Copy the model above. Then use it to show how many marbles should fall into the third compartment. Explain your answer.

B. Use a model to show how many marbles should fall into the fourth compartment.

EXERCISES

Guided Practice

▶ **CRITICAL THINKING about the Lesson**

1. In the expansion of $(x + y)^n$, describe the pattern for the exponents with base x.

2. Describe two methods you could use to expand the binomial $(x + 5)^4$.

3. Identify the binomial coefficients of the expansion of $(x + y)^7$ shown below.

   $$x^7 + 7x^6y + 21x^5y^2 + 35x^4y^3 + 35x^3y^4 + 21x^2y^5 + 7xy^6 + y^7$$

4. Which of the following is equal to $\binom{11}{5}$? Explain.

   a. $\dfrac{11 \cdot 10 \cdot 9 \cdot 8 \cdot 7}{5 \cdot 4 \cdot 3 \cdot 2 \cdot 1}$ **b.** $\dfrac{11 \cdot 10 \cdot 9 \cdot 8 \cdot 7}{6 \cdot 5 \cdot 4 \cdot 3 \cdot 2 \cdot 1}$

5. Which row in Pascal's Triangle is given by the following binomial coefficients?

   $$\binom{6}{0} \quad \binom{6}{1} \quad \binom{6}{2} \quad \binom{6}{3} \quad \binom{6}{4} \quad \binom{6}{5} \quad \binom{6}{6}$$

6. Write the expansions for $(x + 7)^4$ and $(x - 7)^4$. How are they similar? How are they different?

Independent Practice

In Exercises 7–14, evaluate the binomial coefficient.

7. $\binom{5}{2}$ **8.** $\binom{5}{3}$ **9.** $\binom{7}{7}$ **10.** $\binom{8}{6}$

11. $\binom{12}{5}$ **12.** $\binom{12}{0}$ **13.** $\binom{12}{7}$ **14.** $\binom{14}{8}$

In Exercises 15–22, use the Binomial Theorem to expand the binomial.

15. $(a + 2)^3$ **16.** $(x - 5)^4$ **17.** $(x + 2)^4$ **18.** $(2x - 1)^4$

19. $(x - 3)^5$ **20.** $(x - 8)^6$ **21.** $(2x + 1)^6$ **22.** $(x + y)^7$

23. Find the coefficient of x^4 in the expansion of $(x + 2)^8$.

24. Find the coefficient of x^6 in the expansion of $(x - 3)^7$.

In Exercises 25–28, use Pascal's Triangle to find the binomial coefficient.

25. $\binom{3}{2}$ **26.** $\binom{6}{0}$ **27.** $\binom{7}{5}$ **28.** $\binom{9}{9}$

In Exercises 29–36, use Pascal's Triangle to expand the binomial.

29. $(4x - y)^3$ **30.** $(3s + 2)^3$ **31.** $(x + 4)^4$ **32.** $(4t - 1)^4$

33. $(2t - s)^5$ **34.** $(x + 7)^5$ **35.** $(2x + y)^6$ **36.** $(x + 2)^6$

Stacking Cubes   **In Exercises 37–39, use the following information.**

The picture at the right shows the different ways to stack four cubes.

37. Sketch the different ways to stack three cubes.

38. Sketch the different ways to stack five cubes. Describe the pattern in the number of ways to stack three, four, and five cubes.

39. In how many different ways could you stack ten cubes? Explain your reasoning.

40. What is the sum of the numbers in Row n of Pascal's Triangle? Explain.

41. What is the sum of the numbers in rows 0 through 20 of Pascal's Triangle?

42. *Finding a Pattern*   Describe the pattern formed by the sums of the numbers along the diagonal segments (shown at the right) of Pascal's Triangle.

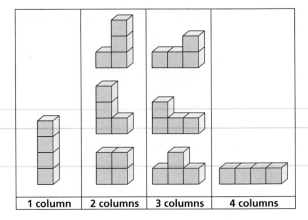

1 column | 2 columns | 3 columns | 4 columns

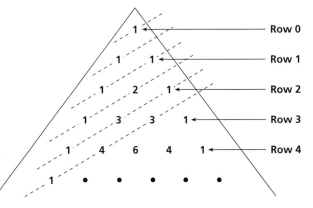

Row 0
Row 1
Row 2
Row 3
Row 4

Integrated Review

In Exercises 43–46, evaluate the expression.

43. $\dfrac{5!}{1! \cdot 4!}$

44. $\dfrac{7!}{4! \cdot 3!}$

45. $\dfrac{9!}{2! \cdot 7!}$

46. $\dfrac{6!}{2! \cdot 4!}$

47. *Wedding Costs*   The average cost of a wedding in 1996 was about $15,000. How much, on the average, was spent on the engagement ring?   *(Source: USA Today)*

48. *Basketball*   What was the percent increase in attendance at Women's NCAA college basketball games from 1990 to 1993?   *(Source: Women's NCAA College Basketball)*

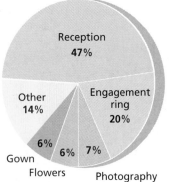

Percent of Wedding Expenses

Reception 47%
Other 14%
Engagement ring 20%
6% Gown
6% Flowers
7% Photography

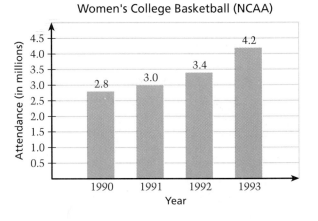

Women's College Basketball (NCAA)

Exploration and Extension

True or False?   In Exercises 49 and 50, decide whether the formula is true or false for all integers *m* and *n* such that $1 \le m \le n$. Explain your reasoning.

49. $\binom{n}{m} = \binom{n}{n-m}$

50. $\binom{n+1}{m} = \binom{n}{m-1} + \binom{n}{m}$

51. *Patterns in Pascal's Triangle*   Use each encircled group of numbers to form a 2×2 matrix. Find the determinant of each matrix. Describe the pattern.

52. *Patterns in Pascal's Triangle*   In the "flowers" below, taken from Pascal's Triangle, fill in the missing numbers. Which rows do the flowers come from?

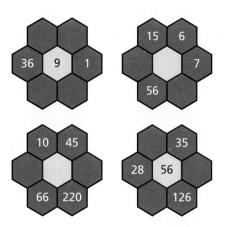

Mixed **REVIEW**

1. Find the inverse of $\begin{bmatrix} 2 & 0 \\ 5 & 1 \end{bmatrix}$. **(4.4)**

2. Evaluate the determinant of $\begin{bmatrix} 4 & -3 \\ 2 & 6 \end{bmatrix}$. **(4.3)**

3. Solve $5x^2 = 245$. **(7.3)**

4. Condense $\log_4 3x - \log_4 y$. **(8.3)**

5. Sketch $y = |3x - 2|$. **(2.6)**

6. Simplify: $\sqrt[3]{27x^3} + 2x$. **(7.4)**

7. Write in exponential form: $\log_4 64 = 3$. **(8.2)**

8. Find the asymptotes of $y = \dfrac{3x^2}{x^2 - 9}$. **(10.1)**

9. Solve $\begin{cases} 5x - 2y = -11 \\ 2x + 5y = -16 \end{cases}$. **(3.2)**

10. Solve $\begin{cases} 3x + 2y - z = -3 \\ 4y + 2z = -12 \\ 5z = 10 \end{cases}$. **(3.6)**

11. Sketch $f(x) = \dfrac{3x + 5}{2x - 3}$. **(10.1)**

12. Multiply: $\dfrac{6x^3 - 18x^2}{x^2 + 5x + 4} \cdot \dfrac{x^2 - 2x - 3}{3x^2 - 9x}$. **(10.3)**

13. Write an equation of the horizontal line through $(-1, 2)$. **(2.2)**

14. Find the focus and directrix of the parabola $x = 8y^2$. **(11.1)**

15. Find the slope of $6x + 2y = 3$. **(2.4)**

16. Sketch $(x + 3)^2 + (y - 4)^2 = 9$. **(11.5)**

17. Classify the conic whose equation is $4x^2 + 24x + y^2 - 4y + 36 = 0$. **(11.5)**

18. Identify the vertices in Exercise 17. **(11.5)**

Exploring Data: The Algebra of Finance

Goal 1   Finding the Balance of an Annuity

In Lesson 7.2, you studied savings plans that involved a *single* deposit. Most people, however, prefer to make several deposits over a long period of time. **Annuities** are savings accounts to which many equal deposits (or withdrawals) are made at regular intervals. Annuities involving equal deposits are **increasing annuities,** and those involving equal withdrawals are **decreasing annuities.** One example of an increasing annuity is a payroll savings plan in which part of an employee's paycheck is deducted each pay period and placed in a savings account.

Example 1   *Constructing an Increasing Annuity Table*

You deposit $50 at the end of each month into a credit union savings plan that pays annual interest of 6%, compounded monthly. What is the balance at the end of six months?

Solution On the last day of the first month, the balance is $50. Then, at the end of the second month, when the second deposit is made, the account will have the following balance.

$$\text{Balance} = \overbrace{50.00}^{\substack{\text{1st} \\ \text{Deposit}}} + \overbrace{\tfrac{1}{12}(0.06)(50.00)}^{\substack{\text{Interest on} \\ \text{1st Deposit}}} + \overbrace{50.00}^{\substack{\text{2nd} \\ \text{Deposit}}} = \$100.25$$

Similarly, at the end of the third month, when the third deposit is made, the balance will be the sum of $100.25 (previous balance), $\tfrac{1}{12}(0.06)(100.25)$ (interest on previous balance), and $50 (new deposit). Continuing, you obtain:

End of Month	Previous Balance	Interest	Deposit	New Balance
1	$ 0.00	$0.00	$50.00	$ 50.00
2	$ 50.00	$0.25	$50.00	$100.25
3	$100.25	$0.50	$50.00	$150.75
4	$150.75	$0.75	$50.00	$201.50
5	$201.50	$1.01	$50.00	$252.51
6	$252.51	$1.26	$50.00	$303.77

The balance after 6 months (and 6 deposits) is $303.77. ∎

Balance of an Increasing Annuity

Consider an increasing annuity with equal periodic deposits of D dollars made n times per year. The annual interest rate is r, and the interest is compounded n times per year. The balance, A, after t years is

$$A = D\left[\frac{(1 + i)^{nt} - 1}{i}\right]$$

where $i = \dfrac{r}{n}$.

For this formula, the total number of deposits is nt. Deposits are made at the *end* of consecutive compounding periods, and the last deposit is made on the last day of the time period (and therefore receives no interest). This type of increasing annuity is called an ordinary *increasing annuity*.

Real Life
Savings

Example 2 · *Finding the Balance of an Increasing Annuity*

You deposit $100 each month into an increasing annuity that pays an annual interest rate of 7.5%, compounded monthly. What is the balance after 40 years? How much of this balance is interest?

Solution   For this increasing annuity, you have $D = 100$, $r = 0.075$, $n = 12$, $i = \frac{0.075}{12} = 0.00625$, and $t = 40$. The balance after 40 years will be

$$A = D\left[\frac{(1 + i)^{nt} - 1}{i}\right]$$

$$= 100\left[\frac{(1 + 0.00625)^{480} - 1}{0.00625}\right]$$

$$= \$302{,}382.22.$$

Since the total amount of money deposited is $480(100) = \$48{,}000$, you can conclude that the total amount of interest earned by the annuity is

$$\text{Interest} = 302{,}382.22 - 48{,}000.00$$
$$= \$254{,}382.22.$$ ■

From Example 2, you can see the primary benefit of a long-term annuity—relatively small deposits can produce very large balances. Because of this, increasing annuities are frequently used as retirement accounts.

Banks take elaborate precautions to safeguard the money and valuables of their customers.

Goal 2 Finding the Deposits Needed

The formula for the balance of an increasing annuity can also be used to determine equal deposits that will produce a given balance.

$$D = A\left[\frac{i}{(1 + i)^{nt} - 1}\right]$$

Real Life

Retirement Planning

Example 3   *How to Save to Become a Millionaire*

What monthly deposits will produce a balance of $1,000,000 after 45 years? Assume that the annual percentage rate is 6.6%, compounded monthly. What is the total amount deposited over the 45-year period?

Solution   Using $A = 1,000,000$, $r = 0.066$, $n = 12$, $i = \frac{0.066}{12} = 0.0055$, and $t = 45$, you can compute the monthly deposit as follows.

$$D = A\left[\frac{i}{(1 + i)^{nt} - 1}\right]$$

$$= 1,000,000\left[\frac{0.0055}{(1 + 0.0055)^{540} - 1}\right]$$

$$= \$299.99$$

The total amount deposited over the 45-year period is

$$540(299.99) = \$161,994.60.$$

The growth of this annuity is shown graphically at the left. ∎

How to Become a Millionaire

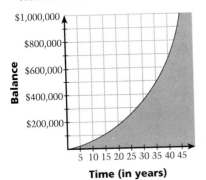

Time (in years)

Communicating about ALGEBRA

▶ **SHARING IDEAS about the Lesson**

The annual interest rate and the length of time can greatly affect the balance of an increasing annuity. Find the following balances.

	Monthly Deposit	Annual Interest	Number of Years
A.	$100	5%	30
B.	$100	8%	30
C.	$200	7.5%	35
D.	$200	7.5%	45

EXERCISES

▶ **CRITICAL THINKING about the Lesson**

1. What is an increasing annuity? Give an example of how an increasing annuity is used.

2. *Savings Plan* You deposit $80 into a savings plan that pays 6% annual interest, compounded monthly. How much interest will your deposit earn in the first month?

3. *Annuity Table* The table below represents an increasing annuity that pays 7.5% annual interest, compounded monthly. Find the missing entries in the table.

End of Month	Previous Balance	Interest	Deposit	New Balance
1	$0.00	$0.00	$100.00	$100.00
2	$100.00	$0.63	$100.00	$200.63
3	$200.63	?	$100.00	?
4	?	$1.89	$100.00	?

4. In an ordinary increasing annuity, when are the monthly deposits made: at the end of the month or at the beginning of the month?

5. Over a 10-year period, you make monthly deposits of $200 into an increasing annuity that pays 6% annual interest, compounded monthly. Identify the values of D, r, n, i, and t.

6. Describe a situation in which you could use the formula

$$D = A\left[\frac{i}{(1 + i)^{nt} - 1}\right].$$

Independent Practice

Constructing an Annuity Table **In Exercises 7–10, construct an annuity table (similar to the one in Exercise 3) showing the deposits and balances for the given savings plan.**

7. At the end of each year for five years, $1000 is invested in an increasing annuity. The annuity pays 8% annual interest, compounded annually.

8. At the end of each quarter for one year, $300 is invested in an increasing annuity. The annuity pays $6\frac{1}{2}\%$ annual interest, compounded quarterly.

9. Twice a year for five years, $500 is invested in an increasing annuity. The annuity pays 6% annual interest, compounded semiannually.

10. At the end of each month for one year, $100 is invested in an increasing annuity. The annuity pays $6\frac{1}{2}\%$ annual interest, compounded monthly.

In Exercises 11–14, find the balance of the increasing annuity.

	Periodic Deposit	Number of Deposits per Year	Number of Years	Annual Interest Rate	Compounding Period
11.	$2000	1	15	12%	Annually
12.	$50	26	2	$6\frac{1}{2}\%$	Biweekly
13.	$40	52	5	6%	Weekly
14.	$75	12	3	$6\frac{1}{2}\%$	Monthly

15. *Saving for College*   The parents of a newborn child decide to deposit $40 a month into a savings account. The account earns 6%, compounded monthly. What is the balance after 15 years?

16. *Saving for a Home*   A newly-married couple are both working and decide to save $1000 a month for a down payment on a home. The account earns $8\frac{1}{2}\%$ annually, compounded monthly. How large a down payment will they have saved in three years? In four years?

17. *Two-Account Savings Plan*   You deposit $30 a month for 20 years into an account that pays 6%, compounded monthly. After 20 years, you leave the money in the account for five more years, but make no more deposits. What is the balance after the 25-year period?

18. *Two-Account Savings Plan*   You deposit $500 a year for 10 years into an account that pays 6.36%, compounded annually. After 10 years, you transfer the money into another account that pays 7%, compounded continuously. The money is left in the second account for eight years. What is the balance after the 18-year period?

19. *Comparing Two Savings Plans*   Which would give you a higher balance in 10 years: monthly deposits of $50 at 10% interest, compounded monthly, or monthly deposits of $80 at 6% interest, compounded monthly?

20. *Comparing Two Savings Plans*   Which would give you a higher balance in 15 years: monthly deposits of $45 at 9% interest, compounded monthly, or monthly deposits of $60 at 5% interest, compounded monthly?

21. *How Much to Deposit?*   How much must be deposited each month into an ordinary annuity paying $7\frac{1}{2}\%$, compounded monthly, to attain a balance of $25,000 after five years?

22. *How Much to Deposit?*   How much must be deposited every other week into an ordinary annuity paying $6\frac{1}{2}\%$, compounded biweekly, to attain a balance of $8000 after three years? (Use 52-week years.)

23. *Comparing Two Savings Plans* You want to save $50,000. Which plan would require a smaller *total* deposit: monthly payments with 5% interest, compounded monthly for 15 years, or monthly payments with $7\frac{1}{2}$% interest, compounded monthly for 10 years?

24. *Comparing Two Savings Plans* You want to save $20,000. Which plan would require a smaller *total* deposit: monthly payments with 8% interest, compounded monthly for 10 years, or monthly payments with 6% interest, compounded monthly for 8 years?

Integrated Review

Retirement Age **In Exercises 25 and 26, use the bar graph at the right, which shows the results of a survey taken in 1991.**

25. What is the ratio of the number of people who said they would retire after age 65 to the number who said they would retire at age 65 or earlier?

26. Of the total number of people who said they would retire at age 65 or earlier, what percent said they would retire at age 54 or earlier?

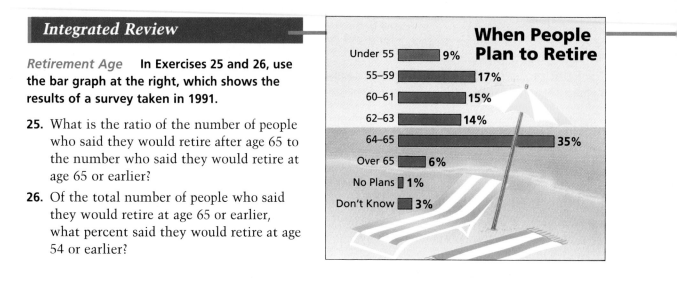

Exploration and Extension

Decreasing Annuity **In Exercises 27 and 28, use the following information.**

A **decreasing annuity** is a savings account that has an initial deposit followed by several equal withdrawals until the account is depleted. A decreasing annuity of n equal withdrawals of W per year for t years is described by the equation

$$W = P\left[\dfrac{i}{1 - \left(\dfrac{1}{1+i}\right)^{nt}}\right]$$

where P is the initial deposit and r is the annual interest rate and $i = \frac{r}{n}$.

27. Your grandparents deposit $50,000 in an account for you to use during college. The account pays $7\frac{1}{2}$% annual interest and is set up to send you equal monthly withdrawals for five years. How much will be sent to you each month? How much will be sent over the five-year period? How much interest will the account have earned?

28. Your grandparents have just retired. They have a balance of $500,000 in an increasing annuity. How much can they withdraw each month in a decreasing annuity that pays 8% annual interest if they plan to deplete the account over a 30-year period?

A programmable calculator can be programmed to calculate the balance of an increasing annuity. To do this, you can program the calculator so that it accepts four inputs.

D = Periodic deposit

r = Annual interest rate

n = Number of deposits (and compoundings) per year

t = Number of years

After these amounts are input, the program can calculate and display the value of A, which is the balance in the annuity after t years. This balance is given by

$$A = D\left[\frac{(1 + i)^{nt} - 1}{i}\right]$$

where $i = \frac{r}{n}$.

Example 1: Finding the Balance of an Increasing Annuity

Complete a table that compares the balances for 30-year increasing annuities in which the annual interest rates are 5%, 6%, 7%, 8%, 9%, and 10%, all compounded monthly. Use monthly deposits of $50, $100, and $200.

Solution

Monthly Deposit	$50.00	$100.00	$200.00
Balance at 5%	$41,612.93	$83,225.86	$166,451.73
Balance at 6%	$50,225.75	$100,451.50	$200,903.01
Balance at 7%	$60,998.55	$121,997.10	$243,994.20
Balance at 8%	$74,517.97	$149,035.94	$298,071.89
Balance at 9%	$91,537.17	$183,074.35	$366,148.70
Balance at 10%	$113,024.40	$226,048.79	$452,097.58

From the table, you can see that for a given interest rate, the balance varies directly with the monthly deposit. For instance, at a 5% interest rate, you can double your balance by doubling your monthly deposit.

From the table, you can also see that for a given monthly deposit, the balance *does not* vary directly with the annual interest rate. For instance, for a given monthly deposit, the balance at 10%, is more than twice the balance at 5%. ■

Example 2: Sketching a Graph of the Balance

Use a graphing calculator to sketch a graph that shows the balance in a 30-year increasing annuity. Use a monthly deposit of $50 and an annual interest rate of 6%, compounded monthly. How does the balance after 15 years compare to the balance after 30 years? Is it half?

Solution For this increasing annuity, the monthly deposit is $D = 50$, the annual interest rate is $r = 0.06$, and the number of compoundings per year is $n = 12$. This implies that $i = 0.005$. To show how the balance, A, increases over time, t, you can sketch the graph of the function

$$A = D\left[\frac{(1 + i)^{nt} - 1}{i}\right] = 50\left[\frac{(1.005)^{12t} - 1}{0.005}\right].$$

The graph is shown at the right. From the graph, you can see that the balance after 15 years is not nearly half of the balance after 30 years. In fact, after 15 years, the annuity has built up a balance that is only about 29% of the 30-year balance. ■

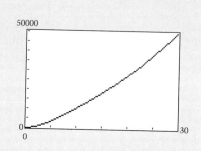

Exercises

In Exercises 1 and 2, use a programmable calculator to complete the table.

1. *20-Year Increasing Annuity*

Monthly Deposit	$50	$100	$200
Balance at 6%	?	?	?
Balance at 8%	?	?	?
Balance at 10%	?	?	?

2. *40-Year Increasing Annuity*

Monthly Deposit	$50	$100	$200
Balance at 6%	?	?	?
Balance at 8%	?	?	?
Balance at 10%	?	?	?

3. *Finding the Periodic Deposit*   Write a program (for a programmable calculator or a computer) that will calculate the periodic deposit that is required to produce a given balance in an increasing annuity.

Finding the Monthly Deposit   **In Exercises 4–6, use the program from Exercise 3 to find the monthly deposit required to produce the balance.**

4. Balance: $100,000
Term: 15 years
Annual interest: 6%
Compounded monthly

5. Balance: $10,000
Term: 5 years
Annual interest: 8%
Compounded monthly

6. Balance: $25,000
Term: 10 years
Annual Interest: 7%
Compounded monthly

7. Use a graphing calculator to sketch a graph that shows the balance in a 40-year increasing annuity. Use a monthly deposit of $100 and an annual interest rate of 8%, compounded monthly. What percent of the balance has accrued after 20 years?

Chapter Summary

What did you learn?

Skills

1. Use summation notation to write a series. **(12.1)**
2. Write a formula for the nth term
   - of an arithmetic sequence. **(12.2)**
   - of a geometric sequence. **(12.3)**
3. Find the sum of a series. **(12.1)**
   - Find the sum of a finite arithmetic series. **(12.2)**
   - Find the sum of a finite geometric series. **(12.3)**
   - Find the sum of an infinite geometric series. **(12.4)**
4. Find binomial coefficients. **(12.5)**
5. Expand a binomial
   - using the Binomial Theorem. **(12.5)**
   - using Pascal's Triangle. **(12.5)**

Strategies

6. Use sequences to solve real-life problems. **(12.2–12.3)**
7. Use series to solve real-life problems. **(12.1–12.4)**

Exploring Data

8. Solve increasing annuity problems. **(12.6)**

Why did you learn it?

Many real-life problems can be modeled with sequences. Often these sequences form patterns that enable you to write a formula for the nth term of the sequence. For instance, suppose your property tax was $2000 in 1991. If your tax increased by 5% each year for 10 years, then a formula for the tax during the nth year would be $a_n = 2000(1.05)^{n-1}$. Because this sequence is geometric, you could find the total property tax paid during the 10 years by using the formula for the sum of a geometric series.

How does it fit into the bigger picture of algebra?

In this chapter, you studied *sequences* of numbers such as

$$2, 5, 8, 11, 14, \ldots \quad \text{and} \quad 2, 4, 8, 16, 32, \ldots .$$

The first of these is an arithmetic sequence, and the second is a geometric sequence. The expression formed by adding the terms in a sequence is the series associated with a sequence. All finite series have a sum, and some infinite series have a sum.

In the chapter, you also studied the Binomial Theorem. This theorem describes patterns for the coefficients of the terms in the expansion of a binomial that is raised to a power.

In Exercises 1–8, write the first five terms of the sequence. Begin with $n = 1$.

1. $a_n = 6 - 2n$

2. $a_n = 10n - n^2$

3. $a_n = \dfrac{10}{n!}$

4. $a_n = \dfrac{n!}{10}$

5. $a_n = (-0.2)^{n-1}$

6. $a_n = \left(-\dfrac{1}{4}\right)^n$

7. $a_n = n^2 + 5$

8. $a_n = (n + 1)^3$

In Exercises 9–12, find the sum.

9. $\displaystyle\sum_{i=0}^{4} (i! + 2)$

10. $\displaystyle\sum_{n=5}^{8} n(2n - 1)$

11. $\displaystyle\sum_{n=1}^{25} n^2$

12. $\displaystyle\sum_{i=1}^{12} i$

In Exercises 13–18, decide whether the sequence is arithmetic, geometric, or neither. If the sequence is arithmetic, state its common difference. If the sequence is geometric, state its common ratio.

13. $22, 28, 34, 40, 46, \ldots$

14. $\dfrac{1}{10}, \dfrac{1}{5}, \dfrac{3}{5}, \dfrac{12}{5}, 12, \ldots$

15. $1, \dfrac{1}{2}, 0, -\dfrac{1}{2}, -1, \ldots$

16. $\dfrac{1}{2}, 2, 8, 32, 128, \ldots$

17. $1, 1, 2, 6, 24, \ldots$

18. $3, \dfrac{11}{3}, \dfrac{13}{3}, 5, \dfrac{17}{3}, \ldots$

19. Write a formula for the nth term of the arithmetic sequence whose common difference is 5 and whose first term is 13.

20. Write the first five terms of the arithmetic sequence whose common difference is 14 and whose third term is 36.

In Exercises 21–26, use sigma notation to write the arithmetic series. Then find the sum of the series.

21. $1 + 7 + 13 + 19 + 25 + 31 + 37$

22. $4 + 6 + 8 + 10 + 12 + 14 + 16$

23. $22 + 16 + 10 + 4 - 2 - 8 - 14 - 20$

24. $\dfrac{3}{2} + 2 + \dfrac{5}{2} + 3 + \dfrac{7}{2} + 4 + \dfrac{9}{2} + 5$

25. $\dfrac{1}{3} + \dfrac{2}{3} + 1 + \dfrac{4}{3} + \dfrac{5}{3} + 2 + \dfrac{7}{3} + \dfrac{8}{3}$

26. $-\dfrac{3}{8} + 0 + \dfrac{3}{8} + \dfrac{3}{4} + \dfrac{9}{8} + \dfrac{3}{2} + \dfrac{15}{8} + \dfrac{9}{4}$

27. Write a formula for the nth term of the geometric sequence whose common ratio is 6 and whose first term is $\dfrac{1}{4}$.

28. Write the first five terms of the geometric sequence whose common ratio is 3 and whose first term is 2.

In Exercises 29–40, find the sum of the series.

29. $\displaystyle\sum_{i=1}^{20} 16(4)^{i-1}$

30. $\displaystyle\sum_{n=1}^{10} \dfrac{1}{2}(3)^{n-1}$

31. $\displaystyle\sum_{n=0}^{15} 6\left(-\dfrac{1}{4}\right)^n$

32. $\displaystyle\sum_{n=0}^{12} 10\left(\dfrac{1}{2}\right)^n$

33. $\displaystyle\sum_{n=1}^{9} \dfrac{1}{10}(2)^{n-1}$

34. $\displaystyle\sum_{i=1}^{20} 2(-2)^{i-1}$

35. $\displaystyle\sum_{i=1}^{\infty} 2\left(\dfrac{3}{5}\right)^{i-1}$

36. $\displaystyle\sum_{i=0}^{\infty} 15\left(\dfrac{2}{9}\right)^i$

37. $\displaystyle\sum_{n=1}^{\infty} 4(-0.2)^{n-1}$

38. $\displaystyle\sum_{n=0}^{\infty} 8(0.15)^n$

39. $\displaystyle\sum_{i=0}^{\infty} 1.4(0.8)^i$

40. $\displaystyle\sum_{i=1}^{\infty} 25(0.5)^{i-1}$

In Exercises 41–44, evaluate the binomial coefficient.

41. $\binom{9}{2}$

42. $\binom{12}{3}$

43. $\binom{11}{11}$

44. $\binom{6}{0}$

In Exercises 45–52, expand the binomial.

45. $(x + 4)^3$

46. $(x + 10)^4$

47. $(x + y)^5$

48. $(y + 3)^6$

49. $(y - 1)^7$

50. $(x + 2)^8$

51. $(x + 2y)^3$

52. $(2x + y)^4$

Annuity Table   In Exercises 53 and 54, construct an annuity table showing interest earned, deposits, and balances for the first six months of the savings plan.

53. You deposit $50 at the end of each month in an increasing annuity that pays 8% annual interest, compounded monthly.

54. You deposit $85 at the end of each month in an increasing annuity that pays 6.5% annual interest, compounded monthly.

55. *Monthly Deposits*   An increasing annuity pays 7.5% annual interest, compounded monthly. What monthly deposits will produce a $5000 balance in 10 years?

56. *Comparing Two Savings Plans*   You want to build a balance of $10,000 in an increasing annuity. Find the monthly deposits for the following plans.
a. A 16-year annuity that earns 6% annual interest, compounded monthly
b. A 14-year annuity that earns 8% annual interest, compounded monthly

Cell Division   In Exercises 57 and 58, use the following information.

In early embryological growth, a human cell divides into two cells, each of which divides into two cells, and so on. The number, a_n, of *new* cells formed after the nth division is $a_n = 2^{n-1}$.

57. Use summation notation to write the series that represents the total number of cells after eight divisions.

58. Find the sum of the series in Exercise 57.

Fibonacci Sequence   In Exercises 59 and 60, use the Golden Ratio, which is $\frac{1}{2}(1 + \sqrt{5})$.

59. Write the first 10 terms of the Fibonacci sequence. Then calculate the ratios of a_{n+1} to a_n for these terms. What do you notice?

60. Calculate the sum:

$$\sum_{n=1}^{10} \left[\frac{1}{2}(1 + \sqrt{5}) \right]^{n-1}.$$

Is it greater than the sum of the first 10 Fibonacci numbers?

61. *Stack of Cannonballs*   The stack of cannonballs shown below is part of a monument in Gettysburg National Park in Gettysburg, Pennsylvania. The stack has the shape of a pyramid with a square base. How many cannonballs are in the stack?

62. *Bouncing Ball*   A bouncing ball is dropped from a height of 10 feet. Each time the ball hits the ground, it bounces to three-fifths of its previous height. Find the total *vertical* distance traveled by the bouncing ball before it comes to rest.

63. *Turntable*   The first second after the power is turned off, a turntable makes 0.8 revolution. Each second after that, the turntable makes $\frac{4}{5}$ as much of a revolution as it did the second before. After a total of 15 seconds, the turntable stops. How many revolutions did it make?

64. *Triangular Numbers*   The nth triangular number is $\frac{1}{2}(n)(n + 1)$ (see page 326). What is the relationship between the triangular numbers and the arithmetic sequence whose nth term is n? The triangular numbers occur as two diagonal rows in Pascal's Triangle. Which diagonal rows are they?

Multiples of Integers   In Exercises 65–67, each of the triangles represents the Rows 0 through 31 of Pascal's Triangle. In one of the triangles, the blue hexagons represent multiples of 2, in another, they represent multiples of 3 and in the other, multiples of 4. Identify the triangles.

65.

66.

67.

68. Using Exercises 65–67 as models, create the Pascal's Triangle pattern for multiples of 5.

Find the Treasure!   **In Exercises 69–71, your goal is to move from the circle marked *Start* to the circle on the bottom. To make each move, you must find the sum of the series and move to the circle represented by the sum. *Only one of the three paths leads to the treasure!* Which path is it?**

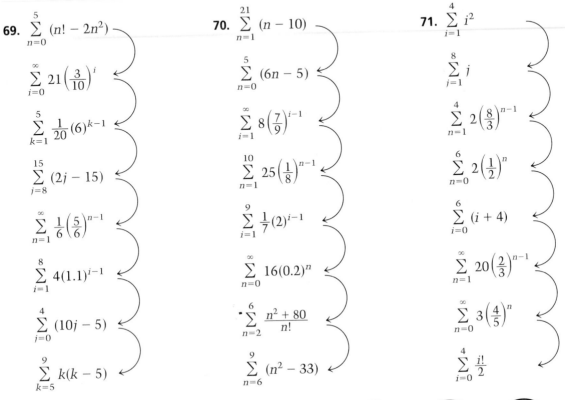

69. $\displaystyle\sum_{n=0}^{5} (n! - 2n^2)$

$\displaystyle\sum_{i=0}^{\infty} 21\left(\frac{3}{10}\right)^i$

$\displaystyle\sum_{k=1}^{5} \frac{1}{20}(6)^{k-1}$

$\displaystyle\sum_{j=8}^{15} (2j - 15)$

$\displaystyle\sum_{n=1}^{\infty} \frac{1}{6}\left(\frac{5}{6}\right)^{n-1}$

$\displaystyle\sum_{i=1}^{8} 4(1.1)^{i-1}$

$\displaystyle\sum_{j=0}^{4} (10j - 5)$

$\displaystyle\sum_{k=5}^{9} k(k - 5)$

70. $\displaystyle\sum_{n=1}^{21} (n - 10)$

$\displaystyle\sum_{n=0}^{5} (6n - 5)$

$\displaystyle\sum_{i=1}^{\infty} 8\left(\frac{7}{9}\right)^{i-1}$

$\displaystyle\sum_{n=1}^{10} 25\left(\frac{1}{8}\right)^{n-1}$

$\displaystyle\sum_{i=1}^{9} \frac{1}{7}(2)^{i-1}$

$\displaystyle\sum_{n=0}^{\infty} 16(0.2)^n$

$\displaystyle\sum_{n=2}^{6} \frac{n^2 + 80}{n!}$

$\displaystyle\sum_{n=6}^{9} (n^2 - 33)$

71. $\displaystyle\sum_{i=1}^{4} i^2$

$\displaystyle\sum_{j=1}^{8} j$

$\displaystyle\sum_{n=1}^{4} 2\left(\frac{8}{3}\right)^{n-1}$

$\displaystyle\sum_{n=0}^{6} 2\left(\frac{1}{2}\right)^n$

$\displaystyle\sum_{i=0}^{6} (i + 4)$

$\displaystyle\sum_{n=1}^{\infty} 20\left(\frac{2}{3}\right)^{n-1}$

$\displaystyle\sum_{n=0}^{\infty} 3\left(\frac{4}{5}\right)^n$

$\displaystyle\sum_{i=0}^{4} \frac{i!}{2}$

72. *How Much Treasure?*   The amount of the treasure is the larger of the following amounts. Which amount is it?
   a. Each month for 100 years, $10 was deposited in an increasing annuity that earned 8% annual interest, compounded monthly.
   b. The sum of all of the numbers in Row 0 through Row 9 of Pascal's Triangle is multiplied by $1000.

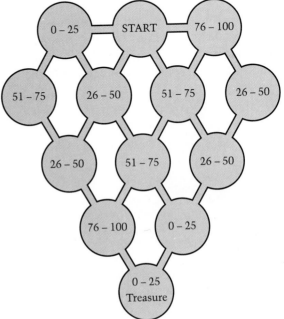

In Exercises 1 and 2, write the formula for the *n*th term of the sequence.

1. $\frac{1}{2}, 2, \frac{7}{2}, 5, \frac{13}{2}, \ldots$

2. $3.6, 3.24, 2.916, 2.6244, 2.36196, \ldots$

In Exercises 3–10, find the sum.

3. $\sum_{i=1}^{3} \frac{i!}{i^2}$

4. $\sum_{n=1}^{5} (2n + 3)$

5. $\sum_{i=1}^{10} i$

6. $\sum_{i=1}^{14} i^2$

7. $\sum_{n=1}^{20} (-4n + 6)$

8. $\sum_{i=0}^{11} (1.5)^i$

9. $\sum_{n=1}^{\infty} \frac{1}{4}\left(\frac{1}{2}\right)^{n-1}$

10. $\sum_{n=1}^{\infty} 5(-0.75)^{n-1}$

In Exercises 11–14, evaluate the binomial coefficient.

11. $\binom{4}{3}$

12. $\binom{10}{8}$

13. $\binom{9}{4}$

14. $\binom{15}{0}$

In Exercises 15–18, use the Binomial Theorem to expand the binomial.

15. $(2x + 3y)^4$

16. $(s + 3t)^3$

17. $(x - 6)^5$

18. $(x - 2y)^2$

In Exercises 19–22, use Pascal's Triangle to expand the binomial.

19. $(2r + 4)^6$

20. $(s + 2t)^3$

21. $(2x - y)^3$

22. $(y - 2)^7$

23. Complete the table below for an increasing annuity that pays 6% annual interest compounded quarterly.

End of Quarter	Previous Balance	Interest	Deposit	New Balance
1	$0.00	$0.00	$250.00	$250.00
2	$250.00	$3.75	$250.00	$503.75
3	$503.75	?	$250.00	?
4	?	$11.42	$250.00	?

24. Which savings plan has a higher balance after 20 years: monthly deposits of $35 at 5% interest compounded monthly, or quarterly deposits of $100 at 6% interest compounded quarterly?

25. For 1985 through 1990 the amount, a_n (in millions of dollars), of food and drink sales at hotel and motel restaurants can be modeled by $a_n = 10,688.1(1.072)^n$ where $n = 0$ represents 1985. Use the model to approximate the total food and drink sales for 1985 through 1990. *(Source: National Restaurant Association)*

26. You release a yo-yo attached to a string whose length is 3 feet. With no further movement of your hand, the yo-yo returns $\frac{4}{5}$ of the way up the string. If this pattern continues, what is the total vertical distance the yo-yo travels before coming to a stop?

In Exercises 1–4, match the function with its graph.

1. $f(x) = \dfrac{-2}{x^2 + 2}$

2. $f(x) = \dfrac{3x}{x^2 - 2x + 1}$

3. $f(x) = \dfrac{x + 6}{x - 3}$

4. $f(x) = \dfrac{6}{4 - x}$

a.

b.

c.

d.

In Exercises 5 and 6, the variables x and y vary inversely. Use the given values to find an equation that relates the variables.

5. $x = 6$, $y = 12$

6. $x = 2$, $y = 11$

In Exercises 7 and 8, the variable z varies jointly with the product of x and y. Use the given values to find an equation that relates the variables.

7. $z = 4$, $x = 2$, $y = 3$

8. $z = 3$, $x = 12$, $y = 7$

In Exercises 9–14, perform the operations and simplify.

9. $\dfrac{3x^2 y}{x - 2} \cdot \dfrac{x^2 + x - 6}{3x - 6} \div (x^2 - 4)$

10. $\dfrac{x - 1}{x^3 + 5x^2 - 6x} \div \dfrac{x^2 - 36}{x + 3} \cdot \dfrac{x^2}{x + 3}$

11. $-3\left(\dfrac{x}{x + 4} + \dfrac{6x}{x^2 - 16}\right) + \dfrac{5}{x - 4}$

12. $\dfrac{x + 2}{x^2 - 6x + 5} - \dfrac{3x}{x - 1} + \dfrac{4}{x + 5}$

13. $\dfrac{\left(\dfrac{6}{x} + \dfrac{3x}{x + 4}\right)}{\left(\dfrac{x + 1}{x - 4} + \dfrac{x - 2}{x + 4}\right)}$

14. $\dfrac{\left(\dfrac{x - 1}{2} - \dfrac{4 - x}{2x}\right)}{\left(\dfrac{6}{x + 3} + \dfrac{3}{x}\right)}$

In Exercises 15–18, match the equation with its graph.

15. $(x + 2)^2 + (y - 4)^2 = 1$

16. $(y + 3)^2 = -4(x + 1)$

17. $\dfrac{(x - 1)^2}{4} + (y + 2)^2 = 1$

18. $\dfrac{(x - 3)^2}{9} - \dfrac{(y - 1)^2}{4} = 1$

a.

b.

c.

d.

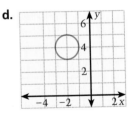

In Exercises 19–26, classify the conic. Write the equation in standard form and then sketch its graph.

19. $x^2 - 4y^2 - 2x - 8y - 7 = 0$

20. $9x^2 + 4y^2 - 18x + 24y + 9 = 0$

21. $x^2 - 6x - 4y + 13 = 0$

22. $x^2 + y^2 - 8x + 15 = 0$

23. $9x^2 + 16y^2 + 36x + 64y - 44 = 0$

24. $y^2 + 8x + 2y + 17 = 0$

25. $x^2 + y^2 + 4x - 2y - 4 = 0$

26. $-9x^2 + y^2 + 36x - 45 = 0$

In Exercises 27–30, find the points of intersection of the graphs.

27. $-9x^2 + 4y^2 + 18x - 45 = 0$
$x^2 + y^2 - 2x - 8 = 0$

28. $x^2 - y^2 - 2x + 2y = 0$
$4x^2 + y^2 - 8x = 0$

29. $9x^2 + 25y^2 + 36x - 200y + 211 = 0$
$x^2 + y^2 + 4x - 8y + 11 = 0$

30. $36x^2 - y^2 + 216x + 4y + 284 = 0$
$2x^2 + 12x + y + 14 = 0$

In Exercises 31–34, write the first five terms of the sequence. Begin with $n = 1$.

31. $a_n = 2n^2 + 3$

32. $a_n = (-1)^n \cdot \dfrac{1}{n}$

33. $a_n = n^3 - n^2$

34. $a_n = \dfrac{1}{4}(n!)$

In Exercises 35–42, evaluate the sum.

35. $\displaystyle\sum_{i=1}^{10} (4i + 2)$

36. $\displaystyle\sum_{n=1}^{20} (10n - 5)$

37. $\displaystyle\sum_{n=1}^{13} n^2$

38. $\displaystyle\sum_{i=1}^{14} i$

39. $\displaystyle\sum_{i=1}^{10} 6\left(\dfrac{1}{3}\right)^{i-1}$

40. $\displaystyle\sum_{n=0}^{12} \left(-\dfrac{3}{4}\right)^n$

41. $\displaystyle\sum_{n=1}^{\infty} 4(0.2)^{n-1}$

42. $\displaystyle\sum_{i=0}^{\infty} 3\left(-\dfrac{1}{5}\right)^i$

43. Write a formula for the nth term of the arithmetic sequence whose common difference is 7 and whose third term is 25.

44. Write a formula for the nth term of the geometric sequence whose common ratio is 4 and whose fourth term is 64.

In Exercises 45–48, evaluate the binomial coefficient.

45. $\dbinom{4}{2}$

46. $\dbinom{3}{1}$

47. $\dbinom{5}{0}$

48. $\dbinom{14}{12}$

49. Expand the binomials: $(2x + 3)^3$, $(x - y)^5$.

In Exercises 50 and 51, find the ratio of the area of the blue region to the total area. Write your result in simplified form.

50.

51.

The number, M, of memberships for the Mountain Top Ski Club for 1980 through 1992 can be modeled by

$$M = \frac{100(3 + 2t)}{3 + 0.5t}$$

where $t = 0$ represents 1980. The cost, C, of a membership can be modeled by

$$C = \frac{225 + 262.5t}{3 + 2t}.$$

52. Write a model for the total amount, A, received in membership fees.

53. Approximate the amount the club received in 1987 from membership fees.

Suzanne's Savings Plan   **In Exercises 54 and 55, use the following information.**

Your friend, Suzanne, wants to buy a car. Her parents agree, *if* for one month she can follow a savings plan they have designed. On the first day, Suzanne must save $0.01. The second day, she must save $0.02, the third day $0.04, and so forth for 30 days.

54. Write a geometric series that represents the amount Suzanne would save in 30 days if she followed the savings plan.

55. Do you think Suzanne can follow her parents' plan? Explain.

Your Savings Plan   **In Exercises 56–59, use the following information.**

You decide to save $25 per month in an increasing annuity that pays an annual interest rate of 6%, compounded monthly.

56. Copy and complete the following table showing the balances and earned interest during the first six months of the annuity.

End of Month	Previous Balance	Interest	Deposit	New Balance
1	$0.00	$0.00	$25.00	$25.00
2	?	?	$25.00	?
3	?	?	$25.00	?
4	?	?	$25.00	?
5	?	?	$25.00	?
6	?	?	$25.00	?

57. What is the balance of your account after two years?

58. What monthly deposit would produce an amount of $1000 after two years?

59. After three years, you have saved enough for the down payment on a car. To purchase the car, however, you need to take out a 3-year loan of $4000 at 11% annual interest. What are your monthly payments? Find the total interest you will pay over the life of the loan.

Solar Oven   **In Exercises 60 and 61, use the following information.**

Located in the Pyrenees mountains of France, the Odieollo Solar Oven can produce temperatures up to 6870°F. Sixty-three flat mirrors, called heliostats, track the sun and reflect its light waves onto the central parabolic mirror, which is composed of 9500 smaller mirrors. The central mirror focuses the light into a small region on the tower that houses the furnace. The resulting solar radiation on the tower is up to 12,000 times more powerful than normal solar radiation.

60. A cross-section of the parabolic mirror can be modeled by $y^2 = 322x$ where x and y are measured in feet. What is the distance between the surface of the mirror and the focus?

61. The surface area, S (in square inches), of each of the heliostats can be found by solving the equation

$$\frac{30{,}240}{S} = \sum_{n=1}^{63} n.$$

What is the surface area of each heliostat?

Galaxies   **In Exercises 62 and 63, use the following information.**

In the 1920's, Edwin P. Hubble classified the galaxies known at that time according to their structural formation: spiral, irregular, or elliptical. Elliptical galaxies contain mostly dying stars. Below are graphs of the structural form of three elliptical galaxies.

62. Write an equation for each of the graphs.

63. Which galaxy has the greatest eccentricity?

a.

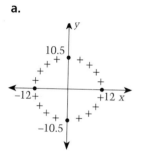

The galaxy NGC4486 is in the Virgo cluster.

b.

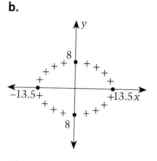

The galaxy NGC147 is in the constellation Cassiopeia.

c.

The galaxy NGC205 is in the constellation Andromeda.

LESSONS

13.1 Right Triangle
Trigonometry ▪ 678

13.2 Angles of Rotation
and Radian
Measure ▪ 685

13.3 Evaluating
Trigonometric
Functions ▪ 693

13.4 Inverse
Trigonometric
Functions ▪ 703

13.5 The Law of
Sines ▪ 709

13.6 The Law of
Cosines ▪ 716

*Molikpaq, a state-of-the-art oil
drilling platform, lies in Alaska's Beaufort Sea, just inside the
Arctic Circle.*

The Arctic Circle has a latitude of 66.55 North, which means that an angle between the equator and the Arctic Circle is 66.55°. Trigonometry can be used to find the circumference of the Arctic Circle. Using Earth's radius as 3960 miles, the radius of the Arctic Circle can be shown to be

3960 cos 66.55° ≈ 1576 miles.

From this, you can determine the circumference of the Arctic Circle to be $2\pi(1576) \approx$ 9902 miles.

13.1

Right Triangle Trigonometry

What you should learn:

Goal 1 How to use trigonometric relationships to evaluate the trigonometric functions of acute angles

Goal 2 How to use trigonometric functions to solve real-life problems

Why you should learn it:

You can use trigonometric functions to solve many real-life problems, such as finding the height of a mountain.

Goal 1 Using Trigonometric Relationships

As derived from the Greek language, the word **trigonometry** means "measurement of triangles." To begin our study of trigonometry, consider a right triangle, one of whose acute angles is θ (the Greek letter *theta*). The three sides of the right triangle are the **hypotenuse,** the **opposite side** (the side opposite the angle θ), and the **adjacent side** (the side adjacent to the angle θ).

Using these three sides, you can form the six **trigonometric functions: sine, cosine, tangent, cosecant, secant,** and **cotangent** (abbreviated as sin, cos, tan, csc, sec, and cot, respectively).

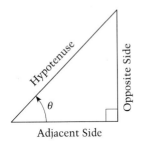

Adjacent Side

Right Triangle Definition of Trigonometric Functions

Let θ be an *acute* angle of a right triangle.

$$\sin \theta = \frac{\text{opp}}{\text{hyp}} \quad \cos \theta = \frac{\text{adj}}{\text{hyp}} \quad \tan \theta = \frac{\text{opp}}{\text{adj}}$$

$$\csc \theta = \frac{\text{hyp}}{\text{opp}} \quad \sec \theta = \frac{\text{hyp}}{\text{adj}} \quad \cot \theta = \frac{\text{adj}}{\text{opp}}$$

The abbreviations *opp, adj,* and *hyp* represent the lengths of the three sides of the right triangle. Note that the ratios in the second row are the *reciprocals* of the ratios in the first row.

Example 1 *Evaluating Trigonometric Functions*

Evaluate the six trigonometric functions of the angle θ shown in the right triangle at the left.

Solution From the Pythagorean Theorem, the length of the hypotenuse is $\sqrt{4^2 + 3^2} = \sqrt{25} = 5$. Using adj = 3, opp = 4, and hyp = 5, you can write the following statements.

$$\sin \theta = \frac{\text{opp}}{\text{hyp}} = \frac{4}{5} \quad \cos \theta = \frac{\text{adj}}{\text{hyp}} = \frac{3}{5} \quad \tan \theta = \frac{\text{opp}}{\text{adj}} = \frac{4}{3}$$

$$\csc \theta = \frac{\text{hyp}}{\text{opp}} = \frac{5}{4} \quad \sec \theta = \frac{\text{hyp}}{\text{adj}} = \frac{5}{3} \quad \cot \theta = \frac{\text{adj}}{\text{opp}} = \frac{3}{4} \quad \blacksquare$$

Example 2   *Evaluating Trig Functions of 45°*

Evaluate sin 45°, cos 45°, and tan 45°.

Solution   Sketch a right triangle having 45° as one of its acute angles. All such triangles are similar. Thus to make the calculations simple, you can choose 1 as the length of the adjacent side. Because the triangle is isosceles, the length of the opposite side is also 1. From the Pythagorean Theorem, the length of the hypotenuse is $\sqrt{1^2 + 1^2} = \sqrt{2}$. Thus you can write the following.

$$\sin 45° = \frac{\text{opp}}{\text{hyp}} = \frac{1}{\sqrt{2}} = \frac{\sqrt{2}}{2} \approx 0.707$$

$$\cos 45° = \frac{\text{adj}}{\text{hyp}} = \frac{1}{\sqrt{2}} = \frac{\sqrt{2}}{2} \approx 0.707$$

$$\tan 45° = \frac{\text{opp}}{\text{adj}} = \frac{1}{1} = 1 \qquad \blacksquare$$

Example 3   *Evaluating Trig Functions of 30° and 60°*

Use the equilateral triangle shown at the left to help you evaluate sin 60°, cos 60°, sin 30°, and cos 30°.

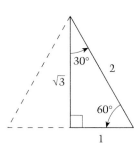

Solution   Try using the Pythagorean Theorem and the equilateral triangle (with sides of length 2) to verify the lengths of the sides given in the figure. For $\theta = 60°$, the length of the adjacent side is 1, the length of the opposite side is $\sqrt{3}$, and the length of the hypotenuse is 2. Thus

$$\sin 60° = \frac{\text{opp}}{\text{hyp}} = \frac{\sqrt{3}}{2} \approx 0.866 \qquad \text{and} \qquad \cos 60° = \frac{\text{adj}}{\text{hyp}} = \frac{1}{2}.$$

For $\theta = 30°$, the length of the adjacent side is $\sqrt{3}$, the length of the opposite side is 1, and the length of the hypotenuse is 2. Thus

$$\sin 30° = \frac{\text{opp}}{\text{hyp}} = \frac{1}{2} \qquad \text{and} \qquad \cos 30° = \frac{\text{adj}}{\text{hyp}} = \frac{\sqrt{3}}{2} \approx 0.866. \qquad \blacksquare$$

Because the angles 30°, 45°, and 60° occur frequently in trigonometry, you should learn to sketch the triangles shown in Examples 2 and 3. The values of the sines, cosines, and tangents of these common angles are summarized below.

$$\sin 30° = \frac{1}{2} \qquad \cos 30° = \frac{\sqrt{3}}{2} \qquad \tan 30° = \frac{\sqrt{3}}{3}$$

$$\sin 45° = \frac{\sqrt{2}}{2} \qquad \cos 45° = \frac{\sqrt{2}}{2} \qquad \tan 45° = 1$$

$$\sin 60° = \frac{\sqrt{3}}{2} \qquad \cos 60° = \frac{1}{2} \qquad \tan 60° = \sqrt{3}$$

Relationships between trigonometric functions are called **trigonometric identities.**

Fundamental Trigonometric Identities

Reciprocal

$$\sin \theta = \frac{1}{\csc \theta} \qquad \cos \theta = \frac{1}{\sec \theta} \qquad \tan \theta = \frac{1}{\cot \theta}$$

$$\csc \theta = \frac{1}{\sin \theta} \qquad \sec \theta = \frac{1}{\cos \theta} \qquad \cot \theta = \frac{1}{\tan \theta}$$

Tangent and Cotangent   **Pythagorean**

$$\tan \theta = \frac{\sin \theta}{\cos \theta} \qquad\qquad \sin^2 \theta + \cos^2 \theta = 1$$
$$1 + \tan^2 \theta = \sec^2 \theta$$
$$\cot \theta = \frac{\cos \theta}{\sin \theta} \qquad\qquad 1 + \cot^2 \theta = \csc^2 \theta$$

Note that $\sin^2 \theta$ is used to represent $(\sin \theta)^2$.

Example 4   *Using Trigonometric Identities*

Let θ be the acute angle such that $\sin \theta = 0.6$. Find $\cos \theta$.

Solution   To find the value of $\cos \theta$, use the Pythagorean Identity that relates the sine and cosine of an angle.

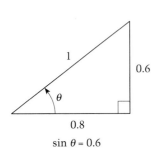

sin θ = 0.6

$\sin^2 \theta + \cos^2 \theta = 1$	*Pythagorean Identity*
$(0.6)^2 + \cos^2 \theta = 1$	*Substitute 0.6 for sin θ.*
$\cos^2 \theta = 1 - (0.6)^2 = 0.64$	
$\cos \theta = \sqrt{0.64} = 0.8$	

Note that you choose the positive square root because the cosine of an acute angle is positive. ∎

A calculator can be used to obtain decimal approximations of the values of trigonometric functions. When doing this, *be sure to set the calculator to the correct mode:* degrees or radians. For instance, using a calculator set to degree mode, you can approximate the value of cos 20° to be 0.940.

Most calculators do not have keys for cosecant, secant, or cotangent. To evaluate these, use the reciprocal key $\boxed{1/x}$ or $\boxed{x^{-1}}$ and the appropriate reciprocal identity. For instance,

$$\sec 20° = \frac{1}{\cos 20°} \approx 1.064.$$

Mt. Everest is in two countries, Nepal and Tibet. Its height first was determined in the Great Trigonometric Survey of India (1849–1850). Modern techniques have verified that the results of the 1850 calculations were correct to within several feet.

Goal 2 Using Trigonometric Functions in Real Life

Connections
Topography

Example 5 *Determining the Height of a Mountain*

You are at an elevation of 25,740 feet. Your position is below the peak of Mt. Everest. Using surveying instruments, you measure the *angle of elevation* to the peak to be 20.5°. The distance between you and the peak is 9388 feet. What is the elevation of the peak?

Solution Using the right triangle at the left, let *a* represent the difference in elevations of the peak and your position.

$$\sin \theta = \frac{\text{opp}}{\text{hyp}} \quad \textit{Definition of sine function}$$

$$\sin 20.5° = \frac{a}{9388} \quad \textit{Let } \theta = 20.5° \textit{ and hyp} = 9388.$$

$$(\sin 20.5°)(9388) = a \quad \textit{Multiply both sides by 9388.}$$

$$3288 \approx a \quad \textit{Use a calculator.}$$

Since your elevation is 25,740 feet, the elevation of the peak is 25,740 + 3288 = 29,028 feet. This elevation, established in 1954, is only 26 feet more than that established in 1850. ∎

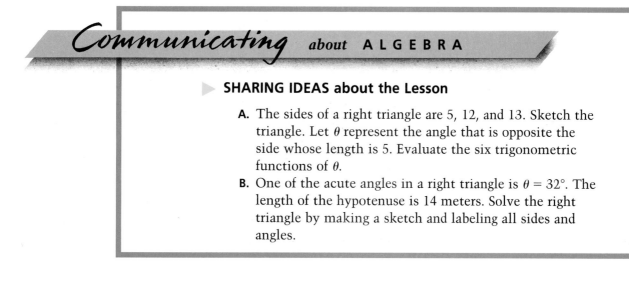

Communicating about ALGEBRA

▷ **SHARING IDEAS about the Lesson**

A. The sides of a right triangle are 5, 12, and 13. Sketch the triangle. Let θ represent the angle that is opposite the side whose length is 5. Evaluate the six trigonometric functions of θ.

B. One of the acute angles in a right triangle is $\theta = 32°$. The length of the hypotenuse is 14 meters. Solve the right triangle by making a sketch and labeling all sides and angles.

EXERCISES

▶ **CRITICAL THINKING about the Lesson**

1. State the full name and the abbreviation of each of the six trigonometric functions.

2. Evaluate the six trigonometric functions of the angle θ in the triangle at the right.

3. Consider a right triangle that has θ as one of its acute angles. The length of the adjacent side is 2, and the tangent of θ is $\frac{1}{4}$. What is the length of the opposite side? What is the length of the hypotenuse?

4. For which acute angle θ is $\cos \theta = \frac{1}{2}$?

5. You are given $\cos \theta = 0.55$, where θ is an acute angle. Explain how to find $\sin \theta$.

6. Use a calculator to approximate the value of $\sec 32°$ to three decimal places.

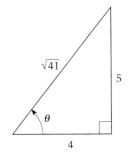

Independent Practice

In Exercises 7–14, evaluate the six trigonometric functions of θ.

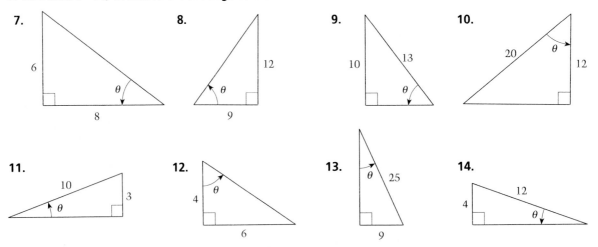

7.

8.

9.

10.

11.

12.

13.

14.

In Exercises 15–22, sketch a right triangle that has θ as one of its acute angles. Then find the values of the five trigonometric functions that are not given.

15. $\sin \theta = \frac{2}{3}$

16. $\cot \theta = 5$

17. $\sec \theta = 2$

18. $\cos \theta = \frac{5}{7}$

19. $\tan \theta = 3$

20. $\csc \theta = \frac{17}{4}$

21. $\cot \theta = \frac{3}{2}$

22. $\sin \theta = \frac{3}{8}$

In Exercises 23–30, evaluate the trigonometric function *without* using a calculator.

23. sec 45°   **24.** sec 30°   **25.** csc 60°   **26.** csc 45°

27. cot 45°   **28.** csc 30°   **29.** cot 60°   **30.** sec 60°

31. Given $\sin \theta = \frac{1}{2}$, find $\cos \theta$.   **32.** Given $\tan \theta = \sqrt{3}$, find $\sin \theta$.

33. Given $\cos \theta = \frac{1}{9}$, find $\sec \theta$.   **34.** Given $\cot \theta = 3$, find $\tan \theta$.

35. Given $\cos \theta = \frac{1}{2}$, find $\cot \theta$.   **36.** Given $\sin \theta = \frac{4}{5}$, find $\cot \theta$.

37. Given $\sin \theta = \frac{1}{3}$, find $\sec \theta$.   **38.** Given $\tan \theta = \frac{1}{3}$, find $\cos \theta$.

39. Given $\cot \theta = \frac{4}{3}$, find $\sin \theta$.   **40.** Given $\sec \theta = 5$, find $\sin \theta$.

In Exercises 41–55, use a calculator to approximate the value of the trigonometric function. Round your result to three decimal places.

41. sin 10°   **42.** csc 80°   **43.** tan 73°

44. cos 29°   **45.** cot 48°   **46.** sec 16°

47. cos 8°   **48.** tan 66°   **49.** sec 31°

50. cot 39°   **51.** csc 50°   **52.** sin 52°

53. sec 62°   **54.** cot 25°   **55.** csc 2°

56. *The Corinth Canal*   The tugboat in the photograph is pulling a ship through the Corinth Canal, which is located near the city of Corinth in southern Greece. Between the points where the two tow lines are fastened to the ship, the ship is 50 feet wide. The angle between the tow lines is 22°. Approximate the length of the tow lines.

The Corinth Canal links the Aegean and Ionian Seas. The canal is 4 miles long and has an average depth of 190 feet.

57. *Grouse Mountain*   The Grouse Mountain ski slope in Avon, Colorado, rises at an angle of about 25.2°. How long is the ski slope?

Grouse Mountain is a ski slope at Beaver Creek in Avon, Colorado. The vertical height of the slope is 1808 feet. Beaver Creek Ski Resort is only ten miles from Vail Ski Resort. Between the two resorts, skiers have a choice of 31 ski lifts and 178 trails.

Duquesne Incline   **In Exercises 58 and 59, use the following information.**

The Duquesne Incline, built in Pittsburgh in 1877, transports people up and down the side of a mountain in cable cars. The original cable cars are still in use, each holding about 20 people. The track is 800 feet long. The top of the incline is 400 feet above the base.

58. What is the angle of inclination of the Duquesne Incline?

59. What is the slope of the track?

Integrated Review

In Exercises 60–63, find the length of the unlabeled side of the triangle.

60.   4   8

61.   3   9

62. $2\sqrt{5}$ 2

63.   10 $5\sqrt{5}$

64. *College Entrance Exam Sample*   Use the diagram to determine the relationship between the lengths of sides AC and AB.
   a. $AC < AB$ **b.** $AC = AB$
   c. $AC > AB$

65. *College Entrance Exam Sample*   The lengths of the sides of five triangles are given. Which is *not* a right triangle?
   a. 5, 12, 13   **b.** 3, 4, 5   **c.** 8, 15, 17
   d. 9, 40, 41   **e.** 12, 15, 18

Exploration and Extension

True or False?   **In Exercises 66–73, decide whether the statement is true or false. Explain your reasoning.**

66. $\sin 60° \csc 60° = 1$

67. $\sec 30° = \csc 60°$

68. $\sin 45° + \cos 45° = 1$

69. $\dfrac{\sin 60°}{\sin 30°} = \sin 2°$

70. $\tan[(0.8)^2] = \tan^2(0.8)$

71. $\tan \theta \csc \theta = \sec \theta$

72. $\cot \theta \sec \theta \sin \theta = 1$

73. $\csc \theta \sec \theta = \tan \theta$

13.2

Angles of Rotation and Radian Measure

What you should learn:

Goal 1 How to measure angles in standard position using degree measure and radian measure

Goal 2 How to use radian measure in real-life problems

Why you should learn it:

You will use radian measure for angles in most courses in science, engineering, and advanced mathematics.

Goal 1 Angles in Standard Position

In Lesson 13.1, the angle θ was always an acute angle—an angle whose measure was between 0° and 90°. In this lesson, you will study *angles of rotation*, whose measures can be any real number. Then, in Lesson 13.3, you will learn how to evaluate trigonometric functions of these angles.

An **angle of rotation** is determined by rotating a ray about its endpoint, or **vertex.** The starting position of the ray is the **initial side** of the angle. The position after rotation is the **terminal side.** In **standard position,** the vertex of the angle in the coordinate plane is at the origin, and the initial side is the positive x-axis.

Because *angles* and *angles of rotation* can be distinguished by how they are used, from now on we will refer to an angle of either type as simply an angle.

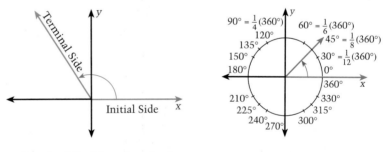

Standard Position of an Angle   **Degree Measure**

The **measure of an angle** is determined by the amount of rotation from the initial side to the terminal side. A measure of **one degree (1°)** is equivalent to $\frac{1}{360}$ of a full revolution. To measure angles, it is convenient to mark degrees on a circle whose center is the origin. A full revolution (counterclockwise) corresponds to 360°, a half revolution to 180°, a quarter revolution to 90°, and so on.

The measure of an **acute** angle is between 0° and 90°. The measure of an **obtuse** angle is between 90° and 180°. **Positive angles** are generated by counterclockwise rotation, and **negative angles** by clockwise rotation.

Coterminal Angles

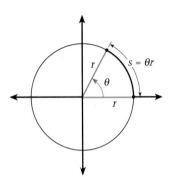

If s = r, then θ = 1 radian.

Two angles are **coterminal** if they have the same initial and terminal sides. For instance, the angles 30° and 390° (shown at the left) are coterminal, as are the angles 240° and −120° (a clockwise rotation of 120°). Coterminal angles have different measures, such as 240° and −120°, but describe the same angle.

The second way to measure angles is in terms of radians. To define a radian, consider a circle of radius r whose center is the origin. One **radian** is the measure of an angle θ whose terminal side intercepts an arc of length r. The *radian measure* of θ, the arc length s, and the radius r are related by the equation $s = \theta r$.

Radian measure of common angles

Two positive angles are **complementary** if the sum of their measures is $\frac{\pi}{2}$ radians (or 90°). Two positive angles are **supplementary** if the sum of their measures is π radians (or 180°).

Example 1 *Complementary, Supplementary, and Coterminal Angles*

a. The complement of $\theta = \frac{\pi}{12}$ is

$\frac{\pi}{2} - \frac{\pi}{12} = \frac{6\pi}{12} - \frac{\pi}{12} = \frac{5\pi}{12}$. (See diagram **a.** below.)

b. The supplement of $\theta = \frac{5\pi}{6}$ is

$\pi - \frac{5\pi}{6} = \frac{6\pi}{6} - \frac{5\pi}{6} = \frac{\pi}{6}$. (See diagram **b.** below.)

c. In radian measure, a coterminal angle is found by adding or subtracting 2π. For $\theta = \frac{17\pi}{6}$, you can find a coterminal angle by subtracting 2π to obtain

$\frac{17\pi}{6} - 2\pi = \frac{17\pi}{6} - \frac{12\pi}{6} = \frac{5\pi}{6}$.

Thus $\frac{17\pi}{6}$ and $\frac{5\pi}{6}$ are coterminal.

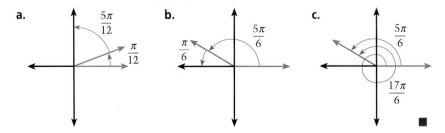

Degree measure and radian measure are related by the equation $360° = 2\pi$ radians, or

$$180° = \pi \text{ radians}.$$

From the latter equation, you can obtain the following conversions between degree and radian measure.

Conversions Between Degrees and Radians

1. To rewrite degrees as radians, multiply by $\dfrac{\pi \text{ radians}}{180°}$.

2. To rewrite radians as degrees, multiply by $\dfrac{180°}{\pi \text{ radians}}$.

Note: When no units of angle measure are specified, *radian measure is implied.* For instance, $\theta = 2$ means $\theta = 2$ radians.

To apply either of these two conversion rules, you simply need to remember the basic relationship $180° = \pi$ radians.

Example 2 *Rewriting Degrees as Radians*

a. $135° = (135 \text{ degrees})\left(\dfrac{\pi \text{ radians}}{180 \text{ degrees}}\right) = \dfrac{3\pi}{4} \text{ radians}$

b. $540° = (540 \text{ degrees})\left(\dfrac{\pi \text{ radians}}{180 \text{ degrees}}\right) = 3\pi \text{ radians}$

c. $-270° = (-270 \text{ degrees})\left(\dfrac{\pi \text{ radians}}{180 \text{ degrees}}\right) = -\dfrac{3\pi}{2} \text{ radians}$

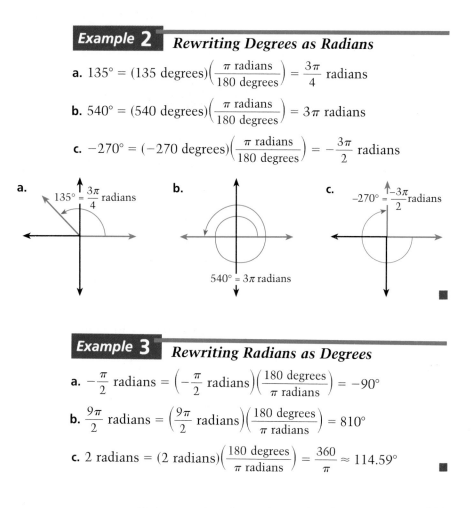

a. $135° = \dfrac{3\pi}{4}$ radians

b. $540° = 3\pi$ radians

c. $-270° = \dfrac{-3\pi}{2}$ radians

Example 3 *Rewriting Radians as Degrees*

a. $-\dfrac{\pi}{2} \text{ radians} = \left(-\dfrac{\pi}{2} \text{ radians}\right)\left(\dfrac{180 \text{ degrees}}{\pi \text{ radians}}\right) = -90°$

b. $\dfrac{9\pi}{2} \text{ radians} = \left(\dfrac{9\pi}{2} \text{ radians}\right)\left(\dfrac{180 \text{ degrees}}{\pi \text{ radians}}\right) = 810°$

c. $2 \text{ radians} = (2 \text{ radians})\left(\dfrac{180 \text{ degrees}}{\pi \text{ radians}}\right) = \dfrac{360}{\pi} \approx 114.59°$

The Seattle Space Needle was built in 1962 for the Seattle World's Fair. The restaurant at the top of the needle is circular, with a radius of 40 feet. The dining part of the restaurant (by the windows) revolves, making one complete revolution per hour.

Goal 2 Using Radian Measure in Real Life

Example 4   *Finding an Angle and Arc Length*

You go to dinner with your family at the Seattle Space Needle. At 6:42 P.M., you take a seat at a window table. You finish dinner at 8:18 P.M. Through what angle did your position rotate during your stay? How many feet did your position revolve?

Solution   You spent a total of 96 minutes at dinner. Because the Space Needle makes one revolution every 60 minutes, your angle of rotation was $\theta = \frac{96}{60}(2\pi) \approx \frac{16}{5}\pi$ radians. Because the radius of the restaurant is 40 feet, your position moved through an arc length of $s = \theta r = \frac{16}{5}\pi (40) \approx 402$ feet.

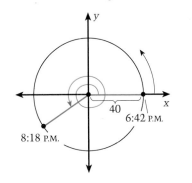

Communicating about ALGEBRA

▶ **SHARING IDEAS about the Lesson**

Match the degree angle measure (**A–D**) with its radian angle measure (**E–H**). Then match the measure with the angle (**I–L**).

A. $20°$ **B.** $420°$ **C.** $-60°$ **D.** $-320°$

E. $-\frac{\pi}{3}$ **F.** $\frac{\pi}{9}$ **G.** $\frac{7\pi}{3}$ **H.** $-\frac{16\pi}{9}$

I.   **J.**   **K.**   **L.**

EXERCISES

▶ **CRITICAL THINKING about the Lesson**

1. What are the locations of the vertex and the initial side of an angle that is in standard position?

2. Match the angle θ with its terminal side.

   a. $\theta = \frac{\pi}{2}$ **b.** $\theta = \pi$ **c.** $\theta = \frac{3\pi}{2}$ **d.** $\theta = 2\pi$

   A. Positive x-axis   **B.** Positive y-axis   **C.** Negative x-axis

   D. Negative y-axis

3. Find two angles, one with positive measure and the other with negative measure, that are coterminal with the angle 60°.

4. A circle has a radius of r. What is the length of the arc corresponding to a central angle of π radians?

5. Find the supplement of $\theta = \frac{\pi}{4}$.

6. Rewrite $\dfrac{3\pi}{2}$ radians as degrees.

Independent Practice

In Exercises 7–14, decide whether the angles are coterminal.

7. 30°, 390°
   8. 30°, −390°
   9. 280°, 640°
   10. 35°, −335°

11. $\dfrac{\pi}{3}, -\dfrac{5\pi}{3}$
   12. $-\dfrac{11\pi}{6}, \dfrac{13\pi}{6}$
   13. $\dfrac{3\pi}{4}, -\dfrac{13\pi}{4}$
   14. $\dfrac{2\pi}{3}, -\dfrac{5\pi}{6}$

In Exercises 15–22, find the complement of the angle.

15. 30°
   16. 45°
   17. 52°
   18. 4°

19. $\dfrac{2\pi}{9}$
   20. $\dfrac{5\pi}{12}$
   21. $\dfrac{\pi}{6}$
   22. $\dfrac{2\pi}{5}$

In Exercises 23–30, find the supplement of the angle.

23. 100°
   24. 150°
   25. 24°
   26. 36°

27. $\dfrac{2\pi}{9}$
   28. $\dfrac{4\pi}{5}$
   29. $\dfrac{\pi}{3}$
   30. $\dfrac{3\pi}{16}$

In Exercises 31–38, find two angles, one with positive measure and the other with negative measure, that are coterminal with the given angle.

31. 50°
   32. 210°
   33. 420°
   34. 840°

35. $\dfrac{13\pi}{3}$
   36. $\dfrac{17\pi}{4}$
   37. $\dfrac{24\pi}{7}$
   38. $\dfrac{26\pi}{3}$

In Exercises 39–46, rewrite the degree measure as radians.

39. 20°
   40. 225°
   41. 150°
   42. 45°

43. −110°
   44. 315°
   45. 320°
   46. 190°

In Exercises 47–54, rewrite the radian measure as degrees.

47. $\frac{5\pi}{3}$

48. $-\frac{3\pi}{2}$

49. $\frac{\pi}{10}$

50. $\frac{\pi}{12}$

51. $\frac{7\pi}{15}$

52. $\frac{9\pi}{2}$

53. $-\frac{7\pi}{6}$

54. $\frac{8\pi}{5}$

In Exercises 55–62, match the measure with the angle.

55. $\frac{5\pi}{4}$

56. $460°$

57. $\frac{7\pi}{3}$

58. $-\frac{13\pi}{3}$

a. **b.** **c.** **d.**

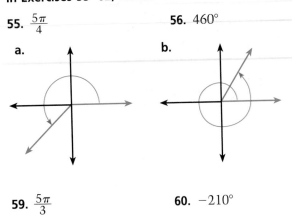

59. $\frac{5\pi}{3}$

60. $-210°$

61. $150°$

62. $-\frac{\pi}{2}$

e. **f.** **g.** **h.**

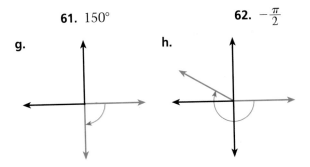

63. *Fire Truck Ladder*   For the ladder on a fire truck to operate properly, the base of the ladder must be almost level. The diagram at the right shows part of a leveling device that is used to determine whether the ladder's base is level enough—the ball of mercury must be within the allowable range. Find the length of the arc that describes the allowable range.

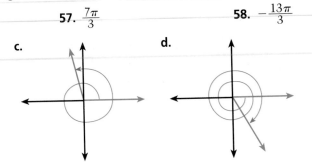

Top View

7 inches

Allowable Range

$\frac{\pi}{8}$

Mercury Ball

64. *Rotating a Bridge*   A rotating bridge is on an island in the middle of a river. Six circular gears, each with a $2\frac{1}{2}$-foot diameter, are attached to the underside of the bridge. As the gears revolve, they roll around the circumference of a stationary circular plate on the island. The circular plate has a diameter of 40 feet. How many revolutions must each of the smaller gears make to rotate the bridge 90°?

90°

Spiral Stairs　**In Exercises 65 and 66, use the following information.**

The freestanding spiral stairs at the right have 13 steps, including the top landing step. Each "pie-shaped" step has a radius of 36 inches and has a central angle of $\frac{\pi}{7}$.

65. What is the arc length of the outer edge of each step?

66. Through what angle would you turn by climbing the stairs? Assume that you start on the ground floor and end on the top landing step.

Integrated Review

67. Complete the table.

θ	$\frac{\pi}{6}$	$\frac{\pi}{4}$	$\frac{\pi}{3}$
$\sin\theta$	?	?	?
$\cos\theta$	?	?	?
$\tan\theta$	?	?	?

68. Complete the table.

θ	$\frac{\pi}{6}$	$\frac{\pi}{4}$	$\frac{\pi}{3}$
$\csc\theta$	?	?	?
$\sec\theta$	?	?	?
$\cot\theta$	?	?	?

69. *Powers of Ten*　Which best estimates the distance (in feet) traveled by a bicycle tire that makes 10 revolutions?
　　a. 6.5×10^{-1}　　**b.** 6.5×10^{0}　　**c.** 6.5×10^{1}　　**d.** 6.5×10^{2}

70. *Powers of Ten*　Which best estimates the angle (in radians) through which Earth rotates on its axis in a week?
　　a. 4.4×10^{0}　　**b.** 4.4×10^{1}　　**c.** 4.4×10^{2}　　**d.** 4.4×10^{3}

Exploration and Extension

71. *Geometry*　Find the angle θ.

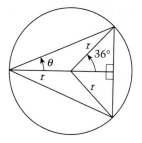

72. *Geometry*　Explain how the result of Exercise 71 can be used to find the angle measure of a point on the star below.

1. Solve $|x + 2| \geq 7$. **(1.7)**

2. Evaluate $\left(\frac{1}{6}\right)^y$ when $y = 4$. **(1.2)**

3. Sketch $y = 3|x - 2| + 4$. **(2.6)**

4. Solve $3x^2 + 8x + 9 = 0$. **(5.4)**

5. Evaluate the determinant: $\begin{vmatrix} 6 & -10 \\ 14 & 12 \end{vmatrix}$.
   (4.3)

6. Solve $\begin{cases} 3x + \frac{1}{4}y = 5 \\ \frac{1}{4}x - 6y = -\frac{93}{8}. \end{cases}$ **(3.2)**

7. Find the median: 12, 3, 9, 14, 27, 36. **(6.7)**

8. Simplify: $3 \log_5 10 + 7 \log_5 4$. **(8.3)**

9. Divide: $x^4 - 256$ by $x + 4$. **(9.4)**

10. Solve $\log_2 x = 6$. **(8.2)**

11. Factor $x^3 + 2x^2 - x - 2$. **(9.3)**

12. Evaluate $\binom{6}{4}$. **(12.5)**

13. Evaluate $\sum\limits_{n=1}^{5} (3n + 2)$. **(12.1)**

14. Solve $\frac{3x}{16} - \frac{3}{2} = -\frac{24}{x}$. **(10.4)**

15. Sketch $(x - 4)^2 + (y + 2)^2 = 4$. **(11.5)**

16. Name the conic: $4x^2 + 9y^2 = 36$. **(11.3)**

17. Write an equation: x and y vary inversely when $x = 6$ and $y = \frac{1}{2}$. **(10.2)**

18. Write an equation for the line through the point $(4, -3)$ with a slope of 0. **(2.2)**

19. Is the inverse of $f(x) = 3x^2 + 2x + 1$ a function? **(6.3)**

20. For $f(1) = 6$ and $f(n + 1) = f(n) + 3n$, find $f(4)$. **(6.6)**

Career Interview

Dermatologist

Michael Bigby is a dermatologist. Dr. Bigby spends 80% of his time on research related to the skin and divides his remaining time teaching resident dermatologists and treating patients.

Q: *What is the focus of your research?*

A: I study T-lymphocytes, which are a group of white blood cells, and their effects on skin diseases, such as poison ivy.

Q: *Does having a math background help you on the job?*

A: It's a tremendous help in my work. The application of math is basic to data collection. My research involves different measurements and calculations. For example, measuring the amount of light absorbed in a solution, or counting cells in a special volume.

Q: *How much of your work is done by computers?*

A: In the technology of research, everything is computerized from counters to spectrophotometers to scanners. Easily 90% of the actual math is done by computers.

Q: *Does this mean you do not need to understand math?*

A: The opposite! You have to understand the math if you want to know what to do with the computers and how to work with the numbers.

13.3

Evaluating Trigonometric Functions

What you should learn:

Goal 1 How to evaluate trigonometric functions of any angle

Goal 2 How to use trigonometric functions to solve real-life problems

Why you should learn it:

You can model many real-life problems with trigonometric functions, such as the horizontal distance that a projectile travels.

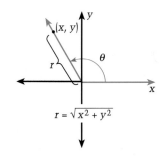

$r = \sqrt{x^2 + y^2}$

Goal 1 Evaluating Functions of Any Angle

In Lesson 13.1, you learned how to evaluate trigonometric functions of an acute angle. In this lesson, you will learn how to evaluate trigonometric functions of *any* angle.

> **Evaluating Trigonometric Functions**
>
> Let θ be an angle in standard position with any point (x, y) (except the origin) on the terminal side of θ. Let $r = \sqrt{x^2 + y^2}$.
>
> $$\sin \theta = \frac{y}{r} \qquad \cos \theta = \frac{x}{r} \qquad \tan \theta = \frac{y}{x}, \quad x \neq 0$$
>
> $$\csc \theta = \frac{r}{y}, \quad y \neq 0 \qquad \sec \theta = \frac{r}{x}, \quad x \neq 0 \qquad \cot \theta = \frac{x}{y}, \quad y \neq 0$$
>
> For acute angles, these definitions give the same values as those given by the definitions in Lesson 13.1.

Because $r = \sqrt{x^2 + y^2}$ cannot be zero, the sine and cosine functions are defined for any angle θ. If $x = 0$, the tangent and secant of θ are undefined. For example, the tangent of 90° $\left(\text{or } \frac{\pi}{2}\right)$ is undefined. Similarly, if $y = 0$, the cotangent and cosecant of θ are undefined.

Example 1 *Evaluating Trigonometric Functions*

Let $(-3, 4)$ be a point on the terminal side of θ. Find the sine, cosine, and tangent of θ.

Solution Using $x = -3$ and $y = 4$, you can determine that

$$r = \sqrt{x^2 + y^2} = \sqrt{(-3)^2 + 4^2} = \sqrt{25} = 5.$$

From these values of x, y, and r, you can write the following.

$$\sin \theta = \frac{y}{r} = \frac{4}{5}$$

$$\cos \theta = \frac{x}{r} = \frac{-3}{5} = -\frac{3}{5}$$

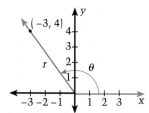

$$\tan \theta = \frac{y}{x} = \frac{4}{-3} = -\frac{4}{3}$$

The values of the trigonometric functions of angles greater than 90° (or less than 0°) can be determined from their values at corresponding acute angles called **reference angles.**

> **The Reference Angle of an Angle**
>
> Let θ be an angle in standard position. Its **reference angle** is the acute angle θ' (read *theta prime*) formed by the terminal side of θ and the *x*-axis.

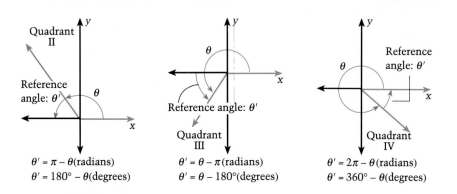

$\theta' = \pi - \theta$(radians)
$\theta' = 180° - \theta$(degrees)

$\theta' = \theta - \pi$(radians)
$\theta' = \theta - 180°$(degrees)

$\theta' = 2\pi - \theta$(radians)
$\theta' = 360° - \theta$(degrees)

Example 2   *Finding Reference Angles*

Find the reference angle θ' for each of the following.

a. $\theta = 300°$ **b.** $\theta = -\dfrac{3\pi}{4}$ **c.** $\theta = 2.3$

Solution

a. Because $\theta = 300°$ lies in Quadrant IV, the reference angle is

$$\theta' = 360° - 300° = 60°.$$

b. First determine that $\theta = -\dfrac{3\pi}{4}$ is coterminal with $\dfrac{5\pi}{4}$, which lies in Quadrant III. The reference angle is

$$\theta' = \frac{5\pi}{4} - \pi = \frac{\pi}{4}.$$

c. Because $\theta = 2.3$ lies between $\dfrac{\pi}{2} \approx 1.57$ and $\pi \approx 3.14$, it follows that θ is in Quadrant II. The reference angle is

$$\theta' = \pi - 2.3 \approx 0.8416.$$

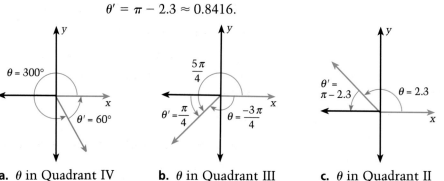

a. θ in Quadrant IV   **b.** θ in Quadrant III   **c.** θ in Quadrant II

The *signs* of the trigonometric function values in the four quadrants can be determined from the definitions of the functions. For instance, because $\cos\theta = \frac{x}{r}$, it follows that $\cos\theta$ is positive wherever $x > 0$, which is in Quadrants I and IV. (Remember, r is always positive.)

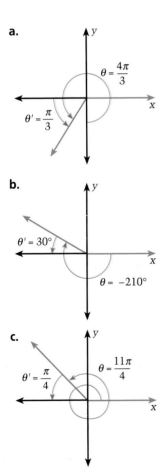

Quadrant II	Quadrant I
$\sin\theta$: +	$\sin\theta$: +
$\cos\theta$: −	$\cos\theta$: +
$\tan\theta$: −	$\tan\theta$: +

Quadrant III	Quadrant IV
$\sin\theta$: −	$\sin\theta$: −
$\cos\theta$: −	$\cos\theta$: +
$\tan\theta$: +	$\tan\theta$: −

Quadrant Signs

Evaluating Trigonometric Functions of Any Angle

Use the following steps to evaluate a trigonometric function of any angle θ.

1. Find the reference angle θ'.
2. Evaluate the trigonometric function for the angle θ'.
3. Use the quadrant in which θ lies to determine the sign of the trigonometric function of θ.

Example 3 *Evaluating Trigonometric Functions of Any Angle*

Evaluate the following.

a. $\cos\frac{4\pi}{3}$ **b.** $\tan(-210°)$ **c.** $\csc\frac{11\pi}{4}$

Solution

a. Because $\theta = \frac{4\pi}{3}$ lies in Quadrant III, the reference angle is

$$\theta' = \frac{4\pi}{3} - \pi = \frac{\pi}{3}.$$

The cosine is negative in Quadrant III, so you can write

$$\cos\frac{4\pi}{3} = -\cos\frac{\pi}{3} = -\frac{1}{2}.$$

b. Because $-210° + 360° = 150°$, it follows that $-210°$ is coterminal with the second-quadrant angle $150°$. The reference angle is

$$\theta' = 180° - 150° = 30°.$$

The tangent is negative in Quadrant II, so you can write

$$\tan(-210°) = -\tan 30° = -\frac{\sqrt{3}}{3}.$$

c. Because $\frac{11\pi}{4} - 2\pi = \frac{3\pi}{4}$, it follows that $\frac{11\pi}{4}$ is coterminal with the second-quadrant angle $\frac{3\pi}{4}$. Therefore, the reference angle is

$$\theta' = \pi - \frac{3\pi}{4} = \frac{\pi}{4}.$$

The cosecant is positive in Quadrant II, so you can write

$$\csc\frac{11\pi}{4} = +\csc\frac{\pi}{4} = \sqrt{2}.$$

The horizontal distance, d (in feet), traveled by a projectile that is launched from ground level with an initial speed, v (in feet per second), is given by

$$d = \frac{v^2}{32} \sin 2\theta$$ *where θ is the angle at which the projectile is launched.*

Goal 2 Using Trig Functions in Real Life

Real Life
Baseball

Example 4 *Finding How Far a Projectile Travels*

You are at bat and hit the baseball so that it has an initial velocity of 100 feet per second. Approximately how far will the ball travel horizontally for the following angles of elevation?

a. 40°   **b.** 45°   **c.** 50°

Solution

a. For θ = 40°, the distance traveled horizontally is

$d = \frac{100^2}{32} \sin(2 \cdot 40°)$ *Substitute 100 for v and 40° for θ.*

$= 312.5 \sin 80°$ *Simplify.*

≈ 307.75 feet.   *Use a calculator.*

b. For θ = 45°, the distance traveled horizontally is

$d = \frac{100^2}{32} \sin(2 \cdot 45°)$ *Substitute 100 for v and 45° for θ.*

$= 312.5 \sin 90°$ *Simplify.*

$= 312.5$ feet.   *Use sin 90° = 1.*

c. For θ = 50°, the distance traveled horizontally is

$d = \frac{100^2}{32} \sin(2 \cdot 50°) = 312.5 \sin 100° \approx 307.75$ feet.   ∎

Communicating about ALGEBRA

▶ **SHARING IDEAS about the Lesson**

What is the minimum initial velocity that you would need to hit a baseball a horizontal distance of at least 400 feet? Explain your reasoning.

EXERCISES

Guided Practice

▶ **CRITICAL THINKING about the Lesson**

1. The point $(x, y) = (-4, -5)$ lies on the terminal side of the angle θ. What is r?

2. The point $(x, y) \neq (0, 0)$ lies on the terminal side of the angle θ. What is $\tan \theta$? For which values of x is $\tan \theta$ undefined? For which values of θ is $\tan \theta$ undefined?

3. What is the maximum value of $\sin \theta$? Explain your reasoning.

4. In which quadrants must θ lie so that $\cos \theta$ is positive?

5. Find the reference angle for $\theta = \frac{7\pi}{4}$.

6. Find the reference angle for $\theta = -120°$.

7. Evaluate $\cos\left(-\frac{4\pi}{3}\right)$.

8. Evaluate $\tan 240°$.

Independent Practice

In Exercises 9–20, you are given a point on the terminal side of an angle θ. Find $\sin \theta$, $\cos \theta$, and $\tan \theta$.

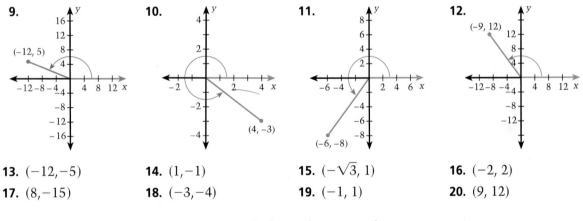

9. 10. 11. 12.

13. $(-12, -5)$ 14. $(1, -1)$ 15. $(-\sqrt{3}, 1)$ 16. $(-2, 2)$

17. $(8, -15)$ 18. $(-3, -4)$ 19. $(-1, 1)$ 20. $(9, 12)$

In Exercises 21–32, sketch the angle. Then find its reference angle.

21. $220°$ 22. $-510°$ 23. $-155°$ 24. $345°$

25. $-\frac{8\pi}{3}$ 26. $\frac{35\pi}{3}$ 27. $\frac{12\pi}{5}$ 28. $\frac{21\pi}{4}$

29. -4.3 30. 6.9 31. 10.6 32. -1.9

In Exercises 33–40, without using a calculator, decide whether the equation is true or false. Then use a calculator to verify your decision.

33. $\sin 174° = \sin 6°$ 34. $\cos 200° = \cos 20°$ 35. $\tan 220° = \tan 40°$ 36. $\cos 300° = \cos 60°$

37. $\tan \frac{5\pi}{3} = \tan \frac{\pi}{3}$ 38. $\tan \frac{7\pi}{4} = \tan \frac{3\pi}{4}$ 39. $\cos \frac{5\pi}{3} = -\cos \frac{\pi}{3}$ 40. $\sin \frac{5\pi}{4} = \sin \frac{3\pi}{4}$

In Exercises 41–56, evaluate the function without using a calculator.

41. $\cos 300°$

42. $\cos(-225°)$

43. $\csc(-120°)$

44. $\tan 225°$

45. $\sec 750°$

46. $\sin 240°$

47. $\cos(-240°)$

48. $\tan(-120°)$

49. $\cot \frac{5\pi}{6}$

50. $\sec \frac{11\pi}{4}$

51. $\sin\left(-\frac{7\pi}{6}\right)$

52. $\cos \frac{2\pi}{3}$

53. $\sin\left(-\frac{13\pi}{6}\right)$

54. $\sin \frac{5\pi}{4}$

55. $\cos \frac{10\pi}{3}$

56. $\csc \frac{17\pi}{3}$

In Exercises 57–68, use a calculator to evaluate the function.

57. $\sin 18°$

58. $\sin 390°$

59. $\sec 29°$

60. $\cot 420°$

61. $\cos \frac{20\pi}{3}$

62. $\cot \frac{10\pi}{3}$

63. $\sec \frac{9\pi}{2}$

64. $\csc \frac{18\pi}{5}$

65. $\tan 3.2$

66. $\csc 2.9$

67. $\cos 5.4$

68. $\tan 2.3°$

69. *Fishing*   You and a friend are fishing. Each of you casts with an initial velocity of 40 feet per second. Your cast was projected at an angle of 45° and your friend's at an angle of 60°. About how much further will your fishing tackle go than your friend's?

70. *Ferris Wheel*   The largest Ferris wheel in operation is the Cosmolock 21 at Yo-kohama City, Japan. It has a diameter of 328 feet. Passengers board the cars at the bottom of the wheel, about 16.5 feet above ground. Imagine that you have boarded the Cosmolock 21. The wheel rotates 300° before it stops. How far above ground are you when your ride on the Cosmolock 21 stops?

71. *Volleyball*   While playing a game of volleyball, you set the ball to your teammate, who sets it to the spiker. You hit the ball with an initial velocity of 24 feet per second at an angle of 70°. About how far away should your teammate be to receive your set?

Tropic of Cancer   **In Exercises 72 and 73, use the following information.**

The Tropic of Cancer is the latitude farthest north of the equator where the sun appears directly overhead and is shown at the right.

72. Find the circumference of the Tropic of Cancer.

73. Imagine that a coordinate plane cuts Earth through its center, as shown in the diagram. If each unit in the coordinate system represents one mile, what are the coordinates of the two points that lie on the Tropic of Cancer?

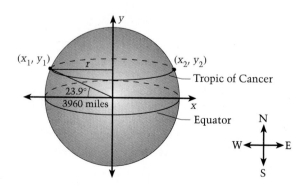

74. *Football Halftime*   Your school's marching band is performing at halftime. At one point in the performance, the band members form a 100-foot-wide circle in the center of the field. As the band begins to march around the circle, you are 100 feet from a goal line. How far from the same goal line will you be after you have marched 300° around the circle?

Tunneling Through Earth   **In Exercises 75 and 76, use the following information.**

The diagram at the right shows the "top view" of the circle of 30° north latitude. Imagine that you travel along this circle from the point at 0° longitude in the Sahara Desert to the point at 120° east longitude, just south of Shanghai, China.

75. Find the distance (in miles) that you travel.

76. Find the coordinates of the point (x, y) just south of Shanghai. Imagine that, instead of traveling around a circular arc, you tunnel through Earth. How many miles long would the tunnel be?

Integrated Review

In Exercises 77–80, use the given value to find the values of the other five trigonometric functions. (Assume θ is an acute angle.)

77. $\tan \theta = \frac{3}{2}$ **78.** $\cos \theta = \frac{2}{3}$ **79.** $\sin \theta = \frac{1}{4}$ **80.** $\cot \theta = 2$

81. *What Went Wrong?*   Your friend used a calculator to evaluate $\sin 10°$ and obtained -0.544. How can you tell this is wrong? What did your friend do wrong?

82. *What Went Wrong?*   Your friend used a calculator to evaluate $\csc 3$ and obtained 0.327. What did your friend do wrong?

Exploration and Extension

83. *Geometry*   The two triangles are similar. Find the six trigonometric functions of θ.

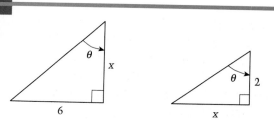

Graphing calculators, such as the *TI-82* or the Casio *fx-9700GE*, can be programmed to perform relatively complicated tasks. The program listed on page 863 takes time to enter, but the result is both fun and instructive.

When the program is run, it prompts you to enter "0" for radians or "1" for degrees. Next, you are prompted to enter an angle—any angle θ can be used. After entering the angle, press ENTER. The calculator then draws the angle in standard position. The point of the terminal side of the angle lies on the *unit circle*. Moreover, the coordinates of the endpoint are $(x, y) = (\cos \theta, \sin \theta)$. *To clear the screen*, press ENTER.

Partner Activity Without showing your partner, use the angle drawing program listed on page 863 to draw an angle. Then, give the graphing calculator to your partner and ask him or her to estimate the value of the angle within 5 degrees. Ask your partner how he or she made the estimate.

After your partner has found the angle, switch roles and repeat the activity.

Two examples of the results of this program are shown below. The screen on the left shows the angle $\theta = 420°$. The screen on the right shows the angle $\theta = -\frac{13\pi}{4}$.

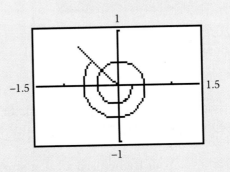

The screen shows an angle of 420°. The "terminal point" is

$(\cos 420°, \sin 420°)$ or $\left(\frac{1}{2}, \frac{\sqrt{3}}{2}\right)$.

The screen shows an angle of $-\frac{13\pi}{4}$. Its "terminal point" is

$\left(\cos\left(-\frac{13\pi}{4}\right), \sin\left(-\frac{13\pi}{4}\right)\right)$ or $\left(-\frac{\sqrt{2}}{2}, \frac{\sqrt{2}}{2}\right)$.

Another nice use of a graphing calculator is to sketch a graph of the unit circle using the calculator's *parametric mode*. On the *TI-82*, you can begin by pressing MODE , cursoring to PAR , and pressing ENTER . Next, press WINDOW and set the bounds for X, Y, and T.

Tmin = 0	Xmin = −1.5	Ymin = −1
Tmax = 6.3	Xmax = 1.5	Ymax = 1
Tstep = .031416	Xscl = 1	Yscl = 1

You are now ready to enter the *x*-coordinates and *y*-coordinates that will trace out the unit circle. Press Y= and enter

$:X_{1T} = \cos T$ and $:Y_{1T} = \sin T$.

Check that the calculator is set to radian mode, then press GRAPH . The screen will appear as shown below. Using the *trace* feature of the calculator, you can move the cursor around the unit circle. The displayed value of T represents the measure of θ in radians. The displayed value of x represents the cosine of θ, and the displayed value of y represents the sine of θ. (When you are done using this program, remember to change the mode back to FUNCTION .)

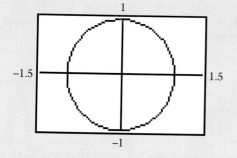

Exercises

In Exercises 1–4, use the angle-drawing program to sketch the angle.

1. $\theta = 500°$ **2.** $\theta = -600°$ **3.** $\theta = \dfrac{11\pi}{3}$ **4.** $\theta = -\dfrac{17\pi}{4}$

In Exercises 5–10, use a graphing calculator set in parametric mode to sketch the unit circle. Then use the trace key to approximate the radian measure of the angle whose cosine and sine are given.

5. $\cos \theta \approx -0.6846$, $\sin \theta \approx 0.7290$

6. $\cos \theta \approx 0.6846$, $\sin \theta \approx -0.7290$

7. $\cos \theta \approx -0.1879$, $\sin \theta \approx 0.9823$

8. $\cos \theta \approx 0.9409$, $\sin \theta \approx 0.3387$

9. $\cos \theta \approx -0.8607$, $\sin \theta \approx -0.5090$

10. $\cos \theta \approx 0.9956$, $\sin \theta \approx -0.0941$

Take this test as you would take a test in class. The answers to the exercises are given in the back of the book.

In Exercises 1–3, evaluate the six trigonometric functions of θ. (13.1)

1.

2.

3.

In Exercises 4–6, find the complement of the angle. (13.2)

4. $37°$

5. $15°$

6. $\frac{3\pi}{8}$

In Exercises 7–9, find the supplement of the angle. (13.2)

7. $120°$

8. $\frac{7\pi}{8}$

9. $\frac{5\pi}{12}$

In Exercises 10–12, find two angles, one with positive measure and the other with negative measure, that are coterminal with the given angle. (13.2)

10. $560°$

11. $-75°$

12. $-\frac{5\pi}{8}$

In Exercises 13–15, you are given a point on the terminal side of an angle θ. Find $\sin \theta$, $\cos \theta$, and $\tan \theta$. (13.3)

13. $(3, 4)$

14. $(-8, 6)$

15. $(-5, -12)$

In Exercises 16–19, decide whether the equation is true or false. (13.3)

16. $\sin 47° = \sin 227°$

17. $\cos 110° = \cos 290°$

18. $\tan \frac{5\pi}{4} = -\tan \frac{\pi}{4}$

19. $\sin 155° = -\sin 35°$

20. The carpenter's square at the right is marked at 12 on the short arm and $3\frac{1}{4}$ and 12 on the long arm. To which angles do these correspond? **(13.1)**

21. The carpenter's square at the right is marked at 12 on the short arm. Where should you place marks on the long arm to correspond to $30°$ and $60°$? **(13.1)**

22. How far will a ball travel horizontally if hit with an initial velocity of 80 feet per second and an angle of elevation of $40°$? Use the formula $d = \frac{1}{32} v^2 \sin 2\theta$. **(13.3)**

13.4

Inverse Trigonometric Functions

What you should learn:

Goal 1 How to evaluate inverse trigonometric functions

Goal 2 How to use inverse trigonometric functions to solve real-life problems

Why you should learn it:

You can solve many problems from real life, such as finding the length of a pulley belt, by using inverse trigonometric functions and trigonometric equations.

Goal 1 Evaluating Inverse Trig Functions

LESSON INVESTIGATION

■ Investigating Inverse Trig Functions

Partner Activity A function f is **one-to-one** if no two values of x correspond to the same value of y.

a. The function $f(x) = \sin x$ is not one-to-one. Why?

b. For a function to have an inverse, it must be one-to-one. Can you find an interval on the real number line in which the sine function is one-to-one? If so, describe the interval.

In this investigation, you may have discovered that the sine function does not have an inverse unless its domain is restricted to an interval over which the sine function is one-to-one. This is also true of the other trigonometric functions.

Study Tip

Not all mathematics texts agree on the definitions of the inverse trigonometric functions. Moreover, other notations such as Arcsin a or $\sin^{-1} a$ are often used. Because of this, whenever you encounter inverse trigonometric functions, you should check the definitions and notations that are being used.

Inverse Trigonometric Functions

1. If $-1 \leq a \leq 1$, then the **inverse sine** of a is

$$\arcsin a = \theta$$

where $\sin \theta = a$ and $-90° \leq \theta \leq 90°$.

2. If $-1 \leq a \leq 1$, then the **inverse cosine** of a is

$$\arccos a = \theta$$

where $\cos \theta = a$ and $0° \leq \theta \leq 180°$.

4. If a is any real number, then the **inverse tangent** of a is

$$\arctan a = \theta$$

where $\tan \theta = a$ and $-90° < \theta < 90°$.

The expression arcsin a is read as "the arcsine of a" or as "the angle whose sine is a." The expressions arccos a and arctan a are read in similar ways. Inverse trigonometric functions corresponding to the secant, cosecant, and cotangent functions can also be defined, but we will not do that in this book.

Example **1** ***Evaluating the Inverse Sine Function***

Evaluate the following, if possible. List your responses in degree measure *and* in radian measure.

a. $\arcsin\left(-\frac{1}{2}\right)$ **b.** $\arcsin\frac{\sqrt{3}}{2}$ **c.** $\arcsin 2$

Solution

a. The value of $\arcsin\left(-\frac{1}{2}\right)$ is the angle θ between $-90°$ and $90°$ whose sine is $-\frac{1}{2}$. Because $\sin(-30°) = -\frac{1}{2}$, you can write

$$\arcsin\left(-\frac{1}{2}\right) = -30°.$$

In radian measure, the angle is $-\frac{\pi}{6}$.

b. The value of $\arcsin\frac{\sqrt{3}}{2}$ is the angle θ between $-90°$ and $90°$ whose sine is $\frac{\sqrt{3}}{2}$. Because $\sin 60° = \frac{\sqrt{3}}{2}$, you can write

$$\arcsin\frac{\sqrt{3}}{2} = 60°.$$

In radian measure, the angle is $\frac{\pi}{3}$.

c. It is not possible to evaluate $\arcsin 2$ because there is no angle whose sine is 2. ■

Example **2** ***Evaluating Inverse Trigonometric Functions***

Evaluate the following, if possible. List your responses in degree measure and in radian measure.

a. $\arccos(-1)$ **b.** $\arctan 0$ **c.** $\arccos 0.3$

Solution

a. Because $\cos 180° = -1$, you can write

$$\arccos(-1) = 180°.$$

In radian measure, the angle is π.

b. Because $\tan 0° = 0$, it follows that

$$\arctan 0 = 0°.$$

In radian measure, the angle is also 0.

c. There is no common angle whose cosine is 0.3. Using a calculator set to *degree mode,* you can approximate the angle to be

$$\arccos 0.3 \approx 72.54°.$$

Using a calculator set to *radian mode,* you can approximate the angle to be

$$\arccos 0.3 \approx 1.27 \text{ radians.} ■$$

Connections

Mechanics

Example 3 *Finding the Length of a Pulley Belt*

Find the length of the pulley belt shown at the left.

Solution To find the length, partition the pulley belt into four parts: the two straight segments, the arc around the small wheel, and the arc around the large wheel.

Two Straight Segments: Each of the straight segments is the side, L, of a right triangle whose hypotenuse is 13 and whose other side is 5. Using the Pythagorean Theorem, you can find the length of each straight segment to be

$$L = \sqrt{13^2 - 5^2} = \sqrt{144} = 12 \text{ inches.}$$

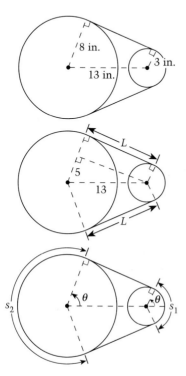

Arc around the Small Wheel: The angle θ is part of a right triangle whose adjacent side has a length of 5 and whose hypotenuse has a length of 13. Therefore, θ is the angle whose cosine is $\frac{5}{13}$. Using the formula for the length of a circular arc, $s = r\theta$, the length of the segment around the small wheel is

$$s_1 = 2\left(3 \arccos \frac{5}{13}\right) = 6 \arccos \frac{5}{13} \text{ inches.}$$

Arc around the Large Wheel: The circumference of the large wheel is $2\pi r = 16\pi$ inches. Therefore, the length of the segment around the large wheel is

$$s_2 = 16\pi - 2\left(8 \arccos \frac{5}{13}\right) = 16\pi - 16 \arccos \frac{5}{13} \text{ inches.}$$

By adding the lengths of the four parts, you can find the length of the pulley.

$$\begin{aligned}
\text{Pulley length} &= 2L + s_1 + s_2 \\
&= 2(12) + 6 \arccos \frac{5}{13} + \left(16\pi - 16 \arccos \frac{5}{13}\right) \\
&= 24 + 16\pi - 10 \arccos \frac{5}{13} \approx 62.5 \text{ inches.}
\end{aligned}$$

Note that when using the formula, $s = r\theta$, for the length of a circular arc, you must use *radian mode.* ■

Communicating *about* **ALGEBRA**

▶ **SHARING IDEAS about the Lesson**

Evaluate the following in degree and radian measure.

A. $\arcsin\left(-\dfrac{\sqrt{2}}{2}\right)$ **B.** $\arccos\left(-\dfrac{\sqrt{2}}{2}\right)$ **C.** $\arctan\left(-\dfrac{\sqrt{2}}{2}\right)$

EXERCISES

Guided Practice

▶ **CRITICAL THINKING about the Lesson**

1. Because $\sin 45° = \dfrac{\sqrt{2}}{2}$, $\arcsin \dfrac{\sqrt{2}}{2} = \boxed{?}$.

2. Because $\tan \dfrac{\pi}{3} = \sqrt{3}$, $\arctan \boxed{?} = \dfrac{\pi}{3}$.

3. Find the degree *and* radian measure of the angle θ in the triangle at the right.

4. Use a calculator to evaluate $\arccos \dfrac{9}{10}$. Write your result in radians and degrees.

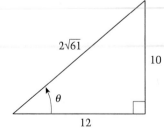

Independent Practice

In Exercises 5–12, write the measure of the angle θ in degrees and in radians.

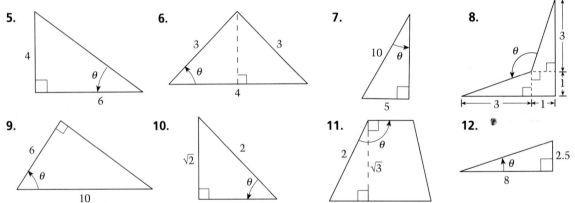

5. **6.** **7.** **8.**

9. **10.** **11.** **12.**

In Exercises 13–28, evaluate the expression without using a calculator. Write the result in degrees and in radians.

13. $\arccos\left(\dfrac{\sqrt{2}}{2}\right)$ **14.** $\arcsin\left(\dfrac{1}{2}\right)$ **15.** $\arcsin(1)$ **16.** $\arccos(0)$

17. $\arctan(\sqrt{3})$ **18.** $\arctan\left(\dfrac{\sqrt{3}}{3}\right)$ **19.** $\arccos\left(-\dfrac{\sqrt{3}}{2}\right)$ **20.** $\arcsin\left(-\dfrac{\sqrt{2}}{2}\right)$

21. $\arcsin(-1)$ **22.** $\arctan(0)$ **23.** $\arctan(-1)$ **24.** $\arccos\left(-\dfrac{1}{2}\right)$

25. $\arcsin\left(-\dfrac{\sqrt{3}}{2}\right)$ **26.** $\arccos\left(-\dfrac{\sqrt{2}}{2}\right)$ **27.** $\arcsin(0)$ **28.** $\arctan(-\sqrt{3})$

In Exercises 29–36, use a calculator to approximate the value. Write the result in degrees and in radians. Round to three decimal places.

29. $\arctan(3.9)$ **30.** $\arccos(0.14)$ **31.** $\arccos(0.22)$ **32.** $\arcsin(0.75)$

33. $\arcsin(-0.6)$ **34.** $\arccos(-0.9)$ **35.** $\arctan(-0.1)$ **36.** $\arctan(2.25)$

37. What Went Wrong? Suppose you used a calculator to evaluate arctan 45, and the calculator displayed 1.000. What did you do wrong? Write the correct answer in degree measure and in radian measure.

38. What Went Wrong? Suppose you used a calculator to evaluate arcsin $\frac{1}{2}$, and the calculator displayed 0.479°. What did you do wrong? Write the correct answer in degree measure and in radian measure.

39. Swimming Pool The swimming pool shown below is 24 feet long. The pool depth ranges from 2 feet to 10 feet. Find the *angle of depression* of the bottom of the pool.

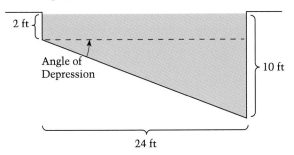

40. Dump Truck The dump truck shown below has a 10-foot bed. When tilted at its maximum angle, the bed reaches a height of 7 feet above its original position. What is the truck bed's maximum angle?

41. Refraction of Light When a light ray enters glass, it bends towards a line perpendicular to the surface of the glass. The *angle of incidence*, θ_1, is the angle between the ray and the perpendicular line before entering the glass (and after leaving the glass). The *angle of refraction*, θ_2, is the angle between the ray and the perpendicular line in the glass. The *index of refraction*, n, of the glass is

$$n = \frac{\sin \theta_1}{\sin \theta_2}.$$

A typical index of refraction for glass is $n = 1.5$. For such glass, if $\theta_1 = 59°$, what is θ_2?

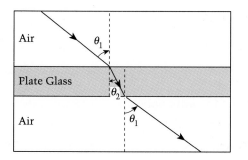

42. Civil Engineering Curves in roads are often constructed as arcs of circles. In the diagram shown below, θ is the central angle of the arc. The radius of the circle is 225 feet, and the length of each "tangent" is 158 feet. Find the degree measure of θ.

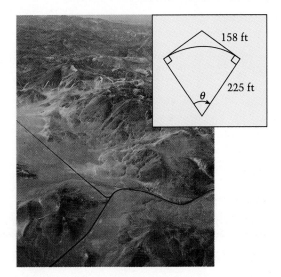

Aerial view of the Pan-American Highway near Arequipa, Peru

Bicycle Chain Length   **In Exercises 43 and 44, use the following information.**

The chain on a one-gear bicycle is turned by two circular sprocket wheels whose centers are 18 inches apart. The front sprocket wheel has 48 teeth, and the rear sprocket wheel has 24 teeth. Each tooth accounts for $\frac{\pi}{6}$ of an inch of its sprocket wheel's circumference.

43. Find the length of the chain.

44. The pedals of the bicycle are attached to the center of the large front sprocket. The diameter of each bicycle wheel is 26 inches. How many inches along the ground does the bike travel with one full revolution of the pedals?

Integrated Review

45. Complete the table.

θ	0	$\frac{\pi}{6}$	$\frac{\pi}{4}$	$\frac{\pi}{3}$	$\frac{\pi}{2}$	π	$\frac{3\pi}{2}$	2π
$\sin\theta$	?	?	?	?	?	?	?	?
$\cos\theta$	?	?	?	?	?	?	?	?
$\tan\theta$	?	?	?	?	?	?	?	?
$\csc\theta$	?	?	?	?	?	?	?	?
$\sec\theta$	?	?	?	?	?	?	?	?
$\cot\theta$	?	?	?	?	?	?	?	?

46. Find the radian measure of two angles that are coterminal with $\arcsin(-1)$.

47. *College Entrance Exam Sample*   In the figure below, the area of square $OABC$ is 2. What is the area of the circle?

a. $\frac{\pi}{4}$ **b.** $\pi\sqrt{2}$ **c.** 2π **d.** 4π **e.** 16π

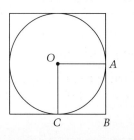

48. *College Entrance Exam Sample*   In the figure below, $AB = 5$, $AC = 3$, and $BC = CD$. What is the length of BE?

a. 1   **b.** 2   **c.** 3   **d.** 4   **e.** 5

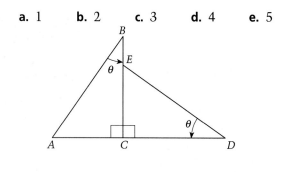

Exploration and Extension

In Exercises 49–52, evaluate the expression. Use a calculator to verify your result.

49. $\arccos\left(\cos\frac{\pi}{3}\right)$

50. $\tan\left(\arctan\frac{4\pi}{3}\right)$

51. $\cos\left(\arcsin\frac{5}{13}\right)$

52. $\sin\left(\arctan\frac{3}{4}\right)$

13.5

The Law of Sines

What you should learn:

Goal 1 How to use the Law of Sines to find the sides and angles of any triangle

Goal 2 How to use the Law of Sines to solve real-life problems

Why you should learn it:

You can use the Law of Sines to solve for many distances that cannot be measured directly.

Goal 1 Using the Law of Sines

In Lesson 13.1, you learned how to solve right triangles. In this lesson and the next, you will learn to solve **oblique triangles**—triangles that have no right angles.

To solve an oblique triangle, you need to know the measure of at least one side and any two other parts of the triangle—either two sides, two angles, or one angle and one side. This breaks down into four possible cases.

1. Two angles and any side (AAS or ASA)
2. Two sides and an angle opposite one of them (SSA)
3. Three sides (SSS)
4. Two sides and their included angle (SAS)

The first two cases can be solved using the **Law of Sines.** The last two cases require the **Law of Cosines** (Lesson 13.6).

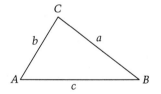

> **Law of Sines**
>
> If ABC is a triangle with sides a, b, and c, then
>
> $$\frac{a}{\sin A} = \frac{b}{\sin B} = \frac{c}{\sin C} \quad \text{or} \quad \frac{\sin A}{a} = \frac{\sin B}{b} = \frac{\sin C}{c}.$$

Example 1 *Given Two Angles and One Side—AAS*

Given a triangle with $C = 102°$, $B = 28°$, and $b = 27$ feet, find the measures of the remaining angle and sides.

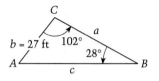

Solution Because the sum of the angles of a triangle is $180°$, you know that the third angle $A = 180° - B - C = 50°$. By the Law of Sines, you can write

$$\frac{a}{\sin 50°} = \frac{b}{\sin 28°} = \frac{c}{\sin 102°}.$$

Because $b = 27$, you can solve for a and c as follows.

$$a = \frac{27}{\sin 28°}(\sin 50°) \approx 44.06 \text{ feet}$$

$$c = \frac{27}{\sin 28°}(\sin 102°) \approx 56.25 \text{ feet}$$ ∎

When solving triangles, a careful sketch is useful as a quick check. Remember that the longest side lies opposite the angle with the greatest measure, and the shortest side lies opposite the angle with the least measure.

Two angles and one side (AAS or ASA) determine exactly one triangle. Two sides and an opposite angle (SSA) may determine no triangle, exactly one triangle, or two triangles.

Example 2   *Single Solution Case—SSA*

Given a triangle with sides $a = 22$ meters and $b = 12$ meters and angle $A = 42°$, find the measure of the remaining side and angles.

Solution   Begin by using the given information to make a careful sketch. Then, using the Law of Sines, you can solve for B.

$$\frac{\sin B}{12} = \frac{\sin 42°}{22} \qquad \textit{Law of Sines}$$

$$\sin B = 12\left(\frac{\sin 42°}{22}\right) \qquad \textit{Multiply both sides by 12.}$$

$$\sin B \approx 0.365 \qquad \textit{Use a calculator in degree mode.}$$

$$B \approx \arcsin 0.365 \qquad \textit{Use arcsine to solve for B.}$$

$$B \approx 21.4° \qquad \textit{Use a calculator in degree mode.}$$

Now you know that $C \approx 180° - 42° - 21.4° = 116.6°$, and you can use the Law of Sines again to find the remaining side of the triangle.

$$\frac{c}{\sin 116.6°} = \frac{22}{\sin 42°}$$

$$c = \sin 116.6°\left(\frac{22}{\sin 42°}\right)$$

$$\approx 29.4 \text{ meters} \qquad \blacksquare$$

The Law of Sines can be used to derive a formula for the area of triangle when you know the lengths of two sides and the measure of the included angle.

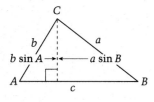

Area of a Triangle

The area of any triangle is given by one half the product of the lengths of two sides times the sine of their included angle.

$$\text{Area} = \frac{1}{2}bc \sin A$$

$$\text{Area} = \frac{1}{2}ab \sin C$$

$$\text{Area} = \frac{1}{2}ac \sin B$$

Real Life
Surveying

Example 3 · *Exploring a Cave*

You are at position *A* and another surveyor is at position *B*. The distance between *A* and *B* is 50 feet. You each locate a point *C* on the ceiling of a cave and measure the angles to be 71° at *A* and 62° at *B*, as shown at the left. Point *C* lies directly above the horizontal line connecting *A* and *B*. Find the height of *C*.

Solution The angle *C* is given by $C = 180 - 71 - 62 = 47°$. Using the Law of Sines, you can find *b*.

$$\frac{b}{\sin B} = \frac{c}{\sin C}$$

$$\frac{b}{\sin 62°} = \frac{50}{\sin 47°}$$

$$b = \sin 62° \left(\frac{50}{\sin 47°}\right)$$

$$b \approx 60.4 \text{ feet}$$

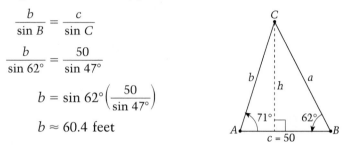

Now, because the height, *h*, is the side of a right triangle, you can use the sine function to solve for *h*.

$$\sin A = \frac{h}{b}$$

$$\sin 71° = \frac{h}{60.4}$$

$$60.4 \sin 71° = h$$

$$57.1 \approx h$$

Therefore, *C* is about 57.1 feet above the horizontal line connecting *A* and *B*. ∎

Calcium deposits have formed beautiful stalactites and stalagmites in the Carlsbad Caverns of New Mexico.

Communicating about **ALGEBRA**

▶ **SHARING IDEAS about the Lesson**

Use the Law of Sines to solve the triangle.

A.

B.

EXERCISES

Guided Practice

▶ **CRITICAL THINKING about the Lesson**

1. State the Law of Sines.

2. Which of the following cannot be solved with the Law of Sines?
   a. AAS **b.** ASA **c.** SSA **d.** SAS

3. Explain why there is no triangle that has sides of $a = 3$, $b = 4$, and $c = 8$.

4. If you are given all three angles of a triangle, is it possible to determine the lengths of its sides? Explain.

5. Find c in the triangle at the right.

6. What is the area of the triangle at the right?

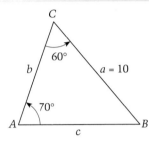

Independent Practice

In Exercises 7–30, solve the triangle. (*Hint:* Some of the "triangles" have no solution and some have two solutions.)

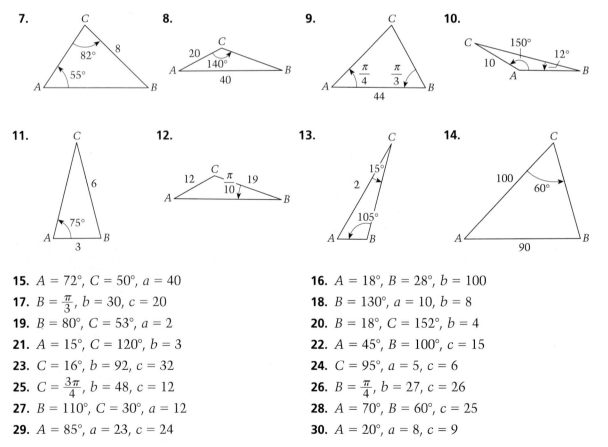

15. $A = 72°$, $C = 50°$, $a = 40$

16. $A = 18°$, $B = 28°$, $b = 100$

17. $B = \frac{\pi}{3}$, $b = 30$, $c = 20$

18. $B = 130°$, $a = 10$, $b = 8$

19. $B = 80°$, $C = 53°$, $a = 2$

20. $B = 18°$, $C = 152°$, $b = 4$

21. $A = 15°$, $C = 120°$, $b = 3$

22. $A = 45°$, $B = 100°$, $c = 15$

23. $C = 16°$, $b = 92$, $c = 32$

24. $C = 95°$, $a = 5$, $c = 6$

25. $C = \frac{3\pi}{4}$, $b = 48$, $c = 12$

26. $B = \frac{\pi}{4}$, $b = 27$, $c = 26$

27. $B = 110°$, $C = 30°$, $a = 12$

28. $A = 70°$, $B = 60°$, $c = 25$

29. $A = 85°$, $a = 23$, $c = 24$

30. $A = 20°$, $a = 8$, $c = 9$

In Exercises 31–46, decide whether there are no solutions, exactly one solution, or two solutions. (You do not need to solve the triangle.)

31.
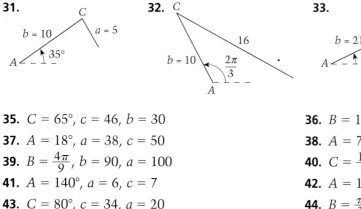

32. C

33.

34. A

35. $C = 65°$, $c = 46$, $b = 30$

36. $B = 105°$, $b = 11$, $a = 5$

37. $A = 18°$, $a = 38$, $c = 50$

38. $A = 70°$, $a = 155$, $c = 160$

39. $B = \frac{4\pi}{9}$, $b = 90$, $a = 100$

40. $C = \frac{11\pi}{36}$, $c = 12$, $b = 16$

41. $A = 140°$, $a = 6$, $c = 7$

42. $A = 16°$, $a = 14$, $c = 10$

43. $C = 80°$, $c = 34$, $a = 20$

44. $B = \frac{\pi}{3}$, $b = 14$, $c = 15$

45. $B = \frac{\pi}{6}$, $b = 12$, $a = 9$

46. $C = 170°$, $c = 10$, $b = 15$

In Exercises 47–56, find the area of the triangle.

47.

48.

49.

50.

51. $A = 60°$, $b = 9$, $c = 12$

52. $B = 25°$, $a = 15$, $c = 31$

53. $C = 130°$, $a = 21$, $b = 17$

54. $A = 85°$, $b = 11$, $c = 18$

55. $B = \frac{\pi}{4}$, $a = 4$, $c = 1$

56. $C = 140°$, $a = 6$, $b = 4$

57. *Aqueduct*   A reservoir supplies water through an aqueduct to Springfield, which is 15 miles southeast of the reservoir. A pumping station at Springfield pumps water 12 miles to Centerville, which is due east of the reservoir. Plans have been made to build an aqueduct directly from the reservoir to Centerville. How long will the aqueduct be?

Hoover Dam, on the Colorado River in Nevada, supplies water for much of southern California through a 240-mile aqueduct.

58. *Measuring an Island* What is the width of the island in the diagram below?

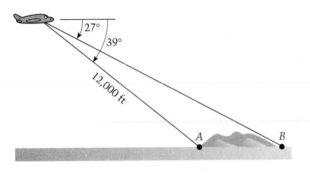

59. *Tracking Stations* What is the altitude of the airplane in the diagram below?

60. *Pythagorean Theorem* The area of the entire enclosed region is given by $A = 2ab + 2c^2$. Verify this formula for the values $a = 5$, $b = 5\sqrt{3}$, and $c = 10$.

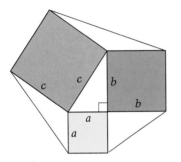

61. *Grand Piano* Use $C = 62°$, $A = 66°$, and $c = 4.5$ feet to find the length, b (in feet), of the longest string of the piano shown below.

62. *Ohio Cities* Use the map below to find the straight-path distance between Toledo and Akron. Then find the straight-path distance between Akron and Columbus. (The straight-path distance between Dayton and Akron is 175 miles.)

Sophie Germain (1776–1831) was a French mathematician who worked in number theory and the theory of elasticity. This statue of her now stands in the courtyard of the École Sophie Germain, a lycée in Paris.

Integrated Review

In Exercises 63–66, find x.

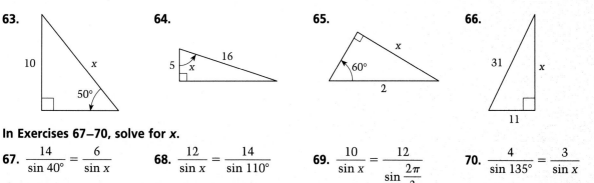

63.

10   x

50°

64.

5   x   16

65.

x

60°

2

66.

31   x

11

In Exercises 67–70, solve for x.

67. $\dfrac{14}{\sin 40°} = \dfrac{6}{\sin x}$

68. $\dfrac{12}{\sin x} = \dfrac{14}{\sin 110°}$

69. $\dfrac{10}{\sin x} = \dfrac{12}{\sin \dfrac{2\pi}{3}}$

70. $\dfrac{4}{\sin 135°} = \dfrac{3}{\sin x}$

Exploration and Extension

71. *Geometry*   Measure the sides of the triangle at the right (in millimeters). Then use a protractor to measure the angles of the triangle.

72. *Geometry*   Use the Law of Sines to check the measurements you obtained in Exercise 71. How closely do your measurements conform to the Law of Sines?

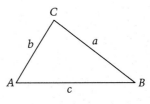

C

b   a

A   B

c

Mixed REVIEW

1. Solve $4n + 2mn = 3mn^2$ for m.   **(1.5)**

2. Graph $3x - 2y = 6$.   **(2.3)**

3. Find the slope: $3y - 2x = 17$.   **(2.3)**

4. Solve $|3t - 8| \le 2$.   **(1.7)**

5. Find the inverse of $\begin{bmatrix} 3 & 1 \\ 4 & 2 \end{bmatrix}$.   **(4.4)**

6. Evaluate $\sum\limits_{n=1}^{\infty} 3\left(\dfrac{1}{4}\right)^{n-1}$.   **(12.4)**

7. Solve $\begin{cases} 3x + y = -11 \\ 2x + 4y = 16 \end{cases}$.   **(3.2)**

8. Sketch the graph of $y = \sqrt{x + 2} - 3$.   **(7.6)**

9. Sketch the graph of $y = 4^x - 5$.   **(8.1)**

10. Expand $\ln\left(\dfrac{3x^2}{4y}\right)$.   **(8.8)**

11. Multiply: $\dfrac{3x + 3}{4x} \cdot \dfrac{x^2}{x + 1}$.   **(10.3)**

12. Solve $x^2 - 10x + 20 = 0$.   **(5.4)**

13. Find the vertex of $y = x^2 + 3x - 2$.   **(5.2)**

14. Factor $4x^3 - 8x^2 - 5x$.   **(9.5)**

15. Find $f(-2)$ for $f(x) = -3x^2$.   **(6.1)**

16. Evaluate $\sin^2 30°$.   **(13.1)**

17. Find the standard deviation of 3, 6, 7, 4, 3, 9, 10, 11, 12.   **(9.7)**

18. Find the nth term of the sequence $1, \dfrac{1}{8}, \dfrac{1}{27}, \dfrac{1}{64}, \dfrac{1}{125}, \ldots$ **(12.1)**

13.6

The Law of Cosines

What you should learn:

Goal 1 How to use the Law of Cosines to find the sides and angles of any triangle

Goal 2 How to use the Law of Cosines to solve problems in real life

Why you should learn it:

You can use the Law of Cosines to solve for many distances that cannot be measured directly, such as the distance from a starting point when a change of direction is involved.

Goal 1 Using the Law of Cosines

Two cases of oblique triangles left to solve are SSS and SAS. Both can be solved with the **Law of Cosines.**

Law of Cosines

Let ABC be a triangle with sides a, b, and c.

Standard Form

$$a^2 = b^2 + c^2 - 2bc \cos A$$

$$b^2 = a^2 + c^2 - 2ac \cos B$$

$$c^2 = a^2 + b^2 - 2ab \cos C$$

Alternative Form

$$\cos A = \frac{b^2 + c^2 - a^2}{2bc}$$

$$\cos B = \frac{a^2 + c^2 - b^2}{2ac}$$

$$\cos C = \frac{a^2 + b^2 - c^2}{2ab}$$

Example 1 *Given Three Sides of a Triangle—SSS*

Find the three angles of the triangle whose sides have lengths $a = 8$ feet, $b = 19$ feet, and $c = 14$ feet.

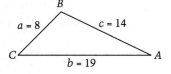

Solution First find the angle opposite the longest side—side b in this case. Using the Law of Cosines, you can write

$$\cos B = \frac{a^2 + c^2 - b^2}{2ac} = \frac{8^2 + 14^2 - 19^2}{2(8)(14)} \approx -0.451.$$

Using the inverse cosine function, you can find B to be the obtuse angle given by $B \approx \arccos(-0.451) \approx 116.8°$. Now use the Law of Sines to solve for A.

$$\frac{\sin A}{a} = \frac{\sin B}{b}$$

$$\sin A = a\left(\frac{\sin B}{b}\right) \approx 8\left(\frac{\sin 116.8°}{19}\right) \approx 0.376$$

Thus $A \approx \arcsin 0.376 \approx 22.1°$. Finally, you can find angle C.

$$C \approx 180° - 22.1° - 116.8° = 41.1°$$ ∎

In Example 1, notice that we solved for the largest angle *first* because then you know whether the triangle is acute or obtuse. After you have found the largest angle, you know that both of the other angles must be acute.

The Law of Cosines can be used to establish the following formula for the area of a triangle. This formula is credited to the Greek mathematician Hero (*circa* 100 B.C.).

Hero's Area Formula

The area of the triangle with sides of length a, b, and c is

$$\text{Area} = \sqrt{s(s-a)(s-b)(s-c)}$$

where $s = \frac{1}{2}(a + b + c)$.

Goal 2 Using the Law of Cosines in Real Life

Real Life
Softball

Example 2 *Given Two Sides and the Included Angle—SAS*

The pitcher's mound on a softball field is 46 feet from home plate. The distance between the bases is 60 feet. How far is the pitcher's mound from first base? How much closer is the pitcher's mound to second base than it is to first base?

Solution Begin by forming the triangle *HPF*. In this triangle, you know that $H = 45°$ because the line *HP* bisects the right angle at home plate. From the given information, you know that $f = 46$ and $p = 60$. Using the Law of Cosines, you can solve for h.

$$
\begin{aligned}
h^2 &= f^2 + p^2 - 2fp \cos H \\
&= 46^2 + 60^2 - 2(46)(60) \cos 45° \\
&\approx 1812.8
\end{aligned}
$$

The approximate distance from the pitcher's mound to first base is

$$h \approx \sqrt{1812.8} \approx 42.58 \text{ feet.}$$

The distance between home plate and second base is $\sqrt{60^2 + 60^2} \approx 84.85$ feet, which implies that the distance between the pitcher's mound and second base is

$$84.85 - 46 \approx 38.85 \text{ feet.}$$

Thus the pitcher's mound is about 4 feet closer to second base than it is to first base. ■

60 ft   *60 ft*
P   *h*
F
f = 46 ft
60 ft   *45°*   *p = 60 ft*
H

Softball Diamond

Example 3 *Given Two Sides and the Included Angle—SAS*

A boat travels 60 miles due east. Then it adjusts its course 15° northward and travels 80 miles, as shown below. How far is the boat from its point of departure?

***The Amoco Procyon** won one of Popular Science's "Best of What's New" awards in 1991. The yacht has many new features including a computer navigation system.*

Solution In the above triangle, you know that $a = 80$, $c = 60$, and

$$B = 180° - 15° = 165°.$$

Using the Law of Cosines, you can find b.

$$\begin{aligned} b^2 &= a^2 + c^2 - 2ac \cos B \\ &= 80^2 + 60^2 - 2(80)(60) \cos 165° \\ &\approx 19{,}273 \end{aligned}$$

Therefore, the distance from the point of departure is

$$b \approx \sqrt{19{,}273} \approx 138.8 \text{ miles.} \qquad \blacksquare$$

Communicating about **ALGEBRA**

▶ **SHARING IDEAS about the Lesson**

You have studied several formulas for the area of a triangle. Find the area of each of the following triangles. In each case, use the formula that you think is most appropriate and explain your choice.

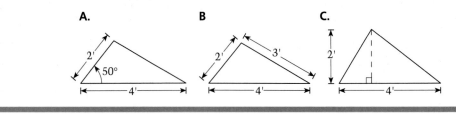

A.   **B**   **C.**

EXERCISES

Guided Practice

▶ **CRITICAL THINKING about the Lesson**

1. Of the triangles represented by AAS, ASA, SSA, SAS, and SSS, which are best solved with the Law of Cosines?

2. Describe how to find angle B in the triangle at the right.

3. Which form of the Law of Cosines would you use to find a, given b, c, and A?

4. A triangle has two sides of lengths 12 feet and 16 feet. The angle between these two sides is 30°. What is the length of the other side?

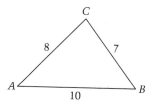

Independent Practice

In Exercises 5–30, find the remaining angles and sides.

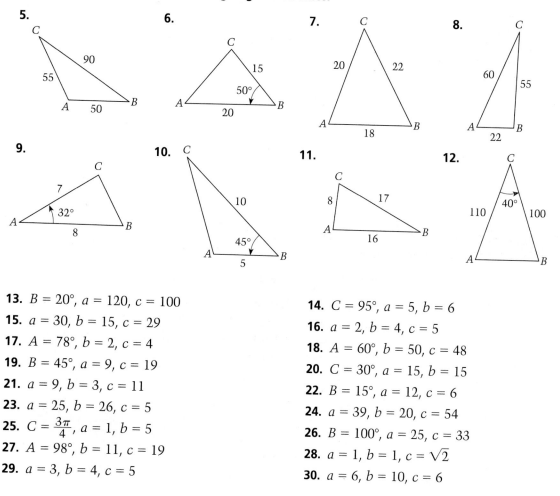

13. $B = 20°$, $a = 120$, $c = 100$

14. $C = 95°$, $a = 5$, $b = 6$

15. $a = 30$, $b = 15$, $c = 29$

16. $a = 2$, $b = 4$, $c = 5$

17. $A = 78°$, $b = 2$, $c = 4$

18. $A = 60°$, $b = 50$, $c = 48$

19. $B = 45°$, $a = 9$, $c = 19$

20. $C = 30°$, $a = 15$, $b = 15$

21. $a = 9$, $b = 3$, $c = 11$

22. $B = 15°$, $a = 12$, $c = 6$

23. $a = 25$, $b = 26$, $c = 5$

24. $a = 39$, $b = 20$, $c = 54$

25. $C = \frac{3\pi}{4}$, $a = 1$, $b = 5$

26. $B = 100°$, $a = 25$, $c = 33$

27. $A = 98°$, $b = 11$, $c = 19$

28. $a = 1$, $b = 1$, $c = \sqrt{2}$

29. $a = 3$, $b = 4$, $c = 5$

30. $a = 6$, $b = 10$, $c = 6$

In Exercises 31–42, find the area of the triangle.

31.

32.

33.

34.

35. $a = 25$, $b = 60$, $c = 45$

36. $a = 11$, $b = 2$, $c = 12$

37. $a = 100$, $b = 55$, $c = 61$

38. $a = 4$, $b = 24$, $c = 26$

39. $a = 2$, $b = \frac{1}{2}$, $c = 2$

40. $a = 20$, $b = 21$, $c = 37$

41. $a = 8$, $b = 8$, $c = 8$

42. $a = 12$, $b = 9$, $c = 5$

43. *Baseball Diamond*   The pitcher's mound on a baseball field is 60.5 feet from home plate. The distance between the bases is 90 feet. How much closer is the pitcher's mound to first base than it is to second base? Explain.

44. *Measuring a Pond*   How long is the pond shown in the diagram at the right?

45. *Distance Between Two Airplanes*   Two airplanes leave the same airport in opposite directions. At 1:00 P.M., the angle of elevation from the airport to the first airplane is 25° and to the second airplane is 16°. The elevation of the first airplane is 8 miles. The elevation of the second airplane is 6 miles. Find the air distance between the two airplanes.

46. *Spaceship Earth*   One of the seven different sizes of panels on *Spaceship Earth* is shown at the right. What are the angles of the outer triangle of the panel? What is the area?

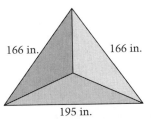

47. *Flying to Orlando*   As your flight is descending to Orlando, the pilot announces that the airplane's elevation is 18,000 feet and the ground distance to the airport is 20 miles. Later the pilot announces that the airplane's elevation is 11,000 feet and the ground distance to the airport is 8 miles. How far (in a straight air path) did the airplane travel between the two announcements?

Spaceship Earth, at Disney World's Epcot Center, is the first completely spherical geodesic dome ever built.

48. *Superdome*   The dome of the *Super-dome* was constructed with a patented configuration composed of hundreds of triangles of various shapes and sizes. Find the angles of the blue triangle at the right.

*The **Superdome** in New Orleans, Louisiana, is the world's largest indoor covered stadium. It can seat over 75,000 people. The dome has a diameter of 680 feet and is 273 feet high at its center.*

Integrated Review

In Exercises 49–56, use the Law of Sines or the Law of Cosines to solve the triangle.

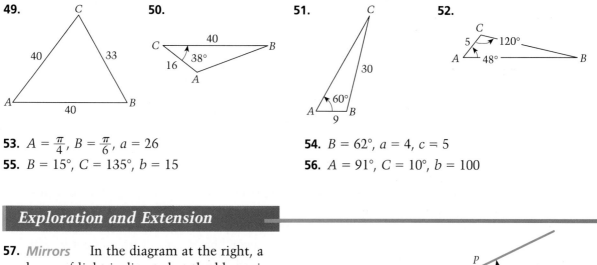

53. $A = \frac{\pi}{4}$, $B = \frac{\pi}{6}$, $a = 26$

55. $B = 15°$, $C = 135°$, $b = 15$

54. $B = 62°$, $a = 4$, $c = 5$

56. $A = 91°$, $C = 10°$, $b = 100$

Exploration and Extension

57. *Mirrors*   In the diagram at the right, a beam of light is directed at the blue mirror, reflected to the red mirror, then reflected back to the blue mirror. Find the length (PT) that the light travels from the red mirror back to the blue mirror given that $OQ = 6$ feet and $OP = 4.7$ feet.

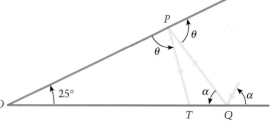

Chapter Summary

What did you learn?

1. Evaluate trigonometric functions
   - of an acute angle. **(13.1)**
   - of any angle. **(13.3)**
2. Use degree and radian measure to measure any angle.
   - Write equivalent degree and radian measures. **(13.2)**
3. Evaluate inverse trigonometric functions. **(13.4)**
4. Solve a triangle.
   - Use trigonometric functions to solve a right triangle. **(13.1)**
   - Use Law of Sines to solve an oblique triangle. **(13.5)**
   - Use Law of Cosines to solve an oblique triangle. **(13.6)**

5. Use trigonometric functions to solve real-life problems. **(13.1–13.6)**
6. Use inverse trigonometric functions to solve real-life problems. **(13.4–13.6)**

Why did you learn it?

Many real-life problems can be solved with trigonometry. The most common type of problem involves a triangle in which some of the sides and angles are *known* and others need to be *determined*. This use of trigonometry is common in surveying, engineering, astronomy, and navigation. For instance, in Example 5 on page 681, you saw how trigonometry could be used to measure the elevation of a mountain.

You also learned how trigonometry can be used to measure circular arcs. For instance, on a tire with a 12-inch radius, a central angle of $\frac{\pi}{3}$ radians corresponds to an arc length of $s = r\theta = 12\left(\frac{\pi}{3}\right) = 8\pi$ inches.

How does it fit into the bigger picture of algebra?

There are two basic types of trigonometry. The type you studied in this chapter deals with trigonometric functions of *angles*. Most of the applications of this type of trigonometry involve triangles or arcs of circles. In the next chapter, you will study the second basic type of trigonometry, which deals with trigonometric functions of *real numbers*.

Almost all practical uses of trigonometry require algebra. To solve the problems in this chapter, you used many algebraic skills, including simplification techniques and techniques for solving equations.

In Exercises 1–4, find the six trigonometric functions of θ. **(13.1)**

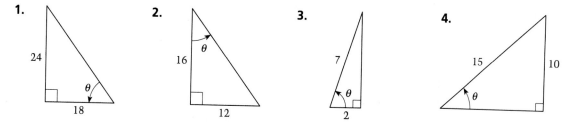

1.
24
18
θ

2.
16
12
θ

3.
7
2
θ

4.
15
10
θ

5. Given $\cos \theta = \frac{5}{13}$, find the other five trigonometric functions of θ. (Assume that θ is acute.) **(13.1)**

6. Given $\tan \theta = \frac{3}{4}$, find the other five trigonometric functions of θ. (Assume that θ is acute.) **(13.1)**

In Exercises 7–12, find the complement of the angle. **(13.2)**

7. 40°

8. 29°

9. $\frac{\pi}{3}$

10. $\frac{2\pi}{11}$

11. $\frac{4\pi}{9}$

12. $\frac{\pi}{7}$

In Exercises 13–18, find the supplement of the angle. **(13.2)**

13. 95°

14. 163°

15. 80°

16. $\frac{6\pi}{7}$

17. $\frac{3\pi}{4}$

18. $\frac{2\pi}{3}$

In Exercises 19–24, find two angles, one with positive measure and the other with negative measure, that are coterminal with the given angle. **(13.2)**

19. 355°

20. $\frac{3\pi}{8}$

21. $-\pi$

22. 114°

23. 66°

24. $-32°$

In Exercises 25–30, rewrite the degree measure as radians. **(13.2)**

25. $-15°$

26. 20°

27. 60°

28. 315°

29. 260°

30. 109°

In Exercises 31–36, rewrite the radian measure as degrees. **(13.2)**

31. $\frac{7\pi}{6}$

32. $\frac{5\pi}{6}$

33. -3π

34. $\frac{4\pi}{15}$

35. $\frac{4\pi}{5}$

36. $\frac{8\pi}{9}$

In Exercises 37–42, sketch the angle. Then find its reference angle. **(13.3)**

37. $\frac{11\pi}{4}$

38. 190°

39. $-115°$

40. $-\frac{17\pi}{15}$

41. 460°

42. 208°

In Exercises 43–58, evaluate the expression without using a calculator.
For Exercises 53–58, write the result in degrees and in radians. (13.3, 13.4)

43. $\sec 60°$

44. $\csc \dfrac{\pi}{6}$

45. $\cot \dfrac{\pi}{4}$

46. $\sin 60°$

47. $\sin 45°$

48. $\cot 45°$

49. $\tan 330°$

50. $\sin 225°$

51. $\csc 120°$

52. $\cos \dfrac{11\pi}{6}$

53. $\arccos 0.5$

54. $\arcsin \dfrac{\sqrt{2}}{2}$

55. $\arcsin \dfrac{1}{2}$

56. $\arctan \dfrac{\sqrt{3}}{3}$

57. $\arctan \sqrt{3}$

58. $\arccos \dfrac{\sqrt{2}}{2}$

In Exercises 59–70, use a calculator to evaluate the expression. Round the result to three decimal places. For Exercises 65–70, write the result in degrees and in radians. (13.3, 13.4)

59. $\cos 43°$

60. $\sin 26°$

61. $\csc \dfrac{10\pi}{11}$

62. $\cot \dfrac{\pi}{9}$

63. $\tan 160°$

64. $\sec 220°$

65. $\arcsin 0.9$

66. $\arctan 51$

67. $\arccos \dfrac{3}{4}$

68. $\arccos 0.42$

69. $\arctan 3$

70. $\arcsin \dfrac{1}{8}$

In Exercises 71–80, solve the triangle. (13.5, 13.6)

71.

72.

73.

74.

75. $A = 53°$, $a = 8$, $b = 3$

76. $B = 40°$, $a = 12$, $c = 10$

77. $B = \dfrac{\pi}{4}$, $C = \dfrac{2\pi}{3}$, $b = 10$

78. $C = \dfrac{3\pi}{4}$, $c = 18$, $a = 5$

79. $a = 8$, $b = 7$, $c = 5$

80. $a = 10$, $b = 15$, $c = 7$

In Exercises 81–90, find the area of the triangle. (13.5)

81.

82.

83.

84.

85. $A = 66°$, $b = 9$, $c = 5$

86. $a = 10$, $b = 5$, $c = 11$

87. $a = 6$, $b = 14$, $c = 9$

88. $C = 28°$, $a = 12$, $b = 8$

89. $a = 5$, $b = 4$, $c = 7$

90. $B = 82°$, $a = 21$, $c = 29$

91. *Fountain Place Tower*   The Bank Tower shown at the right is about 700 feet tall and has 60 floors. The figure below shows dimensions of the section between the 13th and 45th floors. Find the angle θ.

92. *Finding a Distance*   You live 4 miles east of your school, and your best friend lives 5 miles northwest of the school. How far does your friend live from you?

93. *Circular Pipe*   Find the inner diameter of the narrowest circular pipe that will fit over the hexagonal nut shown at the right.

94. *The Star Sirius*   The *parallax* of a star can be measured by comparing pairs of photographs taken several months apart. The parallax for Sirius, the brightest star that can be seen from Earth, is

$\theta = 1.04 \times 10^{-4}$ degree.

What is the distance between Earth and Sirius in astronomical units? (An *astronomical unit* is the mean distance between Earth and the sun.)

The Bank Tower at Fountain Place in Dallas

95. *Submarine Torpedo*   In World War II, a submarine tracked a ship on a course 10° west of north. As the ship passed directly west of the submarine, the submarine fired a torpedo that traveled three times as fast as the ship. At what angle did the torpedo have to be fired to hit the ship?

The fan casing for the jet engine's fan blades has a diameter of 6 feet. (Each of the fan blades extends to the end of the fan casing.)

96. *Jet Engine*   Use the above photo to find the angle between each pair of consecutive fan blades.

97. *Jet Engine*   Approximate the distance between the outer tips of two consecutive fan blades.

98. *Jet Engine*   The tip of one of the fan blades starts at the lowest position. The fan blade then rotates 75° counterclockwise. How far did the tip move horizontally? How far did it move vertically?

Jet Airplane   **In Exercises 99–102, use the following information.**

The diagram below shows a top view of a DC-10 jet airplane. The length of the airplane is 182 feet, and the length from one wingtip to the other is 161 feet.

99. Find *AB*, the distance between a wingtip and the nose of the airplane.

100. Find the length of the front edge of each wing.

101. Find the angle, *θ*, that the wing makes with the airplane.

102. Find *CD*, the distance between a wingtip and the tail of the airplane.

In Exercises 1–3, evaluate the expression.

1. $\csc \frac{\pi}{4}$

2. $\tan 135°$

3. $\cos \frac{11\pi}{6}$

In Exercises 4–6, evaluate the expression. Write the result in degrees and in radians.

4. $\arccos 0.5$

5. $\arcsin\left(-\frac{\sqrt{2}}{2}\right)$

6. $\arctan(-1)$

In Exercises 7–12, solve the triangle.

7.

8.

9.

10. $a = 7$, $C = 35°$, $b = 14$

11. $A = 29°$, $B = 130°$, $a = 5$

12. $a = 6$, $b = 12$, $c = 9$

In Exercises 13–18, find the area of the triangle.

13.

14.

15.

16. $b = 4$, $c = 9$, $A = 36°$

17. $a = 5$, $c = 10$, $B = \frac{3\pi}{4}$

18. $a = 3$, $b = 6$, $C = \frac{3\pi}{8}$

19. A boat travels 50 miles due west before adjusting its course 30° northward and traveling an additional 25 miles. How far is the boat from its point of departure?

20. A bike has tires with radii of 13 inches. How many degrees of revolution does each tire go through when the bike travels 10 feet?

21. The kitchen work triangle at the right has acute angles of 20° each. The longest side of the triangle measures 10 feet. What are the lengths of the two legs of the triangle?

22. Find the total length of the sides of a work triangle that contains an angle of 67° with adjoining sides of 5 feet and 9 feet. For the greatest efficiency, the total length of the sides of the work triangle should be less than 26 feet. Is this kitchen work triangle efficient?

CHAPTER

14

Trigonometric Graphs, Identities, and Equations

LESSONS

14.1 Graphs of Sine and Cosine Functions ▪ 730

14.2 Translations of Graphs ▪ 737

14.3 Trigonometric Identities ▪ 744

14.4 Solving Trigonometric Equations ▪ 753

14.5 Sum and Difference Formulas ▪ 760

14.6 Double- and Half-Angle Formulas ▪ 766

Exercising vigorously, as these cross-country runners are, increases your pulse rate. One effect of this on your blood pressure is shown in the graphs on the opposite page.

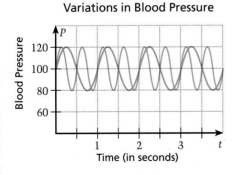

Real Life

Sports Medicine

The graph of $P = 100 + 20 \sin 2\pi t$ is shown in green at the left. It represents a person's blood pressure, P (in millimeters of mercury), where t is the time in seconds. The *amplitude* of this graph is 20—the blood pressure oscillates 20 millimeters above and below 100 millimeters, which means that the person's blood pressure is 120/80. The graph has a *period* of 1 second, which means that the person's heart beats 60 times per minute.

When you exercise, your pulse rate increases. The graph of $P = 100 + 20 \sin 4\pi t$ (in blue) represents a blood pressure of 120/80 for a person whose pulse rate is 120 heartbeats per minute.

Variations in Blood Pressure

14.1

Graphs of Sine and Cosine Functions

What you should learn:

Goal 1 How to sketch the graphs of the sine and cosine functions

Goal 2 How to use sine and cosine functions as models of real-life problems

Why you should learn it:

You can model wave patterns, such as sound waves, with the sine and cosine functions.

Goal 1 — Graphing Sine and Cosine Functions

LESSON INVESTIGATION

■ **Investigating Sine and Cosine Graphs**

Partner Activity Use a graphing calculator to sketch the graph of the sine function, $y = \sin x$. Set the calculator to radian mode and choose an appropriate viewing rectangle. With your partner, describe the graph. What is its domain? Its range? Repeat this activity for the cosine function. Then compare the graphs of the two functions.

In this investigation, you may have discovered the following.

1. The *domain* of each function is all real numbers.
2. The *range* of each function is $-1 \le y \le 1$.
3. Each of the graphs below has a period of 2π.
4. The maximum value of $y = \sin x$ occurs when $x = \frac{\pi}{2} + 2n\pi$, where n is an integer. The maximum value of $y = \cos x$ occurs when $x = 2n\pi$.
5. The minimum value of $y = \sin x$ occurs when $x = \frac{3\pi}{2} + 2n\pi$, where n is an integer. The minimum value of $y = \cos x$ occurs when $x = (2n + 1)\pi$.

> **Study Tip**
> A function is **periodic** if its graph has a pattern that repeats indefinitely. The shortest repeating portion is a **cycle**. The horizontal length of each cycle is the **period**.

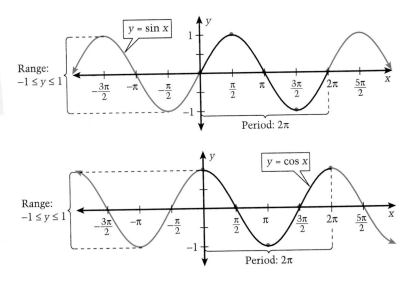

On the interval from 0 to 2π, the graphs of the basic sine and cosine functions have five key points: the x-intercepts, the maximum, and the minimum. These are shown in the graphs below.

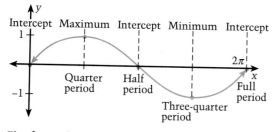

Five key points on graph of $y = \sin x$

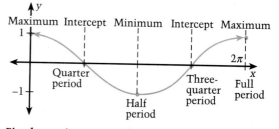

Five key points on graph of $y = \cos x$

Amplitude and Period of Sine and Cosine Graphs

The **amplitude** of the graph of $y = a \sin bx$ or $y = a \cos bx$ is the amount by which it varies above and below the x-axis. The **period** of each graph is the length of the shortest interval on the x-axis over which the graph repeats.

$$\text{Amplitude} = |a| \quad \text{and} \quad \text{Period} = \frac{2\pi}{|b|}$$

Example 1 **Using Amplitude and Period to Sketch a Graph**

Sketch the graph of $y = 2 \sin x$.

Solution Because $a = 2$, the graph has an amplitude of 2. Because $b = 1$, the graph has a period of 2π. Thus, it cycles once from 0 to 2π with one maximum of 2, one minimum of -2, and three x-intercepts.

Intercept	Maximum	Intercept	Minimum	Intercept
$(0, 0),$	$\left(\frac{\pi}{2}, 2\right),$	$(\pi, 0),$	$\left(\frac{3\pi}{2}, -2\right),$	$(2\pi, 0)$

Note how the graph of $y = 2 \sin x$ is like the graph of $y = \sin x$. Each has the same x-intercepts, but $y = 2 \sin x$ has an amplitude that is twice the amplitude of $y = \sin x$. ∎

Example 2 · Using Amplitude and Period

Sketch the graph of $y = \frac{1}{2} \cos x$ and $y = 3 \cos x$.

Solution For $y = \frac{1}{2} \cos x$, the amplitude is $\frac{1}{2}$ and the period is 2π. Between 0 and 2π, the five key points on the graph are

$$
\overbrace{\left(0, \tfrac{1}{2}\right)}^{\text{Maximum}}, \quad \overbrace{\left(\tfrac{\pi}{2}, 0\right)}^{\text{Intercept}}, \quad \overbrace{\left(\pi, -\tfrac{1}{2}\right)}^{\text{Minimum}}, \quad \overbrace{\left(\tfrac{3\pi}{2}, 0\right)}^{\text{Intercept}}, \quad \overbrace{\left(2\pi, \tfrac{1}{2}\right)}^{\text{Maximum}}.
$$

For $y = 3 \cos x$, the amplitude is 3 and the period is 2π. Between 0 and 2π, the five key points on the graph are

$$
\overbrace{(0, 3)}^{\text{Maximum}}, \quad \overbrace{\left(\tfrac{\pi}{2}, 0\right)}^{\text{Intercept}}, \quad \overbrace{(\pi, -3)}^{\text{Minimum}}, \quad \overbrace{\left(\tfrac{3\pi}{2}, 0\right)}^{\text{Intercept}}, \quad \overbrace{(2\pi, 3)}^{\text{Maximum}}.
$$

The graphs of both functions are shown at the left with the graph $y = \cos x$.

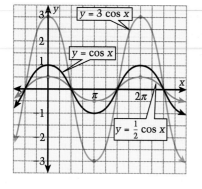

Example 3 · Comparing Graphs with Other Periods

In the graphs below, note that the one with the least period oscillates most frequently, and the one with the greatest period oscillates least frequently (over intervals of the same length).

a. The graph of $y = \sin 2x$ has a period of $\frac{2\pi}{2} = \pi$.

b. The graph of $y = \sin x$ has a period of 2π.

c. The graph of $y = \sin \frac{x}{2}$ has a period of $\frac{2\pi}{1/2} = 4\pi$.

Musical notes are classified by their frequency. For instance, the musical note A above middle C has a frequency of 440 hertz (cycles per second), and the A above A-440 has a frequency of 880 hertz. The sound waves of musical notes can be modeled by sine functions. The frequency is the reciprocal of the period.

Goal 2 Using Trig Functions in Real Life

Real Life
Music

Example 4 *Amplitude and Frequency of Musical Sound*

The amplitude of a sound wave is a measure of its *intensity*. Which of the following sine functions, where t is the time in seconds, models the musical note A-220? A-440? A-880? Which note has the greatest intensity?

a. $y = 3 \sin 440\pi t$ **b.** $y = 4 \sin 880\pi t$ **c.** $y = 2 \sin 1660\pi t$

Solution

a. The amplitude of this sound wave is 3. Its period is

$$\frac{2\pi}{|b|} = \frac{2\pi}{440\pi} = \frac{1}{220} \text{ second.}$$

The frequency is 220 hertz. Thus the note is A-220.

b. The amplitude of this sound wave is 4. Its period is

$$\frac{2\pi}{|b|} = \frac{2\pi}{880\pi} = \frac{1}{440} \text{ second.}$$

The frequency is 440 hertz. Thus the note is A-440.

c. The amplitude of this sound wave is 2. Its period is

$$\frac{2\pi}{|b|} = \frac{2\pi}{1660\pi} = \frac{1}{880} \text{ second.}$$

The frequency is 880 hertz. Thus the note is A-880.

The second note has the greatest intensity. ∎

Communicating about ALGEBRA

▶ **SHARING IDEAS about the Lesson**

Sketch the graphs of the functions. Explain your steps.

A. $y = 2 \sin 3x$ **B.** $y = \cos \frac{x}{3}$ **C.** $y = \sin 2\pi x$

EXERCISES

Guided Practice

▶ **CRITICAL THINKING about the Lesson**

1. Which x-value does *not* give a maximum of $y = \sin x$?

   a. $x = -\frac{3\pi}{2}$ **b.** $x = -\frac{\pi}{2}$ **c.** $x = \frac{\pi}{2}$

2. What is the domain and range of the sine and cosine functions?

3. What is the period of the graph at the right?

4. What is the period of $y = \cos \pi x$?

5. What is the amplitude of $y = 5 \sin x$?

Independent Practice

In Exercises 6–15, find the amplitude and period of the graph.

6.

7.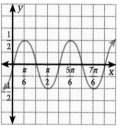

8. $y = 2 \sin 2x$

9. $y = \frac{1}{2} \cos 2x$

10. $y = 3 \cos \frac{1}{2}x$

11. $y = \sin 4x$

12. $y = \frac{1}{4} \cos \pi x$

13. $y = 4 \cos 2\pi x$

14. $y = 3 \sin \frac{1}{2}\pi x$

15. $y = \frac{1}{3} \sin 4\pi x$

In Exercises 16–19, match the equation with its graph.

16. $y = 2 \cos 2x$ **17.** $y = 2 \sin 2x$ **18.** $y = 2 \sin \frac{1}{2}x$ **19.** $y = 2 \cos \frac{1}{2}x$

a.

b.

c.

d.

In Exercises 20–31, sketch two cycles of the graph of the function.

20. $y = \sin \frac{1}{3}x$

21. $y = \cos \frac{1}{5}x$

22. $y = \frac{1}{2} \sin x$

23. $y = 6 \cos x$

24. $y = 5 \cos x$

25. $y = 10 \sin x$

26. $y = 4 \cos 2x$

27. $y = \frac{1}{3} \sin 4x$

28. $y = \frac{1}{3} \sin \pi x$

29. $y = 3 \sin 2\pi x$

30. $y = 2 \cos 6\pi x$

31. $y = \frac{1}{2} \cos \frac{1}{4}\pi x$

Technology   **In Exercises 32 and 33, the graph was sketched with a graphing calculator, but it is *incorrect*. Can you see what went wrong?**

32. $y = 3 \cos(2x)$

33. $y = \frac{1}{2} \sin x$

In Exercises 34–37, write an equation of the indicated function. (Use $a > 0$ and $b > 0$.)

34. $y = a \sin bx$
Amplitude: 4
Period: 3π

35. $y = a \sin bx$
Amplitude: 3
Period: $\frac{\pi}{3}$

36. $y = a \cos bx$
Amplitude: 1
Period: 4

37. $y = a \cos bx$
Amplitude: $\frac{5}{2}$
Period: π

In Exercises 38 and 39, write two x-values at which the function has a minimum. Write two x-values at which it has a maximum.

38. $y = 2 \cos 3x$

39. $y = \frac{1}{2} \sin 4x$

In Exercises 40 and 41, which graph oscillates most frequently?

40. a. $y = \sin \frac{1}{4}x$ **b.** $y = 2 \sin \frac{1}{2}x$ **c.** $y = \frac{1}{4} \sin x$ **d.** $y = \sin 3x$

41. a. $y = \frac{1}{4} \cos 2x$ **b.** $y = 2 \cos \frac{1}{3}x$ **c.** $y = 4 \cos \frac{5}{2}x$ **d.** $y = \cos \frac{1}{2}x$

Sound Waves   **In Exercises 42 and 43, use the following information.**

Plucking or striking a stretched string such as a violin string causes sound waves. Sound waves can be modeled on the screen of an **oscilloscope** as shown, and by sine functions of the form $y = a \sin bx$, where x is measured in seconds.

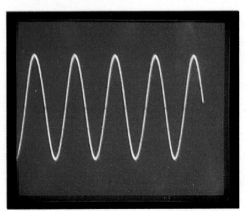

42. Write an equation of a sound wave whose amplitude is 2 and whose period is $\frac{1}{264}$ second.

43. What is the frequency of the sound wave described in Exercise 42?

44. Pendulum Motion   The motion of a pendulum can be modeled by

$$y = A \cos \frac{\sqrt{32}t}{L}.$$

In this model, y is the *directed* length (in feet) of the arc, A is the length (in feet) of the arc from which the pendulum is released, L is the length (in feet) of the pendulum, and t is the time in seconds. How many seconds does it take a 2-foot-long pendulum that is released with an initial arc of 4 inches to swing through one complete cycle?

45. Spring Motion   The motion of a simple spring can be modeled by $y = A \cos kt$, where y is the vertical displacement (in feet), A is the initial displacement (in feet), k is a constant that measures the elasticity of the spring, and t is the time in seconds. Find the amplitude and period of a spring for which $A = \frac{1}{2}$ foot and $k = 6$.

Integrated Review

In Exercises 46–49, evaluate the expression.

46. $\sin \frac{3\pi}{4}$ **47.** $\cos \frac{7\pi}{3}$ **48.** $\tan \frac{7\pi}{4}$ **49.** $\sec \frac{5\pi}{6}$

Estimating Latitude   **In Exercises 50 and 51, use the following information.**

You can estimate the latitude of your location on Earth by pointing one arm at the North Star and the other at the horizon directly below the North Star. The latitude of your location is approximately equal to the angle (in degrees) between your two arms.

50. One of the people pictured is in Portland, Maine. The other is in San Antonio, Texas. Which is which? Explain.

51. Use a protractor to estimate the latitudes of Portland and San Antonio.

Exploration and Extension

52. Copy and complete the table. Round each value to two decimal places. Sketch the graph of $y = \tan x$ for $-\frac{\pi}{2} < x < \frac{\pi}{2}$. What is the period of the graph?

x	$-\frac{11\pi}{24}$	$-\frac{5\pi}{12}$	$-\frac{\pi}{3}$	$-\frac{\pi}{4}$	$-\frac{\pi}{6}$	0	$\frac{\pi}{6}$	$\frac{\pi}{4}$	$\frac{\pi}{3}$	$\frac{5\pi}{12}$	$\frac{11\pi}{24}$
tan x	?	?	?	?	?	?	?	?	?	?	?

14.2 Translations and Reflections of Graphs

What you should learn:

Goal 1 How to graph vertical and horizontal shifts and reflections of the graphs of the sine and cosine functions

Goal 2 How to use sine and cosine functions to solve real-life problems

Why you should learn it:

You can model many cyclical relationships, such as average daily temperature, using translations or reflections of the sine and cosine function.

Goal 1 | Graphing Shifts and Reflections

In Lesson 14.1, you learned how to sketch the graphs of functions of the form $y = a \sin bx$ and $y = a \cos bx$ where a is positive. In this lesson, you will study the graphs of functions of the form $y = a \sin(bx + c) + d$ and $y = a \cos(bx + c) + d$ where a is any real number.

Shifts of Sine and Cosine Graphs

To obtain the graph of

$$y = a \sin(bx + c) + d \qquad \text{or} \qquad y = a \cos(bx + c) + d$$

shift the graph of $y = a \sin bx$ or $y = a \cos bx$ as follows.

1. If $d > 0$, shift d units up.
2. If $d < 0$, shift $|d|$ units down.
3. If $\dfrac{c}{b} > 0$, shift $\dfrac{c}{b}$ units to the left.
4. If $\dfrac{c}{b} < 0$, shift $\left|\dfrac{c}{b}\right|$ units to the right.

The *amplitude* of the resulting graph is $|a|$ and the *period* is $\dfrac{2\pi}{|b|}$.

Example 1 | *Using a Vertical Shift to Sketch a Graph*

Sketch the graph of $y = 2 + 3 \sin 2x$.

Solution The amplitude of the graph is 3, and the period is π. Because the graph is shifted two units up, it oscillates about the line $y = 2$ rather than about the x-axis. One way to sketch the graph is to sketch the graph of $y = 3 \sin 2x$ first, and then shift the graph up two units. Another way is to locate five key points within one period (between 0 and π). At three of the points, the graph intersects the line $y = 2$. The other two represent the maximum and minimum values of the graph.

$$
\underbrace{(0, 2),}_{y = 2} \quad \underbrace{\left(\tfrac{\pi}{4}, 5\right),}_{\text{Maximum}} \quad \underbrace{\left(\tfrac{\pi}{2}, 2\right),}_{y = 2} \quad \underbrace{\left(\tfrac{3\pi}{4}, -1\right),}_{\text{Minimum}} \quad \underbrace{(\pi, 2)}_{y = 2}
$$

The graph of the function is shown at the left. ■

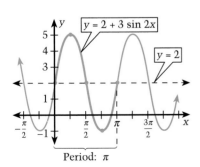

Period: π

Example 2 — *Graphing Horizontal Shifts*

Sketch the graph of $y = \cos\left(x - \frac{\pi}{2}\right)$.

Solution The amplitude of the graph is 1, and the period is 2π. One way to sketch the graph is to first sketch the graph of $y = \cos x$, and then shift that graph $\frac{\pi}{2}$ units to the right. Another way is to locate five key points within one period (between 0 and 2π).

Intercept	Maximum	Intercept	Minimum	Intercept
$(0, 0),$	$\left(\frac{\pi}{2}, 1\right),$	$(\pi, 0),$	$\left(\frac{3\pi}{2}, -1\right),$	$(2\pi, 0)$

The graph is shown below in blue. The black curve is the graph $y = \cos x$.

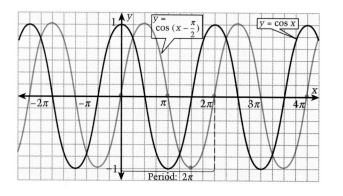

Example 3 — *Using a Reflection to Sketch a Graph*

Sketch the graph of $y = -3 \cos x$.

Solution The amplitude of the graph is 3, and the period is 2π. One way to sketch the graph is to graph $y = 3 \cos x$ first, and then reflect it in the x-axis. Another way is to locate five key points in the interval between 0 and 2π.

Minimum	Intercept	Maximum	Intercept	Minimum
$(0, -3),$	$\left(\frac{\pi}{2}, 0\right),$	$(\pi, 3),$	$\left(\frac{3\pi}{2}, 0\right),$	$(2\pi, -3)$

The graph is shown below in blue. The black curve is the graph $y = 3 \cos x$.

Real Life
Meteorology

The Riverfront Plaza in down-town Louisville

Example 4 — *Using a Temperature Model*

A model for the average daily temperature, T (in degrees Fahrenheit), in Louisville, Kentucky, is given by

$$T = 55.2 + 22.8 \sin\left(\tfrac{1}{6}\pi t + 4.2\right)$$

where $t = 0$ represents January 1, $t = 1$ represents February 1, and so on. What is the period of this function? Which months have the highest and lowest average daily temperatures?

Solution The period of the function is

$$\frac{2\pi}{|b|} = \frac{2\pi}{\tfrac{1}{6}\pi} = 12.$$

Thus the temperature cycle repeats every 12 months. By calculating temperatures, you can sketch the graph shown below. The highest and lowest average temperatures are

$$55.2 + 22.8 = 78°F \quad \text{and} \quad 55.2 - 22.8 = 32.4°F$$

which occur around the first of July and the first of February, respectively.

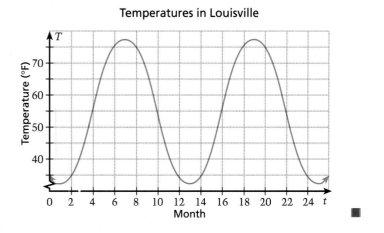

Temperatures in Louisville

(vertical axis: Temperature (°F); horizontal axis: Month, t)

Communicating about ALGEBRA

▶ **SHARING IDEAS about the Lesson**

Sketch the graph of each function from 0 to 4π. Explain the effects of the constants a, b, c, and d in $y = a \sin(bx + c) + d$.

A. $y = 3 \sin x$ **B.** $y = 3 \sin 2x$

C. $y = 3 \sin(2x - 2\pi)$ **D.** $y = -2 + 3 \sin(2x - 2\pi)$

EXERCISES

Guided Practice

▶ **CRITICAL THINKING about the Lesson**

In Exercises 1–4, state whether the graph of the function is a vertical
shift, a horizontal shift, or a reflection of the graph of $y = 6 \cos 2x$.

1. $y = 1 + 6 \cos 2x$ **2.** $y = -6 \cos 2x$ **3.** $y = 6 \cos(2x - 3)$ **4.** $y = 6 \cos(2x + 1)$

5. Sketch the graph of $y = \sin\left(x + \frac{\pi}{2}\right)$. **6.** Sketch the graph of $y = 2 + 3 \cos(x + \pi)$.

Independent Practice

In Exercises 7–18, describe how the graphs of $y = \sin x$ or $y = \cos x$ can be
shifted to produce the graph of the function.

7. $y = 1 + \sin x$ **8.** $y = 6 + \cos x$ **9.** $y = -3 + \cos x$

10. $y = -5 + \sin x$ **11.** $y = \cos\left(x + \frac{\pi}{2}\right)$ **12.** $y = \sin(x + \pi)$

13. $y = \sin(x - \pi)$ **14.** $y = \cos\left(x - \frac{\pi}{2}\right)$ **15.** $y = 4 + \cos\left(x - \frac{\pi}{4}\right)$

16. $y = -2 + \cos\left(x + \frac{3\pi}{4}\right)$ **17.** $y = -1 + \cos(x - \pi)$ **18.** $y = 3 + \cos(x + \pi)$

In Exercises 19–24, match the equation to its graph.

19. $y = \cos(x + \pi)$ **20.** $y = 1 + \sin \frac{1}{2}x$ **21.** $y = -2 + \cos x$

22. $y = -2 + \sin(2x + \pi)$ **23.** $y = -\cos(x + \pi)$ **24.** $y = 1 + 2 \cos\left(\frac{1}{2}x + \frac{\pi}{2}\right)$

25. The graph of $y = 2 \sin 3x$ is drawn and then shifted up two units.
Write an equation of the resulting graph.

26. The graph of $y = 2 \sin x$ is drawn and then shifted π units to the
right. Write an equation of the resulting graph.

In Exercises 27–44, sketch the graph of the function.

27. $y = 4 + \sin \frac{1}{2}x$

28. $y = \cos\left(x - \frac{\pi}{2}\right)$

29. $y = -2 + \cos 3x$

30. $y = 3 + \sin 2x$

31. $y = 1 + \sin(x + \pi)$

32. $y = -1 + \cos(x - \pi)$

33. $y = 3 + 2 \cos(2x - \pi)$

34. $y = 2 + 3 \sin(4x + \pi)$

35. $y = -4 \cos \frac{1}{4}x$

36. $y = -\frac{1}{2} \sin 4x$

37. $y = -1 + 2 \sin(x - \pi)$

38. $y = -8 + 6 \cos\left(2x - \frac{\pi}{2}\right)$

39. $y = 10 + \sin\left(\frac{1}{4}x + \pi\right)$

40. $y = -2 + \cos\left(2x + \frac{\pi}{2}\right)$

41. $y = 2 - \sin x$

42. $y = 1 - \cos x$

43. $y = 1 + 5 \cos(x - \pi)$

44. $y = 5 + 10 \sin\left(x + \frac{3\pi}{2}\right)$

45. What are the minimum and maximum values of $y = -1 + 2 \sin 6x$? Write two x-values at which the minimum occurs. Write two x-values at which the maximum occurs.

46. What are the minimum and maximum values of the function $y = 4 - 3 \cos\left(x + \frac{\pi}{2}\right)$? Write two x-values at which the minimum occurs. Write two x-values at which the maximum occurs.

In Exercises 47 and 48, write an equation of the graph.

47.

48.

Coyotes and Rabbits **In Exercises 49 and 50, use the following information.**

Sine functions are used in biology to model oscillations in predator and prey populations. The population, R, of rabbits and the population, C, of coyotes in a region are modeled by

$$R = 25{,}000 + 15{,}000 \cos \frac{2\pi t}{24}$$

$$C = 5000 + 2000 \sin \frac{2\pi t}{24}$$

where t is the time in months.

49. Find the amplitude and period of each graph.

50. Sketch both of these functions on the same coordinate plane and explain the oscillations in the size of each population.

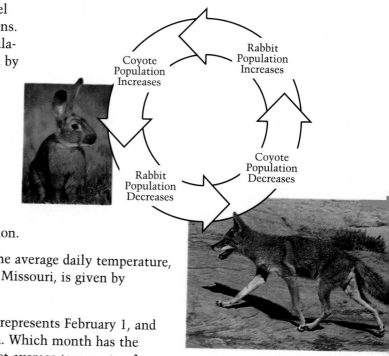

51. *Average Temperature*   A model for the average daily temperature, T (degrees Fahrenheit), in Kansas City, Missouri, is given by

$$T = 54 + 25.2 \sin\left(\frac{2\pi}{12}t + 4.3\right)$$

where $t = 0$ represents January 1, $t = 1$ represents February 1, and so on. Sketch the graph of this function. Which month has the highest average temperature? The lowest average temperature?

Sunrise, Sunset   **In Exercises 52 and 53, use the following information.**

Cheyenne (Wyoming), DuBois (Pennsylvania), Ft. Wayne (Indiana), and Omaha (Nebraska) all have a latitude of 41° north. On this latitude, the position of the sun at sunrise (and sunset) can be modeled by

$$T = 31 \sin\left(\tfrac{2\pi}{365}t - 1.4\right)$$

where t is the time in days with $t = 1$ representing January 1. In this model, T represents the number of degrees north or south of due east (and west) that the sun rises (and sets).

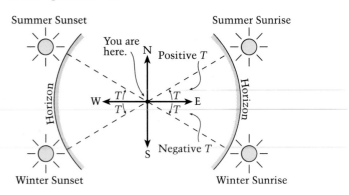

52. Sketch the graph of this function.

53. Locate the spring equinox, the summer solstice, the fall equinox, and the winter solstice on the graph. Which of these four days has the most hours of sunlight? Which has the least?

54. *Blood Pressure*   The blood pressure, P (in millimeters of mercury), of a certain person is given by $P = 100 - 20 \cos \frac{8\pi}{3}t$, where t is the time in seconds. Sketch the graph of this function. What is this person's pulse rate in heartbeats per minute?

Integrated Review

In Exercises 55–60, sketch the graph of the function.

55. $y = 6 \sin 4x$

56. $y = 5 \cos 6x$

57. $y = \frac{1}{3} \cos 5x$

58. $y = \frac{1}{2} \sin 2x$

59. $y = 3 \cos\left(\frac{1}{4}x\right)$

60. $y = \cos\left(\frac{1}{3}x\right)$

61. *College Entrance Exam Sample*   In the figure below, line PQ is parallel to line RS. What is the degree measure of θ?

a. 90° **b.** 100° **c.** 110° **d.** 120° **e.** 130°

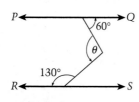

62. *College Entrance Exam Sample*   In the figure below, what is the length of $\overline{NP}$?

a. 3 **b.** 8 **c.** 9 **d.** 12 **e.** 15

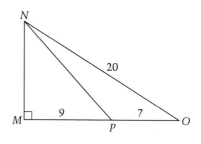

Exploration and Extension

63. Find a value of c for which the graphs of $y = \sin x$ and $y = \cos(x - c)$ are the same.

64. Find a value of c for which the graphs of $y = \cos x$ and $y = \sin(x - c)$ are the same.

1. Solve $\frac{3}{4}x^2 - 6 = 8$. **(5.2)**
2. Solve $3x + 2 \leq -3$. **(1.6)**
3. Find the mean: 0, 2, 3, 6, 5, 4, 2. **(6.7)**
4. Find the inverse of $y = \frac{1}{3}x^3 - 3$. **(6.3)**
5. Simplify: $6^2 x^2 y^{-3} \cdot 2^{-2} xy^4$.
6. Complete the square: $3x^2 + 3x - 4$. **(5.3)**
7. Condense $2 \log_4 x + 4 \log_4 y$. **(8.3)**
8. Sketch the graph of $y = e^{-2x}$. **(8.1)**
9. Sketch the graph of $y^2 - 4x = 0$. **(11.1)**
10. Find the complement of $\frac{3\pi}{13}$. **(13.2)**
11. Sketch the graph of $4x^2 + 6y^2 = 24$. **(11.3)**
12. Sketch the graph of $y = x^2 + 5x + 6$. **(11.1)**
13. What is the reciprocal of the $\cos \theta$? **(13.1)**
14. Sketch the graph of $y \leq 2x^2 + 5x + 3$. **(5.7)**
15. Factor $4x^5 + 3x^2 + x$. **(9.3)**
16. True or False? $1 + \tan^2 \theta = \sec^2 \theta$ **(13.1)**
17. Solve $\frac{3y}{x} + 2y = x^2$ for y. **(1.5)**
18. Solve for a: $\dfrac{5}{\sin 30°} = \dfrac{a}{\sin 60°}$. **(13.5)**
19. Find the area of a triangle whose sides have lengths of 2, 4, and 5. **(13.6)**
20. Identify the conic whose equation is $4x^2 + 8x - 2y^2 + 8y = 6$. **(11.6)**

Milestones UNSOLVED PROBLEMS

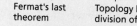

| 600 | 400 | 200 | B.C. A.D. | 200 | 400 | 600 | 800 | 1000 | 1200 | 1400 | 1600 | 1800 | 2000 | 2200 | 2400 | 26 |

Euclid's proof of the number of primes

Fermat's last theorem

Topology becomes a division of mathematics

Some of the questions raised in the study of mathematics are answered, while others raise new questions. Around 300 B.C., Euclid proved that the number of primes is infinite, but no one has found a formula for the next larger prime number for any given prime. Other questions arise from new areas of research, such as the topological question, How many ways can a rubber sphere be wrapped around another sphere?

In the 1600's, Pierre de Fermat made the assertion that the equation $x^n + y^n = z^n$ has no solution in the positive integers when $n > 2$. "Fermat's last theorem," as it is called, has been proven true for all values of $n < 100,000$, and certain other values of n, but it has not yet been proven (or disproven) for *all* the positive integers greater than 2. In his notes describing the theorem, Fermat asserted, ". . . I have assuredly found an admirable proof of this, but the margin is too narrow to contain it." The proof has not been found in any of his other writings, leading many people to believe that he later found a flaw in it.

Find out what topology is.

Pierre de Fermat was a lawyer by profession and a mathematician in his spare time.

14.3 Trigonometric Identities

What you should learn:

Goal 1 How to use trigonometric identities to simplify trigonometric expressions and how to verify trigonometric identities

Goal 2 How to use trigonometric identities to solve real-life problems

Why you should learn it:

In real-life problems, trigonometric expressions often occur in unsimplified forms. You can use trigonometric identities to simplify these expressions.

Goal 1 Using Trigonometric Identities

In Lesson 13.1 (page 680), you studied three of the five types of fundamental trigonometric identities: reciprocal identities, tangent and cotangent identities, and Pythagorean identities. Two other types are *cofunction identities* and *negative angle identities*.

Cofunction Identities:

$$\sin\left(\frac{\pi}{2} - x\right) = \cos x \quad \tan\left(\frac{\pi}{2} - x\right) = \cot x \quad \sec\left(\frac{\pi}{2} - x\right) = \csc x$$

$$\cos\left(\frac{\pi}{2} - x\right) = \sin x \quad \cot\left(\frac{\pi}{2} - x\right) = \tan x \quad \csc\left(\frac{\pi}{2} - x\right) = \sec x$$

Negative Angle Identities:

$$\sin(-x) = -\sin x \qquad \cos(-x) = \cos x \qquad \tan(-x) = -\tan x$$

$$\csc(-x) = -\csc x \qquad \sec(-x) = \sec x \qquad \cot(-x) = -\cot x$$

Example 1 Simplifying a Trigonometric Expression

Simplify $\cos x - \cos x \sin^2 x$.

Solution

$$\cos x - \cos x \sin^2 x = \cos x(1 - \sin^2 x) \quad \textit{Factor.}$$

$$= \cos x(\cos^2 x) \qquad \textit{Pythagorean identity:}$$
$$\textit{sin}^2 \textit{ x} + \textit{cos}^2 \textit{ x} = 1$$

$$= \cos^3 x \qquad \textit{Simplify.} \qquad ■$$

Example 2 Simplifying a Trigonometric Expression

Simplify $\sin\left(\frac{\pi}{2} - x\right) \tan x$ for $x \neq \frac{\pi}{2}, \frac{3\pi}{2}$.

Solution

$$\sin\left(\frac{\pi}{2} - x\right) \tan x = \cos x \tan x \qquad \textit{Cofunction identity}$$

$$= \cos x \frac{\sin x}{\cos x} \qquad \textit{Tangent identity}$$

$$= \cos x \frac{\sin x}{\cos x} \qquad \textit{Divide by common factor.}$$

$$= \sin x \qquad \textit{Simplify.} \qquad ■$$

A *verification* of a statement is a logical argument that the statement is true. The fundamental trigonometric identities can be used to verify other trigonometric identities.

Example 3 Verifying a Trigonometric Identity

Verify the identity $\frac{\cot^2 x}{\csc x} = \csc x - \sin x$.

Solution

$$\frac{\cot^2 x}{\csc x} = \frac{\csc^2 x - 1}{\csc x} \qquad \textit{Pythagorean identity}$$

$$= \frac{\csc^2 x}{\csc x} - \frac{1}{\csc x} \qquad \textit{Write as separate fractions.}$$

$$= \frac{\csc^{\cancel{2}} x}{\cancel{\csc} x} - \frac{1}{\csc x} \qquad \textit{Divide by common factor.}$$

$$= \csc x - \frac{1}{\csc x} \qquad \textit{Simplify.}$$

$$= \csc x - \sin x \qquad \textit{Reciprocal identity} \qquad \blacksquare$$

Example 4 Verifying a Trigonometric Identity

Verify the identity $\cos^2 x - \sin^2 x = 2 \cos^2 x - 1$.

Solution

$$\cos^2 x - \sin^2 x = \cos^2 x - (1 - \cos^2 x) \qquad \textit{Pythagorean identity}$$

$$= \cos^2 x - 1 + \cos^2 x \qquad \textit{Simplify.}$$

$$= 2 \cos^2 x - 1 \qquad \textit{Simplify.} \qquad \blacksquare$$

Example 5 Verifying a Trigonometric Identity

Verify the identity $\frac{\sin x}{1 - \cos x} = \frac{1 + \cos x}{\sin x}$.

Solution

$$\frac{\sin x}{1 - \cos x} = \frac{\sin x(1 + \cos x)}{(1 - \cos x)(1 + \cos x)} \qquad \textit{Multiply numerator and}$$
$$\textit{denominator by (1 + cos x).}$$

$$= \frac{\sin x(1 + \cos x)}{1 - \cos^2 x} \qquad \textit{Simplify denominator.}$$

$$= \frac{\sin x(1 + \cos x)}{\sin^2 x} \qquad \textit{Pythagorean identity}$$

$$= \frac{\cancel{\sin x}(1 + \cos x)}{\sin^{\cancel{2}} x} \qquad \textit{Divide by common factor.}$$

$$= \frac{1 + \cos x}{\sin x} \qquad \textit{Simplify.} \qquad \blacksquare$$

Goal 2 Using Trig Identities in Technology

Most graphing calculators have two graphing modes: *function* mode and *parametric* mode. In function mode, you must enter y as a function of x. In parametric mode, you enter x and y as functions of a *parameter t*. In either case, the resulting graph is in the standard xy-coordinate plane.

Connections
Technology

Example 6 *Sketching an Ellipse*

Show that the graph of these parametric equations is an ellipse: $x = 2 \cos t$ and $y = 3 \sin t$.

Solution To get an idea of the shape of the graph, you can substitute several values of t and plot the resulting points (x, y).

t	0	$\dfrac{\pi}{4}$	$\dfrac{\pi}{2}$	$\dfrac{3\pi}{4}$	π	$\dfrac{5\pi}{4}$	$\dfrac{3\pi}{2}$	$\dfrac{7\pi}{4}$
(x, y)	$(2, 0)$	$\left(\sqrt{2}, \dfrac{3\sqrt{2}}{2}\right)$	$(0, 3)$	$\left(-\sqrt{2}, \dfrac{3\sqrt{2}}{2}\right)$	$(-2, 0)$	$\left(-\sqrt{2}, -\dfrac{3\sqrt{2}}{2}\right)$	$(0, -3)$	$\left(\sqrt{2}, -\dfrac{3\sqrt{2}}{2}\right)$

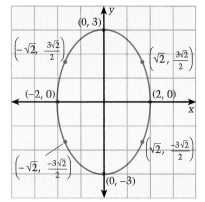

By plotting the points in the table, it appears that each point lies on an ellipse. You can use a trig identity to verify this.

$$\sin^2 t + \cos^2 t = 1 \quad \textit{Pythagorean identity}$$

$$\left(\frac{y}{3}\right)^2 + \left(\frac{x}{2}\right)^2 = 1 \quad \textit{Substitute for sin t and cos t.}$$

$$\frac{y^2}{3^2} + \frac{x^2}{2^2} = 1 \quad \textit{Simplify.}$$

From the last equation, you can recognize that the graph of the equations is an ellipse. If you have a graphing calculator, try using it in parametric mode to sketch this ellipse. ∎

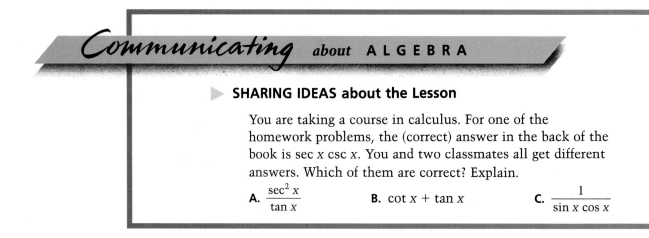

Communicating about **A L G E B R A**

▶ SHARING IDEAS about the Lesson

You are taking a course in calculus. For one of the homework problems, the (correct) answer in the back of the book is sec x csc x. You and two classmates all get different answers. Which of them are correct? Explain.

A. $\dfrac{\sec^2 x}{\tan x}$ **B.** $\cot x + \tan x$ **C.** $\dfrac{1}{\sin x \cos x}$

EXERCISES

Guided Practice

▶ CRITICAL THINKING about the Lesson

1. Write the six cofunction identities.
2. A function is *odd* if $f(-x) = -f(x)$. A function is *even* if $f(-x) = f(x)$. Which of the six trigonometric functions are odd? Which are even?
3. Simplify $\cos\left(\frac{\pi}{2} - x\right) \cot x$. Which identities did you use?
4. Complete the verification shown at the right.

$$\tan^2 x = \frac{\sin^2 x}{\cos^2 x}$$
$$= \frac{\boxed{?}}{\cos^2 x}$$
$$= \boxed{?} - 1$$
$$= \sec^2 x - 1$$

Independent Practice

In Exercises 5–22, simplify the expression.

5. $\sec x \cos(-x) - \sin^2 x$

6. $\dfrac{\cot(-x)}{\csc(-x)}$

7. $\cos\left(\dfrac{\pi}{2} - x\right) \csc x$

8. $\cos x(1 + \tan^2 x)$

9. $\sec^2\left(\dfrac{\pi}{2} - x\right) - 1$

10. $\dfrac{\cos^2 x \cot^2\left(\frac{\pi}{2} - x\right) - 1}{\cos^2 x}$

11. $-1 + \sin^2 x + \sec^2(-x)$

12. $\cot\left(\dfrac{\pi}{2} - x\right) \cot x$

13. $(1 - \cos^2 x)(\cot^2(-x) + 1)$

14. $\dfrac{\csc x \sin^2 x - \csc x}{\sec\left(\frac{\pi}{2} - x\right)}$

15. $\dfrac{\sin(-x)}{\csc x} + \cos^2(-x)$

16. $\sec(-x) - \sec(-x) \sin^2 x$

17. $\csc^2(-x) \tan^2\left(\dfrac{\pi}{2} - x\right)$

18. $\dfrac{\cos^2(-x)}{\cot^2 x}$

19. $\dfrac{\cos\left(\frac{\pi}{2} - x\right) - 1}{1 + \sin(-x)}$

20. $\dfrac{\sec x \tan x}{\sin(-x) \cot\left(\frac{\pi}{2} - x\right)}$

21. $\dfrac{\cos x \cot x + \tan\left(\frac{\pi}{2} - x\right)}{1 + \cos x}$

22. $\tan x \cot\left(\dfrac{\pi}{2} - x\right) - \sec^2 x$

In Exercises 23–38, verify the identity.

23. $\cos^2 x - \sin^2 x = 1 - 2\sin^2 x$

24. $\csc^4 x - \cot^4 x = 2\csc^2 x - 1$

25. $\cot^2 x(\sec^2 x - 1) = 1$

26. $4\tan^4 x + \tan^2 x - 3 = \sec^2 x(4\tan^2 x - 3)$

27. $\sin x \csc x = 1$

28. $\tan y \cot y = 1$

29. $\tan^2 x + 4 = \sec^2 x + 3$

30. $2 - \sec^2 x = 1 - \tan^2 x$

31. $\sin^2 x - \sin^4 x = \cos^2 x - \cos^4 x$

32. $\cos x + \sin x \tan x = \sec x$

33. $\dfrac{1 + \sin x}{\cos x} + \dfrac{\cos x}{1 + \sin x} = 2\sec x$

34. $\dfrac{1}{\cot x + 1} + \dfrac{1}{\tan x + 1} = 1$

35. $\dfrac{\cos(-x)}{1 + \sin(-x)} = \sec x + \tan x$

36. $\dfrac{1 + \sec(-x)}{\sin(-x) + \tan(-x)} = -\csc x$

37. $\cos\left(\dfrac{\pi}{2} - x\right) \csc x = 1$

38. $\dfrac{\cos\left(\frac{\pi}{2} - x\right)}{\sin\left(\frac{\pi}{2} - x\right)} = \tan x$

In Exercises 39 and 40, show that the equation is not an identity (for *all* values of *x*) by finding a value of *x* for which the equation is not true.

39. $\sin x = \sqrt{1 - \cos^2 x}$

40. $\sqrt{\tan^2 x} = \tan x$

Technology   In Exercises 41–43, use a graphing calculator in parametric mode to sketch the graph represented by the parametric equations. Use a trigonometric identity to verify that the graph is a circle, an ellipse, or a hyperbola. (Use a calculator setting of $-6 \le x \le 6$ and $-4 \le y \le 4$.)

41. $x = 4 \cos t,\ y = 4 \sin t$ **42.** $x = 3 \sec t,\ y = \tan t$ **43.** $x = 2 \cos t,\ y = 3 \sin t$

44. *Wheel Spokes*   The diagram below shows a wheel with 12 equally-spaced spokes. Each pair of consecutive spokes meets at an angle of $\theta = \frac{\pi}{6}$. Use the trigonometric identity $\tan\left(\frac{\pi}{2} - x\right) = \cot x$ to show that $\cot \theta = \tan 2\theta$.

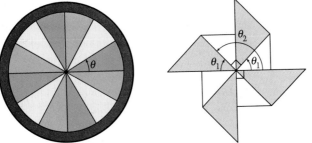

45. *Propeller*   The diagram above shows a toy propeller. Use the identity $\sec\left(\frac{\pi}{2} - x\right) = \csc x$ and a negative angle identity to show that $\sec \theta_1 = \csc \theta_2$.

46. *Up the Down Staircase*   Each of the handrails on the up and down spiral stairs of the Statue of Liberty has the shape of a *helix*. The *projection* of the *down* handrail onto an *xy*-plane can be modeled by $y = 3.5 \sin \frac{\pi}{7}x$, where *x* and *y* are measured in feet. Which of the following models represents the projection of the *up* handrail? Explain.

a. $y = 3.5 \cos\left(-\frac{\pi}{7}x\right)$ **b.** $y = 3.5 \sin\left(-\frac{\pi}{7}x\right)$

c. $y = 3.5 \cos\left(\frac{\pi}{2} - \frac{\pi}{7}x\right)$

KEY
Down Staircase
Up Staircase

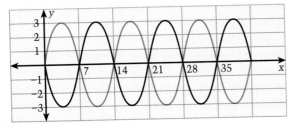

Inside the Statue of Liberty there are two 112-foot spiral stairs—one for people walking up and the other for people walking down.

Integrated Review

In Exercises 47–54, evaluate the indicated trigonometric function. $\left(\text{Assume } 0 \le x \le \frac{\pi}{2}.\right)$

47. Given $\cos x = \frac{4}{5}$, find $\sin x$.

48. Given $\sin x = \frac{2}{3}$, find $\csc x$.

49. Given $\tan x = 10$, find $\sec x$.

50. Given $\cot x = 1$, find $\cos\left(\frac{\pi}{2} - x\right)$.

51. Given $\cos x = \frac{1}{2}$, find $\csc\left(\frac{\pi}{2} - x\right)$.

52. Given $\tan x = 3$, find $\sec\left(\frac{\pi}{2} - x\right)$.

53. Given $\sin x = \frac{1}{3}$, find $\csc x$.

54. Given $\cos x = \frac{1}{5}$, find $\tan x$.

55. *Archerfish* The archerfish at the right is shooting a jet of water into the air to catch the beetle. The beetle is 12 in. above and 11 in. to one side of the fish. At what angle must the archerfish aim to hit the beetle?

56. *Angelfish* Approximate the length of the angelfish shown below.

Exploration and Extension

In Exercises 57–60, substitute the given value of x into the radical expression. Then use a trigonometric identity to rewrite the expression so that it contains no radical.

57. $\sqrt{25 - x^2}$
$x = 5\sin\theta$

58. $\sqrt{16 - 4x^2}$
$x = 2\sin\theta$

59. $\sqrt{1 - (x - 1)^2}$
$x = 1 + \cos\theta$

60. $\sqrt{x^2 + 9}$
$x = 3\tan\theta$

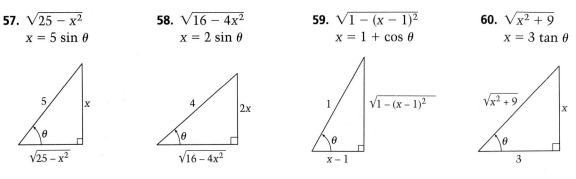

A graphing calculator can be used to verify trigonometric identities graphically. For instance, to verify the Pythagorean identity $\sin^2 x + \cos^2 x = 1$, you can sketch the graph of

$$y = \sin^2 x + \cos^2 x$$

over the interval $0 \le x < 2\pi$. From the graph, you can see that $y = 1$ for all values of x in the interval. Then, using the fact that the sine and cosine functions each have a period of 2π, you can conclude that $y = 1$ for *any* value of x.

Example 1: Discovering Trigonometric Identities

Sketch the graph of

$$y = \sin x + \cos x.$$

From the graph, can you see how to represent this function as a single sine or cosine function?

Solution   From the graph, as shown at the right, it looks like the sum of $\sin x$ and $\cos x$ is itself a sine or cosine function. Suppose you guess that the function is of the form $y = a \cos(bx + c)$. Using the trace key, the minimum and maximum values appear to be $-1.414 \approx -\sqrt{2}$ and $1.414 \approx \sqrt{2}$, which would imply that $a = \sqrt{2}$. Because the period of the function is 2π, you can conclude that $b = 1$. Finally, because the graph appears to have been shifted $\frac{\pi}{4}$ units to the right, you can conclude that $\frac{c}{b} = -\frac{\pi}{4}$, which implies that $c = -\frac{\pi}{4}$. Thus an equation for the graph appears to be

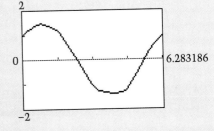

$$y = \sqrt{2} \cos\left(x - \frac{\pi}{4}\right).$$

You can verify this by sketching both graphs on the same screen. Because both equations have the same graph, you have discovered the following trigonometric identity.

$$\sin x + \cos x = \sqrt{2} \cos\left(x - \frac{\pi}{4}\right) \quad \blacksquare$$

Another important use of a graphing calculator in trigonometry is to sketch graphs of functions that would be very tedious to sketch by hand.

Example 2: Sketching a Graph of a Function

Since 1957, the Mauna Loa Climate Observatory in Hawaii has been collecting data on the carbon dioxide level of Earth's atmosphere. A model that represents the data is given by

$$y = (316 + 0.654t + 0.0216t^2) + 2.5 \sin 2\pi t$$

where y represents the carbon dioxide concentration (in parts per million) and $t = 0$ represents 1960 (January 1). Sketch a graph of this function and explain the oscillations in the graph.

Solution The graph of the function is shown below. From the graph, you can see that the carbon dioxide level fluctuates each year. The low level each year, which occurs toward the end of summer in the northern hemisphere, is caused by the intake of carbon dioxide by growing plants. ∎

Carbon Dioxide Levels

Mauna Loa Climate Observatory

Exercises

In Exercises 1–4, sketch the graphs of all three functions on the same display screen. Which two graphs are the same? What trigonometric identity have you discovered?

1. a. $y = \sin^2 x$
   b. $y = \frac{1}{2}(1 - \cos 2x)$
   c. $y = \frac{1}{2}(1 + \cos 2x)$

2. a. $y = 2 \cos^2 x$
   b. $y = 1 - \cos 2x$
   c. $y = 1 + \cos 2x$

3. a. $y = 2 \sin x \cos 2x$
   b. $y = \sin 3x + \sin x$
   c. $y = \sin 3x - \sin x$

4. a. $y = \sin 2x$
   b. $y = 2 \sin x$
   c. $y = 2 \sin x \cos x$

5. *Carbon Dioxide* Sketch the graph of the model from Example 2 for $28 \le t \le 30$. Between January 1, 1988 and January 1, 1990, what were the highest and lowest levels of carbon dioxide? When did each occur?

Take this test as you would take a test in class. The answers to the exercises are given in the back of the book.

In Exercises 1–3, find the amplitude and period of the graph. **(14.1, 14.2)**

1. $y = \frac{5}{2} \sin 2x$

2. $y = 3 + 4 \cos \pi x$

3. $y = \frac{1}{2} - 3 \sin 4x$

In Exercises 4–6, sketch two cycles of the graph of the function. **(14.1, 14.2)**

4. $y = -\sin 2\pi x$

5. $y = 2 + \sin \frac{x}{2}$

6. $y = -2 + \cos 3x$

In Exercises 7–9, write an equation of the function, where $a > 0$ and $b > 0$. **(14.1)**

7. $y = a \sin bx$
   Amplitude: 6
   Period: $\frac{1}{2}$

8. $y = a \sin bx$
   Amplitude: $\frac{4}{3}$
   Period: 3π

9. $y = a \cos bx$
   Amplitude: $\frac{2}{5}$
   Period: π

In Exercises 10–12, simplify the expression. **(14.3)**

10. $\dfrac{-\sec(-x)}{\csc(-x)}$

11. $\sin x + \cos x \cot x$

12. $\dfrac{\sin x \cos x - \tan x}{\tan(-x) \sin^2 x}$

In Exercises 13–15, verify the identity. **(14.3)**

13. $\dfrac{\cos^2(-x)}{\sin(-x)} = \dfrac{\cos x}{\tan(-x)}$

14. $\sin^2 x + \dfrac{1}{\sec^2 x} = 1$

15. $\cos x + \sin x \tan x = \sec x$

16. The graph of $y = 3 \sin 4x$ is shifted down 3 units. Write an equation of the resulting graph. **(14.2)**

17. The graph of $y = \frac{1}{4} \cos 2x$ is shifted $\frac{\pi}{2}$ units to the left. Write an equation of the resulting graph. **(14.2)**

18. The average daily temperature, T (in degrees Fahrenheit), in Spartanburg, South Carolina, can be modeled by $T = 71.2 + 19.2 \sin\left(\frac{1}{6}\pi t + 4.7\right)$, where $t = 0$ represents 1, $t = 1$ represents February 1, and so on. Sketch the graph of this model. **(14.2)**

19. In Exercise 18, which month has the highest average daily temperature? Which has the lowest? **(14.2)**

20. Which of the following equations represents the graph of a person's blood pressure? Simplify that equation. **(14.2)**

   a. $P = 120 + 40 \sin\left(2\pi t - \frac{\pi}{2}\right)$

   b. $P = 100 - 20 \cos\left(2\pi t - \frac{\pi}{2}\right)$

   c. $P = 100 + 20 \sin\left(\frac{\pi}{2} - 2\pi t\right)$

   d. $P = 120 + 20 \sin\left(\pi t - \frac{\pi}{2}\right)$

14.4 Solving Trigonometric Equations

What you should learn:

Goal 1 How to solve a trigonometric equation

Goal 2 How to solve trigonometric equations that model real-life problems

Why you should learn it:

You can use trigonometric equations to find the measure of the angles in many complex geometric figures.

Goal 1 Solving a Trigonometric Equation

In Lesson 14.3, you learned to *verify* a trigonometric identity. In this lesson, you will learn to solve a trigonometric equation. To see the difference, consider the following two equations: $\sin^2 x + \cos^2 x = 1$ and $\sin x = 1$. The first equation is an identity because it is true for all real values of x. The second equation, however, is true only for some values of x. When you find these values, you are solving the equation.

Example 1 Solving a Trigonometric Equation

Solve $2 \sin x - 1 = 0$.

Solution

$2 \sin x - 1 = 0$ *Rewrite original equation.*

$2 \sin x = 1$ *Add 1 to both sides.*

$\sin x = \frac{1}{2}$ *Divide both sides by 2.*

The equation $\sin x = \frac{1}{2}$ has solutions $x = \frac{\pi}{6}$ and $x = \frac{5\pi}{6}$ in the interval $0 \le x < 2\pi$. Moreover, because $\sin x$ has a period of 2π, there are infinitely many other solutions, which can be written as

$$x = \frac{\pi}{6} + 2n\pi \quad \text{and} \quad x = \frac{5\pi}{6} + 2n\pi \quad \textit{General solution}$$

where n is an integer.

To see that the equation $\sin x = \frac{1}{2}$ has infinitely many solutions, consider the graph. Each x-value at which the graph intersects the line $y = \frac{1}{2}$ is a solution.

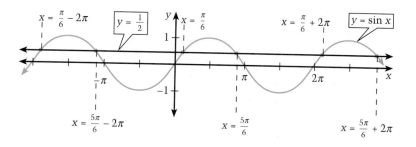

Example 2 Collecting Like Terms

Solve $\cos x + \sqrt{2} = -\cos x$.

Solution

$$\cos x + \sqrt{2} = -\cos x \qquad \textit{Rewrite original equation.}$$

$$\cos x + \cos x = -\sqrt{2} \qquad \textit{Add cos x to both sides.}$$

$$2\cos x = -\sqrt{2} \qquad \textit{Collect like terms.}$$

$$\cos x = -\frac{\sqrt{2}}{2} \qquad \textit{Divide both sides by 2.}$$

Because $\cos x$ has a period of 2π, first find all solutions in the interval $0 \le x < 2\pi$. These are $x = \frac{3\pi}{4}$ and $x = \frac{5\pi}{4}$. Adding $2n\pi$ to each of these solutions produces the general solution

$$x = \frac{3\pi}{4} + 2n\pi \qquad \text{and} \qquad x = \frac{5\pi}{4} + 2n\pi$$

where n is an integer. ∎

Examples 1 and 2 used the fact that the sine and cosine functions have a period of 2π. The periods of the other four trigonometric functions are as follows.

Tangent function:	Period is π.
Cotangent function:	Period is π.
Secant function:	Period is 2π.
Cosecant function:	Period is 2π.

Example 3 Finding Square Roots

Solve $3\tan^2 x - 1 = 0$.

Solution

$$3\tan^2 x - 1 = 0 \qquad \textit{Rewrite original equation.}$$

$$3\tan^2 x = 1 \qquad \textit{Add 1 to both sides.}$$

$$\tan^2 x = \frac{1}{3} \qquad \textit{Divide both sides by 3.}$$

$$\tan x = \pm\frac{1}{\sqrt{3}} \qquad \textit{Find square roots.}$$

$$\tan x = \pm\frac{\sqrt{3}}{3} \qquad \textit{Simplify.}$$

Because $\tan x$ has a period of π, first find all solutions in the interval $0 \le x < \pi$. These are $x = \frac{\pi}{6}$ and $x = \frac{5\pi}{6}$. Adding $n\pi$ to each produces the general solution

$$x = \frac{\pi}{6} + n\pi \qquad \text{and} \qquad x = \frac{5\pi}{6} + n\pi$$

where n is an integer. ∎

Example **4** *Factoring*

Solve $\cot x \csc^2 x = 2 \cot x$ in the interval $0 \le x < \pi$.

Solution

$$\cot x \csc^2 x = 2 \cot x \qquad \textit{Rewrite original equation.}$$

$$\cot x \csc^2 x - 2 \cot x = 0 \qquad \textit{Subtract 2 cot x from both sides.}$$

$$\cot x(\csc^2 x - 2) = 0 \qquad \textit{Factor.}$$

Use the Zero Product Property to obtain the solutions. From $\cot x = 0$, you obtain $x = \frac{\pi}{2}$. From $\csc^2 x - 2 = 0$, you obtain $\csc x = \pm\sqrt{2}$, which has $x = \frac{\pi}{4}$ and $x = \frac{3\pi}{4}$ as solutions. Check each of these solutions in the original equation. ∎

If you have a graphing calculator, try using it to sketch the graphs of $y = \cot x \csc^2 x$ and $y = 2 \cot x$, as shown at the left. If your calculator does not have cotangent and cosecant keys, you can enter these functions as

$$y = \frac{1}{\tan x \sin^2 x} \qquad \text{and} \qquad y = \frac{2}{\tan x}.$$

Note that the graphs intersect at three points between 0 and π.

$y = \cot x \csc^2 x$

$(\frac{\pi}{4}, 2)$

$(\frac{\pi}{2}, 0)$

$y = 2 \cot x$ $(\frac{3\pi}{4}, -2)$

Example **5** *Solving an Equation of Quadratic Type*

Solve $2 \sin^2 x - \sin x = 1$ in the interval $0 \le x < 2\pi$.

Solution   Treat the equation as a quadratic in $\sin x$.

$$2 \sin^2 x - \sin x = 1 \qquad \textit{Rewrite original equation.}$$

$$2 \sin^2 x - \sin x - 1 = 0 \qquad \textit{Subtract 1 from both sides.}$$

$$(2 \sin x + 1)(\sin x - 1) = 0 \qquad \textit{Factor.}$$

Setting each factor equal to zero produces the following.

$$2 \sin x + 1 = 0 \qquad\qquad \text{and} \qquad \sin x - 1 = 0$$

$$\sin x = -\frac{1}{2} \qquad\qquad\qquad\qquad \sin x = 1$$

$$x = \frac{7\pi}{6}, \frac{11\pi}{6} \qquad\qquad\qquad\qquad x = \frac{\pi}{2} \qquad ∎$$

When an equation contains more than one trigonometric function, you may want to begin by rewriting the equation in terms of a single trigonometric function. Here is an example.

$$-2 \cos^2 x - \sin x + 1 = 0 \qquad \textit{Original equation}$$

$$-2(1 - \sin^2 x) - \sin x + 1 = 0 \qquad \textit{Pythagorean identity}$$

$$2 \sin^2 x - \sin x - 1 = 0 \qquad \textit{Simplify.}$$

This equation is the same as that solved in Example 5.

Top view of honeycomb (left) Cross section of honeycomb (right)

Goal 2 Solving Trig Equations in Real Life

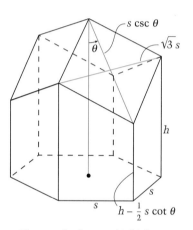

The top (or bottom) of a honeycomb cell is composed of three congruent rhombi. The sides of the cell are trapezoids. Each rhombus has an area of $\frac{\sqrt{3}}{2}s^2 \csc \theta$. Each trapezoid has an area of $hs - \frac{1}{4}s^2 \cot \theta$. (s, θ, and h are shown in the diagram above.)

Example 6   *Surface Area of a Honeycomb Cell*

The total surface area of a honeycomb cell is $6hs + \frac{3}{\sqrt{2}}s^2$.

Find the angle, θ, at which the face of each rhombus meets the vertical line passing through the center of the cell.

Solution   Because the total surface area consists of the area of three rhombi and six trapezoids, you can use the areas given above to write the following.

$$6hs + \frac{3}{\sqrt{2}}s^2 = 3\left(\frac{\sqrt{3}}{2}s^2 \csc \theta\right) + 6\left(hs - \frac{1}{4}s^2 \cot \theta\right)$$

This equation simplifies to $\sqrt{2} \sin \theta = \sqrt{3} - \cos \theta$, which can be solved as follows.

$$\sqrt{2} \sin \theta = \sqrt{3} - \cos \theta \qquad \textit{Simplified equation}$$

$$2 \sin^2 \theta = 3 - 2\sqrt{3} \cos \theta + \cos^2 \theta \qquad \textit{Square both sides.}$$

$$2(1 - \cos^2 \theta) = 3 - 2\sqrt{3} \cos \theta + \cos^2 \theta \qquad \textit{Pythagorean identity}$$

$$0 = 1 - 2\sqrt{3} \cos \theta + 3 \cos^2 \theta \qquad \textit{Simplify.}$$

$$0 = (1 - \sqrt{3} \cos \theta)^2 \qquad \textit{Factor.}$$

This means that the angle θ is as follows.

$$\cos \theta = \frac{1}{\sqrt{3}} \qquad \textit{Zero Product Property}$$

$$\theta = \arccos \frac{1}{\sqrt{3}} \approx 54.7°$$

■

Communicating about **ALGEBRA**

▶ **SHARING IDEAS about the Lesson**

Show that the first equation in the solution to Example 6 simplifies to $\sqrt{2} \sin \theta = \sqrt{3} - \cos \theta$.

EXERCISES

Guided Practice

▶ **CRITICAL THINKING about the Lesson**

1. What makes a trigonometric equation an identity?

2. Solve $2 \cos x + 4 = 5$ for $0 \leq x < 2\pi$. Show your result graphically.

3. Write the general solution of the equation in Exercise 2.

4. State the period of each of the six trigonometric functions.

5. Solve the equation $\tan^2 x = \sec x \tan^2 x$ for $0 \leq x < \pi$. Explain.

6. Use a trigonometric identity to rewrite $1 + \cot^2 x = 2 \csc x - 1$ in terms of a single trigonometric function. Explain how to solve the resulting equation.

Independent Practice

In Exercises 7–12, verify that the *x*-value is a solution of the equation.

7. $3 - 2 \cot x - 1 = 0$, $x = \frac{\pi}{4}$

8. $\csc x - 2 = 0$, $x = \frac{5\pi}{6}$

9. $4 \cos^2 2x - 3 = 0$, $x = \frac{\pi}{12}$

10. $3 \tan^3 4x - 3 = 0$, $x = \frac{\pi}{16}$

11. $2 \sin^4 x - \sin^2 x = 0$, $x = \frac{5\pi}{4}$

12. $2 \cot^4 x - \cot^2 x - 15 = 0$, $x = \frac{13\pi}{6}$

In Exercises 13–34, solve the equation for $0 \leq x < 2\pi$.

13. $\sqrt{2} \cos x - 1 = 0$

14. $7 \sec x - 7 = 0$

15. $3 \sin x = \sin x + 1$

16. $5 \cos x - \sqrt{3} = 3 \cos x$

17. $2 \csc x + 17 = 15 + \csc x$

18. $\cos x - 1 = -\cos x$

19. $4 \sin^2 x - 2 = 0$

20. $\tan^2 x - 3 = 0$

21. $3 \tan^2 x - 1 = 0$

22. $3 \sec^2 x - 4 = 0$

23. $\sec x \csc x - 2 \csc x = 0$

24. $\sqrt{2} \cos x \sin x - \cos x = 0$

25. $4 \sin^2 x - 3 = 0$

26. $3 \tan^3 x - \tan x = 0$

27. $\cos^3 x = \cos x$

28. $3 \sin x \sec x - 2\sqrt{3} \sin x = 0$

29. $\sqrt{3} \tan x = 3 \tan x \csc x - \sqrt{3} \tan x$

30. $2 \csc x - \sqrt{2} \cos x \csc x = 3 \csc x$

31. $\sqrt{3} \tan^2 x + 4 \tan x + \sqrt{3} = 0$

32. $\csc^2 x - \csc x - 2 = 0$

33. $2 \cos^2 x - \sin x - 1 = 0$

34. $2 \cot x + \sec^2 x = 0$

In Exercises 35–40, use a graphing calculator to approximate the solutions in the interval $0 \leq x < 2\pi$.

35. $3 \tan x + 1 = 13$

36. $9 \cos x + 2 = 3$

37. $\csc^2 x + \cot x = 7$

38. $\tan^2 x + 6 = 4 \sec x$

39. $\sin x + \cos x \tan^2 x = 30 \cos x$

40. $2 \cos^2 x + \sin^2 x \cot x = \sin^2 x$

In Exercises 41 and 42, find the *x*-intercepts of the graph in the interval $0 \le x \le 2\pi$.

41. $y = 2 \cos x + 1$

42. $y = 2 \tan^2 x - 6$

In Exercises 43–48, find the intersection points of the two graphs in the interval $0 \le x \le 2\pi$.

43. $y = \sqrt{3} \tan^2 x$
$y = \sqrt{3} - 2 \tan x$

44. $y = 9 \cos^2 x$
$y = \cos^2 x + 8 \cos x - 2$

45. $y = 2 \sec^2 x$
$y = 3 - \tan^2 x$

46. $y = \sin^2 x$
$y = 2 \sin x - 1$

47. $y = \sin x \tan x$
$y = 2 - \cos x$

48. $y = 4 \cos^2 x$
$y = 4 \cos x - 1$

49. In calculus, it can be shown that the function $y = \sin x - \cos x$ has minimum or maximum values when

$$\cos x + \sin x = 0.$$

Find all solutions of $\cos x + \sin x = 0$ in the interval $0 \le x < 2\pi$. Verify your solutions with a graphing calculator.

50. In calculus, it can be shown that the function $y = 2 \sin x + \cos 2x$ has minimum or maximum values when

$$2 \cos x - 4 \sin x \cos x = 0.$$

Find all solutions of $2 \cos x - 4 \sin x \cos x = 0$ in the interval $0 \le x < 2\pi$. Verify your solutions with a graphing calculator.

51. *Soap Film*   A wire tetrahedron has sides of *x* inches each. When the tetrahedron is dipped into soapy water, six triangular soap films form within the tetrahedron as shown at the right. The six triangular soap films meet at four liquid edges, and all have a common vertex. Each triangular soap film has an area of $\frac{\sqrt{2}}{8}x^2$, and the base of each of these triangles is an edge of the tetrahedron frame. The height of each triangular soap film is equal to $\frac{x}{2} \tan \theta$. Find θ.

52. *Geometry*   The diameter of a circle can be found by drawing any triangle whose vertices all lie on the circle. The diameter is then equal to the ratio of any side of the triangle to the sine of its opposite angle. For a triangle inscribed in a 5-meter radius circle, find the angle, θ, whose opposite side is 6 meters.

53. *Kite*   Find the angle θ in the kite shown at the right by solving the equation $\cot \theta = 16 \tan \theta$.

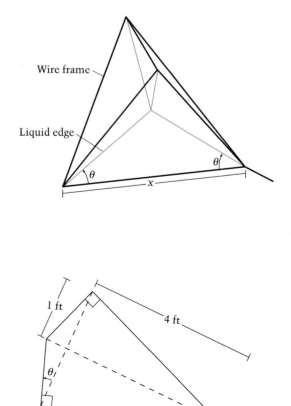

54. *High Tide*   The depth of the Atlantic Ocean at a channel buoy off the coast of Maine can be modeled by

$$y = 5 - 3 \cos\left(\frac{\pi}{6}t\right)$$

where y is the water depth in feet and t is the time in hours. Consider a day in which $t = 0$ represents 12:00 midnight. For that day, when do the high and low tides occur?

Channel marker off the Maine coast

Integrated Review

In Exercises 55–60, find the period and amplitude of the function.

55. $y = 10 \sin \frac{1}{2}x$

56. $y = 6 \cos 3x$

57. $y = -4 \cos(x - \pi)$

58. $y = -5 + \sin\left(\frac{1}{3}x + \pi\right)$

59. $y = 8 + 3 \cos\left(3x - \frac{\pi}{2}\right)$

60. $y = -12 \sin(2x + \pi)$

In Exercises 61–66, sketch the graph of the function.

61. $y = 3 \cos 3x$

62. $y = -2 \sin(-2x + \pi)$

63. $y = 5 + 2 \sin 4x$

64. $y = -2 + \cos\left(\frac{1}{2}x + \pi\right)$

65. $y = -4 \cos\left(x - \frac{\pi}{2}\right)$

66. $y = 1 - 3 \sin\left(x - \frac{\pi}{2}\right)$

67. *Powers of Ten*   Which best estimates the angle (in radian measure) of the tip of a sharpened pencil?
  a. 2.7×10^{-1} **b.** 2.7×10^{0} **c.** 2.7×10^{1} **d.** 2.7×10^{2}

68. *Powers of Ten*   Which best estimates the number of times a ten-pin bowling ball revolves as it rolls down a bowling lane?
  a. 2.7×10^{-1} **b.** 2.7×10^{0} **c.** 2.7×10^{1} **d.** 2.7×10^{2}

Exploration and Extension

Computer Graphics   **In Exercises 69 and 70, use the following information.**

Matrix multiplication can be used to rotate a point (x, y) an angle of θ around the origin. The coordinates of the resulting point, (x', y'), are determined by the following matrix equation.

$$\begin{bmatrix} \cos \theta & -\sin \theta \\ \sin \theta & \cos \theta \end{bmatrix} \begin{bmatrix} x \\ y \end{bmatrix} = \begin{bmatrix} x' \\ y' \end{bmatrix}$$

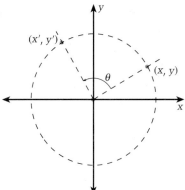

69. The point $(4, 1)$ is rotated an angle of $\frac{\pi}{6}$ about the origin. What are the coordinates of the "resulting point"?

70. Through what angle θ must the point $(2, 4)$ be rotated to produce

$$(x', y') = (-2 + \sqrt{3}, \ 1 + 2\sqrt{3})?$$

14.5

Sum and Difference Formulas

What you should learn:

Goal 1 How to use the sum and difference formulas to evaluate trigonometric functions of the sum or difference of two angles

Goal 2 How to use sum and difference formulas to solve real-life problems

Why you should learn it:

You can model many real-life situations, such as the angle of refraction of water or glass, using the sum or difference of two angles.

Goal 1 Using Sum and Difference Formulas

In this lesson, you will study formulas that will allow you to evaluate trigonometric functions of the sum or difference of two angles.

Sum and Difference Formulas

$\sin(u + v) = \sin u \cos v + \cos u \sin v$

$\sin(u - v) = \sin u \cos v - \cos u \sin v$

$\cos(u + v) = \cos u \cos v - \sin u \sin v$

$\cos(u - v) = \cos u \cos v + \sin u \sin v$

$\tan(u + v) = \dfrac{\tan u + \tan v}{1 - \tan u \tan v}$

$\tan(u - v) = \dfrac{\tan u - \tan v}{1 + \tan u \tan v}$

Note that $\sin(u + v) \neq \sin u + \sin v$. Similar statements can be made for $\cos(u + v)$ and $\tan(u + v)$.

Example 1 *Evaluating a Trigonometric Function*

Find the exact value of sin 75° and sin 15°.

Solution Use the fact that $75° = 45° + 30°$ and $15° = 45° - 30°$.

$$\sin 75° = \sin(45° + 30°)$$
$$= \sin 45° \cos 30° + \cos 45° \sin 30°$$
$$= \frac{\sqrt{2}}{2}\left(\frac{\sqrt{3}}{2}\right) + \frac{\sqrt{2}}{2}\left(\frac{1}{2}\right) = \frac{\sqrt{6} + \sqrt{2}}{4}$$

$$\sin 15° = \sin(45° - 30°)$$
$$= \sin 45° \cos 30° - \cos 45° \sin 30°$$
$$= \frac{\sqrt{2}}{2}\left(\frac{\sqrt{3}}{2}\right) - \frac{\sqrt{2}}{2}\left(\frac{1}{2}\right) = \frac{\sqrt{6} - \sqrt{2}}{4}$$

Try checking these results with a calculator. For instance, evaluate sin 75° and $\dfrac{\sqrt{6} + \sqrt{2}}{4}$ to check that both have the same value. ∎

Example 2 **Evaluating a Trigonometric Function**

Find the exact value of $\cos \frac{\pi}{12}$.

Solution Use the fact that $\frac{\pi}{12} = \frac{\pi}{3} - \frac{\pi}{4}$.

$$\cos \frac{\pi}{12} = \cos \left(\frac{\pi}{3} - \frac{\pi}{4} \right)$$

$$= \cos \frac{\pi}{3} \cos \frac{\pi}{4} + \sin \frac{\pi}{3} \sin \frac{\pi}{4}$$

$$= \frac{1}{2} \left(\frac{\sqrt{2}}{2} \right) + \frac{\sqrt{3}}{2} \left(\frac{\sqrt{2}}{2} \right)$$

$$= \frac{\sqrt{2} + \sqrt{6}}{4}$$

■

Example 3 **Evaluating a Trigonometric Expression**

Find the exact value of $\dfrac{\tan 80° + \tan 55°}{1 - \tan 80° \tan 55°}$.

Solution Use the fact that $55° + 80° = 135°$.

$$\frac{\tan 80° + \tan 55°}{1 - \tan 80° \tan 55°} = \tan(80° + 55°)$$

$$= \tan 135°$$

$$= -\tan 45°$$

$$= -1$$

■

Example 4 **Solving a Trigonometric Equation**

Solve $\sin \left(x + \frac{\pi}{4} \right) + 1 = \sin \left(\frac{\pi}{4} - x \right)$ for $0 \le x < 2\pi$.

Solution $\sin \left(x + \frac{\pi}{4} \right) + 1 = \sin \left(\frac{\pi}{4} - x \right)$

$$\sin x \cos \frac{\pi}{4} + \cos x \sin \frac{\pi}{4} + 1 = \sin \frac{\pi}{4} \cos x - \cos \frac{\pi}{4} \sin x$$

$$2 \sin x \cos \frac{\pi}{4} = -1$$

$$2(\sin x) \left(\frac{\sqrt{2}}{2} \right) = -1$$

$$\sin x = -\frac{1}{\sqrt{2}}$$

$$\sin x = -\frac{\sqrt{2}}{2}$$

In the interval $0 \le x < 2\pi$, the solutions are

$$x = \frac{5\pi}{4} \qquad \text{and} \qquad x = \frac{7\pi}{4}.$$

■

The graphs at the left are a visual check for the solutions obtained in Example 4.

$y = \sin \left(x + \frac{\pi}{4} \right) + 1$

$y = \sin \left(\frac{\pi}{4} - x \right)$

When light passes from one medium to another, such as from water to air, it is refracted, or bent. To demonstrate this, place a penny at the same position in two cups. Fill one cup with water and place the cups side by side. By looking down at the right angle, you will see the penny in the water but not the other penny.

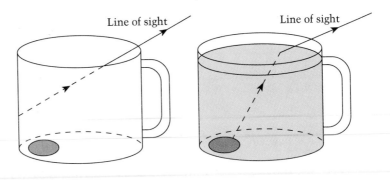
Line of sight   Line of sight

Goal 2 Using Sum and Difference Formulas

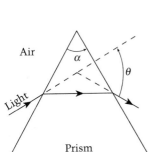

Air
α
θ
Light
Prism

Example 5 Measuring the Index of Refraction

The *index of refraction, n,* of a transparent material is the ratio of the speed of light in a vacuum to the speed of light in the material. Some common indexes are air (1.00), water (1.33), glass (1.5), and diamond (2.4). Triangular prisms are often used to measure the index of refraction using the formula

$$n = \frac{\sin\left(\frac{\theta}{2} + \frac{\alpha}{2}\right)}{\sin\frac{\theta}{2}}.$$

For the prism at the left, $\alpha = 60°$. Write the index of refraction as a function of $\cot\frac{\theta}{2}$.

Solution

$$n = \frac{\sin\left(\frac{\theta}{2} + 30°\right)}{\sin\frac{\theta}{2}} \qquad \textit{Substitute } \alpha = 60°.$$

$$= \frac{\sin\frac{\theta}{2}\cos 30° + \cos\frac{\theta}{2}\sin 30°}{\sin\frac{\theta}{2}} \qquad \textit{Sine of sum of two angles}$$

$$= \frac{\left(\sin\frac{\theta}{2}\right)\left(\frac{\sqrt{3}}{2}\right) + \left(\cos\frac{\theta}{2}\right)\left(\frac{1}{2}\right)}{\sin\frac{\theta}{2}} \qquad \textit{Evaluate } \sin 30° \textit{ and } \cos 30°.$$

$$= \frac{\sqrt{3}}{2} + \frac{1}{2}\cot\frac{\theta}{2} \qquad \textit{Simplify.} \qquad ■$$

Communicating about ALGEBRA

▶ **SHARING IDEAS about the Lesson**

For the diagram in Example 5, find the angle θ for each material: water, glass, diamond.

EXERCISES

Guided Practice

▶ **CRITICAL THINKING about the Lesson**

1. Explain how to use a sum or difference formula to find the exact value of tan 240°.

2. The sum and difference formulas can be written as follows. Explain why "∓" rather than "±" occurs in the cosine and tangent formulas.

$$\sin(u \pm v) = \sin u \cos v \pm \cos u \sin v$$

$$\cos(u \pm v) = \cos u \cos v \mp \sin u \sin v$$

$$\tan(u \pm v) = \frac{\tan u \pm \tan v}{1 \mp \tan u \tan v}$$

3. Find the exact value of $\sin(-15°)$.

4. Solve $\cos\left(x - \frac{\pi}{6}\right) = 1 + \cos\left(x + \frac{\pi}{6}\right)$ for $0 \leq x < 2\pi$.

Independent Practice

In Exercises 5–16, find the exact value of the expression.

5. $\cos 105°$

6. $\tan 195°$

7. $\tan 75°$

8. $\sin 345°$

9. $\cos 255°$

10. $\cos 375°$

11. $\tan \frac{11\pi}{12}$

12. $\sin \frac{13\pi}{12}$

13. $\sec \frac{19\pi}{12}$

14. $\cos \frac{17\pi}{12}$

15. $\cot \frac{5\pi}{12}$

16. $\cot \frac{7\pi}{12}$

In Exercises 17–20, simplify the expression. Do not evaluate it.

17. $\cos 35° \cos 15° - \sin 35° \sin 15°$

18. $\sin 110° \cos 50° + \cos 110° \sin 50°$

19. $\sin 4 \cos 2.2 - \cos 4 \sin 2.2$

20. $\sin \frac{\pi}{9} \sin \frac{\pi}{3} + \cos \frac{\pi}{9} \cos \frac{\pi}{3}$

In Exercises 21–26, evaluate the expression.

21. $\sin 30° \cos 45° + \cos 30° \sin 45°$

22. $\cos \frac{\pi}{4} \cos \frac{\pi}{3} - \sin \frac{\pi}{4} \sin \frac{\pi}{3}$

23. $\sin 240° \cos 45° - \cos 240° \sin 45°$

24. $\dfrac{\tan 60° - \tan 45°}{1 + \tan 60° \tan 45°}$

25. $\cos \frac{5\pi}{3} \cos \frac{\pi}{4} + \sin \frac{5\pi}{3} \sin \frac{\pi}{4}$

26. $\sin 420° \cos 45° + \cos 420° \sin 45°$

In Exercises 27–32, solve the equation for $0 \leq x < 2\pi$.

27. $\sin\left(x + \frac{\pi}{3}\right) + \sin\left(x - \frac{\pi}{3}\right) = 1$

28. $\sin\left(x + \frac{\pi}{4}\right) - \sin\left(x - \frac{\pi}{4}\right) = 1$

29. $\cos\left(x + \frac{\pi}{4}\right) + \cos\left(x - \frac{\pi}{4}\right) = 1$

30. $\cos\left(x + \frac{\pi}{6}\right) - \cos\left(x - \frac{\pi}{6}\right) = 1$

31. $\tan(x + \pi) + 2\sin(x + \pi) = 0$

32. $\tan(x + \pi) - \cos\left(x + \frac{\pi}{2}\right) = 0$

In Exercises 33–36, evaluate the expression. Use the fact that $\sin u = -\frac{12}{13}$ with $\pi < u < \frac{3\pi}{2}$ and $\cos v = \frac{3}{5}$ with $\frac{3\pi}{2} < v < 2\pi$.

33. $\cos(u + v)$ **34.** $\sin(u + v)$ **35.** $\sin(v - u)$ **36.** $\cos(u - v)$

Angle Between Two Lines   **In Exercises 37 and 38, use the following information.**

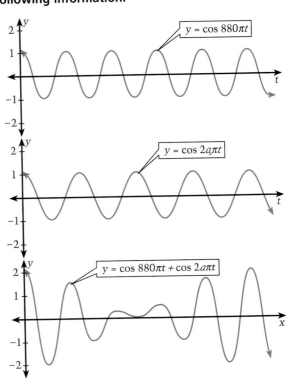

In the figure at the right, the acute angle of intersection, $\theta_2 - \theta_1$, of two lines with slopes m_1 and m_2 is given by the formula

$$\tan(\theta_2 - \theta_1) = \frac{m_2 - m_1}{1 + m_1 m_2}.$$

37. Find the acute angle of intersection between the lines $y = \frac{1}{2}x + 3$ and $y = 2x - 3$.

38. Find the acute angle of intersection between the lines $y = x + 2$ and $y = 3x + 1$.

Tuning a Guitar   **In Exercises 39 and 40, use the following information.**

A guitar is being tuned by using a piano that is known to be in tune. The note A-440 is struck on the piano producing sound waves given by the model

$$y = \cos 880\pi t$$

where t is measured in seconds. Then the note that is supposed to be A-440 is struck on the guitar. If the guitar note has a frequency of a, then the guitar produces sound waves given by the model

$$y = \cos 2a\pi t.$$

If the guitar is not in tune, then the sound from both notes has a beat (or pulse) that is represented by the graph of

$$y = \cos 880\pi t + \cos 2a\pi t.$$

As a gets closer and closer to 440, the beat occurs less frequently. Finally, when the beat disappears, you know that a is equal to 440 and the guitar is in tune.

39. Use the trigonometric formula

$$\cos u + \cos v = 2 \cos\left(\frac{u + v}{2}\right) \cos\left(\frac{u - v}{2}\right)$$

to rewrite $y = \cos 880\pi t + \cos 2a\pi t$.

40. Use the result of Exercise 39 to rewrite the sound from *both* notes as

$$y = 2(\cos^2 440\pi t \, \cos^2 a\pi t - \sin^2 440\pi t \, \sin^2 a\pi t).$$

In Exercises 41–44, find the values of the other five trigonometric functions of θ. $\left(\text{Assume } 0 < \theta < \frac{\pi}{2}.\right)$

41. $\cot \theta = \sqrt{6}$

42. $\csc \theta = \dfrac{2\sqrt{3}}{3}$

43. $\sin \theta = \dfrac{\sqrt{2}}{2}$

44. $\cos \theta = \dfrac{1}{2}$

In Exercises 45–50, simplify the expression.

45. $\sec x - \sec x \tan^2 x$

46. $\sin^2\left(\dfrac{\pi}{2} - x\right) + \sin^2 x$

47. $\dfrac{\sin x}{\cos x} + \sec x \tan x$

48. $\left(\dfrac{1}{\sin x}\right)^2 - \left(\dfrac{1}{\tan x}\right)^2$

49. $\dfrac{\cos x \csc x}{\tan x}$

50. $\dfrac{\cos x}{1 - \sin x} - \tan x$

Exploration and Extension

51. *Diamond or Zircon?* Diamond has an index of refraction of 2.4. Zircon has an index of refraction of 1.9. One of the prisms shown below is diamond; the other is zircon. Which is which?

Mixed REVIEW

1. Solve $8x^3 = -27$. **(7.3)**

2. Write the nth term: $\dfrac{1}{2}$, 0, $-\dfrac{1}{2}$, -1, ... **(12.1)**

3. Evaluate $\binom{7}{5}$. **(12.5)**

4. Sketch $(x - 3)^2 + (y + 3)^2 = 16$. **(11.5)**

5. Write in terms of radians: $75°$. **(13.2)**

6. Write in terms of degrees: $\dfrac{5\pi}{4}$. **(13.2)**

7. Solve $\log_a 16 = 4$ for a. **(8.3)**

8. Evaluate $e^{\ln 5}$. **(8.5)**

9. Solve $\sqrt{x - 2} = 5$. **(7.5)**

10. Write the inverse of $y = 3x + 2$. **(6.3)**

11. Find the reference angle of $-\dfrac{5\pi}{12}$. **(13.3)**

12. Divide $(x^3 + 3x^2 - x - 3)$ by $(x + 1)$. **(9.4)**

13. Evaluate $f(-1)$ for $f(x) = 3^x - 2$. **(7.1)**

14. True or False? $\sec \theta = \dfrac{1}{\tan \theta}$ **(13.1)**

15. Sketch $y \le |3x - 2| + 3$. **(2.5)**

16. Classify the conic: $9x^2 - 4y^2 = 36$. **(11.6)**

17. Solve $|4 - t| > 10$. **(1.7)**

18. Evaluate $\begin{vmatrix} 4 & -4 \\ 6 & 3 \end{vmatrix}$. **(4.3)**

19. Write an equation of the line passing through $\left(-3, -\dfrac{1}{2}\right)$ and $(-1, 6)$. **(2.2)**

20. Write a quadratic model that represents the points $(1, 3)$, $(0, 0)$, and $(-1, 3)$. **(6.6)**

14.6 Double- and Half-Angle Formulas

What you should learn:

Goal 1 How to use double-angle and half-angle formulas

Goal 2 How to use trigonometry to solve real-life problems

Why you should learn it:

You can model many real-life situations with double-angle and half-angle relationships, such as the path of a projectile launched at an initial angle θ.

Goal 1 Double- and Half-Angle Formulas

In this lesson, you will use formulas for double angles (angles of measure 2θ) and half angles (angles of measure $\frac{1}{2}\theta$).

Three formulas for $\cos 2u$ are listed below. All three formulas are equivalent, and you can use whichever one is most convenient in a problem.

Double-Angle Formulas

$$\sin 2u = 2 \sin u \cos u \qquad\qquad \cos 2u = \cos^2 u - \sin^2 u$$

$$\qquad\qquad\qquad\qquad\qquad\qquad \cos 2u = 2 \cos^2 u - 1$$

$$\tan 2u = \frac{2 \tan u}{1 - \tan^2 u} \qquad\qquad \cos 2u = 1 - 2 \sin^2 u$$

Note that $\sin 2u \neq 2 \sin u$. Similar statements can be made for $\cos 2u$ and $\tan 2u$.

Example 1 Solving a Trigonometric Equation

Solve $2 \cos x + \sin 2x = 0$ for $0 \leq x < 2\pi$.

Solution Begin by rewriting the equation using functions of x rather than $2x$. Then factor and solve as usual.

$$2 \cos x + \sin 2x = 0 \qquad \textit{Rewrite original equation.}$$

$$2 \cos x + 2 \sin x \cos x = 0 \qquad \textit{Double-angle formula}$$

$$2 \cos x(1 + \sin x) = 0 \qquad \textit{Factor.}$$

Using the Zero Product Property, set each factor equal to zero and solve for x.

$$\cos x = 0 \qquad\qquad\qquad 1 + \sin x = 0$$

$$x = \frac{\pi}{2}, \; x = \frac{3\pi}{2} \qquad\qquad \sin x = -1$$

$$\qquad\qquad\qquad\qquad\qquad x = \frac{3\pi}{2}$$

In the interval $0 \leq x < 2\pi$, the equation has two solutions, $\frac{\pi}{2}$ and $\frac{3\pi}{2}$. Check these in the original equation. Or, if you have a graphing calculator, use a graphing check, as shown at the left.

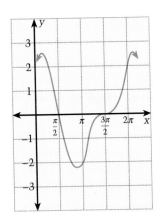

Half-Angle Formulas

$$\sin \frac{u}{2} = \pm\sqrt{\frac{1 - \cos u}{2}} \qquad \cos \frac{u}{2} = \pm\sqrt{\frac{1 + \cos u}{2}}$$

$$\tan \frac{u}{2} = \frac{1 - \cos u}{\sin u} \qquad \tan \frac{u}{2} = \frac{\sin u}{1 + \cos u}$$

The signs of $\sin \frac{u}{2}$ and $\cos \frac{u}{2}$ depend on the quadrant in which $\frac{u}{2}$ lies.

Example 2 *Using a Half-Angle Formula*

Find the exact value of $\tan \frac{\pi}{8}$.

Solution Use the fact that $\frac{\pi}{8}$ is half of $\frac{\pi}{4}$.

$$\tan \frac{\pi}{8} = \frac{1 - \cos \frac{\pi}{4}}{\sin \frac{\pi}{4}}$$

$$= \frac{1 - \frac{\sqrt{2}}{2}}{\frac{\sqrt{2}}{2}}$$

$$= \frac{2 - \sqrt{2}}{\sqrt{2}}$$

$$= \sqrt{2} - 1$$

Try checking this result with a calculator by evaluating $\tan \frac{\pi}{8}$ and $\sqrt{2} - 1$. ∎

Example 3 *Using a Half-Angle Formula*

Use $\cos 72° = \frac{-1 + \sqrt{5}}{4}$ to find the exact value of $\cos 36°$.

Solution Because $36°$ lies in the first quadrant, $\cos 36°$ is positive.

$$\cos 36° = \sqrt{\frac{1 + \cos 72°}{2}}$$

$$= \sqrt{\frac{1 + \frac{-1 + \sqrt{5}}{4}}{2}}$$

$$= \sqrt{\frac{\frac{3 + \sqrt{5}}{4}}{2}}$$

$$= \sqrt{\frac{3 + \sqrt{5}}{8}}$$

Try checking this result with a calculator. ∎

The path traveled by an object that is projected at an initial height of h feet, an initial velocity of v (in feet per second), and an initial angle of θ is given by

$$y = -\frac{16}{v^2 \cos^2 \theta} x^2 + (\tan \theta)x + h$$

where y is the height of the object (in feet), and x is the horizontal distance (in feet).

Connections

Physics

Example 4   *Path of a Projectile*

In Lesson 13.3 (page 696), the horizontal distance traveled by an object that is projected from ground level at an angle of θ is given as $\frac{1}{32}v^2 \sin 2\theta$. Use the equation above to verify this.

Solution   Because the object starts at ground level, you know that $h = 0$. You can find the horizontal distance that the object travels by letting y be equal to 0 and solving for x.

$$-\frac{16}{v^2 \cos^2 \theta} x^2 + (\tan \theta)x = 0 \quad \textit{Let y = 0.}$$

$$(-x)\left(\frac{16}{v^2 \cos^2 \theta} x - \tan \theta\right) = 0 \quad \textit{Factor.}$$

$$\frac{16}{v^2 \cos^2 \theta} x - \tan \theta = 0 \quad \textit{Zero Product Property}$$

$$\frac{16}{v^2 \cos^2 \theta} x = \tan \theta$$

$$x = \frac{1}{16}v^2 \cos^2 \theta \tan \theta$$

$$x = \frac{1}{16}v^2 \cos \theta \sin \theta$$

$$x = \frac{1}{32}v^2 (2 \cos \theta \sin \theta)$$

$$x = \frac{1}{32}v^2 \sin 2\theta$$

The last step uses the double-angle formula for $\sin 2\theta$. ∎

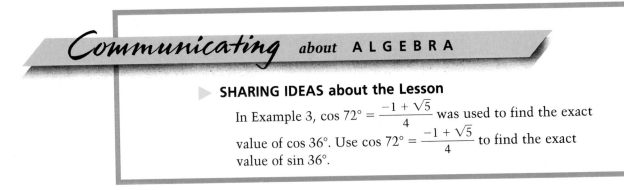

Communicating about ALGEBRA

▶ **SHARING IDEAS about the Lesson**

In Example 3, $\cos 72° = \dfrac{-1 + \sqrt{5}}{4}$ was used to find the exact value of $\cos 36°$. Use $\cos 72° = \dfrac{-1 + \sqrt{5}}{4}$ to find the exact value of $\sin 36°$.

EXERCISES

Guided Practice

▶ **CRITICAL THINKING about the Lesson**

1. Rewrite $\tan x$ as a function of $\tan \frac{x}{2}$.

2. Use $\cos \frac{4\pi}{9} \approx 0.174$ to approximate $\cos \frac{8\pi}{9}$.

3. Use $\sin \frac{4\pi}{9} \approx 0.985$ to approximate $\cos \frac{8\pi}{9}$. Do your answers for Exercises 2 and 3 agree?

4. Use $\sin 105° = \frac{1}{4}(\sqrt{2} + \sqrt{6})$ and $\cos 105° = \frac{1}{4}(\sqrt{2} - \sqrt{6})$ to find the exact value of $\tan 52.5°$.

5. Solve $\cos 2x + 3 \sin^2 x - 2 = 0$ for $0 \le x < 2\pi$.

6. Which of the following is the graph of $y = \cos 2x + 3 \sin^2 x - 2$? Explain.

a.   b.   c.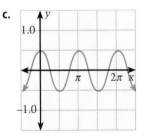

Independent Practice

In Exercises 7–12, rewrite each expression without double angles. Simplify the expression.

7. $\tan 2x(1 + \tan x)$

8. $\cos 2x - 4 \sin^4 x$

9. $\cot x \tan 2x$

10. $\dfrac{\sin 2x}{\sin x}$

11. $\dfrac{\cos 2x}{\cos^2 x}$

12. $\dfrac{-1 + \sqrt{2} \cos x}{\cos 2x}$

In Exercises 13–24, solve the equation for $0 \le x < 2\pi$.

13. $\cos 2x = -1$

14. $\cos 2x - \cos x = 0$

15. $\sin 2x \sin x = \cos x$

16. $\cos 2x = -2 \cos^2 x$

17. $\cot x = \tan 2x$

18. $\sin 2x + \sin x = 0$

19. $2 \tan x = \tan 2x$

20. $\sin 2x = \tan x$

21. $\cos 2x - 3 \sin x = 2$

22. $\dfrac{3}{2} \tan 2x = 2$

23. $\dfrac{\cos 2x + \sqrt{2} \cos x}{\cos^2 x} = 1$

24. $\dfrac{\tan x \sin 2x + 2 \sin^2 x}{-1 + 4 \sin x} = 1$

In Exercises 25–30, find the exact value of the expression.

25. $\tan \dfrac{\pi}{12}$

26. $\sin \dfrac{7\pi}{12}$

27. $\cos(-22.5°)$

28. $\cos \dfrac{7\pi}{8}$

29. $\tan \dfrac{3\pi}{8}$

30. $\tan\left(-\dfrac{7\pi}{8}\right)$

In Exercises 31–33, use the given value to find the exact value of the indicated expression. Check your result with a calculator.

31. $\cos 195° = -\dfrac{1}{2}\sqrt{2 + \sqrt{3}}$

$\sin 97.5° = \boxed{?}$

32. $\sin 105° = \dfrac{\sqrt{6} + \sqrt{2}}{4}$

$\cos 105° = \dfrac{\sqrt{2} - \sqrt{6}}{4}$

$\tan 52.5° = \boxed{?}$

33. $\sin \dfrac{\pi}{12} = \dfrac{\sqrt{6} - \sqrt{2}}{4}$

$\cos \dfrac{\pi}{12} = \dfrac{\sqrt{6} + \sqrt{2}}{4}$

$\tan \dfrac{\pi}{24} = \boxed{?}$

In Exercises 34–39, find the exact values of $\sin \dfrac{u}{2}$, $\cos \dfrac{u}{2}$, and $\tan \dfrac{u}{2}$.

34. $\cos u = \dfrac{3}{5}$, $0 \le u < \dfrac{\pi}{2}$

35. $\tan u = 2$, $0 \le u < \dfrac{\pi}{2}$

36. $\sin u = \dfrac{1}{3}$, $\dfrac{\pi}{2} \le u < \pi$

37. $\sin u = -\dfrac{9}{10}$, $\dfrac{3\pi}{2} \le u < 2\pi$

38. $\tan u = \dfrac{1}{2}$, $0 \le u < \dfrac{\pi}{2}$

39. $\sin u = \dfrac{4}{5}$, $0 \le u < \dfrac{\pi}{2}$

In Exercises 40–43, match the equation with its graph.

40. $y = \sin x \cos x$

41. $y = \cos^2 2x - \sin^2 2x$

42. $y = 1 - 2\sin^2 x$

43. $y = \sin \dfrac{1}{2}x \cos \dfrac{1}{2}x$

a.

b.

c.

d.

Inca Dwelling   **In Exercises 44 and 45, use the following information.**

The picture at the right is a drawing of an Inca dwelling. This dwelling was in the Inca city of Machu Picchu, about 50 miles northwest of Cusco, Peru. All that remains of the ancient city today are stone ruins.

44. Express the area of the triangular portion of the right side of the dwelling as a function of $\sin \dfrac{\theta}{2}$ and $\cos \dfrac{\theta}{2}$.

45. Express the area found in Exercise 44 as a function of $\sin \theta$. Then solve for θ using an area of 132 square feet.

46. Mach Number The *mach number, M,* of an airplane is the ratio of its speed to the speed of sound. When an airplane travels faster than the speed of sound, the sound waves form a cone behind the airplane. The mach number is related to the apex angle of the cone by $\sin \frac{\theta}{2} = \frac{1}{M}$. Find the angle θ that corresponds to a mach number of 4.5.

47. Railroad Track When two railroad tracks merge, the overlapping portions of the tracks are in the shape of circular arcs. The radius of the arcs, r (in feet), the width of the track, x (in feet), and the angle, θ, are related by $\frac{x}{2} = 2r \sin^2 \frac{\theta}{2}$. Write a formula for x in terms of $\cos \theta$.

Integrated Review

In Exercises 48–50, solve the equation for $0 \leq x < 2\pi$.

48. $2 \sin^2 x = 1$

49. $2 \cos^2 x - 9 \cos x = 5$

50. $2 \sin^2 x - \sin x = 1$

Exploration and Extension

Carpet Area **In Exercises 51 and 52, use the following information.**

The following parametric equations can be used to model a cross section of one roll of carpeting.

$$x = \left(1 + \frac{1}{2\pi}t\right)\cos t \qquad y = \left(1 + \frac{1}{2\pi}t\right)\sin t$$

In this model, x and y are measured in inches.

51. Use a graphing calculator to sketch the graph given by the parametric equations. Let the parameter, t, vary between 0 and 20π and use a calculator setting of $-15 \leq x \leq 15$ and $-10 \leq y \leq 10$.

52. Using calculus, the length of the rug in feet (when unrolled) can be shown to be

$$\frac{1}{4\pi}(11a - b) - \frac{1}{4\pi^2} \ln\left(\frac{22\pi + a}{2\pi + b}\right) \text{ where}$$

$a = \sqrt{1 + (22\pi)^2}$ and $b = \sqrt{1 + (2\pi)^2}$.
What is the length of the rug?

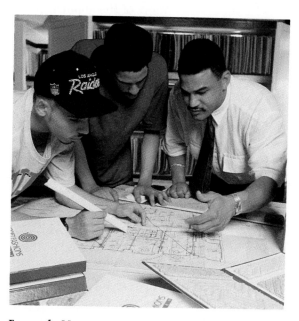

Fernando Mateo owns two successful carpet stores in Manhattan. He has won several civic awards for his work in helping young people help themselves. "I rose from nowhere—so can others," says Mateo.

14

Chapter Summary

What did you learn?

Skills

1. Sketch graphs of sine and cosine functions. **(14.1)**
   - Find the amplitude of sine and cosine graphs. **(14.1)**
   - Find the period of sine and cosine graphs. **(14.1)**
   - Use horizontal shifts to sketch sine and cosine graphs. **(14.2)**
   - Use vertical shifts to sketch sine and cosine graphs. **(14.2)**
   - Use reflections to sketch sine and cosine graphs. **(14.2)**
2. Use trigonometric identities to simplify expressions. **(14.3)**
3. Verify trigonometric identities. **(14.3)**
4. Solve trigonometric equations. **(14.4)**
5. Use sum and difference formulas. **(14.5)**
6. Use double- and half-angle formulas. **(14.6)**

Strategies

7. Use trigonometric functions to solve real-life problems. **(14.1–14.6)**

Why did you learn it?

In Chapters 13 and 14, you have studied many types of real-life problems that can be modeled with trigonometry. Most of these fall into two categories: those dealing with angles and those dealing with periodic behavior. Many of the applications in this chapter have been of the second type.

For instance, in this chapter, you learned that heartbeats, sound waves, and temperatures are periodic and can therefore be modeled with trigonometric functions.

How does it fit into the bigger picture of algebra?

In this chapter, you have seen many examples of the use of algebra in trigonometry. For instance, to solve the trigonometric equation in Example 5 on page 755,

$$2 \sin^2 x - \sin x = 1$$

you used the same basic procedure used to solve the algebraic equation,

$$2u^2 - u = 1.$$

That is, you subtracted 1 from both sides, factored the left side, and used the Zero Product Property to solve for the variable.

If you go on to study higher-level algebra, you will see other connections between trigonometry and algebra. For instance, trigonometry is used in algebra to find the complex nth roots of a real number.

In Exercises 1–9, find the amplitude and period of the function. **(14.1)**

1. $y = 4 \sin \frac{1}{2}x$

2. $y = \sin \frac{2\pi}{3}x$

3. $y = \cos \frac{\pi}{4}x$

4. $y = 10 \cos 8x$

5. $y = \frac{3}{2} \sin 2\pi x$

6. $y = 1.2 \cos \pi x$

7. $y = 1 - 2 \sin 2x$

8. $y = 6 \sin 4\pi x - 2$

9. $y = 1 + \frac{1}{3} \cos\left(2x - \frac{\pi}{2}\right)$

In Exercises 10–18, match the equation with its graph. **(14.1, 14.2)**

10. $y = 1 - 3 \cos(x + 2\pi)$

11. $y = 3 \sin \frac{1}{2}x$

12. $y = 1 + 3 \cos \frac{1}{2}x$

13. $y = 3 \cos\left(x - \frac{\pi}{2}\right)$

14. $y = 3 \sin(x + \pi)$

15. $y = 1 + 3 \sin\left(2x + \frac{\pi}{4}\right)$

16. $y = 3 \sin \frac{\pi}{2}x$

17. $y = -3 \cos(x + \pi)$

18. $y = -3 \sin(2x - 3\pi)$

a.

b.

c.

d.

e.

f.

g.

h.

i.

In Exercises 19–27, sketch the graph of the function. **(14.1, 14.2)**

19. $y = 4 - \sin x$

20. $y = -1 + \cos 4x$

21. $y = 2 \cos \pi x$

22. $y = \frac{1}{2} \sin 8x$

23. $y = 6 \cos\left(x - \frac{\pi}{2}\right)$

24. $y = 5 \sin(2x + \pi)$

25. $y = 2 + \sin\left(\frac{1}{2}x + 2\pi\right)$

26. $y = 3 + 3 \cos\left(\frac{1}{2}x + 2\pi\right)$

27. $y = -4 \cos(x - \pi)$

In Exercises 28–33, simplify the expression. **(14.3)**

28. $\cos^2 x + \sin(-x)$

29. $\tan(-x) \cos(-x)$

30. $\sin^2\left(\frac{\pi}{2} - x\right) - 2 \sin^2 x + 1$

31. $\cot^2\left(\frac{\pi}{2} - x\right) - \sec^2(-x)$

32. $\csc^2(-x) \cos^2\left(\frac{\pi}{2} - x\right)$

33. $-1 + \tan(-x)\dfrac{\cos\left(\frac{\pi}{2} - x\right)}{\sin\left(\frac{\pi}{2} - x\right)}$

In Exercises 34–37, verify the identity. (14.3)

34. $\cot^2 x(\tan^2 x + 1) = 1 + \cot^2 x$

35. $\cot x + \tan x = \sec x \csc x$

36. $\sin^2(-x) = \dfrac{\tan^2 x}{\tan^2 x + 1}$

37. $1 - \cos^2 x = \tan^2(-x) \cos^2 x$

In Exercises 38–47, solve the equation for $0 \le x < 2\pi$. (14.4)

38. $2 \sin^2 x \tan x - \tan x = 0$

39. $\cos x \csc^2 x + 3 \cos x = 7 \cos x$

40. $2 \sin^2 x - \sin x - 1 = 0$

41. $\sec^2 x - 2 = 0$

42. $\sin\left(x + \dfrac{\pi}{2}\right) - \sqrt{3} = \sin\left(x - \dfrac{\pi}{2}\right)$

43. $\sin\left(x - \dfrac{\pi}{3}\right) + \sqrt{3} \cos x = \sin\left(\dfrac{\pi}{3} - x\right) + 1$

44. $\tan\left(x + \dfrac{\pi}{4}\right) + \tan x + 2 = 0$

45. $\sin x \tan(x + \pi) - \sin(x + \pi) = 0$

46. $\cos 2x + 2 \sin^2 x - \sin x = 0$

47. $(\sin 2x + \cos 2x)^2 - 1 = 0$

In Exercises 48–55, find the exact value of the expression. (14.5)

48. $\sin 285°$

49. $\cos 195°$

50. $\tan \dfrac{7\pi}{12}$

51. $\cot\left(-\dfrac{\pi}{12}\right)$

52. $\dfrac{\tan 145° - \tan 55°}{1 + \tan 145° \tan 55°}$

53. $\cos 226° \cos 136° + \sin 226° \sin 136°$

54. $\sin \dfrac{\pi}{5} \cos \dfrac{\pi}{30} - \sin \dfrac{\pi}{30} \cos \dfrac{\pi}{5}$

55. $\dfrac{\tan \dfrac{7\pi}{12} - \tan \dfrac{\pi}{4}}{1 + \tan \dfrac{7\pi}{12} \tan \dfrac{\pi}{4}}$

56. *Seasonal Sales* For 1990, the national monthly sales, S (in thousands of units), of *Easy Glide* lawn furniture can be modeled by $S = 74.50 + 43.75 \sin \dfrac{\pi}{6} t$ where t represents the time in months, with $t = 1$ corresponding to January. In which months did sales exceed 100,000 units? Sketch the graph of this function for one year.

57. *Biorhythms* A popular but unproven theory called *biorhythms* explains the ups and downs of everyday life with three cycles that begin at birth.

Physical: $P = \sin \dfrac{2\pi}{23} t$

Emotional: $E = \sin \dfrac{2\pi}{28} t$

Intellectual: $I = \sin \dfrac{2\pi}{33} t$

Positive values indicate high-energy days, and negative values indicate low-energy days. Consider a person who was born on August 16, 1967. Describe this person's three energy levels on May 3, 1995 (the 10,122nd day of the person's life).

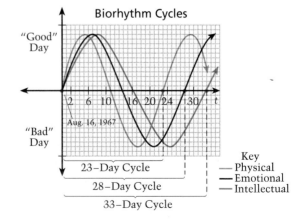

Biorhythm Cycles

"Good" Day

Aug. 16, 1967

"Bad" Day

23–Day Cycle
28–Day Cycle
33–Day Cycle

Key
— Physical
— Emotional
— Intellectual

Many mathematicians have worked at finding ways to compute the decimal form of π. Here are three well-known series.

James Gregory (1638–1675):

$$\pi \approx 4\left(1 - \frac{1}{3} + \frac{1}{5} - \frac{1}{7} + \cdots + \frac{(-1)^{n+1}}{2n-1}\right)$$

John Machin (1680–1751): (For n = 4)

$$\pi \approx 16\left(\frac{1}{5} - \frac{1}{3 \cdot 5^3} + \frac{1}{5 \cdot 5^5} - \frac{1}{7 \cdot 5^7}\right)$$

$$- 4\left(\frac{1}{5} - \frac{1}{3 \cdot 239^3} + \frac{1}{5 \cdot 239^5} - \frac{1}{7 \cdot 239^7}\right)$$

Srinivasa Ramanujan (1877–1920): (For n = 2)

$$\pi \approx \frac{9801}{\sqrt{8}}\left(\frac{1}{1103 + 24(1103 + 26,390)394^{-4}}\right)$$

58. Find the sum of Gregory's series for $n = 11$ and $n = 15$. Average the two results. How close is the answer to π?

59. Evaluate Machin's approximation for $n = 4$. How close is the answer to π?

60. Evaluate Ramanujan's approximation for $n = 2$. How close is the answer to π?

Srinivasa Ramanujan developed methods of calculating π with extraordinary efficiency. His approach is now incorporated in computer algorithms that yield millions of digits of π.

61. *Cofunction Identities* Use the triangle below to verify the six cofunction identities for an *acute* angle.

62. *x-Intercepts of a Graph* Find the x-intercepts of the graph of $y = \sin 2x + \sin x$ in the interval $0 \le x < 2\pi$.

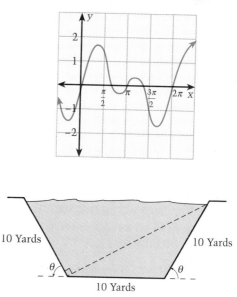

63. *Canal Construction* A canal is being constructed with a cross section in the shape of an isosceles trapezoid, as shown at the right. What angle θ is required for the cross-sectional area of the canal to be $75\sqrt{3}$ square yards?

10 Yards   10 Yards

10 Yards

Blanket Pattern In Exercises 64–73, match the equation with its graphs in the blanket. Then state the amplitude and period of each "matched graph." (The equations match all 22 graphs in the blanket except C, H, K, L, O, and T.)

64. $y = d + \frac{1}{4} \cos 2x$

65. $y = d - \frac{1}{4} \cos 2x$

66. $y = d + 2 \sin x$

67. $y = d - \sin x$

68. $y = d + 2 \cos\left(x + \frac{3\pi}{4}\right)$

69. $y = d + 2 \cos\left(x + \frac{\pi}{4}\right)$

70. $y = d - 2 \sin x$

71. $y = d + \sin x$

72. $y = d + 2 \cos\left(x + \frac{5\pi}{4}\right)$

73. $y = d + 2 \cos\left(x + \frac{7\pi}{4}\right)$

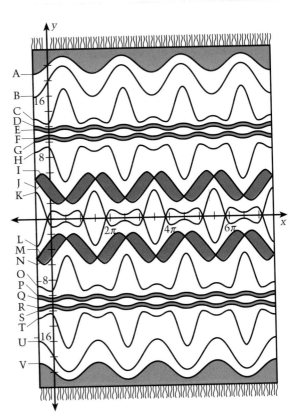

74. Which of the following is *not* an equation of the graph labeled U?

   a. $y = -18 + 2 \sin(x + \pi)$

   b. $y = -18 + 2 \sin(-x)$

   c. $y = -18 + 2 \cos\left(x + \frac{\pi}{2}\right)$

   d. $y = -18 + 2 \cos\left(x + \frac{3\pi}{2}\right)$

75. Which of the following is *not* an equation of the graph labeled D?

   a. $y = 12 + \frac{1}{4} \cos(2x + 2\pi)$

   b. $y = 12 - \frac{1}{4} \cos(2x + 2\pi)$

   c. $y = 12 - \frac{1}{4} \sin\left(2x + \frac{\pi}{2}\right)$

   d. $y = 12 + \frac{1}{4} \sin\left(2x + \frac{3\pi}{2}\right)$

76. How many periods of the graph labeled D appear on the blanket?

77. The graph labeled K has the following equation.

$$y = \frac{1}{2} + 2 \sin(x - \pi) - \cos(2x - 2\pi)$$

The graph labeled C is a translation of K: 13.5 units up and π units to the left. Find an equation for C. Then find all x-values on the blanket at which C is 17.

78. The graph labeled L is also a translation of K. Find an equation for L.

In Exercises 1–3, sketch the graph of the function.

1. $y = 4 + 2 \sin x$

2. $y = -1 - \sin\left(x + \dfrac{\pi}{2}\right)$

3. $y = 3 + 6 \cos(x - \pi)$

In Exercises 4–6, simplify the expression.

4. $2 \sin^2 u \cot u$

5. $\dfrac{4 \sin x \cos x - 2 \sin x \sec x}{2 \tan x}$

6. $\dfrac{1}{\csc x + \cot x}$

In Exercises 7–9, verify the identity.

7. $\csc u - \cot u = \tan \dfrac{u}{2}$

8. $\cos^2 u - \sin^2 u = 1 - 2 \sin^2 u$

9. $-2 \cos^2 u \tan(-u) = \sin 2u$

In Exercises 10–13, solve the equation for $0 \le x \le 2\pi$.

10. $-6 + 10 \cos x = -1$

11. $\tan^2 x - 2 \tan x + 1 = 0$

12. $\cos x - \sin x \sin 2x = 0$

13. $4 - 3 \csc^2 x = 0$

In Exercises 14–17, find the exact value of the expression.

14. $\dfrac{\tan 175° + \tan 140°}{1 - \tan 175° \tan 140°}$

15. $\dfrac{\tan 160° - \tan 40°}{1 + \tan 160° \tan 40°}$

16. $\sin \dfrac{2\pi}{3} \cos \dfrac{5\pi}{3} + \cos \dfrac{2\pi}{3} \sin \dfrac{5\pi}{3}$

17. $\cos \dfrac{13\pi}{12} \cos \dfrac{11\pi}{12} + \sin \dfrac{13\pi}{12} \sin \dfrac{11\pi}{12}$

18. On a horseshoe-pitching court, the two stakes tilt towards each other, 40 feet apart. Use the diagram at the right to find the angle, θ, that a horseshoe stake makes with the ground.

19. Find the length of the stake above the ground. Round the result to one decimal place.

3-inch tilt toward opposite stake

15 inches

20. The depth of the ocean at a swim buoy can be modeled by

$$y = 4 + 2 \sin\left(\frac{\pi}{6} t\right)$$

where y is the water depth in feet and t is the time in hours. Consider a day in which $t = 0$ represents 12:00 midnight. For that day, when do high and low tides occur?

21. A ball thrown and caught at a height of 4 feet with an initial velocity of 30 feet per second traveled 14 feet. Use the formula

$$x = \tfrac{1}{16} v^2 \cos \theta \sin \theta$$

to determine the angle of the throw.

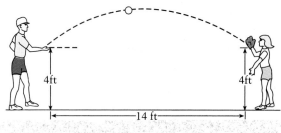

4ft

4ft

14 ft

In Exercises 1–4, find the complement and supplement of the angle.

1. $25°$　　　　**2.** $89°$　　　　**3.** $\dfrac{\pi}{12}$　　　　**4.** $\dfrac{3\pi}{8}$

In Exercises 5–8, find two angles, one with positive measure and the other with negative measure that are coterminal with the given angle.

5. $195°$　　　　**6.** $-47°$　　　　**7.** $\dfrac{4\pi}{3}$　　　　**8.** $-\dfrac{9\pi}{2}$

In Exercises 9–12, evaluate the expression without using a calculator. For Exercises 11 and 12, write the answer in degrees and radians.

9. $\csc\dfrac{13\pi}{4}$　　　　**10.** $\cot\left(-\dfrac{\pi}{4}\right)$　　　　**11.** $\arccos\dfrac{\sqrt{3}}{2}$　　　　**12.** $\arcsin\left(-\dfrac{1}{2}\right)$

In Exercises 13–16, solve the triangle.

13. $A = 47°,\ B = 20°,\ c = 4$　　　　**14.** $b = 4,\ c = 5,\ C = 110°$

15. $a = 6,\ b = 10,\ c = 7$　　　　**16.** $a = 4,\ B = 100°,\ c = 6$

In Exercises 17 and 18, find the area of the triangle.

17. $a = 3,\ B = \dfrac{\pi}{6},\ C = \dfrac{2\pi}{3}$　　　　**18.** $a = 7,\ b = 4,\ c = 6$

In Exercises 19–24, sketch the graph of the function.

19. $y = 4 + 3\sin 3x$　　　　**20.** $y = -\cos\dfrac{1}{2}x$

21. $y = -2 - \cos(x + \pi)$　　　　**22.** $y = -4\sin\left(x + \dfrac{\pi}{2}\right)$

23. $y = 3 + \cos(x - \pi)$　　　　**24.** $y = -\sin 3x$

In Exercises 25–30, simplify the expression.

25. $\sin^2 x\sec^2\left(\dfrac{\pi}{2} - x\right) - \sin^2(-x)$　　　　**26.** $2\sin\left(\dfrac{x}{2}\right)\sin\left(\dfrac{\pi}{2} - x\right)\cos\dfrac{1}{2}x$

27. $\left(\dfrac{\sin 4x}{1 + \cos 4x}\right)^2 + 1$　　　　**28.** $\tan(-x) + \tan x\sec^2 x$

29. $2\sin x\cos^3 x - 2\sin^3 x\cos x$　　　　**30.** $\dfrac{\cos^2 x}{\cos^2\left(\dfrac{\pi}{2} - x\right)} + 1 + \sin^2 x$

In Exercises 31–34, verify the identity.

31. $\dfrac{\sin\left(\dfrac{\pi}{2} - x\right)}{\sin x} = \cot x$　　　　**32.** $2\cos^2 x - 1 = 1 - 2\sin^2 x$

33. $\csc 2x - \cot 2x = \tan x$　　　　**34.** $\tan x\sec x - \csc x\sec^2 x = -\csc x$

In Exercises 35–38, solve the equation for $0 \le x < 2\pi$.

35. $3\sin x = \sqrt{3} + 5\sin x$　　　　**36.** $\tan^2 x - \tan x - \sqrt{3}\tan x + \sqrt{3} = 0$

37. $4\cos^2 x - 1 = 0$　　　　**38.** $4\sin\left(\dfrac{\pi}{2} - x\right) = 3\sec x$

In Exercises 39–42, find the exact value of the expression.

39. $\cos \dfrac{5\pi}{12}$

40. $\tan\!\left(\dfrac{\pi}{12}\right)$

41. $\sin 65° \cos 355° + \sin 355° \cos 65°$

42. $\cos \dfrac{5\pi}{3} \cos \dfrac{3\pi}{2} - \sin \dfrac{5\pi}{3} \sin \dfrac{3\pi}{2}$

Shuffleboard   **In Exercises 43 and 44, use the shuffleboard diagram.**

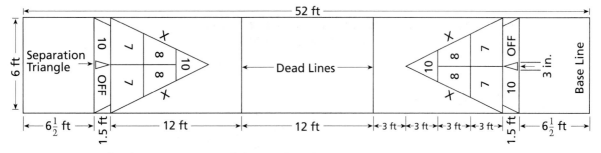

43. Determine the degree measure of the angles of the scoring triangles.

44. Find the length, x (in feet), of the scoring triangles.

Cloverleaf   **In Exercises 45 and 46, use the following information.**

A car is traveling on a circular portion of a cloverleaf at a highway interchange. The radius of one ramp of the cloverleaf is 150 feet.

45. Through what angle has the car driven after the "inside tires" of the car have traveled 600 feet on the cloverleaf? (List your result in degrees.)

46. The inside and outside tires of the car are 5 feet apart. How much farther did the outside tires of the car travel?

Throwing a Softball   **In Exercises 47 and 48, use the following equation for the path of a projectile. (In this equation, *y* is the height in feet, *x* is the horizontal distance in feet, *v* is the initial velocity, *h* is the initial height, and *θ* is the initial angle at which the projectile is launched.)**

$$y = -\frac{16}{v^2 \cos^2 \theta}x^2 + (\tan \theta)x + h$$

47. You and a teammate are warming up for a softball game. You throw the ball at an initial height of 6 feet, an initial velocity of 30 feet per second, and an angle of 30°. The ball lands at your teammate's feet. How far away is your teammate?

48. Your teammate returns the ball, releasing it at a height of 6 feet with an initial velocity of 40 feet per second. You catch the ball 6 feet above the ground. At what angle was the ball thrown?

LESSONS

15.1 Introduction to
Probability ▪ 782

15.2 Counting Methods:
Permutations ▪ 788

15.3 Counting Methods:
Combinations ▪ 796

15.4 Probability, Unions,
and Intersections
▪ 805

15.5 Independent
Events ▪ 811

15.6 Expected Value
▪ 817

*The gleaming roof of white
ceramic tiles belongs to the
Sydney Opera House of
Sydney, Australia, which
was designed by the
Danish architect, Jorn
Utzon. Completed in
1973, it houses five
auditoriums for the performing
arts in a complex that
covers $4\frac{1}{2}$ acres.*

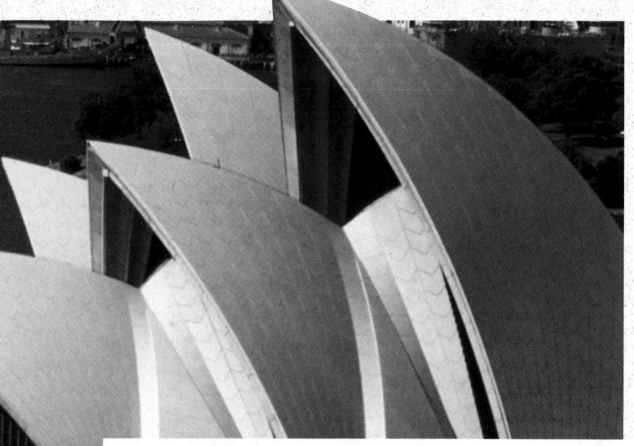

Probability of Rain during 3 Days

Day 1	Day 2	Day 3	
		$\frac{15}{29} \to \approx 0.151$	
	$\frac{16}{30}$	$\frac{14}{29} \to \approx 0.141$	
$\frac{17}{31}$		$\frac{16}{29} \to \approx 0.141$	
	$\frac{14}{30}$	$\frac{13}{29} \to \approx 0.115$	
		$\frac{16}{29} \to \approx 0.141$	
	$\frac{17}{30}$	$\frac{13}{29} \to \approx 0.115$	
$\frac{14}{31}$		$\frac{17}{29} \to \approx 0.115$	
	$\frac{13}{30}$	$\frac{12}{29} \to \approx 0.081$	

A travel agent is taking a tour group to Australia in January, a warm summer month there. The agent wonders if scheduling three days in Sydney would normally give the group at least two days without rain to photograph the sights. A guidebook states that Sydney averages 17 days without rain (and 14 days with rain) in the month of January. Using the tree diagram at the left, the travel agent concludes that the probability of having at least two days without rain is

$$0.151 + 3(0.141) = 0.574.$$

Because this is greater than one half, the group should be able to expect at least two days without rain during their stay.

15.1 Introduction to Probability

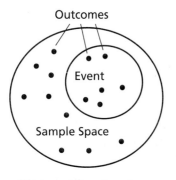

What you should learn:

Goal 1 How to find the probability of an event

Goal 2 How to use probability to answer questions about real-life situations

Why you should learn it:

You can use probability to solve many real-life problems, such as those involving survey results or Punnett squares.

Goal 1 Finding the Probability of an Event

The **probability of an event** is a number between 0 and 1 that indicates the likelihood the event will occur. An event that is certain to occur has a probability of 1. An event that *cannot* occur has a probability of 0. An event that is *equally likely* to occur or not occur has a probability of $\frac{1}{2}$, or 0.5.

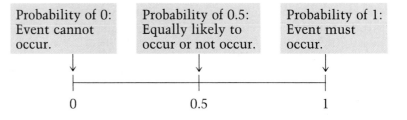

| Probability of 0: Event cannot occur. | Probability of 0.5: Equally likely to occur or not occur. | Probability of 1: Event must occur. |

```
|----------+----------+----------|
0         0.5         1
```

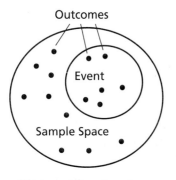

Outcomes

Event

Sample Space

This event has six outcomes, and the sample space has 15 outcomes.

Finding the Probability of an Event

Consider a set, *S*, called a **sample space,** that is composed of a finite number of outcomes, each of which is equally likely to occur. A subset, *E*, of the sample space is an **event.** The probability, *P*, that an outcome in *E* will occur is the ratio of the number of outcomes in *E* to the number of outcomes in *S*.

$$P = \frac{\text{Number of outcomes in event}}{\text{Number of outcomes in sample space}}$$

Example 1 *Finding the Probability of an Event*

a. You are dialing a friend's phone number, but can't remember the last digit. If you choose a digit at random, what is the probability that you dial the correct number?

$$P = \frac{\text{Number of correct digits}}{\text{Number of possible digits}} = \frac{1}{10}$$

b. On a multiple-choice test, you know the answer to Question 8 is not **a** or **d**, but you are not sure about **b**, **c**, and **e**. If you guess, what is the probability that you are *wrong?*

$$P = \frac{\text{Number of wrong answers}}{\text{Number of possible answers}} = \frac{2}{3}$$

■

Real Life
Polling

Underweight
366
Good weight 3082
1776
Overweight
Female

Underweight
1057
Good weight 4389
961
Overweight
Male

Example 2 _Conducting a Poll_

In 1990, the Centers for Disease Control took a survey of 11,631 high school students. The students were asked whether they considered themselves to be at a good weight, under-weight, or overweight. The results of the survey are shown at the left.

a. If you choose a female at random from those surveyed, the probability that she said she was underweight is

$$P = \frac{\text{Number who answered ``underweight''}}{\text{Number of females in survey}}$$

$$= \frac{366}{3082 + 366 + 1776}$$

$$= \frac{366}{5224} \approx 0.07.$$

b. If you choose a person who answered "underweight" from those surveyed, the probability that the person is female is

$$P = \frac{\text{Number of females who answered ``underweight''}}{\text{Number in survey who answered ``underweight''}}$$

$$= \frac{366}{366 + 1057} = \frac{366}{1423} \approx 0.26.$$ ∎

Polls like the one described in Example 2 are often used to make inferences about a population that is larger than the sample. For instance, from Example 2, you might infer that 7% of _all_ high school girls consider themselves to be under-weight. When you make such an inference, it is important that those surveyed are representative of the entire population.

Connections
Geometry

Example 3 _Using Area to Find Probability_

You have just stepped into the tub to take a shower when one of your contact lenses falls out. (You have not yet turned on the shower.) Assuming that the lens is equally likely to land anywhere on the bottom of the tub, what is the probability that it landed in the drain? Use the dimensions shown at the left to answer the question.

Solution Because the area of the tub bottom is $(26)(50) = 1300$ square inches and the area of the drain is $\pi(1^2) = \pi$ square inches, the probability that the lens landed in the drain is about

Drain
} 2 in.
26 in.
50 in.

$$P = \frac{\pi}{1300} \approx 0.0024.$$ ∎

Example 4   *The Probability of Inheriting Genes*

Common parakeets have genes that can produce four feather colors: green (BBCC, BBCc, BbCC, or BbCc), blue (BBcc or Bbcc), yellow (bbCC or bbCc), or white (bbcc). Use the *Punnett square* below to find the probability that an offspring of two green parents (both with BbCc feather genes) will be yellow. Note that each parent passes along a B or b gene and a C or c gene.

	BC	Bc	bC	bc
BC	BBCC	BBCc	BbCC	BbCc
Bc	BBCc	BBcc	BbCc	Bbcc
bC	BbCC	BbCc	bbCC	bbCc
bc	BbCc	Bbcc	bbCc	bbcc

Solution $P = \dfrac{\text{Number of yellow possibilities}}{\text{Number of possibilities}} = \dfrac{3}{16}$ ∎

Communicating about ALGEBRA

▶ **SHARING IDEAS about the Lesson**

	Bc	bc	Bc	bc
bC	?	?	?	?
bc	?	?	?	?
bC	?	?	?	?
bc	?	?	?	?

A. In Example 1a, suppose you remembered that the last digit is even. If you choose an even digit at random, what is the probability that you dial the correct number?

B. In Example 2, if you choose a person who answered "overweight" from those surveyed, what is the probability that the person is male?

C. Use Example 4 as a model to copy and complete the Punnett square at the left for a blue parent (Bbcc) and a yellow parent (bbCc). For these parents, what is the probability that an offspring will be yellow?

EXERCISES

Guided Practice

▶ **CRITICAL THINKING about the Lesson**

1. One of your friends says that there is a 110% chance of snow to-morrow. Why is this statement not mathematically correct?

2. Is it possible that the probability of an event is negative?

3. *Marbles*   A jar contains three red marbles and four blue marbles. One of the marbles is drawn at random. How many possible out-comes are in the sample space: two or seven? Explain.

4. *Picking a Pencil*   There are six pencils, eraser end up, in a pencil can. Two are newly sharpened. Because all have the same length, you can't tell which are sharpened. If you choose one of the pencils, what is the probability that it is sharpened?

5. *Punnett Square*   Draw a Punnett square that represents the possi-ble combinations of color genes for the offspring of a green parakeet (BBCc) and a yellow parakeet (bbCc). What is the probability that one of the offspring is green?

Independent Practice

In Exercises 6–9, use the sample space {1, 2, . . . , 20} to find the probability of the event.

6. An even number is chosen.

7. A prime number is chosen.

8. A perfect square is chosen.

9. A number with at least four factors is chosen.

Geometry   **In Exercises 10–15, find the probability that the marble will come to rest in the indicated region.**

A marble is dropped into a large box whose base is painted different colors, as shown at the right. Because the base *a* is a horizontal surface, the marble has an equal likelihood of coming to rest at any point on the base.

10. The red center

11. The orange ring

12. The yellow ring

13. The green ring

14. The blue ring

15. The purple border

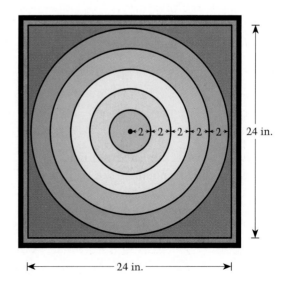

16. *Picking a Penguin*   Estimate the probability that a penguin that is chosen randomly in the photo will be an adult penguin. (The baby penguins are brown.)

17. *Unemployed Workers*   In October, 1991, of the 5,711,000 American workers who had recently left their jobs, 4,722,000 left because they had been laid off. If you randomly choose one of the workers who had recently left his or her job, what is the probability that the person left because he or she was laid off? *(Source: Bureau of Labor Statistics)*

18. *Giving a Speech*   You are sitting in English class, and your teacher is drawing names to see which student will give the first speech. There are 31 students in your class. What is the probability that the first name drawn will be yours? Four speeches are given each day. What is the probability that you will have to give your speech on the first day?

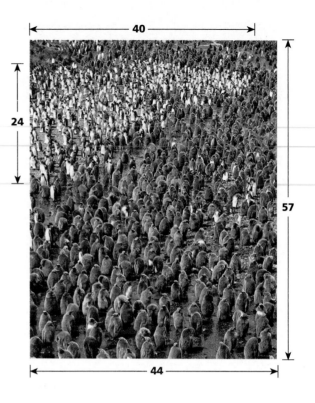

19. *Girl or Boy?*   The genes that determine the sex of humans are denoted as XX (female) and XY (male). Copy and complete the Punnett square below. Then use the result to explain why the probability that a newborn baby will be a boy or a girl is equally likely.

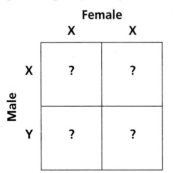

20. *Blood Types*   There are four basic human blood types: A (AA or Ao), B (BB or Bo), AB (AB), and O (oo). Copy and complete the Punnett square below. What is the blood type of each parent? What is the probability that their offspring will have blood type A? B? AB? O?

	A	o
B	?	?
o	?	?

21. *Paris, France*   One line from Edna St. Vincent Millay's poem at the right is chosen at random. What is the probability that the line contains a word with the letter "i"? What is the probability that the line contains a word with the letter "p"?

Look, Edwin! Do you see that boy
Talking to the other boy?
No, over there by those two men—
Wait, don't look now—now look again.
No, not the one in navy-blue:
That's the one he's talking to.
Sure you see him? Stripéd pants?
Well, he was born in Paris, France.

United States Blood Types   In Exercises 22 and 23, use the following information.

The circle graph at the right shows the number of people in the United States in 1990 with each blood type. *(Source: American Association of Blood Banks)*

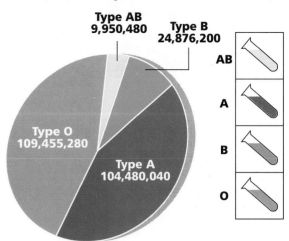

Type AB
9,950,480

Type B
24,876,200

Type O
109,455,280

Type A
104,480,040

AB

A

B

O

22. A person is selected at random from the United States population. What is the probability that the person does *not* have blood type B?

23. What is the probability that a person selected at random from the United States population *does* have blood type B? How is this probability related to the probability found in Exercise 22?

Integrated Review

In Exercises 24–27, find the area of the shaded region.

24.

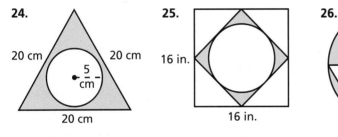

20 cm   20 cm

$\frac{5}{cm}$

20 cm

25.

16 in.

16 in.

26.

10 m

10 m

10 m

10 m

10 m

10 m

27.

4 yd

|← 5 yd →|← 5 yd →|

28. *College Entrance Exam Sample*   In the figure at the right, what percent of the area of rectangle *PQRS* is shaded blue?
a. 20%   **b.** 25%   **c.** 30%   **d.** $33\frac{1}{3}$%   **e.** 40%

29. *College Entrance Exam Sample*   How many of the whole numbers between 100 and 300 begin or end with 2?
a. 20   **b.** 40   **c.** 100   **d.** 110   **e.** 180

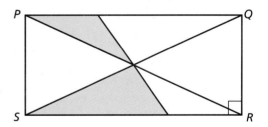

P   *Q*

S   *R*

Exploration and Extension

30. *Choose a Number*   Studies have shown that when people are asked to choose one of the integers 1, 2, 3, or 4, more than half of the people choose the same number. Conduct this experiment by asking several people to choose one of the four integers. Which number was chosen most often? Use this result to explain why asking a person to choose a number is *not* the same as randomly selecting a number.

15.2

Counting Methods: Permutations

What you should learn:

Goal 1 How to use the Fundamental Counting Principle to find probabilities

Goal 2 How to use permutations to find probabilities

Why you should learn it:

You can use the Fundamental Counting Principle to find many real-life probabilities, such as the probability of guessing a number correctly.

Goal 1 The Fundamental Counting Principle

From Lesson 15.1, you know that a basic skill needed to find probabilities is to be able to count the number of outcomes in an event and in a sample space. Sometimes this can be done by simply listing all possible outcomes. At other times, when there are too many outcomes to list, it is more efficient to use a formula to count the number of outcomes.

Almost all "counting formulas" are based on the following **Fundamental Counting Principle.**

Fundamental Counting Principle

If one event can occur in m ways and another event can occur in n ways, then the number of ways that both events can occur is equal to $m \cdot n$.

This principle can be extended to three or more events. For instance, if three events can occur in m, n, and k ways, then the number of ways that all three can occur is $m \cdot n \cdot k$.

Example 1 Using the Fundamental Counting Principle

How many different three-letter "words" from the English alphabet are possible?

Solution This experiment has three events. The first event is the choice of the first letter, the second event is the choice of the second letter, and the third event is the choice of the third letter. Because the English alphabet contains 26 letters, it follows that each event can occur in 26 ways.

Three-letter "words": ⬜ ⬜ ⬜
                       26 26 26

Using the Fundamental Counting Principle, it follows that the number of three-letter "words" is $26 \cdot 26 \cdot 26 = 17,576$. ∎

A gnu, or wildebeest

Example 2 — *Finding a Probability*

You are using a word processor to prepare a term paper. The word processor has a spelling checker that contains all commonly used English words, including 522 three-letter words. You are unsure of the correct spelling for *gnu*, so you type three letters at random. What is the probability that the spelling checker will identify this "word" as misspelled?

Solution From Example 1, you know there are 17,576 possible three-letter "words." Of these, $17{,}576 - 522 = 17{,}054$ would be flagged as incorrect by the spelling checker. Therefore, the probability that your word will be flagged is

$$\frac{\text{Number of incorrect words}}{\text{Number of possible words}} = \frac{17{,}054}{17{,}576} \approx 0.970 \text{ or } 97\%. \qquad \blacksquare$$

Example 3 — *Applying the Fundamental Counting Principle*

Telephone numbers in the United States have ten digits. The first three form the *area code* and the next seven form the *local telephone number.* What is the maximum number of local telephone numbers that are possible within each of the states shown in blue on the map? (A local telephone number cannot have 0 or 1 as its first or second digit.)

Solution There are only eight choices for the first two digits, because neither can be 0 or 1. For each of the other digits, there are ten choices.

Area code   Local number

     8   8 10   10 10 10 10

Using the Fundamental Counting Principle, the number of telephone numbers possible within each area code is

$8 \cdot 8 \cdot 10 \cdot 10 \cdot 10 \cdot 10 \cdot 10 = 6{,}400{,}000.$

Each of these states had, at most, 6.4 million phone numbers in 1990. $\blacksquare$

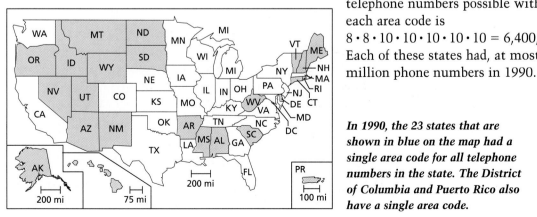

In 1990, the 23 states that are shown in blue on the map had a single area code for all telephone numbers in the state. The District of Columbia and Puerto Rico also have a single area code.

Goal 2 Using Permutations to Find Probabilities

The Fundamental Counting Principle can be used to determine the number of ways that *n* elements can be arranged *in order*. Such an ordering of *n* elements is a **permutation** of the elements.

Example 4 *Listing Permutations*

Write all the permutations of the letters A, B, and C.

Solution The three letters can be arranged in six ways.

ABC, ACB, BAC, BCA, CAB, CBA

In Example 4, the number of permutations could also have been found using the Fundamental Counting Principle. To do this, note that there are three choices for the first letter, two choices for the second, and only one choice for the third.

Permutations of three letters

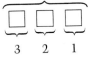

3   2   1

Thus the number of permutations is $3 \cdot 2 \cdot 1 = 3! = 6$.

Example 5 *Finding the Number of Permutations of n Different Elements*

How many permutations of the letters A, B, C, D, E, and F are possible?

Solution There are six choices for the first letter, five for the second, four for the third, and so on.

Permutations of six letters

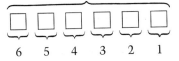

6   5   4   3   2   1

Using the Fundamental Counting Principle, the number of permutations of the six letters is $6 \cdot 5 \cdot 4 \cdot 3 \cdot 2 \cdot 1 = 6! = 720$.

Number of Permutations of *n* Elements

The number of permutations of *n* elements is given by

$$n! = n \cdot (n-1) \cdot \cdots \cdot 4 \cdot 3 \cdot 2 \cdot 1.$$

Real Life
Test Taking

First Ten Elements of the Periodic Table

Name	Symbol
Beryllium	Be
Boron	B
Carbon	C
Fluorine	F
Helium	He
Hydrogen	H
Lithium	Li
Neon	Ne
Nitrogen	N
Oxygen	O

Example 6 *Probability of Guessing Correctly*

You are taking a chemistry test and are asked to list the first ten elements *in order* as they appear in the periodic table of elements. Suppose you have no idea of the correct order and simply guess. What is the probability that you guess correctly?

Solution   You have ten choices for the first element, nine choices for the second, eight choices for the third, and so on.

Order of first ten elements

10 9 8 7 6 5 4 3 2 1

The number of different orders is $10! = 3{,}628{,}800$, so your probability of guessing correctly is $P = \dfrac{1}{3{,}628{,}800}$. ∎

Communicating about **A L G E B R A**

▶ **SHARING IDEAS about the Lesson**

The diagram below represents the 36 possible outcomes when rolling two six-sided dice.

A. What is the probability that the total is 7?

B. Roll a pair of dice 90 times and record each total. Use the results to estimate the probability of rolling a 7. How closely does the probability agree with the probability you found in part A?

EXERCISES

▶ **CRITICAL THINKING about the Lesson**

1. When you use the Fundamental Counting Principle, what are you counting?

2. Use the Fundamental Counting Principle to explain why there are 1000 three-digit numbers from 000 to 999.

3. A coin is tossed six times. Explain why the number of ways the coin can land heads up or tails up is 2^6. Is this an example of a permutation? (*Hint:* Three ways the coin can land are HHHHHH, THHHHH, and HTHHHH.)

4. Find the number of permutations of the letters ARST. How many of these are English words? If one of the permutations is chosen at random, what is the probability that it is an English word?

5. In how many orders can six people be arranged in a line?

6. How many three-digit numbers have only even digits?

Independent Practice

In Exercises 7–10, find the number of permutations of the given letters. Then, find the number of "words" of the same length that can be formed with the given letters if you are allowed to repeat letters. (For instance, from STOP, you could form SSSS, SSST, SSTT, and so on.)

7. STOP   **8.** SMILE   **9.** PENCIL   **10.** FORMULA

11. *Taking a Trip*   Four people are taking a long trip in a car. Two sit in the front seat and two in the back seat. Three of the people agree to share the driving. In how many different arrangements can the four people sit?

12. *Morse Code*   In Morse code, all characters are transmitted using a sequence of *dots* and *dashes*. How many different characters can be formed with a sequence of four symbols, each of which is a dot or a dash? How many can be formed with a sequence of one, two, or three symbols?

13. *Holiday Lights*   You are decorating the living room window with a string of holiday lights. You have four red, four blue, four green, four yellow, and four white lights. In how many different patterns can you string the lights so that matching colors are five lights apart?

14. Batting Order   A baseball coach is determining the batting order for the team. The team has nine members, but the coach does not want the pitcher to be one of the first four to bat. How many batting orders are possible?

15. School Lunch   Your school cafeteria offers three salads, four main courses, two vegetables, and three desserts. How many different combinations of a salad, main course, vegetable, and dessert are possible?

16. Combination Lock   You have forgotten the combination of the lock on your school locker. There are 40 numbers on the lock, and the correct combination is "R ☐ – L ☐ – R ☐." How many combinations may it be necessary to try in order to get the correct combination? (Numbers may be repeated, such as 8-8-8.)

17. Combination Lock   In Exercise 16, suppose you remember that the first part of the combination is "Right 16." Now how many combinations may it be necessary to try in order to get the correct combination?

18. Scheduling Classes   Next year you are taking math, English, history, keyboarding, chemistry, physics, and physical education. Each class is offered during each of the seven periods in the day. In how many different orders can you schedule your classes?

19. Scheduling Classes   Your best friend is taking four of the seven courses you are taking. She has already scheduled her classes. In how many ways can you schedule your classes so that you and your friend share four classes? (Assume that each of the nonshared classes is offered during each of the periods in the day.)

Boston Computer Museum   **In Exercises 20–22, use the following information.**

You visited the Boston Computer Museum and bought four different robots—one for each of your four cousins. When you bought the robots, you intended a specific one for each cousin. After wrapping the packages, however, you realize that you don't know which robot is in which package. You don't want to unwrap the packages, so you randomly assign names to the packages.

20. What is the probability that all four cousins receive the robot you intended?

21. What is the probability that exactly three receive the robot you intended?

22. What is the probability that exactly two receive the robot you intended? Exactly one? None?

23. *Sydney Opera House*   You are attending a concert at the Sydney Opera House. As you are walking in, you see a friend you haven't seen in years. Your friend is attending the same concert. What is the probability that your friend will be sitting in one of the two seats beside you?

24. *Car License Number*   You witnessed a hit-and-run automobile accident. You remember the license number of the automobile, except for the last two digits. You do remember that the license is from your state, that the last two symbols are digits (not letters of the alphabet), and that they are *not* the same. With this information, how many automobile license numbers would the police have to check?

The Opera House in Sydney, Australia, has a seating capacity of 1547.

25. *Mobile Home*   You are buying a new mobile home. You have seven choices of carpet and four choices of wall paneling for each of six rooms. In how many different ways can you choose carpeting and paneling for the six rooms?

Integrated Review

In Exercises 26–31, evaluate the expression.

26. 4!   **27.** 3!   **28.** 6!

29. 7!   **30.** 5!   **31.** 8!

Geometry   **In Exercises 32 and 33, use the figure at the right.**

32. What is the probability that a point chosen randomly inside the circle will also be inside the square?

33. What is the probability that a point chosen randomly inside the square will also be inside the circle?

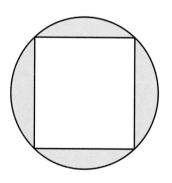

Exploration and Extension

34. *Dance Recital*   For a dance recital, five beginner groups, eight intermediate groups, and six advanced groups are to perform. The director wants to set up the program so that all the beginner groups perform first, then the intermediate groups, then the advanced groups. How many orders are possible?

1. Solve $3a^2b + c = bc$ for a. **(1.5)**

2. Solve $25 - 3t < 20$. **(1.6)**

3. Find the reference angle of $\frac{11}{8}\pi$. **(13.2)**

4. Factor $x^3 - 3x^2 + 4x - 12$. **(9.3)**

5. Solve $|4 - t| \geq 10$. **(1.7)**

6. Sketch $y = |4x| + 7$. **(2.6)**

7. Complete the square: $x^2 - x + 9$. **(5.3)**

8. Solve $\begin{cases} 5x - y = -14 \\ -5x + 2y = 13 \end{cases}$. **(3.2)**

9. Find the inverse of $y = 4x^2 - \frac{1}{4}$. **(6.3)**

10. Add: $(x^2 + x) + (x^3 - x^2 + 2)$. **(9.1)**

11. Solve $\sqrt[3]{27r} + 15 = 0$. **(7.5)**

12. Find the amplitude of $y = 3 \sin 2x$. **(14.1)**

13. Classify: $4x^2 - 4x + 4y^2 + 2y = 8$. **(11.5)**

14. Find the mean: 17, 21, 6, 15, 17, 19. **(6.7)**

15. Simplify: $(3x^0 b^{-1}) \cdot \left(\frac{1}{6}x^2 y^{-2}\right) \div b^2$. **(7.1)**

16. Find the period of $y = \cos 2\pi\theta$. **(14.1)**

17. Solve $\log_2 16 = x$. **(8.6)**

18. Sketch $y = 2 \sin(3x - 2)$. **(14.1)**

19. Write an equation of the vertical line passing through the point $\left(\frac{3}{4}, \frac{1}{2}\right)$. **(2.2)**

20. Find $g(f(x))$ for $g(x) = x - 2$ and $f(x) = x^3$. **(6.2)**

Career Interview

Illustrator

Lily Yamamoto designs and illustrates print material such as brochures, books, catalogs, manuals, and even menus. Most of her work is done through desktop publishing.

Q: What led you into this career?

A: I was attracted to my career by my love for art, particularly with drawing, painting, visual communication, and problem solving.

Q: Does having a math background help you on the job?

A: To create different colors, I need to combine percentages of cyan, magenta, yellow, and black. To position art, I need to consider proportion in relation to space and text. I am constantly converting between picas, a unit of measure used in publishing, and inches. I knew math was needed to do daily tasks, like banking and shopping, but was I surprised to discover how much math can be applied to graphic design.

Q: Do you use calculators?

A: Complicated resizing of art is usually done first with a calculator. However, you still need to understand math in order to do it correctly. Also, understanding the math allows me to compute mentally when I do not have the luxury of time.

15.3 Counting Methods: Combinations

What you should learn:

Goal 1 How to use combinations to count the number of ways an event can happen

Goal 2 How to use combinations to find probabilities

Why you should learn it:

You can solve many real-life probability problems using combinations, such as the probability that you will be dealt a particular five-card hand.

Goal 1 Counting Combinations

For some counting problems, order is important. For instance, when counting phone numbers, 454-5526 and 454-5562 are not the same. These are called permutations. For other counting problems, order is not important. For instance, in most card games, the order in which your cards are dealt is not important. Reordering the cards that are dealt does not change your "card hand." These are called combinations.

Choosing *m* elements from a set that has *n* elements is called forming a **combination of *n* elements taken *m* at a time.**

Example 1 Combination of n Elements Taken m at a Time

In how many ways can three letters be chosen from the letters A, B, C, D, and E? Their order is not important.

Solution The following subsets represent the combinations of three letters that can be chosen from five letters.

{A, B, C}   {A, B, D}   {A, B, E}   {A, C, D}   {A, C, E}
{A, D, E}   {B, C, D}   {B, C, E}   {B, D, E}   {C, D, E}

Thus there are ten ways that three letters can be chosen from five letters. ∎

Combinations of *n* Elements Taken *m* at a Time

The number of combinations of *n* elements taken *m* at a time is

$$\binom{n}{m} = \frac{n!}{(n-m)!\,m!}.$$

Note that this formula is the same one given for binomial coefficients in Lesson 12.5. Applying the formula to Example 1 produces the original result

$$\binom{5}{3} = \frac{5!}{2! \cdot 3!} = \frac{5 \cdot 4}{2} = 10.$$

Connections
Game Theory

Standard 52 - Card Deck			
A ♠	A ♥	A ♦	A ♣
K ♠	K ♥	K ♦	K ♣
Q ♠	Q ♥	Q ♦	Q ♣
J ♠	J ♥	J ♦	J ♣
10 ♠	10 ♥	10 ♦	10 ♣
9 ♠	9 ♥	9 ♦	9 ♣
8 ♠	8 ♥	8 ♦	8 ♣
7 ♠	7 ♥	7 ♦	7 ♣
6 ♠	6 ♥	6 ♦	6 ♣
5 ♠	5 ♥	5 ♦	5 ♣
4 ♠	4 ♥	4 ♦	4 ♣
3 ♠	3 ♥	3 ♦	3 ♣
2 ♠	2 ♥	2 ♦	2 ♣

Real Life
Polling

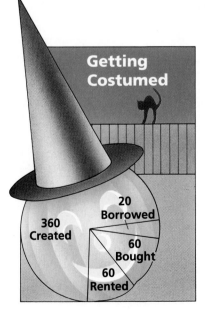

Example 2 *The Probability of a Run of Cards*

Five cards are dealt at random from a standard deck of 52 playing cards. What is the probability that the cards are 10–J–Q–K–A of the same suit?

Solution The number of five-card hands possible from a deck of 52 cards is given by the number of combinations of 52 elements taken five at a time.

$$\binom{52}{5} = \frac{52!}{47! \cdot 5!} = \frac{52 \cdot 51 \cdot 50 \cdot 49 \cdot 48}{5 \cdot 4 \cdot 3 \cdot 2 \cdot 1} = 2{,}598{,}960$$

Because only four of these five-card hands are 10–J–Q–K–A of the same suit, the probability that the hand contains these cards is

$$P = \frac{4}{2{,}598{,}960} = \frac{1}{649{,}740}.$$ ∎

Example 3 *Conducting a Survey*

In 1990, a survey was conducted of 500 adults who have worn Halloween costumes. Each person was asked how he or she acquired a Halloween costume: created it, rented it, bought it, or borrowed it. The results are shown at the left. What is the probability that the first four people who were polled all created their costumes?

Solution To answer this question you need to use the formula for the number of combinations *twice.* First, find the number of ways to choose four people from the 360 who created their own costumes.

$$\binom{360}{4} = \frac{360 \cdot 359 \cdot 358 \cdot 357}{4 \cdot 3 \cdot 2 \cdot 1} = 688{,}235{,}310$$

Next, find the number of ways to choose four people from the 500 who were surveyed.

$$\binom{500}{4} = \frac{500 \cdot 499 \cdot 498 \cdot 497}{4 \cdot 3 \cdot 2 \cdot 1} = 2{,}573{,}031{,}125$$

The probability that all of the first four people surveyed created their own costumes is the ratio of these two numbers.

$$P = \frac{\text{Number of ways to choose 4 from 360}}{\text{Number of ways to choose 4 from 500}}$$

$$= \frac{688{,}235{,}310}{2{,}573{,}031{,}125} \approx 0.267$$ ∎

Example 4 Forming a Committee

To obtain input from 200 company employees, the management of a company selected a committee of 5. Of the 200 employees, 56 are from minority groups. None of the 56, however, were selected to be on the committee. Does this indicate that the management's selection was biased?

Solution Part of the solution is similar to that of Example 3. If the 5 committee members were selected at random, the probability that all 5 would be nonminorities is

$$P = \frac{\text{Number of ways to choose 5 from 144 nonminorities}}{\text{Number of ways to choose 5 from 200 employees}}$$

$$= \frac{\binom{144}{5}}{\binom{200}{5}}$$

$$= \frac{481{,}008{,}528}{2{,}535{,}650{,}040}$$

$$\approx 0.19.$$

Thus if the committee were chosen at random (that is, without bias), then the likelihood that it would have no minority members is about 0.19. While this does not *prove* there was bias, it does suggest it.

Communicating about ALGEBRA

▶ **SHARING IDEAS about the Lesson**

A. Six pennies are tossed in the air and land on a table—either heads up or tails up. The $\binom{6}{3}$ ways that exactly three of the pennies can land heads up are as follows.

HHHTTT	HHTHTT	HHTTHT	HHTTTH	HTHHTT
HTHTHT	HTHTTH	HTTHHT	HTTHTH	HTTTHH
TTTHHH	TTHTHH	TTHHTH	TTHHHT	THTTHH
THTHTH	THTHHT	THHTTH	THHTHT	THHHTT

Explain how this number could be found using the formula for the number of combinations.

B. Eight pennies are tossed in the air and land on a table. What is the probability that exactly four of them land heads up?

EXERCISES

Guided Practice

▶ **CRITICAL THINKING about the Lesson**

1. How many different *combinations* of four letters can be chosen from the letters A, B, C, D, E, F, and G?

2. In the portion of Pascal's Triangle shown below, which entry is $\binom{7}{2}$?

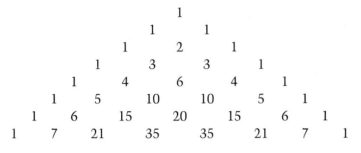

```
                    1
                1       1
            1       2       1
        1       3       3       1
    1       4       6       4       1
1       5      10      10       5       1
1   6      15      20      15       6       1
1   7   21      35      35      21       7       1
```

Disc Jockey   **In Exercises 3 and 4, use the following information.**

By winning a contest on a local radio station, you get to be the disc jockey for two hours. During your time, you must play 20 songs, 17 of which are selected by the station and 3 of which are your own choice.

3. Six of your favorite songs are not among the 17 chosen by the station. In how many ways can you choose 3 songs from the 6?

4. If the 20 songs are played in random order, what is the probability that your 3 choices will be played first?

Independent Practice

5. *Study Questions*   Your history teacher gives your class a list of eight study questions. Five of the eight will be on the next test. How many different combinations of five test questions can your teacher choose from the eight study questions?

6. *Basketball Lineup*   A high school basketball team has 15 players. In how many different ways can the coach choose the starting lineup? (Assume each player can play each position.)

7. *First-String Team*   A high school football team has 2 centers, 9 linemen (who can play either guard or tackle), 2 quarterbacks, 5 halfbacks, 5 ends, and 6 fullbacks. The coach uses 1 center, 4 linemen, 2 ends, 2 halfbacks, 1 quarterback, and 1 fullback to form an offensive unit. In how many ways can the offensive unit be selected?

8. *Pizza Toppings*   A pizza shop offers nine toppings. How many different "three-topping pizzas" can be formed with the nine toppings? (Assume no topping is used twice.)

9. *Geometry*   Three points that are not on a line determine three lines. How many lines are determined by seven points, no three of which are on a line?

10. *Geometry*   How many circles are determined by seven points, no four of which are on a circle? (Assume no three of the points lie on a line.)

11. *Microwave Shipment*   Fifty microwave ovens were shipped to an appliance store. Four of the fifty were defective. What is the probability that exactly two of the first five sold are defective?

12. *100-Yard Dash*   You, your friend, and five other high school students are running in the 100-yard dash at the state finals. In how many different orders can the seven runners finish? In how many of these are you and your friend in first and second place, respectively? (Assume there are no ties.)

13. *Television Game Show*   A contestant on a game show must choose 2 of 16 boxes. Of the 16 boxes, 3 contain money, 5 contain prizes, and 8 are empty. What is the probability that both boxes chosen by a contestant contain money? What is the probability that both are empty?

14. *Selecting a Card*   Two cards are selected at random from a standard deck of 52 playing cards. What is the probability that both are hearts?

15. *Pizza*   The graph below shows the percents of different types of pizza sold in 1990. Suppose 3 pizzas are randomly chosen from 100 pizzas. What is the probability that all 3 have thin crusts? (Assume the 100 pizzas are represented by the circle graph.) *(Source: National Restaurant Association)*

Types of Pizza Sold

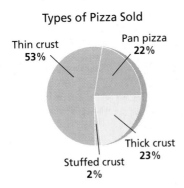

16. *Bank Loans*   The graph below shows the percents of different types of bank loans in 1992. Suppose 4 loans are randomly chosen from 1000 loans. What is the probability that all 4 are auto loans? (Assume the 1000 loans are represented by the circle graph.) *(Source: Federal Reserve System)*

Types of Bank Loans

Hospital Inspection   **In Exercises 17 and 18, use the following information.**

As part of a monthly inspection at a hospital, the inspection team randomly selects reports from 8 of the 84 nurses who are on duty.

17. What is the probability that none of the reports selected will be from the 10 most experienced nurses on duty?

18. What is the probability that all of the reports selected will be from the 20 least experienced nurses on duty?

19. *Jelly Beans*   A bag of 4340 jelly beans contains equal numbers of red, green, purple, yellow, black, white, and orange. You pick 7 jelly beans at random. What is the probability that at least 1 is orange?

20. *Jelly Beans*   In Exercise 19, what is the probability that none of the 7 you choose are orange?

Integrated Review

In Exercises 21–26, evaluate the expression.

21. $\binom{8}{2}$

22. $\binom{5}{4}$

23. $\binom{30}{26}$

24. $\binom{1000}{2}$

25. $\binom{55}{6}$

26. $\binom{103}{3}$

In Exercises 27 and 28, identify each situation as involving permutations, combinations, or neither.

27. The number of ways a 5-person volleyball team can be chosen from 15 people

28. The number of orders in which five people can stand in line

Exploration and Extension

29. *Probability Demonstrator*   What is the probability that the marble at the right will land in each of the four compartments at the bottom of the "probability demonstrator"?

30. *Probability Demonstrator*   You are constructing a probability demonstrator similar to the one shown at the right, except that your probability demonstrator has eight bottom compartments. What is the probability that a marble will land in each of the eight compartments?

Most graphing calculators have a random number generator that can be used to perform probability experiments. Each time the random number generator is used, it selects a real number between 0 and 1. (The number selected is greater than 0 and less than 1.) If you want the calculator to randomly select an *integer* x, such that $n \le x \le m$, you can enter the following keystrokes.

iPart $((m - n + 1)$ rand $+ n)$

Choose the integer part of the number

Select a random number between 0 and 1.

Specific keystroke instructions for a *TI-82*, Casio *fx-9700GE*, and Sharp *EL-9300C* are listed on page 865.

Example: Tossing a Die with a Graphing Calculator

Use one of the calculator programs on page 865 to simulate the tossing of a six-sided die 120 times. Record the number of times you obtain 1, 2, 3, 4, 5, and 6.

Solution Theoretically, you would expect each number to occur 20 times. *Experimentally*, however, you shouldn't expect this exact result. Here are the results we obtained.

Number	1	2	3	4	5	6
Tally	20	20	22	23	25	10

From these results, it appears that the probability of obtaining each number is as follows.

$1: \dfrac{20}{120}$ $\quad 2: \dfrac{20}{120}$ $\quad 3: \dfrac{22}{120}$ $\quad 4: \dfrac{23}{120}$ $\quad 5: \dfrac{25}{120}$ $\quad 6: \dfrac{10}{120}$

A probability that is determined by this method is called an **experimental probability.** As you can see from this example, experimental probabilities can differ from theoretical probabilities. By conducting an experiment with a larger number of trials, you will obtain experimental results that are closer to the theoretical results. For instance, running the dice-rolling program 10,000 times produced the results shown in the following table.

Number	1	2	3	4	5	6
Tally	1633	1670	1663	1644	1698	1692

From this table, you obtain experimental probabilities that differ from the theoretical ones by less than 0.004. ∎

In 1978, 32 students in a mathematics class at the Pennsylvania State University at Erie each tossed a standard six-sided playing die 1000 times. The results of the 32,000 tosses are shown in the table.

Number	1	2	3	4	5	6
Tally	5057	5186	5292	5401	5491	5573

A six-sided die with recessed indicia is slightly unbalanced. Higher numbers are more likely to turn up than lower numbers.

The experimental probabilities for each of the numbers from 1 through 6 can be obtained by dividing each tally by 32,000.

1: 0.158,   2: 0.162,   3: 0.165
4: 0.169,   5: 0.172,   6: 0.174

With such a large number of trials, why were the results not closer to the theoretical probability of $\frac{1}{6}$ (0.167)? The answer is that standard six-sided playing dice are made with recessed *indicia* (or dots), causing them to be unbalanced. The side with only one recessed dot is the heaviest, the side with only two recessed dots is the next heaviest, and so on. The lightest sides, those with six and five recessed dots, tend to land up more often than the sides with one and two dots.

To overcome this problem, Ron Larson (one of the authors of this book) devised a new type of die, called *Duo-Dice*.* These dice also have recessed dots, but because each die is 12-sided, it is perfectly balanced—a 1 is opposite a 1, a 2 is opposite a 2, and so on. Using *Duo-Dice*, the experiment described above was repeated with the following results.

A 12-sided Duo-Die is perfectly balanced. Each number is equally likely to turn up.

Number	1	2	3	4	5	6
Tally	5288	5316	5373	5271	5402	5350

*Duo-Dice are patented by Roland E. Larson, Patent #4,465,279.

Exercises

1. *Experimental Probability*   Use a graphing calculator to perform the experiment described in the example on page 802. How closely do your experimental results agree with the theoretical results?

2. *Duo-Dice*   If a single *Duo-Die* is tossed, what is the probability that a given number turns up?

3. *Duo-Dice*   The game *Monopoly* requires two standard dice. Explain why this game would also require two *Duo-Dice*.

4. *Duo-Dice*   In the experiment described above in which *Duo-Dice* were tossed 32,000 times, what is the experimental probability for each number? How much does it differ from the theoretical probability of $\frac{1}{6}$?

Take this test as you would take a test in class. The answers to the exercises are given in the back of the book.

1. A bunch of balloons contains 1 red, 2 blue, 2 white, and 2 yellow balloons. You randomly choose one of the strings that are attached to the balloons. What is the probability that you choose a red one? A yellow one? **(15.1)**

2. An archer shoots an arrow at the target shown at the right. Suppose that the arrow is equally likely to hit any point on the target. What is the probability that the arrow hits the bull's eye? What is the probability that the arrow hits the blue ring? **(15.1)**

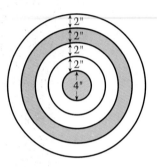

3. The notepapers in a memo cube alternate from pink to yellow to blue to green. (The cube contains the same number of each color.) You take a piece of notepaper from the cube. What is the probability that it is pink? **(15.1)**

4. A 5-disc CD player randomly selects the order in which the discs are played. How many sequences can the CD player select? **(15.2)**

5. In how many ways can the letters A, E, L, M, S be arranged? **(15.2)**

6. You and your sister rent 3 VCR movies from the corner store. In how many orders can the three tapes be viewed? **(15.2)**

7. The softball coach is determining the batting order for the nine-member team. The catcher and pitcher will bat 5th and 9th, respectively. How many batting orders can the coach form? **(15.2)**

8. A committee consisting of 12 girls and 8 boys is planning the senior prom. The committee randomly selects six members to form a subcommittee to be in charge of decorating. What is the probability that the subcommittee will have 2 girls and 4 boys? **(15.3)**

9. A deck of UNO® cards is made up of 108 cards. (Twenty-five each are red, yellow, blue, and green, and 8 are wild cards.) Each player is randomly dealt a seven-card hand. What is the probability that a hand will have 2 wild cards? What is the probability that a hand will have 2 wild cards, 2 red cards, and 3 blue cards? **(15.3)**

10. A sales clerk in a shoe store is setting up a display using 6 different colors of socks. The clerk wants to display all 2-color combinations of socks (a 2-color combination consists of two socks, each of a *different* color). How many *pairs* of socks are needed to form all possible 2-color combinations? **(15.3)**

11. You have time to listen to 3 selections from a CD that contains 12 songs. How many combinations of songs do you have to choose from? **(15.3)**

12. Twenty-five television sets are delivered to the appliance store. Three of these sets are defective. What is the probability that exactly one of the first five sold is defective? **(15.3)**

15.4

Probability, Unions, and Intersections

What you should learn:

Goal 1 How to use unions to find probabilities

Goal 2 How to use complements and intersections to find probabilities

Why you should learn it:

You can solve many probability problems using unions and intersections, such as the probability that one event or another will not happen.

Goal 1 Using Unions to Find Probabilities

The **union** of two events, A and B, written as $A \cup B$, consists of all outcomes that are in A *or* in B (or in both A and B). The **intersection** of A and B, written as $A \cap B$, consists of all outcomes that are in A *and* B.

Union and Intersection

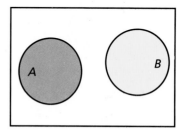

Mutually exclusive events

> **The Probability of the Union of Two Events**
>
> If A and B are events in the same sample space, then the probability of A *or* B occurring is $P(A \cup B) = P(A) + P(B) - P(A \cap B)$. If $A \cap B$ is empty, then A and B are called **mutually exclusive events** and $P(A \cup B) = P(A) + P(B)$.

Connections

Game Theory

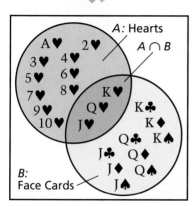

Example 1 *Using Unions to Find Probability*

One card is selected from a standard deck of 52 playing cards. What is the probability that the card is a heart *or* a face card?

Solution Let event A represent selecting a heart and event B represent selecting a face card. Because there are 13 hearts and 12 face cards, you can conclude that $P(A) = \frac{13}{52}$ and $P(B) = \frac{12}{52}$. Also, because three of the cards, $J\heartsuit$, $Q\heartsuit$, and $K\heartsuit$, are both hearts *and* face cards, you know that $P(A \cap B) = \frac{3}{52}$. Using this information, you can find the probability of selecting a heart *or* a face card.

$$P(A \cup B) = P(A) + P(B) - P(A \cap B)$$

$$= \frac{13}{52} + \frac{12}{52} - \frac{3}{52} = \frac{22}{52} \approx 0.423$$

∎

Using Complements and Intersections

If A is an event in a sample space S, then the event consisting of all outcomes in S that are not in A is called the **complement** of A. The complement of A is written as A'.

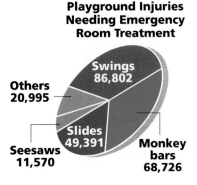

> **The Probability of the Complement of an Event**
> The probability of the complement of A is
>
> $$P(A') = 1 - P(A).$$

Real Life
Safety

Example 2 *Finding the Probability of a Complement*

In 1990, emergency rooms treated 237,484 cases of playground injuries involving children. You work for the United States Consumer Product Safety Commission and have used a computer to randomly select one of the cases for study. What is the probability that the injury involved playground equipment other than swings, monkey bars, slides, and seesaws? *(Source: U.S. Consumer Product Safety Commission)*

**Playground Injuries
Needing Emergency
Room Treatment**

**Others
20,995**

**Swings
86,802**

**Slides
49,391**

**Seesaws
11,570**

**Monkey
bars
68,726**

Solution From the information given at the left, the probability that the case involved swings, monkey bars, slides, or seesaws is

$$P(A) = \frac{86{,}802 + 68{,}726 + 49{,}391 + 11{,}570}{237{,}484} \approx 0.9116.$$

The probability that the case involved playground equipment other than swings, monkey bars, slides, and seesaws is

$$P(A') = 1 - P(A) \approx 1 - 0.9116 = 0.0884. \quad \blacksquare$$

Real Life
Meteorology

Example 3 *Finding the Probability of a Complement*

A television meteorologist announces that your area has a 50% chance of rain tomorrow and a 20% chance of snow. What is the probability that it will not rain or snow tomorrow? (Assume that it will not rain *and* snow.)

Solution Let event A represent rain tomorrow and event B represent snow. Because $P(A) = 0.5$ and $P(B) = 0.2$, you can use the assumption that A and B are mutually exclusive to conclude that the probability that it will rain *or* snow is

$$P(A \cup B) = P(A) + P(B) = 0.5 + 0.2 = 0.7.$$

This means that the probability that it will not rain or snow is

$$P((A \cup B)') = 1 - 0.7 = 0.3. \quad \blacksquare$$

Example 4   *Using Intersection to Find Probability*

In 1992, your company paid overtime wages *or* hired temporary help during 27 weeks. Overtime wages were paid during 21 weeks, and temporary help was hired during 12 weeks. At the end of the year, an auditor checks your accounting records and randomly selects one week to check your company's payroll. What is the probability that the auditor will select a week in which you paid overtime wages *and* temporary help?

Solution   Let event *A* represent the weeks during which overtime wages were paid and let event *B* represent the weeks during which temporary help was hired. From the given information, you know that

$$P(A) = \frac{21}{52}, \quad P(B) = \frac{12}{52}, \quad \text{and} \quad P(A \cup B) = \frac{27}{52}.$$

The probability that the selected week comes from event *A* *and* event *B* is $P(A \cap B)$.

$$P(A \cup B) = P(A) + P(B) - P(A \cap B)$$
$$\frac{27}{52} = \frac{21}{52} + \frac{12}{52} - P(A \cap B)$$
$$P(A \cap B) = \frac{21}{52} + \frac{12}{52} - \frac{27}{52}$$
$$P(A \cap B) = \frac{6}{52}$$

Therefore, the probability that the auditor will select a week in which you paid both overtime and temporary help is $P(A \cap B) = \frac{6}{52} \approx 0.1154$.   ■

Communicating about **ALGEBRA**

▶ SHARING IDEAS about the Lesson

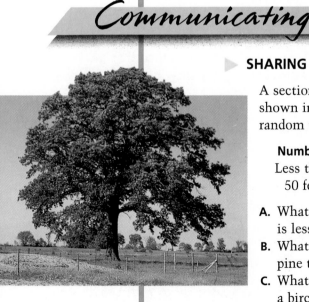

A section of forest is composed of three species of trees as shown in the matrix below. One of the trees is selected at random to be cut down.

Number of Trees	Birch	Pine	Oak
Less than 50 feet	123	165	214
50 feet or more	56	189	78

A. What is the probability that the selected tree is an oak or is less than 50 feet?

B. What is the probability that the selected tree is not a pine that is 50 feet or more?

C. What is the probability that the selected tree is an oak or a birch?

EXERCISES

Guided Practice

▶ **CRITICAL THINKING about the Lesson**

In Exercises 1 and 2, consider the integers from 1 through 12. One of the integers is chosen at random. Let event *A* represent choosing an even integer. Let event *B* represent choosing a multiple of three.

1. Describe the event $A \cup B$. What is the probability of this event?

2. Describe the event $A \cap B$. What is the probability of this event?

3. State an example of two events that are mutually exclusive.

4. *Doing Your Homework*   Let event *A* represent completing your homework tonight. What is *A'*? If $P(A) = 0.95$, what is $P(A')$?

5. *A* and *B* are mutually exclusive events such that $P(A) = 0.1$ and $P(B) = 0.2$. What is $P(A \cup B)$? What is $P(A \cap B)$?

6. *A* and *B* are events in the same sample space such that $P(A) = \frac{1}{4}$, $P(B) = \frac{2}{5}$, and $P(A \cup B) = \frac{1}{2}$. What is $P(A \cap B)$?

Independent Practice

In Exercises 7–12, find the indicated probability. State whether *A* and *B* are mutually exclusive.

7. $P(A) = 0.55$
$P(B) = 0.30$
$P(A \cup B) = 0.65$
$P(A \cap B) = \boxed{?}$

8. $P(A) = 0.5$
$P(B) = 0.30$
$P(A \cup B) = \boxed{?}$
$P(A \cap B) = 0.2$

9. $P(A) = 0.25$
$P(B) = \boxed{?}$
$P(A \cup B) = 0.90$
$P(A \cap B) = 0$

10. $P(A) = 0.75$
$P(B) = 0.20$
$P(A \cup B) = \boxed{?}$
$P(A \cap B) = 0$

11. $P(A) = \frac{11}{15}$
$P(B) = \frac{8}{15}$
$P(A \cup B) = \boxed{?}$
$P(A \cap B) = \frac{4}{15}$

12. $P(A) = \frac{1}{3}$
$P(B) = \frac{1}{4}$
$P(A \cup B) = \frac{1}{3}$
$P(A \cap B) = \boxed{?}$

13. If $P(A) = 0.64$, what is $P(A')$?

14. If $P(A) = 0.19$, what is $P(A')$?

15. Find $P(A')$ using the figure below. (The sample space has 60 outcomes.)

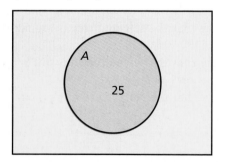

16. Find $P(A \cup B)$ using the figure below. (The sample space has 800 outcomes.)

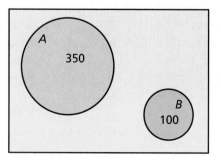

17. *Hockey or Swimming* The probability that Mick will make the hockey team is $\frac{2}{3}$. The probability that he will make the swimming team is $\frac{3}{4}$. If the probability that he makes both teams is $\frac{1}{2}$, what is the probability that he makes at least one of the teams? That he makes neither team?

18. *Aquarium* An aquarium at a pet store contains 30 orange swordtails (12 females and 18 males) and 48 green swordtails (32 females and 16 males). You randomly net one of the fish. What is the probability that it is a female or a green swordtail?

19. *Class Election* Three people are running for class president. From a poll that was taken, the probability that Candidate A will win is estimated to be 0.3. The probability that Candidate B will win is estimated to be 0.55. Given a reasonable estimate of the probability that Candidate C will win.

20. *Probability of Rain* The probability that it will rain today is 0.4, and the probability that it will rain tomorrow is 0.2. The probability that it will rain both days is 0.1. What is the probability that it will rain today *or* tomorrow?

21. *Picking a Pie* The freezer case at a grocery store contains several frozen pies: 10 apple, 4 peach, 6 blueberry, 5 pumpkin, 3 peanut butter, and some pecan. You are shopping in a hurry and pick one of the pies from the freezer without looking at the type. The probability that the pie you picked is apple or pecan is $\frac{13}{22}$. How many pecan pies are in the freezer case?

22. *Picking a Cola* A picnic cooler contains several types of colas: 12 regular, 8 cherry, 10 diet, 6 diet cherry, 8 caffeine-free, and some caffeine-free diet. You pick one of the colas without looking at the type. The probability that it is a diet drink is $\frac{5}{12}$. How many caffeine free diet colas are in the picnic cooler?

23. *Holiday Shopping* In 1995 a survey was conducted to find when people do their holiday shopping. The results are shown in the graph at the right. If one of those indicated in the graph is chosen at random, what is the probability that the person said that he or she shops on the day before Christmas? *(Source: USA Today)*

24. *Holiday Shopping* If two of those surveyed in Exercise 23 are chosen at random, what is the probability that both said that they shop in the last two weeks of November?

When People Shop

Category	Value
Already done / don't know	40
Last 2 weeks of November	112
Day after Thanksgiving	32
First 2 weeks of December	280
Evenly through the season	176
Last 2 weeks of December	104
Day before Christmas	56

25. *Honors Banquet*   Of 148 students honored at an academic awards banquet, 40 won awards for mathematics and 82 for English. Twelve of these students won awards in both mathematics and English. One of the 148 students is chosen at random to be interviewed for a newspaper article. What is the probability that the student won an award in mathematics or English?

26. *Art Gallery*   An art gallery has scheduled 38 shows during the year: 18 that feature painters and 20 that feature sculptors. Some of the shows are scheduled for one week, and the others are scheduled for two weeks. Each week, only one painter or sculptor is shown. If you attend one show at random, the probability that it is a two-week show of paintings is $\frac{2}{13}$. What is the probability that it is a one-week show of sculptures?

Integrated Review

Salary Expectations   **In Exercises 27–29, use the following information.**

In 1991, a survey was conducted to determine salary expectations of high school students. In the survey, 1879 "A" and "B" students were asked what they expected to earn in their first job after completing their education. The salary expectations of the 1728 who responded are shown in the graph at the right.

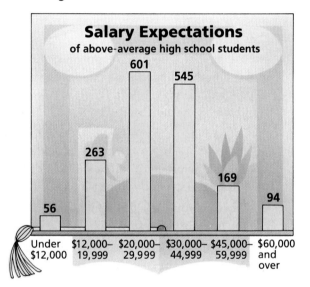

Salary Expectations
of above-average high school students

56	263	601	545	169	94
Under $12,000	$12,000–19,999	$20,000–29,999	$30,000–44,999	$45,000–59,999	$60,000 and over

27. One of the 1728 students who responded is chosen at random. What is the probability that this student expects to earn between $30,000 and $44,999?

28. Five of the 1728 students who responded are chosen at random. What is the probability that all five students expect to earn between $30,000 and $44,999?

29. One of the 1728 students who responded is chosen at random. What is the probability that this student expects to earn $60,000 or more? $12,000 or more?

Exploration and Extension

Odds   **In Exercises 30 and 31, use the following information.**

The odds of an event *A* occurring are the ratio of the probability that the event will occur to the probability that the event will not occur.

30. A jar contains three red marbles and five green marbles. What are the odds that a randomly chosen marble is green?

31. A jar contains three red marbles and some green marbles. The odds are "3 to 1" that a randomly chosen marble is green. How many green marbles are in the jar?

15.5

Independent Events

What you should learn:

Goal 1 How to find the probability of independent events

Goal 2 How to use the complement of an event to find the probability of the event

Why you should learn it:

You can solve many probability problems in real life using independent events, such as finding the probability that in a group of 35 people, at least two will have the same birthday.

Goal 1 **Independent Events**

Two events are **independent** if the occurrence of one has no effect on the occurrence of the other. For instance, if two coins are tossed, the outcomes (heads or tails) are independent. Two events are **dependent** if the occurrence of one *does* affect the occurrence of the other.

> **Probability of Independent Events**
> If A and B are independent events, then the probability that both A and B occur is $P(A \cap B) = P(A) \cdot P(B)$.

Example 1 *Random Number Generator*

You use a graphing calculator to randomly select two integers between 1 and 20. What is the probability that both integers are less than 6?

Solution   Let event A represent selecting a first number that is less than 6. Let event B represent selecting a second number than is less than 6. Each of these outcomes has a probability of $\frac{5}{20} = \frac{1}{4}$. Because the program randomly selects numbers, the two events are independent. Therefore, the probability that both numbers are less than 6 is

$$P(A \cap B) = P(A) \cdot P(B) = \frac{1}{4} \cdot \frac{1}{4} = \frac{1}{16}. \qquad \blacksquare$$

Study Tip

In Example 1, the events are independent. Here is a similar experiment in which the events are dependent. A box contains 20 pieces of paper numbered from 1 to 20. Two pieces are drawn from the box (the second is drawn without replacing the first). The probability that both numbers are less than 6 is

$$P = \frac{5}{20} \cdot \frac{4}{19} = \frac{1}{19}.$$

Can you see why?

LESSON INVESTIGATION

■ **Investigating Random Numbers**

Partner Activity Use a graphing calculator to randomly select two integers between 1 and 20. (See page 865 for keystrokes.) Repeat the experiment several times and record your results. How many times were both numbers less than 6? Compare your result with the result obtained in Example 1 above.

Goal 2 Using Complements to Find Probabilities

Sometimes it is easier to find the probability that an event A *does not* occur than it is to find the probability that it *does* occur. In such cases, you can still find the probability of the event occurring by using the formula $P(A') = 1 - P(A)$.

Example 2 Using the Complement to Find a Probability

You work in the quality control department of a company that manufactures fluorescent lights. Suppose that 1% of the lights in a shipment of 10,000 lights are defective. If you make 100 random tests of the lights (each time choosing a light, testing it, and replacing it), what is the probability that at least one of the tests reveals a defective light?

Solution Let event A represent selecting a light that is defective. Then event A' represents selecting a good light. Because there are 9900 good lights, the probability of A' is

$$P(A') = \frac{9900}{10,000} = 0.99. \qquad \textit{Select 1 good light.}$$

Because each light is replaced after it is tested, the selection of the next light is independent of the selection of the first. This means that the probability that the first two selections are good lights is $[P(A')]^2$. By similar reasoning, you can conclude that the probability of selecting 100 good lights is

$$[P(A')]^{100} = (0.99)^{100} \approx 0.366. \qquad \textit{Select 100 good lights.}$$

Finally, you can conclude that the probability of selecting at least one defective light is

$$P(A) = 1 - (0.99)^{100} \approx 0.634. \qquad \textit{Select at least 1 bad light.} \ \blacksquare$$

Connections

Birthday Problem

Of the approximately 35 people shown in the square in the photo, the probability that at least 2 have the same birthday is 0.813.

Example 3	*Using the Complement*

A famous probability problem, called the *Birthday Problem*, can be stated as follows.

Thirty-five people are chosen at random. What is the probability that at least two of them have the same birthday?

Solve this problem. (Assume there are 366 different birthdays in a year.)

Solution   Let event A represent each of the 35 people having *different* birthdays. The probability that the first 2 people have different birthdays is

$$\frac{366}{366} \cdot \frac{365}{366},$$ *First 2 birthdays are different.*

that the first 3 people have different birthdays is

$$\frac{366}{366} \cdot \frac{365}{366} \cdot \frac{364}{366},$$ *First 3 birthdays are different.*

and that the first 4 people have different birthdays is

$$\frac{366}{366} \cdot \frac{365}{366} \cdot \frac{364}{366} \cdot \frac{363}{366}.$$ *First 4 birthdays are different.*

By continuing this pattern, you can reason that the probability that all 35 people have different birthdays is

$$\frac{366}{366} \cdot \frac{365}{366} \cdot \ldots \cdot \frac{332}{366} \approx 0.187.$$ *All 35 birthdays are different.*

The probability that at least 2 of the 35 people have the same birthday is $P(A') = 1 - P(A) \approx 1 - 0.187 = 0.813$. ∎

Communicating about ALGEBRA

▶ **SHARING IDEAS about the Lesson**

A. You are tossing a coin five times. What is the probability that the coin lands heads up all five times?

B. You are tossing a coin five times. What is the probability that the coin lands heads up at least once?

C. A bookbinding machine at a printing company has a probability of 0.005 of producing a defective book. Your school has ordered 300 books that were bound on this machine. What is the probability that at least 1 of the books is defective? Explain.

EXERCISES

Guided Practice

▶ **CRITICAL THINKING about the Lesson**

In Exercises 1–4, state whether events *A* and *B* are independent or dependent.

1. Event *A* is rolling a 5 on a die.
   Event *B* is rolling a 3 on the same die.

2. Event *A* is drawing a queen from a standard deck of cards.
   Event *B* is drawing a king from the remaining cards in the same deck.

3. Event *A* is getting a red gumball from a gumball machine.
   Event *B* is getting a yellow gumball from the remaining gumballs in the same machine.

4. Event *A* is getting 0.25 inches of snow on Monday.
   Event *B* is getting 0.45 inches of snow on Tuesday.

In Exercises 5 and 6, *A* and *B* are independent events. Evaluate *P(A ∩ B)*.

5. $P(A) = 0.29$, $P(B) = 0.80$

6. $P(A) = \frac{1}{2}$, $P(B) = \frac{5}{6}$

Independent Practice

In Exercises 7–10, *A* and *B* are independent events. Find the indicated probability.

7. $P(A) = \frac{2}{3}$
   $P(B) = \frac{7}{8}$
   $P(A \cap B) = \boxed{?}$

8. $P(A) = 0.1$
   $P(B) = 0.1$
   $P(A \cap B) = \boxed{?}$

9. $P(A) = 0.5$
   $P(B) = \boxed{?}$
   $P(A \cap B) = 0.01$

10. $P(A) = \boxed{?}$
    $P(B) = \frac{2}{5}$
    $P(A \cap B) = \frac{1}{4}$

11. *Six Girls*   Consider all families that have exactly six children. If one of these families is chosen at random, what is the probability that all six children are girls?

12. *SCRABBLE*[R]   You and your friend are playing SCRABBLE[R]. The distribution of letters is shown at the right. If you pick your seven letters first, what is the probability that you will pick three vowels and four consonants? (Count "Y" as a vowel.)

A: 9	G: 3	M: 2	S: 4	Y: 2
B: 2	H: 2	N: 6	T: 6	Z: 1
C: 2	I: 9	O: 8	U: 4	Blank: 2
D: 4	J: 1	P: 2	V: 2	
E: 12	K: 1	Q: 1	W: 2	
F: 2	L: 4	R: 6	X: 1	

13. *Numbers in a Hat*   There are 25 pieces of paper, numbered 1 to 25, in a hat. You pick a piece of paper, replace it, and then pick another piece of paper. What is the probability that each number is greater than 20 or less than 4?

14. *Pick a Prize*   There are 30 gifts for 30 people at a party. To determine who gets which gift, numbers from 1 to 30 are drawn. Starting with the person who drew the number 1, each person opens a gift. As each person opens a gift, he or she can retain the gift or switch with any previously opened gift. (At the end, the person who drew the number 30 has a choice of any of the 30 gifts.) What is the probability that you and your best friend will draw numbers 29 and 30 (in either order).

15. *Baby Shower*   There are 7 prizes at a baby shower. Each person at the shower places a tag by 3 prizes. You choose the first 3 prizes and, including your tags, there are 10 tags by the first prize, 8 tags by the second prize, and 18 tags by the third prize. To determine the winner of each prize, a tag beside the prize is chosen at random. What is the probability that you will win all 3 prizes? What is the probability that you won't win any of the prizes?

16. *Wrong Number*   A friend of yours works as a telephone operator. From past records, your friend has a probability of about 0.001 of connecting a caller to an incorrect number. Last Tuesday, your friend connected 906 callers. What is the probability that at least 1 was connected to an incorrect number?

17. *American Travelers*   In 1990, three percent of all Americans who took trips traveled outside the United States. Twenty Americans who took a trip in 1990 are chosen at random. What is the probability that at least one traveled out of the United States?

18. *Birthdays*   If there are 26 people in your algebra class, what is the probability that at least 2 of you have the same birthday?

19. *Technology*   Modify the graphing calculator program shown on page 811 to choose random numbers from 1 through 366. Use the program to choose 26 numbers. What is the probability that at least 2 of the numbers are the same? Are at least 2 of the numbers the same?

20. *Popping Balloons*   Your school is having a fair. At the sundae bar, the price of a sundae is determined by choosing a balloon with a price inside. When you get to the sundae bar, there are 20 balloons left, 3 of which contain tags marked "FREE." If you and two of your friends get sundaes, what is the probability that at least one of you gets a free sundae?

21. *Ping Pong Balls*   Marcus had 4 table tennis balls with small cracks. His friend, Sasha, accidentally mixed them in with 16 good ones. If Marcus randomly picks 3 table tennis balls, what is the probability that at least 1 is cracked?

In Exercises 22 and 23, use the following information.

You and your friends are playing a game. Each player receives a card that has 25 different numbers from 1 through 75. Your card is shown at the right. One player randomly draws numbers from 1 through 75 from a basket (without replacement). As your number is called, you mark the appropriate space on your card. The goal is to mark five squares in a row on your card, either horizontally, vertically, or diagonally.

5	16	41	48	72
1	30	44	49	69
10	28	39	50	65
4	19	42	55	73
2	20	35	59	75

22. The numbers that have been drawn so far are 5, 39, 55, 2, 72, 1, 73, 19, and 30. What is the probability that you will win the game with the next number called?

23. The numbers that have been drawn so far are 49, 39, 4, 42, 72, 69, 55, and 19. What is the probability that you will win the game with the next number called?

Exploration and Extension

24. *Choosing Marbles*   If A and B are *dependent* events, then the probability that event B will occur given that event A has occurred is given by $P(B|A)$ and read as "the probability of B given A." This probability is

$$P(B|A) = \frac{P(A \cap B)}{P(A)}$$

where $P(A \cap B)$ is the probability that *both* A and B occur. A jar contains eight white marbles numbered 1 through 8 and six blue marbles numbered 1 through 6. What is the probability that a randomly chosen marble is white, given that the number on the marble is 4?

Mixed REVIEW

1. Does $\sin(-x) = -\sin x$?   **(14.3)**

2. Evaluate $\frac{1}{2} \cdot 4 \cdot 3 \cdot \sin \frac{\pi}{4}$.   **(13.6)**

3. Sketch $y = (x - 3)^2 + 2$.   **(11.5)**

4. Solve $3xy^2 - 3xy = 7y$ for x.   **(1.5)**

5. Solve $3s + 4 \le 5s - 6$.   **(1.6)**

6. Sketch $|x - 4| < 5$.   **(1.6)**

7. Solve for θ: $\tan \theta = \sqrt{3}$.   **(13.4)**

8. Solve $|3x - 2| = 12$.   **(1.7)**

9. Solve $0 = \frac{3}{2}x^2 - \frac{3}{4}x + 1$.   **(5.6)**

10. Sketch $y > x^2 + x - 12$.   **(5.7)**

11. Solve $\frac{1}{5}x^2 = 180$.   **(7.1)**

12. Sketch $y = \sqrt{x} + 2$.   **(7.6)**

13. Find the cofunction of $\cot\left(\frac{\pi}{2} - x\right)$.   **(14.3)**

14. Find the x-intercepts of $y = 3x^2 + 4$.   **(5.5)**

15. Multiply: $(3x^2 - x + 2) \cdot (x + 1)$.   **(9.1)**

16. Evaluate $f(-3)$ for $f(x) = -x^2 + x^3$.   **(6.1)**

17. Find $f(g(x))$ for $f(x) = 2x^2$ and $g(x) = x + 1$.

18. Write in standard form: $x^2 + 25y^2 = 25$.   **(11.3)**

15.6

Expected Value

What you should learn:

Goal 1 How to find the expected value of a sample space

Goal 2 How to use expected value to answer questions about real-life situations

Why you should learn it:

You can use expected value to calculate how much you will win in games in which winners are determined randomly, such as random drawing.

Goal 1 Finding an Expected Value

Suppose you and a friend are playing a game. You flip a coin. If the coin lands heads up, your friend scores 1 point, and you lose 1 point. If the coin lands tails up, you score 1 point, and your friend loses 1 point. After playing the game many times, would you expect to have more, fewer, or the same number of points as when you started? The answer is that you should expect to end up with about the same number. You can expect to lose a point about half the time and win a point about half the time. Your *expected value* for this game is 0.

Expected Value of a Sample Space

A sample space is partitioned into *n* events, no two of which have any outcomes in common. The probabilities of the *n* events occurring are $P_1, P_2, P_3, \ldots, P_n$ and the **payoffs** for the *n* events are $x_1, x_2, x_3, \ldots, x_n$. The **expected value,** *V*, of the sample space is

$$V = P_1 x_1 + P_2 x_2 + P_3 x_3 + \cdots + P_n x_n$$

where $P_1 + P_2 + P_3 + \cdots + P_n = 1$.

Connections
Game Theory

Example 1 *Finding the Expected Value of a Game*

You and a friend each flip a coin. If both coins land heads up, then your friend scores 3 points, and you lose 3 points. If one or two coins land tails up, then you score 1 point, and your friend loses 1 point. What is the expected value of this game?

Solution When two coins are tossed, four outcomes are possible: HH, HT, TH, TT.

Let event *A* be HH. Then event *A′* is HT, TH, *or* TT. The probability of *A* is $\frac{1}{4}$, and the probability of *A′* is $\frac{3}{4}$. *From your point of view,* the payoff for event *A* is −3 and the payoff for event *A′* is 1. Therefore, the expected value of the game is

$$V = P(A) \cdot (-3) + P(A') \cdot (1) = \frac{1}{4}(-3) + \frac{3}{4}(1) = 0.$$

The game is called **fair** because its expected value is 0. ∎

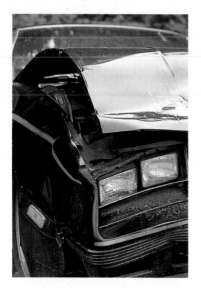

*In 1993, there were 121,100,000
cars in use in the United States.
That year, there were 14,100,000
automobile accidents.*

Connections
Game Theory

Example 2 *Finding an Expected Value*

The average premium paid in 1993 for automobile collision insurance was $638, and the average automobile collision claim paid by insurance companies was $1796. What was the expected value of the insurance coverage for a person who paid $638 for collision insurance in 1993?

Solution   Let event A represent having an automobile accident. Then event A' represents not having an automobile accident. In 1993, the probability of having an automobile accident was

$$P(A) = \frac{14,100,000}{121,100,000} \approx 0.116$$

which means $P(A') \approx 0.884$. You can calculate the payoffs for A and A' as follows. If the person had an accident, he or she paid $638 and received $1796, so the person received $1796 − $638 = $1158. If the person didn't have an accident, he or she paid $638. Thus the expected value was

$$V = P(A) \cdot (1158) + P(A') \cdot (-638)$$
$$= 0.116(1158) - 0.884(638) \approx -\$429.66.$$

The $429.66 represents an average amount paid by each policy-holder to cover insurance company expenses (and produce a profit for the insurance companies).   ∎

Example 3 *Entering a Contest*

A fast-food restaurant chain is having a contest. No purchase is necessary to enter. The contest has five prizes. What is the expected value for a contest ticket?

Prize	Value	Probability of Winning
Soda Pop	$0.69	0.01
Hamburger	$1.29	0.005
Double Cheeseburger	$2.59	0.002
Scholarship	$1,000.00	0.000005
New Home	$100,000.00	0.00000004

Solution   Let event A represent not winning a prize. Because you paid nothing for the ticket, it is not necessary to compute the probability of A. The expected value is as follows.

$$V = 0.01(0.69) + 0.005(1.29) + 0.002(2.59) + 0.000005(1000)$$
$$+ 0.00000004(100,000)$$
$$= 0.0069 + 0.00645 + 0.00518 + 0.005 + 0.004$$
$$= 0.02753$$

Thus the average amount won per ticket is about $2\frac{3}{4}$ cents.   ∎

Goal 2 Using Expected Value in Real Life

Real Life
Sales

Example 4 *Estimating Sales*

You are a sales representative for a publisher that sells college textbooks. It is March, and your regional manager has asked you to prepare a "top-20 list." (A top-20 list contains your 20 largest potential sales for next fall.) With each potential sale, you are asked to estimate the probability that you will get the sale. Your top-20 list is shown below. What is the expected value of each entry on the list? What is the total expected value of the list?

Text	Price	Copies	Prob.	Text	Price	Copies	Prob.
B	$39.95	3000	0.40	G	$45.95	900	0.70
A	$35.95	2500	0.90	A	$35.95	900	0.95
C	$46.95	2000	0.75	C	$46.95	800	0.25
C	$46.95	2000	0.25	D	$42.95	750	0.40
E	$28.95	1750	0.50	A	$35.95	700	0.30
A	$35.95	1500	0.50	E	$28.95	600	0.80
D	$42.95	1500	0.60	E	$28.95	500	0.75
D	$42.95	1200	0.75	G	$45.95	500	0.90
E	$28.95	1100	0.70	B	$39.95	400	0.60
F	$37.95	1000	0.90	A	$35.95	400	0.50

Expected Values

$47,940.00	$28,948.50
$80,887.50	$30,737.25
$70,425.00	$9,390.00
$23,475.00	$12,885.00
$25,331.25	$7,549.50
$26,962.50	$13,896.00
$38,655.00	$10,856.25
$38,655.00	$20,677.50
$22,291.50	$9,588.00
$34,155.00	$7,190.00

Solution The expected value of each potential sale can be found by multiplying the price by the number of copies by the probability. For instance, the expected value of the first text on the list is $V = (39.95)(3000)(0.40) = \$47,940$. The expected values of all 20 potential sales are shown at the left. The expected value of the list is the total of these 20 expected values, or $560,495.75. ∎

Communicating about ALGEBRA

▶ **SHARING IDEAS about the Lesson**

The spinner at the left is used in a game for two people: the Blue Player and the Green Player. Whichever color the spinner points to is the player who receives the indicated number of points from the other player.

A. What is the expected value for the Blue Player?
B. What is the expected value for the Green Player?
C. What number of points should be in the "southeast" region to make the game fair?

Guided Practice

▶ **CRITICAL THINKING about the Lesson**

1. A sample space has five equally likely outcomes. The payoffs for the outcomes are 1, 2, 3, 4, and 5. What is the expected value of the sample space?

2. A sample space has five equally likely outcomes. The payoffs for four of the outcomes are 1, 2, 3, and 4. The expected value of the sample space is 5. What is the payoff for the fifth outcome?

3. Two people are playing a *fair* game. What is the expected value for each player? Why is the game called "fair"?

4. Two people are playing a game in which they exchange points, depending on the outcomes in the game. The expected value for one player is 3 points. What is the expected value for the other player?

Independent Practice

In Exercises 5 and 6, a sample space has five outcomes, each with the indicated payoff and probability. Find the expected value.

5.

Payoff	$3	$5	$1	−$3	−$2
Probability	0.10	0.12	0.50	0.10	0.18

6.

Payoff	$0	$10	$20	$30	$40
Probability	0.9955	0.0030	0.0010	0.0004	0.0001

Game Theory   **In Exercises 7–10, consider a game in which each of two people simultaneously chooses an integer: 1, 2, or 3. Find the expected value for player _A_ and the expected value for player _B_. Is each game fair?**

7. If the sum of the two numbers is odd, then player A loses that sum of points, and player B wins that sum. If the sum of the two numbers is even, player B loses 4 points, and player A wins 4 points.

8. If both players choose the same number, then no points are exchanged. Otherwise, the player with the higher number wins a point, and the other player loses a point.

9. If both players choose the same number, then no points are exchanged. If the two numbers differ by one, then the player with the higher number wins two points and the other player loses two points. If the two numbers differ by two, then the player with the higher number wins one point and the other player loses one point.

10. If both players choose the same number, then no points are exchanged. If the sum of the two numbers is even, the player with the higher number wins two points and the other player loses two points. If the sum of the numbers is odd, the player with the lower number wins two points and the other player loses two points.

11. *Fair Game?*   Two players play *Stone, Scissors, Paper*, a game in which each player simultaneously represents either a stone, a pair of scissors, or a sheet of paper using one hand. If there is a tie, then neither player receives any points. When stone "breaks" scissors, scissors must give stone two points. When paper "covers" stone, stone must give paper three points. When scissors "cut" paper, paper must give scissors four points. Find the expected value to determine whether this game is fair.

12. *Board Game*   You are playing a board game. To advance around the board, you must first draw a card, roll a die three times, and add up the points you receive for each number rolled. (The card tells you the number of points each roll receives.) If the sum of the points is positive, you must advance that many spaces around the board; if it is negative, you must move backwards. Find the expected value for each of the four cards below.

a.

Number Rolled	Points
1	4
2	3
3	−5
4	2
5	1
6	−3

b.

Number Rolled	Points
1	3
2	−3
3	2
4	2
5	−3
6	1

c.

Number Rolled	Points
1	6
2	−5
3	−1
4	2
5	0
6	3

d.

Number Rolled	Points
1	−3
2	4
3	−1
4	−1
5	3
6	−1

13. *Buying Insurance*   You have purchased a one-year policy to insure your contact lenses. The insurance fee is $18. If you have to replace a pair of contact lenses, the insurance will pay $30 toward the cost. Your optician told you that of 1000 people who purchase your type of contact lens, about 400 need to replace their lenses within a year. What is the expected value for this insurance policy?

14. *Roofing Jobs*   You are a roofer and have six potential customers. The list below shows the price per square of shingles, the number of squares of shingles, and the probability that you will get the job. What is the expected income for these jobs?

Job	Price Installed	Number of Squares	Probability
A	$90	12	0.9
B	$130	9	0.5
C	$125	10	0.3
D	$100	7	0.1
E	$140	10	0.8
F	$110	8	0.6

15. *Selling Yearbooks*   You are a sales representative for a company that prints high school yearbooks. The following is a list of 16 potential customers, the prices of the books, the estimated sales, and the probability that you will make the sale. What is the expected value of your sales this year?

School	Price	Copies	Probability	School	Price	Copies	Probability
1	12.95	225	0.60	9	15.95	25	0.95
2	11.00	450	0.85	10	14.00	175	0.80
3	10.50	100	0.80	11	18.00	500	0.75
4	13.00	200	0.65	12	16.00	400	0.80
5	15.00	100	0.70	13	12.00	750	0.80
6	11.00	600	0.90	14	12.50	450	0.65
7	11.50	50	0.60	15	14.50	80	0.90
8	14.00	75	0.85	16	10.50	400	0.80

Integrated Review

16. *Contract Bidding*   Ten construction companies are bidding for a job. Three are local companies, three have state-wide operations, and four have national operations. Each company is equally likely to win the contract. What is the probability that the contract will be awarded to a local company?

17. *Boy or Girl?*   There are two children in a family. At least one of them is a boy. What is the probability that both children are boys? (*Hint:* The sample space is BB, BG, and GB.)

18. *College Entrance Exam Sample*   In the figure, what is the value of z?
a. 80   **b.** 100   **c.** 110   **d.** 120   **e.** 130

19. *College Entrance Exam Sample*   In the figure, what is the value of $x + y$?
a. 140   **b.** 130   **c.** 120   **d.** 110   **e.** 100

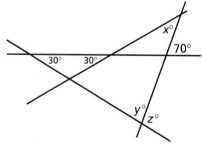

Exploration and Extension

Tossing Coins   In Exercises 20 and 21, consider an experiment in which five coins are tossed.

20. Copy and complete the table that gives the probabilities for 0, 1, 2, 3, 4, or 5 heads turning up.

Number of Heads	0	1	2	3	4	5
Probability	?	?	?	?	?	?

21. Find the expected number of heads that will turn up.

Chapter Summary

What did you learn?

Skills

1. Find the probability of an event. **(15.1)**

2. Count the number of outcomes in an event
- by making a list. **(15.1)**
- by using the Fundamental Counting Principle. **(15.2)**
- by using permutations. **(15.2)**
- by using combinations. **(15.3)**

3. Find the probability of the union of two events. **(15.4)**

4. Find the probability of the complement of an event. **(15.5)**

5. Find the probability of the intersection of two events. **(15.4)**

6. Find the probability of independent events. **(15.5)**

7. Find the expected value of a sample space. **(15.6)**

Strategies

8. Use probability to solve real-life problems. **(15.1–15.6)**

Why did you learn it?

We all have to cope with the uncertainties of life. When you plan a picnic, you consider the probability that it will rain. When you drive a car, you consider the probability that you will be involved in an accident. When you enter a contest, you consider the probability that you will win.

Understanding the basic principles of probability can help you make decisions. For instance, in Lesson 15.6 you saw how a sales representative can use probability to forecast sales. This can help the sales representative decide whether to expect a bonus.

Using probability to make decisions can be difficult. A common error is to think that probabilities have "memories." For instance, a person who has just tossed a coin that lands heads up might reason that the next toss must be tails up, because heads and tails occur half the time. This reasoning is not correct. Regardless of how many times the coin has been tossed, the probability that the next toss will be heads is still one half.

How does it fit into the bigger picture of algebra?

In this chapter, and for that matter, in the entire book, you have learned that there are many connections between the many areas of mathematics. Algebra is connected to geometry, to trigonometry, to statistics, and to probability. For instance, in Chapter 12 you studied Pascal's Triangle as it related to binomial coefficients. In this chapter, you saw that Pascal's Triangle is connected to probability.

In Exercises 1 and 2, find the probability of a successful event given the number of successes and the number of possibilities.

1. Number of successes: 16
Number of possibilities: 360

2. Number of successes: 3
Number of possibilities: 135

3. *Choosing a Calculator*   A calculator is chosen randomly from a display case that contains four solar calculators and eight battery-operated calculators. What is the probability that the calculator is solar?

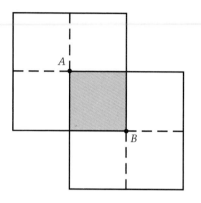

4. *Geometry*   The two larger squares in the figure on the right have the same dimensions. The centers of these squares are labeled *A* and *B*. What is the probability that a randomly chosen point inside the figure will lie in the shaded region?

5. *Payroll Error*   The employees of a company are in six departments: 31 are in sales, 54 are in research, 42 are in marketing, 20 are in engineering, 47 are in finance, and 58 are in production. If one employee's paycheck is lost, what is the probability that the employee is in the research department?

6. *Defective Units*   A shipment of 12 microwave ovens contains 3 defective units. A vending company has ordered 4 of these units, and since each is identically packaged, the selection will be at random. What is the probability that all 4 units are good? Exactly 2 units are good? At least 2 units are good?

7. *Permuting Letters*   In how many ways can you order the letters A, B, C, and D?

8. *Permuting Letters*   How many permutations are possible for the letters in the word HOUSE?

9. *Making a Key*   The key blank at the right has five notches, each of which has four possible heights. How many different keys can be made using this key blank?

10. *Trying a Key*   You have found a key that was made from a key blank like the one at the right. You recognize that the key to your apartment was made from the same type of blank. What is the probability that the key you found will open your door?

11. *Random Number Generator*   A computer generates random integers from 1 through 20. What is the probability that the first two numbers are 5 or less?

12. *School Pictures*   There are 34 students
in your homeroom. Numbers from 1
through 34 are randomly assigned to the
students to determine the order in which
your school pictures will be taken. What
is the probability that you and your best
friend will be the first and second to get
your pictures taken (in either order)?

13. *Supreme Court*   The Supreme Court of
the United States has nine justices. On a
certain case, the justices voted 5 to 4 in
favor of the defendant. In how many ways
could this have occurred?

14. *Supreme Court*   On a certain case, the
justices of the Supreme Court voted 7 to
2 in favor of the plaintiff. In how many
ways could this have occurred? In which
row of Pascal's Triangle does the number
of ways occur?

*In 1981, Sandra Day O'Connor became the first
woman to serve as a justice of the United States
Supreme Court.*

In Exercises 15 and 16, find the indicated probability.

15. $P(A) = \frac{1}{4}$

$P(B) = \frac{1}{5}$

$P(A \cap B) = \frac{2}{15}$

$P(A \cup B) = \boxed{?}$

16. $P(A) = \frac{2}{5}$

$P(B) = \frac{1}{10}$

$P(A \cap B) = \boxed{?}$

$P(A \cup B) = \frac{1}{2}$

**In Exercises 17 and 18, you are given the probability that an event will
happen. Find the probability that the event will not happen.**

17. $P = 0.04$

18. $P = 0.63$

19. *Asian-Americans*   The circle graph at
the right is representative of the relative
percents of Asian-Americans living in the
United States in 1990. If 2 people are chosen randomly from this group of 219
people, what is the probability that both
are Asian-Indians? *(Source: United States Bureau of Census)*

20. *Asian-Americans*   If a random sample of
219 Asian-Americans are polled, what is
the probability that the first 3 people are
Japanese-Americans?

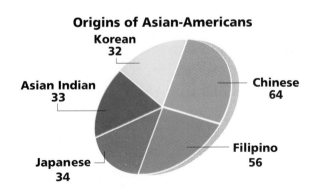

Origins of Asian-Americans

Korean 32

Asian Indian 33

Chinese 64

Japanese 34

Filipino 56

21. Soccer or Baseball You play soccer and baseball during the summer (June 1 through August 15). On 22 days you play soccer, and on 26 days you play baseball. On 36 days, you play soccer or baseball. On how many days do you play both?

22. YAHTZEE^R In the game of *YAHTZEE^R*, 5 six-sided dice are rolled. A "yahtzee" is when all 5 dice show the same number. What is the probability of this happening on a single roll of the 5 dice?

23. Family Trip Your family decides to visit the local amusement park twice during the summer (June 1 through August 15). During the summer, your city averages 32 days with rain and 10 days when the temperature is under 70°F. There are 37 days with rain *or* a temperature under 70°F. What is the probability that it will rain and be under 70°F on at least 1 of the days planned for your visits?

The World's Children **In Exercises 24 and 25, use the following information.**

In 1990, 33% of the world's population were under the age of 15 and 6% were over 65. Suppose that 20 people are chosen at random.

24. What is the probability that none of the 20 chosen are under the age of 15?

25. What is the probability that none of the 20 chosen are over the age of 65?

26. The World's Languages The graph at the right shows the percents of people in the world who speak the world's most-used languages as their primary language. (The "other" includes, in descending order of frequency, Bengali, Portuguese, Indonesian, Japanese, German, French, and 200 other languages.) In a random sample of two people, what is the probability that both people speak Spanish *or* English as their primary language?

Languages of the World's Population

Mandarin 16.5% Russian 5.8% Arabic 3.7% Spanish 6.4% English 8.6% Hindi/Urdu 8.3% Other 50.7%

27. Care Package Your mother is sending a "care package" to your brother at college. She insures delivery of the package by paying $1.60 extra. If the package is lost in the mail, your mother will collect $60.00. The probability that the package will be lost is 0.001. What is the expected value of this insurance?

28. Pascal's Triangle Write the entire row of Pascal's triangle in which $\binom{8}{4}$ appears.

29. Tossing Coins Eight coins are tossed. Explain how to use Pascal's triangle to decide which of the following is most likely.
  a. 0 heads and 8 tails   **b.** 1 head and 7 tails   **c.** 2 heads and 6 tails
  d. 3 heads and 5 tails   **e.** 4 heads and 4 tails   **f.** 5 heads and 3 tails
  g. 6 heads and 2 tails   **h.** 7 heads and 1 tail   **i.** 8 heads and 0 tails

Collie Colors **In Exercises 30 and 31, use the following information.**

There are six basic types of coloring in registered collies: sable (SSmm), tricolor (ssmm), trifactored sable (Ssmm), blue merle (ssMm), sable merle (SSMm), and trifactored sable merle (SsMm).

30. Copy and complete the following Punnett square, which shows the possible colorings of offspring of a trifactored sable merle collie and a trifactored sable collie.

	SM	Sm	sM	sm
Sm				
Sm				
sm				
sm				

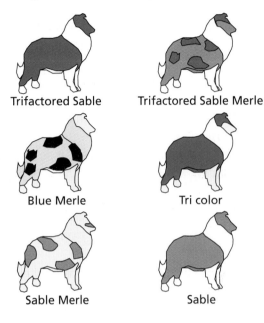

Trifactored Sable   Trifactored Sable Merle

Blue Merle   Tri color

Sable Merle   Sable

31. Use the results of Exercise 30 to find the probability of obtaining each of the six basic collie colorings in the offspring of the two collies described by the Punnett square.

32. *Choosing a Dog* Two breeds of dogs are randomly chosen from the following list. What is the probability that both breeds are spaniels?

Boston Terrier
Cocker Spaniel
Golden Retriever
Doberman Pinscher
Scottish Terrier
Labrador Retriever

Collie
Beagle
Great Dane
King Charles
    Spaniel

33. *Dog Show* The fee for entering a dog in a dog show is $50. The owner of the winning dog receives $1000. Forty dogs are entered in the show. What is the expected value for each contestant? (Assume each contestant is equally likely to win.)

34. *Dog Show* In how many different orders can the 40 dogs in Exercise 33 be shown?

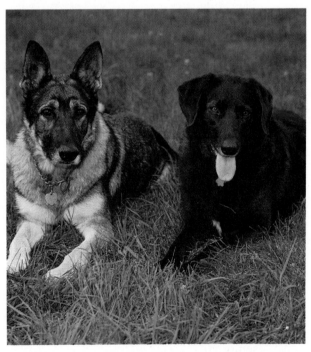

1. A radio is tuned to one of the radio stations in the United States. What is the probability that the radio station is an "oldies" station? What is the probability that it is a "country" station?

Radio Formats

There are 10,924 AM and FM radio stations in the USA.

2. A quiz consists of ten true or false questions. Each question is answered true or false. In how many ways can this be done?

3. How many two-person teams can be chosen from eight tennis players?

4. Of the 15 players on a basketball team, six play guard, six play forward, and three play center. How many starting lineups can be formed from 15 players? (A starting lineup has two guards, two forwards, and one center.)

5. The directions on a snack cake mix instruct you to add the cake mix, water, oil, and eggs in a bowl. In how many orders can you put the ingredients into the bowl?

In Exercises 6–8, find the indicated probability.

6. $P(A) = 0.61$
$P(B) = 0.39$
$P(A \cup B) = 0.75$
$P(A \cap B) = \boxed{?}$

7. $P(A) = \boxed{?}$
$P(B) = \frac{3}{8}$
$P(A \cup B) = \frac{7}{16}$
$P(A \cap B) = \frac{1}{16}$

8. $P(A) = \frac{5}{16}$
$P(B) = \boxed{?}$
$P(A \cup B) = \frac{3}{4}$
$P(A \cap B) = 0$

9. Your mom claims that 90% of incoming phone calls are for you. Assuming that this claim is true, what is the probability that all of the next three phone calls are for you?

10. You want to invest $500 in the stock of a new company. There is a 0.25 probability of receiving a profit of $1000 in a year and a 0.75 probability of losing the $500. What is the expected value of this investment?

11. If $P(A) = 0.71$, what is $P(A')$?

12. If $P(A) = \frac{7}{12}$, what is $P(A')$?

In Exercise 13, use the following information.

One of the students from a high school will be chosen to attend a statewide meeting of high school students. The table at the right shows the composition of the high school.

13. What is the probability that the student chosen is a junior or senior? not a sophomore boy? a junior boy or a senior girl?

	Boys	Girls
Freshmen	178	150
Sophomores	188	185
Juniors	150	147
Seniors	143	166

Properties	830
Models	831
Transformations	832
Formulas	833
Glossary	836
Handbook of Mathematical Connections	846
Technology Appendix	856
Selected Answers	868
Index	937
Credits	952

Basic Properties		**Addition**	**Multiplication**
	Closure	$a + b$ is a real number	$a \cdot b$ is a real number
	Commutative	$a + b = b + a$	$ab = ba$
	Associative	$(a + b) + c = a + (b + c)$	$(ab)c = a(bc)$
	Identity	$a + 0 = a,\ 0 + a = a$	$a(1) = a,\ 1(a) = a$
	Inverse	$a + (-a) = 0$	$a \cdot \dfrac{1}{a} = 1,\ a \neq 0$
	Distributive	$a(b + c) = ab + ac$ or $(a + b)c = ac + bc$	

Properties of Exponents

Product of Powers	$a^m \cdot a^n = a^{m+n}$
Power of a Power	$(a^m)^n = a^{m \cdot n}$
Power of a Product	$(a \cdot b)^m = a^m \cdot b^m$
Quotient of Powers	$\dfrac{a^m}{a^n} = a^{m-n},\ a \neq 0$
Power of a Quotient	$\left(\dfrac{a}{b}\right)^m = \dfrac{a^m}{b^m},\ b \neq 0$
Negative Exponent	$a^{-n} = \dfrac{1}{a^n},\ a \neq 0$
Zero Exponent	$a^0 = 1,\ a \neq 0$

Properties of Radicals

Product Property	$\sqrt{ab} = \sqrt{a} \cdot \sqrt{b}$
Quotient Property	$\sqrt{\dfrac{a}{b}} = \dfrac{\sqrt{a}}{\sqrt{b}}$

Properties of Matrices

Equal Matrices	$\begin{bmatrix} a & b \\ c & d \end{bmatrix} = \begin{bmatrix} e & f \\ g & h \end{bmatrix}$ then $a = e,\ b = f,\ c = g,$ and $d = h.$
Adding Matrices	$\begin{bmatrix} a & b \\ c & d \end{bmatrix} + \begin{bmatrix} e & f \\ g & h \end{bmatrix} = \begin{bmatrix} a + e & b + f \\ c + g & d + h \end{bmatrix}$
Multiplying Matrices	$\begin{bmatrix} a & b \\ c & d \end{bmatrix} \cdot \begin{bmatrix} e & f \\ g & h \end{bmatrix} = \begin{bmatrix} ae + bg & af + bh \\ ce + dg & cf + dh \end{bmatrix}$

Properties of Matrix Multiplication

Associative Property	$A(BC) = (AB)C$ $\quad A,\ B,$ and C are matrices.
Distributive Property	$A(B + C) = AB + AC$
Distributive Property	$(A + B)C = AC + BC$
Scalar Multiplication	$c(AB) = (cA)B = A(cB)$

Special Products and their Factors

Sum and Difference Pattern	$(a + b)(a - b) \longleftrightarrow a^2 - b^2$
Square of a Binomial Pattern	$(a + b)^2 \longleftrightarrow a^2 + 2ab + b^2$
	$(a - b)^2 \longleftrightarrow a^2 - 2ab + b^2$
Sum of Cubes	$a^3 + b^3 \longleftrightarrow (a + b)(a^2 - ab + b^2)$
Difference of Cubes	$a^3 - b^3 \longleftrightarrow (a - b)(a^2 + ab + b^2)$

Properties of Logarithms

Let a, u, and v be positive numbers such that $a \neq 1$.

Product Property	$\log_a (uv) = \log_a u + \log_a v$
Quotient Property	$\log_a \dfrac{u}{v} = \log_a u - \log_a v$
Power Property	$\log_a u^n = n \log_a u$

MODELS

A Problem-Solving Plan	**Ask** yourself what you need to know to solve the problem. Then **write a verbal model** that will give you what you need to know. **Assign labels** to each part of your verbal model. Use the labels to **write an algebraic model** based on your verbal model. **Solve** the algebraic model. **Answer** the original question. **Check** that your answer is reasonable.
Summary of Equations of Lines in Two Variables	**Slope of a Line through Two Points** $\quad m = \dfrac{(y_2 - y_1)}{(x_2 - x_1)}$ **Standard Form** $\quad Ax + By = C$ **Intercept Form** $\quad \dfrac{x}{a} + \dfrac{y}{b} = 1$ **Slope-intercept Form** $\quad y = mx + b$ **Point-slope Form** $\quad y - y_1 = m(x - x_1)$
Algebraic Models	**Linear** $\quad f(x) = mx + b$ **Quadratic** $\quad f(x) = ax^2 + bx + c \quad$ or $\quad f(x) = a(x - h)^2 + k$ **Rational** $\quad f(x) = \dfrac{a}{x - h} + k$ **Exponential Growth Model, $a > 1$, $C > 0$** $\quad y = Ca^x$ **Exponential Decay Model, $0 < a < 1$, $C > 0$** $\quad y = Ca^x$
Models for Conic Sections	In a parabola the point (h, k) is the vertex, and p is the distance from the focus to the vertex. For the other conics, (h, k) is the center. **Circle** $\quad (x - h)^2 + (y - k)^2 = r^2$ $\qquad\qquad$ Focus (or foci) on $x = h \qquad$ Focus (or foci) on $y = k$ **Parabola** $\quad (y - k)^2 = 4p(x - h) \qquad (x - h)^2 = 4p(y - k)$ **Ellipse** $\quad \dfrac{(x - h)^2}{a^2} + \dfrac{(y - k)^2}{b^2} = 1 \qquad \dfrac{(x - h)^2}{b^2} + \dfrac{(y - k)^2}{a^2} = 1$ **Hyperbola** $\quad \dfrac{(x - h)^2}{a^2} - \dfrac{(y - k)^2}{b^2} = 1 \qquad \dfrac{(y - k)^2}{a^2} - \dfrac{(x - h)^2}{b^2} = 1$
Models for Trigonometric Functions	Let θ be an angle in standard position with any point (x, y) (except the origin) on the terminal side of θ. Let $r = \sqrt{x^2 + y^2}$. $\sin \theta = \dfrac{y}{r} \qquad\qquad \cos \theta = \dfrac{x}{r} \qquad\qquad \tan \theta = \dfrac{y}{x},\ x \neq 0$ $\csc \theta = \dfrac{r}{y},\ y \neq 0 \qquad \sec \theta = \dfrac{r}{x},\ x \neq 0 \qquad \cot \theta = \dfrac{x}{y},\ y \neq 0$
Models for Direct and Inverse Variation	**1.** The variables x and y vary directly if, for a constant k, $\qquad \dfrac{y}{x} = k$ or $y = kx$ **2.** The variables x and y vary inversely if, for a constant k, $\qquad yx = k$ or $y = \dfrac{k}{x}$ In both cases, the number k is the constant of variation.

TRANSFORMATIONS

Using Transformations to Solve Equations, Inequalities, and Systems

Transformations that Produce Equivalent Equations
1. Add or subtract the same number to *both* sides.
2. Multiply or divide *both* sides by the same nonzero number.
3. Interchange the two sides.
4. Raise *both* sides to the same power. (Be careful, this may give an extraneous solution.)

Transformations that Produce Equivalent Inequalities
1. Add or subtract the same number to *both* sides.
2. Multiply or divide *both* sides by the same *positive* number.
3. Multiply or divide *both* sides by the same *negative* number and reverse the inequality sign.

Transformations of Absolute Value Inequalities
1. The inequality $|ax + b| < c$ means that $ax + b$ is between $-c$ and c. This is equivalent to $-c < ax + b < c$.
2. The inequality $|ax + b| > c$ means that $ax + b$ is not between $-c$ and c inclusive. This is equivalent to $ax + b < -c$ or $ax + b > c$.

Equivalent Systems of Equations
Each of the following **row operations** on a system of linear equations produces an equivalent system of linear equations.
1. Interchange two equations.
2. Multiply one of the equations by a nonzero constant.
3. Add a multiple of one of the equations to another equation to replace an equation.

Using Transformations to Graph Related Functions

Vertical and Horizontal Shifts
Let c be a positive real number. **Vertical** and **horizontal** shifts of the graph of f are represented as follows.
1. Vertical shift of c units upward: $\qquad g(x) = f(x) + c$
2. Vertical shift of c units downward: $\qquad g(x) = f(x) - c$
3. Horizontal shift of c units to the right: $\quad g(x) = f(x - c)$
4. Horizontal shift of c units to the left: $\quad\; g(x) = f(x + c)$

Reflection in the x-Axis
If $g(x) = -f(x)$, then the graph of g is a reflection in the x-axis of the graph of f.

Shifts of Sine and Cosine Graphs
To graph $y = a \sin(bx + c) + d$ or $y = a \cos(bx + c) + d$, shift the graph of $y = a \sin bx$ or $y = a \cos bx$ as follows.
1. If $d > 0$, shift d units up.
2. If $d < 0$, shift $|d|$ units down.
3. If $\dfrac{c}{b} > 0$, shift, $\dfrac{c}{b}$ units to the left.
4. If $\dfrac{c}{b} < 0$, shift, $\left|\dfrac{c}{b}\right|$ units to the right.

FORMULAS

The Inverse of a 2 × 2 Matrix	The inverse of the matrix $A = \begin{bmatrix} a & b \\ c & d \end{bmatrix}$ is $$A^{-1} = \frac{1}{|A|} \begin{bmatrix} d & -b \\ -c & a \end{bmatrix} = \frac{1}{ad - cb} \begin{bmatrix} d & -b \\ -c & a \end{bmatrix}, \ ad - cb \neq 0.$$
Cramer's Rule	Consider a linear system whose coefficient matrix has a determinant D. If $D \neq 0$, then the system has exactly one solution. **1.** The solution of $\begin{cases} ax + by = c \\ dx + ey = f \end{cases}$ is $$x = \frac{\begin{vmatrix} c & b \\ f & e \end{vmatrix}}{\begin{vmatrix} a & b \\ d & e \end{vmatrix}} \text{ and } y = \frac{\begin{vmatrix} a & c \\ d & f \end{vmatrix}}{\begin{vmatrix} a & b \\ d & e \end{vmatrix}}$$ **2.** The solution of $\begin{cases} ax + by + cz = d \\ ex + fy + gz = h \\ ix + jy + kz = l \end{cases}$ is $$x = \frac{\begin{vmatrix} d & b & c \\ h & f & g \\ l & j & k \end{vmatrix}}{\begin{vmatrix} a & b & c \\ e & f & g \\ i & j & k \end{vmatrix}}, \ y = \frac{\begin{vmatrix} a & d & c \\ e & h & g \\ i & l & k \end{vmatrix}}{\begin{vmatrix} a & b & c \\ e & f & g \\ i & j & k \end{vmatrix}}, \text{ and } z = \frac{\begin{vmatrix} a & b & d \\ e & f & h \\ i & j & l \end{vmatrix}}{\begin{vmatrix} a & b & c \\ e & f & g \\ i & j & k \end{vmatrix}}$$
The Quadratic Formula	Let a, b, and c be real numbers such that $a \neq 0$. The solutions of the quadratic equation $ax^2 + bx + c = 0$ are $$x = \frac{-b \pm \sqrt{b^2 - 4ac}}{2a}$$
Interest	An initial principal of P is deposited in an account that pays interest at an annual rate of r. The balance, A, in the account after t years is as follows. **Compounded n times per year:** $A = P\left(1 + \dfrac{r}{n}\right)^{nt}$. **Continuously compounded:** $A = Pe^{rt}$
The Distance Formula	The distance d between the points (x_1, y_1) and (x_2, y_2) is $$d = \sqrt{(x_2 - x_1)^2 + (y_2 - y_1)^2}$$
Standard Deviation of a Collection of Numbers	The standard deviation of $x_1, x_2, x_3, \ldots, x_n$ is $$s = \sqrt{\frac{(x_1 - \bar{x})^2 + (x_2 - \bar{x})^2 + \cdots + (x_n - \bar{x})^2}{n}}$$ $$= \sqrt{\frac{x_1^2 + x_2^2 + \cdots + x_n^2}{n} - \bar{x}^2}$$ where $\bar{x}$ is the mean of $x_1, x_2, \ldots,$ and x_n.

Conic Sections	**Ellipse** If a, b, and c represent the distances from the center of an ellipse to a vertex, covertex, and a focus, respectively, then: $a^2 = b^2 + c^2$. **Hyperbola** If a and c are the distances from the center (h, k) to a vertex and a focus, respectively, then b is related to the hyperbola by the equation $a^2 + b^2 = c^2$, and the equations for the asymptotes are: $y - k = \pm\dfrac{b}{a}x - h$ when the transverse axis is horizontal, or $y - k = \pm\dfrac{a}{b}x - h$ when the transverse axis is vertical.
Formulas for Special Series	**1.** $\displaystyle\sum_{i=1}^{n} 1 = n$ **2.** $\displaystyle\sum_{i=1}^{n} i = \frac{1}{2}(n)(n + 1)$ **3.** $\displaystyle\sum_{i=1}^{n} i^2 = \frac{1}{6}(n)(n + 1)(2n + 1)$
Sum of a Series	• The sum of an arithmetic series with n terms is $$\sum_{i=1}^{n} a_i = n\left(\frac{a_1 + a_n}{2}\right) \text{ or } \frac{1}{2}n(2a_1 + (n - 1)d).$$ • The sum of the geometric series $a_1 + a_1r + a_1r^2 + a_1r^3 + \cdots + a_1r^{n-1}$ with common ratio $r \neq 1$ is $$\sum_{i=1}^{n} a_1r^{i-1} = a_1\left(\frac{1 - r^n}{1 - r}\right).$$ • If $|r| < 1$, then the sum of the infinite geometric series $a_1 + a_1r + a_1r^2 + a_1r^3 + \cdots + a_1r^{n-1} + \cdots$ is $$\sum_{i=1}^{\infty} a_1r^{i-1} = \frac{a_1}{1 - r}.$$ If $|r| \geq 1$, then the series has no sum.

Fundamental Trigonometric Identities	**Reciprocal** $\sin\theta = \dfrac{1}{\csc\theta}$ $\quad \cos\theta = \dfrac{1}{\sec\theta} \quad$ $\tan\theta = \dfrac{1}{\cot\theta}$ $\csc\theta = \dfrac{1}{\sin\theta} \quad \sec\theta = \dfrac{1}{\cos\theta} \quad \cot\theta = \dfrac{1}{\tan\theta}$ **Tangent and Cotangent** $\quad \tan\theta = \dfrac{\sin\theta}{\cos\theta} \quad \cot\theta = \dfrac{\cos\theta}{\sin\theta}$ **Pythagorean** $\quad \sin^2\theta + \cos^2\theta = 1 \qquad 1 + \tan^2\theta = \sec^2\theta$ $\qquad\qquad\qquad\qquad\qquad\qquad\qquad\quad 1 + \cot^2\theta = \csc^2\theta$
Sum and Difference Formulas	$\sin(u+v) = \sin u \cos v + \cos u \sin v \quad \tan(u+v) = \dfrac{\tan u + \tan v}{1 - \tan u \tan v}$ $\sin(u-v) = \sin u \cos v - \cos u \sin v \quad \tan(u-v) = \dfrac{\tan u - \tan v}{1 + \tan u \tan v}$ $\cos(u+v) = \cos u \cos v - \sin u \sin v$ $\cos(u-v) = \cos u \cos v + \sin u \sin v$
Double- and Half-Angle Formulas	$\sin 2u = 2\sin u \cos u \qquad\qquad \cos 2u = \cos^2 u - \sin^2 u$ $\tan 2u = \dfrac{2\tan u}{1 - \tan^2 u} \qquad\qquad\quad = 2\cos^2 u - 1$ $\qquad\qquad\qquad\qquad\qquad\qquad\quad = 1 - 2\sin^2 u$ $\sin\dfrac{u}{2} = \pm\sqrt{\dfrac{1 - \cos u}{2}} \qquad \cos\dfrac{u}{2} = \pm\sqrt{\dfrac{1 + \cos u}{2}}$ $\tan\dfrac{u}{2} = \dfrac{1 - \cos u}{\sin u} \qquad\qquad \tan\dfrac{u}{2} = \dfrac{\sin u}{1 + \cos u}$ The signs of $\sin\dfrac{u}{2}$ and $\cos\dfrac{u}{2}$ depend on the quadrant in which $\dfrac{u}{2}$ lies.
Law of Sines	If ABC is a triangle with sides a, b, and c, then $\dfrac{a}{\sin A} = \dfrac{b}{\sin B} = \dfrac{c}{\sin C} \quad$ or $\quad \dfrac{\sin A}{a} = \dfrac{\sin B}{b} = \dfrac{\sin C}{c}$.
Law of Cosines	Let ABC be a triangle with sides a, b, and c, then $a^2 = b^2 + c^2 - 2bc\cos A$, $b^2 = a^2 + c^2 - 2ac\cos B$, and $c^2 = a^2 + b^2 - 2ab\cos C$.
The Binomial Theorem	The binomial expansion of $(x+y)^n$ is $(x+y)^n = x^n + nx^{n-1}y + \cdots + \dbinom{n}{m}x^{n-m}y^m + \cdots + nxy^{n-1} + y^n$ where $\dbinom{n}{m} = \dfrac{n!}{(n-m)!m!}$

absolute value of a real number (44, 101) The distance between the origin and the point representing the real number. For example: $|3| = 3$, $|-3| = 3$, or $|0| = 0$.

acute angle (678) An angle whose measure is greater than 0° and less than 90°.

additive identity (4) See Properties page 830.

algebraic expression (9) A collection of numbers, variables, operations, and grouping symbols.

algebraic model (9) An algebraic expression or equation used to represent a real-life situation.

amortization (555) The process of repaying an installment loan.

amplitude (730, 737) The amount by which a sine or cosine graph varies above and below its axis.

annuities (658) Savings accounts that involve many equal deposits (or withdrawals) at regular intervals over a long period of time.

associative property (4, 259) See Properties on page 830.

associative property of matrices (175, 181) See Properties on page 830.

asymptote (421) A line to which a graph becomes arbitrarily close as $|x|$ or $|y|$ increases without bound.

augmented matrix (210) A matrix containing the coefficients and constants of a system of linear equations.

axis of symmetry of a parabola (236) The vertical line passing through the vertex of a parabola and dividing the parabola into two parts that are mirror images of each other.

bar graph (11) A graph that organizes a collection of data by using horizontal or vertical bars to display how many times each number occurs in the collection.

base of a logarithm (405) In logarithmic notation, $\log_a x$, a is the base.

base of an exponent (10, 346) The number or variable that is used as a factor in repeated multiplication. For example, in the expression 4^6, 4 is the base.

best-fitting line (107) A line that best fits the data points on a scatter plot.

binomial (456) A polynomial that has only two terms.

box-and-whisker plot (328) A plot used to present a graphic summary of information. The quartiles and extreme values of a set of data displayed using a number line.

branches (518) Two portions of a graph that are not connected.

catenary (249) A U-shaped curve that resembles a parabola.

centroid (33) The point at which a plane figure will balance.

change of base formula (406) A formula which makes it possible to use a calculator to evaluate logarithms in bases other than base 10.

$$\log_a x = \frac{\log_{10} x}{\log_{10} a}$$

circle graph (51) A circle partitioned into sectors used to show the relative size of different portions of a whole.

closure property (4) See Properties on page 830.

coefficient (456) In a term that is the product of a number and a variable, the number is the coefficient of the variable.

coefficient matrix (216) A matrix representation of the coefficients of the variables in a system of equations.

collinearity test (193) A test which involves finding the area of the "triangle" formed by three points to determine if those points are collinear (lie on the same line). If the area is zero, the points are collinear.

column matrix (174) A matrix that has only one column.

combinations (796) Any choice of *m* elements from a set of *n* elements.

common difference (629) The difference between successive terms in an arithmetic sequence.

common logarithmic function (406) A logarithmic function with base 10.

common ratio (637) The ratio of successive terms in a geometric sequence.

commutative property (4, 259) See Properties on page 830.

commutative property for adding matrices (175) See Properties on page 830.

complement of an event (806) If an event *A* is in a sample space *S*, then the complement of *A* consists of all outcomes in *S* that are not in *A*.

completed-square form (250) A quadratic equation in the form "perfect square = *k*," $k \geq 0$; a quadratic function in the form $f(x) = a(x - h)^2 + k$. The vertex of the parabola is the point (h, k).

completing the square (245) A process which can be used to solve any quadratic equation.

complex conjugate (496) A complex number of the form $a + bi$ is $a - bi$.

complex fraction (549) A fraction that contains at least one fraction in its numerator and/or denominator.

complex number (259) A number that is the sum of a real number and an imaginary number. Each complex number can be written in the standard form, $a + bi$.

complex plane (260) A plane formed by a real number line and an imaginary number line intersecting at a right angle. The horizontal axis is the real axis and the vertical axis is the imaginary axis.

composition of two functions (292) The composition of the function *f* with the function *g* is given by $h(x) = f(g(x))$.

compound function (306) A function that may be represented by a combination of equations.

compound inequality (38) Two inequalities connected by *and* or *or*.

compound interest (35, 352) Interest paid on the original principal and on interest that becomes part of the account.

constant of variation (88, 526) The constant *k* in the relationships of variation.

constant term (456) A monomial without a variable. For example, in $x^2 + 2x + 5$ the number 5 is the constant term.

constraints (151) The system of linear inequalities in a linear programming problem.

continuous function (463) A function whose graph has no breaks.

coordinate plane (64) A plane formed by two real number lines intersecting at a right angle.

correlation coefficient (110) A statistical measure used to determine how well a collection of data points can be modeled by a line. Correlation coefficients range between -1 and $+1$.

cosecant (678) See Formulas on pages 833–835.

cosine (678) See Formulas on pages 833–835.

cotangent (678) See Formulas on pages 833–835.

Cramer's rule (216) See Formulas on pages 833–835.

cycle (730) The shortest repeating portion of a periodic function.

data (50) The facts, or numbers, that describe something.

definition of division (4) For all real numbers *a* and *b*, division is defined as multiplying by the reciprocal, $\frac{a}{b} = a \cdot \frac{1}{b}$.

definition of subtraction (4) For all real numbers *a* and *b*, subtraction is defined as adding the opposite, $a - b = a + (-b)$.

degree of a monomial (456) The integer *k* is the degree of ax^k.

denominator (9) The divisor in a quotient expressed in fraction form. For example, 2 is the denominator of $\frac{5x}{2}$.

dependent events (811) Two events where the occurrence of one affects the occurrence of the other.

determinant (187) A real number associated with each square matrix. For example, $ad - cb$ is the determinant of the matrix.

diagonal method (189) A method used to evaluate the determinant of a 3×3 matrix, where the first and second columns of the matrix form fourth and fifth columns. The determinant is then obtained by adding the products of three diagonals and subtracting the products of three diagonals.

difference (4) The result obtained when numbers or expressions are subtracted. The difference of a and b is defined as $a - b$.

difference of two cubes (474) See Properties on page 830.

difference of two squares (458) See Properties on page 830.

direct variation (88) A function whose equation has the form $y = kx$ or $\frac{x}{y} = k$.

directrix (570) A fixed line from which all the points of a parabola are equidistant.

discriminant (253) The expression $b^2 - 4ac$ is for a quadratic equation $ax^2 + bx + c = 0$.

distance formula (376) The distance, d, between any two points, (x_1, y_1) and (x_2, y_2), is given by $d = \sqrt{(x_2 - x_1)^2 + (y_2 - y_1)^2}$.

distributive property (4) See Properties on page 830.

distributive property for matrices (175, 181) See Properties on page 830.

dividing rational expressions (534) To divide one rational expression by another, multiply the first by the reciprocal of the second. $\frac{a}{b} \div \frac{c}{d} = \frac{a}{b} \cdot \frac{d}{c}$

domain, or input, of a function (284) The x-values of a function $y = f(x)$.

domain of a rational expression (518) The set of all real numbers, except those for which the denominator is zero.

eccentricity of an ellipse (585) The measure of the ovalness of an ellipse.

elementary row operations (210) Row operations which when performed on an augmented matrix produce a matrix that is row-equivalent to the original matrix.

ellipse (583) The set of all points (x, y) such that the sum of the distances between (x, y) and two distinct fixed points, the focuses or foci, is a constant.

equal complex numbers (259) Two complex numbers, $a + bi$ and $c + di$, are equal if $a = c$ and $b = d$.

equal matrices (174) Matrices are equal if the entries in corresponding positions are equal.

equally-likely outcome (782) An event that is as likely to happen as not to happen.

equation (18) A statement formed when an equality symbol is placed between two equal expressions.

equivalent equations (18) Equations with the same solution set.

equivalent inequalities (37) Inequalities with the same solution set.

equivalent systems of equations (158) Two linear systems are equivalent if they have the same set of solutions.

Euler number (420) The natural base e.

evaluate a function (286) To find $f(x)$ for a given value of x is to evaluate the function f.

evaluate an algebraic expression (9) To find the value of an algebraic expression by replacing each variable in the expression by a number.

expansion by minors (188) A method that can be used to find the value of any third or higher order determinant. It expresses the determinant of a 3×3 matrix in terms of three 2×2 determinants.

expected value (817) The sum of the probabilities of n events occurring, each multiplied by its payoff.

experimental probability (802) A probability determined by performing a number of trials.

exponent (10, 346) The number or variable that represents the number of times the base is used as a factor. For example, in the expression 4^6, 6 is the exponent.

exponential decay (354) A situation in which the original amount is repeatedly multiplied by a change factor less than one.

exponential form of a power (346) The expression 4^6 is the exponential form of $4 \cdot 4 \cdot 4 \cdot 4 \cdot 4 \cdot 4$.

exponential growth (354) A situation in which the original amount is repeatedly multiplied by a change factor greater than one.

extraneous solutions (375, 542) A solution of a transformed equation that is not a solution of the original equation.

Factor Theorem (482) A polynomial $f(x)$ has a factor $(x - k)$ if and only if $f(k) = 0$.

factorial function (321) The function defined by the equation $f(n) = n!$ The product of the positive integers from n to 1. 0! is defined to be 1.

factors (473) The numbers and variables that are multiplied in an expression. For example, 4 and x are factors of $4x$.

Fibonacci sequence (323) The sequence 1, 1, 2, 3, 5, 8, 13, ... This special sequence, discovered by Leonardo Fibonacci, is often found in nature.

finite sequence (622) A sequence with a limited number of terms.

first differences of a recursive function (322) The first differences of a recursive function are found by subtracting consecutive values of the function.

FOIL pattern (457) A method used to multiply two binomials in a single step. Find the sum of the products of the **F**irst terms, **O**uter terms, **I**nner terms, and **L**ast terms.

formula (17) An algebraic expression that represents a relationship in real-life situations.

fractal (261) Pictures that are drawn using the complex plane.

frequency distribution (50) A table that organizes a collection of data by counting how many times each number occurs in the collection.

function (285) A special type of relationship between two values in which each input value corresponds to exactly one output value. A relation in which no two ordered pairs (x, y) have the same x-value.

Fundamental Counting Principle (788) If one event can occur in m ways and another in n ways, then the number of ways that both can occur is $m \cdot n$.

Fundamental Theorem of Algebra (495) Counting complex and repeated solutions, an nth-degree polynomial equation has exactly n solutions.

Gaussian elimination (158) The process of rewriting a system of linear equations into triangular form.

general form of a linear equation (78) See Models on page 831.

general form of a second-degree equation (606) See Models on page 831.

geometric mean (375) The geometric mean of a and b is $\sqrt{ab}$.

geometric sequence (637) A sequence in which each term after the first is the product of the preceding term and a constant, r. The constant is called the common ratio.

geometric series (639) The expression formed by adding the terms of a geometric sequence.

golden ratio (377, 668) The golden ratio is $\dfrac{\sqrt{5} + 1}{2}$.

graph of an equation (64) A visual model of an equation.

greatest common monomial factor (473) The greatest monomial factor that can be factored from the terms of a polynomial.

half-plane (94) In a plane, the region on either side of a boundary.

horizontal shift of a graph (314) See Transformations on page 832.

Hero's Area Formula (717) The area of the triangle with sides of length a, b, and c, is Area = $\sqrt{s(s - a)(s - b)(s - c)}$ where $s = \frac{1}{2}(a + b + c)$.

hyperbola (590) The graph of a rational function $f(x) = \dfrac{a}{(x - h)} + k$, whose center is (h, k).

identity matrix (196) For a 2×2 matrix the multiplicative identity is $I = \begin{bmatrix} 1 & 0 \\ 0 & 1 \end{bmatrix}$.

identity property (4) See Properties on page 830.

imaginary number (258) If a is a positive number, then $\sqrt{-a}$ is an imaginary number and $\sqrt{-a} = i\sqrt{a}$.

independent events (811) Two events where the occurrence of one has no effect on the occurrence of the other.

index of a radical (369) In the radical expression $c\sqrt[n]{a}$, the number n is the index.

index of summation (623) In the summation $\sum\limits_{i=1}^{n} a_i$, i is the index of summation.

inequality (37) An open sentence formed when an inequality symbol is placed between two expressions.

infinite series (645) A series that has no upper limit of summation.

integers (2) The set of numbers $\{\ldots, -3, -2, -1, 0, 1, 2, 3, \ldots\}$.

intercept form of an equation of a line (79) See Models on page 831.

intersection of two events (805) The intersection of two events consists of all outcomes that are in both A and B.

inverse of a matrix (196) Two 2×2 matrices are inverses of each other if their product (in both orders) is the identity matrix.

inverse of a relation (298) The set of ordered pairs obtained by switching the coordinates of each ordered pair in the relation.

inverse property (4) See Properties on page 830.

inverse property of exponents and logarithms (434) See Properties on page 830.

inverse variation (526) A function defined by an equation of the form $xy = k$ or $y = \dfrac{k}{x}$.

irrational number (2) A real number that cannot be expressed as the quotient of two integers. For example, the square roots of numbers that are not perfect squares ($\sqrt{2}$, $\sqrt{3}$, $\sqrt{5}$, and $\sqrt{6}$). When expressed as a decimal, it neither repeats nor terminates.

joint variation (528) A joint variation occurs when a quantity varies directly as the product of two or more other quantities. An equation of the form $z = kxy$ where k is a nonzero constant.

Law of Cosines (716) If ABC is a triangle with sides a, b, and c, then $a^2 = b^2 + c^2 - 2bc \cos A$, $b^2 = a^2 + c^2 - 2ac \cos B$ and $c^2 = a^2 + b^2 - 2ab \cos C$.

Law of Sines (709) If ABC is a triangle with sides a, b, and c, then $\dfrac{a}{\sin A} = \dfrac{b}{\sin B} = \dfrac{c}{\sin C}$ or $\dfrac{\sin A}{a} = \dfrac{\sin B}{b} = \dfrac{\sin C}{c}$.

leading coefficient (230, 456) The coefficient of the first term in a polynomial written in standard form.

least common multiple of polynomials (541) The simplest polynomial that is a multiple of each of the original polynomials.

like radicals (369) Two radical expressions are like radicals if they have the same index and the same radicand.

linear combination method (131) A method of solving systems of equations that involves adding multiples of the given equations.

Linear Factorization Theorem (496) A polynomial of degree n has exactly n linear factors $f(x) = a_n(x - k_1)(x - k_2) \ldots (x - k_n)$, where $k_1, k_2, \ldots, k_n$ are complex numbers and a_n is the leading coefficient of $f(x)$.

linear function (285) A function defined by the equation $f(x) = mx + b$.

linear model (24) An equation of a line that is used to represent a real-life situation.

linear programming (151) A type of optimization process for finding the maximum or minimum value of an objective quantity by using a system of constraints.

literal equation (31) An equation which uses more than one letter as a variable. For example, $3x + y = 4$ is a literal equation.

logarithm (405) If $a > 0$ and $x > 0$, $y = \log_a x$ if and only if $x = a^y$.

logarithmic function (405) The inverse of an exponential function.

logistics growth models (441) Models used to represent populations or quantities whose rate of growth changes from an increasing rapid growth to a decreasing rapid growth.

major axis of an ellipse (31, 583) The major axis is the longer of the two line segments that form the axes of symmetry for an ellipse.

Mandelbrot set (261) A set of famous fractal pictures.

mapping diagram (284) A diagram that pictures a correspondence between two sets.

matrix (174) A rectangular arrangement of numbers into rows and columns.

matrix multiplication (180) If A is an $m \times n$ matrix and B is an $n \times p$ matrix, then the product AB is an $m \times p$ matrix.

mean (327) The sum of a set of numbers divided by the number of numbers in the set.

measures of central tendency (327) The mean, median, and mode of a distribution.

median (327) The middle number of an odd collection of numbers; the average of the two middle numbers in an even collection of numbers.

minor axis of an ellipse (31, 583) The line segment perpendicular to the major axis at the center.

mode (327) The number that occurs most frequently in a collection of numbers. If two numbers tie for most frequent occurrence, the collection is said to be bimodal.

modeling (9) Writing algebraic expressions or equations to represent real-life situations.

monomial (456) A polynomial with only one term.

multiplicative identity (4) See Properties on page 830.

multiplying rational expressions (534) To multiply two rational expressions, multiply the numerators, multiply the denominators, and write the new fraction in simplest form.

mutually exclusive events (805) Events which have no outcomes in common.

natural base (404, 426) The number $e \approx 2.71828$ is called the natural base.

negative correlation (110) Data points on a scatter plot that approximate a line with a negative slope.

negative numbers (2) Numbers represented by points to the left of the origin on the real number line. Numbers less than 0.

negative power property (346) See Properties on page 830.

numerator (9) The dividend in a quotient expressed in fraction form. For example, $5x$ is the numerator of $\dfrac{5x}{2}$.

objective quantity (151) In linear programming, the quantity or expression to be maximized or minimized.

obtuse angle (685) An angle whose measure is between 90° and 180°.

odds (810) The ratio of the number of ways an event can occur to the number of ways the event cannot occur.

opposites (3) Two points on the real number line that are the same distance from the origin but on opposite sides of the origin. For example, 3 and -3 are opposites.

optimization (151) Finding the minimum or maximum value of a quantity.

order of a matrix (174) The number of rows of the matrix "by" the number of columns of the matrix. For example, a 2×3 matrix has 2 rows and 3 columns.

ordered pair (64) A pair of real numbers used to locate each point in a coordinate plane.

origin of the coordinate plane (64) The point in the coordinate plane at which the horizontal axis intersects the vertical axis. The point (0, 0).

origin of the real number line (2) The point that represents 0 on the real number line.

parabola (236, 570) The graph of a quadratic equation.

paraboloid (574) A shape that is made up of vertical cross sections that are parabolas and horizontal cross sections that are circles.

parallelogram rule (261) To add (or subtract) two complex numbers, add (or subtract) the real and imaginary parts of the numbers.

Pascal's Triangle (652) A convenient triangular pattern for writing binomial coefficients. The first and last number in each row is 1. Each of the other entries in any row is formed by adding the two numbers immediately above it.

perfect square trinomial (245) A trinomial that factors into the square of a binomial.

perimeter of a polygon (35) The sum of the lengths of the sides of the polygon.

period (730) The horizontal length of each cycle of a periodic function.

periodic function (730) A function whose graph has a repeating pattern that continues indefinitely.

permutation (790) The number of ways that n elements can be arranged in order.

point-slope form of the equation of a line (86) See Models on page 831.

polynomial (456) An expression whose terms are of the form $a_k x^k$, where k is a nonnegative integer, is a polynomial in x.

polynomial function (463) A function of the form $f(x) = a_n x^n + a_{n-1} x^{n-1} + \cdots + a_1 x + a_0$, $a_n \neq 0$.

positive correlation (110) Data points on a scatter plot that approximate a line with a positive slope.

positive numbers (2) Numbers represented by the points to the right of the origin on the real number line. Numbers greater than 0.

power (346) The result of repeated multiplication. For example, in the expression $4^2 = 16$, 16 is the power.

power of a power property (346) See Properties on page 830.

power of a product property (346) See Properties on page 830.

power of a quotient property (346) See Properties on page 830.

power property of logarithms (413) See Properties on page 830.

principal (352, 555) The initial amount of money invested or borrowed.

probability (782) The ratio of successful outcomes to the total number of outcomes of the event.

probability of an event (782) A number between 0 and 1 that indicates the likelihood the event will occur.

probability of independent events (811) If A and B are independent events, then the probability that both A and B occur is $P(A \cap B) = P(A) \cdot P(B)$.

product (4) The result obtained when numbers or expressions are multiplied. The product of a and b is $a \cdot b$, or ab.

properties See page 830.

Pythagorean Identity (680) See Formulas on pages 833–835.

Pythagorean Theorem (32) For any right triangle, the sum of the squares of the lengths of the legs, a and b, equals the square of the length of the hypotenuse, c. For example, $a^2 + b^2 = c^2$.

quadrant (64) In the coordinate plane, one of the four parts into which the axes divide the plane.

quadratic equation (230) An equation in x that can be written in the standard form $ax^2 + bx + c = 0$, $a \neq 0$.

quadratic formula (252) See Formulas on pages 833–835.

quartile (328) The values in a collection of numbers that separate the data into four equal parts.

quotient (4) The result obtained when numbers or expressions are divided. The quotient of a and b is $\dfrac{a}{b}$, where a and b are real numbers, and $b \neq 0$.

radian (686) A unit of angle, arc, or rotation measure such that π radians = 180°.

radicand (230, 369) The number or expression under a radical symbol.

range, or output, of a function (284) The y-values of a function $y = f(x)$.

rate of change (70) A relationship such as distance over time, often described by using a slope.

rational equation (541) An equation that involves rational expressions with the variable occurring in the denominator(s).

rational expressions (548) Fractions whose numerators and denominators are polynomials.

rational function (518) A function of the form $f(x) = \dfrac{p(x)}{q(x)}$, $q(x) \neq 0$.

rational numbers (2) Any number that can be written in the form $\dfrac{a}{b}$, where a and b are integers and $b \neq 0$.

real number line (2) A horizontal line that pictures real numbers as points.

real numbers (2) The set of numbers consisting of the positive numbers, the negative numbers, and zero.

reciprocal (4) If $\dfrac{a}{b}$ is a non-zero number then its reciprocal is $\dfrac{b}{a}$.

recursive function (321) A function whose domain is the set of nonnegative integers and which can be defined by stating the value of the function at 0 and a formula relating each of the other values to the preceding value.

reference angle (694) The acute angle formed by the terminal side of an angle and the x-axis.

reflection (316) See Transformations on page 832.

reflection of the graph (298) See Transformations on page 832.

relation (284) A set of ordered pairs (x, y).

Remainder Theorem (482) If a polynomial $f(x)$ is divided by $(x - k)$, then the remainder is $r = f(k)$.

rotation (600) See Transformations on page 832.

round-off error (23) The error produced when a decimal result is rounded in order to provide a meaningful answer.

row-equivalent matrices (210) Two matrices are row equivalent if one can be obtained from the other by a sequence of elementary row operations.

row matrix (174) A matrix that has only one row.

sample space (782) The set of all possible outcomes of an experiment.

scalar (175) In matrix algebra, a real number is called a scalar.

scatter plot (109) The plot, or graph, of the points that correspond to the ordered pairs in a collection.

secant (678) See Formulas on pages 833–835.

second differences of a recursive function (322) The second differences of a recursive function are found by subtracting consecutive first differences.

sequence (622) A function whose domain is the set of positive integers. Each value is a term of the sequence.

series (623) The expression formed by adding the first n terms of a sequence.

set (2) A well-defined collection of objects.

sigma notation (623) The Greek letter Σ.

simple interest (352) The amount paid or earned for the use of money for a unit of time.

sine (678) See Formulas on pages 833–835.

slope of a line (70) The ratio of the vertical change to the horizontal change; the ratio of the change in y to the corresponding change in x.

slope-intercept form (79) See Models on page 831.

solution (18, 37) A replacement for a variable that makes an equation or inequality true.

solution of a system (122, 145, 204) An ordered pair that is a solution of each of the equations in the system.

solution of a system of equations in *x, y, z* (157) An ordered triple (x, y, z) that is a solution of each of the equations in the system.

speed (254) The absolute value of the velocity of an object; the rate of motion given by distance traveled over time.

square matrix (174) A matrix that has the same number of rows and columns.

square root (2) If $b^2 = a$, then b is a square root of a.

standard deviation (502) For any set of data, x_1, x_2, x_3, ..., x_n, the standard deviation is

$$s = \sqrt{\frac{(x_1 - \overline{x})^2 + (x_2 - \overline{x})^2 + ... + (x_n - \overline{x})^2}{n}}$$

where $\overline{x}$ is the mean of x_1, x_2, ..., and x_n.

standard form of a polynomial (456) A polynomial in which the terms are written in descending order, from the greatest degree to the smallest degree.

standard form of an equation (576) See Models on page 831.

statistics (107) A field of mathematics that organizes large collections of data in ways that can be used to understand trends and make predictions.

substitution method (130) A method of solving a system of equations in which one variable is written in terms of other variables in one equation and the resulting expression is substituted into the other equation.

sum (4) The result obtained when numbers or expressions are added. The sum of a and b is $a + b$.

summation notation (623) The Greek letter Σ.

supplementary (686) Two positive angles are supplementary if the sum of their measures is π radians (or 180°).

synthetic division (480) A method that uses only coefficients to display the process of dividing a polynomial in x by $x \pm k$.

system of equations (122, 157) A set of equations in the same variables.

system of inequalities (147) A set of inequalities in the same variables.

tangent (678) See Formulas on pages 833–835.

terms of an expression (9) In an expression such as $3x + 2$, $3x$ and 2 are called terms.

three-dimensional coordinate system (164) A system that begins with the xy-coordinate plane in a horizontal position and then adds the z-axis as a vertical line through the origin.

time-line graph (52) A graph used to represent events that occur in a given sequence in time.

transformations (314) See Transformations on page 832.

transverse axis (590) The line segment joining the vertices of a hyperbola.

triangular form (157) A linear system in which the equations follow a stair-step pattern and each equation has 1 as the coefficient of its first nonzero term.

trigonometric identities (680) See Formulas on pages 833–835.

trigonometry (678) The study of the measurements of triangles.

trinomial (456) A polynomial that has only three terms.

union of two events (805) The union of two events, A and B, consists of all outcomes that are in A or B (or in both A and B).

variable (9) A letter that is used to represent one or more numbers.

velocity (254) The speed and direction in which an object is traveling.

vertex of a parabola (236) The lowest point of a parabola that opens up and the highest point of a parabola that opens down.

vertical shift of a graph (314) See Transformations on page 832.

vertices of a hyperbola (590) The line through the foci intersects the hyperbola at two points, the vertices.

vertices of an ellipse (583) The line through the foci intersects the ellipse at two points, the vertices.

whole numbers (2) The set of numbers $\{0, 1, 2, 3, 4, ...\}$.

x-axis (64) The horizontal axis in the coordinate plane.

x-coordinate (64) The first number of an ordered pair, the horizontal coordinate.

x-intercept (78) The value of x when $y = 0$.

y-axis (64) The vertical axis in the coordinate plane.

y-coordinate (64) The second number of an ordered pair, the vertical coordinate.

y-intercept (78) The value of y when $x = 0$.

zero factor property (577) See Properties on page 830.

zero matrix (174) A matrix whose entries are all zero.

zero power property (346) See Properties on page 830.

zero product property (475) See Properties on page 830.

▶ Handbook of Mathematical Connections

You may have taken a geometry course in which some geometric properties (called theorems) were proved using other theorems and basic assumptions (called postulates). The proofs show how the geometric properties are interrelated and help convince us that the proved properties are correct.

In this handbook, we will show how various properties of algebra are related to other properties in algebra, in geometry, and in trigonometry.

▶ THE QUADRATIC FORMULA

Lesson 5.4, page 252

The quadratic formula can be derived by completing the square of the general quadratic equation written in standard form. In completing the square, we use properties of addition and multiplication (see page 4) and transformations that produce equivalent equations (see page 18).

$$ax^2 + bx + c = 0 \qquad \textit{Standard form}$$

$$x^2 + \frac{b}{a}x + \frac{c}{a} = 0 \qquad \textit{Divide both sides by a, (a} \neq \textit{0).}$$

$$x^2 + \frac{b}{a}x = -\frac{c}{a} \qquad \textit{Subtract } \frac{c}{a} \textit{ from both sides.}$$

$$x^2 + \frac{b}{a}x + \left(\frac{b}{2a}\right)^2 = -\frac{c}{a} + \left(\frac{b}{2a}\right)^2 \qquad \textit{Complete the square by adding the square of half the coefficient of x to both sides.}$$

$$\left(x + \frac{b}{2a}\right)^2 = \frac{b^2 - 4ac}{4a^2} \qquad \textit{Simplify.}$$

$$x + \frac{b}{2a} = \pm\sqrt{\frac{b^2 - 4ac}{4a^2}} \qquad \textit{Take the square root of both sides.}$$

$$x = -\frac{b}{2a} \pm \sqrt{\frac{b^2 - 4ac}{4a^2}} \qquad \textit{Subtract } \frac{b}{2a} \textit{ from both sides.}$$

$$x = \frac{-b \pm \sqrt{b^2 - 4ac}}{2a} \qquad \textit{Simplify.}$$

Try this. Solve the quadratic equation $3x^2 + 5x + 2 = 0$ by completing the square. Compare each step in your solution with the steps in the above proof.

▶ PROPERTIES OF LOGARITHMS

Lesson 8.3, page 413

Since logarithms are defined in terms of exponents:

$$\log_a x = y \quad \text{if and only if} \quad a^y = x,$$

the properties of logarithms can be derived directly from the properties of exponents which were developed in Lesson 7.1.

Properties of Logarithms
1. $\log_a(uv) = \log_a u + \log_a v$
2. $\log_a \dfrac{u}{v} = \log_a u - \log_a v$
3. $\log_a(u^n) = n \log_a u$

Properties of Exponents
1. $a^n a^m = a^{n+m}$
2. $\dfrac{a^n}{a^m} = a^{n-m}$
3. $(a^n)^m = a^{nm}$

For example, to derive the first property of logarithms, let

$$n = \log_a u \quad \text{and} \quad m = \log_a v.$$

Then,

$$u = a^n \quad \text{and} \quad v = a^m. \qquad \textit{Definition of logarithm}$$

Multiplying, we obtain

$$uv = a^{n+m} \qquad \textit{First property of exponents}$$

Taking the logarithm of both sides, we obtain

$$\log_a(uv) = \log_a(a^{n+m})$$

$$= n + m \qquad \textit{Definition of logarithm}$$

$$= \log_a u + \log_a v. \qquad \textit{Substitution}$$

Try this. The second property of logarithms would be derived in a very similar fashion. The difference would be in dividing u and v instead of multiplying. Write the derivation. Which property of exponents is used?

The third property of logarithms depends on the third property of exponents as follows.

Let $\quad m = \log_a u.$

Then $\quad u = a^m. \qquad \textit{Definition of logarithm}$

$$u^n = (a^m)^n \qquad \textit{Raise both sides to the same power.}$$

$$\log_a u^n = \log_a(a^m)^n \qquad \textit{Take the logarithm of both sides.}$$

$$\log_a u^n = \log_a(a^{mn}) \qquad \textit{Third property of exponents}$$

$$= mn \qquad \textit{Definition of logarithm}$$

$$= n \log_a u \qquad \textit{Substitution}$$

▶ CHANGE OF BASE FORMULAS

Pages 406 and 427

The Change of Base Formula can be stated in terms of logarithms to the base 10, base e, or, in general, any base b:

$$\log_a x = \frac{\log_{10} x}{\log_{10} a} \qquad\qquad \log_a x = \frac{\ln x}{\ln a} \qquad\qquad \log_a x = \frac{\log_b x}{\log_b a}$$

The formulas can be derived from the properties of logarithms. Here is a derivation of the first formula.

Let $u = \log_a x$.

$a^u = x$	*Definition of logarithm*
$\log_{10} a^u = \log_{10} x$	*Take the logarithm of both sides.*
$u \log_{10} a = \log_{10} x$	*3rd property of logarithms*
$u = \dfrac{\log_{10} x}{\log_{10} a}$	*Solve for u.*
$\log_a x = \dfrac{\log_{10} x}{\log_{10} a}$	*Substitution*

Try this. What changes would you make in the above derivation to derive the other two change of base formulas?

▶ EQUATION OF A PARABOLA

Lesson 11.1, page 570

Using the geometric definition of a parabola and the distance formula, we can derive the equation of a parabola.

Definition: A parabola is the set of all points (x, y) that are equidistant from a fixed line, the directrix, and a fixed point, the focus.

Let the coordinates of the focus be $(0, p)$ and the equation of the directrix be $y = -p$ as in this diagram. Notice that $(0, 0)$ is p units from the focus and also p units from the directrix. Therefore $(0, 0)$ is on the parabola.

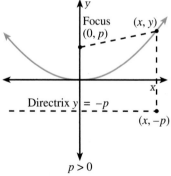

For any point (x, y) on the parabola,

distance from (x, y) to $(0, p)$ = distance from (x, y) to $y = -p$	*Definition of a parabola*
$\sqrt{(x - 0)^2 + (y - p)^2} = \sqrt{(x - x)^2 + (y - (-p))^2}$	*Distance formula*
$\sqrt{(x^2 + (y - p)^2)} = \sqrt{(y + p)^2}$	*Simplify.*
$x^2 + (y - p)^2 = (y + p)^2$	*Square both sides.*
$x^2 + y^2 - 2yp + p^2 = y^2 + 2yp + p^2$	*Multiply.*
$x^2 = 4yp$	*Subtract $y^2 - 2yp + p^2$ from both sides.*

848

In the diagram on the previous page, we assumed that p was positive. If p were negative, the focus would be below the x-axis and the directrix would be above it. However, there would be no change in the proof.

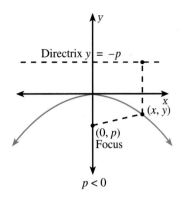

Directrix $y = -p$

(x, y)

$(0, p)$
Focus

$p < 0$

So, if p is positive in the equation $x^2 = 4py$, the parabola opens upward; if p is negative, it opens downward.

The proof that $y^2 = 4px$ is the equation of a parabola that opens to the left or right is similar to the proof on page 848.

Try this. Derive the formula for the set of all points (x, y) that are the same distance from $(0, 5)$ as they are from $y = -5$. Compare your derivation with each step in the proof on page 848.

▶ EQUATION OF AN ELLIPSE

Lesson 11.3, page 583

Using the geometric definition of an ellipse and the distance formula, we can derive the equation of an ellipse.

Definition: An ellipse is the set of all points (x, y) such that the sum of the distances between (x, y) and two distinct points, the foci, is a constant.

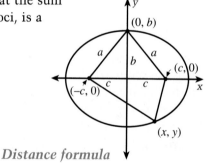

$(0, b)$

a b a

$(c, 0)$

$(-c, 0)$ c c x

(x, y)

Let the two foci have coordinates $(-c, 0)$ and $(c, 0)$. Let $(0, b)$ be the point where the ellipse intersects the positive y-axis. Let the distance from $(0, b)$ to each focus be a. Then the sum of the distances from any point (x, y) on the ellipse to the two foci must be $2a$. So,

$$\sqrt{(x - (-c))^2 + (y - 0)^2} + \sqrt{(x - c)^2 + (y - 0)^2} = 2a. \quad \textit{Distance formula}$$

By squaring both sides and simplifying, we can obtain

$$4a\sqrt{(x - c)^2 + y^2} = 4a^2 - 4cx.$$

Again, squaring both sides and simplifying, we can obtain

$$\frac{(a^2 - c^2)x^2}{a^2} + y^2 = a^2 - c^2.$$

Since a, b, and c are sides of a right triangle, $a^2 - c^2 = b^2$. Substituting, we obtain

$$\frac{b^2x^2}{a^2} + y^2 = b^2 \quad \text{or} \quad \frac{x^2}{a^2} + \frac{y^2}{b^2} = 1.$$

We now have the equation of an ellipse whose center is (0, 0). We know that the length of the vertical axis of the ellipse, the distance from (0, b) to (0, −b), is 2b. But what is the length of the other axis? Let (d, 0) be the intersection of the ellipse with the positive x-axis.

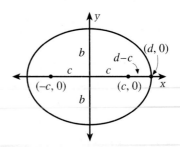

Then, distance from (d, 0) to (−c, 0) plus distance from (d, 0) to (c, 0) is 2a.

$$[c + c + (d - c)] + (d - c) = 2a$$
$$2d = 2a$$
$$d = a$$

Therefore, the ellipse intersects the x-axis at (−a, 0) and (a, 0) and the length of the horizontal axis of the ellipse is 2a.

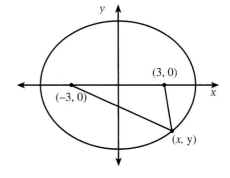

Try this. Derive the formula for the set of all points (x, y) such that the sum of the distances between (x, y) and the two points (−3, 0) and (3, 0) is 10. Compare your derivation with each step in the above proof.

▶ **EQUATION OF A HYPERBOLA**
Lesson 11.4, page 590

Using the geometric definition of a hyperbola and the distance formula, we can derive the equation of a hyperbola.

Definition: A hyperbola is the set of all points (x, y) such that the difference of the distances between (x, y) and two distinct points, the foci, is a constant.

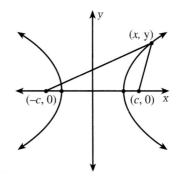

Let the two foci have coordinates (−c, 0) and (c, 0). Let 2a be the constant difference in distances.

Then,

$$\sqrt{(x - (-c))^2 + (y - 0)^2} - \sqrt{(x - c)^2 + (y - 0)^2} = \pm 2a.$$

Squaring both sides and simplifying, we can obtain

$$\frac{cx}{a} - a = \pm\sqrt{(x - c)^2 + y^2}.$$

Again, squaring both sides and simplifying we can obtain

$$\frac{(c^2 - a^2)x^2}{a^2} - y^2 = c^2 - a^2.$$

Let $b^2 = c^2 - a^2$ and substitute to obtain

$$\frac{b^2 x^2}{a^2} - y^2 = b^2 \quad \text{or} \quad \frac{x^2}{a^2} - \frac{y^2}{b^2} = 1.$$

This diagram shows how a, b, and c are related to the hyperbola. The vertices of the hyperbola are at $(a, 0)$ and $(-a, 0)$. The lines $y = \frac{b}{a}x$ and $y = -\frac{b}{a}x$ are the asymptotes of the hyperbola—the lines which the branches of the hyperbola approach.

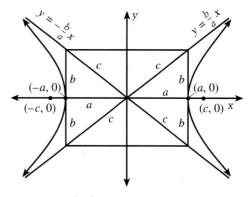

Try this. Derive the formula for the set of all points (x, y) such that the difference of the distances from (x, y) to the points $(5, 0)$ and $(-5, 0)$ is ± 10. Compare your derivation with each step in the above proof.

▶ FORMULA FOR THE SUM OF AN ARITHMETIC SERIES

Lesson 12.2, page 631

Think of an arithmetic series in geometric terms and think of a duplicate arithmetic series stacked on top as in the diagram. The height of each bar is $a_1 + a_n$ and there are n of them.

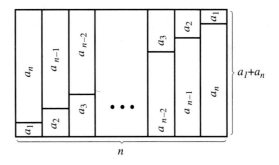

Algebraically we can write this as
$S_n = a_1 + (a_1 + d) + (a_1 + 2d) + \ldots + (a_1 + (n-1)d)$.

Each term is d larger than the previous one.

$S_n = a_n + (a_n - d) + (a_n - 2d) + \ldots + (a_n - (n-1)d)$

In reverse order, each term is d less than the previous one.

Adding we get
$2S_n = (a_1 + a_n) + (a_1 + a_n) + (a_1 + a_n) + \ldots + (a_1 + a_n)$.

Where the term $(a_1 + a_n)$ occurs n times.

Therefore, $2S_n = n(a_1 + a_n)$ or $S_n = \frac{n}{2}(a_1 + a_n)$.

Try this. Find the sum of this arithmetic series by using the techniques in the above derivation; that is by adding the series to itself with the order reversed.

$7 + 10 + 13 + \ldots + 178 + 181 + 184$ (60 terms)

▶ FORMULA FOR THE SUM OF A GEOMETRIC SERIES

Lesson 12.3, page 639

This derivation is similar to the one for an arithmetic series in that it adds two related series. However, it does not lend itself to a geometric representation.

In expanded form, the sum of a geometric series, S_n, is

$$S_n = a_1 + a_1 r + a_1 r^2 + \ldots + a_1 r^{n-2} + a_1 r^{n-1}.$$

Multiply both sides by $-r$ to obtain:

$$-rS_n = -a_1 r - a_1 r^2 - \ldots - a_1 r^{n-2} - a_1 r^{n-1} - a_1 r^n.$$

Adding gives:

$$S_n - rS_n = a_1 - a_1 r^n$$
$$S_n(1 - r) = a_1(1 - r^n)$$
$$S_n = a_1\left(\frac{1 - r^n}{1 - r}\right) \quad (r \neq 1).$$

Try this. Find the sum of the geometric series by using the techniques used in the above derivation; that is, multiply each term by -3, add the two series, etc.

$$2 + 6 + 18 + \ldots + 1458 + 4374 \text{ (8 terms)}$$

▶ **TRIGONOMETRIC PYTHAGOREAN IDENTITIES**

Lesson 13.1, page 680

The trigonometric Pythagorean Identities can be derived directly from the Pythagorean Theorem.

$a^2 + b^2 = c^2$

Since $\sin \theta = \frac{a}{c}$ and $\cos \theta = \frac{b}{c}$,

$$\sin^2 \theta + \cos^2 \theta = \left(\frac{a}{c}\right)^2 + \left(\frac{b}{c}\right)^2 = \frac{a^2 + b^2}{c^2} = \frac{c^2}{c^2} = 1.$$

Since $\tan \theta = \frac{a}{b}$ and $\sec \theta = \frac{c}{b}$,

$$1 + \tan^2 \theta = 1 + \left(\frac{a}{b}\right)^2 = \frac{b^2 + a^2}{b^2} = \frac{c^2}{b^2} = \left(\frac{c}{b}\right)^2 = \sec^2 \theta.$$

Try this. Use the definitions of $\cot \theta$ and $\csc \theta$ and the Pythagorean Theorem to show that $1 + \cot^2 \theta = \csc^2 \theta$.

▶ **LAW OF SINES**

Lesson 13.5, page 709

This law can be derived directly from the formula for the area of a triangle.

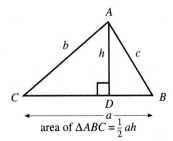

area of $\triangle ABC = \frac{1}{2}ah$

In $\triangle CAD$, $\sin C = \frac{h}{b}$. So, $h = b \sin C$. Therefore, area of $\triangle ABC = \frac{1}{2}ab \sin C$. In a similar manner, area of $\triangle ABC = \frac{1}{2}ac \sin B$ and area of $\triangle ABC = \frac{1}{2}bc \sin A$. Therefore, $\frac{1}{2}ab \sin C = \frac{1}{2}ac \sin B = \frac{1}{2}bc \sin A$. Multiplying by $\frac{2}{abc}$ gives $\frac{\sin C}{c} = \frac{\sin B}{b} = \frac{\sin A}{a}$.

Try this. Use the ideas in the proof on page 852 to find the area of this triangle.

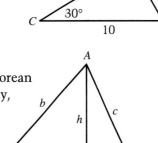

▶ **LAW OF COSINES**

Lesson 13.6, page 716

The Law of Cosines can be derived from the Pythagorean Theorem and the trigonometric Pythagorean Identity, $\sin^2 \theta + \cos^2 \theta = 1$.

Suppose that C is an acute angle as shown.

$$c^2 = h^2 + (a - x)^2$$

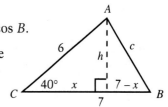

Since $\sin C = \frac{h}{b}$ and $\cos C = \frac{x}{b}$, $h = b \sin C$ and $x = b \cos C$. Substitute into the first equation to get $c^2 = (b \sin C)^2 + (a - b \cos C)^2$. Simplifying and replacing $\sin^2 C + \cos^2 C$ with 1 gives $c^2 = a^2 + b^2 - 2ab \cos C$.

The same result is obtained if C is an obtuse angle, and similar arguments establish that

$$a^2 = b^2 + c^2 - 2bc \cos A \quad \text{and} \quad b^2 = a^2 + c^2 - 2ac \cos B.$$

Try this. Given $\triangle ABC$ with $a = 7$, $b = 6$, and $C = 40°$, use the Pythagorean Theorem, $\sin^2 \theta + \cos^2 \theta = 1$, and the procedure used in the above derivation to show that

$$c^2 = 36 + 49 - 84 \cos 40°.$$

▶ **SUM AND DIFFERENCE FORMULAS**

Lesson 14.5, page 760

The formula for the cosine of the difference of two angles can be derived using the Law of Cosines, the distance formula, and the identity $\sin^2 \theta + \cos^2 \theta = 1$. The other sum and difference formulas can be derived from the formula for the cosine of the difference.

Draw two angles whose sides are the x-axis, as shown in the diagram. Let v be the measure of the smaller angle and u be the measure of the larger angle. Choose points P and Q on the sides of the angles so that they are each 1 unit from the origin. Then the sides of the right triangles have length $\sin v$, $\cos v$, $\sin u$ and $\cos u$ as labeled. Therefore, the coordinates of P are $(\cos v, \sin v)$ and the coordinates of Q are $(\cos u, \sin u)$.

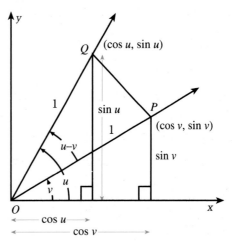

By the distance formula,

$$PQ = \sqrt{(\cos u - \cos v)^2 + (\sin u - \sin v)^2}.$$

By the Law of Cosines applied to $\triangle QOP$,

$$PQ^2 = 1^2 + 1^2 - 2(1)(1)\cos(u - v).$$

By squaring the first formula, substituting into the second one, and simplifying we can obtain

$$\cos(u - v) = \cos u \cos v + \sin u \sin v.$$

The same argument can be used for P and Q in any quadrants.

Try this. Derive the formula for the cosine of a sum of two angles by substituting $-v$ for v in the above formula and using the fact that $\cos(-v) = \cos v$ and $\sin(-v) = -\sin v$.

▶ SINE OF A SUM

Lesson 14.5, page 760

Since sine and cosine are cofunctions, $\sin\left(\frac{\pi}{2} - u\right) = \cos u$ and $\cos\left(\frac{\pi}{2} - u\right) = \sin u$.

$$
\begin{aligned}
\text{So, } \sin(u + v) &= \cos\left(\frac{\pi}{2} - (u + v)\right) \\
&= \cos\left(\left(\frac{\pi}{2} - u\right) - v\right) \\
&= \cos\left(\frac{\pi}{2} - u\right)\cos v + \sin\left(\frac{\pi}{2} - u\right)\sin v \quad \textit{Cosine of a difference} \\
&= \sin u \cos v + \cos u \sin v.
\end{aligned}
$$

Try this.

1. Derive the formula for the sine of a difference of two angles by replacing v in the above formula by $-v$.

2. Derive the formulas for the tangent of a sum and difference of two angles from the sine and cosine formulas and the fact that $\tan \theta = \frac{\sin \theta}{\cos \theta}$.

▶ DOUBLE-ANGLE FORMULAS

Lesson 14.6, page 766

The double-angle formulas are obtained from the sum formulas. In the formula for the cosine of the sum of two angles:

$$\cos(u + v) = \cos u \cos v - \sin u \sin v,$$

replace v by u:

$$
\begin{aligned}
\cos(u + u) &= \cos u \cos u - \sin u \sin u \\
\cos 2u &= \cos^2 u - \sin^2 u.
\end{aligned}
$$

Try this. Use the formula on page 854 and $\sin^2 u + \cos^2 u = 1$ to derive the other two formulas for $\cos 2u$. Derive the formulas for $\sin 2u$ and $\tan 2u$ from the sum formulas.

▶ HALF-ANGLE FORMULAS

Lesson 14.6, page 767

The half-angle formulas are obtained from the double-angle formulas. In the formula for $\cos 2u$:

$$\cos 2u = 2\cos^2 u - 1$$

replace $2u$ by u and replace u by $\frac{u}{2}$.

$$\cos u = 2\cos^2 \frac{u}{2} - 1$$

$$\cos^2 \frac{u}{2} = \frac{\cos u + 1}{2}$$

$$\cos \frac{u}{2} = \pm\sqrt{\frac{\cos u + 1}{2}}$$

Try this.

1. Derive the formula for $\sin \frac{u}{2}$ from the formula $\cos 2u = 1 - 2\sin^2 u$.

2. When deriving $\tan \frac{u}{2}$ from $\sin \frac{u}{2}$ and $\cos \frac{u}{2}$ we get

$$\tan \frac{u}{2} = \pm\sqrt{\frac{1 - \cos u}{1 + \cos u}}.$$

First, simplify this radical by multiplying numerator and denominator of the fraction by $1 + \cos u$. Then, simplify this radical by multiplying the numerator and denominator of the fraction by $1 - \cos u$.

Keystrokes for page 17

You can use your graphing calculator as a programmable calculator. This means you can *write*, *store*, and *execute* programs using your calculator. For example, you can write a program that calculates the volume of a right circular cylinder. The formula for the volume is

$V = \pi r^2 h$

where r is the radius and h is the height.

The following programs use a Texas Instruments *TI-82*, a Casio *fx-9700GE*, and a Sharp *EL-9300C* to find the volume of a right circular cylinder. When you execute, or run, the programs, you will be prompted to enter the radius and height of a cylinder. The program will then calculate the cylinder's volume.

TI-82	**Casio *fx-9700GE***	**Sharp *EL-9300C***
PROGRAM:VOLUME	VOLUME	volume
:Disp "ENTER RADIUS"	"ENTER RADIUS"	——————REAL
:Input R	?→R	Print "enter radius"
:Disp "ENTER HEIGHT"	"ENTER HEIGHT"	Input r
:Input H	?→H	Print "enter height"
:$\pi * R^2 * H{\rightarrow}V$	$\pi * R^2 * H{\rightarrow}V$	Input h
:Disp "THE VOLUME IS"	"THE VOLUME IS"	$v = \pi r^2 h$
:Disp V	V	Print "the volume is"
		Print v

Exercises

1. Enter a program listed above on your graphing calculator. (See your owner's manual to learn how to enter a program.) Then use the program to find the volume of several cylinders, including the one shown below.

2. Write a graphing calculator program that calculates the volume of a rectangular prism. Then use the program to find the volume of several prisms, including the one shown below.

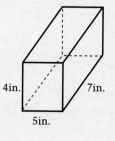

Keystrokes for page 84

A graphing calculator can be used to sketch the graph of an equation. Here we show how to use a Texas Instruments *TI-82*, a Casio *fx-9700GE*, and a Sharp *EL-9300C* to sketch the graph of $x + 2y = 4$.

Using a graphing calculator is fairly easy, but you must remember four things:

- Set the calculator mode to rectangular.
- Solve the equation for y in terms of x.
- Set the viewing window (the range) by entering the least and greatest x- and y-values and the scale (units per tick mark).
- Use parentheses if you are unsure of the calculator's order of operations.

Before sketching the graph of the equation, solve the equation for y: $y = -\frac{1}{2}x + 2$.

Graph of $x + 2y = 4$

Xmin=−10	Ymin=−10
Xmax=10	Ymax=10
Xscl=1	Yscl=1

TI-82

WINDOW ▽ (Set window.)

Y= CLEAR

((−) 1 ÷ 2) X,T,θ + 2

GRAPH   CLEAR (Clear screen.)

Sharp *EL-9300C*

⌐⌐ RANGE (Set range.)

QUIT CL

((−) 1 ÷ 2) X/θ/T + 2 ⌐⌐

QUIT (Clear screen.)

Casio *fx-9700GE*

In MAIN MENU, enter 1.

Range (Set range.) EXIT

SHIFT F5 EXE

Graph

((−) 1 ÷ 2) X,θ,T + 2

EXE

SHIFT F5 EXE (Clear screen.)

If you want a closeup view of the point where the line $y = -\frac{1}{2}x + 2$ crosses the x-axis, you could enter a new range setting to obtain the graph shown at the right.

Xmin=−1	Ymin=−1
Xmax=5	Ymax=3
Xscl=1	Yscl=1

Refer to page 85 for an example of using a graphing calculator to approximate the solution of an equation and for related exercises.

Keystrokes for page 128

A graphing calculator can be used to graph a system of equations. Here we show how to use a *TI-82*, a Casio *fx-9700GE*, and a Sharp *EL-9300C* to graph the following system.

$$\begin{cases} 3x - 4y = 2 & \textbf{Equation 1} \\ 5x + 6y = 16 & \textbf{Equation 2} \end{cases}$$

The display at the right shows the graph of the system. Note that the two lines appear to intersect at the point (2, 1). To check this, substitute 2 for x and 1 for y in each equation.

The first step in using a graphing calculator to sketch the graph of a linear system is to solve each equation for y.

$$\begin{cases} y = \frac{3}{4}x - \frac{1}{2} & \textbf{Equation 1} \\ y = -\frac{5}{6}x + \frac{8}{3} & \textbf{Equation 2} \end{cases}$$

Next find a window setting that shows the point of intersection. For this particular system, use the window setting shown at the right.

TI-82

WINDOW ▽ (Set window.)

Y= CLEAR

(3 ÷ 4) X,T,θ − (1 ÷ 2)

ENTER CLEAR

((−) 5 ÷ 6) X,T,θ + (8 ÷ 3)

GRAPH

CLEAR (Clear screen.)

Casio *fx-9700GE*

In MAIN MENU, enter 1.

Range (Set range.) EXIT

SHIFT F5 EXE

Graph

(3 ÷ 4) X,θ,T − (1 ÷ 2) EXE

Graph

((−) 5 ÷ 6) X,θ,T + (8 ÷ 3) EXE

SHIFT F5 EXE (Clear screen.)

Sharp *EL-9300C*

⌐┴ RANGE (Set range.)

QUIT CL

(3 ÷ 4) X/θ/T − (1 ÷ 2)

ENTER CL

((−) 5 ÷ 6) X/θ/T + (8 ÷ 3)

⌐┴ QUIT (Clear screen.)

Refer to page 129 for an example of using a graphing calculator to approximate the solution of a linear system and for related exercises.

Keystrokes for page 194

Most graphing calculators can perform matrix algebra. That is, they can add, subtract, and multiply matrices, multiply a matrix by a scalar, find the determinant of a matrix, and find the inverse of a matrix. (The inverse of a matrix is introduced in Lesson 4.4.) Here we show how to use a Texas Instruments *TI-82*, a Casio *fx-9700GE*, and a Sharp *EL-9300C* to perform the following matrix operation.

$$\begin{bmatrix} 5 & -1 & 0 \\ 7 & 2 & -1 \end{bmatrix} + \begin{bmatrix} 2 & 0 & -2 \\ 1 & -2 & -4 \end{bmatrix} = \begin{bmatrix} 7 & -1 & -2 \\ 8 & 0 & -5 \end{bmatrix}$$

TI-82

$\boxed{MATRX}$

Cursor to EDIT, $\boxed{1}$

2 $\boxed{ENTER}$ 3 $\boxed{ENTER}$

Input 1st matrix in [A].
[A] 2 × 3
1,1=5   2,1=7
1,2=−1 2,2=2
1,3=0   2,3=−1

$\boxed{MATRX}$

Cursor to edit, $\boxed{2}$

2 $\boxed{ENTER}$ 3 $\boxed{ENTER}$

Input 2nd matrix in [B].
[B] 2 × 3
1,1=2   2,1=1
1,2=0   2,2=−2
1,3=−2 2,3=−4

$\boxed{2nd}$ $\boxed{QUIT}$

$\boxed{MATRX}$ $\boxed{1}$ $\boxed{+}$ $\boxed{MATRX}$ $\boxed{2}$

$\boxed{ENTER}$

Display will be
[[7 −1 −2]
[8   0 −5]]

Casio *fx-9700GE*

In MAIN MENU, enter 5.

$\boxed{F4}$ $\boxed{F2}$ 2 $\boxed{EXE}$ 3

$\boxed{EXIT}$ $\boxed{F1}$

Input 1st matrix in [A].

$\boxed{EXIT}$ Cursor to Mat B.

$\boxed{F2}$ 2 $\boxed{EXE}$ 3

$\boxed{EXIT}$ $\boxed{F1}$

Input 2nd matrix in [B].

$\boxed{EXIT}$ $\boxed{EXIT}$

$\boxed{F1}$ $\boxed{ALPHA}$ $\boxed{A}$ $\boxed{+}$

$\boxed{F1}$ $\boxed{ALPHA}$ $\boxed{B}$ $\boxed{EXE}$

Display will be

Ans	1	2	3
1	7	−1	−2
2	8	0	−5

Sharp *EL-9300C*

$\boxed{⊞}$ $\boxed{MENU}$ $\boxed{3}$

$\boxed{MENU}$ Cursor to C DIM.

$\boxed{ENTER}$ $\boxed{ENTER}$

2 $\boxed{ENTER}$ 3 $\boxed{ENTER}$

Input 1st matrix in [A].
A[1,1]=5   A[2,1]=7
A[1,2]=−1 A[2,2]=2
A[1,3]=0   A[2,3]=−1

$\boxed{MENU}$ $\boxed{ENTER}$

Cursor to matrix B. $\boxed{ENTER}$

2 $\boxed{ENTER}$ 3 $\boxed{ENTER}$

Input 2nd matrix in [B].
B[1,1]=2   B[2,1]=1
B[1,2]=0   B[2,2]=−2
B[1,3]=−2 B[2,3]=−4

$\boxed{QUIT}$

$\boxed{2nd\,F}$ $\boxed{MAT}$ $\boxed{A}$ $\boxed{+}$

$\boxed{2nd\,F}$ $\boxed{MAT}$ $\boxed{B}$ $\boxed{ENTER}$

Display will be
Ans [1, 1]=7
Ans [2, 1]=8

Cursor to see entire display.

Refer to page 195 for an example of using a graphing calculator to solve problems involving matrices and for related graphing exercises.

Keystrokes for page 205

Example 2

Use a matrix equation and a graphing calculator to solve the linear system.

$$\begin{cases} 2x + 3y + z = -1 \\ 3x + 3y + z = 1 \\ 2x + 4y + z = -2 \end{cases}$$

Solution The matrix equation that represents the system is

$$\underbrace{\begin{bmatrix} 2 & 3 & 1 \\ 3 & 3 & 1 \\ 2 & 4 & 1 \end{bmatrix}}_{A} \underbrace{\begin{bmatrix} x \\ y \\ z \end{bmatrix}}_{X} = \underbrace{\begin{bmatrix} -1 \\ 1 \\ -2 \end{bmatrix}}_{B}.$$

Using a graphing calculator, you can find the inverse of the matrix A to be

$$A^{-1} = \begin{bmatrix} -1 & 1 & 0 \\ -1 & 0 & 1 \\ 6 & -2 & -3 \end{bmatrix}.$$

To find the solution, multiply B (on the left) by A^{-1}.

$$X = A^{-1}B = \begin{bmatrix} -1 & 1 & 0 \\ -1 & 0 & 1 \\ 6 & -2 & -3 \end{bmatrix} \begin{bmatrix} -1 \\ 1 \\ -2 \end{bmatrix} = \begin{bmatrix} 2 \\ -1 \\ -2 \end{bmatrix} = \begin{bmatrix} x \\ y \\ z \end{bmatrix}$$

The solution $x = 2$, $y = -1$, and $z = -2$. ■

The keystrokes for the *TI-82*, the Casio *fx-9700GE*, and the Sharp *EL-9300C* for Example 2 are given below.

TI-82

Enter matrix A in [A] and matrix B in [B]. (See p. 859.)

| MATRX | 1 | x^{-1} |

| MATRX | 2 | ENTER |

Casio *fx-9700GE*

In matrix mode, enter matrix A in [A] and matrix B in [B]. (See p. 859.)

Sharp *EL-9300C*

In matrix mode, enter matrix A in [A] and matrix B in [B]. (See p. 859.)

Refer to Exercises on page 207 and 208 for practice using a graphing calculator to solve linear systems.

Keystrokes for page 266

If you have a graphing calculator, you can write a program that will find the real solutions of a quadratic equation. The following programs for the *TI-82*, the Casio *fx-9700GE*, and the Sharp *EL-9300C* will find the real solutions of the quadratic equation $ax^2 + bx + c = 0$.

TI-82

```
PROGRAM:QUADRTIC            :Goto 1
:Disp "Enter A"            :(−B+√D)/(2A)→S
:Input A                   :Disp S
:Disp "ENTER B"           :(−B−√D)/(2A)→S
:Input B                   :Disp S
:Disp "ENTER C"           :Stop
:Input C                   :Lbl 1
:B²−4AC→D                  :Disp "NO REAL SOLUTION"
:If D<0                    :Stop
```

Casio *fx-9700GE*

```
QUADRATIC                 S◢
"A="?→A                   (−B−√D)÷(2A)→S
"B="?→B                   S
"C="?→C                   Goto 2
B²−4AC→D                  Lbl 1
D<0⇒Goto 1                "NO REAL SOLUTION"
(−B+√D)÷(2A)→S            Lbl 2
```

Sharp *EL-9300C*

```
quadratic                 s=(−b+√d)/(2a)
───────────────REAL       Print s
Input a                   s=(−b−√d)/(2a)
Input b                   Print s
Input c                   End
d=b²−4a∗c                 Label 1
If d<0 Goto 1             Print "no real solutions"
```

Refer to page 266 for an example of using a graphing calculator to find real solutions of a quadratic equation. Also, refer to exercises on pages 268 and 269 for practice.

Keystrokes for page 389

Example 2: Finding a Mathematical Model

Most graphing calculators can fit power models of the form $y = ax^b$ to data. For instance, the *TI-82*, the Casio *fx-9700GE*, and the Sharp *EL-9300C* all have this capability programmed into their statistical features. Use a graphing calculator to find a model that relates the diameter, y (in inches), to the length, x (in inches), of a common nail.

Length, *x*	1.00	2.00	3.00	4.00	5.00	6.00
Diameter, *y*	0.070	0.111	0.146	0.176	0.204	0.231

Solution To solve this problem, enter the keystrokes shown below.

TI-82

STAT 4 2nd L1 ,
2nd L2 ENTER
STAT 1

Enter data.

L1(1)=1 L2(1)=.070
L1(2)=2 L2(2)=.111
L1(3)=3 L2(3)=.146
L1(4)=4 L2(4)=.176
L1(5)=5 L2(5)=.204
L1(6)=6 L2(6)=.231

STAT Cursor to CALC.
ALPHA B
2nd L1 , 2nd L2
ENTER

Casio *fx-9700GE*

In MAIN MENU, enter 4.

F2 F3 F1
SHIFT SET UP

Cursor to STAT GRAPH. F2
Cursor to REG MODEL. F4

EXIT

Enter data.

1   F3 .070 F1
2   F3 .111 F1
3   F3 .146 F1
4   F3 .176 F1
5   F3 .204 F1
6   F3 .231 F1

F6 F6
F1 EXE
F2 EXE

Sharp *EL-9300C*

≡ MENU
D 2
ENTER 3

Enter data.

X1=1   Y1=.070
X2=2   Y2=.111
X3=3   Y3=.146
X4=4   Y4=.176
X5=5   Y5=.204
X6=6   Y6=.231

2nd ⋯
F 5
MENU ENTER

From each display, you obtain $a \approx 0.07$ and $b \approx 0.66$. Because $2/3 \approx 0.66$, you can write the following model.

$$y = 0.07x^{2/3}$$

Refer to Exercise 5 on page 389 for a related graphing exercise.

Keystrokes for page 700

The following programs for the *TI-82* and the Casio *fx-9700GE* are angle drawing programs. When you run the program, you are prompted to enter an angle. The calculator then draws the angle in standard position. The point of the terminal side of the angle lies on the unit circle. The coordinates of the endpoint are $(x, y) = (\cos \theta, \sin \theta)$.

TI-82

PROGRAM:ANGLE	$:-1.5 \to$ Xmin	$:1 \to$ S
:Disp "ENTER MODE"	$:1.5 \to$ Xmax	:If T<0
:Disp "0, RADIAN"	$:1 \to$ Xscl	$:-1 \to$ S
:Disp "1, DEGREE"	$:-1 \to$ Ymin	:"(.25+.04T)cos T" $\to X_{1T}$
:Input M	$:1 \to$ Ymax	:"S(.25+0.4T)sin T" $\to Y_{1T}$
:Disp "ENTER ANGLE"	$:1 \to$ Yscl	:DispGraph
:Input T	$:0 \to$ Tmin	:Line(0,0,A,B)
:If M=1	:abs T $\to$ Tmax	:Pause
$:\pi$T/180 $\to$ T	$:.1 \to$ Tstep	:Func
:Radian	:cos T $\to$ A	:FnOn
:ClrDraw	:sin T $\to$ B	:Stop
:FnOff	:Param	

Casio *fx-9700GE*

ANGLE	Range $-1.5,1.5,1,-1,1,1,0$,Abs T,.15
Lbl 1	cosT $\to$ A
"ENTER MODE"	sinT $\to$ B
"0=RADIAN"	$1 \to$ S
"1=DEGREE"	T<0 $\Rightarrow -1 \to$ S
? $\to$ M	Graph(X,Y)=((.25+.04T)cos T,S (.25+.04T)sin T)
"ENTER ANGLE"	Plot 0,0
? $\to$ T	Plot A,B
M=1 $\Rightarrow \pi$T$\div$180 $\to$ T	Line
Rad	Goto 1
Cls	

Note: Before running the program, set the calculator in parametric mode. To do so, enter the following keystrokes.

In MAIN MENU, enter 1. | SHIFT | | SET UP | | F3 | | EXIT |

Refer to Exercises 1–4 on page 701 for practice using this program.

Keystrokes for page 701

Another nice use of a graphing calculator is to sketch a graph of the unit circle using the calculator's *parametric* mode. The keystrokes listed below show how to sketch the graph of the unit circle using a *TI-82*, a Casio *fx-9700GE*, and a Sharp *EL-9300C*.

The graph of the unit circle is shown at the right. Remember, after graphing the unit circle, change the calculator back to *function* mode.

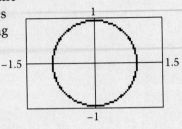

TI-82

MODE Cursor to Radian. ENTER

Cursor to Par. ENTER

WINDOW ▽ (Set window.)

Tmin=0	Xmin=−1.5	Ymin=−1
Tmax=6.3	Xmax=1.5	Ymax=1
Tstep=.031416	Xscl=1	Yscl=1

Y= CLEAR

COS X,T,θ

ENTER CLEAR

SIN X,T,θ

GRAPH

Sharp *EL-9300C*

↲ SET UP

ALPHA B 2

ALPHA E 3 QUIT

RANGE (Set range.)

Tmin=0	Xmin=−1.5	Ymin=−1
Tmax=6.3	Xmax=1.5	Ymax=1
Tstp=Do not set.	Xscl=1	Yscl=1

QUIT MENU 1 CL

cos X/θ/T ENTER

CL sin X/θ/T

↲

Casio *fx-9700GE*

In MAIN MENU, enter 1.

SHIFT SET UP F3 EXIT

SHIFT DRG F2 EXE

Range (Set range.)

Xmin:−1.7	Ymin:−1
Xmax:1.7	Ymax:1
Xscale:1	Yscale:1

EXE (or cursor down)

T,θ

   min:0

   max:6.3

   pitch:0.031416

EXIT

Graph

cos X,θ,T SHIFT , sin X,θ,T) EXE

Refer to Exercises 5–10 on page 701 for practice using this feature.

Keystrokes for page 802

Most graphing calculators, such as the *TI-82*, the Casio *fx-9700GE*, and the Sharp *EL-9300C*, have a random number generator that can be used to perform probability experiments. Each time the random number generator is used, it selects a number between 0 and 1. (The number selected is greater than 0 and less than 1.) If you want the calculator to randomly select an integer x, such that $n \leq x \leq m$, you must follow an algorithm similar to the one shown below.

Integer Part of $[(m - n + 1) \times (\text{random number}) + 1]$

For example, to generate a random number between 1 and 6, enter the following keystrokes on your calculator.

TI-82: MATH ▷ 2 (6 MATH ◁ 1 + 1) ENTER

Casio *fx-9700GE*: SHIFT MATH F3 F2 (6 SHIFT MATH F2 F4 + 1) EXE

Sharp *EL-9300C*: MATH 3 (6 MATH 8 + 1) ENTER

Often when performing probability experiments, you want to generate many random numbers. This is a simple task when using the programming features of a graphing calculator. For example, each program listed below simulates the roll of a six-sided die. Every time you press enter, the program generates a number between 1 and 6.

TI-82	Casio *fx-9700GE*	Sharp *EL-9300C*
PROGRAM:RANDOM	RANDOM	random
:Lbl 1	Lbl 1	——————REAL
:iPart (6rand+1)→X	Int (6Ran#+1)→X	Label 1
:Disp X	X◢	X=ipart (6random+1)
:Pause	Goto 1	Print X
:Goto 1		Wait
		Goto 1

To exit the program enter ON 2.	To exit the program, enter AC$^{/ON}$ AC$^{/ON}$.	To exit the program, enter ON CL.

Refer to pages 802 and 803 for an example of using these programs to generate random numbers and for related exercises.

TECHNOLOGY APPENDIX

USING THE COMMUNICATION LINK

The *TI-82,* the Casio *fx-9700GE,* and the Sharp *EL-9300C* all have a port that allows you to communicate, or link, with a similar calculator. That is, this feature allows you to send and receive programs, data, and other information to and from a calculator of the same type. Instructions for using the communication link to send and receive a program are given below.

TI-82

The link port is located at the bottom center of the calculator. Insert the link cable in each calculator port.

To send a program:

$\boxed{2nd}$ $\boxed{LINK}$ $\boxed{2}$ Cursor to program

name. $\boxed{\triangleright}$ $\boxed{ENTER}$

To receive a program:

$\boxed{2nd}$ $\boxed{LINK}$ $\boxed{\triangleright}$ $\boxed{ENTER}$

Casio *fx-9700GE*

The link port is located at the bottom right of the calculator. Turn both calculators off and insert the link port in each calculator. Turn the calculators on.

To send a program:

In *MAIN MENU,* enter $\boxed{B}$.

$\boxed{F1}$ Cursor to program. $\boxed{EXE}$

$\boxed{F2}$ Cursor to program name. $\boxed{EXE}$

To receive a program:

In *MAIN MENU,* enter $\boxed{ALPHA}$ $\boxed{B}$.

$\boxed{F2}$ Cursor to program. $\boxed{EXE}$

$\boxed{F2}$ Cursor to empty program location.

$\boxed{EXE}$

Note: The parameters of both calculators must be identical. To determine the parameters, press $\boxed{F6}$. Change as necessary.

Sharp *EL-9300C*

The link port is located at the bottom center of the calculator. Insert the link cable in each calculator port.

To send a program:

$\boxed{:\!\mathbb{Z}}$ $\boxed{2ndF}$ $\boxed{OPTION}$

$\boxed{G}$ $\boxed{ENTER}$

$\boxed{ENTER}$ Cursor to program name.

$\boxed{ENTER}$

To receive a program:

$\boxed{:\!\mathbb{Z}}$ $\boxed{2ndF}$ $\boxed{OPTION}$

$\boxed{G}$ $\boxed{ENTER}$

$\boxed{C}$ $\boxed{ENTER}$

Use with Lesson 5.4, pp. 252–257

Some graphing calculators can be used to solve equations with tables. The following shows how to use the table features of a Texas Instruments *TI-82* and a Casio *fx-9700GE* to solve the equation

$$-2x^2 + 4x + 7 = 0.$$

X	Y1	
-5	-63	
-4	-41	
-3	-23	
-2	-9	
-1	1	
0	7	
1	9	

X= -5

TI-82

| Y= | | CLEAR |

| (−) | 2 | X,T,θ | x² | + | 4 | X,T,θ | + | 7 |

| 2nd | | TblSet |

   TblMin = −5

    △Tbl = 1

   Indpnt: Auto

   Depend: Auto

| 2nd | | TABLE |

A possible table is shown above. Use $\triangle$ and $\triangledown$ to scroll through the table. A solution occurs when the *y*-value is 0. From the table, it appears that one solution occurs when *x* is between −2 and −1. Alter the table by changing TblMin to −2 and △Tbl to 0.1. Continue to alter TblMin and △Tbl until you can approximate the solution *x* = −1.121 (accurate to three decimal places).

Casio *fx-9700GE*

In MAIN MENU, enter 8.

| F1 | F1 | F1 | (Clears any functions.)

| (−) | 2 | X,θ,T | x² | + | 4 | X,θ,T | + | 7 |

| F2 | (RANGE)

   Start: −5

   End : 10

   Pitch: 1

| F1 |

A possible table is shown above. Use $\triangle$ and $\triangledown$ to scroll through the table. A solution occurs when the *y*-value is 0. From the table, it appears that one solution occurs when *x* is between −2 and −1. Alter the table by changing the Start to −2, End to −1, and Pitch to 0.1. (To do so, enter | F2 | F2 |.) Continue to alter the Start, End, and Pitch until you can approximate the solution *x* = −1.121 (accurate to three decimal places).

Exercises

1. Find the second solution to the equation $-2x^2 + 4x + 7 = 0$.

In Exercises 2–4, use a table to find the solutions to the equation. Each equation has two solutions. Your solution should be accurate to three decimal places.

2. $3x^2 + 4x - 5$

3. $-5x^2 - 7x + 3$

4. $0.25x^2 - 2x - 1$

CHAPTER 1

■ 1.1 Communicating About Algebra p. 5
A. ≈483,516   **B.** ≈2,752,294 barrels of oil

■ 1.1 Guided Practice p. 6
1. Neither, yes   **2.** See page 2.   **3.** d, $\frac{1}{4}$ is not an integer.
4. d, On a number line, 16 is not to the right of 16.   **5.** a,
c, b is not true because $(8 - 3) - 2 \neq 8 - (3 - 2)$, d is not
true because $(12 \div 6) \div 2 \neq 12 \div (6 \div 2)$.   **6.** $\frac{\text{dollars}}{\text{square foot}}$,
The other units cancel.

■ 1.1 Independent Practice pp. 6–8
7. $\frac{1}{2}$

9. $\sqrt{3}$

11. $\sqrt{5}$

13. $9, 1, \frac{1}{3}, -\sqrt{3}, -4$ **15.** $4, \frac{3}{2}, 0, -\sqrt{5}, -\frac{5}{2}$
17. Associative for x **19.** Commutative for +
21. Inverse for +   **23.** Left distributive   **25.** 59   **27.** −24
29. 24   **31.** 6   **33.** George Halas, Don Shula, Tom Landry,
Earl Lambeau, Paul Brown, Chuck Noll, Bud Grant,
Chuck Knox, Steve Owen, Hank Stram. Halas   **35.** 75°F;
−15°F

■ 1.1 Integrated Review p. 8
37. Rational   **39.** Irrational   **41.** <   **43.** <   **45.** −14
47. $\sqrt{5}$ **49.** $-\frac{1}{31}$ **51.** $-\frac{7}{5}$ **53.** 73.3 feet per second

■ 1.2 Communicating About Algebra p. 11

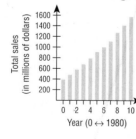

■ 1.2 Guided Practice p. 12
1. Answers vary; x^2, $|x|$ **2.** Terms are parts of an
expression that are added, factors are multiplied.   **3.** $6x^3$,
$-17x, 5$ **4.** $10, x, y$ **5.** Square the sum of x cubed and 1.
6. $3 - 8^2 \div 4 + 1$
$$\underset{3^{rd}}{\uparrow}\ \underset{1^{st}}{\uparrow}\ \underset{2^{nd}}{\uparrow}\ \underset{4^{th}}{\uparrow}$$

■ 1.2 Independent Practice pp. 12–13
7. −2   **9.** 66   **11.** 65   **13.** 2.8   **15.** 3   **17.** 14   **19.** 18
21. 77.72   **23.** 248.25   **25.** y^2 **27.** x^3 **29.** z^6 **31.** 144
33. 40   **35.** 1100   **37.** 4   **39.** 24   **41.** 24   **43.** −138
45. $\frac{1}{2}n(10 + n), 3600$ **47.** $(x + y)^2, 169$ **49.** $51,400
51. $\frac{A}{P} = \frac{2.2t + 25}{2.6t + 29}$ **53.** 1,162,500

■ 1.2 Integrated Review p. 14
55. 3.05   **57.** 17.59   **59.** 8052   **61.** 36 cm³
63. ≈113.10 ft³   **65.** b

■ 1.2 Mixed Review p. 15
1. $\frac{1}{4}$ **3.** $\frac{1}{6}$ **5.** 4.9   **7.** 5   **9.** 31.25   **11.** 16   **13.** 6
15. $-3, -2, 0, 1, 3$ **17.** No   **19.** 2^2x^3

■ 1.3 Communicating About Algebra p. 20
46; Use the verbal model in Example 5 and the 1-week
earnings of 318.50 to write the equation: $6.50(40) +$
$1.5(6.50)(t - 40) = 318.50$, then solve the equation.

■ 1.3 Guided Practice p. 21
1. No   **2.** Yes   **3.** c; −2 is a solution of the new equation
but is not a solution of the original equation   **4.** yes,
$2x + 9 = 1$ is equivalent to $2x = -8$, which is equivalent
to $x = -4$

■ 1.3 Independent Practice pp. 21–23
5. Subtract 8.   **7.** Multiply by $-\frac{2}{5}$.   **9.** Multiply by 3.
11. It is.   **13.** It is not.   **15.** It is.   **17.** $\frac{1}{2}$ **19.** 2   **21.** $\frac{1}{2}$
23. 4   **25.** −18   **27.** 32   **29.** −10   **31.** −12   **33.** $\frac{13}{4}$
35. $\frac{8}{7}$ **37.** $\frac{4}{7}$ **39.** 0   **41.** 36 by 14   **43.** 12   **45.** 50
47. 10,000   **49.** −109.3°F

■ 1.3 Integrated Review p. 23
51. −24   **53.** −23   **55.** −26   **57.** $-x + 12$
59. $36x + 107$ **61.** $3x + 4$ **63.** e

■ 1.4 Communicating About Algebra p. 26
A. 18.0 ft, The exterior dining room wall is the
hypotenuse of an isosceles right triangle as indicated in
the diagram. If each leg is a, then $a^2 + a^2 = x^2$ and
$a = \frac{\sqrt{2}x}{2}$. Then the distance between opposite walls is
$\left(\frac{\sqrt{2}x}{2} + x + \frac{\sqrt{2}x}{2}\right)$ ft.   **B.** 1570 ft²

1.4 Guided Practice p. 27

1. Boxes sold = 6
   Price per box = 2.60   (dollars per box)
   Total sales = 130   (dollars)
   Boxes to be sold = x
2. $6(2.60) + x(2.60) = 130$ **3.** 44 **4.** 44

1.4 Independent Practice pp. 27–29

5. Distance traveled = 547   (km)
   Rate of boat = 32   (km per hour)
   Time traveled = t (hours)
7. ≈ 17.1
9. Your rate = 5.5   (yards per second)
   Your time = t (seconds)
   Opponent's rate = 5   (yards per second)
   Opponent's time = $t + 16$ (seconds)
11. 160 **13.** $83\frac{1}{3}$ mph **15.** 1st: \$60, others: \$40 **17.** ≈ 0.79

1.4 Integrated Review p. 29

19. meters **21.** feet **23.** yards **25.** ≈ 13.9 **27.** ≈ -0.25
29. 1.5

1.4 Mid-Chapter Self-Test p. 30

1. $-3, -2, -\frac{3}{2}, 0, \frac{1}{2}, 3, 4$ **2.** -2 **3.** $-\frac{4}{9}$ **4.** 0 **5.** 7
6. 12 **7.** -20 **8.** 2 **9.** $\frac{5}{8}$ **10.** $\frac{5}{3}$ **11.** 34.58 **12.** 0.59
13. -4 **14.** 2 **15.** $\frac{5}{2}$ **16.** 4 **17.** 9 cm^2 **18.** $\approx 86 \text{ ft}^2$
19. 6 ft^2 **20.** 1996

1.5 Communicating About Algebra p. 33

Hands on experiment

1.5 Guided Practice p. 34

1. a, $t = \frac{20}{s}$ **2.** b; b, length of the side of the base, h,
height **3.** c; r, radius of the base, h, height **4.** a; r, radius

1.5 Independent Practice pp. 34–36

5. b; a, length of the major axis, b, length of the minor
axis **7.** c; b, length of the base, h, height **9.** d; b, length
of the base, h, height **11.** $h = \frac{V}{\pi r^2}$ **13.** $r = \frac{C}{2\pi}$
15. $b_2 = \frac{2A}{h} - b_1$ **17.** $F = \frac{9}{5}C + 32$ **19.** $P = \frac{A}{1 + rt}$
21. $p = \frac{A}{2\pi w}$; ≈ 1.8 cm **23.** $r = \frac{P - 2x}{2\pi t}$; ≈ 5.6 ft
25. 1314 gal **27.** 26.28

1.5 Integrated Review p. 36

29. -6 **31.** 4 **33.** 3 **35.** 13 **37.** 940 **39.** $\frac{61}{5}$

1.6 Communicating About Algebra p. 40

A. $x \le \frac{5}{3}$

B. $x \ge 3$

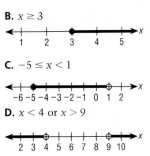

C. $-5 \le x < 1$

D. $x < 4$ or $x > 9$

1.6 Guided Practice p. 41

1. $x \le -5$ **2.** $-2 \le x < 7$ **3.** False for multiplying by 0
4. All real numbers greater than -1
5.

6.

1.6 Independent Practice pp. 41–42

7. $x < 9$ **9.** $4 < x < 6$ **11.** c **13.** d **15.** It is not.
17. It is. **19.** It is. **21.** $t > \frac{2}{3}$ **23.** $k > 5$ **25.** $h \ge 3$
27. $0 \le x \le 9$ **29.** $-\frac{10}{3} \le x \le -\frac{5}{3}$ **31.** $-2 \le x < 1$
33. $-1 \le r \le 0$

35. $x < 4$ or $x \ge 10$

37. $m \le -\frac{7}{2}$ or $m > 1$

39. $0 \le n \le 2160$
41. $2 \le x \le 7$

43. $10,000 \le b \le 120,000$ **45.** If you scream, the bat will
hear you only if the frequency of the scream is between
1000 and 1100 cycles per second. If the bat screams, you
will hear the bat only if the frequency of the scream is
between 10,000 and 20,000 cycles per second.

1.6 Integrated Review p. 43

47. $\frac{5}{14}$ **49.** $-\frac{14}{3}$ **51.** $\frac{18}{5}$ **53.** b **55.** e

1.6 Mixed Review p. 43

1. 24 **3.** 1.10 **5.** $-\frac{3}{2}$ **7.** 1.54×10^6 **9.** No **11.** $\frac{8}{7}$

13. 27 in.³ **15.** Yes

17. $-1 < x \le 1$

1.7 Communicating About Algebra p. 46

A. $|x| \le 3$ **B.** $|x| \ge 2$ **C.** $|x - 3| < 3$ **D.** $|x - 4| > 4$

1.7 Guided Practice p. 47

1. If a is negative, $-a$ is positive. **2.** $|-3| = 3$, $|4| = 4$
3. All real numbers that are within one unit of 4 **4.** All real numbers that are more than 4 units from -2

1.7 Independent Practice pp. 47–48

5. No **7.** Yes **9.** $x - 10 = 17$ or $x - 10 = -17$

11. $4x + 1 = \frac{1}{2}$ or $4x + 1 = -\frac{1}{2}$ **13.** $-1, -8$ **15.** 60, 12

17. $\frac{13}{3}$, 9 **19.** $-3 < y + 5 < 3$ **21.** $7 - 2h \le -9$ or
$7 - 2h \ge 9$ **23.** $-7 \le d \le 5$ **25.** $x > \frac{22}{5}$ or $x < \frac{6}{5}$

27. $x \le -\frac{29}{2}$ or $x \ge \frac{23}{2}$ **29.** $-21 < j < -17$

31.

33.

35. $|s - x| \le \frac{3}{16}$, $4\frac{15}{16} \le x \le 5\frac{5}{16}$

37.

39. $|t - 98.6| \le 1.0$ **41.** $|x - 57.5| \le 7.5$

1.7 Integrated Review p. 49

43. d **45.** f **47.** b **49.** $\frac{9}{28}$ **51.** -6 **53.** $\frac{1}{7}$ **55.** $x \ge -13$

57. $x > -2$ **59.** $x < \frac{38}{3}$

1.8 Communicating About Algebra p. 52

A. Double bar, to compare countries for numbers of two kinds of medals received

B. Bar graph, to compare number of countries participating in various years

C. Time line, to compare years when various sports became Olympic events

D. Circle graph, to compare portions of the total number of medals won by each continent

1.8 Guided Practice p. 53

1. Answers will vary.

2. Bar graph, to compare candidates for numbers of votes received; or a circle graph, to compare candidates for parts of a total number of votes received

3. Bar graph **4.** A bar graph, because there will probably be eight different prices

1.8 Independent Practice pp. 53–54

5.

Number	Tally	Frequency
1				2
2					3
3						4
4						4
5					3
6					3
7				2

7.

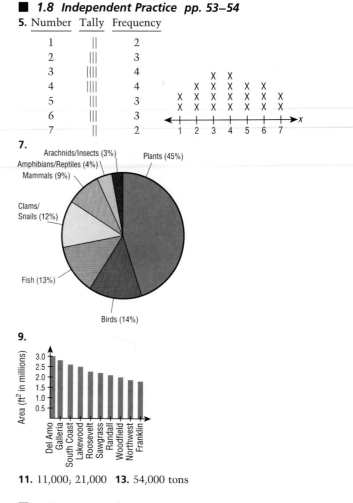

9.

11. 11,000; 21,000 **13.** 54,000 tons

1.8 Integrated Review p. 55

15. $\approx 3.7\%$ **17.** $x > -2$ **19.** $-\frac{3}{7} \le x \le \frac{1}{7}$

21. $-18 < x < 24$

1.8 Chapter Review pp. 57–60

1. $\frac{3}{4}$ **3.** -3 **5.** $\sqrt{3}$ **7.** $-2, -1.5, -0.5, 0, 0.5, 1$

9. $-\frac{1}{2}, -\frac{1}{4}, -\frac{1}{8}, \frac{1}{3}, \frac{2}{5}, \frac{2}{3}$

11. $-1.42, -\sqrt{2}, -1.41, 1.41, \sqrt{2}, 1.42$ **13.** $22\frac{2}{9}$ m per

second **15.** -8 **17.** 12 **19.** -1 **21.** -18 **23.** 11

25. 14 cm² **27.** ≈ 6.0 cm² **29.** -3 **31.** -7 **33.** $-3, 3$

35. $-1, 4$ **37.** $x < 4$

39. $-2 \le x < 2$

41. $-2 < x < 7$

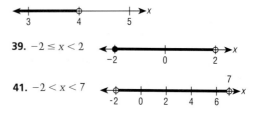

43. ≈1439.4 mi **45.** 1995 **47.** ≈1436.76 cm³
49. ≈384.85 m³ **51.** $y = -\frac{7}{3}x + 3$ **53.** $-17 \le G \le 113$
55. 48

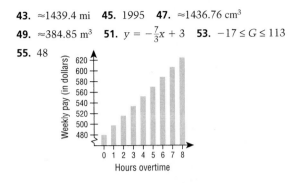

57. Georgia: 5,632,000; Maryland: 3,560,000; New
Mexico: 1,421,000 **59.** 667 **61.** January 17, 1912
63. $-89\frac{2}{9} \le C \le 10$ **65.** $K = 33, E = 66$

CHAPTER 2

■ 2.1 Communicating About Algebra p. 66

A.
B.

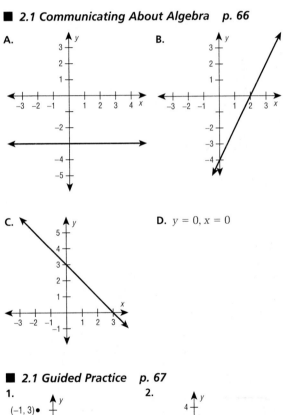

C.
D. $y = 0, x = 0$

■ 2.1 Guided Practice p. 67

1.
2.

3. No, because it is endless. One can choose any value
for x, and find a value for y.

4. One of the four parts into which a plane is divided by
two perpendicular lines **5.** Draw a vertical line through
the point −5 on the x-axis. **6.** Draw a horizontal line
through the point 2 on the y-axis.

■ 2.1 Independent Practice pp. 67–69

7. IV

9. III

11. None

13. $(0, 5), (-2, 3), (1, 6)$ **15.** $(0, -1), (-1, -6), (2, 9)$
17. $(0, 4), (-2, 10), (1, 1)$ **19.** e **21.** c **23.** f
25.

27.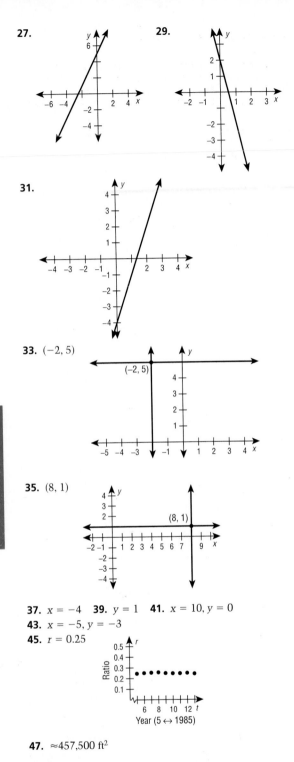

29.

31.

33. $(-2, 5)$

35. $(8, 1)$

37. $x = -4$ **39.** $y = 1$ **41.** $x = 10, y = 0$
43. $x = -5, y = -3$
45. $r = 0.25$

47. $\approx 457{,}500 \text{ ft}^2$

■ 2.1 Integrated Review p. 69
49. -28 **51.** -7 **53.** 11 **55.** $-14, -11, -8, -5, -2, 1, 4$
57. $y = -4x + 10$ **59.** $y = -3x + \frac{9}{2}$

■ 2.2 Communicating About Algebra p. 73
A. $\dfrac{-16 \text{ degrees}}{3 \text{ hours}}$ **B.** $\dfrac{68 \text{ miles}}{9 \text{ minutes}}$

■ 2.2 Guided Practice p. 74
1. The slope of a nonvertical line is a change in y divided by a corresponding change in x, which is equivalent to the rise or fall per unit of horizontal change, as the definition says.
2. It is negative; it is positive; 0 **3.** b **4.** They are parallel if their slopes are equal. They are perpendicular if their slopes are negative reciprocals.

■ 2.2 Independent Practice pp. 74–76
5. 0 **7.** $-\frac{1}{3}$

9.

11.

13.

15. $-\frac{5}{3}$

17. $-\frac{11}{14}$

19. $-\frac{4}{5}$

21. $-\frac{1}{18}$

23. $-\frac{1}{2}$

25. $\frac{12}{5}$

27. b **29.** d **31.** b **33.** parallel **35.** Neither
37. 4 dollars per hour **39.** 40 mph **41.** 11.2
43. 0.73% per year

■ 2.2 Integrated Review p. 76

45.

47. •$(-14, 3)$ $(-\frac{1}{2}, 3)$•

49.
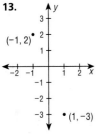

51. $(0, 6)$, $(-4, 5)$ **53.** $(0, -4)$, $(1, 2)$ **55.** $(0, 3)$, $(1, -6)$
57. c

■ 2.2 Mixed Review p. 77

1. 2.58×10^6 **3.** $11x - 24$ **5.** 27 **7.** $\frac{1}{2}$ **9.** 20 **11.** 2, 5

13.
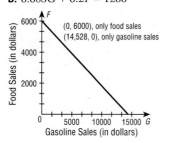

15. $\frac{12}{3x^2 + 2}$ **17.** -324 **19.** $-\frac{9}{5}$

■ 2.3 Communicating About Algebra p. 80

A. gas: $1464.13 food: $4392.39
B. $0.083G + 0.2F = 1200$

■ 2.3 Guided Practice p. 81

1. Because its graph is a line.
2. The x-intercept is the value of x when y is zero; the y-intercept is the value of y when x is zero. To find the x-intercept, let $y = 0$ and solve the equation of the line for x; to find the y-intercept, let $x = 0$ and solve for y.
3. x-intercept: 4, y-intercept: -2 **4.** -4, -2 **5.** Using intercepts, because 24 can be divided mentally by both 3 and 4. **6.** Using slope and y-intercept, because the equation is already in slope-intercept form.

■ 2.3 Independent Practice pp. 81–82

7. $\frac{1}{2}$, 4 **9.** 3, $-\frac{9}{8}$ **11.** $-\frac{1}{3}$, -1 **13.** e **15.** c **17.** a

31. $y = -4x + \frac{1}{2}$; -4, $\frac{1}{2}$ **33.** $y = 13x + 2$; 13, 2
35. $y = \frac{1}{2}x - 4$; $\frac{1}{2}$, -4

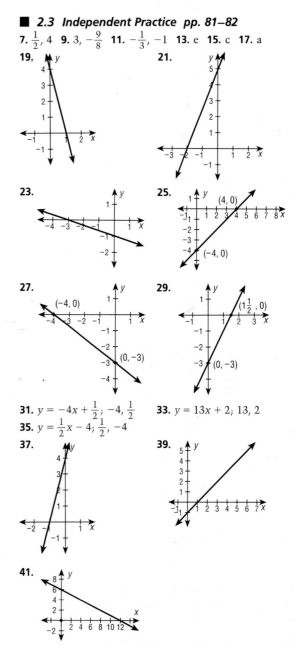

43. ≈ 3.9, the ladder is apt to tip back **45.** $2s + 5n = 6800$

■ 2.3 Integrated Review p. 83

47. No **49.** 8 **51.** $-2\frac{1}{2}$ **53.** -9 **55.** $y = \frac{3}{2}x - 4$

57. $y = \frac{5}{3}x + 3$ **59.** $y = \frac{1}{4}x - \frac{5}{2}$

61. 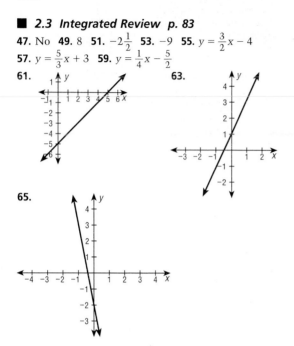 **63.**

65.

■ 2.4 Communicating About Algebra p. 89

A. Yes, because $0 = k(0)$ **B.** k; constant of variation

C. 8; $\frac{y}{x} = k$, $\frac{24}{3} = 8$

■ 2.4 Guided Practice p. 90

1. Use the point-slope form of the equation, $y - y_1 = m(x - x_1)$, where m is the slope and x_1 and y_1 are coordinates of the given point.

2. Use the slope-intercept form of the equation, $y = mx + b$, where m is the slope and b is the y-intercept.

3. Use the coordinates of the intercepts to find the slope, then use the point-slope form of the equation with the slope just found and the coordinates of either of the two points.

4. Answers vary; for example, distance and miles per hour

■ 2.4 Independent Practice pp. 90–91

5. $y = -3x + 6$ **7.** $y = \frac{4}{5}x + 4$ **9.** $y = x + 10$

11. $y = -\frac{1}{2}x + 3$ **13.** $y = 10x + 81$ **15.** $y = -\frac{4}{3}x - \frac{4}{3}$

17. $y = 3x - 15$ **19.** $y = -\frac{8}{9}x + 1$ **21.** $y = -\frac{3}{2}x$

23. $y = \frac{1}{4}x$ **25.** $y = 0.5x$ **27.** $c = \frac{3}{2}t$; 6 hours, $3\frac{1}{3}$ minutes

29. $m = \frac{820}{11}t + 1456$; 2574 **31.** $\approx 0.055\%$

■ 2.4 Integrated Review p. 92

33. 5 **35.** $-\frac{1}{7}$ **37.** 0 **39.** b **41.** a **43.** $-21, \frac{21}{8}$

45. $1, -\frac{5}{9}$ **47.** $-\frac{10}{3}, -\frac{5}{3}$ **49.** c

■ 2.4 Mid-Chapter Self-Test p. 93

1.

$(-3, 5)$ $(0, 2)$ $(4, -1)$

2.

x	-3	-2	-1	0	1	2	3
y	24	20	16	12	8	4	0

3. $\frac{3}{2}$ **4.** $-\frac{6}{5}$ **5.** 0 **6.** 135 mph **7.** parallel

8. perpendicular **9.** x-intercept: -9; y-intercept: 6 **10.** x-intercept: 4; y-intercept: 20

11. $-\frac{1}{2}, -\frac{5}{2}$ **12.** $\frac{5}{4}, 10$

13.

14.

15. $y = -\frac{1}{3}x - \frac{2}{3}$ **16.** $y = \frac{1}{4}x + 4$ **17.** $y = \frac{1}{5}x - \frac{13}{5}$

18. 4.58 **19.** $w = \frac{1}{3}A$ or $A = 3w$ **20.** \$2 per year

■ 2.5 Communicating About Algebra p. 96

A.

B.

C.

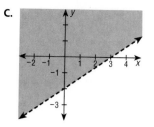

A–C. Sketch the solid or dashed line of the corresponding equality; shade the half-plane that is seen to contain solutions after a point in one of them has been tested.

■ 2.5 Guided Practice p. 97

1. Because its boundary is a line.

2. No, $6\left(\frac{5}{6}\right) + 0$ is not less than 5.

3. Dashed line for $ax + by < c$, solid line for $ax + by \leq c$; the solid line means the points on the line satisfy the inequality, the dashed line means the points on the line do not satisfy the inequality.

4. True; (0, 0) lies below the line and satisfies the inequality.

■ 2.5 Independent Practice pp. 97–98

5. Only $(-5, 1)$ is.   **7.** Only $(0, 2)$ is.   **9.** Only $(3, -9)$ is.

11. Neither is.   **13.** $y = -2x + \frac{2}{5}$ **15.** $y = -\frac{2}{3}x - \frac{1}{3}$

17. **19.**

21. **23.**

25. d **27.** a

29. **31.**

33. **35.**

37.

39. (12, 220), yes

41.

■ 2.5 Integrated Review p. 99

43. Neither is.   **45.** Neither is.   **47.** $y = -7x + \frac{1}{2}$

49. $y = -3x - 4$

51. **53.**

■ 2.5 Mixed Review p. 100

1. 0.00613   **3.** $-\frac{5}{3}$ **5.** $\frac{4}{3}$ **7.** $\frac{4}{7}$ **9.** $\frac{9}{4}x$ **11.** $\frac{16}{3}, -\frac{8}{3}$

13. $\frac{4}{2m^2 - m}$ **15.** $\frac{5}{3}$ **17.** 2040 ft   **19.** $y = -\frac{17}{7}x - \frac{33}{7}$

2.6 Communicating About Algebra p. 103

A–C.

A. Shifts 2 units to the right.
B. Shifts 2 units to the right and 1 unit up.
C. Shifts 2 units to the right and reflects in x-axis.

2.6 Guided Practice p. 104

1. The absolute value of x is the same as x if x is either positive or zero. If x is a negative number, its absolute value is opposite of that negative number. For example, $|-7| = -(-7)$, or 7.

2. a; when a is positive the graph opens upward to show a minimum value for y, when a is negative the graph opens downward to show a maximum value for y.

3. 5; 5, and values to the left and right of 5.

4.

2.6 Independent Practice pp. 104–105

5. b; this is the graph of $y = |x|$, shifted up 4 units. **7.** c; this is the graph of $y = |x|$, shifted left 4 units. **9.** (0, 1)
11. (1, 3) **13.** (2, −12) **15.** (−2, 3) **17.** (6, 6) **19.** $\left(\frac{5}{2}, 6\right)$
21. b **23.** a **25.** 3, 2, 1, 0, 1, 2, 3; symmetric about $x = -2$ **27.** 9, 7, 5, 3, 5, 7, 9; symmetric about $x = 1$
29.   **31.**

33.   **35.**

37.   **39.**

41.   **43.**

45.

47. No; the total sales would equal the area of the rectangle between the line $s = 20$ and the t-axis, which is only 880,000.

2.6 Integrated Review p. 106

49. $y = |x - 2| - 1$ **51.** $y = -|x| - 1$

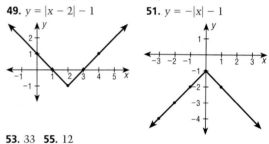

53. 33 **55.** 12

2.7 Communicating About Algebra p. 110

A–B.

A. Positive correlation
B. $m = 15,125t + 91$
C. \$317.88 million

■ 2.7 Guided Practice p. 111

1. Positive, the best-fitting line has a positive slope.

2. $y = \frac{3}{4}x + 2$ **3.** Positive correlation; taller men tend to have larger feet. **4.** Negative correlation; the larger the income, the smaller the percent spent on food

■ 2.7 Independent Practice pp. 111–112

5. Negative correlation **7.** No correlation

9–18. Equations vary. **9.** $y = \frac{5}{4}x + 1$ **11.** $y = \frac{1}{4}x + \frac{1}{2}$

13. $y = -\frac{4}{3}x + \frac{3}{2}$

15. $c = \frac{7}{2}t - 8$, ≈38 million **17.** $p = \frac{13}{3}t - 20$, ≈41%

■ 2.7 Integrated Review p. 113

19. 16 **21.** $-\frac{1}{10}$ **23.** $y = 7x - 47$ **25.** $y = \frac{13}{3}x - \frac{76}{3}$

■ 2.7 Chapter Review pp. 115–118

1. I, none

3. IV, I

5. IV, I

7. \$4,000 per year

9.

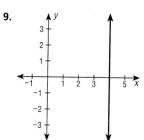

11.

13.

15. 2 **17.** $-\frac{1}{2}$ **19.** 10, −4 **21.** −16, 4

23. $y = x - 9$

25. $y = -\frac{1}{4}x + 3$

27. $y = -\frac{3}{7}x - \frac{1}{7}$

29. $y = 3x - 21$ **31.** $y = \frac{9}{5}x - \frac{62}{5}$ **33.** $y = \frac{3}{11}x + \frac{31}{11}$

35. $y = 10x$

37.

39.

41.

43.

45.

47. e **49.** j **51.** g **53.** b **55.** h **57.** f **59.** -875 per year
61. In the buried chamber **63.** 1 **65.** 87.5 liters
67. 10 ft^2
69. Too high; the standard tire has a smaller diameter than the low-profile tire, so the speedometer would assume a greater distance was being traveled for each revolution of tires.

CHAPTER 3

■ 3.1 Communicating About Algebra p. 124

A. (3, 1); if the two graphs intersect, the point of intersection is the solution.

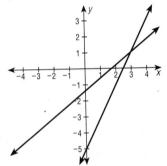

B. Any point on the line $3x - 4y = 5$; if the two graphs coincide, any point on the line is a solution.

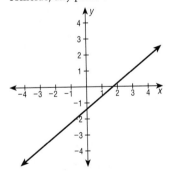

C. No solution; if the two graphs are parallel, there is no solution.

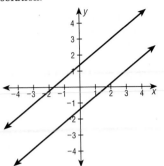

■ 3.1 Guided Practice p. 125

1. If the graphs of the equations intersect, the system has one solution, if the graphs of the equations do not intersect, the system has no solutions; if the graphs of the equations coincide, the system has many solutions.
2. It is impossible for two lines to intersect in exactly two points.
3. $(4, -1)$; $4 + 5(-1) = -1$, $4 + 4(-1) = 0$

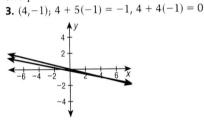

4. c, 1 **5.** a, none **6.** b, infinitely many

■ 3.1 Independent Practice pp. 125–127

7. Infinitely many **9.** 1 **11.** None **13.** It is. **15.** It is not.
17. It is. **19.** It is not. **21.** It is. **23.** It is.
25. $(2, -1)$

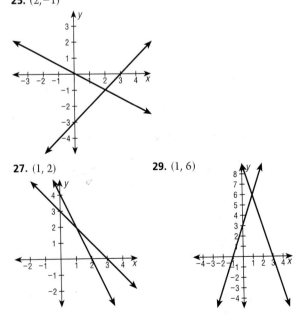

27. $(1, 2)$ **29.** $(1, 6)$

31. $(12, 0)$

33. $(-2,-1)$

35. $(3, 2)$

37. 4%: $1500, 5%: $3000 **39.** $141\frac{2}{3}$

41. $y = 2x - 4$, $y = \frac{2}{3}x - 2$; $\left(\frac{3}{2}, -1\right)$

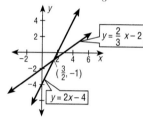

43. About 1972.

■ 3.1 Integrated Review p. 127

45. It is not. **47.** It is not. **49.** It is. **51.** $y = \frac{7}{2}x + 3$

53. $y = 4x - 13$

55.

■ 3.2 Communicating About Algebra p. 133

A. $\left(\frac{1}{23}, -\frac{14}{23}\right)$, the linear combination method is easiest to use.

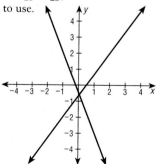

B. $(1, 2)$, the substitution method is easiest to use.

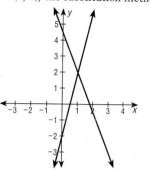

■ 3.2 Guided Practice p. 134

1. Solve the second equation for x in terms of y, substitute the resulting expression into the first equation and solve for y; substitute the value for y into the revised second equation and solve for x; check.

2. Multiply the first equation by 2 and the second equation by 3, add the equations, and solve for y; substitute the value for y into either equation and solve for x; check.

3. There are infinitely many solutions. **4.** There is no solution.

5. Linear combination; neither variable in either equation has a coefficient of 1.

6. Substitution; the second equation contains a variable with a coefficient of 1.

■ 3.2 Independent Practice pp. 134–135

7. $(4, 1)$ **9.** $(-2,-3)$ **11.** $\left(\frac{87}{5}, \frac{-68}{5}\right)$ **13.** $(9, 4)$

15. $(-6, 2)$ **17.** $\left(1, \frac{1}{5}\right)$

19. $(5,-5)$ **21.** $(1,-1)$

23. $\left(-\frac{19}{3}, \frac{35}{12}\right)$

25. 1, graphs have different slopes **27.** none, derived equation is false **29.** 1980 **31.** $(4, 11)$

■ 3.2 Integrated Review p. 136

33. 1 **35.** $-\frac{2}{3}$ **37.** 2 **39.** It is not. **41.** It is.

43. It is not. **45.** $y = -\frac{2}{9}x + 4$ **47.** $y = -\frac{16}{3}x + 8$

49. $y = \frac{1}{2}x + \frac{7}{5}$ **51.** $\approx 0.37, \approx 0.42, \approx 0.42, \approx 0.67$; they increase

■ 3.2 Mixed Review p. 137

1. -7 **3.** $31,400$ **5.** -4

7.

9.

11. 66.15 **13.** $2 \cdot 3 \cdot 5$ **15.** $y = \dfrac{8}{3x + 4}$ **17.** $y = 6$

19. $y = -x - 1$

■ 3.3 Communicating About Algebra p. 140

A. 1987, once Wal-Mart's revenues began increasing at a linear rate of about $5 billion per year.

B. $43 billion; $58 billion; fit a line to the data and substituted for t in the equation for the line.

■ 3.3 Guided Practice p. 141

1. $12 \cdot$ Cost of double cone $+ 8 \cdot$ Cost of single cone $= 17$
Cost of double cone $=$ Cost of single cone $+ 0.25$

2. Cost of single cone $= s$ (dollars)
Cost of double cone $= d$ (dollars)

3. $12d + 8s = 17$
$d = s + 0.25$

4. $s = 0.70$, $d = 0.95$; single: $0.70, double: $0.95

■ 3.3 Independent Practice pp. 141–143

5. 60 mph **7.** Round: 1, rectangular: 4 **9.** $32.50

11. Liability: $200,000; deductible: $250

13. 1985, they increased

■ 3.3 Integrated Review p. 143

15. $(-1, 7)$ **17.** $(-3, -2)$

19. $(-1, 2)$ **21.** $\left(\dfrac{-54}{7}, \dfrac{17}{7}\right)$ **23.** $(-1, -2)$

■ 3.3 Mid-Chapter Self-Test p. 144

1. a, one solution **2.** c, many solutions **3.** b, no solutions

4. $(2, 1)$

5. Any point on the line $-x + y = 3$

6. No solution

7. $\left(\dfrac{10}{11}, -\dfrac{9}{11}\right)$ **8.** $\left(-\dfrac{49}{13}, \dfrac{32}{13}\right)$ **9.** No solution **10.** $(5, 2)$

11. $(6, 4)$ **12.** $(2, -1)$ **13.** 6%: $7200, 8%: $5400

14. 1910 **15.** $36°, 54°$ **16.** 115,000

■ 3.4 Communicating About Algebra p. 147

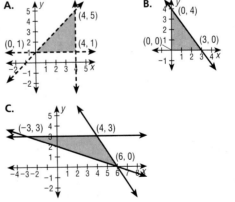

A–C. Graph the inequalities on the same coordinate plane to get 3 half-planes that intersect in a common region.

1.

2. It is not. **3.** It is not. **4.** It is. **5.** It is not.
6. Find the region that is the intersection of the half-planes; the vertices are the corner points of that region and are the intersections of the edges of half-planes.

3.4 Independent Practice *pp. 148–150*

7. c **9.** f **11.** a

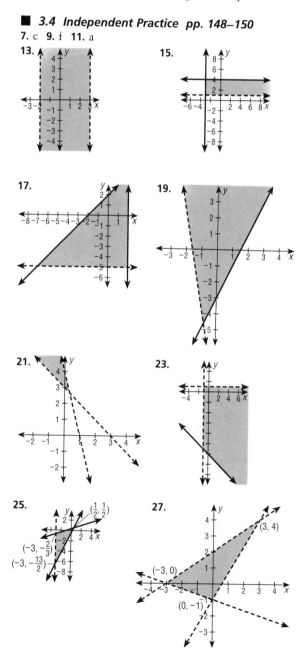

13.

15.

17.

19.

21.

23.

25.

27.

29.

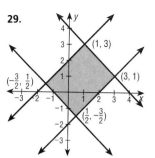

31. $x \geq 1$, $x \leq 8$, $y \leq 3$, $y \geq -5$ **33.** $y \leq \frac{9}{10}x + \frac{42}{5}$, $y \geq 3x$, $y \geq \frac{2}{3}x + 7$

35. $x \geq 40$, $y \geq 40$, $0.10x + 0.40y \leq 26$

Drink Boxes

Boxes of Raisins

37. $y > -\frac{1}{7}x$, $y \geq -10$, $x < 90$, $y \leq 0$

3.4 Integrated Review *p. 150*

39.

41.

43.

45. $(4, -6)$ **47.** $(1, 9)$ **49.** $(-12, 7)$ **51.** a

3.5 Communicating About Algebra *p. 153*
A. A: 380, B: 200 **B.** A: 400, B: 0

3.5 Guided Practice *p. 154*
1. It is evaluated at the vertices formed by the constraints; they define the region of possible answers.
2. Coordinates of the vertices. **3.** (4, 0), (2, 4), (0, 3), (0, 0) **4.** Min: 0, Max: 38

3.5 Independent Practice *pp. 154–155*
5. $-56, 40$ **7.** $-34, 27$ **9.** $-9, 13$ **11.** 12, 52 **13.** 8, 10
15. 0, 17 **17.** 12, $\frac{169}{3}$ **19.** 6, 29 **21.** A: 300 units, B: 400 units **23.** \$3000

25. **27.**

29.

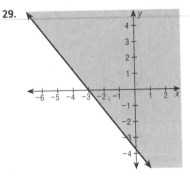

31. c

■ **3.5 Mixed Review p. 156**

1. $2x + 17$ **3.** ≈ 0.162 mi **5.** $-\dfrac{7}{6}$ **7.** 4.046 **9.** $x \geq 4$ or $x \leq -2$ **11.** 18, 19

13.

15. 96 **17.** $\dfrac{3}{5}$ **19.** $\left(\dfrac{1}{2}, -1\right)$

■ **3.6 Communicating About Algebra p. 160**

A–B. Methods vary.

A. $(4, -3, 2)$ Add -3 times $x - 3z = -2$ to $3x + y - 2z = 5$, to get $y + 7z = 11$; add -2 times $x - 3z = -2$ to $2x + 2y + z = 4$, to get $2y + 7z = 8$; solve the linear system in y and z; solve for x in the original system.

B. $(1, 2, 3)$ Add -2 times $x + y + z = 6$ to $2x - y + z = 3$, to get $-3y - z = -9$; add -3 times $x + y + z = 6$ to $3x - z = 0$, to get $-3y - 4z = -18$; solve the linear system in y and z; solve for x in the original system.

■ **3.6 Guided Practice p. 161**

1. $(3, 3, 1)$ **2.** $(4, 2, 2)$ **3.** Eliminates the x-term.
4. Eliminates the y-term. **5–6.** Triangular forms vary.

5. $x + 5y + z = 3$
    $y + z = 1$
        $z = 2$

6. $x + 5y - 3z = 2$
    $y - \dfrac{1}{2}z = 0$
        $z = 2$

■ **3.6 Independent Practice pp. 161–163**

7. $(1, 2, 3)$ **9.** $(-9, 1, 4)$ **11.** $(-3, 4, -1)$

13. $x + y - z = 39$
    $-2x + 2y - z = 12$
    $4x + y - 3z = 19$

15. $x - 3y + 4z = 24$
    $7y - 10z = -18$
    $-3x - 2y + z = 46$

17–20. Triangular forms may vary.

17. $x - y + 2z = 15$
    $y + 2z = 9$
        $z = 5$

19. $x - y - 3z = 1$
    $y + 2z = -5$
        $z = -1$

21. $(-18, 4, 2)$ **23.** $(8, -2, -4)$ **25.** $(4, 3, 1)$ **27.** $(-1, 5, 5)$
29. String: 50, Wind: 20, Percussion: 8 **31.** Mild: 180 lb,
Medium: 140 lb, Sharp: 80 lb

■ **3.6 Integrated Review p. 163**

33. $(1, -1)$ **35.** $(5, -3)$ **37.** $(3, 9)$ **39.** 20 **41.** 23

■ **3.6 Chapter Review pp. 166–168**

1. It is not. **3.** It is.

5. $(-1, 5)$

7. $(8, -3)$ **9.** $(-2, 0)$ **11.** $(-2, -1)$
13. $(0, 12), (8, 8), (10, 0), (0, 0)$

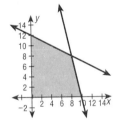

15. $(0, 3), (5, 3), (5, 0), (0, 0)$

17. $-\dfrac{16}{3}, 144$ **19.** $(23, -3, 4)$ **21.** $(1, 0, -3)$

23. $x + y + z = 2{,}433{,}000$
    $y + z = 2{,}040{,}000$
        $z = 1{,}350{,}000$
    $(393000, 690000, 1350000)$

25. $s \geq 0, t \geq 0, 4s + t \leq 39, \dfrac{6}{5}s + t \geq 32$ **27.** 0.4 in.

29. $\dfrac{1}{30}$ mm

1. $\frac{1}{5}$ **3.** $-\frac{11}{3}, \frac{19}{3}$ **5.** $r = \frac{A-P}{Pt}$; 0.05 or 5%

7. $-\frac{23}{2} \le x \le \frac{29}{2}$

9.

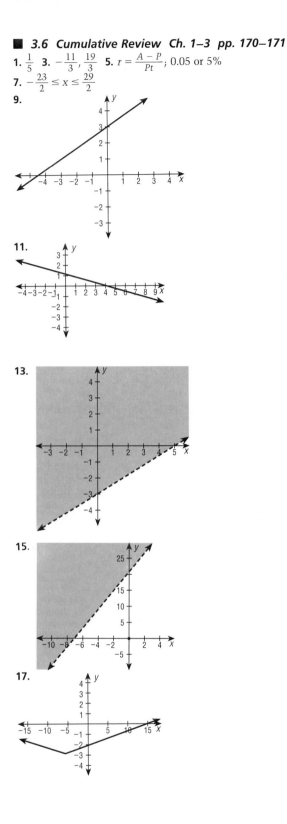

11.

13.

15.

17.

19. $\left(\frac{5}{2}, -\frac{3}{2}\right)$ **21.** (3, 2) **23.** (4, 2, 4)

25.

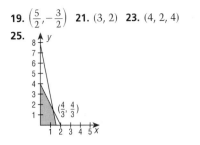

$\left(\frac{4}{3}, \frac{4}{3}\right)$

27. 145 calories, 120 calories, 110 calories **29.** Positive correlation **31.** ≈$16,000 million

33. Process A: 600
Process B: 1200

CHAPTER 4

■ *4.1 Communicating About Algebra p. 176*

A. $2\left(\begin{bmatrix} 4 & -5 \\ -2 & 8 \end{bmatrix} + \begin{bmatrix} -3 & 7 \\ 8 & 2 \end{bmatrix}\right) \overset{?}{=} 2\begin{bmatrix} 4 & -5 \\ -2 & 8 \end{bmatrix} + 2\begin{bmatrix} -3 & 7 \\ 8 & 2 \end{bmatrix}$

$2\begin{bmatrix} 1 & 2 \\ 6 & 10 \end{bmatrix} \overset{?}{=} \begin{bmatrix} 8 & -10 \\ -4 & 16 \end{bmatrix} + \begin{bmatrix} -6 & 14 \\ 16 & 4 \end{bmatrix}$

$\begin{bmatrix} 2 & 4 \\ 12 & 20 \end{bmatrix} = \begin{bmatrix} 2 & 4 \\ 12 & 20 \end{bmatrix}$

B. $c\left(\begin{bmatrix} d_{11} & d_{12} \\ d_{21} & d_{22} \end{bmatrix} + \begin{bmatrix} e_{11} & e_{12} \\ e_{21} & e_{22} \end{bmatrix}\right) \overset{?}{=}$

$c\begin{bmatrix} d_{11} & d_{12} \\ d_{21} & d_{22} \end{bmatrix} + c\begin{bmatrix} e_{11} & e_{12} \\ e_{21} & e_{22} \end{bmatrix}$

For any d and e: $c(d + e) = cd + ce$.

■ *4.1 Guided Practice p. 177*

1. $[1 \ \ 5 \ \ -3], \begin{bmatrix} -1 \\ 0 \\ 2 \end{bmatrix}, \begin{bmatrix} 1 & 0 & -2 \\ 6 & 3 & 0 \\ -4 & 7 & 5 \\ 0 & 9 & 3 \end{bmatrix}$

2. Must be the same **3.** 3×4 **4.** No, $-2 \ne 2$

5. $[2 \ \ -3 \ \ 6 \ \ 3]$ **6.** $\begin{bmatrix} -8 & -12 \\ -2 & 0 \end{bmatrix}$

■ *4.1 Independent Practice pp. 177–179*

7. 3×3 **9.** 2×4 **11.** $\begin{bmatrix} 2 & 7 \\ -1 & 1 \end{bmatrix}$

13. $\begin{bmatrix} 8 & -3 & -3 \\ 0 & 16 & 8 \\ 1 & 15 & 0 \end{bmatrix}$ **15.** $\begin{bmatrix} -5 & -12 \\ 1 & -5 \\ 3 & 7 \end{bmatrix}$

17. Different number of rows and columns

19. $\begin{bmatrix} -3 & 9 & -18 \\ -27 & 3 & -12 \end{bmatrix}$ **21.** $\begin{bmatrix} 0 & -4 \\ 16 & 8 \\ -32 & -24 \end{bmatrix}$

23. $\begin{bmatrix} 1 & 7 \\ -5 & 9 \end{bmatrix}$ **25.** $\begin{bmatrix} -16 & 28 & 4 \\ 0 & -24 & 4 \\ 24 & -40 & -4 \end{bmatrix}$

27. $\begin{bmatrix} 6 & -14 & 2 \\ 24 & 11 & 15 \\ 0 & -7 & 12 \end{bmatrix}$

29. 6 **31.** $(6, 2, -1)$ **33.** 48,000 **35.** 40,770 ft^2

37. $92,819

■ **4.1 Integrated Review p. 179**
39. −4 **41.** −4 **43.** 215 **45.** 75%

■ **4.2 Communicating About Algebra p. 182**

Multiply the given matrix by $\begin{bmatrix} 25,000 \\ 30,000 \\ 45,000 \end{bmatrix}$.

$\begin{bmatrix} 0.70 & 0.15 & 0.15 \\ 0.20 & 0.80 & 0.15 \\ 0.10 & 0.05 & 0.70 \end{bmatrix} \begin{bmatrix} 25,000 \\ 30,000 \\ 45,000 \end{bmatrix} = \begin{bmatrix} 28,750 \\ 35,750 \\ 35,500 \end{bmatrix}$

■ **4.2 Guided Practice p. 183**

1. Yes, the number of columns in the first matrix is equal to the number of rows in the second. **2.** 6 **3.** AB, the number of columns in the first matrix is equal to the number of rows in the second. **4.** False; the products, $\begin{bmatrix} 10 & 3 \\ -6 & 5 \end{bmatrix}$ and $\begin{bmatrix} 10 & 6 \\ -3 & 5 \end{bmatrix}$, are not equal.

■ **4.2 Independent Practice pp. 183–185**

5. It is, 2×1. **7.** It is not. **9.** It is, 5×2. **11.** It is, 8×4.

13. $\begin{bmatrix} 4 & -1 \\ -16 & -7 \end{bmatrix}$ **15.** $\begin{bmatrix} 2 & 6 & 21 \\ -8 & 2 & -46 \\ -13 & 8 & 2 \end{bmatrix}$

17. Not defined, the number of columns in the first matrix is not equal to the number of rows in the second.

19. $\begin{bmatrix} -10 \\ 10 \end{bmatrix}$ **21.** $\begin{bmatrix} 20 & 10 & -50 \\ 0 & 0 & 0 \\ 4 & 2 & -10 \end{bmatrix}$

23. 2, −8 **25.** $\begin{bmatrix} 8 & -24 \\ 12 & -60 \end{bmatrix}$

27. $\begin{bmatrix} -18 & -24 \\ -12 & -6 \end{bmatrix}$ **29.** $\begin{bmatrix} 44 & 3 & 31 \\ -51 & 7 & -23 \\ 39 & 35 & 49 \end{bmatrix}$

31. $\begin{bmatrix} 3 \\ 1.25 \\ 4 \end{bmatrix} [6 \quad 4 \quad 3] = [35]$, $\$35 \div 2 = \$17.50$

33. $\begin{bmatrix} 0.166 & 0.372 & 0.136 \\ 0.087 & 0.189 & 0.017 \\ 0.172 & 0.005 & 0.026 \\ 0.106 & 0.013 & 0.436 \end{bmatrix} \begin{bmatrix} 535,842 \\ 475,533 \\ 480,609 \end{bmatrix} \approx$

$\begin{bmatrix} 331,210.9 \\ 144,664.3 \\ 107,038.3 \\ 272,526.7 \end{bmatrix} \begin{matrix} \text{China} \\ \text{India} \\ \text{S.U.} \\ \text{U.S.} \end{matrix}$

■ **4.2 Integrated Review p. 185**
35. 3×3 **37.** 2×5 **39.** Not possible, orders do not match. **41.** Possible, 2×3 **43.** Possible, 1×4

■ **4.2 Mixed Review p. 186**
1. 3 **3.** 26 **5.** $4\frac{2}{15}$ **7.** $\frac{2}{3}$ **9.** $-\frac{5}{3}$ **11.** $-\frac{2}{3}$

13. $\begin{bmatrix} 7 & 5 \\ -1 & -4 \end{bmatrix}$ **15.** $1 < x < 7$

17. **19.** $\left(\dfrac{40}{17}, \dfrac{21}{17}\right)$

■ **4.3 Communicating About Algebra p. 190**

A. $(2)\begin{vmatrix} 0 & 2 \\ 3 & 4 \end{vmatrix} - (3)\begin{vmatrix} -1 & 1 \\ 3 & 4 \end{vmatrix} + (2)\begin{vmatrix} -1 & 1 \\ 0 & 2 \end{vmatrix} =$
$2(-6) - 3(-7) + 2(-2) = 5,$
$-4 + 9 + 0 - 12 + 12 - 0 = 5$

B. 0; by expanding by minors along that row, each product in the expansion becomes zero.

■ **4.3 Guided Practice p. 191**

1. −6 **2.** $\begin{bmatrix} 8 & 7 \\ 2 & 3 \end{bmatrix}$ and $\begin{bmatrix} 6 & -4 \\ -1 & 1 \end{bmatrix}$

3. $(1)\begin{vmatrix} 0 & -3 \\ 1 & -2 \end{vmatrix} - (-2)\begin{vmatrix} 0 & -3 \\ 2 & -2 \end{vmatrix} + 4\begin{vmatrix} 0 & 0 \\ 2 & 1 \end{vmatrix} =$
$(1)(3) + (2)(6) + 4(0) = 15,$
$-(0)\begin{vmatrix} -2 & 4 \\ 1 & -2 \end{vmatrix} + (0)\begin{vmatrix} 1 & 4 \\ 2 & -2 \end{vmatrix} - (-3)\begin{vmatrix} 1 & -2 \\ 2 & 1 \end{vmatrix} =$
$(0)(0) + (0)(-10) + 3(5) = 15;$
expanding by minors along the second row, two products in the expansion become zero.
4. $20 + 12 + 0 - (-12) - (20) - 0 = 24$

■ **4.3 Independent Practice pp. 191–193**

5. 0 **7.** 19 **9.** −5 **11.** 1 **13.** −11 **15.** 12 **17.** −10 **19.** 110 **21.** −170 **23.** 10 **25.** −222 **27.** The determinant of a 3×3 matrix with a column of zeros is 0.

29. $(-1)\begin{vmatrix} 2 & 3 \\ 4 & 6 \end{vmatrix} - (0)\begin{vmatrix} 1 & 3 \\ 2 & 6 \end{vmatrix} + (8)\begin{vmatrix} 1 & 2 \\ 2 & 4 \end{vmatrix} =$
$(-1)(0) - (0)(0) + (8)(0) = 0,$
one row is a multiple of another.

31. $(5)\begin{vmatrix} -4 & -4 \\ 3 & 3 \end{vmatrix} - (-3)\begin{vmatrix} 2 & 2 \\ 3 & 3 \end{vmatrix} + (8)\begin{vmatrix} 2 & 2 \\ -4 & -4 \end{vmatrix} =$
$(5)(0) - (-3)(0) + (8)(0) = 0$, two columns are the same.
33. 17 **35.** 7 **37.** $\frac{33}{2}$ **39.** 446,218 mi^2

■ **4.3 Integrated Review p. 193**
41. $AB = \begin{bmatrix} 72 & 4 \\ 15 & -5 \end{bmatrix}$, $|AB| = -420$; $|A| = 21$,
$|B| = -20$, $|A|\,|B| = -420$ **43.** b **45.** a

■ **4.4 Communicating About Algebra p. 199**
BEAM ME UP SCOTTY

■ **4.4 Guided Practice p. 200**

1. $\begin{bmatrix} 1 & 0 \\ 0 & 1 \end{bmatrix}$, $\begin{bmatrix} 1 & 0 & 0 \\ 0 & 1 & 0 \\ 0 & 0 & 1 \end{bmatrix}$

2. Both must equal I. **3.** Yes, $AB = I$ and $BA = I$
4. $\begin{bmatrix} 2 & -3 \\ 3 & -4 \end{bmatrix}$ **5.** No, its determinant is 0.
6. Multiply both sides of the equation by A^{-1} on the left.

7. Yes **9.** $\begin{bmatrix} 3 & 4 \\ 5 & 7 \end{bmatrix}$ **11.** $\begin{bmatrix} -2 & =17 \\ 1 & 8 \end{bmatrix}$ **13.** $\begin{bmatrix} -1 & 1 \\ -\frac{7}{2} & 3 \end{bmatrix}$

15. $\begin{bmatrix} -\frac{1}{4} & \frac{5}{4} \\ -\frac{3}{4} & \frac{11}{4} \end{bmatrix}$ **17.** $\begin{bmatrix} -37 & 5 \\ 14 & -2 \end{bmatrix}$ **19.** $\begin{bmatrix} -4 & 2 & -7 \\ 3 & -1 & 5 \end{bmatrix}$

21. $\begin{bmatrix} 1 & -3 \\ 0 & 1 \end{bmatrix}$ **23.** It has not. **25.** It has. **27.** They are.
29. They are not.

31. $\begin{bmatrix} 0 & 1 & 0 \\ 7 & 66 & -9 \\ -3 & -29 & 4 \end{bmatrix}$ **33.** $\begin{bmatrix} -4 & -\frac{7}{2} & 2 \\ -5 & -5 & 3 \\ 2 & 2 & -1 \end{bmatrix}$

35. $-16, 50, 4, -7, 11, -22, 1, -2, 7, -9, 7, -14$
37. $19, 31, 40, 60, 51, 79, 36, 60, 19, 38, 45, 75, 28, 42$
39. IVORY PENDANT, b **41.** BONE NEEDLES, d

■ **4.4 Integrated Review p. 202**

43. $\begin{bmatrix} -12 & -24 & -16 \\ -36 & -16 & -12 \\ 8 & -4 & -8 \end{bmatrix}$ **45.** $\begin{bmatrix} 14 & 7 & 0 \\ 26 & 5 & -3 \\ -22 & 10 & 1 \end{bmatrix}$
47. 25 **49.** 22

■ **4.4 Mid-Chapter Self-Test p. 203**

1. $\begin{bmatrix} 6 & 2 & 5 \\ -2 & -1 & 6 \end{bmatrix}$ **2.** $\begin{bmatrix} 5 & 0 \\ 0 & 3 \end{bmatrix}$ **3.** $\begin{bmatrix} 20 & -12 & 24 \\ 36 & -16 & 0 \\ -8 & 12 & 28 \end{bmatrix}$

4. $\begin{bmatrix} -8 \\ 5 \\ 4 \end{bmatrix}$ **5.** $\begin{bmatrix} -1 & -12 \\ 38 & -12 \end{bmatrix}$ **6.** $\begin{bmatrix} -2 & 7 & 9 \\ 4 & -2 & -7 \\ 9 & 8 & 2 \end{bmatrix}$ **7.** 16

8. -3 **9.** $\begin{bmatrix} \frac{5}{2} & -\frac{3}{2} \\ 2 & -1 \end{bmatrix}$ **10.** $\begin{bmatrix} 5 \\ 6 \end{bmatrix}$ **11.** $\begin{bmatrix} 0 & \frac{1}{2} & -\frac{1}{2} \\ 1 & -\frac{1}{2} & -\frac{1}{2} \\ -1 & \frac{1}{2} & \frac{3}{2} \end{bmatrix}$

12. $\frac{41}{2}$

	Profit (\$)
13. Store 1	$\begin{bmatrix} 220,000 \\ 170,000 \end{bmatrix}$
Store 2	

	Inventory value (\$)
14. Store 1	$\begin{bmatrix} 1474 \\ 882 \end{bmatrix}$
Store 2	

■ **4.5 Communicating About Algebra p. 206**
A. $(-1, 13)$ **B.** $(19.65, 1.2, 5.25)$

■ **4.5 Guided Practice p. 207**
1. $\begin{bmatrix} 6 & -1 \\ 1 & 3 \end{bmatrix}\begin{bmatrix} x \\ y \end{bmatrix} = \begin{bmatrix} 0 \\ 5 \end{bmatrix}$

2. Yes, $\begin{bmatrix} 3 & 7 & 2 \\ -2 & -5 & -1 \\ 0 & 1 & -2 \end{bmatrix}\begin{bmatrix} 28 \\ -10 \\ -7 \end{bmatrix} = \begin{bmatrix} 0 \\ 1 \\ 4 \end{bmatrix}$

3. $A^{-1}B$

4. $\begin{bmatrix} x \\ y \\ z \end{bmatrix} = \begin{bmatrix} -3 & 1 & 5 \\ 1 & 0 & -1 \\ 0 & 2 & 3 \end{bmatrix}^{-1}\begin{bmatrix} 2 \\ 1 \\ 2 \end{bmatrix}$

■ **4.5 Independent Practice pp. 207–208**
5. $\begin{bmatrix} 2 & -4 \\ -3 & 1 \end{bmatrix}\begin{bmatrix} x \\ y \end{bmatrix} = \begin{bmatrix} 7 \\ 12 \end{bmatrix}$

7. $\begin{bmatrix} 2 & -5 \\ 1 & -3 \end{bmatrix}\begin{bmatrix} x \\ y \end{bmatrix} = \begin{bmatrix} 12 \\ -3 \end{bmatrix}$ **9.** $\begin{bmatrix} 3 & -1 & 4 \\ 2 & 4 & -1 \\ 1 & -1 & 3 \end{bmatrix}\begin{bmatrix} x \\ y \\ z \end{bmatrix} = \begin{bmatrix} 16 \\ 10 \\ 31 \end{bmatrix}$
11. $(1, 2)$ **13.** $(5, -9)$ **15.** $(4, 6)$ **17.** $(-1, -4)$ **19.** $(4, 4)$
21. $(-18, 4, 2)$ **23.** $(5, -1, 0)$ **25.** $(-1, 5, 5)$ **27.** $(-1, 4, 3)$
29. $e + c + s = 1162$,
  $e = c + s$,
  $s = 0.14(1162)$;
Operating expenses (e): \$581 million
Facilities construction (c): \$418.32 million
Surplus (s): \$162.68 million
31. X: \$5000, Y: \$7500, Z: \$7500

■ **4.5 Integrated Review p. 209**
33. $(-2, 5)$ **35.** $(9, 0, -2)$ **37.** $\begin{bmatrix} -1 \\ 2 \end{bmatrix}$

■ **4.5 Mixed Review p. 209**
1. 2 **3.** -3 **5.** 20 **7.** $x \geq 6$
9.

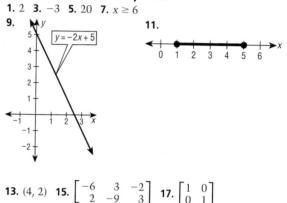

11.

13. $(4, 2)$ **15.** $\begin{bmatrix} -6 & 3 & -2 \\ 2 & -9 & 3 \end{bmatrix}$ **17.** $\begin{bmatrix} 1 & 0 \\ 0 & 1 \end{bmatrix}$

■ **4.6 Communicating About Algebra p. 212**
A–B. Elementary row operations vary.
A. $2R_1 + R_2 \to$ new R_2, $-\frac{1}{10}R_2$; $(-4, -3)$
B. $-3R_1 + R_2 \to$ new R_2, $-2R_1 + R_3 \to$
new R_3; $(1, 2, -1)$

■ **4.6 Guided Practice p. 213**
1–2. See page 210.
3. Yes; $2R_1 + R_2 \to$ new R_2, $-R_1 + R_3 \to$ new R_3
4. -3 times the first row added to the third row;
either Row 1 or Row 3

■ **4.6 Independent Practice pp. 213–214**
5. $\begin{bmatrix} 1 & 3 & -1 & : & 16 \\ 4 & -6 & 0 & : & 9 \\ 0 & 2 & -3 & : & 12 \end{bmatrix}$ **7.** $\begin{bmatrix} 2 & -1 & 3 & : & 4 \\ -3 & 0 & -1 & : & 1 \\ 1 & -3 & 1 & : & 5 \end{bmatrix}$
9. $(-5, -2, 0)$ **11.** $(16, -5, 2)$
13. $\left(\frac{-13}{2}, \frac{35}{6}, \frac{-11}{6}\right)$ **15.** $(-1, -2, 3)$
17. $(-16, 12, 10)$ **19.** $(-6, 4, 4)$
21. You: 5000, Jamie: 5200, Lan: 4900 **23.** X: 6600g,
Y: 7500g, Z: 8800g

■ **4.6 Integrated Review p. 215**

25. $(4,-1, 3)$ **27.** $(-1, 3, 1)$

29. $x + 2y - 2z = -13$
  $3x - 2y + 4z = 9$
  $2x + y + z = -3$

31. $-2y + 5z = 19$ **33.** They do. **35.** They do.

■ **4.7 Communicating About Algebra p. 218**

A. $\left(-\frac{5}{2}, -\frac{8}{3}\right)$ **B.** $(1, -7)$ **C.** $\left(2, 1, -\frac{1}{3}\right)$

■ **4.7 Guided Practice p. 219**

1. Not equal to 0. **2.** 4, 1; 4, 1; $\left(\frac{6}{7}, \frac{11}{7}\right)$ **3.** $(-26, -20)$
4. 3, 1, −1; 3, 1, −1; 3, 1, −1; $x = \frac{28}{84} = \frac{1}{3}$,
$y = \frac{-56}{84} = -\frac{2}{3}$, $z = \frac{-28}{84} = -\frac{1}{3}$; $\left(\frac{1}{3}, -\frac{2}{3}, -\frac{1}{3}\right)$

■ **4.7 Independent Practice pp. 219–221**

5. 15 **7.** 1 **9.** $(2, -5)$ **11.** $\left(\frac{1}{2}, 4\right)$ **13.** $\left(-\frac{11}{2}, -\frac{9}{2}\right)$

15. $x = \dfrac{\begin{vmatrix} 3 & 0 & 2 \\ -1 & 2 & 5 \\ 10 & 1 & -7 \end{vmatrix}}{\begin{vmatrix} 4 & 0 & 2 \\ -1 & 2 & 5 \\ 3 & 1 & -7 \end{vmatrix}}$, $y = \dfrac{\begin{vmatrix} 4 & 3 & 2 \\ -1 & -1 & 5 \\ 3 & 10 & -7 \end{vmatrix}}{\begin{vmatrix} 4 & 0 & 2 \\ -1 & 2 & 5 \\ 3 & 1 & -7 \end{vmatrix}}$,

$z = \dfrac{\begin{vmatrix} 4 & 0 & 3 \\ -1 & 2 & -1 \\ 3 & 1 & 10 \end{vmatrix}}{\begin{vmatrix} 4 & 0 & 2 \\ -1 & 2 & 5 \\ 3 & 1 & -7 \end{vmatrix}}$

17. $(-1, 4, 3)$ **19.** $(0, 5, 4)$ **21.** $\left(-\frac{2}{3}, -34, -12\right)$
23. $\left(\frac{3}{4}, \frac{1}{4}, 0\right)$ **25.** $\left(\frac{1}{3}, 1, -\frac{2}{3}\right)$ **27.** $(5, 2, -1)$ **29.** $(2, 1, 1)$
31. $(3, -3, 0)$

33. $x = \dfrac{\begin{vmatrix} 41.6 & 1 \\ 31.2 & -1 \end{vmatrix}}{\begin{vmatrix} 1 & 1 \\ 1 & -1 \end{vmatrix}} = \frac{-72.8}{-2} = 36.4$ million

$y = \dfrac{\begin{vmatrix} 1 & 41.6 \\ 1 & 31.2 \end{vmatrix}}{\begin{vmatrix} 1 & 1 \\ 1 & -1 \end{vmatrix}} = \frac{-10.4}{-2} = 5.2$ million

Color: 36.4 million, Black-and-white: 5.2 million
35. $0.18x + 0.10y + 0.02z = 200.40$;
  $0.10x + 0.12y + 0.03z = 154.50$;
  $0.16x + 0.26y + 0.16z = 361.80$;
$780 million; $450 million; $750 million

■ **4.7 Integrated Review p. 221**

37. 14 **39.** −13 **41.** 434

■ **4.7 Chapter Review pp. 223–226**

1. $\begin{bmatrix} 10 & 4 & 6 \\ 2 & 9 & 9 \end{bmatrix}$ **3.** $\begin{bmatrix} -1 & -6 & 7 \\ -1 & -14 & -6 \\ 1 & 4 & 2 \end{bmatrix}$

5. $\begin{bmatrix} 12 & 18 & -3 \\ 30 & -15 & 6 \\ 6 & 33 & 3 \end{bmatrix}$ **7.** $\begin{bmatrix} -2 & 12 \\ 2 & 0 \end{bmatrix}$

9. $\begin{bmatrix} -1 & 1 \\ 23 & 22 \end{bmatrix}$ **11.** $\begin{bmatrix} -6 & -6 & 30 \\ 4 & -37 & 3 \end{bmatrix}$

13. $[23]$ **15.** 12 **17.** 21 **19.** 16 **21.** 4 **23.** 20

25. $\begin{bmatrix} -2 & 3 \\ 5 & -7 \end{bmatrix}$

27. $\begin{bmatrix} \frac{3}{4} & -\frac{1}{2} \\ -\frac{1}{4} & \frac{1}{2} \end{bmatrix}$ **29.** $\begin{bmatrix} \frac{1}{2} & -\frac{3}{4} \\ 1 & -2 \end{bmatrix}$

31. They are.

33. $\begin{bmatrix} -\frac{4}{11} \\ \frac{21}{11} \end{bmatrix}$ **35.** $\begin{bmatrix} -5 \\ 9 \end{bmatrix}$

37. 51, 2, 39, 10, −1, 2, −23, 46, 17, 38, 32, 0 **39.** AN APPLE A DAY **41.** $(4, -2)$ **43.** $(20, 21, 9)$ **45.** $(-15, 9, 2)$
47. $(-4, 3)$ **49.** $(1, -2, 1)$ **51.** X: $6000, Y: $4000, Z: $8000 **53.** 15 units^2

55. $\begin{bmatrix} 8 & 7 & 1 \\ 3 & 9 & 5 \\ 4 & 6 & 2 \end{bmatrix}$

57. $\begin{bmatrix} 2 & 3 & 8 \\ 1 & 7 & 6 \\ 5 & 9 & 4 \end{bmatrix}$

CHAPTER 5

■ **5.1 Communicating About Algebra p. 232**
A. $\sqrt{52}$ cm, 7.21 cm **B.** $\sqrt{109}$ cm, 10.44 cm

■ **5.1 Guided Practice p. 233**
1. $4x^2 - 2x + 3 = 0, 4$ **2.** No real number solutions, the square of a number cannot be negative. **3.** 0 **4.** ±2

■ **5.1 Independent Practice pp. 233–235**
5. ±4 **7.** $\pm\sqrt{12}$ **9.** $\pm\frac{\sqrt{14}}{2}$ **11.** $\pm\sqrt{5}$ **13.** $\pm\sqrt{13}$
15. $\pm\sqrt{18}$ **17.** $\approx \pm 1.07$ **19.** $\approx \pm 2.16$ **21.** $\approx \pm 1.87$
23. ≈ 7.37 m **25.** 4 **27.** 1.25 seconds **29.** ≈ 3.5 seconds
31. 3 miles **33.** 1990 **35.** ≈ 11.3 in., ≈ 56.6 in.

■ **5.1 Integrated Review p. 235**
37. 50 **39.** −5 **41.** $\frac{1}{2}$ **43.** 3 **45.** −24 **47.** 5 **49.** c

■ **5.2 Communicating About Algebra p. 238**
A. $(250, 0), (-250, 0); (0, -300)$ **B.** 100,000
C. about right

■ **5.2 Guided Practice p. 239**
1. U-shaped parabola **2.** Up; the leading coefficient, 3, is positive.
3. $(2, 4); -\frac{b}{2a} = -\frac{4}{2(-1)} = 2, y = -x^2 + 4x = -2^2 + 4 \cdot 2 = 4$

4. An x-intercept is the value of x when $y = 0$.
A y-intercept is the value of y when $x = 0$.

◾ 5.2 Independent Practice pp. 239–241

5. Down **7.** Up **9.** Up **11.** $\left(\frac{5}{4}, -\frac{55}{8}\right)$, $x = \frac{5}{4}$ **13.** $\left(\frac{1}{4}, \frac{3}{4}\right)$, $x = \frac{1}{4}$ **15.** $(1, -25)$, $x = 1$ **17.** x-intercepts: $(-3, 0)$, $(1, 0)$; y-intercept: $(0, 3)$ **19.** x-intercepts: $(-2, 0)$, $(2, 0)$; y-intercept: $(0, -12)$ **21.** x-intercepts: $(2, 0)$, $(6, 0)$; y-intercept: $(0, 12)$ **23.** b **25.** e **27.** a

29. 31. 33.

35. 37. 39.

41. $576{,}000$ mi^2; area $= \frac{2}{3}bh = \frac{2}{3}(24 \times 60)(10 \times 60)$
43. 15 yd, 38-yd line **45.** 1st: $(0, 5)$, 2nd: $(2100, 5)$

◾ 5.2 Integrated Review p. 241

47. 49. 51.

53. $\pm\sqrt{3}$ **55.** 0 **57.** ± 4 **59.** b

◾ 5.2 Mixed Review p. 244

1. $2x^2 - 8x + 21$ **3.** $4 < x < 10$ **5.** 5.4 **7.** $\frac{1}{4}$
9. $-5 < x < -1$ **11.** $\frac{x}{2x + 3}$
13.

15. $-9 \leq x \leq -5$ **17.** $\begin{bmatrix} 6 & 15 \\ -3 & 9 \end{bmatrix}$ **19.** ≈ 3.82 in.

◾ 5.3 Communicating About Algebra p. 247

A. $4 \pm \sqrt{6}$; subtract 10 from both sides, add the square of half of -4 to both sides, find square roots

B. $-1, -3$; add 6 to both sides, divide both sides by -2, add the square of half of 4 to both sides, find square roots

◾ 5.3 Guided Practice p. 248

1. a, 4 is the square of half of -4 **2.** $(x - 4)^2$
3. Subtract 2 from both sides, add the square of half of 8 to both sides; 4
4. 25
5. $\left(x + \frac{3}{2}\right)^2 = \frac{13}{4}$; divide both sides by 2, add the square of half of 3 to both sides, write the binomial squared
6. Algebraic method: substitute the values found for x into the equation and simplify; geometric method: set the equation equal to zero, then substitute y for zero and graph the equation to find the x-intercepts.

◾ 5.3 Independent Practice pp. 248–249

7. $(x - 1)^2$ **9.** $(x + 7)^2$ **11.** $\left(x - \frac{1}{2}\right)^2$ **13.** $-6, -4$
15. $-3, 5$ **17.** $-3 \pm \sqrt{13}$
19. $\frac{3}{2} \pm \frac{\sqrt{19}}{2}$

21. $-\frac{3}{2} \pm \sqrt{\frac{23}{12}}$ **23.** $-\frac{1}{2} \pm \sqrt{\frac{41}{20}}$

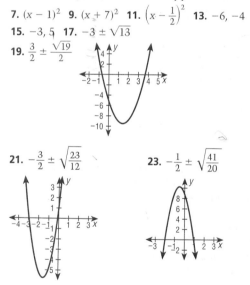

25. 4 cm, 6 cm **27.** ≈ 271 m, ≈ 129 m **29.** ≈ 73.5 ft
31. 30 and 660, 630 ft

◾ 5.3 Integrated Review p. 250

33. $x^2 + 12x + 36$
35. $x^2 - \frac{2}{3}x + \frac{1}{9}$ **37.** $4x^2 - 4x + 1$ **39.** It is.

41. It is not. **43.** It is not.

45. **47.** **49.**

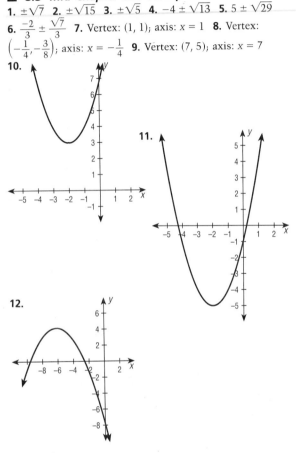

5.3 Mid-Chapter Self-Test p. 251

1. $\pm\sqrt{7}$ **2.** $\pm\sqrt{15}$ **3.** $\pm\sqrt{5}$ **4.** $-4 \pm \sqrt{13}$ **5.** $5 \pm \sqrt{29}$

6. $\frac{-2}{3} \pm \frac{\sqrt{7}}{3}$ **7.** Vertex: $(1, 1)$; axis: $x = 1$ **8.** Vertex:

$\left(-\frac{1}{4}, -\frac{3}{8}\right)$; axis: $x = -\frac{1}{4}$ **9.** Vertex: $(7, 5)$; axis: $x = 7$

10.

11.

12.

13. 16 **14.** $y = (x + 6)^2 - 7$ **15.** 4.47 in. **16.** 3400 ft
17. 21.8 ft **18.** 36 square units **19.** 0.01 sec **20.** 9.5 mi

5.4 Communicating About Algebra p. 254

A. No solution: $c > 16$, one: $c = 16$, two $c < 16$
B. Number of x-intercepts is the number of solutions.

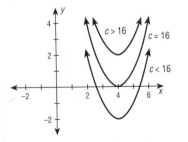

5.4 Guided Practice p. 255

1. Solutions are the opposite of b, plus or minus the square root of b squared minus $4ac$, all divided by $2a$.
2. $b^2 - 4ac$
If positive, there are two solutions;
if zero, there is one solution;
if negative, there are no real number solutions.
3. $-10, 2, -5$; two, the discriminant is positive
4. The first h is the height of an object after it is dropped, the second h is the height of an object after it is thrown.

5.4 Independent Practice pp. 255–256

5. $4x^2 + 7x - 5 = 0$ **7.** $30x^2 + 12x - 5 = 0$ **9.** -80

11. 40 **13.** 0 **15.** None **17.** None **19.** None

21. $-\frac{3}{2} \pm \frac{\sqrt{425}}{10}$ **23.** $\frac{1}{2} \pm \frac{\sqrt{117}}{18}$ **25.** $-\frac{1}{3}, -\frac{1}{5}$

27. No real solution. **29.** $-1, \frac{2}{3}$ **31.** $0.18, -0.11$

33. $2.75, -1.72$ **35.** $c < 9, c = 9, c > 9$ **37.** $c < 16$,
$c = 16, c > 16$ **39.** 5.1 in., 11.4 in. **41.** ≈ 1.6 seconds
43. ≈ 0.46 second

5.4 Integrated Review p. 257

45. ± 0.77 **47.** $0.55, -0.09$ **49.** $0.67, 1$ **51.** $0.06, -4.53$
53. ± 2.65 **55.** d

5.5 Communicating About Algebra p. 261

A. Yes, a real number can be written as $a + bi$ with $b = 0$.
B. They are the vertices of a parallelogram.

5.5 Guided Practice p. 262

1. No, yes; the solutions, $\pm i$, are not real numbers. **2.** $2i$
3. -2 **4.** $2 + i$ **5.** $-2 - 2i$ **6.** $6 - 2i$
7. Yes, $(-i\sqrt{2})^2 + 2 = i^2 \cdot 2 + 2 = -2 + 2 = 0$
8.

5.5 Independent Practice pp. 262–263

9. $3i$ **11.** $-5i$ **13.** $i\sqrt{5}$ **15.** -2 **17.** 1 **19.** -10
21. It is. **23.** It is. **25.** It is not. **27.** $\pm 2i$ **29.** $\pm i\sqrt{2}$
31. $\pm i$ **33.** $12 + 3i$ **35.** $-8 + 2i$ **37.** $6 - 4i$ **39.** $-7 - 4i$
41. $9 - 7i$ **43.** $4 - 10i$ **45.** $-1 + i$ **47.** $2 - 5i$
49. $-2 + 12i$ **51.** $5 + 5i$ **53.** $6 + 7i$ **55.** $-19 - 17i$
57. $2 + 6i$ **59.** $1 - 7i$ **61.** $80 + 120i$

63.

65.

67.

■ 5.5 Integrated Review p. 264

73. $-6x - 9$

75. $\frac{1}{2}s^2 - \frac{3}{2}s$

77. $-3x^2 + x$

79. $1 \pm \sqrt{2}$

81. $\pm\frac{1}{2}$ **83.** $\frac{1}{6} \pm \frac{\sqrt{220}}{60}$

■ 5.5 Mixed Review p. 264

1. ± 2 **3.** $(0, 8)$ **5.** $10\frac{2}{3}$ square units **7.** 5.32×10^6

9. $x < -1$ or $x > \frac{7}{3}$ **11.** $\pm\frac{2}{3}$

13.

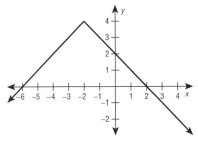

15. $y = (x + 2)^2 - 11$ **17.** 64 ft **19.** $\begin{bmatrix} 1 & 13 \\ -4 & 8 \end{bmatrix}$

■ 5.6 Communicating About Algebra p. 267

A. Answers vary; $y = -x^2 + x - 1$ **B.** Answers vary; $y = x^2 + x + 1$

■ 5.6 Guided Practice p. 268

1. c, b, a **2.** $\frac{2}{3} \pm \frac{\sqrt{2}}{6}i$ **3.** $-\frac{3}{2} \pm \frac{1}{2}i$ **4.** No month, the discriminant is negative and $(4, 63)$ is the highest point on the graph.

■ 5.6 Independent Practice pp. 268–269

5. It is. **7.** It is. **9.** It is. **11.** $\frac{5}{2} \pm \frac{\sqrt{11}}{2}i$ **13.** $-1 \pm \frac{\sqrt{24}}{2}i$

15. $\frac{3}{4} \pm \frac{\sqrt{12}}{8}i$ **17.** $-\frac{5}{6} \pm \frac{\sqrt{11}}{6}i$ **19.** $-\frac{8}{21} \pm \frac{\sqrt{80}}{42}i$

21. $\frac{1}{6} \pm \frac{\sqrt{35}}{6}i$ **23.** 0.5, 0.125 **25.** No real solutions

27. No real solutions **29.** No, area $= \frac{1}{2}(b_1 + b_2)h =$ $\frac{1}{2}(x + [550 - 2x])x = 43,560$. No real solution.

31. It was never down to 300; there are no real number solutions because the discriminant is negative, and the minimum point on the graph is at $(20, 312)$.

33.

Year	Amount	Year	Amount
1980	822.51	1988	859.31
1981	790.99	1989	910.35
1982	769.79	1990	971.71
1983	758.91	1991	1043.39
1984	758.35	1992	1125.39
1985	768.11	1993	1217.71
1986	788.19	1994	1320.35
1987	818.59		

No, there are no real number solutions.

■ 5.6 Integrated Review p. 270

35. $\pm i\sqrt{\frac{7}{5}}$ **37.** $\pm\frac{3}{2}i$ **39.** $\pm\sqrt{15}$ **41.** 0, 2 **43.** 2, $-1\frac{2}{3}$

45.   **47.**   **49.**

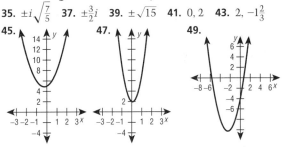

■ 5.7 Communicating About Algebra p. 273

A. I **B.** III **C.** II

A–C. $(0, 0)$ is only on graph I and $(0, 0)$ is only a solution of inequality A; $(4, 0)$ is only on graph II and $(4, 0)$ is only a solution of inequality C; then graph III must match with inequality B.

■ 5.7 Guided Practice p. 274

1. $\left(\frac{3}{8}, \frac{7}{16}\right)$

2–4. Test points will vary.

■ 5.7 Independent Practice pp. 274–276

5. It is. **7.** It is not. **9.** It is. **11.** c **13.** f **15.** d

17.   **19.**   **21.**

23.   **25.**

27.

29.

31.

33.

35. b, a **37.** Less; the predicted use was 516.865 billion gallons.

5.7 Integrated Review p. 276

39.

41.

43. It is not. **45.** It is not. **47.** It is.

49.

51.

53.

5.7 Chapter Review pp. 278–280

1. ± 6 **3.** $\pm\sqrt{2}$

5.

7.

9.

11. $-\dfrac{3}{2} \pm \dfrac{\sqrt{17}}{2}$ **13.** $1 \pm \sqrt{2}$ **15.** $-2 \pm \sqrt{3}$ **17.** 1

19. $-\dfrac{5}{18} \pm \dfrac{\sqrt{61}}{18}$ **21.** $-1, 2$ **23.** $\approx 0.03, \approx 1.33$

25. $-\dfrac{1}{14} \pm \dfrac{\sqrt{141}}{14}$ **27.** 1 **29.** $-\dfrac{1}{3} \pm \dfrac{\sqrt{28}}{6}$ **31.** $-2 - 2i$

33. $-3 + 4i$ **35.** $-16 - 3i$ **37.** $-1 + 5i$ **39.** $1 + 7i$

41.

43. $-\dfrac{3}{4} \pm \dfrac{\sqrt{23}}{4}i$ **45.** $-\dfrac{7}{6} \pm \dfrac{\sqrt{71}}{6}i$ **47.** $-3 \pm \sqrt{11}$

49.

51.

53.

55. ≈ 53.9 ft, ≈ 67.1 ft **57.** 1981; when $M = 28$, $t \approx 11$; the point $(11, 28)$ is on the graph

59. 12 mm, 0.36 mm

61. 2000 **63.** 500 ft; 156.25 ft; 26 million ft^3

CHAPTER 6

6.1 Communicating About Algebra p. 287

A. No, one input corresponds to more than one output.

B. Yes, each input corresponds to exactly one output.

6.1 Guided Practice p. 288

1. Yes, they both describe the same ordered pairs: $(-3, 0)$, $(-2, 1)$, $(-1, 2)$, $(-1, -2)$, $(0, -2)$, $(1, -2)$, $(2, 3)$. **2.** A relation is a function if each input corresponds to exactly one output. **3.** Yes, there is no vertical line that passes through two points of the relation when it is graphed. **4.** B; in A the x-value 1 corresponds to the y-values 6 and 7, and in B each x-value corresponds to exactly one y-value.

6.1 Independent Practice pp. 288–290

5. Domain: $\{-2, -1, 0, 1, 2\}$, range: $\{4, 5, 8\}$ **7.** Domain: $\{3, 4, 7\}$, range: $\{-2, -1, 0, 1, 2\}$

9.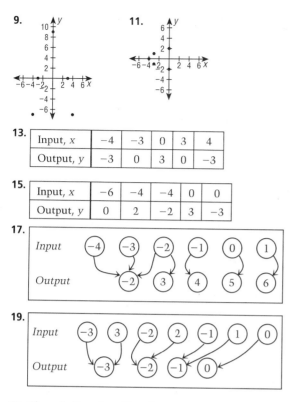

11.

13.

Input, x	-4	-3	0	3	4
Output, y	-3	0	3	0	-3

15.

Input, x	-6	-4	-4	0	0
Output, y	0	2	-2	3	-3

17.

19.

21. Those in Exercises **13** and **16**. **23.** It is not. **25.** It is.
27. -6 **29.** 12 **31.** $-3\frac{1}{2}$ **33.** $-4\frac{3}{4}$ **35.** 125, the volume of the cube with an edge of length 5. **37.** Yes, each y-value corresponds to exactly one P-value.

■ 6.1 Integrated Review p. 290
39. 41, 10, -7, -10, 1, 26 **41.** 5, 9, 11, 11, 9, 5, -1
43. **45.**

■ 6.2 Communicating About Algebra p. 293
Sale price with rebate of \$1200: $f(x) = x - 1200$
Sale price with discount of 15%: $g(x) = 0.85x$
Rebate first: $g(f(x)) = g(x - 1200) = 0.85(x - 1200)$
Discount first: $f(g(x)) = f(0.85x) = 0.85x - 1200$
Rebate first: \$14,620; discount first: \$14,440; \$180

■ 6.2 Guided Practice p. 294
1. All real numbers **2.** All real numbers except $x = 5$
3. Addition, subtraction, multiplication, division, composition **4.** $f(g(x)) = 3x + 1$, $g(f(x)) = 3x + 3$; no

■ 6.2 Independent Practice pp. 294–296
5. All real numbers, all real numbers **7.** All real numbers, all real numbers $\geq \frac{7}{8}$ **9.** All real numbers ≥ 3, all real numbers ≥ 0 **11.** All real numbers except -1, all real numbers except 0 **13.** $h(x) = 3x + 1$ **15.** $h(x) = 2$
17. $h(x) = 2x^2 + 2x$ **19.** $h(x) = \frac{2x}{x+1}$ **21.** $f(g(x)) = 2x + 1$, $g(f(x)) = 2x + 2$ **23.** $f(g(x)) = x^2 - 2x + 1$, $g(f(x)) = x^2 - 1$ **25.** $f(g(x)) = x$, $g(f(x)) = x$ **27.** $h(x) = 4x - 16$, all real numbers **29.** $h(x) = x^2 - 2x + 8$, all real numbers
31. $h(x) = \frac{2x - 8}{x^2}$, all real numbers except 0 **33.** $h(x) = 2x^2 - 8$, all real numbers **35.** $f(x) = x - 50$, $g(x) = 0.8x$
37. b, you must subtract first **39.** $60(50t) + 750 = 3000t + 750$, $0 \leq t \leq 40$; cost: \$750 to \$120,750
41. $(0.875t + 46.25) + (2.5t + 38) = 3.375t + 84.25$, total number of dogs and cats in the U.S. in a given year
43. 1, represents 100% of people polled

■ 6.2 Integrated Review p. 296
45. -8 **47.** 10 **49.** 1 **51.** 0 **53.** 10 **55.** 5 **57.** c

■ 6.2 Mixed Review p. 297
1. $\{-3, -2, -1, 0, 1, 2\}$ **3.** 3×10^3, or 3000
5.

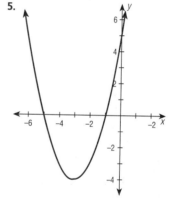

7. $(4a + 10b + 3c)$ **9.** $-\frac{by}{a-c}$ or $\frac{by}{c-a}$
11. y: -6, x: -3, 2 **13.** $\pm 7i$ **15.** 0.246 **17.** $y = \frac{3}{4}x - \frac{1}{2}$
19. $\begin{bmatrix} 3 & -2 \\ 1 & 0 \end{bmatrix}$

■ 6.3 Communicating About Algebra p. 301
A. $x = \frac{2}{3}y - 4$, yes **B.** $x = \frac{1}{2}y^2 + 3$, no

1. Switch the coordinates of each ordered pair, for example: {(−3, 4), (−1, 2)} → {(4,−3), (2,−1)} 2. Switch x and y, for example: $y = 3x − 1 \rightarrow x = 3y − 1$

3. $x = \frac{1}{2}y − 4$ or $g(x) = 2x + 8$, yes

4. No, its graph does not pass the vertical line test.
5. They are reflections of each other in the line $y = x$.
6. $f(g(x)) = 2\left(\frac{1}{2}x − 2\right) + 4 = x$,
$g(f(x)) = \frac{1}{2}(2x + 4) − 2 = x$

7. {(5, 1), (−3, 4), (9, 1), (−1, 0)} 9. {(1,−3), (2,−2), (0,−1), (3, 3)} 11. c 13. d 15. $x = −3y + 5$
17. $x = y + 4$ 19. $x = 12y − 6$ 21. $x = 4y − 1$
23. Yes 25. Yes

27. No 29. No

31. Yes 33. No

35. $f(g(x)) = (x − 9) + 9 = x$, $g(f(x)) = (x + 9) − 9 = x$
37. $f(g(x)) = 2\left(\frac{1}{2}x + \frac{1}{2}\right) − 1 = x$, $g(f(x)) = \frac{1}{2}(2x − 1) + \frac{1}{2} = x$ 39. $f(g(x)) = −3\left(−\frac{1}{3}x + \frac{1}{6}\right) + \frac{1}{2} = x$,
$g(f(x)) = −\frac{1}{3}\left(−3x + \frac{1}{2}\right) + \frac{1}{6} = x$ 41. $C = \frac{5}{9}(F − 32)$
43. $A = 200 − \frac{H}{0.8}$, 160 45. a

47. $y = \frac{1}{2}x + \frac{3}{2}$ 49. $y = x − 2$
51. Yes 53. No

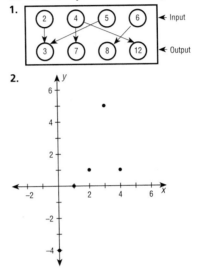

55. $f(g(x)) = \frac{3}{2}x + 1$
57. $f(g(x)) = 100x^2 − 6$

1.

2.

3. b 4. 5 5. No. −1 maps to 2 and 3. 6. Domain: {−4,−3,−2,−1, 0}, Range: {1, 2, 3, 4, 5} 7. All real numbers except −2 8. All real numbers 9. All real numbers ≥7 10. All real numbers ≥9 11. All real numbers ≥3 12. All real numbers ≥−16
13. $h(x) = x^2 − 4x + 6$ 14. $h(x) = 16x^2 − 48x + 36$
15. $h(x) = \frac{1}{4}x + \frac{3}{2}$ 16. $P(x) = 1.5x$ 17. $C(x) = 1.905x$
18. $9.53 19. $f(x) = \left(\frac{x + 7}{75}\right)(100)$ 20. $g(x) = \frac{75x}{100} − 7$, 60

A. Lightly draw each graph for all values of x, then darken the portion that is the graph of the compound function.

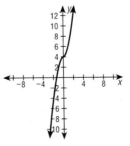

B. Draw horizontal line segments, each with a solid dot on the left and an open dot on the right.

■ 6.4 Guided Practice p. 309

1. Answers vary. $f(x) = \begin{cases} x, & x \geq 0 \\ -x, & x < 0 \end{cases}$

2. $f(x) = \begin{cases} 10 - 2x, & x < 5 \\ -(10 - 2x), & x \geq 5 \end{cases}$ or $f(x) = \begin{cases} 10 - 2x, & x \leq 5 \\ -(10 - 2x), & x > 5 \end{cases}$

3. 4, 2

4. Answers vary. $f(x) = \begin{cases} -1, & 0 \leq x < 2 \\ 0, & 2 \leq x < 4 \\ 1, & 4 \leq x < 6 \end{cases}$

■ 6.4 Independent Practice pp. 309–311

5. -3 **7.** 1 **9.** -3 **11.** -9

13.

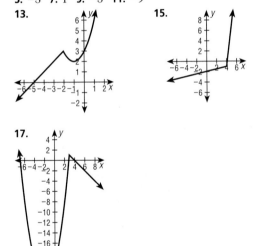

15.

17.

19. d **21.** b

23. $f(x) = \begin{cases} -(x + 2), & x < -2 \\ x + 2, & x \geq -2 \end{cases}$ or $f(x) = \begin{cases} -(x + 2), & x \leq -2 \\ x + 2, & x > -2 \end{cases}$

25. $f(x) = \begin{cases} -2x - 6, & x < -3 \\ -(-2x - 6), & x \geq -3 \end{cases}$ or $f(x) = \begin{cases} -2x - 6, & x \leq -3 \\ -(-2x - 6), & x > -3 \end{cases}$

27. $f(x) = \begin{cases} -\left(\frac{1}{3}x - 1\right), & x < 3 \\ \frac{1}{3}x - 1, & x \geq 3 \end{cases}$ or

$f(x) = \begin{cases} -\left(\frac{1}{3}x - 1\right), & x \leq 3 \\ \frac{1}{3}x - 1, & x > 3 \end{cases}$

29.

31.

33. $C = \begin{cases} 10 + 8.5x, & x \leq 25 \\ 10 + 7.75x, & x > 25 \end{cases}$

35.

37. Second graph; $133 billion, $422.5 billion

■ 6.4 Integrated Review p. 311

39.

41.

43.

45. 1 **47.** 2 **49.** 73

37. **39.**

41.

■ 6.5 Communicating About Algebra   p. 317
A. $g(x) = x^2 + 2$, vertical shift 2 units up   **B.** $g(x) = -x^2$, reflection   **C.** $g(x) = (x + 4)^2$, horizontal shift 4 units to the left

■ 6.5 Guided Practice   p. 318
1. Vertical up, vertical down, horizontal to the right, horizontal to the left.   **2.** They are reflections of each other.

3.   **4.**

5. d **6.** a **7.** c **8.** b

■ 6.5 Independent Practice   pp. 318–319
9. $g(x)$ is $f(x)$ shifted up 3.   **11.** $g(x)$ is $f(x)$ shifted down 1.
13. $g(x)$ is $f(x)$ shifted to the right 8.   **15.** $g(x)$ is $f(x)$ shifted to the left 5.   **17.** $g(x) = f(x + 1)$
19. $g(x) = f(x) - 3$ **21.** b   **23.** c

25.   **27.**

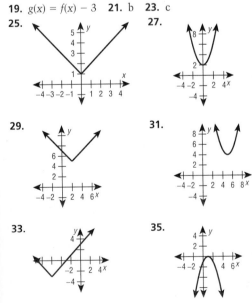

29.   **31.**

33.   **35.**

---

43. d **45.** c
47. $C(t) = 14(t + 10)^2 + 63.2(t + 10) + 2500$
49. 11,360

■ 6.5 Integrated Review   p. 320
51.   **53.**   **55.**

57. d

■ 6.5 Mixed Review   p. 320
1. $\frac{2}{15}$ **3.** $x < -2$ or $x > 6$ **5.** $x: 3 \pm \sqrt{5}, y: 4$
7.

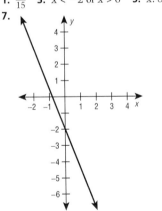

9. $3x + 6y + 1$ **11.** $h(x) = 3x - 3$ **13.** $h(x) = 6x^2 - 18x$
15. $h(x) = \frac{1}{3}x + 3$ **17.** $\frac{2y^3}{3x^3}$ **19.** 128 ft/sec

■ 6.6 Communicating About Algebra   p. 323
Fibonacci numbers: 1, 1, 2, 3, 5, 8, 13, 21, 34, 55; First differences: 0, 1, 1, 2, 3, 5, 8, 13, 21; Second differences: 1, 0, 1, 1, 2, 3, 5, 7; No, neither the first nor the second differences are all the same number.

■ 6.6 Guided Practice   p. 324
1. Answers vary. $f(1) = 2, f(n) = f(n - 1) + 4$ **2.** 11   **3.** 21
4. −1, 1, 3, 5, 7; 2, 2, 2, 2

5. Yes, a quadratic model, the second differences are all the same.

6. Quadratic model, the second differences are all the same.

■ 6.6 Independent Practice pp. 324–326

7. 1, 3, 5, 7, 9 **9.** 0, 1, 5, 14, 30 **11.** 2, 5, 26, 677, 458,330 **13.** 10, 40, 160, 640, 2560 **15.** 4, 0, 10, 8, 20
17. 0, 2, 2, 6, 10 **19.** 3, −2, 6, 3, 13, 12, 24; −5, 8, −3, 10, −1, 12 **21.** 0, 3, 6, 9, 12, 15, 18; 3, 3, 3, 3, 3, 3
23. −2, −2, −7, −9, −16, −20, −29; 0, −5, −2, −7, −4, −9 **25.** 3, 1, −2, −6, −11, −17, −24; −1, −1, −1, −1, −1 **27.** 0, 5, −10, 35, −100, 305, −910; −20, 60, −180, 540, −1620 **29.** 9, 21, 41, 71, 113, 169, 241; 8, 10, 12, 14, 16 **31.** Quadratic **33.** Linear **35.** Neither
37. $f(n) = 2n - 1$ **39.** $f(n) = -2n + 9$ **41.** $f(n) = 5n - 4$
43. $f(n) = n^2 - n + 3$ **45.** $f(n) = \frac{1}{2}n^2 + n - 3$
47. $f(n) = -3n^2 - 3n + 4$ **49.** $f(n) = 2n^2 + 5n - 3$
51. $f(n) = 2n + 2$ **53.** $f(n) = 2n^2 + 2n - 4$
55. $f(n) = -n^2 - n$ **57.** 0, 2, 5, 9, 14, 20; $f(n) = \frac{1}{2}n^2 - \frac{3}{2}n$
59. \$20, \$40.10, \$60.30, \$80.60, \$101.00, \$121.51, \$142.12, \$162.83, \$183.64, \$204.56, \$225.58, \$246.71; quadratic model

■ 6.6 Integrated Review p. 326

61. −9 **63.** 10 **65.** 7 **67.** (1,−4) **69.** (−40,−15)
71. (4,−1, 3)

■ 6.7 Communicating About Algebra p. 329

Answers vary. Americans aged 18-to-29 use more time to wash and dress than Americans aged 12-to-17.

■ 6.7 Guided Practice p. 330

1. See page 327. **2.** 34.35, 34, 34 **3.** 32.5, 34, 36
4.

■ 6.7 Independent Practice pp. 330–332

5. Preamble: ≈5.15, Green Eggs and Ham: ≈3.04; the Preamble has a higher reading level **7.** Mean: ≈\$331.67, median: \$340, mode: \$400
9. Answers vary.

11. 8, 17, 21.5 **13.** ≈2.8%, 1.25%
15. Either the mean (972.9) or the median (971) best describes the average weight, the mode (925) is too low.

■ 6.7 Integrated Review p. 332

17. a

■ 6.7 Chapter Review pp. 334–338

1. It is. **3.** It is not. **5.** −8 **7.** −11 **9.** −5 **11.** All real numbers except 1 **13.** All real numbers ≥ 0 **15.** All real numbers **17.** $h(x) = 3x - 5$ **19.** $h(x) = -x - 1$
21. $h(x) = 2x^2 - 6x + 4$ **23.** $h(x) = \frac{x - 1}{2x - 4}$ **25.** $h(x) = 2x - 5$ **27.** $x = \frac{1}{2}(y - 10)$

35. $f(g(x)) = 2\left(\frac{1}{2}x + \frac{5}{2}\right) - 5 = x$, $g(f(x)) = \frac{1}{2}(2x - 5) + \frac{5}{2} = x$
37. $f(g(x)) = 3\left(\frac{1}{3}x - 2\right) + 6 = x$, $g(f(x)) = \frac{1}{3}(3x + 6) - 2 = x$ **39.** −17

51.

53.

33.

55.

57.

35. c **37.** b **39.** $h(x) = 5x$
41. $h(x) = -12x^2 - 9x + 3$
43.

$y = 4x + 24$

$y = \frac{1}{4}x - 6$

59. 4, 12, 21, 31, 42 **61.** 1, 2, 5, 26, 677 **63.** $c, f(n) = 2n$
65. $d, f(n) = -\frac{1}{2}n^2 - \frac{1}{2}n + 10$ **67.** e **69.** c **71.** b
73. g **75.** $\approx$72.8, 72.5, 60.6 and 92.3 **77.** $3\sqrt{3}, r(18)$ is
the radius of a circle inscribed in an equilateral triangle
with a side of length 18. **79.** $P = 1.2(t + 28)^2 + 430$
81. $8360 million **83.** $60,478 million **85.** 1840, West
Virginia **87.** 1990, Missouri **89.** 1790, Maryland
91. 1920, Indiana

45. 4, 2, 0, -2, -4 **47.** 120 **49.** 5040
51. $[500 \ \ 500]\begin{bmatrix} 0.34 & 0.28 & 0.13 \\ 0.18 & 0.33 & 0.15 \end{bmatrix} = [260 \ \ 305 \ \ 140]$
53. $\approx$1.6 seconds **55.** No **57.** 575.25 **59.** $343 billion
61.

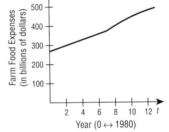

■ 6.7 Cumulative Review for Chapters 1–6
pp. 340–343

1. $\begin{bmatrix} 7 & 2 & \frac{17}{2} \\ -\frac{57}{2} & 25 & 13 \end{bmatrix}$

3. $\begin{bmatrix} 6 & 12 \\ 12 & 6 \\ 4 & 29 \end{bmatrix}$

5. $-10;$ $\begin{bmatrix} -\frac{1}{10} & \frac{7}{10} \\ \frac{1}{5} & -\frac{2}{5} \end{bmatrix}$

7. 407 **9.** Yes **11.** $(-3, -1)$ **13.** $(1, -2, -1)$ **15.** -6
17. $-\frac{1}{3} \pm \frac{\sqrt{24}}{6}$ **19.** Two real solutions **21.** One real
solution

23.

25.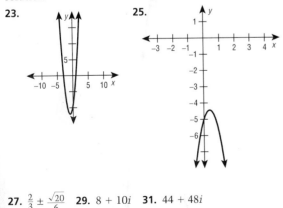

63. $f(t) = 0.14(t + 10)^2 - 6.76(t + 10) + 1040$

CHAPTER 7

■ 7.1 Communicating About Algebra   p. 348

A. $\dfrac{180 \cdot \frac{4}{3}\pi\left(\frac{3}{10}\right)^3}{\pi\left(\frac{3}{2}\right)^2\left(\frac{11}{2}\right)} = \dfrac{180 \cdot \frac{4}{3}\pi\left(\frac{27}{1000}\right)}{\pi\left(\frac{9}{4}\right)\left(\frac{11}{2}\right)}$ Power of Quotient
Property

$= \dfrac{180 \cdot 4 \cdot 27 \cdot 4 \cdot 2}{3 \cdot 1000 \cdot 9 \cdot 11} = \dfrac{144}{275}$ Simplifying

B. 8000, $\dfrac{1000}{n} = \dfrac{6^3}{12^3}$, $n = 8000$

■ 7.1 Guided Practice   p. 349
1. "x to the third power divided by y to the fourth
power" **2.** $2a^8$; Product of Powers Property **3.** $\frac{1}{a^4}$;
Negative Power Property, Product of Powers Property
4. a^6; Power of a Power Property **5.** a^2; Power of a
Quotient Property, Negative Power Property **6.** 212.36

27. $\frac{2}{3} \pm \frac{\sqrt{20}}{6}$ **29.** $8 + 10i$ **31.** $44 + 48i$

■ 7.1 Independent Practice   pp. 349–351

7. 3; 4   **9.** x; 3   **11.** 256   **13.** 1   **15.** x^2 **17.** 4096   **19.** $\frac{1}{x^{15}}$
21. $x^{12}y^4$ **23.** $9x^4$ **25.** $\frac{4y}{x}$ **27.** $3y^4$ **29.** 16   **31.** $\frac{y^3}{x^4}$
33. $\frac{6y}{5x^4}$ **35.** $-9x^2y^2$ **37.** $10x^{10}y^4$ **39.** 3   **41.** 4   **43.** 12
45. 3   **47.** $\frac{1}{10}, -\frac{1}{10}$ **49.** $36\pi x^8$ **51.** $\approx 121{,}940$ days
53. 102.1 in.   **55.** $\approx\$147.26$ billion, $\$146.57$ billion

■ 7.1 Integrated Review   p. 351

57. 48   **59.** -312 **61.** a

■ 7.2 Communicating About Algebra   p. 355

A. $\$1132.05$ **B.** $\$1130.53$ A, because use of $A =$
$P\left(1 + \frac{r}{n}\right)^{nt}$.

■ 7.2 Guided Practice   p. 356

1. See page 352.   **2.** b; It is compounded more frequently.

a. $3000\left(1 + \frac{0.06}{2}\right)^{2\cdot 1} = 3000(1.03)^2 = 3182.70$

b. $3000\left(1 + \frac{0.06}{4}\right)^{4\cdot 1} = 3000(1.015)^4 = 3184.09$

3. $\$2979.69$ **4.** $\$2938.66$ **5.** Growth, $\frac{6}{5} > 1$
6. Decay, $\frac{3}{4} < 1$

■ 7.2 Independent Practice   pp. 356–358

7. $\$1129.27$ **9.** $\$4081.54$ **11.** $\$620.07$ **13.** $\$19{,}553.40$
15. Growth   **17.** Growth   **19.** c   **21.** b
23. 32, 16, 8, 4, 2, 1   **25.** $\frac{1}{81}, \frac{1}{27}, \frac{1}{9}, \frac{1}{3}, 1, 3, 9$

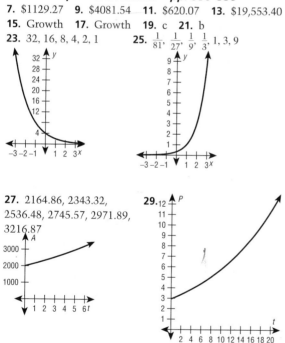

27. 2164.86, 2343.32,
2536.48, 2745.57, 2971.89,
3216.87

29.

31. Yes, the inflation graph is below the salary graph.

■ 7.2 Integrated Review   p. 358

33. $\frac{384}{125}$ **35.** ≈ 599.14 **37.** a

■ 7.2 Mixed Review   p. 359

1. 20%   **3.** $-2, 6$ **5.** x: 7, y: 3   **7.** 3
9. All real numbers > 4 **11.** 1.36×10^4 **13.** $(3, 8)$
15. $y = 5x - 14$ **17.** $\left(-3\frac{1}{2}, 4\frac{1}{3}\right)$

■ 7.3 Communicating About Algebra   p. 363

A. ≈ 2.41 ft   **B.** ≈ 4.08 in.   **C.** ≈ 8.99 knots

■ 7.3 Guided Practice   p. 364

1. Yes, $4^3 = 64$; no, $(-4)^3 \neq 64$ **2.** Yes, $4^2 = 16$; yes,
$(-4)^2 = 16$ **3.** 5, 10   **4.** -5, does not exist   **5.** ≈ 70 ft
6. $\frac{1}{9}$

■ 7.3 Independent Practice   pp. 364–366

7. $12^{1/5}$ **9.** $16^{1/9}$ **11.** $2^{1/4}$ **13.** $\sqrt[3]{4}$ **15.** $\sqrt[6]{10}$ **17.** $\sqrt[4]{3}$
19. $\sqrt[3]{3}$ **21.** $\pm\sqrt[6]{9}$ **23.** $\pm\sqrt[4]{10}$ **25.** 5   **27.** -8 **29.** 4
31. 5   **33.** -3 **35.** 4   **37.** ≈ 1.73 **39.** ≈ 2.60 **41.** ≈ 1.35
43. $\frac{1}{64}$ **45.** 27   **47.** 25   **49.** -81 **51.** 4   **53.** 1000
55. ≈ 2.520 **57.** ≈ 0.464 **59.** ≈ 0.109 **61.** ≈ 2.13 cm
63. ≈ 3.18 cm   **65.** 1988   **67.** $\frac{150}{\pi}$

■ 7.3 Integrated Review   p. 366

69. $2\sqrt{5}$ **71.** $3\sqrt{6}$ **73.** 256   **75.** 64   **77.** $\pm\frac{5}{4}$ **79.** ± 2

■ 7.3 Mid-Chapter Self-Test   p. 367

1. $\frac{a^2b^7}{c^4}$ **2.** $\frac{1}{b^{13}}$ **3.** $a^{11}b^6$ **4.** 4   **5.** $\frac{1}{27}$ **6.** 2   **7.** $\frac{1}{3^5}$
8. $\frac{2^3}{3}$ **9.** 2^3 **10.** $(-2, 9), (-1, 6), (0, 4), \left(1, \frac{8}{3}\right), \left(2, \frac{16}{9}\right)$
11. $\left(-2, \frac{3}{16}\right), \left(-1, \frac{3}{4}\right), (0, 3), (1, 12), (2, 48)$ **12.** $\sqrt{3}$
13. $7^{\frac{1}{3}}$ **14.** $\pm\sqrt[4]{90}$ **15.** $\approx 21{,}611$ **16.** $\$3{,}638.79$
17. $\$1499.97$ **18.** ≈ 84.09 grams, 20 years   **19.** ≈ 8.2
million   **20.** ≈ 2.43 billion

■ 7.4 Communicating About Algebra   p. 370

A. ≈ 0.38 **B.** ≈ 3.29 **C.** ≈ 0.29

■ 7.4 Guided Practice   p. 371

1. 2   **2.** 64   **3.** $x^{\frac{4}{5}}$ **4.** 2   **5.** No; $3 \neq 4$ (The radicands
are not equal.)   **6.** $\sqrt[4]{7}, 7, 4$

■ 7.4 Independent Practice   pp. 371–373

7. 3   **9.** 2   **11.** $\left(\frac{1}{3}\right)^{4/5}$ **13.** $4^{3/4}$ **15.** $-6^{4/7}$ **17.** $6x^{1/4}$
19. $3y^{1/5}$ **21.** $\frac{1}{2}$ **23.** $\frac{15{,}625}{4096}$ **25.** 3   **27.** $4\sqrt[4]{x}$ **29.** 2
31. $\sqrt{6}$ **33.** $4^{7/6}$ **35.** 6   **37.** $|x|\sqrt[4]{6}$ **39.** $2x$ **41.** $x^2\sqrt[3]{2}$
43. ≈ 5.67 **45.** ≈ 6.56 **47.** ≈ 0.000129 **49.** ≈ 1.31
51. ≈ 1.53 **53.** ≈ 2.74 **55.** $5\sqrt[4]{5}$ **57.** $-2\sqrt[9]{6}$ **59.** $\sqrt[4]{3}$
61. $5\sqrt[3]{10}$ **63.** $7\sqrt[5]{7}$ **65.** $-\sqrt[8]{5}$ **67.** $\frac{\sqrt{3}}{2}$ **69.** Spruce, bone
71. $9 + 2\sqrt{2} + 3\sqrt{5}$ **73.** ≈ 175 vibrations per second,
≈ 932 vibrations per second

75. x^{11} **77.** x^{15} **79.** $\frac{1}{x}$ **81.** $\frac{1}{x^7}$ **83.** ≈ -1.44 **85.** ≈ 1.59
87. ≈ 5.85 **89.** ≈ 1.93

7.5 Communicating About Algebra p. 377

A. $b = (\sqrt{5} - 2) - (-1) = \sqrt{5} - 1$
$a = 1 - (\sqrt{5} - 2) = -\sqrt{5} + 3$
$$\frac{\sqrt{5} - 1}{-\sqrt{5} + 3} \overset{?}{=} \frac{\sqrt{5} + 1}{2}$$
$$2\sqrt{5} - 2 \overset{?}{=} -5 + 3\sqrt{5} - \sqrt{5} + 3$$
$$2\sqrt{5} - 2 = 2\sqrt{5} - 2$$
B. $\frac{2}{\sqrt{5} - 1} \cdot \frac{\sqrt{5} + 1}{\sqrt{5} + 1} = \frac{2(\sqrt{5} + 1)}{5 - 1} = \frac{2(\sqrt{5} + 1)}{4} = \frac{\sqrt{5} + 1}{2}$

7.5 Guided Practice p. 378

1. Isolate the radical on one side, raise both sides to the same power to eliminate the radical, solve the resulting equation.
2. $\sqrt[3]{2x + 10} = 2$ Isolate the radical by subtracting 1 from both sides.
$2x + 10 = 8$ Raise both sides to the third power to eliminate the radical.
$x = -1$ Solve the resulting equation.
3. $\sqrt{18}$
4. $d = \sqrt{(6 - (-2))^2 + (1 - 5)^2} = \sqrt{80}$;
$d^2 = (6 - (-2))^2 + (1 - 5)^2$, $d^2 = 80$, $d = \sqrt{80}$

7.5 Independent Practice pp. 378–379

5. It is. **7.** It is. **9.** It is. **11.** 400 **13.** 343 **15.** 128
17. 525 **19.** No solution. **21.** $\frac{44}{3}$ **23.** 623 **25.** $-\frac{2}{3}$
27. 4 **29.** No solution. **31.** 7 **33.** -15 **35.** 8 **37.** 1, 3
39. $\frac{1}{2}$ **41.** 27 **43.** $\sqrt{17}$ **45.** 10 **47.** 0, 4 **49.** h is the geometric mean of x and y.
$$(x + y)^2 = a^2 + b^2$$
$$x^2 + 2xy + y^2 = x^2 + h^2 + y^2 + h^2$$
$$2xy = 2h^2$$
$$xy = h^2$$
$$\sqrt{xy} = h$$
$$h = y$$

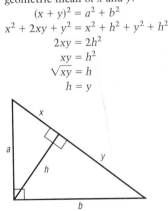

51. ≈ 166 miles, ≈ 44.3 minutes **53.** 1982

7.5 Integrated Review p. 380

55. $9x^2$ **57.** $216^{\frac{1}{5}}x^{\frac{9}{5}}$ **59.** 4 **61.** $\frac{1}{13}$ **63.** b

7.5 Mixed Review p. 380

1. x^9 **3.** 24 **5.** 16 **7.** 0.05 **9.** $\frac{8x^2}{27y^6z^2}$ **11.** 3^{-4} **13.** $(2, -3)$

15.

17. $f(x) = \frac{1}{2}x^2 + \frac{3}{2}x - 2$

7.6 Communicating About Algebra p. 383

A. Translate the graph of $\sqrt{x}$ down 2 units and to the right 5 units.

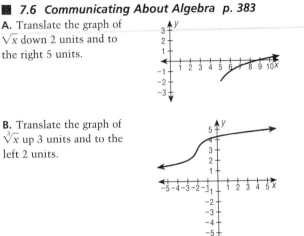

B. Translate the graph of $\sqrt[3]{x}$ up 3 units and to the left 2 units.

7.6 Guided Practice p. 384

1. b, a; only the cube root function has negative roots
2. g is a translation of f to the right 10 units **3.** 0, -1, $-\sqrt{2}$, $-\sqrt{3}$, -2; $x \geq -2$, $y \leq 0$
4.

7.6 Independent Practice pp. 384–386

5. g is a reflection of f in the x-axis, to the left 16 units
7. g is a reflection of f in the x-axis, down 9 units. **9.** g is a translation of f to the right 10 units and down 1 unit.
11. b **13.** a **15.** e **19.** All real numbers, all real numbers
17. $x \geq 1$, $y \geq 0$

21. All real numbers, all real numbers

23. $x \geq 1$, $y \geq 7$

25. All real numbers, all real numbers

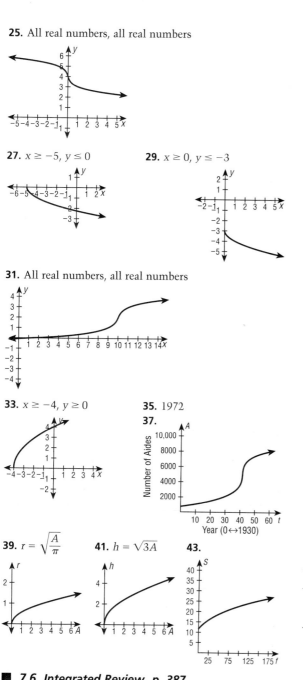

27. $x \geq -5$, $y \leq 0$

29. $x \geq 0$, $y \leq -3$

31. All real numbers, all real numbers

33. $x \geq -4$, $y \geq 0$

35. 1972

37.

39. $r = \sqrt{\dfrac{A}{\pi}}$ **41.** $h = \sqrt{3A}$ **43.**

7.6 Integrated Review p. 387
45. 5   **47.** 9   **49.** −4   **51.** f   **53.** e   **55.** d

7.6 Chapter Review pp. 391–394
1. 390,625   **3.** $\dfrac{1}{x}$ **5.** $\dfrac{1}{y^{12}}$ **7.** $36x^2$ **9.** $3y$ **11.** $\dfrac{1}{x^2}$ **13.** $\dfrac{3y^5}{x^5}$

15. $\dfrac{2x}{y^2}$ **17.** $701.28   **19.** $450.53   **21.** 8, 4, 2, 1, $\dfrac{1}{2}$

23. $\dfrac{4}{27}, \dfrac{2}{9}, \dfrac{1}{3}, \dfrac{1}{2}, \dfrac{3}{4}$ **25.** 5   **27.** 3   **29.** $\dfrac{1}{8}$ **31.** 2   **33.** $\dfrac{1}{25}$

35. $\sqrt[3]{4}$ **37.** $25^{\frac{1}{3}}$ **39.** 864   **41.** $-6\sqrt[3]{6}$ **43.** $9\sqrt[4]{7}$ **45.** 1

47. 8   **49.** No solution   **51.** −4   **53.** 32   **55.** $4 \pm \sqrt{11}$

57. −2, 22   **59.** c   **61.** e   **63.** b

65.

67.

69.

71.

73.

75.

77. $94,000   **79.** 1984   **81.** ≈279.7 knots   **83.** 58,000
85. 514 million   **87.** 1667

CHAPTER 8

■ 8.1 Communicating About Algebra p. 401
A. Shift the graph of 2^x two units to the right and one unit down.

B. Reflect the graph of 3^x in the x-axis, then shift the graph one unit to the left and 4 units up.

■ 8.1 Guided Practice p. 402
1. The graph of g is the graph of f shifted 3 units down.
2. The graph of g is the graph of f reflected in the x-axis and shifted 2 units to the left.   **3.** 16.242   **4.** 2^π

■ 8.1 Independent Practice pp. 402–404
5. The graph of g is the graph of f shifted 2 units down.
7. The graph of g is the graph of f shifted 6 units up.
9. The graph of g is the graph of f reflected in the x-axis and shifted 4 units to the left.   **11.** The graph of g is the graph of f shifted 4 units to the right and 5 units up.
13. h   **15.** g   **17.** f   **19.** c

21.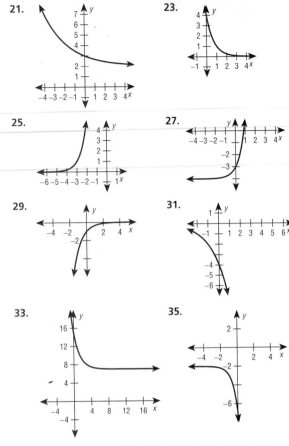

23.

25.

27.

29.

31.

33.

35.

59.

61. Exponential decay   **63.** Exponential growth   **65.** c

8.2 Communicating About Algebra   *p. 408*
A. 3, the graph includes (3, 1)
B. 1, the graph includes (4, 1)
C. 2, the graph includes (5, 1)

8.2 Guided Practice   *p. 409*
1. $\log_2 3$ **2.** $3^{1.7} = x$ **3.** $\log_4 8 = x$ **4.** $\frac{1}{2}$ **5.** ≈ 1.086
6. At left: f, at right: g

8.2 Independent Practice   *pp. 409–411*
7. $3^3 = 27$ **9.** $6^2 = 36$ **11.** $2^5 = 32$ **13.** $5^3 = 125$
15. $\log_3 243 = 5$ **17.** $\log_4 \frac{1}{4} = -1$ **19.** $\log_4 64 = 3$
21. $\log_9 4.327 \approx \frac{2}{3}$ **23.** 2   **25.** 0   **27.** $\frac{5}{6}$ **29.** 1   **31.** -3
33. No solution   **35.** Between 1 and 2, ≈ 1.161
37. Between 0 and 1, ≈ 0.613 **39.** 3.170   **41.** 6.843
43. 2.727   **45.** No solution   **47.** 4   **49.** $\frac{1}{6}$ **51.** 243   **53.** 4
55. 2   **57.** 1   **59.** $g(x) = 6^x$ **61.** $g(x) = \log_{\frac{1}{3}} x$ **63.** c   **65.** d

67.

69.

71.

73.

37. 36.555   **39.** 278.378   **41.** 3.322   **43.** 4.270   **45.** e
47. $v = 380(1.08)^t$ where $t = 0$ represents 1985
49. $10,393.16, $6610.63

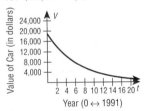

51. ≈ 36 million, tape cassettes became more popular

8.1 Integrated Review   *p. 404*
53.

55.

75.

77.

79. 56 in.   **81.** 4.6   **83.** 17,100 years

57.

■ 8.2 Integrated Review p. 411

85.

87.

89. b

■ 8.2 Mixed Review p. 412

1. $\dfrac{c^2}{a^3 b^3}$ **3.** -3 **5.** $3^{2/5}$ **7.** $-6i$ **9.** IV **11.** $(7, 5)$ **13.** -8
15. 8 **17.** 2 **19.** \$1930.12

■ 8.3 Communicating About Algebra p. 415

$\approx 7.08 \times 10^{23}$ ergs, $\approx 1.12 \times 10^{22}$ ergs

■ 8.3 Guided Practice p. 416

1. a, because of the quotient and power properties of logarithms **2.** 15 **3.** 3.907 **4.** c, logarithm properties refer to products and quotients, not sums

■ 8.3 Independent Practice pp. 416–418

5. 0.602 **7.** 1.556 **9.** $\log_2 3 + \log_2 x$
11. $\log_{10} 2 + 3 \log_{10} x$ **13.** $\log_4 6 - \log_4 5$
15. $\log_6 10 - \log_6 3$
17. $\log_{10} 7 + 3 \log_{10} x + \log_{10} y + \log_{10} z$
19. $\frac{1}{2} \log_2 x + 3 \log_2 y$ **21.** $\frac{1}{2} \log_{10} x$ **23.** $\frac{2}{3} \log_{10} x$
25. $\log_5 \frac{6}{4}$ **27.** $\log_{10} 5x^2$ **29.** $\log_3 \left(\frac{19}{38}\right)^3$ **31.** $\log_{10} 8xy^2$
33. $\log_8 64x^2 y^2$ **35.** $\log_{10} 16x^{10}$ **37.** $\log_5 9$ **39.** 3 **41.** 2
43. 3 **45.** 2 **47.** $E = \log_{10} \left(\frac{C_2}{C_1}\right)^{1.4}$ **49.** ≈ 1.09 kilocalories
per gram molecule **51.** 1.000, 2, 3.000, 4, 5.000, 6, 7.000, 8; pattern for s: consecutive integers **53.** 10^{-11} watts per square centimeter **55.** 10^{-4} watts per square centimeter

■ 8.3 Integrated Review p. 418

57. 5 **59.** 2 **61.** 4 **63.** 5 **65.** ≈ 0.70 **67.** ≈ 1.43
69. ≈ 1.63

■ 8.3 Mid-Chapter Self-Test p. 419

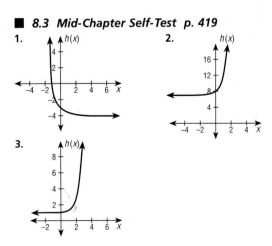

4. $2^3 = 8$ **5.** $5^1 = 5$ **6.** $7^0 = 1$ **7.** $\log_6 1 = 0$
8. $\log_7 7 = 1$ **9.** $\log_4 64 = 3$ **10.** 5 **11.** Not defined
12. -3 **13.** 1 **14.** Not defined **15.** 1.230 **16.** $\log_{10} 6 +$
$\log_{10} x$ **17.** $\log_{10} 3 - \log_{10} a$ **18.** $4 \log_{10} x$ **19.** $\log_{10} 3x$
20. $\log_{10} \frac{7}{b}$ **21.** $\log_{10} y^4$ **22.** 64 **23.** 2 **24.** 83 **25.** $3\frac{1}{5}$
26. 2 **27.** 27
28.

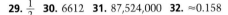

29. $\frac{1}{2}$ **30.** 6612 **31.** 87,524,000 **32.** ≈ 0.158

■ 8.4 Communicating About Algebra p. 422

A. Exponential growth   **B.** Exponential decay

■ 8.4 Guided Practice p. 423

1. False, e is irrational **2.** $\frac{e^5}{4}$ **3.**
3. Exponential growth

4. $y = -2$

■ 8.4 Independent Practice pp. 423–424

5. 148.413 **7.** 0.472 **9.** 1.649 **11.** 24.533 **13.** e^6
15. $4e^{3x+1}$ **17.** $\frac{4}{e^{3x}}$ **19.** $\frac{e^{3x}}{3}$ **21.** $4e^{10x}$ **23.** $2e\sqrt{x}$
25. Exponential growth **27.** Exponential decay **29.** c
31. d

41.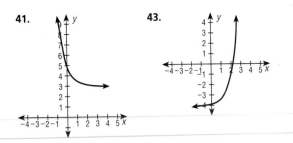

43.

45. \$851.44 **47.** Quarterly: \$4930.86, continuously: \$4946.16; continuously compounded interest pays \$15.30 more **49.** ≈4.6 lb per in.^{2}, answers vary

51.

8.4 Integrated Review p. 425

53. 5^x **55.** 4^{10x} **57.** a. $g(x)$, b. $h(x)$, c. $f(x)$, d. $k(x)$; the larger the base, the steeper the curve

59. The value of A when $t = 0$ is the same for the model and the graph; the value of A when $t = 10$ is 1,149,254 for the model and 1,149,159 for the graph; the model does not show the slight decline from 1981 to 1982 shown on the graph.

8.5 Communicating About Algebra p. 428

(i) $kt = \ln \frac{15.7}{28.6} \approx -0.5997$, $kt + \frac{1}{2}k = \ln \frac{12.8}{28.6} \approx -0.8040$

(ii) $\left(kt + \frac{1}{2}k\right) - kt \approx -0.8040 - (-0.5997)$
$$\frac{1}{2}k \approx -0.2043$$
$$k \approx -0.4086$$

(iii) $kt \approx -0.5997$
$$-0.4086t \approx -0.5997$$
$$t \approx 1.4677$$

(iv) $k \approx -0.4$, $t \approx 1.5$

8.5 Guided Practice p. 429

1. Let $\ln e = \log_e e = x$, then $e^x = e$ and $x = 1$. **2.** Let $\ln e^6 = \log_e e^6 = x$, then $e^x = e^6$ and $x = 6$.
3. $x > 0$, all real numbers; it is the reflection of $\ln x$ in the x-axis

4. $\log_6 10 = \dfrac{\ln 10}{\ln 6}$

8.5 Independent Practice pp. 429–431

5. 4 **7.** −3 **9.** ≈2.7081 **11.** ≈6.6542 **13.** ≈5.4657
15. ≈3.4657 **17.** $\ln 8 - \ln 6 - \ln x$ **19.** $\ln 16 + 2 \ln x$
21. $\ln 2 + 7 \ln y - 3 \ln x$ **23.** $\ln 4$ **25.** $\ln 25$
27. $\ln 10x^3 y$ **29.** a **31.** c

33. **35.**

37. **39.**

41. **43.**

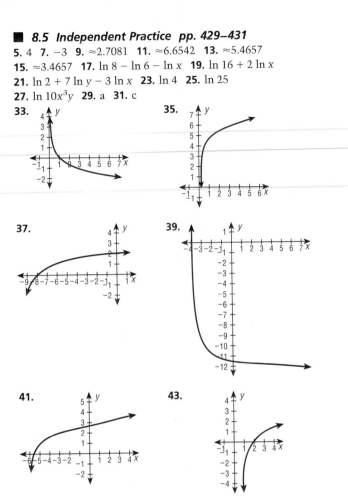

45. $\dfrac{\ln 9}{\ln 2} \approx 3.170$ **47.** $\dfrac{\ln 4.2}{\ln 5} \approx 0.892$ **49.** $\dfrac{\ln 3^{\frac{1}{2}}}{\ln 8} \approx 0.264$
51. ≈ −0.157 **53.** ≈2.84 hours **55.** ≈\$354 million

8.5 Integrated Review p. 431

57. $x = -5$ **59.** $y = -2$ **61.** $2 \log_{10} x - 2 \log_{10} y$
63. $\log_6 81 + 2 \log_6 y$ **65.** 1 **67.** $\log_{10} 32$

8.6 Communicating About Algebra p. 437

A. ≈0.631; subtract 4 from both sides, divide both sides by 2, take log with base 3 of both sides, simplify, divide both sides by 2, use a calculator

B. ≈15.18; add 3 to both sides, divide both sides by 2, exponentiate both sides, simplify, add 3 to both sides, use a calculator

8.6 Guided Practice p. 438

1. $2^x = 10$, $\log_2 2^x = \log_2 10$, $x \approx 3.322$ **2.** $\log_{10} x = 2.4$; $10^{\log_{10} x} = 10^{2.4}$; $x \approx 251.19$ **3.** b; you need to use 3, not e, as the base **4.** $\ln x = 0.5$, $e^{\ln x} = e^{0.5}$, $x \approx 1.649$

8.6 Independent Practice pp. 438–439

5. It is. **7.** It is. **9.** It is. **11.** 2.485 **13.** 1.5 **15.** ≈0.693
17. ≈0.589 **19.** ≈2.48 **21.** ≈8.982 **23.** ≈0.635
25. ≈−0.164 **27.** ≈2.603 **29.** ≈ 54.598 **31.** ≈15.811

33. 2187 **35.** ≈12.182 **37.** ≈−33.115 **39.** 25 **41.** 256
43. ≈49.471 **45.** ≈1627.548 **47.** ≈8.11 years
49. ≈9.90 years **51.** 1986 **53.** 1.0234 g per cm³;
1.0241 g per cm³

■ 8.6 Integrated Review p. 440
55. ≈17.974 **57.** ≈20.392 **59.** ≈0.195 **61.** $1.04

■ 8.6 Mixed Review p. 440
1. x **3.** $2a^2b^4\sqrt[3]{3b^2}$ **5.** $23 + 2i$ **7.** $\frac{1}{2}$ **9.** $g(x) = \frac{1}{3}(x + 1)$
11. 9 **13.** $4a^4$ **15.**
17. $\dfrac{b^{11}c^4}{a^6}$
19. $5395.40

■ 8.7 Communicating About Algebra p. 443
A–B. Make a table of values, plot the points, connect the
points with a smooth curve.
A. $y = 0$, $y = 2$ **B.** $y = 0$, $y = 5$

■ 8.7 Guided Practice p. 444
1. 0.049, 0.131, 0.337, 0.8, 1.618, 2.595, 3.336
2. Logistics growth **3.** $y = 0$, $y = 4$ **4.** All real numbers,
$0 < y < 4$

■ 8.7 Independent Practice pp. 444–446
5. Logarithmic **7.** Logistics growth **9.** Exponential
growth **11.** a **13.** b
15. $y = 0$, $y = 1$ **17.** $y = 0$, $y = 5$

19. $y = 0$, $y = 4$ **21.** $y = -4$, $y = 6$

23. $y = 4$, $y = 12$

25. $y = -6$, $y = 0$

27. 10,000 trout;
the denominator must be
at least 1

29. Decrease, $238,860.58 **31.** ≈$110,000 thousand,
≈$590,000 thousand, ≈$1,300,000 thousand

■ 8.7 Integrated Review p. 446
33. c; all real numbers, $y > -3$ **35.** b; all real numbers,
$y > 3$ **37.** e

■ 8.7 Chapter Review pp. 449–452
1. 687.291 **3.** 1.285 **5.** 1.386 **7.** 66.686 **9.** 22.459
11. 3 **13.** −3 **15.** 0 **17.** $3^4 = 81$ **19.** $\log_2 32 = 5$
21. $\log_{25} \frac{1}{5} = -\frac{1}{2}$ **23.** $8e^{x^2+2x+1}$ **25.** $\frac{1}{3}e^{-2x-3}$ **27.** $9e^{20x}$
29. $\ln 8 - 3 \ln x$ **31.** $\log_3 6 + \log_3 x + 2 \log_3 y$
33. $5 \ln x - \ln 2 - 3 \ln y$ **35.** $\log_2 3x$ **37.** $\log_6 2xy^2$
39. $\log_{10} \frac{1}{8} x^{-\frac{3}{2}}$ **41.** ≈148.413 **43.** ≈0.633 **45.** 9
47. ≈1.461 **49.** Logistics growth **51.** Logarithmic
53. Exponential decay **55.** b; all real numbers, $y > -1$
57. a; all real numbers, $y < 4$ **59.** f; $x > -3$, all real
numbers **61.** c; all real numbers $0 < y < 2$

63. **65.**

67. **69.**

71. **73.**

75. $2873.31 **77.** ≈ 11.55 years, no, the formula shows that $1000 would also double in ≈ 11.55 years **79.** ≈ 3.26 **81.** ≈ 0.00079 moles per liter **83.** $\approx 50{:}1$ **85.** ≈ 1.002, 4th **87.** ≈ 46656, 10th **89.** ≈ 10.920, 8th **91.** ≈ 2.718, 6th **93.** ≈ 0.292, 3rd

CHAPTER 9

■ *9.1 Communicating About Algebra* *p. 459*

A. $3x^3 + 3x^2 + 2x + 5$, add the numerical coefficients of like terms with the same degree

B. $6x^2 - 33x + 45$, use the distributive property

C. $-3x^2 - 2x$, change the signs of the second polynomial and add the numerical coefficients of like terms with the same degree

D. $2x^3 - x^2 - 50x + 25$, use the distributive property

■ *9.1 Guided Practice* *p. 460*

1. $3; -3, 1, 1$ **2.** Answers vary; $-3x^2 + x$ and $3x^2$
3. $14x^2 + 19x - 3$ **4.** $12x^3 - 16x^2 + 9x + 2$ **5.** $x^2 + 4x + 4$ **6.** $x^3 - 3x^2 + 3x - 1$ **7.** $4x^2 - 1$ **8.** $x^2 - 6x + 9$

■ *9.1 Independent Practice* *pp. 460–462*

9. Not a polynomial **11.** Not a polynomial **13.** Not a polynomial **15.** Polynomial **17.** $13x^2 + x + 14, 2$
19. $6x^3 + x^2 - 1, 3$ **21.** $-x^3 - 3x^2 + 3, 3$ **23.** $11x^2 - 3$
25. $-4x + 4$ **27.** $-12x^3 - 2x^2 + x + 4$ **29.** $4x^2 - 13x - 4$ **31.** $-5x^3 - x^2 + 5x - 9$ **33.** $-10x^3 - 3x^2 - 6x + 15$
35. $20x^3 + 9x^2 - 15x - 30$ **37.** $x^3 + 9x^2 - 5x$
39. $-2x^2 - 8x$ **41.** $x^2 - 6x + 8$ **43.** $x^3 + 2x^2 - x + 6$
45. $6x^4 - 3x^3 - 2x^2 + 7x - 3$ **47.** $x^3 + 7x^2 - 12x + 54$
49. $x^2 - 81$ **51.** $x^2 + 10x + 25$ **53.** $x^3 - 12x^2 + 48x - 64$ **55.** $x^3 + 3x^2 + 3x + 1$ **57.** $4x^2 - 4x + 1$ **59.** $\frac{5}{2}x^2 + \frac{25}{2}x$ **61.** $y = 3.53t^2 + 1753t + 200{,}843; 218{,}726$ thousand **63.** 165 ft, 1127 ft

■ *9.1 Integrated Review* *p. 462*

65. e^2 **67.** 3^{x+2} **69.** c **71.** $7y^2 + 3y + 3$ **73.** $-x + 5$
75. $-x^3 + x^2 + 3x + 4$

■ *9.2 Communicating About Algebra* *p. 466*

No; they gave more money to charity than Americans whose income was lower, even though they gave a lower percent of their income than Americans whose income was lower.

■ *9.2 Guided Practice* *p. 467*

1. A continuous graph is a graph that has no breaks—you could sketch the graph without lifting your pencil from the paper.
2. The graph $f(x) = |x|$ does not have only smooth turns; it's shaped like a V.
3. The graph rises to the right, the leading coefficient is positive.
4. a, the graph rises to the right since the leading coefficient is positive.

5. The graph of g is the graph of f shifted up 3 units.
6. $-5, 3$

■ *9.2 Independent Practice* *pp. 467–469*

7. The graph of f is the graph of g shifted to the right 5 units.
9. The graph of f is the graph of g reflected in the x-axis.
11. 4 **13.** 3
15. The graph falls to the left and falls to the right.
17. The graph rises to the left and rises to the right.
19. The graph falls to the left and falls to the right.
21. The graph falls to the left and rises to the right.
23. The graph falls to the left and rises to the right.
25. a **27.** e **29.** c

31.   **33.**

35.   **37.**

39.   **41.**

43.

45.

47.

49. ≈ 0.42, ≈ -9.42 **51.** ≈ -2.64, ≈ 1.14
53. ≈ 6086

55. $V = x(12 - 2x)(10 - 2x)$, 1.81 in.

9.2 Integrated Review p. 469

57.

59.

61.

63. b

9.2 Mixed Review p. 472

1.

3. $\dfrac{18}{35}$ **5.** $-5 + 12i$ **7.** 8

9.

11. $\dfrac{1}{2}$

13.

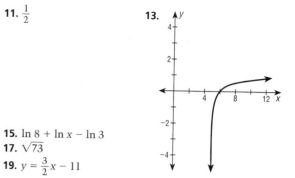

15. $\ln 8 + \ln x - \ln 3$
17. $\sqrt{73}$
19. $y = \dfrac{3}{2}x - 11$

9.3 Communicating About Algebra p. 476

A. -3, 2, 3; write the equation in standard form, factor by grouping, factor the difference of two squares, use the Zero-Product property

B. -5, -2, 2, 5; factor the trinomial, factor the difference of two squares twice, use the Zero-Product property

9.3 Guided Practice p. 477

1. It cannot be factored further using integer coefficients; example: $x^2 + 1$ **2.** $(9x^2 + 1)(3x + 1)(3x - 1)$ **3.** $16x(x + 2)(x - 2)$ **4.** $(1 - 4x)(1 + 4x + 16x^2)$ **5.** $(2x^2 + 3)(x - 4)$
6. The Zero-Product property must be used for each factor; the fourth step should be: $2x^2 = 0 \rightarrow x = 0$.

9.3 Independent Practice pp. 477–479

7. $10x^2$ **9.** $2x^2 + 3$ **11.** $x + 2$ **13.** $3x^2 + 2$ **15.** $(3x + 2)(3x - 2)$ **17.** $(x - 2)(x^2 + 2x + 4)$ **19.** $(6x + 1)(36x^2 - 6x + 1)$ **21.** $50(2x + 1)(2x - 1)$ **23.** $2(4x - 1)(16x^2 + 4x + 1)$ **25.** $3(x + 3)(x^2 - 3x + 9)$ **27.** $(x^2 + 1)(x + 1)$ **29.** $(x^2 + 5)(x + 2)$ **31.** $(9x^2 + 7)(x + 2)$ **33.** $2(x^2 + 2)(x + 2)$ **35.** $(2x^2 + 5)(x - 1)$ **37.** $(5x^2 + 3)(x - 4)$ **39.** $7x(x + 1)^2$ **41.** $(2x^2 - 3)(x - 2)$ **43.** $3(x - 2)(x^2 + 2x + 4)$ **45.** $3x^2(x + 10)(x - 10)$ **47.** $3x(x^2 + 2)(x + 1)$ **49.** $2(5x^2 - 1)(x - 2)$ **51.** 0, 3 **53.** -4 **55.** 5 **57.** $\dfrac{3}{2}$, -1 **59.** $\pm\sqrt{2}$, -3 **61.** -2, ± 1 **63.** 6.75, 7.5, 8.25, 9, 9.75, ≈ 15.49, ≈ 13.68, 12, ≈ 9.80, ≈ 6.93, **65.** ≈ 0.95 sec
67. 16 ft by 10 ft

9.3 Integrated Review p. 479

69. $x^2 + 8x + 16$ **71.** $x^3 - 9x^2 + 27x - 27$
73. $x^3 + 27x^2 + 243x + 729$ **75.** -6, 5 **77.** $\dfrac{3}{4}$, -1

9.4 Communicating About Algebra p. 483

$\approx \$22$ million, $\approx \$32$

9.4 Guided Practice p. 484

1. $2x^2 + 3x - 1 + \dfrac{1}{x - 1}$ **2.** No, there is a remainder of $6x$. **3.** Of the form $x \pm k$ **4.** $(2x^3 + 6x^2 - 8) \div (x - 1) = 2x^2 + 8x + 8$ **5.** 0 **6.** $2(x - 1)(x + 2)^2$

9.4 Independent Practice pp. 484–486

7. $x + 9 + \dfrac{16}{x - 2}$ **9.** $3x + \dfrac{1}{x + 3}$ **11.** $4x^2 - 4 + \dfrac{9}{x^2 + 1}$
13. $2x^2 + 3 + \dfrac{6}{3x^2 + x - 2}$ **15.** $2x + 3 - \dfrac{1}{x^2 - 2}$

17. $5x^2 + 3x + 1$ **19.** $x^2 + 2x - 3$ **21.** $4x - 1 - \dfrac{2}{x+1}$

23. $2x + 11 + \dfrac{30}{x-2}$ **25.** $x - 3 + \dfrac{18}{x+3}$

27. $10x^3 - 5x^2 + 9x - 9$

29. $2x^3 + x - \dfrac{3}{x-3}$ **31.** 29 **33.** 29 **35.** 50 **37.** $(x-6)$,
$(x+2)$ **39.** $(x-2)$, $(x+1)$ **41.** $3(x+2)$, $(x-1)$
43. $3x - 10$ **45.** $2x + 5$ **47.** $(1, 14), (2, 16), (-2, -16)$,
$(-3, -34)$ **49.** ≈ 0.92 million

■ **9.4 Integrated Review p. 486**
51. $3(x+3)(x-3)$ **53.** $2(x-10)(x+1)$
55. $3(4x^2 + 1)(x - 1)$ **57.** \$533 million, \$195 million

■ **9.4 Mid-Chapter Self-Test p. 487**
1. $3x^3 + x^2 - 7x + 3$ **2.** $7x^4 + 5x^3 + 7x - 2$
3. $6x^5 - 12x^4 + 15x^2$ **4.** $6x^2 - 11x - 7$
5. **6.**

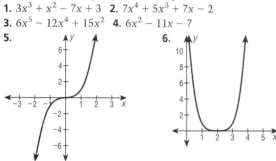

7. $(4x - 3)(4x + 3)$ **8.** $3x^2(2x - 7)$ **9.** $(2x - 5)^2$
10. $(2x - 5)(4x^2 + 10x + 25)$ **11.** $-\dfrac{5}{4}, \dfrac{2}{3}$ **12.** $\pm\dfrac{3}{2}$
13. $5x + 2$ **14.** $4x^2 - 3$ **15.** $3x^3 - 5x + 2$ **16.** $x^2 + x + 3$
17. -62 **18.** $(x - 4)(x - 3)(x + 2)$ **19.** $h(t) = 3.73t + 38.1$
20. $x + 3$ **21.** $p = -2x^3 + 12x$

■ **9.5 Communicating About Algebra p. 490**
A. $-2, -1, 3$ **B.** None

■ **9.5 Guided Practice p. 491**
1. $\dfrac{\pm 1, \pm 2}{\pm 1, \pm 3}$ **2.** $(x - 1)(x - 4)(x + 2)$
3. $(x - 1)(x + 1)(x + 4)$ **4.** $-1, \dfrac{3}{2}, \dfrac{5}{2}$ **5.** $-\dfrac{1}{4}, 1, 3$
6. $\dfrac{2}{3}, 2, 4$

■ **9.5 Independent Practice pp. 491–492**
7. $\dfrac{\pm 1, \pm 3}{\pm 1}$ **9.** $\dfrac{\pm 1, \pm 2, \pm 4, \pm 8, \pm 16}{\pm 1, \pm 2}$ **11.** $-4, -1, 3$
13. $-3, 1, 10$ **15.** $-2, 4, 5$ **17.** $-2, \pm 1$ **19.** $-2, \dfrac{1}{2}, 4$
21. $-1, \pm\sqrt{2}$ **23.** $\pm 3, -2$ **25.** $\pm 4, \dfrac{1}{2}$ **27.** $-8, -1, \pm\sqrt{3}$
29. $-3, -1, \pm\sqrt{5}$ **31.** 2000 **33.** 1988

■ **9.5 Integrated Review pp. 492–493**
35. **37.** **39.**

41. $x^3 - x^2 + 3x + 4$ **43.** $x^2 - x + 1$ **45.** $x^5 - x^2 + 3$
47. $(x - 2)(x + 1)(x - 1)$ **49.** $(x - 2)(x - 3)(x + 1)$ **51.** b

■ **9.5 Mixed Review p. 493**
1. $8x^2 - 2x - 15$ **3.** $(3x - 5)(5x - 2)$
5. $\pm 3, \pm 3i$ **7.**

9. 3 **11.** 3 **13.** $\ln \dfrac{x^5\sqrt{y}}{2}$
15. $\dfrac{\ln 7 + 4}{3}$, or ≈ 1.982
17. 8 **19.** $\left(-\dfrac{7}{5}, \dfrac{13}{5}\right)$

■ **9.6 Communicating About Algebra p. 497**
1,100; yes, two roots are not real

■ **9.6 Guided Practice p. 498**
1. 6; $(-r_1)(-r_2)(-r_3) = 96$, $r_3 = 6$ **2.** 5, every fifth degree
equation has exactly 5 solutions **3.** $\pm 2i, \pm\sqrt{3}$ **4.** See
page 496. **5.** 4, 0

■ **9.6 Independent Practice pp. 498–500**
7. It is not. **9.** It is. **11.** It is. **13.** $f(x) = (x - 1)(x +$
$3)(x - 4)$ **15.** $f(x) = (x - 6)(x + 2)(x - 2)$ **17.** $f(x) = (x^2 +$
$9)(x - 4)$ **19.** $f(x) = (x^2 + 1)(x^2 + 4)$ **21.** $f(x) = (x +$
$2)(x - 5)$ **23.** $f(x) = (x - 9)(x + 1)$ **25.** $(x + 1)(x - 2)(x +$
$2)(x + 2)$ **27.** $(x + 3)(x - 3)(x + 5)$ **29.** $(x - 1)(x +$
$3i)(x - 3i)$ **31.** $(x + 3)(x + 5i)(x - 5i)$ **33.** $(x + 1)(x -$
$2)(x + 2i)(x - 2i)$ **35.** $(x - 2)(x + 5i)(x - 5i)$ **37.** In the
fourth and tenth years **39.** 4, 4 times **41.** 5, 500 species
43. 10, 10,000 **45.** No, the minimum value of the
function is $\approx$\$305 million.

■ **9.6 Integrated Review p. 500**
47. $-2, -\dfrac{1}{2}, 1$ **49.** $-6, -1$ **51.** $-2, \pm 1$ **53.** $-3, -2, 1, 4$
55. e

■ **9.7 Communicating About Algebra p. 503**
A. 64, ≈ 18.47 **B.** 5.8, ≈ 1.68

■ **9.7 Guided Practice p. 504**
1. Example with range 3: 4, 4, 5, 7.
Example with range 7: 1, 5, 6, 8.
The collection with range 7.
2. a, 3 and 10 are farther apart than 5 and 11 **3.** a, the
data in **a** are not spread as far apart as the data in **b**
4. ≈ 2.65, no

■ **9.7 Independent Practice pp. 504–506**
5. 0.5, ≈ 0.15 **7.** 0.8, ≈ 0.29 **9.** 10, ≈ 3.37 **11.** \$48.25,
$\approx$\$195.64 **13.** 27 **15.** ≈ 10.85 **17.** Roll #2 **19.** 4, 2;
Roswell

■ **9.7 Integrated Review p. 507**
21. c **23.** 46.2¢

9.7 Chapter Review pp. 509–512

1. $4x^3 + 3x^2 + x - 4$ **3.** $8x^2 - 5x - 3$ **5.** $2x^3 + 6x^2 - 8x$
7. $x^2 - 36$ **9.** $x^3 - 2x^2 - 10x + 21$ **11.** $x^2 + 18x + 81$
13. $x^3 - 21x^2 + 147x - 343$ **15.** b **17.** a **19.** f

21. **23.** **25.**

27. **29.** **31.**

33. $16(x - 3)(x + 3)$ **35.** $(5x - 2)(25x^2 + 10x + 4)$
37. $(x - 11)(x + 2)$ **39.** $(2x - 1)(x - 2)$ **41.** $(x^2 + 5)(x - 1)$ **43.** $(x^2 + 2)(2x - 3)$ **45.** $-3, 9$ **47.** $-3, \pm 1$
49. $-1, \pm 4$ **51.** $\frac{3}{2}, \pm 3$ **53.** $x^2 - 7x + 6$ **55.** $2x^2 + x + 6$
57. $x^4 - x + 3 - \frac{3}{x + 3}$ **59.** $2x^3 + 5x^2 + 5x + 6 - \frac{3}{x - 1}$
61. $3x^2 - 13x + 64 - \frac{316}{x + 5}$ **63.** $x^5 - 2x^4 + 4x^3 - 5x^2 + 4x - 8 + \frac{23}{x + 2}$ **65.** $9, \pm 7i$ **67.** $1, \pm 4i$ **69.** $-3, 1, \pm 2i$
71. $1, \frac{1}{2}, \pm\sqrt{3}i$ **73.** $T = (0.09t^2 - 1.6t + 172.5)(-0.5t^2 + 90t + 1190)$, \$310,733.88 million **75.** $N = 143t^2 + 582t + 10,650$, \$56,570 million **77.** 70% **79.** 3, 15 in. by 8 in. by 19 in. **81.** 2, 1900's **83.** 10, 1980's **85.** 7, 1950's
87. 9, 1970's **89.** 4, 1920's

9.7 Cumulative Review for Chapters 7–9 pp. 514–515

1. $7\sqrt[5]{5}$ **3.** $-10\sqrt[4]{5}$ **5.** 3 **7.** $\frac{100}{9}$ **9.** -2 **11.** 4

13. **15.** 8 **17.** ≈ 0.9808
19. ≈ 0.8959 **21.** $\log_{10} 3 + 2 \log_{10} x + 3 \log_{10} y$
23. $\ln 6 + \ln x - \ln 5 - \ln y$
25. $\ln \frac{3^{1/4}}{4}$

27.

29.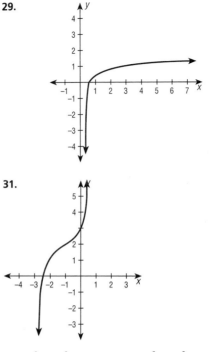

31.

33. $5x^3 + 6x^2 + 3x + 4$ **35.** $3x^3 - 4x^2 + 5x + 5$
37. $2x^4 + x^3 + 4x^2 - 4x - 3$ **39.** $x^2 + 7x + 52 + \frac{366}{x - 7}$
41. $2x^2 + 14x + 67 + \frac{336}{x - 5}$ **43.** $-\frac{3}{2}, 1, 2$
45. $-2, -1, 1, \frac{3}{2}$ **47.** \$10,800 **49.** About \$1922
51. 0.001 mole per liter **53.** 1989

CHAPTER 10

10.1 Communicating About Algebra p. 520

A. 88.25, 11.75, 4.1, 3.335 **B.** $y = 3.25$; the club needs to charge at least \$3.25 per calendar.

10.1 Guided Practice p. 521

1. See page 518.
2. ≈ 0.607, 1.25, ≈ 3.179, -37, -1, -0.25, -1, -37, ≈ 3.179, 1.25, ≈ 0.607

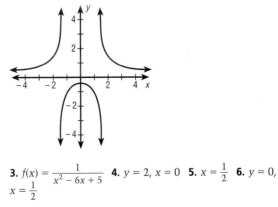

3. $f(x) = \dfrac{1}{x^2 - 6x + 5}$ **4.** $y = 2$, $x = 0$ **5.** $x = \dfrac{1}{2}$ **6.** $y = 0$, $x = \dfrac{1}{2}$

7. All real numbers except $x = -16$ **9.** All real numbers except $x = -1$ **11.** All real numbers except $x = 1$
13. $0, -1, -3, 5, 3, 2$ **15.** $y = 0; x = 5$ **17.** $y = 0; x = -1$
19. $x = 1$ **21.** $y = \frac{3}{2}; x = 0$ **23.** $y = 4; x = 0$ **25.** $y = 0;$
$x = -1, x = 2, x = 0$ **27.** b **29.** d

31.

33.

35.

37.

39.

41.

43. $A = \dfrac{3m + 180}{m}$; $A = 3$; when the VCR is paid for, $3 will be spent for each movie.

Average Cost per Movie (in dollars) / Number of Movies

45. No, it is unlikely that costs will decrease to the level of 1970 in 2010.

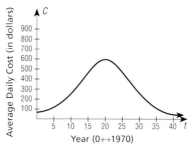

Average Daily Cost (in dollars) / Year (0↔1970)

47. $6x^2 - 24x + 105 - \dfrac{424}{x + 4}$
49. $2x^3 - 5x^2 + 4x - 4 + \dfrac{13}{x + 1}$ **51.** $(x - 1)(x + 3)(x^2 + 9)$
53. $3(x + 2)(x - 2)(x^2 + 1)$ **55.** $\dfrac{13}{487}$

■ 10.2 Communicating About Algebra p. 528

2375, direct variation, the number of solar cells varies directly with horsepower.

■ 10.2 Guided Practice p. 529

1. Inversely **2.** Inversely **3.** Directly **4.** Directly

5. Inversely, rt is a constant **6.** Directly, $\frac{d}{r}$ is a constant

■ 10.2 Independent Practice pp. 529–531

7. $yx = -6$ **9.** $yx = 5$ **11.** $z = -\frac{3}{40}xy$ **13.** $rt = 2000$

15. $R = \frac{\pi \cdot L}{500{,}000\,A}$ **17.** $6\frac{2}{3}$ ft **19.** \$318.75 **21.** 187.5 luxes **23.** 1470 Joules

■ 10.2 Integrated Review p. 531

25.

27.

29.

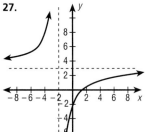

31. c

■ 10.2 Mixed Review p. 532

1. $3x^3 - 7x$ **3.** 16

5.

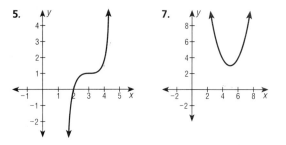

7.

9. $-4 < x < -1$ **11.** $x < 3$ or $x > 7$ **13.** $(3x + 2)(2x - 5)$

15. 324 **17.** $f(x) = \frac{1}{2}x^2 + \frac{1}{2}x - 4$ **19.** -7

■ 10.3 Communicating About Algebra p. 536

A. A mouse has a larger ratio of surface area to volume and, so, has a larger air resistance.

B. A parachute has a very large ratio of surface area to volume and, so, has a very large air resistance.

■ 10.3 Guided Practice p. 537

1. $\frac{x}{x^2 + 7}$ **2.** Not possible **3.** $\frac{x + 1}{x^2}$ **4.** $\frac{1}{3x}$

■ 10.3 Independent Practice pp. 537–539

5. $\frac{x + 3}{x - 3}$ **7.** $\frac{x + 1}{x - 4}$ **9.** $\frac{y^3}{2x^3}$ **11.** $\frac{x^5}{25y^4}$

13. $\frac{x - 4}{2(x + 1)}$ **15.** $\frac{3(x + 4)}{x + 3}$ **17.** $\frac{3(x - 1)}{x + 1}$

19. $\frac{16(x + 4)(x^2 - 4)}{x - 4}$ **21.** $\frac{2(x + 5)}{x}$ **23.** $\frac{(x + 4)(x - 2)}{x + 2}$

25. $\frac{1}{(x + 2)^2}$ **27.** $\frac{x + 4}{3x(x + 1)}$ **29.** $\frac{x(x + 3)}{x - 10}$ **31.** $(x + 5)(x - 15)$

33. $\frac{1}{2(x + 3)}$ **35.** $3(x + 2)$ **37.** $(x + 4)(x + 3)$ **39.** $\frac{1}{3}$

41. $\frac{7}{6x(x + 5)}$ **43.** $A = \frac{500(t + 20)}{1 - 0.05t}$; \$23,333.33 **45.** π

■ 10.3 Integrated Review p. 539

47. $(x^2 + 5)(x - 9)$ **49.** $(x^2 + 9)(x - 4)$

51. $(x^2 + 1)(2x - 3)$ **53.** $\frac{3y^2}{x^3}$ **55.** $\frac{-3y}{x^3}$ **57.** c

■ 10.3 Mid-Chapter Self-Test p. 540

1.

2.

3.

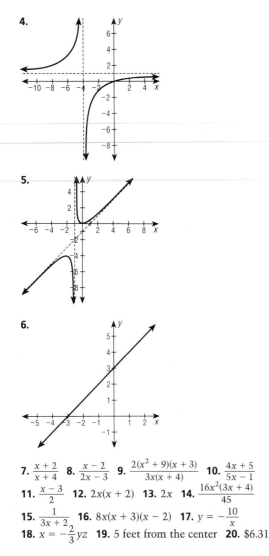

4.

5.

6.

7. $\dfrac{x+2}{x+4}$ **8.** $\dfrac{x-2}{2x-3}$ **9.** $\dfrac{2(x^2+9)(x+3)}{3x(x+4)}$ **10.** $\dfrac{4x+5}{5x-1}$

11. $\dfrac{x-3}{2}$ **12.** $2x(x+2)$ **13.** $2x$ **14.** $\dfrac{16x^2(3x+4)}{45}$

15. $\dfrac{1}{3x+2}$ **16.** $8x(x+3)(x-2)$ **17.** $y=-\dfrac{10}{x}$

18. $x=-\dfrac{2}{3}yz$ **19.** 5 feet from the center **20.** \$6.31

■ **10.4 Communicating About Algebra p. 544**
A. $\dfrac{15}{2}$ **B.** $5,-1$

■ **10.4 Guided Practice p. 545**
1. Multiplying by the least common denominator and cross multiplying; multiplying by the least common denominator; it works for any rational equation
2. $x(x+3)(x+2)$ **3.** $\pm\sqrt{5}$ **4.** $-5,6$

■ **10.4 Independent Practice pp. 545–546**
5. $3(x+3)(x-3)$ **7.** $4x^3(x-1)$ **9.** $2x^2(x+2)(x-2)$
11. It is not. **13.** It is not. **15.** It is not. **17.** -2
19. None **21.** $2,-2$ **23.** $-5,\dfrac{1}{2}$ **25.** $\dfrac{3}{4}$ **27.** $-\dfrac{3}{2},5$
29. $-\dfrac{3}{2},2$ **31.** -5 **33.** No solution **35.** 5 **37.** $2,5$
39. -1 **41.** $1,3$ **43.** $\dfrac{1}{3},2$ **45.** $1,\dfrac{3}{2}$ **47.** 5 **49.** 12,000
51. 1984

■ **10.4 Integrated Review p. 547**
53. d **55.** c **57.** $\approx 40\%$ **59.** $\approx\$4.4$ billion

■ **10.5 Communicating About Algebra p. 550**
A–B. Rewrite fractions using least common denominator, simplify, add or subtract fractions
A. $\dfrac{x^2-16x-17}{(x+3)(x-5)}$ **B.** $\dfrac{-x^3+x^2+18x-15}{3x(x-1)}$

■ **10.5 Guided Practice p. 551**
1. $2x(x+4)$, $\dfrac{2x^2+17x+68}{2x(x+4)}$
2. a, b, the numerator must be multiplied by the reciprocal of the sum of the fractions in the denominator (not by the sum of the reciprocals)

3–4. $\dfrac{x^2+20}{5x+6}$

■ **10.5 Independent Practice pp. 551–553**
5. $2x(x+1)$ **7.** $x(x-5)(x+2)$ **9.** $-\dfrac{43}{28x}$
11. $\dfrac{x-5}{(x+2)(x-2)}$ **13.** $\dfrac{-20x-25}{(x-6)(x+5)}$ **15.** $\dfrac{12x^2-x-39}{3(x+11)}$
17. $\dfrac{8x^3-15x^2+9x+12}{x(x+1)(2x-3)}$ **19.** $\dfrac{-4x^2+3x-1}{(x+10)(x-1)}$
21. $\dfrac{-6x+7}{(x+5)(x-2)}$ **23.** $\dfrac{x(x-12)}{3(5x+1)}$ **25.** $\dfrac{5(x+3)}{2x(5x-2)}$ **27.** $\dfrac{20}{x+7}$
29. $\dfrac{1}{4x}$ **31.** $\dfrac{(x+3)(x+1)}{3}$ **33.** $\dfrac{(-11x+5)(x-5)}{2(x+5)(x^2+x-5)}$
35. $-\dfrac{2}{5},2$ **37.** -1 **39.** $1,\dfrac{10}{7}$ **41.** $I=$
$\dfrac{-1374t^2-20,461t+1,627,410}{(85-t)(55-2t)}$
43. $N=\dfrac{17,510(41+5t)}{20+t}-\dfrac{174,720(148+5t)}{1174-t}$

■ **10.5 Integrated Review p. 553**
45. $x^2(x-7)(x+7)$ **47.** $x(x+1)(x-1)$ **49.** $x^2(x+1)$
51. $\dfrac{1}{3},3$ **53.** 2 **55.** 5, 2 **57.** c

■ **10.5 Mixed Review p. 554**
1. $25x^2-20x+4$
3.

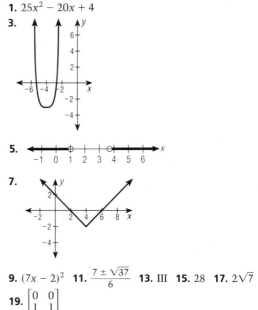

5.

7.

9. $(7x-2)^2$ **11.** $\dfrac{7\pm\sqrt{37}}{6}$ **13.** III **15.** 28 **17.** $2\sqrt{7}$
19. $\begin{bmatrix} 0 & 0 \\ 1 & 1 \end{bmatrix}$

A. $391.70; $1601.20   **B.** $415.18; $2446.48   **C.** $451.90; $3768.40

■ **10.6** *Guided Practice* **p. 558**
1. $177.70   **2.** $20   **3.** $157.70   **4.** $1842.30

■ **10.6** *Independent Practice* **pp. 558–560**

5.

Payment number	Balance before payment	Payment	Interest payment	Principal payment	Balance after payment
1	$1200.00	$139.23	$10.50	$128.73	$1071.27
2	$1071.27	$139.23	$ 9.37	$129.86	$ 941.41
3	$ 941.41	$139.23	$ 8.24	$130.99	$ 810.42
4	$ 810.42	$139.23	$ 7.09	$132.14	$ 678.28
5	$ 678.28	$139.23	$ 5.93	$133.30	$ 544.98
6	$ 544.98	$139.23	$ 4.77	$134.46	$ 410.52
7	$ 410.52	$139.23	$ 3.59	$135.64	$ 274.88
8	$ 274.88	$139.23	$ 2.41	$136.82	$ 138.06
9	$ 138.06	$139.27	$ 1.21	$138.06	$ 0.00

7.

Payment number	Balance before payment	Payment	Interest payment	Principal payment	Balance after payment
1	$5000	$434.94	$33.33	$401.61	$4598.39
2	$4598.39	$434.94	$30.66	$404.28	$4194.11
3	$4194.11	$434.94	$27.96	$406.98	$3787.13
4	$3787.13	$434.94	$25.25	$409.69	$3377.44
5	$3377.44	$434.94	$22.52	$412.42	$2965.02
6	$2965.02	$434.94	$19.77	$415.17	$2549.85
7	$2549.85	$434.94	$17.00	$417.94	$2131.91
8	$2131.91	$434.94	$14.21	$420.73	$1711.18
9	$1711.18	$434.94	$11.41	$423.53	$1287.65
10	$1287.65	$434.94	$ 8.58	$426.36	$ 861.29
11	$ 861.29	$434.94	$ 5.74	$429.20	$ 432.09
12	$ 432.09	$434.97	$ 2.88	$432.09	$ 0.00

9. $909.28   **11.** $674.79   **13.** $100,745.60
15. $164,261.60   **17.** $143.56   **19.** $202.28   **21.** $177.70
23. $132.40, $2132.40; $195.28, $2195.28   **25.** e, only **e**
has a monthly payment of at most $100   **27.** b
29. $8,482.17, $88,415.13

■ **10.6** *Integrated Review* **p. 560**
31. $625.50   **33.** ≈7 million

■ **10.6** *Chapter Review* **pp. 562–566**
1. $y = 0$; $x = 0$ **3.** $y = \frac{3}{4}$; $x = -1, x = 1$ **5.** $x = 3$ **7.** c
9. d

11.

13.

15.

17.

19.

21.

23. $xy = 5$ **25.** $z = \frac{1}{3}xy$ **27.** Inversely   **29.** $\frac{x-5}{x-2}$
31. $\frac{1}{x-9}$ **33.** $16y^4$ **35.** $x(x-10)$ **37.** $\frac{(x+1)(x-1)}{x+4}$
39. $\frac{2x}{x+1}$ **41.** $\frac{8x}{5}$ **43.** x **45.** $-2, 5$ **47.** $\frac{3}{2}$
49. No solution   **51.** $0, 3$ **53.** 4 **55.** $\frac{x^3 + 2x + 24}{(x^2 - 4)(x + 4)}$
57. $\frac{5x^2 - x + 9}{x(x+3)}$ **59.** $\frac{x^2 - x + 4}{(x-1)(x+3)}$ **61.** $\frac{6x - 8}{x(x+4)(x-4)}$
63. $\frac{5x^2 - 9x - 8}{2(x-2)(x+1)}$ **65.** $\frac{-7x^2 + x + 6}{(4x-3)(x+2)}$
67. $\frac{(-x^2 + 5x - 5)(x+1)}{(x^2 + 6x + 6)(x-1)}$ **69.** $\frac{x(x^2 + 2x + 16)}{(-x^2 + 5x - 10)(x+2)}$
71. $\frac{-9x(2x - 1)}{(x+4)(x^2 + 2x - 30)}$ **73.** $\frac{2x^2 + 4x}{9x^2 + 36x} = \frac{2x + 4}{9x + 36}$

75.

Payment number	Balance before payment	Payment	Interest payment	Principal payment	Balance after payment
1	$900.00	79.12	$7.50	$71.62	$828.38
2	$828.38	79.12	$6.90	$72.22	$756.16
3	$756.16	79.12	$6.30	$72.82	$683.34
4	$683.34	79.12	$5.69	$73.43	$609.91
5	$609.91	79.12	$5.08	$74.04	$535.87
6	$535.87	79.12	$4.47	$74.65	$461.22
7	$461.22	79.12	$3.84	$75.28	$385.94
8	$385.94	79.12	$3.22	$75.90	$310.04
9	$310.04	79.12	$2.58	$76.54	$233.50
10	$233.50	79.12	$1.95	$77.17	$156.33
11	$156.33	79.12	$1.30	$77.82	$78.51
12	$78.51	79.16	$0.65	$78.51	$0.00

77. $1020.77   **79.** $Fr^2 \approx 6.67 \times 10^{-11} m_1 m_2$

81. $\dfrac{6(5407 - 121t)(126t + 878)}{t(1 - 0.038t)}$; $8,648,607.31 thousand

83.

85. 1962, no   **87.** $\dfrac{t^3(40 - t)}{18,750(t + 330)}$

89. A greater percentage of paper used is being recycled.

CHAPTER 11

■ 11.1 Communicating About Algebra   p. 572
A–D. Isolate the second-degree variable, then set the coefficient of the first-degree variable equal to $4p$ and solve for p.
A. $(0, p) = \left(0, \frac{1}{8}\right), y = -p = -\frac{1}{8}$ **B.** $(0, p) = \left(0, -\frac{1}{24}\right),$
$y = -p = \frac{1}{24}$ **C.** $(p, 0) = \left(\frac{1}{2}, 0\right), x = -p = -\frac{1}{2}$
D. $(p, 0) = \left(-\frac{1}{48}, 0\right), x = -p = \frac{1}{48}$

■ 11.1 Guided Practice   p. 573
1. The vertex is the midpoint of the distance between the focus and the directrix.
2. Horizontal   **3.** $y = -1$ **4.** $(0, -2)$ **5.** Opens up.
6. $x^2 = 12y$

■ 11.1 Independent Practice   pp. 573–575
7. $x^2 = 4\left(\frac{1}{20}\right)y$ **9.** $x^2 = 4\left(-\frac{1}{8}\right)y$ **11.** $y^2 = 4\left(\frac{1}{6}\right)x$
13. $y^2 = 4\left(\frac{1}{56}\right)x$ **15.** Vertical   **17.** Horizontal
19. $\left(0, -\frac{1}{8}\right), y = \frac{1}{8}$ **21.** $(0, 2), y = -2$ **23.** $(-4, 0), x = 4$

25. $(0, -3), y = 3$ **27.** $(0, 1), x = -1$ **29.** $(0, 6), y = -6$
31. $y^2 = 4(5)x$ **33.** $y^2 = 4(-3)x$ **35.** $y^2 = 4(-4)x$
37. $x^2 = 4(-1)y$ **39.** c   **41.** b
43.

45.   **47.**

49.

51.   **53.**

55. $x^2 = 16y$, signals hit the parabolic dish and reflect into the focus.
57. $x^2 = 8y$. The distance from F to the gold bar is the same as the distance from the gold bar to the bottom of the screen, $x^2 = 8y$.
59. The distance from the pole to the zipper clasp is equal to the distance from tab A to the zipper clasp. Tab A is the focus and the pole is the directrix.

11.1 Integrated Review p. 575

61.

63.

65.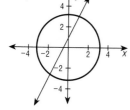

67. b

11.2 Communicating About Algebra p. 578

$$\frac{I}{(\sqrt{(x-10)^2+(y-0)^2})^2} = \frac{2I}{(\sqrt{(x-20)^2+(y-0)^2})^2}$$

$$\frac{I}{(x-10)^2+y^2} = \frac{2I}{(x-20)^2+y^2}$$

$$\frac{I}{x^2-20x+100+y^2} = \frac{2I}{x^2-40x+400+y^2}$$

$$\frac{1}{x^2-20x+100+y^2} = \frac{2}{x^2-40x+400+y^2}$$

$$x^2-40x+400+y^2 = 2x^2-40x+200+2y^2$$

$$-x^2-y^2 = -200$$

$$x^2+y^2 = 200$$

11.2 Guided Practice p. 579

1. 1, (0, 0) **2.** $x^2+y^2=52$, $r^2=(6-0)^2+(-4-0)^2=52$
3. Yes, 2

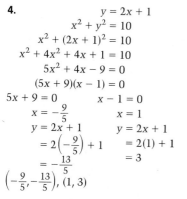

4.
$$y = 2x + 1$$
$$x^2 + y^2 = 10$$
$$x^2 + (2x+1)^2 = 10$$
$$x^2 + 4x^2 + 4x + 1 = 10$$
$$5x^2 + 4x - 9 = 0$$
$$(5x+9)(x-1) = 0$$

$$5x+9=0 \qquad x-1=0$$
$$x = -\frac{9}{5} \qquad x = 1$$
$$y = 2x+1 \qquad y = 2x+1$$
$$= 2\left(-\frac{9}{5}\right)+1 \qquad = 2(1)+1$$
$$= -\frac{13}{5} \qquad = 3$$
$$\left(-\frac{9}{5}, -\frac{13}{5}\right), (1, 3)$$

11.2 Independent Practice pp. 579–580

5. $x^2+y^2=16$ **7.** $x^2+y^2=3$ **9.** $x^2+y^2=20$

11. $x^2+y^2=26$ **13.** b **15.** a

17.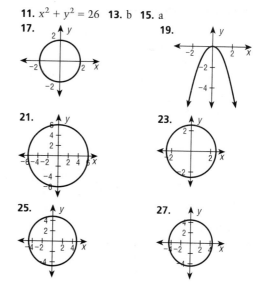

19.

21.

23.

25.

27.

29. $(-1, 0)$, $(0, -1)$ **31.** (6, 8), (8, 6)
33. $\left(\frac{1+\sqrt{7}}{2}, \frac{-1+\sqrt{7}}{2}\right)$, $\left(\frac{1-\sqrt{7}}{2}, \frac{-1-\sqrt{7}}{2}\right)$ **35.** $(-8, 8)$,
$(0, 0)$

37. $x^2+y^2=\frac{2,400,000}{\pi}$

39. $x^2+y^2=128$ **41.** The points that lie on the line
segments with end points $\left(\frac{4}{5}, -\frac{3}{5}\right)$ and $\left(-\frac{3}{5}, -\frac{4}{5}\right)$, but not
including the endpoints.

11.2 Integrated Review p. 580

43. $\sqrt{26}$ **45.** $\sqrt{17}$ **47.** $\sqrt{82}$ **49.** $(5, -2)$ **51.** (0, 4)
53. $(1, -2)$ **55.** d

11.2 Mixed Review p. 582

1.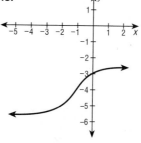

3. 372,000 **5.** 27 **7.** x-intercept: -4, y-intercept: -1
9. $f(x) = \frac{3}{2}x + 7\frac{1}{2}$ **11.** $\frac{1}{6}$
13.

15. -1 **17.** $-4, 3$ **19.** 99

11.3 Communicating About Algebra p. 585

A. ≈ 7.375 billion km **B.** $\frac{x^2}{5.909^2} + \frac{y^2}{5.724^2} = 1$ where x
and y are billions of kilometers

■ **11.3 Guided Practice** *p. 586*

1. Segment with $(0,-3)$ and $(0, 3)$ as its endpoints.
2. Segment with $(-2, 0)$ and $(2, 0)$ as its endpoints.
3. $(0,-3)$ and $(0, 3)$ **4.** $(-2, 0)$ and $(2, 0)$ **5.** $(0,-\sqrt{5})$ and $(0, \sqrt{5})$ **6.** $\dfrac{x^2}{4} + \dfrac{y^2}{9} = 1$

■ **11.3 Independent Practice** *pp. 586–588*

7. $(-3, 0)$, $(3, 0)$; $(-5, 0)$, $(5, 0)$ **9.** $(0, -4\sqrt{2})$, $(0, 4\sqrt{2})$, $(0,-\sqrt{32})$, $(0, \sqrt{32})$; $(0,-6)$, $(0, 6)$ **11.** $(0,-2\sqrt{2})$, $(0, 2\sqrt{2})$; $(0,-\sqrt{8})$, $(0, \sqrt{8})$; $(0,-3)$, $(0, 3)$
13. $\dfrac{x^2}{16} + \dfrac{y^2}{49} = 1$; $(0,-\sqrt{33})$, $(0, \sqrt{33})$; $(0, -7)$, $(0, 7)$
15. $\dfrac{x^2}{\frac{25}{4}} + \dfrac{y^2}{\frac{25}{9}} = 1$; $\left(\dfrac{-5\sqrt{5}}{6}, 0\right)$, $\left(\dfrac{5\sqrt{5}}{6}, 0\right)$; $\left(-\dfrac{5}{2}, 0\right)$, $\left(\dfrac{5}{2}, 0\right)$
17. $\dfrac{x^2}{90,000} + \dfrac{y^2}{315,000} = 1$; $(0,150\sqrt{10})$, $(0,150\sqrt{10})$; $(0,-150\sqrt{14})$, $(0, 150\sqrt{14})$
19. $\dfrac{x^2}{25} + \dfrac{y^2}{36} = 1$ **21.** $\dfrac{x^2}{16} + \dfrac{y^2}{9} = 1$ **23.** $\dfrac{x^2}{16} + \dfrac{y^2}{7} = 1$
25. c **27.** d

29. **31.** **33.** **35.** **37.** **39.**

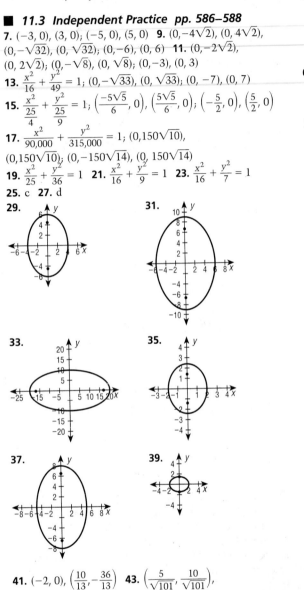

41. $(-2, 0)$, $\left(\dfrac{10}{13}, -\dfrac{36}{13}\right)$ **43.** $\left(\dfrac{5}{\sqrt{101}}, \dfrac{10}{\sqrt{101}}\right)$, $\left(-\dfrac{5}{\sqrt{101}}, -\dfrac{10}{\sqrt{101}}\right)$ **45.** $(0, 2)$, $\left(-\dfrac{16}{5}, -\dfrac{6}{5}\right)$ **47.** The sum of the distances between any point on the path and the two thumbtacks is a constant. **49.** $\dfrac{x^2}{4^2} + \dfrac{y^2}{\left(\frac{15}{4}\right)^2} = 1$ or $\dfrac{x^2}{\left(\frac{15}{4}\right)^2} + \dfrac{y^2}{4^2} = 1$ **51.** 15π in.^{2} **53.** ≈ 84.26 ft **55.** ≈ 0.4326

■ **11.3 Integrated Review** *p. 588*
57. $y = \pm 2\sqrt{1 - x^2}$ **59.** $y = \pm\dfrac{3}{2}\sqrt{4 - x^2}$

61. $y = \pm\dfrac{9}{10}\sqrt{100 - x^2}$
63. **65.** **67.**

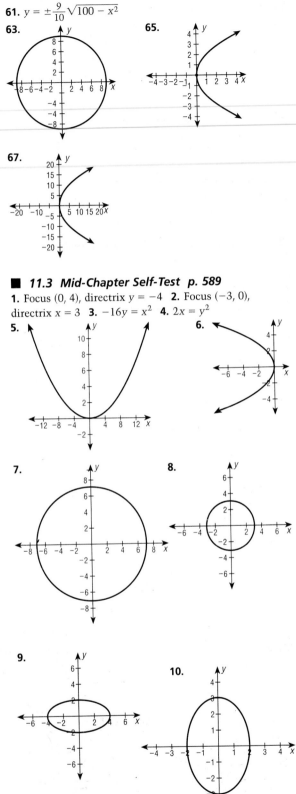

■ **11.3 Mid-Chapter Self-Test** *p. 589*
1. Focus $(0, 4)$, directrix $y = -4$ **2.** Focus $(-3, 0)$, directrix $x = 3$ **3.** $-16y = x^2$ **4.** $2x = y^2$
5. **6.** **7.** **8.** **9.** **10.**

11. $x^2 + y^2 = 25$ **12.** $x^2 + y^2 = 17$ **13.** Foci $(0, 4)$, $(0, -4)$, Vertices $(0, 5)$, $(0, -5)$ **14.** Foci $(-\sqrt{7}, 0)$, $(\sqrt{7}, 0)$, Vertices $(-4, 0)$, $(4, 0)$ **15.** $\left(-4, \frac{4}{3}\right)$, $\left(2, \frac{1}{3}\right)$ **16.** $\left(-\frac{8}{5}, -\frac{3}{5}\right)$, $(0, 1)$ **17.** $(3, 4)$, $(5, 0)$ **18.** $\frac{x^2}{36} + \frac{y^2}{16} = 1$ **19.** ≈ 0.0559 **20.** $y = -\frac{2}{5}x^2$ **21.** $x^2 + y^2 = 100$, $x^2 + y^2 = 256$

■ **11.4 Communicating About Algebra p. 593**
A. 1, $(1, 0)$ is only on graph 1 **B.** 2, $(2, 0)$ is only on graph 2 **C.** 3, $(0, 1)$ is only on graph 3

■ **11.4 Guided Practice p. 594**
1. $(-4, 0)$, $(4, 0)$; $(-6, 0)$, $(6, 0)$ **2.** $y = 0$ **3.** $\frac{x^2}{16} - \frac{y^2}{20} = 1$ **4.** $y = \pm\frac{\sqrt{5}}{2}x$ **5.** $\frac{y^2}{36} - \frac{x^2}{9} = 1$ **6.** b

■ **11.4 Independent Practice pp. 594–596**
7. $(-3, 0)$, $(3, 0)$; $(-\sqrt{58}, 0)$, $(\sqrt{58}, 0)$ **9.** $(-4, 0)$, $(4, 0)$; $(-2\sqrt{5}, 0)$, $(2\sqrt{5}, 0)$
11. $(0, -5)$, $(0, 5)$; $(0, -\sqrt{26})$, $(0, \sqrt{26})$
13. $\frac{x^2}{4} - \frac{y^2}{25} = 1$; $(-\sqrt{29}, 0)$, $(\sqrt{29}, 0)$; $(-2, 0)$, $(2, 0)$

15. $\frac{y^2}{\frac{1}{4}} - \frac{x^2}{\frac{9}{4}} = 1$; $\left(0, -\frac{\sqrt{10}}{2}\right)$, $\left(0, \frac{\sqrt{10}}{2}\right)$; $\left(0, -\frac{1}{2}\right)$, $\left(0, \frac{1}{2}\right)$

17. $\frac{y^2}{4} - \frac{x^2}{100} = 1$; $(0, -2\sqrt{26})$, $(0, 2\sqrt{26})$; $(0, -2)$, $(0, 2)$

19. $\frac{x^2}{1} - \frac{y^2}{3} = 1$ **21.** $\frac{x^2}{4} - \frac{y^2}{77} = 1$ **23.** $\frac{y^2}{49} - \frac{x^2}{32} = 1$
25. b **27.** d
29. $y = \pm\frac{12}{5}x$ **31.** $y = \pm\frac{4}{3}x$

33. $y = \pm\frac{3}{13}x$ **35.** $y = \pm\frac{55}{6}x$

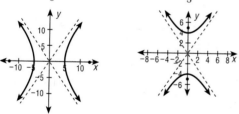

37. $y = \pm\frac{1}{2}x$ **39.** $y = \pm\frac{5}{4}x$

41. $(-\sqrt{10}, 0)$, $(\sqrt{10}, 0)$ **43.** $(0, -\sqrt{26})$, $(0, \sqrt{26})$
45. $(0, -10)$, $(0, 10)$
47. $\frac{y^2}{8} - \frac{x^2}{8} = 1$ **49.** $\frac{x^2}{\frac{225}{64}} - \frac{y^2}{\frac{31}{64}} = 1$ **51.** $(\approx 6.54, \approx 3.46)$

■ **11.4 Integrated Review p. 596**
53. Ellipse   **55.** Hyperbola

57. Ellipse   **59.** Circle

61. d

■ **11.5 Communicating About Algebra p. 600**
A. $\frac{x^2}{\frac{3}{4}} + \left(y - \frac{1}{2}\right)^2 = 1$ **B.** $\left(x + \frac{1}{2}\right)^2 + \frac{y^2}{\frac{3}{4}} = 1$

C. $\frac{x^2}{\frac{3}{4}} + \left(y + \frac{1}{2}\right)^2 = 1$

■ **11.5 Guided Practice p. 601**
1. To graph a conic whose only vertex or center is not at the origin. **2.** Circle, $(1, 2)$ **3.** Hyperbola, $(-1, 1)$
4. Ellipse, $(10, -2)$ **5.** Parabola, $(1, 4)$
6. $(x - 5)^2 + (y + 6)^2 = 24$, complete the square for the x- and y-terms, circle

■ **11.5 Independent Practice pp. 601–603**
7. g **9.** c **11.** f **13.** a **15.** $(x - 9)^2 + (y - 3)^2 = 16$

17. $(x - 1)^2 = 12(y + 2)$ **19.** $\frac{(x + 2)^2}{8} + \frac{\left(y + \frac{1}{2}\right)^2}{\frac{81}{4}} = 1$

21. $\frac{y^2}{16} - \frac{(x - 8)^2}{20} = 1$
23. $(x - 1)^2 + (y + 3)^2 = 1$; 1, $(1, -3)$

25. $(x + 3)^2 - (y - 4)^2 = 1$; 1, (3, 4)

27. $(y - 2)^2 = 4(-3)(x - 1)$; (1, 2), (-2, 2)

29. $(x + 2)^2 = 4(2)(y - 1)$; (-2, 1), (-2, 3)

31. $\dfrac{(x - 2)^2}{1} + \dfrac{(y - 1)^2}{25} = 1$; (2, 6), (2, -4);
(2, 1 + 2√6), (2, 1 - 2√6);

33. $\dfrac{(x - 8)^2}{36} + \dfrac{(y - 1)^2}{1} = 1$; (14, 1), (2, 1); (8 + √35, 1),
(8 - √35, 1)

35. $\dfrac{(x - 7)^2}{25} - \dfrac{(y - 2)^2}{1} = 1$; (12, 2), (2, 2); (7 + √26, 2),
(7 - √26, 2)

37. $\dfrac{(y - 2)^2}{36} - \dfrac{(x + 2)^2}{16} = 1$; (-2, -4), (-2, 8);
(-2, 2 + 2√13), (-2, 2 - 2√13)

39. $\dfrac{x^2}{100^2} + \dfrac{(y - 85)^2}{85^2} = 1$; 8500π yd^2

11.5 Integrated Review p. 603
41. $y = x$ **43.** $-2 \pm \sqrt{5}$ **45.** $3 \pm \sqrt{5}$
47.   **49.**

11.5 Mixed Review p. 603
1. $\dfrac{14}{15}$ **3.** $6|x|y\sqrt{2y}$ **5.** $3(x - 2)^2 - 5$
7.

9. $2x^2 - 2x + 10$ **11.** $\dfrac{2 \pm \sqrt{4 - 3c}}{3}$ **13.** $x < -2$ or $x > 1$
15. $-3\sqrt{10}$ **17.** $\left(\dfrac{1}{4}, 0\right)$ **19.** 3, 8

11.6 Communicating About Algebra p. 609
A. Ellipse **B.** Hyperbola **C.** (-1, 1), (5, 1)

11.6 Guided Practice p. 610
1. See page 606 **2.** See page 606 **3. a.** Intersecting lines;
b. line; **c.** point **4.** $B = 0$ **5.** (0, 0); substitute $-y$ for x^2
in the first equation and solve for y, then solve for x by
using $x^2 = -y$. **6.** (0, 0), (3, √3), (3, -√3)

11.6 Independent Practice pp. 610–613
7. Ellipse **9.** Hyperbola **11.** Ellipse **13.** Hyperbola

15. Parabola **17.** Ellipse **19.** Circle **21.** Hyperbola
23. b **25.** d **27.** c **29.** g

31.
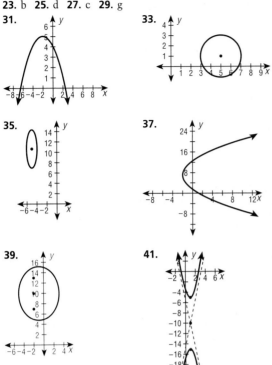

33.

35.

37.

39.

41.

43. $(-2, 8)$, $(5, 8 + 4\sqrt{21})$, $(5, 8 - 4\sqrt{21})$ **45.** $(2, 4)$, $(2, 2)$
47. $(-10, 12)$ **49.** $(0, 0)$ **51.** $(0, 6)$, $(12, 6)$ **53.** $(1, 0)$
55. Hyperbola; plane through cone is vertical
57. Circles in Relation to Tangent Circle

	Small	Medium	Large
given	outside	inside	outside
given	outside	inside	inside
1	inside	outside	outside
2	outside	outside	inside
3	inside	inside	outside
4	inside	outside	inside
5	inside	inside	inside
6	outside	outside	outside

59. $(3, 4)$; draw a circle from each seismograph's location, then write the coordinates of the point where all three circles intersect.

■ *11.6 Integrated Review p. 613*
61. ≈95% **63.** a

■ *11.6 Chapter Review pp. 615–618*
1. $x^2 + y^2 = 25$ **3.** $(y - 2)^2 = -8(x - 3)$
5. $\frac{(x-2)^2}{4} + \frac{(y-2)^2}{1} = 1$ **7.** $\frac{(x-2)^2}{3} + \frac{(y-2)^2}{4} = 1$
9. $\frac{(y)^2}{9} - \frac{(x-2)^2}{16} = 1$ **11.** $(0, 0)$, $\left(0, \frac{1}{8}\right)$, $y = -\frac{1}{8}$
13. $(0, 0)$, $\left(\frac{3}{4}, 0\right)$, $x = -\frac{3}{4}$ **15.** $(-3, 2)$, $\left(-\frac{13}{4}, 2\right)$, $x = -\frac{11}{4}$
17. $(0, 0)$; $(0, -13)$, $(0, 13)$; $(0, -5)$, $(0, 5)$ **19.** $(5, 0)$; $(1, 0)$, $(9, 0)$; $(5 - \sqrt{7}, 0)$, $(5 + \sqrt{7}, 0)$ **21.** $(-3, 1)$; $(-3, -5)$, $(-3, 7)$; $(-3, 1 - \sqrt{11})$, $(-3, 1 + \sqrt{11})$ **23.** $(0, 0)$; $(-6, 0)$, $(6, 0)$; $(-2\sqrt{10}, 0)$, $(2\sqrt{10}, 0)$; $y = \pm\frac{1}{3}x$ **25.** $(-1, 4)$; $(-13, 4)$, $(11, 4)$; $(-14, 4)$, $(12, 4)$; $y = \frac{5}{12}x + \frac{43}{12}$, $y = -\frac{5}{12}x + \frac{43}{12}$
27. $(-3, 1)$; $\left(-3, \frac{1}{2}\right)$, $\left(-3, \frac{3}{2}\right)$; $\left(-3, 1 - \frac{\sqrt{13}}{6}\right)$, $\left(-3, 1 + \frac{\sqrt{13}}{6}\right)$; $y = \frac{3}{2}x + \frac{11}{2}$, $y = -\frac{3}{2}x - \frac{7}{2}$ **29.** d **31.** a

33.

35.

37.

39.

41. $(x + 4)^2 = 4(2)y$ **43.** $(y - 5)^2 = 4(4)(x + 2)$
45. $(x - 5)^2 + (y + 1)^2 = 100$ **47.** $(x + 2)^2 + (y + 4)^2 = 1$
49. $\frac{(x+4)^2}{1} + \frac{(y-1)^2}{9} = 1$ **51.** $\frac{(x-1)^2}{4} + \frac{(y-5)^2}{\frac{25}{4}} = 1$
53. $\frac{(y-9)^2}{1} - \frac{(x+1)^2}{\frac{1}{4}} = 1$ **55.** $\frac{(x+1)^2}{25} - \frac{(y+1)^2}{\frac{49}{4}} = 1$
57. Circle **59.** Hyperbola **61.** Ellipse **63.** Parabola
65. $(6, -8)$, $(12, -16)$ **67.** $(-1, 1)$, $(-4, 2)$
69. $(4, 1)$
71. Parabola; the distance between a point on the curve and the focus is the same as the distance between the point and the bottom edge of the paper.
73.

75. $(0, 125)$, 49 ft **77.** $\frac{x^2}{18.12^2} + \frac{y^2}{4.39^2} = 1$ **79.** Pluto: ≈0.2500, Venus: ≈0.0067, Venus **81.** Hyperbolic, 13.5 million miles

CHAPTER 12

12.1 Communicating About Algebra   p. 625
A. 120   **B.** 385

12.1 Guided Practice   p. 626
1. a is a sequence, **b** is a series; a series is the sum of the terms of a sequence.   **2.** 2, 4, 6, 8, 10, 12   **3.** 1, -1, 1, -1, 1, -1 **4.** 12

12.1 Independent Practice   pp. 626–628
5. $-2, 1, 4, 7, 10$ **7.** 3, 6, 11, 18, 27   **9.** 2, 4, 8, 16, 32
11. $-\frac{1}{2}, \frac{1}{4}, -\frac{1}{8}, \frac{1}{16}, -\frac{1}{32}$ **13.** $\frac{1}{2}, \frac{2}{3}, \frac{3}{4}, \frac{4}{5}, \frac{5}{6}$ **15.** $-2, 4,$
$-8, 16, -32$ **17.** $-1, 0, 4, 22, 118$ **19.** $3, \frac{9}{2}, \frac{9}{2}, \frac{27}{8}, \frac{81}{40}$
21. 2, 4, 12, 48, 240   **23.** 1, 1, 2, 6, 24   **25.** 3, 5, 3, 5, 3
27. 3, 5, 3, 5, 3   **29.** 1, 1, 2, 3, 5, 8   **31.** $0 + 1 + 4 + 9 +$
$16 = 30$ **33.** $2 + 5 + 10 + 17 + 26 = 60$ **35.** $2 + 6 +$
$12 + 20 = 40$ **37.** $0 + 3 + 20 + 115 + 714 = 852$ **39.** $2 +$
$\frac{3}{2} + \frac{4}{3} + \frac{5}{4} + \frac{6}{5} = \frac{437}{60}$ **41.** $11 + 11 + 12 + 16 + 34 + 130 +$
$730 = 944$ **43.** $\sum_{i=1}^{6} 2i$ **45.** $\sum_{i=1}^{5} 3^i$ **47.** 24   **49.** 25,585
51. $\sum_{i=1}^{n}(2^i - 1)$, 63   **53.** $\frac{180}{7}, 45, 60, 72, \frac{900}{11}$

12.1 Integrated Review   p. 628
55. 40,320   **57.** 0   **59.** 3   **61.** 1, 2, 4, 8, 16, 32
63. 0, 1, 1, 0, -1, -1

12.2 Communicating About Algebra   p. 632
A. $a_n = 6 + 0.5n$
B. $S = \frac{1}{2}n(a_1 + a_n)$
$= \frac{1}{2} \cdot 100(1 + 199)$
$= 50(200)$
$= 10,000$

12.2 Guided Practice   p. 633
1. A common difference between consecutive terms.
2. 2   **3.** $a_n = 2n + 7$ **4.** 22   **5.** 5   **6.** 160

12.2 Independent Practice   pp. 633–635
7. It is.   **9.** It is.   **11.** It is.   **13.** 8, 45   **15.** $\frac{1}{6}, \frac{7}{6}$ **17.** $-\frac{5}{4}$,
$-\frac{11}{4}$ **19.** $a_n = 4n - 3$ **21.** $a_n = -2n + 13$ **23.** 15
25. 30, 20, 10, 0, -10 **27.** $-61, -52, -43, -34$ **29.** b
31. a   **33.** 1850   **35.** 23   **37.** 20.5   **39.** 16,100   **41.** 1312
43. $25.42   **45.** 126   **47.** $S_n = 1500n + 26,000$, $187,500

12.2 Integrated Review   p. 635
49. 8, 11, 14, 17, 20   **51.** $\frac{1}{2}, \frac{1}{3}, \frac{1}{4}, \frac{1}{5}, \frac{1}{6}$ **53.** 97, 94, 91, 88, 85
55. 1, 1, 1, 1, 1   **57.** Linear   **59.** Neither   **61.** b

12.2 Mixed Review   p. 636
1. $g(x) = \sqrt[3]{x} - 2$ **3.** $\frac{y}{3x}$ **5.** $(x + 2)(x + 6)(x - 3)$
7. $\frac{3}{4} \le x \le \frac{9}{4}$ **9.** $\begin{bmatrix} -2 & 13 \\ 3 & 7 \end{bmatrix}$ **11.** 1

13. $\log_6 3 + 2\log_6 x - \log_6 4$ **15.** $n = \frac{m - 2}{3m - 1}$
17. $x + y = -1$ **19.** $x^3 - x^2 + 4x - 4 = 0$

12.3 Communicating About Algebra   p. 640
A. $a_n = 2n - 1$, $100 million   **B.** $a_n \approx 1.387^{n-1}$, $\approx$$65.5 million

12.3 Guided Practice   p. 641
1. A common ratio of consecutive terms   **2.** $a_n = a_1 r^{n-1}$
3. 3   **4.** a   **5.** ≈ 5.99 **6.** ≈ 11.99

12.3 Independent Practice   pp. 641–642
7. Geometric   **9.** Arithmetic   **11.** Geometric   **13.** $-3, 81$
15. 5, 1250   **17.** $-\frac{1}{2}, \frac{5}{16}$ **19.** 2, 6, 18, 54, 162   **21.** 6, 12,
24, 48, 96   **23.** 1, $-\frac{1}{4}, \frac{1}{16}, -\frac{1}{64}, \frac{1}{256}$ **25.** $\frac{1}{128}$
27. $-\frac{2}{59,049}$ **29.** 25,600   **31.** $a_n = \left(\frac{3}{2}\right)^{n-1}$
33. $a_n = 4\left(\frac{3}{2}\right)^{n-1}$ **35.** $a_n = 3\left(\frac{1}{2}\right)^{n-1}$ **37.** $-\frac{1}{177,147}$
39. 8748 or -8748 **41.** $\frac{1}{4}$ or $-\frac{1}{4}$ **43.** $a_n = 32\left(\frac{1}{2}\right)^{n-1}$
or $a_n = 32\left(-\frac{1}{2}\right)^{n-1}$ **45.** 4095   **47.** ≈ 7.50
49. -85 **51.** $\frac{28,394}{729}$ **53.** 126 in.^{2}

12.3 Integrated Review   p. 643
55. Geometric   **57.** Arithmetic   **59.** Neither   **61.** Neither
63. Neither   **65.** $\frac{4202}{625}$ **67.** -10 **69.** $\approx 7\%$

12.3 Mid-Chapter Self-Test   p. 644
1. Neither   **2.** Arithmetic   **3.** Geometric   **4.** 5, 8, 11, 14,
17   **5.** $-1, -10, -25, -46, -73$ **6.** $1, \frac{1}{2}, \frac{2}{3}, \frac{3}{2}, \frac{24}{5}$
7. $a_n = 6n - 2$ **8.** $a_n = 6(2)^{n-1}$ **9.** $a_n = \frac{n + 9}{3}$ **10.** -4
11. -2 **12.** 25   **13.** $a_n = 10\left(\frac{1}{5}\right)^{n-1}$ **14.** 4374   **15.** -2
16. 990   **17.** $\frac{121}{81}$ **18.** 496   **19.** $1442.22 billion
20. $35,100.76 million   **21.** $48.6 billion

12.4 Communicating About Algebra   p. 647
No, it can come closer and closer to the top, but it never quite makes it.

12.4 Guided Practice   p. 648
1. ∞ **2.** $\sum_{i=1}^{\infty} a_i$ **3.** $|r| < 1$ **4.** 6

12.4 Independent Practice   pp. 648–649
5. It does not.   **7.** It does.   **9.** It does.   **11.** It does not.
13. 2   **15.** $\frac{2}{3}$ **17.** $\frac{16}{3}$ **19.** It has none.   **21.** $-\frac{1}{9}$ **23.** $\frac{25}{336}$
25. 100   **27.** 2   **29.** Finite, $\frac{a_1}{1 - r} = \frac{160}{1 - \frac{16}{25}} = \frac{4000}{9}$;
infinite, $r = 1$ so that $\frac{a_1}{1 - r}$ is undefined for the series of
heights.   **31.** 85 ft   **33.** $\frac{I}{3}$, $\frac{a_1}{1 - r} = \frac{\frac{I}{4}}{1 - \frac{1}{4}} = \frac{I}{3}$

12.4 Integrated Review   p. 650
35. 45   **37.** 19,530   **39.** 1456   **41.** $\frac{1023}{1024}$ **43.** d   **45.** c

■ 12.5 Communicating About Algebra   p. 654

```
                128
            64      64
        32      64      32
    16      48      48      16
        32      48      32      8
            40      40      20      4
                40      30      12
                   |35|    |21|
                    B.      A.
```

■ 12.5 Guided Practice   p. 655

1. The exponents with base x decrease by 1 from term to term.   **2.** Binomial Theorem of Pascal's Triangle   **3.** 1, 7, 21, 35, 35, 21, 7, 1   **4.** a, $\binom{11}{5} = \frac{11!}{6!5!} = \frac{11 \cdot 10 \cdot 9 \cdot 8 \cdot 7}{5!}$
5. Row 6   **6.** $x^4 + 28x^3 + 294x^2 + 1372x + 2401$, $x^4 - 28x^3 + 294x^2 - 1372x + 2401$; absolute values of the coefficients are the same for like terms, the even-numbered terms have opposite signs.

■ 12.5 Independent Practice   pp. 655–656

7. 10   **9.** 1   **11.** 792   **13.** 792   **15.** $a^3 + 6a^2 + 12a + 8$
17. $x^4 + 8x^3 + 24x^2 + 32x + 16$ **19.** $x^5 - 15x^4 + 90x^3 - 270x^2 + 405x - 243$ **21.** $64x^6 + 192x^5 + 240x^4 + 160x^3 + 60x^2 + 12x + 1$ **23.** 1120   **25.** 3   **27.** 21
29. $64x^3 - 48x^2y + 12xy^2 - y^3$ **31.** $x^4 + 16x^3 + 96x^2 + 256x + 256$ **33.** $32t^5 - 80t^4s + 80t^3s^2 - 40t^2s^3 + 10ts^4 - s^5$ **35.** $64x^6 + 192x^5y + 240x^4y^2 + 160x^3y^3 + 60x^2y^4 + 12xy^5 + y^6$
37.

1 column   2 columns   3 columns

39. 512, *add the numbers in row 9 of Pascal's Triangle*
41. 2,097,151

■ 12.5 Integrated Review   p. 656

43. 5   **45.** 36   **47.** $3000

■ 12.5 Mixed Review   p. 657

1. $\begin{bmatrix} \frac{1}{2} & 0 \\ -\frac{5}{2} & 1 \end{bmatrix}$ **3.** ± 7

5.

7. $4^3 = 64$ **9.** $(-3, -2)$
11.

13. $y = 2$ **15.** -3 **17.** Ellipse

■ 12.6 Communicating About Algebra   p. 660

A. $83,225.86   **B.** $149,035.94   **C.** $406,152.40
D. $893,406.19

■ 12.6 Guided Practice   p. 661

1. See page 658; as a retirement account   **2.** $0.40
3. $1.25; $301.88; $301.88; $403.77   **4.** at the end of the month   **5.** $D = 200$, $r = 0.06$, $n = 12$, $i = 0.005$, $t = 10$
6. To determine equal deposits that will produce a given balance

■ 12.6 Independent Practice   pp. 661–663

7.

End of year	Previous balance	Interest	Deposit	New balance
1	$0.00	$0.00	$1000.00	$1000.00
2	$1000	$80.00	$1000.00	$2080.00
3	$2080	$166.40	$1000.00	$3246.40
4	$3246.40	$259.71	$1000.00	$4506.11
5	$4506.11	$360.49	$1000.00	$5866.60

9.

End of half	Previous balance	Interest	Deposit	New balance
1	$0.00	$0.00	$500.00	$500.00
2	$500.00	$15.00	$500.00	$1015.00
3	$1015.00	$30.45	$500.00	$1545.45
4	$1545.45	$46.36	$500.00	$2091.81
5	$2091.81	$62.75	$500.00	$2654.56
6	$2654.56	$79.64	$500.00	$3234.20
7	$3234.20	$97.03	$500.00	$3831.23
8	$3831.23	$114.94	$500.00	$4446.17
9	$4446.17	$133.39	$500.00	$5079.56
10	$5079.56	$152.39	$500.00	$5731.95

11. $74,559.43   **13.** $12,120.35   **15.** $11,632.75
17. $18,696.72   **19.** Monthly deposits of $80 at 6% interest compounded monthly   **21.** $344.70   **23.** Monthly payments with 5% interest compounded monthly for 15 years

■ 12.6 Integrated Review   p. 663

25. $\frac{1}{15}$

■ 12.6 Chapter Review   pp. 667–670

1. 4, 2, 0, -2, -4 **3.** 10, 5, $\frac{5}{3}$, $\frac{5}{12}$, $\frac{1}{12}$ **5.** 1, -0.2, 0.04, -0.008, 0.0016   **7.** 6, 9, 14, 21, 30   **9.** 44   **11.** 5525
13. Arithmetic, 6   **15.** Arithmetic, $-\frac{1}{2}$ **17.** Neither
19. $a_n = 5n + 8$ **21.** $\sum_{n=1}^{7} (6n - 5) = 133$
23. $\sum_{n=1}^{8} (28 - 6n) = 8$ **25.** $\sum_{n=1}^{8} \frac{1}{3}n = 12$ **27.** $a_n = \frac{1}{4}(6)^{n-1}$
29. $\approx 5.864 \times 10^{12}$ **31.** ≈ 4.800 **33.** 51.1   **35.** 5   **37.** $\frac{10}{3}$
39. 7   **41.** 36   **43.** 1   **45.** $x^3 + 12x^2 + 48x + 64$
47. $x^5 + 5x^4y + 10x^3y^2 + 10x^2y^3 + 5xy^4 + y^5$
49. $y^7 - 7y^6 + 21y^5 - 35y^4 + 35y^3 - 21y^2 + 7y - 1$

51. $x^3 + 6x^2y + 12xy^2 + 8y^3$

53.

End of month	Previous balance	Interest	Deposit	New balance
1	$0.00	$0.00	$50.00	$50.00
2	$50.00	$0.33	$50.00	$100.33
3	$100.33	$0.67	$50.00	$151.00
4	$151.00	$1.01	$50.00	$202.01
5	$202.01	$1.35	$50.00	$253.36
6	$253.36	$1.69	$50.00	$305.05

55. $28.10 **57.** $1 + \sum_{n=1}^{8} 2^{n-1}$ **59.** 1, 1, 2, 3, 5, 8, 13, 21, 34, 55; 1, 2, 1.5, $\approx$1.667, 1.6, 1.625, $\approx$1.615, $\approx$1.619, $\approx$1.618; the ratios get closer and closer to the Golden Ratio. **61.** 55 **63.** $\approx$3.86 **65.** Multiples of 4 **67.** Multiples of 3

69.
44
30
$\frac{311}{4}$
64
1
45.74
75
80

71.
30
36
59.5
3.97
49
60
15
17

12.6 Cumulative Review For Chapters 7–12 pp. 672–675

1. c **3.** a **5.** $xy = 72$ **7.** $\frac{z}{xy} = \frac{2}{3}$ **9.** $\frac{x^2y(x+3)}{(x-2)^2(x+2)}$

11. $\frac{-3x^2 - x + 20}{(x+4)(x-4)}$ **13.** $\frac{3x^3 - 6x^2 - 96}{2x^3 - x^2 + 12x}$ **15.** d **17.** b

19. Hyperbola, $\frac{(x-1)^2}{4} - (y+1)^2 = 1$

21. Parabola, $(x-3)^2 = 4(y-1)$

23. Ellipse; $\frac{(x+2)^2}{16} + \frac{(y+2)^2}{9} = 1$

25. Circle; $(x+2)^2 + (y-1)^2 = 9$

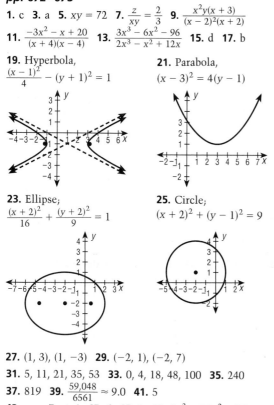

27. $(1, 3), (1, -3)$ **29.** $(-2, 1), (-2, 7)$
31. 5, 11, 21, 35, 53 **33.** 0, 4, 18, 48, 100 **35.** 240
37. 819 **39.** $\frac{59,048}{6561} \approx 9.0$ **41.** 5
43. $a_n = 7n + 4$ **45.** 6 **47.** 1 **49.** $8x^3 + 36x^2 + 54x + 27$; $x^5 - 5x^4y + 10x^3y^2 - 10x^2y^3 + 5xy^4 - y^5$ **51.** $\frac{21x + 8}{24x + 8}$

53. $31,730.77 **55.** no **57.** $635.80 **59.** $130.95, $714.20 **61.** 15 in.^{2} **63.** c

CHAPTER 13

13.1 Communicating About Algebra p. 681

A. $\sin \theta = \frac{5}{13}$, $\cos \theta = \frac{12}{13}$, $\tan \theta = \frac{5}{12}$, $\csc \theta = \frac{13}{5}$, $\sec \theta = \frac{13}{12}$, $\cot \theta = \frac{12}{5}$

B.

13.1 Guided Practice p. 682

1. Sine, sin; cosine, cos; tangent, tan; cosecant, csc; secant, sec; cotangent, cot
2. $\sin \theta = \frac{5}{\sqrt{41}}$, $\cos \theta = \frac{4}{\sqrt{41}}$, $\tan \theta = \frac{5}{4}$, $\csc \theta = \frac{\sqrt{41}}{5}$, $\sec \theta = \frac{\sqrt{41}}{4}$, $\cot \theta = \frac{4}{5}$
3. $\frac{1}{2}$, $\frac{\sqrt{17}}{2}$ **4.** $60°$ **5.** $\sin^2 \theta + \cos^2 \theta = 1$, $\sin^2 \theta + (0.55)^2 = 1$, $\sin \theta \approx 0.8352$ **6.** 1.179

13.1 Independent Practice pp. 682–684

7. $\sin \theta = \frac{3}{5}$, $\cos \theta = \frac{4}{5}$, $\tan \theta = \frac{3}{4}$, $\csc \theta = \frac{5}{3}$, $\sec \theta = \frac{5}{4}$, $\cot \theta = \frac{4}{3}$ **9.** $\sin \theta = \frac{10}{13}$, $\cos \theta = \frac{\sqrt{69}}{13}$, $\tan \theta = \frac{10}{\sqrt{69}}$, $\csc \theta = \frac{13}{10}$, $\sec \theta = \frac{13}{\sqrt{69}}$, $\cot \theta = \frac{\sqrt{69}}{10}$ **11.** $\sin \theta = \frac{3}{10}$, $\cos \theta = \frac{\sqrt{91}}{10}$, $\tan \theta = \frac{3}{\sqrt{91}}$, $\csc \theta = \frac{10}{3}$, $\sec \theta = \frac{10}{\sqrt{91}}$, $\cot \theta = \frac{\sqrt{91}}{3}$ **13.** $\sin \theta = \frac{9}{25}$, $\cos \theta = \frac{4\sqrt{34}}{25}$, $\tan \theta = \frac{9}{4\sqrt{34}}$, $\csc \theta = \frac{25}{9}$, $\sec \theta = \frac{25}{4\sqrt{34}}$, $\cot \theta = \frac{4\sqrt{34}}{9}$

15. $\cos \theta = \frac{\sqrt{5}}{3}$, $\tan \theta = \frac{2}{\sqrt{5}}$, $\csc \theta = \frac{3}{2}$, $\sec \theta = \frac{3}{\sqrt{5}}$, $\cot \theta = \frac{\sqrt{5}}{2}$

17. $\sin \theta = \frac{\sqrt{3}}{2}$, $\cos \theta = \frac{1}{2}$, $\tan \theta = \sqrt{3}$, $\csc \theta = \frac{2}{\sqrt{3}}$, $\cot \theta = \frac{1}{\sqrt{3}}$

19. $\sin \theta = \frac{3}{\sqrt{10}}$, $\cos \theta = \frac{1}{\sqrt{10}}$, $\csc \theta = \frac{\sqrt{10}}{3}$, $\sec \theta = \sqrt{10}$, $\cot \theta = \frac{1}{3}$

$$\sin \theta = \frac{2}{\sqrt{13}}, \cos \theta = \frac{3}{\sqrt{13}},$$
$$\tan \theta = \frac{2}{3}, \csc \theta = \frac{\sqrt{13}}{2},$$
$$\sec \theta = \frac{\sqrt{13}}{3}$$

23. $\sqrt{2}$ **25.** $\frac{2\sqrt{3}}{3}$ **27.** 1 **29.** $\frac{\sqrt{3}}{3}$ **31.** $\frac{\sqrt{3}}{2}$

33. 9 **35.** $\frac{1}{\sqrt{3}}$ **37.** $\frac{3}{2\sqrt{2}}$ **39.** $\frac{3}{5}$ **41.** 0.174 **43.** 3.271
45. 0.900 **47.** 0.990 **49.** 1.167 **51.** 1.305 **53.** 2.130
55. 28.654 **57.** ≈4246.3 ft **59.** ≈0.577

■ **13.1 Integrated Review p. 684**
61. $3\sqrt{10}$ **63.** 5 **65.** e

■ **13.2 Communicating About Algebra p. 688**
A,F,K; B,G,I; C,E,L; D,H,J

■ **13.2 Guided Practice p. 689**
1. Origin, positive x-axis **2.** a, B; b, C; c D; d, A **3.** 420°,
−300° **4.** πr **5.** $\frac{3\pi}{4}$ **6.** 270°

■ **13.2 Independent Practice pp. 689–691**
7. They are. **9.** They are. **11.** They are. **13.** They are.
15. 60° **17.** 38° **19.** $\frac{5\pi}{18}$ **21.** $\frac{\pi}{2}$ **23.** 80° **25.** 156°
27. $\frac{7\pi}{9}$ **29.** $\frac{2\pi}{3}$ **31.** 410°, −310° **33.** 60°, −300° **35.** $\frac{\pi}{3}$,
$-\frac{5\pi}{3}$ **37.** $\frac{10\pi}{7}$, $-\frac{4\pi}{7}$ **39.** $\frac{\pi}{9}$ **41.** $\frac{5\pi}{6}$ **43.** $-\frac{11\pi}{18}$ **45.** $\frac{16\pi}{9}$
47. 300° **49.** 18° **51.** 84° **53.** −210° **55.** a **57.** b **59.** f
61. e **63.** $\frac{7\pi}{8}$ **65.** $\frac{36\pi}{7}$ in.

■ **13.2 Integrated Review p. 691**
67. $\frac{1}{2}$, $\frac{\sqrt{2}}{2}$, $\frac{\sqrt{3}}{2}$; $\frac{\sqrt{3}}{2}$, $\frac{\sqrt{2}}{2}$, $\frac{1}{2}$; $\frac{\sqrt{3}}{3}$, 1, $\sqrt{3}$ **69.** c

■ **13.2 Mixed Review p. 692**
1. $x \le -9$ or $x \ge 5$

3.

5. 212 **7.** 13 **9.** $x^3 - 4x^2 + 16x - 64$
11. $(x - 1)(x + 1)(x + 2)$ **13.** 55
15.

17. $xy = 3$ **19.** No

■ **13.3 Communicating About Algebra p. 696**
≈113.14 ft per second

■ **13.3 Guided Practice p. 697**
1. $\sqrt{41}$ **2.** $\frac{y}{x}$; 0; 90; 270° **3.** 1; $\sin \theta = \frac{y}{r}$, $y \le r$ **4.** I, IV
5. $\frac{\pi}{4}$ **6.** 60° **7.** $-\frac{1}{2}$ **8.** $\sqrt{3}$

■ **13.3 Independent Practice pp. 697–699**
9. $\frac{5}{13}$, $-\frac{12}{13}$, $-\frac{5}{12}$ **11.** $-\frac{4}{5}$, $-\frac{3}{5}$, $\frac{4}{3}$ **13.** $-\frac{5}{13}$, $-\frac{12}{13}$, $\frac{5}{12}$
15. $\frac{1}{2}$, $-\frac{\sqrt{3}}{2}$, $-\frac{1}{\sqrt{3}}$ **17.** $-\frac{15}{17}$, $\frac{8}{17}$, $-\frac{15}{8}$ **19.** $\frac{1}{\sqrt{2}}$, $-\frac{1}{\sqrt{2}}$, -1

21. 40°   **23.** 25°

25. $\frac{\pi}{3}$ **27.** $\frac{2\pi}{5}$

29. ≈1.16   **31.** ≈1.18

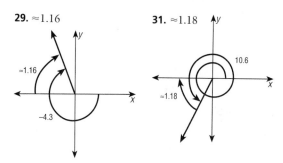

33. True **35.** True **37.** False **39.** False **41.** $\frac{1}{2}$
43. $-\frac{2\sqrt{3}}{3}$ **45.** $\frac{2\sqrt{3}}{3}$ **47.** $-\frac{1}{2}$ **49.** $-\sqrt{3}$ **51.** $\frac{1}{2}$ **53.** $-\frac{1}{2}$
55. $-\frac{1}{2}$ **57.** ≈0.3090 **59.** 1.14 **61.** −0.5 **63.** Undefined
65. ≈0.0585 **67.** 0.635 **69.** ≈6.70 ft **71.** ≈11.57 ft
73. ≈(−3620.4, 1604.4), ≈(3620.4, 1604.4)
75. ≈7182.7 mi

■ **13.3 Integrated Review p. 699**
77. $\sin \theta = \frac{3}{\sqrt{13}}$, $\cos \theta = \frac{2}{\sqrt{13}}$, $\csc \theta = \frac{\sqrt{13}}{3}$, $\sec \theta = \frac{\sqrt{13}}{2}$,
$\cot \theta = \frac{2}{3}$ **79.** $\cos \theta = \frac{\sqrt{15}}{4}$, $\tan \theta = \frac{1}{\sqrt{15}}$, $\csc \theta = 4$,
$\sec \theta = \frac{4}{\sqrt{15}}$, $\cot \theta = \sqrt{15}$ **81.** The sin 10° is positive.
The calculator is in radian mode.

1. $\sin \theta = \frac{3}{\sqrt{13}}$, $\cos \theta = \frac{2}{\sqrt{13}}$, $\tan \theta = \frac{3}{2}$, $\csc \theta = \frac{\sqrt{13}}{3}$, $\sec \theta = \frac{\sqrt{13}}{2}$, $\cot \theta = \frac{2}{3}$ **2.** $\sin \theta = \frac{1}{\sqrt{5}}$, $\cos \theta = \frac{2}{\sqrt{5}}$, $\tan \theta = \frac{1}{2}$, $\cot \theta = 2$, $\sec \theta = \frac{\sqrt{5}}{2}$, $\csc \theta = \sqrt{5}$ **3.** $\sin \theta = \frac{1}{2}$, $\cos \theta = \frac{\sqrt{3}}{2}$, $\tan \theta = \frac{1}{\sqrt{3}}$, $\cot \theta = \sqrt{3}$, $\sec \theta = \frac{2}{\sqrt{3}}$, $\csc \theta = 2$ **4.** 53° **5.** 75° **6.** $\frac{\pi}{8}$ **7.** 60° **8.** $\frac{\pi}{8}$ **9.** $\frac{7\pi}{12}$ **10.** 200°, −160° **11.** 285°, −435° **12.** $\frac{11\pi}{8}$, $\frac{-21\pi}{8}$ **13.** $\sin \theta = \frac{4}{5}$, $\cos \theta = \frac{3}{5}$, $\tan \theta = \frac{4}{3}$ **14.** $\sin \theta = \frac{3}{5}$, $\cos \theta = -\frac{4}{5}$, $\tan \theta = -\frac{3}{4}$ **15.** $\sin \theta = -\frac{12}{13}$, $\cos \theta = -\frac{5}{13}$, $\tan \theta = \frac{12}{5}$ **16.** False **17.** False **18.** False **19.** False **20.** ≈17.35°, ≈45° **21.** $6\frac{7}{8}$ in., $20\frac{3}{4}$ in. **22.** ≈197 ft

■ **13.4 Communicating About Algebra p. 705**
A. $-45°$, $-\frac{\pi}{4}$ **B.** 135°, $\frac{3\pi}{4}$ **C.** ≈−35.3°, ≈−0.615

■ **13.4 Guided Practice p. 706**
1. 45° **2.** $\sqrt{3}$ **3.** ≈39.8°, ≈0.695 **4.** ≈25.8°, ≈0.451

■ **13.4 Independent Practice pp. 706–708**
5. ≈33.7°, ≈0.588 **7.** 30°, ≈0.524 **9.** ≈53.1°, ≈0.927 **11.** 120°, ≈2.094 **13.** 45°, $\frac{\pi}{4}$ **15.** 90°, $\frac{\pi}{2}$ **17.** 60°, $\frac{\pi}{3}$ **19.** 150°, $\frac{5\pi}{6}$ **21.** −90°, $-\frac{\pi}{2}$ **23.** −45°, $-\frac{\pi}{4}$ **25.** −60°, $\frac{-\pi}{3}$ **27.** 0°, 0 **29.** 75.619°, 1.320 **31.** 77.291°, 1.349 **33.** −36.870°, −0.644 **35.** −5.711°, ≈−0.100 **37.** You didn't push the second function key in the degree mode and found tan 45 instead of arctan 45; ≈88.7°, ≈1.549 **39.** ≈18.4° **41.** ≈34.9° **43.** ≈53.29 in.

■ **13.4 Integrated Review p. 708**
45. $0, \frac{1}{2}, \frac{1}{\sqrt{2}}, \frac{\sqrt{3}}{2}, 1, 0, -1, 0; 1, \frac{\sqrt{3}}{2}, \frac{1}{\sqrt{2}}, \frac{1}{2}, 0, -1, 0, 1; 0, \frac{1}{\sqrt{3}}, 1, \sqrt{3}, *, 0, *, 0; *, 2, \sqrt{2}, \frac{2}{\sqrt{3}}, 1, *, -1, *; 1, \frac{2}{\sqrt{3}}, \sqrt{2}, 2, *, -1, *, 1; *, \sqrt{3}, 1, \frac{1}{\sqrt{3}}, 0, *, 0, *$ * mean function is not defined **47.** c

■ **13.5 Communicating About Algebra p. 711**
A. $\angle B = 80°$, $a \approx 4.45$, $b \approx 6.82$ **B.** $\angle B = 37°$, $\angle C = 85°$, $c = 8.3$

■ **13.5 Guided Practice p. 712**
1. See page 709. **2.** d **3.** The length of the longest side must be less than the sum of the lengths of the other two sides.
4. No; for example: If you are given that the three angles are 40°, 60°, and 80°, then many triangles of different sizes are possible.

5. ≈9.22 **6.** ≈35.31

■ **13.5 Independent Practice pp. 712–714**
7. $\angle B = 43°$, $b \approx 6.66$, $c \approx 9.67$ **9.** $\angle C = \frac{5\pi}{12}$, $a \approx 32.21$, $b \approx 39.45$ **11.** $C \approx 28.9°$, $B \approx 76.1°$, $b \approx 6.03$ **13.** $A = 60°$, $a \approx 1.79$, $c \approx 0.54$ **15.** $B = 58°$, $b \approx 35.67$, $c \approx 32.22$ **17.** $A \approx 1.47$, $C \approx 0.62$, $a \approx 34.47$ **19.** $A = 47°$, $b \approx 2.69$, $c \approx 2.18$ **21.** $B = 45°$, $a \approx 1.10$, $c \approx 3.67$ **23.** $A \approx 111.6°$, $B \approx 52.4°$, $a \approx 107.95$; $A \approx 36.4°$, $B \approx 127.6°$, $a \approx 68.89$ **25.** No solution **27.** $A = 40°$, $b \approx 17.54$, $c \approx 9.33$ **29.** No solution **31.** No solution **33.** Two solutions **35.** Exactly one solution **37.** Two solutions **39.** No solutions **41.** No solutions **43.** Exactly one solution **45.** Exactly one solution **47.** ≈54.38 **49.** ≈12.99 **51.** ≈46.77 **53.** ≈136.74 **55.** ≈1.41 **57.** ≈16.22 mi **59.** ≈11.17 mi **61.** ≈4.0 ft

■ **13.5 Integrated Review p. 715**
63. ≈13.05 **65.** $\sqrt{3}$ **67.** ≈16.0° **69.** ≈0.806

■ **13.5 Mixed Review p. 715**
1. $m = \frac{-4}{2 - 3n}$ **3.** $\frac{2}{3}$ **5.** $\begin{bmatrix} 1 & -\frac{1}{2} \\ -2 & \frac{3}{2} \end{bmatrix}$ **7.** $(-6, 7)$
9.

11. $\frac{3x}{4}$ **13.** $\left(-\frac{3}{2}, -\frac{17}{4}\right)$ **15.** −12 **17.** ≈3.26

■ **13.6 Communicating About Algebra p. 718**
A. ≈3.06 ft², use the formula derived from the Law of Sines because two sides and the included angle are given. **B.** ≈2.90 ft², use Heron's formula because three sides are given **C.** 4 ft², use the formula involving the height and the base because they are given

■ **13.6 Guided Practice p. 719**
1. SAS and SSS **2.** Use the formula $\cos B = \frac{a^2 + c^2 - b^2}{2ac}$, substituting for a, b, and c and solving for B. **3.** $a^2 = b^2 + c^2 - 2bc \cos A$ **4.** ≈8.21 ft

■ **13.6 Independent Practice pp. 719–721**
5. $A \approx 117.9°$, $B \approx 32.7°$, $C \approx 29.4°$ **7.** $A \approx 70.5°$, $B \approx 59.0°$, $C \approx 50.5°$ **9.** $a \approx 4.24$, $B \approx 61.0°$, $C \approx 87.1°$ **11.** $A \approx 83.0°$, $B \approx 27.8°$, $C \approx 69.2°$ **13.** $b \approx 42.98$, $A \approx 107.3°$, $C \approx 52.7°$ **15.** $A \approx 79.0°$, $B \approx 29.4°$, $C \approx 71.6°$ **17.** $a \approx 4.08$, $B \approx 28.6°$, $C \approx 73.4°$ **19.** $b \approx 14.15$, $A \approx 26.7°$, $C \approx 108.3°$ **21.** $A \approx 42.1°$, $B \approx 12.9°$, $C \approx 125.0°$ **23.** $A \approx 73.0$, $B \approx 96.0$, $C \approx 11.0°$ **25.** $C \approx 5.75$, $A \approx 0.123$, $B \approx 0.662$ **27.** $a \approx 23.24$, $B \approx 28.0°$, $C \approx 54.0$ **29.** $A \approx 36.9°$, $B \approx 53.2°$, $C \approx 89.9°$ **31.** ≈116.31 **33.** ≈404.54 **35.** ≈509.90 **37.** ≈1467.05 **39.** ≈0.50 **41.** ≈27.71 **43.** 3.06 ft **45.** ≈38.14 mi **47.** ≈12.07 mi

49. $A \approx 48.8°$, $B \approx 65.6°$, $C \approx 65.6°$ **51.** $b \approx 33.47$,
$B \approx 104.9°$, $C \approx 15.1°$ **53.** $C = \frac{7\pi}{12}$, $b \approx 18.38$, $c \approx 35.52$
55. $A = 30°$, $a \approx 28.98$, $c \approx 40.98$

■ *13.6* Chapter Review *pp. 723–726*

1. $\sin \theta = \frac{4}{5}$, $\cos \theta = \frac{3}{5}$, $\tan \theta = \frac{4}{3}$, $\csc \theta = \frac{5}{4}$, $\sec \theta = \frac{5}{3}$,
$\cot \theta = \frac{3}{4}$ **3.** $\sin \theta = \frac{3\sqrt{5}}{7}$, $\cos \theta = \frac{2}{7}$, $\tan \theta = \frac{3\sqrt{5}}{2}$,
$\csc \theta = \frac{7}{3\sqrt{5}}$, $\sec \theta = \frac{7}{2}$, $\cot \theta = \frac{2}{3\sqrt{5}}$ **5.** $\sin \theta = \frac{12}{13}$,
$\tan \theta = \frac{12}{5}$, $\csc \theta = \frac{13}{12}$, $\sec \theta = \frac{13}{5}$, $\cot \theta = \frac{5}{12}$ **7.** 50°
9. $\frac{\pi}{6}$ **11.** $\frac{\pi}{18}$ **13.** 85° **15.** 100° **17.** $\frac{\pi}{4}$ **19.** 715°, −5°
21. π, -3π **23.** 426°, −294° **25.** $-\frac{\pi}{12}$ **27.** $\frac{\pi}{3}$ **29.** $\frac{13\pi}{9}$
31. 210° **33.** −540° **35.** 144°

37. $\frac{\pi}{4}$

39. 65°

41. 80°

43. 2 **45.** 1 **47.** $\frac{1}{\sqrt{2}}$ **49.** $\frac{-1}{\sqrt{3}}$ **51.** $\frac{2}{\sqrt{3}}$ **53.** 60°, $\frac{\pi}{3}$
55. 30°, $\frac{\pi}{6}$ **57.** 60°, $\frac{\pi}{3}$ **59.** 0.731 **61.** 3.549
63. −0.364 **65.** 64.158°, 1.120 **67.** 41.410°, 0.723
69. 71.565°, 1.249 **71.** $C = 98°$, $a \approx 9.68$, $c \approx 18.10$
73. $A \approx 25.8°$, $B \approx 28.2$, $a \approx 6.46$ **75.** $B \approx 17.4°$,
$C \approx 109.6°$, $c \approx 9.44$ **77.** $A = \frac{\pi}{12}$, $a \approx 3.66$, $c \approx 12.25$
79. $A \approx 81.8$, $B = 60$, $C \approx 38.2$ **81.** ≈ 164.40 **83.** ≈ 26.83
85. ≈ 20.55 **87.** ≈ 18.41 **89.** ≈ 9.80 **91.** 13.26°
93. ≈ 1.27 cm **95.** $\approx 19.2°$ **97.** ≈ 0.50 ft **99.** 148.7 ft
101. 127.2°

CHAPTER 14

■ *14.1* Communicating About Algebra *p. 733*

A. The amplitude is 2 and the period is $\frac{2\pi}{3}$.

B. The amplitude is 1 and the period is 6π.

C. The amplitude is 1 and the period is 1.

■ *14.1* Guided Practice *p. 734*

1. b **2.** All real numbers, $-1 \leq y \leq 1$ **3.** 4π **4.** 2 **5.** 5

■ *14.1* Independent Practice *p. 734–736*

7. $\frac{1}{2}$, $\frac{2\pi}{3}$ **9.** $\frac{1}{2}$, π **11.** 1, $\frac{\pi}{2}$ **13.** 4, 1 **15.** $\frac{1}{3}$, $\frac{1}{2}$ **17.** d
19. c

21.

23.

25.

27.

29.

31.

33. "cos x" was entered instead of "sin x" **35.** $y = 3 \sin 6x$ **37.** $y = \frac{5}{2} \cos 2x$ **39.** $\frac{3\pi}{8}, \frac{7\pi}{8}; \frac{\pi}{8}, \frac{5\pi}{8}$ **41.** c
43. 264 hertz (cycles per second) **45.** $\frac{1}{2}, \frac{\pi}{3}$

■ 14.1 Integrated Review p. 736
47. $\frac{1}{2}$ or 0.5 **49.** $-\frac{2}{\sqrt{3}}$ or ≈ -1.155 **51.** Portland, $\approx 44°$, San Antonio $\approx 29°$

■ 14.2 Communicating About Algebra p. 739

A.

B.

C. same as in **B**

D.

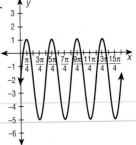

A–D.

	a indicates amplitude is	indicates period is	c indicates	d indicates
A.	3	2π	no horizontal shift	no vertical shift
B.	3	π	no horizontal shift	no vertical shift
C.	3	π	a shift of π units to the right	no vertical shift
D.	3	π	a shift of π units to the right	a shift of 2 units down

■ 14.2 Guided Practice p. 740
1. Vertical shift **2.** Reflection **3.** Horizontal shift
4. Horizontal shift

5.

6.

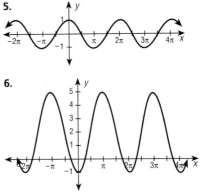

■ 14.2 Independent Practice p. 740–742
7. 1 unit up **9.** 3 units down **11.** $\frac{\pi}{2}$ units left **13.** π units right **15.** $\frac{\pi}{4}$ units right, 4 units up **17.** π units right, 1 unit down **19.** e **21.** f **23.** c **25.** $y = 2 + 2 \sin 3x$

27.

29.

31.

33.

35.

37.

39.

41.

43.

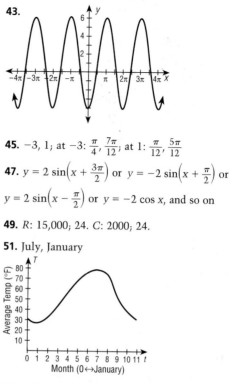

45. -3, 1; at -3: $\dfrac{\pi}{4}$, $\dfrac{7\pi}{12}$; at 1: $\dfrac{\pi}{12}$, $\dfrac{5\pi}{12}$

47. $y = 2 \sin\left(x + \dfrac{3\pi}{2}\right)$ or $y = -2 \sin\left(x + \dfrac{\pi}{2}\right)$ or

$y = 2 \sin\left(x - \dfrac{\pi}{2}\right)$ or $y = -2 \cos x$, and so on

49. R: 15,000; 24. C: 2000; 24.

51. July, January

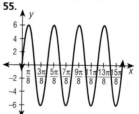

53. Spring equinox: Day 79, March
Summer solstice: Day 172, June, most sunlight,
Fall equinox: Day 265, September
Winter solstice: Day 355, December, least sunlight.

■ *14.2 Integrated Review p. 742*

55.

57.

59.

61. c

1. $\pm 2\sqrt{\dfrac{14}{3}}$ **3.** $\dfrac{22}{7}$ **5.** $9x^3y$ **7.** $\log_4 x^2y^4$

9. **11.**

13. $\sec\theta$ **15.** $x(4x^4 + 3x + 1)$ **17.** $y = \dfrac{x^3}{3 + 2x}$ **19.** $\dfrac{\sqrt{231}}{4}$

■ **14.3 Communicating About Algebra p. 746**

A. $\dfrac{\sec^2 x}{\tan x} = \dfrac{1}{\cos^2 x}\cdot\dfrac{\cos x}{\sin x} = \dfrac{1}{\cos x\sin x} = \sec x\csc x$, **A** is correct

B. $\cot x + \tan x = \dfrac{\cos x}{\sin x} + \dfrac{\sin x}{\cos x} = \dfrac{\cos^2 x + \sin^2 x}{\sin x\cos x} =$

$\dfrac{1}{\sin x\cos x} = \csc x\sec x$, **B** is correct

C. $\dfrac{1}{\sin x\cos x} = \csc x\sec x$, **C** is correct

■ **14.3 Guided Practice p. 747**

1. See page 744. **2.** Odd: sine, tangent, cosecant, cotangent; even: cosine, secant **3.** $\cos x$, cofunction, and cotangent **4.** $1 - \cos^2 x$, $\dfrac{1}{\cos^2 x}$

■ **14.3 Independent Practice p. 747–748**

5. $\cos^2 x$ **7.** 1 **9.** $\cot^2 x$ **11.** $\sec^2 x - \cos^2 x$ **13.** 1

15. $1 - 2\sin^2 x$ or $2\cos^2 x - 1$ **17.** $\csc^2 x\cot^2 x$ or $\dfrac{\cos^2 x}{\sin^4 x}$

19. -1 **21.** $\cot x$

23. $\cos^2 x - \sin^2 x \overset{?}{=} 1 - 2\sin^2 x$
$(1 - \sin^2 x) - \sin^2 x \overset{?}{=} 1 - 2\sin^2 x$
$1 - 2\sin^2 x = 1 - 2\sin^2 x$

25. $\cot^2 x(\sec^2 x - 1) = \cot^2 x(\tan^2 x)$
$\qquad = \dfrac{1}{\tan^2 x}(\tan^2 x)$
$\qquad = 1$

27. $\sin x\csc x = \sin x\dfrac{1}{\sin x}$
$\qquad\quad = 1$

29. $\tan^2 x + 4 = (\sec^2 x - 1) + 4$
$\qquad\qquad = \sec^2 x + 3$

31. $\sin^2 x - \sin^4 x = \sin^2 x(1 - \sin^2 x)$
$\qquad\qquad = (1 - \cos^2 x)\cos^2 x$
$\qquad\qquad = \cos^2 x - \cos^4 x$

33. $\dfrac{1 + \sin x}{\cos x} + \dfrac{\cos x}{1 + \sin x} = \dfrac{(1 + \sin x)^2 + \cos^2 x}{\cos x(1 + \sin x)}$

$\qquad\qquad = \dfrac{1 + 2\sin x + \sin^2 x + \cos^2 x}{\cos x(1 + \sin x)}$

$\qquad\qquad = \dfrac{2 + 2\sin x}{\cos x(1 + \sin x)}$

$\qquad\qquad = \dfrac{2(1 + \sin x)}{\cos x(1 + \sin x)}$

$\qquad\qquad = 2\sec x$

35. $\dfrac{\cos(-x)}{1 + \sin(-x)} = \dfrac{\cos x}{1 - \sin x}$

$\qquad = \dfrac{\cos x}{1 - \sin x}\cdot\dfrac{1 + \sin x}{1 + \sin x}$

$\qquad = \dfrac{\cos x(1 + \sin x)}{1 - \sin^2 x}$

$\qquad = \dfrac{\cos x + \sin x\cos x}{\cos^2 x}$

$\qquad = \dfrac{\cos x}{\cos^2 x} + \dfrac{\sin x\cos x}{\cos^2 x}$

$\qquad = \dfrac{1}{\cos x} + \dfrac{\sin x}{\cos x}$

$\qquad = \sec x + \tan x$

37. $\cos\left(\dfrac{\pi}{2} - x\right)\csc x = \sin x\csc x$

$\qquad\qquad\qquad = \sin x\dfrac{1}{\sin x}$

$\qquad\qquad\qquad = 1$

39. $x = \dfrac{3\pi}{2}$, $\sin x = -1 \neq \sqrt{1 - \cos^2 x}$

41. Circle, $x^2 + y^2 = 16\cos^2 t + 16\sin^2 t$
$\qquad\qquad\qquad = 16(\cos^2 t + \sin^2 t)$
$\qquad\qquad\qquad = 16$

43. Ellipse, $\dfrac{x^2}{4} + \dfrac{y^2}{9} = \cos^2 t + \sin^2 t = 1$

45. Because $\dfrac{\pi}{2} + \theta_1 + \theta_2$,

$\qquad \sec\theta_1 = \sec\left(\theta_1 - \dfrac{\pi}{2}\right)$

$\qquad\qquad = \sec\left(\dfrac{\pi}{2} - \theta_2\right)$

$\qquad\qquad = \csc\theta_2$

■ **14.3 Integrated Review p. 749**

47. $\dfrac{3}{5}$ **49.** $\sqrt{101}$ **51.** 2 **53.** 3 **55.** $\approx 47.5°$

■ **14.3 Mid-Chapter Self-Test p. 752**

1. $\dfrac{5}{2}$, π **2.** 4, 2 **3.** 3, $\dfrac{\pi}{2}$

4.

5. **6.**

7. $y = 6 \sin 4\pi x$ **8.** $y = \frac{4}{3} \sin \frac{2}{3} x$ **9.** $y = \frac{2}{5} \cos 2x$
10. $\tan x$ **11.** $\csc x$ **12.** 1 **13.** $-\cos x \cot x$ **14.** 1
15. $\sec x$ **16.** $y = -3 + 3 \sin 4x$ **17.** $y = \frac{1}{4} \cos\left(2x + \frac{\pi}{2}\right)$
18.

Month (0↔January 1)

19. July, January **20.** c., $P = 100 + 20 \cos(2\pi t)$

■ **14.4 Communicating About Algebra p. 756**

$6hs + \dfrac{3}{\sqrt{2}}s^2 = 3\left(\dfrac{\sqrt{3}}{2}s^2 \csc \theta\right) + 6\left(hs - \dfrac{1}{4}s^2 \cot \theta\right)$

$6hs + \dfrac{3}{\sqrt{2}}s^2 = 3\left(\dfrac{\sqrt{3}}{2}s^2 \csc \theta\right) + 6hs - \dfrac{3}{2}s^2 \cot \theta$

$\dfrac{3}{\sqrt{2}}s^2 = \dfrac{3\sqrt{3}}{2}s^2 \csc \theta - \dfrac{3}{2}s^2 \cot \theta$

$\dfrac{2}{\sqrt{2}} = \sqrt{3} \csc \theta - \cot \theta$

$\sqrt{2} = \sqrt{3} \cdot \dfrac{1}{\sin \theta} - \dfrac{\cos \theta}{\sin \theta}$

$\sqrt{2} \sin \theta = \sqrt{3} - \cos \theta$

■ **14.4 Guided Practice p. 757**
1. It is true for all real values of the variables.

2. $y = 2 \cos x - 1$, $\frac{\pi}{3}$ and $\frac{5\pi}{3}$

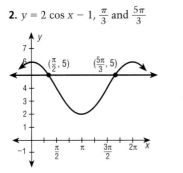

3. $x = \frac{\pi}{3} + 2n\pi$ or $x = \frac{5\pi}{3} + 2n\pi$ **4.** sin, csc, sec, and cos: 2π; tan and cot: π **5.** $x = 0$; get all terms on one side, factor, set each factor equal to zero, and solve for x with $0 \le x < \pi$. **6.** $\csc^2 x = 2 \csc x - 1$; get all terms on one side, factor, take the square root, and solve for x.

■ **14.4 Independent Practice pp. 757–759**
7. $\cot x = 1$ **9.** $\cos 2x = \frac{\sqrt{3}}{2}$, $2x = \frac{\pi}{6}$ **11.** $\sin x = 0$,
$\pm\frac{1}{\sqrt{2}}$, $\sin \frac{5\pi}{4} = -\frac{1}{\sqrt{2}}$ **13.** $\frac{\pi}{4}, \frac{7\pi}{4}$ **15.** $\frac{\pi}{6}, \frac{5\pi}{6}$
17. $\frac{7\pi}{6}, \frac{11\pi}{6}$ **19.** $\frac{\pi}{4}, \frac{3\pi}{4}, \frac{5\pi}{4}, \frac{7\pi}{4}$ **21.** $\frac{\pi}{6}, \frac{5\pi}{6}, \frac{7\pi}{6}, \frac{11\pi}{6}$
23. $\frac{\pi}{3}, \frac{5\pi}{3}$ **25.** $\frac{\pi}{3}, \frac{2\pi}{3}, \frac{4\pi}{3}, \frac{5\pi}{3}$ **27.** $0, \frac{\pi}{2}, \pi, \frac{3\pi}{2}$

29. $0, \frac{\pi}{3}, \frac{2\pi}{3}, \pi$ **31.** $\frac{2\pi}{3}, \frac{5\pi}{6}, \frac{5\pi}{3}, \frac{11\pi}{6}$ **33.** $\frac{\pi}{6}, \frac{5\pi}{6}, \frac{3\pi}{2}$
35. $\approx 1.33, \approx 4.47$ **37.** $\approx 0.46, \approx 2.82, \approx 3.61, \approx 6.00$
39. $\approx 1.37, \approx 1.74, \approx 4.51, \approx 4.88$ **41.** $\approx 2.09, \approx 4.19$
43. $\left(\frac{\pi}{6}, \frac{\sqrt{3}}{3}\right), \left(\frac{7\pi}{6}, \frac{\sqrt{3}}{3}\right), \left(\frac{2\pi}{3}, 3\sqrt{3}\right), \left(\frac{5\pi}{3}, 3\sqrt{3}\right)$
45. $\left(\frac{\pi}{6}, \frac{8}{3}\right), \left(\frac{5\pi}{6}, \frac{8}{3}\right), \left(\frac{7\pi}{6}, \frac{8}{3}\right), \left(\frac{11\pi}{6}, \frac{8}{3}\right)$
47. $\left(\frac{\pi}{3}, \frac{3}{2}\right), \left(\frac{5\pi}{3}, \frac{3}{2}\right)$ **49.** $\frac{3\pi}{4}, \frac{7\pi}{4}$ **51.** $\theta \approx 35.26°$
53. $\approx 14.0°$ or ≈ 0.24

■ **14.4 Integrated Review p. 759**
55. 4π, 10 **57.** 2π, 4 **59.** $\frac{2\pi}{3}$, 3
61.

63.

65.

67. a

■ **14.5 Communicating About Algebra p. 762**
Water $\approx 94.3°$, Glass $\approx 76.5°$, Diamond $\approx 36.1°$

■ **14.5 Guided Practice p. 763**
1. $\tan 240° = \tan(180° + 60°) = \dfrac{\tan 180° + \tan 60°}{1 - \tan 180° \tan 60°}$

$= \dfrac{0 + \sqrt{3}}{1 - 0 \cdot \sqrt{3}} = \sqrt{3}$

2. The top sign on the left side corresponds to the top sign on the right side. **3.** $\dfrac{\sqrt{2} - \sqrt{6}}{4}$ **4.** $\dfrac{\pi}{2}$

■ **14.5 Independent Practice p. 763–764**
5. $\dfrac{\sqrt{2} - \sqrt{6}}{4}$ **7.** $\dfrac{1 + \sqrt{3}}{-1 + \sqrt{3}}$ **9.** $\dfrac{\sqrt{2} - \sqrt{6}}{4}$ **11.** $\dfrac{1 - \sqrt{3}}{1 + \sqrt{3}}$
13. $\dfrac{4}{\sqrt{6} - \sqrt{2}}$ **15.** $\dfrac{-1 + \sqrt{3}}{1 + \sqrt{3}}$ **17.** $\cos 50°$ **19.** $\sin 1.8$
21. $\dfrac{\sqrt{2} + \sqrt{6}}{4}$ **23.** $\dfrac{\sqrt{2} - \sqrt{6}}{4}$ **25.** $\dfrac{\sqrt{2} - \sqrt{6}}{4}$ **27.** $\dfrac{\pi}{2}$
29. $\frac{\pi}{4}, \frac{7\pi}{4}$ **31.** $0, \frac{\pi}{3}, \pi, \frac{5\pi}{3}$ **33.** $-\frac{63}{65}$ **35.** $\frac{56}{65}$ **37.** $\approx 36.9°$
39. $y = 2 \cos(440\pi t + a\pi t) \cos(440\pi t - a\pi t)$

41. $\sin \theta = \frac{1}{\sqrt{7}}$, $\cos \theta = \frac{\sqrt{6}}{\sqrt{7}}$, $\tan \theta = \frac{1}{\sqrt{6}}$, $\csc \theta = \sqrt{7}$,

$\sec \theta = \frac{\sqrt{7}}{\sqrt{6}}$ **43.** $\cos \theta = \frac{\sqrt{2}}{2}$, $\tan \theta = 1$, $\csc \theta = \frac{2}{\sqrt{2}}$,

$\sec \theta = \frac{2}{\sqrt{2}}$, $\cot \theta = 1$ **45.** $2 \sec x - \sec^3 x$

47. $\tan x(1 + \sec x)$ **49.** $\cot^2 x$

■ **14.5 Mixed Review** *p. 765*

1. $-\frac{3}{2}$ **3.** 21 **5.** $\frac{5\pi}{12}$ **7.** $a = 2$ **9.** 27 **11.** $\frac{5\pi}{12}$ **13.** $-\frac{5}{3}$

15.

17. $t < -6$ or $t > 14$
19. $-13x + 4y = 37$

■ **14.6 Communicating About Algebra** *p. 768*

$\sqrt{\frac{5 - \sqrt{5}}{8}}$

■ **14.6 Guided Practice** *p. 769*

1. $\tan x = \dfrac{2 \tan \frac{x}{2}}{1 - \tan^2 \frac{x}{2}}$ **2.** -0.939 **3.** ≈ -0.940;

agree to 0.01

4. $\dfrac{\sqrt{2} + \sqrt{6}}{4 + \sqrt{2} - \sqrt{6}}$ or $\dfrac{4 - \sqrt{2} + \sqrt{6}}{\sqrt{2} + \sqrt{6}}$ or $\sqrt{\dfrac{4 - \sqrt{2} + \sqrt{6}}{4 + \sqrt{2} - \sqrt{6}}}$

5. $\frac{\pi}{2}, \frac{3\pi}{2}$ **6.** b, the graph is the same as the graph of

$y = -\frac{1}{2} \cos 2x - \frac{1}{2}$

■ **14.6 Independent Practice** *p. 769–771*

7. $\frac{2 \tan x}{1 - \tan x}$ **9.** $\frac{2}{1 - \tan^2 x}$ **11.** $2 - \sec^2 x$ **13.** $\frac{\pi}{2}, \frac{3\pi}{2}$

15. $\frac{\pi}{4}, \frac{3\pi}{4}, \frac{5\pi}{4}, \frac{7\pi}{4}, \frac{\pi}{2}, \frac{3\pi}{2}$ **17.** $\frac{\pi}{6}, \frac{5\pi}{6}, \frac{7\pi}{6}, \frac{11\pi}{6}, \frac{\pi}{2}, \frac{3\pi}{2}$

19. $0, \pi$ **21.** $\frac{7\pi}{6}, \frac{11\pi}{6}, \frac{3\pi}{2}$ **23.** $\approx 1.026, \approx 5.256$ **25.** $2 -$

$\sqrt{3}$ **27.** $\frac{\sqrt{2 + \sqrt{2}}}{2}$ **29.** $\sqrt{2} + 1$ **31.** $\frac{\sqrt{2 + \sqrt{2 + \sqrt{3}}}}{2}$

33. $\frac{4 - \sqrt{6} - \sqrt{2}}{\sqrt{6} - \sqrt{2}}$ or $\frac{\sqrt{6} - \sqrt{2}}{4 + \sqrt{6} + \sqrt{2}}$

35. $\sqrt{\frac{\sqrt{5} - 1}{2\sqrt{5}}}$, $\sqrt{\frac{\sqrt{5} + 1}{2\sqrt{5}}}$, $\frac{\sqrt{5} - 1}{2}$ or $\frac{2}{\sqrt{5} + 1}$ or $\sqrt{\frac{\sqrt{5} - 1}{\sqrt{5} + 1}}$

37. $\frac{\sqrt{10 - \sqrt{19}}}{2\sqrt{5}}$, $-\frac{\sqrt{10 + \sqrt{19}}}{2\sqrt{5}}$, $\frac{10 - \sqrt{19}}{-9}$ or $\frac{-9}{10 + \sqrt{19}}$ or

$-\sqrt{\frac{10 - \sqrt{19}}{10 + \sqrt{19}}}$ **39.** $\sqrt{\frac{1}{5}}$, $\sqrt{\frac{4}{5}}$, $\frac{1}{2}$ **41.** a **43.** b

45. $162 \sin \theta$, $\approx 54.6°$ **47.** $x = 2r(1 - \cos \theta)$

49. $\frac{2\pi}{3}, \frac{4\pi}{3}$

■ **14.6 Chapter Review** *p. 773–776*

1. $4, 4\pi$ **3.** $1, 8$ **5.** $\frac{3}{2}, 1$ **7.** $2, \pi$ **9.** $\frac{1}{3}, \pi$ **11.** a **13.** c
15. g **17.** e
19.   **21.**

23. **25.**

27.
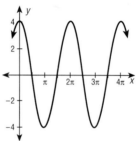

29. $-\sin x$ **31.** -1 **33.** $-\sec^2 x$

35. $\cot x + \tan x = \dfrac{\cos x}{\sin x} + \dfrac{\sin x}{\cos x}$

$= \dfrac{\cos^2 x + \sin^2 x}{\sin x \cos x}$

$= \dfrac{1}{\sin x \cos x} = \sec x \csc x$

37. $\tan^2(-x) \cos^2 x = \tan^2 x \cos^2 x$

$= \dfrac{\sin^2 x}{\cos^2 x} \cos^2 x$

$= \sin^2 x = 1 - \cos^2 x$

39. $\frac{\pi}{2}, \frac{3\pi}{2}, \frac{\pi}{6}, \frac{5\pi}{6}, \frac{7\pi}{6}, \frac{11\pi}{6}$ **41.** $\frac{\pi}{4}, \frac{3\pi}{4}, \frac{5\pi}{4}, \frac{7\pi}{4}$ **43.** $\frac{\pi}{2}$

45. $0, \pi, \frac{3\pi}{4}, \frac{7\pi}{4}$ **47.** $0, \pi, \frac{\pi}{2}, \frac{3\pi}{2}, \frac{\pi}{4}, \frac{3\pi}{4}, \frac{5\pi}{4}, \frac{7\pi}{4}$

49. $\frac{-\sqrt{6} - \sqrt{2}}{4}$ **51.** $\frac{1 + \sqrt{3}}{1 - \sqrt{3}}$ **53.** 0 **55.** $\sqrt{3}$ **57.** Physical:

high, Emotional: neutral, Intellectual: low
59. 2.358328177, within 0.8

61. $\sin\left(\frac{\pi}{2} - \theta_1\right) = \sin\theta_2 = \frac{b}{c} = \cos\theta_1$

$\cos\left(\frac{\pi}{2} - \theta_1\right) = \cos\theta_2 = \frac{a}{c} = \sin\theta_1$

$\tan\left(\frac{\pi}{2} - \theta_1\right) = \tan\theta_2 = \frac{b}{a} = \cot\theta_1$

$\cot\left(\frac{\pi}{2} - \theta_1\right) = \cot\theta_2 = \frac{a}{b} = \tan\theta_1$

$\sec\left(\frac{\pi}{2} - \theta_1\right) = \sec\theta_2 = \frac{c}{a} = \csc\theta_1$

$\csc\left(\frac{\pi}{2} - \theta_1\right) = \csc\theta_2 = \frac{c}{b} = \sec\theta_1$

63. $60°$ **65.** D, E, P, Q; $\frac{1}{4}$, π **67.** V, 1, 2π **69.** I, 2, 2π
71. A, 1, 2π **73.** M, 2, 2π **75.** a **77.** $y = 14 + 2\sin x - \cos 2x$; $\frac{\pi}{2}, \frac{5\pi}{2}, \frac{9\pi}{2}, \frac{13\pi}{2}$

■ **Cumulative Review for Chapters 13–14 pp. 778–779**
1. $65°$, $155°$ **3.** $\frac{5\pi}{12}, \frac{11\pi}{12}$ **5.** $555°$, $-165°$ **7.** $\frac{10\pi}{3}, -\frac{2\pi}{3}$
9. $-\sqrt{2}$ **11.** $30°$, $\frac{\pi}{6}$ **13.** $\angle C = 113°$, $a \approx 3.18$, $b \approx 1.49$
15. $\angle A \approx 36.18°$, $\angle B \approx 100.28°$, $\angle C \approx 43.54°$ **17.** $\frac{9\sqrt{3}}{4}$
19.

21.

23.

25. $\cos^2 x$ **27.** $\sec^2 2x$ **29.** $\sin 2x\cos 2x$

31. $\dfrac{\sin\left(\frac{\pi}{2} - x\right)}{\sin x} = \dfrac{\cos x}{\sin x} = \cot x$

33. $\csc 2x - \cot 2x = \dfrac{1}{\sin 2x} - \dfrac{\cos 2x}{\sin 2x}$

$= \dfrac{1 - \cos^2 x + \sin^2 x}{\sin 2x}$

$= \dfrac{\sin^2 x + \sin^2 x}{\sin 2x} = \dfrac{2\sin^2 x}{2\sin x\cos x} = \dfrac{\sin x}{\cos x}$

$= \tan x$

35. $\frac{4\pi}{3}, \frac{5\pi}{3}$ **37.** $\frac{\pi}{3}, \frac{2\pi}{3}, \frac{4\pi}{3}, \frac{5\pi}{3}$ **39.** $\frac{\sqrt{6} - \sqrt{2}}{4}$ **41.** $\frac{\sqrt{3}}{2}$
43. $\approx 71.57°$, $\approx 71.57°$, $\approx 36.86°$ **45.** $229.2°$ **47.** ≈ 32 ft

CHAPTER 15

■ **15.1 Communicating About Algebra p. 784**
A. $\frac{1}{5}$ **B.** ≈ 0.35

C. $\frac{1}{4}$

	Bc	bc	Bc	bc
bC	BbCc	bbCc	BbCc	bbCc
bc	Bbcc	bbcc	Bbcc	bbcc
bC	BbCc	bbCc	BbCc	bbCc
bc	Bbcc	bbcc	Bbcc	bbcc

■ **15.1 Guided Practice p. 785**
1. The probability of an event always occurring is 1 or 100%. **2.** No **3.** 7, any one of the 7 marbles may be drawn at random **4.** $\frac{1}{3}$

5. $\frac{3}{4}$

	BC	Bc	BC	Bc
bC	BbCC	BbCc	BbCC	BbCc
bc	BbCc	Bbcc	BbCc	Bbcc
bC	BbCC	BbCc	BbCC	BbCc
bc	BbCc	Bbcc	BbCc	Bbcc

■ **15.1 Independent Practice pp. 785–787**
7. $\frac{7}{20}$ **9.** $\frac{9}{20}$ **11.** $\frac{\pi}{48}$ **13.** $\frac{7\pi}{144}$ **15.** $1 - \frac{25\pi}{144}$ **17.** $\frac{4722}{5711}$

19. Each probability is $\frac{1}{2}$ **21.** $\frac{7}{8}, \frac{1}{4}$ **23.** $\frac{1}{10}$; $\frac{9}{10} + \frac{1}{10} = 1$
25. $128 - 32\pi$ **27.** 20 yd^2 **29.** d

■ **15.2 Communicating About Algebra p. 791**
A. $\frac{1}{6}$ **B.** Depends on experiment.

■ **15.2 Guided Practice p. 792**
1. The number of ways 2 or more events can occur
2. There are 10 choices for the first digit, 10 choices for the second digit, and 10 choices for the third digit. So, $10 \cdot 10 \cdot 10 = 1000$.

3. Consider each toss an event that has 2 possible choices, heads or tails; then the number of ways the coin can land is $2 \cdot 2 \cdot 2 \cdot 2 \cdot 2 \cdot 2 = 2^6$. No.
4. 24, 5, STAR, ARTS, RATS, TARS, and TSAR; $\frac{5}{24}$
5. 720 **6.** 125

■ 15.2 Independent Practice pp. 792–794
7. 24, 256 **9.** 720; 46,656 **11.** 18 **13.** 120 **15.** 72
17. 1600 **19.** 6 **21.** 0 **23.** $\frac{1}{773}$ **25.** 28^6 or 481,890,304

■ 15.2 Integrated Review p. 794
27. 6 **29.** 5040 **31.** 40,320 **33.** 1

■ 15.2 Mixed Review p. 795
1. $a = \pm\sqrt{\frac{bc - c}{3b}}$ **3.** $\frac{3\pi}{8}$ **5.** $t \le -6$ or $t \ge 14$
7. $\left(x - \frac{1}{2}\right)^2 + \frac{35}{4}$ **9.** $y = \pm\frac{\sqrt{4x + 1}}{4}$ **11.** -125 **13.** circle
15. $\frac{x^2}{2b^3y^2}$ **17.** 4 **19.** $x = \frac{3}{4}$

■ 15.3 Communicating About Algebra p. 798
A. $\binom{6}{3} = \frac{6!}{(6 - 3)!3!} = 20$ **B.** $\frac{35}{128}$

■ 15.3 Guided Practice p. 799
1. 35 **2.** 21 **3.** 20 **4.** $\frac{1}{1140}$

■ 15.3 Independent Practice pp. 799–801
5. 56 **7.** 302,400 **9.** 21 **11.** $\frac{99}{2303}$ **13.** $\frac{1}{40}, \frac{7}{30}$
15. $\frac{11,713}{80,850}$ **17.** ≈ 0.346 **19.** 0.6604

■ 15.3 Integrated Review p. 801
21. 28 **23.** 27,405 **25.** 28,989,675 **27.** Combinations

■ 15.3 Mid-Chapter Self-Test p. 804
1. $\frac{1}{7}, \frac{2}{7}$ **2.** 0.04, 0.28 **3.** $\frac{1}{4}$ **4.** 120 **5.** 120 **6.** 6
7. 5040 **8.** ≈ 0.12 **9.** $\approx 0.076, \approx 0.00069$ **10.** 30
11. 220 **12.** ≈ 0.413

■ 15.4 Communicating About Algebra p. 807
A. $\frac{116}{165}$ **B.** $\frac{212}{275}$ **C.** $\frac{157}{275}$

■ 15.4 Guided Practice p. 808
1. $A \cup B$ is the event of choosing an integer that is either even or a multiple of three. $\frac{2}{3}$ **2.** $A \cap B$ is the event of choosing an integer that is even and a multiple of three. $\frac{1}{6}$ **3.** Answers vary. **4.** A' is not completing your homework, 0.05 **5.** 0.3, 0 **6.** 0.15

■ 15.4 Independent Practice pp. 808–810
7. 0.20, not mutually exclusive **9.** 0.65, mutually exclusive **11.** 1, not mutually exclusive **13.** 0.36
15. $\frac{7}{12}$ **17.** $\frac{11}{12}, \frac{1}{12}$ **19.** 0.15 **21.** 16 pecan pies
23. $\frac{56}{800}$ or 0.07 **25.** $\frac{55}{74}$

■ 15.4 Integrated Review p. 810
27. $\frac{545}{1728}$ **29.** $\frac{47}{864}, \frac{209}{216}$

■ 15.5 Communicating About Algebra p. 813
A. $\frac{1}{32}$ **B.** $\frac{31}{32}$ **C.** ≈ 0.778

■ 15.5 Guided Practice p. 814
1. Independent **2.** Dependent **3.** Dependent
4. Independent **5.** 0.232 **6.** $\frac{5}{12}$

■ 15.5 Independent Practice pp. 814–816
7. $\frac{7}{12}$ **9.** 0.02 **11.** $\frac{1}{64}$ **13.** $\frac{64}{625}$ **15.** $\frac{1}{1440}, \frac{119}{160}$
17. ≈ 0.456 **19.** Answers will vary. **21.** ≈ 0.509

■ 15.5 Integrated Review p. 816
23. ≈ 0.299

■ 15.5 Mixed Review p. 816
1. Yes
3.

5. $s \ge 5$ **7.** $60°$ or $\frac{\pi}{3}$ **9.** $\frac{3 \pm i\sqrt{87}}{12}$ **11.** ± 30 **13.** $\tan x$
15. $3x^3 + 2x^2 + x + 2$ **17.** $2(x + 1)^2$

■ 15.6 Communicating About Algebra p. 819
A. $\frac{1}{4}$ **B.** $-\frac{1}{4}$ **C.** 4

■ 15.6 Guided Practice p. 820
1. 3 **2.** 15 **3.** Zero, neither person has an advantage.
4. -3

■ 15.6 Independent Practice pp. 820–822
5. $0.74 **7.** A: $\frac{4}{9}$, B: $-\frac{4}{9}$, No **9.** A: 0, B: 0, Yes **11.** 0, the game is fair. **13.** $-\$6$ **15.** $46,182.31

■ 15.6 Integrated Review p. 822
17. $\frac{1}{3}$ **19.** c

■ 15.6 Chapter Review pp. 824–827
1. $\frac{2}{45}$ **3.** $\frac{1}{3}$ **5.** $\frac{3}{14}$ **7.** 24 **9.** 1024 **11.** $\frac{1}{16}$ **13.** 126
15. $\frac{19}{60}$ **17.** 0.96 **19.** ≈ 0.022 **21.** 12 **23.** 0.127
25. 0.290 **27.** $-\$1.54$ **29.** e **31.** sable: $\frac{1}{8}$, tricolor: $\frac{1}{8}$, trifactored sable: $\frac{1}{4}$, bluemerle: $\frac{1}{8}$, sable merle: $\frac{1}{8}$, trifactored sable merle: $\frac{1}{4}$ **33.** $-\$25$

A

Abscissa, 64
Absolute value
  equations, 44, 47, 49, 58, 101–107,
    581
  evaluating expressions, 106
  function, 44, 101
  graph of, 101–107
  inequalities, 44–49, 58, 103
  model, 105
  problem solving, 103, 105–106
  vertex, 101–102, 104
Addition
  identity element, 4
  polynomials, 456, 459–460
  properties, 4
  radicals, 369, 371
  real numbers, 4, 6–8
  solving equations, 19–23
  solving inequalities, 37–43
  transforming equations, 18
Additive inverse, 4, 6
Algebraic definition, 4
Algebraic expression, 9–15, 20, 30
Angle(s)
  acute, 678, 680, 682, 685, 689
  complementary, 686, 689, 723
  degree measure, 685, 687, 689–690,
    694–701, 704, 706, 723
  depression, 707
  elevation, 681, 696
  incidence, 707
  inclination, 684
  obtuse, 685
  refraction, 707
  rotation, 600, 685–686, 688–689
  radian measure, 686–691, 694–695,
    697–701, 704–706, 723
  reference, 694–695, 697, 723
  supplementary, 686, 689, 723
  trigonometric functions, 678–726
Annuities, 658–665, 668, 670
Applications, *See also* Problem solving
  accounting, 20, 22, 28, 807, 824
  advertising, 127, 155, 214, 337, 451
  aerospace, 351, 393, 720
  agriculture, 22, 83, 112, 135, 163,
    185, 451, 459, 580
  animal/insect studies, 8, 23, 35, 42,
    46, 48, 53, 167, 193, 323, 332,
    382, 386, 388–389, 410, 425, 445,
    451, 504, 507, 511, 741, 749, 786,
    809, 827
  archaeology, 238, 497
  architecture, 106, 241, 249, 462,
    476, 479
  arts, 147, 220, 272, 356, 520, 603,
    617, 688, 691, 721, 725, 794, 810
  astronomy, 234, 350, 370, 505, 585,
    588, 618, 628, 649, 720, 725
  banking, 326, 422, 424, 437, 439,
    450, 553, 560, 800

biology, 36, 46, 167, 366, 668, 741,
  756, 784, 786, 827
business, 26, 51, 83, 98, 124, 126,
  142, 153, 155, 179, 184, 195, 214,
  221, 234, 256, 290, 294–295, 307,
  310, 351, 358, 365, 403–404, 430,
  433, 447, 451, 468, 471, 483,
  485–486, 490, 506, 523, 632,
  634–635, 640, 807, 812, 824
chemistry, 14, 23, 40, 166, 212, 214,
  411, 417, 424, 439, 451, 525, 530,
  791
communications, 247, 267, 270,
  310, 337, 580, 789, 799–800
construction, 25, 256, 707, 821–
  822
consumer, 8, 75, 82, 142, 148, 166,
  184, 293, 307, 310, 317, 505, 546
cryptography, 198–199, 201
earth science, 713, 751
economics, 166, 176, 195, 290, 295,
  353
education, 13, 73, 176, 179, 296,
  327, 330, 358, 394, 446, 793, 810,
  825
electronics, 418, 526, 529
engineering, 393, 497, 531, 600,
  690, 707
entertainment, 42, 98, 105, 141–
  142, 155, 218, 225, 290, 319, 330,
  379, 445, 522, 538, 574, 627, 656,
  698
environmental science, 5, 28, 54,
  133, 190, 355, 447, 525, 528, 566,
  572, 751
finance, 22, 82, 91, 108, 126, 135,
  139, 141–142, 174, 273, 287,
  293–294, 303–304, 326, 352–353,
  356, 401, 437, 439, 450, 468, 546,
  555–560, 564, 642, 658–665,
  668–669, 800, 807, 818, 824
forensic science, 428
fractals, 261, 263
game theory, 797, 802–803, 814,
  816–818, 820–821
geography, 42, 66, 68, 75, 98, 192,
  240, 281, 336, 506, 699, 714, 736,
  742
geology/mining, 68, 276, 415
geometry, 14, 26, 31, 33–35, 42, 69,
  99, 126–127, 147, 179, 189–190,
  192–193, 233, 240, 243, 249, 261,
  269, 285, 289, 295, 301, 303–304,
  325, 336, 350–351, 362, 364–365,
  372, 377, 379, 385, 458, 462,
  468–469, 476, 478, 485, 497, 512,
  529–530, 538–539, 564, 574, 587,
  602–603, 612, 627, 642, 648, 691,
  699, 715, 748, 758, 764, 770–771,
  775, 783, 785, 794, 800, 824
government, 52, 89, 221, 269, 385,
  424, 439, 492, 505, 798, 806, 825
history, 75, 117, 505, 512

home economics, 98, 372
insurance, 818, 821
law enforcement, 76
library science, 394
mechanics, 705, 726
medical, 49, 68, 214, 279, 311, 357,
  379, 442, 446, 522, 552, 801
meteorology, 7, 42, 88, 103, 303,
  336, 383, 386, 410, 478, 543, 595,
  739, 741, 806, 826
military, 492, 523
music, 53, 150, 162, 373, 525, 546,
  554, 714, 733, 764
nautical science, 363
navigation, 609, 718
nutrition/fitness, 65, 91, 112, 184,
  499
oceanography, 24, 48, 393, 408, 439
optics, 735, 762, 765
photography, 220, 417, 547
physics, 36, 91, 143, 231, 234, 254,
  269, 337, 373, 393, 417–418, 424,
  430, 478, 520, 528–531, 536,
  564–565, 574–575, 578, 580, 593,
  612, 647, 649, 669, 707, 721, 733,
  748, 768
physiology, 48, 98, 109, 388, 536,
  742, 774
population, 13, 140, 166, 202, 269,
  281, 319, 328–329, 331, 338, 431,
  439, 461, 501, 505, 523, 550, 643,
  741, 783, 787, 797, 825
publishing, 9, 11, 91, 149, 327, 461
recreation, 27, 160, 357
retailing, 8, 75, 80, 82, 91, 138, 142,
  148, 166, 184, 268–269, 293, 461,
  490, 499–500, 510, 625, 774, 819,
  822
sociology, 50, 466
sports, 7, 27–28, 32, 48, 52–54, 96,
  105, 112, 142, 150, 166, 178, 182,
  208, 218, 221, 225, 234, 240, 249,
  256, 303, 332, 365, 404, 425, 478,
  500, 503, 539, 544, 587, 596, 602,
  627, 656, 696, 698, 708, 717, 720,
  792, 799–800, 809, 826
technology, 85, 205–206, 243, 246,
  266, 313, 361, 432, 470–471, 490,
  492, 524, 539, 746, 748, 759, 811,
  815, 824
testing, 123, 417, 504, 511, 791
time management, 329
topography, 3, 7, 681, 683–684, 711
transportation, 127, 135, 527, 565,
  609, 720
travel, 162, 225, 232, 235, 357, 379,
  815
Approximation(s)
  best-fitting line, 107–112, 129
  calculator, 129, 361, 471
  distance, 717, 726
  irrational square root, 2
  solutions, 2, 9, 32, 54, 65–66, 68–

69, 75, 91, 108–109, 112, 117, 122–126, 129, 140, 168, 192, 231–235, 238, 240–243, 246, 249, 252, 256, 337, 348, 350, 361–366, 379, 421–422, 424, 428, 432–433, 439, 469, 471, 483, 499, 507, 544, 552, 588, 632, 656–657, 680, 683, 704, 736, 757, 775, 809, 819

Area
  circle, 34, 295
  circular ring, 34–35
  ellipse, 31, 34, 256
  Hero's, 717
  octagon, 26
  parabolic region, 238
  parallelogram, 34
  rectangle, 34, 248, 256, 478
  surface, 34–35, 370
  triangle, 34, 189–190, 192, 248, 710, 717
  trapezoid, 34–35
Arithmetic sequence, 629–630, 633–635, 643, 667
Asymptote(s), 421, 426–427, 441, 444, 519–521, 523, 562
Average, 75–76, 112–113, 116, 124, 220, 308, 332, 350, 358, 417, 466, 520, 522, 538, 543, 546, 565, 640, 739, 741, 749, 818
Automatic grapher, See Calculator
Axioms, 4, 259
Axis(es)
  coordinate, 64–69, 74
  imaginary, 260
  real, 260
  symmetry, 236–237, 239, 570, 573

B

Bar graph, See Graphs
Base of a power, 404, 406, 420–425, 447
Best-fitting line, 107–112, 129
Binomial(s)
  cube of, 458, 461
  difference, two cubes, 474, 477–479
  difference, two squares, 473, 475, 477–479
  dividing by, 480–486
  expansion coefficients, 651–656, 668
  FOIL algorithm, 457, 460
  multiplying, 458–461, 651–657, 668–670
  Pascal's triangle, 652–653, 655–657, 669–670, 799, 825–826
  product of sum/difference, 458–461
  squares of, 458–461
  theorem, 651, 653, 655, 667
Biographical/historical note
  Abel and Galois, 532
  algebraic symbols, 77
  Anasazi Indians, 238
  ancient libraries, 394
  area codes, 789
  Aztec cosmos, 452
  Briggs, Henry, 412
  Burgi, Jobst, 412

Canady, Alexa, 379
Cayley, Arthur, 186
Corinth Canal, 683
Cramer, Gabriel, 216
Curie, Marie and Pierre, 424
David, Jacques-Louis, 142
Escher, M. C., 520
Euler, Leonhard, 420
Fibonacci numbers, 323
food sources, 459
Garcia, Donald, 254
Gauss, Carl Friederich, 495
Germain, Sophie, 714
Gregory, James, 775
Godel, Kurt, 636
golden ratio, 377, 668
hailstorms, 88
Hero, 717
home computers, 490
Homestead Act, 66
Indian etching, 411
influenza epidemic, 442
Jamestown, Virginia, 439
Japanese magic circle, 635
Kowa, Seki, 635
Laplace, Pierre-Simon, 412
Lechuguilla Cave, 711
Leonardo of Pisa, 323
Machin, John, 775
Mandelbrot, Benoit, 261
Napier, John, 412
Olympias, 363
Pascal, Blaise, 652
Penrose, Roger, 377
pi, 775
port of Caesarea, 497
railroad construction, 25
Ramanujan, Srinivasa, 775
Reiter, Ashley, 261
Stone of the Fifth Sun, 453
unsolved problems, 743
Viking I, 234
Young, Thomas, 372
women elected, 89
Boundary line, half-plane, 94, 145–150, 272, 276
Box-and-whisker plot, 328, 330–332, 504

C

Calculator
  approximations, 361, 365, 471, 680, 683, 704, 757
  best-fitting line, 129
  drawing angles, 700–701
  evaluate expressions, 361–365, 371, 423, 429, 441, 449, 706–708, 724
  exponential equations, 434–437
  exponential regression, 432–433
  graphing, 16–17, 84–85, 128–129, 164, 194–195, 205–206, 242–243, 246, 266, 268, 312, 388–389, 420, 432–433, 440, 447, 470–471, 497, 500, 507, 524, 539, 541–542, 604–605, 664–665, 746, 748, 750–751, 755–759, 766, 771, 802–803

irrational exponents, 400, 403
matrix operations, 194–195, 201, 205–206, 207
minimum, 84
quadratic equations, 266
random number generator, 802–803, 815
solving equations, 231–232, 242–243, 246, 266, 268, 697–698, 706
trigonometric identities, 748, 750–751, 755–759, 766–767, 770–771
Calculator keys
  base e key, 420
  change sign key, 16
  data key, 389
  enter key, 16
  execute key 84
  exponent key, 16
  fraction key, 84
  function key, 701
  graph key, 84
  inverse key, 205
  IPart key, 802
  ln key, 426
  log key, 406
  matrix key, 194
  maximum key, 84
  mode key, 194
  natural base key, 420
  negative key, 16
  parametric mode key, 701, 748
  powers key, 16, 361
  pre key, 194
  quit key, 194
  rand key, 802
  range key, 84, 539
  scale key, 84
  shift key, 84
  square root key, 361
  square setting, 312–313
  stat key, 389
  zoom feature, 242
Career interviews
  air traffic controller, 137
  architect, 15
  contractor, 359
  dermatologist, 692
  epidemiologist, 244
  illustrator, 795
  nursing home director, 472
  sales coordinator, 582
Central tendency, measures of, 113, 327–332
Chapter Review, See Reviews
Chapter Summary, 56, 114, 165, 222, 277, 333, 390, 448, 508, 561, 614, 666, 722, 772, 823
Chapter Test, See Tests
Circle
  area, 34, 295
  circumference, 35, 699, 705
  distance formula, 376–379, 576, 578
  equation of, 576–581, 597–598, 601–605
  graph, 51, 53, 295, 440, 787, 825
  graphing, 577, 579–580
  problem solving, 578, 580
  standard form, 576, 579

Closed half-plane, 94, 145–150, 272, 276
Coefficient(s)
    expansion, 651–656, 668
    leading, 230, 236, 245–246, 456, 465, 488
    matrix, 204, 206–207, 216, 219
College Entrance Exam, *See* Tests
Collinearity test, 193
Combinations, 796–801, 824–827
Common denominator, 541, 545, 548, 551
Common monomial factoring, 473–475, 477–479
Completing the square, 245, 248–250
Complex fractions, 548, 551–552, 564
Complex numbers
    adding/subtracting, 259, 262
    conjugates, 496
    equations, 262, 265–270
    expressions, 260, 262–263
    fractals, 260–261, 263
    imaginary numbers, 258–259, 262, 264
    properties, 259
    Mandelbrot set, 261
    multiplying, 260, 263
    parallelogram rule, 261
    plane, 260
    plotting, 260–261, 263
    standard form, 259
Compound interest, 35, 352–353, 355–356, 422, 424, 437, 555–560, 564, 658–665, 668, 670
Computer(s)
    analyzing data, 507
    exponential equations, 447
    graphing equations, 84–85, 128–129
    home computers, 490
    linear equations, 84–85
    logarithmic equations, 447
    quadratic equations, 266
    system of equations, 128–129
Conics
    asymptotes, 591–592, 594–595
    classifying, 606–613, 616–618
    equations, 570–618
    graphing, 571, 573–574, 577, 580–581, 584–588, 592–596, 598–599, 601, 603–605, 607–613, 615–617
    model, 572, 617
    problem solving, 572, 574–575, 577–578, 580–581, 584–585, 587–588, 593, 595–596, 600, 602–603, 609, 612–613, 616–618
Constant
    rate of change, 73, 75–76, 308
    variation, 88–89, 526
Converse, 72
Coordinate
    plane, 64–69, 74
    three-dimensional system, 164
Correlations, 110–113
Cosecant, 678, 680, 682–684, 691, 695, 723
Cosine(s)
    function, 678–680, 682–684, 691, 695, 723, 730–742
    law of, 716–721, 724

Cotangent, 678, 680, 682–684, 691, 723
Critical thinking, 6, 12, 21, 27, 34, 41, 47, 53, 67, 74, 81, 90, 97, 104, 111, 125, 134, 141, 148, 154, 161, 177, 183, 191, 200, 207, 213, 219, 233, 239, 248, 255, 262, 268, 274, 288, 294, 302, 309, 318, 324, 330, 349, 356, 364, 371, 378, 384, 402, 409, 416, 423, 429, 438, 444, 460, 467, 477, 484, 491, 498, 504, 521, 529, 537, 545, 551, 558, 573, 579, 586, 594, 601, 610, 626, 633, 641, 648, 655, 661, 682, 689, 697, 706, 712, 719, 734, 740, 747, 757, 763, 769, 785, 792, 799, 808, 814, 820
Cumulative Review, *See* Reviews
Cylinder
    right circular, 35
    surface area, 34–35
    volume, 17, 35, 539

D

Data analysis, 50–55, 107–113, 151–156, 174–179, 327–332, 352–358, 441–446, 501–507, 511, 555–560, 658–665, 668, 670
Degree
    measure, 685, 687, 689–690, 694–701, 704, 706, 723
    monomial, 456
    polynomial, 456, 460
Determinants
    expansion by minors, 188–192
    form of linear equation, 193, 216–221
    matrix, 187–193, 202, 216–221
Difference, *See also* Subtraction
    definition, 4
    two cubes, 474, 477–479
    two squares, 473, 475, 477–479
    real numbers, 4, 6–8
Direct variation, 88–91, 526, 528–531, 562
Discrete mathematics, *See also* Probability, Sets, *and* Statistics
    linear programming, 151–156
Discriminant, 253–256
Distance
    between two points, 376–379, 576, 578
    rate/time, 27, 75, 141, 529
Division
    Factor theorem, 482
    long, 480, 484
    polynomial by a binomial, 480–486
    polynomial by a monomial, 473–479
    powers, 346
    property of, 4
    quotient, 4
    radicals, 368–371
    real numbers, 4, 6–8
    Remainder theorem, 482
    solving equations, 18–23
    synthetic, 480–486, 488–489
Domain, 284–286, 288, 291, 294,

334, 381–382, 384–385, 426–427, 450, 518, 521, 730, 734

E

Ellipse, 583–588, 597, 599–603, 746
    area, 31, 34, 256, 587
    eccentricity, 585, 587–588
    equation, 583–588, 597, 599–603, 746
    graphing, 584, 586–587
    problem solving, 584–585, 587–588
    standard form, 583, 586
Equally-likely outcomes, 782, 786, 824–827
Error analysis, 699, 707
Evaluating an expression, 9–14, 347, 349, 361
    using a calculator, 361–365, 371, 423, 429, 441, 449, 706–708, 724
Event, 806, 808–809, 811–816, 824–827
Expand binomial squares, 651–656, 668
Expansion by minors, 188–192
Experimental probability, 802–803
Exploration and Extension, 8, 14, 23, 29, 36, 43, 49, 55, 69, 76, 83, 92, 99, 106, 113, 127, 136, 143, 150, 156, 163, 179, 185, 193, 202, 209, 215, 221, 235, 241, 250, 257, 264, 270, 276, 290, 296, 304, 311, 320, 326, 332, 351, 358, 366, 373, 380, 387, 404, 411, 418, 425, 431, 440, 446, 462, 469, 479, 486, 492, 500, 507, 523, 531, 539, 547, 554, 560, 575, 581, 588, 596, 603, 612, 628, 635, 643, 650, 657, 663, 684, 691, 699, 708, 715, 721, 736, 742, 749, 759, 765, 771, 787, 794, 801, 810, 816, 822
Exploring data, *See* Data analysis
Exponent(s)
    expressions, 347, 349, 361
    irrational, 400
    meaning, 346
    model, 348, 354, 357, 363, 365, 382, 386, 388–389, 393–394, 401, 403–404, 422, 424–425, 432–433
    negative, 346–347, 349, 361
    problem solving, 348, 350–353, 355–358, 362–363, 365–366, 370–373, 377, 379, 383, 385–386, 389, 393–394, 401–404
    properties, 346–349, 361, 400, 413, 434
    rational, 348, 350–351, 360–366
    variable, 351–352, 354–358
    zero, 346, 349
Exponential
    equations, 434–439
    form, 405, 435, 449
    properties, 436
Exponential functions
    base e, 404, 420–425, 447
    graph, 354, 357–358, 398–404, 432–433, 447
    growth/decay, 352–358, 398–404,

421–424, 441
model, 348, 354–357, 363, 365–366, 382, 386, 388–389, 393–394, 401, 403–404, 422, 424–425
problem solving, 401, 403–404, 421–422, 424–425, 432–433, 437, 439
Expression(s), *See also* Rational expressions
algebraic, 9–14
evaluating, 347, 349, 361–365, 371, 421, 423, 429, 441, 449, 706–708, 724
exponents, 347, 349, 361
radical, 369–373
trigonometric, 678–679, 683, 695, 698, 704–708, 736, 744–747, 749, 761–765, 767–769, 773–774
Extraneous roots, 375, 378, 542

F

Factor
missing, 477, 485
monomial, 473–475, 477–479
theorem, 482
Factorial, 321, 335, 425, 623, 626, 628, 651, 652, 656, 667, 670
Factoring
common monomial, 473–475, 477–479
complete the square, 245, 248, 250
difference of cubes, 474, 477–479
difference of squares, 473, 475, 477–479
grouping, 474, 476–479
Linear Factorization theorem, 496
perfect square trinomials, 245, 248–250, 473, 477–479
polynomials, 473–512
quadratic trinomials, 473, 477–479
solving equations, 475, 477–479, 755–759
sum of two cubes, 474, 477–479
zero product property, 475
Fibonacci numbers, 323, 626, 668
FOIL algorithm, 457, 460
Formula, *See also* Area, Surface Area, *and* Volume
change of base, 406
circumference, circle, 35
compound interest, 35, 352, 422, 437
correlation coefficient, 110
diagonals of polygon, 325
discount, 35
distance, 376, 576, 578
distance/rate/time, 27, 141
Double-Angle, 766
Doyle log rule, 366
Half-Angle, 767
height of falling object, 231
Newton's Law of Cooling, 428
period, pendulum, 234
Pythagorean Theorem, 232
Pythagorean Theorem of baseball, 32

profit, 35
quadratic, 252
simple interest, 35
slope, 70
sum/difference, 760
sum of angles, *n*-gon, 301
temperature, 35, 40
vertical motion, 254
Fractal geometry, 260–261, 263
Fractions, *See* Rational expressions *and* Complex fractions
Frequency distribution, 50–55
Function(s)
absolute value, 307
base *e* exponential, 404, 420–424
calculators, 312–313
composite of two, 292–296, 300, 304
compound, 306–311
continuous, 463–500
cube root, 382, 384–386
definition, 284
domain, 284–286, 288, 291, 294, 334, 381–382, 384–385, 426–427, 450, 518, 521, 730, 734
evaluating, 286–311
exponential, 352–358, 388–389, 398–404, 420–425, 441, 443
graphs, 284–285, 288, 298–299, 301–303, 306–310, 312–319, 334, 381–386, 388–389, 392, 398–404, 407–411, 418, 420–427, 429–433, 441–446, 450, 463–465, 467–471, 494, 498, 500, 509, 518–525, 539, 542–544, 547, 562, 566
input/output, 284, 286, 290, 301
inverse, 298–304, 334, 338
linear, 284–320
logarithmic, 405–411, 426–431, 441
mapping diagram, 284, 287–290
models, 287, 293, 295, 301, 308, 311, 317, 319, 322–323, 325, 337, 466, 471, 476, 478–479, 483, 490, 492, 497, 499–500, 510–511
natural logarithms, 426–431
notation, 286, 289, 292–296, 306–311
operations, 291–296
polynomial, 463–500
quadratic, 284–320
range, 284–285, 288, 294, 381–382, 384–385, 427, 450, 501–505, 730, 734
rational, 518–566
recursive, 321–326, 335, 425, 628
square root, 381–386
transformations, 298, 312–319
trigonometric, 678–726, 730–776
values, 284, 287–290
vertex, 236–237, 239, 250, 271, 591–596
x-intercept, 78–79, 81–83, 237–239, 242–243, 246, 249, 260, 267, 494, 496–497, 731–732, 737–738, 775
y-intercept, 78–79, 81–83, 237–239, 306
Fundamental Counting Principle, 788–789, 824–827

G

Game theory, 817–822, 824–827
Gaussian, 441
Geographical note, 27, 683, 713
Geometric
mean, 375, 378–379
reflections, 298, 312–313, 318–319, 335, 387, 401–403, 464, 467, 737–742
rotations, 600, 685–686, 688–689
sequence, 637–638, 641–643, 667
translations, 314–315, 317–319, 464, 467, 737–742
Geometry, *See also* Area formula(s) *and* Volume
acute angle, 678, 680, 682, 685, 689
circle graph, 51, 53, 295, 440, 787, 825
circumference, circle, 35, 699, 705
distance formula, 376–379, 576, 578
equation of, 576–581
graphing, 577, 579–580
model, 536
parallel lines, 71–72, 92
perimeter, 35
perpendicular lines, 71–72, 92, 312
problem solving, 14, 26, 31, 33–35, 42, 69, 99, 126–127, 147, 179, 189–190, 192–193, 233, 240, 243, 249, 261, 269, 285, 289, 295, 301, 303–304, 325, 336, 350–351, 364–365, 372, 377, 379, 385, 458, 462, 468–469, 476, 478, 485, 462, 497, 512, 529–530, 538–539, 564, 574, 587, 602–603, 612, 627, 642, 648, 691, 699, 715, 748, 758, 764, 770–771, 775, 783, 785, 794, 800, 824
Pythagorean Theorem, 232–233, 243, 247–249
Glossary, 834–847
Graph(s)
absolute value, 101–107
bar, 11, 51, 54, 218, 221, 327, 330–331, 503, 640
box-and-whisker plot, 328, 330–332, 504
calculator, 16–17, 84–85, 128–129, 164, 194–195, 205–206, 242–243, 246, 266, 268, 312, 388–389, 420, 432–433, 440, 447, 470–471, 497, 500, 507, 524, 539, 541–542, 604–605, 664–665, 746, 748, 750–751, 755–759, 766, 771, 802–803
choose, 52
circle, 51, 53, 295, 440, 787, 825
compare, 384, 402
conics, 571, 573–574, 577, 580–581, 584–588, 592–596, 598–599, 601, 603–605, 607–613, 615–617
coordinate, 64–65, 67, 74, 260
cube root function, 382, 384–385
exponential, 354, 357–358, 398–404, 432–433, 447

frequency distribution, 50, 53
functions, 284–285, 288, 298–299
    301–303, 306–310, 312–319, 334,
    381–386, 388–389, 392, 398–404,
    407–411, 418, 420–427, 429–433,
    441–447, 450, 463–465, 467–471,
    494, 498, 500, 509, 518–525, 539,
    542–544, 547, 562, 566
horizontal shifts, 298, 312–313,
    316, 318–319, 335, 399, 401–403
hyperbola, 592, 594–596
linear equations, 18–24, 64–69,
    72–76, 78–82, 84–92, 101–109,
    111–112, 193
linear inequalities, 94–95, 97–100
logarithmic, 418, 420–427, 429–
    433, 440, 447
logistics growth, 441–445
number line, 2–3, 41–42, 47–49
ordered pairs, 64–65, 67, 74
polynomial, 463–471, 494, 498,
    500, 509
quadratic equations, 236–237, 239,
    241–243, 246, 248–250,
    269–270, 306, 308, 381
quadratic inequalities, 271–274
rational functions, 518–525, 539,
    542–544, 547, 562, 566
reflections, 298, 312–319, 335,
    398–399, 401–403
relations, 284–285, 288, 298–299
    301–303, 306–310, 312–319, 334
scatter plot, 109, 111–113, 433
square root function, 381, 383–385
systems, inequalities, 145–156
systems, linear, 122–144
time line, 52, 55
trigonometric function, 732–742,
    746, 748, 750–751, 753, 755–759,
    764, 766–767, 770–771
vertex, 101–102, 104
vertical shifts, 314–315, 317–319,
    398, 401–403
Graphing calculator, *See* Calculator
Greatest monomial factor, 474–475
    477–479

H

Half-plane, 94, 145–150
Hero's Area formula, 717
Horizontal asymptote, 421, 426,
    441, 444, 519–521, 562
Horizontal coordinate, 64–69, 74
Horizontal line
    equation, 65–69
    slope, 71
Horizontal shifts, 298, 312–313, 316,
    318–319, 335, 399, 401–403
Hyperbola
    asymptotes, 591–592, 594–595
    equation, 590–597, 599, 601–603, 605
    graphing, 592, 594–596
    problem solving, 591–593, 595–596
    vertex, 590–596

I

Imaginary
    axis, 260
    numbers, 258–259, 262, 264
    plane, 260
Inequality, *See also* Solving
    inequalities
    absolute value, 44–49, 58, 103
    compound, 38–43
    equivalent, 37–43
    graph of linear, 94–100
    graph of quadratic, 271–274
    graph of systems of linear, 94–100,
        145–156
    model, 46, 96
    problem solving, 40, 42, 46, 48–49,
        96, 98, 100, 103, 105–106, 147,
        149–150
    quadratic, 271–276
    slope-intercept form, 95, 97
    symbols, 3
    systems, 147–150
    transformations, 37–43
Installment loans, 555–560
Integer(s)
    addition, 4, 6–7
    division, 4, 6–7
    multiplication, 4, 6–7
    negative, 2
    positive, 2
    subtraction, 4, 6–7
Integrated Review, *See* Reviews
Intercepts, 78–83, 237–239, 242–243,
    246, 249, 260, 267, 306, 494,
    496–497, 731–732, 737–738, 775
Interest
    compound, 35, 352–353, 355–356,
        422, 424, 437, 555–560, 564,
        658–665, 668, 670
    simple, 35, 126, 174, 437, 450, 530
Intersection
    half-planes, 94, 145–150, 272, 276
    points of, 65, 68, 122, 485, 577
Inverse variation, 526–531, 562
Inverses, 4
Investigations, 37, 107, 145, 196, 266,
    314, 346, 400, 473, 533, 577, 652,
    703, 730, 811
Irrational numbers, 2

L

Least common denominator, 541,
    548, 551
Least common multiple, 541
Line(s)
    boundary, 94, 145–150, 272, 276
    fitting to data, 107–112, 129
    graphing, 64–69
    horizontal, 65–69, 71
    intersecting, 65, 68
    parallel, 71–72
    perpendicular, 71–72
    slope of, 70–72, 79, 764
    vertical, 65–69, 71

x-intercept, 78–79, 81–83
y-intercept, 78–79, 81–83, 306
Linear combination method, 131
Linear equation(s), *See also* System(s)
    fit to data, 107–112, 129
    given two points, 70–76, 86,
        89–91, 108–109
    graph, 18–28, 64–69, 72–76, 78–82,
        84–92, 101–106, 107–109,
        111–112, 193
    model, 24–28, 33, 65, 80, 88–89,
        91, 325, 358
    point-slope, 86–87, 90–91, 109
    problem solving, 20, 22–29, 65–66,
        68–69, 73, 75–76, 80–83, 88–89,
        91–92, 108–110, 112–113
    slope-intercept, 79–83, 86–87, 89
    standard form, 78
Linear Factorization Theorem, 496
Linear inequality, *See also* System(s)
    graph, 94–100
    half-plane, 94, 145–150, 272, 276
    model, 46, 96
    problem solving, 40, 42, 46, 48–49,
        96, 98, 100, 103, 105–106, 147,
        149–150
    slope-intercept form, 95, 97
    transformations, 37–43
Linear programming, 151–156
    constraints, 151
Linear systems, *See* System(s)
Literal equations, 31–36
Logarithm(s)
    inverse properties, 434
    natural, 426–431, 447
    products, 414, 416
    properties, 406, 413, 415–416
Logarithmic
    equations, 434–439
    expressions, 414–418, 426–431
    form, 405, 449
    functions, 405–411, 426–431
    graphs, 418, 420–427, 429–433,
        440, 447
    models, 415, 417–418, 428, 430–
        433, 439, 447
    problem-solving, 408, 410–411, 415,
        417–418, 428, 430–433, 437, 439
Logistics growth, 441–446, 451–452

M

Maintaining skills, *See* Reviews *and*
    Tests
Mandelbrot set, 261
Mapping, 284, 287–290
Math in other disciplines, *See* Appli-
    cations *and* Career interviews
Mathematical model, *See* Models
Matrix (matrices)
    addition, 175–179
    augmented, 210–215
    calculator, 194–195, 201, 205, 208
    coefficient, 204, 206–207, 216, 219
    column, 174, 178

INDEX

constant, 204, 206
Cramer's rule, 216–221
definition, 174
determinants, 187–193, 202, 216–221
diagonals method, 189, 191
dimensions, 174
entries, 174
equal, 174
equation(s), 193, 196–221, 224, 759
expansion by minors, 188–192
history, 216
identity, 196–197, 200
inverse, 196–202, 204–207, 209
model, 174, 182, 190, 195, 198–199, 206
multiplication, 180–185, 198–199, 201
order, 174, 177, 185, 759
problem solving, 81–83, 85–86, 94, 112, 174, 176, 178–179, 182, 184–185, 190, 192–193, 195, 198–199, 201–202, 206, 208–209, 212, 214, 218, 220–221, 224–226
properties, 175, 181
row equivalent, 210, 213
row operations, 158, 161, 210–214
scalar multiplication, 175–179
solving linear systems, 204–221
square, 174–178, 187
subtraction, 175–179
zero, 174
Maximum value, 151–156, 730, 732, 735, 737–738, 741, 750, 758
Mean(s)
    arithmetic, 327, 329–332
    deviations from, 503, 505–507
    distribution, 327, 329–332
    geometric, 375, 378–379
Measures of central tendency
    comparing, 327
    mean, 327, 329–332
    median, 327–328, 330–332
    mode, 327, 330–332
Measures of dispersion, 501–507
Median, 327–328, 330–332
Mid-Chapter Self-Test, See Tests
Milestones, See Biographical/historical note
Minimum value, 151–156, 730, 732, 735, 737–738, 741, 750, 758
Mixed expression(s), 6, 12, 15–17
Mixed Review, See Reviews
Mixture problems, See Problem-solving
Mode, 327, 330–332
Model(s)
    absolute value, 105
    algebraic expression, 9, 11, 13, 20, 30
    exponential, 348, 354–357, 363, 365, 382, 386, 388–389, 393–394, 401, 403–404, 422, 424–425, 432–433

geometric, 536
inequality, 46, 96
linear, 24–28, 33, 65, 80, 88–89, 91, 325, 358
logarithmic, 415, 417–418, 428, 430–433, 439, 447
matrix, 174, 182, 190, 195, 198–199, 206
parabolas, 572
polynomials, 458–459, 461, 466, 471, 476, 478–479, 483, 490, 492, 497, 499–500, 510–511
probability, 783–784, 819
quadratic, 231, 234, 238, 241, 247, 254, 256–257, 265, 267–269, 272–274, 279–280, 311, 317, 319, 322–323, 335
rational function, 520, 522–523, 525, 538, 543–544, 546, 550, 553, 565–566
real-life situations, 11, 20, 40, 88, 96, 123–124, 133, 135, 138–140, 147, 153, 160, 174, 190, 195, 198–199, 206, 231, 238, 247, 254, 267, 272, 348, 353, 355, 363, 370, 382–383, 401, 408, 415, 422, 428, 437, 442–443, 451, 459, 466, 476, 483, 490, 497, 520, 536, 550, 572, 584, 593, 600, 624, 632, 640, 646, 654, 681, 688, 696, 705, 711, 717, 733, 739, 756, 762, 768, 783, 819
sequence/series, 624, 632, 640, 642, 646
systems, linear, 123–124, 133, 138–140, 147, 153, 160, 174, 190, 195, 198–199, 206
trigonometric, 733, 735–736, 739, 741, 748, 751, 756, 759, 762, 764, 768, 771, 774
variation, 526–528
verbal, 20, 24–28, 33, 80, 247, 476, 497
Monomial(s), 456, 473–479
    common factor, 473–475, 477–479
Multiplication
    binomial squares, 473, 475, 477–479
    binomials, 458–461, 651–657, 668–670
    difference of two cubes, 474, 477–479
    difference of two FOIL algorithms, 457, 460
    geometric models, 456
    identity element, 4
    polynomial by a monomial, 457, 460
    polynomials, 457–460
    radical expressions, 368–373
    real numbers, 4, 6–8
    solving equations, 18–23
Multiplication method for solving a system, 131
Multiplicative inverse, 4
Mutually exclusive events, 805–810, 824–827

N

Negative number(s)
    absolute value, 44, 101
    square roots, 230, 258, 262, 291
Negative rate of change, 354–356
Notation, function, 286, 289, 292–296, 306–311
Number(s)
    absolute value, 44, 101
    comparing, 3
    Fibonacci, 323, 626, 668
    integers, 2
    irrational, 2
    opposite, 3
    ordering, 3, 6
    rational, 2
    real, 2
    reciprocal, 4
    triangular, 326, 669
    whole, 2, 4, 6–7
Number line
    coordinate, point, 1–3, 6
    graphing inequalities, 41–42, 47–49
    origin, 2
    plotting points, 2–3
Numerical coefficient, 230, 236, 245–246, 456, 465, 488
Numerical expression, 6, 12, 15–17

O

Octagon, 26
Odds, 810
Open half-plane, 94, 145–150, 272, 276
Operations
    order of, 10
    row, 158, 161, 210–214
Opposites, 3
Order
    operations, 10
    rational numbers, 3, 6
    real numbers, 2–3, 6, 8
    symbols, 3
    terms in a polynomial, 456
Ordered pairs
    coordinates, 64–69, 74
    graph of, 64–65, 67, 74
Ordered triple, 157–159
Ordinate, 64
Origin, 2, 64
Outcome, equally-likely, 782, 786, 824–827

P

Parabola(s)
    axis of symmetry, 236–237, 239, 570, 573
    directrix, 570–575
    equations, 570–575, 597–598, 601–603

focus, 570–575

graphing, 571, 573–574

maximum point, 151–156, 730, 732, 735, 737–738, 741, 750, 758

minimum point, 151–156, 730, 732, 735, 737–738, 741, 750, 758

models, 572

problem solving, 572, 574–575

standard equation, 570–571, 573–575

vertex, 236–237, 239, 250, 271

Pascal's Triangle, 652–653, 655–657, 669–670, 799, 825–826

Pattern(s), *See also* Problem-solving strategies

difference of two cubes, 474, 477–479

difference of two squares, 473, 475, 477–479

factoring trinomials, 473, 477–479

perfect square trinomial, 245, 248–250, 473, 477–479

of symmetry, 105

Percent, *See* Problem-solving

Perfect square(s), trinomial, 245, 248–250, 473, 477–479

Perimeter, 35

Permutations, 790–794, 801, 824–827

Perpendicular lines, 72, 92, 312

Pi (π), 775

Point(s)

coordinates, 1–3, 64–69, 74

distance between two, 376–379, 576, 578

intersection, 65, 68, 122, 485

number line, 1–3, 6

plotting, 64–65, 67, 74

slope form, 86–87, 90–91, 109

Polynomial(s)

addition/subtraction, 456, 459–460

classifying, 456

constant term, 456

cube of a binomial, 458, 461

degree of, 456, 460

difference of two squares, 473, 475, 477–479

division, binomial, 480–486

division, monomial, 473–479

equations, 473–512

evenly divisible, 480

factoring, 473–512

FOIL pattern, 457, 460

greatest monomial factor, 473

leading coefficient, 456, 465, 488

linear factorization, 496–500

long division, 480, 484

models, 458–459, 461, 466, 471, 476, 478–479, 483, 490, 492, 497, 499–500, 510–511

monomial factors, 473–479

multiplication, polynomials, 456–457, 460

problem solving, 458–459, 461–462, 466, 468–469, 470–471, 476, 478–479, 483, 485–486, 490, 492, 497, 499–500, 501, 503–506, 510–512

solutions, number of, 494–500

square of a binomial, 458–461

standard form, 456, 460

sum/difference, binomials, 458–461

synthetic division, 480–486, 488–489

trinomials, 473, 477–479

Polynomial equation(s), 473–512

Positive number(s)

absolute value, 44, 101

Positive rate of change, 352–356

Positive square root, 2, 230

Power(s), *See also* Exponents

power, 346

product, 346

quotient, 345

ten, 92, 193, 235, 320, 462, 493, 531, 553, 581, 596, 635, 649–650, 691, 759

Principal, 35, 126, 174, 352, 422, 437, 439, 450, 530, 555–560, 564, 658–665, 668, 670

Principal square root, 2, 230

Probability

combinations, 796–801, 824–827

complement of an event, 806, 808–809, 811–816, 824–827

dependent events, 811–816, 824–827

equally-likely outcome, 782, 786, 824–827

expected value, 817–822, 824–827

experimental, 802–803

Fundamental Counting Principle, 788–789, 824–827

game theory, 817–822, 824–827

independent events, 811–816, 824–827

model, 783–784, 819

mutually exclusive events, 805–810, 824–827

odds, 810

one event, 782–787, 789–794, 797–798, 800–801, 807, 824–827

permutations, 790–794, 801, 824–827

problem solving, 782–787, 789, 791–794, 797–803, 805–807, 809–822, 824–827

random number generator, 787, 802–803, 811, 815, 824–827

sample space, 782, 785, 808, 817, 825

two events, 805, 808–810, 824–827

Problem solving, *See also* Applications

absolute value, 103, 105–106

approximating solutions, 9, 32, 54, 65–66, 68–69, 75, 91, 108–109, 112, 117, 129, 140, 168, 192, 231–235, 238, 240–243, 249, 256, 337, 348, 350, 362, 366, 379, 421–422, 424, 428, 432–433, 439, 469, 483, 499, 507, 544, 552, 588, 632, 656–657, 683, 736, 775, 809, 819

average, 75–76, 112–113, 116, 124, 220, 308, 332, 350, 417, 466, 520, 522, 538, 543, 546, 565, 640, 739, 741, 749, 818

coin, 486

cost/income/value, 124, 126, 138–139, 142, 149, 153, 155, 167, 174, 176, 182, 184, 293–294, 308, 403, 483, 485–486, 490, 520, 522–523, 546, 565

discount/markup/tax, 135, 293–294, 303–304, 560

distance/rate/time, 27, 75, 141, 529

elapsed time, 646

equations, three variables, 160, 162–163

exponential, 348, 350–353, 355–358, 362–363, 365–366, 370–373, 377, 379, 383, 385–386, 389, 393–394, 401–404, 421–422, 424–425, 432–433, 437, 439

formula, 31–36, 587, 627

geometry, 14, 26, 31, 33–35, 42, 69, 99, 126–127, 147, 179, 189–190, 192–193, 233, 240, 243, 249, 261, 269, 285, 289, 295, 301, 303–304, 325, 336, 350–351, 362, 364–365, 372, 377, 379, 385, 458, 462, 468–469, 476, 478, 485, 497, 512, 529–530, 538–539, 564, 574, 578, 580, 584–585, 587–588, 602–603, 612, 627, 642, 648, 691, 699, 715, 748, 758, 764, 770–771, 775, 783, 785, 794, 800, 824

hyperbola, 591–593, 595–596

installment loans, 555–560

interest, 35, 126, 174, 352, 422, 424, 437, 439, 450, 530, 555–560, 564, 658–665, 668, 670

investment, 206, 208, 326, 352–353, 356, 433, 450, 510, 555–560

linear equations, 20, 22–29, 65–66, 68–69, 73, 75–76, 80–83, 88–89, 91–92, 108–110, 112–113

linear inequalities, 40, 42, 46, 48–49, 96, 98, 100, 103, 105–106

linear programming, 153, 155–156

logarithmic, 408, 410–411, 415, 417–418, 428, 430–433, 437, 439

matrices, 81–83, 85–86, 94, 112, 174, 176, 178–179, 182, 184–185, 190, 192–193, 195, 198–199, 201–202, 206, 208–209, 212, 214, 218, 220–221, 224–226

mean/median/mode, 327, 329–330

mixture, 212, 214

parabolas, 572, 574–575 574–575

percent, 5, 14, 54, 73, 80, 98, 126, 135–136, 143, 155, 162–163, 167, 174, 178–179, 184, 206, 208, 214, 221, 225, 293–294, 296, 303, 326, 348, 352–353, 355–356, 401, 403, 424, 433, 437, 439, 450, 506, 523, 547, 555–560, 564, 643, 658–665,

668, 670

polynomials, 458–459, 461–462, 466, 468–469, 470–471, 476, 478–479, 483, 485–486, 490, 492, 497, 499–500, 501, 503–506, 510–512

probability, 782–787, 789, 791–794, 797–803, 805–807, 809–822, 824–827

proportion/variation, 526–531

quadratic equations, 231–232, 234–235, 238, 240–241, 243, 247, 249, 254, 256–257, 279–280, 308, 317, 756, 758, 759

quadratic inequalities, 272–275

radicals, 362–366, 370, 372–373, 377, 379, 382–383, 385–386, 393–394

rate/ratio, 5, 13, 36, 66, 73, 75–76, 82, 88–91, 103, 108–109, 116, 118, 123–124, 126–127, 133, 135–136, 140, 308, 312–313, 327, 330, 348, 350, 358, 362, 370, 377, 386, 424, 451, 536, 539, 564, 637–639, 641, 650, 668, 681, 683–684, 696, 698–699, 705, 707–708, 711, 714–715, 717–718, 720–721, 725–726, 758, 771, 782–787, 789, 791–794, 797–803, 805–807, 809–822, 824–827

rational equations, 543–544, 546

rational expressions, 536, 538–539, 550, 552–553

rational functions, 520, 522–523, 524–525

statistics, 50–55, 107–110, 112, 167, 327–332, 394, 501, 503–507, 511

systems, equations, 123–124, 126–127, 129, 133, 135, 138–143

systems, inequalities, 147, 149–150

technology, 16–17, 84–85, 128–129, 164, 194–195, 205–206, 242–243, 246, 266, 268, 312, 388, 432–433, 447, 432–433, 447, 490, 497, 507, 511, 524–525, 664–665, 802–803

trigonometry, 681, 683–684, 696, 698–699, 705, 707–708, 711, 714–715, 717–718, 720–721, 725–726, 733, 735–736, 739, 741–742, 746, 748–749, 756, 758–759, 762, 764–765, 768, 770–771, 774–776

unsolved problems, 743

velocity, 478, 768

work, 531

Problem-solving strategies

draw/use a diagram/picture, 3, 24–26, 35, 46, 281, 284, 287–290, 323, 350, 377, 379, 575, 585, 587, 600, 616, 654, 656, 681, 690, 699, 705, 710, 714, 720–721, 725–726, 748, 762, 770, 775, 783–786, 789, 791–794, 799–801

find/recognize a pattern, 112, 180, 323, 373, 417, 626, 643, 654, 656–657, 776

guess/check/revise, 24

make/use, graph, 3, 32, 38–40, 45, 47–52, 54–55, 64–69, 74–76, 78–83, 86, 87, 88–89, 91–92, 94–109, 111–113, 123–124, 127, 129, 153, 218, 221, 243, 268–269, 272, 276, 279, 285, 307–308, 310–311, 317, 354, 382, 403–404, 425, 432–433, 437, 440, 442, 446, 466, 468–469, 470, 750, 787

make/use, table, 7, 24, 49, 51, 53, 64–65, 68, 108–110, 112, 153, 155, 160, 162–163, 176, 179, 198, 212, 231, 237, 284, 287–290, 304, 328–332, 336, 350, 355, 372, 417–418, 432–433, 505–506, 520, 555, 558, 584, 595, 624, 646, 664–665, 746, 819–822

unit analysis, 5–6, 118

work backwards, 199

Product(s), *See* Multiplication

Properties

complex numbers, 259

exponential equations, 436

exponents, 346, 361, 400, 413, 434

logarithmic equations, 434

logarithms, 413

radicals, 368, 374

real numbers, 3–4

zero product, 475, 755–756, 768

Properties, Models, Transformations, Formulas, 830–835

Proportion(s), *See also* Variation

direct variation, 88–91, 526–531, 562

inverse variation, 526–527, 529–531, 562

joint variation, 528–531, 562

problem solving, 28, 526–531

Pythagorean distance formula, 376–379, 576, 578

Pythagorean identity, 680, 744–746, 755–756

Pythagorean Theorem, 232–233, 243, 247–249, 678–679, 705, 714

Q

Quadrants, 64

Quadratic equation(s)

axis of symmetry, 236–237, 239, 570, 573

discriminant, 253–256

finding *x*-intercept, 237–239, 242–243, 246, 249, 260, 267

finding *y*-intercept, 237–239

graphs, 236–237, 239, 241–243, 246, 248–250, 269–270, 306, 308, 381

leading coefficient, 230, 236, 245–246

model, 231, 234, 238, 241, 247, 254, 256–257, 265, 267–269, 272, 279–280, 311, 317, 319, 322–323, 335

parabolas, 236–241, 267, 306, 308, 311, 381

perfect square trinomial, 245, 248–250, 473, 477–479

problem solving, 231–232, 234–235, 238, 240–241, 243, 247, 249, 254, 256–257, 279–280

properties, 236

quadratic formula, 252–256

solving, 230–240, 242–250, 252–257, 265–270, 755–758

solving, calculator, 231–232, 242–243, 246, 266, 268

solving, completing the square, 245, 248–250

solving, square roots, 230–235

square of binomial, 245–249

standard form, 230

vertex, 236–237, 239, 250, 271, 590–596

Quadratic functions, 284–320

Quadratic inequality

graphing, 271–274

intersection, 272, 276

models, 272–274

problem solving, 272–275

solving, 271–274

vertex, 271

Quadratic trinomials, *See* Factoring

Quartile, 328, 330–332

Quotient(s), *See also* Division

polynomials, 473–486

powers of, 346

property of radicals, 368, 374

real numbers, 4, 6–8

R

Radical(s)

addition/subtraction, 369, 371

equations, 373–379

extraneous roots, 375, 378, 542

index, 369

like, 369

multiplication/division, 368–373

notation, 354, 360–361

problem solving, 362–366, 370, 372–373, 377, 379, 382–383, 385–386, 393–394

properties, 368, 374

simplifying, 369–373

trigonometric functions, 749–750

Radicand, 230, 369

Random number generator, 787, 802–803, 811, 815, 824–827

Range, 501–505

Rate(s) *See also* Problem Solving

of change, 73–76, 103, 116, 308, 358

distance/rate/time, 27, 75, 141, 529

Ratio(s), *See also* Problem Solving

common, 637–639, 641

golden, 377, 668

trigonometric, 678, 703–776

using, 88–91, 312–313, 370, 377, 386, 637–643, 650

Rational equations

common denominator, 541, 545, 548, 551

cross multiplying, 543, 545

extraneous solutions, 542

least common multiple, 541, 545

problem solving, 542–544, 546–547
solving, 541–547, 552, 563
Rational expressions
adding/subtracting, 548, 550–552, 563
dividing, 535–539, 563
least common denominator, 548, 551
multiplying, 534, 537–539, 563
problem solving, 536, 538–539, 550, 552–553
simplifying, 533–539, 564
Rational function(s), *See also* Polynomials
asymptotes, 421, 426–427, 441, 444, 519–521, 523, 562
domain, 518, 521
graphing, 518–525, 539, 542–544, 547, 562, 566
inverse variation, 526–527, 529–531, 562
joint variation, 528–531, 562
LCD, model, 520, 522–523, 525, 538, 543–544, 546, 550, 553, 565–566
problem solving, 520, 522–525
Rational number(s)
definition, 2, 4, 6–7
decimal forms, 2
Rational-Zero Test, 488–493
Real number(s) 2–8
Rectangle
area, 34, 248, 256, 478
Recursive functions
classifying, 321–322
differences, 322–326
evaluating, 321–326
factorial, 321
Fibonacci numbers, 323
linear model, 325
quadratic model, 322–323, 335
triangular numbers, 326, 669
Reflections, *See* Transformations
Relation(s), 284–337
graphs, 284–285, 288, 298–299, 301–303, 306–310, 312–319, 334
Remainder Theorem, 482
Reviews
Chapter Review, 57–60, 115–118, 166–168, 223–226, 278–280, 334–337, 391–394, 449–452, 509–512, 562–566, 615–618, 667–670, 723–726, 773–776, 824–827
Cumulative Review, 170–171, 340–343
Integrated Review, 8, 14, 23, 29, 36, 43, 49, 55, 69, 76, 83, 92, 99, 106, 113, 127, 136, 143, 150, 156, 163, 179, 185, 193, 202, 209, 215, 221, 235, 241, 250, 257, 264, 270, 276, 290, 296, 304, 311, 320, 326, 332, 351, 358, 366, 373, 380, 387, 404, 411, 418, 425, 431, 440, 446, 462, 469, 479, 486, 492, 500, 507, 523, 531, 539, 547, 553, 560, 575, 581, 588, 596, 603, 613, 628, 635, 643, 650, 656, 663, 684, 691, 699,

708, 715, 721, 736, 742, 749, 759, 765, 771, 787, 794, 801, 810, 816, 822
Mixed Review, 15, 43, 77, 100, 137, 156, 186, 209, 244, 264, 297, 320, 359, 380, 412, 440, 472, 493, 532, 554, 582, 603, 636, 657, 692, 715, 743, 765, 795, 816
Right triangles
Pythagorean Theorem, 232–233, 243, 247–249, 678–679, 705, 714
trigonometric ratios, 678–776
Root(s), *See also* Solution(s) *and* Radicals
extraneous, 375, 378, 542
*n*th, 360–366, 382–384
properties, 368
quadratic equations, 230–235
square, 230, 381, 383–384
Rotation, *See* Transformations
Round-off error, 503
Rule(s)
Cramer's, 216–221
Doyle Log, 366
order of operations, 10
parallelogram, 261
transforming equations, 18
transforming inequalities, 37

S

Sample space, 782, 785, 808, 817, 825
Scatter plot, 107–112
Science, *See* Applications *and* Formula
Scientific notes, 24, 28, 46, 109, 190, 193, 212, 350, 355, 370, 372, 377, 383, 386, 415, 424, 428, 431, 762
Series
arithmetic, 631–634, 667
geometric, 639–643, 645–650, 667
infinite, 645–650
model, 632, 640, 642, 646
special, 625, 627
summation notation, 623–627, 667, 670
Selected Answers, 856–926
Sequence
arithmetic, 629–630, 633–635, 643, 667
factorials, 623, 626, 628, 668
Fibonacci, 626, 668
finding terms, 624, 626–628, 667
finite, 622–630, 637–638, 641–643, 667
geometric, 637–638, 641–643, 667
models, 624
Set(s)
complex numbers, 259
imaginary numbers, 258, 262
integers, 2
irrational numbers, 2
Mandelbrot, 261
rational numbers, 2
real numbers, 2
whole numbers, 2
Simple interest, 35, 126, 174, 437, 439, 450, 530

Simplifying
polynomials, 456–457, 462
radical expressions, 369–373
sides of an equation, 18
Simultaneous equations, *See* System(s)
Sine(s)
function, 678–684, 691, 696, 723, 730–742
graphs, 732–742
law of, 709–715, 721
Slant asymptotes, 523
Slope
horizontal line, 71
interpreting, 71
line, 70–72, 764
negative, 71
parallel lines, 71–72
perpendicular, 71–72
positive, 71
vertical lines, 71
zero, 71
Slope-intercept form
linear equations, 79–83, 86–87, 89
linear inequalities, 95, 97
Solution(s), *See also* Root(s)
linear equations, 64–92
linear inequalities, 94–100
quadratic equations, 233–280
quadratic inequalities, 271–274
system, equations, 122–129, 130–135, 138–143, 157–164, 204–221, 224
system, inequalities, 145–150
Solving problems, *See* Problem solving *and* Problem-solving strategies
Square(s)
binomials, 458–461
difference of two, 473, 475, 477–479
perfect, trinomial, 245, 248–250, 473, 477–479
Square root(s)
approximating, 2, 231–235, 246, 252
evaluating with a calculator, 231–232
finding, 230–235, 246, 252–256
imaginary numbers, 258, 262
irrational numbers, 2
negative, 230, 258, 262, 291
principal, 2, 230
product property, 230
trigonometric functions, 754
Standard deviation, 502–507, 511
Standard form
complex number, 259
equation of circle, 576, 579
equation of ellipse, 583, 586
linear equation, 78
polynomial equation, 456, 460
quadratic equation, 230
Statistics *See also* Graphs
analyzing data, 507
bar graph, 11, 51, 54, 218, 221, 327, 330–331, 503, 640
box-and-whisker, 328, 330–332

INDEX

circle graph, 51, 53, 295, 440, 787, 825
correlations, 110–113
fitting a line to data, 107–112, 129
frequency distribution, 50–55
mean, 503, 505–507
measures of central tendency, 113, 327–332
problem solving, 50–55, 107–110, 112, 327–332, 394, 501, 503–507, 511
quartiles, 328, 330–332
range, 501–505
scatter plot, 109, 111–113
standard deviation, 502–507, 511
table, 51, 53–54, 108–109
Student Handbook, 848–855
Substitution method, 130
Subtraction, *See also* Difference
  definition, 3
  polynomials, 456, 459–460
  radicals, 369, 371
  real numbers, 4, 6–8
  transforming equations, 18
  transforming inequalities, 37
Surface area
  cylinder, 34–35
  sphere, 370
Symbol(s)
  absolute value, 44
  approximately equal to, 2
  braces, 2
  equality/inequality, 3
  pi, 775
  square root, 2
Symmetry
  parabola, 236–237, 239, 570, 573
  pattern, 105
System(s), linear equations
  algebraic, 130–135, 138–143, 157–164
  Cramer's rule, 216–221
  equivalent, 158
  matrices, 204–221, 224
  matrix inverses, 196–202, 204–207, 209
  model, 733, 735–736, 739, 741, 748, 751, 756, 759, 762, 764, 768, 771, 774
  number of solutions, 122–135, 138–143, 159–164
  problem solving, 123–124, 126–127, 133, 135, 138–143, 160, 162–163, 174, 176, 178–179, 182, 184–185, 190, 192–193, 195, 198–199, 201–202, 206, 208–209, 212, 214, 218, 220–221, 224–226
  three variables, 157–164
  triangular form, 157–162
  two variables, 122–135, 138–143
System(s), linear inequalities
  graphing, 145–147, 149–150
  half-plane, 145–150, 272, 276
  intersection, 145

problem solving, 147, 149–150
vertex, 145

Tangent
  function, 678–680, 682–684, 691, 695, 723
Technology, *See* Calculator, Computer, *and* Problem solving
Technology Appendix, 856–867
Term(s)
  constant, 456
  expression, 9
  polynomial, 456
  sequence, 624, 626–628, 667
  variation, 88–89, 526
Tests
  Chapter Test, 61, 119, 169, 227, 281, 338, 395, 453, 513, 567, 619, 671, 727, 777, 828
  College Entrance Exam, 14, 23, 43, 76, 150, 193, 241, 257, 296, 332, 358, 380, 411, 446, 469, 500, 507, 539, 575, 613, 650, 684, 708, 742, 787, 822
  Mid-Chapter Self-Test, 30, 93, 144, 203, 251, 305, 367, 419, 487, 540, 589, 644, 702, 752, 804
Transformation(s)
  equations, 18
  formulas, 31–36
  inequalities, 37
  reflections, 298, 312–313, 316, 318–319, 335, 387, 401–403, 464, 467, 737–742
  rotations, 600, 685–686, 688–689
  translations, 314–315, 317–319, 464, 467, 737–742
Trapezoid, 34–35
Triangle(s)
  AAS, 709–710, 712
  ASA, 709–710, 712
  area, 34, 189–190, 192, 248, 710, 712–714, 717, 724
  Hero's Area formula, 717
  Pascal's, 652–653, 655–657, 669–670, 799, 825–826
  SAS, 709–710, 712, 717–718
  SSA, 709–710, 712
  SSS, 709–710, 712
  trigonometry, 709–714, 719, 724
Triangular form, 157–162
Triangular numbers, 326, 669
Trigonometric functions
  cosecant, 678, 680, 682–684, 691, 695, 723
  cosine, 678–680, 682–684, 691, 695, 723, 730–742
  cotangent, 678, 680, 682–684, 691, 723
  equations, 693, 695–699, 730–776
  graphing, 732–742, 746, 748, 750–751, 753, 755–759, 764, 766–767, 770–771
  inverse, 703–708

  model, 733, 735–736, 739, 741, 748, 751, 756, 759, 762, 764, 768, 771, 774
  problem solving, 681, 683–684, 696, 698–699, 705, 707–708, 711, 714–715, 717–718, 720–721, 725–726, 733, 735–736, 739, 741–742, 746, 748–749, 756, 758–759, 762, 764–765, 768, 770–771, 774–776
  Pythagorean Theorem, 678–679, 705, 714
  reflections, 737–742
  secant, 678, 680, 682–684, 691, 723
  sine, 678–684, 691, 696, 723, 730–742
  sum/difference, 760–765
  tangent, 678–680, 682–684, 691, 695, 723
  translations, 737–742
Trigonometric identities, 680, 683–684, 744–752
Trinomial(s)
  factoring, 245, 248, 250, 473–479
  perfect square, 245, 248–250, 473, 477–479
  quadratic, 473, 477–479

Value(s)
  expected, 817–822, 824–827
  expression, 9–12
  function, 284, 287–290
  maximum, 151–156, 730, 732, 735, 737–738, 741, 750, 758
  minimum, 151–156, 730, 732, 735, 737–738, 741, 750, 758
Variable, 9–12
Variation, *See also* Proportion(s)
  constant of, 88–89, 526
  direct, 88–91, 526–531, 562
  equations, 88–91, 526–531, 563
  inverse, 526–527, 529–531, 562
  joint, 528–531, 562
  model, 526–528
Verbal model, 20, 24–28, 33, 80, 247, 476, 497
Vertex (vertices)
  absolute value, 101–102, 104
  hyperbolas, 590–596
  parabola, 236–237, 239
Vertical asymptote, 421, 426–427, 519, 521, 562
Vertical coordinate, 64–65, 67, 74
Vertical line
  equation of, 65–69
  slope of, 71
Vertical shifts, 314–315, 317–319, 398, 401–403
Volume
  cone, 14, 34–35, 529
  cube, 289
  cylinder, 17, 539
  octahedron, 362
  prism, 14, 458, 476, 539
  pyramid, 34

rectangular solid(s), 14, 458, 476, 539
right circular cylinder, 35
sphere, 14, 34, 289, 333, 370

Whole number(s), 2, 4, 6–7

x-axis, 64, 66
x-intercept 78–79, 81–83, 237–239, 242–243, 246, 249, 260, 267, 494, 496–497, 731–732, 737–738, 775

y-axis, 64, 66
y-intercept, 78–79, 81–83, 237–239, 306

Zero
exponent property, 346
identity for addition, 4
product property, 475, 755–756, 768

Appreciation to the following art/photo production staff:

Leslie Concannon, Pam Daly, Irene Elios, Julie Fair, Martha Friedman, Susan Geer, Aimee Good, Carmen Johnson, Judy Kelly, Maureen Lauran, Mark MacKay, Helen McDermott, Penny Peters, Nina Whitney, Bonnie Yousefian.

from the Fractal Geometry of Nature by Benoit B. Mandelbrot, 1982. 301: Arthur Hustwitt (Leo deWys). 303: Antman (The Image Works). 307: Nicholas Foster (The Image Bank). 308: Steve Proehl (The Image Bank). 310: The Image Works. 316: Don Landwehrle (The Image Bank). 319: Benn Mitchell (The Image Bank). 323: Paulette Crowley. 328: Bob Daemmerich (The Image Works). 329: Paul Conklin (Monkmeyer Press). 331: Mimi Forsyth (Monkmeyer Press). 332: Dan Guravich (Photo Researchers, Inc.). 337: John P. Kelly (The Image Bank). 338: The Bettmann Archive. 342: Gazuit (Photo Researchers, Inc.). 342: Paolo Koch (Photo Researchers, Inc.). 343: Grant Heilman (Grant Heilman Photography).

CHAPTER 7 344–345: Pixar. 348: Margot Granitsas (The Image Works). 350: Jet Propulsion Lab, NASA. 351: Renee Lynn (David Madison). 357: Dan Helme (Duomo). 359: Susan Doheny/© D.C. Health. 362: Breck Kent (Animals, Animals). 363 t: Christy Hill. 363 b: Christy Hill. 364: Henryk T. Kaiser (The Picture Cube). 365 t: Ulrike Welsch (Photo Researchers, Inc.). 365 b: Stuart Dee (The Image Bank). 366: Del Mulkey (Photo Researchers, Inc.). 370 t: NASA. 370 b: David Madison. 373: David Madison. 379: Courtesy Children's Hospital of Michigan. 382: E.R. Degginger. 385: Everett C. Johnson (Leo de Wys). 388: Tom McHugh (Photo Researchers, Inc.). 389: Anup & Manoj Shah (Animals, Animals). 391: Margot Granitsas (Photo Researchers, Inc.). 393: Superstock. 394: Churchill & Klehr (Tony Stone Worldwide).

CHAPTER 8, 396–397: George Zimbel (Monkmeyer Press). 403: The Bettmann Archive. 408: W. Gregory Brown (Animals, Animals). 410: The Image Works. 411: Harry Casey. 412: Culver Pictures. 415: Superstock. 417all: Susan A. Anderson/© D.C. Heath. 418 l: Howard Dratch (Leo deWys). 418 cr: Read D. Brugger (The Picture Cube). 418 r: The Image Works. 418 lc: Hal Clason (Tom Stack & Assoc.). 419: AP/Wide World. 422: Will & Demi McIntyre (Photo Researchers, Inc.). 424: Culver Pictures. 428: Richard Wood (The Picture Cube). 430: Renee Lynn (David Madison). 431: Thomas R. Taylor (Photo Researchers, Inc.). 433: Grant LeDuc (Monkmeyer Press). 437: Frank Siteman (The Picture Cube). 442: The American Red Cross. 443: Audrey Gottlieb (Monkmeyer Press). 445: Treat Davidson (Photo Researchers, Inc.). 451 t: Don Carl Steffen (Photo Researchers, Inc.). 451 b: Chet Seymore (The Picture Cube). 452: Susan A. Anderson/ © D.C. Heath.

CHAPTER 9 456–457: George Loehr (The Image Bank). 459: Julian Calder (Tony Stone Worldwide). 462: Steve Elmore (The Stock Market). 472: Susan Doheny/© D.C. Heath. 476: Robert Isear (Photo Researchers, Inc.). 478: Susan A. Anderson/© D.C. Heath. 479 i: Adam Woolfitt/Daily Telegraph Magazine (Woodfin Camp).

479: Bill Bachmann (The Image Works). 483: Gale Zucker (Stock Boston). 490: Michael L. Abramson (Woodfin Cam). 493: Walter E. Harvey (Photo Researchers, Inc.). 495: Historical Pictures Service. 497: William Curtsinger © National Geographic Society. 499 l: Cary Wolinski (Stock Boston). 499 r: Cary Wolinski (Stock Boston). 500: Vandystadt (Photo Researchers, Inc.). 501: Davies/Pashko (Envision). 503: John Cancalosi (Stock Boston). 504: William Johnson (Stock Boston). 505: ASP/Science Source (Photo Researchers, Inc.). 506 at: Joseph Nettis (Stock Boston). 506 b: Robert Frerck (Woodfin Camp). 511: Tom & Pat Leeson (Photo Researchers, Inc.). 512 t: Culver Pictures. 512 l: North Winds Picture Archive. 512 lt: George E. Jones (Photo Researchers, Inc.). 512 c: UPI/Bettmann. 512 cb: George Holton (Photo Researchers, Inc.). 512 cr: Bettmann Archive.

CHAPTER 10 516–517: Carleton Ray (Photo Researchers, Inc.). 520: National Gallery of Art, Washington, Cornelius Van S. Roosevelt Collection. 522: Sybil Shackman (Monkmeyer Press). 525: William Curtsinger (Photo Researchers, Inc.). 527: John Coletti (Tony Stone Worldwide). 528: Courtesy GM Hughes Electronics. 529: Diane M. Lowe (Stock Boston). 530: Francoise Sauze (Photo Researchers, Inc.). 531: Bob Daemmerich (Stock Boston). 532 t: The Bettmann Archive. 532 b: The Bettmann Archive. 536: Ellis Herwig (Stock Boston). 539: Bob Daemmerich (The Image Works). 543: Dennis J. Cipnic (Photo Researchers, Inc.). 544: Bob Daemmerich (Stock Boston). 547: Stephen G. Maka. 550: Blair Seitz (Photo Researchers, Inc.). 552: Bob Daemmerich (Stock Boston). 553 t: Crandall (The Image Works). 553 b: Walt Anderson (Visuals Unlimited). 557: The Image Works. 559: The Image Works. 560: Paul Barton (The Stock Market). 560: John Coletti (Stock Boston). 565: Science Source (Photo Researchers, Inc.). 566: The Image Works.

CHAPTER 11 568–569: Peter Pearson (Tony Stone Worldwide). 572: Hank Morgan (Photo Researchers, Inc.). 575: The Bettman Archive. 580: Derek Bayes (Tony Stone Worldwide). 582: Susan Doheny/© D.C. Heath. 588: Superstock. 602: Gatha Ashvin (Leo DeWys). 609: Robert Kristofik (The Image Bank). 617: J.B. Bidner. 618: NASA.

CHAPTER 12 620–621: Thomas W. Martin, APSA (Photo Researchers, Inc.). 626: Scott Camazine (Photo Researchers, Inc.). 627: David Madison. 632: Eric Lars Bakke. 635: Ken Kaminsky (The Picture Cube). 636: Alfred Eisenstaedt, Life Magazine © Time Warner Inc. 643: PIP/LGI. 647: Mary Clay (Tom Stack & Assoc.). 650: Ken O'Donoghue/© D.C. Heath. 659: Robert Essel (The Stock Market). 662: Bob Daemmerich (Stock Boston). 668: C.W. Brown (Photo Researchers, Inc.). 669 l: Phil Degginger (Tony Stone Worldwide). 669 r: Richard Megna (Fundamental Photos). 675: Gazuit (Photo Researchers, Inc.).

CHAPTER 13   676–677: Dan Guravich (Photo Researchers, Inc.).   681: Ira Kirschenbaum (Stock Boston). 683: Isreal Talby (Woodfin Camp).   684: Walt Urbina. 688: Alain Thomas (Photo Researchers, Inc.).   691: R.P. Kingston (Stock Boston).   692: Susan Doheny/© D.C. Heath.   696: David Madison.   707: Geoff Tompkinson (Aspect Picture Library).   711: Dave Brown (Stock Market).   713: D. & J. Heaton (Stock Boston). 714: Steve Murez (Black Star).   718: Courtesy of Amoco Chemical Company.   720: Brian Parker (Tom Stack & Assoc.).   721: Walter Looss (The Image Bank). 725: Wes Thompson (The Stock Market).   726: Bill Gallery (Stock Boston).

CHAPTER 14   728–729: Bob Daemmerich (The Image Works).   733: Steve Dunwell (The Image Bank). 735: Alvis Upitis (The Image Bank).   741 l: Charles Mahaux (The Image Bank).   741 b: Joe Van Os (The Image Bank).   743: The Bettmann Archive.   749: Roy Pinney (Photo Researchers, Inc.).   751: Anne La Bastille (Photo Researchers, Inc.).   765: Treat Davidson (Photo Researchers, Inc.).   759: Jim Hamilton (The Picture Cube).   756: Michel Tcherevkoff (The Image Bank). 771: People Weekly © Mario Ruiz.   775: John Moss, Courtesy of the Royal Society of London. 779: Beringer/Dratch (The Image Bank).

CHAPTER 15   780–781: Peter Hendrie (The Image Bank). 784: Treat Davidson (Photo Researchers, Inc.). 786: Mark Jones (Hedgehog House of New Zealand). 789: Tim Davis (Photo Researchers, Inc.).   792: Hank deLespinasse (The Image Bank).   793: Susan A. Anderson/© D.C. Heath.   794: Matt Kelly.   795: Susan Doheny/© D.C. Heath.   798: t: Stephen Wilkes (The Image Bank).   798 b: Murray Alcosser (The Image Bank).   801: Hank deLespinasse (The Image Bank). 807: Dr. Wm. M. Harlow (Photo Researchers, Inc.). 809: Robert Frerck (The Stock Market).   812: Gary Gladstone (The Image Bank).   813: Steve Dunwell (The Image Bank).   814: Susan A. Anderson/© D.C. Heath. 815: Richard Gross (The Stock Market).   817: Fred Lyon (Photo Researchers, Inc.).   818: Gabe Palmer/Mug Shots (The Stock Market).   819: Jeff Smith (The Image Bank). 825: AP/Wide World Photos.   827: Ralph A. Reinhold (Animals, Animals).

In appreciation to the following editorial staff at Larson Texts:

Richard Bambauer, Linda Bollinger, Laurie Brooks, Patti Jo Campbell, Jordan Feidler, Linda Kifer, Deanna Larson, Patricia Larson, Timothy Larson, Amy Marshall, John Musser, Scott O'Neil, Louis Rieger, Paula Sibeto, Kristin Smith, and Evelyn Wedzikowski